THE New PHILLIES ENCYCLOPEDIA

Rich Westcott and Frank Bilovsky

THE *New* PHILLIES ENCYCLOPEDIA

Temple University Press | Philadelphia

Temple University Press, Philadelphia, PA 19122
Copyright © 1993 by Temple University
All rights reserved
Published 1993

⊗ The paper used in this publication meets the minimum
requirements of American National Standard for Information
Sciences—Permanence of Paper for Printed Library Materials,
ANSI Z39.48-1984

Printed in Canada

Library of Congress Cataloging-in-Publication Data

Westcott, Rich.
    The new Phillies encyclopedia / Rich Westcott and Frank Bilovsky.
        p.   cm.
    Rev. ed. of: The Phillies encyclopedia / Frank Bilovsky. c1984.
    ISBN 1–56639–045–1
    1. Philadelphia Phillies (Baseball team)—History.   2. Philadelphia
Phillies (Baseball team)—Records.   I. Bilovsky, Frank. Phillies
encyclopedia.   II. Title.
GV875.P45B55   1993
796.357′64′0974611—dc20   93–18387
                                                                            CIP

Contents

Foreword

Dear Phillies Fans:

All baseball fans, especially Phillies fans, should enjoy reading *The New Phillies Encyclopedia*. It is without a doubt the most comprehensive and best-researched history of Phillies baseball ever written.

As a player and broadcaster, I have been associated with the Phillies organization for 45 years, and the authors brought back a lot of pleasant memories for me.

I particularly enjoyed reading about the era of the Whiz Kids of which I was a part in the late 1940s and 1950s. It warmed my heart to recall our playing days with Robin Roberts, Del Ennis, Puddin' Head Jones, Granny Hamner, Curt Simmons, Putsy Caballero, Andy Seminick, and many, many more. And it brought back fond memories of the best manager I ever saw or played for, "The Squire of Valley Forge Mountain," Eddie Sawyer.

In their long history, the Phillies have had 30 Hall of Famers come through Baker Bowl and Shibe Park/Connie Mack Stadium. And Veterans Stadium will be included when Mike Schmidt and Steve Carlton are inducted soon.

Frank Bilovsky and Rich Westcott are to be commended for writing what was obviously a labor of love.

I loved the book, and I know you will love it also.

Rich Ashburn

Introduction

If success is measured by victories, the franchise of the Philadelphia Phillies has been a dismal failure.

This, after all, is a team that has reached baseball's mountaintop just once in its history. And it took 98 years to get there.

That 1980 season, when three players with Hall of Fame credentials and a supporting cast that was the envy of baseball took the franchise to its only World Championship, remains a source of pride to long-suffering Phillies fans, who once went 35 years between post-season appearances and 65 seasons between World Series victories.

During the majority of their seasons, though, victories for the Phillies have been far less common than defeats, and heartache has been an affliction that has accompanied the team through many of its summers.

The oldest, continuous, one-name, one-city franchise in the major leagues has broken more hearts over more seasons than it ever could mend with that one glorious moment on October 21, 1980, when Tug McGraw struck out Willie Wilson and sent a city into an elongated fit of delirium.

The Phillies had left the bitter taste of defeat in countless mouths before Hall of Famer–to–be Mike Schmidt told the City of Brotherly Love to "take this victory and savor it" the day after the 1980 Series had been won.

So many losses . . . so much time. So many bumblers . . . so few superstars. Decrepit ball parks. Terrible managers. Horrendous trades. Owners who gave new meaning to the word *incompetent*.

But sometimes success means more than won-lost records. Sometimes, it is based on intangibles.

In these terms, the Phillies have indeed been successful. In the long and occasionally glorious history of the franchise, no team has been more entertaining, more interesting, more colorful . . . and less dull.

Or more unpredictable.

The Phillies, after all, once lost 23 games in a row. Who else can say that? In 1964 they lost a pennant that appeared to be already theirs by blowing a six-and-one-half-game lead with 12 games left to play. Sixteen years later, they won a pennant that they had just about lost by falling six games off the pace in mid-August. They won 13 of 16 games on their way to clinching the flag on the next-to-last day of the season. And capped it by winning the deciding League Championship contest after trailing Nolan Ryan by three runs with six outs to go in the game.

They won a pennant in extra innings on the last day of the 1950 season after nearly blowing all of a nine-and-one-half-game lead. They sent a pitcher to the mound to start the World Series opener that year, even though he hadn't started a game all season. Three decades later, they entrusted the starting assignment in the opening game of the World Series to a rookie pitcher who during his professional career had gone to the mound without a glove and to the plate without a bat.

Both pitchers performed admirably. Who would have expected that?

But then again, Phillies fans had come to demand a lot but expect very little. Still, the Phillies often provided spectacular moments, even in their most unspectacular times.

They are a team that once hit five home runs in one inning; that in one

Tug McGraw's jubilant leap in 1980 represented the most memorable moment in Phillies history.

season had four outfielders who hit .400 or better; that had three players—Ed Delahanty, Chuck Klein, and Schmidt—hit four home runs in one game, a feat no other team can boast; that had a pitcher with the unlikely name of Grover Cleveland Alexander pitch the wondrous total of 16 shutouts in one season; and that had four outfielders each record perfect 1.000 fielding percentages during single seasons.

The Phillies had the game's only long-term lefthanded catcher, a pitcher who relied on an undertaker to diagnose his problems on the mound, and two owners who were banned from the league for life.

Billy Sunday, who later became a world-famous evangelist, often beginning his sermons by running across the stage and sliding into the pulpit, played with the Phillies. So did Earle (Greasy) Neale, who went on to a highly successful career as a Hall of Fame coach with the Philadelphia Eagles, and Bill Hulen, a lefthander who played more games at shortstop than any other southpaw in major league history.

The Phillies had a pitcher, Stan Baumgartner, who later covered the team for many years for the *Philadelphia Inquirer,* often wearing his Phillies cap in the press box. One of the club's pitchers, Lowell Palmer, liked to take the mound wearing sunglasses. Another hurler, Flint Rhem, once refused to pitch a game until groundskeepers built a new mound. Still another moundsman, Russ Meyer, angered about being removed from a game, heaved a resin bag high in the air, only to have it land squarely on his head.

Ty Cobb once tried to buy the Phillies. So did Bill Veeck, whose plan in 1943 was to stock the club with star players from the Negro Leagues, but who was rebuffed in that attempt by Commissioner Kenesaw Mountain Landis. The Carpenter family bought the team in 1943 for $400,000 and sold it in 1981 for $30 million.

The Phillies are a team that traded away a rookie pitcher named Ferguson Jenkins because the manager (Gene Mauch) said he couldn't throw hard enough, and a minor league infielder named Ryne Sandberg, who the brass thought wouldn't make it in the big leagues as a regular. One is now in the Hall of Fame; the other doubtless will join it later.

On the other hand, the Phillies are also the club that pirated Steve Carlton away from the St. Louis Cardinals, and that landed both 1950 pennant hero Dick Sisler and 1960s outfield stalwart Johnny Callison in deals for utility infielders.

In 1964 the Phillies acquired Vic Power for a player to be named later. A few months afterward, that player turned out to be Vic Power. Another time, the Phils landed catcher Clyde Kluttz in a swap in the morning, and traded him away in the afternoon.

Five Phillies—Howie Schultz, Frankie Baumholtz, Dick Groat, Gene Conley, and Ron Reed—played professional basketball. Outfielder Chuck Essegian played for Stanford in the Rose Bowl, and infielder Al Dark was an All-American halfback at Louisiana State in the same backfield as Steve VanBuren.

Outfielder Sherry Magee, known for his fun-loving spirit and hot temper, once dropped a bag full of water out of a sixth-floor window onto the head of pitcher Eppa Rixey. Real cutup, that Sherry. He and fellow outfielder Dode Paskert had a fistfight in the dugout after Paskert had hit a home run. It seems that everybody in the park cheered the feat except Magee's two sons, who booed lustily from the stands. When Paskert reached the dugout, he went right for Magee in the continuation of a long-standing family feud.

Magee was suspended for most of the 1911 season after punching an umpire. He later became an umpire, one of at least six Phillies who made the big leagues as arbitrators after their playing days ended.

The Phillies' third baseman in the mid-1880s was a player named Joe Mulvey. No defensive wizard, he made 135 errors over a two-year period. In 1921, first baseman Gene Paulette was banned from baseball for associating with gamblers. In 1939 pitcher Hal Kelleher gave up 12 runs in one inning. Nine years later, Charlie Bicknell surrendered four home runs and 18 total bases in one inning.

Five years after that, Tom Qualters, whom the Phillies had chosen instead of Al Kaline, and who was a $100,000 bonus baby who should have been in the minors, made his only appearance by facing seven batters and allowing six to reach base. They all scored, giving Qualters an earned run average of 162.00 for the season.

In the 1960s the Phillies could have had an outfield of Kaline, Carl Yastrzemski, and Hank Aaron. The Phils could have signed Yastrzemski if they'd given him the $10,000 more his father wanted. And after giving Aaron a tryout in the early 1950s, they told him, "Don't call us, we'll call you," which, of course, they never did.

The Phillies of old were never very good with minorities. No team in the National League gave Jackie Robinson a harder time when he joined the Brooklyn Dodgers in 1947. And the Phillies were the next-to-last team in the big leagues to sign black players, an exquisite example of bigotry and shortsightedness that for years kept the club from being competitive in a league in which black players were often dominant.

In 1946 the Phillies did hire a 33-year-old ex-Wave and former ladies professional baseball player, Edith Houghton, as baseball's first female scout. Eleven years later—10 years after Robinson entered the big leagues—the first black player joined the Phillies.

Shortstop Mickey Doolan and manager Doc Prothro were both practicing dentists. In the 1880s first baseman Sid Farrar, more widely noted later in life as the father of prominent opera star Geraldine Farrar, batted ninth throughout his seven-year career. In 1899 outfielder Roy Thomas became the first player in the majors to wear sliding gloves. Another player, Kid Gleason, who later managed the 1919 Black Sox, won 62 games as a pitcher for the Phillies over a two-year period, then returned 12 seasons later and was the club's regular second baseman for four years.

A former Phillies third baseman, Eddie Grant, was the first big league player killed in World War I. Pitcher Hugh Mulcahy was the first big league player drafted into military service in World War II.

Mulcahy's nickname was Losing Pitcher. The Phillies had a magnificent collection of nicknames. One of the best was Death to Flying Things, a name given to the team's first manager, Bob Ferguson, because of his ability as a player to catch nearly every ball in the air that was hit to him.

Ranking just behind that delicious sobriquet were such treasures as Pearce (What's the Use) Chiles, Togie (Horse Face) Pittinger, Benny (Earache) Meyer, John (Tight Pants) Titus, Charles (She) Donahue, Hubert (Shucks) Pruett, Ed (The Only) Nolan, Phil (Fidgety Phil) Collins, Claude (Weeping Willie) Willoughby, and Norm (The Tabasco Kid) Elberfeld.

Of course, there was also Walter (Boom Boom) Beck, John (Phenomenal) Smith, Bill (Wagon Tongue) Keister, Willie (Puddin' Head) Jones, Dick (Stone Fingers) Stuart, John (Brewery Jack) Taylor, Bob (Whirlybird) Walk, and the ever-popular Chester (Squack) Crist.

Like their preponderance of nicknames, the Phillies were rarely lost for words, even though they weren't always on target. "Nobody's gonna make a scrapgoat out of me," intoned manager Frank Lucchesi after he was fired in 1972. "Even Napoleon had his Watergate," advised skipped Danny Ozark as the Phillies' ship was sinking late one season.

Dick Allen once said of Astroturf, "If a horse can't eat it, I don't want to play on it." And Mike Schmidt, revealing what it was like to be a professional athlete in his adopted city, declared that "Philadelphia is the only city where you can experience the thrill of victory and the agony of reading about it the next morning."

If you wanted color, the Phillies certainly had it. From their first year in 1883 on up to the present, the Phils have been a team that has seldom strayed far from the bizarre. But often through the lean years, that was what kept the Phillies interesting—and so endearing to their fans.

No one would ever mistake the Phillies for being one of the glamour teams of the big leagues. Until recent years, in fact, the Phils have been strictly blue-collar, laboring away in the trenches of the National League with a club that was much more often brushed by the agony of defeat than it was the thrill of victory.

The team that entered the world in 1883 as outcasts, an odd collection of misfits and rejects who were thrown together by the spastic gyrations of the still-fledging National League, has won just four pennants and one World Series. It has finished either first, second, or third only 28 times.

Conversely, the Phillies have finished in sixth place or below 50 times, including 29 times in the basement, far more than any other team in baseball. From 1918 through 1948, the Phillies were the hallmark of ineptitude, finishing in the first division just once when they placed fourth in 1932. In 24 of those 31 seasons, the team wound up either seventh or eighth, sinking the Phils to a level of futility that is virtually unequaled in professional sports.

There have been times when the franchise dipped to such low levels that one owner had to borrow money just to send the team to spring training. In fact, that beleaguered executive, a hardworking but often penniless unfortunate named Gerry Nugent, occasionally had to sell the office furniture just to make ends meet.

During Nugent's luckless era, mostly in the 1930s, good players arrived regularly in Philadelphia. But they usually didn't stay long as Nugent, a former underling of previous owner William Baker who had parlayed enough stock to gain control of the club, sired one bad trade after another. Usually, Nugent was fleeced, surrendering an established player for someone of far less standing and the obligatory bundle of cash, some of which went toward hotel bills, players' salaries, or simply the purchase of baseballs.

"We had players coming and going all the time," remembered ex-pitcher Bucky Walters, himself a part of one of Nugent's trades. "Sometimes, you could hardly tell who was on the team. But because the team never had any money, the owner used to have to scramble to pay the bills. If the bank wanted a payment, the club often had to sell somebody to get the cash."

The Phillies of much of the first part of the 20th century were so woebegone that players, when they were traded, regarded their liberation from the club with the same relief as a prisoner getting out of jail.

Such was the case in 1921 when Casey Stengel was traded by the Phillies to the New York Giants. Stengel got the news in the locker room while the teams waited out a rain delay. Immediately, he raced half-clothed into the deluge and onto the soaked and muddy playing field of Baker Bowl. Once there, the irrepressible Casey circled the bases, sliding into each bag. By the time he reached home plate, Stengel was covered with mud, but grinning from ear to ear. It was his way, he explained, of celebrating his liberation from the awful Phillies.

Baker Bowl was one of the four parks the Phillies have called home. The club began in Recreation Park, but after four years there, moved to what was at the time the most magnificent stadium in the world. Later named Baker Bowl, the Phillies stayed there for 51½ years before moving into Shibe Park/Connie Mack Stadium, the club's home for another 32½ years. That residency was followed by a move in 1971 to Veterans Stadium, the team's present headquarters.

The Phils never had much luck in their first three ballparks. Once, a part of Baker Bowl collapsed, resulting in the deaths of 12 people and injuries to 232 more. The Phils were unlucky in many other ways, too. In the 1880s their great pitcher Charlie Ferguson died of typhoid fever after winning 99 games in four seasons. Promising young catcher Walter (Peck) Lerian died in 1929 after being hit by a truck, and second baseman Mickey Finn succumbed after undergoing surgery for an ulcer in 1933. The 1949 incident in which first baseman Eddie Waitkus was shot by a deranged fan and the 1991 accident in which center fielder Len Dykstra crashed his car into a couple of trees didn't enhance Phillies fortunes, either.

The club's lucklessness had been so omnipresent over the years that in a game in 1971 the Phillies' two catchers, Tim McCarver and Mike Ryan, broke their hands in the same inning, leaving the team without a receiver.

Over the years, Phillies' pitchers have had the worst earned run averages in the league (for pitchers with more than 100 innings) 24 times. The club has also had more than its share of sub-.200 hitters and bumbling fielders.

The Phillies, though, have had their share of great players and memorable moments. The franchise has had 30 Hall of Famers associated with it, including four—Delahanty, Alexander, Klein, and Robin Roberts—who earned their credentials primarily as Phillies. Two others—Carlton and Schmidt—will soon join that category, and a third, Pete Rose, should, but won't, at least for now.

Other players such as Billy Hamilton, Nap Lajoie, Sam Thompson, Elmer Flick, Eppa Rixey, and Dave Bancroft also enjoyed banner seasons with the Phillies en route to their enshrinements at Cooperstown.

Still other players such as Cy Williams, Gavvy Cravath, Magee, Roy Thomas, Jimmie Wilson, Pinky Whitney, Del Ennis, Richie Ashburn, Granny Hamner, Dick Allen, Callison, Jim Bunning, Larry Bowa, Garry Maddox, Bob Boone, and Greg Luzinski wore the Phillies uniform with the utmost distinction and certainly belong in the team's small galaxy of stars.

Phillies have won nine batting championships, 24 home run crowns, and 21 RBI titles. Phillies pitchers have led the league in wins 16 times, in ERA eight times, and in strikeouts 17 times. The club has had 32 Gold Glove winners, five Most Valuable Players, six Cy Young Award winners, and eight stolen base champs.

The Phillies have had eight no-hitters pitched for them, and 17 thrown against them. The club's first hitless game was pitched in 1885 by Ferguson. The last was in 1991 by Tommy Greene. In between, Phils no-hitters have been registered by Red Donahue (1898), Chick Fraser (1903), John Lush (1906), Bunning (1964, the only perfect game in Phillies history), Rick Wise (1971), and Terry Mulholland (1990).

Although Bunning's perfect game, the first one during the regular season in the major leagues in 42 years, was unquestionably the finest mound performance ever turned in by a Phillies pitcher in a single game, brilliant playing often has been a staple of Phillies games. In addition to the superb work usually turned in by the club's big three of Alexander, Roberts, and Carlton, who combined for 665 Phillies victories and 13 one-hitters, a Phils quartet of Roberts, Ken Johnson, Bubba Church, and Russ Meyer pitched four straight shutout games in 1951. In 1965, Chris Short struck out 18 New York Mets in a 15-inning game, and in 1961 Art Mahaffey fanned 17 Chicago Cubs in a nine-inning contest. In 1952 and 1953, Roberts hurled 28 straight complete games. Kent Tekulve appeared in 90 games in 1987, and Tully Sparks and Joe Oeschger each pitched 20 innings in games in 1905 and 1919, respectively.

For Phillies pitchers, four seasons stand out above the rest. Alexander's 1916 campaign in which he posted a 33–12 record with a 1.55 ERA, 38 complete games, and 16 shutouts, leading the league in all those categories in addition to strikeouts, innings pitched, and games started, ranks as the finest single season for a Phillies pitcher.

Next come Roberts' 1952 campaign when he compiled a 28–7 record over 330 innings and with 30 complete games; the 1950 season of Jim Konstanty when he won the Most Valuable Player award with a 16–7 record and 22 saves in a then-record 74 games; and Carlton's 1972 Cy Young season when he was 27–10 with a 1.98 ERA while striking out 310 in 346⅓ innings for a last-place team that won just 59 games all year.

The Phillies also had numerous big hitting performances. Delahanty (1896), Klein (1936), and Schmidt (1976) each hit four home runs in one game. Kitty Bransfield in 1910, Cravath in 1915, and Willie Jones in 1958 drove in eight runs apiece in single games. In 1953, Connie Ryan lashed six hits in one game to match a feat accomplished in 1894 by Delahanty. And in 1900, Harry Wolverton achieved the unusual distinction of hitting three triples in one game.

Probably the greatest individual season for a Phillies batter occurred in 1894 when Hamilton hit .404 with 220 hits and 87 RBI, and led the league with a record-setting 192 runs, 98 stolen bases, and 361 putouts. Close behind that was the 1895 season of Thompson when he led the league with 165 RBI, 18 home runs, and a .654 slugging average while batting .392 with 211 hits and 131 runs.

Delahanty's 1899 season in which he led the league in hitting with a .410 average, in hits with 238, RBI with 137, and slugging average with .585 also ranks high. So does the 1929 season of Lefty O'Doul with a league-leading 254 hits and .398 batting average, plus 122 RBI, 152 runs, and a .622 slugging average; the 1933 triple-crown season of Klein when he led the league in hitting (.368), RBI (120), home runs (28), hits (223), and slugging average (.602); and the 1980 campaign of Schmidt who had league-leading totals in RBI (121), home runs (48), and slugging average (.624) while hitting .286 and scoring 104 runs.

The Phillies played in the first National League game at Ebbets Field, defeating the Brooklyn Dodgers, 1–0, in 1913. In 1919 they played the first legal Sunday game in New York, beating the New York Giants, 4–3. The Phils also participated in the first night game in the major leagues, bowing to the Cincinnati Reds, 2–1, in 1935 at Crosley Field. And in 1965 they participated in the first game at the Astrodome, downing the Houston Astros, 2–0.

Over the years the club won games by scores of 24–0, 29–4, and 26–7 and lost games by scores of 29–1, 28–6, and 20–16. One of the most notable wins in Phillies history was the club's 26–24 victory over the Cubs in the "shootout in Chicago" game. In another memorable game, a 20–14 win over the St. Louis Cardinals in 1923, the two teams combined for 10 home runs.

There have been other great moments in Phillies history. Who can forget the final game of the 1950 season when Dick Sisler's three-run home run in the top of the 10th inning gave the weary Phillies a 4–1 victory over the Brooklyn Dodgers at Ebbets Field and the club's first National League pennant in 35 years? Or Robin Roberts' gritty 10-inning pitching performance? Or Richie Ashburn's throw that nailed Cal Abrams at the plate in the bottom of the ninth?

How ironic that the manager of that Dodger team was Burt Shotton, the only successful Phillies skipper in the club's previous 34 years, and that the coach who made the injudicious decision to send Abrams home was Milt Stock, the Phils' third baseman on the club's last pennant winner in 1915. Both were unceremoniously dumped by the Dodgers after that heartbreaking loss to the Phillies.

Unquestionably, the most memorable moment in Phillies history, though, happened October 21, 1980, when the club—fresh from winning its first pennant in 30 years and only its third flag ever—defeated the Kansas City Royals in six games of the World Series.

To hundreds of thousands of Phillies fans, who for too many years had suffered excruciating frustration and heartbreak, the image of McGraw leaping high into the autumn night after the last out will last a lifetime.

McGraw's jubilant leap was to Phillies rooters of all ages at least comparable to the great scenes of World Series past. More than just a World Series victory, though, the pitcher's emotional outburst signified a much deeper dimension that only a Phillies fan could understand. In its boyish simplicity, it represented a celebration that for decades had been forbidden to happen.

McGraw did it on the mound after striking out Wilson for the last out of the Series (on the previous play, first baseman Rose had reached under the mitt of catcher Boone to catch a bobbled foul pop in front of the Phillies' dugout). But what McGraw's joyous leap stood for among Phillies fans was a release of stored emotion that had endured for years, decades, nearly a century of broken dreams, of false hopes, of bitter disappointments. And so it was all right for hundreds of grown men and women, superficially hardened by all the seasons of failure, to stand silently as the fireworks exploded at Veterans Stadium, tears streaming down their cheeks.

Shortstop Bowa put the feeling into as good a perspective as anyone could have. "We had some ghosts to put to sleep," he said. "And tonight we did it."

The Phillies' 1980 World Series triumph did, indeed, put some ghosts to sleep—97 years worth. In the process, it erased some stigmas that had cursed Phillies teams through most of those years.

But in their own way, even though that marvelous 1980 season stood as the zenith of Phillies accomplishments, they had been rich years; years that always began with hope; years that in many ways often provided fans with some measure of satisfaction, despite the unpleasantness of losing.

There is no rich tradition of victory with this team. But it has not always been the loser that its records suggest, either. Instead, it has been a team on which the unusual has been usual, the unpredictable common. And never—but never—has it ever been dull.

Surely, that statement cannot be made about all other professional sports teams.

Down Through the Seasons

The game of baseball was popular in Philadelphia long before the Phillies came into existence in 1883.

As early as the 1830s a version of the game, called town ball by those who played it, was a widely accepted form of recreation in the city, particularly among the upper crust. By the 1850s the city had an abundance of club teams, most of which had their fields in North and West Philadelphia.

One of the leading club teams in Philadelphia was called the Athletics. By the 1860s the Athletics had not only surpassed the levels of the other teams, but in 1863 they signed their first and the sport's first professional player. His name was Al Reach, and later he would play a prominent role in Phillies history.

Reach led the Athletics to a national championship in 1866. By then the team had added more professional players to its ranks, and with the Brooklyn Atlantics and the Cincinnati Red Stockings ranked among the nation's finest baseball aggregations.

The Athletics claimed another national championship in 1870. It followed a late-season victory over the Red Stockings and four out of five wins over the Atlantics, the team that earlier in the season had stopped Cincinnati's miraculous 87-game winning streak under manager Harry Wright, another major contributor to Phillies' history.

A year later the Athletics became a charter member of the new National Association of Professional Baseball Players. Formed officially March 17, 1871, the league also included Boston, Chicago, Cleveland, Fort Wayne, New York, Rockford, and two teams from Washington. The admission fee for the league was $10.

Using a field at 25th and Jefferson Streets as their home grounds, the Athletics won the first league championship with a 22–7 record.

In 1873 another team from Philadelphia joined the league, this one called the Quakers. The team, which also played at 25th and Jefferson, was formed by a group of local politicians. Much of the team was stocked through raids on existing league teams, particularly the Athletics.

The Quakers, considered by some to be ancestors of the Phillies, finished second in their first season. The club might have won the pennant had it not cooled off substantially following a rollicking mid-summer vacation in Cape May, New Jersey, that was sponsored by the Quakers' owners.

By 1875 the National Association had expanded to 13 teams. Philadelphia was the backbone of the league, and the hottest baseball city in the country. The Athletics were led by Cap Anson, one of the early giants of the game and a Hall of Fame inductee in 1939. In addition to the Quakers, a third team from the city, the Centennials, entered the league late in the season.

It was, however, to be the National Association's last season. Thugs, gambling, drinking, and general rowdyism had permeated the league, ultimately causing its demise after the 1875 campaign.

From the ashes of the National Association, a better and stronger league was formed. Absorbing the best of the disbanded league, it took the name National League. The new circuit had eight teams: Boston, Chicago, Cincinnati, St. Louis, Hartford, New York, Louisville, and Philadelphia.

Chuck Klein's Most Valuable Player Award in 1932 occurred during the finest five-season period of any Phillies batter.

The Athletics were awarded the Philadelphia franchise. And on April 22, 1876, they played in the first National League game, facing the Boston Red Stockings before 3,000 at 25th and Jefferson Streets. Boston won, 6–5, behind the pitching of Joe Borden, later the first National Leaguer to hurl a no-hitter.

Although the Athletics had the league's first home run champion—George Hall with five—the club won only 14 of 59 games, and was in seventh place as the end of the season approached. The Athletics were scheduled for one final western road trip, but having insufficient funds and not wanting to spend any more on a futile season, the club refused to go. The Athletics were immediately expelled from the league.

The Athletics continued in subsequent years as an independent club, but Philadelphia was without a major league franchise until 1882 when the American Association formed as a six-team league. The circuit was established as a rival of the National League, and player raids, Sunday baseball, and ticket prices reduced from 50 to 25 cents made it competitive with the older loop.

The Athletics were charter members of the new league, joining other National League castoffs St. Louis, Louisville, and Cincinnati along with Pittsburgh and Baltimore.

The Athletics remained in the American Association until it disbanded after the 1891 season. Meanwhile, in 1883 the National League moved its Worcester, Massachusetts, franchise to Philadelphia.

The new team was called the Phillies. What follows is a year-by-year summary of that team's first 110 seasons.

NOTE: Parentheses around items in the statistical tables indicate the player led the league in that category for the year.

1883

Record: 17–81
Finish: Eighth
Games Behind: 46
Managers: Bob Ferguson, Blondie Purcell

At 1:30 P.M., May 1, 1883, at Recreation Park, 24th and Columbia Avenues, the Philadelphia Phillies Base Ball Club was born. On that date, the new team opened play in the National League in a game against the Providence Grays.

An estimated 1,200 spectators witnessed the occasion. With John Coleman on the mound pitted against Providence's great hurler Charles (Old Hoss) Radbourne—a future Hall of Famer who would win 48 games in 1883 and 60 the next season—the Phillies led 3–0 after seven innings. But a four-run rally in the top of the eighth inning by Providence propelled the visitors to a 4–3 victory.

Despite the loss, it was a respectable beginning for the new team. Disaster, however, was close at hand.

Having built a team from scratch after obtaining the Worcester, Massachusetts, franchise, owners Al Reach and John Rogers had put together a club made up mostly of ex–minor leaguers and players they were able to coax away from other National League teams. The first Phillies squad, therefore, was an odd and somewhat disorganized collection of players.

By the time the team had played its 17th game, winning only four of them, manager Bob Ferguson quit the post and took a job in the club's business office. He was replaced by Bill (Blondie) Purcell, a pitcher-outfielder on the team.

Poor Blondie's team could win only 13 of 81 games. And the club finished with a record so bad that most people never expected to see the Phillies again.

The Phillies' winning percentage was .173. During the season, the team was subjected to an assortment of atrocities that no team has ever again encountered.

The Phillies lost one game to Boston, 29–4. It dropped another, 28–0, to Providence in the highest scoring shutout victory in major league history. It was no-hit by Hugh Dailey of Cleveland in a 1–0 loss. And in one other game against Providence, the Phillies made 27 errors, although walks, wild pitches, and passed balls counted as errors in those days.

Pitcher Coleman established a record that may stand forever by losing 48 games (he won 13). Coleman pitched in 65 games and worked 538 innings, third best in the league in each category.

	W	L	G	CG	IP	H	BB	K	ERA
Alonzo Breitenstein	0	1	1	0	5	8	2	0	9.00
John Coleman	13	48	65	59	538	772	48	159	4.87
Bob Ferguson	0	0	1	0	1	2	0	0	9.00
Art Hagan	1	14	17	15	137	207	33	39	5.45
Hardie Henderson	0	1	1	1	9	26	2	2	19.00
Charlie Hilsey	0	3	3	3	26	36	4	8	5.54
Jack Neagle	1	7	8	6	61	88	21	13	6.93
Blondie Purcell	2	6	11	7	80	110	12	30	4.39
Edgar Smith	0	1	1	0	7	18	3	2	15.43
	17	81	99	91	864	1,267	125	253	5.34

Shutouts: Coleman (3)

	G	AB	R	H	2B	3B	HR	RBI	AVG
Art Benedict	3	15	3	4	1	0	0	4	.267
John Coleman	90	354	33	83	12	8	0	32	.234
Conny Doyle	16	68	3	15	3	2	0	3	.221
Sid Farrar (1B)	99	377	41	88	19	8	0	29	.233
Bob Ferguson (2B)	86	329	39	85	19	2	0	27	.258
Bill Gallagher	2	8	1	0	0	0	0	0	.000
Buck Gladman	1	4	1	0	0	0	0	0	.000
Emil Gross (C)	57	231	39	71	25	7	1	25	.307
Bill Harbridge	73	280	32	62	12	3	0	21	.221
Charlie Kelly	2	7	1	1	0	1	0	0	.143
Kick Kelly	1	3	0	0	0	0	0	0	.000
Fred Lewis (CF)	38	160	21	40	7	0	0	15	.250
Jack Manning (RF)	98	420	60	112	31	5	0	37	.267
Joe Mulvey	3	12	2	6	1	0	0	3	.500
Bill McClellan (SS)	80	326	42	75	21	4	1	33	.230
Jack Neagle	18	73		12					.164
Dick Pierre	5	19	1	3	0	0	0	0	.158
Blondie Purcell (LF)	97	425	70	114	20	5	1	32	.268
Frank Ringo	60	221	24	42	10	1	0	12	.190
Charlie Waitt	1	3	0	1	0	0	0	0	.333
Piggy Ward	1	5	0	0	0	0	0	0	.000
Fred Warner (3B)	39	141	13	32	6	1	0	13	.227
C. B. White	1	1	0	0	0	0	0	0	.000
	99	3,576	437	859	181	48	3		.240

The team had a .240 batting average, the lowest in the league. Only one regular, catcher Emil Gross, hit over .300 with a .307 average.

Art Hagen, the Phillies' number-two pitcher, had a 1–14 record. But the Phils' staff tied for second in the league in complete games with 91.

A fter the disastrous season they had the year before, it was inevitable that the Phillies would make some major changes in 1884.

The biggest change was in the managerial department. English-born Harry Wright, a one-time cricket player, was lured to the Phillies. President Al Reach called Wright the greatest manager in the country.

Reach, of course, was the supreme optimist. Following the 1883 season when some were urging Reach to give up, he had said, "Some day the Philadelphia National League club will be famous—more famous than the Athletics."

With Wright, though, there was good cause for optimism. Harry had been manager of the first professional baseball team, the Cincinnati Red Stockings, and he later won six pennants with two different Boston teams. By the time he came to the Phillies from Providence, he was regarded as the game's premier pilot.

It takes more than a manager, however, to make a team click. But Reach took care of that, too, bringing in a fresh band of talented, young players. Foremost of the group was a 21-year-old Virginian, Charlie Ferguson.

Ferguson became not only the team's best pitcher, but also its best hitter and best base-runner. When he wasn't pitching, he played the outfield.

Ferguson had a 21–25 record on the mound in his rookie season. One of his best efforts was a 7–2 victory over Boston, which snapped that club's 21-game winning streak.

1884

Record: 39–73
Finish: Sixth
Games Behind: 45
Manager: Harry Wright

	W	L	G	CG	IP	H	BB	K	ERA
John Coleman	5	15	21	14	154	216	22	37	4.91
Charlie Ferguson	21	25	50	46	417	443	93	194	3.54
Jim Fogarty	0	0	1	0	1	2	0	1	0.00
Joe Knight	2	4	6	6	51	66	21	8	5.47
Cyclone Miller	0	1	1	1	9	17	6	1	10.00
Sparrow Morton	0	2	2	2	17	16	11	5	5.29
Con Murphy	0	3	3	3	26	37	6	10	6.58
Jim McElroy	1	12	13	13	111	115	54	45	4.84
Blondie Purcell	0	0	1	0	4	3	0	1	2.25
Shadow Pyle	0	1	1	1	9	9	6	4	4.00
Bill Vinton	10	10	21	20	182	166	35	105	2.23
	39	73	113	106	981	1,090	254	411	3.93

Shutouts: Ferguson (2), Coleman

	G	AB	R	H	2B	3B	HR	RBI	AVG
Hezekiah Allen	1	3	0	2	0	0	0	0	.667
Ed Andrews (2B)	109	420	74	93	21	2	0	23	.221
Jack Clements	9	30	3	7	0	0	0	0	.233
John Coleman	43	171	16	42	7	2	0	22	.246
Bill Conway	1	4	0	0	0	0	0	0	.000
Paul Cook	3	12	0	1	0	0	0	0	.083
John Crowley (C)	48	168	26	41	7	3	0	19	.244
Tony Cusick	9	29	2	4	0	0	0	1	.138
Mike Dupaugher	4	10	0	2	0	0	0	0	.200
Sid Farrar (1B)	111	428	62	105	16	6	1	45	.245
Charlie Ferguson	52	203	19	50	6	3	0		.246
Jim Fogarty (CF)	97	378	42	80	12	6	1	37	.212
Lew Hardie	3	8	0	3	2	0	0	0	.375
Buster Hoover	10	42	6	8	1	0	1	4	.190
Joe Kappel	4	15	1	1	0	0	0	0	.067
Tom Lynch	13	48	7	15	4	2	0	3	.313
Jack Manning (RF)	104	424	71	115	29	4	5	52	.271
Bill McClellan (SS)	111	450	71	116	13	2	3	33	.258
Joe Mulvey (3B)	100	401	47	92	11	2	2	32	.229
Blondie Purcell (LF)	103	428	67	108	11	7	1	31	.252
Jack Remsen	12	43	9	9	2	0	0	3	.209
Frank Ringo	26	91	4	12	2	0	0	6	.132
Ed Sixsmith	1	2	0	0	0	0	0	0	.000
Gene Vadeboncoeur	4	14	1	3	0	0	0	3	.214
	113	3,998	549	934	149	39	14		.234

Harry Wright became manager in 1884 and molded the Phillies into a perennial contender late in the 19th century.

There were only four starters back from the previous year's team, first baseman Sid Farrar, one of the few nonpitchers to bat ninth in the order, shortstop Bill McClellan, and outfielders Blondie Purcell and John Manning. Right fielder Manning had the team's highest batting average with .271.

Among the newcomers who would later shine for the Phillies were third baseman Joe Mulvey and center fielder Jim Fogarty. Neither had very impressive rookie seasons, however. Mulvey led National League third basemen with 73 errors. But that wasn't even high for the club. McClellan claimed that honor with 83 miscues. Yet, the Phillies did not lead the league in errors, or even rank lowest in fielding percentage, despite their .888 mark.

In general, the team was vastly improved over the previous year, moving up two notches in the standings and winning 22 more games. The surge gave the Phillies good reason to look ahead with optimism.

1885

Record: 56–54
Finish: Third
Games Behind: 30
Manager: Harry Wright

By their third season in the National League, the Phillies had not only become respectable, they were downright good.

Only two teams, the Chicago White Stockings and the New York Giants, finished ahead of them as the Phillies vaulted all the way to third place. The Phillies did, however, finish a distant 30 games out of first, a situation directly attributable to Chicago's glittering 87–25 record.

That matter notwithstanding, in 1885 the Phillies arrived as a legitimate first-division club. In fact, the team would not finish out of the first division again until 1896.

The heart of the club was its pitching staff, led by the brilliant Charlie

	W	L	G	CG	IP	H	BB	K	ERA
Ed Daily	26	23	50	49	440	370	90	140	2.21
Charlie Ferguson	26	20	48	45	405	345	81	197	2.22
Edward Nolan	1	5	7	6	54	55	24	20	4.17
Bill Vinton	3	6	9	8	77	90	23	21	3.04
	56	54	110	108	976	860	218	378	2.39

Shutouts: Ferguson (5), Daily (4)

	G	AB	R	H	2B	3B	HR	RBI	AVG
Ed Andrews (LF)	103	421	77	112	15	3	0	23	.266
Charlie Bastian (SS)	103	389	63	65	11	5	4	29	.167
Jack Clements (C)	52	188	14	36	11	3	1	14	.191
Tony Cusick	39	141	12	25	1	0	0	5	.177
Ed Daily	50	184	22	38	8	2	1		.207
Sid Farrar (1B)	111	420	49	103	20	3	3	36	.245
Charlie Ferguson	61	235	42	72	8	3	1		.306
Jim Fogarty (CF)	111	427	49	99	13	3	0	39	.232
Charlie Ganzel	34	125	15	21	3	1	0	6	.168
John Hiland	3	9	0	0	0	0	0	0	.000
Tom Lynch	13	53	7	10	3	0	0	1	.189
Jack Manning (RF)	107	445	61	114	24	4	3	40	.256
Joe Mulvey (3B)	107	443	74	119	25	6	6	64	.269
Al Myers (2B)	93	357	25	73	13	2	1	28	.204
Edward Nolan	7	26	1	2	1	0	0		.077
	110	3,893	513	891	156	35	20		.229

Ferguson. Although only 22, Ferguson was a 20-game winner for the second straight season and was inching his way up the ladder toward the ranks of the elite pitching members of the National League.

During the season Ferguson pitched the first no-hitter in the Phillies' history when he beat the Providence Grays, 1–0.

The achievement was accorded one lone paragraph in the next morning's *Philadelphia Inquirer.* "Ferguson, the pitcher of the Philadelphia Base Ball Club," the account read, "accomplished the feat of retiring the Providence nine without a hit in a full nine inning game at Recreation Park. The visitors retired from the field defeated by the score of 1 to 0."

Charlie posted a 26–20 record in 1885. He and Ed Daily, a youngster the Phillies had purchased from the Harrisburg club, alternated on the mound nearly every game. Daily finished the season with a 26–23 record, which gave the two all but four of the Phillies' wins.

Unusual as that was, it was nothing compared to the Phillies' catcher. Newcomer Jack Clements was lefthanded. One of the few southpaw backstops in big league history, Clements was a Philadelphia native who would enjoy an illustrious 13-year career with the Phillies.

He didn't hit much in his first year (.191), but neither did most of the Phillies. Only Ferguson reached .300, hitting .306 while seeing action in the outfield when he wasn't on the mound.

1886

The Phillies in 1886 established a winning percentage of .623, which ranked as the highest mark in club history until tied by the 1976 and 1977 teams.

Yet the 1886 Phillies finished in only fourth place. "Our final position looks rather silly when contrasted to our percentage," manager Harry Wright remarked.

The reason for the imbalance was that the Chicago White Stockings and the Detroit Wolverines were so far ahead of everybody else in the league that it was ridiculous. Chicago won the pennant again, this time with a 90–34 record. Detroit wasn't far behind with an 87–36 log.

Thus, in spite of such a splendid record, the Phillies were mere also-rans. "But I'll tell you one thing, Al," Wright said to president Reach. "We now really have a ball team. It's only a matter of time before I can give you a championship. I make you that promise."

As it turned out, it didn't quite happen that way. But the Phillies had made

Record: 71–43
Finish: Fourth
Games Behind: 14
Manager: Harry Wright

Charlie Ferguson (left) and Cannonball Titcomb (standing) were two of the Phillies pitchers in 1886 (third player is unidentified).

huge strides since joining the National League in 1883, and they were on the verge of becoming a legitimate contender for the title.

By now they had eclipsed the rival Athletics of the American Association as the hometown favorites. The Phillies outdrew the Athletics by a large margin at home, and they were just as popular an attraction on the road.

Several key additions had bolstered the club since the previous season. One new plus was shortstop Art Irwin, who was picked up from the Providence Grays after they folded in 1885. Irwin, the Grays' captain, was the first infielder to wear a glove, an invention he patented and from which he eventually made a great deal of money.

In addition, the Phillies had also obtained pitcher Dan Casey, outfielder George Wood, and catcher David McGuire from Detroit. Wood's .273 average was second only to Jim Fogarty's .293.

Casey was a mediocre pitcher before coming to Philadelphia, but after his arrival he blossomed. His record in 1886 was 24–18, which when combined with those of Charlie Ferguson (30–9) and Ed Daily (16–9), gave the club an outstanding pitching threesome.

By now Ferguson was the darling of Philadelphia fans, as well as one of the premier hurlers in the league. His 1.98 ERA was by far the best in the league. He had even pitched two complete game victories in one day during the season. Along with Daily, he was being used in the outfield nearly every day he didn't pitch.

The Phillies raced to the conclusion of the season with 13 wins in their final 15 decisions. In one of the games against Washington, a string-bean rookie catcher made his league debut for the opponents. He was listed in the lineup as Cornelius McGillicuddy, a name the Phillies would come across again.

	W	L	G	CG	IP	H	BB	K	ERA
Dan Casey	24	18	44	39	369	326	104	193	2.41
Ed Daily	16	9	27	22	218	211	59	95	3.06
Charlie Ferguson	30	9	48	43	396	317	69	212	(1.98)
Jim Fogarty	0	1	1	0	6	7	0	4	0.00
Tommy McCarthy	0	0	1	0	1	0	1	1	0.00
John Strike	1	1	2	1	15	19	7	11	4.80
Cannonball Titcomb	0	5	5	5	41	43	24	24	3.73
	71	43	119	110	1,046	923	264	540	(2.45)

Shutouts: Ferguson (4), Casey (4), Daily

	G	AB	R	H	2B	3B	HR	RBI	SB	AVG
Ed Andrews (CF)	107	437	93	109	15	4	2	28	(56)	.249
Charlie Bastian (2B)	105	373	46	81	9	11	2	36	29	.217
Jack Clements	54	185	15	38	5	1	0	11	4	.205
Tony Cusick	29	104	10	23	5	1	0	4	1	.221
Ed Daily	79	309	40	70	17	1	4	50	23	.227
Sid Farrar (1B)	118	439	55	109	19	7	5	50	10	.248
Jack Farrell	17	60	7	11	0	1	0	3	1	.183
Charlie Ferguson	72	261	56	66	9	1	2	25	9	.253
Jim Fogarty (RF)	77	280	54	82	13	5	3	47	30	.293
Charlie Ganzel	1	3	0	0	0	0	0	0	0	.000
Art Irwin (SS)	101	373	51	87	6	6	0	34	24	.233
Tommy McCarthy	8	27	6	5	2	1	0	3	1	.185
Deacon McGuire (C)	50	167	25	33	7	1	2	18	2	.198
Joe Mulvey (3B)	107	430	71	115	16	10	2	53	27	.267
George Wood (LF)	108	450	81	123	18	15	4	50	9	.273
	119	4,072	621	976	145	66	26		226	.240

1887

Record: 75–48
Finish: Second
Games Behind: 3½
Manager: Harry Wright

In just the fifth season after they joined the National League, the Phillies arrived as a definite threat to win the pennant.

The 1887 campaign was a banner year in virtually every respect for the Phillies. But the best part of it was the club's season-long seesaw battle with the Detroit Wolverines for the flag. The two moved in and out of the lead in a brutal tussle that captivated the nation's baseball followers.

Along with their pennant race, the Phillies had another landmark event. It was the year they moved out of Recreation Park into a new stadium at Broad Street and Lehigh Avenue.

	W	L	G	CG	IP	H	BB	K	ERA
Charlie Buffinton	21	17	40	35	332	352	92	160	3.66
Dan Casey	28	13	45	43	390	377	115	119	(2.86)
Ed Daily	0	4	6	4	41	52	25	7	7.24
Jim Devlin	0	2	2	2	18	20	10	6	6.00
Charlie Ferguson	22	10	37	31	297	297	47	125	3.00
Jim Fogarty	0	0	1	0	3	3	1	1	9.00
Al Maul	4	2	7	4	50	72	15	18	5.58
	75	48	128	119	1,133	1,173	305	435	(3.47)

Shutouts: Casey (4), Ferguson (2), Buffinton

	G	AB	R	H	2B	3B	HR	RBI	SB	AVG
Ed Andrews (CF)	104	464	110	151	19	7	4	67	57	.325
Charlie Bastian	60	221	33	47	11	1	1	21	11	.213
Charlie Buffinton	66	269	34	72	12	1	1	46	8	.268
Jack Clements (C)	66	246	48	69	13	7	1	47	7	.280
Tony Cusick	7	24	3	7	1	0	0	5	0	.292
Ed Daily	26	106	18	30	11	1	1	17	8	.283
Sid Farrar (1B)	116	443	83	125	20	9	4	72	24	.282
Charlie Ferguson	72	264	67	89	14	6	3	85	13	.337
Jim Fogarty (RF)	126	495	113	129	26	12	8	50	102	.261
Tom Gunning	28	104	22	27	6	1	1	16	18	.260
Art Irwin (SS)	100	374	65	95	14	8	2	56	19	.254
Harry Lyons	1	4	0	0	0	0	0	0	0	.000
Tommy McCarthy	18	70	7	13	4	0	0	6	15	.186
Deacon McGuire	41	150	22	46	6	6	2	23	3	.307
Barney McLaughlin (2B)	50	205	26	45	8	3	1	26	2	.220
Joe Mulvey (3B)	111	474	93	136	21	6	2	78	43	.287
George Wood (LF)	113	491	118	142	22	19	14	66	19	.289
	128	4,630	901	1,269	213	89	47		355	.274

Originally called the Philadelphia Base Ball Park, the stadium that would later be known as Baker Bowl was a magnificent wooden structure considered to be the finest park of its time. The Phillies opened the 1887 season there before an estimated crowd of 20,000. In a game preceded by a parade and other festivities, the Phillies defeated the New York Giants (or Metropolitans, as they were originally called) 19–10.

The stadium was a boon to the Phillies' coffers as huge crowds jammed into the park to watch what was far and away Philadelphia's favorite team. Of course, the blistering pennant race helped.

The race might not have been so hot if the Chicago White Stockings, champions in each of the last two years, had not sold their great slugger, King Kelly, to the Boston Beaneaters. The departure of Kelly, the premier player of the era, assured Chicago of not repeating as the pennant winner.

"That will eliminate Chicago," Phillies' manager Harry Wright said upon hearing of the sale. "I know I've got a better team than (Jim) Mutrie in New

When it opened in 1887, Philadelphia Ball Park—later called Baker Bowl—was a showplace for baseball.

York. The club we've got to beat now is Detroit. If we can finish ahead of them, we'll celebrate our new park with a pennant."

Wright's prediction was perfect. A four-team race, with Boston not far behind in fifth, raged all season.

The Phillies had some memorable moments. In back-to-back outings, pitcher Charlie Buffinton, a 47-game winner in 1884 who was bought before the season from Boston, pitched one-hitters, beating Indianapolis and Chicago.

The Phillies reeled off 16 wins in a row, although in one game during their season they were destroyed by the New York Giants, 29–1, which tied an 1883 record for most runs scored against the Phillies and became the most lopsided defeat in club history.

Buffinton, Dan Casey, and Charlie Ferguson gave the club a superb pitching trio. Casey led the league in earned run average with a 2.86 mark while posting a 28–13 record. Buffinton was 21–17, and Ferguson was 22–10, his fourth straight 20-win season.

With the success enjoyed by the other two, Ferguson was used with increasing frequency at second base. He was the club's top hitter with a .337 average.

Center fielder Ed Andrews, who had been a regular with the club since 1884, had the best season of his career with a .325 batting mark.

1888

Record: 69–61
Finish: Third
Games Behind: 14½
Manager: Harry Wright

The 1888 season got under way under a cloud of gloom. During spring training, the Phillies' ace pitcher-hitter Charlie Ferguson was stricken with typhoid fever. Although he was at first expected to recover, Ferguson's condition worsened, and nine days after the season began he died at the age of 25.

It was a tragedy beyond definition. The biggest sports hero in the city had died at the height of his career, a career in which he won 99 games in just four seasons. Not only did the the whole city grieve, the entire baseball world did.

Nobody mourned Charlie's loss more than the Phillies, of course. The club

	W	L	G	CG	IP	H	BB	K	ERA
Charlie Buffinton	28	17	46	43	400	324	59	199	1.91
Dan Casey	14	18	33	31	286	298	48	108	3.15
Kid Gleason	7	16	24	23	200	199	53	89	2.84
Ben Sanders	19	10	31	28	275	240	33	121	1.90
Jim Tyng	0	0	1	0	4	8	2	2	4.50
George Wood	0	0	2	0	2	3	1	0	4.50
	69	61	131	125	1,167	1,072	196	519	2.38

Shutouts: Sanders (4), Buffinton (3), Casey, Gleason

	G	AB	R	H	2B	3B	HR	RBI	SB	AVG
Ed Andrews (CF)	124	528	75	126	14	4	3	44	35	.239
Charlie Bastian (2B)	80	275	30	53	4	1	1	17	12	.193
Cupid Childs	2	4	0	0	0	0	0	0	0	.000
Jack Clements (C)	86	326	26	80	8	4	1	32	3	.245
Ed Delahanty	74	290	40	66	12	2	1	31	38	.228
Sid Farrar (1B)	131	508	53	124	24	7	1	53	21	.244
Jim Fogarty (RF)	121	454	72	107	14	6	1	35	58	.236
Gid Gardner	1	3	0	2	0	0	0	1	0	.667
Kid Gleason	24	83	4	17	2	0	0	5	3	.205
John Grim	2	7	0	1	0	0	0	0	0	.143
Bill Hallman	18	63	5	13	4	1	0	6	1	.206
Art Irwin (SS)	125	448	51	98	12	4	0	28	19	.219
Deacon McGuire	12	51	7	17	4	2	0	11	0	.333
Joe Mulvey (3B)	100	398	37	86	12	3	0	39	18	.216
Ben Sanders	57	236	26	58	11	2	1	25	13	.246
Pop Schriver	40	134	15	26	5	2	1	23	2	.194
Woodie Wagenhorst	2	8	2	1	0	0	0	0	0	.125
George Wood (LF)	106	433	67	99	19	6	6	15	20	.229
	131	4,528	535	1,021	151	46	15		246	.225

tried gamely to overcome its grief, as well as to overcome the loss on the field of its top player.

"We've got to win now, just for poor Charlie's sake," the players told each other.

In an attempt to fill Ferguson's spot on the mound—a virtual impossibility—the Phillies signed a tough little 21-year-old from Camden, New Jersey. His name was Kid Gleason, and he would go on to an outstanding 22-year career, first as a pitcher and then as a second baseman. But the bantam hurler, who would also achieve notoriety as the manager of the 1919 Chicago Black Sox, could post only a 7–16 record in his first year.

Charlie Buffinton (28–17), Dan Casey (14–18), and another new hurler, Ben Sanders (19–10), bought from Canton, handled the pitching chores. But without Ferguson, it was not the same.

To compound the problem, manager Harry Wright had declared at the outset of spring training, "Ferguson will play second base in any game that he doesn't pitch. We're always stronger with Charlie at second; he's the best second baseman in the league."

Neither that statement nor the fact that he had to fill in at second for a hero did much for the confidence of Charlie Bastian, the man who was assigned to play second. Bastian hit below .200 and fielded poorly.

"We've got to get somebody in there for Bastian," Wright said. "He's losing too many games for us."

"There's a fellow playing for Wheeling in the Tri-State league that's going very well," president Al Reach replied. "They tell me he is quite a hitter. His name is Delahanty."

"You better get him quick," Wright said. "We need somebody who can hit."

In July, Reach shelled out an uncommonly high sum for the era, $1,900, to buy the minor league hotshot. Ed Delahanty was hitting .408 at the time. When he reported to the Phillies, he was immediately inserted into the lineup at second base.

Delahanty didn't hit well his first season, registering only a .228 average. In fact, the whole team hit poorly, ranking next to last in the league in home runs and average.

The New York Giants walked off with the pennant, with the Chicago White Stockings finishing a distant second and the Phillies third. The Phillies had an especially tough time with the Giants, losing 14 of 19 games, including eight of nine at the Polo Grounds.

When Reach asked Wright how he accounted for so many losses, the manager had a quick answer. "Those Giants," he said, "always seemed to finish with the most runs."

1889

For the fifth year in a row the Phillies finished in the first division in 1889. That wasn't bad for a former expansion team.

Despite their fourth-place status, the season was a disappointment for the club, though, its record dipping under .500 for the first time since 1884.

Manager Harry Wright still hadn't figured out how to score more runs than the New York Giants. The Polo Grounders won their second straight pennant, and again handled the Phillies easily, winning 12 out of 18 games, including seven out of eight at Coogan's Bluff.

Probably the most important matter in which the Phillies were involved all year was the acquisition of Sam Thompson from the Detroit Wolverines. Although they had won the pennant in 1887, the Detroits folded after the 1888 season. Before they did, the club's owners sold off their top players.

The Phillies landed Thompson in what was considered a tremendous coup. Big Sam had hit .372 the year Detroit won the title, and was regarded as one of the league's finest hitters.

Although his .296 average was not up to par for him, Thompson maintained his reputation as an excellent power hitter in his first year with the

Record: 63–64
Finish: Fourth
Games Behind: 20½
Manager: Harry Wright

	W	L	G	CG	IP	H	BB	K	ERA
Dave Anderson	0	1	5	1	23	30	14	8	7.43
Charlie Buffinton	28	16	47	37	380	390	121	153	3.24
Dan Casey	6	10	20	15	153	170	72	65	3.76
Bill Day	0	3	4	2	19	16	23	20	5.21
Jim Fogarty	0	0	4	0	4	4	2	0	9.00
Kid Gleason	9	15	29	15	205	242	97	64	5.58
Ben Sanders	19	18	44	34	350	406	96	123	3.55
George Wood	0	0	1	0	1	2	0	2	18.00
Pete Wood	1	1	3	2	19	28	3	8	5.21
	63	64	130	106	1,153	1,288	428	443	4.00

Shutouts: Buffinton (2), Casey, Sanders

	G	AB	R	H	2B	3B	HR	RBI	SB	AVG
Ed Andrews	10	39	10	11	1	0	0	7	7	.282
Jack Clements (C)	78	310	51	88	17	1	4	35	3	.284
Harry Decker	11	30	4	3	0	0	0	2	1	.100
Ed Delahanty	56	246	37	72	13	3	0	27	19	.293
Sid Farrar (1B)	130	477	70	128	22	2	3	58	28	.268
Jim Fogarty (CF)	128	499	107	129	15	17	3	54	(99)	.259
Bill Hallman (SS)	119	462	67	117	21	8	2	60	20	.253
Art Irwin	18	73	9	16	5	0	0	10	6	.219
Joe Mulvey (3B)	129	544	77	157	21	9	6	77	23	.289
Al Myers (2B)	75	305	52	82	14	2	0	28	8	.269
Pop Schriver	55	211	24	58	10	0	1	19	5	.265
Sam Thompson (RF)	128	533	103	158	36	4	(20)	111	24	.296
Piggy Ward	7	25	0	4	1	0	0	4	3	.160
George Wood (LF)	97	422	77	106	21	4	5	53	17	.251
	130	4,695	742	1,248	215	52	44		353	.266

Phillies by leading the league in home runs. Thompson's 20 homers were the most ever hit up to that point in the National League.

The purchase of Thompson meant that the Phillies now had two-thirds of the group that would become known as one of the greatest outfields of all time. Ed Delahanty, the first of the three future Hall of Famers to arrive, was still struggling in 1889, though.

Plagued by injuries, Delahanty played in only 56 games. But at least he was starting to hit more. His average climbed to .293.

Third baseman Joe Mulvey (.289) and lefthanded catcher Jack Clements (.284) also had decent years at the plate, and center fielder Jim Fogarty led the National League with an eye-popping 42 assists.

Charlie Buffinton (28–16) and Ben Sanders (19–18) were the only pitchers to perform respectably. In his last season in the National League, Dan Casey would continue his slide, falling to a 6–10 record. And Kid Gleason, still learning the game, had only a 9–15 mark.

The season was also marked by an internal dispute. Art Irwin, the shortstop and captain, feuded with Wright. Irwin's discontent with his manager resulted first in his being benched, and then in his being sold to Washington.

1890

Record: 78–54
Finish: Third
Games Behind: 9½
Managers: Harry Wright, Jack Clements, Al Reach, Bob Allen

There have been other years of turmoil in the major leagues, but 1890 ranks at the top of the list, right up there with 1919 and 1981. It was the year of the first substantial players' revolt, and it had a lasting effect on the Phillies as well as the entire National League.

A long-simmering feud between players and owners involving salaries finally broke out in 1890. The players had formed a union called the National Brotherhood of Professional Baseball Players. With substantial financial backing, the union had formed its own league, the Players' League, and signed many of the men from the National League.

The Players' League awarded itself franchises in most of the existing National League cities. Naturally, Philadelphia got a team. With the Athletics in the American Association still hanging on, the city had three professional ball clubs.

Although the Phillies lost a number of key players to the union league, they didn't lose as many as some teams. Nevertheless, the jumpers included Charlie Buffinton, the players' team representative who was actually awarded the new franchise, Jim Fogarty, one of the leaders in the union revolt, Sid Farrar, George Wood, Ben Sanders, Billy Hallman, Joe Mulvey, and Ed Delahanty. The last two became known as triple jumpers, infuriating Phillies' owners Al Reach and John Rogers by going to the Players' League, being lured back to the Phillies with bigger contracts, then upping the ante and going back to the Players' League.

The Phillies would have lost more players, but a few such as Sam Thompson, Jack Clements, and Al Myers were persuaded to return to the club with higher salaries after originally signing with the rebel league.

Kid Gleason was one of the few players who remained loyal to the Phillies. "Harry Wright gave me my chance two years ago when I was just a fresh kid playing coal towns, and I'm not running out on him now," Gleason said.

It was a good thing for the Phillies that he didn't. As virtually the only experienced pitcher on the team, Gleason came of age with a 38–17 record, working 60 games and 506 innings, and hurling 54 complete games. To Gleason's record, newcomer Tom Vickery added a 24–22 mark.

Even without the players' rebellion, it would still have been a season of torment. Teams were coming and going in the National League, and in 1890 the Brooklyn Dodgers and Cincinnati Red Stockings left the dying American Association to join the Nationals. In this year of depleted rosters, Brooklyn won the pennant after having won the flag the year before in the AA.

Compounding the Phillies' problems was the fact that Wright missed a large part of the season because of a serious eye problem. Harry piloted the team at the beginning and at the end of the season, but in between the Phillies used three other managers, including owner Al Reach and players Jack Clements and Bob Allen, who managed for a combined total of 65 games.

The Phillies, as did all teams, had patched together a lineup, but they had a 16-game winning streak, and stayed in the race until nearly the end of the season.

One of the team's key reserves, purchased at mid-season from the financially troubled Pittsburgh club, was outfielder Billy Sunday. An eight-year veteran who hit .261 in a Phillies uniform, Sunday left baseball at the end of the

	W	L	G	CG	IP	H	BB	K	ERA
Dave Anderson	1	1	3	1	19	31	11	7	7.58
Sumner Bowman	0	0	1	0	8	11	2	2	7.88
John Coleman	0	1	1	0	2	4	3	2	27.00
Bill Day	1	1	4	2	24	26	12	9	3.00
Duke Esper	5	0	5	4	41	40	17	15	3.07
Kid Gleason	38	17	60	54	506	479	167	222	2.63
John McFetridge	1	0	1	1	9	5	2	4	1.00
Phenomenal Smith	8	12	24	19	204	209	89	81	4.28
Billy Sunday	0	0	1	0	0	2	0	0	∞
Tom Vickery	24	22	46	41	382	405	184	162	3.44
	78	54	133	122	1,195	1,210	486	507	3.32

Shutouts: Gleason (6), Smith, Vickery

	G	AB	R	H	2B	3B	HR	RBI	SB	AVG
Bob Allen (SS)	133	456	69	103	15	11	1	57	13	.226
Eddie Burke (CF)	100	430	85	113	16	11	4	50	38	.263
Jack Clements (C)	97	381	64	120	23	8	7	74	10	.315
Harry Decker	5	19	5	7	1	0	0	2	4	.368
Bill Grey	34	128	20	31	8	4	0	21	5	.242
Billy Hamilton (LF)	123	496	133	161	13	9	2	49	(102)	.325
Ed Mayer (3B)	117	484	49	117	25	5	1	70	20	.242
Al McCauley (1B)	112	418	63	102	25	7	1	42	8	.244
Frank Motz	1	2	1	0	0	0	0	3	1	.000
Al Myers (2B)	117	487	95	135	29	7	2	81	44	.277
Pop Schriver	57	223	37	61	9	6	0	35	9	.274
Billy Sunday	31	119	26	31	3	1	0	18	26	.261
Sam Thompson (RF)	132	549	116	(172)	(41)	9	4	102	25	.313
	133	4,707	823	1,267	(220)	78	23		335	(.269)

season and embarked on a career that would earn him international acclaim as an evangelist.

Another newcomer to the Phillies was a blazing-fast outfielder picked up from the American Association's Kansas City team. His name was Billy Hamilton and he would become the third of the Phillies Hall of Fame outfield.

Hamilton, later to be rated as one of the finest base stealers ever to play the game, swiped 102 bases and led the Phillies with a .325 average. Clements (.315) and Thompson (.313) were right behind.

Despite their difficulties, the Phillies had an exciting squad, one that fans flocked to see, even with competition from the other two Philadelphia teams. The Phillies franchise was considered the strongest organization in the league in 1890, and many credited the club with holding up the rest of the league in the face of numerous faltering franchises and poor attendance in most other cities.

1891

Record: 68–69
Finish: Fourth
Games Behind: 18½
Manager: Harry Wright

With baseball returning to normal, the Players' League having folded after one season, the Phillies figured that 1891 would be their year.

One of the reasons was that for the first time the club would be able to put its brilliant outfield on the field together. In the previous year, Billy Hamilton had staked a claim as one of the superior outfielders in the league. Sam Thompson had long been established, and Ed Delahanty had come back to the team.

After a year in the Players' League, Delahanty and Jim Fogarty were the only two players taken back by the Phillies. The team's management refused to allow the others back into the fold, which proved to be their downfall.

"Fogarty stays on the payroll," co-owner John Rogers said. "But I don't want any of the others, Buffinton, Wood, Farrar—above all, not Buffinton."

Fogarty was ill and was re-signed for sentimental reasons. But he died of tuberculosis at age 27 before he was able to suit up again for the Phillies.

In Delahanty's case, Big Ed had finally begun to hit well and was simply too

	W	L	G	CG	IP	H	BB	K	ERA
Ed Cassian	1	3	6	3	38	40	16	10	2.84
Duke Esper	20	15	39	25	296	302	121	108	3.56
Kid Gleason	24	22	53	40	418	431	165	100	3.51
Ed Gormley	0	1	1	1	8	10	5	2	5.63
Timothy Keefe	3	6	11	9	78	84	28	35	3.92
Mike Kilroy	0	2	3	0	10	15	4	3	9.90
Bill Kling	4	2	12	4	75	90	32	26	4.32
Lefty Saylor	0	0	1	0	3	2	0	0	6.00
John Schultze	0	1	6	0	15	18	11	4	6.60
Phenomenal Smith	1	1	3	0	19	20	8	3	4.26
John Thornton	15	16	37	23	269	268	115	52	3.68
	68	69	138	105	1,229	1,280	505	343	3.73

Shutouts: Esper, Gleason, Thornton

	G	AB	R	H	2B	3B	HR	RBI	SB	AVG
Bob Allen (SS)	118	438	46	97	7	4	1	51	12	.221
Charlie Bastian	1	0	0	0	0	0	0	0	0	.000
Willard Brown (1B)	115	441	62	107	20	4	0	50	7	.243
Jack Clements (C)	107	423	58	131	29	4	4	75	3	.310
Ed Delahanty (CF)	128	543	92	132	19	9	5	86	25	.243
Jerry Denny	19	73	5	21	1	1	0	11	1	.288
Joe Donohue	6	22	2	7	1	0	0	2	0	.318
Jocko Fields	8	30	4	7	2	1	0	5	0	.233
Lew Graulich	7	26	2	8	0	0	0	3	0	.308
Bill Grey	23	75	11	18	0	0	0	7	3	.240
Billy Hamilton (LF)	133	527	(141)	(179)	23	7	2	60	(111)	(.340)
Ed Mayer	68	268	24	50	2	4	0	31	7	.187
Harry Morelock	4	14	1	1	0	0	0	0	0	.071
Al Myers (2B)	135	514	67	118	27	2	2	69	8	.230
Walt Plock	2	5	2	2	0	0	0	0	0	.400
Bill Shindle (3B)	103	415	68	87	13	1	0	38	17	.210
Sam Thompson (RF)	133	554	108	163	23	10	7	90	29	.294
	138	4,929	756	1,244	180	51	21		232	.252

promising for the Phillies to let slip away. While playing in 1890 at Cleveland, he had been used mostly at shortstop. But when he returned to Philadelphia, he was shifted to center field, and Hamilton was moved to left.

Hamilton hit .340, which was good enough to lead the league in batting. It was the first batting championship for a Phillies player. In addition to his hitting exploits, Sliding Billy stole 111 bases, a National League record that still stands.

The Phillies got good pitching from Kid Gleason (24–22) and Duke Esper (20–15), but they didn't have much after that. Manager Harry Wright used 11 pitchers during the season, an unheard of number for that era. The Phillies even tried the once-great hurler Tim Keefe, purchased from the New York Giants, but he was a flop with a 3–6 mark.

Because of their weak pitching, the Phillies pulled in a distant fourth while the Boston Beaneaters ran off with the pennant. The Phillies' finish launched a streak of four straight times in fourth place.

Just as the Players' League had folded the year before, the American Association ended its 10-year existence in 1892 and merged with the National League.

That gave the Phillies undisputed possession of Philadelphia. The rival Athletics of the old AA were merged with the Washington club.

The merger of the two leagues also resulted in some strange player transfers, one of which sent ace pitcher Kid Gleason to the St. Louis Browns, one of the new entries from the old AA. The Phillies, however, picked up several players from the Athletics, including their former triple-jumping third baseman Joe Mulvey, pitcher Gus Weyhing, and catcher-infielder-outfielder Lave Cross, who had the distinction during his 21-year career of playing for four Philadelphia professional teams—the Athletics of the AA, the Quakers of the Players' League, the Phillies, and the Athletics of the American League.

The Phillies also grabbed pitcher Wilfred (Kid) Carsey from Washington. Carsey would have several fine seasons with the Phillies, and 1892 was one of them. He posted a 19–16 record.

The main hurler was Weyhing, whose 32–21 record gave him four straight 30-win seasons. To go along with that, Tim Keefe, who had once won 19 games in a row for the Giants, made a comeback with a 19–16 mark.

1892

Record: 87–66
Finish: Fourth
Games Behind: 16½
Manager: Harry Wright

	W	L	G	CG	IP	H	BB	K	ERA
Kid Carsey	19	16	43	30	318	320	104	76	3.11
Duke Esper	11	6	21	14	160	171	58	45	3.43
Timothy Keefe	19	16	39	31	313	264	100	127	2.36
Phil Knell	5	5	11	7	80	87	35	43	4.05
Jack Taylor	1	0	1	1	8	4	3	3	1.13
John Thornton	0	2	3	1	12	16	17	2	12.75
Gus Weyhing	32	21	59	46	470	411	168	202	2.66
	87	66	155	131	1,379	1,297	492	502	2.93

Shutouts: Weyhing (6), Keefe (3), Carsey

	G	AB	R	H	2B	3B	HR	RBI	SB	AVG
Bob Allen (SS)	152	563	77	128	20	14	2	64	15	.227
Jack Clements (C)	109	402	50	106	25	6	8	76	7	.264
Roger Connor (1B)	155	564	123	166	(37)	11	12	73	22	.294
Jerry Connors	1	3	0	0	0	0	0	0	0	.000
Lave Cross	140	541	84	149	15	10	4	69	18	.275
Ed Delahanty (CF)	123	477	79	146	30	(21)	6	91	29	.306
Tom Dowse	16	54	3	10	0	0	0	6	1	.185
Bill Hallman (2B)	138	586	106	171	27	10	2	84	19	.292
Billy Hamilton (LF)	139	554	132	183	21	7	3	53	57	.330
Harry Morelock	1	3	0	0	0	0	0	0	0	.000
Joe Mulvey	25	98	9	14	1	1	0	4	2	.143
Charlie Reilly (3B)	91	331	42	65	7	3	1	24	13	.196
Dummy Stephenson	8	37	4	10	3	0	0	5	0	.270
Sam Thompson (RF)	153	609	109	186	28	11	9	104	28	.305
	155	5,413	860	1,420	(225)	95	(50)		216	(.262)

The most prominent development, though, was that for the first time all three outfield stars hit over .300. Billy Hamilton's .330 was second in the league to Dan Brouther's .335, Sam Thompson was second in the circuit in RBI (104) and hits (186) to Brouthers in each category while batting .305, and Ed Delahanty led the loop in slugging average (.495) and triples (21) while hitting .306.

Roger Connor, a veteran first baseman bought from the Giants, hit .294 and led the club with 12 home runs, and second baseman Bill Hallman added a .292 average. All the hitting helped to give the Phillies a tie for first place in team batting average and undisputed possession of first place in slugging average.

Yet in spite of all their big bats, good pitching, a record-tying 16-game winning streak, and the presence of five future Hall of Famers—Connor, Keefe, Delahanty, Hamilton, and Thompson—the Phillies managed to finish only fourth again in the overall standings, trailing the Boston Beaneaters, Cleveland Spiders, and Brooklyn Dodgers. The club was especially weak on the road, even losing five out of seven to the 11th-place St. Louis Browns, a point which irked co-owner John Rogers.

"Why are we so terrible on the road?" Rogers quizzed manager Harry Wright. "Once the team gets away from Broad and Huntington, it acts like a bunch of stray, befuddled cats."

"The home team," answered the ever-patient Wright, "always has the edge."

1893

Record: 72–57
Finish: Fourth
Games Behind: 14
Manager: Harry Wright

Before 1893 the distance between home plate and the pitcher's mound was 50 feet. Between that and the so-called dead ball, pitchers had a decided edge on hitters.

But the low-scoring, low-hitting games that often resulted had a way of boring even the fans of the Gay Nineties. Baseball, they complained, had become so dominated by the pitchers and so devoid of offense that it was dull.

As questionable as that attitude might be considered today, the National League leaders took it seriously enough that they moved the mound back to 60 feet, 6 inches, with the start of the 1893 season.

The immediate effect was to liberate the hitters to the point that the advantage swung to them. Nowhere was that more evident than in Philadelphia.

	W	L	G	CG	IP	H	BB	K	ERA
Kid Carsey	20	15	39	30	318	375	124	50	4.81
Timothy Keefe	10	7	22	17	178	202	79	53	4.40
Gus McGinnis	1	3	5	4	37	39	17	12	4.38
Frank O'Connor	0	0	3	0	4	2	9	0	11.25
John Sharrott	4	2	12	2	56	53	33	11	4.50
Jack Taylor	10	9	25	14	170	189	77	41	4.24
Tom Vickery	4	5	13	7	80	100	37	15	5.40
Gus Weyhing	23	16	42	33	345	399	145	101	4.75
	72	57	133	107	1,189	1,359	521	283	4.68

Shutouts: Weyhing (2), Carsey, McGinnis

	G	AB	R	H	2B	3B	HR	RBI	SB	AVG
Bob Allen (SS)	124	471	86	126	19	12	8	90	8	.268
Jack Boyle (1B)	116	504	105	144	29	9	4	81	22	.286
Jack Clements (C)	94	376	64	107	20	3	17	80	3	.285
Lave Cross	96	415	81	124	17	6	4	78	18	.299
Ed Delahanty (LF)	132	595	145	219	35	18	(19)	(146)	37	.368
Bill Hallman (2B)	132	596	119	183	28	7	5	76	22	.307
Billy Hamilton (CF)	82	355	110	135	22	7	5	44	43	(.380)
Charlie Reilly (3B)	104	416	64	102	16	7	4	56	13	.245
Jack Sharrott	50	152	25	38	4	3	1	22	6	.250
Sam Thompson (RF)	131	600	130	(222)	(37)	13	11	126	18	.370
Tuck Turner	36	155	32	50	4	3	1	13	7	.323
	133	5,151	(1,011)	(1,553)	(246)	90	(80)		202	(.301)

The fearsome outfield trio hit like it never had before. With Billy Hamilton, shifted back to center field, again leading the league in hitting, the Phillies captured the top three spots in the National League batting race. Hamilton hit .380, Sam Thompson hit .370, and Ed Delahanty hit .368.

Delahanty led the league for the first time in home runs (19), RBI (146), total bases (347), and slugging average (.583). Thompson finished first in hits (222) and doubles (37).

Altogether, Phillie players won each of the seven main hitting categories, and placed second in five of the seven.

And there was more to the offense than that provided by the three outfielders. Catcher Jack Clements hit 17 home runs, second in the league, second baseman Bill Hallman had a .307 average, reserve outfielder Tuck Turner hit .323, and a new first baseman, Honest John Boyle, obtained in a trade with the New York Giants for Roger Connor, added a .286 average which included six hits in six at bats in an 11-inning game with the Chicago White Stockings.

It was an awesome attack. The Phillies as a team led the league in home runs (80), batting average (.301), slugging average (.430), runs (1,011), and doubles (246). The team also had the fewest errors and paced the circuit in fielding percentage.

Yet it was still stuck in a rut in fourth place. The Boston Beaneaters won their third consecutive pennant, and the Pittsburgh Pirates vaulted into second place, with the Cleveland Spiders finishing third.

The Phillies finished only one and one-half games out of third. Perhaps with a stronger number-three pitcher, they could have finished higher. As it was, though, only Gus Weyhing (23–16) and Kid Carsey (20–15) gave the club consistent winning efforts. The aging Tim Keefe and a youngster, Jack Taylor, won 10 apiece.

Man for man, the Phillies thought they had the best team in the National League. Yet year in and year out they knocked on the door of the league lead, but never quite made it to the top.

By 1894 the Phillies' owners had had enough of such near misses. It was time, they decided, to get a new manager.

Reluctantly, they fired Harry Wright, the old baseball pioneer who had been the club's skipper since 1884. He was replaced by Arthur Irwin, a former Phillies shortstop and captain whose feuding with Wright had led to his being sent to Washington in 1889. Since then, Irwin had managed Washington in the National League and Boston in the American Association, winning the pennant with the latter. But never had he piloted the kinds of hitters he inherited in Philadelphia.

The 1894 Phillies hit a league-leading .349, far and away the highest team batting average in major league history. As usual, the Phillies' hitting attack was led by the outfield threesome of Billy Hamilton, Ed Delahanty, and Sam Thompson.

This season the trio was particularly awesome. Hamilton, who had a 36-game hitting streak and stole seven bases in one game during the season, batted .404.

Thompson hit .407 and Delahanty registered .404. But neither had the highest average on the team, much less among Phillies' outfielders. Reserve Tuck Turner belted out a .416 average, second in the league to Hugh Duffy's .438. Turner played frequently, because of injuries to Thompson and Delahanty.

The Phillies captured four of the five top spots in the batting race. Hamilton set an all-time major league record that still stands with 192 runs. He also led the circuit in stolen bases with 98. Thompson (141) and Delahanty (131) ranked second and third in the league in RBI, Duffy also winning that title as well as most of the other major hitting categories that year.

1894

Record: 71–57
Finish: Fourth
Games Behind: 18
Manager: Arthur Irwin

	W	L	G	CG	IP	H	BB	K	ERA
Al Burris	0	0	1	0	5	14	2	0	18.00
Nixey Callahan	1	2	9	1	34	64	17	9	10.06
Kid Carsey	18	12	35	26	277	349	102	41	5.56
Jack Fanning	1	3	5	2	33	45	20	7	8.16
Frank Figgemeyer	0	1	1	1	8	12	4	2	11.25
George Haddock	4	3	10	5	56	63	34	7	5.79
George Harper	6	6	12	7	86	128	49	24	5.34
John Johnson	1	1	4	2	33	44	15	10	6.27
Alex Jones	1	0	1	1	9	10	0	2	2.00
Al Lukens	0	1	3	1	15	26	10	0	10.20
Jack Scheible	0	1	1	0	⅓	6	2	0	189.00
Jack Taylor	23	13	41	31	298	347	96	76	4.08
Tuck Turner	0	0	1	0	6	9	2	3	7.50
Gus Weyhing	16	14	38	25	266	365	116	81	5.82
	71	57	131	102	1,125	1,482	469	262	5.64

Shutouts: Weyhing (2), Taylor

	G	AB	R	H	2B	3B	HR	RBI	SB	AVG
Bob Allen	40	149	26	38	10	3	0	19	4	.255
Jack Boyle (1B)	114	495	98	149	21	10	4	88	21	.301
Dick Buckley	43	160	18	47	7	3	1	26	0	.294
Jack Clements (C)	45	159	26	55	6	5	3	36	6	.346
Lave Cross (3B)	119	529	123	204	34	9	7	125	21	.386
Ed Delahanty (LF)	114	489	147	199	39	18	4	131	21	.407
Tom Delahanty	1	4	0	1	0	0	0	0	0	.250
Mike Grady	60	190	45	69	13	8	0	40	3	.363
Bill Hallman (2B)	119	505	107	156	19	7	0	66	36	.309
Billy Hamilton (CF)	129	544	(192)	220	25	15	4	87	(98)	.404
Art Irwin	1	0	0	0	0	0	0	0	0	.000
Tom Murray	1	2	0	0	0	0	0	0	0	.000
Charlie Reilly	39	135	21	40	1	2	0	19	9	.296
Joe Sullivan (SS)	75	304	63	107	10	8	3	63	10	.352
Sam Thompson (RF)	99	437	108	178	29	27	13	141	24	.407
Tuck Turner	80	339	91	141	21	9	1	82	11	.416
Joe Yingling	1	4	0	1	0	0	0	0	0	.250
	131	4,967	1,143	(1,732)	252	131	40		273	(.349)

The outfielders weren't the only Phillies to hit. Lave Cross hit .386. In fact, the lowest average among regulars was John Boyle's .301.

In one game against the Louisville Colonels, the Phillies unleashed all their batting fury, smashing 36 hits, getting 49 total bases, and rolling to a 29–4 win. It was the third time in their history the Phillies scored that many runs. Thompson hit for the cycle with a homer, triple, double, and three singles in seven trips to the plate. Amazingly, losing pitcher Jack Wadsworth pitched the whole game.

Despite all the lusty hitting, which also included a six-for-six game by Delahanty, the Phillies again failed to advance above fourth place. Brewery Jack Taylor was the top pitcher with a 23–13 record, Kid Carsey posted an 18–12 mark, and Gus Weyhing was 16–14. But the team's ERA of 5.64 ranked among the highest in the league.

The Phillies, who had to endure a fire that partially destroyed their stadium, were in and out of second place through the early months, but went into a slump, and by the end of July had plummeted to seventh place. A 10-game winning streak in August helped to push them back to fourth. They could get no higher, however, as a final road trip resulted in their losing 11 of 17 games, including the last five contests of the season.

The Baltimore Orioles, featuring such players as John McGraw, Hughie Jennings, Dan Brouthers, Willie Keeler, and Kid Gleason, won the pennant, three games ahead of the New York Giants. The defending champion Boston Beaneaters placed third.

"I always thought when Boston was stopped we'd be the club to stop them," said Phillies' co-owner John Rogers, who had pretty much taken over the operation of the team. "Now the pennant goes to an upstart team of rowdies."

1895

After four seasons in a row in fourth place, the Phillies finally escaped their rut in 1895. They finished third.

The Phillies made a decent run for the pennant all season long before finally settling behind the front-running Baltimore Orioles and runner-up Cleveland Spiders.

It might have been a different order had the Phillies' pitching staff not pulled its usual stunt and come up short. Once again Kid Carsey (24–16) and Jack Taylor (26–14) were the big winners. But there was no consistent winner after them.

One of the main problems was the uselessness of Gus Weyhing. The slender righthander had given the Phillies 71 wins in the previous three seasons, but in 1895 he developed arm trouble and could hardly pitch. After losing decisions in his only two outings, Weyhing was sold to Pittsburgh, which sent him to Louisville.

To fill his spot, the Phillies tried an assortment of young hurlers. The one with the most promise was a big righthander whom the Phillies purchased during the season for $1,000 from Lynchburg of the Virginia League. His name was Al Orth, and he would become an outstanding pitcher for the Phillies and later in the American League.

Orth had an 8–1 record. He was undefeated until the Brooklyn Dodgers beat him in his final start of the season.

As troubled as they were on the mound, the Phillies performed their usual devastation at the plate. Again, the club led the league in hitting with a .330 average, home runs (61), and runs (1,068).

Catcher Jack Clements, who hit well throughout most of his days with the Phillies but who took a back seat to his outfield teammates, joined the ranks of the big hitters with a .394 average. That gave the Phillies three of the loop's top four hitters, Delahanty hitting .404 and Thompson .392.

Thompson led the league in home runs with 18, in RBI with 165, in total bases with 352, and in slugging average with .654. Billy Hamilton, who hit .389, topped the circuit in runs (166) and stolen bases (97).

So devastating was the Phillies' attack that during the season they extended their streak of games without being shut out to 182.

Record: 78–53
Finish: Third
Games Behind: 9½
Manager: Arthur Irwin

	W	L	G	CG	IP	H	BB	K	ERA
Ernie Beam	0	2	9	1	25	33	25	3	11.52
Kid Carsey	24	16	44	35	342	460	118	64	4.92
George Hodson	1	2	4	1	17	27	9	6	9.53
Henry Lampe	0	2	7	2	44	68	33	18	7.57
Con Lucid	6	3	10	7	70	80	35	19	5.91
Willie McGill	10	8	20	13	146	177	81	70	5.55
Al Orth	8	1	11	9	88	103	22	25	3.89
Tom Smith	2	3	11	4	68	76	53	21	6.88
Jack Taylor	26	14	41	33	335	403	83	93	4.49
Gus Weyhing	0	2	2	0	9	23	13	5	20.00
Deke White	1	0	3	1	17	17	13	6	10.06
	78	53	133	106	1,161	1,467	485	330	5.47

Shutouts: Taylor

	G	AB	R	H	2B	3B	HR	RBI	SB	AVG
Jack Boyle (1B)	133	565	90	143	17	4	0	67	13	.253
Dick Buckley	38	112	20	28	6	1	0	14	2	.250
Jack Clements (C)	88	322	64	127	27	2	13	75	3	.394
Lave Cross (3B)	125	535	95	145	26	9	2	101	21	.271
Ed Delahanty (LF)	116	480	149	194	(49)	10	11	106	46	.404
Mike Grady	46	123	21	40	3	1	1	23	5	.325
Bill Hallman (2B)	124	539	94	169	26	5	1	91	16	.314
Billy Hamilton (CF)	123	517	(166)	201	22	6	7	74	(97)	.389
Art Madison	11	34	6	12	3	0	0	8	4	.353
Charlie Reilly	49	179	28	48	6	1	0	25	7	.268
Joe Sullivan (SS)	94	373	75	126	7	3	2	50	15	.338
Sam Thompson (RF)	119	538	131	211	45	21	(18)	(165)	27	.392
Tuck Turner	59	210	51	81	8	6	2	43	14	.386
	133	5,037	(1,068)	(1,664)	(272)	73	(61)		276	(.330)

PHILADELPHIA BASE BALL CLUB, 1895.

The 1895 Phillies.

1896

Record: 62–68
Finish: Eighth
Games Behind: 28½
Manager: Billy Nash

The 1896 season was one in which luck, stupidity, and the breakup of the Phillies all had a significant part.

The season's unusual sequence of events began when manager Arthur Irwin took an offer to manage the New York Giants. Dissatisfied with his performance, the Phillies were probably going to dump him anyway; thus Irwin switched clubs without resistance from the Phillies.

Soon afterward, Billy Hamilton requested a modest raise. But instead of getting more money, he found himself traded to the Boston Beaneaters for their aging captain–third baseman Billy Nash.

A sparkplug on Boston's three pennant-winning teams of the early 1890s, Nash was named to replace Irwin as the Phillies' manager. It wouldn't have mattered what kind of manager Nash became; unloading the brilliant Hamilton ranked as one of the least intelligent trades the Phillies ever made.

The loss of Hamilton spelled disaster. Without their base-stealing leadoff man, the Phillies' offense lost a lot of its thrust. Moreover, Sam Thompson was growing older and slipped to a .298 average.

About the only constant was Ed Delahanty. Still going strong, Big Ed belted out a .397 average in 1896 with 13 home runs and a league-leading RBI total of 126. He also enjoyed the finest game of his career when on July 13 he lashed four home runs and a single and drove in six runs in a game at Chicago. It was only the second time in major league history that a batter had poled four homers in a game. Indicative of the way the Phillies were going, however, they lost the game, 9–8.

It was a strange year in many other respects for the Phillies. They played most of the season with the only lefthanded regular shortstop in baseball history, Billy Hulen. Their first baseman that year was Dan Brouthers, the aging future Hall of Famer whom the Phillies had bought from the Louisville Colonels. Brouthers played only one season for the Phillies, hitting .344 in a limited role.

Delahanty had been filling in a good deal for Brouthers at first. Needing outfield help, the Phillies uncovered a player named Phil Geier whose hitting exploits for the Fall River of New England League were getting rave reviews. After some haggling, the Phillies decided to purchase the outfielder for $1,500, but at the insistence of Fall River owner Charley Marston, they had to take another player named Nap Lajoie, too.

Lajoie became perhaps the most successful throw-in in history. Geier never did much for the Phillies, but Lajoie became an immediate success. Talked into playing first base by Delahanty, Lajoie hit .326 after joining the team at

	W	L	G	CG	IP	H	BB	K	ERA
Kid Carsey	11	11	27	18	187	273	72	36	5.63
Ned Garvin	0	1	2	1	13	19	7	4	7.62
Ad Gumbert	5	3	11	7	77	99	23	14	4.56
Bill Hallman	0	0	1	0	2	4	2	0	18.00
Bert Inks	0	1	3	0	10	21	5	2	8.10
Charlie Jordan	0	0	2	0	5	9	2	3	9.00
Harry Keener	3	11	16	11	113	144	39	28	5.89
Con Lucid	1	4	5	5	42	75	17	3	8.36
Willie McGill	5	4	12	7	80	87	53	29	5.40
Jerry Nops	1	0	1	1	7	11	1	1	5.14
Al Orth	15	10	25	19	196	244	46	23	4.41
Jack Taylor	20	21	45	35	359	459	112	97	4.79
George Wheeler	1	1	3	2	16	18	5	2	3.94
Bill Whitrock	0	1	2	1	9	10	3	1	3.00
	62	68	131	107	1,117	1,473	387	243	5.21

Shutouts: Carsey, Gumbert, Taylor

	G	AB	R	H	2B	3B	HR	RBI	SB	AVG
Jack Boyle	40	154	17	43	4	1	1	28	3	.297
Dan Brouthers (1B)	57	218	42	75	13	3	1	41	7	.344
Jack Clements	57	184	35	66	5	7	5	45	2	.359
Duff Cooley (CF)	64	287	63	88	6	4	2	22	18	.307
Lave Cross	106	406	63	104	23	5	1	73	8	.256
Ed Delahanty (LF)	123	499	131	198	(44)	17	13	(126)	37	.397
Ben Ellis	4	16	0	1	0	0	0	0	0	.063
Bill Gallagher	14	49	9	15	2	0	0	6	0	.306
Phil Geier	17	56	12	13	0	1	0	6	3	.232
Mike Grady (C)	71	242	49	77	20	7	1	44	10	.318
Bill Hallman (2B)	120	469	82	150	21	3	2	83	16	.320
Bill Hulen (SS)	88	339	87	90	18	7	0	38	23	.265
Napoleon Lajoie	39	175	36	57	12	7	4	42	7	.326
Dan Leahy	2	6	0	2	1	0	0	1	0	.333
Sandow Mertes	37	143	20	34	4	4	0	14	19	.238
Billy Nash (3B)	65	227	29	56	9	1	3	30	3	.247
Joe Sullivan	48	191	45	48	5	3	2	24	9	.251
Sam Thompson (RF)	119	517	103	154	28	7	12	100	12	.298
Tuck Turner	13	32	12	7	2	0	0	8	6	.219
	131	4,680	890	1,382	(234)	84	(49)		191	.295

mid-season. Although just 21 years old, he demonstrated awesome talent, both as a hitter and a fielder.

Lajoie went on to become a Hall of Famer, one of four future Hall of Famers on the 1896 Phillie team.

Despite such talent, the Phillies finally ended their long run in the first division. After 11 straight years in the top division, the Phillies tumbled all the way to eighth place. It was the lowest they'd finished since their first year in baseball.

It was obvious after the previous season's eighth-place finish that Billy Nash wasn't the answer to the Phillies' managerial needs. So Billy was sent back to third base, and the club named a new skipper, George Stallings.

A one-time medical school student and the son of a Confederate general, Stallings was a polished gentleman off the field. On the field, he was a raving, swearing tyrant.

Nearly two decades later, Stallings would be the manager of Boston's Miracle Braves in 1914. But in 1897, his first season of running a club, he was strictly an oppressive, devious upstart whose methods and manners quickly became the objects of the players' hatred.

Under such a cloud, it was little wonder that the Phillies finished a sorry 10th in their 12-team league. The players' dislike for the manager and their frequent explosions with him proved more defeating than any enemy pitcher.

Although baseball players of that era were not the most genteel people, even they were appalled by Stallings' tirades, his profanity, and his abusive habits.

1897

Record: 55–77
Finish: Tenth
Games Behind: 38
Manager: George Stallings

	W	L	G	CG	IP	H	BB	K	ERA
Bob Becker	0	2	5	2	24	32	7	10	5.63
Kid Carsey	2	1	4	2	28	35	16	1	5.14
Davey Dunkle	5	2	7	7	62	72	23	9	3.48
Jack Fifield	5	18	27	21	211	263	80	38	5.55
Tom Johnson	1	2	5	1	29	39	12	7	4.66
Tom Lipp	0	1	1	0	3	8	2	1	15.00
Al Orth	14	19	36	29	282	349	82	64	4.63
Tully Sparks	0	1	1	1	8	12	4	0	10.13
Jack Taylor	16	20	40	35	317	376	76	88	4.23
George Wheeler	11	10	26	17	191	229	62	35	3.96
	55	77	134	115	1,155	1,415	364	253	4.61

Shutouts: Orth (2), Taylor (2)

	G	AB	R	H	2B	3B	HR	RBI	SB	AVG
Ed Abbaticchio	3	10	0	3	0	0	0	0	0	.300
Jack Boyle (C)	75	288	37	73	9	1	2	36	3	.253
Jack Clements	55	185	18	44	4	2	6	36	3	.238
Duff Cooley (CF)	133	566	124	186	14	13	4	40	31	.329
Lave Cross (2B)	88	344	37	89	17	5	3	51	10	.259
Ed Delahanty (LF)	129	530	109	200	40	15	5	96	26	.377
Tommy Dowd (RF)	91	391	68	114	14	4	0	43	30	.292
Phil Geier	92	316	51	88	6	2	1	35	19	.278
Sam Gillen (SS)	75	270	32	70	10	3	0	27	2	.259
Mike Grady	4	13	1	2	0	0	0	0	0	.154
Bill Hallman	31	126	16	33	3	0	0	15	1	.262
Napoleon Lajoie (1B)	127	545	107	197	40	23	9	127	20	.361
Kohly Miller	3	11	2	2	0	0	0	1	0	.182
Ed McFarland	38	130	18	29	3	5	1	16	2	.223
Billy Nash (3B)	104	337	45	87	20	2	0	39	4	.258
Frank Shugart	40	163	20	41	8	2	5	25	5	.252
George Stallings	2	9	1	2	1	0	0	0	0	.222
Sam Thompson	3	13	2	3	0	1	0	3	0	.231
	134	4,756	752	1,392	213	83	40		163	.293

The Phillies had some talent still on the scene, too. In his first full season in the majors, Nap Lajoie hit .361, was second in the league in home runs with 19, drove in 127 runs, and led the circuit in slugging average (.578) and total bases (315).

The French cab driver from Woonsocket, Rhode Island, was obviously a player with considerable talent, and it took him only a short time to attract a following in Philadelphia.

Meanwhile, the old hero, Ed Delahanty, continued to roll along, posting a .377 average and ranking among the league leaders in many hitting categories.

Center fielder Duff Cooley, picked up during the previous season from the St. Louis Browns, was the only other regular above .300 with a .329 average.

The pitching left much to be desired. Jack Taylor was still the club's top hurler. After a 20–21 season the year before, he was 16–20 in 1897. Al Orth was 14–19.

Generally, though, the whole season was a disaster. The only teams to finish below the Phillies were the soon-to-be-extinct Louisville Colonels and the St. Louis Browns, who that season had four different managers.

1898

Record: 78–71
Finish: Sixth
Games Behind: 24
Managers: George Stallings, Billy Shettsline

Throughout baseball history, there have been teams that disliked their managers. But few clubs ever hated their skipper more than the Phillies did George Stallings.

The players couldn't stand the very ground he walked on. So intense was their dislike for the heavy-handed pilot that in 1898 the Phillies became the first team in baseball annals to go on strike against their manager.

It happened in mid-June. The players hated Stallings so passionately that they formed a committee to meet with owners Al Reach and John Rogers. The players told the owners that they would not play again for the abusive tyrant.

After the meeting, center fielder Duff Cooley, who headed the group, released a statement. It said, "We are fed up with the way Stallings has been riding us and we decided we had enough of him and would regard him as our manager no longer. For weeks he's been handling us like a lot of cattle. We may not be the best team in the league, but we don't intend to put up with Stallings' tactics."

Reach and Rogers responded to the players' resentment the only way they could. Although Stallings had a year-and-one-half left on his contract, they fired him, reaching a settlement on the remainder of the pact.

In Stallings' place, the Phillies installed Billy Shettsline, a likeable fellow who had worked in a variety of jobs for the club, including secretary, ticket-taker, and bookkeeper, and who eventually became the team's president.

The Phillies had only a 19–27 record when Stallings departed. Under Shettsline, they put together a 59–44 log that was good enough to bring the club home in sixth place, a marked improvement over the previous year.

Before being dethroned, Stallings had made one move that had lasting effects. He pulled Nap Lajoie off first base and converted him into a second baseman, the position at which he would earn Hall of Fame honors.

Once he took command, Shettsline made some important decisions, too. Among his early moves was the purchase of pitcher Frank (Red) Donahue from the St. Louis Browns. The year before Donahue had led the league with 33 losses. With the Phillies, though, it was a different story. Donahue pitched a no-hitter, the second in Phillies' history, beating the Boston Beaneaters, 5–0. He wound up the season with a 17–17 record.

The Phillies also picked up a batch of other players, including pitcher Bill Duggleby, who hit a grand slam home run in his first at bat, and right fielder Elmer Flick, another future Hall of Famer, who had four superb seasons with the Phillies before they peddled him.

Flick was brought in to take the place of the aging Sam Thompson who was in his last year with the Phillies. The rookie hit .302. To that, Ed Delahanty

	W	L	G	CG	IP	H	BB	K	ERA
Bob Becker	0	0	1	0	5	6	5	0	10.80
Bert Conn	0	1	1	0	7	13	2	3	6.43
Red Donahue	17	17	35	33	284	327	80	57	3.55
Bill Duggleby	3	3	9	4	54	70	18	12	5.50
Davey Dunkle	1	4	12	4	68	83	38	21	7.01
Jack Fifield	11	9	21	18	171	170	60	31	3.32
Ed Murphy	1	2	7	2	30	41	10	8	5.10
Al Orth	15	13	32	25	250	290	53	52	3.02
Wiley Piatt	24	14	39	33	306	285	97	121	3.18
George Wheeler	6	8	15	10	112	155	36	20	4.18
	78	71	150	129	1,288	1,440	399	325	3.72

Shutouts: Piatt (6), Fifield (2), Donahue, Orth

	G	AB	R	H	2B	3B	HR	RBI	SB	AVG
Ed Abbaticchio	25	92	9	21	4	0	0	14	4	.228
Jack Boyle	6	22	0	2	0	1	0	3	0	.091
Duff Cooley (CF)	149	629	123	196	24	12	4	55	17	.312
Monte Cross (SS)	149	525	68	135	25	5	1	50	20	.257
Ed Delahanty (LF)	144	548	115	183	36	9	4	92	(58)	.334
Klondike Douglass (1B)	146	582	105	150	26	4	2	48	18	.258
Kid Elberfeld	14	38	1	9	4	0	0	7	0	.237
Newt Fisher	9	26	0	3	1	0	0	0	1	.115
Elmer Flick (RF)	134	453	84	137	16	13	8	81	23	.302
Dave Fultz	19	55	7	10	2	2	0	5	1	.182
Napoleon Lajoie (2B)	147	608	113	197	(43)	11	6	(127)	25	.324
Bill Lauder (3B)	97	361	42	95	14	7	2	67	6	.263
Ed McFarland (C)	121	429	65	121	21	5	3	71	4	.282
Morgan Murphy	25	86	6	17	3	0	0	11	0	.198
Billy Nash	20	70	9	17	2	1	0	9	0	.243
George Stallings	1	0	1	0	0	0	0	0	0	.000
Sam Thompson	14	63	14	22	5	3	1	15	2	.349
	150	5,118	823	1,431	(238)	81	33		182	.280

added his usual outstanding season with a .334 average, while Lajoie hit .324 and led the league with 127 RBI.

A rookie pitcher, Wiley Piatt, was the club's top winner with a 24–14 record. He also tied for the league lead in shutouts with six.

Another new player, veteran shortstop Monte Cross (no relation to the Phils' former third baseman Lave Cross), made 93 errors, but it was 13 less than the National League record set five years earlier by Washington's Joe Sullivan.

1899

Record: 94–58
Finish: Third
Games Behind: 9
Manager: Billy Shettsline

Following a three-year hiatus in the National League dungeon, the Phillies made a brilliant comeback in 1899 with what some called the greatest all-around team in the club's history.

It was a team that had everything—strong pitching, outstanding hitting, and the ability to run and field. It was a squad with hardly a noticeable flaw.

The Phillies won more games in 1899 than any team in club history until the 1976 club won 101. Although it finished in third place, it was in the pennant race throughout the season, and was beaten out of second by the Boston Beaneaters by just one game. The Brooklyn Dodgers walked away with the pennant with a team led by Wee Willie Keeler and Joe Kelley.

After a long period of mediocrity, the pitching staff finally came together. It had three 20-game winners, including Wiley Piatt (23–15), Red Donahue (21–8), and Chick Fraser (21–12), acquired from Cleveland. A fourth hurler, Al Orth (14–3), had the league's lowest ERA with a 2.48.

The Phillies' outfield was almost as devastating as the ones of the early 1890s. Ed Delahanty had the finest season of his career, winning his first batting title with a .410 average, his third .400-plus season. Big Ed also led the league in RBI (137), slugging (.585), total bases (335), hits (238), and doubles (55) in one of the most glittering seasons any Phillie ever had.

The other two outfielders also had superb seasons. In his second year Elmer Flick hit a lusty .342 with 98 RBI, and rookie Roy Thomas, who moved from the University of Pennsylvania nine to the Phillies' starting lineup, added a .325 mark. Thomas, a pesky leadoff batter known for his ability to foul off pitches, would go on to a memorable nine-year career with the Phillies. He was

	W	L	G	CG	IP	H	BB	K	ERA
Bill Bernhard	6	6	21	10	132	120	36	23	2.66
Red Donahue	21	8	35	27	279	292	63	51	3.39
Jack Fifield	3	8	14	9	93	110	36	8	4.06
Chick Fraser	21	12	35	29	271	278	85	68	3.35
Bill Magee	3	5	9	7	70	82	32	4	5.66
Al Orth	14	3	21	13	145	149	19	35	(2.48)
Wiley Piatt	23	15	39	31	305	323	86	89	3.45
George Wheeler	3	1	6	3	39	44	13	3	6.00
	94	58	154	129	1,333	1,398	370	281	3.47

Shutouts: Donahue (4), Fraser (4), Orth (3), Piatt (2), Bernhard, Fifield

	G	AB	R	H	2B	3B	HR	RBI	SB	AVG
Pearce Chiles	97	338	57	108	28	7	2	76	6	.320
Duff Cooley (1B)	94	406	75	112	15	8	1	31	15	.276
Henry Croft	2	7	0	1	0	0	0	0	0	.143
Monte Cross (SS)	154	557	85	143	25	6	3	65	26	.257
Ed Delahanty (LF)	146	581	135	(238)	(55)	9	9	(137)	30	(.410)
Joe Dolan	61	222	27	57	6	3	1	30	3	.257
Klondike Douglass	77	275	26	70	6	6	0	27	7	.255
Elmer Flick (RF)	127	485	98	166	22	11	2	98	31	.342
Dave Fultz	2	5	0	2	0	0	0	0	1	.400
Bill Goeckel	37	141	17	37	3	1	0	16	6	.262
Napoleon Lajoie (2B)	77	312	70	118	19	9	6	70	13	.378
Bill Lauder (3B)	151	583	74	156	17	6	3	90	15	.268
Ed McFarland (C)	96	324	59	108	22	10	1	57	9	.333
Red Owens	8	21	0	1	0	0	0	1	0	.048
Roy Thomas (CF)	150	547	137	178	12	4	0	47	42	.325
	154	5,353	(916)	(1,613)	(241)	84	30		212	(.301)

The 1899 Phillies were no dogs, finishing in third place in the National League.

the first major leaguer to wear sliding gloves, which protected his hands on head-first slides.

Catcher Ed McFarland, another player plucked from the St. Louis Browns, added a .333 average, while second baseman Nap Lajoie hit .378, although his season was limited by injuries. Many felt that had Lajoie played a full season instead of about half of it, the Phillies would have won the pennant in a runaway.

Overall, the Phillies hit .301 as a team, leading the league in average as well as runs.

The club was so strong in every department that as late as the 1950s, *The Sporting News* called it the greatest of all Phillies teams, even better than the 1915 and 1950 championship clubs.

The Phillies fans of 1899 were justifiably proud of their team, and they supported it in large numbers. When the season ended, most people had the feeling that the Phillies' time had finally come. As the 20th century began, a pennant seemed to be the club's next step.

In the last year of the calm before the American League storm, it seems as if the Phillies should have done better.

They started a lineup with Hall of Famers at first base, second base, and right field. The right fielder, Elmer Flick, led the National League in RBI with 110, one more than the first baseman, Ed Delahanty. The second baseman, Nap Lajoie, chipped in with 92.

The batting averages of the threesome were outstanding, too. Flick's .367 was runnerup to Honus Wagner and Lajoie's .337 was sixth best in the NL. Delahanty's .323 was, for him, an off-season. Center fielder Roy Thomas batted .316 and catcher Ed McFarland finished at .305 as the Phillies batted .290 as a team, second in the league by three points to champion Brooklyn.

One problem the Phillies had was fielding. Their 125 errors led the league. Particularly disappointing was shortstop Monte Cross, who made 62 errors and didn't redeem himself at bat (.202).

Another problem was the pitching staff, which lacked a 20-game winner and a real stopper, although Chick Fraser and Strawberry Bill Bernhard each won 15 games and Al Orth 14.

A newcomer who would make his mark in the future was third baseman Harry Wolverton, who came over from Chicago and batted .282.

1900

Record: 75–63
Finish: Third
Games Behind: 8
Manager: Billy Shettsline

	W	L	G	CG	IP	H	BB	K	ERA
Bill Bernhard	15	10	32	20	219	284	74	49	4.77
Bert Conn	0	2	4	1	17	29	16	2	8.47
Red Donahue	15	10	32	21	240	299	50	41	3.60
Jack Dunn	5	5	10	9	80	87	29	12	4.84
Chick Fraser	15	9	29	22	223	250	93	58	3.15
Al Maul	2	3	5	3	38	53	3	6	6.16
Warren McLaughlin	0	0	1	0	6	4	6	1	4.50
Al Orth	14	14	33	24	262	302	60	68	3.78
Wiley Piatt	9	10	22	16	161	194	71	47	4.70
Roy Thomas	0	0	1	0	3	4	0	0	3.00
	75	63	141	116	1,249	1,506	402	284	4.13

Shutouts: Donahue (2), Dunn, Fraser, Piatt

	G	AB	R	H	2B	3B	HR	RBI	SB	AVG
Pearce Chiles	33	111	13	24	6	2	1	23	4	.216
Monte Cross (SS)	131	466	59	94	11	3	3	62	19	.202
Ed Delahanty (1B)	131	539	82	174	32	10	2	109	16	.323
Joe Dolan	74	257	39	51	7	3	1	27	10	.198
Klondike Douglass	50	160	23	48	9	4	0	25	7	.300
Elmer Flick (RF)	138	545	106	200	32	16	11	(110)	35	.367
Fred Jacklitsch	5	11	0	2	1	0	0	3	0	.182
Napoleon Lajoie (2B)	102	451	95	152	33	12	7	92	22	.337
Ed McFarland (C)	94	344	50	105	14	8	0	38	9	.305
Morgan Murphy	11	36	2	10	0	1	0	3	0	.278
Bert Myers	7	28	5	5	1	0	0	2	1	.179
Shorty Slagle (LF)	141	574	115	165	16	9	0	45	34	.287
Roy Thomas (CF)	140	531	(132)	168	4	3	0	33	37	.316
Harry Wolverton (3B)	101	383	42	108	10	8	3	58	4	.282
Charlie Ziegler	3	11	0	3	0	0	0	1	0	.273
	141	4,969	810	(1,439)	187	82	29		205	.290

1901

Record: 83–57
Finish: Second
Games Behind: 7½
Manager: Billy Shettsline

The Phillies finished second twice this season. On the field they were seven-and-one-half games behind the Pittsburgh Pirates. Off the field, they were much farther behind the upstart American League, which went whole hog after the Phillies' stars.

The new league managed to sign pitchers Bill Bernhard, Chick Fraser, and Wiley Piatt and—most importantly—future Hall of Famer Napoleon Lajoie. All four hopped to Connie Mack's rival Athletics. But Reach and Rogers were able to fend off the advances made on Ed Delahanty by paying him $3,000, which was $600 more than the National League ceiling.

When Lajoie, who had agreed to a $2,600 salary, found out that Delahanty was making more than he was, he stormed into the front office and demanded

	W	L	G	GS	CG	IP	H	BB	K	ERA
Red Donahue	21	13	35	34	34	304	307	60	89	2.61
Bill Duggleby	19	12	34	28	25	276	294	40	94	2.87
Jack Dunn	0	1	2	2	0	5	11	7	1	19.80
Al Orth	20	12	35	33	30	282	250	32	92	2.27
Jack Townsend	9	6	19	16	14	144	118	64	72	3.44
Doc White	14	13	31	27	22	237	241	56	132	3.19
	83	57		140	125	1,247	1,221	259	480	2.87

Shutouts: Orth (6), Duggleby (5), Townsend (2), Donahue

	G	AB	R	H	2B	3B	HR	RBI	SB	AVG
Shad Barry	67	252	35	62	10	0	1	22	13	.246
George Browne	8	26	2	5	1	0	0	4	2	.192
Bert Conn	5	18	2	4	1	0	0	0	0	.222
Monte Cross (SS)	139	483	49	95	14	1	1	44	24	.197
Ed Delahanty (LF)	138	542	106	192	38	16	8	108	28	.354
Joe Dolan	10	37	0	3	0	0	0	2	0	.081
Klondike Douglass	51	173	14	56	6	1	0	23	10	.324
Elmer Flick (RF)	138	540	112	180	32	17	8	88	30	.333
Billy Hallman (2B)	123	445	46	82	13	5	0	38	13	.184
Fred Jacklitsch	33	120	14	30	4	3	0	24	2	.250
Hughie Jennings (1B)	81	302	38	83	22	2	1	39	13	.274
Ed McFarland (C)	74	295	33	84	14	2	1	32	11	.285
Shorty Slagle	48	183	20	37	6	2	1	20	5	.202
Roy Thomas (CF)	129	479	102	148	5	2	1	28	27	.309
Harry Wolverton (3B)	93	379	42	117	15	4	0	43	13	.309
		4,793	668	1,275	194	58	24	553	199	.266

equal pay. Rogers refused, and Nap jumped to the A's where he hit .424, an all-time league record.

Despite the losses of players, the Phillies had a successful year at the gate, drawing 234,937, even with the opposition from the Athletics. And, although they never made a real run at the Pirates, they finished second for the first time in 14 years.

They were able to overcome the loss of three good pitchers because two holdovers won big. Red Donahue won 21 times and Al Orth 20.

Delahanty, moved from first base to left field when the Phils dealt for Hughie Jennings in June, made his last year with the Phillies as successful as ever, batting .354 and driving in 108 runs. His two outfield mates, Roy Thomas and Elmer Flick, were also .300-plus hitters. But at season's end, two questions remained:

—Could the Phillies have won it all with Lajoie and the three pitchers they lost?

—Would the team challenge for the pennant again in 1902?

The answers, in order, were perhaps and no.

The 1902 season gave the American League, and Connie Mack in particular, the chance to send the second shock wave through the Phillies organization.

Mack loosened his purse strings again, and future Hall of Famer Elmer Flick, shortstop Monte Cross, and 19-game winner Bill Duggleby reached for the dollars inside.

The St. Louis Browns convinced 21-game winner Red Donahue to cast his lot with them, and Donahue won 22 games.

But the worst news came from Washington. The Senators were able to

1902

Record: 56–81
Finish: Seventh
Games Behind: 46
Manager: Bill Shettsline

	W	L	G	GS	CG	IP	H	BB	K	ERA
Bill Duggleby	11	17	33	28	25	259	282	57	60	3.37
Harry Felix	1	3	9	5	3	45	61	11	10	5.60
Henry Fox	0	0	1	0	0	1	2	1	1	18.00
Chick Fraser	12	13	27	26	24	224	238	74	97	3.42
Ham Iburg	11	18	30	30	20	236	286	62	106	3.89
Bill Magee	2	4	8	6	6	54	61	18	15	3.67
Barney McFadden	0	1	1	1	1	9	14	7	3	8.00
Bill Salisbury	0	0	2	1	0	6	15	2	0	13.50
Cy Vorhees	3	3	10	4	3	54	63	20	24	3.83
Doc White	16	20	36	35	34	306	277	72	185	2.53
Jesse Whiting	0	1	1	1	1	9	13	6	0	5.00
Bill Wolfe	0	1	1	1	1	9	11	4	3	4.00
	56	81		138	118	1,211	1,323	334	504	3.50

Shutouts: Fraser (3), White (3), Iburg, Vorhees

	G	AB	R	H	2B	3B	HR	RBI	SB	AVG
Shad Barry (RF)	138	543	65	156	20	6	3	58	14	.287
Joe Berry	1	4	0	1	0	0	0	1	1	.250
George Browne (LF)	70	281	41	73	7	1	0	26	11	.260
Pete Childs (2B)	123	403	25	78	5	0	0	25	6	.194
Bill Clay	3	8	1	2	0	0	0	1	0	.250
Red Dooin (C)	94	333	20	77	7	3	0	35	8	.231
Klondike Douglass	109	408	37	95	12	3	0	37	6	.233
Tom Fleming	5	16	2	6	0	0	0	2	0	.375
Patsy Greene	19	65	6	11	1	0	0	1	2	.169
Billy Hallman (3B)	73	254	14	63	8	4	0	35	9	.248
Rudy Hulswitt (SS)	128	497	59	135	11	7	0	38	12	.272
Fred Jacklitsch	38	114	8	23	4	0	0	8	2	.202
Hughie Jennings (1B)	78	289	31	80	16	3	1	32	8	.277
Henry Krug	53	198	20	45	3	3	0	14	2	.227
Frank Maher	1	1	0	0	0	0	0	0	0	.000
Tom Maher	1	0	0	0	0	0	0	0	0	.000
Nap Shea	3	8	1	1	0	0	0	0	0	.125
Roy Thomas (CF)	138	500	89	143	4	7	0	24	17	.286
Bill Thomas	6	17	1	2	0	0	0	0	0	.118
Ed Watkins	1	3	0	0	0	0	0	0	0	.000
Doc White	61	179	17	47	3	1	1	15	5	.263
Harry Wolverton	34	136	12	40	3	2	0	16	3	.294
		4,615	484	1,139	110	43	5	389	108	.247

convince four Phillies that the new league was right for them. Pitchers Al Orth and Jack Townsend and third baseman Harry Wolverton, a .309 hitter the season before, were tough enough losses. But the killer was Ed Delahanty, who immediately won the American League batting title.

The Phillies didn't win much of anything. Of all their stars, only center fielder Roy Thomas remained faithful to Rogers and Reach. The team slipped to seventh place in what never was a National League race, the Pirates outdistancing runner-up Brooklyn by 27½ games.

The Phils slipped dreadfully even though two of the players they had lost to the A's, Fraser (in 1901) and Duggleby, returned to the fold after the Pennsylvania Supreme Court ruled that all players who had jumped to the American League in 1901 had to play for the Phillies if they were to play professional baseball. The ruling applied only to games played in Pennsylvania. Ban Johnson, the American League president, wasn't about to allow the credibility that he had acquired from the National League to disappear. He assigned the contracts of Nap Lajoie, Flick, and Bill Bernhard to Cleveland. It meant that trio could not play against the Athletics in 1902, but that all three of them could play against all other American League teams.

Not only that, but the A's won the American League flag. The fans began shifting their attention to Connie Mack's upstarts. The Phillies' attendance dipped more than 50 percent to 112,066.

In reality, with the exception of a handful of seasons, the course of history had been plotted. The Phillies would be Philadelphia's weak-sister major league team until the Carpenter family and the Whiz Kids changed it all.

1903

Record: 49–86
Finish: Seventh
Games Behind: 39½
Manager: Chief Zimmer

Mark this season down as one of the most disastrous in the Phillies' history. Reach and Rogers sold the Phillies to a socialite named Jimmy Potter, who knew little about baseball and cared less.

Chief Zimmer was installed as manager, not as much by Potter as by Pirates' owner Barney Dreyfuss, who had advanced the Phillies money during the fight with the American League and who was pulling the strings behind the scenes in what today would be viewed as an unbelievable conflict of interest.

	W	L	G	GS	CG	IP	H	BB	K	ERA
Fred Burchell	0	3	6	3	2	44	48	14	12	2.86
Bill Duggleby	13	18	36	30	28	264	318	79	57	3.75
Chick Fraser	12	17	31	29	26	250	260	97	104	4.50
Fred Mitchell	11	15	28	28	24	227	250	102	69	4.48
Jack McFetridge	1	11	14	13	11	103	120	49	31	4.89
Warry McLaughlin	0	2	3	2	2	23	38	11	3	7.04
Tully Sparks	11	15	28	28	27	248	248	56	88	2.72
Libe Washburn	0	4	4	4	4	35	44	11	9	4.37
Pop Williams	1	1	2	2	2	18	21	6	8	3.00
	49	86		139	(126)	1,212	1,347	425	381	3.97

Shutouts: Duggleby (3), Fraser, Mitchell

	G	AB	R	H	2B	3B	HR	RBI	SB	AVG
Shad Barry (LF)	138	550	75	152	24	5	1	60	26	.276
Roy Brashear	20	75	9	17	3	0	0	4	2	.227
Red Dooin	62	188	18	41	5	1	0	14	9	.218
Klondike Douglass (1B)	105	377	43	96	5	4	1	36	6	.255
Kid Gleason (2B)	106	412	65	117	19	6	1	49	12	.284
Billy Hallman	63	198	20	42	11	2	0	17	2	.212
Rudy Hulswitt (SS)	138	519	56	128	22	9	1	58	10	.247
Bill Keister (RF)	100	400	53	128	27	7	3	63	11	.320
Frank Roth (C)	68	220	27	60	11	4	0	22	3	.273
Dutch Rudolph	1	1	0	0	0	0	0	0	0	.000
Roy Thomas (CF)	130	477	88	156	11	2	1	27	17	.327
John Titus	72	280	38	80	15	6	2	34	5	.286
John Walsh	1	3	0	0	0	0	0	0	0	.000
Harry Wolverton (3B)	123	494	72	152	13	12	0	53	10	.308
Chief Zimmer	37	118	9	26	3	1	1	19	3	.220
		4,781	618	1,283	186	62	12	500	120	.268

Chief Zimmer's only season as manager produced a seventh-place finish in 1903.

And on August 6 a balcony behind the left field bleachers collapsed. One dozen people died and 232 were injured. The Phillies moved their games to the Athletics' home field at Columbia Park, but a continuous rain forced nine straight postponements. Eventually the Phillies got to play, posting a 6–9–1 record at Columbia Park before returning to Baker Bowl.

The team was wretched. Although it finished seventh for the second straight season, it won seven less games than the previous team. For some unexplained reason, though, attendance jumped to 151,729, even as the Athletics were finishing a strong second in an American League that the National League now recognized.

Other than Roy Thomas' .327 average and Harry Wolverton's .308 upon his return to the fold, there was precious little to get excited about. None of the regular pitchers could make the positive side of .500, although Chick Fraser did pitch a no-hitter, beating the Chicago Cubs, 10–0. At the end of the season, Zimmer made one of the most unorthodox moves in big league history. He left managing and became a big league umpire.

Maybe Chief Zimmer was lucky. No matter what insult the fans hurled at him when he made a controversial umpiring decision, at least he didn't have to suffer on the Phillies bench watching the team sink to its first last-place finish since the 1883 inaugural.

That torturous assignment befell one Hugh Duffy, who just three seasons before had been one of the leading American League headhunters in the raiding of National League talent. Although his raids were conducted in New England, not Philadelphia, managing this particular collection of tumblers and jugglers had to serve as purgatory on earth for the Boston Irishman.

Amazingly enough, 140,771 masochists chose to pay their way into the stadium to see this team. Perhaps they were lured by a hair-shirt day promotion.

Whatever the reason, the fans were treated to some awful baseball. But if they looked hard enough, they could also see light at the end of the tunnel—and it wasn't an oncoming train. A rookie named Sherry Magee batted .277. He would become an all-time Phillie by the time his career ended.

But this was a year in which no regular hit .300 and the ace of the pitching

1904

Record: 52–100
Finish: Eighth
Games Behind: 53½
Manager: Hugh Duffy

	W	L	G	GS	CG	IP	H	BB	K	ERA
Tom Barry	0	1	1	1	0	.2	6	1	1	40.50
John Brackinridge	0	1	7	1	0	34	37	16	11	5.56
Ralph Caldwell	2	3	6	5	5	41	40	15	30	4.17
Frank Corridon	6	5	12	11	11	94	88	28	44	2.20
Bill Duggleby	12	14	32	27	22	224	265	53	55	3.78
Chick Fraser	14	24	42	36	32	302	287	100	127	3.25
Johnny Lush	0	6	7	6	3	43	52	27	27	3.56
Fred Mitchell	4	7	13	13	11	109	133	25	29	3.39
John McPherson	1	10	15	12	11	128	130	46	32	3.66
Tully Sparks	7	16	26	25	19	201	208	43	67	2.64
Jack Sutthoff	6	13	19	18	17	164	172	71	46	3.68
	52	100		155	131	1,339	(1,418)	425	469	3.39

Shutouts: Sparks (3), Duggleby (2), Fraser (2), Corridon, McPherson

	G	AB	R	H	2B	3B	HR	RBI	SB	AVG
Shad Barry	35	122	15	25	2	0	0	3	2	.205
She Donahue	58	200	21	43	4	0	0	14	7	.215
Red Dooin (C)	108	355	41	86	11	4	6	36	15	.242
Klondike Douglass	3	10	1	3	0	0	0	1	0	.300
Jack Doyle (1B)	66	236	20	52	10	3	1	22	4	.220
Hugh Duffy	18	46	10	13	1	1	0	5	3	.283
Tom Fleming	3	6	0	0	0	0	0	0	0	.000
Kid Gleason (2B)	153	587	61	161	23	6	0	42	17	.274
Bob Hall	46	163	11	26	4	0	0	17	5	.160
Rudy Hulswitt (SS)	113	406	36	99	11	4	1	36	8	.244
Herman Long	1	4	0	1	0	0	0	0	0	.250
Sherry Magee (RF)	95	364	51	101	15	12	3	57	11	.277
Doc Marshall	8	20	1	2	0	0	0	1	0	.100
Jesse Purnell	7	19	2	2	0	0	0	1	1	.105
Butch Rementer	1	2	0	0	0	0	0	0	0	.000
Frank Roth	81	229	28	59	8	1	1	20	8	.258
Roy Thomas (CF)	139	496	92	144	6	6	3	29	28	.290
John Titus (LF)	146	504	60	148	25	5	4	55	15	.294
Deacon Van Buren	12	43	2	10	2	0	0	3	2	.205
Harry Wolverton (3B)	102	398	43	106	15	5	0	49	18	.266
		5,103	571	1,268	170	54	23	469	159	.248

staff, Chick Fraser, finished at 14–24. In other words, it was a year that would be duplicated many times in the '20s, '30s, and '40s.

1905

Record: 83–69
Finish: Fourth
Games Behind: 21½
Manager: Hugh Duffy

The Phillies showed dramatic improvement this season, winning 31 more games than they had in 1904 and rising from last place to fourth.

Duffy worked with a nearly brand new infield. Kitty Bransfield came from Pittsburgh and took over at first base. Kid Gleason held down second as usual, but the left side consisted of newcomers Mickey Doolan at shortstop and Ernie Courtney at third. Those two complemented each other quite nicely, since Courtney could hit but had little range, which was Doolan's strong suit.

But the most exciting thing about the Phillies this year was their outfield. Sherry Magee was with the club the entire year and hit .299 with 98 RBI. The other two starters were .300-plus hitters as Roy Thomas smacked the ball at a .317 clip and Silent John Titus averaged .308. The team lifted its collective average from .248 to .260.

Bill Shettsline also made a trade that got him a pitching ace. Third baseman Harry Wolverton was dealt to Boston for Togie Pittinger, who had a big season with a 23–14 record in a league-leading 46 mound appearances.

In mid-season, the Phillies signed Kid Nichols, who had been released by the Cardinals. The future Hall of Famer won 10 of 16 decisions and had a fine 2.27 ERA. Other hurlers included Bill Duggleby (18–17), Tully Sparks (14–11), and Frank Corridon (10–13).

The catcher was dependable Red Dooin.

The Phillies were a hit at the box office this season, too. They more than doubled the previous season's attendance as they drew a record 317,932.

	W	L	G	GS	CG	IP	H	BB	K	ERA
Charlie Brady	1	1	2	2	2	13	19	2	3	3.46
Ralph Caldwell	1	1	7	2	1	34	44	7	29	4.24
Frank Corridon	10	13	35	26	18	212	203	57	79	3.48
Bill Duggleby	18	17	38	36	27	289	270	83	75	2.46
Harry Kane	1	1	2	2	2	17	12	8	12	1.59
Johnny Lush	2	0	2	2	1	17	12	8	8	1.59
Kid Nichols	10	6	17	16	15	139	129	28	50	2.27
Togie Pittinger	23	14	(46)	37	29	337	311	104	136	3.10
Tully Sparks	14	11	34	26	20	260	217	73	98	2.18
Jack Sutthoff	3	4	13	6	4	78	82	36	26	3.81
Buck Washer	0	0	1	0	0	3	4	5	0	6.00
	83	69		155	119	1,399	1,303	411	516	2.81

Shutouts: Pittinger (4), Sparks (3), Corridon, Duggleby, Nichols, Sutthoff

	G	AB	R	H	2B	3B	HR	RBI	SB	AVG
Fred Abbott	42	128	9	25	6	1	0	12	4	.195
Kitty Bransfield (1B)	151	580	55	150	23	9	3	76	27	.259
Ernie Courtney (3B)	155	601	77	165	14	7	2	77	17	.275
Red Dooin (C)	113	380	45	95	13	5	0	36	12	.250
Mickey Doolan (SS)	136	492	53	125	27	11	1	48	17	.254
Hugh Duffy	15	40	7	12	2	1	0	3	0	.300
Kid Gleason (2B)	155	608	95	150	17	7	1	50	16	.247
Mike Kahoe	16	51	2	13	2	0	0	4	1	.255
Oompaul Krueger	46	114	10	21	1	1	0	12	1	.184
Sherry Magee (LF)	155	603	100	180	24	17	5	98	48	.299
Red Munson	9	26	1	3	1	0	0	2	0	.115
Roy Thomas (CF)	147	562	118	178	11	6	0	31	23	.317
John Titus (RF)	147	548	99	169	36	14	2	89	11	.308
		(5,243)	708	1,362	187	82	16	567	180	.260

The Phillies had their second successive fourth-place finish, but here the similarity between 1905 and 1906 ends. While the 1905 squad finished 14 games over .500, the 1906 squad was 11 games under the break-even point.

By this time, people were confusing Mickey Doolan and Red Dooin, a pair of players who led the league in errors at their positions. Catcher Dooin had 32, shortstop Doolan an astronomical 66.

The Phillies slipped 19 points at the plate, batting just .241. And the

1906

Record: 71–82
Finish: Fourth
Games Behind: 45½
Manager: Hugh Duffy

	W	L	G	GS	CG	IP	H	BB	K	ERA
Bill Duggleby	13	19	42	30	22	280	241	66	83	2.25
Harry Kane	1	3	6	3	2	28	28	18	14	3.86
Johnny Lush	18	15	37	35	24	281	254	119	151	2.37
Walter Moser	0	4	6	4	4	43	49	15	17	3.56
John McCloskey	3	2	9	4	3	41	46	9	6	2.85
Kid Nichols	0	1	4	2	1	11	17	13	1	9.82
Togie Pittinger	8	10	20	16	9	130	128	50	43	3.39
Lew Richie	9	11	33	22	14	206	170	79	65	2.40
Charlie Roy	0	1	7	1	0	18	24	5	6	5.00
Tully Sparks	19	16	42	37	29	317	244	62	114	2.16
	71	82		154	108	1,354	1,201	436	500	2.58

Shutouts: Sparks (6), Duggleby (5), Lush (4), Richie (3), Pittinger (2)

	G	AB	R	H	2B	3B	HR	RBI	SB	AVG
Kitty Bransfield (1B)	140	524	47	144	28	5	1	60	12	.275
Ernie Courtney (3B)	116	398	53	94	12	2	0	42	6	.236
Ches Crist	6	11	1	0	0	0	0	0	0	.000
Jerry Donovan	61	166	11	33	4	0	0	15	2	.199
Red Dooin (C)	113	351	25	86	19	1	0	32	15	.245
Mickey Doolan (SS)	154	535	41	123	19	7	1	55	16	.230
Kid Gleason (2B)	135	494	47	112	17	2	0	34	17	.227
Harry Houston	2	4	0	0	0	0	0	0	0	.000
Sherry Magee (LF)	154	563	77	159	36	8	6	67	55	.282
Paul Sentelle	63	192	19	44	5	1	1	14	15	.229
Roy Thomas (CF)	142	493	81	125	10	7	0	16	22	.254
John Titus (RF)	145	484	67	129	22	5	1	57	12	.267
Joe Ward	35	129	12	38	8	6	0	11	2	.295
		4,911	530	1,183	(197)	47	12	444	180	.241

The 1906 Phillies included: (top row from left) Gleason, Doolin, Ritchie, Moren, Duggleby, Kane, Titus, and Nichols; (middle row) Bransfield, Ward, Dooin, Sparks, Duffy, Pittinger, Lush, and McCloskey; and (bottom row) Sentelle, Donovan, Magee, Thomas, and Crist.

pitching slipped almost as drastically as the hitting. Kid Nichols was hardly any use, and Togie Pittinger slipped from 23 wins to eight. Bill Duggleby dipped from 18 to 13. Tully Sparks (19–16) and Johnny Lush (18–15) carried the bulk of the pitching load. Lush also pitched a no-hitter, beating Brooklyn, 6–0.

No regular hit higher than Sherry Magee's .282. Run production dropped from 708 to 530. And when the season was over, Hugh Duffy packed his managerial bags and headed for Providence.

The Phillies' fans were no fools, either. Attendance dropped to 294,680, probably because there was no National League race to speak of as the Tinker-to-Evers-to-Chance Chicago Cubs won 116 games and outdistanced the second-place defending champ New York Giants by 20 games.

1907

Record: 83–64
Finish: Third
Games Behind: 21½
Manager: Billy Murray

The Phillies' new manager was Billy Murray, a likeable sort from Massachusetts, who had developed quite a reputation for excellence in the minor leagues. He proved himself quickly at the major league level by leading the Phillies to a dozen more victories and a third-place finish, best for the club since 1901.

The big change this season was at second base. Kid Gleason, who was 40, opened the season there but was soon replaced by Otto Knabe, who fielded spectacularly and hit .255.

Sherry Magee was the offensive star once again. He batted .328, and his 85 RBI led the league. He finished second to Honus Wagner in the National League batting race.

Tully Sparks, meanwhile, had a terrific season on the mound with a 22–8 record and a 2.00 ERA. Frank Corridon went 18–14, and little Lew Moren pitched much better than his 11–18 record.

	W	L	G	GS	CG	IP	H	BB	K	ERA
Buster Brown	9	6	21	16	13	130	118	55	38	2.42
Frank Corridon	18	14	37	32	23	274	228	89	131	2.46
Harry Coveleskie	1	0	4	0	0	20	10	3	6	0.00
Bill Duggleby	0	2	5	2	2	29	43	11	20	7.45
Johnny Lush	3	5	8	8	5	57	48	21	20	3.00
Lew Moren	11	18	37	31	21	255	202	101	98	2.54
John McCloskey	0	0	3	0	0	9	15	6	3	7.00
George McQuillan	4	0	6	5	5	41	21	11	28	0.66
Togie Pittinger	9	5	16	12	8	102	101	35	37	3.00
Lew Richie	6	6	25	12	9	117	88	38	40	1.77
Tully Sparks	22	8	33	31	24	265	221	51	90	2.00
	82	64		149	110	1,299	1,095	422	499	2.43

Shutouts: Brown (4), Corridon (3), Moren (3), McQuillan (3), Sparks (3), Lush (2), Richie (2), Pittinger

	G	AB	R	H	2B	3B	HR	RBI	SB	AVG
Kitty Bransfield (1B)	94	348	25	81	15	2	0	38	8	.233
Ernie Courtney (3B)	130	440	42	107	17	4	2	43	6	.243
Red Dooin (C)	101	313	18	66	8	4	0	14	10	.211
Mickey Doolan (SS)	145	509	33	104	19	7	1	47	18	.204
Kid Gleason	36	126	11	18	3	0	0	6	3	.143
Eddie Grant	74	268	26	65	4	3	0	19	10	.243
Fred Jacklitsch	73	202	19	43	7	0	0	17	7	.213
Otto Knabe (2B)	129	444	67	113	16	9	1	34	18	.255
Sherry Magee (LF)	140	503	75	165	28	12	4	(85)	46	.328
Ossie Osborn	56	163	22	45	2	3	0	9	4	.276
Paul Sentelle	3	3	0	0	0	0	0	0	0	.000
Roy Thomas (CF)	121	419	70	102	15	3	1	23	11	.243
John Titus (RF)	145	523	72	144	23	12	3	63	9	.275
		4,725	514	1,113	(162)	65	12	424	154	.236

Corridon had an eight-inning one-hitter and an 8–0 lead in the season's opening game against the New York Giants at the Polo Grounds. The game, however, went in the record book as a 9–0 win for the Phillies after umpire Bill Klem forfeited the contest because Giants fans piled onto the field and refused to leave.

Late in the season, the Phillies bought a couple of pitchers of exceptional promise. One was George McQuillan, who was 4–0 and had a 0.66 ERA in 41 innings, including 25 straight scoreless innings. The other was Harry Coveleskie, who worked 20 scoreless innings.

Even though the Cubs again ran away with the pennant race, the Phillies drew 341,216 fans, a substantial improvement over the previous season.

The Phillies slipped back to fourth in the second season of Billy Murray's stewardship, but the 1908 season will be long remembered for what Harry Coveleskie did the last week of the season. He knocked the Giants right out of a sure pennant and into a playoff, which they lost to the Cubs.

Because of it, Harry picked up the nickname "Giant Killer," and, even though he won 20 or more games three straight seasons with the Detroit Tigers later in his career, he is best remembered for beating the Giants in three games in a six-day stretch.

It began on September 27. Coveleskie had been recalled that month from Lancaster, where he had won 22 games. In his first start against John McGraw's Giants, Coveleskie threw a 7–0 shutout. Four days later, he won, 6–3. And two days after that, he triumphed, 3–2.

McGraw was furious. "No manager in a tight race has the right to play favorites," he said. "It was a lousy trick, pitching that young lefthander out of turn in his efforts to beat us out of a pennant."

"In this game, you're out to win ball games," Murray responded.

The Phillies won 83 ballgames that season and drew 420,660 fans to their

1908

Record: 83–71
Finish: Fourth
Games Behind: 16
Manager: Billy Murray

	W	L	G	GS	CG	IP	H	BB	K	ERA
Buster Brown	0	0	3	0	0	7	9	5	3	2.57
Frank Corridon	14	10	27	24	18	208	178	48	50	2.51
Harry Coveleskie	4	1	6	5	5	44	29	12	22	1.23
Bill Foxen	7	7	22	16	10	147	126	53	52	1.96
Harry Hock	2	1	3	3	2	26	20	13	4	2.77
Earl Moore	2	1	3	3	3	26	20	8	16	0.00
Lew Moren	8	9	28	16	9	154	146	49	72	2.92
George McQuillan	23	17	48	42	32	360	263	91	114	1.52
Lew Richie	7	10	25	15	13	158	125	49	58	1.82
Tully Sparks	16	15	33	31	24	263	251	51	85	2.60
	83	71		155	116	1,393	1,167	379	476	(2.10)

Shutouts: McQuillan (7), Moren (4), Corridon (2), Coveleskie (2), Foxen (2), Richie (2), Sparks (2), Moore

	G	AB	R	H	2B	3B	HR	RBI	SB	AVG
Kitty Bransfield (1B)	144	527	53	160	25	7	3	71	30	.304
Wally Clement	16	36	0	8	3	0	0	1	2	.222
Ernie Courtney	60	160	14	29	3	0	0	6	1	.181
Pep Deininger	1	0	0	0	0	0	0	0	0	.000
Red Dooin (C)	133	435	28	108	17	4	0	41	20	.248
Mickey Doolan (SS)	129	445	29	104	25	4	2	49	5	.234
Kid Gleason	2	1	0	0	0	0	0	0	0	.000
Eddie Grant (3B)	147	(598)	69	146	13	8	0	32	27	.244
Fred Jacklitsch	37	86	6	19	3	0	0	7	3	.221
Charlie Johnson	6	16	2	4	0	1	0	2	0	.250
Otto Knabe (2B)	151	555	63	121	26	8	0	27	27	.218
Sherry Magee (LF)	143	508	79	144	30	16	2	57	40	.283
Moose McCormick	11	22	0	2	0	0	0	2	0	.091
Ossie Osborn (CF)	152	555	62	148	19	12	2	44	16	.267
Dave Shean	14	48	4	7	2	0	0	2	1	.146
Roy Thomas	6	24	2	4	0	0	0	0	0	.167
John Titus (RF)	149	539	75	154	24	5	2	48	27	.286
		5,012	503	1,223	194	68	11	400	200	.244

Harry Coveleski pitched the Giants right out of the 1908 pennant when he beat them three times in six days down the stretch.

home games. George McQuillan was the talk of the league as he won 23 of 40 decisions and pitched 360 innings with a sparkling 1.52 ERA.

Tully Sparks won 16 games and Frank Corridon 14.

Although Sherry Magee's average dipped to .283, Kitty Bransfield had a great season, finishing fourth in the league with a .304 average.

The Phillies allowed fewer runs (446) than any team in the National League, and the pitching staff topped the league with a 2.10 earned run average.

1909

Record: 74–79
Finish: Fifth
Games Behind: 36½
Manager: Billy Murray

The Phillies slipped out of the first division for the first time in five years, and their fans showed their displeasure by slipping into the stadium at a much lower rate than they had the previous year.

Attendance dropped more than 25 percent to 303,177. And the pitching dropped off almost as sharply as the fans.

George McQuillan had been the shining light the previous season, but he apparently got caught up in the glare of night lights and his work suffered as a result. His record slipped to 13–16.

Both Frank Corridon and Tully Sparks also had off-years. Earl Moore (18–12) and Lew Moren (16–15) carried the staff.

No regular hit .300. Sherry Magee dipped to .270 and drove in only 66 runs and, in fact, was almost traded to the Giants for aging holdout Mike Donlin before Billy Murray vetoed it. "That deal will be made over my dead body," Murray fumed. He pointed out that his contract stipulated that no deals could be made without his sanction.

Unfortunately for Billy, the team changed hands again, and new boss Horace Fogel was quick to dismiss the manager after three seasons.

	W	L	G	GS	CG	IP	H	BB	K	ERA
Buster Brown	0	0	7	1	0	25	22	16	10	3.24
Frank Corridon	11	7	27	19	11	171	147	61	69	2.11
Harry Coveleskie	6	10	24	17	8	122	109	49	56	2.73
Bill Foxen	3	7	18	7	5	83	65	32	37	3.36
Earl Moore	18	12	38	34	24	300	238	(108)	173	2.10
Lew Moren	16	15	40	31	19	258	226	93	110	2.65
George McQuillan	13	16	41	28	16	248	202	54	96	2.14
Lew Richie	1	1	11	1	0	45	40	18	11	2.00
Frank Scanlan	0	0	6	0	0	11	8	5	5	1.64
Tully Sparks	6	11	24	16	6	122	126	32	40	2.95
Ben Van Dyke	0	0	2	0	0	7	7	4	5	3.86
	74	79		154	89	1,391	1,190	472	612	2.44

Shutouts: Moore (4), McQuillan (4), Corridon (3), Coveleskie (2), Moren (2), Foxen, Sparks

	G	AB	R	H	2B	3B	HR	RBI	SB	AVG
Johnny Bates (CF)	77	266	43	78	11	1	1	15	22	.293
Kitty Bransfield (1B)	140	527	47	154	27	6	1	59	17	.292
Wally Clement	3	3	0	0	0	0	0	0	0	.000
Pep Deininger	55	169	22	44	9	0	0	16	5	.260
Red Dooin (C)	141	468	42	105	14	1	2	38	14	.224
Mickey Doolan (SS)	147	493	39	108	12	10	1	35	10	.219
Ben Froelich	1	1	0	0	0	0	0	0	0	.000
Eddie Grant (3B)	154	(631)	75	170	18	4	1	37	28	.269
Fred Jacklitsch	20	32	6	10	1	1	0	1	1	.313
Otto Knabe (2B)	114	402	40	94	13	3	0	34	9	.234
Sherry Magee (LF)	143	522	60	141	33	14	2	66	38	.270
Marty Martel	24	41	1	11	3	1	0	7	0	.268
Ed McDonough	1	1	0	0	0	0	0	0	0	.000
Ossie Osborn	58	189	14	35	4	1	0	19	6	.185
Dave Shean	36	112	14	26	2	2	0	4	3	.232
Charlie Starr	3	3	0	0	0	0	0	0	0	.000
John Titus (RF)	151	540	69	146	22	6	3	46	23	.270
Joe Ward	74	184	21	49	8	2	0	23	7	.266
		5,036	515	1,228	185	53	12	417	185	.244

The switch in managers from Billy Murray to popular catcher Charlie (Red) Dooin seemed to revitalize the Phillies in 1910.

They bounced back on the good side of .500 with a 78–75 record and advanced one notch to fourth in the National League race, although they were badly outdistanced by 25½ games by the Chicago Cubs.

Sherry Magee won his first batting title with a .331 average and also topped the National League in RBI with 123. It was the first time in four seasons that Honus Wagner was denied the batting championship.

Shortstop Mickey Doolan also had an outstanding season. He batted .263, drove in 57 runs and sparkled in the field, topping the league shortstops in assists (500), double plays (71), and fielding percentage (.948).

Outfielder Johnny Bates, picked up from Boston, batted .305.

The pitching staff was another matter.

George McQuillan led the league in ERA with 1.60, but wasn't nearly as good off the field as he was on it. Dooin suspended him for a time early in the season for a flagrant violation of training rules, but George continued on his playful way and eventually in August was suspended for the balance of the season by president Horace Fogel.

Earl Moore, who was suspended along with McQuillan by Dooin, realized the error of his ways, however, and won 22 games, his best season ever.

With Tully Sparks useless, the staff did get a big boost from Bob Ewing. Purchased from Cincinnati, Ewing won 16 games and kept the Phillies from sliding into the second division.

The fans were, at best, apathetic. The attendance for the season was 296,579, down marginally from the previous season.

1910

Record: 78–75
Finish: Fourth
Games Behind: 25½
Manager: Charlie Dooin

	W	L	G	GS	CG	IP	H	BB	K	ERA
Ad Brennan	3	0	19	5	2	73	72	28	28	2.34
George Chalmers	1	1	4	3	2	22	21	11	12	5.32
Bill Culp	0	0	4	0	0	7	8	4	4	7.71
Bob Ewing	16	14	34	32	20	255	235	86	102	3.00
Patsy Flaherty	0	0	1	0	0	1	1	1	0	0.00
Bill Foxen	5	5	16	9	5	78	73	40	33	2.54
Charlie Girard	0	2	7	1	0	27	33	12	11	6.34
Bert Humphries	0	0	5	0	0	10	13	3	3	4.50
Jim Maroney	1	2	12	2	1	42	43	11	13	2.14
Earl Moore	22	15	46	35	19	283	228	121	(185)	2.58
Lew Moren	13	14	34	26	12	205	207	82	74	3.56
George McQuillen	9	6	24	17	13	152	109	50	71	(1.60)
Lou Schettler	2	6	27	7	3	107	96	51	62	3.20
Barney Slaughter	0	1	8	1	0	18	21	11	7	5.50
Tully Sparks	0	2	3	3	0	15	22	2	4	6.00
Eddie Stack	6	7	20	16	7	117	115	34	48	4.00
	78	75		157	84	1,411	1,297	547	657	3.05

Shutouts: Moore (6), Ewing (4), McQuillan (3), Moren, Stack

	G	AB	R	H	2B	3B	HR	RBI	SB	AVG
Johnny Bates (CF)	135	498	91	152	26	11	3	61	31	.305
Kitty Bransfield (1B)	123	427	39	102	17	4	3	52	10	.239
John Castle	3	4	1	1	0	0	0	0	1	.250
Harry Cheek	2	4	1	2	1	0	0	0	0	.500
Red Dooin (C)	103	331	30	80	13	4	0	30	10	.242
Mickey Doolan (SS)	148	536	58	141	31	6	2	57	16	.263
Eddie Grant (3B)	152	579	70	155	15	5	1	67	25	.268
Fred Jacklitsch	25	51	7	10	3	0	0	2	0	.196
Otto Knabe (2B)	137	510	73	133	18	6	1	44	15	.261
Fred Luderus	21	68	10	20	5	4	0	14	2	.294
Sherry Magee (LF)	154	519	(110)	172	39	17	6	(123)	49	(.331)
Pat Moran	68	199	13	47	7	1	0	11	6	.236
Ed McDonough	5	9	1	1	0	0	0	0	0	.111
Roy Thomas	23	71	7	13	0	2	0	4	4	.183
John Titus (RF)	143	535	91	129	26	5	3	35	20	.241
Jimmy Walsh	88	242	28	60	8	3	3	31	5	.248
Joe Ward	48	124	11	18	2	1	0	13	1	.145
		(5,171)	674	1,319	(223)	71	22	565	199	.255

1911

Record: 79–73
Finish: Fourth
Games Behind: 19½
Manager: Charlie Dooin

Despite a big four-for-four trade before the season began that had president Horace Fogel talking pennant, the Phillies finished in their familiar fourth-place surroundings and improved their record by only a game and one-half over the previous season.

Fogel's trade—which rid the club of third baseman Eddie Grant, troublesome pitcher George McQuillan, center fielder Johnny Bates, and pitcher Lew Moren, replacing them with Hans Lobert, Dode Paskert and pitchers Jack Rowan and Fred Beebe—did get the fans excited, though. They showed up in near record numbers to see the new-look Phillies. Their attendance of 416,000 was less than 5,000 lower than the record set three seasons earlier.

Many of them were attracted to the ballpark by a young righthanded pitcher who had the sharpest breaking curve ball anyone had ever seen and uncanny control. His name was Grover Cleveland Alexander, and by the time the season was over, he had a league-leading 28 victories and a 2.57 ERA with 367 innings pitched, also best in the National League.

If Alex had gotten any help from his mound mates, the Phillies might have finished a notch or two higher. But the only regular pitcher to win more than he lost was George Chalmers (13–10).

Manager Dooin batted an unlikely .328, but Sherry Magee slipped 43 points from his league-leading figure of the previous season and also dipped by 29 RBI. Newcomers played key roles, however. First baseman Fred Luderus (22 errors) was a defensive liability, but he batted .301 with a team-leading 99 RBI; Paskert hit .273 and caught anything hit his way; and Lobert led the league's third basemen in putouts and batted .285 with 72 RBI.

Rowan and Beebe were major disappointments, however. Each finished at 3–4.

	W	L	G	GS	CG	IP	H	BB	K	ERA
Grover C. Alexander	(28)	13	48	37	(31)	(367)	285	129	227	2.57
Fred Beebe	3	4	9	8	3	48	52	24	20	4.50
Ad Brennan	3	1	5	3	1	23	22	12	12	3.52
Bill Burns	4	7	21	14	8	121	132	26	47	3.42
George Chalmers	13	10	38	22	11	209	196	101	101	3.10
Cliff Curtis	2	1	8	5	3	45	45	15	13	2.60
Bob Ewing	0	2	4	3	1	24	29	14	12	7.88
Bert Hall	0	1	7	1	0	18	19	13	8	4.00
Bert Humphries	3	1	11	5	2	41	56	10	13	4.17
Earl Moore	15	(19)	42	36	21	308	265	164	174	2.63
Troy Puckett	0	0	1	0	0	2	4	2	1	13.50
Jack Rowan	3	4	12	6	2	45	59	20	17	4.70
Toots Schultz	0	3	5	3	2	25	30	15	9	9.36
Jake Smith	0	0	2	0	0	5	3	2	1	0.00
Eddie Stack	5	5	13	10	5	78	67	41	36	3.57
Buck Stanley	0	1	4	0	0	11	14	9	5	6.54
Jimmy Walsh	0	1	1	0	0	3	7	1	1	12.00
	79	73		153	90	1,373	1,285	598	697	3.30

Shutouts: Alexander (7), Moore (5), Burns (3), Chalmers (3), Curtis, Stack

	G	AB	R	H	2B	3B	HR	RBI	SB	AVG
Fred Beck	66	210	26	59	8	3	3	25	3	.281
Kitty Bransfield	23	43	4	11	1	1	0	3	1	.256
Dick Cotter	20	46	2	13	0	0	0	5	1	.283
Red Dooin (C)	74	247	18	81	15	1	1	16	6	.328
Mickey Doolan (SS)	146	512	51	122	23	6	1	49	14	.238
Bill Killefer	6	16	3	3	0	0	0	2	0	.188
Red Kleinow	4	8	0	1	0	0	0	0	0	.125
Otto Knabe (2B)	142	528	99	125	15	6	1	42	23	.237
Clarence Lehr	23	27	2	4	0	0	0	2	0	.148
Hans Lobert (3B)	147	541	94	154	20	9	9	72	40	.285
Fred Luderus (1B)	146	551	69	166	24	11	16	99	6	.301
Tom Madden	28	76	4	21	1	1	0	4	0	.276
Sherry Magee (LF)	121	445	79	128	32	5	15	94	22	.288
Paddy Mayes	5	5	0	1	0	0	0	0	0	.200
Hughie Miller	1	0	0	0	0	0	0	0	0	.000
Pat Moran	34	103	2	19	3	0	0	8	0	.184
Dode Paskert (CF)	153	560	96	153	18	5	4	47	28	.273
John Quinn	1	2	0	0	0	0	0	0	0	.000
Tubby Spencer	11	32	2	5	1	0	1	3	0	.156
Roy Thomas	21	30	5	5	2	0	0	2	0	.167
John Titus (RF)	76	236	35	67	14	1	8	26	3	.284
Jimmy Walsh	94	289	29	78	20	3	1	31	5	.270
Harry Welchonce	26	66	9	14	4	0	0	6	0	.212
		5,044	658	1,307	214	56	(60)	564	153	.259

For a good part of the season, it appeared that the Phillies might just fulfill their owner's prediction and win the pennant. They were in first place from July 13 to August 3.

They faded mightily, however, when Sherry Magee was suspended for slugging an umpire and Dooin, off to the best start of his career, was sidelined with a broken leg in late July. Silent John Titus had broken his leg earlier in the season. With so much manpower out of the lineup, the Phillies dropped 19½ games behind the champion New York Giants, but looked forward eagerly to the following season when everyone would be healthy again.

A not-so-funny thing happened to the Phillies on their way to the 1912 pennant. More injuries. They thought they had suffered more than their share in 1911, but that was just the beginning.

Meanwhile, the fans again turned apathetic. Only a quarter million of them showed up to watch Red Dooin's squad play ball amid the aches and pains. That was a drop of 166,000 customers from the previous season.

The problems began quickly in the City Series with the two-time American League champ Athletics. Sherry Magee broke his wrist and missed the first month of the season. And soon after his return to the lineup, he collided with Dode Paskert and was out for another spell.

1912

Record: 73–79
Finish: Fifth
Games Behind: 30½
Manager: Charlie Dooin

	W	L	G	GS	CG	IP	H	BB	K	ERA
Grover C. Alexander	19	17	46	34	26	(310)	289	105	(195)	2.82
Ad Brennan	11	9	27	19	13	174	185	49	78	3.57
George Chalmers	3	4	12	8	3	58	64	37	22	3.26
Cliff Curtis	2	5	10	8	2	50	55	17	20	3.24
Happy Finneran	0	2	14	4	0	46	50	10	10	2.55
Rube Marshall	0	1	2	1	0	3	12	1	2	21.00
Erskine Mayer	0	1	7	1	0	21	27	7	5	6.43
Earl Moore	9	14	31	24	10	182	186	77	79	3.31
Red Nelson	2	0	4	2	1	19	25	6	2	3.79
Frank Nicholson	0	0	2	0	0	4	8	2	1	4.75
Hank Ritter	0	0	3	0	0	6	5	5	1	4.50
Eppa Rixey	10	10	23	20	10	162	147	54	49	2.50
Toots Schultz	1	4	22	4	1	59	75	35	20	4.58
Tom Seaton	16	12	44	27	16	255	246	106	118	3.28
Huck Wallace	0	0	4	0	0	5	7	4	4	0.00
	73	79		152	82	1,355	1,381	515	616	3.25

Shutouts: Alexander (3), Rixey (3), Seaton (2), Brennan, Moore

	G	AB	R	H	2B	3B	HR	RBI	SB	AVG
Jack Boyle	15	25	4	7	1	0	0	2	0	.280
Dode Brinker	9	18	1	4	1	0	0	2	0	.222
George Browne	6	5	0	1	0	0	0	0	0	.200
Gavvy Gravath (RF)	130	436	63	124	30	9	11	70	15	.284
John Dodge	30	92	3	11	1	0	0	3	2	.129
Cozy Dolan	11	50	8	14	2	2	0	7	3	.280
Red Dooin	69	184	20	46	9	0	0	22	8	.234
Mickey Doolan (SS)	146	532	47	137	26	6	1	62	6	.258
Tom Downey	54	171	27	50	6	3	1	23	3	.292
Peaches Graham	24	59	6	17	1	0	1	4	1	.288
Bill Killefer (C)	85	268	18	60	6	3	1	21	6	.224
Otto Knabe (2B)	126	426	56	120	11	4	0	46	16	.282
Mike Loan	1	2	1	1	0	0	0	0	0	.500
Hans Lobert (3B)	65	257	37	84	12	5	2	33	13	.327
Fred Luderus (1B)	148	572	77	147	31	5	10	69	8	.257
Sherry Magee (LF)	132	464	79	142	25	9	6	66	30	.306
George Mangus	10	25	2	5	3	0	0	3	0	.200
Doc Miller	67	177	24	51	12	5	0	21	3	.288
Pat Moran	13	26	1	3	1	0	0	1	0	.115
Dode Paskert (CF)	145	540	102	170	37	5	2	43	36	.315
Jim Savage	2	3	1	0	0	0	0	0	0	.000
Gene Steinbrenner	3	9	0	2	1	0	0	1	0	.222
John Titus	45	157	43	43	9	5	3	22	6	.274
Jim Walsh	51	150	16	40	6	3	2	19	3	.267
		5,077	660	1,354	244	68	43	570	159	.267

Third baseman Hans Lobert cracked a rib, then a kneecap. His replacement, Runt Walsh, broke his ankle. Otto Knabe broke his hand. Dooin was nailed by a major intestinal ailment.

Red's pitching staff didn't escape the wrath of fate, either. Earl Moore had his arm broken by a batted ball. George Chalmers tore ligaments in his shoulder. Ad Brennan developed diphtheria.

Gavvy Cravath, a 31-year-old, was picked up from Minneapolis and was a plus, as were pitchers Tom Seaton and Eppa Rixey. But the season was one of disappointment.

1913

Record: 88–63
Finish: Second
Games Behind: 12½
Manager: Charlie Dooin

The two-year injury bugaboo finally dissipated and the Phillies played the kind of ball they had been expecting in 1913. They led the National League through much of April and from May 3 to June 30 before dropping behind the New York Giants. They stayed in second place the rest of the way and finished 12½ games behind John McGraw's club.

The pitching staff was outstanding. Tom Seaton had 27 wins and 322 innings pitched, both National League bests. Grover Cleveland Alexander rebounded from 19–17 to 22–8. Ad Brennan, healthy again, won 14 games; Eppa Rixey and Erskine Mayer nine each.

Bill Killefer, in his second year as the regular catcher, led the league in assists and double plays at his position. Shortstop Mickey Doolan did likewise. Hans Lobert rebounded from his succession of injuries to play a full season at third base and bat .300, and Fred Luderus, while slipping to .262 at the plate, led the league's first basemen in putouts, assists, and errors.

The Phillies also put on an awesome display of power for the times. They hit 73 home runs, 14 more than the second-best team in the league, and had three of the top four homer-hitting individuals in champion Gavvy Cravath (19), runner-up Luderus (18), and Sherry Magee (11).

Cravath was particularly outstanding. In addition to leading the National League in homers, he finished second in hitting (.341), first in RBI (128), and first in hits (179).

This was a year when the fans came back to the park—and it almost cost the Phillies a game. For the season, 470,000 fans paid their way into the ballpark (which was fast going downhill). In a late-season game, some bleacher patrons among a capacity crowd flashed mirrors in the Giants' faces when the New Yorkers were batting. The umpire behind the plate requested that it stop. When it didn't, he awarded a forfeit to the Giants.

Club president William F. Baker appealed the decision and won a reversal. The game was ordered replayed from the point of stoppage, but it didn't really matter, since the Giants won anyway.

	W	L	G	GS	CG	IP	H	BB	K	ERA
Grover C. Alexander	22	8	47	35	23	306	288	75	159	2.79
Ad Brennan	14	12	40	25	12	207	204	46	94	2.39
Howie Camnitz	3	3	9	5	1	49	49	23	21	3.67
George Chalmers	3	10	26	13	4	116	133	51	46	4.81
Happy Finneran	0	0	3	0	0	5	12	2	0	7.20
Jim Haislip	0	0	1	0	0	3	4	3	0	6.00
Ray Hartranft	0	0	1	0	0	1	3	1	1	9.00
Doc Imlay	0	0	9	0	0	14	19	7	7	7.07
Rube Marshall	0	1	14	3	0	45	54	22	18	4.60
Erskine Mayer	9	9	39	20	7	171	172	46	51	3.11
Earl Moore	1	3	12	4	0	52	50	40	24	5.02
Red Nelson	0	0	2	0	0	8	9	4	3	2.25
Eppa Rixey	9	5	35	19	9	156	148	56	75	3.11
Tom Seaton	(27)	12	52	35	21	(322)	262	(136)	(168)	2.60
	88	63		159	77	(1,455)	1,407	(512)	(667)	3.16

Shutouts: Alexander (7), Seaton (6), Mayer (2), Rixey (2), Brennan

	G	AB	R	H	2B	3B	HR	RBI	SB	AVG
Beals Becker	88	306	53	99	19	10	9	44	11	.324
Ed Burns	17	30	3	6	3	0	0	3	2	.200
Bobby Byrne	19	58	9	13	1	0	1	4	2	.224
Ralph Capron	2	1	1	0	0	0	0	0	0	.000
Gavvy Cravath (RF)	147	525	78	(179)	34	14	(19)	(128)	10	.341
Josh Devore	23	39	9	11	1	0	0	5	0	.282
John Dodge	3	3	0	1	0	0	0	0	0	.333
Cozy Dolan	55	126	15	33	4	0	0	8	9	.262
Red Dooin	5	129	6	33	4	1	0	13	1	.256
Mickey Doolan (SS)	151	518	32	113	12	6	1	43	17	.218
Vern Duncan	8	12	3	5	1	0	0	1	0	.417
Dan Howley	26	32	5	4	2	0	0	2	3	.125
Bill Killefer (C)	120	360	25	88	14	3	0	24	2	.244
Otto Knabe (2B)	148	571	70	150	25	7	2	53	14	.263
Hans Lobert (3B)	150	573	98	172	28	7	11	55	41	.300
Fred Luderus (1B)	155	588	67	154	32	7	18	86	5	.262
Sherry Magee (LF)	138	470	92	144	36	6	11	70	23	.306
Doc Miller	69	87	9	30	6	0	0	11	2	.345
Pat Moran	1	1	0	0	0	0	0	0	0	.000
Dode Paskert (CF)	124	454	83	119	21	9	4	29	12	.262
Milt Reed	13	24	4	6	1	0	0	0	1	.250
Jimmy Walsh	26	30	3	10	4	0	0	5	1	.333
		(5,400)	693	(1,433)	(257)	78	(73)	597	156	.265

1914

Record: 74–80
Finish: Sixth
Games Behind: 20½
Manager: Charlie Dooin

If one thing doesn't get the Phillies, something else does, or so it seems. This time, it wasn't injuries that caused the team to tumble four places in the standings. It was a new league and a stingy owner.

The league was the Federal League, and the owner was William F. Baker. Just as the American League had spoiled a good Phillies team at the turn of the century, so, too, did the Federal League threaten to do it this time.

Baker tied the purse strings securely around the club's budget, and, when the Feds came with much bigger bucks, the Phillies jumped ship in droves. The keystone combination of many years—Otto Knabe and Mickey Doolan—left. So did great young pitchers Tom Seaton and Ad Brennan. Dooin himself was seeing less and less action behind the plate. The Phillies were a shadow of their former selves.

Two pitchers carried the team. Grover Cleveland Alexander led the league with 27 victories and 355 innings pitched. Erskine Mayer won 21 times and worked 321 frames.

The Phillies still led the league in home runs, but their total of 62 was 11 fewer than in 1913. Gavvy Cravath topped the league with 19, and his 100 RBI was second in the NL to teammate Sherry Magee (103). But the team missed its young starting pitchers and its keystone combination. Also its fans. Apparently disgusted with Baker's refusal to pay the price to keep his talent, they looked elsewhere with their entertainment dollar. Only 138,474 went to Baker Bowl. At the end of the season, Red Dooin was fired as manager.

	W	L	G	GS	CG	IP	H	BB	K	ERA
Grover C. Alexander	(27)	15	46	39	(32)	(355)	(327)	76	(214)	2.38
Stan Baumgartner	3	2	15	3	2	60	60	16	24	3.30
George Chalmers	0	3	3	2	1	18	23	15	6	5.50
Elmer Jacobs	1	3	14	7	1	51	65	20	17	4.76
Rube Marshall	6	7	27	19	7	134	144	50	49	3.76
Eddie Matteson	3	2	15	3	2	58	58	23	28	3.10
Erskine Mayer	21	19	48	39	24	321	308	91	116	2.58
Joe Oeschger	4	8	32	10	5	124	129	54	47	3.77
Eppa Rixey	2	11	24	15	2	103	124	45	41	4.37
Ben Tincup	7	10	28	17	9	155	165	62	108	2.61
	74	80		154	85	1,379	(1,403)	452	650	3.06

Shutouts: Alexander (6), Mayer (4), Tincup (3), Baumgartner

	G	AB	R	H	2B	3B	HR	RBI	SB	AVG
Beals Becker (LF)	138	514	76	167	25	5	9	66	16	.325
Ed Burns	70	139	8	36	3	4	0	16	5	.259
Bobby Byrne (2B)	126	467	61	127	12	1	0	26	9	.272
Gavvy Cravath (RF)	149	499	76	149	27	8	(19)	100	14	.299
Josh Devore	30	53	5	16	2	0	0	7	0	.302
Red Dooin	53	118	10	21	2	0	1	8	4	.178
Frank Fletcher	1	1	0	0	0	0	0	0	0	.000
Pat Hilly	8	10	2	3	0	0	0	1	0	.300
Grump Irelan	67	165	16	39	8	0	1	16	3	.236
Bill Killefer (C)	98	299	27	70	10	1	0	27	3	.234
Hans Lobert (3B)	135	505	83	139	24	5	1	52	31	.275
Fred Luderus (1B)	121	443	55	110	16	5	12	55	2	.248
Sherry Magee	146	544	96	(171)	(39)	11	15	(103)	25	.314
Jack Martin (SS)	83	292	26	74	5	3	0	21	6	.253
Fred Mollenkamp	3	8	0	1	0	0	0	0	0	.125
Pat Moran	1	0	0	0	0	0	0	1	0	.000
Dummy Murphy	9	26	1	4	1	0	0	3	0	.154
George McAvoy	1	1	0	0	0	0	0	0	0	.000
Dode Paskert (CF)	132	451	59	119	25	6	3	44	23	.264
Milt Reed	44	107	10	22	2	1	0	2	4	.206
		5,110	651	1,345	211	52	(62)	564	145	.263

When the first National League championship finally came to Philadelphia, the most remarkable thing was how easily it was attained.

If the pennant race of 1915 were to be compared to a horse race, it was a matter of the Phillies battling a so-so sprinter in the early going, putting that one away about midway through the race, and breezing home effortlessly the rest of the way.

The only team to give the Phillies trouble in Pat Moran's first season at the helm was the Cubs. The Phillies jumped on top almost from the outset of the season, stayed there until mid-May, ran second to the Cubs until June 8, shifted back and forth with Chicago until July 14, and then pulled away and led the rest of the way.

In fact, the Cubs faded badly and finished in fourth place, 17 games behind. The Boston defending champions got off to a dismal start, closed strongly, and finished second, seven games back, but were never a real factor.

The season was a remarkable tribute to the managerial abilities of Moran. Never since the turn of the century had a manager taken over an established major league team with no previous experience as a manager and led it to the pennant. But Moran, who had been a catcher with the Phillies for the five previous seasons and whose playing career spanned 14 big league seasons, had learned the tricks of managing while sitting on the bench, something he normally did in Philadelphia. Moran, appointed by William F. Baker to succeed Red Dooin after the 1914 season, had acted in the capacity of coach as well as reserve catcher under Dooin.

Before the 1915 season began, Baker and Moran considered trades to strengthen the team that had slipped to sixth place the season before. One trade sent Sherry Magee, a fixture in the Philadelphia outfield, to Boston for

1915

Record: 90–62
Finish: First
Games Ahead: 7
Manager: Pat Moran

The starting outfield for the 1915 National League champions was (from left) Possum Whitted, Dode Paskert, and Gavvy Cravath.

	W	L	G	GS	CG	IP	H	BB	K	ERA
Grover C. Alexander	(31)	10	49	42	(36)	(376)	253	64	(241)	(1.22)
Stan Baumgartner	0	2	16	1	0	48	38	23	27	2.44
George Chalmers	8	9	26	20	13	170	159	45	82	2.49
Al Demaree	14	11	32	26	13	210	201	58	69	3.04
Erskine Mayer	21	15	43	33	20	275	240	59	114	2.36
George McQuillan	4	3	9	7	5	64	60	11	13	2.11
Joe Oeschger	1	0	6	1	1	24	21	9	8	3.38
Eppa Rixey	11	12	29	22	10	177	163	64	88	2.39
Ben Tincup	0	0	10	0	0	31	26	9	10	2.03
	90	62		153	(98)	1,374	1,161	342	652	(2.17)

Shutouts: Alexander (12), Demaree (3), Mayer (2), Rixey (2), Chalmers

	G	AB	R	H	2B	3B	HR	RBI	SB	AVG
Jack Adams	24	27	1	3	0	0	0	2	0	.111
Dave Bancroft (SS)	153	563	85	143	18	2	7	30	15	.254
Beals Becker	112	338	38	83	16	4	11	35	12	.246
Ed Burns	67	174	11	42	5	0	0	16	1	.241
Bobby Byrne (3B)	105	387	50	81	6	4	0	21	4	.209
Gavvy Cravath (RF)	150	522	(89)	149	31	7	(24)	(115)	11	.285
Oscar Dugey	42	39	4	6	1	0	0	0	2	.154
Bill Killefer (C)	105	320	26	76	9	2	0	24	5	.238
Fred Luderus (1B)	141	499	55	157	36	7	7	62	9	.315
Bert Niehoff (2B)	148	529	61	126	27	2	2	49	21	.238
Dode Paskert (CF)	109	328	51	80	17	4	3	39	9	.244
Milt Stock	69	227	37	59	7	3	1	15	6	.260
Bud Weiser	37	64	6	9	2	0	0	8	2	.141
Possum Whitted (LF)	128	448	46	126	17	3	1	43	24	.281
		4,916	589	1,216	202	39	(58)	486	121	.247

Possum Whitted. Hans Lobert was shipped off to John McGraw's Giants for Al Demaree, a pitcher who would win 14 games, and Milt Stock, a young third baseman who would play every day down the stretch. Red Dooin was moved to Cincinnati for Bert Niehoff, who became the second baseman and filled one of the infield holes up the middle that had been created by the Federal League raids. For the other, the Phillies bought a young shortstop from the Pacific Coast League. His name was Dave Bancroft, and he is a member of baseball's Hall of Fame.

All the holes in the lineup were filled with quality, or at least adequate, personnel. The next job for Moran was teaching them to play the game as a unit. Spring training in St. Petersburg was no picnic. The players walked the three miles each way from their hotel to Coffee Pot Park and back again. Almost every hour in camp was spent on fundamentals. The Phillies learned to hit the cutoff man, to throw to the right base, to mask their signals so they couldn't be stolen.

And Moran kept drilling the same message into his team from the day spring training opened. "This is not a sixth-place ball club," he told them.

The Phillies wasted little time taking that message to heart. Behind the pitching of Alexander, they opened the season with a 3–0 victory over the defending champion Boston Braves at South End Field, then won their first eight games in a row and 11 of their first 12.

The club held first place from the start of the season until May 22, when it was displaced briefly by the Chicago Cubs. Then, after holding down the lead in 41 of the next 50 days, the Phillies took over first place for good on July 13 when Alexander beat the St. Louis Cardinals, 8–0.

During the season Alexander was the dominant force for the Phillies. Whenever they needed a victory, Ol' Pete always seemed to come up with one. He pitched three one-hitters in one month, beating the Cardinals on June 5, the Dodgers on June 26, and the Giants on July 5.

Alexander pitched a record-setting fourth one-hitter of the season on September 29, beating Boston at Braves Field, 5–0. The victory, coming in the Phillies' 148th game of the season, clinched the team's first pennant. Ironically, the only hit of the game was a single by Sherry Magee, who one year earlier had been traded away by the Phillies.

During the season the Phillies had never been lower than second place.

The infielders who helped the Phillies to their first pennant included (from left) Dave Bancroft, Oscar Dugey, Fred Luderus, Milt Stock, Bobby Byrne, and Bert Niehoft.

With his first of three straight 30-win seasons, Alexander finished with a 31–10 record and led the league with a 1.22 earned run average and 12 shutouts. Erskine Mayer won 21 games, Demaree had his 14 wins, including six over the Giants, and Rixey, nowhere near the pitcher he would become, was 11–12.

Fred Luderus had, for him, a remarkable season with the glove, making only 11 errors at first and fielding .993. He also batted .315. Gavvy Cravath led the league with 24 homers, 115 RBI, and 28 outfield assists. And Bill Killefer was simply the most outstanding defensive catcher in the National League.

It was, all in all, a team that finally could make the National League fans in Philadelphia proud after Connie Mack's American League Athletics had stolen their thunder for a time. The pride lasted one year. It would be 35 more before it returned.

The fans turned out to Baker Bowl in record numbers for the season. The 449,898 head count was more than triple what it had been the previous season.

Part of the pitching staff that faced the Boston Red Sox in the 1915 World Series: (from left) Ben Tincup, Erskine Mayer, Eppa Rixey, and Stan Baumgartner.

1916

Record: 91–62
Finish: Second
Games Behind: 2½
Manager: Pat Moran

The Phillies made a valiant, if futile, bid for their second straight pennant in 1916. They actually finished with one more win than they had the previous season. They held first place as late as September 8. But they wound up 2½ games behind the Brooklyn Dodgers.

Many people have pointed to the slump of Erskine Mayer as the reason for the Phillies failing to repeat. While Mayer slipped from 21 victories to seven, he wasn't the only guilty party. Gavvy Cravath's home run production dipped from 24 to 11, and his RBI production plunged from 115 to 70. Fred Luderus returned to his old ways defensively and dropped 34 points in batting. And the Phillies infield had an atrocious season with the gloves. Luderus (28 errors), second baseman Bert Niehoff (49), and shortstop Dave Bancroft (60) all led their National League position peers in errors.

With all this evidence, the more logical question may be: How did the Phillies manage to finish second?

With Pat Moran's strong point, his ability to handle pitchers, that's how. Of course, if Grover Cleveland Alexander is on your staff, it makes the job that much easier, especially when Ol' Pete is setting a major league record with 16 shutouts on his way to 33 victories and a 1.55 ERA.

Eppa Rixey finally scratched the surface of his potential with 22–10, and Al Demaree was 19–14. But the rest of the staff tumbled badly. Mayer was 7–7, so was Chief Bender, and George McQuillan slipped to 1–7. Still, the city remained excited. A record 515,365 paid their way into Phillies' home games. It would be the year after World War II before that attendance record would fall.

	W	L	G	GS	CG	IP	H	BB	K	ERA
Grover C. Alexander	(33)	12	48	(45)	(38)	(389)	(323)	50	(167)	(1.55)
Stan Baumgartner	0	0	1	0	0	4	5	1	0	2.25
Chief Bender	7	7	27	13	4	123	137	34	43	3.73
George Chalmers	1	4	12	8	2	54	49	19	21	3.17
Al Demaree	19	14	39	35	25	285	252	48	130	2.62
Gary Fortune	0	1	1	1	0	5	2	4	3	3.60
Erv Kantlehner	0	0	3	0	0	4	7	3	2	9.00
Erskine Mayer	7	7	28	16	7	140	148	33	62	3.15
George McQuillan	1	7	21	3	1	62	58	15	22	2.76
Joe Oeschger	1	0	14	0	0	30	18	14	17	2.40
Eppa Rixey	22	10	38	33	20	287	239	74	134	1.85
	91	62		154	(97)	1,382	1,238	295	601	2.36

Shutouts: Alexander (16), Demaree (3), Rixey (3), Mayer (2)

	G	AB	R	H	2B	3B	HR	RBI	SB	AVG
Jack Adams	11	13	2	3	0	0	0	1	0	.231
Dave Bancroft (SS)	142	477	53	101	10	0	3	33	15	.212
Ed Burns	78	219	14	51	8	1	0	14	3	.233
Bobby Byrne	48	141	22	33	10	1	0	9	6	.234
Claude Cooper	56	104	9	20	2	0	0	11	1	.192
Gavvy Cravath (RF)	137	448	70	127	21	8	11	70	9	.283
Oscar Dugey	41	50	9	11	3	0	0	1	3	.220
Bob Gandy	1	2	0	0	0	0	0	0	0	.000
Wilbur Good	75	136	25	34	4	3	1	15	7	.250
Bill Killefer (C)	97	286	22	62	5	4	3	27	2	.217
Fred Luderus (1B)	146	508	52	143	26	3	5	53	8	.281
Billy Maharg	1	1	0	0	0	0	0	0	0	.000
Bert Niehoff (2B)	146	548	65	133	(42)	4	4	61	20	.243
Dode Paskert (CF)	149	555	82	155	30	7	8	46	22	.279
Milt Stock (3B)	132	509	61	143	25	6	1	43	21	.281
Bud Weiser	4	10	1	3	1	0	0	1	0	.300
Possum Whitted (LF)	147	526	68	148	20	12	6	68	29	.281
		4,985	581	1,244	(223)	53	42	486	149	.250

Manager Pat Moran (center, wearing sweater and carrying ball bag) watches the defending National League champs work out at St. Petersburg's Coffee Pot Park in 1916.

Erosion began setting in fast for the Phillies in 1917. The team again finished second, but was hardly as competitive as the 1916 group. The New York Giants ran away with the pennant by 10 games.

The Phillies ran a good race for a while. They held first place as late as June 24 before losing it to the Giants for good. They stayed close for a while after that, but a pitching collapse in late July made a late-season run at McGraw's Giants impossible.

Grover Cleveland Alexander was, once again, phenomenal. He won 30 games, led the league in earned run average (1.86) and innings pitched (388), and completely dominated the National League. But his major helpers from 1916 faded. Eppa Rixey dipped to 16–21. Al Demaree was gone to the Cubs. Chief Bender rebounded to 8–2, and Erskine Mayer was 11–6, but even Joe Oeschger's 15–14 record wasn't enough to save the cause.

Catcher Bill Killefer had a magnificent season. He batted .274 and led the NL catchers with 617 putouts and 14 double plays, as well as a .984 fielding percentage. Gavvy Cravath's dozen home runs were enough to lead the league, but the franchise was fading fast. The team batting average of .248 was in the middle of the pack, and, without Alexander, the team ERA would have ballooned from 2.46. In fact, it did just that the following year, which was played without Alexander.

The announcement hit Philadelphia like an earthquake. The National League meetings were being held in New York City on December 11. World War I was on and Alexander had been drafted and told to be ready for call-up. William F. Baker, able to use the excuse that he feared for Alex's safe return from the European battlefields, made a trade with the Chicago Cubs. Alexander and Bill Killefer went to Chicago. The Phillies received pitcher Mike Pendergast, catcher Pickles Dilhoefer, and $60,000.

Pressed about it later, Baker admitted that the war was not his main consideration in dealing the best pitcher in his league. "I needed the money," he said.

1917

Record: 87–65
Finish: Second
Games Behind: 10
Manager: Pat Moran

	W	L	G	GS	CG	IP	H	BB	K	ERA
Grover C. Alexander	(30)	13	45	(44)	(35)	(388)	(336)	58	(201)	(1.86)
Chief Bender	8	2	20	10	8	113	84	26	43	1.67
Paul Fittery	1	1	17	2	1	56	69	27	13	4.50
Jimmy Lavender	6	8	28	14	7	129	119	44	52	3.56
Erskine Mayer	11	6	28	18	11	160	160	33	64	2.76
Joe Oeschger	15	14	42	30	18	262	241	72	123	2.75
Eppa Rixey	16	(21)	39	36	23	281	249	67	121	2.27
	87	65		154	103	1,389	1,258	327	617	2.46

Shutouts: Alexander (8), Oeschger (5), Rixey (4), Bender (4), Mayer

	G	AB	R	H	2B	3B	HR	RBI	SB	AVG
Jack Adams	43	107	4	22	4	1	1	7	0	.206
Dave Bancroft (SS)	127	478	56	116	22	5	4	43	14	.243
Ed Burns	20	49	2	10	1	0	0	6	2	.204
Bobby Byrne	13	14	1	5	0	0	0	0	0	.357
Claude Cooper	24	29	5	3	1	0	0	1	0	.103
Gavvy Gravath (RF)	140	503	70	141	29	16	(12)	83	6	.280
Oscar Dugey	44	72	12	14	4	1	0	9	2	.194
Johnny Evers	56	183	20	41	5	1	1	12	8	.224
Bill Killefer (C)	125	409	28	112	12	0	0	31	4	.274
Fred Luderus (1B)	154	522	57	136	24	4	5	72	5	.261
Patsy McGaffigan	19	60	5	10	1	0	0	6	1	.167
Bert Niehoff (2B)	114	361	30	92	17	4	2	42	8	.255
Dode Paskert (CF)	141	546	78	137	27	11	4	43	19	.251
Harry Pearce	7	16	2	4	3	0	0	2	0	.250
Frank Schulte	64	149	24	32	10	0	1	15	4	.215
Milt Stock (3B)	150	564	76	149	27	6	3	53	25	.264
Possum Whitted (LF)	149	553	69	155	24	9	3	70	19	.280
		5,084	578	1,262	(225)	60	38	526	109	.248

It marked the start of the end of the Phillies' era of "goodness." Until the Phils won the National League East three times in a row from 1976 to 1978, the franchise could not claim anything close to the pennant-second-second achieved during 1915–17.

You can't fool all the people all the time. Attendance dropped drastically to 354,428, beginning a trend. The team didn't top that figure again until 1943.

1918

Record: 55–68
Finish: Sixth
Games Behind: 26
Manager: Pat Moran

It is impossible to subtract 30 victories from the pitching staff and expect to do as well as the season before.

It is more than impossible to subtract 46, which includes the two top pitchers from the staff. But that was the dilemma facing Pat Moran when he gathered his team for spring training in 1918.

Grover Cleveland Alexander, who had carried the franchise on his back since 1911, went from Philadelphia to Chicago to France (after three games with the Cubs). Eppa Rixey, who would later join him in the Hall of Fame, joined Ol' Pete in Europe for World War I. Alex had won 30 and Eppa 16 the previous season.

The pitcher the Phillies got for Ol' Pete, Mike Pendergast, pitched well and went 13–14, and Bradley Hogg was 13–13. But Joe Oeschger flopped to 6–18. Gavvy Cravath led the NL in homers with eight, but the Philadelphia scoring output faded to 430. Nobody hit .300. The Phillies finished sixth, 13 games under .500 and only four games out of the basement they were about to occupy regularly.

On July 17, the Phillies played their longest game in club history, falling to the Chicago Cubs, 2–1, in 21 innings at Cubs Park.

Two outstanding outfielders, Cy Williams and Irish Meusel, joined the team. Unfortunately for Pat Moran, the only salvation would have been Cy Young and Stan Musial. It didn't matter that William F. Baker "needed the money," because he obviously didn't need the manager who might have been the greatest in the franchise's history. Moran had ripped the owner for the Alexander deal, which constituted good judgment on Pat's part.

The old expression reads: "If you want to dance, you've got to pay the piper." With the 1918 Phillies, it should have read: "If you want to dance,

	W	L	G	GS	CG	IP	H	BB	K	ERA
Dixie Davis	0	2	17	2	1	47	43	30	18	3.06
Gary Fortune	0	2	5	2	1	31	41	19	10	8.13
Brad Hogg	13	13	29	25	17	228	201	61	81	2.53
Elmer Jacobs	9	5	18	14	12	123	91	42	33	2.41
Alex Main	2	2	8	4	1	35	30	16	14	4.63
Erskine Mayer	7	4	13	13	7	104	108	26	16	3.12
Joe Oeschger	6	(18)	30	23	13	184	159	83	60	3.03
Mike Prendergast	13	14	33	30	20	252	257	46	41	2.89
Ben Tincup	0	1	8	1	0	17	24	6	6	7.41
Milt Watson	5	7	23	11	6	113	126	36	29	3.42
Frank Woodward	0	0	2	0	0	6	6	4	4	6.00
	55	68		125	78	1,140	1,086	369	312	3.15

Shutouts: Hogg (3), Jacobs (3), Oeschger (2), Main

	G	AB	R	H	2B	3B	HR	RBI	SB	AVG
Jack Adams (C)	84	227	10	40	4	0	0	12	5	.176
Dave Bancroft (SS)	125	499	69	132	19	4	0	26	11	.265
Ed Burns	68	184	10	38	1	1	0	9	1	.207
Gavvy Cravath (RF)	121	426	43	99	27	5	(8)	54	7	.232
Mickey Devine	4	8	0	1	1	0	0	0	0	.125
Pickles Dillhoefer	8	11	0	1	0	0	0	0	2	.091
Justin Fitzgerald	66	133	21	39	8	0	0	6	3	.293
Ed Hemingway	33	108	7	23	4	1	0	12	4	.213
Fred Luderus (1B)	125	468	54	135	23	2	5	67	4	.288
Patsy McGaffigan(2B)	54	192	17	39	3	2	1	8	3	.203
Irish Meusel (LF)	124	473	47	132	25	6	4	62	18	.279
Harry Pearce	60	164	16	40	3	2	0	18	5	.244
Ty Pickup	1	1	0	1	0	0	0	0	0	1.000
Milt Stock (3B)	123	481	62	132	14	1	1	42	20	.274
Possum Whitted	24	86	7	21	4	0	0	3	4	.244
Cy Williams (CF)	94	351	49	97	14	1	6	39	10	.276
		4,192	430	1,022	158	28	25	376	97	.244

you've got to pay the piker." Moran refused to pay lip service to stingy Baker. So, at the end of the season, Moran was discharged as manager. It was as if Baker had pulled the plug on moderate success and all that was left was a whirlpool headed down the drain.

For almost three decades, the whirlpool swirled.

1919

Record: 47–90
Finish: Eighth
Games Behind: 47½
Managers: Jack Coombs, Gavvy Cravath

The Phillies began paying the price for their bad front office moves almost immediately. They plunged to the bottom of the National League four years after they had won the championship. Worse yet, they wound up 47½ games behind the man who had managed them the previous season as Pat Moran guided the Cincinnati Reds to the National League title.

The new manager for the Phillies was Jack Coombs, who had starred as a pitcher for Connie Mack's Athletics in their glory years of 1910–11 and who was a popular man in Philadelphia.

A dignified man with a degree from Colby College, Coombs lasted until July 4 when he had his last blowup with Baker. Coombs was replaced by Gavvy Cravath as manager, but the team limped home last.

Baker made deal after deal in an attempt to put together what he had ripped apart in the two previous seasons. One trade yielded Specs Meadows, who was a quality pitcher, but too many others dealt mediocrity for mediocrity.

The Phillies were weak enough to finish seven games out of seventh place, but in one August game, the bookies were getting a big play on the Phillies to beat the third-place Chicago Cubs. A couple of Chicago baseball writers got anonymous calls that the game was fixed. The rumors were so strong that the Cubs switched pitchers, sending Grover Cleveland Alexander out to face his former mates.

Meadows was the stronger pitcher that day, however, and beat Alex, 3–0. And that night, *Philadelphia Bulletin* writer Bill Brandt called manager Cravath for his reaction to the fix story.

Gavvy's reply was a classic:

	W	L	G	GS	CG	IP	H	BB	K	ERA
Red Ames	0	2	3	2	1	16	26	3	4	6.19
Mike Cantwell	1	3	5	3	2	27	36	9	6	5.67
Larry Cheney	2	5	9	6	5	57	69	28	25	4.58
Rags Faircloth	0	0	2	0	0	2	5	0	0	9.00
Brad Hogg	5	12	22	19	13	150	163	55	48	4.44
Elmer Jacobs	6	10	17	15	13	129	150	44	37	3.84
Lee Meadows	8	10	18	17	15	149	128	49	88	2.48
Pat Murray	0	2	8	2	1	34	50	12	11	6.35
Joe Oeschger	0	1	5	4	2	38	52	16	5	5.92
Gene Packard	6	8	21	16	10	134	167	30	24	4.16
Mike Prendergast	0	1	5	0	0	15	20	10	5	8.40
Eppa Rixey	6	12	23	18	11	154	160	50	63	3.97
George Smith	5	11	31	20	11	185	194	46	42	3.21
Milt Watson	2	4	8	4	3	47	51	19	12	5.17
Lefty Weinert	0	0	1	0	0	4	11	2	0	18.00
Frank Woodward	6	9	17	12	6	101	109	35	27	4.72
	47	90		138	93	1,243 (1,391)		408	397	4.17

Shutouts: Meadows (3), Packard, Rixey, Smith

	G	AB	R	H	2B	3B	HR	RBI	SB	AVG
Jack Adams (C)	78	232	14	54	7	2	1	17	4	.233
Doug Baird	66	242	33	61	13	3	2	30	13	.252
Dave Bancroft (SS)	92	335	45	91	13	7	0	25	8	.272
Lena Blackburne (3B)	72	291	32	58	10	5	2	19	2	.199
Hick Cady	34	98	6	21	6	0	1	19	1	.214
Leo Callahan (RF)	81	235	26	54	14	4	1	9	5	.230
Pat Cavanaugh	1	1	0	0	0	0	0	0	0	.000
Nig Clarke	26	62	4	15	3	0	0	2	1	.242
Gavvy Cravath	83	214	34	73	18	5	(12)	45	8	.341
Bevo LeBourveau	17	63	4	17	0	0	0	0	0	.270
Fred Luderus (1B)	138	509	60	149	30	6	5	49	6	.293
Irish Meusel (LF)	135	521	65	159	26	7	5	59	24	.305
Mike Pasquariello	1	1	1	1	0	0	0	0	0	1.000
Gene Paulette (2B)	67	243	20	63	8	3	1	31	10	.259
Harry Pearce	68	244	24	44	3	3	0	9	6	.180
Lou Raymond	1	2	0	1	0	0	0	0	0	.500
Eddie Sicking	61	185	16	40	2	1	0	15	4	.216
Walt Tragesser	35	114	7	27	7	0	0	8	4	.237
Possum Whitted	78	289	32	72	14	1	3	32	5	.249
Cy Williams (CF)	109	435	54	121	21	1	9	39	9	.278
Bert Yeabsley	3	0	0	0	0	0	0	0	0	.000
Doc Wallace	2	4	0	1	0	0	0	0	0	.250
		4,746	510	1,191 (208)		50	(42)	436	114	.251

"Sure I heard something about it," he said, "but I don't know anything about it. Jeez, I don't know why they gotta bring a thing like this up just because we win one. Gee, we're likely to win a game most anytime."

As fans for the next three decades would learn, the Phillies were more likely to lose a game most anytime. And 1919 was just the start by which futility could be measured. None of the starting pitchers won more than they lost, and about the only offensive plus was Cravath, who led the league with 12 home runs in just 214 at bats and who batted .341.

In their most noteworthy game of the year, the Phillies battled Brooklyn to a 9–9 tie in 20 innings, the longest tie game in National League history. Joe Oeschger pitched all the way for the Phils.

1920

Record: 62–91
Finish: Eighth
Games Behind: 30½
Manager: Gavvy Cravath

Gavvy Cravath, in his first (and last) full year as Phillies' manager, uttered the big lie that would be spoken over and over again by a bevy of his successors. Just before the season began, he said, "We're not a last-place club."

It took until the last day of the season to prove Gavvy wrong. The Phillies were edged by half a game by the Braves for seventh place.

Cravath's beliefs were based on what he considered an excellent outfield— Cy Williams, Irish Meusel, and Casey Stengel. And he was right. The problem was that the Phillies had very little going for them elsewhere in their lineup.

Williams led the league with 15 home runs and batted .325, fifth best in the

	W	L	G	GS	CG	IP	H	BB	K	ERA
Huck Betts	1	1	27	4	1	88	86	33	18	3.58
Mike Cantwell	0	3	5	1	0	23	25	15	8	3.91
Red Causey	7	14	35	26	11	181	203	79	30	4.33
Johnny Enzmann	2	3	16	1	1	59	79	16	35	3.82
Bert Gallia	2	6	18	5	1	72	79	29	35	4.50
Bill Hubbell	9	9	24	20	9	150	176	42	26	3.84
Jim Keenan	0	0	1	0	0	3	3	1	2	3.00
Lee Meadows	16	14	35	33	19	247	249	90	95	2.84
Eppa Rixey	11	(22)	41	33	25	284	288	69	109	3.48
George Smith	13	18	43	28	10	251	265	51	561	3.44
Lefty Weinert	1	1	10	2	0	22	27	19	10	6.14
	62	91		153	77	1,381	1,480	444	419	3.63

Shutouts: Meadows (3), Smith (2), Causey, Hubbell, Rixey

	G	AB	R	H	2B	3B	HR	RBI	SB	AVG
Dave Bancroft	42	171	23	51	7	2	0	5	1	.298
Gavvy Gravath	46	45	2	13	5	0	1	11	0	.289
Art Fletcher (SS)	102	379	36	112	25	7	4	38	4	.296
Bevo LeBourveau	84	261	29	67	7	2	3	12	9	.257
Fred Luderus	16	32	1	6	2	0	0	4	0	.156
Irish Meusel (LF)	138	518	75	160	27	8	14	69	17	.309
Dots Miller	98	343	41	87	12	2	1	27	13	.254
Ralph Miller (3B)	97	338	28	74	14	1	0	28	3	.219
Gene Paulette (1B)	143	562	59	162	16	6	1	36	9	.288
Johnny Rawlings (2B)	98	384	39	90	19	2	3	30	9	.234
Casey Stengel (RF)	129	445	53	130	25	6	9	50	7	.292
Walt Tragesser	62	176	17	37	11	1	6	26	4	.210
Walt Walsh	2	0	0	0	0	0	0	0	0	.000
Mack Wheat (C)	78	230	15	52	10	3	3	20	3	.226
Cy Williams (CF)	148	590	88	192	36	10	(15)	72	18	.325
Frank Withrow	48	132	8	24	4	1	0	12	0	.182
Russ Wrightstone	76	206	23	54	6	1	3	17	3	.262
		5,264	565	1,385	229	54	(64)	483	100	.263

NL. Meusel batted .309 with Stengel coming in at .292. Cravath also pointed out on the eve of the season that he believed he had a fine first baseman in Gene Paulette, who was taking over for Fred Luderus, and baseball's best shortstop in Dave Bancroft.

The Phillies of 1920 stand at attention during playing of the National Anthem at Baker Bowl. They are: (from left) Dave Bancroft, Frank Withrow, Lee Meadows, coach Jesse Tannehill, and Cecil Causy.

Two months later, he didn't have Bancroft, and, a year later, the Phillies didn't have Paulette. Baker, in one of his worst trades, sent Bancroft to the Giants for aging shortstop Art Fletcher, pitcher Bill Hubbell, and $100,000. Fletcher batted .296 but had the range of Billy Penn's statute atop City Hall. Paulette hit .288 but was thrown out of baseball before the next season began for his previous close association with gamblers.

Lee Meadows pitched excellent baseball and was 16–14, but no other starter had a winning record. Eppa Rixey lost 22 games and was on his way to Cincinnati and the Hall of Fame.

The fans still showed up at the ball park, 330,998 in fact. Never again in the eras of Baker or Gerald Nugent would the franchise see those kinds of numbers again.

1921

Record: 51–103
Finish: Eighth
Games Behind: 43½
Managers: Wild Bill Donovan,
Kaiser Wilhelm

The manager William F. Baker chose to replace Gavvy Cravath was Wild Bill Donovan, a Philadelphian since childhood and a fine major league pitcher with 18 years service and 187 big league wins.

As manager with the Phillies, he fell 162 victories below his playing standard. This proved to be Donovan's last managing job at the major league level. He had managed the Yankees for three so-so years from 1915 to 1917.

Donovan lasted for 102 games before Baker fired him with the following terse announcement:

	W	L	G	GS	CG	IP	H	BB	K	ERA
Stan Baumgartner	3	6	22	7	2	67	103	22	13	6.98
Petie Behan	0	1	2	2	1	11	7	1	3	5.73
Huck Betts	3	7	32	2	1	101	141	14	28	4.46
Red Causey	3	3	7	7	4	51	58	11	8	2.82
Bill Hubbell	9	16	36	30	15	220	269	38	43	4.34
Jim Keenan	1	2	15	2	0	32	48	15	7	6.75
Lee Meadows	11	16	28	27	15	194	226	62	52	4.31
Jimmy Ring	10	19	34	30	21	246	258	88	88	4.25
Duke Sedgwick	1	3	16	5	1	71	81	32	21	4.94
George Smith	4	(20)	39	28	12	221	303	52	45	4.76
Lefty Weinert	1	0	8	0	0	12	8	5	2	1.50
Kaiser Wilhelm	0	0	4	0	0	8	11	3	1	3.38
Jesse Winters	5	10	18	14	10	114	142	28	22	3.64
	51	103		154	82	1,349	(1,665)	371	333	4.48

Shutouts: Meadows (2), Hubbell, Smith

	G	AB	R	H	2B	3B	HR	RBI	SB	AVG
Frank Bruggy (C)	86	277	28	86	11	2	5	28	6	.310
Butch Henline	33	111	8	34	2	0	0	8	1	.306
Lee King	64	216	25	58	19	4	4	32	1	.269
Ed Konetchy (1B)	72	268	38	86	17	4	8	59	3	.321
Bevo LeBourveau (RF)	93	281	42	83	12	5	6	35	4	.295
Cliff Lee	88	286	31	88	14	4	4	29	5	.308
Irish Meusel (LF)	89	343	59	121	21	7	12	51	8	.353
Dots Miller	84	320	37	95	11	3	0	25	3	.297
Ralph Miller	57	204	19	62	10	0	3	26	3	.304
John Monroe	41	133	13	38	4	2	1	8	2	.286
Greasy Neale	22	57	7	12	1	0	0	1	3	.211
Frank Parkinson (SS)	108	391	36	99	20	2	5	32	3	.253
John Peters	55	155	7	45	4	0	3	23	1	.290
Don Rader	9	32	4	9	2	0	0	3	0	.281
Goldie Rapp	52	202	28	56	7	1	1	10	6	.277
Johnny Rawlings	60	254	20	74	14	2	1	16	4	.291
Lance Richbourg	10	5	2	1	1	0	0	0	1	.200
Jimmy Smith (2B)	67	247	31	57	8	1	4	22	2	.231
Casey Stengel	24	59	7	18	3	1	0	4	1	.305
Curt Walker	21	77	11	26	2	1	0	8	0	.338
Mack Wheat	10	27	1	5	2	1	0	4	0	.185
Cy Williams (CF)	146	562	67	180	26	6	18	75	5	.320
Russ Wrightstone (3B)	109	372	59	110	13	4	9	51	4	.296
		5,329	617	1,512	238	50	(88)	573	66	.284

"Donovan's activities with the Philadelphia National League club for the balance of the season will be limited to the endorsement of his pay check every two weeks—provided, however, that he does not break the rules of Organized Baseball."

As it turned out, it was Baker who skirted the rules of organized baseball in setting up the trade of Irish Meusel to the Giants. Baker stated that Donovan had reported Meusel for being indifferent and, as a result, Baker had suspended the outfield star. When Donovan was fired, Commissioner Landis intervened, asking Wild Bill for his side of the Meusel story. Donovan declared that he had never reported Irish for indifference. Landis then ripped Baker to shreds in an off-the-record meeting with newspapermen.

The commissioner, however, never negated the deal and, although he ordered Baker to honor the financial part of Donovan's contract, he didn't tell Baker he had to rehire the manager. So Baker landed himself Kaiser Wilhelm, who signed on for small bucks, a fact that endeared him to the heart of Baker.

Big bucks, small bucks. Donovan, Wilhelm. None of it mattered. John McGraw could have been the manager with Walter Alston and Earl Weaver as his coaches, and the Phillies still would have been pathetic.

Cy Williams hit 18 homers and batted .320, and third baseman Russ Wrightstone batted .296 and fielded like a cigar store Indian. Lee Meadows was the ace of the staff with 11–16. Columbia George Smith lost a league-topping 20 games. He won four.

The Phillies finished 13½ games out of seventh place, although they set a new major league record with 88 home runs. In one game, Meadows and shortstop Ralph Miller each hit grand slams in an 11–6 win over the Boston Braves at Baker Bowl.

George Smith's 20 losses led the league in 1921.

1922

Record: 57–96
Finish: Seventh
Games Behind: 35½
Manager: Kaiser Wilhelm

This was the year of the first "shootout in Chicago," which was even worse than the infamous one in May 1979. That one wound up with the Phillies winning, 23–22, but never really recovering from it, so much so that they dropped from three straight division championships into fourth place.

In 1922 the Phillies lost the shootout in Chicago. The final score was 26–23, and the 49 runs still stand as the all-time record for most runs in a major league game.

After four innings, the Phillies were losing by a 25–6 score. They almost bounced back, scoring 14 runs in their final two innings. But this year, the Phillies had no lofty perch from which to fall as a result of the shootout. Instead, they escaped the basement for the first time in four seasons, finishing seventh, four games ahead of the Boston Braves.

The Phillies began to develop their good-hit, no-pitch tradition of the late '20s and early '30s about this time. The 1922 club could hit—116 league-leading homers and a .282 team batting average. But the pitching staff had an earned run average of 4.64.

Cy Williams hit 26 home runs, making him runner-up to Rogers Hornsby's 42. He batted .308, which was lowest among the outfield regulars, with Curt Walker hitting .337 and Cliff Lee .322. Catcher Butch Henline, later a major league umpire, hit .316.

Jimmy Ring and Lee Meadows, both 12–18, were the aces of the staff. No one else won more than eight games. And at the end of the season Wilhelm was dropped by Baker.

	W	L	G	GS	CG	IP	H	BB	K	ERA
Stan Baumgartner	1	1	6	1	0	10	18	5	2	6.30
Petie Behan	4	2	7	5	3	47	49	14	13	2.49
Huck Betts	1	0	7	0	0	15	23	8	4	9.60
Bill Hubbell	7	15	35	24	11	189	257	41	33	5.00
Lee Meadows	12	18	33	33	19	237	264	71	62	4.02
Lerton Pinto	0	1	9	0	0	25	31	14	4	5.04
Jimmy Ring	12	18	40	33	17	249	292	(103)	116	4.59
John Singleton	1	10	22	9	3	93	127	38	27	5.90
George Smith	5	14	42	8	6	194	250	35	44	4.78
Tom Sullivan	0	0	3	0	0	8	16	5	2	11.25
Lefty Weinert	8	11	34	22	10	167	189	70	58	3.39
Jesse Winters	6	6	34	9	4	138	176	56	29	5.35
	57	96		154	73	1,372	(1,692)	460	394	4.64

Shutouts: Meadows (2), Behan, Hubell, Singleton, Smith

	G	AB	R	H	2B	3B	HR	RBI	SB	AVG
Stan Benton	6	19	1	4	1	0	0	3	0	.211
Art Fletcher (SS)	110	396	46	111	20	5	7	53	3	.280
Butch Henline (C)	125	430	57	136	20	4	14	64	2	.316
Lee King	19	53	8	12	5	1	2	13	0	.226
Bevo LeBourveau	74	167	24	45	8	3	2	20	0	.269
Cliff Lee (LF)	122	422	65	136	29	6	17	77	2	.322
Roy Leslie (1B)	141	513	44	139	23	2	6	60	3	.271
John Mokan	47	151	20	38	7	1	3	27	1	.252
Frank Parkinson (2B)	141	545	86	150	18	6	15	70	3	.275
John Peters	55	143	15	35	9	1	4	24	0	.245
Goldie Rapp (3B)	119	502	58	127	26	3	0	38	6	.253
Jimmy Smith	38	114	13	25	1	0	1	6	1	.219
Curt Walker (RF)	148	581	102	196	36	11	12	89	11	.337
Cy Williams (CF)	151	584	98	180	30	6	26	92	11	.308
Frank Withrow	10	21	3	7	2	0	0	3	0	.333
Russ Wrightstone	99	331	56	101	18	6	5	33	4	.305
	5,459	738	1,537	268	55	(116)	685	48		.282

1923

Record: 50–104
Finish: Eighth
Games Behind: 45½
Manager: Art Fletcher

The new manager was William F. Baker's favorite, Art Fletcher. He was the shortstop that Baker had acquired in the Dave Bancroft deal. Now Baker was asking him to lead the team from the depths of the National League standings.

Again the Phillies led the league in home runs (112). Again they put together a fine team batting average (.278). And again the pitching was awful, except that this season was even worse than 1922 (5.30 team ERA).

The lively ball and the short right field fence in Baker Bowl were becoming a two-edged sword for anyone who pitched for the Phillies for a living. Considering all of this, plus the fact that he was a wild pitcher, Jimmy Ring had an extraordinary season. His record was 18–16 and his ERA 3.76. Fletcher had no one else who could come close to those figures as Ring accounted for 36 percent of his team's victories.

Cy Williams poked 41 homers to lead the league and drove in 114 runs. Four Phillie regulars hit over .300, topped by Butch Henline's .324.

On May 11 the Phillies beat the St. Louis Cardinals, 20–14, in a game in which the teams combined for 10 home runs, two by Johnny Mokan. Two months later the Phils scored 12 runs in the sixth inning of a 17–4 win over the Chicago Cubs. That was a club record.

This was also the year the Phillies bought shortstop Heinie Sand. Sand's keystone mate, Cotton Tierney, came to the Phillies from Pittsburgh early in the season and hit .317 with 11 homers and 65 RBI. But the price for him was high, pitcher Lee Meadows.

	W	L	G	GS	CG	IP	H	BB	K	ERA
Petie Behan	3	12	31	17	5	131	182	57	37	5.50
Huck Betts	2	4	19	4	3	84	100	14	18	3.11
Jim Bishop	0	3	15	0	0	33	48	11	5	6.27
Johnny Couch	2	4	11	7	2	65	91	21	18	5.26
Art Gardiner	0	0	1	0	0	0	1	0	0	0.00
Whitey Glazner	7	14	28	23	12	161	195	63	51	4.70
Jim Grant	0	0	2	0	0	4	10	4	0	13.50
Ralph Head	2	9	35	13	5	132	185	57	24	6.68
Walter Holke	0	0	1	0	0	1	1	0	0	0.00
Bill Hubbell	1	6	22	5	1	55	102	17	8	8.35
Broadway Jones	0	0	3	0	0	8	5	7	1	9.00
Lee Meadows	1	3	8	5	0	20	40	15	10	13.05
Red Miller	0	0	1	0	0	2	6	1	0	27.00
Clarence Mitchell	9	10	29	19	8	139	170	46	42	4.73
Pat Ragan	0	0	1	0	0	3	6	0	0	6.00
Jimmy Ring	18	16	39	36	23	313	336	(115)	112	3.76
Lefty Weinert	4	17	38	20	8	156	207	81	46	5.42
Jesse Winters	1	6	21	6	1	78	116	39	23	7.38
	50	104		155	68	1,385	(1,801)	(549)	384	5.30

Shutouts: Glazner (2), Mitchell

	G	AB	R	H	2B	3B	HR	RBI	SB	AVG
Joe Bennett	1	0	0	0	0	0	0	0	0	.000
Tod Dennehy	9	24	4	7	2	0	0	2	0	.292
Butch Henline (C)	111	330	45	107	14	3	7	46	7	.324
Walter Holke (1B)	147	562	64	175	31	4	7	70	7	.311
Freddy Leach	52	104	5	27	4	0	1	16	1	.260
Cliff Lee	107	355	54	114	20	4	11	47	3	.321
Carl Lord	17	47	3	11	2	0	0	2	0	.234
Lenny Metz	12	37	4	8	0	0	0	3	0	.216
Johnny Mokan (LF)	113	400	76	125	23	3	10	48	6	.313
Mickey O'Brien	15	21	3	7	2	0	0	0	0	.333
Dixie Parker	4	5	0	1	0	0	0	1	0	.200
Frank Parkinson	67	219	21	53	12	0	3	28	0	.242
Goldie Rapp	47	179	27	47	5	0	1	10	1	.263
Heinie Sand (SS)	132	470	85	107	16	5	4	32	7	.228
Cotton Tierney (2B)	121	480	68	152	31	1	11	65	3	.317
Curt Walker (RF)	140	527	66	148	26	5	5	66	12	.281
Cy Williams (CF)	136	535	98	157	22	3	(41)	114	11	.293
Jimmie Wilson	85	252	27	66	9	0	1	25	4	.262
Andy Woehr	13	41	3	14	2	0	0	3	0	.341
Russ Wrightstone (3B)	119	392	59	107	21	7	7	57	5	.273
		5,491	748	1,528	259	39	(112)	677	70	.278

The Phillies, improved by five victories, climbed out of the National League basement and into seventh place in their second year under Art Fletcher. They appeared to be making some progress. In reality, they weren't. It was just a case of the Braves, under new manager Dave Bancroft, slipping below them.

William F. Baker could have patted himself on the back after this season. After all, he had traded Fletcher for Bancroft, and Art had outmanaged Dave by three games. But Baker was too busy trying to meet the payroll without dipping into his personal fortune to worry about such things. Over 71,000 more people paid their way into Baker Bowl than had the previous season.

Jimmy Ring and Bill Hubbell each won 10 games to lead a staff that still surrendered almost five runs a game. Cy Williams slipped from 41 to 24 home runs but led the team with a .328 average. First baseman Walt Holke batted .300, and Russ Wrightstone hit. 307.

Toward the end of the season, Giant rookie Jimmy O'Connell foolishly tried to bribe Heinie Sand. The shortstop reported the bribe and Commissioner Landis banned O'Connell from organized baseball. Also banned was New York coach Cozy Dolan, but three future Hall of Famers, Frankie Frisch, Ross Youngs, and George Kelly, were exonerated.

After the season, Fletcher was rehired for his third season as manager, first since Pat Moran to achieve that tenure at the Phils' helm.

1924

Record: 55–96
Finish: Seventh
Games Behind: 37
Manager: Art Fletcher

Owner William Baker (right) and manager Art Fletcher couldn't talk the Phillies out of the second division between 1923 and 1926.

	W	L	G	GS	CG	IP	H	BB	K	ERA
Huck Betts	7	10	37	9	2	144	160	42	46	4.31
Jim Bishop	0	1	7	1	0	17	24	7	3	6.35
Hal Carlson	8	17	38	24	12	204	267	55	66	4.85
Johnny Couch	4	8	37	6	3	137	170	39	23	4.73
Whitey Glazner	7	16	35	24	8	157	210	63	41	5.85
Earl Hamilton	0	1	3	0	0	6	9	2	2	10.50
Bill Hubbell	10	9	36	22	9	179	233	45	30	4.83
Bert Lewis	0	0	12	0	0	18	23	7	3	6.00
Clarence Mitchell	6	13	30	26	9	165	223	58	36	5.62
Joe Oeschger	2	7	19	8	0	65	88	16	8	4.43
Lerton Pinto	0	0	3	0	0	4	7	0	1	9.00
Jimmy Ring	10	12	32	31	16	215	236	(108)	72	3.98
Ray Steineder	1	1	9	0	0	29	29	16	11	4.34
Lefty Weinert	0	1	8	1	0	15	10	11	7	2.40
	55	96		152	59	1,355	(1,689)	469	349	4.87

Shutouts: Glazner (2), Hubbell (2), Carlson, Mitchell, Ring

	G	AB	R	H	2B	3B	HR	RBI	SB	AVG
Spoke Emery	5	3	3	2	0	0	0	0	0	.667
Hod Ford (2B)	145	530	58	144	27	5	3	53	1	.272
George Harper (RF)	109	411	68	121	26	6	16	55	10	.294
Butch Henline (C)	115	289	41	82	18	4	5	35	1	.284
Fritz Henrich	36	90	4	19	4	0	0	4	0	.211
Walter Holke (1B)	148	563	60	169	23	6	6	64	3	.300
Freddy Leach	8	28	6	13	2	1	2	7	0	.464
Cliff Lee	21	56	4	14	3	2	1	7	0	.250
Lenny Metz	7	7	1	2	0	0	0	1	0	.286
Johnny Mokan (LF)	96	366	50	95	15	1	7	44	7	.260
Frank Parkinson	62	156	14	33	7	0	1	19	3	.212
Heinie Sand (SS)	137	539	79	132	21	6	6	40	5	.245
Joe Schultz	88	284	35	80	15	1	5	29	6	.282
Curt Walker	24	71	11	21	6	1	1	8	0	.296
Lew Wendell	21	32	3	8	1	0	0	2	0	.250
Cy Williams (CF)	148	558	101	183	31	11	24	93	7	.328
Jimmie Wilson	95	280	32	78	16	3	6	39	5	.279
Andy Woehr	50	152	11	33	4	5	0	17	2	.217
Russ Wrightstone (3B)	118	388	55	119	24	4	7	58	5	.307
		5,306	676	1,459	256	56	94	615	57	.275

1925

Record: 68–85
Finish: Sixth (tie)
Games Behind: 27
Manager: Art Fletcher

For the first time in almost a decade, Philadelphia began to get excited about the Phillies. Fletcher, in his third year as manager, seemed to be building a team that might challenge for the first division before long. In 1925 the Phillies finished just nine games out of fourth place and batted .295 as a team. But the earned run average swelled to 5.02, even though two pitchers had good seasons.

Jimmy Ring had a 14–16 record, and spitballer Hal Carlson was 13–14. The other pitchers were undependable, winning this time, losing the next.

But the hitting was terrific. First baseman Chicken Hawks batted .322 and was never heard from at the major league level again. Sand lifted his average to .278. Williams slipped to 13 home runs in an injury-riddled season but batted .331. The new outfield hitting star was George Harper with 18 homers and a .349 average. Catcher Jimmie Wilson hit .328, and utility man Russ Wrightstone batted .346 with 14 homers and 61 RBI in only 286 at-bats.

The Phillies also managed to snap a 20-game winning streak against them by Cincinnati Reds pitcher Pete Donohue with a 5–4 victory.

The fans eagerly awaited a higher climb in 1926. So did Fletcher. All were sorely disappointed.

	W	L	G	GS	CG	IP	H	BB	K	ERA
Huck Betts	4	5	35	7	1	97	146	38	28	5.57
Hal Carlson	13	14	35	32	18	234	281	52	80	4.23
Johnny Couch	5	6	34	7	2	94	112	39	11	5.46
Ray Crumpler	0	0	3	1	0	5	8	2	1	7.20
Art Decatur	4	13	25	15	4	128	172	34	31	5.27
Dana Fillingim	1	0	5	1	0	9	19	6	2	10.00
Bill Hubbell	0	0	2	0	0	3	5	1	0	0.00
Jack Knight	7	6	3	11	4	105	161	36	19	6.86
Clarence Mitchell	10	17	32	26	12	199	245	51	46	5.29
Skinny O'Neal	0	0	11	1	0	20	35	12	6	9.45
Ray Pierce	5	4	23	8	4	90	134	24	18	5.50
Jimmy Ring	14	16	38	37	21	270	(325)	(119)	93	4.37
Dutch Ulrich	3	3	21	4	2	65	73	12	29	3.05
Bob Vines	0	0	3	0	0	4	9	3	0	11.25
Claude Willoughby	2	1	3	3	1	23	26	11	6	1.96
	68	85		153	69	1,351	(1,753)	444	371	5.02

Shutouts: Carlson (4), Couch, Mitchell, Ring, Ulrich

	G	AB	R	H	2B	3B	HR	RBI	SB	AVG
George Burns (LF)	88	349	65	102	29	1	1	22	4	.292
George Durning	5	14	3	5	0	0	0	1	0	.357
Lew Fonseca	126	467	78	149	39	5	7	60	6	.319
Barney Friberg (2B)	91	304	41	82	12	1	5	22	1	.270
George Harper (CF)	132	495	86	173	35	7	18	97	10	.349
Chicken Hawks (1B)	105	320	52	103	15	5	5	45	3	.322
Butch Henline	93	263	43	80	12	5	8	48	3	.304
Walter Holke	39	86	11	21	5	0	1	17	0	.244
Clarence Huber (3B)	124	436	46	124	28	5	5	54	3	.284
Wally Kimmick	70	141	16	43	3	2	1	10	0	.305
Freddy Leach	65	292	47	91	15	4	5	28	1	.312
Lenny Metz	11	14	1	0	0	0	0	0	0	.000
Benny Meyer	1	1	1	1	1	0	0	0	0	1.000
Johnny Mokan	75	209	30	69	11	2	6	42	3	.330
Heinie Sand (SS)	148	496	69	138	30	7	3	65	1	.278
Joe Schultz	24	64	10	22	6	0	0	8	1	.344
Lew Wendell	18	26	0	2	0	0	0	3	0	.077
Cy Williams (RF)	107	314	78	104	11	5	13	60	4	.331
Jimmie Wilson (C)	108	335	42	110	19	3	3	54	5	.328
Russ Wrightstone	92	286	48	99	18	5	14	61	0	.346
		5,412	812	1,598	288	58	100	731	48	.295

The Phillies had one stickout this season, pitcher Hal Carlson. The righthander, who still threw the outlawed spitball because he was a bonafide user of the pitch at the time it was deemed illegal, baffled hitters with it. Lefthanded hitters were unable to pull it over the short right field porch at Baker Bowl.

The result was that Carlson won 17 games out of 29 decisions, completed 20, had a 3.23 ERA, and was named to the National League All-Star team at the end of the season by the Baseball Writers' Association.

Carlson was one bright spot in a dismal season in which the Phillies, under Art Fletcher, won 10 fewer games than they had the previous season, slipped from sixth place to eighth, and lost all the momentum they had been building.

Cy Williams hit 18 homers, and outfielder Fred Leach added 11. No other Phillie topped seven. The team average skidded 14 points to .281. Russ Wrightstone accounted for nine runs in one game, with six RBI and three runs scored.

In September, Fletcher was placed under indefinite suspension by John Heydler after an argument with umpire Bill Klem. Baker fired Fletcher during his period of suspension. Once again, Baker would dip into the grab bag of Philadelphia baseball legends to replace his manager. Once again, the experiment would fail miserably.

1926

Record: 58–93
Finish: Eighth
Games Behind: 29½
Manager: Art Fletcher

	W	L	G	GS	CG	IP	H	BB	K	ERA
Ed Baecht	2	0	28	1	1	56	73	28	14	6.11
Jack Bentley	0	2	7	3	0	25	37	12	8	8.28
Hal Carlson	17	12	38	34	20	267	293	47	55	3.24
Wayland Dean	8	16	33	26	15	164	245	89	52	6.09
Art Decatur	0	0	2	1	0	3	6	2	0	6.00
Mike Kelly	0	0	4	0	0	7	9	4	2	9.00
Jack Knight	3	12	35	15	5	143	206	48	29	6.61
Ernie Maun	1	4	14	5	0	38	57	18	9	6.39
Clarence Mitchell	9	14	28	25	12	179	232	55	52	4.58
Ray Pierce	2	7	37	7	1	85	128	35	18	5.61
Pete Rambo	0	0	1	0	0	4	6	4	4	13.50
Lefty Taber	0	0	6	0	0	8	8	5	0	7.88
Dutch Ulrich	8	13	45	17	8	148	178	37	52	4.07
Claude Willoughby	8	12	47	18	6	168	218	71	37	5.95
Rusty Yarnall	0	1	1	0	0	1	3	1	0	18.00
	58	93		152	68	1,294	(1,699)	454	331	5.19

Shutouts: Carlson (3), Dean, Ulrich

	G	AB	R	H	2B	3B	HR	RBI	SB	AVG
Dick Attreau	17	61	9	14	1	1	0	5	0	.230
Jack Bentley (1B)	75	240	19	62	12	3	2	27	0	.258
Joe Buskey	5	8	1	0	0	0	0	0	0	.000
Ed Cotter	17	26	3	8	0	1	0	1	1	.308
Wayland Dean	63	102	11	27	4	0	3	19	0	.265
Lee Dunham	5	4	0	1	0	0	0	1	0	.250
Barney Friberg (2B)	144	478	38	128	21	3	1	51	2	.268
Ray Grimes	32	101	13	30	5	0	0	15	0	.297
George Harper	56	194	32	61	6	5	7	38	6	.314
Butch Henline	99	283	32	80	14	1	2	30	1	.283
Clarence Huber (3B)	118	376	45	92	17	7	1	34	9	.245
Bubber Jonnard	19	34	3	4	1	0	0	2	0	.118
Chick Keating	4	2	0	0	0	0	0	0	0	.000
Wally Kimmick	20	28	0	6	2	1	0	2	0	.214
Freddy Leach (CF)	129	492	73	162	29	7	11	71	6	.329
Johnny Mokan (LF)	127	456	68	138	23	5	6	62	4	.303
Al Nixon	93	311	38	91	18	2	4	41	5	.293
Bob Rice	19	54	3	8	0	1	0	10	0	.148
Heinie Sand (SS)	149	567	99	154	30	5	4	37	2	.272
Denny Sothern	14	53	5	13	1	0	3	10	0	.245
George Stutz	6	9	0	0	0	0	0	0	0	.000
Lew Wendell	1	4	0	0	0	0	0	0	0	.000
Cy Williams (RF)	107	336	63	116	13	4	18	53	2	.345
Jimmy Wilson (C)	90	279	40	85	10	2	4	32	2	.305
Russ Wrightstone	112	368	55	113	23	1	7	57	5	.307
		5,254	687	1,479	244	50	75	632	47	.281

1927

Record: 51–103
Finish: Eighth
Games Behind: 43
Manager: Stuffy McInnis

Philadelphia baseball hero Jack Coombs had been tapped by William F. Baker to replace Pat Moran as manager in 1919. Coombs lasted less than one season.

Philadelphian Wild Bill Donovan had been picked by Baker to replace Gavvy Cravath in 1921. Donovan lasted less than one year.

So maybe Stuffy McInnis should have considered himself successful in 1927. Connie Mack's former first baseman was another Philadelphia baseball institution chosen by Baker to lead the Phillies out of the wilderness. And he lasted a whole season before Baker dismissed him.

It was not the kind of season that Philadelphians remember with fondness. The Phillies had a 14-game losing streak and wound up nine games out of seventh place and 34½ out of the first division. Except for Cy Williams' National League–leading 30 home runs, there was little to cheer for the 305,120 fans who paid their way into Baker Bowl.

Hal Carlson was traded to the Cubs after winning four and losing five. George Harper was traded to the Giants in a three-cornered deal that brought Fresco Thompson (.303 at second base) and Jack Scott (9–21 on the mound). The team ERA reached a lofty 5.35. And the team, which at one stretch was the National League home run leader, accounted for only 57 round-trippers, 52 behind the Giants.

Little wonder that McInnis was let go at the end of the season.

	W	L	G	GS	CG	IP	H	BB	K	ERA
Ed Baecht	0	1	1	1	0	6	12	2	0	12.00
Hal Carlson	4	5	11	9	4	64	80	18	13	5.20
Wayland Dean	0	1	2	0	0	3	6	2	1	12.00
Art Decatur	3	5	29	3	0	97	130	20	27	7.24
Alex Ferguson	8	16	31	31	16	227	280	65	73	4.84
Tony Kaufmann	0	3	5	5	1	19	37	8	4	10.42
Russ Miller	1	1	2	2	1	15	21	3	4	5.40
Clarence Mitchell	6	3	13	12	8	95	99	28	17	4.07
Skinny O'Neal	0	0	2	0	0	5	9	2	2	9.00
Hub Pruett	7	17	31	28	12	186	238	89	90	6.05
Jack Scott	9	(21)	(48)	25	17	233	304	69	69	5.10
Les Sweetland	2	10	21	13	6	104	147	53	21	6.14
Lefty Taber	0	1	3	1	0	3	8	5	0	21.00
Dutch Ulrich	8	11	32	18	14	193	201	40	42	3.17
Augie Walsh	0	1	1	1	1	10	12	5	0	4.50
Claude Willoughby	3	7	35	6	1	98	126	51	14	6.52
	51	103		155	81	1,357	(1,710)	462	377	5.35

Shutouts: Mitchell, Pruett, Scott, Ulrich, Willoughby

	G	AB	R	H	2B	3B	HR	RBI	SB	AVG
Dick Attreau	44	83	17	17	1	1	1	11	1	.205
Henry Baldwin	6	16	1	5	0	0	0	1	0	.313
Jimmy Cooney	78	259	33	70	12	1	0	15	4	.270
Bill Dietrick	5	6	1	1	0	0	0	0	0	.167
Barney Friberg (3B)	111	335	31	78	8	2	1	28	3	.233
Bill Hohman	7	18	1	5	0	0	0	0	0	.278
Bubber Jonnard	53	143	18	42	6	0	0	14	0	.294
Freddy Leach (CF)	140	536	69	164	30	4	12	83	2	.306
Johnny Mokan	74	213	22	61	13	2	0	33	5	.286
Stuffy McInnis	1	0	0	0	0	0	0	0	0	.000
Al Nixon	54	154	18	48	7	0	0	18	1	.312
Harry O'Donnell	16	16	1	1	0	0	0	2	0	.063
Heinie Sand (SS)	141	535	87	160	22	8	1	49	5	.299
Jack Scott	83	114	6	33	6	0	1	17	0	.289
Dick Spalding (LF)	115	442	68	131	16	3	0	25	5	.296
Fresco Thompson (2B)	153	597	78	181	32	14	1	70	19	.303
Cy Williams (RF)	131	492	86	135	18	2	(30)	98	0	.274
Jimmie Wilson (C)	128	443	50	122	15	2	2	45	13	.275
Russ Wrightstone (1B)	141	533	62	163	24	5	6	75	9	.306
		5,317	678	1,487	216	46	57	617	68	.280

New manager Stuffy McInnis (left) got some tips from his ex-boss, Connie Mack, after taking over the Phillies in 1927.

In the 110 years of Phillies baseball, some horrible teams have represented the franchise. This was, from a percentage standpoint, the fourth worst.

Baker finally made a sound baseball move as far as hiring a manager. He stopped trying the local angle and instead signed Burt (Barney) Shotton, a Branch Rickey protege with a load of managerial know-how. And although he was unable to show much of it his first year, he would exhibit it later in his career.

But while the Phillies finished 42 games out of the first division, at one point losing 12 games in a row on the road, they began to use players who would make a positive impact in the future. One was third baseman Pinky Whitney, who enjoyed a banner rookie season with a .301 average and 103 RBI. Another was powerful first baseman Don Hurst, who contributed a team-topping 19 home runs. Catcher Peck Lerian hit .272 and impressed everyone with his defensive ability, but Lerian would die a year later in Baltimore when hit by a truck and pinned to the side of a building.

The most important addition, however, didn't arrive until mid-season from Fort Wayne, the team that sold the Phillies his contract for $5,000. He was six feet tall, weighed 195 pounds, and appeared clumsy when he reported to Shotton.

"I'm Klein," he said. "They call me Chuck Klein."

Shotton wasn't overly thrilled.

"All right, Klein, get in uniform," he said. "They tell me you can hit. Goodness knows, we need hitters." Then Shotton mumbled to himself, "We need everything."

Klein was everything a manager could want offensively. He stepped into

1928

Record: 43–109
Finish: Eighth
Games Behind: 51
Manager: Burt Shotton

	W	L	G	GS	CG	IP	H	BB	K	ERA
Ed Baecht	1	1	9	1	0	24	37	9	10	6.00
Ray Benge	8	18	40	28	12	202	219	88	68	4.54
Earl Caldwell	1	4	5	5	1	35	46	17	6	5.66
Alex Ferguson	5	10	34	19	5	132	162	48	50	5.66
June Green	0	0	1	0	0	2	5	0	0	9.00
Ed Lennon	0	0	5	0	0	12	19	10	6	9.00
Russ Miller	0	12	33	12	1	108	137	34	19	5.42
John Milligan	2	5	13	7	3	68	69	32	22	4.37
Clarence Mitchell	0	0	3	0	0	6	13	2	0	9.00
Bob McGraw	7	8	39	3	0	132	150	56	28	4.64
Hub Pruett	2	4	13	9	4	71	78	49	35	4.56
Jimmy Ring	4	17	35	25	4	173	214	103	72	6.40
Les Sweetland	3	15	37	18	5	135	163	97	23	6.60
Marty Walker	0	1	1	1	0	0	2	3	0	∞
Augie Walsh	4	9	38	11	2	122	160	40	38	6.20
Claude Willoughby	6	5	35	13	5	131	180	83	26	5.29
	43	109		152	42	1,353	(1,654)	(671)	403	5.52

Shutouts: Benge, Caldwell, Ferguson, Willoughby

	G	AB	R	H	2B	3B	HR	RBI	SB	AVG
Spud Davis	67	163	16	46	2	0	3	18	0	.282
Bill Dietrick	52	100	13	20	6	0	0	7	1	.200
Barney Friberg	52	94	11	19	3	0	1	7	0	.202
Don Hurst (1B)	107	396	73	113	23	4	19	64	3	.285
Art Jahn	36	94	8	21	4	0	0	11	0	.223
Bill Kelly	23	71	6	12	1	1	0	5	0	.169
Chuck Klein (RF)	64	253	41	91	14	4	11	34	0	.360
Freddy Leach (LF)	145	588	83	179	36	11	13	96	4	.304
Walt Lerian (C)	96	239	28	65	16	2	2	25	1	.272
Harvey MacDonald	13	16	0	4	0	0	0	2	0	.250
Al Nixon	25	64	7	15	2	0	0	7	1	.234
Heinie Sand (SS)	141	426	38	90	26	1	0	38	1	.211
Johnny Schulte	65	113	14	28	2	2	4	17	0	.248
Denny Sothern (CF)	141	579	82	165	27	5	5	38	17	.285
Fresco Thompson (2B)	152	634	99	182	34	11	3	50	19	.287
Pinky Whitney (3B)	151	595	73	176	35	4	10	103	3	.301
Cy Williams	99	238	31	61	9	0	12	37	0	.256
Jimmie Wilson	21	70	11	21	4	1	0	13	3	.300
Russ Wrightstone	33	91	7	19	5	1	1	11	0	.209
		5,234	660	1,396	257	47	85	606	53	.267

the lineup immediately and batted .360. He replaced a legend in right field, Cy Williams, and quickly replaced Cy in the hearts of Phillies fans.

Now if only they could have replaced the pitching staff!

Staff ace Ray Benge finished 8–18. Jimmy Ring, back for a second time, was 4–17. Les Sweetland won three of 18, making his two-year record 5–25. Russ Miller had 12 decisions, all losses. Only 182,168 fans showed up to see the pitchers get hammered game after game. The pitching turned even worse the following season. The team turned far better.

1929

Record: 71–82
Finish: Fifth
Games Behind: 27½
Manager: Burt Shotton

It figured! The year the stock market crashed, the Phillies made a remarkable upswing. For a change, the rich got poorer, and the poor got richer.

The Phillies tested the giddy heights of fifth place despite a pitching staff on which the leading starter had an ERA of 4.99.

This was a team that lived by the bat and died by the arm. The Phillies led the league in hitting with a .309 average and in home runs with 153. They scored 897 runs, which sounds impressive until you realize the pitchers allowed 1,032.

While Connie Mack's Athletics were winning the World Series, the Phillies were carving their little niche in the hearts of Philadelphians. Despite the hard economic times and the fact that Baker Bowl was becoming an increasingly dangerous place to watch a baseball game, attendance jumped almost 100,000 to 281,200. The fans came to see new hitting heroes like second-year men Chuck Klein, Pinky Whitney, Don Hurst, and newcomer Lefty O'Doul, who came to town from the Giants for Fred Leach and $20,000.

	W	L	G	GS	CG	IP	H	BB	K	ERA
Ray Benge	11	15	38	27	9	199	255	77	78	6.29
Phil Collins	9	7	43	11	3	153	172	83	61	5.77
Sam Dailey	2	2	20	5	0	51	74	23	18	7.59
Hal Elliott	3	7	40	8	2	114	146	59	32	6.08
Alex Ferguson	1	2	5	4	1	13	19	10	3	11.77
June Green	0	0	5	0	0	14	33	9	4	19.29
Jim Holloway	0	0	3	0	0	5	10	5	1	12.60
Lou Koupal	5	5	15	12	3	87	106	29	18	4.76
Elmer Miller	0	1	8	2	0	11	12	21	5	11.45
John Milligan	0	1	8	3	0	10	29	10	2	16.20
Bob McGraw	5	5	41	4	0	86	113	43	22	5.76
Luther Roy	3	6	21	12	1	89	137	37	16	8.39
Harry Smyth	4	6	19	7	2	69	94	15	12	5.22
Les Sweetland	13	11	43	25	10	204	255	87	47	5.12
Claude Willoughby	15	14	49	34	14	243	288	108	50	4.99
	71	82		154	45	1,348	(1,743)	(616)	369	6.13

Shutouts: Benge (2), Sweetland (2), Willoughby

	G	AB	R	H	2B	3B	HR	RBI	SB	AVG
Spud Davis	98	263	31	90	18	0	7	48	1	.342
Barney Friberg	128	455	74	137	21	10	7	55	1	.301
Don Hurst (1B)	154	589	100	179	29	4	31	125	10	.304
Chuck Klein (RF)	149	616	126	219	45	6	(43)	145	5	.356
Walt Lerian (C)	105	273	28	61	13	2	6	25	0	.223
Terry Lyons	1	0	0	0	0	0	0	0	0	.000
Lefty O'Doul (LF)	154	638	152	(254)	35	6	32	122	2	(.398)
Joe O'Rourke	3	3	0	0	0	0	0	0	0	.000
Homer Peel	53	156	16	42	12	1	0	19	1	.269
Tripp Sigman	10	29	8	15	1	0	2	9	0	.517
Denny Sothern (CF)	76	294	52	90	21	3	5	27	13	.306
George Susce	17	17	5	5	3	0	1	1	0	.294
Tommy Thevenow (SS)	90	317	30	72	11	0	0	35	3	.227
Fresco Thompson (2B)	148	623	115	202	41	3	4	53	16	.324
Pinky Whitney (3B)	154	612	89	200	43	14	8	115	7	.327
Cy Williams	66	65	11	19	2	0	5	21	0	.292
		5,484	897	(1,693)	305	51	(153)	841	59	(.309)

O'Doul led the National League in hitting with a .398 average, slugged 32 homers, and drove in 122 runs. Klein's figures were even more impressive. Included in a .356 average were 43 homers and 145 RBI. Hurst pounded 31 homers, drove in 125 runners, and batted .304.

While not in the slugger class of that trio, Whitney managed to hit .327 and drive in 115 runs with just eight homers.

And that wasn't all. Catcher Spud Davis hit .342, and second baseman Fresco Thompson was good for .324. The Phillies needed every hit they could get.

They lost one game 28–6 to the St. Louis Cardinals. That was the most runs scored in one game by a single National League team after 1900.

Claude Willoughby, the staff ace with the 4.99 ERA, was 15–14. Les Sweetland reversed his previous two seasons and finished 13–11. Ray Benge was 11–15. The staff led the National League with 24 saves, mainly because it was dead last in complete games with 45. On July 6, it gave up a National League record number of runs in a 28–6 loss to the St. Louis Cardinals. Baker Bowl was truly a hitter's dream and a pitcher's nightmare. The following season would prove it even more conclusively.

The Phillies never had a stranger season than this one. They had the third-highest team hitting average (.315) in National League history, five regulars hit above .300, and Chuck Klein had one of his greatest seasons, hitting .386 with 40 home runs, 170 RBI, and two 26-game hitting streaks.

The club set all-time Phillies records that still stand in hits, singles, doubles, total bases, runs, RBI, and at-bats. Yet the Phillies were buried so far into the cellar that even the seventh-place Cincinnati Reds were seven games ahead of them.

Lefty O'Doul (left) and Chuck Klein were a dynamic duo as 1929–30 batsmen.

1930

Record: 52–102
Finish: Eighth
Games Behind: 40
Manager: Burt Shotton

	W	L	G	GS	CG	IP	H	BB	K	ERA
Grover C. Alexander	0	3	9	3	0	22	40	6	6	9.00
Ray Benge	11	15	38	29	14	226	305	81	70	5.69
Hap Collard	6	12	30	15	4	127	188	39	25	6.80
Phil Collins	16	11	47	25	17	239	287	86	87	4.78
Hal Elliott	6	11	(40)	11	2	117	191	58	37	7.69
Snipe Hansen	0	7	22	9	1	84	123	38	25	6.75
Lou Koupal	0	4	13	4	1	37	52	17	11	8.51
John Milligan	1	2	9	2	1	28	26	21	7	3.21
Chet Nichols	1	2	16	5	1	60	76	16	15	6.75
Buz Phillips	0	0	14	1	0	44	68	18	9	7.98
Harry Smyth	0	3	25	3	0	50	84	31	9	7.74
Byron Speece	0	0	11	0	0	20	41	4	9	13.05
Les Sweetland	7	15	34	25	8	167	271	60	36	7.71
Claude Willoughby	4	17	41	24	5	153	241	68	38	7.59
	52	102		156	54	1,373	(1,993)	(546)	384	6.71

Shutouts: Collins, Willoughby

	G	AB	R	H	2B	3B	HR	RBI	SB	AVG
Fred Brickell	53	240	33	59	12	6	0	17	1	.246
Spud Davis (C)	106	329	41	103	16	1	14	65	1	.313
Barney Friberg	105	331	62	113	21	1	4	42	1	.341
Don Hurst (1B)	119	391	78	128	19	3	17	78	6	.327
Chuck Klein (RF)	156	648	(158)	250	(59)	8	40	170	4	.386
Harry McCurdy	80	148	23	49	6	2	1	25	0	.331
Lefty O'Doul (LF)	140	528	122	202	37	7	22	97	3	.383
Tony Rensa	54	172	31	49	11	2	3	31	0	.285
Monk Sherlock	92	299	51	97	18	2	0	38	0	.324
Tripp Sigman	52	100	15	27	4	1	4	6	1	.270
Denny Sothern (CF)	90	347	66	97	26	1	5	36	6	.280
Jim Spotts	3	2	1	0	0	0	0	0	0	.000
Tommy Thevenow (SS)	156	573	57	164	21	1	0	78	1	.286
Frenco Thompson (2B)	122	478	77	135	34	4	4	46	7	.282
Pinky Whitney (3B)	149	606	87	207	41	5	8	117	3	.342
Cy Williams	21	17	1	8	2	0	0	2	0	.471
		(5,667)	944	(1,783)	345	44	126	884	34	.315

The horrible record was wholly attributable to a horrible pitching staff. Phils hurlers had a combined earned run average of 6.71. Three of the top six moundsmen had ERAs above 7.50, and the staff yielded an all-time major league record 1,199 runs. Only Fidgety Phil Collins was respectable, posting a 16–11 record.

Asked how he could finish last with hitters such as Klein, Lefty O'Doul who

The Phillies batted .315 as a team in 1930. Four of the regulars were (from left) right fielder Chuck Klein, first baseman Don Hurst, catcher Spud Davis, and third baseman Pinky Whitney.

had a .383 average, Pinky Whitney (.342), Don Hurst (.327), and Spud Davis (.313), manager Burt Shotton said: "Have you looked at my pitching staff by any chance?"

There wasn't a shutout pitched in 1930 at Baker Bowl. And in 77 games there, the Phillies were outscored by the opposition 8–7 on the average. In one game, the Phillies walloped the Cincinnati Reds, 18–0, getting 21 hits but no home runs, and in another they beat the Pittsburgh Pirates, 15–14.

Phillie fielders weren't much better than the pitchers. The club finished last in the league in fielding, a dishonor it would hold in seven years of the decade.

The return to the club of former Phillies great Grover Cleveland Alexander didn't help. Alex was ineffective in his last season in the majors.

A fter the inglorious 1930 season, nobody clamored to break up the Phillies. But president William Baker did anyway.

Although he died of a heart attack during the winter, Baker made two key trades before then. The key players he brought in were fiery shortstop Dick Bartell from the Pittsburgh Pirates and pitcher Jumbo Elliott from the Brooklyn Dodgers.

Baker paid a steep price, especially in parting with the slugging Lefty O'Doul, who had become testy when denied a pay raise. But something had to be done, particularly to bolster a horrendous pitching staff.

Elliott did just that. He led the league in wins (19) and games (52), and combined with Phil Collins (12), who had tossed a one-hitter at the New York Giants, and Ray Benge (14) to give the Phils three pitchers with double-figure wins.

1931

Record: 66–88
Finish: Sixth
Games Behind: 35
Manager: Burt Shotton

	W	L	G	GS	CG	IP	H	BB	K	ERA
Bob Adams	0	1	1	1	0	6	14	1	3	9.00
Ray Benge	14	18	38	31	16	247	251	61	117	3.17
Sheriff Blake	4	5	14	9	1	71	90	35	31	5.58
Stew Bolen	3	12	28	16	2	99	117	63	55	6.36
Phil Collins	12	16	42	27	16	240	268	83	73	3.86
Clise Dudley	8	14	30	24	8	179	206	56	50	3.52
Hal Elliott	0	2	16	4	0	33	46	19	8	9.55
Jumbo Jim Elliott	(19)	14	(52)	30	12	249	288	83	99	4.27
Ed Fallenstein	0	0	24	0	0	42	56	26	15	7.07
John Milligan	0	0	3	0	0	8	11	4	6	3.38
Chet Nichols	0	1	3	0	0	6	10	1	1	9.00
Dutch Schesler	0	0	17	0	0	38	65	18	14	7.34
Ben Shields	1	0	4	0	0	5	9	7	0	16.20
Lil Stoner	0	0	7	1	0	14	22	5	2	6.43
Frank Watt	5	5	38	12	5	123	147	49	25	4.83
Hal Wiltse	0	0	1	0	0	1	3	0	0	9.00
	66	88		155	60	1,360	(1,603)	511	499	4.58

Shutouts: Benge (2), Collins (2), Jumbo Elliott (2)

	G	AB	R	H	2B	3B	HR	RBI	SB	AVG
Buzz Arlett (RF)	121	418	65	131	26	7	18	72	3	.313
Dick Bartell (SS)	135	554	88	169	43	7	0	34	6	.289
Fred Brickell (CF)	130	514	77	130	14	5	1	31	5	.253
Gene Connell	6	12	1	3	0	0	0	0	0	.250
Spud Davis (C)	120	393	30	128	32	1	4	51	0	.326
Barney Friberg	103	353	33	92	19	5	1	26	1	.261
Don Hurst (1B)	137	489	63	149	37	5	11	91	8	.305
Chuck Klein (LF)	148	594	(121)	200	34	10	(31)	(121)	7	.337
Fred Koster	76	151	21	34	2	2	0	8	4	.225
Hal Lee	44	131	13	29	10	0	2	12	0	.221
Les Mallon (2B)	122	375	41	116	19	2	1	45	0	.309
Harry McCurdy	66	150	21	43	9	0	1	25	2	.287
Tony Rensa	19	29	2	3	1	0	0	2	0	.103
Bobby Stevens	12	35	3	12	0	0	0	4	0	.343
Doug Taitt	38	151	13	34	4	2	1	15	0	.225
Pinky Whitney (3B)	130	501	64	144	36	5	9	74	6	.287
Hugh Willingham	23	35	5	9	2	1	1	3	0	.257
		5,375	684	1,502	299	52	81	649	42	.279

As usual Chuck Klein tore National League pitching apart, leading the circuit in home runs (31) and RBI (121) and batting .337. Chuck won *The Sporting News'* Most Valuable Player award.

Spud Davis (.326), who had by now established himself as a first-rate catcher, was joined in the .300 circle by right fielder Buzz Arlett, who hit .313 in his only big league season, second baseman Les Mallon (.309), and first baseman Don Hurst (.305).

The Phillies didn't hit anything like they had as a team the previous year—they tumbled to a mere .279—but the improved pitching staff was enough to kick the club into sixth place, despite one game in which they gave up 28 hits to the New York Giants and lost, 23–8.

1932

Record: 78–76
Finish: Fourth
Games Behind: 12
Manager: Burt Shotton

Little did the Phillies know at the time, but 1932 was to hold a special place in the club's annals. The Phillies' fourth-place finish was the only time the team finished in the first division between 1917 and 1949.

It was a glorious year for the victory-starved Phils, who ended the season one game ahead of the fifth place Boston Braves. Six Phillies hitters wound up with averages above .300, and six pitchers won in double figures.

The Phillies had the National League's top three men in RBI with Don Hurst leading the circuit with 143, followed by Chuck Klein (137) and Pinky Whitney (124). Klein, who tied with the New York Giants' Mel Ott for the home run crown with 38, combined with Hurst for 737 total bases.

Such slugging invited comparison between the Phillies' one-two punch and the New York Yankees' famed duo of Babe Ruth and Lou Gehrig, who combined for 672 total bases for the World Champion Yanks.

Klein, who also led the league in hits (226), total bases (420), slugging percentage (.646), and stolen bases (20), was both the Baseball Writers'

	W	L	G	GS	CG	IP	H	BB	K	ERA
Bob Adams	0	0	4	0	0	6	7	2	2	1.50
Ray Benge	13	12	41	28	13	222	247	58	89	4.05
Jack Berly	1	2	21	1	1	46	61	21	15	7.63
Stew Bolen	0	0	5	0	0	16	18	10	3	2.81
Phil Collins	14	12	43	21	6	184	231	65	66	5.28
Clise Dudley	1	1	13	0	0	18	23	8	5	7.00
Hal Elliott	2	4	16	7	0	58	70	38	13	5.74
Jumbo Jim Elliott	11	10	39	22	8	166	210	47	62	5.42
Reggie Grabowski	2	2	14	2	0	34	38	22	15	3.71
Snipe Hansen	10	10	39	23	5	191	215	51	56	3.72
Ed Holley	11	14	34	30	16	228	247	56	87	3.95
Ad Liska	2	0	8	0	0	27	22	10	6	1.67
Chet Nichols	0	2	11	0	0	19	23	14	5	7.11
Flint Rhem	11	7	26	20	10	169	177	49	35	3.75
	78	76		154	59	1,384	(1,589)	450	459	4.47

	G	AB	R	H	2B	3B	HR	RBI	SB	AVG
Dick Bartell (SS)	154	614	118	189	48	7	1	53	8	.308
Rube Bressler	27	83	9	19	6	1	0	6	0	.229
Fred Brickell	45	66	9	22	6	1	0	2	2	.333
Kiddo Davis (CF)	137	576	100	178	39	6	5	57	16	.309
Spud Davis (C)	125	402	44	135	23	5	14	70	1	.336
Eddie Delker	30	62	7	10	1	1	1	7	0	.161
Barney Friberg	61	154	17	37	8	2	0	14	0	.240
Cliff Heathcote	30	39	7	11	2	0	1	5	0	.282
Don Hurst (1B)	150	579	109	196	41	4	24	(143)	10	.339
Chuck Klein (RF)	154	650	(152)	(226)	50	15	(38)	137	(20)	.348
George Knothe	6	12	2	1	1	0	0	0	0	.083
Hal Lee (LF)	149	595	76	180	42	10	18	85	6	.303
Les Mallon (2B)	103	347	44	90	16	0	5	31	1	.259
Harry McCurdy	62	136	13	32	6	1	1	14	0	.235
Russ Scarritt	11	0	2	0	0	0	0	0	0	.182
Doug Taitt	4	2	0	0	0	0	0	0	0	.000
Al Todd	33	70	8	16	5	0	0	9	1	.229
Pinky Whitney (3B)	154	624	93	186	33	1	13	124	6	.298
Hugh Willingham	4	2	0	0	0	0	0	0	0	.000
		5,510	(844)	(1,608)	(330)	67	(122)	(780)	71	(.292)

Association and *The Sporting News'* Most Valuable Player. He also hit three grand slam homers during the year.

Hurst (.339), Spud Davis (.336), a rookie former Yankee farmhand named Kiddo Davis (.309), Dick Bartell (.308), and Hal Lee (.303) all went over the .300 mark, despite the presence that year of a deadened ball. As a result of all the lusty hitting, the Phillies led the league in team average (.292), runs (844), and home runs (122). The club's runs total was 124 more than the runs scored by the pennant-winning Chicago Cubs.

Despite all their scoring, the Phillies also gave up a heavy total of runs. The pitching staff gave up the most runs (796) in the league. It also had the highest ERA (4.47), the fewest complete games (59), and the most walks (450).

Some new blood, however, pumped life into the staff. Flint Rhem, a character who was purchased from the St. Louis Cardinals, and Edgar Holley, bought from the Kansas City club, each won 11, Ray Benge 13, and Snipe Hansen 10. Phil Collins led the staff with 14 victories.

Rhem's antics were often as effective as his pitching. On one occasion, the South Carolina native, who was said to have a "big thirst," refused to pitch until the groundskeeper built him a new mound.

The 1933 season was the year of the big upheaval. The Phillies began the year with a new owner. And by the time 1933 was over, they had practically a new team, too.

In between, the club slipped back to seventh place, erasing the hopes the previous season had inspired. Attendance, which since 1929 had ranged between 269,000 and 299,000 for the season, fell to 156,421.

Prior to the season's opener, new club president Gerald P. Nugent traded dependable pitcher Ray Benge and promising outfielder Kiddo Davis. During

1933

Record: 60–92
Finish: Seventh
Games Behind: 31
Manager: Burt Shotton

	W	L	G	GS	CG	IP	H	BB	K	ERA
Jack Berly	2	3	13	6	1	50	62	22	4	5.04
Charlie Butler	0	0	1	0	0	1	1	2	0	9.00
Phil Collins	8	13	42	13	5	151	178	57	40	4.11
Jumbo Jim Elliott	6	10	35	21	6	162	188	49	43	3.83
Reggie Grabowski	1	3	10	5	4	48	38	10	9	2.44
Snipe Hansen	6	14	32	22	8	168	199	30	47	4.45
Ed Holley	13	15	30	28	12	207	219	62	56	3.52
John Jackson	2	2	10	7	1	54	74	35	11	6.00
Ad Liska	3	1	45	1	0	76	96	26	23	4.50
Cy Moore	8	9	36	18	9	161	177	42	53	3.75
Frank Pearce	5	4	20	7	3	82	78	29	18	3.62
Clarence Pickrel	1	0	9	0	0	14	20	3	6	3.86
Frank Ragland	0	4	11	5	0	38	51	10	4	6.87
Flint Rhem	5	14	28	19	3	125	182	33	27	6.62
	60	92		152	52	1,338	(1,563)	410	341	4.34

Shutouts: Holley (3), Moore (3), Berly, Collins, Grabowski, Pearce

	G	AB	R	H	2B	3B	HR	RBI	SB	AVG
Dick Bartell (SS)	152	587	78	159	25	5	1	37	6	.271
Fred Brickell	8	13	2	4	1	1	0	1	0	.308
Alta Cohen	19	32	6	6	1	0	0	1	0	.188
Spud Davis (C)	141	495	511	173	28	3	9	65	2	.349
Eddie Delker	25	41	6	7	3	1	0	1	0	.171
Gus Dugas	37	71	4	12	3	0	0	9	0	.169
Mickey Finn	51	169	15	40	4	1	0	13	2	.237
Chick Fullis (CF)	151	(647)	91	200	31	6	1	45	18	.309
Mickey Haslin	26	89	3	21	2	0	0	9	1	.236
Don Hurst (1B)	147	550	58	147	27	8	8	76	3	.267
Chuck Klein (RF)	152	606	101	(223)	(44)	7	(28)	(120)	15	(.368)
Fritz Knothe	41	113	10	17	2	0	0	11	2	.150
Hal Lee	46	167	25	48	12	2	0	12	1	.287
Harry McCurdy	73	54	9	15	1	0	2	12	0	.278
Jim McLeod (3B)	67	232	20	45	6	1	0	15	1	.194
Wes Schulmerich (LF)	97	365	53	122	19	4	8	59	1	.334
Al Todd	73	136	13	28	4	0	0	10	1	.206
Jack Warner (2B)	107	340	31	76	15	1	0	22	1	.224
Pinky Whitney	31	121	12	32	4	0	3	19	1	.264
Hugh Willingham	1	1	0	0	0	0	0	0	0	.000
		5,261	617	1,413	224	51	62	566	55	.274

the season, he swapped popular third baseman Pinky Whitney. And after the season, he dealt away catcher Spud Davis and—to the great dismay of Phillies fans—the future Hall of Famer Chuck Klein.

Nugent got hardly anything in return, except for aging catcher Jimmie Wilson, who would become the Phils' manager the following year (after Nugent dumped Burt Shotton, too) and center fielder Chick Fullis, who had a 22-game hitting streak during the season.

Klein went out like a firecracker. He won the Triple Crown, leading the league in batting (.368), home runs (28), and RBI (120), as well as hits (223), total bases (365), and slugging average (.602). He and shortstop Dick Bartell were starters on the National League's first All-Star team. Bartell in 1933 became the first player in the league to hit four consecutive doubles in a nine-inning game.

On the mound, only Edgar Holley pitched semi-effectively. There was no one else on the staff who came close to rivaling his 13–15 record.

1934

Record: 56–93
Finish: Seventh
Games Behind: 37
Manager: Jimmie Wilson

Several significant events occurred in 1934, one of which was the advent of Sunday baseball in Philadelphia. On April 29 the Phillies lost to the Brooklyn Dodgers, 8–7, in the first legal Sunday National League game in the city.

Sunday baseball, however, didn't help attendance, which continued to sag. Nor did it help the Phillies' record, despite the presence of new manager Jimmie Wilson.

	W	L	G	GS	CG	IP	H	BB	K	ERA
Phil Collins	13	18	45	32	15	254	277	87	72	4.18
George Darrow	2	6	17	8	2	49	57	28	14	5.51
Curt Davis	19	17	(51)	31	18	274	283	60	99	2.95
Jumbo Jim Elliott	0	1	3	1	0	5	8	4	1	10.80
Reggie Grabowski	1	3	27	5	0	65	114	23	13	9.28
Snipe Hansen	6	12	50	16	5	151	194	61	40	5.42
Ed Holley	1	8	15	13	2	73	85	31	14	7.15
Syl Johnson	5	9	42	10	4	134	122	24	54	3.49
Ted Kleinhans	0	0	5	0	0	6	11	3	2	9.00
Bill Lohrman	0	1	4	0	0	6	5	1	2	4.50
Cy Malis	0	0	1	0	0	4	4	2	1	4.50
Euel Moore	5	7	20	16	3	122	145	41	38	4.06
Cy Moore	4	9	35	15	3	127	163	65	55	6.45
Frank Pierce	0	2	7	1	0	20	25	5	4	7.20
Bucky Walters	0	0	2	1	0	7	8	2	7	1.29
	56	93		149	52	1,297	1,501	437	416	4.76

Shutouts: Davis (3), Johnson (3), Hansen (2)

	G	AB	R	H	2B	3B	HR	RBI	SB	AVG
Ethan Allen (LF)	145	581	87	192	(42)	4	10	85	6	.330
Dick Bartell (SS)	146	604	102	187	30	4	0	37	13	.310
Ed Boland	8	30	2	9	1	1	0	5	1	.300
Dolph Camilli (1B)	102	378	52	100	20	3	12	68	3	.265
Lou Chiozza (2B)	134	484	66	147	28	5	0	44	9	.304
Bud Clancy	20	49	8	12	0	0	1	7	0	.245
Kiddo Davis (CF)	100	393	50	115	25	5	3	48	1	.293
Fred Frink	2	0	0	0	0	0	0	0	0	.000
Chick Fullis	28	102	8	23	6	0	0	12	2	.225
Mickey Haslin	72	166	28	44	8	2	1	11	1	.265
Gink Hendrick	59	116	12	34	8	0	0	19	0	.293
Andy High	47	68	4	14	2	0	0	7	1	.206
Joe Holden	10	14	1	1	0	0	0	0	0	.071
Marty Hopkins	10	25	6	3	2	0	0	3	0	.120
Don Hurst	40	130	16	34	9	0	2	21	1	.262
Irv Jeffries	56	175	28	43	6	0	4	19	2	.246
Johnny Moore (RF)	116	458	68	157	34	6	11	93	7	.343
Prince Oana	6	21	3	5	1	0	0	3	0	.238
Art Ruble	19	54	7	15	4	0	0	8	0	.278
Wes Schulmerich	15	52	2	13	1	0	0	1	0	.250
Al Todd (C)	91	302	33	96	22	2	4	41	3	.318
Bucky Walters (3B)	83	300	36	78	20	3	4	38	1	.260
Jimmie Wilson	91	277	25	81	11	0	3	35	1	.292
Hack Wilson	7	20	0	2	0	0	0	3	0	.100
		5,218	675	1,480	286	35	56	634	52	.284

A Philadelphia native, Wilson was a favorite of club president Gerry Nugent, who had landed him in a trade the previous year. The easygoing Wilson was nearing the end of a career as one of the National League's top catchers, and had returned to the Phillies, after leaving the club in 1928, with the expressed intent of being handed the managerial reins.

Jimmie couldn't do much with the club's place in the standings. As usual, the pitching was poor and the hitting, at least at friendly Baker Bowl, was terrific. In one six-game stretch with the Brooklyn Dodgers and Boston Braves, the Phillies scored 63 runs to the oppositions' 55.

The Phils did come up with another outstanding pitcher in Curt Davis. The young righthander won 19 games and posted a 2.95 ERA, third best in the league and the lowest for a Phils' regular since 1920.

During the season, Nugent continued his trading frenzy, sending Don Hurst to the Chicago Cubs for a young player named Dolph Camilli. He also landed pitcher Syl Johnson and outfielder Johnny Moore in a swap with the Cincinnati Reds.

There was a steady parade of players moving in and out of Philadelphia in the 1930s as the team's financially unstable owners made a practice of getting rid of good players once they attained some value. From that standpoint, it was business as usual in 1935.

During the off-season, the Phillies had traded standout shortstop Dick Bartell and, for the second time, outfielder Kiddo Davis. The team remained centered on a pair of fine-hitting outfielders, Ethan Allen and Johnny Moore,

1935

Record: 64–89
Finish: Seventh
Games Behind: 35½
Manager: Jimmie Wilson

	W	L	G	GS	CG	IP	H	BB	K	ERA
Jim Bivin	2	9	47	14	0	162	220	65	54	5.78
Joe Bowman	7	10	33	17	6	148	157	56	58	4.26
Phil Collins	0	2	3	3	0	15	24	9	4	11.40
Curt Davis	16	14	44	27	19	231	264	47	74	3.66
Snipe Hansen	0	1	2	1	0	4	8	5	0	13.50
Syl Johnson	10	8	37	18	8	175	182	31	89	3.55
Orville Jorgens	10	15	(53)	24	6	188	216	96	57	4.84
Hal Kelleher	2	0	3	3	2	25	26	12	12	1.80
Euel Moore	1	6	15	8	1	40	63	20	15	7.88
Hugh Mulcahy	1	5	18	5	0	53	62	25	11	4.75
Frank Pearce	0	0	5	0	0	13	22	6	7	8.31
Pretzels Pezzullo	3	5	41	7	2	84	115	45	24	6.43
Ray Prim	3	4	29	6	1	73	110	15	27	5.79
Tommy Thomas	0	1	4	1	0	12	15	5	3	5.25
Bucky Walters	9	9	24	22	8	151	68	78	40	4.17
	64	89		156	53	1,375	(1,652)	(505)	475	4.76

Shutouts: Davis (3), Walters (2), Bowman, Johnson, Kelleher

	G	AB	R	H	2B	3B	HR	RBI	SB	AVG
Ethan Allen (CF)	156	645	90	198	46	1	8	63	5	.307
Ed Boland	30	47	5	10	0	0	0	4	1	.213
Art Bramhall	2	1	0	0	0	0	0	0	0	.000
Dolph Camilli (1B)	156	603	88	157	23	5	25	83	9	.261
Dino Chiozza	2	0	1	0	0	0	0	0	0	.000
Lou Chiozza (2B)	124	472	71	134	26	6	3	47	5	.284
Chile Gomez	67	222	24	51	3	0	0	16	2	.230
Mickey Haslin (SS)	110	407	53	108	17	3	3	52	5	.265
Joe Holden	6	9	0	1	0	0	0	0	1	.111
Bubber Jonnard	1	1	0	0	0	0	0	0	0	.000
Fred Lucas	20	34	1	9	0	0	0	2	0	.265
Johnny Moore (RF)	153	600	84	194	33	3	19	93	4	.323
Blondy Ryan	39	129	13	34	3	0	1	10	1	.264
Al Todd (C)	107	328	40	95	18	3	3	42	3	.290
Johnny Vergez (3B)	148	546	56	136	27	4	9	63	8	.249
Bucky Walters	49	96	14	24	2	1	0	6	0	.250
George Watkins (LF)	150	600	80	162	25	5	17	76	3	.270
Jimmie Wilson	93	290	38	81	20	0	1	37	4	.279
		5,442	685	1,466	249	32	92	624	52	.269

who hit .323 for the season, and Dolph Camilli, a young power-hitter at first base, who clubbed 25 home runs.

Once again, with the exception of Curt Davis, the Phillies had little pitching. But in 1935 they had at least one thing in their favor. The Boston Braves were in the league, too.

The Braves—or Bees as they were then called—were so bad they lost 115 games. They finished 61½ games out of first and 26 games back of the seventh-place Phillies.

Manager Jimmie Wilson was the starting catcher in the All-Star Game, although he didn't catch as much that year for the Phillies as Al Todd. Aside from that, the club had two notable occurrences.

One was the arrival of reserve infielder Chile Gomez, who secured a place on the roster, and became the first Latin American to play for the Phillies.

The other was the conversion of third baseman Bucky Walters to pitcher. Purchased the previous year from the Boston Red Sox, Walters and his strong arm attracted the attention of Wilson, who by bringing Bucky to the mound helped launch a long and successful pitching career.

Another occurrence during the season was the death of Mickey Finn, the team's regular second baseman. Finn died in an Allentown hospital while being treated for ulcers.

The Phillies got a small measure of solace from the season by participating in the first night game in major league history. The Phillies bowed to the Reds, 2–1, at Cincinnati's Crosley Field. Paul Derringer pitched a six-hitter to beat Joe Bowman. The Reds got just four hits. Some 20,422 were in attendance for the game, which began with President Franklin D. Roosevelt pressing a key in the White House that turned on the lights.

There was one other achievement worth noting. The 1935 season was the only one from 1918 to 1942 in which the Phillies' pitching staff did not finish eighth in the league in ERA. This time it wound up seventh.

1936

Record: 54–100
Finish: Eighth
Games Behind: 38
Manager: Jimmie Wilson

After three straight years in seventh place, the 1936 Phillies broke the monotony. They finished eighth—even with the return of Chuck Klein, who came back from the Chicago Cubs in a swap that sent pitcher Curt Davis to the Windy City. Klein hit .309 for the Phillies. He also hit four home runs in a 10-inning game at Pittsburgh's Forbes Field, thereby becoming the third National Leaguer and second Phillie (Ed Delahanty was the first) to accomplish that feat.

The Phillies also brought back third baseman Pinky Whitney, who had been exiled to the Boston Bees and who hit .294 on his joyful return. And they landed a young pitcher named Claude Passeau in a trade that sent catcher Al Todd to the Cubs.

Dolph Camilli erupted with 28 home runs, 102 RBI, and a .315 batting average as he moved toward becoming one of the league's top hitters. Reliable Johnny Moore had his usual good season with a .328 average. And Lou Chiozza, moved to center field from second base, gave the Phillies his third straight respectable year at the plate.

But no pitcher, not even the two future standouts, Passeau and Bucky Walters, could win more than 11 games. Walters lost 21, Joe Bowman dropped 20, and the Phillies again anchored the bottom of the league in mound work.

Surprisingly, attendance increased to 249,219, its highest level since the fourth-place finish in 1932.

The Phillies lost 14 games in a row at one point. The streak set a record that stood until 1961.

	W	L	G	GS	CG	IP	H	BB	K	ERA
Ray Benge	1	4	15	6	0	46	70	19	13	4.70
Lefty Bertrand	0	0	1	0	0	2	3	2	1	9.00
Joe Bowman	9	20	40	28	12	204	243	53	80	5.03
Elmer Burkart	0	0	2	2	0	8	4	12	2	3.38
Curt Davis	2	4	10	8	3	60	71	19	18	4.65
Herb Harris	0	0	4	0	0	7	14	5	0	10.29
Syl Johnson	5	7	39	8	1	111	129	29	48	4.30
Orville Jorgens	8	8	39	21	4	167	196	69	59	4.80
Hal Kelleher	0	5	14	4	1	44	60	29	13	5.32
Fabian Kowalik	1	5	22	8	2	77	100	31	19	5.38
Euel Moore	2	3	20	5	1	54	76	12	19	7.00
Hugh Mulcahy	1	1	3	2	2	23	20	12	2	3.13
Claude Passeau	11	15	49	21	8	217	247	55	85	3.48
Pretzels Pezzullo	0	0	1	0	0	2	1	6	0	4.50
Pete Sivess	3	4	17	6	2	65	84	36	22	4.57
Bucky Walters	11	(21)	40	33	15	258	284	115	66	4.26
Tom Zachary	0	3	7	2	0	10	28	11	8	8.10
	54	100		154	51	1,365	(1,630)	515	454	4.64

Shutouts: Walters (4, led league), Passeau (2)

	G	AB	R	H	2B	3B	HR	RBI	SB	AVG
Ethan Allen	30	125	21	37	3	1	1	9	4	.296
Morrie Arnovich	13	48	4	15	3	0	1	7	0	.313
Bill Atwood	71	192	21	58	9	2	2	29	0	.302
Walt Bashore	10	10	1	2	0	0	0	0	0	.200
Dolph Camilli (1B)	151	530	106	167	29	13	28	102	5	.315
Lou Chiozza (CF)	144	572	83	170	32	6	1	48	17	.297
Gene Corbett	6	21	1	3	0	0	0	2	0	.143
Chile Gomez (2B)	108	332	24	77	4	1	0	28	0	.232
Earl Grace (C)	86	221	24	55	11	0	4	32	0	.249
Mickey Haslin	16	64	6	22	1	1	0	6	0	.344
Joe Holden	1	1	0	0	0	0	0	0	0	.000
Chuck Klein (RF)	117	492	83	152	30	7	20	86	6	.309
Johnny Moore (LF)	124	472	85	155	24	3	16	68	1	.328
Leo Norris (SS)	154	581	64	154	27	4	11	76	4	.265
Charlie Sheerin	39	72	4	19	4	0	0	4	0	.264
Stan Sperry	20	37	2	5	3	0	0	4	0	.135
Ernie Sulik	122	404	69	116	14	4	6	36	4	.287
Johnny Vergez	15	40	4	11	2	0	1	5	0	.275
Bucky Walters	64	121	12	29	10	1	1	16	0	.240
George Watkins	19	70	7	17	4	0	2	5	2	.243
Pinky Whitney (3B)	114	411	44	121	17	3	6	59	2	.294
Jimmie Wilson	85	230	25	64	12	0	1	27	5	.278
		5,465	726	1,538	250	46	(103)	682	50	.281

With Dolph Camilli, Chuck Klein, and Pinky Whitney bludgeoning opposing pitchers, the Phillies' hitting attack looked like it did at the beginning of the decade.

Camilli, by now one of the most feared swatters in the league, ripped off 27 home runs to go with his .339 average. Klein added a .325 mark with 15 homers, and Whitney soared with a .341 average. Added to that was some fine hitting by outfielders Morrie Arnovich (.290) and Hersh Martin (.283).

All the lusty bats were enough to ship the Phillies all the way up to seventh place.

The trouble was, of course, pitching, or lack of it. For the third of what would become five straight years, the staff gave up more than 800 runs. Naturally, the Phillies scored less often. They even lost one game, 21–10, to the Cincinnati Reds.

Despite such a troubled situation, the Phillies got satisfactory performances from Claude Passeau and Bucky Walters, each of whom won 14. A third hurler, Wayne LaMaster, posted a 15–19 mark in his first and next-to-last big league season. Another youngster, Hugh Mulcahy, got in his first full big league season and led National League pitchers in games. His 8–18 record started him on a 40–76 log over the next four years.

1937

Record: 61–92
Finish: Seventh
Games Behind: 34½
Manager: Jimmie Wilson

Catcher Bill Atwood and pitcher Bucky Walters go over the signs before a 1937 game.

Walters even went so far as to lose two games in one day. The St. Louis Cardinals and Si Johnson beat him, 10–3, in the first game of a doubleheader. In the second game, Walters lost in relief in an 18–10 fracas. The winner of that game was also Johnson.

	W	L	G	GS	CG	IP	H	BB	K	ERA
Bob Allen	0	1	3	1	0	12	18	8	8	6.75
Elmer Burkart	0	0	7	0	0	16	20	9	4	6.19
Bobby Burke	0	0	2	0	0	0	1	2	0	∞
Larry Crawford	0	0	6	0	0	6	12	1	2	15.00
Syl Johnson	4	10	32	15	4	138	155	22	46	5.02
Orville Jorgens	3	4	52	11	1	141	159	68	34	4.40
Hal Kelleher	2	4	27	2	1	58	72	31	20	6.67
Wayne LaMaster	15	(19)	50	30	10	220	255	82	135	5.32
Walt Masters	0	0	1	0	0	1	5	1	0	36.00
Hugh Mulcahy	8	18	(56)	25	9	216	256	(97)	54	5.13
Claude Passeau	14	18	50	(34)	18	(292)	(348)	79	135	4.35
Leon Pettit	0	1	3	1	0	4	6	4	0	11.25
Pete Sivess	1	1	6	2	1	23	30	11	4	8.10
Bucky Walters	14	15	37	(34)	15	246	292	86	87	4.76
	61	92*		154	59	1,371	(1,629)	501	529	5.06

Shutouts: Walters (3), LaMaster, Mucahy, Passeau
*Includes one loss by forfeit.

	G	AB	R	H	2B	3B	HR	RBI	SB	AVG
Bill Andrus	3	2	0	0	0	0	0	0	0	.000
Morrie Arnovich (LF)	117	410	60	119	27	4	10	60	5	.290
Bill Atwood (C)	87	279	27	68	15	1	2	32	3	.244
Earl Browne	105	332	42	97	19	3	6	52	4	.292
Dolph Camilli (1B)	131	475	101	161	23	7	27	80	6	.339
Gene Corbett	7	12	4	4	2	0	0	1	0	.333
Howie Gorman	13	19	3	4	1	0	0	1	1	.211
Earl Grace	80	223	19	47	10	1	6	29	0	.211
Chuck Klein (RF)	115	406	74	132	20	2	15	57	3	.325
Hersh Martin (CF)	141	579	102	164	35	7	8	49	11	.283
Johnny Moore	96	307	46	98	16	2	9	59	2	.319
Leo Norris	116	381	45	98	24	3	9	36	3	.257
George Scharein (SS)	146	511	44	123	20	1	0	57	13	.241
Walter Stephenson	10	23	1	6	0	0	0	2	0	.261
Fred Tauby	11	20	2	0	0	0	0	3	1	.000
Bucky Walters	56	137	15	38	6	0	1	16	1	.277
Pinky Whitney (3B)	138	487	56	166	19	4	8	79	6	.341
Jimmie Wilison	39	87	15	24	3	0	1	8	1	.276
Del Young (2B)	109	360	36	70	9	2	0	24	6	.194
		5,424	724	1,482	258	37	103	668	66	.273

In the Phils' lineup for opening day 1938 were: (from left) Chuck Klein, Emmett Mueller, Bill Atwood, Hersh Martin, Earl Browne, Pinky Whitney, George Scharein, and Morrie Arnovich.

On June 30, 1938, the Phillies played their last game at Baker Bowl. It was the end of a legendary era which had been dominated by many incidents and awful teams.

Hardly a soul shed a tear. For more than 50 years the Phillies had played at Baker Bowl, and their move to Shibe Park was viewed with great expectations. In greeting his new tenants, Connie Mack of the A's remarked, "I'm sure the Phillies will play better at Shibe Park."

He was dead wrong. In 1938 the Phillies began what would turn into a streak of five straight years of last-place finishes and more than 100 losses a season.

1938

Record: 45–105
Finish: Eighth
Games Behind: 43
Managers: Jimmie Wilson, Hans Lobert

Phil Weintraub (left), the starting first baseman in his only season with the Phillies, relaxes with Buck Jordan and Tuck Stainback before a 1938 game.

	W	L	G	GS	CG	IP	H	BB	K	ERA
Elmer Burkart	0	1	2	1	1	10	12	3	1	4.50
Max Butcher	4	8	12	12	11	98	94	31	29	2.94
Bill Hallahan	1	8	21	10	1	89	107	45	22	5.46
Ed Heusser	0	0	1	0	0	1	2	1	0	27.00
Al Hollingsworth	5	16	24	21	11	174	177	77	80	3.83
Syl Johnson	2	7	22	6	2	83	87	11	21	4.23
Hal Kelleher	0	0	6	0	0	7	16	9	4	19.29
Wayne LaMaster	4	7	18	12	1	64	80	31	35	7.73
Tom Lanning	0	1	3	1	0	7	9	2	2	6.43
Hugh Mulcahy	10	(20)	46	34	15	267	294	120	90	4.62
Claude Passeau	11	18	44	33	15	239	281	93	100	4.52
Tommy Reis	0	1	4	0	0	5	8	8	2	18.00
Pete Sivess	3	6	39	8	2	116	143	69	32	5.51
Al Smith	1	4	37	1	0	86	115	40	46	6.28
Bucky Walters	4	8	12	12	9	83	91	42	28	5.20
	45	105		151	68	1,329	(1,516)	(582)	492	4.93

Shutouts: Hollingsworth, LaMaster, Walters

	G	AB	R	H	2B	3B	HR	RBI	SB	AVG
Morrie Arnovich (LF)	139	502	47	138	29	0	4	72	2	.275
Bill Atwood (C)	102	281	27	55	8	1	3	28	0	.196
Gib Brack	72	282	40	81	20	4	4	28	2	.287
Earl Browne	21	74	4	19	4	0	0	8	0	.257
Cap Clark	52	74	11	19	1	1	0	4	0	.257
Gene Corbett	24	75	7	6	1	0	2	7	0	.080
Spud Davis	70	215	11	53	7	0	2	23	1	.247
Eddie Feinberg	10	20	0	3	0	0	0	0	0	.150
Howie Gorman	1	1	0	0	0	0	0	0	0	.000
Buck Jordan	87	310	31	93	18	1	0	18	1	.300
Chuck Klein (RF)	129	458	53	113	22	2	8	61	7	.247
Hersh Martin (CF)	120	466	58	139	36	6	3	39	8	.298
Emmett Mueller (2B)	136	444	53	111	12	4	4	34	2	.250
Alex Pitko	7	19	2	6	1	0	0	2	1	.316
Art Rebel	7	9	2	2	0	0	0	1	0	.222
George Scharein	117	390	47	93	16	4	1	29	11	.238
Tuck Stainback	30	81	9	21	3	0	1	11	1	.259
Ray Stoviak	10	10	1	0	0	0	0	0	0	.000
Phil Weintraub (1B)	100	351	51	109	23	2	4	45	1	.311
Pinky Whitney (3B)	102	300	27	83	9	1	3	38	0	.277
Jimmie Wilson	3	2	0	0	0	0	0	0	0	.000
Del Young (SS)	108	340	27	78	13	2	0	31	0	.229
		5,192	550	1,318	233	29	40	503	38	.254

Manager Tommy Prothro (center) is flanked by catcher Spud Davis (left) and pitcher Claude Passeau in 1938.

1939

Record: 45–106
Finish: Eighth
Games Behind: 50½
Manager: Doc Prothro

During the season, money-starved president Gerry Nugent traded two of his stars, Dolph Camilli (to the Brooklyn Dodgers) and Bucky Walters (to the Cincinnati Reds), getting little in return except aging catcher Spud Davis and lots of cash.

Pitchers Claude Passeau and Hugh Mulcahy were the top winners, combining for 21 victories as well as 38 losses. Passeau got the Phillies' first win at Shibe Park. On the opposite end of the scale was Hal Kelleher. So ineffective was he that he allowed 12 runs in the eighth inning of a 21–2 loss to the Reds.

For the first time in years, the Phillies didn't have a rousing hitting attack. They finished next to last in the league in hitting, a result some said of their move to Shibe Park. Only first baseman Phil Weintraub (.311) hit above .300 among the regulars.

With two games left to play in the season, manager Jimmie Wilson threw in the sponge. After five years at the helm, the beleaguered Wilson had had enough of lousy teams and the constant practice of trading good players.

The man the Phillies chose to pilot the team in 1939 was a former major league player and minor league manager who practiced dentistry in the off-season. But James (Doc) Prothro could drill no winning habits into his forlorn charges.

As a team, the Phillies had the league's lowest batting average and tied for the lowest fielding average. The pitching staff brought up the rear in earned run average and most other categories.

Only one man played the entire season and hit over .300. Spunky left fielder Morrie Arnovich, who represented the Phillies in the All-Star Game, hit .324. No one on the team had more than nine home runs.

Early in the season, the club traded pitcher Claude Passeau to the Chicago Cubs. One of the players the Phillies received in return was fireballing Kirby Higbe, who led the Phils with 10 wins. Passeau, meanwhile, went on to lead the league in strikeouts.

About the only thing the Phillies accomplished during this otherwise dismal season was that they played in their first home night game. On the evening of June 1, Rip Sewell and the Pittsburgh Pirates beat Higbe and the Phillies, 5–2.

At one point during the season, the Phillies lost 11 games in a row. Indicative of the way their season went, the Phils gave up four home runs in one inning in an 11–2 loss to the New York Giants. Pitcher Bill Kerksieck was touched for all four of the homers.

President Gerry Nugent (left) hired Johnny Ogden to help run the farm system in 1939.

	W	L	G	GS	CG	IP	H	BB	K	ERA
Boom-Boom Beck	7	14	34	16	12	183	203	64	77	4.72
Roy Bruner	0	4	4	4	2	27	38	13	11	6.67
Elmer Burkart	1	0	5	0	0	8	11	2	2	4.50
Max Butcher	2	13	19	16	3	104	131	51	27	5.63
Bud Hafey	0	0	2	0	0	1	7	1	1	45.00
Ray Harrell	3	7	22	10	4	95	101	56	35	5.40
Jim Henry	0	1	9	1	0	23	24	8	7	5.09
Kirby Higbe	10	14	34	26	14	187	208	(101)	79	4.86
Bill Hoffman	0	0	3	0	0	6	8	7	1	13.50
Al Hollingsworth	1	9	15	10	3	60	78	27	24	5.85
Syl Johnson	8	8	22	14	6	111	112	15	37	3.81
Bill Kerksieck	0	2	23	2	1	63	81	32	13	7.14
Joe Marty	0	0	1	0	0	4	2	3	1	4.50
Hugh Mulcahy	9	16	38	31	14	226	246	93	59	4.98
Claude Passeau	2	4	8	8	4	53	54	25	29	4.24
Ike Pearson	2	13	26	13	4	125	144	56	29	5.76
Jennings Poindexter	0	0	11	1	0	30	29	15	12	4.20
Gene Schott	0	1	4	0	0	11	14	5	1	4.91
Al Smith	0	0	5	0	0	9	11	5	2	4.00
	45	106		152	67	1,327	1,502	(579)	447	5.17

Shutouts: Higbe, Mulcahy, Passeau

	G	AB	R	H	2B	3B	HR	RBI	SB	AVG
Morrie Arnovich (LF)	134	491	68	159	25	2	5	67	7	.324
Bill Atwood	4	6	0	0	0	0	0	1	1	.000
Bud Bates	15	58	8	15	2	0	1	2	1	.259
Stan Benjamin	13	50	4	7	2	1	0	2	1	.140
Jack Bolling	69	211	27	61	11	0	3	13	6	.289
Gib Brack	91	270	40	78	21	4	6	41	1	.289
Dave Coble	15	25	2	7	1	0	0	0	0	.280
Spud Davis (C)	87	202	10	62	8	1	0	23	0	.307
Eddie Feinberg	6	18	2	4	1	0	0	0	0	.222
Len Gabrielson	5	18	3	4	0	0	0	1	0	.222
Roy Hughes (2B)	65	237	22	54	5	1	1	16	4	.228
Chuck Klein	25	47	8	9	2	1	1	9	1	.191
Joe Kracher	5	5	1	1	0	0	0	0	0	.200
Charlie Letchas	12	44	2	10	2	0	1	3	0	.227
Hersh Martin (CF)	111	393	59	111	28	5	1	22	4	.282
Joe Marty (RF)	91	299	32	76	12	6	9	44	1	.254
Pinky May (3B)	135	464	49	133	27	3	2	62	4	.287
Wally Millies	84	205	12	48	3	0	0	12	0	.234
Emmett Mueller	115	341	46	95	19	4	9	43	4	.279
Les Powers	19	52	7	18	1	1	0	2	0	.346
George Scharein (SS)	118	399	35	95	17	1	1	33	4	.238
LeGrant Scott	76	232	31	65	15	1	1	26	5	.280
Jim Shilling	11	33	3	10	2	3	0	4	0	.303
Gus Suhr (1B)	60	198	21	63	12	2	3	24	1	.318
Bennie Warren	18	56	4	13	0	0	1	7	0	.232
Cliff Watwood	2	6	0	1	0	0	0	0	0	.167
Pinky Whitney	34	75	9	14	0	1	1	6	0	.187
Del Young	77	217	22	57	9	2	3	20	1	.263
	5,133	533	1,341	232	40	49	510	47		.261

1940

Record: 50–103
Finish: Eighth
Games Behind: 50
Manager: Doc Prothro

When Doc Prothro had taken the job as Phillies manager in 1939, he said, "The Phillies are down, but they still are the major leagues."

After his second straight season of more than 100 losses, even the good dentist had reason to doubt his own statement.

The 1940 Phillies played what had become their typical brand of terrible baseball. They hit an anemic .238 as a team and the pitching ranked last in the league. Worst of all, Dolph Camilli, Claude Passeau, and Bucky Walters, three recent Phillies, were now among the top players in the league—with other teams.

The Phillies did find one diamond in the haystack. Late in the season, they signed a young college graduate named Danny Litwhiler. In the remaining 36 games of the season, Litwhiler spanked the ball for a .345 average while reeling off a hitting streak of 21 games.

The 1940 season was also the one in which Chuck Klein, released by the Pittsburgh Pirates, returned to the Phillies for the third time. But the faded slugger could hit only .218.

Meanwhile, Kirby Higbe was the only bright spot on the mound, posting a

	W	L	G	GS	CG	IP	H	BB	K	ERA
Boom-Boom Beck	4	9	29	15	4	129	147	41	38	4.33
Cy Blanton	4	3	13	10	5	77	82	21	24	4.32
Lloyd Brown	1	3	18	2	0	38	58	16	16	6.16
Roy Bruner	0	0	2	0	0	6	5	6	4	6.00
Charlie Frye	0	6	15	5	1	50	58	26	18	4.68
Kirby Higbe	14	19	41	36	20	283	242	(121)	(137)	3.72
Frank Hoerst	1	0	6	0	0	12	12	8	3	5.25
Si Johnson	5	14	37	14	5	138	145	42	58	4.89
Syl Johnson	2	2	17	2	2	41	37	5	13	4.17
Art Mahan	0	0	1	0	0	1	1	0	0	0.00
Paul Masterson	0	0	2	0	0	5	5	2	3	7.20
Hugh Mulcahy	13	(22)	36	36	21	280	(283)	91	82	3.60
Ike Pearson	3	14	29	20	5	145	160	57	43	5.46
Johnny Podgajny	1	3	4	4	3	35	33	1	12	2.83
Lefty Smoll	2	8	33	9	0	109	145	36	31	5.37
Maxie Wilson	0	0	3	0	0	7	16	2	3	12.86
	50	103		153	66	1,357	1,429	475	485	4.40

Shutouts: Mulcahy (3), Higbe, Pearson

	G	AB	R	H	2B	3B	HR	RBI	SB	AVG
Morrie Arnovich	39	141	13	28	2	1	0	12	0	.199
Bill Atwood	78	203	7	39	9	0	0	22	0	.192
Stan Benjamin	8	9	1	2	0	0	0	1	0	.222
Wally Berger	20	41	3	13	2	0	1	5	1	.317
Bobby Bragan (SS)	132	474	36	105	14	1	7	44	2	.222
Sam File	7	13	0	1	0	0	0	1	0	.077
Roy Hughes	1	0	0	0	0	0	0	0	0	.000
George Jumonville	11	34	0	3	0	0	0	0	0	.088
Chuck Klein (RF)	116	354	39	77	16	2	7	37	2	.218
Ed Levy	1	0	0	0	0	0	0	0	0	.000
Danny Litwhiler	36	142	10	49	2	2	5	17	1	.345
Art Mahan (1B)	146	544	55	133	24	5	2	39	4	.244
Hal Marnie	11	34	4	6	0	0	0	4	0	.176
Hersh Martin	33	83	10	21	6	1	0	5	1	.253
Joe Marty (CF)	123	455	52	123	21	8	13	50	2	.270
Pinky May (3B)	136	501	59	147	24	2	1	48	2	.293
Mel Mazzera	69	156	16	37	5	4	0	13	1	.237
Wally Millies	26	43	1	3	0	0	0	0	0	.070
Al Monchak	19	14	1	2	0	0	0	0	1	.143
Emmett Mueller	97	263	24	65	13	2	3	28	2	.247
Johnny Rizzo (LF)	103	367	53	107	12	2	20	53	2	.292
George Scharein	7	17	0	5	0	0	0	0	0	.294
Ham Schulte (2B)	120	436	44	103	18	2	1	21	3	.236
Neb Stewart	10	31	3	4	0	0	0	0	0	.129
Gus Suhr	10	25	4	4	0	0	2	5	0	.160
Bennie Warren (C)	106	289	33	71	6	1	12	34	1	.246
Del Young	15	33	2	8	0	1	0	1	0	.242
		5,137	494	1,225	180	35	75	459	25	.238

Lots of rain fell into the lives of the 1939 Phillies, who won just 45 times. (From left) Emmett Mueller, Morrie Arnovich, Joe Marty, and Gus Suhr check out the weather conditions.

14–19 record. Hugh Mulcahy led the league with 22 defeats (13 wins), which included a 12-game losing streak.

Johnny Rizzo, acquired in a trade for Morrie Arnovich, wound up with 20 home runs and a .292 average to lead Phils regulars.

The most amazing thing about the 1941 season is that the Phillies actually attracted 231,401 fans to their games. P. T. Barnum was right, after all.

The 1941 Phils etched their names in infamy, losing more games than any other team in the club's history. They finished no less than 19 games out of seventh place.

To make matters worse, Hugh Mulcahy had become the first major league player drafted into the military, and Kirby Higbe had been traded to the Brooklyn Dodgers. That left Chester native Johnny Podgajny and Tommy Hughes as the big winners on the pitching staff with nine wins apiece. Hughes also hurled a one-hitter during the season, beating the Chicago Cubs, 7–0.

The Phillies did have a couple of up-and-coming new infielders in second baseman Danny Murtaugh, a hustling Irishman also from nearby Chester, and first baseman Nick Etten, a former Villanova student. Etten led the team with a .311 batting average, and Murtaugh led the National League with 18 stolen bases.

It was also the first full season for left fielder Danny Litwhiler. The Bloomsburg State grad hit .305 with 18 home runs, including one in every park. With Etten he provided the club with virtually its only punch at the plate.

At one point during the season, the team went 28 innings without scoring a run. The streak was symbolic of the futility of the whole season.

1941

Record: 43–111
Finish: Eighth
Games Behind: 57
Manager: Doc Prothro

Catcher Bennie Warren chats with pitcher-turned-soldier Hugh Mulcahy, who came home on leave to visit his former teammates.

	W	L	G	GS	CG	IP	H	BB	K	ERA
Boom-Boom Beck	1	9	34	7	2	95	104	35	34	4.64
Cy Blanton	6	12	28	25	7	164	186	57	64	4.50
Roy Bruner	0	3	13	1	0	29	37	25	13	4.97
Bill Crouch	2	3	20	5	1	59	65	17	26	4.42
Lee Grissom	2	13	29	18	2	131	120	70	74	3.99
Bill Harman	0	0	5	0	0	13	15	8	3	4.85
Frank Hoerst	3	10	37	11	1	106	111	50	33	5.18
Tommy Hughes	9	14	34	24	5	170	187	82	59	4.45
Si Johnson	5	12	39	21	6	163	207	54	80	4.53
Dale Jones	0	1	2	1	0	8	13	6	2	7.88
Gene Lambert	0	1	2	1	0	9	11	2	3	2.00
Paul Masterson	1	0	2	1	1	11	11	6	8	4.91
Rube Melton	1	5	25	5	2	84	81	47	57	4.71
Ike Pearson	4	14	46	10	0	136	139	70	38	3.57
Johnny Podgajny	9	12	34	24	8	181	191	70	53	4.62
Vito Tamulis	0	1	6	1	0	12	21	7	5	9.00
	43	111		155	35	1,372	(1,499)	(606)	552	4.50

Shutouts: Hughes (2), Blanton, Johnson

	G	AB	R	H	2B	3B	HR	RBI	SB	AVG
Stan Benjamin (RF)	129	480	47	113	20	7	3	27	17	.235
Bobby Bragan (SS)	154	557	37	140	19	3	4	69	7	.251
Paul Busby	10	16	3	5	0	0	0	2	0	.313
Jim Carlin	16	21	2	3	1	0	1	2	0	.143
Nick Etten (1B)	151	540	78	168	27	4	14	79	9	.311
George Jumonville	6	7	1	3	0	0	1	2	0	.429
Chuck Klein	50	73	6	9	0	0	1	3	0	.123
Danny Litwhiler (LF)	151	590	72	180	29	6	18	66	1	.305
Mickey Livingston	95	207	16	42	6	1	0	18	2	.203
Hal Marnie	61	158	12	38	3	3	0	11	0	.241
Joe Marty (CF)	137	477	60	128	19	3	8	39	6	.268
Pinky May (3B)	142	490	46	131	17	4	0	39	2	.267
Wally Millies	1	2	0	0	0	0	0	0	0	.000
Emmett Mueller	93	233	21	53	11	1	1	22	2	.227
Danny Murtaugh (2B)	85	347	34	76	8	1	0	11	(18)	.219
Bill Nagle	17	56	2	8	1	1	0	6	0	.143
Johnny Rizzo	99	235	20	51	9	2	4	24	1	.217
Bennie Warren (C)	121	345	34	74	13	2	9	35	0	.214
		5,233	501	1,277	188	38	64	467	65	.244

1942

Record: 42–109
Finish: Eighth
Games Behind: 62½
Manager: Hans Lobert

The previous season may have been the worst in Phillies history, but 1942 wasn't much better. In fact, in some respects it was worse.

The Phillies under new manager Hans Lobert, a long-time coach, played three fewer games than the 1941 club, thus depriving themselves of a record-setting number of losses. But they did succeed in reaching all-time depths with the fewest runs (394) and lowest batting average (.232) in club history. Over one stretch they also lost 13 straight games and went 30 innings in a row without scoring a run.

What salvaged an otherwise horrendous season was the play of Danny Litwhiler in left field. After leading National League outfielders in errors the year before, Litwhiler went through the entire 1942 season without making a miscue. No outfielder had ever done that before, and only three other outfielders (Curt Flood, Rocky Colavito, Terry Puhl) have since matched the feat in 150 games or more.

Although his average dropped to .271 and his home runs fell to nine, Litwhiler still led the team in both categories. Etten tumbled to a .264 mark, while rookie Ron Northey showed promise with a strong throwing arm and a live bat.

Also on the team in 1942 was rickety old Lloyd Waner, a future Hall of Famer nearing the end of his career. Waner, picked up as a free agent after playing for three teams in 1941, hit .261 in his only year as a Phillie.

In addition, the Phillies included among their number a wild, young pitcher named Rube Melton. Considered a top prospect, he lost 20 games for the Phillies, one more than Si Johnson and two more than Tommy Hughes.

	W	L	G	GS	CG	IP	H	BB	K	ERA
Boom-Boom Beck	0	1	26	1	0	53	69	17	10	4.75
Cy Blanton	0	4	6	3	0	22	30	13	15	5.73
Hilly Flitcraft	0	0	3	0	0	3	6	2	1	9.00
George Hennessey	1	1	5	1	0	17	11	10	2	2.65
Frank Hoerst	4	16	33	22	5	151	162	78	52	5.19
Tommy Hughes	12	18	40	31	19	253	224	99	77	3.06
Si Johnson	8	19	39	26	10	195	198	72	78	3.69
Apples Lapihuska	0	2	3	2	0	21	17	13	8	5.14
Paul Masterson	0	0	4	0	0	8	10	5	3	6.75
Rube Melton	9	20	42	29	10	209	180	(114)	107	3.70
Sam Nahem	1	3	35	2	0	75	72	40	38	4.92
Earl Naylor	0	5	20	4	1	60	68	29	19	6.15
Ike Pearson	1	6	35	7	0	85	87	50	21	4.55
Johnny Podgajny	6	14	43	23	6	187	191	63	40	3.90
	42	109		151	51	1,341	1,328	(605)	472	4.12

Shutouts: Johnson, Melton

	G	AB	R	H	2B	3B	HR	RBI	SB	AVG
Stan Benjamin	78	210	24	47	8	3	2	8	5	.224
Bobby Bragan (SS)	109	335	17	73	12	2	2	15	0	.218
Bill Burich	25	80	3	23	1	0	0	7	2	.288
Benny Culp	1	0	0	0	0	0	0	0	0	.000
Nick Etten (1B)	139	459	37	121	21	3	8	41	3	.264
Ed Freed	13	33	3	10	3	1	0	1	1	.303
Al Glossop (2B)	121	454	33	102	15	1	4	40	3	.225
Bert Hodge	8	11	0	2	0	0	0	0	0	.182
Chuck Klein	14	14	0	1	0	0	0	0	0	.071
Ernie Koy	91	258	21	63	9	3	4	26	0	.244
Danny Litwhiler (LF)	151	591	59	160	25	9	9	56	2	.271
Mickey Livingston	89	239	20	49	6	1	2	8	5	.224
Hal Marnie	24	30	3	5	0	0	0	0	1	.167
Pinky May (3B)	115	345	25	82	15	0	0	18	3	.238
Ed Murphy	13	28	2	7	2	0	0	4	0	.250
Danny Murtaugh	144	506	48	122	16	4	0	27	13	.241
Earl Naylor	76	168	9	33	4	1	0	14	1	.196
Ron Northey (RF)	127	402	31	101	13	2	5	31	2	.251
Bill Peterman	1	1	0	1	0	0	0	0	0	1.000
Lloyd Waner (CF)	101	287	23	75	7	3	0	10	1	.261
Bennie Warren (C)	90	225	19	47	6	3	7	20	0	.209
		5,060	394	1,174	168	37	44	354	37	.232

Outfielder Ron Northy (left) and pitcher Al Gerheauser share one of the few laughs that the wartime Phillies enjoyed.

Another pitcher, George Hennessey, was only available for home games. Hennessey held down a full-time job as an airplane mechanic in Trenton, New Jersey. His 2-B classification prevented him from participating in road trips or spring training.

On the whole, the team was so bad that wins were usually quite unexpected when they arrived. "When we won a few games in a row," second baseman Danny Murtaugh recalled, "it might have been cause for a Congressional investigation. They probably thought the opponent was throwing games. I know it's hard to look back and wonder how any club could be that bad, but we were."

With their 109 losses, the Phillies became the only National League team ever to lose 100 or more games in a season for five straight years.

At the request of manager Lobert, the team officially changed its name in 1942 to Phils. Hans thought that sounded better than the name Phillies, which because of years of losing had a negative image, he said. The new handle, however, was dropped before the next season.

1943

Record: 64–90
Finish: Seventh
Games Behind: 41
Managers: Bucky Harris, Freddie Fitzsimmons

In 1943 the Phillies were almost as active off the field as they were on it.

To begin with, after six eighth-place finishes in the last seven years and a decade of hapless and mostly spiritless play, the club was deeply in debt and beginning to attract the resentment of the other teams. Owner Gerry Nugent was forced to surrender the team to the National League, which, after taking it over briefly, found a buyer in William D. Cox, a businessman-sportsman from New York City.

Cox promptly hired veteran manager Bucky Harris to run the team. Only trouble was, Harris had few players. In fact, when the club opened spring training at Hershey, Pennsylvania, only 14 players appeared. The shortage soon reached a ridiculous level with old Chuck Klein, a player-coach, performing at first base, newly acquired pitcher Schoolboy Rowe playing shortstop, and even owner Cox dabbling on the mound.

Before he left, Nugent had traded Nick Etten. Then Cox swapped Danny Litwhiler, getting back three so-so outfielders. One, Buster Adams, would "make Philadelphia fans think Dode Paskert is back playing center field," said Cox.

Rowe, however, was an especially good bargain, the big pitcher having

New owner William Cox took part in spring training with his club in 1943.

	W	L	G	GS	CG	IP	H	BB	K	ERA
Dick Barrett	10	9	23	20	10	169	137	51	65	2.40
Boom-Boom Beck	0	0	4	0	0	14	24	5	3	9.64
Dick Conger	2	7	13	10	2	55	72	24	18	6.05
Dutch Dietz	1	1	21	0	0	36	42	15	10	6.50
Deacon Donahue	0	0	2	0	0	4	4	1	1	4.50
George Eyrich	0	0	9	0	0	19	23	9	5	3.32
Charlie Fuchs	2	7	17	9	4	78	76	34	12	4.27
Al Gerheauser	10	19	38	31	11	215	222	70	92	3.60
Si Johnson	8	3	21	14	9	113	110	25	46	3.27
Andy Karl	1	2	9	2	0	27	44	11	4	7.00
Newt Kimball	1	6	34	6	2	90	85	42	33	4.10
Tex Kraus	9	15	34	25	10	200	197	78	48	3.15
Apples Lapihuska	0	0	1	0	0	2	5	3	0	27.00
Bill Lee	1	5	13	7	2	61	70	21	17	4.57
Rogers McKee	1	0	4	1	1	13	12	5	1	6.23
Dale Matthewson	0	3	11	1	0	26	26	8	8	4.85
Johnny Podgajny	4	4	13	5	3	64	77	16	13	4.22
Ken Raffensberger	0	1	1	1	1	8	7	2	3	1.13
Schoolboy Rowe	14	8	27	25	11	199	194	29	52	2.94
Manny Salvo	0	0	1	0	0	1	2	1	0	27.00
Bill Webb	0	0	1	0	0	1	1	1	0	9.00
	64	90		157	66	1,393	1,430	451	431	3.79

Shutouts: Rowe (3), Barrett (2), Gerheauser (2), Fuchs, Johnson, Kraus

	G	AB	R	H	2B	3B	HR	RBI	SB	AVG
Buster Adams (CF)	111	418	48	107	14	7	4	38	2	.256
Charlie Brewster	49	159	13	35	2	0	0	12	1	.220
Paul Busby	26	40	13	10	1	0	0	5	2	.250
Benny Culp	10	24	4	5	1	0	0	2	0	.208
Babe Dahlgren	136	508	55	146	19	2	5	56	2	.287
Garton DelSavio	4	11	0	1	0	0	0	0	0	.091
Bob Finley	28	81	9	21	2	0	1	7	0	.259
Ray Hamrick	44	160	12	32	3	1	0	9	0	.200
Chuck Klein	12	20	0	2	0	0	0	3	1	.100
Danny Litwhiler	36	139	23	36	6	0	5	17	1	.259
Mickey Livingston (C)	84	265	25	66	9	2	3	18	1	.249
Pinky May (3B)	137	415	31	117	19	2	1	48	2	.282
Dee Moore	37	113	13	27	4	1	1	8	0	.239
Danny Murtaugh (2B)	113	451	65	123	17	4	1	35	4	.271
Earl Naylor	33	120	12	21	2	0	3	14	1	.175
Ron Northey (RF)	147	586	72	163	31	5	16	68	2	.278
Tom Padden	17	41	5	12	0	0	0	1	0	.293
Andy Seminick	22	72	9	13	2	0	2	5	0	.181
Glen Stewart (SS)	110	336	23	71	10	1	2	24	1	.211
Coaker Triplett (LF)	105	360	45	98	16	4	14	52	2	.272
Jimmy Wasdell (1B)	141	522	54	136	19	6	4	67	6	.261
		5,297	571	1,320	186	36	66	529	29	.249

been purchased at Harris' insistence from the Brooklyn Dodgers, who thought he was washed up. By late July, Rowe had helped the Phillies climb to fifth place, a position to which they were totally unaccustomed.

At the end of the month, though, a long-simmering feud between Cox and Harris erupted with the owner's sudden firing of the manager and replacing him with former Giants pitching star Freddie Fitzsimmons. The players were irate. They refused to take the field for a game at St. Louis. Only at the urging of Harris did the players end their brief strike and go back to the game.

The firing, however, eventually backfired on Cox. A remark to the press by Harris about the owner's gambling habits resulted in Cox's being banned that winter from baseball by Commissioner Landis.

Through all the turmoil, the Phillies managed to finish with their best record since 1935. Rowe was the first regular pitcher in eight seasons to win more than he lost (14–8). The club also got occasional good pitching from Al Gerheauser, Dick Barrett, and Tex Kraus.

Babe Dahlgren had the best batting average (.287), but Pinky May, Ron Northey, Danny Murtaugh, and Coaker Triplett all hit above .270. Adams hit .256.

The club also set a National League record by playing in the most doubleheaders in one season. The Phils engaged in 43 twin bills.

	W	L	G	GS	CG	IP	H	BB	K	ERA
Dick Barrett	12	18	37	27	11	221	223	88	74	3.87
Chet Covington	1	1	19	0	0	39	46	8	13	4.62
Deacon Donahue	0	2	6	0	0	9	18	2	2	8.00
John Fick	0	0	4	0	0	5	3	3	2	3.60
Al Gerheauser	8	16	30	29	10	183	210	65	66	4.57
Andy Karl	3	2	38	0	0	89	76	21	26	2.32
Vern Kennedy	1	5	12	7	3	55	60	20	23	4.25
Bill Lee	10	11	31	28	11	208	199	57	50	3.16
Lou Lucier	0	0	1	0	0	2	3	2	1	13.50
Dale Matthewson	0	0	17	1	0	32	27	16	8	3.94
Barney Mussill	0	1	16	0	0	19	20	13	5	6.16
Rogers McKee	0	0	1	0	0	2	2	1	0	4.50
Ken Raffensberger	13	20	37	31	18	259	257	45	136	3.06
Charlie Ripple	0	0	1	1	0	2	6	4	2	18.00
Charley Schanz	13	16	40	30	13	241	231	103	84	3.32
Harry Shuman	0	0	18	0	0	27	26	11	4	4.00
Al Verdel	0	0	1	0	0	1	0	0	0	0.00
	61	92		154	66	1,395	1,407	459	496	3.64

Shutouts: Lee (3), Raffensberger (3), Gerheauser (2), Barrett, Schanz

	G	AB	R	H	2B	3B	HR	RBI	SB	AVG
Buster Adams (CF)	151	584	86	165	35	3	17	64	2	.283
Joe Antolik	4	6	1	2	0	0	0	0	0	.333
Putsy Caballero	4	4	0	0	0	0	0	0	0	.000
Ted Cieslak	85	220	18	54	10	0	2	11	1	.245
Benny Culp	4	2	1	0	0	0	0	0	0	.000
Bob Finley (C)	94	281	18	70	11	1	1	21	1	.249
Nick Goulish	1	0	0	0	0	0	0	0	0	.000
Granny Hamner	21	77	6	19	1	0	0	5	0	.247
Ray Hamrick (SS)	74	292	22	60	10	1	1	23	1	.205
Heinie Heltzel	11	22	1	4	1	0	0	0	0	.182
Chuck Klein	4	7	1	1	0	0	0	0	0	.143
Charlie Letchas	116	396	29	94	8	0	0	33	0	.237
Tony Lupien (1B)	153	597	82	169	23	9	5	52	18	.283
Moon Mullen (2B)	118	464	51	124	9	4	0	31	4	.267
Ron Northey (RF)	152	570	72	164	35	9	22	104	1	.288
Johnny Peacock	83	253	21	57	9	3	0	21	1	.225
Lee Riley	4	12	1	1	1	0	0	1	0	.083
Andy Seminick	22	63	9	14	2	1	0	4	2	.222
Merv Shea	7	15	2	4	0	0	1	1	0	.267
Glen Stewart (3B)	118	377	32	83	11	5	0	29	0	.220
Coaker Triplett	84	184	15	43	5	1	1	25	1	.234
Turkey Tyson	1	1	0	0	0	0	0	0	0	.000
Jimmy Wasdell (LF)	133	451	47	125	20	3	3	40	0	.277
		5,301	539	1,331	199	42	55	495	32	.251

1944

Record: 61–92
Finish: Eighth
Games Behind: 43½
Manager: Freddie Fitzsimmons

A new era in Phillies' baseball dawned in 1944 as the club found itself now owned by the millionaire Carpenter family of Wilmington, Delaware.

Robert R.M. Carpenter, Jr., was installed by his father as the club president, and he soon hired former pitching great Herb Pennock to be the team's first official general manager. It may not have been too obvious at the time, but the Phillies at long last were pointed back toward respectability.

The picture was still hazy at field level, though. A steady stream of players moved in and out of the lineup as World War II took its toll on big league rosters. The names were mostly those belonging to unknown players—names such as Hamrick, Stewart, Finley, Cieslak, Letchas, and Schanz. In many cases, they played one year or less and then were gone.

The batting attack featured Ron Northey with a .288 average, 22 home runs, and 104 RBI, as well as Buster Adams (.283), Tony Lupien (.283), and Jimmy Wasdell (.277). Northey also led National League outfielders in assists with 24.

The pitching staff was led by lefthander Ken Raffensberger, who had a deceptive 13–20 record with a 3.06 ERA. The York, Pennsylvania, native was the winning pitcher that year in the All-Star Game, the only Phillies pitcher ever to win that game.

In 1944, Carpenter also initiated a contest to rename the Phillies. The winning entry would win a $100 bond.

From 5,064 entries, the name Blue Jays was chosen. It was officially declared the team's new nickname. But about the only reaction it provoked was from students at Johns Hopkins University in Baltimore. At the time, Hopkins athletic teams had been called Blue Jays for 68 years.

The Hopkins student council passed a resolution, which it sent to Carpenter. It called his use of the name Blue Jays "a reprehensible act which brought disgrace and dishonor to the good name of Johns Hopkins University."

Sproull, Mauney, Flager, Powell, Daniels, Mott, Antonelli—players with unfamiliar names continued to drift through the Phillies' clubhouse. Their combined efforts sent the Phillies careening into the depths they had known a few years earlier.

The 1945 team was a pitiful aggregation that seemed to negate the progress the team had made in the previous two years. "Owners change, managers change, but it's the same old tailender," Phillies fans lamented.

After Freddie Fitzsimmons won only 18 out of the first 69 games, he was replaced by a firebrand former American League outfielder, Ben Chapman, who had been suspended the previous year for punching an umpire in the minor leagues.

Chapman ignited his new club somewhat, but it couldn't go far on what it had. The team had five players under 21 years of age and nine over 35. That included the aging ex-Athletics great Jimmie Foxx, who hit the final seven of the 534 home runs of his illustrious career in a Phillies' uniform. Another old-timer, Gus Mancuso, caught some games, but hit only .199.

Jimmy Wasdell (.300) and Vance Dinges (.287) were the team's top hitters. Vince DiMaggio, lesser-known brother of Joe and Dom who had come in a trade in the spring, hit four grand slam home runs during the season. A young catcher, Andy Seminick, got in some playing time. And Rene Monteagudo, a tiny Cuban, got 18 pinch hits.

1945

Record: 46–108
Finish: Eighth
Games Behind: 52
Managers: Freddie Fitzsimmons, Ben Chapman

Jimmie Foxx (left) was playing out the string and ex-A's teammate Al Simmons (third from left) was already retired when he visited with manager Freddie Fitzsimmons (right) and coach Merv Shea in 1945.

	W	L	G	GS	CG	IP	H	BB	K	ERA
Dick Barrett	8	(20)	36	30	8	191	216	92	72	5.42
Ben Chapman	0	0	3	0	0	7	7	6	4	7.71
Mitch Chetkovich	0	0	4	0	0	3	2	3	0	0.00
Dick Coffman	2	1	14	0	0	26	39	2	2	5.19
Jimmie Foxx	1	0	9	2	0	23	13	14	10	1.57
Don Grate	0	1	4	2	0	8	18	12	6	18.00
Oscar Judd	5	4	23	9	3	83	80	40	36	3.80
Andy Karl	8	8	(67)	2	1	181	175	50	51	2.98
Vern Kennedy	0	3	12	3	0	36	43	14	13	5.50
Tex Kraus	4	9	19	13	0	82	96	40	28	5.38
Bill Lee	3	6	13	13	2	77	107	30	13	4.68
Izzy Leon	0	4	14	4	0	39	49	19	11	5.31
Lou Lucier	0	1	13	0	0	20	14	5	5	2.25
Dick Mauney	6	10	20	16	6	123	127	27	35	3.07
Rene Monteagudo	0	0	14	0	0	46	67	28	16	7.43
Hugh Mulcahy	1	3	5	4	1	28	33	9	2	3.86
Ken Raffensberger	0	3	5	4	1	24	28	14	6	4.50
Charlie Ripple	0	1	4	0	0	8	7	10	5	6.75
Charley Schanz	4	15	35	21	5	145	165	87	56	4.34
Lefty Scott	0	2	8	2	0	22	29	12	5	4.50
Charlie Sproull	4	10	34	19	2	130	158	80	47	5.95
Whit Wyatt	0	7	10	10	2	51	72	14	10	5.29
	46	108		154	31	1,353	(1,545)	(608)	433	4.64

Shutouts: Mauney (2), Judd, Schanz

	G	AB	R	H	2B	3B	HR	RBI	SB	AVG
Buster Adams	14	56	6	13	3	1	2	8	0	.232
Stan Andrews	13	33	3	11	2	0	1	6	1	.333
John Antonelli (3B)	125	504	50	129	27	2	1	28	1	.256
Putsy Caballero	9	1	1	0	0	0	0	1	0	.000
Ben Chapman	24	51	4	16	2	0	0	4	0	.314
Glen Crawford	82	302	41	89	13	2	2	24	5	.295
Fred Daniels (2B)	76	230	15	46	3	2	0	10	1	.200
Vince DiMaggio (CF)	127	452	64	116	25	3	19	84	12	.257
Vance Dinges (RF)	109	397	46	114	15	4	1	36	5	.287
Wally Flager	49	168	21	42	4	1	2	15	1	.250
Jimmie Foxx	89	224	30	60	11	1	7	38	0	.268
Nick Goulish	13	11	4	3	0	0	0	2	0	.273
Granny Hamner	14	41	3	7	2	0	0	6	0	.171
Garvin Hamner	32	101	12	20	3	0	0	5	2	.198
Don Hasenmayer	5	18	1	2	0	0	0	1	0	.111
Tony Lupien	15	54	1	17	1	0	0	3	2	.315
Gus Mancuso	70	176	11	35	5	0	0	16	2	.199
Rene Monteagudo	114	193	26	58	6	0	0	15	2	.301
Bitsy Mott (SS)	90	289	21	64	8	0	0	22	2	.221
Johnny Peacock	33	74	6	15	6	0	0	6	1	.203
Nick Picciuto	36	89	7	12	6	0	0	6	0	.135
Jake Powell	48	173	13	40	5	0	1	14	1	.231
Andy Seminick (C)	80	188	18	45	7	2	6	26	3	.239
Hal Spindel	36	87	7	20	3	0	0	8	0	.230
Coaker Triplett (LF)	120	363	36	87	11	1	7	46	6	.240
Ed Walczak	20	57	6	12	3	0	0	2	0	.211
Jimmy Wasdell (1B)	134	500	65	150	19	8	7	60	7	.300
		5,203	548	1,278	197	27	56	503	54	.246

No less than 19 pitchers were involved in the Phillies' 154 decisions. Even Chapman pitched in three games. And Foxx pitched in nine.

1946

Record: 69–85
Finish: Fifth
Games Behind: 28
Manager: Ben Chapman

If a single season could be regarded as a turning point in the modern fortunes of the Phillies, the 1946 campaign was surely it. The season was one in which the Phillies finally entered the realm of the respectable. It was the start of a trail that would lead to the National League pennant five years later.

The year 1946 was actually very special for all of baseball. World War II had ended, the troops had returned, and there was a wholesome, enthusiastic spirit reaching across the country. Much of this enthusiasm carried over to the nation's ballparks where record crowds flocked to see the game played at all levels.

For the first time in five seasons, the major league teams were at full strength. And with old stars returning and new ones emerging, the 1946 season was one of major league baseball's finest and most exciting years.

As for the Phillies, for the first time since 1932 they finally had a decent unit on the field. It was comprised of talented veterans such as Frank McCormick, Emil Verban, Jim Tabor, and Schoolboy Rowe who had been picked up from other teams, young and up-and-coming players such as Del Ennis, Andy Seminick, and Johnny Wyrostek, and a few good players from the war-era Phillies such as Ron Northey and Ken Raffensberger.

The team had an entirely different infield and outfield from the previous year. Despite their unfamiliarity with each other, the players hustled throughout the season.

Eventually, they wound up in fifth place, along the way beating the

	W	L	G	GS	CG	IP	H	BB	K	ERA
Ben Chapman	0	0	1	0	0	1	1	0	1	0.00
Blix Donnelly	3	4	12	8	2	76	64	24	38	2.96
Don Grate	1	0	3	0	0	8	4	2	2	1.13
Eli Hodkey	0	1	2	1	0	4	9	5	0	13.50
Frank Hoerst	1	6	18	7	2	68	77	36	17	4.61
Tommy Hughes	6	9	29	13	3	111	123	44	34	4.38
John Humphries	0	0	10	1	0	25	24	9	10	3.96
Si Johnson	0	0	1	0	0	3	7	0	2	3.00
Oscar Judd	11	12	30	24	12	173	169	90	65	3.54
Al Jurisch	4	3	13	10	2	68	71	31	34	3.71
Andy Karl	3	7	39	0	0	65⅓	84	22	15	4.96
Dick Koecher	0	1	1	1	0	3	7	1	2	9.00
Art Lopatka	0	1	4	1	0	6	13	4	4	18.00
Dick Mauney	6	4	24	7	3	90	98	18	31	2.70
Al Milnar	0	0	1	1	0	⅓	2	2	0	108.00
Hugh Mulcahy	2	4	16	5	1	63	69	33	12	4.43
Dick Mulligan	2	2	19	5	1	55	61	27	16	4.75
Ike Pearson	1	0	5	2	1	14	19	8	6	3.86
Lou Possehl	1	2	4	4	0	14	19	10	4	5.93
Ken Raffensberger	8	15	39	23	14	196	203	39	73	3.63
Charlie Ripple	1	0	6	0	0	3	5	6	3	12.00
Schoolboy Rowe	11	4	17	16	9	136	112	21	51	2.12
Charley Schanz	6	6	32	15	4	116	130	71	47	5.82
Charley Stanceu	2	4	14	11	1	70	71	39	23	4.24
	69	85		155	55	1,369 (1,442)	542	490		3.99

Shutouts: Hughes (2), Raffensberger (2), Rowe (2), Judd, Jurisch, Mauney, Pearson

	G	AB	R	H	2B	3B	HR	RBI	SB	AVG
Bill Burich	2	1	1	0	0	0	0	0	0	.000
Glenn Crawford	1	1	0	0	0	0	0	0	0	.000
Vince DiMaggio	6	19	1	4	1	0	0	0	0	.211
Vance Dinges	50	104	7	32	5	1	1	10	2	.308
Del Ennis (LF)	141	540	70	169	30	6	17	73	5	.313
Charlie Gilbert	88	260	34	63	5	2	1	17	3	.242
Granny Hamner	2	7	0	1	0	0	0	0	0	.143
Don Hasenmayer	6	12	0	1	1	0	0	0	0	.083
Rollie Hemsley	49	139	7	31	4	1	0	11	0	.223
Roy Hughes	89	276	23	65	11	1	0	22	7	.236
Charlie Letchas	6	13	1	3	0	0	0	0	0	.231
Frank McCormick (1B)	135	504	46	143	20	2	11	66	2	.284
Dee Moore	11	13	2	1	0	0	0	1	0	.077
Danny Murtaugh	6	19	1	4	1	0	1	3	0	.211
Skeeter Newsome (SS)	112	375	35	87	10	2	1	23	4	.232
Ron Northey (RF)	128	438	55	109	24	5	16	62	1	.249
Lou Novikoff	17	23	0	7	1	0	0	3	0	.304
John O'Neil	46	94	12	25	3	0	0	9	0	.266
Ken Richardson	6	20	1	3	1	0	0	2	0	.150
Andy Seminick (C)	124	406	55	107	15	5	12	52	2	.264
Hal Spindel	1	3	0	1	0	0	0	1	0	.333
Jim Tabor (3B)	124	463	53	124	15	2	10	50	3	.268
Emil Verban (2B)	138	473	44	130	17	5	0	34	5	.275
Jimmy Wasdell	26	51	7	13	0	2	1	5	0	.255
Johnny Wyrostek (CF)	145	545	73	153	30	4	6	45	7	.281
		5,233	560	1,351	209	40	80	517	41	.258

Manager Ben Chapman (right) and players return from victorious road trip in 1946.

pennant-bound St. Louis Cardinals eight times and the defending champion Chicago Cubs in 10 games.

The fans responded by coming to Shibe Park in droves. Encouraged by the new regime of Bob Carpenter, 1,045,247 spectators watched the Phillies at home. It was not only an all-time club attendance record, but nearly twice as many people as had set the old mark way back in 1916.

One of the focal points of the fans' interests was Ennis, a Philadelphia native. Playing in his first season, the slugging left fielder hit a sparkling .313 with 17 home runs. At the end of the season, *The Sporting News* made him its Rookie of the Year.

The Phillies also got a sterling season from first baseman McCormick, a former National League MVP. Frank went 131 straight games without an error and ended the season with a record-setting .999 fielding percentage.

Rowe was the ace of the pitching staff, posting an 11–4 record before being sidelined for the season with a back injury. Oscar Judd added an 11–12 mark. While the pitching staff still ranked last in the league in ERA, at least it was a respectable 3.99. The catching of the rapidly developing Seminick had a lot to do with it.

In the early part of the season, the Phillies idled in last place. But in late June they caught fire, moving from eighth to sixth. Their final fifth-place finish was the highest level for the club since 1932.

1947

Record: 62–92
Finish: Seventh (tie)
Games Behind: 32
Manager: Ben Chapman

Under normal circumstances, the Phillies' slide back to the lower regions of the National League in 1947 would have been typical of the way the club had performed over the past three decades. But neither the club ownership nor the team's fans, who came out in numbers bettering 900,000, were particularly bothered by the Phillies' seventh place tie.

They were aware that better days were ahead. Quietly but quickly, president Bob Carpenter and general manager Herb Pennock were building for the future, stocking their farm system with young players with big league potential.

Therefore, the 1947 team, despite a dismal record reminiscent of days gone by, was merely there to hold the fort, to kill time until the youngsters on the vine were ripe.

The '47 season, however, was not without some bright spots. Harry Walker, one of the heroes of the St. Louis Cardinals' 1946 World Series victory who had been to spring training with the Phillies in 1939, came to Philadelphia in a trade for Ron Northey. A leadoff batter and center fielder, Walker ran away with the National League batting title, hitting .363, vanquishing second place Bob Elliott of the Boston Braves by 46 points.

Second baseman Emil Verban was the class of the league at his position and, together with Walker, was in the starting lineup for the All-Star Game. Ancient pitcher Dutch Leonard, purchased from the Washington Senators, used his knuckle ball to befuddle opposing hitters while ranking as one of the league's top moundsmen. The 38-year-old hurler had a 17–12 record, and his 2.68 ERA was fourth best in the circuit.

Probably the most incredible development of the season was the attendance on May 11 at a doubleheader with the Brooklyn Dodgers. Some 41,660 (40,952 paid) jammed Shibe Park, about 8,000 beyond its listed capacity, to see the Phillies beat the pennant-bound Dodgers, 7–3 and 5–4, behind the pitching of Leonard and Schoolboy Rowe, who had a 14–10 record for the season. It was the largest crowd ever to see a game up to that point in Philadelphia baseball history.

Another memorable event occurred when 18-year-old, $65,000 bonus

In a celebrated pose, photographers coaxed Jackie Robinson (left) and Phillies manager Ben Chapman to get together before a 1947 game. Robinson had been the target of Chapman's verbal abuse earlier in the season, his first in the major leagues.

	W	L	G	GS	CG	IP	H	BB	K	ERA
Blix Donnelly	4	6	38	10	5	121	113	46	31	2.98
Ken Heintzelman	7	10	24	19	8	136	144	46	55	4.04
Frank Hoerst	1	1	4	1	0	11	19	3	0	8.18
Tommy Hughes	4	11	29	15	4	127	121	59	44	3.47
Oscar Judd	4	15	32	19	8	147	155	69	54	4.59
Al Jurisch	1	7	34	12	5	118	110	52	48	4.96
Dick Koecher	0	2	3	2	1	17	20	10	4	4.76
Dutch Leonard	17	12	32	29	19	235	224	57	103	2.68
Dick Mauney	0	0	9	1	0	16	15	7	6	3.94
Lou Possehl	0	0	2	0	0	4	5	0	1	4.50
Ken Raffensberger	2	6	10	7	3	41	50	8	16	5.49
Schoolboy Rowe	14	10	31	28	15	196	232	45	74	4.32
Charley Schanz	2	4	34	6	1	102	107	47	42	4.15
Fred Schmidt	5	8	29	5	0	77	76	43	24	4.68
Curt Simmons	1	0	1	1	1	9	5	6	9	1.00
Homer Spragins	0	0	4	0	0	5	3	3	3	7.20
	62	92		155	70	1,362	1,399	501	514	3.96

Shutouts: Leonard (3), Donnelly, Hughes, Judd, Raffensberger, Rowe

	G	AB	R	H	2B	3B	HR	RBI	SB	AVG
Buster Adams	69	182	21	45	11	1	2	15	2	.247
Jack Albright	41	99	9	23	4	0	2	5	1	.232
Putsy Caballero	2	7	2	1	0	0	0	0	0	.143
Del Ennis (LF)	139	541	71	149	25	6	12	81	9	.275
Nick Etten	14	41	5	10	4	0	1	8	0	.244
Lou Finney	4	4	0	0	0	0	0	0	0	.000
Charlie Gilbert	83	152	20	36	5	2	2	10	1	.237
Granny Hamner	2	7	1	2	0	0	0	0	0	.286
Lee Handley (3B)	101	277	17	70	10	3	0	42	1	.253
Rollie Hemsley	2	3	0	1	0	0	0	1	0	.333
Willie Jones	18	62	5	14	0	1	0	10	2	.226
Al Lakeman	55	182	11	29	3	0	6	19	0	.159
Ralph LaPointe	56	211	33	65	7	0	1	15	8	.308
Jesse Levan	2	9	3	4	0	0	0	1	0	.444
Frank McCormick	15	40	7	9	2	0	1	8	0	.225
Skeeter Newsome (SS)	95	310	36	71	8	2	2	22	4	.229
Ron Northey	13	47	7	12	3	0	0	3	1	.255
Don Padgett	75	158	14	50	8	1	0	24	0	.316
Hugh Poland	4	8	0	0	0	0	0	0	0	.000
Howie Schultz (1B)	114	403	30	90	19	1	6	35	0	.223
Andy Seminick (C)	111	337	48	85	16	2	13	50	4	.252
Jim Tabor	75	251	27	59	14	0	4	31	2	.235
Emil Verban (2B)	155	540	50	154	14	8	0	42	5	.285
Harry Walker (CF)	130	488	79	181	28	(16)	1	41	13	(.371)
Johnny Wyrostek (RF)	128	454	68	124	24	7	5	51	7	.273
		5,256	589	1,354	210	52	60	544	60	.258

Dutch Leonard and Schoolboy Rowe were the winning pitchers as the Phillies swept a doubleheader from the Dodgers in 1947 at Shibe Park before 41,660.

baby Curt Simmons stopped the power-hitting New York Giants, 3–1, with a five-hitter in the last game of the season.

1948

Record: 66–88
Finish: Sixth
Games Behind: 25½
Managers: Ben Chapman, Dusty Cooke, Eddie Sawyer

The 1948 season was the one in which the Phillies began fitting the pieces together that would lead to a National League pennant. It was still not a successful year in the standings, but the players who would lead the club to the top were beginning to be assembled at Shibe Park.

Richie Ashburn, Granny Hamner, Curt Simmons, and Robin Roberts arrived in 1948 from the farm system. Dick Sisler came in a trade with the St. Louis Cardinals. Andy Seminick was already there. And at mid-season a former New York Yankee farmhand and off-season college professor, Eddie Sawyer, became the team's manager.

It was to be the season in which the Phillies got their act together before they made their move upward.

During the winter, general manager Herb Pennock had died of a cerebral hemorrhage. It was a crushing blow to the Phils because Pennock had been the chief architect of the promising young club.

The Phillies continued to make trades, however, adding veterans Bert Haas and Eddie Miller. With pitchers Dutch Leonard (with a 12–17 record and the league's second best ERA, 2.51) and Schoolboy Rowe (10–10) still on the scene, this group formed an aging quartet to go along with the fuzzy-cheeked youngsters.

Defending batting champion Harry Walker and sterling second baseman Emil Verban were still on the club, but neither could crack the starting lineup and would be gone before the next season.

In their places were Ashburn, a speedster who could hit, and Hamner, a fiery hustler who could also handle the bat. By the time the season was over,

	W	L	G	GS	CG	IP	H	BB	K	ERA
Charlie Bicknell	0	1	17	1	0	26	29	17	5	5.88
Blix Donnelly	5	7	26	19	8	132	125	49	46	3.68
Walt Dubiel	8	10	37	17	6	150	139	58	42	3.90
Paul Erickson	2	0	4	2	0	17	19	17	5	5.29
Lou Grasmick	0	0	2	0	0	5	3	8	2	7.20
Ken Heintzelman	6	11	27	16	5	130	117	45	57	4.29
Ed Heusser	3	2	33	0	0	74	89	28	22	4.99
Oscar Judd	0	2	4	1	0	14	19	11	7	7.07
Dick Koecher	0	1	3	0	0	6	4	3	2	3.00
Jim Konstanty	1	0	6	0	0	10	7	2	7	0.90
Al Lakeman	0	0	1	0	0	1	1	0	0	9.00
Dutch Leonard	12	17	34	31	16	226	226	54	92	2.51
Sam Nahem	3	3	28	1	0	59	68	45	30	7.02
Lou Possehl	1	1	3	2	1	15	17	4	7	4.80
Al Porto	0	0	3	0	0	4	2	1	1	0.00
Robin Roberts	7	9	20	20	9	147	148	61	84	3.18
Schoolboy Rowe	10	10	30	20	8	148	167	31	46	4.07
Curt Simmons	7	13	31	22	7	170	169	108	86	4.87
Nick Strincevich	0	1	6	1	0	17	26	10	4	9.00
Jocko Thompson	1	0	2	2	1	13	10	9	7	2.77
	66	88		155	61	1,362	1,385	561	552	4.08

Shutouts: Dubiel (2), Heintzelman (2), Donnelly, Leonard

	G	AB	R	H	2B	3B	HR	RBI	SB	AVG
Richie Ashburn (CF)	117	463	78	154	17	4	2	40	(32)	.333
John Blatnik (LF)	121	415	56	108	27	8	6	45	3	.260
Putsy Caballero (3B)	113	351	33	86	12	1	0	19	7	.245
Bert Haas	95	333	35	94	9	2	4	34	8	.282
Del Ennis (RF)	152	589	86	171	40	4	30	95	2	.290
Granny Hamner (2B)	129	446	42	116	21	5	3	48	2	.260
Willie Jones	17	60	9	20	2	0	2	9	0	.333
Al Lakeman	32	68	2	11	2	0	1	4	0	.162
Jackie Mayo	12	35	7	8	2	1	0	3	1	.229
Eddie Miller (SS)	130	468	45	115	20	1	14	61	1	.246
Don Padgett	36	74	3	17	3	0	0	7	0	.230
Bama Rowell	77	196	15	47	16	2	1	22	2	.240
Howie Schultz	6	13	0	1	0	0	0	1	0	.077
Andy Seminick (C)	125	391	49	88	11	3	13	44	4	.225
Dick Sisler (1B)	121	446	60	122	21	3	11	56	1	.274
Emil Verban	55	169	14	39	5	1	0	11	0	.231
Hal Wagner	3	4	0	0	0	0	0	0	0	.000
Harry Walker	112	332	34	97	11	2	2	23	4	.292
		5,287	591	1,367	227	39	91	548	68	.259

Ashburn would set a National League rookie record by hitting in 23 straight games while batting .333 and winning Rookie of the Year honors from *The Sporting News*. Hamner would hit a solid .260, and in one game drive in seven runs in an 11–10 victory over the Cardinals.

In July president Bob Carpenter, tiring of Ben Chapman and his volatile habits, fired the manager. Coach Dusty Cooke took over the team until Carpenter could appoint Sawyer, a fatherly individual who had a way with young players.

In June the Phillies had brought up Roberts. In his big league debut, the hard-throwing righthander pitched a five-hitter but lost to the Pittsburgh Pirates, 2–0.

In addition to Ashburn's second-highest average in the league, Ennis clouted 30 home runs, the most for a Phillie since Chuck Klein hit 38 in 1932. Del hit .290 with 95 RBI.

One of the Phillies' top pitching efforts in years was turned in by lefty Ken Heintzelman, whom the team had purchased the previous year. Heintzelman hurled a one-hitter, beating the New York Giants, 8–1. The only hit was a triple by Whitey Lockman.

Conversely, one of the worst performances on the mound was given by Charlie Bicknell, a short-term righthander. In an 11–1 loss to St. Louis, Bicknell gave up four home runs and 18 total bases in one inning.

1949

Record: 81–73
Finish: Third
Games Behind: 16
Manager: Eddie Sawyer

At long last, the promised land was in sight. The Phillies rounded the final bend in 1949.

By then, most of the pieces of the puzzle were in place. Over the winter, the team had added Eddie Waitkus, Russ Meyer, and Bill Nicholson in three separate trades with the Chicago Cubs. Jim Konstanty had been rescued from the minors. And the Carolina hotshot, Willie Jones, had finally nailed down a regular position on the team.

All that was left now was the final assault on the National League summit. But that was still a year away. The Phillies of 1949 still had some rough edges.

In fact, as late as mid-August, the team was languishing in fifth place. Eddie Sawyer knew the club should have been higher in the standings. One morning in New York he shared his views with the rest of the team.

It was an epic tirade. Enraged because his team was taking life too easy, especially after he spotted Andy Seminick eating a heavy breakfast in his room and several young players lobster-red from an off-day at the beach, Sawyer called his troops together at the Hotel Commodore where they were staying.

"We've come to the crossroads, yours and mine," Eddie began. "For the past month and a half, we've been going downhill steadily. We're slipping not only in our play on the field but in our thinking, and in our conduct after we leave the ballpark. There is only one result, another year in the second division.

"Now, we are going to do an about-face," Sawyer roared. "Or you guys can guess the rest."

The outburst from the usually mild-mannered manager worked like magic. Over the next three days the Phillies won three games from the pennant-bound Brooklyn Dodgers. By Labor Day, they had moved into third, passing the defending league champion Boston Braves and the New York Giants.

The team won 16 of its last 26 games and finished the season with its best finish and most wins since 1917.

The Phillies finally had an excellent pitching staff. Robin Roberts began to show signs of his forthcoming prowess with a 15–15 record. Ken Heintzelman was the ace of the staff with a 17–10 record, which included three 1–0 wins, 32⅔ scoreless innings, and some of the best pitching that had been seen in a Phillies suit in years. Meyer, who hurled a one-hit, 3–1 win over the Boston Braves, also won 17, capturing eight victories in a row at the end of the season. And Hank Borowy, who had also come from the Cubs, added a 12–12 mark.

It was a season in which the name Blue Jays, which had lingered as an

Eddie Waitkus visits the Phillies clubhouse late in the 1949 season after being shot by a deranged woman in Chicago hotel room in June.

	W	L	G	GS	CG	IP	H	BB	K	ERA
Charlie Bicknell	0	0	13	0	0	28	32	17	4	7.71
Hank Borowy	12	12	28	28	12	193	188	63	43	4.20
Blix Donnelly	2	1	23	10	1	78	84	40	36	5.08
Ken Heintzelman	17	10	33	32	15	250	239	93	65	3.02
Jim Konstanty	9	5	53	0	0	97	98	29	43	3.25
Russ Meyer	17	8	37	28	14	213	199	70	78	3.08
Bob Miller	0	0	3	0	0	3	2	2	0	0.00
Robin Roberts	15	15	43	31	11	227	229	75	95	3.69
Schoolboy Rowe	3	7	23	6	2	65	68	17	22	4.85
Curt Simmons	4	10	38	14	2	131	133	55	83	4.60
Jocko Thompson	1	3	8	5	1	31	38	11	12	6.97
Ken Trinkle	1	1	42	0	0	74	79	30	14	4.04
	81	73*		154	58	1,392	1,389	502	495	3.89

Shutouts: Heintzelman (5), Roberts (3), Borowy (2), Meyer (2)
*Includes one loss by forfeit.

	G	AB	R	H	2B	3B	HR	RBI	SB	AVG
Richie Ashburn (CF)	154	(662)	84	188	18	11	1	37	9	.284
John Blatnik	6	8	3	1	0	0	0	0	0	.125
Buddy Blatner	64	97	15	24	6	0	5	21	0	.247
Putsy Caballero	29	68	8	19	3	0	0	3	0	.279
Del Ennis (LF)	154	610	92	184	39	11	25	110	2	.302
Bill Glynn	8	10	0	2	0	0	0	1	0	.200
Mike Goliat	55	189	24	40	6	3	3	19	0	.212
Bert Haas	2	1	0	0	0	0	0	0	0	.000
Granny Hamner (SS)	154	(662)	83	174	32	5	6	53	6	.263
Stan Hollmig	81	251	28	64	11	6	2	26	1	.255
Willie Jones (3B)	149	532	71	130	35	1	19	77	3	.244
Stan Lopata	83	240	31	65	9	2	8	27	1	.271
Jackie Mayo	45	39	3	5	0	0	0	2	0	.128
Eddie Miller (2B)	85	266	21	55	10	1	6	29	1	.207
Bill Nicholson (RF)	98	299	42	70	8	3	11	40	1	.234
Ed Sanicki	7	13	4	3	0	0	3	7	0	.231
Andy Seminick (C)	109	334	52	81	11	2	24	68	0	.243
Ken Silvestri	4	4	1	0	0	0	0	0	0	.000
Dick Sisler (1B)	121	412	42	119	19	6	7	50	0	.289
Hal Wagner	1	4	0	0	0	0	0	0	0	.000
Eddie Waitkus	54	209	41	64	16	3	1	28	3	.306
		5,307	662	1,349	232	(55)	122	622	27	.254

alternate nickname although it had never been accepted by the public, the press, or anybody else, was officially dropped. And it was a season in which fans hurled bottles, cans, and other missiles onto the field to protest a call in which a line drive by the Giants' Joe Lafata had been ruled trapped by Richie Ashburn. The game was forfeited to the Giants.

In June, Waitkus was shot and critically injured by a deranged girl in a hotel room in Chicago. He missed the rest of the season, but Dick Sisler did an excellent job filling in for him at first.

An explosion of a different kind occurred in the same month when the Phillies slammed six home runs, including five in one inning, in a 12–3 triumph over the Cincinnati Reds. Seminick hit three homers, including two in the eighth inning when he was joined by round-trip blasts by Del Ennis, Jones, and Schoolboy Rowe.

Ennis had another superb season, driving in 110 runs with 25 homers and a .302 batting average. Sisler added a .289 mark, while Ashburn hit .284.

A s the Phillies assembled for spring training in 1950, there was a feeling on the club that this could finally be the year that the elusive pennant came to Philadelphia.

Most of the sportswriters around the country picked the team to finish third or fourth, but the Phillies had been the hottest club in the National League at the end of 1949, and, despite the team's youth, it was a confident group that met March 1 at Clearwater, Florida.

The confidence was understandable. The Phillies had a solid everyday lineup and what seemed to be a strong pitching staff, headed by 17-game

1950

Record: 91–63
Finish: First
Games Ahead: 2
Manager: Eddie Sawyer

winners Ken Heintzelman and Russ Meyer and 15-game winner Robin Roberts.

Of course, there were a few question marks. Although Eddie Waitkus had labored hard all winter to overcome his gunshot wounds, no one knew for sure how he would respond on the playing field. If Waitkus couldn't make it back, Dick Sisler would have to play at first base again, which would leave a hole in left field. Second base was unsolved, with Mike Goliat's hitting an uncertainty.

On the other hand, the Phillies' farm system was producing players like cherries on a tree. Since taking over as president, Bob Carpenter had poured some $2 million into a long-range improvement plan for the club. Twenty-five percent of that went in bonuses to young prospects. Most of it went toward building the farm system from one team in 1943—a working agreement with Trenton—to 11 minor league clubs by 1950.

In the years since 1946 a steady flow of young players had emerged from the system. In 1950 the influx continued, especially in the persons of pitchers Bob Miller and Bubba Church.

The 1950 team even had a new image. Having dumped the lingering and never-popular nickname Blue Jays once and for all in 1949, the Phillies became known as the Whiz Kids. The name symbolized the youthfulness of the club (average age 26) and was quickly accepted by the fans and the press.

The name tied in well with the Phillies' new uniforms. The club abandoned the red, white, and blue home livery of the 1940s, appearing in snazzy new white flannels with red pinstripes, trim, caps, and socks.

The club was all set, therefore, for its first real run at the pennant as spring training opened. But some kinks developed. The Phillies won only 12 of 23 exhibition games, ending the grapefruit season with a grueling string of games in Texas and Louisiana.

In the opening game of the regular season, the Phillies whipped the

	W	L	G	GS	CG	IP	H	BB	K	ERA
Hank Borowy	0	0	3	0	0	6	5	4	3	6.00
John Brittin	0	0	3	0	0	4	2	3	3	4.50
Milo Candini	1	0	18	0	0	30	32	15	10	2.70
Bubba Church	8	6	31	18	8	142	113	56	50	2.73
Blix Donnelly	2	4	14	1	0	21	30	10	10	4.29
Ken Heintzelman	3	9	23	17	4	125	122	54	39	4.10
Ken Johnson	4	1	14	8	3	61	61	43	32	3.98
Jim Konstanty	16	7	(74)	0	0	152	108	50	56	2.68
Russ Meyer	9	11	32	25	3	160	193	67	74	5.29
Bob Miller	11	6	35	22	7	174	190	57	44	3.57
Steve Ridzik	0	0	1	0	0	3	3	1	2	6.00
Robin Roberts	20	11	40	(39)	21	304	282	77	146	3.02
Curt Simmons	17	8	31	27	11	215	178	88	146	3.39
Paul Stuffel	0	0	3	0	0	5	4	1	3	1.80
Jocko Thompson	0	0	2	0	0	4	1	4	2	0.00
	91	63		157	57	(1,406)	1,324	530	620	(3.50)

Shutouts: Roberts (5), Church (2), Miller (2), Simmons (2), Heintzelman, Johnson

	G	AB	R	H	2B	3B	HR	RBI	SB	AVG
Richie Ashburn (CF)	151	594	84	180	25	(14)	2	41	14	.303
John Blatnik	4	4	0	1	0	0	0	0	0	.250
Jimmy Bloodworth	54	96	6	22	2	0	0	13	0	.229
Putsy Caballero	46	24	12	4	0	0	0	0	1	.167
Del Ennis (RF)	153	595	92	185	34	8	31	(126)	2	.311
Mike Goliat (2B)	145	483	49	113	13	6	13	64	3	.234
Granny Hamner (SS)	157	637	78	172	27	5	11	82	2	.270
Stan Hollmig	11	12	1	3	2	0	0	1	0	.250
Willie Jones (3B)	157	610	100	163	28	6	25	88	5	.267
Stan Lopata	58	129	10	27	2	2	1	11	1	.209
Jackie Mayo	18	36	1	8	3	0	0	3	0	.222
Bill Nicholson	41	58	3	13	2	1	3	10	0	.224
Andy Seminick (C)	130	393	55	113	15	3	24	68	0	.288
Ken Silvestri	11	20	2	5	0	1	0	4	0	.250
Dick Sisler (LF)	141	523	79	155	29	4	13	83	1	.296
Eddie Waitkus (1B)	154	641	102	182	32	5	2	44	3	.284
Dick Whitman	75	132	21	33	7	0	0	12	1	.250
	(5,426)	722	1,440	225	55	125	673	33	.265

Starting outfield for the 1950 Whiz Kids: (from left) Dick Sisler, Richie Ashburn, and Del Ennis.

Brooklyn Dodgers, 9–1. But then they lost five of their next six games. By the end of April, the club was languishing in sixth place.

On May 6 the team finally pulled up to .500 with an 11–7 victory over the St. Louis Cardinals. The win launched the club on a six-game winning streak that temporarily lifted the Phillies into first place.

By now, the Phillies were starting to come together as a team. Thanks to hard work and the efforts of trainer Frank Weichec, Waitkus had made a strong comeback, although there were some who said he never fully recovered from the shooting. Goliat was proving to be a good hitter in the clutch. And rookies Miller and Church displaced veterans Meyer and Heintzelman in the starting rotation.

Moreover, the Phillies were getting surprisingly strong pitching from Curt Simmons. Despite his $65,000 bonus in 1947, Simmons had never had a winning season for the Phillies. Suddenly in 1950, though, Curt turned into the pitcher the Phillies had envisioned, and for the first half of the season he was the best pitcher on the team.

For good measure, the Phillies added another lefthander to their staff, picking up Ken Johnson from the Cardinals in a swap for outfielder Johnny Blatnik. Johnson would win a key game down the stretch for the Phillies.

From mid-May until mid-July, the Phillies were in and out of first place six more times. They were locked in a feverish pennant race with the Dodgers, Cardinals, New York Giants, and Boston Braves.

On Memorial Day the Phillies dropped a doubleheader to the Dodgers, losing 7–6 and 6–4 and tumbling all the way to third place. But they bounced back with a successful road trip. Upon their return home, the Whiz Kids lost a two-game series to St. Louis, and the Cardinals took the lead. Then the Phils won five of their next six games against the Cincinnati Reds and Pittsburgh Pirates.

It was a tense time for the Phillies and their followers as the club bobbed up and down like a cork in a stormy sea. For those who doubted the Phillies' legitimacy, a weekend series at Shibe Park with Brooklyn proved that the club was for real. The Phillies hammered Don Newcombe and Preacher Roe on June 30, winning, 8–5. Then, behind Miller and Jim Konstanty, the Phils took the Saturday game, 6–4.

A doubleheader with the Dodgers followed the next day. In the first game, Bill Nicholson's eighth-inning pinch-hit two-run homer gave the Phillies another 6–4 triumph. In the second game, Simmons had a no-hitter and an 8–0 lead in the seventh inning, but the Dodgers got to him to tie the score at 8–8 before the game was halted by Philadelphia's Sunday curfew.

The Phillies were in first place, and they stayed there after a five-game winning streak in early July against the Giants and Dodgers. But a week later, the club lost five in a row to the Cardinals and Chicago Cubs, one of three times they lost that many games in a row during the campaign.

At that point, the pennant race couldn't have been closer. Brooklyn was in fourth place, but only one game out of first. Meanwhile, the Phillies were bouncing back and forth between first and third.

On July 25 the Phillies opened a 16-game home stand with a doubleheader with the Cubs. Church won the first game, 7–0. Roberts, the National League's All-Star Game starting pitcher a few weeks earlier, captured the second outing, 1–0. The twin victories put the Phillies in first place again, and they never vacated the spot for the rest of the season.

Two days later, during what would become another five-game winning streak, the Phillies blasted the Cubs, 13–3. Del Ennis drove in seven runs with a three-run double and a grand slam homer. All the runs crossed in the seventh and eighth innings.

The spree climaxed what had been a fantastic month for the slugging right fielder. During the month, he drove in 41 runs. There was no hitter in the National League who was better in the clutch. Del would finish the season with the league lead in RBI with 126, 31 homers, and .311 batting average.

Although his easygoing style often attracted boos from the fans, Ennis, like all of the Whiz Kids, hustled 100 percent of the time.

"We had more incentive than anyone," Ennis said. "We had some real good pitchers and eight guys who wanted to play. You couldn't get any of them out of the lineup."

The night Ennis drove in his seven runs, Simmons left the club to spend two weeks of summer training with the National Guard. With the Korean War

Pitchers who helped Phillies win the 1950 pennant were: (from left) Russ Meyer, Robin Roberts, Ken Heintzelman, Bubba Church, and Jim Konstanty.

heating up, the Phillies feared that Curt might be drafted, and had suggested he join the Guard instead.

Simmons' departure left the Phillies with a huge hole in the pitching staff. At that point he had won more games than Roberts, and as Robbie himself said, "was pitching like a Hall of Famer."

Even with the loss of Simmons, though, the pitching staff was performing brilliantly. The rookie Miller had won his first eight decisions. When Heintzelman couldn't win, Church was moved into the rotation in mid-July, and promptly won three straight games.

But the biggest surprise on the staff was the veteran reliever Konstanty. No one had expected the bespectacled hurler to have the kind of season he was having. But it seemed that Konstanty was either winning or saving a game nearly every other day. Jim went on to win 16 games, save 22 more, and become the league's Most Valuable Player.

"He wanted to show everybody that he was the best pitcher on the staff," said manager Eddie Sawyer. "There was a rivalry between all of the pitchers, and Jim had a burning desire to be the best. He had a disposition that went right along with it. And he couldn't wait to take the ball away from Roberts or Simmons or Church or Meyer."

Konstanty's assortment of slow-breaking pitches, the most effective of which was a palm ball that baffled the hitters in 1950, bailed the Phillies out of one jam after another. At one point over a one-month stretch, he allowed no runs and only seven hits in 22⅓ innings. Konstanty and his seemingly rubber arm rarely made it necessary to use any other relief pitcher. As a result, the rest of the Phils' bullpen staff, which essentially included Blix Donnelly, Milo Candini, and spot starter Ken Johnson, rarely got to work.

One pitcher who did get to work long and often was the tireless Roberts. In 1950 the great righthander was in his second full season, and was rapidly establishing himself as one of the National League's superior pitchers. His blazing fastball mixed with a sharp curve and pinpoint control made him a hitters' nightmare, especially Brooklyn batters whom he had a way of beating. During one stretch, he pitched three straight shutouts and won seven games in a row.

As the Phillies swung into August, they held first place by three games over the Cardinals and three and one-half games over the Dodgers and Braves. The Giants had faded temporarily out of the race, although they would be back in September.

The Phillies by this time had attracted a national following, their youth, fighting spirit, and hustle having caught the attention of baseball fans far beyond the city limits. They even had a large following abroad of servicemen who got to know the club through games broadcast over Radio Free Europe.

It was a club that was easy to like. Center fielder Richie Ashburn (.303 for the season) was an outstanding hitter, a superb fielder, and a speed demon on the bases. Shortstop Granny Hamner (.270) was a fiery team leader and a fine clutch hitter. Third baseman Willie Jones (.267, 25 home runs) was ranked behind Ennis as the team's second-best power hitter, and he was an excellent man with the glove. Goliat (.234) didn't hit for high average, but he hit in the clutch (ultimately producing 13 game-winning hits), and he did especially well against Brooklyn. Waitkus (.284) was the smooth fielding, line-drive hitting first sacker. Sisler (.296) was a solid everyday performer who had his best season at the plate. And Andy Seminick (.288, 24 home runs) was a tough catcher who handled pitchers with superior skill and who also had his best year in 1950.

Behind this group was a bench that saw little action but was highly dependable. Outfielders Bill Nicholson, Dick Whitman, Stan Hollmig, and late in the season Jackie Mayo, could all hit when called upon. Infielders Jimmy Bloodworth and Putsy Caballero weren't much at the plate, but were versatile, good fielding replacements. And catchers Stan Lopata, a youngster on the way up, and Ken Silvestri, a veteran who spent most of his time in the bullpen, were both handy men to have on the team.

The Whiz Kids stormed through August like a runaway truck. At one point

Glum Curt Simmons stares into locker after pitching his last game in 1950 before joining National Guard unit.

they won 12 of 16 games at home. By the end of the month the club had won 20 of 28 contests and had stretched its lead to seven games over the Dodgers and 9½ over the Braves.

During the winning spree Simmons returned from the National Guard and promptly turned in six wins. Roberts also won six games in August.

About the only interruption in the otherwise steady rush toward the pennant was an incident that occurred in mid-August while the Phillies were playing the Giants. It involved the hard-playing but usually mild-mannered Seminick.

After a series of incidents initiated the day before by New York second baseman Eddie Stanky's arm-waving tactics while Seminick was at bat, the Phillies' catcher slid hard into the Giants' Bill Rigney at second base. The two came up swinging in what developed as one of the rougher brawls in Shibe Park history. Eventually, both teams emptied onto the field, and police had to be summoned to quell the battle.

It was the second major brawl of the season for the Phillies. The first one also developed after a hard slide at second in which Jones barreled into Cincinnati's Connie Ryan. A slugging match ensued with the Phils and Reds pouring onto the field to join the fracas.

The Phillies came by their nickname, Fightin' Phils, honestly. But as September began the main fight was against overconfidence. The team, its fans, and even its adoring press, some of whose members often wore their Phillies caps and T-shirts in the press box, figured the club would wrap up the flag by the middle of the month.

On September 3 the Phillies returned home from a road trip in which they had won 11 of 14 games. Some 30,000 fans waited several hours in the rain to greet the Phillies when they arrived at Philadelphia Airport.

"There are still 27 games left," Sawyer told the crowd. "We don't have this pennant won yet."

How right he was. A day later, as their bats suddenly turned silent, the Phillies' world began to crumble. In a Labor Day doubleheader with the red-hot Giants, the Phillies suffered two shutouts, first at the hands of Jim Hearn, then Sal Maglie. After an off-day, the Phils dropped another twin bill, this time to the Dodgers, 2–0 and 3–2. The following day, they lost again to Brooklyn, 3–2.

The losing streak was finally halted in the fourth game of the series with Brooklyn when Meyer pitched a gutty 4–3 victory. It was a win of major importance, and it launched the Phillies on a spurt in which they won eight of their next 11 games. The lead that had shrunk to four and one-half games was back to seven.

All was not well in Philadelphia, however. On September 10, Simmons had to leave the club to report to active duty. It was just what the Phillies had tried to prevent. Curt's unit was recalled and sent to Germany, and he was lost to the Phils for the season.

Just five days after Simmons' departure, the Phillies were dealt another low blow. A line drive off the bat of the Reds' Ted Kluszewski smashed into Church's face. The pitcher was badly injured and did not pitch for the next week.

Then a day later, Miller, who earlier in the season had hurt his back when he slipped on steps at the train station in Boston, injured his arm in the midst of a pitching duel with the Reds' Ewell Blackwell.

Sawyer suddenly found himself with a badly depleted pitching staff. "Until then, everything was going according to plan," he said. "But I didn't plan on losing the three pitchers."

Neither Miller nor Church pitched effectively for the rest of the season. To make matters worse for the Phillies, Seminick suffered a badly injured ankle while guarding the plate on a hard slide by the Giants' Monte Irvin. It was an extremely painful injury, and Andy would be hobbled the rest of the season, although he played on courageously, shot full of Novocain before each game.

The main burden of the pitching staff fell to Roberts. But Meyer chipped in with two more key victories. And on September 15, Donnelly and

Heintzelman won an important doubleheader against the Reds, winning 2–1 and 8–7 in 19 innings, the longest game of the season. "Some Whiz Kids," Blix said. "They're taking us old men out of camphor to win."

With 11 games left in the season, the Phillies enjoyed what seemed to be a comfortable seven-game lead. On September 23 the Dodgers came to Philadelphia for a two-game series. Although Brooklyn was a distant second, Burt Shotton's club was on a hot streak and had been winning right along with the Phillies.

Brooklyn took the series, 3–2 and 11–0, with Newcombe besting Roberts in the first game and Church getting pounded in the second while Erv Palica two-hit the Phils. The Phillies' lead was cut to five games, and the club was faced with a season-ending, nine-game road trip against the other first-division teams.

There was a brief burst of optimism as the Phillies took two out of three games from the Braves. But two consecutive doubleheaders loomed at the Polo Grounds against a Giants team that had clawed its way up to third place with a September hot streak.

In the first game, the Phillies scored five runs in the eighth inning to gain a 7–7 tie, but the Giants won in the 10th, 8–7. Then Hearn blanked the Phillies for the third time in the season with a 5–0 triumph in the nightcap.

The next day Maglie beat the Phillies, 3–1, and Sheldon Jones downed Roberts, also 3–1. The second loss was particularly unsettling because the winning margin came on a two-out, bases-loaded seventh-inning bloop single by Whitey Lockman in which the Giants batter had been trying to get out of the way of an inside pitch. In the ninth, the Giants preserved the win when first baseman Irvin made a spectacular catch of a Hamner line drive with two on and none out, then doubled the runner at first.

The Phillies' lead was fortunately cut just to three games as the Dodgers managed only to split two doubleheaders with the Braves. But the Whiz Kids were in trouble. The bats that had scorched clutch hits all season turned cold. People were beginning to say, "Maybe this wasn't the Phillies' year, after all."

There was no game for the Phillies on the last Friday of the season, so the club huddled by radios and listened painfully as the Dodgers jolted the Braves in both ends of a doubleheader. The wins meant that Brooklyn had narrowed the gap to two games as the Phillies headed into the final weekend at Ebbets Field. At least the Phillies could do no worse than tie for first, forcing a best-of-three playoff.

The Dodgers had won 12 of their last 15 games, while the Phillies had lost seven out of nine. About the only number on the Phillies' side was that they had beaten the Dodgers more times at Ebbets Field in 1950 than the Dodgers had beaten them.

On Saturday, with Miller starting for the Phillies, Duke Snider poled a two-run homer, Roy Campanella knocked a three-run four-bagger, and Palica and Brooklyn triumphed, 7–3. That reduced the Phillies' lead to a scant one game as the teams headed into the last game of the regular season.

Sawyer selected Roberts as his pitcher. The big righthander had been masterful down the stretch, and the fact that he had lost some games was mainly attributable to his teammates not getting any runs. For Robbie, it would be his third start in the last five games and his fourth start in the last eight games, and he would be working with just two days' rest.

"He could pitch with little rest," Sawyer said. "He threw so few pitches that you could use him like that. Besides, he hadn't pitched a bad ball game all year in Brooklyn, despite the size of their park and the club they had."

Roberts was making his sixth attempt to win 20 games. His opponent, the towering Newcombe, was also going for his 20th.

It was a mild, sunny day as the Phillies filed into Ebbets Field. A standing-room-only crowd of 35,073 jammed into the ancient ballpark. It was estimated that another 30,000 fans had been turned away. Although a sizable contingent of Philadelphia fans got into the game, it seemed that back home the whole city was glued to radios.

The Phillies scored first when Jones singled to left to score Sisler in the sixth inning. The Dodgers came back with the tying run in the bottom half of the inning as Pee Wee Reese hit a controversial home run that lodged at the base of a wire screen in right-center.

The score was still 1–1 when the Dodgers came to bat in the bottom of the ninth. Cal Abrams opened with a walk and Reese singled him to second. Then Snider rifled a liner to center. Ashburn fielded the ball on one hop, and with Abrams streaking toward home, fired to the plate. Catcher Stan Lopata gloved the throw and Abrams was out by 15 feet.

The throw was unquestionably the most memorable peg in Phillies history. But before the inning could end, Roberts walked Jackie Robinson intentionally, then retired Carl Furillo on a pop-up and Gil Hodges on a fly to right.

In the top of the 10th, Roberts led off with a single up the middle. Waitkus followed with a looping single to center. Then Ashburn, trying to sacrifice, forced Roberts at third.

That brought up Sisler, who already had three singles in the game. With the count one ball, two strikes, Dick belted a high, outside fast ball to deep left. The ball carried into the stands. The Phillies had a 4–1 lead and three outs to go.

Roberts set down the Dodgers in order in the bottom of the 10th. When pinch-hitter Tommy Brown fouled out to Waitkus to end the game, the Phillies jubilantly exploded onto the field in possession of the club's first pennant in 35 years.

The famine was over. And back in Philadelphia, a celebration erupted like none the city had ever seen. The Whiz Kids had done it. After all the miserable teams and all the horrendous records, the Phillies—the Philadelphia Phillies—were champions of the National League.

1951

Record: 73–81
Finish: Fifth
Games Behind: 23½
Manager: Eddie Sawyer

After the Phillies won the pennant in 1950, it was assumed by mostly everyone following or connected with the team that it would be a genuine pennant contender for years to come. While the fans spoke of a dynasty, many of the sports writers picked the club to repeat as National League champions.

The 1951 Phillies fooled them all. Exhibiting one of the greatest flops of a defending champion, the team tumbled all the way to fifth place and was never in contention for the flag.

The team was a shell of its former self as slumps, inflated egos, and an attitude that it could win by merely stepping on the field carved a path to destruction.

Only Richie Ashburn, Dick Sisler, and Willie Jones among the hitters, and Robin Roberts and Bubba Church among the pitchers, repeated or improved upon their good works of 1950. The rest of the club generally played like the Phillies of olden days.

It was a damaging blow, of course, to lose Curt Simmons to the army for the entire season. But just as damaging was the way the club had slipped away from manager Eddie Sawyer's control. A year earlier Sawyer had been a father figure to the players and would listen patiently to their problems, dreams, and opinions. But in 1951 it was almost as if the players had become too good for that. They disregarded Sawyer's attempts to maintain rapport.

In late June the team was all the way down in seventh place. Sawyer coaxed and screamed, but it was useless. Even though the Phillies got as high as third place in early August, a tailspin in the closing months of the season pushed them back to fifth.

The season did, at least, end dramatically. For the third year in a row, the Phillies and Brooklyn Dodgers battled into extra innings in a game that had a marked bearing on the pennant. The Dodgers needed a win to tie the New York Giants for the flag, but the Phils took an early 6–1 lead off Preacher Roe, a 22–3 hurler that season. The Phils led, 8–5, after five, but Brooklyn fought to an 8–8 tie to send the game into overtime. In the 12th, Jackie Robinson made a sensational diving catch of an Eddie Waitkus liner to keep the Phils from

	W	L	G	GS	CG	IP	H	BB	K	ERA
John Brittin	0	0	3	0	0	4	5	6	3	9.00
Milo Candini	1	0	15	0	0	30	33	18	14	6.00
Bubba Church	15	11	38	33	15	247	246	90	104	3.53
Leo Cristante	1	1	10	1	0	22	28	9	6	4.91
Karl Drews	1	0	5	3	1	23	29	7	13	6.26
Andy Hansen	3	1	24	0	0	39	34	7	11	2.54
Ken Heintzelman	6	12	35	12	3	118	119	53	55	4.19
Ken Johnson	5	8	20	18	4	106	103	68	58	4.48
Niles Jordan	2	3	5	5	2	37	35	8	11	3.16
Jim Konstanty	4	11	58	1	0	116	127	31	27	4.03
Russ Meyer	8	9	28	24	7	168	172	55	65	3.48
Bob Miller	2	1	17	3	0	34	47	18	10	6.88
Lou Possehl	0	1	2	1	0	6	9	3	6	6.00
Robin Roberts	21	15	44	(39)	22	(315)	284	64	127	3.03
Jocko Thompson	4	8	29	14	3	119	102	59	60	3.86
	73	81		154	57	1,385	1,373	496	570	3.81

Shutouts: Roberts (6), Church (4), Johnson (3), Meyer (2), Thompson (2), Henitzelman, Jordan

	G	AB	R	H	2B	3B	HR	RBI	SB	AVG
Richie Ashburn (CF)	154	643	92	(221)	31	5	4	63	29	.344
Jimmy Bloodworth	21	42	2	6	0	0	0	1	1	.143
Tommy Brown	78	196	24	43	2	1	10	32	1	.219
Putsy Caballero (2B)	84	161	15	30	3	2	1	11	1	.186
Mel Clark	10	31	2	10	1	0	1	3	0	.323
Del Ennis (RF)	144	532	76	142	20	5	15	73	4	.267
Mike Goliat	41	138	14	31	2	1	4	15	0	.225
Granny Hamner (SS)	150	589	61	150	23	7	9	72	10	.255
Stan Hollmig	2	2	0	0	0	0	0	0	0	.000
Willie Jones (3B)	148	564	79	161	28	5	22	81	6	.285
Stan Lopata	3	5	0	0	0	0	0	0	0	.000
Jackie Mayo	9	7	1	1	0	0	0	0	0	.143
Bill Nicholson	85	170	23	41	9	2	8	30	0	.241
Eddie Pellagrini	86	197	31	46	4	5	5	30	5	.234
Ed Sanicki	13	4	1	2	1	0	0	1	1	.500
Andy Seminick (C)	101	291	42	66	8	1	11	37	1	.227
Ken Silvestri	4	9	2	2	0	0	0	1	0	.222
Dick Sisler (LF)	125	428	46	123	20	5	8	52	1	.287
Eddie Waitkus (1B)	145	610	65	157	27	4	1	46	0	.257
Dick Whitman	19	17	0	2	0	0	0	0	0	.118
Del Wilber	84	245	30	68	7	3	8	34	0	.278
Dick Young	15	68	7	16	5	0	0	2	0	.235
		5,322	648	1,384	199	47	108	609	63	.260

scoring. Jackie, who had knocked himself out on the catch, came back to homer off Roberts in the 14th to win for the Dodgers, 9–8.

Roberts had an outstanding season otherwise, ending with a 21–15 record and leading the league in innings pitched. Church also pitched well, finishing with a 15–11 record that included a one-hit, 5–1 win over the Pittsburgh Pirates. It was one of two one-hitters during the campaign, the other resulting from the combined efforts of Russ Meyer and Jim Konstanty in a game in which Pee Wee Reese's third-inning, two-run triple gave the Dodgers a 2–0 win.

During the season the pitching staff also had one other distinguished act. It worked 41 consecutive scoreless innings, including four straight complete game shutouts pitched by Roberts, Ken Johnson, Church, and Meyer. Roberts beat the St. Louis Cardinals, 2–0; Johnson blanked the Redbirds, 7–0; Church topped the Chicago Cubs, 2–0; and Meyer downed the Bruins, 1–0.

Konstanty was a big disappointment. The previous year's MVP was largely ineffective, careening to a 4–11 record and reaching the point where the Phillies were reluctant to use him in critical situations.

Bob Miller, another 1950 standout, was equally ineffective, and wound up back in the minors, as did second baseman Mike Goliat, whom Sawyer had disciplined for violations in spring training.

Del Ennis, Granny Hamner, Waitkus, and Andy Seminick all dropped off drastically in their batting production, especially Ennis, who tumbled to a .267

average with only 15 homers and 73 RBI, and Seminick, who dove to a .227 mark.

The one shining light in the batting attack was Ashburn, who by now had established himself as one of the top center fielders in the majors. The fleet Nebraskan had a magnificent season, hitting .344, second-best in the league. Richie, who had eight hits in a doubleheader against the Pirates, led the league in hits (221), was second in stolen bases, and led all outfielders in putouts.

Jones took over the role as the club's big power hitter, slamming 22 homers and driving in 81 runs while hitting .285. Sisler added a .287 mark, but the rest of the team was far behind.

1952

Record: 87–67
Finish: Fourth
Games Behind: 9½
Managers: Eddie Sawyer, Steve O'Neill

There was no way the Phillies were going to repeat their debacle of the previous year in 1952. At least, that's how Eddie Sawyer and the club's management felt.

To make sure of that, the Phillies instituted what would become known as their "austerity program," a set of rigid rules that were designed to combat the players' indifference shown in 1951. Launched in spring training, the program banned wives, autos, swimming, golf, and a series of other pleasures that had been standard fare in Florida.

The program was a miserable failure. All it succeeded in doing was making the players more indifferent and more unhappy. What's more, a lot of them smuggled their wives and cars to camp anyway.

The Phillies were in a rebellious mood as the season began. Yet it was supposed to be a year in which the club reclaimed its place among the league's top contenders.

Realizing he needed a second baseman, Sawyer had arranged a trade in which the club obtained Connie Ryan from the Cincinnati Reds. The Phils paid a high price, giving up Andy Seminick and Dick Sisler as the main figures in the deal. But they also landed Smoky Burgess in return.

Also returning was Curt Simmons from his army stint. With Robin Roberts, he was expected to give the Phillies one of the top right-left pitching punches in the majors.

For Roberts, 1952 was his most spectacular season. The ace hurler registered a 28–7 record, the highest number of wins in the majors since Dizzy Dean won that many in 1935. At one stage, Roberts won nine games in a row. Early in the season, he also lost four straight.

He led the league in innings pitched (330) and complete games (30), allowed only 45 walks the whole season, and beat the league champion Brooklyn Dodgers six times. *The Sporting News* named him Major League Player of the Year.

The rest of the team, however, wasn't even close to having the same kind of season as Roberts. And with its big guns, Richie Ashburn, Del Ennis, and Willie Jones all floundering, the Phils got off to a miserable start. Even the acquisition of Johnny Wyrostek, a former Phil, in another trade with the Reds for Bubba Church, who had fallen into Sawyer's doghouse and pitched poorly, didn't help.

In early June, owner Bob Carpenter held a meeting with the team in St. Louis following a particularly grating loss to the Cardinals. It was a stormy session in which Carpenter both praised and berated his team. One of the outcomes of the session was the removal of Granny Hamner as team captain.

"If we don't win from now on, we won't draw flies when we get back to Philadelphia," Carpenter said after the meeting.

The session was futile. The Phillies returned to their losing habits. By late June, the club was mired in sixth place with a 28–35 record.

On June 28, after Simmons blanked the New York Giants, 6–0, Carpenter fired Sawyer after the game. In his place came Steve O'Neill, a former American League manager.

Immediately upon joining the team, O'Neill relaxed the rules. And with Steve's easygoing manner seeming to remove the tension in the clubhouse, the Phillies began playing the way they had been expected to play.

	W	L	G	GS	CG	IP	H	BB	K	ERA
Bubba Church	0	0	2	1	0	5	11	1	3	10.80
Karl Drews	14	15	33	30	15	229	213	52	96	2.71
Howie Fox	2	7	13	11	2	62	70	26	16	5.08
Andy Hansen	5	6	43	0	0	77	76	27	18	3.27
Ken Heintzelman	1	3	23	1	0	43	41	12	20	3.14
Jim Konstanty	5	3	42	2	2	80	87	21	16	3.94
Russ Meyer	13	14	37	32	14	232	235	65	92	3.14
Bob Miller	0	1	3	1	0	9	13	1	2	6.00
Kent Peterson	0	0	3	0	0	7	2	2	7	0.00
Lou Possehl	0	1	4	1	0	13	12	7	4	4.85
Steve Ridzik	4	2	24	9	2	93	74	37	43	3.00
Robin Roberts	(28)	7	39	(37)	(30)	(330)	(292)	45	148	2.59
Curt Simmons	14	8	28	28	15	201	170	70	141	2.82
Paul Stuffel	1	0	2	1	0	6	5	7	3	3.00
	87	67		154	(80)	1,387	1,301	373	609	(3.07)

Shutouts: Simmons (6), Drews (5), Roberts (3), Meyer, Konstanty

	G	AB	R	H	2B	3B	HR	RBI	SB	AVG
Richie Ashburn (CF)	154	613	93	173	31	6	1	42	16	.282
Tom Brown	18	25	2	4	1	0	1	2	0	.160
Smoky Burgess (C)	110	371	49	110	27	3	6	56	3	.296
Putsy Caballero	35	42	10	10	3	0	0	6	1	.238
Mel Clark	47	155	20	52	6	4	1	15	2	.335
Del Ennis (LF)	151	592	90	171	30	10	20	107	6	.289
Granny Hamner (SS)	151	596	74	164	30	5	17	87	7	.275
Nippy Jones	8	30	3	5	0	0	1	5	0	.167
Willie Jones (3B)	147	541	60	135	12	3	18	72	5	.250
Jack Lohrke	25	29	4	6	0	0	0	1	0	.207
Stan Lopata	57	179	25	49	9	1	4	27	1	.274
Jackie Mayo	50	119	13	29	5	0	1	4	1	.244
Bill Nicholson	56	88	17	24	3	0	6	19	0	.273
Connie Ryan (2B)	154	577	81	139	24	6	12	49	13	.241
Eddie Waitkus (1B)	146	499	51	144	29	4	2	49	2	.289
Del Wilber	2	2	0	0	0	0	0	0	0	.000
Johnny Wyrostek (RF)	98	321	45	88	16	3	1	37	1	.274
Dick Young	5	9	3	2	1	0	0	0	1	.222
		5,205	657	1,353	237	45	93	606	60	.260

For the last three months of the season, the Phillies were the hottest club in either league, winning 59 games and losing only 32.

Coming down the stretch, Roberts was magnificent. He received help on the mound from All-Star Game starter Simmons (14–8), who had been sporadic in the early season, and Karl Drews (14–15), a New York Yankee castoff picked up before the season. Russ Meyer also chipped in with 13 wins. About the only real disappointments were Jim Konstanty, who continued to suffer indignities at the hands of opposing batters, and Howie Fox, a pitcher who came with Ryan and Burgess.

Burgess was a pleasant surprise with the bat, collecting the highest average (.296) of the regulars. Rookie outfielder Mel Clark also hit extremely well after getting a chance to play. The Ohio University graduate batted .335 and reeled off a 17-game hitting streak.

In addition, Ashburn (.282), Ennis (.289 with 20 home runs and 107 RBI), Eddie Waitkus (.289), and Hamner (.275) all began pounding the ball again.

When the team ended the season in fourth place, just one game out of third, there was good reason to believe that the Phillies were on the right track to another pennant.

Entering the 1953 season, there was no team more optimistic about its chances than the Phillies. Having finished the last season as the hottest team in the majors, the Phillies seemed likely to make a strong run for the National League pennant.

All of the pieces seemed to be in order. Robin Roberts had become one of the top pitchers in the big leagues; Curt Simmons was joining the ranks of premier lefthanders; and the team had a potent hitting attack spearheaded by the resurgent bats of Del Ennis, Richie Ashburn, and Granny Hamner and bolstered by Smoky Burgess and Johnny Wyrostek.

1953

Record: 83–71
Finish: Third (tie)
Games Behind: 22
Manager: Steve O'Neill

	W	L	G	GS	CG	IP	H	BB	K	ERA
Karl Drews	9	10	47	27	6	185	218	50	72	4.52
Andy Hansen	0	2	30	1	0	51	60	24	17	4.06
Thornton Kipper	3	3	20	3	0	46	59	12	15	4.70
Jim Konstanty	14	10	48	19	7	171	198	42	45	4.42
Johnny Lindell	1	1	5	3	2	23	22	23	16	4.30
Bob Miller	8	9	35	20	8	157	169	42	63	4.01
Kent Peterson	0	1	15	0	0	27	26	21	20	6.67
Tom Qualters	0	0	1	0	0	⅓	4	1	0	162.00
Steve Ridzik	9	6	42	12	1	124	119	48	53	3.77
Robin Roberts	(23)	16	44	(41)	(33)	(347)	(324)	61	(198)	2.75
Curt Simmons	16	13	32	30	19	238	211	82	138	3.21
Paul Stuffel	0	0	2	0	0	0	0	4	0	0.00
	83	71		156	(76)	1,369	1,410	410	637	3.80

Shutouts: Roberts (5), Simmons (4), Miller (3)

	G	AB	R	H	2B	3B	HR	RBI	SB	AVG
Richie Ashburn (CF)	156	622	110	(205)	25	9	2	57	14	.330
Smoky Burgess (C)	102	312	31	91	17	5	4	36	3	.292
Mel Clark	60	198	31	59	10	4	0	19	1	.298
Del Ennis (LF)	152	578	79	165	22	3	29	125	1	.285
Tommy Glaviano	53	74	17	15	1	2	3	5	2	.203
Granny Hamner (2B)	154	609	90	168	30	8	21	92	2	.276
Willie Jones (3B)	149	481	61	108	16	2	19	70	1	.225
Ted Kazanski (SS)	95	360	39	78	17	5	2	27	1	.217
Johnny Lindell	11	18	3	7	1	0	0	2	0	.389
Jack Lohrke	12	13	3	2	0	0	0	0	0	.154
Stan Lopata	81	234	34	56	12	3	8	31	3	.239
Jackie Mayo	5	4	0	0	0	0	0	0	0	.000
Bill Nicholson	38	62	12	13	5	1	2	16	0	.210
Stan Palys	2	2	0	0	0	0	0	0	0	.000
Connie Ryan	90	247	47	73	14	6	5	26	5	.296
Earl Torgeson (1B)	111	379	58	104	25	8	11	64	7	.274
Eddie Waitkus	81	247	24	72	9	2	1	16	1	.291
Johnny Wyrostek (RF)	125	409	42	111	14	2	6	47	0	.271
		5,290	716	1,400	228	(62)	115	657	42	.265

In addition, the club had beefed up its lineup by trading Russ Meyer for veteran first baseman Earl Torgeson, and its pitching staff was improved with the emergence of a fireballing young hurler named Steve Ridzik.

The optimism appeared to be legitimate when the Phillies opened the season with nine victories in their first 11 games. But misfortune was just around the corner.

In late May the Phillies lost five games in a row, including one game to Brooklyn in which the Dodgers scored 12 runs in one inning before an out was made en route to a 16–2 win. A week later, a much more cruel blow was dealt. While mowing his lawn, Simmons accidentally cut off the end of one of his big toes. At the time Curt appeared to be headed for his best season. A few weeks earlier he had even pitched a one-hitter, yielding a leadoff single to Billy Bruton before retiring 27 Milwaukee Braves in a row in a 3–0 victory.

The accident seemed to take some of the wind out of the Phillies' sails. But they battled on gamely.

Only trouble was, it happened to be a year in which the Brooklyn Dodgers ran away with the pennant. The second place Milwaukee Braves, in their first season since moving from Boston, also had a great year and finished nine games ahead of the Phillies, who tied for third with the St. Louis Cardinals. It was a lost cause for the Phillies, despite their having a better record than the previous year's fourth-place finish.

There were, however, some sparkling individual performances. Connie Ryan got six hits in one game in a 14–12 loss to the Pittsburgh Pirates. In that game, the Phillies scored nine runs and the Pirates six in the same inning.

Ryan, who had come to the Phillies with the hope of plugging a big hole at second base, hit .296 for the season. But he wasn't the second baseman the Phillies had hoped he would be, and the club brought up bonus baby Ted Kazanski at mid-season. Kazanski went in at shortstop, and Hamner was moved to second base shortly after he had been the National League All-Star team's starting shortstop.

Celebrating National League All-Star game victory in 1953 at Crosley Field were: (from left) Murry Dickson, Charlie Dressen, Pee Wee Reese, Enos Slaughter, Warren Giles, Curt Simmons, and Robin Roberts.

Simmons, who missed a month of the season, came back to finish with a 16–13 record. Ridzik was a somewhat disappointing 9–6. And Jim Konstanty, after a two-year hiatus, made a comeback with a 14–10 record. The reliever was used 19 times during the season as a starting pitcher.

Roberts was a 20-game winner for the fourth straight season, and led the league in wins (23), innings (347), strikeouts (198), and complete games (33). Extending from the previous year, Robbie pitched 28 consecutive complete games before his streak was stopped in the 1953 season. For the second year in a row, he was named Major League Pitcher of the Year by *The Sporting News*.

Ashburn came back with a banner season, hitting .330 and leading the league with 205 hits. Ennis maintained his status as one of the league's finest power hitters with 29 home runs and 125 RBI to go along with a batting average of .285. And Burgess (.292), Hamner (.276), Torgeson (.274), and Wyrostek (.271) added punch to the lineup, while Mel Clark (.298) and Eddie Waitkus (.291) hit well coming off the bench.

As far as the Phillies were concerned, the 1954 season belonged essentially to Robin Roberts.

The team slid below the .500 mark, although it finished in the first division, and it abruptly changed managers during the season. But all that was somewhat secondary to the performance by the great righthanded pitching ace.

For the fifth straight year, Roberts was a 20-game winner, cranking out a 23–15 record. Robbie led the league in wins, strikeouts (185), innings pitched (337), and complete games (29) while recording a 2.97 earned run average, the loop's sixth best.

During the season, Roberts hurled two one-hitters. He beat Warren Spahn and the Milwaukee Braves, 4–0, allowing only a third-inning double to Del Crandall. And he downed the Cincinnati Reds, 8–1, retiring 27 men in a row after serving a leadoff home run to Bobby Adams.

Roberts also went the distance to win a 15-inning, 3–2 victory over the St.

1954

Record: 75–79
Finish: Fourth
Games Behind: 22
Managers: Steve O'Neill, Terry Moore

Louis Cardinals. And in one six-day period, he captured three wins, surrounding a four-hit victory over the Braves with two-and-one-third and six-inning relief stints against the Cardinals and Chicago Cubs.

For the fourth time in five years, Robbie was also the starting pitcher for the National League in the All-Star Game.

While the season belonged mostly to Roberts, there were a few other activities of note. With the hiring of Roy Hamey, the club had its first general manager since the death of Herb Pennock in 1948.

One of Hamey's first big acts was to fire manager Steve O'Neill in mid-July. It was a surprise move, the Phillies holding a 40–37 record and third place at the time. But what was even more surprising was the appointment of former Cardinal center fielder Terry Moore as the new pilot. The Phillies slipped to a 35–42 mark under Moore, and he was fired at the end of the season.

The close of the season also represented the end of a streak for Richie Ashburn. In the last game of the season, Ashburn played in his 730th straight game. A spring training injury in 1955 prevented him from playing in the season's opener, thus ending the streak.

Ashburn was, as usual, the Phillies' top hitting regular. He smacked out a .313 average and, for the sixth year in a row, led National League outfielders in putouts.

Smoky Burgess hit .368 in a part-time role. He shared catching duties with Stan Lopata, a big, strong fellow who had been with the club for the better part of seven seasons, and finally blossomed in '54 with a .290 average and 14 home runs.

Del Ennis continued his heavy RBI production with 119, although his average dipped to .261. Granny Hamner added a strong .299 with 89 RBI. And Willie Jones and Earl Torgeson each hit .271.

Overall, though, the Phils' hitting was not consistently strong. That was

	W	L	G	GS	CG	IP	H	BB	K	ERA
Murry Dickson	10	(20)	40	31	12	226	256	73	64	3.78
Karl Drews	1	0	8	0	0	16	18	8	6	5.63
Bob Greenwood	1	2	11	4	0	37	28	18	9	3.16
Thornton Kipper	0	0	11	0	0	14	22	12	5	7.71
Jim Konstanty	2	3	33	1	0	50	62	12	11	3.78
Bob Miller	7	9	30	16	5	150	176	39	42	4.56
Ron Mrozinski	1	1	15	4	1	48	49	25	26	4.50
Paul Penson	1	1	5	3	0	16	14	14	3	4.50
Steve Ridzik	4	5	35	6	0	81	72	44	45	4.11
Robin Roberts	(23)	15	45	(38)	(29)	(337)	(289)	56	(185)	2.97
Curt Simmons	14	15	34	33	21	253	226	98	125	2.81
Herm Wehmeier	10	8	25	17	10	138	117	51	49	3.85
	75*	79		153	(78)	1,365	1,329	450	570	3.59

Shutouts: Dickson (4), Roberts (4), Simmons (3), Wehmeier (2)
*Includes one win by forfeit.

	G	AB	R	H	2B	3B	HR	RBI	SB	AVG
Richie Ashburn (CF)	153	559	111	175	16	8	1	41	11	.313
Floyd Baker	23	22	0	5	0	0	0	0	0	.227
Smoky Burgess (C)	108	345	41	127	27	5	4	46	1	.368
Mel Clark	83	233	26	56	9	7	1	24	0	.240
Jim Command	9	18	1	4	1	0	1	6	0	.222
Del Ennis (LF)	145	556	73	145	23	2	25	119	2	.261
Granny Hamner (2B)	152	596	83	168	39	11	13	89	1	.299
Stan Jok	3	3	0	0	0	0	0	0	0	.000
Willie Jones (3B)	142	535	64	145	28	3	12	56	4	.271
Ted Kazanski	39	104	7	14	2	0	1	8	0	.135
Johnny Lindell	7	5	0	1	0	0	0	2	0	.200
Stan Lopata	86	259	42	75	14	5	14	42	1	.290
Bobby Micelotta	13	3	2	0	0	0	0	0	0	.000
Bobby Morgan (SS)	135	455	58	119	25	2	14	50	3	.262
Gus Nairhos	3	5	0	1	0	0	0	0	0	.200
Stan Palys	2	4	0	1	0	0	0	0	0	.250
Danny Schell (RF)	92	272	25	77	14	3	7	33	0	.283
Earl Torgeson (1B)	135	490	63	133	22	6	5	54	7	.271
Johnny Wyrostek	92	259	28	62	12	4	3	28	0	.239
		5,184	659	1,384	243	(58)	102	620	30	.267

evident when an undistinguished Milwaukee pitcher, Jim Wilson, no-hit the club, 2–0.

The pitching staff had weak spots, too. After Roberts, Curt Simmons was the best hurler, but he had an erratic season as reflected in his 14–15 record.

Two veteran pitchers, Murry Dickson, landed in a trade with the Pittsburgh Pirates, and Herm Wehmeier, purchased from the Reds, could only contribute 10 wins apiece. Dickson, who lost 10 straight at one stage of the season, led the league in losses with 20.

1955

When the Phillies gathered for spring training in 1955, they were greeted by their fourth manager in less than three years. During the off-season, new general manager Roy Hamey fired Terry Moore and hired a former New York Yankee associate of his, Mayo Smith.

Record: 77–77
Finish: Fourth
Games Behind: 21½
Manager: Mayo Smith

Smith, whose entire big league experience consisted of playing 73 games as an outfielder for the Philadelphia A's in 1945, had been a manager in the Yankee chain for six years. He was an unknown; yet the Phillies, after flirting with being a pennant contender in the previous three seasons, had high hopes of giving the title a thorough chase in 1955.

As it turned out, however, the season revolved largely around Richie Ashburn's quest for the batting title. The club was never really in contention after launching a 13-game losing streak on April 30.

The same day the streak began, the Phillies also said goodbye to Smoky Burgess. The roly-poly, hard-hitting catcher was among those dealt to the Cincinnati Reds in a trade in which the Phillies got back Andy Seminick. Also involved in the six-player deal was Jim Greengrass, a hard-hitting outfielder who had socked 47 home runs in the last two years.

Greengrass was expected to join with Del Ennis and Willie Jones to give the Phillies a three-way power punch that would make opposing pitchers tremble. But it wasn't to happen. Greengrass, saddled with leg problems, contributed only 12 home runs and 37 RBI, and the load, as usual, fell on the broad shoulders of Ennis, who had another big year with 29 home runs, 120 runs batted in, and a .296 batting average.

The loudest bat, though, belonged to Ashburn. Richie carried a hot bat throughout the season, finishing with a .338 average to beat Willie Mays and Stan Musial for the batting championship, each by 19 points. The last Phillie to win a batting crown had been Harry Walker, the man Ashburn displaced in center field, in 1947.

During the season, the Phillies did bounce back from their devastating losing streak, which finally ended when Robin Roberts beat the Milwaukee Braves, 9–1. At one point the club had an 11-game winning streak, the longest one since 1892. Included in the streak was a string of five straight complete games by Phillie pitchers. The team also won 40 of its last 70 games.

Ennis, in driving in more than 100 runs for the sixth time in seven years, hit three home runs and collected seven RBI in a 7–2 triumph over the St. Louis Cardinals.

Aside from Del and Richie, the club had few other big bats. One, however, was carried by Stan Lopata. The big catcher had been inching toward regular status for several years, and despite the return of Seminick, Stan saw considerable action in 1955. He responded with 22 homers and a .271 average, and was named to the All-Star team.

Meanwhile, Seminick had gone downhill. So had the infield. Willie Jones held forth at third, and although he had 16 homers and 81 RBI, he hit only .258. After starting at shortstop and second base, Granny Hamner was shuttled around the infield without a regular position. Much of the time the Phillies lined up with Roy Smalley at short, Bobby Morgan at second, and Marv Blaylock at first.

Roberts had his sixth straight 20-game season with a 23–14 record, again led the league in wins, innings (305), and complete games (26), and got the nod from *The Sporting News* for his third Major League Pitcher of the Year award.

	W	L	G	GS	CG	IP	H	BB	K	ERA
Dave Cole	0	3	7	3	0	18	21	14	6	6.50
Murry Dickson	12	11	36	28	12	216	189	82	92	3.50
Bob Greenwood	0	0	1	0	0	2	7	0	0	18.00
Thornton Kipper	0	1	24	0	0	40	47	22	15	4.95
Bub Kuzava	1	0	17	4	0	32	47	12	13	7.31
Lynn Lovenguth	0	1	14	0	0	18	17	10	14	4.50
Jack Meyer	6	11	50	5	0	110	75	66	97	3.44
Bob Miller	8	4	40	0	0	90	80	28	28	2.40
Ron Mrozinski	0	2	22	1	0	34	38	19	18	6.62
Ron Negray	4	3	19	10	2	72	71	21	30	3.50
Jim Owens	0	2	3	2	0	9	13	7	6	8.00
Steve Ridzik	0	1	3	1	0	11	7	8	6	2.45
Robin Roberts	(23)	14	41	(38)	(26)	(305)	(292)	53	160	3.28
Saul Rogovin	5	3	12	11	5	73	60	17	27	3.08
Curt Simmons	8	8	25	22	3	130	148	50	58	4.92
Jack Spring	0	1	2	0	0	3	2	1	2	6.00
Herman Wehmeier	10	12	31	29	10	194	176	67	85	4.41
	77	77		154	58	1,357	1,291	477	657	3.93

Shutouts: Dickson (4), Rogovin (2), Roberts, Wehmeier

	G	AB	R	H	2B	3B	HR	RBI	SB	AVG
Richie Ashburn (CF)	140	533	91	180	32	9	3	42	12	(.338)
Floyd Baker	5	8	0	0	0	0	0	0	0	.000
Marv Blaylock (1B)	113	259	30	54	7	7	3	24	6	.208
Bob Bowman	3	3	0	0	0	0	0	0	0	.000
Smoky Burgess	7	21	4	4	2	0	1	1	0	.190
Mel Clark	10	32	3	5	3	0	0	1	0	.156
Jim Command	5	5	0	0	0	0	0	0	0	.000
John Easton	1	0	0	0	0	0	0	0	0	.000
Del Ennis (LF)	146	564	82	167	24	7	29	120	4	.296
Glen Gorbous	91	224	25	53	9	1	4	23	0	.237
Jim Greengrass (RF)	94	323	43	88	20	2	12	37	0	.272
Granny Hamner	104	405	57	104	12	4	5	43	0	.257
Willie Jones (3B)	146	516	65	133	20	3	16	81	6	.258
Ted Kazanski	9	12	1	1	0	0	1	1	0	.083
Stan Lopata	99	303	49	82	9	3	22	58	4	.271
Peanuts Lowrey	54	106	9	20	4	0	0	8	2	.189
Bobby Micelotta	4	4	0	0	0	0	0	0	0	.000
Bobby Morgan (2B)	136	483	61	112	20	2	10	49	6	.232
Gus Nairhos	7	9	1	1	0	0	0	0	0	.111
Stan Palys	15	52	8	15	3	0	1	8	1	.288
Danny Schell	2	2	0	0	0	0	0	0	0	.000
Andy Seminick (C)	93	289	32	71	12	1	11	34	1	.246
Roy Smalley (SS)	92	260	33	51	11	1	7	39	0	.196
Earl Torgeson	47	150	29	40	5	3	1	17	2	.267
Fred Van Dusen	1	0	0	0	0	0	0	0	0	.000
Eddie Waitkus	33	107	10	30	5	0	2	14	0	.280
Jim Westlake	1	1	0	0	0	0	0	0	0	.000
		5,092	675	1,300	214	50	132	631	44	.255

Phillies also came up with an outstanding reliever in rookie Jack Meyer, a local boy from Penn Charter. Converted to relief pitching after blazing through the minors as a starter, the speedballing Meyer led the league in saves with 16 while winning six games.

The rest of the staff was a disappointment. Curt Simmons won only eight games, Herm Wehmeier picked up 10, and Murry Dickson had the team's second best record with 12–11.

1956

Record: 71–83
Finish: Fifth
Games Behind: 22
Manager: Mayo Smith

The National League in the mid-1950s was loaded with strong, talented teams, starting with the Brooklyn Dodgers and continuing on through the Milwaukee Braves, St. Louis Cardinals, Cincinnati Reds, and New York Giants.

Overall, the league was probably as strong as it had ever been. It was no wonder, then, that the Phillies found it hard to make any headway.

In overall team talent, the Phillies could hardly compare to some of the other teams. It was always a case of the Phillies having a few outstanding players, but not enough strength in other places to make a solid run at the title.

By 1956, however, the talent the Phillies did have was starting to erode rather seriously. As they had done in previous years, the club tried to patch the deteriorating parts by picking up players from other teams. In most cases, they were players who had seen better days.

The 1956 roster included names such as Stu Miller, Saul Rogovin, Harvey Haddix, Elmer Valo, Frankie Baumholtz, and Solly Hemus, all players who had been added to the team by either trades, purchases, or free agent signings.

The club was not what could be called a pennant contender. That became particularly clear after the Phillies opened the season with 10 losses in a row, then dropped 15 of their first 20 games.

About the brightest spot during the season was Stan Lopata's arrival as a power hitter. The big backstop clouted 32 home runs and drove in 95.

But there were disappointments galore. Haddix, obtained in a trade with the Cardinals, did not give the club the pitching boost it had hoped for, winning only 12 games. Roberts, hampered by a leg injury, failed to win 20 games for the first time in seven years, settling for a 19–18 record. He lost his bid for a 20th on the last day of the season, winding up instead with the league lead in losses. Robbie also set a major league record by serving 46 home run pitches, a feat that had a marked bearing on his 4.45 ERA.

The Phillies gave Ted Kazanski another crack at winning a regular job, moving him to second and putting Granny Hamner back at shortstop. But neither produced at the plate, nor did their even weaker-hitting occasional replacements, Hemus and Roy Smalley.

	W	L	G	GS	CG	IP	H	BB	K	ERA
Murry Dickson	0	3	3	3	0	23	20	12	1	5.09
Dick Farrell	0	1	1	1	0	4	6	3	0	13.50
Ben Flowers	0	2	32	0	0	41	54	10	22	5.71
Harvey Haddix	12	8	31	26	11	207	196	55	154	3.48
Granny Hamner	0	1	3	1	0	8	10	2	4	4.50
Angelo LiPetri	0	0	6	0	0	11	7	3	8	3.27
Jack Meyer	7	11	41	7	2	96	86	51	66	4.41
Bob Miller	3	6	49	6	3	122	115	34	53	3.25
Stu Miller	5	8	24	15	2	107	109	51	65	4.46
Ron Negray	2	3	39	4	0	67	72	24	44	4.16
Jim Owens	0	4	10	5	0	30	35	22	22	7.20
Duane Pillette	0	0	20	0	0	23	32	12	10	6.65
Robin Roberts	19	(18)	43	37	(22)	297	(238)	40	157	4.45
Saul Rogovin	7	6	22	18	3	107	122	27	48	4.96
Bob Ross	0	0	3	0	0	3	4	2	4	9.00
Jack Sanford	1	0	3	1	0	13	7	13	6	1.38
Curt Simmons	15	10	33	27	14	198	186	65	88	3.36
Herm Wehmeier	0	2	3	3	0	20	18	11	8	4.05
	71	83		154	57	1,377	(1,407)	437	750	4.20

Shutouts: Haddix (2), Miller, Roberts

	G	AB	R	H	2B	3B	HR	RBI	SB	AVG
Richie Ashburn (CF)	154	628	94	190	26	8	3	50	10	.303
Frank Baumholtz	76	100	13	27	0	0	0	9	0	.270
Marv Blaylock (1B)	136	460	71	117	14	8	10	50	5	.254
Ed Bouchee	9	22	0	6	2	0	0	1	0	.273
Bob Bowman	6	16	2	3	0	1	1	2	0	.188
Mack Burk	15	1	3	1	0	0	0	0	0	1.000
Del Ennis (LF)	153	630	80	164	23	3	26	95	7	.260
Glen Gorbous	15	33	1	6	0	0	0	1	0	.182
Jim Greengrass	86	215	24	44	9	2	5	25	0	.205
Granny Hamner (SS)	122	401	42	90	24	3	4	42	2	.224
Solly Hemus	78	187	24	54	10	4	5	24	1	.289
Willie Jones (3B)	149	520	88	144	20	4	17	78	5	.277
Ted Kazanski (2B)	117	379	35	80	11	4	4	34	0	.211
Joe Lonnett	16	22	2	4	0	0	0	0	0	.182
Stan Lopata (C)	146	535	96	143	33	7	32	95	5	.267
Bobby Morgan	8	25	1	5	0	0	0	1	0	.200
Andy Seminick	60	161	16	32	3	1	7	23	3	.199
Roy Smalley	65	168	14	38	9	3	0	16	0	.226
Elmer Valo (RF)	98	291	40	84	13	3	5	37	7	.289
Wally Westlake	5	4	0	0	0	0	0	0	0	.000
		5,204	668	1,313	207	49	121	616	45	.252

Richie Ashburn did his usual excellent job of hitting, registering a .303 mark, and Del Ennis collected 26 home runs and 95 RBI. Willie Jones also had a good year, hitting .277 with 17 homers and 78 RBI, and Valo played well, hitting .289 after taking over in right field.

The one serious blemish on the Phils' hitters occurred when they were subjected to a no-hitter by Sal Maglie in a 5–0 loss to the Dodgers.

The Phillies' pitching staff, on the other hand, was the least effective in the league, ranking last in ERA. The top accomplishment on the staff was the comeback of Curt Simmons, who checked in with a 15–10 record.

The team played winning baseball from June through August. But with a tight, three-team race among the Dodgers, Braves, and Reds, they finished 20 games back of third-place Cinci.

1957

Record: 77–77
Finish: Fifth
Games Behind: 18
Managers: Mayo Smith

By 1957 it had become obvious that the Phillies weren't going anywhere with the combination of Whiz Kids still on the scene and veterans acquired from other teams. It was clearly the time for some drastic changes on the roster.

Fortunately, the Phillies had most of these changes waiting in their farm system. Thus 1957 became the year of the Phillies' youth movement.

Out of the minors, the Phillies brought pitchers Jack Sanford, Don Cardwell, Dick Farrell, and Seth Morehead, first baseman Ed Bouchee, and outfielders Harry Anderson and Bob Bowman. It was an extremely talented group, one that was reminiscent of the bright young band the club had assembled in the late 1940s.

To this fresh group, the Phillies added in trades a much-needed shortstop in Chico Fernandez, who became the first black player in a Phillies regular season lineup, a veteran pitcher in Jim Hearn, and an outfielder who always clobbered Phillies pitchers, Rip Repulski. Rip came in a controversial swap with the St. Louis Cardinals in which Del Ennis departed after giving the Phillies 11 seasons of first-rate slugging.

In the opening months of the season, it looked as though the youth movement was paying early dividends. The Phillies were in the thick of a five-team pennant race. In early July, they won 12 of 14 games, and, after a 6–2 victory over the Cardinals, went roaring into first place. It was the first time a Phillie team had been in first place that late in the season since 1950. The Phils were the fifth team to take the lead.

Their stay at the top lasted just two days. A three-game sweep by the Milwaukee Braves knocked them out of first, and although they remained in

Harvey Haddix (center) welcomes rookies Ed Bouchee and Chico Fernandez to the big leagues in 1957.

	W	L	G	GS	CG	IP	H	BB	K	ERA
Don Cardwell	4	8	30	19	5	128	122	42	92	4.92
Dick Farrell	10	2	52	0	0	83	74	36	54	2.39
Warren Hacker	4	4	20	10	1	74	72	18	33	4.50
Harvey Haddix	10	13	27	25	8	171	176	39	136	4.05
Granny Hamner	0	0	1	0	0	1	1	0	1	0.00
Jim Hearn	5	1	36	4	1	74	79	18	46	3.65
Jack Meyer	0	2	19	2	0	38	44	28	34	5.68
Bob Miller	2	5	32	1	0	60	61	17	12	2.70
Seth Morehead	1	1	34	1	1	59	57	20	36	3.66
Tom Qualters	0	0	6	0	0	7	12	4	6	7.71
Robin Roberts	10	(22)	39	32	14	250	246	43	128	4.07
Saul Rogovin	0	0	4	0	0	8	11	3	0	9.00
Jack Sanford	19	8	33	33	15	237	194	94	(188)	3.08
Curt Simmons	12	11	32	29	9	212	214	50	92	3.44
	77	77		156	54	1,401	1,363	412	858	3.80

Shutouts: Sanford (3), Roberts (2), Simmons (2), Cardwell, Haddix

	G	AB	R	H	2B	3B	HR	RBI	SB	AVG
Harry Anderson (LF)	118	400	53	107	15	4	17	61	2	.268
Richie Ashburn (CF)	156	626	93	186	26	8	0	33	13	.297
Frank Baumholtz	2	2	0	0	0	0	0	0	0	.000
Marv Blaylock	37	26	5	4	0	0	2	4	0	.154
Ed Bouchee (1B)	154	574	78	168	35	8	17	76	1	.293
Bob Bowman	99	237	31	63	8	2	6	23	0	.266
Chico Fernandez (SS)	149	500	42	131	14	4	5	51	18	.262
Glen Gorbous	3	2	1	1	1	0	0	1	0	.500
Granny Hamner (2B)	133	502	59	114	19	5	10	62	3	.227
Chuck Harmon	57	86	14	22	2	1	0	5	7	.256
Solly Hemus	70	108	8	20	6	1	0	5	1	.185
Willie Jones (3B)	133	440	58	96	19	2	9	47	1	.218
Ted Kazanski	62	185	15	49	7	1	3	11	1	.265
John Kennedy	5	2	1	0	0	0	0	0	0	.000
Don Landrum	2	7	1	1	1	0	0	0	0	.143
Joe Lonnett	67	160	12	27	5	0	5	15	0	.169
Stan Lopata (C)	116	388	50	92	18	2	18	67	2	.237
Bobby Morgan	2	0	0	0	0	0	0	0	0	.000
Ron Northey	33	26	1	7	0	0	1	5	0	.269
Rip Repulski (RF)	134	516	65	134	23	4	20	68	7	.260
Andy Seminick	8	11	0	1	0	0	0	0	0	.091
Roy Smalley	28	31	5	5	0	1	1	1	0	.161
		5,241	623	1,311	213	44	117	569	57	.250

contention for the rest of the month, a 9–19 slump in August jettisoned the Phillies from the race.

Despite their final resting spot of fifth place, a few breaks here and there could have given the club a first-division berth. It would've helped, too, if the Phillies had hit better and if Robin Roberts hadn't encountered a year in which he lost a league-leading 22 of 32 decisions.

As it was, though, the rookie crop performed admirably. Bouchee hit .293 with 17 home runs and 76 RBI, and was named Rookie of the Year by *The Sporting News*. Sanford was one of the best pitchers in the league, registering a 19–8 record, leading the league in strikeouts (188), and earning *The Sporting News* honors as Rookie Pitcher of the Year as well as the Baseball Writers' Association Rookie of the Year award.

Anderson added 17 homers and a .268 average, Bowman demonstrated one of the best throwing arms in the league, and Farrell turned out to be one of the league's top relievers with a 10–2 record.

Repulski led the club in home runs with 20, and Richie Ashburn hit .297. But the Phils were an otherwise weak-hitting bunch with the second-lowest team batting average in the circuit. Three of the regulars—Willie Jones, Granny Hamner, who had tried pitching, and Stan Lopata—hit below .240. Jones had been seriously injured in spring training when he was hit in the face by a thrown ball while sliding into second trying to break up a double play.

After Sanford, the pitching staff also suffered a letdown. Curt Simmons slipped to 12 wins, Haddix collected 10, Cardwell produced only four, and relief ace Jack Meyer wound up back in the minors.

1958

Record: 69–85
Finish: Eighth
Games Behind: 23
Manager: Mayo Smith, Eddie Sawyer

If any season had the potential for driving a manager out of his wits, the 1958 campaign was surely it. It was one of those weird seasons which had some high points and some low points and ended with a totally unexpected result.

On the plus side, Richie Ashburn won his second National League batting crown, this time hitting .350. He had to win it on the last day of the season, getting three hits in four at bats to edge Willie Mays. Ashburn also led the league in hits (215), walks, triples, and outfield putouts in what was one of the finest seasons of any player in modern Phillies history.

The Phillies also came up with another talented rookie pitcher, righthander Ray Semproch, who posted a 13–11 record. Unfortunately, he won only two games after mid-July.

Semproch's collapse was typical of the Phillies' season. The bad news began even before spring training when their 1957 rookie hotshot Ed Bouchee was arrested on a morals charge in January. Bouchee underwent treatment, and didn't return to the team until close to mid-season.

During the winter, the Phillies had landed the slugging Wally Post in an off-season trade with the Cincinnati Reds for Harvey Haddix. Although Post hit .282 for the season, his 12 home runs were less than half his normal production of past years.

In spite of all the setbacks, the Phillies got off to a flying start. Throughout the first half of the season, they were in the thick of the battle for the pennant.

	W	L	G	GS	CG	IP	H	BB	K	ERA
John Anderson	0	0	5	1	0	16	26	4	9	7.88
Don Cardwell	3	6	16	14	3	108	99	37	77	4.50
Bob Conley	0	0	2	2	0	8	9	1	0	7.88
Don Erickson	0	1	9	0	0	12	11	9	9	4.50
Dick Farrell	8	9	54	0	0	94	84	40	73	3.35
John Gray	0	0	15	0	0	17	12	14	10	4.24
Warren Hacker	0	1	9	1	0	17	24	8	4	7.41
Jim Hearn	5	3	39	1	0	73	88	27	33	4.19
Angelo LiPetri	0	0	4	0	0	4	6	0	1	11.25
Hank Mason	0	0	1	0	0	5	7	2	3	10.80
Jack Meyer	3	6	37	5	1	90	77	33	87	3.60
Bob Miller	1	1	17	0	0	22	36	9	9	11.86
Seth Morehead	1	6	27	11	0	92	121	26	54	5.87
Jim Owens	1	0	1	1	0	7	4	5	3	2.57
Tom Qualters	0	0	1	0	0	2	2	1	0	4.50
Robin Roberts	17	14	35	34	21	270	270	51	130	3.23
Jack Sanford	10	13	38	27	7	186	197	81	106	4.45
Ray Semproch	13	11	36	30	12	204	211	58	92	3.93
Curt Simmons	7	14	29	27	7	168	196	40	78	4.39
	69	85		154	51	(1,397)	(1,480)	446	778	4.32

Shutouts: Sanford (2), Semproch (2), Roberts, Simmons

	G	AB	R	H	2B	3B	HR	RBI	SB	AVG
Harry Anderson (LF)	140	515	80	155	34	6	23	97	0	.301
Richie Ashburn (CF)	152	615	98	(215)	24	(13)	2	33	30	(.350)
Ed Bouchee (1B)	89	334	55	86	19	5	9	39	1	.257
Bob Bowman	91	184	31	53	11	2	8	24	0	.288
Mack Burk	1	1	0	0	0	0	0	0	0	.000
Jim Coker	2	6	0	1	0	0	0	0	0	.167
Chuck Essegian	39	114	15	28	5	2	5	16	0	.246
Chico Fernandez (SS)	148	522	38	120	18	5	6	51	12	.230
Granny Hamner	35	133	18	40	7	3	2	18	0	.301
Jim Hegan	25	59	5	13	6	0	0	6	0	.220
Solly Hemus (2B)	105	334	53	95	14	3	8	36	3	.284
Pancho Herrera	29	63	5	17	3	0	1	6	1	.270
Willie Jones (3B)	118	398	52	108	15	1	14	60	1	.271
Ted Kazanski	95	289	21	66	12	2	3	35	2	.228
Joe Lonnett	17	50	0	7	2	0	0	2	0	.140
Stan Lopata (C)	86	258	36	64	9	0	9	33	0	.248
Dave Philley	91	207	30	64	11	4	3	31	1	.309
Wally Post (RF)	110	379	51	107	21	3	12	62	0	.282
Rip Repulski	85	238	33	58	9	4	13	40	0	.244
Carl Sawatski	60	183	12	42	4	1	5	12	0	.230
Roy Smalley	1	2	0	0	0	0	0	0	0	.000
Bobby Young	32	60	7	14	1	1	1	4	0	.233
		(5,363)	664	(1,424)	238	56	124	630	51	(.266)

Right before the All-Star break, they reeled off seven wins in a row to move to within two and one-half games of first.

In mid-July, a seven-game losing streak, during which they lost the first four games by one run, plunged the Phillies out of the pack of contenders. Nearing the end of the month, they had slipped to eight and one-half games back, and manager Mayo Smith was fired.

He was replaced by a familiar figure, Eddie Sawyer, who was urged back to the club by president Bob Carpenter. Sawyer, though, fared even worse than his predecessor. The Phillies won only 28 of their final 69 games and plummeted all the way to the National League cellar, a position last occupied by the club in 1945. It was little consolation that the Phils' 69 wins were the most any major league cellar-dweller ever had.

Their collapse notwithstanding, the Phillies did have some special individual performances. Jack Meyer struck out the first six batters he faced, a major league record for relief pitchers, in a 14-inning game in which Phillies hurlers fanned 21 Pittsburgh Pirates while winning 3–2.

Willie Jones tied an all-time club record with eight RBI in one game, a 12–2 victory over the St. Louis Cardinals. Willie had a single, double, and two three-run homers.

And Dave Philley, bought from the Detroit Tigers, set a major league record with eight consecutive pinch-hits en route to an 18 pinch-hit season.

Second-year man Harry Anderson had an outstanding season, hitting .301 with 23 homers and 97 RBI. But the other 1957 rookie phenoms, Bouchee (.257 after he returned), Sanford (10–13), and Farrell (8–9), slipped drastically.

The top pitcher on the staff was Robin Roberts, who returned from the previous year's disaster to post a 17–14 record.

For a decade that began so brightly, the 1950s certainly ended dismally. In fact, it was almost as though the Phillies had gone into a time warp, and had slipped back into the late 1930s.

1959

Record: 64–90
Finish: Eighth
Games Behind: 23
Manager: Eddie Sawyer

Gene Freese touches home plate after hitting one of his three grand slams in 1959. Freese hit five pinch-hit home runs that season.

	W	L	G	GS	CG	IP	H	BB	K	ERA
Bob Bowman	0	1	5	0	0	6	5	5	0	6.00
Don Cardwell	9	10	25	22	5	153	135	65	106	4.06
Gene Conley	12	7	25	22	12	180	159	42	102	3.00
Dick Farrell	1	6	38	0	0	57	61	25	31	4.74
Ruben Gomez	3	8	20	12	2	72	90	24	37	6.10
Jim Hearn	0	2	6	0	0	11	15	6	1	5.73
Ed Keegan	0	3	3	3	0	9	19	13	3	18.00
Jack Meyer	5	3	47	1	1	94	76	53	71	3.35
Seth Morehead	0	2	3	3	0	10	15	3	8	9.90
Jim Owens	12	12	31	30	11	221	203	73	135	3.22
Taylor Phillips	1	4	32	3	1	63	72	31	35	5.00
Robin Roberts	15	17	35	35	19	257	267	35	137	4.27
Humberto Robinson	2	4	31	4	1	73	70	24	32	3.33
Freddy Rodriguez	0	0	1	0	0	2	4	0	1	13.50
Al Schroll	1	1	3	0	0	9	12	6	4	9.00
Ray Semproch	3	10	30	18	2	112	119	59	54	5.38
Chris Short	0	0	3	2	0	14	19	10	8	8.36
Curt Simmons	0	0	7	0	0	10	16	0	4	4.50
	64	90		.155	54	1,354	1,357	474	769	4.27

Shutouts: Conley (3), Roberts (2), Cardwell, Gomez, Owens

	G	AB	R	H	2B	3B	HR	RBI	SB	AVG
Sparky Anderson (2B)	152	477	42	104	9	3	0	34	6	.218
Harry Anderson (LF)	142	508	50	122	28	6	14	63	1	.240
Richie Ashburn (CF)	153	564	86	150	16	2	1	20	9	.266
Jim Bolger	35	48	1	4	1	0	0	1	0	.083
Ed Bouchee (1B)	136	499	75	142	29	4	15	74	0	.285
Bob Bowman	57	79	7	10	0	0	2	5	0	.127
Solly Drake	67	62	10	9	1	0	0	3	5	.145
John Easton	3	3	0	0	0	0	0	0	0	.000
Chico Fernandez	45	123	15	26	5	1	0	3	2	.211
Gene Freese (3B)	132	400	60	107	14	5	23	70	8	.268
Granny Hamner	21	64	10	19	4	0	2	6	0	.297
Harry Hanebrink	57	97	10	25	3	1	1	7	0	.258
Jim Hegan	25	51	1	10	1	0	0	8	0	.196
Willie Jones	47	160	23	43	9	1	7	24	0	.269
Joe Koppe (SS)	126	422	68	110	18	7	7	28	7	.261
Joe Lonnett	43	93	8	16	1	0	1	10	0	.172
Dave Philley	99	254	32	74	18	2	7	37	0	.291
Wally Post (RF)	132	468	62	119	17	6	22	94	0	.254
Carl Sawatski (C)	74	198	15	58	10	0	9	43	0	.293
Valmy Thomas	66	140	5	28	2	0	1	7	1	.200
		5,109	599	1,237	196	38	113	560	39	.242

In 1959, for the second of what would become four straight years, the team finished in last place. Such an ending would have seemed hardly possible a few years earlier, but by the time the 1950s exited, the club had receded to such a level that it was once again the league's softest touch.

The Whiz Kids were now just a pleasant memory. By the end of the 1959 season, only Robin Roberts, Richie Ashburn, and Curt Simmons were left from the 1950 club. During the season, Willie Jones, Granny Hamner, and Stan Lopata departed, all shipped away in trades made by the new general manager John Quinn.

Quinn, who had built pennant-winning teams for the Boston Braves in 1948 and the Milwaukee Braves in 1957 and 1958, was brought in to replace Roy Hamey. A heavy trader, he pulled off one deal after another in an effort to restore the Phillies to the level of pennant contender.

Prior to Quinn's arrival in January, the Phillies made two other swaps, each of which would rank among the team's worst deals. The club shipped away Jack Sanford to the San Francisco Giants for two players of little worth, Ruben Gomez and Valmy Thomas, and it sent Rip Repulski and two minor leaguers to the Los Angeles Dodgers for Sparky Anderson.

Anderson, a minor league flash whom the Phillies hoped would fill a big hole at second base, was a flop. He hit only .218 in what would be his only big league season. As for the other two, they did even less. In fact, of all the trades that went into the formation of the 1959 team, none produced any players of substance for the Phillies except 6-foot, 8-inch pitcher Gene Conley, who doubled as a pro basketball player, and light-hitting shortstop Joe Koppe.

Thus the 1959 Phillies, save for a few members of the roster, comprised a dreary gang that ranked last in the league in hitting as well as fielding. In one game during the season, the Los Angeles Dodgers' Sandy Koufax struck out 16 Phillies.

The best hitter on the club was Ed Bouchee, who stroked out a .285 average. No other regular finished above .270, although Gene Freese hit 23 home runs, and Wally Post hit 22 with 94 RBI.

Post hit a home run in every stadium in the league. And Freese, obtained in a late-season trade in 1958, slammed five pinch-hit home runs, including two grand slams. Another pinch-hit specialist, Dave Philley, extended his major league consecutive pinch-hit record to nine.

Ashburn, who faded to a .266 mark, put the finishing touches on a brilliant Phillies career—he would be traded the next winter—by setting a club record for hits with 2,217.

The pitching staff received commendable efforts from Roberts (15–17), Conley (12–7), and Jim Owens (12–12). But the rest of the crew had little to offer. Especially disappointing were the previous year's rookie flash, Ray Semproch (3–10), Gomez (3–8 with a 6.10 ERA), and Dick Farrell (1–6).

You want to know who threw out the first ball in the first World Series game the Phillies won in 65 years?

Eddie Sawyer, that's who.

You want to know why Eddie Sawyer was around at the age of 69 to throw out the first ball?

Possibly because of a decision he made in April 1960. Sawyer was the Phillies' manager for the opening game of the 1960 season. The team lost to the Reds, 9–4, one of 95 losses for the Phillies that season.

1960

Record: 59–95
Finish: Eighth
Games Behind: 36
Managers: Eddie Sawyer, Andy Cohen, Gene Mauch

The Phillies lineup in 1960 coming out of spring training included: (from left) Johnny Callison, Tony Curry, Bobby Gene Smith, Joe Koppe, Alvin Dark, Ken Walters, Bobby Del Greco, Ed Bouchee and Jim Coker.

	W	L	G	GS	CG	IP	H	BB	K	ERA
John Buzhardt	5	16	30	29	5	200	198	68	73	3.87
Don Cardwell	1	2	5	4	0	28	28	11	21	4.50
Gene Conley	8	14	29	25	9	183	192	42	117	3.69
Dick Farrell	10	6	59	0	0	103	88	29	70	2.71
Ruben Gomez	0	3	22	1	0	52	68	9	24	5.37
Dallas Green	3	6	23	10	5	109	100	44	51	4.05
Art Mahaffey	7	3	14	12	5	93	78	34	56	2.31
Hank Mason	0	0	3	0	0	6	9	5	3	9.00
Jack Meyer	3	1	7	4	0	25	25	11	18	4.32
Al Neiger	0	0	6	0	0	13	16	4	3	5.45
Jim Owens	4	14	31	22	6	150	182	64	83	5.04
Taylor Phillips	0	1	10	1	0	14	21	4	6	8.36
Robin Roberts	12	16	35	33	13	237	256	34	122	4.03
Humberto Robinson	0	4	33	1	0	50	48	22	31	3.42
Chris Short	6	9	42	10	2	107	101	52	54	3.95
Curt Simmons	0	0	4	2	0	4	13	6	4	18.00
	59	95		154	45	1,375 (1,423)	439	736		4.01

Shutouts: Conley (2), Roberts (2), Green, Mahaffey

	G	AB	R	H	2B	3B	HR	RBI	SB	AVG
Ruben Amaro (SS)	92	264	25	61	9	1	0	16	0	.231
Harry Anderson	38	93	10	23	2	0	5	12	0	.247
Ed Bouchee	22	65	1	17	4	0	0	8	0	.262
Johnny Callison (LF)	99	288	36	75	11	5	9	30	0	.260
Jim Coker (C)	81	252	18	54	5	3	6	34	0	.214
Tony Curry	95	245	26	64	14	2	6	34	0	.261
Clay Dalrymple	82	158	11	43	6	2	4	21	0	.272
Alvin Dark (3B)	55	198	29	48	5	1	3	14	1	.242
Bobby Del Greco (CF)	100	300	48	71	16	4	10	26	1	.237
Tony Gonzalez	78	241	27	72	17	5	6	33	2	.299
Pancho Herrera (1B)	145	512	61	144	26	6	17	71	2	.281
Joe Koppe	58	170	13	29	6	1	1	13	3	.171
Ted Lepcio	69	141	16	32	7	0	2	8	0	.227
Bobby Malkmus	79	133	16	28	4	1	1	12	2	.211
Joe Morgan	26	83	5	11	2	2	0	2	0	.133
Cal Neeman	59	160	13	29	6	2	4	13	0	.181
Dave Philley	14	15	2	5	2	0	0	4	0	.333
Wally Post	34	84	11	24	6	1	2	12	0	.286
Bobby Gene Smith	98	217	24	62	5	2	4	27	2	.286
Tony Taylor (2B)	127	505	66	145	22	4	4	35	24	.287
Lee Walls	65	181	19	36	6	1	3	19	3	.199
Ken Walters (RF)	124	426	42	102	10	0	8	37	4	.239
Bobby Wine	4	14	1	2	0	0	0	0	0	.143
Jim Woods	11	34	4	6	0	0	1	3	0	.176
		5,169	546	1,235	196	44	99	503	45	.239

Andy Cohen was the manager for the second game. Sawyer resigned after the opener with one terse comment: "I'm 49 years old and I want to live to be 50."

Bob Carpenter and John Quinn dipped into Minneapolis to get the manager for the third game. He was Gene Mauch; he was 34 years old, and he would live to regret 1964. But in 1960 he was eager. He wasn't overmatched. His team was.

Robin Roberts, nearing the end of a brilliant career in Philadelphia, had a 12–16 record. No other starter won more than eight games. Reliever Dick Farrell was 10–6, and lefty Chris Short showed some promise with a 6–9 record. But, more than anything, this was a club that was living off Whiz Kid memories—and dying as a result.

It needed new direction, which Mauch provided. After losing three straight games by 1–0 scores and going 29 scoreless innings, the team limped along in eighth place most of the season, rose to seventh for a little over a month in late July and early August, then faded and finished a game behind the seventh-place Cubs.

The Phillies and Cubs engineered a major trade in May. Philadelphia sent Ed Bouchee and Don Cardwell to the Cubs for catcher Cal Neeman and second baseman Tony Taylor, who led the team with a .287 average. First baseman

Pancho Herrera had 17 homers and 71 RBI but established a National League record with 136 strikeouts.

Outfielder Johnny Callison, obtained during the off-season for Gene Freese, showed some promise and hit .260, while a catcher drafted from the Pacific Coast League named Clay Dalrymple had his moments. And in July, the Phillies called up Art Mahaffey, who put together a 7–3 record and a 2.31 earned run average.

The 59 victories for the Phillies was their lowest total since 1945, and the 862,205 fans who ventured to Connie Mack Stadium figured things had bottomed out and couldn't get any worse.

They were dead wrong.

John Buzhardt won six games in 1961. One of them was at Connie Mack Stadium on July 28 when John pitched the Phillies to a 4–3 victory over the Giants in the second game of a doubleheader. Another was on August 20 when he scored a 7–4 victory over the Braves in Milwaukee County Stadium, again in a doubleheader nightcap.

What happened in between became major league history.

The Phillies lost 23 straight games. It is a record that may never be broken.

1961

Record: 47–107
Finish: Eighth
Games Behind: 46
Manager: Gene Mauch

	W	L	G	GS	CG	IP	H	BB	K	ERA
Jack Baldschun	5	3	(65)	0	0	100	90	49	59	3.87
Paul Brown	0	1	5	1	0	10	13	8	1	8.10
John Buzhardt	6	18	41	27	6	202	200	65	92	4.50
Dick Farrell	2	1	5	0	0	10	10	6	10	6.30
Don Ferrarese	5	12	42	14	3	139	120	68	89	3.76
Dallas Green	2	4	42	10	1	128	160	47	51	4.85
Ken Lehman	1	1	41	2	0	63	61	25	27	4.29
Art Mahaffey	11	(19)	36	32	12	219	205	70	158	4.11
Jack Meyer	0	0	1	0	0	2	2	2	2	9.00
Jim Owens	5	10	20	17	3	107	119	32	38	4.46
Robin Roberts	1	10	26	18	2	117	154	23	54	5.85
Chris Short	6	12	39	16	1	127	157	71	80	5.95
Frank Sullivan	3	16	49	18	1	159	161	55	144	4.30
	47	107		155	29	1,383	1,452	521	775	4.61

Shutouts: Mahaffey (3), Buzhardt, Ferrarese, Green, Sullivan

	G	AB	R	H	2B	3B	HR	RBI	SB	AVG
Ruben Amaro (SS)	135	381	34	98	14	9	1	32	1	.257
Johnny Callison (RF)	138	455	74	121	20	11	9	47	10	.266
Jim Coker	11	25	3	10	1	0	1	4	1	.400
Choo-Choo Coleman	34	47	3	6	1	0	0	4	0	.128
Wes Covington	57	165	23	50	9	0	7	26	0	.303
Tony Curry	15	36	3	7	0	0	0	3	0	.194
Clay Dalrymple (C)	129	378	23	83	11	1	5	42	0	.220
Bobby Del Greco	41	112	14	29	5	0	2	11	0	.259
Don Demeter (LF)	106	382	54	98	18	4	20	68	2	.257
Tony Gonzalez (CF)	126	426	58	118	16	8	12	58	15	.277
Pancho Herrera (1B)	126	400	56	103	17	2	13	51	5	.258
Darrell Johnson	21	61	4	14	1	0	0	3	0	.230
Al Kenders	10	23	0	4	1	0	0	1	0	.174
Joe Koppe	6	7	1	0	0	0	0	0	0	.000
Bobby Malkmus	121	342	39	79	8	2	7	31	1	.231
Cal Neeman	19	31	0	7	1	0	0	2	1	.226
Bob Sadowski	16	54	4	7	0	0	0	0	1	.130
Bobby Gene Smith	79	174	16	44	7	0	2	18	0	.253
Charley Smith (3B)	112	411	43	102	13	4	9	47	3	.248
Tony Taylor (2B)	106	400	47	100	17	3	2	26	11	.250
Elmer Valo	50	43	4	8	2	0	1	8	0	.186
Lee Walls	91	261	32	73	6	4	8	30	2	.280
Ken Walters	86	180	23	41	8	2	2	14	2	.228
George Williams	17	36	4	9	0	0	0	1	0	.250
Jim Woods	23	48	6	11	3	0	2	9	0	.229
		5,213	584	1,265	185	50	103	549	56	.243

Gene Mauch was a fiery leader of the 1960s Phillies as he shows here in an argument with umpire Shag Crawford.

John Buzhardt was the winning pitcher when the Phillies ended their 23-game losing streak in 1961.

Even the wretched 1962 Mets never lost 23 straight games. Seventeen of the losses came on the road, and eight were by one run. It was the bottom, but Gene Mauch would say later that it was the catalyst for the team's road to recovery. Mauch explained that the team used the disastrous losing streak as a means of rallying around each other.

It was a team that needed plenty of rallying. It finished 17 games out of seventh place, reminding old-time Phillie fans of some of the awful teams of the 1920s, '30s, and '40s. But there was a nucleus around which Mauch would build. Don Demeter came from Los Angeles and hit 20 home runs while playing the outfield. Tony Gonzalez and John Callison, the other two outfielders, looked like they might be stars once they learned to play at the major league level.

Among the pitchers, Art Mahaffey was the closest thing to a bona fide prospect. His record was 11–19, with the losses tying him for the National League lead. But he had a fastball that crackled, and in one game against the Chicago Cubs struck out 17 hitters.

Robin Roberts played his final season with the Phillies. He finished 1–10 and didn't see eye-to-eye with Mauch about much of anything. When asked about Roberts, Mauch said of the future Hall of Famer, "He throws like Betsy Ross." Roberts was sold to the Yankees after the season and later enjoyed a rejuvenated career with the Orioles and the Astros.

The Phillies were about to do some rejuvenating of their own, thanks in part to the expansion teams, in 1962.

1962

Record: 81–80
Finish: Seventh
Games Behind: 20
Manager: Gene Mauch

The New York Mets and Houston Colt 45s were born this season. The Phillies, who had been battered so badly the previous season, turned the tables. They hammered the expansion teams on their way to a 34-win improvement.

A big off-season trade with the White Sox sent third baseman Charlie Smith and pitcher John Buzhardt to the Windy City for first baseman Roy Sievers, an aging power hitter. Gene Mauch felt the Phillies needed a home run hitter to bring them one step closer to being competitive in the National League.

For half a season, the trade appeared to be a dud. Sievers struggled to get above the .200 mark and was the target of abuse from Connie Mack Stadium fans. But he woke up in August and so did the team.

John Callison was rested on the last day of the season by Mauch to save his .300 average. Gonzalez hit two points higher, and they combined for 43 home runs. Sievers had 21 and Don Demeter, playing third base on a regular basis for the first time in his career, topped the team with 29 round-trippers. Even catcher Clay Dalrymple chipped in with 11 homers while batting .276.

Art Mahaffey won 19 games and was an All-Star. Cal McLish and Chris Short each won 11, while rookies Jack Hamilton and Dennis Bennett scored nine victories each. Jack Baldschun had a 12–7 record with 13 saves in 67 trips out of the bullpen.

Mauch's reputation as a managerial genius was growing at a rapid rate. It would continue to expand the following season when the Phillies would rise from curiosities to contenders after a terrible start.

	W	L	G	GS	CG	IP	H	BB	K	ERA
Jack Baldschun	12	7	67	0	0	113	95	58	95	2.95
Dennis Bennett	9	9	31	24	7	175	144	68	149	3.81
John Boozer	0	0	9	0	0	20	22	10	13	5.85
Paul Brown	0	6	23	9	0	64	74	33	29	5.91
Don Ferrarese	0	1	5	0	0	7	9	3	6	7.71
Dallas Green	6	6	37	10	2	129	145	43	58	3.84
Jack Hamilton	9	12	41	26	4	182	185	(107)	101	5.09
Ed Keegan	0	0	4	0	0	8	6	5	5	2.25
Bobby Locke	1	0	5	0	0	16	16	10	9	5.63
Art Mahaffey	19	14	41	39	20	274	253	81	177	3.94
Cal McLish	11	5	32	24	5	155	184	45	71	4.24
Jim Owens	2	4	23	12	1	70	90	33	21	6.30
Chris Short	11	9	47	12	4	142	149	56	91	3.42
Bill Smith	1	5	24	5	0	50	59	10	26	4.32
Frank Sullivan	0	2	19	0	0	23	38	12	12	6.26
	81	80		161	43	1,427	1,469	574	863	4.28

Shutouts: Bennett (2), Mahaffey (2), McLish, Hamilton

	G	AB	R	H	2B	3B	HR	RBI	SB	AVG
Ruben Amaro	79	226	24	55	10	0	0	19	5	.243
Johnny Callison (RF)	157	603	107	181	26	(10)	23	83	10	.300
Jim Coker	5	3	0	0	0	0	0	1	0	.000
Billy Consolo	13	5	3	2	0	0	0	0	0	.400
Wes Covington	116	304	36	86	12	1	9	44	0	.283
Clay Dalrymple (C)	123	370	40	102	13	3	11	54	1	.276
Jacke Davis	48	75	9	16	0	1	1	6	1	.213
Don Demeter (3B)	153	550	85	169	24	3	29	107	2	.307
Tony Gonzalez (CF)	118	437	76	132	16	4	20	63	17	.302
John Herrnstein	6	5	0	1	0	0	0	1	0	.200
Billy Klaus	102	248	30	51	8	2	4	20	1	.206
Bobby Malkmus	8	5	3	1	1	0	0	0	0	.200
Bob Oldis	38	80	9	21	1	0	1	10	0	.263
Mel Roach	65	105	9	20	4	0	0	8	0	.190
Ted Savage (LF)	127	335	54	89	11	2	7	39	16	.266
Roy Sievers (1B)	144	477	61	125	19	5	21	80	2	.262
Tony Taylor (2B)	152	625	87	162	21	5	7	43	20	.259
Frank Torre	108	168	13	52	8	2	0	20	1	.310
Sammy White	41	97	7	21	4	0	2	12	0	.216
Bobby Wine (SS)	112	311	30	76	15	0	4	25	2	.244
		5,420	705	1,410	199	39	142	658	79	.260

1963

Record: 87–75
Finish: Fourth
Games Behind: 12
Manager: Gene Mauch

The quote was Buzzy Bavasi's. The Dodger general manager, looking at the 1963 World Series against the Yankees, suggested that maybe the Dodgers weren't the proper team to represent the National League.

"Aw, we just ought to let the Phillies go," he said. "They played the best ball in the league the last two months."

Indeed they had. The team that had lost 23 straight games two seasons before had now grown to the point where the top teams in the league were showing their respect.

The way 1963 started, it was like 1961 all over again. The Phillies stumbled out of the starting blocks and were mired in eighth place until mid-July. At the end of June, they were six games under .500. But from June 25 to the end of the season, they were 56–35. And they accomplished that, for the most part, without Art Mahaffey, who tore up his right ankle in July and didn't pitch again until the last week of the season. He was 7–10.

The slack was picked up by rookie Ray Culp (14–11), Cal McLish (13–11), and Dennis Bennett, who came off the disabled list in June and was 9–5 the rest of the way. Jack Baldschun was terrific out of the bullpen again and got some help from veteran John Klippstein.

	W	L	G	GS	CG	IP	H	BB	K	ERA
Jack Baldschun	11	7	65	0	0	114	99	42	89	2.29
Dennis Bennett	9	5	23	16	6	119	102	39	82	2.65
John Boozer	3	4	26	8	2	83	67	33	69	2.93
Paul Brown	0	1	6	2	0	15	15	5	11	4.20
Ray Culp	14	11	34	30	10	203	148	(102)	176	2.97
Ryne Duren	6	2	33	7	1	87	65	52	84	3.31
Dallas Green	7	5	40	14	4	120	134	38	68	3.23
Jack Hamilton	2	1	19	1	0	30	22	17	23	5.40
John Klippstein	5	6	49	1	0	112	80	46	84	1.93
Bobby Locke	0	0	9	0	0	11	10	5	7	5.73
Marcelino Lopez	1	0	4	2	0	6	8	7	2	6.00
Art Mahaffey	7	10	26	22	6	149	143	48	97	3.99
Cal McLish	13	11	32	32	10	210	184	56	98	3.26
Chris Short	9	12	38	27	6	198	185	69	160	2.95
	87	75		162	45	1,457	1,262	(553)	1,052	3.09

Shutouts: Culp (5), Short (3), McLish (2), Bennett, Mahaffey

	G	AB	R	H	2B	3B	HR	RBI	SB	AVG
Dick Allen	10	24	6	7	2	1	0	2	0	.292
Ruben Amaro	115	217	25	47	9	2	2	19	0	.217
Earl Averill	47	71	8	19	2	0	3	8	0	.268
Johnny Callison (RF)	157	626	96	178	36	11	26	78	8	.284
Wes Covington (LF)	119	353	46	107	24	1	17	64	1	.303
Clay Dalrymple (C)	142	452	40	114	15	3	10	40	0	.252
Don Demeter	154	515	63	133	20	2	22	83	1	.258
Cal Emery	16	19	0	3	1	0	0	0	0	.158
Tony Gonzalez (CF)	155	555	78	170	36	12	4	66	13	.306
Wayne Graham	10	22	1	4	0	0	0	0	0	.182
Mickey Harrington	1	0	0	0	0	0	0	0	0	.000
John Herrnstein	15	12	1	2	0	0	1	1	0	.167
Don Hoak (3B)	115	377	35	87	11	3	6	24	5	.231
Billy Klaus	11	18	1	1	0	0	0	0	0	.056
Jim Lemon	31	59	6	16	2	0	2	6	0	.271
Bob Oldis	47	85	8	19	3	0	0	8	0	.224
Cookie Rojas	64	77	18	17	0	1	1	2	4	.221
Roy Sievers (1B)	138	450	46	108	19	2	19	82	0	.240
Tony Taylor (2B)	157	640	102	180	20	10	5	49	23	.281
Frank Torre	92	112	8	28	7	2	1	10	0	.250
Bobby Wine (SS)	142	418	29	90	14	3	6	44	1	.215
		5,524	642	1,390	228	54	126	599	56	.252

Wes Covington was still a feared slugger after the Phillies obtained him from the Milwaukee Braves.

Although Roy Sievers slipped to .240, he drove in 80 runs in his last big season. John Callison hit 26 homers, and part-timer Wes Covington batted .303 with 17 homers. Tony Gonzalez hit .306, Tony Taylor rebounded to .281, and in September a young man came up from Little Rock and batted .292 while playing seven games in the outfield and one at third base. He had never played third base in his life.

The following season he would. Dick Allen, then called Richie, would almost lead the Phillies to the pennant in 1964 before embarking on the stormy part of his career.

1964

Record: 92–70
Finish: Second (tie)
Games Behind: 1
Manager: Gene Mauch

U ntil 1980 and redemption, the 1964 season was the most memorable in Phillies history for what hadn't happened instead of what had taken place.

The Phillies hadn't won the pennant after 162 games. Through 150 games, they had. Clinching the first flag in 14 years appeared to be a mere formality. They had a 6½-game lead with 12 to play.

Up to then, everything manager Gene Mauch had done was right. He pulled the strings, and the Phillies, like puppets, acted out the game perfectly.

There was one gaping hole on the roster as the team prepared for the season. The team lacked a starting pitcher who could go out and give the team a chance to win every fourth game, a veteran who could be the mortar to hold the young pitchers together. Mauch and general manager John Quinn found the pitcher they wanted in Detroit, where Jim Bunning was coming off a 12–13 season and was being offered by the Tigers. But the price was high—utility man Don Demeter and pitcher Jack Hamilton.

The Phillies paid the price and found themselves with a gaping hole at third. Not to worry, Mauch said. And he spent the spring working to convert young outfielder Dick Allen into a third baseman.

Considering his lack of experience, Allen did well. Although he led the league with 41 errors, it can also be pointed out that Ken Boyer, the MVP and a great defensive third baseman, had 24 for the Cardinals. And Dick, or Richie as he was called at the time, more than made up for it with his bat. He shattered the Phillies' rookie home run record by 10, with his 29 home runs easily surpassing Don Hurst's 1928 figures. He drove in 91 runs batting behind Johnny Callison for most of the season.

Callison finally realized his enormous potential with 31 home runs and 104 RBI, including a three-homer game down the stretch when the season was coming apart for the team.

Three good reasons the Phillies made a run at the 1964 pennant were (from left) Johnny Callison, Jim Bunning, and Cookie Rojas.

	W	L	G	GS	CG	IP	H	BB	K	ERA
Jack Baldschun	6	9	71	0	0	118	111	40	96	3.13
Dave Bennett	0	0	1	0	0	1	2	0	1	9.00
Dennis Bennett	12	14	41	32	7	208	222	58	125	3.68
John Boozer	3	4	22	3	0	60	64	18	51	5.10
Jim Bunning	19	8	41	39	13	284	248	46	219	2.63
Ray Culp	8	7	30	19	3	135	139	56	96	4.13
Ryne Duren	0	0	2	0	0	3	5	1	5	6.00
Dallas Green	2	1	25	0	0	42	63	14	21	5.79
John Klippstein	2	1	11	0	0	22	22	8	13	4.09
Gary Kroll	0	0	2	0	0	3	3	2	2	3.00
Bobby Locke	0	0	8	0	0	19	21	6	11	2.84
Art Mahaffey	12	9	34	29	2	157	161	82	80	4.53
Cal McLish	0	1	2	1	0	5	6	1	6	3.60
Ed Roebuck	5	3	60	0	0	77	55	25	42	2.22
Bobby Shantz	1	1	14	0	0	32	23	6	18	2.25
Chris Short	17	9	42	31	12	221	174	51	181	2.20
Morrie Steevens	0	0	4	0	0	3	5	1	3	3.00
Rick Wise	6	3	25	8	0	69	78	25	39	4.04
	90	72		162	37	1,460	1,402	440	1,009	3.37

Shutouts: Bunning (5), Short (4), Bennett (2), Mahaffey (2), Culp

	G	AB	R	H	2B	3B	HR	RBI	SB	AVG
Dick Allen (3B)	162	632	(125)	201	38	(13)	29	91	3	.318
Ruben Amaro	129	299	31	79	11	0	4	34	1	.264
John Briggs	61	66	16	17	2	0	1	6	1	.258
Johnny Callison (RF)	162	654	101	179	30	10	31	104	6	.274
Danny Cater	60	152	13	45	9	1	1	13	1	.296
Pat Corrales	2	1	1	0	0	0	0	0	0	.000
Wes Covington (LF)	129	339	37	95	18	0	13	58	0	.280
Clay Dalrymple (C)	127	382	36	91	16	3	6	46	0	.238
Tony Gonzalez (CF)	131	421	55	117	25	3	4	40	0	.278
John Herrnstein (1B)	125	303	38	71	12	4	6	25	1	.234
Don Hoak	6	4	0	0	0	0	0	0	0	.000
Alex Johnson	43	109	18	33	7	1	4	18	1	.303
Adolfo Phillips	13	13	4	3	0	0	0	0	0	.231
Vic Power	18	48	1	10	4	0	0	3	0	.208
Cookie Rojas	109	340	58	99	19	5	2	31	1	.291
Costen Shockley	11	35	4	8	0	0	1	2	0	.229
Roy Sievers	49	120	7	22	3	1	4	16	0	.183
Tony Taylor (2B)	154	570	62	143	13	6	4	46	13	.251
Frank Thomas	39	143	20	42	11	0	7	26	0	.294
Gus Triandos	73	188	17	47	9	0	8	33	0	.250
Bobby Wine (SS)	126	283	28	60	8	3	4	34	1	.212
		5,493	693	1,415	241	51	130	649	30	.258

Tony Taylor played second, Ruben Amaro and Bobby Wine shared shortstop, and John Herrnstein saw the most action among nine first basemen.

Tony Gonzalez stopped hitting home runs but played a solid center field. Wes Covington played left field against righthanded pitching; Cookie Rojas settled into the spot against lefties. Rojas developed into an invaluable utility man. Clay Dalrymple caught against righthanded pitchers; Gus Triandos, who dubbed it "The Year of the Blue Snow" before the snow turned a dismal gray, caught against lefty pitchers. It was Triandos, who had come from Detroit as a throw-in with Bunning, who caught Jim's perfect game on Father's Day.

Everything the Phillies did was right until the bitter end. They even reeled off three triple plays. Danny Cater played some first base and right field and was batting .296 when he broke his ankle in late July. Quinn made a deal with the Mets for Frank Thomas a week later, and Thomas went on a tear. In 34 games as the Phillies' first baseman, he drove in 26 runs before breaking his thumb sliding into first base on September 8.

Quinn went to the American League California Angels to get a replacement, Vic Power, but the fancy fielder was unable to supply the hitting punch that Thomas had. Still, on the morning of September 21, the Phillies had a 6½-game lead and a magic number of seven.

Seven was unlucky.

The Phillies stayed there for what seemed like months. It was actually only about a week. But during that period the Phils lost every game they played while the Cards and Reds won every one of their games. The Phils' losing streak reached 10 at a time when the Reds won nine in a row, the Cards eight, and the Giants, who had been Philadelphia's main competition through most of the season, won seven of nine. The race became so tight that National League President Warren Giles was forced to work out details in case of a two-way, three-way, or even four-way tie.

Mauch has often been accused of giving the ball only to Bunning and Chris Short down the stretch. While there is no question that Jim (19–8) and Chris (17–9) were his only two reliable pitchers at that point, Mauch has been unfairly labeled as having used just two pitchers as starters over a 12-game period. What he had done was used Bunning and Short three different times each with only two days rest. Dennis Bennett got two starts and so did Art Mahaffey during that period.

In fact, Mahaffey pitched the best game of anyone in the 10-game losing streak. It was the first loss and, had the Phillies beaten the Cincinnati Reds that night, the race almost surely would have been over.

For the record, and at the risk of breaking Phillies fans' hearts one more time, here's how it came apart at the end of 1964:

SEPTEMBER 21—Cincinnati's Chico Ruiz steals home with Frank Robinson at bat in the sixth inning off Art Mahaffey, and the Reds beat the Phillies, 1–0.

SEPTEMBER 22—The Reds pound Chris Short for four third-inning runs on their way to a 9–2 victory.

SEPTEMBER 23—Vada Pinson smacks two home runs against Dennis Bennett as the Reds complete a three-game sweep at Connie Mack Stadium with a 6–4 victory.

SEPTEMBER 24—Joe Torre's three RBI are the difference as the Braves beat Jim Bunning, 5–3.

SEPTEMBER 25—Reliever John Boozer loses to Braves in the 12th inning, 7–5.

SEPTEMBER 26—Rico Carty's three-run triple off reliever Bobby Shantz in the ninth beats the Phils, 6–4.

SEPTEMBER 27—Callison hits three home runs but the Braves pound Bunning in 14–8 victory for a four-game series sweep at Connie Mack Stadium. Phils trail Reds by one game, lead Cards by one-half.

SEPTEMBER 28—Phillies fall to third place in St. Louis as Bob Gibson outpitches Chris Short, 5–1.

SEPTEMBER 29—Ray Sadecki tops Dennis Bennett in 4–2 Cardinal victory.

SEPTEMBER 30—Former Phillie Curt Simmons hands the team its 10th straight loss with 8–5 victory over Bunning.

OCTOBER 1—Day off.

On October 2, Mauch started Short, but Ed Roebuck got credit for a 4–3 victory over Cincinnati. And when the Phils and Cincinnati sat idly by on Saturday, October 3, and watched the Mets knock off the Cards again, the Phillies had new life. They trailed the Cards and Reds by one game. If they could beat Cincy on Sunday and the Mets could knock off the Cards again, the first three-way tie in major league history would be the result.

The Phillies did their part, stomping the Reds, 10–0, behind Bunning's shutout pitching and Allen's slugging. But the Cards beat the Mets handily and took the 1964 pennant.

Philadelphia fans, an ever-optimistic lot, couldn't wait for next year. Unfortunately, the front office at Mauch's request began to trade prospects for veterans, trying to get the present pennant at the risk of bankrupting the future.

It was a philosophy that worked for George Allen in football. It failed miserably for Mauch and Quinn.

Gene Mauch said Frank Thomas' thumb injury in September 1964 was the main reason the Phillies didn't win the pennant.

1965

Record: 85–76
Finish: Sixth
Games Behind: 11½
Manager: Gene Mauch

Dick Stuart. Bo Belinsky. Ray Herbert.

Those were the three new faces that the Phillies made deals to get. Manager Gene Mauch liked Stuart's home run bat, Belinsky's live arm, and Herbert's pitching guile.

But nobody liked Dr. Strangeglove, which is what Stuart was called when he pulled on his first baseman's mitt. And nobody could tame the wildness that was Belinsky's nature. And everybody could figure out Herbert's assortment of junkballs.

Stuart hit .234 with 28 home runs and 95 RBI after coming to the Phillies for pitcher Dennis Bennett. Stuart was gone before the next season began.

Belinsky won four of 13 decisions, argued constantly with Mauch, and was released to the San Diego team in the Pacific Coast League early the following season.

Herbert gave up 162 hits in 131 innings, was 5–8, stuck around one more year, and retired at the age of 37.

And, although John Callison (32 HR, 101 RBI), Dick Allen (20 HR, 85 RBI, .302), Jim Bunning (19–9), Chris Short (18–11), and Ray Culp (14–10) had good seasons, the Phillies sank all the way to sixth place in the National League.

It was also the year of the Dick Allen–Frank Thomas fight. Thomas was needling Allen during batting practice on July 3. Allen motioned to Thomas to fight; Thomas hit Allen on the shoulder with a bat and was released after the game, in which he ironically hit the game-winning home run.

	W	L	G	GS	CG	IP	H	BB	K	ERA
Jack Baldschun	5	8	65	0	0	99	102	42	81	3.82
Bo Belinsky	4	9	30	14	3	110	103	48	71	4.83
Jim Bunning	19	9	39	39	15	291	253	62	260	2.60
Lew Burdette	3	3	19	9	1	71	95	17	23	5.45
Ray Culp	14	10	33	30	11	204	188	78	134	3.22
Ryne Duren	0	0	6	0	0	11	10	4	6	3.27
Ray Herbert	5	8	25	19	4	131	162	19	51	3.85
Grant Jackson	1	1	6	2	0	14	17	5	15	7.07
Fergy Jenkins	2	1	7	0	0	12	7	2	10	2.25
Art Mahaffey	2	5	22	9	1	71	82	32	52	6.21
Ed Roebuck	5	3	44	0	0	50	55	15	29	3.42
Chris Short	18	11	47	40	15	297	260	89	237	2.82
Morrie Steevens	0	1	6	0	0	3	5	4	3	15.00
Gary Wagner	7	7	59	0	0	105	87	49	91	3.00
	85	76		162	50	1,469	1,426	466	1,071	3.53

Shutouts: Bunning (7), Short (5), Culp (2), Herbert

	G	AB	R	H	2B	3B	HR	RBI	SB	AVG
Dick Allen (3B)	161	619	93	187	31	14	20	85	15	.302
Ruben Amaro	118	184	26	39	7	0	0	15	1	.212
Johnny Briggs	93	229	47	54	9	4	4	23	3	.236
Johnny Callison (RF)	160	619	93	162	25	(16)	32	101	6	.262
Pat Corrales	63	174	16	39	8	1	2	15	0	.224
Wes Covington	101	235	27	58	10	1	15	45	0	.247
Clay Dalrymple (C)	103	301	14	64	5	5	4	23	0	.213
Bobby Del Greco	8	4	1	0	0	0	0	0	0	.000
Tony Gonzales (CF)	108	370	48	109	19	1	13	41	3	.295
John Herrnstein	63	85	8	17	2	0	1	5	0	.200
Alex Johnson (LF)	97	262	27	77	9	3	8	28	4	.294
Adolfo Phillips	41	87	14	20	4	0	3	5	3	.230
Cookie Rojas	142	521	78	158	25	3	3	42	5	.303
Bill Sorrell	10	13	2	5	0	0	1	2	0	.385
Dick Stuart (1B)	149	538	53	126	19	1	28	95	1	.234
Tony Taylor (2B)	106	323	41	74	14	3	3	27	5	.229
Frank Thomas	35	77	7	20	4	0	1	7	0	.260
Gus Triandos	30	82	3	14	2	0	0	4	0	.171
Bobby Wine (SS)	139	394	31	90	8	1	5	33	0	.228
		5,528	654	1,380	205	53	144	608	46	.250

The team, however, finished just 11½ games behind the champion Los Angeles Dodgers and only 4½ in back of the third-place Pittsburgh Pirates.

The logic was this: A couple more veteran players, more professional than the freewheeling Stuart and the freedom-loving Belinsky, and the National League pennant would fly over Connie Mack Stadium once more.

The first shock waves were heard in late October 1965, shortly after the World Series. The Phillies and the St. Louis Cardinals made the deal. Veterans for prospects. To Philadelphia came one of baseball's top first basemen, Bill White, and shortstop Dick Groat along with catcher Bob Uecker. In White and Groat, Mauch got himself a couple of consummate professionals. Both went about their work with an attitude that approached reverence. And while Uecker couldn't hit for average, his bat had some sting in it—seven HR, 30 RBI in 207 at bats. The price for the trio: Alex Johnson, Art Mahaffey, and Pat Corrales. The Cardinals said Alex Johnson was the key. For them, the trade was a flop.

1966

Record: 87–75
Finish: Fourth
Games Behind: 8
Manager: Gene Mauch

	W	L	G	GS	CG	IP	H	BB	K	ERA
Bo Belinsky	0	2	9	1	0	15	14	5	8	3.00
John Boozer	0	0	2	2	0	5	8	3	5	7.20
Bob Buhl	6	8	32	18	1	132	156	39	59	4.77
Jim Bunning	19	14	43	(41)	16	314	260	55	252	2.41
Roger Craig	2	1	14	0	0	32	31	5	13	5.48
Ray Culp	7	4	34	12	1	111	106	53	100	5.03
Terry Fox	3	2	36	0	0	44	57	17	22	4.50
Ray Herbert	2	5	23	2	0	50	55	14	15	4.32
Grant Jackson	0	0	2	0	0	2	2	3	0	4.50
Larry Jackson	15	13	35	33	12	247	243	58	107	2.99
Fergy Jenkins	0	0	1	0	0	2	3	1	2	4.50
Darold Knowles	6	5	69	0	0	100	98	46	88	3.06
John Morris	1	1	13	0	0	14	15	3	8	5.14
Steve Ridzik	0	0	2	0	0	2	5	1	0	9.00
Ed Roebuck	0	2	6	0	0	6	9	2	5	6.00
Chris Short	20	10	42	39	19	272	257	68	177	3.54
Joe Verbanic	1	1	17	0	0	14	12	10	7	5.14
Gary Wagner	0	1	5	1	0	6	8	5	2	9.00
Rick Wise	5	6	22	13	3	99	100	24	58	3.73
	87	75		162	(52)	1,460	1,439	412	928	3.57

Shutouts: Bunning (5), L. Jackson (5), Short (4)

	G	AB	R	H	2B	3B	HR	RBI	SB	AVG
Dick Allen (3B)	141	524	112	166	25	10	40	110	10	.317
Jackie Brandt	82	164	16	41	6	1	1	15	0	.250
Johnny Briggs (CF)	81	255	43	72	13	5	10	23	3	.282
Johnny Callison (RF)	155	612	93	169	(40)	7	11	55	8	.276
Doug Clemens	79	121	10	31	1	0	1	15	1	.256
Clay Dalrymple (C)	114	331	30	81	13	3	4	39	0	.245
Tony Gonzalez (LF)	132	384	53	110	20	4	6	40	2	.286
Dick Groat (SS)	155	584	58	152	21	4	2	53	2	.260
John Herrnstein	4	10	0	1	0	0	0	1	0	.100
Harvey Kuenn	86	159	15	47	9	0	0	15	0	.296
Phil Linz	40	70	4	14	3	0	0	6	0	.200
Adolfo Phillips	2	3	1	0	0	0	0	0	0	.000
Cookie Rojas (2B)	156	626	77	168	18	1	6	55	4	.268
Jimmie Schaffer	8	15	2	2	1	0	1	4	0	.133
Gary Sutherland	3	3	0	0	0	0	0	0	0	.000
Tony Taylor	125	434	47	105	14	8	5	40	8	.242
Bob Uecker	78	207	15	43	6	0	7	30	0	.208
Bill White (1B)	159	577	85	159	23	6	22	103	16	.276
Bobby Wine	46	89	8	21	5	0	0	5	0	.236
		5,607	696	1,448	224	49	117	628	56	.258

Soon after the season began, Mauch decided he needed a strong third starter to go along with Bunning and Short. Again he picked an absolute pro. Larry Jackson came from the Cubs along with Bob Buhl, who would be the fourth starter. The cost was center fielder Adolfo Phillips, who was the key to the deal as far as Chicago manager Leo Durocher was concerned, first baseman John Herrnstein, and a lightly regarded pitcher whose fastball the Phillies considered suspect. His name was Ferguson Jenkins.

Mauch was convinced he had just traded for the pennant. He told the press after the Jackson deal: "Gentlemen, we just got a diamond and a ruby for three bags of garbage."

Jackson, the diamond, was genuine enough, but the ruby (Buhl) was aged beyond polishing, and one of the bags of garbage (Jenkins) wound up in the Hall of Fame. Still, it wasn't a bad trade for the Phillies. In the end, they were simply outdistanced eight games by a better ball club, the Los Angeles Dodgers.

One factor was the sudden hitting tailspin of John Callison, who dipped to 11 homers and 55 RBI while batting 612 times. Dick Allen had his biggest season as a Phillie with 40 HR and 110 RBI along with a .317 average, but Dick got help in the power department from White (22 HR, 103 RBI) and no one else.

Chris Short won 20 games for the first time, Jim Bunning won 19 for the third straight season, and Larry Jackson added 15 victories, but Ray Culp was next with just seven wins.

The Phillies' .982 fielding percentage was best in the league. The team was fundamentally sound, just not quite good enough.

But Mauch wasn't about to give up. With 11 games left, the Phillies were 11 behind the Dodgers. Mauch was asked about it. He stuck out his jaw defiantly and announced:

"We'll play for the tie."

1967

Record: 82–80
Finish: Fifth
Games Behind: 19½
Manager: Gene Mauch

It was now time to begin paying the price for robbing the farm system to trade for veterans. The veterans began to fade badly (Dick Groat) or get hurt (Bill White) or lose more games than they won (Larry Jackson). And, with the exception of Rick Wise (11–11), there was no help coming up from the minors.

This was also the year of the famous Dick Allen–versus–car episode. The car won. Allen was pushing it up the street near his home in Mount Airy when his hand broke through the headlamp. He nearly lost the use of his hand for good. His season, and the Phillies' hopes, were dashed.

Chris Short slipped to 9–11 although he pitched well. Jim Bunning was 17–15 with a 2.29 ERA. His season included five 1–0 defeats. Larry Jackson was 13–15.

The season was a disaster before it began. White, playing paddleball back in St. Louis, tore his Achilles tendon. When he returned to the team in May, he was still limping badly. He never hit stride, getting just eight home runs in 308 at-bats.

While Tony Gonzalez finished second in the batting race to Roberto Clemente with a .339 mark, Johnny Callison continued his batting slump. And nothing was more pathetic than those innings when the Phillies batted seven-eight-nine, meaning Clay Dalrymple (.172), Bobby Wine (.190), and the pitcher.

	W	L	G	GS	CG	IP	H	BB	K	ERA
John Boozer	5	4	28	7	1	75	86	24	48	4.08
Bob Buhl	0	0	3	0	0	3	6	2	1	12.00
Jim Bunning	17	15	40	(40)	16	(302)	241	73	(253)	2.29
Dick Ellsworth	6	7	32	21	3	125	152	36	45	4.39
Dick Farrell	9	6	50	1	0	92	76	15	68	2.05
Dallas Green	0	0	8	0	0	15	25	6	12	9.00
Ruben Gomez	0	0	7	0	0	11	8	7	9	4.09
Dick Hall	10	8	48	1	1	86	83	12	49	2.20
Grant Jackson	2	3	43	4	0	84	86	43	83	3.86
Larry Jackson	13	15	40	37	11	262	242	54	139	3.09
Larry Loughlin	0	0	3	0	0	5	9	4	5	16.20
Pedro Ramos	0	0	6	0	0	8	14	8	1	9.00
Cookie Rojas	0	0	1	0	0	1	1	0	0	0.00
Chris Short	9	11	29	26	8	199	163	74	142	2.40
Dick Thoenen	0	0	1	0	0	1	2	0	0	9.00
Gary Wagner	0	0	1	0	0	2	1	0	1	0.00
Rick Wise	11	11	36	25	6	181	177	46	111	3.28
	82	80		162	46	1,453	1,372	403	967	3.10

Shutouts: Bunning (6), L. Jackson (4), Wise (3), Short (2), Ellsworth

	G	AB	R	H	2B	3B	HR	RBI	SB	AVG
Dick Allen (3B)	122	463	89	142	31	10	23	77	20	.307
Jackie Brandt	16	19	1	2	1	0	0	1	0	.105
Johnny Briggs (CF)	106	332	47	77	12	4	9	30	3	.232
Johnny Callison (RF)	149	556	62	145	30	5	14	64	6	.261
Doug Clemens	69	73	2	13	5	0	0	4	0	.178
Billy Cowan	34	59	11	9	0	0	3	6	1	.153
Clay Dalrymple (C)	101	268	12	46	7	1	3	21	1	.172
Tito Francona	27	73	7	15	1	0	0	3	0	.205
Tony Gonzalez (LF)	149	508	74	172	23	9	9	59	10	.339
Dick Groat	10	26	3	3	0	0	0	1	0	.115
Terry Harmon	2	0	0	0	0	0	0	0	0	.000
Chuck Hiller	31	43	4	13	1	0	0	2	0	.302
Rick Joseph	17	41	4	9	2	0	1	5	0	.220
Phil Linz	23	18	4	4	2	0	1	5	0	.222
Don Lock	112	313	46	79	13	1	14	51	9	.252
Gene Oliver	85	263	29	59	16	0	7	34	2	.224
Cookie Rojas (2B)	147	528	60	137	21	2	4	45	8	.259
Jimmie Schaffer	2	2	1	0	0	0	0	0	0	.000
Gary Sutherland	103	231	23	57	12	1	1	19	0	.247
Tony Taylor	132	462	55	110	16	6	2	34	10	.238
Bob Uecker	18	35	3	6	2	0	0	7	0	.171
Bill White (1B)	110	308	29	77	6	2	8	33	6	.250
Bobby Wine (SS)	135	363	27	69	12	5	2	28	3	.190
		5,401	612	1,306	221	47	103	553	79	.242

The Dick Allen–Gene Mauch fight went from simmer to boil, cost Mauch his job, and turned the fans against Allen worse than ever.

It began in spring training when Allen took off and flew home without permission. He returned two days later and was fined.

On April 30 he overslept and missed the team bus from Philadelphia to New York, then got caught in New York traffic and arrived at Shea Stadium late for the game. Mauch benched him.

Then, on May 29, Allen pulled a muscle while horseback riding and was taken out of the Phillies' lineup by Mauch. Two weeks later he announced that he was ready to play and had, in fact, been ready to play all along.

By then, it was obvious that Mauch and Allen could not coexist peacefully. One of them had to go. On June 14 owner Bob Carpenter made his decision. He fired Mauch and replaced him with Bob Skinner, who had been managing the Phillies' Triple-A team in San Diego.

The move did little to smooth over the relations on the team. It had been

1968

Record: 76–86
Finish: Seventh (tie)
Games Behind: 21
Managers: Gene Mauch, George Myatt, Bob Skinner

	W	L	G	GS	CG	IP	H	BB	K	ERA
John Boozer	2	2	38	0	0	69	76	15	49	3.65
Paul Brown	0	0	2	0	0	4	6	1	4	9.00
Larry Colton	0	0	1	0	0	2	3	0	2	4.50
Dick Farrell	4	6	54	0	0	83	83	32	57	3.47
Woodie Fryman	12	14	34	32	10	214	198	64	151	2.78
Dick Hall	4	1	32	0	0	46	53	5	31	4.89
Grant Jackson	1	6	33	6	1	61	59	20	49	2.95
Larry Jackson	13	17	34	34	12	244	229	60	127	2.77
Jeff James	4	4	29	13	1	116	112	46	83	4.27
Jerry Johnson	4	4	16	11	2	81	82	29	40	3.22
Chris Short	19	13	42	36	9	270	236	81	202	2.93
Gary Wagner	4	4	44	0	0	78	69	31	43	3.00
Rick Wise	9	15	30	30	7	182	210	37	97	4.55
	76	86		162	42	1,448	(1,416)	421	935	3.36

Shutouts: Fryman (5), L. Jackson (2), Short (2), James, Wise

	G	AB	R	H	2B	3B	HR	RBI	SB	AVG
Dick Allen (LF)	152	521	87	137	17	9	33	90	7	.263
Howie Bedell	9	7	0	1	0	0	0	1	0	.143
Johnny Briggs	110	338	36	86	13	1	7	31	8	.254
Johnny Callison (RF)	121	398	46	97	18	4	14	40	4	.244
Doug Clemens	29	57	6	12	1	1	2	8	0	.211
Clay Dalrymple	85	241	19	50	9	1	3	26	1	.207
Tony Gonzalez (CF)	121	416	45	110	13	4	3	38	6	.264
Larry Hisle	7	11	1	4	1	0	0	1	0	.364
Rick Joseph	66	155	20	34	5	0	3	12	0	.219
Don Lock	99	248	27	52	7	2	8	34	3	.210
Don Money	4	13	1	3	2	0	0	2	1	.231
Bobby Pena (SS)	138	500	56	130	13	2	1	38	3	.260
Cookie Rojas (2B)	152	621	53	144	19	0	9	48	4	.232
Mike Ryan (C)	96	296	12	53	6	1	1	15	0	.179
John Sullivan	12	18	0	4	0	0	0	1	0	.222
Gary Sutherland	67	138	16	38	7	0	0	15	0	.275
Tony Taylor (3B)	145	547	59	137	20	2	3	38	22	.250
Bill White (1B)	127	385	34	92	16	2	9	40	0	.239
Bobby Wine	27	71	5	12	3	0	2	7	0	.169
		5,372	543	1,253	178	30	100	505	58	.233

26–27 under Mauch and was a 2–0 under acting manager George Myatt. Under Skinner, it went 48–59 to finish 10 games below .500.

The team finally reversed its trading policy before the season began, sending aging Jim Bunning to the Pirates for Woodie Fryman and young infielder Don Money, whom the Phillies called the key to the deal.

Except for Chris Short's 19–13 record and Allen's 33 home runs, there was little in this ball club to excite the fans. As a result, only 664,546 bothered to show up at Connie Mack Stadium. The high crime rate in the neighborhood and the lack of parking facilities were two of the problems. The boring team was a much bigger one.

1969

Record: 63–99
Finish: Fifth (East)
Games Behind: 37
Managers: Bob Skinner, George Myatt

Baseball was celebrating its 100th anniversary this season. The All-Star Game was played in Washington's RFK Stadium. The Phillies had one representative on the National League team, Grant Jackson. He warmed up in the bullpen late in the game but didn't play.

That's how far things had sunk, just five years after the Phillies had kicked away a sure pennant. In 1969 only the presence of the expansion Montreal Expos, managed by Gene Mauch, kept the Phils from sliding into last place.

Dick Allen and Bob Skinner were the new act in town. Allen missed a flight to St. Louis one morning, then missed the same flight the next morning. He missed one whole game and part of another. He arrived late at Shea Stadium once again. He moved out of the team's dressing area at Connie Mack

	W	L	G	GS	CG	IP	H	BB	K	ERA
John Boozer	1	2	46	2	0	82	91	36	47	4.28
Billy Champion	5	10	23	20	4	117	130	63	70	5.00
Dick Farrell	3	4	46	0	0	74	92	27	40	4.01
Woodie Fryman	12	15	36	35	10	228	243	89	150	4.42
Jeff James	2	2	6	5	1	32	36	14	21	5.34
Grant Jackson	14	18	38	35	13	253	237	92	180	3.34
Jerry Johnson	6	13	33	21	4	147	151	57	82	4.29
Barry Lersch	0	3	10	0	0	18	20	10	13	7.00
Lowell Palmer	2	8	26	9	1	90	91	47	68	5.20
Luis Peraza	0	0	8	0	0	9	12	2	7	6.00
Al Raffo	1	3	45	0	0	72	81	25	38	4.13
Chris Short	0	0	2	2	0	10	11	4	5	7.20
Gary Wagner	0	3	9	2	0	19	31	7	8	8.05
Billy Wilson	2	5	37	0	0	62	53	36	48	3.34
Rick Wise	15	13	33	31	14	220	215	61	144	3.23
	63	99		162	47	1,434	(1,494)	570	921	4.14

Shutouts: Jackson (4), Wise (4), Champion (2), Johnson (2), Fryman, Palmer
Saves: Boozer (6), Wilson (6), Farrell (3), Lersch (2), Raffo, Champion, Jackson, Johnson

	G	AB	R	H	2B	3B	HR	RBI	SB	AVG
Dick Allen (1B)	118	438	79	126	23	3	32	89	9	.288
Rich Barry	20	32	4	6	1	0	0	0	0	.188
Johnny Briggs (LF)	124	361	51	86	20	3	12	46	9	.238
Johnny Callison (RF)	134	495	66	131	29	5	16	64	2	.265
Terry Harmon	87	201	25	48	8	1	0	16	1	.239
Larry Hisle (CF)	145	482	75	128	23	5	20	56	18	.266
Deron Johnson	138	475	51	121	19	4	17	80	4	.255
Rick Joseph	99	264	35	72	15	0	6	37	2	.273
Don Lock	4	4	0	0	0	0	0	0	0	.000
Don Money (SS)	127	450	41	103	22	2	6	42	1	.229
Leroy Reams	1	1	0	0	0	0	0	0	0	.000
Scott Reid	13	19	5	4	0	0	0	0	0	.211
Cookie Rojas (2B)	110	391	35	89	11	1	4	30	1	.228
Vic Roznovsky	13	13	0	3	0	0	0	1	0	.231
Mike Ryan (C)	133	446	41	91	17	2	12	44	1	.204
Gene Stone	18	28	4	6	0	1	0	0	0	.214
Ron Stone	103	222	22	53	7	1	1	24	3	.239
Tony Taylor (3B)	138	557	68	146	24	5	3	30	19	.262
Dave Watkins	69	148	17	26	2	1	4	12	2	.176
		5,408	645	1,304	227	35	137	593	73	.241

Stadium and into a broom closet. He began scratching messages into the dirt around first base with his spikes.

Skinner was fired in mid-season, and George Myatt took over. Myatt was asked if he could handle Dick Allen. "God Almighty Hisself couldn't handle that man," Myatt said.

Neither could National League pitchers. Allen played first, batted 438 times, and crushed 32 home runs. Rookie Larry Hisle had 20 and John Callison 16. Utilityman Deron Johnson added 17.

The first three starting pitchers were adequate, as Grant Jackson finished 14–18, Woodie Fryman 12–15, and Rick Wise 15–13. After that, the pitching staff was a disaster.

In August the Phils recorded four consecutive shutout victories. Jerry Johnson and Fryman beat the Atlanta Braves, 7–0 and 6–0, respectively, and Jackson and Wise blanked the Houston Astros, 1–0 and 7–0.

At the end of the season, owner Bob Carpenter knew that changes had to be made. Despite his enormous talent, Allen would have to be traded. And a new manager would have to be found, one who could change the image and direction of the team. The Phillies would be moving to their new Veterans Stadium home after the 1970 season and it had to reverse the attendance trend in a hurry. In 1969 only 519,414 paid their way into Connie Mack Stadium, lowest season total for the Phillies since 1945.

As Willie Mays watches, Tim McCarver leaves the field with a broken hand suffered from a foul tip in May 1970. Moments later, Mike Ryan, who replaced McCarver at catcher, also broke his hand.

1970

Record: 73–88
Finish: Fifth (East)
Games Behind: 15½
Manager: Frank Lucchesi

The story wasn't even entered in the World Series record book about the Miracle Mets when the Phillies decided to make some headlines of their own.

On October 8, 1970, they called a press conference at the Philadelphia Marriott Hotel to announce a major trade. Dick Allen was being dealt to the St. Louis Cardinals—that was the immediate news that impacted Philadelphia. The far-reaching implications for baseball had to do with the players the Phillies were getting in return. One was Tim McCarver, who would eventually become Steve Carlton's personal catcher. Another was Curt Flood, one of baseball's finest center fielders.

It was Flood's inclusion in the trade that shook the very foundations upon which the game of baseball had been built. The reserve clause bound a man to a team that held his contract from the first day he signed until his final moment in the game.

Flood simply did not want to play in Philadelphia. The city had a decided racist reputation that was not totally unfounded. Flood challenged the reserve clause in the courts, and, although he lost, it opened the way for free agency and the escalation of salaries.

When the Phillies realized they could not sign Flood, they asked for and received compensation from the Cardinals in a limping first baseman with a fancy glove and a live bat. He was Willie Montanez, and he would become immensely popular.

Two weeks before the Allen-Flood-McCarver deal, which also sent Cookie Rojas and Jerry Johnson to St. Louis and brought Joe Hoerner and Byron Browne to Philadelphia, the Phillies had selected their new manager. He was Frank Lucchesi, a 19-year member of the Phillies' minor league organization. If ever the Phillies picked a man to clean up their image, Lucchesi was it. He visited sick kids in hospitals. He wept emotionally when he received an ovation

	W	L	G	GS	CG	IP	H	BB	K	ERA
Jim Bunning	10	15	34	33	4	219	233	56	147	4.11
Billy Champion	0	2	7	1	0	14	21	10	12	9.00
Woodie Fryman	8	6	27	20	4	128	122	43	97	4.08
Joe Hoerner	9	5	44	0	0	58	53	20	39	2.64
Grant Jackson	5	15	32	23	1	150	170	61	104	5.28
Mike Jackson	1	1	5	0	0	6	6	4	4	1.50
Bill Laxton	0	0	2	0	0	2	2	2	2	13.50
Barry Lersch	6	3	42	11	3	138	119	47	92	3.26
Lowell Palmer	1	2	38	5	0	102	98	55	85	5.47
Ken Reynolds	0	0	4	0	0	2	3	4	1	0.00
Dick Selma	8	9	73	0	0	134	108	59	153	2.75
Chris Short	9	16	36	34	7	199	211	66	133	4.30
Fred Wenz	2	0	22	0	0	30	27	13	24	4.50
Billy Wilson	1	0	37	0	0	58	57	33	41	4.81
Rick Wise	13	14	35	34	5	220	253	65	113	4.17
	73	88		161	24	1,461	1,483	538	1,047	4.17

Shutouts: Fryman (3), Short (2), Wise
Saves: Selma (22), Hoerner (9), Lersch (3), Short, Wenz

	G	AB	R	H	2B	3B	HR	RBI	SB	AVG
Del Bates	22	60	1	8	2	0	0	1	0	.133
Larry Bowa (SS)	145	547	50	137	17	6	0	34	24	.250
Johnny Briggs (LF)	110	341	43	92	15	7	9	47	5	.270
Bryon Browne	104	270	29	67	17	2	10	36	1	.248
Mike Compton	47	110	8	18	0	1	1	7	0	.164
Denny Doyle (2B)	112	413	43	86	10	7	2	16	6	.208
Doc Edwards	35	78	5	21	0	0	0	6	0	.269
Oscar Gamble	88	275	31	72	12	4	1	19	5	.262
Terry Harmon	71	129	16	32	2	4	0	7	6	.248
Larry Hisle (CF)	126	405	52	83	22	4	10	44	5	.205
Jim Hutto	57	92	7	17	2	0	3	12	0	.185
Deron Johnson (1B)	159	574	66	147	28	3	27	93	0	.256
Rick Joseph	71	119	7	27	2	1	3	10	0	.227
Joe Lis	13	37	1	7	2	0	1	4	0	.189
Greg Luzinski	8	12	0	2	0	0	0	0	0	.167
Tim McCarver (C)	44	164	16	47	11	1	4	14	2	.287
Don Money (3B)	120	447	66	132	25	4	14	66	4	.295
Willie Montanez	18	25	3	6	0	0	0	3	0	.240
Sam Parilla	11	16	0	2	1	0	0	0	0	.125
Scott Reid	25	49	5	6	1	0	0	1	0	.122
Mike Ryan	46	134	14	24	8	0	2	11	0	.179
Ron Stone (RF)	123	321	30	84	12	5	3	39	5	.262
Tony Taylor	124	439	74	132	26	9	9	55	9	.301
John Vukovich	3	8	1	1	0	0	0	0	0	.125
		5,456	594	1,299	224	58	101	553	72	.238

on opening day. Mostly, he took the attention away from a team that could barely play the game above the Triple-A level.

Chris Short went 9–16 and was on the downslide, and Jim Bunning, back for a second tour of duty, was 10–15. Rick Wise was the closest thing the Phillies had to a winning pitcher at 13–14, although Dick Selma was an overpowering reliever.

McCarver conducted himself professionally behind the plate until he broke his hand against the Giants on May 2 on a foul tip off the bat of Willie Mays. Later that same inning, Mike Ryan suffered exactly the same injury while tagging a sliding Willie McCovey out at the plate. Lucchesi patched with the likes of Mike Compton, Jim Hutto, Del Bates, and Doc Edwards.

Larry Hisle slumped terribly in center field as a second-year player, but Deron Johnson hit 27 home runs at first base. Tony Taylor batted .301. And the first seed of what would become the 1980 World Championship team was planted when Lucchesi put Larry Bowa at shortstop and refused to lift him even though he was hitting below .200 after two full months. Bowa responded with a .250 season. His development would become Lucchesi's finest legacy to the organization.

1971

Record: 67–95
Finish: Sixth (East)
Games Behind: 30
Manager: Frank Lucchesi

On April 10, 1971, an event that had been awaited for almost two decades came to fruition. Veterans Stadium, at Broad and Pattison in South Philadelphia, was opened. It was a moment many Philadelphians had become convinced would never happen. They seemed resigned to the fact that they would spend season after season watching the Phillies play terrible baseball in the musty old stadium at 21st and Lehigh.

One out of two ain't bad.

The stadium wasn't musty, but the team was awful enough to finish 4½ games behind Gene Mauch's expansion Expos. A pre-season deal with the Orioles in which they acquired Roger Freed was supposed to give them 20-plus home run power in the outfield. Freed hit the first Vet homer but had only five more for the season.

Larry Bowa proved for a second straight year that he was a defensive shortstop par excellence, and Deron Johnson powered 34 homers, including four in four at-bats over a two-game stretch. Willie Montanez, the replacement in the Curt Flood deal, played center field for the first time in his life, made several sensational defensive plays, and walloped 30 home runs with 99 RBI in a terrific rookie season. But, except for Rick Wise, who had a no-hitter among his 17 victories, the pitching was putrid. The crowds weren't. Lured by the new stadium, the Phillies were able to attract a team-record 1,511,223 patrons.

	W	L	G	GS	CG	IP	H	BB	K	ERA
Darrell Brandon	6	6	52	0	0	83	81	47	44	3.90
Jim Bunning	5	12	29	16	1	110	126	37	58	5.48
Billy Champion	3	5	37	9	0	109	100	48	49	4.38
Woodie Fryman	10	7	37	17	3	149	133	46	104	3.38
Joe Hoerner	4	5	49	0	0	73	57	21	57	1.97
Barry Lersch	5	14	38	30	3	214	203	50	113	3.79
Manny Muniz	0	1	5	0	0	10	9	8	6	7.20
Lowell Palmer	0	0	3	1	0	15	13	13	6	6.00
Ken Reynolds	5	9	35	25	2	162	163	82	81	4.50
Dick Selma	0	2	17	0	0	25	21	8	15	3.24
Chris Short	7	14	31	26	5	173	182	63	95	3.85
Wayne Twitchell	1	0	6	1	0	16	8	10	15	0.00
Billy Wilson	4	6	38	0	0	59	39	22	40	3.05
Rick Wise	17	14	38	37	17	272	261	70	155	2.88
	67	95		162	31	1,471	1,396	525	838	3.71

Shutouts: Wise (4), Fryman (2), Short (2), Reynolds
Saves: Hoerner (9), Wilson (7), Brandon (4), Fryman (2), Bunning, Selma, Short

	G	AB	R	H	2B	3B	HR	RBI	SB	AVG
Mike Anderson	26	89	11	22	5	1	2	5	0	.247
Larry Bowa (SS)	159	(650)	74	162	18	5	0	25	28	.249
Johnny Briggs	10	22	3	4	1	0	0	3	0	.182
Byron Browne	58	68	5	14	3	0	3	5	0	.206
Denny Doyle (2B)	95	342	34	79	12	1	3	24	4	.231
Roger Freed (RF)	118	348	23	77	12	1	6	37	0	.221
Oscar Gamble (LF)	92	280	24	62	11	1	6	23	5	.221
Terry Harmon	79	221	27	45	4	2	0	12	3	.204
Larry Hisle	36	76	7	15	3	0	0	3	1	.197
Deron Johnson (1B)	158	582	74	154	29	0	34	95	0	.265
Pete Koegel	12	26	1	6	1	0	0	3	0	.231
Joe Lis	59	123	16	26	6	0	6	10	0	.211
Greg Luzinski	28	100	13	30	8	0	3	15	2	.300
Tim McCarver (C)	134	474	51	132	20	5	8	46	5	.278
Don Money	121	439	40	98	22	8	7	38	4	.223
Willie Montanez (CF)	158	599	78	153	27	6	30	99	4	.255
Bobby Pfeil	44	70	5	19	3	0	2	9	1	.271
Mike Ryan	43	134	9	22	5	1	3	6	0	.164
Ron Stone	95	185	16	42	8	1	2	23	2	.227
Tony Taylor	36	107	9	25	2	1	1	5	2	.234
John Vukovich (3B)	74	217	11	36	5	0	0	14	2	.166
Rick Wise	39	97	14	23	2	1	6	15	0	.237
		5,538	558	1,289	209	35	123	522	63	.233

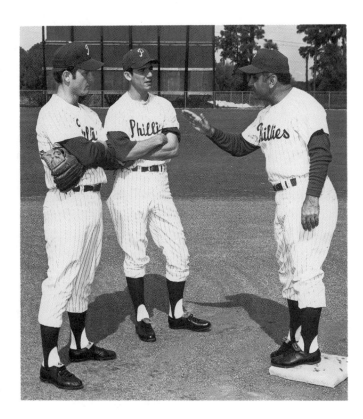

Manager Frank Lucchesi instructs the left side of his infield, third baseman Don Money (left) and shortstop Larry Bowa, in spring training of 1971.

These were the days when the owners still controlled the purse strings of baseball. There were two National League pitchers who wanted to get their fingers a little deeper into the till. One was Rick Wise, the only pitcher remotely resembling a star in the Phillies' system. The other was Cardinal Steve Carlton, who wasn't to be rewarded by Gussie Busch for winning 20 games in 1971.

Neither team would budge in its ceilings. When neither pitcher would stoop to the numbers, John Quinn called Bing Devine in St. Louis and suggested that they swap their reluctant hurlers. Devine agreed, the even-up swap was made, and the Phillies had finally gotten even for the Grover Cleveland Alexander deal over one-half century before.

If Larry Bowa was the first seed of the 1980 World Championship, Carlton was the most important. And it took him no time to prove what he was made of, as he put together perhaps the greatest season a pitcher has ever had under the circumstances.

The circumstances were that he was pitching for a wretched team. He won 46 percent of his team's 59 games (27–10). His earned run average was 1.98. He had 310 strikeouts and completed 30 of 41 starts. He won 15 straight decisions from June 1 to August 21. The streak was stopped by Phil Niekro and the Braves, 2–1, in 11 innings.

At the end of the season, the man called The Franchise was named the unanimous winner of the Cy Young Award.

More importantly from the front office viewpoint, his function was to draw attention away from just how bad the team was, just as Frank Lucchesi had in 1970 and the Vet had in 1971.

Lucchesi, meanwhile, had another chance to drop emotional tears. He was fired in mid-July and replaced by his old buddy Paul Owens, the general manager who wanted to look around and see what his team needed. He found out quickly—nearly everything. Wayne Twitchell looked like he might help, young left fielder Greg Luzinski (.281, 18 HR, 68 RBI) was on his way to

1972

Record: 59–97
Finish: Sixth (East)
Games Behind: 37½
Managers: Frank Lucchesi, Paul Owens

	W	L	G	GS	CG	IP	H	BB	K	ERA
Darrell Brandon	7	7	42	6	0	104	106	46	67	3.46
Steve Carlton	(27)	10	41	(41)	(30)	(346)	257	87	(310)	(1.98)
Billy Champion	4	14	30	22	2	133	155	54	54	5.08
Dave Downs	1	1	4	1	1	23	25	3	5	2.74
Woodie Fryman	4	10	23	17	3	120	131	39	69	4.35
Joe Hoerner	0	2	15	0	0	22	21	5	12	2.05
Barry Lersch	4	6	36	8	3	101	86	33	48	3.03
Jim Nash	0	8	9	8	0	37	46	17	15	6.32
Gary Neibauer	0	2	9	2	0	19	17	14	7	5.21
Ken Reynolds	2	15	33	23	2	154	149	60	87	4.27
Mac Scarce	1	2	31	0	0	37	30	20	40	3.41
Dick Selma	2	9	46	10	1	99	91	73	58	5.55
Chris Short	1	1	19	0	0	23	24	8	20	3.91
Bob Terlecki	0	0	9	0	0	13	16	10	5	4.85
Wayne Twitchell	5	9	49	15	1	140	138	56	112	4.05
Billy Wilson	1	1	23	0	0	30	26	11	18	3.30
	59	97		156	43	1,400	1,318	536	927	3.66

Shutouts: Carlton (8), Fryman (2), Downs, Lersch, Twitchell
Saves: Scarce (4), Selma (3), Hoerner (3), Brandon (2), Fryman, Short, Twitchell

	G	AB	R	H	2B	3B	HR	RBI	SB	AVG
Mike Anderson	36	103	8	20	5	1	2	5	1	.194
John Bateman (C)	78	252	10	56	9	0	3	16	0	.222
Bob Boone	16	51	4	14	1	0	1	4	1	.275
Larry Bowa (SS)	152	579	67	145	11	(13)	1	31	17	.250
Byron Browne	21	21	2	4	0	0	0	0	0	.190
Denny Doyle	123	442	33	110	14	2	1	26	6	.249
Roger Freed	73	129	10	29	4	0	6	18	0	.225
Oscar Gamble	74	135	17	32	5	2	1	13	0	.237
Terry Harmon	73	218	35	62	8	2	2	13	3	.284
Tommy Hutton (1B)	134	381	40	99	16	2	4	38	5	.260
Deron Johnson	96	230	19	49	4	1	9	31	0	.213
Pete Koegel	41	49	3	7	2	0	0	1	0	.143
Joe Lis	62	140	13	34	6	0	6	18	0	.243
Greg Luzinski (LF)	150	563	66	158	33	5	18	68	0	.281
Tim McCarver	45	152	14	36	8	0	2	14	1	.237
Don Money (3B)	152	536	54	119	16	2	15	52	5	.222
Willie Montanez (CF)	147	531	60	131	(39)	3	13	64	1	.247
Bill Robinson (RF)	82	188	19	45	9	1	8	21	2	.239
Craig Robinson	5	15	1	3	1	0	0	0	0	.200
Mike Ryan	46	106	6	19	4	0	2	10	0	.179
Mike Schmidt	13	34	2	7	0	0	1	3	0	.206
Ron Stone	41	54	3	9	0	1	0	3	0	.167
		5,248	503	1,240	200	36	98	469	41	.236

stardom, and Bill Robinson, rescued from the minors, seemed to get the key hit or make the key defensive play every time Carlton took the mound.

In September the Phillies brought some of their top minor leaguers up for a look. Two of them would become stars—third baseman Mike Schmidt and catcher Bob Boone.

1973

Record: 71–91
Finish: Sixth (East)
Games Behind: 11½
Manager: Danny Ozark

Paul Owens knew what he needed after spending a few months as field manager of the Phillies. Now the general manager went after it.

He needed starting pitching, so he made a deal with Milwaukee, giving up Don Money, who never quite lived up to expectations, and getting Ken Brett and Jim Lonborg. The third base job was inherited by Mike Schmidt, who had a good glove but struck out far too often, although he could put a charge into a pitch when he hit it.

Owens needed a first baseman, so he moved Willie Montanez back to his natural position. And he gave the Indians Oscar Gamble and Roger Freed for Del Unser, who could handle center field in a professional manner. Bob Boone became the regular catcher.

The Phillies were not quite ready for prime time, but they were getting closer. They approached Labor Day weekend only five games out of first place but soon became the sixth team in a five-team dogfight for the National League East title.

Danny Ozark, the new manager who would be much maligned later in his successful career, was credited for making the Phillies a far better team. He had spent the entire spring training drilling them in fundamentals, and the reward was 12 more victories than the previous year. In fact, the Phillies might have had a genuine shot at stealing the division title if Steve Carlton hadn't skidded from 27–10 to 13–20.

Brett, Lonborg, and Wayne Twitchell each won 13 games. Twitchell tore up his knee in September or he might have won 15. Brett set a record with home runs in four straight games in which he pitched.

Greg Luzinski and Bill Robinson supplied most of the power with 29 and 25 home runs. Schmidt batted only .196 but hit 18 homers and drove in 52 runs. He also struck out 136 times in 367 at bats, an alarming ratio. Unser batted .289, and Boone did a splendid job behind the plate for a rookie and hit .261 with 61 RBI.

It became obvious to baseball people that the Phillies were a team headed in the right direction. Philadelphians recognized it, too, as 1,475,934 went to the Vet, 132,000 more than the previous season when Carlton was the major attraction.

Not only did Ken Brett win 13 games in 1973, he set a record for a pitcher by hitting home runs in four straight starts.

	W	L	G	GS	CG	IP	H	BB	K	ERA
Darrell Brandon	2	4	36	0	0	56	54	25	25	5.46
Ken Brett	13	9	31	25	10	212	206	74	111	3.44
Steve Carlton	13	20	40	(40)	(18)	(293)	(293)	113	223	3.90
Larry Christenson	1	4	10	9	1	34	53	20	11	6.62
George Culver	3	1	14	0	0	19	26	15	7	4.74
Ron Diorio	0	0	23	0	0	19	18	6	11	2.37
Barry Lersch	3	6	42	4	0	98	105	27	51	4.41
Jim Lonborg	13	16	38	30	6	199	218	80	106	4.88
Dick Ruthven	6	9	25	23	3	128	125	75	98	4.22
Mac Scarce	1	8	52	0	0	71	54	47	57	2.41
Dick Selma	1	1	6	0	0	8	6	5	4	5.63
Wayne Twitchell	13	9	34	28	10	223	172	99	169	2.50
Dave Wallace	0	0	4	0	0	4	13	2	2	20.25
Mike Wallace	1	1	20	3	1	33	38	15	20	3.82
Billy Wilson	1	3	44	0	0	49	54	29	24	6.61
	71	91		162	(49)	1,447	1,435	632	919	3.99

Shutouts: Twitchell (5), Carlton (3), Brett, Ruthven
Saves: Scarce (12), Wilson (4), Brandon (2), Lersch, Diorio, M. Wallace, Ruthven

	G	AB	R	H	2B	3B	HR	RBI	SB	AVG
Mike Anderson	87	193	32	49	9	1	9	28	0	.254
Bob Boone (C)	145	521	42	136	20	2	10	61	3	.261
Larry Bowa (SS)	122	446	42	94	11	3	0	23	10	.211
Ken Brett	37	80	6	20	5	0	4	16	0	.250
Larry Cox	1	0	0	0	0	0	0	0	0	.000
Denny Doyle (2B)	116	370	45	101	9	3	3	26	1	.273
Jim Essian	2	3	0	0	0	0	0	0	0	.000
Billy Grabarkewitz	25	66	12	19	2	0	2	7	3	.288
Terry Harmon	72	148	17	31	3	0	0	8	1	.209
Tommy Hutton	106	247	31	65	11	0	5	29	3	.263
Deron Johnson	12	36	3	6	2	0	1	5	0	.167
Greg Luzinski (LF)	161	610	76	174	26	4	29	97	3	.285
Willie Montanez (1B)	146	552	69	145	16	5	11	65	2	.263
Jose Pagan	46	78	4	16	5	0	0	5	0	.205
Bill Robinson (RF)	124	452	62	130	32	1	25	65	5	.288
Craig Robinson	46	146	11	33	7	0	0	7	1	.226
Mike Rogodzinski	66	80	13	19	3	0	2	7	0	.238
Mike Ryan	28	69	7	16	1	2	1	5	0	.232
Mike Schmidt (3B)	132	367	43	72	11	0	18	52	8	.196
Cesar Tovar	97	328	49	88	18	4	1	21	6	.268
Del Unser (CF)	136	440	64	127	20	4	11	52	5	.289
		5,546	642	1,381	218	29	134	592	51	.249

1974

Record: 80–82
Finish: Third (East)
Games Behind: 8
Manager: Danny Ozark

Leadership . . . that was the next ingredient Paul Owens wanted to add to the Phillies. They needed a positive thinking player, a guy who under no circumstances would let them get down on themselves.

At the winter meeting, Owens thought of the perfect man, Dave Cash. He got the Pirate second baseman for Ken Brett, straight up, then tried to fill the pitching void by getting Ron Schueler from the Atlanta Braves.

This was the season in which Mike Schmidt was transformed from a suspect to a superstar. He led the league with 36 home runs, drove in 116 runs, and batted .282. The Phillies needed everything they could get from him, since Greg Luzinski tore up his knee in early June, didn't return to action until late August, and hit just seven home runs.

Cash led the league in at-bats (687), batted .300, and so inspired Larry Bowa that the shortstop lifted his average 64 points to .275. Willie Montanez had his first .300 season (.304), Unser did another nice job in center, and Boone dipped a bit at bat but was still more than adequate behind the plate. Mike Anderson took over in right field for Bill Robinson, who had a personality clash with manager Danny Ozark.

Steve Carlton rebounded to 16–13, and Jim Lonborg had a big year at 17–13. The other two starters, Dick Ruthven and Ron Schueler, were 9–13 and

	W	L	G	GS	CG	IP	H	BB	K	ERA
Steve Carlton	16	13	39	39	17	291	249	(136)	(240)	3.22
Larry Christenson	1	1	10	1	0	23	20	15	18	4.30
George Culver	1	0	14	0	0	22	20	16	9	6.55
Ron Diorio	0	0	2	0	0	1	2	1	0	18.00
Ed Farmer	2	1	14	3	0	31	41	27	20	8.42
Gene Garber	4	0	34	0	0	48	39	31	27	2.06
Jesus Hernaiz	2	3	27	0	0	41	53	25	16	5.93
Frank Linzy	3	2	22	0	0	25	27	7	12	3.24
Jim Lonborg	17	13	39	39	16	283	280	70	121	3.21
Pete Richert	2	1	21	0	0	20	15	4	9	2.25
Dick Ruthven	9	13	35	35	6	213	182	116	153	4.01
Mac Scarce	3	8	58	0	0	70	72	35	50	5.01
Ron Schueler	11	16	44	27	5	203	202	98	109	3.72
Erskine Thomason	0	0	1	0	0	1	0	0	1	0.00
Wayne Twitchell	6	9	25	18	2	112	122	65	72	5.22
Tommy Underwood	1	0	7	0	0	13	15	5	8	4.85
Dave Wallace	0	1	3	0	0	3	4	3	3	9.00
Mike Wallace	1	0	8	0	0	8	12	2	1	5.63
Eddie Watt	1	1	42	0	0	38	39	26	23	4.03
	80	82		162	46	1,447	1,394	682	892	3.91

Shutouts: Lonborg (3), Carlton
Saves: Watt (6), Scarce (5), Garber (4), Christenson (2), Hernaiz, Schueler

	G	AB	R	H	2B	3B	HR	RBI	SB	AVG
Mike Anderson (RF)	145	395	35	99	22	2	5	34	2	.251
Alan Bannister	26	25	4	3	0	0	0	1	0	.120
Bob Boone (C)	146	488	41	118	24	3	3	52	3	.242
Larry Bowa (SS)	162	669	97	184	19	10	1	36	39	.275
Ollie Brown	43	99	11	24	5	2	4	13	0	.242
Dave Cash (2B)	162	(687)	89	206	26	11	2	58	20	.300
Larry Cox	30	53	5	9	2	0	0	4	0	.170
Jim Essian	17	20	1	2	0	0	0	0	0	.100
Billy Grabarkewitz	34	30	7	4	0	0	1	2	3	.133
Terry Harmon	27	15	5	2	0	0	0	0	0	.133
Tommy Hutton	96	208	32	50	6	3	4	33	2	.240
Jay Johnstone	64	200	30	59	10	4	6	30	5	.295
Greg Luzinski (LF)	85	302	29	82	14	1	7	48	3	.272
Jerry Martin	13	14	2	3	1	0	0	1	0	.214
Willie Montanez (1B)	143	527	55	160	33	1	7	79	3	.304
Bill Robinson	100	280	32	66	14	1	5	29	5	.236
Mike Rogodzinski	17	15	1	1	0	0	0	1	0	.067
Mike Schmidt (3B)	162	568	108	160	28	7	(36)	116	23	.282
John Stearns	1	2	0	1	0	0	0	0	0	.500
Tony Taylor	62	64	5	21	4	0	2	13	0	.328
Del Unser (CF)	142	454	72	120	18	5	11	61	6	.264
		(5,494)	676	1,434	233	(50)	95	636	115	.261

11–16. Wayne Twitchell never came back fully from his knee injury and finished 6–9.

The Phillies led the National League East through much of the early going, were tied with the Pirates atop the division as late as August 1 and trailed by just 1½ games on August 21 before finishing third, eight lengths behind.

It also marked the first of four straight years in which the Phillies would break their own attendance record as 1,808,648 saw them play at the Vet.

T his was the year Danny Ozark refused to say die. If one date could be picked which changed Ozark's image among the fans of Philadelphia, it would be September 22, 1975.

That night Bruce Kison beat Tommy Underwood, knocking the Phillies seven games behind the Pirates with six to play. Afterward, D. Byron Yake, then the Pittsburgh AP bureau chief and later the sports editor for the entire AP system, asked Ozark how it felt to be out of it.

Danny responded with an incredulous look. Pressed on the matter, Ozark insisted that the Phillies were not out of it. "If we win all our games and they lose all theirs. . .," he began.

Later, he said he was only kidding, that he thought Yake was "some

1975

Record: 86–76
Finish: Second (East)
Games Behind: 6½
Manager: Danny Ozark

	W	L	G	GS	CG	IP	H	BB	K	ERA
Cy Acosta	0	0	6	0	0	9	9	3	2	6.00
Steve Carlton	15	14	37	37	14	255	217	104	192	3.56
Larry Christenson	11	6	29	26	5	172	149	45	88	3.66
Gene Garber	10	12	(71)	0	0	110	103	27	69	3.60
Tom Hilgendorf	7	3	53	0	0	97	82	38	52	2.13
Joe Hoerner	0	0	25	0	0	21	25	8	20	2.57
Jim Lonborg	8	6	27	26	6	159	161	45	72	4.13
Tug McGraw	9	6	56	0	0	103	84	36	55	2.97
John Montague	0	0	3	0	0	5	8	4	1	9.00
Dick Ruthven	2	2	11	7	0	41	37	22	26	4.17
Ron Schueler	4	4	46	6	1	93	88	40	69	5.23
Wayne Simpson	1	0	7	5	0	31	31	11	19	3.19
Wayne Twitchell	5	10	36	20	0	134	132	78	101	4.43
Tom Underwood	14	13	35	35	7	219	221	84	123	4.15
	86	76		162	33	1,455	1,353	546	897	3.82

Shutouts: Carlton (3), Christenson (2), Lonborg (2), Underwood (2)
Saves: McGraw (14), Garber (14), Acosta, Christenson

	G	AB	R	H	2B	3B	HR	RBI	SB	AVG
Dick Allen (1B)	119	416	54	97	21	3	12	62	11	.233
Mike Anderson	115	247	24	64	10	3	4	28	1	.259
Alan Bannister	24	61	10	16	3	1	0	0	2	.262
Bob Boone (C)	97	288	28	71	14	2	2	20	1	.246
Larry Bowa (SS)	136	583	79	178	18	9	2	38	24	.305
Ollie Brown	84	145	19	44	12	0	6	26	1	.303
Ron Clark	1	1	0	0	0	0	0	0	0	.000
Dave Cash (2B)	162	(699)	111	(213)	40	3	4	57	13	.305
Larry Cox	11	5	0	1	0	0	0	1	1	.200
Jim Essian	2	1	1	1	0	0	0	1	0	1.000
Larry Fritz	1	1	0	0	0	0	0	0	0	.000
Don Hahn	9	5	0	0	0	0	0	0	0	.000
Terry Harmon	48	72	14	13	1	2	0	5	0	.181
Tommy Hutton	113	165	24	41	6	0	3	24	2	.248
Jay Johnstone (RF)	122	350	50	115	19	2	7	54	7	.329
Greg Luzinski (LF)	161	596	85	179	35	3	34	(120)	3	.300
Garry Maddox (CF)	101	371	39	109	25	8	4	45	24	.294
Jerry Martin	57	113	15	34	7	1	2	11	2	.212
Tim McCarver	47	59	6	15	2	0	1	7	0	.254
Willie Montanez	21	84	9	24	8	0	2	16	1	.286
John Oates	90	269	28	78	13	1	0	24	1	.286
Mike Rogodzinski	16	19	3	5	1	0	0	4	0	.263
Mike Schmidt (3B)	158	562	93	140	34	3	(38)	95	29	.249
Tony Taylor	79	103	13	25	5	1	1	17	3	.243
		5,592	735	1,506	(283)	42	125	687	126	.269

bumpkin." He would have been better off letting it go without trying to excuse himself. He lost a bit of credibility and the fans never let him forget it.

Later, Ozark could remind people that during the following three years, the Phillies were never out of it in the National League East. But this year, they ran second most of the way. They grabbed a share of the lead on August 18 when they beat knuckleballer Phil Niekro, but they lost to the Braves the following night and never got back on top.

It was also the year that Dick Allen came back to Philadelphia. He played in his first game on May 14 and singled to center in his first at-bat before slumping to a career-low .233 with just 12 home runs.

Mike Schmidt led the league again with 38 home runs and Greg Luzinski topped the NL with 120 RBI while hitting 34 out of the park. Another early season deal sent popular Willie Montanez to San Francisco for Garry Maddox, baseball's best center fielder. Johnny Oates, who came from Atlanta with Allen, helped Bob Boone with the catching and batted .286. And the keystone combination really put on a show both defensively and offensively with Bowa batting .305 and Cash putting up the same numbers with 699 at-bats.

Larry Christenson, who had won his first start in the majors in 1973, then was shipped back to the minors, returned with an 11–6 record to help a staff led by Steve Carlton (15–14) and Tommy Underwood (14–13).

Owens was doing terrific work at reclamation. His best righthanded reliever was Gene Garber, who won 10 and saved 14 while appearing in a league-leading 71 games. Tug McGraw, who would be the World Series hero five years later, came from the Mets and was 9–6 with 14 saves.

And a couple of outfielders, Ollie Brown and Jay Johnstone, established themselves in right. Both hit over .300, and they combined for 13 home runs and 80 RBI.

1976

Record: 101–61
Finish: First (East)
Games Ahead: 9
Manager: Danny Ozark

The nation was celebrating its bicentennial, and Philadelphia was called the Cradle of Liberty. The celebration lasted all summer, and one of the highlights was the All-Star Game party.

Vice President Bill Giles rented an area of Independence Mall. The Liberty Bell and Independence Hall were in the background. The party was held on Monday, July 12, the night before the All-Star Game at the Vet. There was a Mummers band, hoagies, soft pretzels—everything that made Philadelphia famous. It was a truly festive occasion, as well it should have been.

The Phillies, who had made Philadelphia famous as losers, were winning big. At the All-Star break, they had a 10-game lead over the Pirates in the NL East. They were breezing to their first League Championship Series and their first post-season action in 26 years.

On August 24, Steve Carlton ran his record to 16–4 with a win over the Braves, and the Phillies were 15½ games on top.

What happened next was that the team went farther south than failed savings and loan stock. In little more than three weeks, the Phillies' lead was cut to three games over the Pirates. The Phillies were threatening to make 1964 seem like a routine loss of the pennant by comparison.

And that's all people wanted to do—compare. Tug McGraw, for one, said he thought it was ridiculous. "None of us were here in 1964," he said.

Tug had theories. One was that the Phillies had a chance to create history if the Pirates should pass them. No team had ever blown that big a lead before and still come back to win it, he reasoned. That was positive thinking.

There was also the Frozen Snowball theory.

"Fifty million years from now the earth will be a frozen snowball and nobody will care who won in 1976," he said. That was loosen-'em-up talk.

In the end, good baseball won it. The Phillies started winning, the Pirates started losing, and, just as suddenly, the Phils were breezing again.

On September 26, in the first game of a doubleheader, Jim Lonborg pitched the Phillies past the Montreal Expos, 4–1, to clinch the East. The

	W	L	G	GS	CG	IP	H	BB	K	ERA
Steve Carlton	20	7	35	35	13	253	224	72	195	3.13
Larry Christenson	13	8	32	29	2	169	199	42	54	3.67
Gene Garber	9	3	59	0	0	93	78	30	92	2.81
Jim Kaat	12	14	38	35	7	228	241	32	83	3.47
Randy Lerch	0	0	1	0	0	3	3	0	0	3.00
Jim Lonborg	18	10	33	32	8	222	210	50	118	3.08
Tug McGraw	7	6	58	0	0	97	81	42	76	2.51
Ron Reed	8	7	59	4	1	128	88	32	96	2.46
Ron Schueler	1	0	35	0	0	50	44	16	43	2.88
Wayne Twitchell	3	1	26	2	0	62	55	18	67	1.74
Tom Underwood	10	5	33	25	3	156	154	63	94	3.52
	101	61		162	34	1,459	1,377	397	918	3.08

Shutouts: Carlton (2), Lonborg, Kaat
Saves: Reed (14), McGraw (11) Garber (11), Schueler (3), Underwood (2), Lerch, Lonborg, Twitchell

	G	AB	R	H	2B	3B	HR	RBI	SB	AVG
Dick Allen (1B)	85	298	52	80	16	1	15	49	11	.268
Fred Andrews	4	6	1	4	0	0	0	0	1	.667
Tim Blackwell	4	8	0	2	0	0	0	1	0	.250
Bob Boone (C)	121	361	40	98	18	2	4	54	2	.271
Rick Bosetti	13	18	6	5	1	0	0	0	3	.278
Larry Bowa (SS)	156	624	71	155	15	9	0	49	30	.248
Ollie Brown	92	209	30	53	10	1	5	30	2	.254
Dave Cash (2B)	160	(666)	92	189	14	(12)	1	56	10	.284
Terry Harmon	42	61	12	18	4	1	0	6	3	.295
Tommy Hutton	95	124	15	25	5	1	1	13	1	.202
Jay Johnstone (RF)	129	440	62	140	38	4	5	53	5	.318
Greg Luzinski (LF)	149	533	74	162	28	1	21	95	1	.304
Garry Maddox (CF)	146	531	75	175	37	6	6	68	29	.330
Jerry Martin	130	121	30	30	7	0	2	15	3	.248
Bill Naharodny	3	5	0	1	1	0	0	0	0	.200
Tim McCarver	90	155	26	43	11	2	3	29	2	.277
John Oates	37	99	10	25	2	0	0	8	0	.253
Mike Schmidt (3B)	160	584	112	153	31	4	(38)	107	14	.262
Tony Taylor	26	23	2	6	1	0	0	3	0	.261
Bob Tolan	110	272	32	71	7	0	5	35	10	.261
		5,528	770	1,505	259	45	110	708	127	.272

regulars celebrated; the minor leaguers and subs played the nightcap. Dick Allen chose not to join the celebration. It brought about some bitter feelings among certain veterans.

On the final day of the season, Carlton beat the team that always gave him trouble, the New York Mets, for his first 20-win season since 1972, and the Phillies wound up nine games up on the Pirates with 101 victories, most in franchise history.

It was a team that got where it did on merit. Besides Carlton, great pitching was turned in by starters Lonborg (18–10), Larry Christenson (13–8), Tom Underwood (10–5), and, through the first half of the season, Jim Kaat (12–14). Relievers McGraw, Gene Garber, and newcomer Ron Reed were superb.

Allen hit 15 homers in 298 at-bats, Mike Schmidt led the majors for the third straight year with 38, including four in an 18–16 Phillies victory over the Chicago Cubs, Greg Luzinski had 21 with a .304 average, Dave Cash again led the league in plate appearances, Garry Maddox batted .330 and might have been the team MVP, Jay Johnstone hit .318, and Larry Bowa was a catalyst with his glove, mouth, and occasionally his bat all season long.

The Phillies won eight of 12 regular season games against the Cincinnati Reds, their LCS opponents. Sparky Anderson, the Cincy manager and ex-Phillies player, warned that the post-season was a different matter altogether.

"The World Series is fun," he said. "We've been to the World Series. That's the fun part. Getting to the World Series is the real pressure. And we've been through it before."

The Phillies hadn't. They lost three straight to the Reds and went home to prepare for next year. So did their 2,480,150 paying fans, first time in the history of the franchise that the two-million barrier was broken.

1977

Record: 101–61
Finish: First (East)
Games Ahead: 5
Manager: Danny Ozark

The Phillies stumbled out of the gate in 1977, looking like anything but a team that had won 101 games the year before. Their only solace early in the season was that they were running as much as 8½ games behind the Chicago Cubs, who had a history of petering out in August and September, no matter how good a start they had.

Once again as the trade deadline approached Paul Owens felt that he had to make a move to get the team a leadoff hitter with some speed. He found just what he wanted in St. Louis where Bake McBride was a part-time player with full-time capabilities. McBride was a lifetime .300 hitter. Owens put together a package of Tommy Underwood, Dane Iorg, and Rick Bosetti for Bake. Danny Ozark put McBride in right field and in the leadoff spot and the Phillies began to fly.

But the Cubs hung tough and still had a four-game lead when they eased their way out of the New York City blackout and into Philadelphia for a four-game series. The Phillies won three of four, including a Friday night twi-nighter that attracted 61,177 fans, and the pattern was set.

The Phillies finally took over first place for the first time with a win over the Los Angeles Dodgers on August 5 in the midst of a modern-record-tying 13-game winning streak, and never looked back. They won over the fast-closing Pirates by five games and equaled the team record for victories.

The pitching staff was carried by two starters and the bullpen. Steve Carlton had his best year since 1972 with 23–10, and Larry Christenson's 19–6 was a career best. Rookie Randy Lerch helped with 10–6, and Jim Lonborg came off the disabled list to go 11–4. The bullpen quartet of Tug McGraw, Ron Reed, Gene Garber, and Warren Brusstar combined for 29 wins and 46 saves.

	W	L	G	GS	CG	IP	H	BB	K	ERA
Warren Brusstar	7	2	46	0	0	71	64	24	46	2.66
Steve Carlton	(23)	10	36	36	17	283	229	89	198	2.64
Larry Christenson	19	6	34	34	5	219	229	69	118	4.07
Gene Garber	8	6	64	0	0	103	82	23	78	2.36
Jim Kaat	6	11	35	27	2	160	211	40	55	5.40
Randy Lerch	10	6	32	28	3	169	207	75	81	5.06
Jim Lonborg	11	4	25	25	4	158	157	50	76	4.10
Tug McGraw	7	3	45	0	0	79	62	24	58	2.62
Ron Reed	7	5	60	3	0	124	101	37	84	2.76
Manny Seoane	0	0	2	1	0	6	11	3	4	6.00
Tom Underwood	3	2	14	0	0	33	44	18	20	5.18
Dan Warthen	0	1	3	0	0	4	4	5	1	0.00
Wayne Twitchell	0	5	12	8	0	46	50	25	37	4.50
	101	61		162	31	1,456	1,451	482	856	3.71

Shutouts: Carlton (2), Christenson, Lonborg
Saves: Garber (19), Reed (15), McGraw (9), Brusstar (3), Underwood

	G	AB	R	H	2B	3B	HR	RBI	SB	AVG
Fred Andrews	12	23	3	4	0	1	0	2	1	.174
Tim Blackwell	1	0	1	0	0	0	0	0	0	.000
Bob Boone (C)	132	440	55	125	26	4	11	66	5	.284
Larry Bowa (SS)	154	624	93	175	19	3	4	41	32	.280
Ollie Brown	53	70	5	17	3	1	1	13	1	.243
Mike Buskey	6	7	1	2	0	1	0	1	0	.286
Barry Foote	18	32	3	7	1	0	1	3	0	.219
Terry Harmon	46	60	13	11	1	0	2	5	0	.183
Richie Hebner (1B)	118	397	67	113	17	4	18	62	7	.285
Tommy Hutton	107	81	12	25	3	0	2	11	1	.309
Dane Iorg	12	30	3	5	1	0	0	2	0	.167
Dave Johnson	78	156	23	50	9	1	8	36	1	.321
Jay Johnstone (RF)	112	363	64	103	18	4	15	59	3	.284
Greg Luzinski (LF)	149	554	99	171	35	3	39	130	3	.309
Garry Maddox (CF)	139	571	85	167	27	10	14	74	22	.292
Jerry Martin	116	215	34	56	16	3	6	28	6	.260
Bake McBride	85	280	55	95	20	5	11	41	27	.339
Tim McCarver	93	169	28	54	13	2	6	30	3	.320
Jim Morrison	5	7	3	3	0	0	0	1	0	.429
Mike Schmidt (3B)	154	544	114	149	27	11	38	101	15	.274
Ted Sizemore (2B)	152	519	64	146	20	3	4	47	8	.281
Bobby Tolan	15	16	1	2	0	0	0	1	0	.125
John Vukovich	2	2	0	0	0	0	0	0	0	.000
		5,546	(847)	(1,548)	266	56	186	(795)	135	(.279)

Greg Luzinski finished second in the MVP, losing after putting up a .309 average with 39 home runs and 130 RBI. Mike Schmidt had 38 homers and 101 RBI. McBride was a sensation with a .339 average, 11 homers, 41 RBI, and 27 stolen bases in 85 games. Garry Maddox slipped to .292 but drove in 74 runs. Free agent Rich Hebner took over first base for Dick Allen and batted .285 with 18 homers. Even Larry Bowa socked four homers, including his first grand slam. Ted Sizemore, who plugged the second base gap created when Dave Cash went the free agent route, batted .281 and led the National League second sackers in double plays (104).

The Phillies' front office privately said that this was the best team the franchise had ever assembled. And everyone felt quite confident after the Phillies beat Los Angeles at Dodger Stadium in the opener of the LCS. But what followed after the Dodgers evened the series at home were two of the most bizarre games in the history of the organization. Both were losses, and the Phillies could only look to next year again.

The Phillies led the National League East for the bulk of the 1978 season, even though they won 11 fewer games than they had in each of the two previous seasons. The race turned into a two-team affair down the stretch, with the Phillies and Pirates battling each other for first and second for the fourth consecutive season.

Once again, general manager Paul Owens put on his trader's hat as the June 15 deadline approached. He heated the trans-American phone cable for days before finally making a couple of deals on the last day possible.

1978

Record: 90–72
Finish: First (East)
Games Ahead: 1½
Manager: Danny Ozark

	W	L	G	GS	CG	IP	H	BB	K	ERA
Dan Boitano	0	0	1	0	0	1	0	1	0	0.00
Warren Brusstar	6	3	58	0	0	89	74	30	60	2.33
Steve Carlton	16	13	34	34	12	247	228	63	161	2.84
Larry Christenson	13	14	33	33	9	228	209	47	131	3.24
Rawly Eastwick	2	1	22	0	0	40	31	18	14	4.05
Gene Garber	2	1	22	0	0	39	26	11	24	1.38
Jim Kaat	8	5	26	24	2	140	159	32	48	4.11
Randy Lerch	11	8	33	28	5	184	183	70	96	3.96
Jim Lonborg	8	10	22	22	1	114	132	45	48	5.21
Tug McGraw	8	7	55	1	0	90	82	23	63	3.20
Horacio Pina	0	0	2	0	0	2	0	0	4	0.00
Ron Reed	3	4	66	0	0	109	87	23	85	2.23
Dick Ruthven	13	5	20	20	9	151	136	28	75	2.98
Dan Larson	0	0	1	0	0	1	1	1	2	9.00
Kevin Saucier	0	1	1	0	0	2	4	1	2	18.00
	90	72		162	38	1,436	1,343	393	813	3.33

Shutouts: Carlton (3), Christenson (3), Ruthven (2), Kaat
Saves: Reed (17), McGraw (9), Garber (3)

	G	AB	R	H	2B	3B	HR	RBI	SB	AVG
Bob Boone (C)	132	435	48	123	18	4	12	62	2	.283
Larry Bowa (SS)	156	654	78	192	31	5	3	43	27	.294
Jose Cardenal	87	201	27	50	12	0	4	33	2	.249
Todd Cruz	3	4	0	2	0	0	0	2	1	.500
Kerry Dineen	5	8	0	2	0	0	0	1	0	.250
Barry Foote	39	57	4	9	0	0	1	4	0	.158
Orlando Gonzalez	26	26	1	5	0	0	0	0	0	.192
Bud Harrelson	71	103	16	22	1	0	0	9	5	.214
Richie Hebner (1B)	137	435	61	123	22	3	17	71	4	.283
Dave Johnson	44	89	14	17	2	0	2	14	0	.191
Jay Johnstone	3 5	56	3	10	2	0	0	4	0	.179
Greg Luzinski (LF)	155	540	85	143	32	2	35	101	8	.265
Pete Mackanin	5	8	0	2	0	0	0	1	0	.250
Garry Maddox (CF)	155	598	62	172	34	3	11	68	33	.288
Jerry Martin	128	266	40	72	13	4	9	36	9	.271
Bake McBride (RF)	122	472	68	127	20	4	10	49	28	.269
Tim McCarver	90	146	18	36	9	1	1	14	2	.247
Keith Moreland	1	2	0	0	0	0	0	0	0	.000
Jim Morrison	53	108	12	17	1	1	3	10	1	.157
Mike Schmidt (3B)	145	513	93	129	27	2	21	78	19	.251
Ted Sizemore (2B)	108	351	38	77	12	0	0	25	8	.219
Lonnie Smith	17	4	6	0	0	0	0	0	4	.000
		5,448	708	1,404	248	32	133	661	152	.258

Dick Ruthven, who had originally signed with the Phillies but who had been traded to the White Sox, then the Braves, was an unhappy young man. He was pitching poorly, and the problem was compounded when Braves owner Ted Turner, according to Dick, made a pass at Ruthven's wife. Owens gave the Braves Gene Garber for Ruthven, then got a relief pitcher to replace Garber in Rawly Eastwick, a former Fireman of the Year who was virtually inactive in the Yankee bullpen. For Eastwick, Owens surrendered Jay Johnstone, who had been one of the most popular Phillies but whose value to the team had dropped dramatically when Bake McBride arrived the year before.

Eastwick never hit his stride, but Tug McGraw, Ron Reed, and Warren Brusstar gave the Phillies more than they needed out of the bullpen. Ruthven, meanwhile, won 13 of 18 decisions and pitched like a man who had been released from prison. Steve Carlton (16–13) and Larry Christenson (13–14) pitched much better than their records indicated. Randy Lerch won 11 games, including the clincher on the next-to-last day of the season. The Phillies, in Pittsburgh, had been swept in a Friday twi-nighter, cutting their lead over the Pirates to one-and-one-half games. On Saturday, Lerch hit two home runs and pitched the Phils to a 10–8 victory.

Greg Luzinski pounded 35 homers, but Mike Schmidt slumped to 21 and was booed by the fans all season. Ted Sizemore was hurt for much of the season and batted only .219. McBride slumped to .269. Bright spots were Larry Bowa (.294), Richie Hebner (.283, 17 HR, 71 RBI), and Bob Boone (.283). Garry Maddox continued to be baseball's best center fielder and hit .288, and Dave Johnson hit two pinch-hit, grand slam home runs, the only Phillies player ever to do that in one season.

The League Championship Series story was more of the same. The Phillies were booed roundly while losing the first two games at home, rallied to win game three in Los Angeles, then lost game four when Maddox, of all people, dropped a 10th-inning fly ball to set up the winning run.

1979

Record: 84–78
Finish: Fourth (East)
Games Behind: 14
Managers: Danny Ozark, Dallas Green

This was an exciting year for the Phillies because of some of the things that happened around the ball club.

It was also a disappointing season because of what happened on the field.

After three straight seasons of NL East championships, the Phillies settled back into fourth. The season, which began with so much promise, ended up costing Danny Ozark his job on August 31.

Dallas Green took over at that point, just as Paul Owens had done in 1972. Farm director Green wanted to take a look at the personnel, see what the team needed, what direction it required. Green wound up staying on and directing the Phillies to their first World Championship the following season.

The excitement had begun on December 5, 1978, when the Phillies, reportedly completely out of the running a week earlier, signed Pete Rose to a four-year contract as a free agent. Rose had said all along that he wanted to sign with the Phillies (Larry Bowa and Greg Luzinski were close friends), but the Phillies couldn't come up with the money until WPHL-TV agreed to kick in extra cash that it would make up with increased advertising revenue for the team's telecasts. Rose's package was for $3.2 million over four seasons.

Owens filled the second base spot with an All-Star, swapping Ted Sizemore, Jerry Martin, Barry Foote, and two minor league pitching prospects to the Cubs for Manny Trillo. Greg Gross and Dave Rader also came in the trade.

With Rose set at first base, Richie Hebner became expendable, so Owens sent him to the Mets for Nino Espinosa.

Through the early part of the season, the Phillies looked like they would

	W	L	G	GS	CG	IP	H	BB	K	ERA
Mike Anderson	0	0	1	0	0	1	2	0	2	0.00
Doug Bird	2	0	32	1	1	61	73	16	33	5.16
Warren Brusstar	1	0	13	0	0	14	23	4	3	7.07
Steve Carlton	18	11	35	35	13	251	202	89	213	3.62
Larry Christenson	5	10	19	17	2	106	118	30	53	4.50
Rawly Eastwick	3	6	51	0	0	83	90	25	47	4.88
Nino Espinosa	14	12	33	33	8	212	211	65	88	3.65
Jim Kaat	1	0	3	1	0	8	9	5	2	4.50
Jack Kucek	1	0	4	0	0	4	6	1	2	9.00
Dan Larson	1	1	3	3	0	19	17	9	9	4.26
Randy Lerch	10	13	37	35	6	214	228	60	92	3.74
Jim Lonborg	0	1	4	1	0	7	14	4	7	11.57
Tug McGraw	4	3	65	1	0	84	83	29	57	5.14
Dickie Noles	3	4	14	14	0	90	80	38	42	3.80
Ron Reed	13	8	61	0	0	102	110	32	58	4.15
Dick Ruthven	7	5	20	20	3	122	121	37	58	4.28
Kevin Saucier	1	4	29	2	0	62	68	33	21	4.21
	84	78		163	33	1,441	1,445	477	787	4.16

Shutouts: Carlton (4), Espinosa (3), Ruthven (2), Lerch
Saves: McGraw (16), Eastwick (6), Reed (5), Saucier, Brusstar

	G	AB	R	H	2B	3B	HR	RBI	SB	AVG
Mike Anderson	79	78	12	18	4	0	1	2	1	.231
Ramon Aviles	27	61	7	17	2	0	0	12	0	.279
Bob Boone (C)	119	398	38	114	21	3	9	58	1	.286
Larry Bowa (SS)	147	539	74	130	17	11	0	31	20	.241
Jose Cardenal	29	48	4	10	3	0	0	9	1	.208
Greg Gross	111	174	21	58	6	3	0	15	5	.333
Bud Harrelson	53	71	7	20	6	0	0	7	3	.282
Greg Luzinski (LF)	137	452	47	114	23	1	18	81	3	.252
Garry Maddox (CF)	148	548	70	154	28	6	13	61	26	.281
Pete Mackanin	13	9	2	1	0	0	1	2	0	.111
Bake McBride (RF)	151	582	82	163	16	12	12	60	25	.280
Tim McCarver	79	137	13	33	5	1	1	12	2	.241
Rudy Meoli	30	73	2	13	4	1	0	6	2	.178
Keith Moreland	14	48	3	18	3	2	0	8	0	.375
John Poff	12	19	2	2	1	0	0	1	0	.105
Dave Rader	31	54	3	11	1	1	1	5	0	.204
Pete Rose (1B)	163	628	90	208	40	5	4	59	20	.331
Mike Schmidt (3B)	160	541	109	137	25	4	45	114	9	.253
Lonnie Smith	17	30	4	5	2	0	0	3	2	.167
Manny Trillo (2B)	118	431	40	112	22	1	6	42	4	.260
Del Unser	95	141	26	42	8	0	6	29	2	.298
John Vukovich	10	15	0	3	1	0	0	1	0	.200
		5,463	683	1,453	250	53	119	641	128	.266

run away with the pennant. After 34 games, they were 24–10. But the 34th game, the 23–22 "shootout in Chicago," seemed to take everything out of the team. They lost 16 of their next 21 games and dropped into fourth place. And this year, Owens was unable to pull out a big deal at the trade deadline.

Trillo had been injured early in May when Dodger pitcher Rick Sutcliffe broke his forearm with a pitch. Manny missed 40 games. Greg Luzinski's average plunged to .252, and, even though Mike Schmidt hit the most home runs in a season in his career up to then (45), he batted just .253.

Steve Carlton won 18 games, and Espinosa added 14, but the other starters had off-years. Randy Lerch was 10–13, Larry Christenson 5–10, and Dick Ruthven, out much of the season with elbow trouble, 7–5. Ron Reed won 13 games in relief, but his ERA swelled to 4.15. McGraw, at 5.14, was even worse.

As for Rose, he was simply sensational. His .331 average was second best in the league, and he played a solid first base, his fifth regular spot in his major league career. Pete's arrival created a box-office stir. More people than ever bought tickets to see the Phillies. The official attendance at the Vet was 2,775,011, but in reality more than 3 million tickets were sold.

1980

Record: 91–71
Finish: First (East)
Games Ahead: 1
Manager: Dallas Green

The Phillies' team that bobbled coming out of the starting gate hardly had the look of a World Champion. Randy Lerch, the pitcher who had looked like such a great prospect a couple of years earlier, lost his first six decisions. Dick Ruthven broke even in his first 10 outings. Larry Christenson underwent elbow surgery at the end of May. Tug McGraw was just so-so before a bout with tendinitis sidelined him in July.

Pete Rose's average was about .300. Greg Luzinski was under .250. So was Bob Boone. Garry Maddox was nowhere near his .290 lifetime mark.

The team tasted first place by percentage points for two days in May, then slipped back, regained the edge by one-half game on July 12, then drifted aimlessly once again.

On the second weekend in August the Phillies were swept in four games by the Pirates. The losses dropped them six games out of first, putting them in third place behind the Montreal Expos and Pittsburgh Pirates. But right there the season turned around.

Between games of the Sunday doubleheader, manager Dallas Green exploded. Dallas's normal speaking voice can be mistaken for a public address

	W	L	G	GS	CG	IP	H	BB	K	ERA
Warren Brusstar	2	2	26	0	0	39	42	13	21	3.69
Marty Bystrom	5	0	6	5	1	36	26	9	21	1.50
Steve Carlton	(24)	9	38	(38)	13	(304)	243	90	(286)	2.34
Larry Christenson	5	1	14	14	0	74	62	27	49	4.01
Mark Davis	0	0	2	1	0	7	4	5	5	2.57
Nino Espinosa	3	5	12	12	1	76	73	19	13	3.79
Lerrin LaGrow	0	2	25	0	0	39	42	17	21	4.15
Dan Larson	0	5	12	7	0	46	46	24	17	3.13
Randy Lerch	4	14	30	22	2	150	178	55	57	5.16
Sparky Lyle	0	0	10	0	0	14	11	6	6	1.93
Tug McGraw	5	4	57	0	0	92	62	23	75	1.47
Scott Munninghoff	0	0	4	0	0	6	8	5	2	4.50
Dickie Noles	1	4	48	3	0	81	80	42	57	3.89
Ron Reed	7	5	55	0	0	91	88	30	54	4.05
Dick Ruthven	17	10	33	33	6	223	241	74	86	3.55
Kevin Saucier	7	3	40	0	0	50	50	20	25	3.42
Bob Walk	11	7	27	27	2	152	163	71	94	4.56
	91	71		162	25	1,480	1,419	530	889	3.43

Shutouts: Carlton (3), Ruthven, Bystrom
Saves: McGraw (20), Reed (9), Noles (6), LaGrow (3), Lyle (2)

	G	AB	R	H	2B	3B	HR	RBI	SB	AVG
Luis Aguayo	20	47	7	13	1	2	1	8	1	.277
Ramon Aviles	51	101	12	28	6	0	2	9	0	.277
Bob Boone (C)	141	480	34	110	23	1	9	55	3	.229
Larry Bowa (SS)	147	540	57	144	16	4	2	39	21	.267
Bob Dernier	10	7	5	4	0	0	0	1	3	.571
Greg Gross	127	154	19	37	7	2	0	12	1	.240
Orlando Isales	3	5	1	2	0	1	0	3	0	.400
Jay Loviglio	16	5	7	0	0	0	0	0	1	.000
Greg Luzinski (LF)	106	368	44	84	19	1	19	56	3	.228
Garry Maddox (CF)	143	549	59	142	31	3	11	73	25	.259
Bake McBride (RF)	137	554	68	171	33	10	9	87	13	.309
Tim McCarver	6	5	2	1	1	0	0	2	0	.200
Don McCormack	2	1	0	1	0	0	0	0	0	1.000
Keith Moreland	62	159	13	50	8	0	4	29	3	.314
Pete Rose (1B)	162	655	95	185	(42)	1	1	64	12	.282
Mike Schmidt (3B)	150	548	104	157	25	8	(48)	(121)	12	.286
Lonnie Smith	100	298	69	101	14	4	3	20	33	.339
Manny Trillo (2B)	141	531	68	155	25	9	7	43	8	.292
Del Unser	96	110	15	29	6	4	0	10	0	.264
Ozzie Virgil	1	5	1	1	1	0	0	0	0	.200
George Vukovich	78	58	6	13	1	1	0	8	0	.224
John Vukovich	49	62	4	10	1	1	0	5	0	.161
		(5,625)	728	1,517	272	54	117	674	140	.270

system. When he yells, it shows up on the Richter scale. This afternoon Dallas yelled louder than ever. He exhausted the book of obscenities as his words somehow drifted through the steel doors that separated the locker room from the corridor in Three Rivers Stadium.

During the second game of the twinbill, Green and reliever Ron Reed almost came to blows in the Phillies dugout. From there on, the team came alive.

Paul Owens got into the act, too. On September 1, before the Phillies were to play the Giants in San Francisco, he called a clubhouse meeting in which he lashed out at the Phillies. "The last month is Ruly Carpenter's and mine," he snarled at the team, which had reached the apex of its carping and pouting.

The Phillies responded. They beat the Giants that day on their way to a sweep and regained first place. But on the next to last Sunday of the season, they lost an 8–3 decision to the Expos and dropped one-half game behind Montreal in the standings.

The following night, the Chicago Cubs broke a 3–3 tie with two runs in the top of the 15th inning. The fans at the Vet booed the team terribly, but the Phillies came back and won the game with three runs in their half of the inning. In the clubhouse afterward, shortstop Larry Bowa could be heard over everything else. "Worse bleeping fans in baseball," he shouted.

The fans responded by booing Bowa for the rest of the season, the playoffs, and the World Series. Bowa responded with some of the best ball he ever played in a Phillies uniform. And the Phillies went into Montreal on Friday, October 3, for the final three-game series of the season; the two teams were dead even atop the National League East.

The Phillies had won 19 of their last 25 games with Mike Schmidt leading the way offensively, but on Friday morning Schmidt got out of bed feverish and weak from flu. So all he did that night was hit a home run and a sacrifice fly as Dick Ruthven won a 2–1 game, his 17th victory of the season.

The next day, rain delayed the start of the game for more than three hours, but 50,794 still showed up at Olympic Stadium and sat for the entire 11 innings before Schmidt broke their hearts with a two-run homer to give the victory to Tug McGraw. Bob Boone, 2-for-25 at the time, had singled home Bake McBride to tie the game in the ninth.

Schmidt's homer was his 48th, and his RBI were numbers 120 and 121, both figures topping the league. The Phillies were National League East champs once again and now had the Houston Astros standing in their path to the World Series. This time, they didn't stumble, beating Houston in five of the most memorable playoff games in baseball history. Six games after that, they were World Champions at last.

Steve Carlton had a brilliant season, going 24–9 with a 2.34 ERA. Ruthven was 17–10, and Bob Walk, recalled from Oklahoma City in late May when Christenson was shelved, was 11–7.

In a season in which none of the regulars, save Manny Trillo (.292) and McBride (.309, 87 RBI), was at the top of his game from a statistical standpoint, two rookies made their presence felt. Lonnie Smith batted .339 in 298 at-bats and stole 33 bases. Keith Moreland was Boone's backup catcher and batted .314.

McGraw was phenomenal down the stretch. Coming off the disabled list on July 17, Tug allowed just three earned runs in the next 52⅓ innings in the regular season, then was the pitching star in both the LCS and the World Series. And the Phillies were World Champions at last, to the delight of 2,651,650 fans who jammed the Vet during the greatest season in the history of the franchise.

The Phillies wouldn't have won the 1980 pennant if rookie Marty Bystrom hadn't won five September games.

1981

Record: 59–48
Finish: First (first half)
Third (second half)
Games Ahead: 1½ (first half)
Games Behind: 4½ (second half)
Manager: Dallas Green

If 1980 was sweet, 1981 was bittersweet. The players' strike, which was allowed to happen by the owners, lasted 50 days. As a result, the season was split in two, and baseball owners foolishly decided on a split season concept with a best-of-three mini-playoff to determine the division champions.

The Phillies' offense was in high gear before the strike. They had a one-and-one-half game lead on the St. Louis Cardinals when the strike was called on June 12.

In the game before the strike, Pete Rose tied Stan Musial's National League record for hits on June 10 against Nolan Ryan. The Phillies won the game, 5–4, on Garry Maddox's three-run homer with two outs in the eighth to insure first place with a 34–21 record. Pete then had to wait more than seven weeks to break Stan the Man's record, which he did on August 10 at the Vet with a single off Mark Littell in the eighth inning.

But something was missing after the end of the strike. The Phillies, and particularly manager Dallas Green, seemed to lack the enthusiasm they had exhibited before the walkout.

One player who was not affected by the layoff was Mike Schmidt. Had the season run its full course, he might have had his greatest year. As it was, he played in 102 games and had 31 homers, 91 RBI, and a .316 batting average.

In spring training, the Phillies had made a valuable move when they traded Bob Walk to the Atlanta Braves for Gary Matthews, an outfielder with a great bat and an attitude to match. Matthews had a splendid September and finished with a .301 average and 67 RBI.

Rose wound up with a .325 average, but Bake McBride had a disappointing

	W	L	G	GS	CG	IP	H	BB	K	ERA
Warren Brusstar	0	1	14	0	0	12	12	10	8	4.50
Marty Bystrom	4	3	9	9	1	54	55	16	24	3.33
Steve Carlton	13	4	24	24	10	190	152	62	179	2.42
Larry Christenson	4	7	20	15	0	107	108	30	70	3.53
Mark Davis	1	4	9	9	0	43	49	24	29	7.74
Nino Espinosa	2	5	14	14	2	74	98	24	22	6.08
Dan Larson	3	0	5	4	1	28	27	15	15	4.18
Sparky Lyle	9	6	48	0	0	75	85	33	29	4.44
Tug McGraw	2	4	34	0	0	44	35	14	26	2.66
Dickie Noles	2	2	13	8	0	58	57	23	34	4.19
Mike Proly	2	1	35	2	0	63	66	19	19	3.86
Jerry Reed	0	1	4	0	0	5	7	6	5	7.20
Ron Reed	5	3	39	0	0	62	54	17	40	3.10
Dick Ruthven	12	7	23	22	5	147	162	54	80	5.14
	59	48		107	19	960	967	347	580	4.05

Shutouts: Carlton
Saves: McGraw (10), Reed (8), Proly (2), Lyle (2), Christenson

	G	AB	R	H	2B	3B	HR	RBI	SB	AVG
Luis Aguayo	45	84	11	18	4	0	1	7	1	.214
Ramon Aviles	38	28	2	6	1	0	0	3	0	.214
Bob Boone (C)	76	227	19	48	7	0	4	24	2	.211
Larry Bowa (SS)	103	360	34	102	14	3	0	31	16	.283
Dick Davis	45	96	12	32	6	1	2	19	1	.333
Bob Dernier	10	4	0	3	0	0	0	0	2	.750
Greg Gross	83	102	14	23	6	1	0	7	0	.225
Garry Maddox (CF)	94	323	37	85	7	1	5	40	9	.263
Gary Matthews (LF)	101	359	62	108	21	3	9	67	15	.301
Len Matuszek	13	11	1	3	1	0	0	1	0	.273
Bake McBride (RF)	58	221	26	60	17	1	2	21	5	.271
Don McCormack	3	4	0	1	0	0	0	0	0	.250
Keith Moreland	61	196	16	50	7	0	6	37	1	.255
Pete Rose (1B)	107	431	73	(140)	18	5	0	33	4	.325
Ryne Sandberg	13	6	2	1	0	0	0	0	0	.167
Mike Schmidt (3B)	102	354	(78)	112	19	2	(31)	(91)	12	.316
Lonnie Smith	62	176	40	57	14	3	2	11	21	.324
Manny Trillo (2B)	94	349	37	100	14	3	6	36	10	.287
Del Unser	62	59	5	9	3	0	0	6	0	.153
Ozzie Virgil	6	6	0	0	0	0	0	0	0	.000
George Vukovich	20	26	5	10	0	0	1	4	1	.385
		3,665	491	1,002	165	25	69	453	102	.273

season. The outfielder had knee trouble all season and batted just 221 times.

Carlton appeared on his way to one of his best seasons when the players hit the bricks. He was 9–1 before the strike and finished 13–4. Ruthven's 12–7 record belied his high 5.14 ERA. Sparky Lyle made the most appearances out of the bullpen (48) but was generally ineffective. Tug McGraw and Ron Reed combined for seven wins and 18 saves.

The Phillies finished third in the second half of the season and met the Expos for the division championship, although the Cardinals had the best overall record in the NL East.

The Expos won the first two games in Montreal, but the Phillies won the next two in Philadelphia, the second on George Vukovich's dramatic home run. In the fifth game, Carlton faced Steve Rogers. This time, Rogers bested Carlton and got the key hits while shutting out the Phillies, 3–0, on six hits.

1982

The Phillies lost loud-spoken, tough-guy Dallas Green after the 1981 season when the Human Thunderstorm decided to join the Chicago Cubs as general manager.

He was replaced by Pat Corrales, soft-spoken but a tough guy, and a man who had two years' experience as manager of the Texas Rangers.

Corrales said at the press conference when he was reintroduced to Philadelphia (he had served as a Phillies backup catcher in the 1960s) that his biggest rule was his simplest: "Be on time." With Dick Allen no longer around, the players had little trouble with that one.

But their timing was a bit off during the season. They got out of the box slowly, and those who had criticized their major deal of the off-season had a field day. In this three-cornered deal with the Cardinals and the Cleveland Indians, the Phillies gave up Lonnie Smith, who wound up in St. Louis, and got catcher Bo Diaz from the Indians.

From the minute the deal was announced, the Phillies took flak. Diaz had a reputation as a malingerer who would let a hangnail sideline him for a month. Bo could catch, but he couldn't run. Smith could run, but he couldn't catch the ball in left field. Since the Phillies weren't exactly the Penn Relays in baseball spikes, the fans weren't thrilled by the trade. They turned the sports talk shows into one-way conversations, which intensified when the Phillies got off to their slow start.

The fans booed Diaz almost from his first at-bat. By late May, however, they were cheering him as he proved that he was a power hitter with a strong enough arm to occasionally make up for baseball's weakest staff (except for Steve Carlton) at holding runners on base.

The Phillies and Cardinals had been picked as a toss-up for second place behind Montreal, which some considered baseball's most talented team. But the Expos spent the season refusing to gain momentum, and on September 13 the Cards visited Philadelphia for a three-game series with the teams dead even.

On Monday night, Steve Carlton overpowered St. Louis. The Phillies had a full game lead. But the next night, Mike Krukow lost to the Cards when Darrell Porter drove in both runs and Bruce Sutter got Mike Schmidt to hit into a double play in a key, bases-loaded situation. The next night, the Cards beat John Denny to take the National League lead, and they never looked back.

Still, it was a good year for the Phillies. Carlton had another superb year at 23–11, and Krukow, obtained from the Cubs in the off-season, won 13. But Dick Ruthven slumped to 11–11 and lost his spot in the starting rotation after throwing his glove into the stands when he was lifted from an August game.

Diaz had a splendid year with 18 homers, 85 RBI, and a .288 season and, in the process, erased all doubts as to his durability.

Record: 89–73
Finish: Second (East)
Games Behind: 3
Manager: Pat Corrales

	W	L	G	GS	CG	IP	H	BB	K	ERA
Porfi Altamirano	5	1	29	0	0	39	41	14	26	4.15
Stan Bahnsen	0	0	8	0	0	13	8	3	9	1.35
Jay Baller	0	0	4	0	0	8	7	2	7	3.38
Warren Brusstar	2	3	22	0	0	23	31	5	11	4.76
Marty Bystrom	5	6	19	16	1	89	93	35	50	4.85
Steve Carlton	(23)	11	38	38	(19)	(296)	253	86	(286)	3.10
Larry Christenson	9	10	33	33	3	223	212	53	145	3.47
John Denny	0	2	4	4	0	22	18	10	19	4.03
Ed Farmer	2	6	47	4	0	76	66	50	58	4.86
Mike Krukow	13	11	33	33	7	208	211	82	138	3.12
Sparky Lyle	3	3	34	0	0	37	50	12	12	5.15
Tug McGraw	3	3	34	0	0	40	50	12	25	4.31
Sid Monge	7	1	47	0	0	72	70	22	43	3.75
Jerry Reed	1	0	7	0	0	9	11	3	1	5.19
Ron Reed	5	5	57	2	0	98	85	24	57	2.66
Dick Ruthven	11	11	33	31	8	204	189	59	115	3.79
	89	73		162	(38)	1,456	1,395	472	(1,002)	3.61

Shutouts: Carlton (6), Krukow (2), Ruthven (2)
Saves: R. Reed (14), Farmer (8), McGraw (5), Altamirano (2), Brusstar (2), Lyle (2), Monge (2)

	G	AB	R	H	2B	3B	HR	RBI	SB	AVG
Luis Aguayo	50	56	11	15	1	2	3	7	1	.268
Dick Davis	28	68	5	19	3	1	2	7	1	.279
Ivan DeJesus (SS)	161	536	53	128	21	5	3	59	14	.239
Bob Dernier	122	370	56	92	10	2	4	21	42	.249
Bo Diaz (C)	144	525	69	151	29	1	18	85	3	.288
Julio Franco	16	29	3	8	1	0	0	3	0	.276
Greg Gross	119	134	14	40	4	0	0	10	4	.299
Garry Maddox (CF)	119	412	39	117	27	2	8	61	7	.284
Gary Matthews (LF)	162	616	89	173	31	1	19	83	21	.281
Len Matuszek	25	39	1	3	1	0	0	3	0	.077
Bob Molinaro	19	14	0	4	0	0	0	2	1	.286
Willie Montanez	18	16	0	1	0	0	0	1	0	.063
Dave Roberts	28	33	2	6	1	0	0	2	0	.182
Bill Robinson	35	69	6	18	6	0	3	19	1	.261
Pete Rose (1B)	162	634	80	172	26	4	3	54	8	.271
Alejandro Sanchez	7	14	3	4	1	0	2	4	0	.286
Mike Schmidt (3B)	148	514	108	144	26	3	35	87	14	.280
Manny Trillo (2B)	149	549	52	149	24	1	0	39	8	.271
Del Unser	19	14	0	0	0	0	0	0	0	.000
Ozzie Virgil	49	101	11	24	6	0	3	8	0	.238
George Vukovich (RF)	123	335	41	91	18	2	6	42	2	.272
		5,454	664	1,417	245	25	112	624	128	.260

Pete Rose hit only .271 and questions were asked about his playing 162 games. Mike Schmidt was sidelined for two weeks with a rib cage muscle pull but still managed 35 home runs. The new shortstop, Ivan DeJesus, batted only .239 but had 59 RBI. Manny Trillo set records for most chances accepted and games played at second base without an error.

Rookie Bob Dernier stole 42 bases but had trouble hitting the outside pitch and wound up at .249; he was replaced by Garry Maddox, who had one of his most productive seasons, in center field. Gary Matthews had his typically solid season.

After the season, the Phillies made one of the biggest, and most controversial, trades in the franchise's history. To get Von Hayes, a great prospect from the Cleveland Indians, they packaged Trillo, who wanted a long-term contract for big dollars, right fielder George Vukovich, infield phenom Julio Franco, and two other prospects.

They also sent Krukow and prospects to the San Francisco Giants for Joe Morgan and Al Holland. The Phillies immediately were dubbed the Wheeze Kids.

I t started long before the season began. Pete Rose was already here, huffing and puffing toward Ty Cobb's record for most hits in a career. Tug McGraw was still here, telling everyone They Gotta Believe. Ron Reed was still here, the legs of an NBA power forward gone but the guts of a top-flight relief pitcher intact.

And here came Joe Morgan, a one-year stopgap at second base between the Latin connection called "Good-bye, Manny Trillo; Hello, Juan Samuel." And then came yet a third member of the former Big Red Machine (along with Morgan and Rose), a power-hitting first baseman named Tony Perez.

The nicknames began shortly thereafter.

First runner-up: "The Big Dead Machine."

And the winner: "The Wheeze Kids."

They were older than Philadelphians had come to expect from the team that 33 years earlier had been nicknamed "The Whiz Kids." Not older, better, the Phillies players insisted. Not better, older, argued the fans who chose either

1983

Record: 90–72
Finish: First (East)
Games Ahead: 6
Managers: Pat Corrales, Paul Owens

	W	L	G	GS	CG	IP	H	BB	K	ERA
Porfi Altamirano	2	3	31	0	0	41	38	15	24	3.70
Larry Andersen	1	0	17	0	0	26	19	9	14	2.39
Marty Bystrom	6	9	24	23	1	119	136	44	87	4.60
Steve Carlton	15	16	37	37	8	(284)	277	84	(275)	3.11
Don Carman	0	0	1	0	0	1	0	0	0	0.00
Larry Christenson	2	4	9	9	0	48	42	17	44	3.91
Steve Comer	1	0	3	1	0	9	11	3	1	5.19
John Denny	(19)	6	36	36	7	243	229	53	139	2.37
Ed Farmer	0	6	12	3	0	27	35	20	16	6.08
Tony Ghelfi	1	1	3	3	0	14	15	6	14	3.14
Kevin Gross	4	6	17	17	1	96	100	35	66	3.56
Willie Hernandez	8	4	63	0	0	96	93	26	75	3.29
Al Holland	8	4	68	0	0	92	63	30	100	2.26
Charles Hudson	8	8	26	26	3	169	158	53	101	3.35
Tug McGraw	2	1	34	1	0	56	58	19	30	3.56
Sid Monge	3	0	14	0	0	12	20	6	7	6.94
Ron Reed	9	1	61	0	0	96	89	34	73	3.48
Dick Ruthven	1	3	7	7	0	34	46	10	26	5.61
	90	72		163	20	1,462	1,429	464	(1,092)	3.34

Shutouts: Carlton (3), Bystrom, Denny, Gross
Saves: Holland (25), Reed (8), Hernandez (7), Carman

	G	AB	R	H	2B	3B	HR	RBI	SB	AVG
Luis Aguayo	2	4	1	0	0	0	0	0	0	.250
Tim Corcoran	3	0	0	0	0	0	0	0	0	.000
Darren Daulton	2	3	1	1	0	0	0	0	0	.333
Ivan DeJesus (SS)	158	497	60	126	15	7	4	45	11	.254
Bob Dernier	122	221	41	51	10	0	1	15	35	.231
Bo Diaz (C)	136	471	49	111	17	0	15	64	1	.236
Kiko Garcia	84	118	22	34	7	1	2	9	1	.288
Greg Gross	136	245	25	74	12	3	0	29	3	.302
Von Hayes (RF)	124	351	45	93	9	5	6	32	20	.265
Steve Jeltz	13	8	0	1	0	1	0	1	0	.125
Joe Lefebvre	101	258	34	80	20	8	8	38	5	.310
Sixto Lezcano	18	39	8	11	1	0	0	7	1	.282
Garry Maddox (CF)	97	324	27	89	14	2	4	32	7	.275
Gary Matthews (LF)	132	446	66	115	18	2	10	50	13	.258
Len Matuszek	28	80	12	22	6	1	4	16	0	.275
Larry Milbourne	41	66	3	16	0	1	0	4	2	.242
Bob Molinaro	19	18	1	2	1	0	1	3	0	.111
Joe Morgan (2B)	123	404	72	93	20	1	16	59	18	.230
Tony Perez	91	253	18	61	11	2	6	43	1	.241
Bill Robinson	10	7	0	1	0	0	0	2	0	.143
Pete Rose (1B)	151	493	52	121	14	3	0	45	7	.245
Juan Samuel	18	65	14	18	1	2	2	5	3	.277
Al Sanchez	8	7	2	2	0	0	0	2	0	.286
Mike Schmidt (3B)	154	534	104	136	16	4	(40)	109	7	.255
Jeff Stone	9	4	2	3	0	2	0	3	4	.750
Ozzie Virgil	55	140	11	30	7	0	6	23	0	.214
		5,426	696	1,352	209	45	125	649	143	.249

Hall of Famer Joe Morgan's hot September bat carried the Phillies to the 1983 pennant.

to watch the games on television, listen to them on radio on the beach, or take a vacation from everything, including the TV and radio. The paid attendance for the year was a disappointing 2,095,055.

The Phillies came away from the gate decently, but quickly went off stride. Fortunately for them, so did the rest of the National League East. In a mile race that went to the quarter pole with no one assuming anything that could be called command, the Phillies ran with the pack. And when Paul Owens went to the whip after replacing Pat Corrales at mid-season, the Phils responded magnificently.

In fact, they never wheezed. When they were supposed to run out of gas, they acted like the former Big Red Machine running on one last tankful.

They won 11 in a row, 14 of their last 16, clinched the National League East pennant on September 28 as former Cub Willie Hernandez got the win in Wrigley Field against his old mates, 13–6. The final three games against the runner-up Pittsburgh Pirates, the three contests that were supposed to provide the last drama among the major league pennant races, were reduced to post-season exhibitions.

It was a year in which everything that seemed so right turned out wrong and everything that seemed so wrong turned out right.

The Von Hayes–for–five trade was hailed as a good one. The Phillies needed youth and power from the left side of the plate. Hayes was going to provide both. He was compared to both Ted Williams and Stan Musial. He wound up the season hitting more like Stan Williams, the former Dodger pitcher, and spent the part of it that mattered mostly on the bench.

The John Denney–for–prospects deal, made in September 1982, was generally looked upon as a bad one, a short-term patch on an inner tube that begged for replacement, not repair. Denny came to town with a deserved reputation as a sore-armed sorehead. A year later, he was a born-again believer deserving of the Cy Young Award.

Dick Ruthven for Willie Hernandez? Did Dallas Green take the dirty linen with him when he went to Chicago? And why do the Phillies need a guy spelled Lefebvre and pronounced La-Fay?

So Hernandez won the clincher, and the Phillies never could have clinched without him. And no matter how you pronounced it, Lefebvre was a tremendous asset.

Then there was the off-season deal, Mike Krukow to the Giants for Joe Morgan. A relatively young starting pitcher for a 40-year-old second baseman? C'mon now. Does it matter that the Phillies are getting a relief pitcher who was Greg Minton's backup when a San Francisco game was on the line?

Mr. Why (Al Holland) became Mr. T, and the Phillies would have been up the track without him as he finished with 25 saves. And even with him, they would have probably run second at best without Morgan, who batted .230, most of it in September, when it mattered.

Going into the season, it was generally felt that the Montreal Expos were the class of the National League, East or West. Close behind in the East were the St. Louis Cardinals, with the Phillies riding behind in third. But St. Louis stumbled in mid-season, Montreal self-destructed (or, if you must say it, choked) down the stretch, and the Phillies had a chance to win the NL East by default. Instead, they took it in style. Their 11-game streak was one of the best in the last 30 years. Their six-game margin seemed preposterous on Labor Day.

They batted .249 as a team (a figure that would haunt them in the World Series). They had only two .300 hitters in Greg Gross, the excellent handyman, and Lefebvre. Mike Schmidt hit 40 home runs but slipped to .255. Rose lost all power. Morgan was batting less than .200 much of the summer.

But the Phillies made just enough noise and showed just enough poise to win. They overcame an injury to Larry Christenson that severely threatened the righthander's career. On superscout Hugh Alexander's recommendation, they recalled Charles Hudson, who filled the third spot in the pitching rotation beautifully. When Ruthven was moved to Chicago, the Phillies eventually called on Kevin Gross, who responded with credible statistics.

On September 23, Steve Carlton beat the Cardinals, 6–2, to become only the 16th pitcher to win 300 games.

Perez carried the team early, Morgan carried the team late, the pitching carried the team in between, and the puzzle that faced Paul Owens before the season was solved, piece by piece, by the Pope, both in the front office and in the dugout.

The season ended with Pete Rose somewhere else, released with honors. Ron Reed was still on the roster, and so were McGraw and Perez.

The Wheeze Kids weren't dead yet, as they proved in the season in which they were written off, but not out.

There was every reason to believe the Phillies would repeat at least as champions of the National League East, if not the entire National League. Even most of the experts felt that way.

After all, wasn't this supposed to be the "team of the '80s"? And wasn't it expected to be even better than the 1983 club, thanks to the addition of veteran lefthander Jerry Koosman and red-hot rookies Juan Samuel and Jeff Stone?

Maybe so, but this was a team without the stabilizing influence of the three expatriates of the Big Red Machine in Cincinnati—Pete Rose, Joe Morgan, and

1984

Record: 81–81
Finish: Fourth
Games Behind: 15½
Manager: Paul Owens

	W	L	G	GS	CG	IP	H	BB	K	ERA
Larry Andersen	3	7	64	0	0	91	85	25	54	2.38
Marty Bystrom	4	4	11	11	0	57	66	22	36	5.08
Bill Campbell	6	5	57	0	0	81	68	35	52	3.43
Steve Carlton	13	7	33	33	1	229	214	79	163	3.58
Don Carman	0	1	11	0	0	13	14	6	16	5.40
John Denny	7	7	22	22	2	154	122	29	94	2.45
Steve Fireovid	0	0	6	0	0	6	4	0	3	1.59
Kevin Gross	8	5	44	14	1	129	140	44	84	4.12
Al Holland	5	10	68	0	0	98	82	30	61	3.39
Charles Hudson	9	11	30	30	1	174	181	52	94	4.04
Jim Kern	0	1	8	0	0	13	20	10	8	10.13
Jerry Koosman	14	15	36	34	3	224	232	60	137	3.25
Renie Martin	0	2	9	0	0	16	17	12	5	4.60
Tug McGraw	2	0	25	0	0	38	36	10	26	3.79
Shane Rawley	10	6	18	18	3	120	117	27	58	3.83
Dave Wehrmeister	0	0	7	0	0	15	18	7	13	7.20
	81	81		162	11	1,458	1,416	448	904	3.62

Shutouts: Hudson, Koosman
Saves: Holland (29), Andersen (4), Campbell, Gross

	G	AB	R	H	2B	3B	HR	RBI	SB	AVG
Luis Aguayo	58	72	15	20	4	0	3	11	0	.278
Tim Corcoran	102	208	30	71	13	1	5	36	0	.341
Ivan DeJesus (SS)	144	435	40	112	15	3	0	35	12	.257
Bo Diaz	27	75	5	16	4	0	1	9	0	.213
Kiko Garcia	57	60	6	14	2	0	0	5	0	.233
Greg Gross	112	202	19	65	9	1	0	16	1	.322
Von Hayes (LF)	152	561	85	164	27	6	16	67	48	.292
Steve Jeltz	28	68	7	14	0	1	1	7	2	.206
Mike Lavalliere	6	7	0	0	0	0	0	0	0	.000
Joe Lefebvre	52	160	22	40	9	0	3	18	0	.250
Sixto Lezcano (RF)	109	256	36	71	6	2	14	40	0	.277
Garry Maddox	77	241	29	68	11	0	5	19	3	.282
Len Matuszek (1B)	101	262	40	65	17	1	12	43	4	.248
Francisco Melendez	21	23	0	3	0	0	0	2	0	.130
Al Oliver	28	93	9	29	7	0	0	14	1	.312
John Russell	39	99	11	28	8	1	2	11	0	.283
Juan Samuel (2B)	160	(701)	105	191	36	(19)	15	69	72	.272
Mike Schmidt (3B)	151	528	93	146	23	3	(36)	(106)	5	.277
Rick Schu	17	29	12	8	2	1	2	5	0	.276
Jeff Stone	51	185	27	67	4	6	1	15	27	.362
Ozzie Virgil (C)	141	456	61	119	21	2	18	68	1	.261
Glenn Wilson (CF)	132	341	28	82	21	3	6	31	7	.240
John Wockenfuss	86	180	20	52	3	1	6	24	1	.289
		5,614	720	1,494	(248)	51	147	673	186	(.266)

Len Matuszek and Juan Samuel were the right side of the Phillies infield to start the 1984 season.

Tony Perez—all key members of the '83 team. Then in spring training another team leader, Gary Matthews, was sent away in a horrendous trade with the Chicago Cubs that gave the Phils next to nothing in return. Outfielder Glenn Wilson was picked up in a swap with the Detroit Tigers, but the Phils had to give up relief pitcher Willie Hernandez, who in 1984 won the American League's Cy Young and Most Valuable Player awards.

Nonetheless, the Phillies began the season in grand style, winning six of their first nine games and climbing briefly into first place. In late April they won back-to-back games against the hated New York Mets by the scores of 12–2 and 12–5.

But by early May the Phillies had tumbled into fifth place after losing 10 of 12 games. They perked up considerably a little while later by winning 10 games in a row, including nine on the West Coast, the first time a Phillies team ever swept its three California rivals on the road.

Along the way Mike Schmidt hit his 400th career home run. And the Phils added two key players in veteran first baseman-outfielder Al Oliver and pitcher Shane Rawley.

From late May until late August the Phillies stayed in the battle for first place. Al Holland kept the club in many games with his sterling relief. Schmidt kept bopping the long ball, and eventually would win the home run (36) and RBI (106) titles.

In early September the Phillies lost five straight games, fell to fourth place, and from then on were out of the pennant race. Their fate was sealed when they lost 14 of their last 16 games, including their final nine games.

Koosman (14–15) wound up the top winner on a pitching staff that included a fading Steve Carlton and '83 Cy Young winner John Denny, who was injured much of the season. Holland finished with 29 saves, at the time a record for a Phillies lefthander.

Two of the biggest hitters for the Phillies were pinch-hit specialists Tim Corcoran (.341) and Greg Gross (.322). Stone hit .362 in limited action after spending the first half of the season in the minors. Juan Samuel showed his huge potential, and Ozzie Virgil was a pleasant surprise after taking over catching duties.

After the season manager Paul Owens decided to give up his duties on the bench and return to the front office. The Phillies made John Felske their new manager.

1985

Record: 75–87
Finish: Fifth
Games Behind: 26
Manager: John Felske

It was supposed to be the year the Phillies stole the pants off their National League brethren. It was going to be the year of the base burglars; the year the Phillies—with a trio of young greyhounds named Juan Samuel, Jeff Stone, and Von Hayes—raced around the bases with searing speed.

A new manager, John Felske, had taken over, too. And with his fresh approach and a squad well-stocked with veterans, the Phillies were going to be one of the main contenders in the NL East.

It never happened. The Phillies got off to a 1–8 start, lost 34 of their first 52 games, 11 games in a row near the end, and were never remotely in contention.

In between the start and the finish, the Phils didn't play too badly. Discounting their 18–45 record at the front and back of the season, they had a respectable mark of 57–42 in the middle, which was the third-best record in the National League over that period.

But because the whole season has to be counted, the Phils finished a dismal fifth. Through much of the season, the Phillies got very little hitting and almost as little pitching. They were eight games under .500 and 9½ games out of first place by the end of May. Only a couple of mid-season spurts, during which they won 20 of 30 games in June and 11 of 17 in August, saved the club from total disaster.

The highlight of the season came on June 11 when the Phils slaughtered the New York Mets, 26–7, in a record-breaking slugfest in which the Phils

	W	L	G	GS	CG	IP	H	BB	K	ERA
Larry Andersen	3	3	57	0	0	73	78	26	50	4.32
Steve Carlton	1	8	16	16	0	92	84	53	48	3.33
Don Carman	9	4	71	0	0	86	52	38	87	2.08
Rocky Childress	0	1	16	1	0	33	45	9	14	6.21
John Denny	11	14	33	33	6	204	252	83	123	3.82
Kevin Gross	15	13	38	31	6	206	194	81	151	3.41
Al Holland	0	1	3	0	0	4	5	4	1	4.50
Charles Hudson	8	13	38	26	3	193	188	74	122	3.78
Jerry Koosman	6	4	19	18	3	99	107	34	60	4.62
Shane Rawley	13	8	36	31	6	199	188	81	106	3.30
Dave Rucker	3	2	39	3	0	79	83	40	41	4.31
Dave Shipanoff	1	2	26	0	0	36	33	16	26	3.22
Dave Stewart	0	0	4	0	0	4	5	4	2	6.23
Rich Surhoff	1	0	2	0	0	1	2	0	1	0.00
Kent Tekulve	4	10	58	0	0	72	67	25	36	2.99
Fred Toliver	0	4	11	3	0	25	27	17	23	4.68
Pat Zachry	0	0	10	0	0	13	14	11	8	4.26
	75	87		162	24	1,447	1,424	596	899	3.68

Shutouts: Denny (2), Gross (2), Rawley (2)
Saves: Tekulve (14), Carman (7), Shipanoff (3), Andersen (3), Holland, Rucker, Toliver

	G	AB	R	H	2B	3B	HR	RBI	SB	AVG
Luis Aguayo	91	165	27	46	7	3	6	21	1	.279
Tim Corcoran	103	182	11	39	6	1	0	22	0	.214
Darren Daulton	36	103	14	21	3	1	4	11	3	.204
Bo Diaz	26	76	9	16	5	1	2	16	0	.211
Tom Foley	46	158	17	42	8	0	3	17	1	.266
Kiko Garcia	4	3	0	0	0	0	0	0	0	.000
Greg Gross	93	169	21	44	5	2	0	14	1	.260
Von Hayes (CF)	152	570	76	150	30	4	13	70	21	.263
Steve Jeltz (SS)	89	196	17	37	4	1	0	12	1	.189
Alan Knicely	7	7	0	0	0	0	0	0	0	.000
Garry Maddox	105	218	22	52	8	1	4	23	4	.239
John Russell	81	216	22	47	12	0	9	23	2	.218
Juan Samuel (2B)	161	663	101	175	31	13	19	74	53	.264
Mike Schmidt (1B)	158	549	89	152	31	5	33	93	1	.277
Rick Schu (3B)	112	416	54	105	21	4	7	24	8	.252
Jeff Stone (LF)	88	264	36	70	4	3	3	11	15	.265
Derrel Thomas	63	92	16	19	2	0	4	12	2	.207
Ozzie Virgil (C)	131	426	47	105	16	3	19	55	0	.246
Glenn Wilson (RF)	161	608	73	167	39	5	14	102	7	.275
John Wockenfuss	32	37	1	6	0	0	0	2	0	.162
		5,477	667	1,343	238	47	141	628	122	.245

clubbed 27 hits, 14 of them for extra bases. No National League team had scored as many runs as the Phillies since 1944.

The big bash was led by Von Hayes, who drilled two home runs in the first inning, one of which was a grand slam. Hayes, who drove in six runs altogether, was only the second Phillies player (the first was Andy Seminick in 1949) to hit two home runs in one inning.

Samuel added five hits and Rick Schu four to the Phillies' attack, which produced nine runs in the first inning and seven in the second.

Aside from their one-day fireworks, the Phillies generated little excitement, although they did finish second in the league in home runs. Mike Schmidt, switched to first base in May in an attempt to perk up his offense and to make room for Schu at third base, led the club with 33 home runs.

Glenn Wilson was the club's top player, driving in 102 runs and leading all NL outfielders in assists with 18, the highest total for a Phils' outfielder since Johnny Callison threw out 21 in 1965.

Don Carman set a Phillies record for most appearances (71) by a lefthanded pitcher. Ozzie Virgil, the only Phillie to make the All-Star team, committed only four errors all season, the fewest among National League catchers.

And the base burglars? Samuel had 53 stolen bases, Hayes 21, and Stone, who spent part of the season back in the minors, 15. It was not quite what had been expected.

1986

Record: 86–75
Finish: Second
Games Behind: 21½
Manager: John Felske

This season the Phillies bid farewell to a couple of old, familiar faces, said hello to a couple of promising new ones, and hoped all along that the club would finally regain its lost sparkle.

Stalwart center fielder Garry Maddox retired in May after nagging back problems had shown no signs of relenting. In June, despite his unwillingness to retire, Steve Carlton was released after club president Bill Giles decided that the aging lefthander was no longer effective.

During the previous winter the Phillies had added relief pitchers Steve Bedrosian and Tom Hume and outfielders Gary Redus and Milt Thompson, four players the club felt could make major contributions to the '86 season. Although it seemed at the time that '85 All-Star Ozzie Virgil, '83 Cy Young winner John Denny, and promising youngsters Pete Smith and Jeff Gray were a lot to give up, none of them made a major dent in the big time after they left Philadelphia.

Carlton's place on the pitching staff was taken by an unassuming young Texan with barely one year of minor league experience. Bruce Ruffin rode into Philadelphia like a tidal wave whipping into a seacoast, and, by the time the

	W	L	G	GS	CG	IP	H	BB	K	ERA
Larry Andersen	0	0	10	0	0	13	19	3	9	4.26
Steve Bedrosian	8	6	68	0	0	90	79	34	82	3.39
Jeff Bittiger	1	1	3	3	0	15	16	7	8	5.52
Steve Carlton	4	8	16	16	0	83	102	45	62	6.18
Don Carman	10	5	50	14	2	134	113	52	98	3.22
Rocky Childress	0	0	2	0	0	3	4	1	1	6.75
Marvin Freeman	2	0	3	3	0	16	6	10	8	2.25
Tom Gorman	0	1	8	0	0	12	21	5	8	7.71
Greg Gross	0	0	1	0	0	1	1	1	2	0.00
Kevin Gross	12	12	37	36	7	242	240	94	154	4.02
Charles Hudson	7	10	33	23	0	144	165	58	82	4.94
Tom Hume	4	1	48	1	0	94	89	34	51	2.77
Mike Jackson	0	0	9	0	0	13	12	4	3	3.38
Randy Lerch	1	1	4	0	0	8	10	7	5	7.88
Mike Maddux	3	7	16	16	0	78	88	34	44	5.42
Shane Rawley	11	7	23	23	7	158	166	50	73	3.53
Dave Rucker	0	2	19	0	0	25	34	14	14	5.76
Bruce Ruffin	9	4	21	21	6	146	138	44	70	2.46
Dan Schatzeder	3	3	25	0	0	29	28	16	14	3.38
Dave Stewart	0	0	8	0	0	12	15	4	9	6.57
Kent Tekulve	11	5	73	0	0	110	99	25	57	2.54
Fred Toliver	0	2	5	5	0	26	28	11	20	3.51
	86	75		161	22	1,452	1,473	553	874	3.85

Shutouts: Gross (2), Carman, Rawley
Saves: Bedrosian (29), Hume (4), Tekulve (4), Carman, Schatzeder

	G	AB	R	H	2B	3B	HR	RBI	SB	AVG
Luis Aguayo	62	133	17	28	6	1	4	13	1	.211
Darren Daulton	49	138	18	31	4	0	8	21	2	.225
Tom Foley	39	61	8	18	2	1	0	5	2	.295
Greg Gross	87	101	11	25	5	0	0	8	1	.248
Von Hayes (1B)	158	610	107	186	46	2	19	98	24	.305
Chris James	16	46	5	13	3	0	1	5	0	.283
Steve Jeltz (SS)	145	439	44	96	11	4	0	36	6	.219
Joe Lefebvre	14	18	0	2	0	0	0	0	0	.111
Gregg Legg	11	20	2	9	1	0	0	1	0	.450
Garry Maddox	6	7	1	3	0	0	0	1	0	.429
Francisco Melendez	9	8	0	2	0	0	0	0	0	.250
Gary Redus (LF)	90	340	62	84	22	4	11	33	25	.247
Ronn Reynolds	43	126	8	27	4	0	3	10	0	.214
Ron Roenicke	102	275	42	68	13	1	5	42	2	.247
John Russell (C)	93	315	35	76	21	2	13	60	0	.241
Juan Samuel (2B)	145	591	90	157	36	12	16	78	42	.266
Mike Schmidt (3B)	160	552	97	160	29	1	(37)	(119)	1	.290
Rick Schu	92	208	32	57	10	1	8	25	2	.274
Jeff Stone	82	249	32	69	6	4	6	19	19	.277
Milt Thompson (CF)	96	299	36	75	7	1	6	23	19	.251
Glenn Wilson (RF)	155	584	70	158	30	4	15	84	5	.271
		5,483	739	1,386	266	39	154	696	153	.253

season was over, he had registered a 9–4 record and was being hailed as the next great lefthander of the Phillies.

In a half season, Ruffin helped to salvage what had begun as another dreary Phillies year. By mid-May, with batters striking out in alarming numbers and all but Shane Rawley struggling on the pitching staff, the Phils had tumbled into the NL East cellar.

Suddenly in June, however, the team came alive. It won 10 of 13 games, hovered near the .500 mark and vaulted all the way up to third place. Not only was Rawley pitching well, but Bedrosian and Kent Tekulve had become a deadly bullpen duo. And Von Hayes and Mike Schmidt were leading a rejuvenated offense.

When Rawley went down with an arm injury and Carlton went out with a dead arm, Ruffin took up the slack. He was joined by second-year twirler Don Carman, who on August 20 pitched a memorable perfect game for eight innings against the San Francisco Giants. Leading off the ninth, Bob Brenly's line drive to left-center just eluded Milt Thompson, bouncing off the end of his glove for a double. Although the perfect game ended, the Phillies went on to capture a pulsating 1–0 victory in 10 innings.

The Phils won 15 of 20 games in August and charged into second place. They stayed there the rest of the season, finishing the campaign in satisfactory fashion, although they were 21½ games behind the front-running and eventual World Champion New York Mets.

Schmidt captured what would be his final home run (37) and RBI (119) crowns, as well as his third Most Valuable Player award. Moved to first base, Hayes finished with a banner .305 batting average and 98 RBI in what would be his crowning season in Philadelphia.

Bedrosian collected 29 saves for a pitching staff whose top winner was Kevin Gross (12–12). Rawley and Tekulve each won 11 and Carman 10.

Mike Schmidt, Von Hayes, Juan Samuel, Glenn Wilson, Lance Parrish, and Mike Easler. Take the best years of this group and lump them into the same season, and you'd have a lineup that would challenge the 1927 Yankees.

That's exactly what the Phillies thought their 1987 club would do, but it never happened. In a tumultuous year in which the Phils did their best imitation of a roller coaster, the team had one of its most bitterly disappointing campaigns in quite a while.

There were some high spots, to be sure. Mike Schmidt hit his 500th career home run with a two-on, two-out blast in the ninth inning that gave the Phillies an 8–6 win over the Pittsburgh Pirates.

Sizzling rookie Mike Jackson pitched a no-hitter for eight innings before giving up two hits in the ninth en route to his first major league win, a 3–1 triumph over the Montreal Expos.

Don Carman gave up an infield hit in the fourth inning to Mookie Wilson. He turned out to be the only New York Met to reach base in a 3–0 victory for Carman and the Phillies.

At the end of the year, after winning five and saving 40, Steve Bedrosian was named winner of the Cy Young Award.

Kent Tekulve pitched in a club record 90 games. And the Phils discovered they had a fine rookie in Chris James. But the offensive onslaught that was supposed to occur never materialized in the way that was expected.

Schmidt had a monster year with a .293 batting average, 35 home runs, and 113 RBI. So did Samuel at .272 with 28 homers and 100 RBI. Hayes batted .277 (21 HR, 84 RBI), which wasn't bad, and unheralded Milt Thompson hit .302.

But Parrish, hotly pursued all spring by the Phillies until he finally signed as a free agent, was a bust. So was Easler, who wound up getting traded back to the New York Yankees before mid-season. And Wilson's slump extended into its second year.

1987

Record: 80–82
Finish: Fourth
Games Behind: 15
Managers: John Felske, Lee Elia

Free agent Lance Parrish was supposed to bring the Phillies the 1987 pennant, but he became a two-year bust.

Steve Bedrosian is all smiles at his Cy Young Award press conference in 1987.

	W	L	G	GS	CG	IP	H	BB	K	ERA
Doug Bair	2	0	11	0	0	14	17	5	10	5.93
Steve Bedrosian	5	3	65	0	0	89	79	28	74	2.83
Jeff Calhoun	3	1	42	0	0	43	25	26	31	1.48
Don Carman	13	11	35	35	3	211	194	69	125	4.22
Joe Cowley	0	4	5	4	0	12	21	17	5	15.43
Todd Frohwirth	1	0	10	0	0	11	12	2	9	0.00
Kevin Gross	9	16	34	33	3	201	205	87	110	4.35
Tom Hume	1	4	38	6	0	71	75	41	29	5.60
Mike Jackson	3	10	55	7	0	109	88	56	93	4.20
Mike Maddux	2	0	7	2	0	17	17	5	15	2.65
Tom Newell	0	0	2	0	0	1	4	3	1	36.00
Shane Rawley	17	11	36	36	4	230	250	86	123	4.38
Wally Ritchie	3	2	49	0	0	62	60	29	45	3.75
Bruce Ruffin	11	14	35	35	3	205	236	73	93	4.35
Dan Schatzeder	3	1	26	0	0	38	40	14	28	4.06
Kent Tekulve	6	4	(90)	0	0	105	96	29	60	3.09
Fred Toliver	1	1	10	4	0	30	34	17	25	5.64
Glenn Wilson	0	0	1	0	0	1	0	0	1	0.00
	80	82		162	13	1,448	1,453	587	877	4.18

Shutouts: Carman (2), Gross, Rawley, Ruffin
Saves: Bedrosian (40), Tekulve (3), Ritchie (3), Calhoun, Jackson

	G	AB	R	H	2B	3B	HR	RBI	SB	AVG
Luis Aguayo	94	209	25	43	9	1	12	21	0	.206
Darren Daulton	53	129	10	25	6	0	3	13	0	.194
Ken Dowell	15	39	4	5	0	0	0	1	0	.128
Mike Easler	33	110	7	31	4	0	1	10	0	.282
Greg Gross	114	133	14	38	4	1	1	12	0	.286
Von Hayes (1B)	158	556	84	154	36	5	21	84	16	.277
Keith Hughes	37	76	8	20	2	0	0	10	0	.263
Ken Jackson	8	16	1	4	2	0	0	2	0	.250
Chris James (LF)	115	358	48	105	20	6	17	54	3	.293
Greg Jelks	10	11	2	1	1	0	0	1	0	.091
Steve Jeltz (SS)	114	293	37	68	9	6	0	12	1	.232
Gregg Legg	3	2	1	0	0	0	0	0	0	.000
Lance Parrish (C)	130	466	42	114	21	0	17	67	0	.245
Ronn Roenicke	63	78	9	13	3	1	1	4	1	.167
John Russell	24	62	5	9	1	0	3	8	0	.145
Juan Samuel (2B)	160	655	113	178	37	(15)	28	100	35	.272
Mike Schmidt (3B)	147	522	88	153	28	0	35	113	2	.293
Rick Schu	92	196	24	46	6	3	7	16	0	.235
Jeff Stone	66	125	19	32	7	1	1	16	3	.256
Milt Thompson (CF)	150	527	86	159	26	9	7	43	46	.302
Glenn Wilson (RF)	154	569	55	150	21	2	14	54	3	.264
		5,477	702	1,390	248	(51)	169	662	111	.254

As a result, the Phillies' vaunted offense was eighth in the league in batting average and fifth in home runs, although the club's 169 round-trippers were the second highest in team history.

With someone other than Steve Carlton (it was Shane Rawley) starting an opening-day game for the Phillies for the first time in 15 years, the club slipped into last place early, then battled back with 18 wins in 26 games in late May and early June. By mid-June, however, the team was mired in another slump and playing listlessly. Manager John Felske was fired, and the job was given to Lee Elia.

Under Elia, the Phils went 51–50 the rest of the way, winning 21 of 31 games at one point. But the Phillies lost 27 of their final 39 contests, tumbling far out of contention and finishing 11 games behind third-place Montreal.

Rawley finished as the top starter with a 17–11 record. Carman was 13–11, but 1986 phenom Bruce Ruffin fell to 11–14.

During the season, Kevin Gross was ejected from a game and suspended for 10 days for having sandpaper in his glove. He denied using it to doctor baseballs.

Also during the season, Carman got his first big league hit after 48 attempts, and Greg Gross slammed his first home run in a Phillies uniform after nine years with the club. He also punched his 1,000th career hit.

Shortly after the 1987 season ended, Woody Woodward was named the Phillies' director of player personnel. But the erstwhile general manager wasn't around long enough to see the fruits of his labor rot on the vine.

Woodward led a parade of dismissals that symbolized the entire woeful Phillies' season.

It was a season that began slowly, and then geared down almost to a stop. The club performed atrociously throughout, mixing one unenthusiastic performance after another with injuries, season-long slumps, and a rash of player moves that did little else but give a lot of people a chance to tell their grandchildren that they once wore a big league uniform.

This team had about as much chance of winning as snow has of falling in Florida. It went into a swoon getting off the airplane from spring training, lost eight of its first 11 games, and never recovered.

Heads rolled. First it was Woodward's and farm director Jim Baumer's in June. Lee Thomas was hired as general manager a few weeks later, and he

1988

Record: 65–96
Finish: Sixth
Games Behind: 35½
Managers: Lee Elia, John Vukovich

	W	L	G	GS	CG	IP	H	BB	K	ERA
Salome Barojas	0	0	6	0	0	9	7	8	1	8.31
Steve Bedrosian	6	6	54	0	0	74	75	27	61	3.75
Jeff Calhoun	0	0	3	0	0	2	6	1	1	15.43
Don Carman	10	14	36	32	2	201	211	70	116	4.29
Danny Clay	0	1	17	0	0	24	27	21	12	6.00
Bill Dawley	0	2	8	0	0	9	16	4	3	13.50
Marvin Freeman	2	3	11	11	0	52	55	43	37	6.10
Todd Frohwirth	1	2	12	0	0	12	16	11	11	8.25
Kevin Gross	12	14	33	33	5	232	209	89	162	3.69
Greg Harris	4	6	66	1	0	107	80	52	71	2.36
Mike Maddux	4	3	25	11	0	89	91	34	59	3.76
Alex Madrid	1	1	5	2	1	16	15	6	2	2.76
Brad Moore	0	0	5	0	0	6	4	4	2	0.00
David Palmer	7	9	22	22	1	129	129	48	85	4.47
Shane Rawley	8	16	32	32	4	198	220	78	87	4.18
Wally Ritchie	0	0	19	0	0	26	19	17	8	3.12
Bruce Ruffin	6	10	55	15	3	144	151	80	82	4.43
Bill Scherrer	0	0	8	0	0	7	7	2	3	5.40
Bob Sebra	1	2	3	3	0	11	15	10	7	7.94
Scott Service	0	0	5	0	0	5	7	1	6	1.69
Kent Tekulve	3	7	70	0	0	80	87	22	43	3.60
	65	96		162	16	1,433	1,447	628	859	4.14

Shutouts: Gross, Palmer, Rawley
Saves: Bedrosian (28), Tekulve (4), Ruffin (3), Harris

	G	AB	R	H	2B	3B	HR	RBI	SB	AVG
Luis Aguayo	49	97	9	24	3	0	3	5	2	.247
Bill Almon	20	26	1	3	2	0	0	1	0	.115
Tommy Barrett	36	54	5	11	1	0	0	3	0	.204
Phil Bradley (LF)	154	569	77	150	30	5	11	56	11	.264
Darren Daulton	58	144	13	30	6	0	1	12	2	.208
Bob Dernier	68	166	19	48	3	1	1	10	13	.289
Greg Gross	98	133	10	27	1	0	0	5	0	.203
Jackie Gutierrez	33	77	8	19	4	0	0	9	0	.247
Von Hayes (1B)	104	367	43	100	28	2	6	45	20	.272
Chris James (RF)	150	566	57	137	24	1	19	66	7	.242
Steve Jeltz (SS)	148	379	39	71	11	4	0	27	3	.187
Ron Jones	33	124	15	36	6	1	8	26	0	.290
Ricky Jordan	69	273	41	84	15	1	11	43	1	.308
Keith Miller	47	48	4	8	3	0	0	6	0	.167
Al Pardo	2	2	0	0	0	0	0	0	0	.000
Lance Parrish (C)	123	424	44	91	17	2	15	60	0	.215
John Russell	22	49	5	12	1	0	2	4	0	.245
Juan Samuel (2B)	157	629	68	153	32	9	12	67	33	.243
Mike Schmidt (3B)	108	390	52	97	21	2	12	62	3	.249
Milt Thompson (CF)	122	378	53	109	16	2	2	33	17	.288
Shane Turner	18	35	1	6	0	0	0	1	0	.171
Mike Young	75	146	13	33	14	0	1	14	0	.226
		5,403	597	1,294	246	31	106	567	112	.239

brought in Lance Nichols as farm director and Jay Hankins as director of scouting. Before the season was over, Thomas had dismissed manager Lee Elia and coaches Claude Osteen, Del Unser, and Dave Bristol.

Woodward had made one major trade, sending outfielder Glenn Wilson and relief pitcher Mike Jackson to the Seattle Mariners for outfielder Phil Bradley. Although Bradley had decent numbers, management didn't like him, and he would soon be gone from Philadelphia.

Cy Young winner Steve Bedrosian missed the first six weeks of the season with pneumonia, but still posted 28 saves. Mike Schmidt missed the last six weeks of the season because of a rotator cuff injury, falling to 12 home runs and 62 RBI.

In mid-season, the Phillies lost 23 of 38 games. By the time the year had ended, they had compiled the worst record for a Phillies team since 1972.

No Phils hitter had 20 home runs, a depth last reached in 1972. No regular starting pitcher had a winning record, a distinction last attained by a Phillies staff in 1961.

The Phils were 11th in the league in hitting and pitching, and 10th in fielding.

About the only bright spots on the team were the performances of two youngsters called up during the season from the minors. Ricky Jordan had a flashy .308 batting average with 11 home runs and 43 RBI in one-half of a season. Ron Jones ripped out a .290 batting average after reporting to the team in late July.

Elia was axed with nine games left in the season. Coach John Vukovich finished the season as interim manager.

1989

Record: 67–95
Finish: Sixth
Games Behind: 26
Manager: Nick Leyva

If ever the expression "You can't tell the players without a program" applied, this was the year.

Players came and went with such regularity that it was nearly impossible to keep track of them. Through trades, sales, and recalls from the minors, the 1989 Phillies were in a constant state of flux as general manager Lee Thomas and manager Nick Leyva groped to find a lineup that could do something besides lose.

Thomas brought in players such as Jeff Parrett, Tommy Herr, Dickie Thon, Floyd Youmans, Steve Lake, and Curt Ford before the season. Then he added John Kruk, Randy Ready, Len Dykstra, Roger McDowell, Terry Mulholland, Dennis Cook, and Charlie Hayes during the season.

All but Thon (signed as a free agent) came in trades as Thomas tinkered constantly with the Phils' roster.

The tinkering didn't do much, though, to help the club's final record. The Phils got off to a good start, but their original pitching staff soon fell apart. The club lost 32 of 44 games and was buried in the basement long before mid-season. Youmans, in particular, was a bust.

On May 30, Mike Schmidt, hitting just .203 with six home runs, announced his decision to retire. Shortly afterward, Thomas ousted farm director Lance Nichols.

The Phils' topsy-turvy season had a little respite on June 8 when the team came from being behind, 10–0, in the first inning, to defeat the Pittsburgh Pirates, 15–11. Von Hayes and Steve Jeltz each hit two home runs, the switch-hitting Jeltz becoming the first player in Phillies history to hit one from each side of the plate in the same game.

Thomas named Del Unser his farm director. Though that was a sound move over the long term, it did nothing to keep the Phils from bouncing aimlessly along the bottom of the division standings.

After a 31–52 first half, the Phils made considerable improvement in the second half with a 36–43 record. There were some bright spots that boded well for the future.

Kruk hit a sizzling .331 after coming to the Phillies. The top draft choice in 1988, Pat Combs, called up in September, fashioned a glittering 4–0 record.

	W	L	G	GS	CG	IP	H	BB	K	ERA
Steve Bedrosian	2	3	28	0	0	34	21	17	24	3.21
Don Carman	5	15	49	20	0	149	152	86	81	5.24
Pat Combs	4	0	6	6	1	39	36	6	30	2.09
Dennis Cook	6	8	21	16	1	106	97	33	58	3.99
Gordon Dillard	0	0	5	0	0	4	7	0	2	6.75
Marvin Freeman	0	0	1	1	0	3	2	5	0	6.00
Todd Frohwirth	1	0	45	0	0	63	56	18	39	3.59
Jason Grimsley	1	3	4	4	0	18	19	19	7	5.89
Greg Harris	2	2	44	0	0	75	64	43	51	3.58
Ken Howell	12	12	33	32	1	204	155	86	164	3.44
Mike Maddux	1	3	16	4	2	43	52	14	26	5.15
Roger McDowell	3	3	44	0	0	57	45	22	32	1.11
Chuck McElroy	0	0	11	0	0	10	12	4	8	1.74
Larry McWilliams	2	11	40	16	2	121	123	49	54	4.10
Terry Mulholland	4	5	20	17	2	104	122	32	60	5.00
Randy O'Neal	0	1	20	1	0	34	46	9	29	6.23
Steve Ontiveros	2	1	6	5	0	31	34	15	12	3.82
Jeff Parrett	12	6	72	0	0	106	90	44	98	2.98
Bruce Ruffin	6	10	24	23	1	126	152	62	70	4.44
Bob Sebra	2	3	6	5	0	34	41	10	21	4.46
Floyd Youmans	1	5	10	10	0	43	50	25	20	5.70
	67	95		163	10	1,433	1,408	613	899	4.04

Shutouts: Combs, Cook, Howell, Maddux, McWilliams, Mulholland
Saves: McDowell (19), Bedrosian (6), Parrett (6), Harris, Maddux

	G	AB	R	H	2B	3B	HR	RBI	SB	AVG
Jim Adduci	13	19	1	7	1	0	0	0	0	.368
Tommy Barrett	14	27	3	6	0	0	0	1	0	.222
Eric Bullock	6	4	1	0	0	0	0	0	0	.000
Darren Daulton (C)	131	368	29	74	12	2	8	44	2	.201
Bob Dernier	107	187	26	32	5	0	1	13	4	.171
Lenny Dykstra (CF)	90	352	39	78	20	3	4	19	17	.222
Curt Ford	108	142	13	31	5	1	1	13	5	.218
Charlie Hayes (3B)	84	299	26	77	15	1	8	43	3	.258
Von Hayes (RF)	154	540	93	140	27	2	26	78	28	.259
Tommy Herr (2B)	151	561	65	161	25	6	2	37	10	.287
Chris James	45	179	14	37	4	0	2	19	3	.207
Steve Jeltz	116	263	28	64	7	3	4	25	4	.243
Ron Jones	12	31	7	9	0	0	2	4	1	.290
Ricky Jordan (1B)	144	523	63	149	22	3	12	75	4	.285
John Kruk (LF)	81	281	46	93	13	6	5	38	3	.331
Steve Lake	58	155	9	39	5	1	2	14	0	.252
Keith Miller	8	10	0	3	1	0	0	0	0	.300
Dwayne Murphy	98	156	20	34	5	0	9	27	0	.218
Tom Nieto	11	20	1	3	0	0	0	0	0	.150
Al Pardo	1	1	0	0	0	0	0	0	0	.000
Randy Ready	72	187	33	50	11	1	8	21	4	.267
Mark Ryal	29	33	2	8	2	0	0	5	0	.242
Juan Samuel	51	199	32	49	3	1	8	20	11	.246
Mike Schmidt	42	148	19	30	7	0	6	28	0	.203
Steve Stanicek	9	9	0	1	0	0	0	1	0	.111
Dickie Thon (SS)	136	435	45	118	18	4	15	60	6	.271
		5,447	629	1,324	215	36	123	594	106	.243

Von Hayes led the club with 26 home runs, while Herr hit a solid .287. Howell at 12–12 and Parrett at 12–6 were the club's leading pitchers.

1990

In 1990 the Phillies shook off the cobwebs and pumped some excitement back into their lives.

Terry Mulholland pitched a no-hitter. Len Dykstra hit over .400 into June and battled all season for the batting title. The Phils landed superstar Dale Murphy in a trade. And a flock of young players with gobs of potential appeared on the scene.

It was almost enough to erase the frustration that had surrounded the team for the previous three years.

Mulholland's no-hitter, the first at home for a Phillies' pitcher in the 20th century, was easily the highlight of the season. The young lefthander, just

Record: 77–85
Finish: Fourth (tie)
Games Behind: 20
Manager: Nick Leyva

Lenny Dykstra became a favorite of the fans when he brought his hustling, aggressive style from the New York Mets.

	W	L	G	GS	CG	IP	H	BB	K	ERA
Darrel Ackerfelds	5	2	71	0	0	93	65	54	42	3.77
Joe Boever	2	3	34	0	0	46	37	16	40	2.15
Don Carman	6	2	59	1	0	87	69	38	58	4.15
Pat Combs	10	10	32	31	3	183	179	86	108	4.07
Dennis Cook	8	3	42	13	2	142	132	54	58	3.56
Jose DeJesus	7	8	22	22	3	130	97	73	87	3.74
Marvin Freeman	0	2	16	3	0	32	34	14	26	5.57
Todd Frohwirth	0	1	5	0	0	1	3	6	1	18.00
Tommy Greene	2	3	10	7	0	39	36	17	17	4.15
Jason Grimsley	3	2	11	11	0	57	47	43	41	3.30
Ken Howell	8	7	18	18	2	107	106	49	70	4.64
Chuck Malone	1	0	7	0	0	7	3	11	7	3.68
Roger McDowell	6	8	72	0	0	86	92	35	39	3.86
Chuck McElroy	0	1	16	0	0	14	24	10	16	7.71
Brad Moore	0	0	3	0	0	3	4	2	1	3.38
Terry Mulholland	9	10	33	26	6	181	172	42	75	3.34
Dickie Noles	0	1	1	0	0	⅓	2	0	0	27.00
Steve Ontiveros	0	0	5	0	0	10	9	3	6	2.70
Jeff Parrett	4	9	47	5	0	82	92	36	69	5.18
Bruce Ruffin	6	13	32	25	2	149	178	62	79	5.38
	77	85		162	18	1,449	1,381	651	840	4.07

Shutouts: Combs (2), Cook, DeJesus, Mulholland, Ruffin
Saves: McDowell (22), Boever (6), Ackerfelds (3), Carman, Cook, Freeman, Parrett

	G	AB	R	H	2B	3B	HR	RBI	SB	AVG
Rod Booker	73	131	19	29	5	2	0	10	3	.221
Sil Campusano	66	85	10	18	1	1	2	9	1	.212
Wes Chamberlain	18	46	9	13	3	0	2	4	4	.283
Darren Daulton (C)	143	459	62	123	30	1	12	57	7	.268
Lenny Dykstra (CF)	149	590	106	(192)	35	3	9	60	33	.325
Darrin Fletcher	9	22	3	3	1	0	0	1	0	.136
Curt Ford	22	18	0	2	0	0	0	0	0	.111
Charlie Hayes (3B)	152	561	56	145	20	0	10	57	4	.258
Von Hayes (RF)	129	467	70	122	14	3	17	73	16	.261
Tommy Herr (2B)	119	447	39	118	21	3	4	50	7	.264
Dave Hollins	72	114	14	21	0	0	5	15	0	.184
Ron Jones	24	58	5	16	2	0	3	7	0	.276
Ricky Jordan (1B)	92	324	32	78	21	0	5	44	2	.241
John Kruk (LF)	142	443	52	129	25	8	7	67	10	.291
Steve Lake	29	80	4	20	2	0	0	6	0	.250
Carmelo Martinez	71	198	23	48	8	0	8	31	2	.242
Louie Meadows	15	14	1	1	0	0	0	0	0	.071
Mickey Morandini	25	79	9	19	4	0	1	3	3	.241
Dale Murphy	57	214	22	57	9	1	7	27	0	.266
Tom Nieto	17	30	1	5	0	0	0	4	0	.167
Randy Ready	101	217	26	53	9	1	1	26	3	.244
Dickie Thon (SS)	149	552	54	141	20	4	8	48	12	.255
Jim Vatcher	36	46	5	12	1	0	1	4	0	.261
		5,535	646	1,410	237	27	103	619	108	.255

starting to emerge as one of the better hurlers in the league, faced the minimum 27 batters while striking out eight and beating the San Francisco Giants, 6–0. His perfect game was marred only by Rick Parker, a one-time Phillies minor leaguer, who hit a hard grounder to Charlie Hayes at third base. Hayes fielded the ball cleanly, but his throw to first pulled John Kruk slightly off the bag, allowing Parker to reach base safely. Hayes was charged with an error, although he later redeemed himself with a sparkling catch of Gary Carter's line drive to end the game. Parker was erased on a double play.

On June 10, Dykstra was hitting .407 with a 23-game hitting streak and was the subject of media attention throughout the nation. He tailed off in the second half of the season but still managed a .325 average, second best in the league, in a controversial batting race. The winner, Willie McGee, finished the season in the American League.

Despite a lockout that closed down half of spring training, the Phillies got off to their best start since 1981, winning 21 of their first 34 games and battling for second place. A slump in June during which they won just 10 of 30 games sent them reeling, and the club went into the All-Star break with a 39–41 record.

Injuries to key players and a fizzling pitching staff took a heavy toll as the season progressed. But a red-hot offense that at one point hit for double figures in 13 of 20 games and the emergence of several young players helped to take up the slack.

A revamped pitching staff featured Mulholland, Pat Combs, Tommy Greene, Jason Grimsley, and Jose DeJesus as the season reached the dog days of August. Only Combs had been in the starting rotation at the beginning of the year.

Darrel Akerfelds and Joe Boever contributed standout efforts from the bullpen, and new outfielder Wes Chamberlain, acquired in a trade after the Pittsburgh Pirates had mistakenly fouled up his waiver status, displayed not only an exciting style but enormous potential as well.

Coming down the home stretch the Phillies won 12 of their last 19 games. They would have had fourth place all to themselves, but using a pieced-together lineup, they dropped their last two games of the season to the Chicago Cubs, thereby ending in a tie with the Bruins.

Dykstra wound up tying Brett Butler for the league lead in hits with 192. Kruk hit .291, and catcher Darren Daulton had a superb second half, finishing with a .268 average and 12 home runs.

Combs, the Phillies' first-round draft choice in 1988 and the first first-rounder to be of use to the club in a number of years, finished as the leading pitcher with a 10–10 record.

It's easy to describe the 1991 Phillies. They were Team Adversity.

Hard times plagued the Phils throughout the season, although amazingly enough, they overcame much of it to attain their highest finish since 1986.

Much of the adversity focused on center fielder Len Dykstra. During spring training he was part of a gambling probe in Mississippi. It was revealed that he had lost $78,000 on golf and poker bets, and commissioner Fay Vincent put him on one year's probation. In May, Dykstra and catcher Darren Daulton were seriously hurt in an auto accident while returning from a bachelor party

1991

Record: 78–84
Finish: Third
Games Behind: 20
Managers: Nick Leyva, Jim Fregosi

Dickie Thon (left) gave the Phillies three years of solid shortstopping in 1989–91, while Dale Murphy provided some power at the bat in 1990–91.

	W	L	G	GS	CG	IP	H	BB	K	ERA
Darrel Ackerfelds	2	3	30	0	0	50	49	27	31	5.26
Andy Ashby	1	5	8	8	0	42	41	19	26	6.00
Joe Boever	3	5	68	0	0	98	90	54	89	3.84
Cliff Brantley	2	2	6	5	0	32	26	19	25	3.41
Amalio Carreno	0	0	3	0	0	3	5	3	2	16.20
Pat Combs	2	6	14	13	1	64	64	43	41	4.90
Danny Cox	4	6	23	17	0	102	98	39	46	4.57
Jose DeJesus	10	9	31	29	3	182	147	128	118	3.42
Tommy Greene	13	7	36	27	3	208	177	66	154	3.38
Jason Grimsley	1	7	12	12	0	61	54	41	42	4.87
Mike Hartley	2	1	18	0	0	26	21	10	19	3.76
Dave LaPointe	0	1	2	2	0	5	10	6	3	16.20
Tim Mauser	0	0	3	0	0	11	18	3	6	7.59
Roger McDowell	3	6	38	0	0	59	61	32	28	3.20
Terry Mulholland	16	13	34	34	8	232	231	49	142	3.61
Wally Ritchie	1	2	39	0	0	50	44	17	26	2.50
Bruce Ruffin	4	7	31	15	1	119	125	38	85	3.78
Steve Searcy	2	1	18	0	0	30	29	14	21	4.15
Mitch Williams	12	5	69	0	0	88	56	62	84	2.34
	78	84		162	16	1,463	1,346	670	988	3.86

Shutouts: Mulholland (3), Greene (2), Ruffin
Saves: Williams (30), McDowell (3), DeJesus, Hartley

	G	AB	R	H	2B	3B	HR	RBI	SB	AVG
Wally Backman	94	185	20	45	12	0	0	15	3	.243
Kim Batiste	10	27	2	6	0	0	0	1	0	.222
Rod Booker	28	53	3	12	1	0	0	7	0	.226
Sil Campusano	15	35	2	4	0	0	1	2	0	.114
Braulio Castillo	28	52	3	9	3	0	0	2	1	.173
Wes Chamberlain (LF)	101	383	51	92	16	3	13	50	9	.240
Darren Daulton (C)	89	285	36	56	12	0	12	42	5	.196
Lenny Dykstra (CF)	63	246	48	73	13	5	3	12	24	.297
Darrin Fletcher	46	136	5	31	8	0	1	12	0	.228
Charlie Hayes (3B)	142	460	34	106	23	1	12	53	3	.230
Von Hayes	77	284	43	64	15	3	0	21	9	.225
Dave Hollins	56	151	18	45	10	2	6	21	1	.298
Ron Jones	28	26	0	4	2	0	0	3	0	.154
Ricky Jordan	101	301	38	82	21	3	9	49	0	.272
John Kruk (1B)	152	538	84	158	27	6	21	92	7	.294
Steve Lake	58	158	12	36	4	1	1	11	0	.228
Jim Lindeman	65	95	13	32	5	0	0	12	0	.337
Doug Lindsey	1	3	0	0	0	0	0	0	0	.000
Mickey Morandini (2B)	98	325	38	81	11	4	1	20	13	.249
John Morris	85	127	15	28	2	1	1	6	2	.220
Dale Murphy (RF)	153	544	66	137	33	1	18	81	1	.252
Randy Ready	76	205	32	51	10	1	1	20	2	.249
Rick Schu	17	22	1	2	0	0	0	2	0	.091
Dickie Thon (SS)	146	539	44	136	18	4	9	44	11	.252
		5,521	629	1,332	248	33	111	590	92	.241

for John Kruk. Dykstra's new $92,000 Mercedes spun off the road and hit two trees. Dykstra, who was later charged with drunk driving and lost his license, suffered the more serious injuries and missed the next 61 games.

If that wasn't enough, soon after he returned to the lineup in August, Dykstra crashed into the unpadded outfield wall at Cincinnati's Riverfront Stadium and rebroke the collarbone he had fractured in the auto accident. His season was over, and he would miss 99 games.

On top of Dykstra's problems, Daulton missed 63 games, Von Hayes was out for 73 games after his wrist was broken by a pitch, and Ken Howell missed the whole season with arm problems.

Injuries weren't the only things to trouble the Phillies. Thirteen games into the regular season, Lee Thomas fired his friend Nick Leyva as manager. At the time the Phils had a 4–9 record.

Jim Fregosi replaced Leyva and immediately revamped the batting order and the roster. It didn't help much as the Phillies struggled to a 39–49 first half with only Kruk hitting consistently well.

By then the Phils had had several major events. Dale Murphy got his 2,000th career hit. The club had its first triple play since 1968 when Randy Ready snared Tony Gwynn's line drive at second, stepped on the bag, then threw to Ricky Jordan at first.

On May 23 the Phils got their second no-hitter in two years when Tommy Greene blanked the Montreal Expos at Olympic Stadium, 2–0. Greene, in only his second start and first complete game of the season, struck out 10 and walked seven.

With Dave Hollins recalled from the minors and supplying some needed offensive punch, the Phillies perked up in the second half. In August reliever Mitch Williams tied a National League record by winning eight games during the month (he also saved five). And the Phillies at one point won 13 games in a row, tying a modern club record, and 16 straight games at home.

By the beginning of September the Phils had won 23 of 32 games. A slight slump slowed them down, but they finished strongly with wins in 11 of their final 18 games to finish in third place.

By the end of the season, 14 different players had spent time on the disabled list. The Phils had played in a club-record-tying 25 extra-inning games (winning 16), and they had 63 one-run games (winning 36).

Kruk became the first hitter since Greg Luzinski in 1977 to lead the team in batting average (.294), home runs (21), and RBI (92). Murphy had 18 home runs and 81 RBI, Hollins hit .298 in the second half, and utility man Jim Lindeman hit .337.

For the first time since 1986, four Phillies pitchers won in double figures. Terry Mulholland, establishing himself as one of the better pitchers in the league, led with a 16–13 record. Greene was 13–7, Williams 12–5, and Jose DeJesus 10–9.

John Kruk developed into an outstanding hitter after being traded from the San Diego Padres.

1992

Record: 70–92
Finish: Sixth
Games Behind: 26
Manager: Jim Fregosi

For the Phillies, the 1992 season was not only one of the most disappointing, it was certainly one of the most peculiar.

The '92 Phils were a team that placed fourth in the National League in runs scored and third in home runs. Darren Daulton led the National League in RBI, John Kruk led the league in hitting much of the season before finishing third and Dave Hollins had a banner season, ranking among the league leaders in runs, RBI and home runs.

Curt Schilling had the lowest batting average against him in the league, Terry Mulholland led the circuit in complete games and Mitch Williams recorded 29 saves.

Yet the Phillies finished dead last in the East Division, despite all of the individual good works.

The season had begun with bright hopes. The Phillies expected to be a contender, a team brimming with good pitching and plenty of offense.

But the season went into the tank almost before it began. Key pitchers Ken Howell and Jose DeJesus came up lame in spring training, and never pitched an inning all season. Then Len Dykstra went out with a broken wrist after getting hit with a Greg Maddux toss on his second pitch of the season. Soon afterward, pitcher Tommy Greene and outfielder Dale Murphy went down with injuries. And the Phillies never even got out of the starting blocks.

They tumbled into last place early and stayed there through much of the season, including all but one day over the final three and one-half months.

All the while, the injuries mounted. Eventually, the Phils wound up with 17 different players on the disabled list, a club record. That forced the team to scramble for replacements, and good ones were simply not available.

The Phillies used 48 players during the season, 19 of them rookies. Fifteen different pitchers were employed as starters.

The highlight of the season was Daulton's becoming only the fourth

	W	L	G	GS	CG	IP	H	BB	K	ERA
Kyle Abbott	1	14	31	19	0	133	147	45	88	5.13
Andy Ashby	1	3	10	8	0	37	42	21	24	7.54
Bob Ayrault	2	2	30	0	0	43	32	17	27	3.12
Jay Baller	0	0	8	0	0	11	10	10	9	8.18
Cliff Brantley	2	6	28	9	0	76	71	58	32	4.60
Brad Brink	0	4	8	7	0	41	53	13	16	4.14
Darren Chapin	0	0	1	0	0	2	2	0	1	9.00
Pat Combs	1	1	4	4	0	19	20	12	11	7.71
Danny Cox	2	2	9	7	0	38	46	19	30	5.40
Jose DeLeon	0	1	3	3	0	15	16	5	7	3.00
Tommy Greene	3	3	13	12	0	64	75	34	39	5.32
Mike Hartley	7	6	46	0	0	55	54	23	53	3.44
Barry Jones	5	6	44	0	0	54	65	24	19	4.64
Greg Mathews	2	3	14	7	0	52	54	24	27	5.16
Terry Mulholland	13	11	32	32	(12)	229	227	46	125	3.81
Wally Ritchie	2	1	40	0	0	39	44	17	19	3.00
Ben Rivera	7	3	20	14	4	102	78	32	66	2.82
Don Robinson	1	4	8	8	0	44	49	4	17	6.18
Curt Schilling	14	11	42	26	10	226	165	59	147	2.35
Steve Searcy	0	0	10	0	0	10	13	8	5	6.10
Keith Shepherd	1	1	12	0	0	22	19	6	10	3.27
Mickey Weston	0	1	1	1	0	4	7	1	0	12.27
Mike Williams	1	1	5	5	1	29	29	7	5	5.34
Mitch Williams	5	8	66	0	0	81	69	64	74	3.78
	70	92		162	27	1,428	1,387	549	851	4.11

Shutouts: Schilling (4), Mulholland (2), Rivera.
Saves: Williams (29), Schilling (2), Shepherd (2), Ritchie.

	G	AB	R	H	2B	3B	HR	RBI	SB	AVG
Ruben Amaro	126	374	43	82	15	6	7	34	11	.219
Wally Backman	42	48	6	13	1	0	0	6	1	.271
Kim Batiste	44	136	9	28	4	0	1	10	0	.206
Juan Bell (SS)	46	147	12	30	3	1	1	8	5	.204
Braulio Castillo	28	76	12	15	3	1	2	7	1	.197
Wes Chamberlain (RF)	76	275	26	71	18	0	9	41	4	.258
Darren Daulton (C)	145	485	80	131	32	5	27	(109)	11	.270
Mariano Duncan (LF)	142	574	71	153	40	3	8	50	23	.267
Lenny Dykstra (CF)	85	345	53	104	18	0	6	39	30	.301
Jeff Grotewold	72	65	7	13	2	0	3	5	0	.200
Dave Hollins (3B)	156	586	104	158	28	4	27	93	9	.270
Stan Javier	74	276	36	72	14	1	0	24	17	.261
Ricky Jordan	94	276	33	84	19	0	4	34	3	.304
John Kruk (1B)	144	507	86	164	30	4	10	70	3	.323
Steve Lake	20	53	3	13	2	0	1	2	0	.245
Jim Lindeman	29	39	6	10	1	0	1	6	0	.256
Tom Marsh	42	125	7	25	3	2	2	16	0	.200
Joe Millette	33	78	5	16	0	0	0	2	1	.205
Mickey Morandini (2B)	127	422	47	112	8	8	3	30	8	.265
Dale Murphy	18	62	5	10	1	0	2	7	0	.161
Julio Peguero	14	9	3	2	0	0	0	0	0	.222
Todd Pratt	16	46	6	13	1	0	2	10	0	.283
Steve Scarsone	7	13	1	2	0	0	0	0	0	.154
Dale Sveum	54	135	13	24	4	0	2	16	0	.178
		5,500	686	1,392	255	36	118	638	127	.253

catcher in major league history to win an RBI title. The heretofore often-maligned Phils catcher drove in 109 runs, the highest total for a catcher since Johnny Bench drove in 129 in 1974 and a new club record for a backstop, as was his home run total of 27.

Kruk had the third highest batting average (.323) in the league after leading much of the way. Hollins, in his first full season as a regular, had a spectacular year with 27 homers, 104 runs, and 93 RBI.

Schilling proved to be the club's best trade of the year, winning 14 games after he was obtained from the Houston Astros and converted into a starter. Mulholland added 13 wins before he, too, came down with an injury.

Darren Daulton reached stardom during the 1992 season after showing promise without tangible results for nearly a decade.

Mickey Morandini grabbed a piece of baseball history by making an unassisted triple play, only the ninth ever recorded and the first during the regular season by a second baseman. It was the first unassisted triple play in the National League in 65 years and the only one ever achieved by a Phillies player.

Another highlight of the season was turned in by Jeff Grotewold, who became the first major leaguer to hit pinch home runs three days in a row.

Player Profiles

In 110 years of baseball, the Phillies fielded just about every kind of team imaginable.

Some of the teams were horrendous losers. A few were gloriously triumphant. And most of them were somewhere in between. But almost all of the clubs had some certain quality that made them interesting.

The main reason for that, of course, was the players themselves. From superstars to bumblers, the Phillies always seemed to have a cast of colorful characters. And whether it was a dramatic home run that won a game or an embarrassing error that lost one, the club usually came up with some way to avoid boring its fans.

More than 1,500 players have worn Phillies uniforms in the years since 1883. The group represents virtually every corner of society. There have been evangelists and thugs, comedians and stoics, city slickers and farmers, and a wholesome conglomeration of Europeans, Canadians, and Latin Americans.

Many extraordinary players have performed for the Phillies, some of whom you are about to meet. This chapter is devoted to profiles on 200 of the best—or in some cases, most interesting—players in Phillies history.

Selections for this section were based on the contributions the player made to the Phillies, and not on their overall career performances.

Profiles in this Chapter

Grover Cleveland Alexander
Dick Allen
Ethan Allen
Ruben Amaro, Sr.
Harry Anderson
Morrie Arnovich
Richie Ashburn
Jack Baldschun
Dave Bancroft
Dick Bartell
Beals Becker
Steve Bedrosian
Ray Benge
Bob Boone
Ed Bouchee
Larry Bowa
Jack Boyle
Kitty Bransfield
Charlie Buffinton
Jim Bunning
Smoky Burgess
Johnny Callison
Dolph Camilli
Hal Carlson
Steve Carlton
Don Carman
Kid Carsey
Dan Casey
Dave Cash

Lou Chiozza
Larry Christenson
Jack Clements
John Coleman
Phil Collins
Gene Conley
Duff Cooley
Frank Corridon
Wes Covington
Gavvy Cravath
Lave Cross
Ray Culp
Clay Dalrymple
Curt Davis
Spud Davis
Ed Delahanty
Al Demaree
Don Demeter
John Denny
Murry Dickson
Frank Donahue
Red Dooin
Mickey Doolan
Bill Duggleby
Jumbo Elliott
Del Ennis
Nick Etten
Sid Farrar
Dick Farrell
Charlie Ferguson

Chico Fernandez
Elmer Flick
Jim Fogarty
Chick Fraser
Barney Friberg
Woodie Fryman
Gene Garber
Kid Gleason
Mike Goliat
Chile Gomez
Tony Gonzalez
Ed Grant
Greg Gross
Kevin Gross
Harvey Haddix
Bill Hallman
Billy Hamilton
Granny Hamner
George Harper
Von Hayes
Richie Hebner
Ken Heintzelman
Walter Henline
Pancho Herrera
Kirby Higbe
Joe Hoerner
Walt Holke
Al Holland
Tommy Hughes
Don Hurst

Grant Jackson
Larry Jackson
Deron Johnson
Syl Johnson
Jay Johnstone
Willie Jones
Oscar Judd
Andy Karl
Ted Kazanski
Bill Killefer
Chuck Klein
Otto Knabe
Jim Konstanty
Napoleon Lajoie
Fred Leach
Cliff Lee
Dutch Leonard
Danny Litwhiler
Hans Lobert
Jim Lonborg
Stan Lopata
Fred Luderus
Greg Luzinski
Garry Maddox
Sherry Magee
Art Mahaffey
Hersh Martin
Gary Matthews
Pinky May
Erskine Mayer

Robin Roberts was on his way to becoming one of the top pitchers in Phillies history when he got a few tips from veteran hurler Dutch Leonard.

Bake McBride	Al Orth	Mike Schmidt	Tuck Turner
Tim McCarver	Dode Paskert	Tom Seaton	Del Unser
Ed McFarland	Claude Passeau	Andy Seminick	Emil Verban
Tug McGraw	Dave Philley	Chris Short	Eddie Waitkus
George McQuillan	Wiley Piatt	Roy Sievers	Curt Walker
Lee Meadows	Togie Pittinger	Curt Simmons	Harry Walker
Emil Meusel	Wally Post	Dick Sisler	Bucky Walters
Jack Meyer	Ken Raffensberger	Ted Sizemore	Jimmy Wasdell
Russ Meyer	Shane Rawley	Lonnie Smith	Gus Weyhing
Bob Miller	Ron Reed	Tully Sparks	Bill White
Johnny Mokan	Jimmy Ring	Milt Stock	Pinky Whitney
Don Money	Eppa Rixey	Jack Taylor	Possum Whitted
Willie Montanez	Robin Roberts	Tony Taylor	Cy Williams
Earl Moore	Cookie Rojas	Kent Tekulve	Glenn Wilson
Johnny Moore	Pete Rose	Roy Thomas	Jimmie Wilson
Hugh Mulcahy	Schoolboy Rowe	Fresco Thompson	Bobby Wine
Joe Mulvey	Dick Ruthven	Sam Thompson	Rick Wise
Danny Murtaugh	Juan Samuel	Dickie Thon	Harry Wolverton
Bill Nicholson	Heinie Sand	John Titus	Russ Wrightstone
Ron Northey	Jack Sanford	Manny Trillo	Johnny Wyrostek
Lefty O'Doul			

Alexander, Grover Cleveland

Phillies: 1911–17; 1930
Pitcher
Nickname: Ol' Pete
Birthplace: Elba, Nebraska
B: February 26, 1887
D: November 4, 1950
Batted right, threw right
Ht. 6–1; **Wt.** 185

He was named after the only United States President to serve two separate terms of office; just from that fact, you get the feeling that Grover Cleveland Alexander's parents knew their son was going to grow up to be unique.

He became known as Ol' Pete and he spent the Prohibition years sneaky-pete-ing his life away when he wasn't driving opposing hitters to drink. The man who was named for a president had his life story posthumously portrayed in a full-length feature film by a man who would later become president (Ronald Reagan). The movie was called "The Winning Team." The team was the 1926 St. Louis Cardinals, and Alexander's great moment came when he supposedly was roused from a post-drunken nap in the St. Louis bullpen and sent in to face Tony Lazzeri with the final game of the World Series on the line. The story line became as clouded as Ol' Pete's mind was supposed to have been when he entered the game. He made a pitch that Lazzeri slammed just barely foul, then struck out the Yankee slugger and became the toast of the town in St. Louis.

Four years later, at the age of 43, he would retire from baseball, failing to win a game in the final season of his second tour of duty with the Phillies at Baker Bowl. In 1938 he would be voted into the Hall of Fame with 373 career victories, a figure surpassed in baseball history only by Cy Young and Walter Johnson. But two years after his induction at Cooperstown, he was discovered working in a flea circus near Times Square in New York City.

"It's better living off the fleas than having them live off you," he said at the time.

He died in November 1950, a month after watching his former team, the Phillies, play in the World Series in Yankee Stadium. The last time the Phils had been in a Series, Alex had been there, too—as a pitcher. In fact, until Steve Carlton won the opening game of the 1980 World Series, Alexander was the only Phillies pitcher in history to record a Series triumph.

While in New York for the 1950 fall classic, Alexander categorically shot down the feat for which he is most famous. He told a writer in his hotel room that he was completely sober when called upon to pitch to Lazzeri with the bases loaded and two outs in the bottom of the seventh inning of that 1926 seventh game.

"I don't want to spoil anyone's story," Alexander said, "but I was cold sober that (evening). There were plenty of other nights before and since that I have not been sober, although I have been cold, but the night before I struck Lazzeri out, I was as sober as a judge should be."

Judge not lest ye be judged, it has been written, so suffice it to say that Grover Cleveland Alexander's life and career were, at the same time, brilliant and tragic. And, although he pitched for 20 years and is best remembered for something he did at age 39, perhaps the most remarkable of all his pitching feats was accomplished early in his major league career with the Phillies at Baker Bowl, which would later become a house of horrors for pitchers of all abilities. But, for seven years, Ol' Pete made Baker Bowl his own personal fun house.

Alexander was discovered toiling in the minor leagues at the relatively old age of 23 during the late summer of 1910 by Patsy O'Rourke, who was a scout of sorts for Phillies owner Horace Fogel. O'Rourke, a Philadelphian, then managed Albany in the same New York State League in which Alexander was playing for Syracuse.

"See anything up there that caught your eye?" Fogel asked O'Rourke.

"You bet, Mr. Fogel," Patsy said. "A fine pitcher. One of the greatest pitching prospects I've ever looked at."

Fogel remained unexcited. "If you're talking about Chalmers, you can save your breath, we've already got him," he said, referring to George Chalmers, who finished that season with a 25–6 record at Scranton.

"Chalmers is good," O'Rourke replied, "but the fella I'm talking about, Alexander, is even better."

Fogel was unimpressed, reminding O'Rourke that everyone he had questioned considered Chalmers the best pitcher in the New York State League.

"Well, all I can say is that you better grab this Alexander before someone else does," O'Rourke said.

O'Rourke's scouting report was impeccable, as was Fogel's luck. Horace rushed Chalmers to the Phillies during 1910 (George lasted seven years with a 29–41 lifetime record), but gambled that he would be able to draft Alexander after the season was over. He was awarded the contract of Grover C. Alexander, of Syracuse, for $750.

It was perhaps the greatest bargain in major league baseball history.

As a rookie, Alex led the league with 28 victories, 31 complete games, and seven shutouts, four of them in succession. No first-year pitcher in history has ever come close to Alex's 28 wins, but that was just a beginning.

He won 19, 22, and league-leading 27 over the next three years, but even that was only a glimpse of what would take place over a three-year stretch beginning with the 1915 pennant season.

Over that period, he worked an awesome 1,153 innings, leading the National League in that category all three seasons. He completed 109 of 131 starts, winning 94 games and losing 35. Thirty-six of the victories were shutouts, including 16 in 1916—a record that should outlive all others, including Joe DiMaggio's 56-game hitting streak. His earned run average in 1915 was 1.22 and, over the next five seasons, it would never surpass 2.00.

Alexander also won the only World Series game the Phillies were to capture in their first 97 years. He defeated the Boston Red Sox in the opener of the 1915 Series, 3–1. He also pitched brilliantly in Game Three before losing, 2–1, when he ignored conventional wisdom and pitched to Duffy Lewis with first base open and the winning run on third with two outs. Lewis singled cleanly up the middle to end it.

Alexander strained his side in that game, which is why he did not pitch in the fifth and final game.

Like the other two Phillie pitchers whose careers are sure to live in Cooperstown, a no-hitter eluded him, just as it did Robin Roberts and Steve Carlton. But in 1915 he threw four one-hitters, an awesome achievement for a man who pitched half his games in Baker Bowl, where pop flies clanged off the right field wall with alarming regularity.

And all of this was accomplished even though Ol' Pete became a heavy drinker soon after he pitched his first big league game.

In the seven seasons of his first tour of duty with the Phillies, Alexander won 190 games. Only Roberts and Carlton have won more, and each needed a

Grover Cleveland Alexander

Grover Cleveland Alexander spent much of his working years after baseball employed by flea circuses and in two-bit vaudeville shows.

lot more seasons to do it. But after the 1917 season, Phillies owner William Baker, fearing that Alex would be drafted, packaged Alexander and his catcher, Bill Killefer, and shipped them to the Chicago Cubs. Philadelphia went into shock and Baker had to explain the move as honestly as possible. "I needed the money," he said.

Alexander spent most of his first year on the Cubs' roster in France as an infantryman during World War I. He developed epilepsy, and his drinking problems escalated. But he led the National League with 27 victories in 1920 and, at the age of 40, was able to win 21 for the Cardinals in 1927.

It was, however, his feat in the 1926 World Series that made Ol' Pete a national celebrity. By then, baseball had reached its pinnacle of popularity, thanks to the Roaring Twenties and Babe Ruth, another man who was known to take a drink but who was establishing hitting records the way Alex had set pitching marks.

The Cardinals, under manager Rogers Hornsby, were driving toward their first National League pennant when they purchased Alex from the Cubs at the end of June. Ol' Pete won nine games during the regular season, took the second game of the World Series to even it for the Cards, then won Game Six to tie it up again. Legend says that Alex, sure that he wouldn't be called upon to work in the seventh game, spent the night on the town. But when he was allegedly roused and came in to pitch to Lazzeri in the bases-loaded situation, he was equal to the task. Gabe Paul, former president of the Cleveland Indians, tells the scene as he remembers it from his seat in the bullpen area of Yankee Stadium.

"I saw them shake Alexander awake and I saw that the pitch was easily foul," said Gabe. "I never knew what the fuss was all about. It was a good pitch."

Alexander, who would later be quoted as saying, "Do you think I would have thrown him the same pitch if I thought he could hit it fair?" could never understand the fuss either.

"Let me tell you what happened," he said to Gerry Hern of the *Boston Post* in 1950. "I was leaving the locker room after the (sixth) game and Hornsby came over and slapped me on the back. He said, 'You were great today and I suppose you want to celebrate. But don't do it. I may need you tomorrow.' And as sure as I'm sitting here, I went back to my room at the Hotel Ansonia that night and didn't leave it—and I didn't celebrate, either.

"I didn't expect to work that day because Jess Haines was going good. But all of a sudden he got in trouble. Hornsby telephoned the bullpen. He asked who was ready. They told him two or three pitchers were. He said, 'I don't care about them. I want Alex.' They said, 'He isn't ready, hasn't even warmed up yet.' 'I don't care, send him anyway,' Hornsby said."

So there Alexander was, facing the clutch-hitting Lazzeri with the bases as loaded as he had ever been. Lazzeri took a called strike, then a ball, then hit the third pitch a mile to left, but foul. On the fourth pitch, Alex said he had the hitter set up perfectly.

"The curve I threw started right at Lazzeri," Alex said. "He stood there. Like I said, he was a tough guy. The ball started breaking about 10 feet in front of the plate. He missed it by two feet."

They may argue whether or not Ol' Pete was sober or hung over when he entered the game, and whether or not Lazzeri's drive was barely foul or way foul. But no one has ever disputed that the pitch that struck Tony out and saved the Cards' first World Championship was about the meanest breaking curve ever seen.

And no one will ever deny that this man who still ranks third on the all-time roster list in wins, second in shutouts (90), and fifth in innings pitched (5,189) was, for his first seven years with the Phillies, the equal of anyone who has ever pitched the game—before or since.

In 1929, Alexander finally won his 373d game, as a Cardinal. At the time, he believed it made him the all-time National League winner, since Christy Matthewson was credited with only 372 at the time. Bill McKechnie, the St. Louis manager, surmised for obvious reasons that Ol' Pete would use the occasion for one of his legendary celebrations and warned the pitcher that missing the midnight curfew would be grounds for his outright release. Alex missed several midnight curfews. By the time he rejoined the team, he found out he had been sold back to the Phillies.

This time Baker Bowl wasn't as kind to its former master. In 1930, Alex pitched nine games, gave up 40 hits in 21 innings, lost all three of his decisions, and quit the game at the age of 43. Those who knew his lifestyle said his longevity was his most astounding statistic.

For the final two decades of his life he fought a losing fight against poverty, alcoholism, and cancer. He drifted from job to job when he worked and finally, in the late 1940s, lived on a $25 a week check that came to him by way of the National League office, courtesy of the estate of Cardinal owner Sam Breadon, who never forgot the man who gave the franchise its first World Series title.

In an interview in 1939 with Frank Yeutter of the *Evening Bulletin,* Alexander waxed melancholy about his career. "I had control of everything but myself," he said. "Control of bats, but none with dollars. But that's the way I've been. I've made promises and broke them, the way I broke a curve outside to the heavy hitters. I've laughed as many times as I've cried so I guess I'm even with life."

Philadelphia remembered him in 1950 when he was invited to be Bob Carpenter's guest at the first World Series involving the team since he had pitched in it. Alex messed up his travel plans from Nebraska and never made it to Shibe Park. But he did show up at Yankee Stadium for the final two games before returning home to die a month later in a cheap hotel room.

Two years later, his career was portrayed on film by a man who would later become president of the United States. For a man who was named after a president, it was life's final irony.

Alexander, Grover Cleveland

Phillies	W	L	Pct	ERA	G	CG	IP	H	BB	SO	ShO
1911	28	13	.683	2.57	43	31	367	285	129	227	7
1912	19	17	.528	2.82	46	26	310	289	105	195	3
1913	22	8	.733	2.79	47	23	306	288	75	159	9
1914	27	15	.643	2.38	46	32	335	327	76	214	6
1915	31	10	.756	1.22	49	36	376	253	64	241	12
1916	33	12	.733	1.55	48	38	389	323	50	167	16
1917	30	13	.698	1.86	45	35	388	336	58	201	8
1930	0	3	.000	9.00	9	0	22	40	6	6	0
Career	373	208	.642	2.56	696	439	5,189	4,868	953	2,199	90

Allen, Dick

Phillies: 1963–69; 1975–76
First baseman, third baseman, outfielder
Nickname: Crash
Birthplace: Wampum, Pennsylvania
B: March 8, 1942
Bats right, throws right
Ht. 5–11; **Wt.** 187

Richard Anthony Allen became eligible for the Hall of Fame in 1982 and didn't come close. Subsequent ballots have also failed to elevate the slugger to a spot in Cooperstown.

The ballot box has become the final irony in the baseball life of a man who was probably his own worst enemy, a talent who insisted upon self-destructing. From the day in 1965 when Frank Thomas attacked him with a baseball bat during some pre-game needling, Allen's baseball career became as famous for things he did off the field as things he did on it. Which is awesome in itself, because Allen did some positively amazing things on the field.

He hit 351 career home runs, some of which were the longest ever seen at Connie Mack Stadium. His lifetime average was .292, and one season he even found time to steal 20 bases. Twice he led his league in home runs, three times in RBI. He also struck out 1,556 times.

And he had a love-hate relationship with most of his managers, including Gene Mauch, whose tenure in Philadelphia finally came to an end in 1968 when it became apparent that Philadelphia wasn't big enough for both him and Allen.

"I never enjoyed a player more than I enjoyed Richie Allen in 1964," Mauch said later. "We both had a lot of fun. It wasn't so much fun at the end."

Ken Boyer won the National League MVP award in 1964, and Johnny Callison finished second. Had justice prevailed, given the term "most valuable player," Allen would have won the award hands down. He was thrown into the pressure of a year-long pennant race at a position which he had hardly ever played before, and with only 24 big league at-bats. He responded incredibly. He had 201 hits, a .318 average, led the league with 125 runs scored and 13 triples, smacked 29 home runs, drove in 91 runs, and played every game at third base. Without him, the Phillies would have been out of the race Father's Day. With him, they almost stole the pennant.

But they would not have come so close to winning the pennant without some fine work also by Frank Thomas at first base and at the plate. And on July 3, 1965, Thomas needled Allen too hard; Allen motioned for Thomas to come get him and Thomas did—with a bat. Thomas hit a game-winning pinch-hit homer that night, was released after the game, and the fans never forgave Allen. They booed him every night after that, even though he kept hitting over .300, hit 40 homers, including three inside-the-park homers, and drove in 110 runs in 1966.

By 1967, Allen's tardiness was becoming a problem. Then, on August 24 of that year, Allen severely cut his right hand and wrist when he said he had punched through a headlight on an old car he was pushing. His season was over and there was speculation that his career might be, too.

But he was back the following year. Although the injury affected Dick's throwing, forcing Mauch to play him in left field, his hitting continued (33 homers). So did his unexcused absences.

By mid-season of 1969, Bob Skinner had come and gone as Mauch's replacement. George Myatt was the manager then, and Allen was still an offensive terror when he showed up at the ball park. But, Myatt was asked, could he handle the slugger? His answer was priceless. "God Almighty hisself couldn't handle that man," he said.

In the off-season, Allen was traded— and even in leaving, he had controversy follow him. The deal with the Cardinals yielded, among others, Curt Flood. Flood refused to report to the Phillies and took his reserve-clause case to the courts. Even though he lost, baseball was changed forever.

Allen lasted a year in St. Louis and a year in Los Angeles before three productive seasons with the Chicago White Sox under his friend Chuck Tanner. Then the Phillies brought him back in a trade with the Atlanta Braves. He had two subpar (for him) years, drove Danny Ozark to a wastebasket-kicking, screaming show on a Sunday afternoon when he didn't play, and closed out his career in 1977 with the Oakland A's.

His career statistics are outstanding. They could have been enough to get him selected to the Hall of Fame if he had taken the game as seriously as some of his less-talented teammates did.

Nobody knew that better than Mauch.

"I can't think of anybody I'd rather have walk up to a mirror, look at himself and say, 'I'm going to take the next five years and do everything I can (in baseball) so I can do what I want to do the next 40 years of my life,' " Frank Dolson quoted Mauch as saying in *The Philadelphia Story*. "And he can do that. Five years of total dedication is not much of a price to pay for 40 years of comfort. . . . I tried. I think my greatest feeling of inadequacy was my inability to convince him how reasonable this thinking is. That feeling of inadequacy finally disappeared when I realized no one on earth could make him feel that way—except himself. He wants independence. Not family. Not job. Not accomplishment. Only independence. You just can't be that way.

"I think I know how he feels. He came from meager circumstances. So did I. He was happy as a poor kid. So was I. Now he probably figures, what do I need all this worry for? But you do have things to worry about."

Allen authored an autobiography, *Crash*, in the 1980s. He also made peace with Frank Thomas in that decade when both were playing in old-timers' games. But he never made the Hall of Fame, despite his enormous talents.

Dick Allen

Allen, Dick

Phillies	G	AB	H	BA	RBI	R	2B	3B	HR	SA	SB
1963	10	24	7	.292	2	6	2	1	0	.458	0
1964	162	632	201	.318	91	125	38	13	29	.557	3
1965	161	619	187	.302	85	93	31	14	20	.494	15
1966	141	524	166	.317	110	112	25	10	40	.632	10
1967	122	463	142	.307	77	89	31	10	23	.566	20
1968	152	521	137	.263	90	87	17	9	33	.520	7
1969	118	438	126	.288	89	79	23	3	32	.573	9
1975	119	416	97	.233	62	54	21	3	12	.385	11
1976	85	298	80	.268	49	52	16	1	15	.480	11
Career	1,749	6,332	1,848	.292	1,119	1,099	320	79	351	.534	133

Allen, Ethan

Phillies: 1934–36
Outfielder
Birthplace: Cincinnati, Ohio
B: January 1, 1904
Bats right, throws right
Ht. 6–1; **Wt.** 180

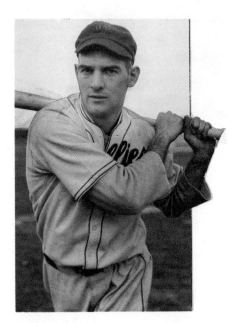

Ethan Allen

Aside from the fact that all his names ended in the letter *n*, Ethan Nathan Allen was one of the more unheralded Phillies of the mid-1930s. Yet he was one of the Phils' top hitters and a fine outfielder who possessed a strong arm.

A rookie in 1926, Allen was sold to the Phillies in 1934 after seeing action with the Cincinnati Reds, New York Giants, and St. Louis Cardinals. His best years had been in 1928 when he hit .305 for the Reds and 1931 when he batted .329 for the Giants.

Allen, who had a bachelor's degree from the University of Cincinnati and a master's from Columbia, was a batting sensation. He hit .330 in his first year in Philadelphia and led the league in doubles with 42. The following year Allen hit .307 with 46 doubles.

Ethan, who played left field and center field, also led the league's outfielders in assists in 1935. He cut down 26 runners.

In 1936, Allen was hitting .296 when the Phillies packed him off to the Chicago Cubs in a trade that brought Chuck Klein back to Philadelphia. After finishing the season with the Cubs, Allen was sold to the St. Louis Browns, for whom he hit .316 in 1937. Ethan played one more year with the Browns before ending his 13-year big league career. His lifetime batting average was .300.

Allen was director of motion picture promotion for the National League from 1939 to 1942. He also wrote several baseball books, including *Major League Baseball* and *Winning Baseball,* and created a popular game, "All-Star Baseball," which was based on players' lifetime records. The game, created in 1941, is still marketed.

At the end of World War II, Allen became head baseball coach at Yale University. In 1947, with George Bush as the first baseman, Yale lost to Jackie Jensen and the University of California in the first NCAA baseball finals. The Elis lost to Southern California in the finals the following year.

Allen remained at Yale through the 1968 season when he retired. Later, he was inducted into the College Baseball Coaches Hall of Fame.

Allen, Ethan

Phillies	G	AB	H	BA	RBI	R	2B	3B	HR	SA	SB
1934	145	581	192	.330	85	87	42	4	10	.468	6
1935	156	645	198	.307	63	90	46	1	8	.419	5
1936	30	125	37	.296	9	21	3	1	1	.360	4
Career	1,281	4,418	1,325	.300	501	623	255	45	47	.410	84

Amaro, Ruben, Sr.

Phillies: 1960–65
Infielder
Birthplace: Vera Cruz, Mexico
B: January 6, 1936
Bats right, throws right
Ht. 5–11; **Wt.** 170

When the Phillies traded Chuck Essegian to the Cardinals in 1958 for a young shortstop named Ruben Amaro, the word was already out on him. "Good field, no hit."

For the most part, it was a correct tag, although Amaro did his part offensively in 1964, the Year the Phillies Almost Won the Pennant, with a .264 average (his career best) in 129 games. He also had career years in home runs (4) and RBI (34). And something that may have been forgotten was the fact that Amaro played 58 games at first base that year, many as a starter and more than any other Phillie at that position.

It's forgotten because when one thinks about Amaro, the image of a sure-handed shortstop with excellent range comes to mind.

Unfortunately for Amaro, there was another sure-handed shortstop with excellent range and a suspect bat in the organization at the same time. And after being the one bright spot in the dismal 1961 season, Amaro found himself in the army at the start of 1962. The Phillies brought up the other shortstop, and Bobby Wine won the regular job. Amaro was released from the service in July of that year and spent the next 2½ years battling Wine. Bobby eventually won the job, and Amaro was traded to the Yankees for Phil Linz after the 1965 season. He wound up his major league career with the California Angels in 1969.

Ruben eventually found his way back to the Phillies organization as both a coach and a scout. It was in the latter position that he might have made his biggest contribution to the club.

Amaro headed the Latin American scouting for the Phillies and was instrumental in discovering Julio Franco, Al Sanchez, and Juan Samuel. He left the team after the 1982 season to take a job with the Chicago Cubs.

He now is a scout and minor league manager with the Detroit Tigers organization. When his son, Ruben, Jr., played in the Phillies' 1992 opener, it marked the first time a father-son combination had ever played for the club.

Ruben Amaro Sr.

Amaro, Ruben, Sr.

Phillies	G	AB	H	BA	RBI	R	2B	3B	HR	SA	SB
1960	92	264	61	.231	16	25	9	1	0	.273	0
1961	135	381	98	.257	32	34	14	9	1	.349	1
1962	79	226	55	.243	19	24	10	0	0	.288	5
1963	115	217	47	.217	19	25	9	2	2	.304	0
1964	129	299	79	.264	34	31	11	0	4	.341	1
1965	118	184	39	.212	15	26	7	0	0	.250	1
Career	940	2,155	505	.234	156	211	75	13	8	.292	11

Anderson, Harry

Phillies: 1957–60
Left fielder, first baseman
Birthplace: Rising Sun, Maryland
B: September 10, 1931
Bats left, throws right
Ht. 6–3; **Wt.** 205

In 1957 the Phillies had one of the finest rookie crops ever to arrive in one season. One of the most promising members of the group was a lanky, free-swinging hitter by the name of Harry Anderson.

Anderson, joined by a collection of other freshmen named Bouchee, Bowman, Cardwell, Farrell, and Sanford, was expected to be the Phillies' ticket back into the ranks of pennant contenders.

It didn't quite work out that way. Anderson played in Philadelphia for nearly three and one-half years, experiencing some high points as well as some low ones.

A graduate of West Chester State College with a degree in physical education, Anderson joined the Phillies farm system in 1953. He hit .323 that year for Terre Haute. A first baseman then, Harry also led his peers in fielding.

Harry divided the next three years between the minors and the military. He came out of the service in 1956 to help Schenectady win the Eastern League championship.

An aggressive hitter who had good power, Anderson had been converted to an outfielder when he reported to the Phillies in 1957. That year he won the regular left field post, and hit .268.

The following season Anderson spurted to a .301 average while leading the last-place Phillies with 23 home runs and 97 RBI. He also led the league in strikeouts with 95. At one point, he lashed five hits in a game against the San Francisco Giants.

In 1959, Harry led National League outfielders (he had played some games at first the previous year) in assists with 17. But his average slipped to .240 and his home run production to 14.

Anderson and the Phillies parted company in June 1960. Harry, outfielder Wally Post, and first baseman Fred Hopke were shipped to the Cincinnati Reds for outfielders Tony Gonzalez and Lee Walls.

It was to be a good trade for the Phillies. As for Anderson, his average continued to plummet, and he was out of the majors by early 1961.

Harry Anderson

Anderson, Harry

Phillies	G	AB	H	BA	RBI	R	2B	3B	HR	SA	SB
1957	118	400	107	.268	61	53	15	4	17	.453	2
1958	140	515	155	.301	97	80	34	6	23	.524	0
1959	142	508	122	.240	63	50	28	6	14	.402	1
1960	38	93	23	.247	12	10	2	0	5	.430	0
Career	484	1,586	419	.264	242	199	82	16	60	.450	3

Arnovich, Morrie

Phillies: 1936–40
Outfielder
Nickname: Snooker
Birthplace: Superior, Wisconsin
B: November 20, 1910
D: July 20, 1959
Batted right, threw right
Ht. 5–10; **Wt.** 168

Morrie Arnovich

With players parading in and out of Philadelphia as though they were caught in a revolving door, anybody who lasted more than three years with the Phillies during the 1930s had to be considered an old-timer by local standards.

On that basis, Morrie Arnovich was that and more. He dressed in a Phillies uniform for nearly five seasons. Arnovich was the Phillies' starting left fielder during the club's lowest period.

A heavy hitter in the minors, he had a .374 average in 1934 and a .327 in 1935. Arnovich joined the Phillies in 1936. He cracked the starting lineup the following year, and hit .290 with 10 home runs, his career high.

Two years later, Morrie had his finest big league campaign when he hit .324. It was the highest average on the eighth-place Phils squad, and the fifth-highest mark in the National League. In June that season, Arnovich led the majors with a .395 average. Arnovich, who had led the club with 72 RBI the previous year, was rewarded for his efforts with a berth on the league All-Star team. He was hitting .375 at the time.

As was usually the case when a player showed too much talent, the Phillies unloaded Arnovich early in the 1940 season, sending him to the Cincinnati Reds for outfielder Johnny Rizzo. It was a lucky stroke for Morrie, although he was no longer a starter. The Reds won the pennant, allowing Arnovich to go from last place to first place in the short span of a few months.

In 1941, Morrie was sold to the New York Giants where he continued his role as a utility outfielder. After four years in the military, he rejoined the Giants briefly in 1946, but played in only one game before retiring.

Arnovich, Morrie

Phillies	G	AB	H	BA	RBI	R	2B	3B	HR	SA	SB
1936	13	48	15	.313	7	4	3	0	1	.438	0
1937	117	410	119	.290	60	60	27	4	10	.449	5
1938	139	502	138	.275	72	47	29	0	4	.357	2
1939	134	491	159	.324	67	68	25	2	5	.413	7
1940	39	141	28	.199	12	13	2	1	0	.227	0
Career	590	2,013	577	.287	261	234	104	12	22	.383	17

Ashburn, Richie

Phillies: 1949–59
Center fielder
Nicknames: Whitey, Putt-Putt
Birthplace: Tilden, Nebraska
B: March 19, 1927
Bats left, throws right
Ht. 5–10; **Wt.** 170

Of the 1,500 men who have worn the uniform of the Phillies since the club's beginning, several stand alone at the top as the team's all-time best players. Richie Ashburn is on that list.

One of the most talented, exciting, and popular players in Phillies history, Ashburn did just about everything during his 12 years with the club. One of the finest center fielders ever to wear the Phils' livery, Richie could hit, run, and field.

He won National League batting championships in 1955 and 1958; he was a perennial league leader in various fielding categories; he was a four-time National League All-Star; he had a lifetime batting average of .308 (.311 with the Phillies) with more than 2,000 hits; and he was one of the key men on the Whiz Kids' 1950 pennant winners.

Playing in an era of great center fielders, Ashburn often had to take a back seat in the public spotlight to Willie Mays and Duke Snider. Except as a long-distance hitter, Richie, it could be and has been argued, was their equal.

Ashburn is one of only four Phillies who has had his number retired by the club. The others are Robin Roberts, Steve Carlton, and Mike Schmidt. It is obvious why Richie's legendary No. 1 holds such an esteemed place.

The blond speedster is second on the team's all-time career list in games, hits, and at-bats. He ranks third in runs, fourth in triples, fifth in total bases and stolen bases, and eighth in batting average. Whitey led the team or tied for the lead in stolen bases 12 times; nine times in games and hits; eight times in batting average and runs; and seven times in triples and at-bats.

He holds the major league record for most years (four) with 500 or more putouts, and he is tied with Max Carey for the major league record for most years (nine) with 400 or more putouts. Ashburn and Carey also share the major league marks for most years leading the league in chances (eight) and most years leading the league in putouts (nine).

Along with Clarence Beaumont, Lloyd Waner, and Maury Wills, Richie shares the National League record for most years (four) leading the league in one-base hits. He also holds the National League standard set in 1959 for fewest RBI (20) in a season while playing in 150 or more games.

Ashburn was also one of the game's most durable players. From June 7, 1950, to September 26, 1954 (the last game of the season), he played in 730 consecutive games. That ranks as the fifth longest streak in National League history. It came to an end on opening day in 1955 when Ashburn was held out of the lineup after suffering injuries from a violent collision with Del Ennis while chasing Mickey Mantle's fly ball in an exhibition game a few days earlier in Wilmington, Delaware, against the New York Yankees.

Between 1949 and 1958, Richie missed only 22 games. During that period, he had three league-leading seasons of more than 200 hits, and he was the league leader in numerous categories in addition to batting average and fielding.

Ironically, despite his skills as a hitter, runner, and fielder, the play for which Richie is probably most remembered was neither a hit, a run, nor a catch.

Richie Ashburn

Dashing home and sliding across the plate safely was a common occurrence for speedy Richie Ashburn.

It was a throw. Without it, there would have been no Dick Sisler home run in 1950 and no Phillies pennant.

Ashburn made the throw in the bottom of the ninth inning in the final game of the season against the Brooklyn Dodgers. With the score tied, 1–1, none out, and men on first and second, the Dodgers' Duke Snider laced a single to center field. Ashburn charged the ball, while Cal Abrams, who had been on second, was being waved home by Brooklyn third base coach Milt Stock. Richie fired a perfect strike to catcher Stan Lopata, who applied the tag on the sliding Abrams.

The throw saved the game for the Phillies and paved the way for Sisler's dramatic pennant-winning homer in the 10th inning.

Although his arm was often taken lightly, as the Dodgers illustrated, Ashburn led National League outfielders in assists in 1952, 1953, and 1957. Originally a catcher, Richie had undergone intense training when he first came to pro ball to learn to throw like an outfielder.

Ashburn had first attracted the attention of big league scouts as a schoolboy in Tilden, Nebraska. As a 16-year-old in 1943, he attended a tryout camp run by the St. Louis Cardinals. Although the Redbirds were impressed, they couldn't sign him because of his age. The following year the Cleveland Indians did sign Richie, but he was still too young, and Commissioner Landis nullified the contract.

A little later, Ashburn signed a Nashville contract for the Chicago Cubs. Again, the pact was voided, this time by minor league commissioner Judge Branham, because of an irregularity in the contract. Soon afterward, the Phillies stepped into the picture, and scout Eddie Krajnik signed the young towhead with the aid of a $7,500 bonus. The New York Yankees had offered a higher price, but Richie figured he could make the big leagues sooner with the Phillies.

Ashburn, who has a twin sister, attended Norfolk Junior College in Nebraska that winter, studying journalism. He reported to the Phils' Utica team in the spring of 1945. That season, Whitey hit .312, and manager Eddie Sawyer converted him from a catcher to a center fielder.

He spent the next year and one-half in the army, receiving his discharge just in time to rejoin Utica. With a .362 average, Ashburn sparked Utica to the Eastern League championship. He also began drawing rave notices about his blinding speed, and his sizzling performance at the plate and in center field. "Another Ty Cobb but without Cobb's meanness," one admirer described him.

Richie was slated for the Triple-A team at Toronto in 1948, but he so impressed Phils manager Ben Chapman that he stayed in spring training with the parent club. Breaking into the starting lineup was a difficult proposition, though. All Richie had to do was to beat out the defending National League batting champion, Harry Walker.

Walker, however, held out briefly, and when he did report to camp he was out of shape. Then Harry got hurt, and Chapman slid the 21-year-old cornhusker into the lineup. Walker never played regular center field for the Phillies again.

Ashburn was the talk of spring training. Farm club director Joe Reardon, calling him one of the fastest kids in the country, said, "He's going to be a great outfielder one day."

Richie didn't disappoint his followers. The clean-cut kid with the wholesome habits tore up the National League in 1948. Beating out bunts and infield hits and slashing drives, mostly to the opposite field, Ashburn had a .333 batting average, which was second to Stan Musial in the race for the batting title. It was also the eighth highest batting average for a rookie in National League history.

At one point, Ashburn, the Phils' leadoff batter, hit in 23 straight games, getting 43 hits in 98 trips to the plate during the streak. The streak tied a National League record for a rookie player. Ashburn was also the starting center fielder for the National League All-Star team.

In late August, Richie broke a finger and was lost for the season. But he still wound up leading the league in stolen bases with 32. And after the season, he was named Rookie of the Year by *The Sporting News*.

The following year, Ashburn suffered a letdown, which he later attributed to a "swelled head." Richie hit only .284, which was at least in part caused by the fact that other teams began looking for his bunts and playing him shallow in the outfield. He did lead the league, however, in at-bats with 662.

The Phillies weren't overjoyed with Ashburn's performance in 1949, and even entertained notions of sending him back to Toronto. But Richie reported to spring training in 1950 with a new attitude and a few new techniques in his batting style.

When he was moved to the number-two position in the batting order, Ashburn's average zoomed to .303. He led the league in triples. And time after time, Richie either started rallies, kept them alive, or in some other fashion sparked the Phillies during their drive to the National League pennant.

Richie also played a key role in center field, flanked as he was by slow-footed teammates, Dick Sisler in left and Del Ennis in right. It was Ashburn's duty to patrol as much of the outfield as possible, and he ranged far to accomplish that assignment.

In the World Series that fall, Ashburn was handcuffed by Yankee pitchers, although he did double home the only Phillies run in the 2–1 second game loss. Richie had three hits in 17 at-bats in the Series.

Ashburn was sometimes called Putt-Putt, a name given him by Ted Williams. The great Boston Red Sox slugger had wisecracked that Richie ran as though he had twin motors in his pants, and went putt-putt, putt-putt.

In 1951, Richie putt-putted to one of the finest seasons of his career. He led the league in hits with a career high 221, placed second to the Boston Braves' Sam Jethroe in stolen bases, and had a batting average of .344, again second in the league to Musial. At one point during the season, Ashburn had eight hits (all singles) in 10 at-bats in a doubleheader. He started in center field for the National League All-Star team.

Ashburn hit another slump in 1952, dropping to a .282 average. It would be the second of only four times in 12 seasons with the Phillies that the lefthanded swinger would hit below .300.

For the next four years, Richie hit at least .300, going .330, .313, .338 and .303. In 1953 he led the league again in hits and made the All-Star team, and in 1954 he was first in bases on balls. That year, he also established an unusual footnote to his record by fouling off 14 consecutive pitches thrown by Cincinnati Reds pitcher Corky Valentine. Eventually, Richie walked.

In 1955, Ashburn won his first batting title with a .338 mark. Mays and Musial tied for second with .319 averages. It was only the eighth batting crown in Phillies history.

After .303 and .297 seasons, Richie won his second batting championship in 1958 with a .350 average. Unlike his first title, which he won easily, Ashburn had to go to the final day of the season this time to clinch the crown. He won it with three hits in four trips to the plate in a 10-inning, 6–4 win over the Pirates. Richie, who had four four-hit games and 16 hits in his last 27 at-bats of the season, edged Mays by three points.

For the third time, Ashburn led the league in hits in 1958. He also won his second triples crown and his third bases on balls title. He was second to Mays in stolen bases. He was named for the fourth time to the National League All-Star team. And his 312 hits and walks ranked as the ninth highest total of this combination in National League history.

Ashburn's average dropped a devastating 84 points in 1959. Although he was still a relatively young man at 32, Ashburn was perceived to be slowing down by the Phillies brass. Indicative of that, perhaps, was the fact that he hit into three double plays in one game that year (Richie hit into only 101 twin killings during his entire career). During the winter of 1960 he was traded to the Chicago Cubs for infielders Al Dark and Jim Wood and pitcher John Buzhardt. It wasn't much of a trade from the Phillies' standpoint, but Ashburn still had some good years left.

He hit .291 in 1960 for the Cubs, leading the league again in walks. In 1961, Richie dipped to .257. Chicago let him go in the expansion draft to the newly formed New York Mets.

Ashburn was a member of the infamous 1962 Mets, a team that lost more games (120) than any other team in baseball history. Through it all, Richie managed to register a .306 batting average, which was by far the best mark on the hapless Mets. Because it turned out to be his final year in the big leagues, the average also gave Ashburn the distinction of being one of only 10 regulars in big league history to hit above .300 in their last full season.

Since 1963, Ashburn has been a member of the Phillies' radio and television team. He also is a writer, having penned a column with the *Philadelphia Bulletin* and the *Philadelphia Daily News*.

Ashburn, Richie

Phillies	G	AB	H	BA	RBI	R	2B	3B	HR	SA	SB
1948	117	463	154	.333	40	78	17	4	2	.400	32
1949	154	662	188	.284	37	84	18	11	1	.349	9
1950	151	594	180	.303	41	84	25	14	2	.402	14
1951	154	643	221	.344	63	92	31	5	4	.426	29
1952	154	613	173	.282	42	93	31	6	1	.357	16
1953	156	622	205	.330	57	110	25	9	2	.408	14
1954	153	559	175	.313	41	111	16	8	1	.376	11
1955	140	533	180	.338	42	91	32	9	3	.448	12
1956	154	628	190	.303	50	94	26	8	3	.384	10
1957	156	626	186	.297	33	93	26	8	0	.364	13
1958	152	615	215	.350	33	98	24	13	2	.441	30
1959	153	564	150	.266	20	86	16	2	1	.307	9
Career	2,189	8,365	2,574	.308	586	1,322	317	109	29	.382	234

Baldschun, Jack

Phillies: 1961–65
Pitcher
Birthplace: Greenville, Ohio
B: October 16, 1936
Bats right, throws right
Ht. 6–1; Wt. 175

In November 1960 the Phillies made an almost-unnoticed move in the minor league drafts. They took a pitcher off the Class A Charleston roster of the Cincinnati Reds organization.

Four years later, the guy almost won a pennant for the Phillies. His name was Jack Baldschun, and for three seasons he was as good a relief pitcher as there was in the National League. Also about as nerve-wracking as you could find.

Between 1962 and 1964, Baldschun won 29 games and saved 50 others for Gene Mauch. He also probably cost the Little General about a decade of his life. Baldschun was a nibbler, a hurler who never really got serious about his task until the hitter had a three-ball count. What Mitch Williams is to the Phillies of the 1990s, Baldschun was to the Phillies of the early 1960s.

His out pitch was a wicked screwball that he discovered in Nashville the season before he was drafted by the Phillies. He had reached bottom—at 24 he was going nowhere.

"My wife wanted me to quit baseball," Baldschun later remembered. "I was warming up. My arm had really gone bad. I started messing with the screwball. The catcher said, 'Stick that scroogie in your pocket, Jack. Your fastball drops just as much.' Just to show him, I really put some stuff on a screwball. It surprised me. It jumped all over the place."

And soon after that, Baldschun's fortunes began to jump upward. Max Macon, his manager at Columbia, assured the Phillies that Jack could win in the bigs, and the Phils took a chance on him in the winter draft.

Mauch fell in love with Baldschun's scroogie from the first day he saw it. And Baldschun was one of the few bright spots in that dismal 1961 season. He led the National League in appearances with 65, posted the only winning record (5–3) among the pitchers, and had a 3.87 ERA.

In the next two seasons, his ERA dropped to 2.95 and 2.29. He started out well enough in 1964. Mauch, however, didn't give him the ball much during the team's 10-game late September losing streak, preferring instead to try to win the pennant with a relief corps that had been in Little Rock the previous month. Still, Baldschun saved 21 games and won six while appearing in 71.

"And I could have worked 20 more," Baldschun insisted the following spring in Clearwater. Instead, he worked six less, saved just half a dozen and was dealt to the Baltimore Orioles for Darold Knowles and Jackie Brandt over the winter. Three days later he was traded to the Reds.

Jack lasted a year and a month in Cincinnati, then resurfaced with the expansion San Diego Padres in 1969. He looked like the Baldschun of old in one Connie Mack Stadium appearance against the Phillies and finished the season 7–2 in 61 games.

After a dozen uninspiring appearances the following season, however, the Padres released him. He could take solace in the fact that his career had lasted a decade longer than anyone would have expected before he was taunted into throwing that first really hard screwball in Nashville.

Jack Baldschun

Baldschun, Jack

Phillies	W	L	Pct	ERA	G	CG	IP	H	BB	SO	ShO
1961	5	3	.625	3.87	65	0	100	90	49	59	0
1962	12	7	.632	2.95	67	0	113	95	58	95	0
1963	11	7	.611	2.29	65	0	114	99	42	89	0
1964	6	9	.400	3.12	71	0	118	111	40	96	0
1965	5	8	.385	3.82	65	0	99	102	42	81	0
Career	48	41	.539	3.70	457	0	704	687	298	555	0

Bancroft, Dave

Phillies: 1915–20
Shortstop
Nicknames: Banny, Beauty
Birthplace: Sioux City, Iowa
B: April 20, 1891
D: October 9, 1972
Batted both, threw right
Ht. 5–9; Wt. 160

When Dave Bancroft was playing shortstop for Portland in the Pacific Coast League in 1914, there were some people who tried to dissuade the Phillies from buying him. He'll never hit major league pitching, the Phillies were told.

Some scouting report! Sixteen years and 2,004 hits later, Bancroft had fashioned a .279 lifetime record and was on his way to baseball's Hall of Fame. In a lot of ways, Beauty's career established a pattern that was repeated several decades later by Larry Bowa, who was also regarded as a nonhitter when he first arrived in the majors but who overcame the knock and was the shortstop for the 1980 World Champions.

As with Bowa, there was never any question about Bancroft's fielding. His hands were terrific, his arm was powerful, and his range in either direction was astounding. And, like Bowa, Banny was a switch-hitter whose sharp clubhouse needling kept things lively around the ballpark.

He and Bowa were within a half-inch in size and five pounds in weight. And their batting averages in their first five seasons were strikingly similar. The difference was that Bowa developed into a fine hitter in Philadelphia, whereas Bancroft did the bulk of his hitting after the Phillies had unwisely traded him to the Giants for a beat-up shortstop named Art Fletcher, who would later manage the Phillies unsuccessfully. It was one of William Baker's worst deals.

Bancroft played splendidly for the Phillies in their championship season as a rookie, batting .254 while scoring 85 runs. The following season, his ankle injury in September might have been the main reason the Phillies didn't repeat as National League champs, the Giants nosing them out by 2½ games.

By 1920, the Phillies had established themselves as a loser, not a winner. Gavvy Cravath, the old slugger, was the manager then, and he knew his assets and his liabilities. "I've still got the best shortstop in baseball in Banny," he announced shortly before the season began.

Two months later, he didn't have him. Bancroft was off to the best hitting

Dave Bancroft

start of his career—.298—but owner Baker found himself short of funds, and Horace Stoneham wanted Bancroft badly. He offered $100,000, Fletcher, and a pitcher named Hubbell. Had it been Carl Hubbell, maybe the deal would have been worth it. Instead, it was journeyman Bill Hubbell.

"I think I made a splendid deal for the Philadelphia ball club," Baker said in announcing the trade. He couldn't have been more wrong. Bancroft continued his amazing fielding and batted over .300 in five of the next six seasons. He managed the Boston Braves from 1924 to 1927 and was named to the Hall of Fame in 1971, the year before he died.

"I never worried about making errors, so I guess that had a lot to do with it," said the man who set a major league record for most chances accepted by a shortstop (984 in 1922) when informed he had made the Hall of Fame. "I guess this is the biggest honor I ever had. I was more surprised than anyone to hear of it."

For those people who had seen his soft hands and quick reflexes operate around shortstop for all those years, the only surprise was that it took the Hall of Fame so long to accept one of baseball's all-time infielders.

Bancroft, Dave

Phillies	G	AB	H	BA	RBI	R	2B	3B	HR	SA	SB
1915	153	563	143	.254	30	85	18	2	7	.330	15
1916	142	477	101	.212	33	53	10	0	3	.252	15
1917	127	478	116	.243	43	56	22	5	4	.335	14
1918	125	499	132	.265	26	69	19	4	0	.319	11
1919	92	335	91	.272	25	45	13	7	0	.352	8
1920	42	171	51	.298	5	23	7	2	0	.363	1
Career	1,913	7,182	2,004	.279	591	1,048	320	77	32	.358	145

Bartell, Dick

Phillies: 1931–34
Shortstop
Nicknames: Rowdy Richard, Pepperpot
Birthplace: Chicago, Illinois
B: November 22, 1907
Bats right, throws right
Ht. 5–9; Wt. 160

Nobody ever accused Dick Bartell of being lackadaisical. As his nicknames suggest, Bartell was a fiery performer who had his share of skirmishes during his 18-year big league career.

One of the early members of a long line of fiercely competitive Phillies shortstops, Bartell was described in his day as a player who "evokes one of the scrapiest dispositions in the majors."

Bartell was also a mighty fine player. He was a standout hitter who hit over .300 five times in his career and whose lifetime batting average was .284. And he was an excellent fielder who covered a wide territory at shortstop and who frequently led the league in various defensive categories at his position.

The sum of this was that Dick was one of the premier shortstops in the National League in the 1930s. In 1933, in the midst of his four-year residence in Philadelphia, he was the starting National League shortstop in the first All-Star Game. Dick was also the circuit's starting shortstop in 1937.

Dick had the best years of his career with the Phillies. He arrived in Philadelphia in November 1930 in a trade in which he was exchanged by the Pittsburgh Pirates for shortstop Tommy Thevenow and pitcher Claude Willoughby.

Born in Chicago, but raised in Alameda, California, Bartell had entered the minors in 1927. The Pirates brought him up at the end of the season. At the time, Pittsburgh had another promising shortstop named Joe Cronin. The Bucs, however, sold the future Hall of Famer to the Washington Senators to make way for Bartell.

After a year as a reserve, Dick became the Pirates' regular shortstop in 1929. He hit .302 that year, then blossomed to .320 the next year. But in one of their best trades of the decade, the Phils pried Dick away after the season.

Bartell quickly became the Phillies' sparkplug and ultimately their captain.

He hit .289 in 1931, then came back with marks of .308, .271, and .310 in succeeding years.

In 1933 he became the first major league player to hit four consecutive doubles in a nine-inning game during a 7–1 win over the Boston Braves.

On defense, Dick led National League shortstops in errors (41) and in double plays in 1931. He ranked first in putouts and assists in 1932, first in putouts and double plays in 1933, and first in putouts, assists, and double plays in 1934. In 1933, with Jack Warner and Mickey Finn alternating as his second base partners, Bartell participated in 100 double plays.

A good base stealer and a player who always drew numerous walks, Bartell was traded by the Phillies in November 1934 to the New York Giants for shortstop Blondy Ryan, third baseman Johnny Vergez, outfielder George Watkins, pitcher Pretzels Pezzulo, and cash.

He spent four seasons in New York, playing on the 1936 and 1937 pennant winners. In 1937 when he hit .306—his only .300 year with the Giants—Bartell was named the National League's and the major league's all-star shortstop. A year later, he had the unusual distinction of hitting two grand slam home runs in one game.

With his talents beginning to erode, Dick was swapped to the Chicago Cubs for the 1939 season. On the same date (December 6) the following year, he was traded to the Detroit Tigers. In 1940, Dick played in his third World Series.

Dick was returned to the Giants early in 1941. With two years out for military service, he played in New York until retiring in 1946.

Dick Bartell

Bartell, Dick

Phillies	G	AB	H	BA	RBI	R	2B	3B	HR	SA	SB
1931	135	554	160	.289	34	88	43	7	0	.392	6
1932	154	614	189	.308	53	118	48	7	1	.414	8
1933	152	587	159	.271	37	78	25	5	1	.336	6
1934	146	604	187	.310	37	102	30	4	0	.373	13
Career	2,016	7,629	2,165	.284	710	1,130	442	71	79	.391	109

The records show that Beals Becker stole a dozen bases for the 1915 National League champs in his third and last season with the Phillies. Actually, he stole 14, but only 12 went into the record book. Twice he stole third that season, only to discover the base already occupied by a teammate.

Becker was already in his eighth year in the majors when the Phils bought him from the Cincinnati Reds early in the 1913 season. He hit .324 in 88 games as the regular left fielder to finish the year at .316, fifth best in the league. And the next season was even better as he lifted the mark to .325, second best in the league to Brooklyn's Jack Daubert (.329).

In the championship season, he played more left field than any other Phillie and had a career-high 11 home runs. But his average slipped to .246 and, by World Series time, he had lost his job to Possum Whitted. During the off-season he was sold to Kansas City in the American Association.

Beals led that league in hitting in both 1916 and 1917 and finally retired when the Blues waived him in the middle of the 1924 season.

Becker, Beals

Phillies: 1913–15
Outfielder
Birthplace: El Dorado, Kansas
B: July 5, 1886
D: August 16, 1943
Batted left, threw left
Ht. 5–9; **Wt.** 170

Beals Becker

Becker, Beals

Phillies	G	AB	H	BA	RBI	R	2B	3B	HR	SA	SB
1913	88	306	99	.324	44	53	19	10	9	.539	11
1914	138	514	167	.325	66	76	25	5	9	.446	16
1915	112	338	83	.246	35	38	16	4	11	.414	12
Career	876	2,764	763	.276	292	367	114	43	45	.397	129

Bedrosian, Steve

Phillies: 1986–89
Pitcher
Nickname: Bedrock
Birthplace: Methuen, Massachusetts
B: December 6, 1957
Bats right, throws right
Ht. 6–3; **Wt.** 200

When the Phillies acquired Steve Bedrosian from the Atlanta Braves along with outfielder Milt Thompson for catcher Ozzie Virgil and pitching prospect Pete Smith, they envisioned Bedrock as a man who could solidify their bullpen.

They got even more than they expected.

By the time they traded Bedrosian to the San Francisco Giants in June 1989, he had appeared in 218 games, all in relief, had saved 103 of them, and had become the sixth Phillies Cy Young Award winner.

Bedrosian joined Steve Carlton (1972, 1977, 1980, 1982) and John Denny (1983) as a Cy Young winner after a terrific 1987 season. He saved a league-leading 40 games that year, including a record 13 in a row, and had a 5–3 record with a 2.83 earned run average in 65 appearances covering 89 innings.

He edged Cubs starter Rick Sutcliffe and Giants starter Rick Reuschel for the award in the closest three-way voting in Cy Young history. Bedrosian received nine first-place votes and 57 points; Sutcliffe had 55 points and four first-place votes; and Reuschel had 54 points and eight first-place votes.

Bedrock earned the honor despite little help from the two hometown writers who had ballots. One had him third; the other did not vote for him at all.

"Winning the award is the ultimate honor," Bedrosian said, "(but) it's an individual honor and I'm a team player. The thing I'd like most is to be in a World Series someday. It's really exciting . . . to be honored in this situation. I'll never forget it as long as I live."

Bedrosian had a hand in 45 of the Phillies' 80 victories that season. He also was named Fireman of the Year by *The Sporting News*, NL pitcher of the year by *Baseball America* and *USA Today*, and he was picked for the *Associated Press* and *Sporting News* All-Star teams.

Bedrosian joined the Phillies after a season in Atlanta in which he had tried to make the transition from reliever to starter. The experiment was a dismal failure. He started 37 games, didn't finish any, and had a 7–15 record and a 3.83 ERA.

But once he joined the Phillies, he returned to the bullpen and achieved immediate success with an 8–6 record and 29 saves.

In 1988 he was 6–6 with 28 saves in 57 appearances. And he had six saves and a 2–3 record in 1989 when the Phillies dealt him to the Giants for pitchers Terry Mulholland and Dennis Cook and third baseman Charlie Hayes.

Bedrosian's 103 saves are the most by a Phillies pitcher.

With the Giants in 1989, Bedrosian achieved his goal when he pitched in the World Series against the Oakland Athletics. In 1991 he was a member of the World Champion Minnesota Twins.

Bedrosian, Steve

Phillies	W	L	Pct	ERA	G	CG	IP	H	BB	SO	ShO
1986	8	6	.571	3.40	68	0	90	79	34	82	0
1987	5	3	.625	2.83	65	0	89	79	28	74	0
1988	6	6	.500	3.77	57	0	74	75	27	61	0
1989	2	3	.400	3.21	28	0	34	21	17	24	0
Career	70	73	.490	3.39	608	0	1,067⅓	911	474	823	0

Steve Bedrosian

Ufortunately for Ray Benge, he pitched most of his career for miserable teams. In nine seasons as a first-line hurler in the big leagues, Benge played for only one first-division squad, the 1932 Phillies.

Despite playing for losers the rest of the time, Ray didn't have as bad a record as might be expected. In fact, he was a double-figure winner for six straight years, and was usually right above or not too far below .500.

Benge labored for five seasons during his first stint in Philadelphia. He was one of the workhorses of the staff—starting, relieving, and nearly always pitching more than 200 innings.

From a won-lost standpoint, his best season was in 1932 when his record was 13–12. Although he started 28 games that year, he was second among the National League's relievers in saves with six.

Ray entered the pro ranks in 1925. Twice over the next two years he was called up temporarily by the Cleveland Indians. In his first major league game in 1925, Benge shut out the Philadelphia A's.

Benge was picked up by the Phillies in time for the 1928 season. Indicative of the kind of team the Phils had that year, Ray led the pitching staff in victories with eight.

The following year Benge had a whopping 6.29 ERA, but managed an 11–15 record. He had the same record in 1930 as a member of the infamous Phils mound corps that allowed an all-time record 1,199 runs. That year Ray was touched for 305 hits in 225⅔ innings and allowed 175 runs, a Phillies record.

After the 1932 season, Benge was traded to the Brooklyn Dodgers for pitcher Austin Moore, second baseman Mickey Finn, and third baseman Jack Warner. He hurled there for three years. In 1936 the Dodgers sent him to the Boston Braves, who sold him back to the Phillies in mid-year for $6,000. Ray retired after the season, then rejoined the active ranks briefly in 1938 with the Cincinnati Reds.

Benge holds spots on two of the Phillies' all-time lists. He ranks 10th in most losses and eighth in highest earned run average.

Benge, Ray

Phillies: 1928–32; 1936
Pitcher
Nickname: Silent Cal
Birthplace: Jacksonville, Texas
B: April 22, 1902
Bats right, throws right
Ht. 5–9½; **Wt.** 160

Ray Benge

Benge, Ray

Phillies	W	L	Pct	ERA	G	CG	IP	H	BB	SO	ShO
1928	8	18	.308	4.55	40	12	201⅔	219	88	68	1
1929	11	15	.423	6.29	38	9	199	255	77	78	2
1930	11	15	.423	5.70	38	14	225⅔	305	81	70	0
1931	14	18	.438	3.17	38	16	247	251	61	117	2
1932	13	12	.520	4.05	41	13	222⅓	247	58	89	2
1936	1	4	.200	4.70	15	0	46	70	19	13	0
Career	101	130	.437	4.52	346	102	1,875⅓	2,177	598	655	12

Bob Boone finished his career by catching more games than any other player in major league history. Ironically, he was signed by the Phillies as a third baseman—their sixth selection in the June 1969 free-agent draft.

That the intelligent Stanford graduate and son of ex-big league infielder Ray Boone, was able to make the transition to baseball's most demanding position was remarkable. It was also overlooked as an achievement while Boone was with the Phillies.

In fact, it was always easy to overlook what Boone meant as part of the foundation of the greatest Phillies teams in their history. His bat didn't compare to Mike Schmidt's, Greg Luzinski's, or even Richie Hebner's. But he managed to hit over .280 for three straight seasons and always drove in a nice share of runs in proportion to his at-bats.

Boone, Bob

Phillies: 1972–81
Catcher
Nickname: Boonie
Birthplace: San Diego, California
B: November 19, 1947
Bats right, throws right
Ht. 6–2½; **Wt.** 195

Although he possessed a strong arm and had the respect of nearly everyone on the pitching staff as a catcher, people remember that Steve Carlton shunned Boone and made Tim McCarver his designated catcher for three seasons.

Being the player representative for the National League in strike-shortened 1981 did little to improve his profile in the mind of baseball-starved fans. And his lack of foot speed was always a subject for discussion.

Still, Boone caught well enough to win Gold Gloves in 1978 and 1979. From 1977 to 1979, his batting averages were .284, .283, and .286. He averaged more than 10 home runs and 62 RBI in that period.

His talents were recognized when he was voted the starting All-Star catcher in 1979. He also was picked as a member of the NL squad in 1976 through 1978. He was 2-for-4 with two RBI in his All-Star appearances.

Although his .229 batting average in 1980 was the worst of his 10-year career with the Phillies, he rebounded to hit .412 with four RBI in the World Series.

Boone, who was named to *The Sporting News* All-Star team in 1976, learned to catch in the minor leagues and, after little more than 200 games behind the plate, he joined the Phillies in September 1972.

In 1973 he had a tremendous rookie season with a last-place team, getting a Phillies-career-high 136 hits, driving in 61 runs and hitting .261. And he was a defensive rock when the Phillies won three straight Eastern Division titles.

But by then injuries were starting to take their toll. After the 1977 season, he underwent knee surgery. In 1979 a home plate collision with Joel Youngblood tore up the ligaments in his left knee, requiring a major operation. Through the 1980 championship year he played in pain and batted just .229. His .412 average and four RBI in the World Series were vital, though.

In 1981, weighed down by a pitching staff (other than Carlton) that had trouble holding runners on the bag, Boone took a lot of heat for all the stolen bases compiled against the Phillies. That was also his year as a spokesman in the player-owner struggle that ended up in a seven-week strike. After that season, he was sold to the California Angels.

Bob Boone

Boone, Bob

Phillies	G	AB	H	BA	RBI	R	2B	3B	HR	SA	SB
1972	16	51	14	.275	4	4	1	0	1	.353	1
1973	145	521	136	.261	61	42	20	2	10	.365	3
1974	146	488	118	.242	52	41	24	3	3	.322	3
1975	97	289	71	.246	20	28	14	2	2	.329	1
1976	121	361	98	.271	54	40	18	2	4	.366	2
1977	132	440	125	.284	66	55	26	4	11	.436	5
1978	132	435	123	.283	62	48	18	4	12	.425	2
1979	119	398	114	.286	58	38	21	3	9	.422	1
1980	141	480	110	.229	55	34	23	1	9	.338	3
1981	76	227	48	.211	24	19	7	0	4	.295	2
Career	2,264	7,245	1,838	.254	826	679	303	26	105	.346	38

Boone played for the Angels for seven seasons and was the catcher on the American League All-Star fielding team in 1982, 1986, 1987, and 1988. He signed with the Kansas City Royals as a free agent for the 1989 season, when he again was named the AL All-Star fielding catcher.

He closed out his playing career in 1990 with the Royals. He passed Al Lopez as the catcher who had played the most games at the position during the 1988 season. He holds major league catching records for most games (2,225), putouts (11,017), chances accepted (12,172), and seasons catching more than 100 games (15).

Boone became a minor league manager at Tacoma in the Triple-A Pacific Coast League. He was in line to manage a major league team in Orlando, Florida, if the city had been granted a franchise.

In 1992, Bob's son Bret joined the Seattle Mariners, making the Boones the first family to send members of three generations to the big leagues.

Bouchee, Ed

Phillies: 1956–60
First baseman
Birthplace: Livingston, Montana
B: March 7, 1933
Bats left, throws left
Ht. 6–0; **Wt.** 200

Not many major league ball players have ever come out of the state of Montana. But Ed Bouchee was one who did, and he enjoyed a mild degree of success with the Phillies during a short although rather eventful career.

A husky lefthander, Bouchee was the National League Rookie of the Year in 1957. At the time, he was one of the most promising players in the Phillies system.

Ed, who had been a fullback with the Washington State College football team, began in the Phillies chain in 1952 with Spokane. He hit .319 there. The following two years were spent in the military. After being discharged, Bouchee put in a year at Schenectady, where he hit .313, and a year at Miami where he led the Marlins in average (.294) and RBI (94) and made the International League All-Star team.

Bouchee became a Phillie in late 1956. In spring training the next season, he won the starting first base job from Marv Blaylock. At the end of the year, he had a .293 average, 17 home runs, and a team-leading total of 76 RBI. He also led the National League in times hit by a pitch (14) and the circuit's first basemen in putouts and errors.

In the balloting for Rookie of the Year, Ed and teammate Jack Sanford wound up tied in the voting. *The Sporting News* gave the award to Bouchee while naming Sanford Rookie Pitcher of the Year.

In 1958, however, what seemed to be a promising career developed problems. Bouchee was arrested during the winter on a morals charge and required treatment. He missed part of the season; when he returned, his average slipped to .257. In one game, Ed tied a major league record by striking out four times in a night game.

The hard-hitting, line-drive specialist made a strong comeback in 1959, stroking opposing pitching for a .285 batting average, the highest on the team. He also socked 15 homers and drove in 74 runs while leading the league's first basemen in putouts and assists.

Early in 1960, with the Phillies sorely in need of a second baseman, Bouchee was traded with pitcher Don Cardwell to the Chicago Cubs for catcher Cal Neeman and second baseman Tony Taylor.

Bouchee had two unspectacular seasons with the Cubs. Eventually, he was drafted by the New York Mets. In 1962 he was a member of the original and infamous Mets. Ed dropped out of the majors after that season.

Ed Bouchee

Bouchee, Ed

Phillies	G	AB	H	BA	RBI	R	2B	3B	HR	SA	SB
1956	9	22	6	.273	1	0	2	0	0	.364	0
1957	154	574	168	.293	76	78	35	8	17	.470	1
1958	89	334	86	.257	39	55	19	5	9	.425	1
1959	136	499	142	.285	74	75	29	4	15	.449	0
1960	22	65	17	.262	8	1	4	0	0	.323	0
Career	670	2,199	583	.265	290	298	114	21	61	.419	5

Bowa, Larry

Phillies: 1970–81
Shortstop
Nicknames: Bo, Gnat
Birthplace: Sacramento, California
B: December 6, 1945
Bats both, throws right
Ht. 5–10; **Wt.** 155

Larry Bowa

Larry Bowa could have told the game of baseball to forget it long before he ever put on a professional uniform.

Like in high school, where he was cut from the team for three years. Or like in 1965, when as a junior college shortstop he went through the entire free agent draft without getting a nibble. But, a few months later, something kept nibbling at Phillies scout Eddie Bockman's mind. The skinny shortstop wouldn't let Bockman rest until he called farm director Paul Owens and asked him to watch some film.

"I'll never forget it," Owens said. "Eddie went out and rented some camera equipment. We went to a motel and he put the bedsheet up on the wall. He started running films of Bowa. I thought he was setting me up for a big bonus, maybe $10,000. I said, 'How much does he want, Eddie?' He said, 'I think I can get him for $1,000.' I said 'Give it to him. I can see that he can hit and field. And the stuff you rented damn near cost $1,000.' We ended up signing him for $1,500."

And Bowa could have packed it in early in 1970, his rookie season, when he was hitting .150 and being compared to a Little Leaguer by some. Instead, he never gave up on himself and neither did his manager, Frank Lucchesi.

"A writer down here asked me what my biggest thrill was," Lucchesi said in Charleston, West Virginia, in 1981, "and I told him, 'The biggest thrill of my career was sticking with Larry Bowa when he was a rookie.' He had a great desire for the game. I could see that desire. Not everybody could, but I stuck with him and he became a star."

In fact, Bowa became a bigger star than even he had a right to expect. He finished his career with more than 2,100 hits, he represented the Phillies in five All-Star games, and he hit .375 in the 1980 World Series.

In 1975 he batted .305. The following year he had this to say about himself: "The only thing I can't do on a baseball field is hit a home run. God gave me the tools to run, to play defense, and to hit for average. But it is as if the Lord said, 'You can't hit a home run.'"

In 1977, Bowa hit four home runs, two in the same game.

His defense was outstanding. He was a double-figure base stealer in all 12 of his seasons with the Phillies. And he will go down in history as the feistiest, most outspoken Phillie of his era.

He was, in fact, the one Phillie who was booed by the home fans during the introductions at the World Series.

The booing stemmed from his comments after a 15-inning victory over the Cubs in September that started the Phillies on their stretch drive to the Eastern Division title. The fans had booed when the Cubs scored two runs in the top of the 15th, and, after the Phils had come back to win the game, Bowa stormed into the clubhouse, screaming at the top of his considerable voice about "bleeping front-runners, the worst fans in baseball."

A month later, as 100,000 cheered at Kennedy Stadium after the victory parade down Broad Street, Bowa yelled into the microphone, "This is probably the greatest moment of my life and I'm glad I can share it with the greatest fans in baseball."

You could make an argument that Bowa was the greatest shortstop of his era, which ended in Philadelphia when he was traded along with Ryne Sandberg to the Chicago Cubs for Ivan DeJesus after the 1981 season. He played three full seasons with the Cubs, helping them win the National League East title in 1984. He was released by the Cubs in August 1985 and signed with the New York Mets. Bowa retired at the end of that season. He managed the San Diego Padres in 1987 and 1988 and rejoined the Phillies as third base coach in 1988.

Bowa was named shortstop on *The Sporting News* National League All-Star team in 1975 and 1978. He was that publication's NL All-Star fielding shortstop in 1972 and 1978. He set NL records for most games played by a shortstop (2,222), fewest errors in a season of 150 or more games (nine in 1972), and most seasons leading the league in fielding percentage by a shortstop (six—1971, 1972, 1974, 1978, 1979, 1983).

He tied a league record for highest fielding percentage by a shortstop when he had a .987 average in both 1971 and 1972, then set the major league record for fielding average by a shortstop at .991 in 1979. The record has since been broken by Cal Ripken, of the Baltimore Orioles, but remains the NL mark.

In the 1980 World Series he set a record by starting seven double plays.

He and Hall of Famer Dave Bancroft were the Phillies' two greatest shortstops of all time, and Larry probably deserves the edge based on longevity.

Not bad for a guy who was signed as an afterthought. Or for a player who couldn't make his high school team.

Bowa, Larry

Phillies	G	AB	H	BA	RBI	R	2B	3B	HR	SA	SB
1970	145	547	137	.250	34	50	17	6	0	.303	24
1971	159	650	162	.249	25	74	18	5	0	.292	28
1972	152	579	145	.250	31	67	11	13	1	.320	17
1973	122	446	94	.211	23	42	11	3	0	.249	10
1974	162	669	184	.275	36	97	19	10	1	.338	39
1975	136	583	178	.305	38	79	18	9	2	.377	24
1976	156	624	155	.248	49	71	15	9	0	.301	30
1977	154	624	175	.280	41	93	19	3	4	.340	32
1978	156	654	192	.294	43	78	31	5	3	.370	37
1979	147	539	130	.241	31	74	17	11	0	.314	20
1980	147	540	144	.267	39	57	16	4	2	.322	21
1981	103	360	102	.283	31	34	14	3	0	.339	16
Career	2,247	8,418	2,191	.260	525	987	262	99	15	.320	318

Boyle, Jack

Phillies: 1893–98
First baseman, catcher
Nickname: Honest Jack
Birthplace: Cincinnati, Ohio
B: March 22, 1866
D: January 7, 1913
Batted right, threw right
Ht. 6–4; Wt. 190

In the long line of occasional Phillies captains, Jack Boyle had one distinction that no one else could claim. He was the first player ever officially designated captain of the Phillies.

Honest Jack, as he was often called, was not only a team leader. He was a pretty fair hitter, who, while playing mostly first base during a six-year stint with the Phillies, had one .300 season and a couple more that weren't far off from that.

He also had a six-hit game on July 6, 1893, his first year with the Phillies. That came in an 11-inning contest in which Boyle touched Chicago pitcher Bill Hutchinson for five singles and a double.

Boyle had come to the Phillies in a trade with the New York Giants.

"I surely would like to have Roger Connor back with me on the Giants," new skipper John Montgomery Ward told Phillies pilot Harry Wright one day during a chance meeting in New York. "It wouldn't seem like the same team if I didn't have Roger at first base," said Montgomery, who had previously been

Jack Boyle

the Giants' shortstop and captain and a teammate of Connor's, a future Hall of Famer.

"Well, that former Browns player, Boyle, would look all right in a Philadelphia uniform," Wright replied. "Give us Boyle, and I think I can talk my bosses into returning Connor."

The deal was done, and Honest Jack moved down the road to Philadelphia, where he became the regular first baseman for three seasons and a valuable utility man for two more.

Boyle, whose brother Eddie had a brief visit to the big leagues in 1896, had been in the big leagues himself since 1886, spending time in the American Association with Cincinnati and St. Louis and in the Players' League in 1890 with Chicago. He joined the National League and the Giants in 1892, then came to the Phillies the next year.

After hitting .286 in 1893, his average climbed to .301 the next season. That was the year the entire Phillies starting lineup hit over .300, with three regulars (Sam Thompson, Billy Hamilton, and Ed Delahanty) and a reserve (Tuck Turner) going over .400.

Boyle's and the Phillies' bats cooled off in 1895, but Honest Jack led the National League in at-bats with 565 while hitting .253. He also led NL first basemen in errors with 36.

In 1896 the Phillies acquired Dan Brouthers, and Boyle lost his job at first to the future Hall of Famer. Jack appeared in only 12 games at first base and 28 at catcher while hitting .297.

After one more season on the bench with the Phillies, he opened the 1898 campaign on the squad, but was released early in the season. That marked the end of Boyle's big league career.

Boyle, Jack

Phillies	G	AB	H	BA	RBI	R	2B	3B	HR	SA	SB
1893	116	504	144	.286	81	105	29	9	4	.403	22
1894	114	495	149	.301	88	98	21	10	4	.408	21
1895	133	565	143	.253	67	90	17	4	0	.297	13
1896	40	145	43	.297	28	17	4	1	1	.359	3
1897	75	288	73	.253	36	37	9	1	2	.313	3
1898	6	22	2	.091	3	0	0	1	0	.182	0
Career	1,086	4,222	1,067	.253	528	668	137	53	24	.327	125

Bransfield, Kitty

Phillies: 1905–11
First baseman
Birthplace: Worcester, Massachusetts
B: January 7, 1875
D: May 1, 1947
Batted right, threw right
Ht. 5–11; **Wt.** 207

Kitty Bransfield was 30 years old and slumping at the plate when the Phillies acquired him along with two other players from the Pittsburgh Pirates for outfielder Del Howard.

It turned out to be one of the best deals ever made by Bill Shettsline. Howard lasted one year with the Pirates and was never a star in his five National League seasons. Bransfield came to Philadelphia and regained his batting stroke well enough to man first base for the Phils for the next six seasons.

Kitty lacked power, never hitting more than three homers in any one season and finishing with just 14 in 4,997 big league at-bats, but he was a productive run producer who drove in 76 in his first season with the Phillies. He also stole 27 bases.

In 1908 he had his best season for the Phils with a .304 average, 71 RBI, and 30 stolen bases. Two years later, he drove in eight runs in an 18–0 victory over the Pirates. But he is best remembered for the slugging he did in his first season in Philadelphia when he and catcher Red Dooin received a message to visit a house near Broad and Columbia so they could hear some news to their advantage. It turned out the occupants were a couple of gamblers.

The gamblers, offering "sure thing" money, were on the third floor when they delivered their message. They wound up on the first floor after Dooin booted them down one flight of stairs and Bransfield down another.

At the age of 36, Bransfield started the 1911 season at first base, but his reflexes were gone. After 23 games, he turned the position over to Fred Luderus, whom the Phillies obtained from the Cubs a year earlier.

He later became a National League umpire, a Phillies scout, and a minor league manager.

Kitty Bransfield

Bransfield, Kitty (William)

Phillies	G	AB	H	BA	RBI	R	2B	3B	HR	SA	SB
1905	151	580	150	.259	76	55	23	9	3	.345	27
1906	140	524	144	.275	60	47	28	5	1	.353	12
1907	94	348	81	.233	38	25	15	2	0	.287	8
1908	144	527	160	.304	71	53	25	7	3	.395	30
1909	140	527	154	.292	59	47	27	6	1	.372	17
1910	123	427	102	.239	52	39	17	4	3	.319	10
1911	23	43	11	.256	3	4	1	1	0	.326	1
Career	1,329	4,997	1,350	.270	637	529	225	74	14	.353	175

You can be sure that Charlie Buffinton wouldn't get along with today's pitchers. As soon as somebody complained about pitching with only three or four days' rest, crusty old Charlie probably would've jumped down his throat.

Buffinton didn't know what rest was. He once pitched 587 innings in one season (1884). Twice during his career he went over 400 innings in a season, and four times he worked more than 300 innings.

It was enough to make most pitchers' arms fall off, but not Charlie's. He toiled for 11 seasons, seven times winning more than 20 games, including 1884 when he won 48.

Charlie was an experienced pitcher when he came to the Phillies in 1887. He had started with Boston in 1882, at one point winning 95 games over a three-year period.

In his first year with the Phillies, Buffinton teamed with Charlie Ferguson and Dan Casey to pitch the club into second place. Buff had a 21–17 record that year, which included consecutive one-hitters against Indianapolis and Chicago. The following year he was 28–17 while working 400 innings.

Charlie was a 20-game winner for the Phillies for the third straight season in 1889 when he logged a 28–16 mark. That gave Buffinton 77 wins in his three years with the Phillies.

Buffinton, who won 232 games in his career, was the Phillies' players' agent—the equivalent of today's union representative. When the Players' League was formed in 1890, naturally he jumped leagues. As the agent, Buffinton was actually the one who was awarded the Philadelphia franchise. During the league's one-year existence, he was also the team's third manager.

Phillies management was adamant about not re-signing Buffinton after the Players' League collapsed. So Charlie went to Boston of the American Association where he posted a 28–9 record in 1891.

In 1892 he was back in the National League with Baltimore, but won only three of 11 decisions. He held out for the entire 1893 season and never again pitched in the majors.

Buffinton, Charlie

Phillies: 1887–89
Pitcher
Birthplace: Fall River, Massachusetts
B: June 14, 1861
D: September 23, 1907
Batted right, threw right
Ht. 6–1; **Wt.** 180

Charlie Buffinton

Buffinton, Charlie

Phillies	W	L	Pct	ERA	G	CG	IP	H	BB	SO	ShO
1887	21	17	.553	3.66	40	35	332⅓	352	92	160	1
1888	28	17	.622	1.91	46	43	400⅓	324	59	199	3
1889	28	16	.636	3.24	47	37	380	390	121	153	2
Career	232	152	.605	2.96	414	351	3,404	3,344	856	1,700	27

Bunning, Jim

Phillies: 1964–67; 1970–71
Pitcher
Birthplace: Southgate, Kentucky
B: October 23, 1931
Bats right, throws right
Ht. 6–3; Wt. 190

Jim Bunning

If there was a word to describe Jim Bunning the pitcher, it was professional. He was a no-nonsense, relatively humorless family man who liked taking his pitching turn every fourth day and always gave a major league effort. Even in his final season with the Phillies (1971), he conducted himself well, although his career was over at age 39. He probably got the hint that he was finished when Willie Stargell hit one of the monster homers in Vet history against him. The ball went through a walkway on the 600 level.

In his first tour with the Phillies, Bunning could throw the ball past Stargell, or anyone else, or get them to hit the ball on the ground to an infielder or to pop routine flies to the outfield.

And on his best day, that's all he did. Father's Day, 1964. Shea Stadium. The New York Mets in the first game of a doubleheader. Twenty-seven up, 27 down. It was the first perfect game during the regular season in the major leagues in 42 years and the first ever in the National League (detailed in Chapter 8).

The perfect game came in Jim Bunning's first season with the Phillies. For 150 games it was the Perfect Season. Then the roof caved in. Manager Gene Mauch overworked Bunning and Chris Short down the stretch. But Gentleman Jim still finished with a 19–8 record and a 2.63 ERA. And he showed in the next three seasons that, while he might have been overworked during that stretch, he wasn't overworked during the season.

From 1965 through 1967, Bunning averaged over 300 innings pitched. His record slipped from 19–9 to 19–14 to 17–15, but his earned run averages dropped each year. He seemed to be getting stronger with age. But after the 1967 season, when he lost five 1–0 decisions, the Phillies decided that Jim, who would be 36 the following season, was about to hit the skids. So they traded him to the Pirates for Don Money and Woodie Fryman, even though he had led the league in innings pitched (302), strikeouts (253), and shutouts (6).

It turned out they were right, too. Bunning slipped to 4–14, then 10–9 in his two seasons with Pittsburgh. Late in the second season, he went to the Los Angeles Dodgers where he was 3–1. He was rewarded with his outright release.

At the time, Bunning had 91 National League victories to go with his 118 in the American League. There is no evidence that Bunning cared about being the first big league pitcher since Cy Young to win 100 games in each league. There was evidence, however, that Bunning still considered himself a big league pitcher. He wrote it himself and sent it by telegram to 22 big league managers.

"I am available to pitch for your club," it read. "I can win 15 games as a starter or save 20 games in relief. I am experienced and healthy." (Signed) Jim Bunning."

Five general managers sent letters, but John Quinn beat them all. He tracked down Bunning's phone number with the help of the Fort Thomas, Kentucky, police and signed Jim.

It should be understood that Bunning, even with a wife and seven children, was not desperate for money, either. He was a successful stockbroker in the off-season, but he didn't want to make the off-season the whole season. Not just yet.

His first year back was the Phillies' last in Connie Mack Stadium. The team was comprised of prospects, rejects, and mostly bad veterans. Bunning won 10 games (giving him 101 in the NL) and lost 15 and was as competitive as he had been, throwing 23 shutouts in his first four years with the team. But by 1971 it was obvious that it was time to try something other than pitching.

He tried managing. But he was fired after five years in the minors "for not developing and communicating with my players." He labeled the reasoning as "hogwash."

Later, he became a player agent before becoming a successful politician in the Commonwealth of Kentucky. Although he failed in a bid to become governor of his home state, he later earned a seat in the United States House of Representatives as a Republican.

Bunning, Jim

Phillies	W	L	Pct	ERA	G	CG	IP	H	BB	SO	ShO
1964	19	8	.704	2.63	41	13	284	248	46	219	5
1965	19	9	.679	2.60	39	15	291	253	62	260	7
1966	19	14	.576	2.41	43	16	314	260	55	252	5
1967	17	15	.531	2.29	40	16	302	241	73	253	6
1970	10	15	.400	4.11	34	4	219	233	56	147	0
1971	5	12	.294	5.48	29	1	110	126	37	58	0
Career	224	184	.549	3.27	591	151	3,760	3,433	1,000	2,855	40

It was once said that if Smoky Burgess was awakened in the middle of the night and sent to the plate, he'd get a hit. Burgess was a masterful hitter, especially when he was called on to bat as a pinch-hitter.

Smoky could walk up to the dish completely cold and blister whoever was pitching. In an 18-year career, Burgess caught his share of games, but he made his reputation as a pinch-hitter. Burgess has the second highest number of pinch-hits (145) in major league history.

Burgess had some of his best years as a regular while playing for the Phillies. He came to Philadelphia and departed from the city in trades involving Andy Seminick each time.

The Phils landed Smoky in the winter of 1951 in a deal that sent Seminick, left fielder Dick Sisler, infielder Eddie Pellagrini, and pitcher Niles Jordan to the Cincinnati Reds for Burgess, second baseman Connie Ryan, and pitcher Howie Fox. Burgess led the Phils' regulars in hitting during each of his three seasons in Philadelphia, batting .296, .292, and .368.

The Phillies declared Burgess the unofficial batting champion of the National League in 1954 after his .368 season. It was, indeed, the highest mark in the league, but Smoky didn't qualify for the title because he had too few appearances at the plate. He did, however, hit safely in all but 30 of the 108 games in which he played.

Smoky was a member of the National League All-Star team in 1954, an honor he repeated in 1955 and 1959. In April 1955, the Phillies shipped Burgess back to Cincinnati along with pitcher Steve Ridzik and outfielder Stan Palys for Seminick and outfielders Jim Greengrass and Glen Gorbous.

Burgess, who had broken into organized ball in 1944 and had appeared in the majors for the first time in 1949 with the Chicago Cubs, went on to a lengthy career after the Phillies traded him. In addition to the Reds, he played for the Pittsburgh Pirates and Chicago White Sox. He hit .333 in the 1960 World Series for the Pirates.

Probably Smoky's finest overall season was the year the Phils swapped him to the Reds. He hit .301 with 21 home runs and 78 RBI, both career highs. That year, Burgess drove in nine runs in one game with two grand slam homers and a solo round-tripper.

In 1961, when he hit .303 for the Pirates, he was named to the National League All-Star team by *The Sporting News*.

The latter part of Burgess's career was spent almost entirely as a

Burgess, Smoky

Phillies: 1952–55
Catcher
Birthplace: Caroleen, North Carolina
B: February 6, 1927
D: September 15, 1991
Batted left, threw right
Ht. 5–8½; **Wt.** 185

Smoky Burgess

pinch-hitter. As a result, Smoky ranks near the top of many all-time pinch-hit lists. His 21 pinch-hits in 1966 rank as the second highest number in American League history. His 16 pinch-hit home runs tie for second on the all-time major league career list.

Burgess, who retired after the 1967 season, also caught two no-hitters. One, with the Reds in 1956, was a combined effort of Johnny Klippstein, Hersh Freeman, and Joe Black. The other, with the Pirates in 1959, was by Harvey Haddix, who hurled 12 perfect innings before being touched in the 13th in a game with the Milwaukee Braves.

Burgess, Smoky (Forrest)

Phillies	G	AB	H	BA	RBI	R	2B	3B	HR	SA	SB
1952	110	371	110	.296	56	49	27	2	6	.429	3
1953	102	312	91	.292	36	31	17	5	4	.417	3
1954	108	345	127	.368	46	41	27	5	4	.510	1
1955	7	21	4	.190	1	4	2	0	1	.429	0
Career	1,718	4,471	1,318	.295	673	485	230	33	126	.446	13

Callison, Johnny

Phillies: 1960–69
Outfielder
Birthplace: Qualls, Oklahoma
B: March 12, 1939
Bats left, throws right
Ht. 5–10; **Wt.** 175

Johnny Callison

Baseball has a habit of pigeonholing its players a certain way. Then, no matter what the player does throughout his career, the tag originally placed on him sticks.

With Johnny Callison, the label was "potential." He could never shake it, even after a 1964 season in which he won the All-Star Game with a dramatic three-run homer and was National League MVP runner-up after he and Dick Allen almost slugged the Phillies into the World Series.

Potential. The Chicago White Sox saw it when they dubbed Callison as "the next Mickey Mantle" in the late 1950s. He was young, like Mantle was when he joined the Yankees. And he was called up and farmed back out, just as Mantle had been in 1951.

After the 1960 season, the Phillies traded their pinch-hit, home-run-hitting hero, Gene Freese, to the White Sox for Callison, and it was time for the Connie Mack Stadium fans to start talking about the potential of the smooth-swinging lefty hitter. They were still saying it after two nondescript seasons. Then, in 1962, Callison hit .300 when Gene Mauch sat him on the last day of the season.

Now the cry became, "He hit .300 and he hasn't even scratched the surface of his potential." Mauch had done Callison a great favor because John never hit .300 again.

In 1964, Gus Triandos's "Year of the Blue Snow" that turned black, Callison hit 31 home runs, drove in 104, scored 101, and batted .274.

He hit the winning three-run home run in the All-Star Game in Shea Stadium in the bottom of the ninth inning, giving the National League a 7–4 victory. And if the Phillies had been able to hang on and win the pennant, he would have been voted the NL's Most Valuable Player. He finished second to Ken Boyer of the St. Louis Cardinals.

The following season he batted just .262 but slammed 32 homers and drove in 101 runs. He was 26 years old, approaching the prime years of his career, and fans couldn't wait until he put it all together—a .300 average, 30-plus homers, 100-plus runs scored, 100-plus RBI. It seemed like it was only a matter of time.

But it never happened. Callison's power disappeared. In his next four Phillie seasons, he never hit more than 16 homers, never drove in more than 65 runs, never batted higher than .276. After the 1969 season, he was moved to the Cubs while Phillie fans bemoaned "all that wasted potential."

Let the record show that John Callison wound up his career in the major leagues with 1,757 hits, 226 home runs, and .264. And those are actual figures, not potential ones.

Callison, Johnny

Phillies	G	AB	H	BA	RBI	R	2B	3B	HR	SA	SB
1960	99	288	75	.260	30	36	11	5	9	.427	0
1961	138	455	121	.266	47	74	20	11	9	.418	10
1962	157	603	181	.300	83	107	26	10	23	.491	10
1963	157	626	178	.284	78	96	36	11	26	.502	8
1964	162	654	179	.274	104	101	30	10	31	.492	6
1965	160	619	162	.262	101	93	25	16	32	.509	6
1966	155	612	169	.276	55	93	40	7	11	.418	8
1967	149	556	145	.261	64	62	30	5	14	.408	6
1968	121	398	97	.244	40	46	18	4	14	.415	4
1969	134	495	131	.265	64	66	29	5	16	.440	2
Career	1,886	6,652	1,757	.264	840	926	321	89	226	.441	74

Camilli, Dolph

Phillies: 1934–37
First baseman
Birthplace: San Francisco, California
B: April 23, 1907
Bats left, throws left
Ht. 5–10; **Wt.** 185

Dolph Camilli

When it comes to the Phillies' trades, Dolph Camilli owns a spot on the list of the worst ones in club history. Camilli was one of the big ones who got away, and mention of his name brings sadness to the eyes of old-timers who remember the way the young Californian plastered the ball during his all-too-short stay in Philadelphia.

If Camilli had remained in a Phillies uniform, he would have been one of the club's all-time greats. Instead, he was traded at the peak of his career and went on to a string of outstanding years with the Brooklyn Dodgers.

While he was in Philadelphia, though, Camilli had his share of success. Traded to the Phillies in 1934 for first baseman Don Hurst (who did little thereafter), Camilli was a real steal for the Phils.

A muscular youngster, who had not played much with the Chicago Cubs despite his being groomed as Charley Grimm's replacement at first, Camilli was immediately inserted into the Phillies' starting lineup. In no time, he took over as the Phils' main power hitter.

In 1934, in what was really his rookie season, Camilli led the Phillies in home runs while batting .265. The following year, his average slipped to .261, but his home run total jumped to 25, which was good enough to rank third in the league behind Wally Berger's pace-setting total of 34. During one game in 1935 against the New York Giants, Dolph drove in seven runs.

During his first two years with the Phillies, Camilli led the league in strikeouts. He would achieve that dubious distinction twice more in his career with Brooklyn.

Camilli really came into his own in 1936 when he blasted the ball for a .315 average while hammering 28 home runs and driving in 102. This time he was second in the league in homers (Mel Ott led with 33) and tied for fifth in RBI.

Dolph continued his torrid pace the following season, teaming for the second straight year with Chuck Klein, who had returned to the Phillies, to give the club a fearsome one-two power punch. For the fourth straight year, Camilli led the Phillies in home runs, hitting 27 (third in the league behind Joe Medwick's front-running 31). Dolph wound up the season with a .339 average, by far the highest of his 12-year career.

With such accomplishments, Camilli's future in a uniform other than that of the Phillies was assured. In the spring of 1938, to the horror of Phillies fans, Dolph was swapped to the Dodgers for a utility outfielder named Eddie Morgan and $50,000. Morgan failed to make the Phillies that season.

Meanwhile, Camilli went on to play six more seasons in Brooklyn and one in 1945 with the Boston Red Sox. He had his greatest year in 1941 when he led the league in home runs (34) and RBI (120) while hitting .285. That year, the Dodgers won the National League pennant and Camilli was named most valuable player.

Camilli, Dolph

Phillies	G	AB	H	BA	RBI	R	2B	3B	HR	SA	SB
1934	102	378	100	.265	68	52	20	3	12	.429	3
1935	156	602	157	.261	83	88	23	5	25	.440	9
1936	151	530	167	.315	102	106	29	13	28	.577	5
1937	131	475	161	.339	80	101	23	7	27	:587	6
Career	1,490	5,353	1,482	.277	950	936	261	86	239	.492	60

Carlson, Hal

Phillies: 1924–27
Pitcher
Birthplace: Rockford, Illinois
B: May 17, 1894
D: May 28, 1930
Batted right, threw right
Ht. 6–0; **Wt.** 180

Hal Carlson was 29 years old and his career seemed over when the Phillies picked him up in the 1923 autumn draft. He had spent seven seasons with the Pirates, but he had pitched only four games in his final season with them before being released to Wichita in the Western Association.

It turned out that Carlson was an absolute steal for the Phillies. One of the few remaining spitball pitchers in the majors, Carlson worked for the Phillies for a little more than three years and compiled a 42–48 record, outstanding when you consider the bad teams for which he played and the short distances in Baker Bowl, where he pitched half his games.

In 1926, pitching for the last-place team, Carlson was 17–12 with a 3.24 ERA and 20 complete games. The season before, his four shutouts were tops in the National League.

All of which set Carlson up as the next star that president William Baker traded in order to keep the franchise solvent. Early in the 1927 season, Carlson was dealt to the Cubs for pitcher Tony Kaufman, infielder Jimmy Cooney and—of utmost importance—a $50,000 check drawn on the Wrigley account.

Hal's ERA soared in Chicago, but he was still considered a vital member of the team when he died suddenly in his hotel room in May 1930 of acute indigestion. He became one of several Phillies and ex-Phillies of that era to die while still active players. Others included pitcher Dutch Ulrich, catcher Peck Lerian, and infielder Mickey Finn.

The Cubs finished in second place in 1930, two games behind the Cards. Late that season, manager Joe McCarthy said Chicago would have won the flag had Carlson not died.

"It was a blow from which the team hasn't yet recovered," McCarthy said in mid-August. "Had Hal lived, we would have had the pennant won by this time. When I needed a game, I just had to tell him, 'Go in today and get this one.' "

Hal Carlson

Carlson, Hal

Phillies	W	L	Pct	ERA	G	CG	IP	H	BB	SO	ShO
1924	8	17	.320	4.85	38	12	204	267	55	66	1
1925	13	14	.481	4.23	35	18	234	281	52	80	4
1926	17	12	.586	3.24	38	20	267	293	47	55	3
1927	4	5	.444	5.20	11	4	64	80	18	13	0
Career	114	120	.487	3.97	377	121	2,002	2,256	498	590	17

Carlton, Steve

Phillies: 1972–86
Pitcher
Nickname: Lefty
Birthplace: Miami, Florida
B: December 22, 1944
Bats left, throws left
Ht. 6–5; **Wt.** 210

Shortly before John Quinn retired in 1972 as general manager of the Phillies, he made a trade with the St. Louis Cardinals. The Phillies gave up pitcher Rick Wise for another pitcher, Steve Carlton.

Although it wasn't immediately apparent, the trade turned out to be the best one the Phillies ever made.

Dealing away the popular and successful Wise resulted in scores of irate calls to the Phillies' office. Little did the callers know at the time that Quinn, the master of the unproductive trade, had in his final swap acquired a pitcher who was destined to become one of the all-time greats in Phillies history and an eventual member of the Hall of Fame.

In the years after that trade, Carlton piled up one milestone after another. He was the premier pitcher in baseball throughout the 1970s and early 1980s, in the process accumulating records that place him among the elite hurlers who have played the game. The Phillies retired his number 32 in 1989.

In those rare moments when he let his feelings be known, Carlton himself admitted that the deal that brought him to Philadelphia had a special significance. "It was," he said, "a blessing in disguise. The turning point of my life was coming here. I didn't know what professional baseball could be until then."

What it turned into for the great lefthander was an unprecedented four Cy Young Awards (1972, 1977, 1980, and 1982), 329 career wins, the second highest number of strikeouts in baseball history, five 20-win seasons with the Phillies, a National League record six one-hitters, and countless other accomplishments, all testimonials to the consistently unhittable offerings Lefty served to opposing batters.

There is no finer description of Carlton's offerings than the one voiced by Hall of Fame hitter Willie Stargell. "Hitting him," said the former Pittsburgh Pirates slugger, "was like trying to drink coffee with a fork."

Tim McCarver, for many years Carlton's special catcher, had an equally apt observation: "When a great pitcher like Steve is getting four different pitches over the plate any time he wants to, the hitters have to be in trouble."

Always a power pitcher, Carlton had exceptional velocity, but also one of the most wicked sliders ever to frustrate a hitter and outstanding control. "He's a power pitcher but he's also a thinking pitcher," former Phils pitching coach Herm Starrette once analyzed.

"Lefty was a craftsman. He was an artist," said Phillies broadcaster and former star center fielder Rich Ashburn. "He was a perfectionist. Lefty never had (Sandy) Koufax's fastball—and nobody else probably did, either—but he painted a ball game. Stroke, stroke, stroke . . . and when he got through, it was a masterpiece."

Carlton was the essence of physical fitness, a towering figure of strength and stamina who worked out religiously on a daily basis. He could do 1,100 situps at a time with 15-pound weights around each wrist and ankle.

"Whoever put that man together genetically did one helluva job," said Phillies strength and conditioning coach Gus Hoefling, the man under whom Carlton developed a fanatical regimen of fitness training. "I've never seen anything like it."

To Carlton, the mental aspect of the game was as important as the physical aspect. Steve relied heavily on the benefits of a strong positive approach to pitching, along with his brilliant left arm, and he had the uncanny ability to block out everything around him.

"The mental game," he said, "is the most important part of my approach. I go out there to win every game.

"I knew what I needed to do to succeed. My job was my performance on the field, so whatever was an intangible or an outside influence that was really not necessary, I just found ways to eliminate them. My obligation to the fans and to the Philadelphia Phillies when I pitched was to give the best of my mental and physical capabilities and performance that I could muster."

So intent was Carlton on blocking out outside influences that he stuffed

Steve Carlton

Steve Carlton got his 1982 Cy Young Award
presented to him by Bill Giles.

cotton in his ears when he pitched. On game days he talked rarely to
teammates, and on all days he talked never to the media.

Stemming from what he considered unfair treatment by one particular
local reporter, although it was an arguable position, Carlton consistently
avoided the press, refusing through most of his years in Philadelphia to talk at
all with reporters. Carlton drastically reduced his public comments in 1973. By
1978 he had stopped giving interviews altogether, except in a few isolated
instances.

As a result, Carlton deprived local fans over the years of knowing either
much about him or how he felt about different situations. "The press is one of
the biggest enemies you have in Philadelphia," Carlton said in the book *The
Team That Wouldn't Die*. "You have to first worry about the opposition, then all
the things that are written in the paper. I just cut all the distractions off."

Carlton also cut off many National League batters from the bases. He was
the model of consistency, rarely deviating from one game to the next except on
those rare days when his pitches simply didn't work.

"His first, last, and middle name should be consistency," former Phillies
manager Dallas Green once remarked.

The sphinxlike Carlton on the mound, emotionless, calculating, a robot in
red pinstripes, was a familiar image to Phillies fans. It was a sight that
dominated the Philadelphia pitching scene for nearly 15 years.

By the time he departed in 1986, Carlton was the Phillies' all-time leader in
wins, games started, strikeouts, and walks, and he ranked second in games,
shutouts, runs, earned runs, innings pitched, hits, and losses.

From 1972 through 1986, except for one year, the Phillies never had
another opening-day starting pitcher. Carlton hurled a National League
record 14 openers.

Carlton's career, which overall extended to 1988, saw him become the
ninth-biggest winner in big league history and the second-winningest
lefthander. He struck out more batters (4,136) than any pitcher but Nolan
Ryan—he also walked the second highest total (1,833)—and he ranked eighth
in innings pitched (5,216⅔).

Carlton easily ranks among the finest lefthanded pitchers of all time, more than holding his own in a class with Warren Spahn, Lefty Grove, Eddie Plank, Carl Hubbell, Whitey Ford, Koufax, Eppa Rixey, and the other great southpaws. Only Spahn with 363 won more games than Carlton.

After joining the Phillies, Carlton led the National League in strikeouts and innings pitched five times, in wins, games started, and hits four times, and in complete games three times.

Originally signed in 1964 for a $5,000 bonus by the St. Louis Cardinals, Carlton spent only his first year entirely in the minors. Although he pitched in just 15 games, he was on the Cards' roster for all of 1965. Steve split the 1966 season between Tulsa and St. Louis, then moved to the Cardinals to stay in 1967.

Over the next five years he posted records of 14–9, 13–11, 17–11, 10–19, and 20–9 in St Louis. In 1969 he set a modern major league record for a nine-inning game (later tied by Tom Seaver, Ryan, and David Cone) by striking out 19 New York Mets. Carlton lost that game, 4–3, to future teammate Tug McGraw.

Steve got into a contract dispute with the Cards following the 1971 season. Unwilling to meet his demands, St. Louis was anxious to trade him, and Quinn was anxious to oblige.

The deal was made, and the Cards got Rick Wise, who was embroiled in a contract squabble with the Phillies. Wise was coming off his finest year, having won 17 games and pitched a no-hitter. The swap was highly unpopular with Phillies fans.

In Carlton's first season with the Phillies, however, he won the fans over with one of the great pitching performances of modern times. Although the Phillies had the worst record in the major leagues, Steve blazed through the season winning nearly one-half of the team's 59 wins. He was nicknamed "The Franchise" and posted a 27–10 record with a 1.98 earned run average and a career-high and league-leading 310 strikeouts. He also won 15 straight games, a Phillies record.

During the season, Carlton pitched a one-hitter against the San Francisco Giants, yielding only a leadoff single to Chris Speier in the first inning. On June 7 he beat the Houston Astros, 3–1, to begin his 15-game winning streak, which came to an end August 21 when he lost to the Atlanta Braves, 2–1, in 11 innings.

Carlton hurled eight shutouts, pitched a career-high 346⅓ innings, and completed 30 of the 41 games he started, at the end of the season walking off with his first Cy Young Award.

The following season, arm miseries and a lingering case of bronchitis reduced Carlton to the level of a mere mortal. He managed only a 13–20 record. Steve followed that with two more average seasons, although he hurled another one-hitter in 1975, beating the New York Mets, 8–1, and allowing only a sixth inning single to Felix Millan.

In 1976, Carlton became a big winner again, going 20–7, beating the Mets, 2–1, on the final game of the season. On July 10 he registered his 2,000th career strikeout by whiffing Dave Winfield of the San Diego Padres.

Carlton repeated as a 20-game winner in 1977 (23–10), 1980 (24–9), and 1982 (23–11). If it hadn't been for some weak offensive support in 1979 and the players' strike in 1981, he probably would have won 20 in those years, too.

Along the way, Carlton was selected for 10 All-Star Games. He was the winning pitcher in 1969, when he was still a Cardinal.

Carlton lost decisions in the 1976 and 1977 League Championship Series games. But he beat the Los Angeles Dodgers in a 1978 LCS game, 9–4, while also hitting a home run. He won again in the 1980 LCS, downing Houston 3–1 in the opener and in 1983, beating the Dodgers twice, including the pennant clincher.

In the 1980 World Series, Carlton was the winning pitcher in the second and sixth games. In the former, he gave up 10 hits and struck out 10 in eight innings of work to beat the Royals, 6–4. Steve scattered four hits over seven innings to get credit for the 4–1 win in the deciding game of the Series.

Carlton was the losing pitcher in Game Three of the 1983 World Series with the Baltimore Orioles.

Carlton pitched two one-hitters during the 1979 season. Jeff Leonard's seventh-inning single was the only Houston hit in an 8–0 Phillies victory. Elliott Maddox slapped a seventh-inning single for the Mets in a 1–0 loss to Carlton.

A fifth one-hitter occurred in 1980 in a 7–0 win over the Cardinals. Ted Simmons got a second-inning single. Carlton almost had a no-hitter that year, working seven and two-thirds innings before he was touched by Bill Nahorodny for a single in what became a three-hit, 7–1 victory for Carlton over the Braves.

In 1981, Carlton added to his list of achievements by winning his first Gold Glove. On April 29 that year, he struck out the Montreal Expos' Tim Wallach, the third whiff of the first inning, to become only the sixth pitcher in major league history to reach 3,000 strikeouts. On September 21, 1981 he fanned the Expos' Andre Dawson to become the National League's all-time strikeout leader.

Carlton lost two games to Montreal in the division series in 1981, one of the few blemishes on his nearly spotless record. The next year, though, he was back as king of the hill when, at 37 years old, he was the major leagues' only 20-game winner while leading the National League in virtually all of the important pitching categories.

That season, Carlton again flirted with the elusive no-hitter he spent a career pursuing but never achieved. With two outs in the eighth inning in what became a 2–0 victory over the San Francisco Giants, Carlton surrendered a single to Bob Brenly.

Steve also struck out 16 Chicago Cubs that season in a 4–2 victory, and won his 200th game in a Phillies uniform with a 5–4 triumph over the Expos.

In 1983, Carlton struck out the Padres' Garry Templeton to move past Walter Johnson and into second place on the all-time strikeout list with 3,503. Two weeks later, his 3,522nd strikeout moved him temporarily past Ryan and into first place on the list.

On September 23, 1983, Carlton became only the 16th 300-game winner in the history of the major leagues when he defeated the Cardinals, 6–2, in St. Louis.

That year, with a nagging back injury reducing his effectiveness, he recorded his first losing record (15–16) since 1973. Nevertheless, he still led the league in strikeouts and innings pitched.

The 1984 season would turn out to be Carlton's last effective year in Philadelphia. He went 13–7. At one point, he hit a grand slam home run off Fernando Valenzuela en route to a 7–2 victory over the Dodgers. He also beat the Expos, 9–5, for his 235th career Phillies win, a club record.

Injuries continued to plague Carlton over the next two years. In 1986, he started his 14th opening game, a National League record. He struck out 10 Mets in a game, running his club record of 10 or more strikeouts in a game to 69. He also set a National League record for most games started (666) when he beat the Giants, 6–2.

Carlton's last win as a Phillie came on June 1, 1986, when he topped the Padres, 16–5. He pitched in his final Phillies game on June 21, ironically against the Cardinals. His final strikeout victim as a Phillies pitcher was Danny Cox.

Having basically lost it, Carlton was asked to retire by the Phillies. But he stubbornly refused. Finally, given no other choice, club president Bill Giles told Carlton he was being released.

"It took me three days to get up enough nerve to tell him," Giles said. "I was convinced that it was not in the best interest of the Phillies for him to continue pitching for us."

Convinced that he could still pitch, Carlton struggled desperately to hang on in the big leagues. He joined the Giants, but was released after six games. Carlton then signed with the Chicago White Sox and in 10 games had a brief resurgence with a 4–3 record.

In 1987, Carlton tried to make it with the Cleveland Indians and the Minnesota Twins. But he had nothing left. He started the 1988 season with the Twins, but lasted just four games.

Carlton's career was over, and everybody knew it but the 44-year-old hurler himself. He went to early spring training with the Phillies in 1989, but that attempt proved to be just as futile as his other efforts of recent years.

Finally, the once-great lefthander saw the light, and hung up his glove. He went out holding a certain ticket to the Hall of Fame, as one of the finest pitchers in baseball history.

Carlton, Steve

Phillies	W	L	Pct	ERA	G	CG	IP	H	BB	SO	ShO
1972	27	10	.730	1.97	41	30	346	257	87	310	8
1973	13	20	.394	3.90	40	18	293	293	113	223	3
1974	16	13	.552	3.22	39	17	291	249	136	240	1
1975	15	14	.517	3.56	37	14	255	217	104	192	3
1976	20	7	.741	3.13	35	13	253	224	72	195	2
1977	23	10	.697	2.64	36	17	283	229	89	198	2
1978	16	13	.552	2.84	34	12	247	228	63	161	3
1979	18	11	.621	3.62	35	13	251	202	89	213	4
1980	24	9	.727	2.34	38	13	304	243	90	286	3
1981	13	4	.765	2.42	24	10	190	152	62	179	1
1982	23	11	.676	3.10	38	19	296	253	86	286	6
1983	15	16	.484	3.11	37	8	284	277	84	275	3
1984	13	7	.650	3.58	33	1	229	214	79	163	0
1985	1	8	.111	3.33	16	0	92	84	53	48	0
1986	4	8	.333	6.18	16	0	83	102	45	62	0
Career	329	244	.574	3.22	741	254	5,217	4,672	1,833	4,136	55

Carman, Don

Don Carman mixed his duties between starting and relieving during his six full years with the Phillies—with mixed results.

At times he was overpowering, like the game in 1986 when he took a perfect game into the ninth inning against the San Francisco Giants or the one-hitter he pitched against the New York Mets a year later. His best season was 1987 when he had a 13–11 record and pitched two of his three career shutouts, including the one-hitter.

At other times he was totally ineffective, like the entire 1989 season in which he failed to complete any of his 20 starts on his way to a 5–15 record and a 5.24 earned run average.

Carman was signed by the Phillies as a free agent after passing through the draft in 1978. He spent six years in the club's minor league system before making the parent team as a reliever in 1985. He won nine games and saved seven with a 2.08 ERA, and his 71 appearances ties for the sixth-highest total by a pitcher and the most ever by a lefthander in team history.

He started the next season in the bullpen but was moved into the starting rotation just before the All-Star break. He was 7–3 with a 2.43 ERA as a starter, losing just one of his last eight starts. On August 20 he retired the first 24 Giants he faced before catcher Bob Brenly led off the ninth inning with a double.

He earned 13 victories in 1987 even though he broke Steve Carlton's club

Phillies: 1983–90
Pitcher
Birthplace: Oklahoma City, Oklahoma
B: August 14, 1959
Bats left, throws left
Ht. 6–3; **Wt.** 195

Don Carman

record for home runs allowed by a lefty with 34. A notoriously poor hitter with an .059 (12-for-204) lifetime average with the Phillies, Carman got his first major league hit in his 50th trip to the plate on May 16, 1987.

Carman slipped to 10–14 the following season, then underwent surgery on his right knee after the season.

In 1989, he was 3–13 as a starter, including nine straight defeats, before he was moved to the bullpen. The following season, his last with the team, he was used as a middle reliever. Carman pitched for the Cincinnati Reds in 1991.

Carman, Don.

Phillies	W	L	Pct	ERA	G	CG	IP	H	BB	SO	ShO
1983	0	0	.000	0.00	1	0	1	0	0	0	0
1984	0	1	.000	5.40	11	0	13	14	6	16	0
1985	9	4	.692	2.08	71	0	86	52	38	87	0
1986	10	5	.667	3.22	50	2	134	113	52	98	1
1987	13	11	.542	4.22	35	3	211	194	69	125	2
1988	10	14	.417	4.29	36	2	201	211	70	116	0
1989	5	15	.250	5.24	49	0	149	152	86	81	0
1990	6	2	.750	4.15	59	0	87	69	38	58	0
Career	53	54	.495	4.09	340	7	920	845	378	596	3

Carsey, Kid

Phillies: 1892–97
Pitcher
Birthplace: New York, New York
B: October 22, 1870
D: March 29, 1960
Batted right, threw right
Ht. 5–7; **Wt.** 168

Kid Carsey

When the Phillies picked up Kid Carsey from Washington after the American Association disbanded, there wasn't any dancing in the streets. After all, Kid had lost 37 games and given up 513 hits in 1891, his first year of major league competition.

But the Phillies soon learned they had themselves a pretty good pitcher, despite his prior statistics. In his first four seasons in Philadelphia, Carsey won 81 games, and he ranked as one of the club's top hurlers of the 1890s.

The elfin moundsman was a 20-game winner twice and a tireless workman during a little more than five seasons with the Phillies.

His best season was in 1895 when he posted a 24–16 record for the third-place Phillies. That year, Carsey gave up a league-leading total of 460 hits in 342 innings of pitching.

After working more than 300 innings—once more than 400—in four of his first five seasons, Carsey began to fade. In 1897 the Phillies unloaded him on St. Louis. Then he bounced from Cleveland to Washington to Brooklyn, never winning more than three games in any season after leaving Philadelphia.

Carsey, Kid (Wilfred)

Phillies	W	L	Pct	ERA	G	CG	IP	H	BB	SO	ShO
1892	19	16	.543	3.11	43	30	317⅔	320	104	76	1
1893	20	15	.571	4.81	39	30	318⅓	375	124	50	1
1894	18	12	.600	5.56	35	26	277	349	102	41	0
1895	24	16	.600	4.92	44	35	342⅓	460	118	64	0
1896	11	11	.500	5.63	27	18	187⅓	273	72	36	1
1897	2	1	.667	5.14	4	2	28	35	16	1	0
Career	116	138	.457	4.95	294	218	2,222	2,780	796	484	4

Casey, Dan

In the pre-1900s, when teams usually got by with only two or three pitchers on the staff, Dan Casey was one of those guys who hurled every second or third game.

He pitched for four years for the Phillies and twice was a 20-game winner. In 1886 he had a 24–18 mark, and in 1887 his record was 28–13.

Casey was only 18 years old when he first came up with Wilmington in the outlaw Union Association in 1884. The next year, he played for Detroit in the National League. He came to the Phillies the following season after having posted only a 5–9 log during his first two years.

With the Phillies, Dan suddenly became an outstanding pitcher. In 1886 he and Charlie Ferguson won all but 17 of the team's victories. Casey and Ferguson tied for second in the National League in shutouts that year with four apiece.

In 1887, Casey was the Phillies' top hurler, and his 2.86 ERA led the National League. While pitching in 45 games that year, he worked in 390 innings. Dan also led the league in shutouts with four.

Casey won only 14 of 32 decisions in 1888. The next year he was down to 6–10. He finished his big league hurling the following season with a 19–22 record at Syracuse of the American Association.

Throughout his life, Casey steadfastly maintained that he was the subject of Ernest Thayer's famous poem "Casey at the Bat." Dan contended that he was immortalized as the Mighty Casey after striking out with the bases loaded in a game in 1887 between the Phillies and New York Giants. The game, of course, was played in Philadelphia instead of Mudville.

As a hitter, Casey in reality was considerably less than mighty. His lifetime batting average was .162 with one home run.

Phillies: 1886–89
Pitcher
Birthplace: Binghamton, New York
B: October 2, 1865
D: February 8, 1943
Batted right, threw left
Ht. 6–0; **Wt.** 180

Dan Casey

Casey, Dan

Phillies	W	L	Pct	ERA	G	CG	IP	H	BB	SO	ShO
1886	24	18	.571	2.41	44	39	369	326	104	193	4
1887	28	13	.683	2.86	45	43	390⅓	377	115	119	4
1888	14	18	.438	3.15	33	31	285⅔	298	48	108	1
1889	6	10	.375	3.76	20	15	152⅔	170	72	65	1
Career	96	90	.516	3.18	201	182	1,680⅓	1,664	543	743	13

Cash, Dave

The slogan was born innocently enough. Dave Cash, the new second baseman, was a dog-racing fan who knew more than a little about handicapping. One night during his first spring training with the Phillies in 1974, Cash took a bundle of his teammates' money to the track with him. The next day in the locker room he was asked if everyone had won.

"Yes we did," Cash said.

The previous September, Tug McGraw had spent the month yelling "You Gotta Believe" in the New York Mets' dressing room, and somehow the team came from the back of the pack to win the National League pennant. And, as spring training wore on in 1974, "Yes we did" somehow became "Yes We Can," which became the slogan of the Phillies' rebirth that ultimately led to the 1980 World Championship.

Cash gave the Phillies much more than a slogan during his three years as the team's second baseman. He made them believe they could win. He provided the steadying influence that turned Larry Bowa into a great shortstop. He gave them All-Star caliber play at a position that had been a traditional problem area. He won over the fans, who had grumbled when Paul

Phillies: 1974–76
Second baseman
Birthplace: Utica, New York
B: June 11, 1948
Bats right, throws right
Ht. 5–11; **Wt.** 170

Dave Cash

Owens traded 13-game-winning pitcher Ken Brett to the Pirates for him even though he had never won a regular job with the Bucs.

And, mostly, he played the game offensively, the way the good citizens in Cook County, Illinois, are alleged to vote. Cash batted early and often.

He handled the troublesome leadoff spot from day one. In all three seasons in the polyester red pinstripes, he led the National League in at-bats. In 1975 he topped the league in hits (213) in a record 699 trips, scored 111 runs, and struck out only 34 times while batting .305. The following year, he topped the NL with 12 triples and struck out just 13 times in 666 official plate appearances as the Phillies made their first post-season appearance in 26 years.

He also asked for, and failed to receive, a long-term contract and opted for the then-new concept of free agency. The Expos signed him, and the Phillies quickly learned how the free-agent game was played.

Cash was never as effective after he left the Phillies. He retired from baseball after the 1980 season at age 32, having left his mark as the player who was most responsible for changing the Phillies' image of the 1970s from losers to winners.

Cash, Dave

Phillies	G	AB	H	BA	RBI	R	2B	3B	HR	SA	SB
1974	162	687	206	.300	58	89	26	11	2	.378	20
1975	162	699	213	.305	57	111	40	3	4	.388	13
1976	160	666	189	.284	56	92	14	12	1	.345	10
Career	1,422	5,554	1,571	.283	426	732	243	56	21	.358	120

Chiozza, Lou

Phillies: 1934–36
Second baseman, third baseman, center fielder
Birthplace: Tallulah, Louisiana
B: May 11, 1910
D: February 28, 1971
Batted left, threw right
Ht. 6–0; **Wt.** 172

Lou Chiozza

Although some of his peers were more prominent, Lou Chiozza put in three solid years for the Phillies in the mid-1930s.

The speedy lefthanded swinger strung together averages of .304, .284, and .297 between 1934 and 1936. He was the Phillies' regular second baseman the first two years, then played mostly in center field in his third year in Philadelphia.

Chiozza, whose brother Dino also appeared briefly for the Phils in 1935, was a good all-around athlete who began his minor league career in 1931. After hitting .325 and .338 in the low minors, he moved to Memphis where he hit .294. The Phillies drafted him from Memphis.

Lou had a fine rookie year with the Phillies in 1934. Although he had been mostly a shortstop in the minors, the Phils used him at second.

Chiozza led National League second basemen in errors in 1934 and 1935. In '35, however, he tied a modern National League record (since broken) with 11 assists in one game. That year he also scored five runs in one game.

The Phillies put Lou in center field in 1936, and he led the league's outfielders with 10 double plays. After the season ended, Chiozza was traded to the New York Giants for shortstop George Sharein and cash. The Giants wanted Lou to be the successor to Travis Jackson at third.

That didn't work out, and eventually New York moved Lou back to the outfield. He had a poor year in 1937, hitting only .232 for the pennant-winning Giants. He broke his leg in each of the next two years, and played sparingly each season. Lou retired in 1940.

Chiozza, Lou

Phillies	G	AB	H	BA	RBI	R	2B	3B	HR	SA	SB
1934	134	484	147	.304	44	66	28	5	0	.382	9
1935	124	472	134	.284	47	71	26	6	3	.383	5
1936	144	572	170	.297	48	83	32	6	1	.379	17
Career	616	2,288	633	.277	197	303	107	22	14	.361	45

Christenson, Larry

Ralph Kiner has startled viewers of his New York Mets telecasts for decades with his outrageous statements. But one of his most outrageous was made off camera in April 1973.

Larry Christenson, a hard-throwing 19-year-old whom the Phillies had drafted as their number-one choice the previous June, had just beaten the Mets, 7–1, in his major league debut.

Kiner was not impressed. After the game in the Veterans Stadium press room, he announced that he didn't think Christenson would ever win another game in the big leagues.

Kiner missed his prediction by 82 victories and would have looked even more foolish if Christenson hadn't been plagued by a series of injuries that brought a premature end to his career in 1983 before he had reached the age of 30.

Christenson scored four consecutive double-figure victory seasons from 1975 to 1978, including a terrific 19–6 season in 1977, forming a formidable one-two punch with teammate Steve Carlton, the Cy Young Award winner.

In 1978, despite a hard-luck 13–14 season, Larry dropped his earned run average from 4.07 to 3.24. That year he established career highs in shutouts (3), complete games (9), and innings pitched (228). His walks-to-strikeouts ratio was a sparkling 47–131. He seemed at the age of 24 to be on the verge of superstardom.

But he broke his collarbone in a bicycle accident the next February and was on the disabled list until May 12. He finished 5–10 in 17 starts and two relief appearances.

In 1980 groin injuries and a second elbow operation limited him to a 5–1 record in 14 starts. He pitched well in his only start in the League Championship Series, a no-decision against the Houston Astros, but didn't survive the first inning against the Kansas City Royals in the fourth game of the World Series.

A groin pull in 1981 sidelined him for 21 days, and he suffered through a 4–7 season. But he was the winning pitcher in Game Three of the NL East Division series with the Montreal Expos.

He underwent his third elbow operation after the 1982 season and called it a career after nine starts and a 2–4 record in 1983.

Phillies: 1973–83
Pitcher
Nickname: L. C.
Birthplace: Everett, Washington
B: November 10, 1953
Bats right, throws right
Ht. 6–4; **Wt.** 215

Christenson, Larry

Phillies	W	L	Pct	ERA	G	CG	IP	H	BB	SO	ShO
1973	1	4	.200	6.62	10	1	34	53	20	11	0
1974	1	1	.500	4.30	10	0	23	20	15	18	0
1975	11	6	.647	3.66	29	5	172	149	45	88	2
1976	13	8	.619	3.67	32	2	169	199	42	54	0
1977	19	6	.760	4.07	34	5	219	229	69	118	1
1978	13	14	.481	3.24	33	9	228	209	47	131	3
1979	5	10	.333	4.50	19	2	106	118	30	53	0
1980	5	1	.833	4.01	14	0	74	62	27	49	0
1981	4	7	.364	3.53	20	0	107	108	30	70	0
1982	9	10	.474	3.47	33	3	223	212	53	145	0
1983	2	4	.333	3.91	9	0	48	42	17	44	0
Career	83	71	.539	3.79	243	27	1,403	1,401	395	781	6

Larry Christenson

Clements, Jack

Phillies: 1884–97
Catcher
Birthplace: Philadelphia, Pennsylvania
B: June 24, 1864
D: May 23, 1941
Batted left, threw left
Ht. 5–8½; **Wt.** 204

Jack Clements

Somewhere along the way, it was decreed that there should be no lefthanded catchers. Today that edict would be called discrimination. In Jack Clements' day, it would've been called horsefeathers.

Clements, you see, was a lefthanded catcher who played in the major leagues for 17 seasons. Squatting behind the plate with his right hand in a mitt never seemed to bother Jack, except at those times when he wanted to snap a throw to first and there was a lefthanded batter in the box.

History has not recorded whether Clements ever put one in any southpaw hitter's breadbasket, but it does note that he was one of the few lefthanded catchers in baseball history. And he also played a little shortstop and third base early in his career, as well as first base and the outfield.

He also commanded another footnote in baseball annals. Clements was one of the first catchers to wear a chest protector.

It was as a catcher that Jack excelled. A Philadelphia native, he ranks third in Phillies annals in number of games played behind the plate (953).

A short, stubby guy, Clements first made the pros in 1884 with the Philadelphia Keystoners of the outlaw Union Association. When that league disbanded before the end of the season, Jack was picked up by the Phillies.

Clements struggled for the first couple of years with the Phillies. But in 1887, having become the regular catcher, his playing began to improve. Jack hit .280 that year.

Always a good handler of pitchers, Clements could also field well. He led National League catchers in fielding average in 1888 and 1892.

Jack hit over .300 five times with the Phillies. He was also one of the league's best home run hitters. He was second in the league in homers with 17 in 1893 and third with 13 in 1895.

Clements was also third in the league's batting races twice: once in 1890 when he hit .315 and once in 1895 when he had his best mark with a .394. His .310 in 1891 was fourth in the circuit.

In 1894, Jack was off to one of his best starts when he broke an ankle. He wound up hitting .346. Two years later he hit .359, but by then was relegated to a reserve role.

He joined the St. Louis Browns in 1898 and again led the league's catchers in fielding as he regained a starting position. Clements played briefly the next season with Cleveland, and then stepped out in 1900 after a short stay with Boston.

Clements, Jack

Phillies	G	AB	H	BA	RBI	R	2B	3B	HR	SA	SB
1884	9	30	7	.233	0	3	0	0	0	.233	
1885	52	188	36	.191	14	14	11	3	1	.298	
1886	54	185	38	.205	11	15	5	1	0	.234	4
1887	66	246	69	.280	47	48	13	7	1	.402	7
1888	86	326	80	.245	32	26	8	4	1	.304	3
1889	78	310	88	.284	35	51	17	1	4	.384	3
1890	97	381	120	.315	74	64	23	8	7	.472	10
1891	107	423	131	.310	75	58	29	4	4	.426	3
1892	109	402	106	.264	76	50	25	6	8	.415	7
1893	94	376	107	.285	80	64	20	3	17	.489	3
1894	45	159	55	.346	36	26	6	5	3	.503	6
1895	88	322	127	.394	75	64	27	2	13	.612	3
1896	57	184	66	.359	45	35	5	7	5	.543	2
1897	55	185	44	.238	36	18	4	2	6	.378	3
Career	1,157	4,283	1,226	.286	673	619	226	60	77	.421	55

John Coleman was the starting pitcher in the first Phillies game in history. That distinction would be enough to earn Coleman a measure of prominence in any discussion about the club's 110 years. But John supplied a little bit more to talk about.

For instance, he was a 48-game loser in 1883, the Phillies' first season. That year, he allowed 544 runs and 772 hits while working 538 innings in 65 games. The losses, runs, and hits are all-time major league records that will never be erased.

Actually, Coleman had a 13–48 record in 1883. The 13 wins weren't so bad, considering the Phillies won only 17 games the entire season (they lost 81). John had a 4.87 ERA that year, and he pitched three shutouts. His 59 complete games ranked third in the league. Remarkably, he never lost more than 12 straight, which, nevertheless, ties an all-time Phillies record.

On May 1, 1883, Coleman was the opening-day pitcher as the Phillies made their debut in the National League against the Providence Grays at Recreation Park. John's opponent was Charley (Old Hoss) Radbourne, a future Hall of Famer who the following season would win 60 games.

The Phillies had a 3–0 lead going into the top of the eighth inning, but Providence erupted with four runs, and held on to win, 4–3. Both Coleman and Radbourne pitched six-hitters with John striking out two and walking two.

Poor old John, whom the Phillies had purchased from Peoria of the Northwestern League, never quite recovered from the tribulations of his 1883 season. In 1884 he withered to a mere 5–15 record with the Phillies before switching to the Philadelphia Athletics of the American Association late in the season.

After that year, Coleman pitched in only 18 more games in the major leagues. He did, however, see a considerable amount of duty out in the field.

As early as 1883, John usually played in the outfield when he wasn't pitching. He hit .234 that year while playing 32 games away from the mound. In 1884 he played 51 games in the outfield, hitting .230 for the season.

By 1885 with the Athletics, John had become the regular right fielder. He also played a little bit at first base, but almost never pitched. Coleman hit .299 that year.

Later, Coleman played the outfield and first base for Pittsburgh, then the

Coleman, John

Phillies: 1883–84
Pitcher
Birthplace: Saratoga Springs, New York
B: March 6, 1863
D: May 31, 1922
Batted left, threw right
Ht. 5–9½; **Wt.** 170

John Coleman

Athletics again, and finally Pittsburgh a second time before ending his big league career in 1890.

He remained a resident of the Philadelphia area, and became a prominent boxing referee and professional wrestler. His descendants still live there.

Coleman, John

Phillies	W	L	Pct	ERA	G	CG	IP	H	BB	SO	ShO
1883	13	48	.200	4.87	65	59	538⅓	772	48	159	3
1884	5	15	.250	4.91	21	14	154	216	22	37	1
Career	24	72	.250	4.68	107	84	842⅔	1,182	102	224	4

Collins, Phil

Phillies: 1929–35
Pitcher
Nickname: Fidgety Phil
Birthplace: Rockford, Illinois
B: August 27, 1900
D: August 14, 1948
Batted right, threw right
Ht. 5–11; **Wt.** 175

Phil Collins

Any pitcher with the nickname Collins had, had to make opposing batters a bit edgy. Fidgety Phil, so named because of his nervous traits on the mound, did indeed keep enemy hitters on edge during a little more than six seasons with the Phillies.

Collins, who preferred the more refined name of Philip E., was an effective hurler, considering that he played all but one year in Philadelphia with second-division clubs.

Phil, a butcher during the off-season, got his first big league exposure in 1923 with the Chicago Cubs, but it was only temporary. Collins toiled in the minors until the Phillies purchased his contract from New Orleans in time for the 1929 season.

Over the next six years, Collins was in double figures in wins four times. His best years were in 1930 when he posted a 16–11 record for a club that won only 52 of 154 games and in 1932 when he was 14–12 as the Phillies climbed all the way to fourth place.

Like all his fellow pitchers laboring in Baker Bowl, Collins never had an outstanding earned run average. Twice, in fact, he exceeded 5.00. But he was a workhorse, hurling in more than 40 games in six straight seasons with the Phils. Collins also relieved on occasion, and his six saves in 1933 led the National League.

He pitched a one-hitter in 1931, beating the New York Giants, 3–0, and yielding only a safety to Shanty Hogan.

Phil, who was sold to the St. Louis Cardinals during the 1935 campaign, his last in the majors, has a spot in several of the Phillies' all-time pitching categories. He ranks seventh in runs allowed, ninth in hits, and eighth in walks.

Perhaps one of Collins' single greatest achievements came as a hitter. In 1930 against the Pittsburgh Pirates, he hit two home runs in one game, one blast coming in the fourth inning and the other in the fifth. That same season, he also hit a grand slam homer against the Boston Braves. Those were the only home runs in Phil's entire major league career.

Collins, Phil

Phillies	W	L	Pct	ERA	G	CG	IP	H	BB	SO	ShO
1929	9	7	.563	5.75	43	3	153⅓	172	83	61	0
1930	16	11	.593	4.78	47	17	239	287	86	87	1
1931	12	16	.429	3.86	42	16	240⅓	268	83	73	2
1932	14	12	.538	5.27	43	6	184⅓	231	65	66	0
1933	8	13	.381	4.11	42	5	151	178	57	40	1
1934	13	18	.419	4.18	45	15	254	277	87	72	0
1935	0	2	.000	11.40	3	0	15	24	9	4	0
Career	80	85	.485	4.66	292	64	1,324⅓	1,541	497	423	4

Conley, Gene

One thing can be said with certainty about Gene Conley. He was no ordinary pitcher. Big Gene stood 6–8, which made him one of the tallest players ever to step onto a major league ballfield. With his size, Conley had the kind of leverage that managers wish every pitcher had.

Conley pitched for two fairly uneventful seasons with the Phillies in the midst of a big league career that lasted 11 years. It was a career that was especially noteworthy because Gene was also a professional basketball player during part of his baseball days.

Gene, who like Ed Bouchee attended Washington State College, came to the Phillies in the spring of 1959. He was part of general manager John Quinn's first deal. The Phils sent catcher Stan Lopata and infielders Ted Kazanski and Johnny O'Brien—an All-American basketball player—to the Milwaukee Braves for Conley and infielders Joe Koppe and Harry Hanebrink.

After an 0–6 record the previous year, Conley had considered quitting baseball to concentrate on basketball. But he changed his mind, and decided to report to the Phils. It was the right move because in 1959 Conley posted a 12–7 record for the last-place Phils. He led the team in ERA (3.00) and was selected to the National League All-Star team for the third time in his career.

In 1960, Gene tumbled to an 8–14 record. During the season, he was involved in a rollicking brawl. It was ignited by Conley's becoming the third batter of the inning to be hit by Cincinnati Reds pitcher Raul Sanchez. As Conley charged the mound, both dugouts erupted onto the field. A huge battle ensued. After order was restored, the Phils went on to a 14–3 win.

At the end of the season, the Phillies traded Conley to the Boston Red Sox for another towering pitcher, 6–7 Frank Sullivan.

Conley, the minor league Player of the Year in 1951 and 1953 when he posted 20–9 and 23–9 records for Hartford and Toledo, respectively, was in the majors briefly with the Boston Braves in 1952. He arrived to stay in 1954 with Milwaukee. Gene had a 14–9 record that year.

After leaving the Phillies, Conley pitched three years with the Red Sox. His best season was in 1962 when he had a 15–14 record.

In pro basketball, Conley was a reserve forward, playing four seasons with the Boston Celtics and two years with the New York Knicks. He broke in with the Celtics in 1952–53, then was out of basketball until rejoining Boston in 1958–59. He played from then through the 1963–64 season, averaging 5.9 points per game in his six years of play.

Phillies: 1959–60
Pitcher
Birthplace: Muskogee, Oklahoma
B: November 10, 1930
Bats right, throws right
Ht. 6–8; **Wt.** 227

Gene Conley

Conley, Gene

Phillies	W	L	Pct	ERA	G	CG	IP	H	BB	SO	ShO
1959	12	7	.632	3.00	25	12	180	159	42	102	3
1960	8	14	.364	3.68	29	9	183⅓	192	42	117	2
Career	91	96	.487	3.82	276	69	1,588⅔	1,606	511	888	13

Cooley, Duff

Duff Cooley was a fine outfielder who hit over .300 in three of his four seasons with the Phillies. But it was as the leader of a rebellion that he gained a niche in Phillies history.

Cooley was starting his second full season with the Phillies in 1898 when he assumed the post of head rabblerouser. He had just come off a .329 season when he led the league with 566 at-bats, and he had gained some stature on the club.

For the previous year and one-half, George Stallings had managed the Phillies the way a dictator runs a banana republic. The tyrannical Stallings was prone to tirades in which his abuse of the players always far exceeded the bounds of mere civility. The abused players suffered the effects of Stallings' tactics for a while, but eventually they grew tired of them. Something, they decided at a secret meeting, had to be done.

Phillies: 1896–99
Outfielder, first baseman
Nickname: Sir Richard
Birthplace: Dallas, Texas
B: March 14, 1873
D: August 9, 1937
Batted left, threw right
Ht. and Wt. unknown

As the leader of a committee, Cooley was charged with the duty of taking some action. Duff headed a delegation that took the problem to Phillies owners Al Reach and John Rogers.

Cooley said not only that the players could not tolerate Stallings, but also that they would henceforth refuse to play for the heavy-handed manager.

Duff followed up with a statement to the press: "We are fed up with the way Stallings has been riding us, and decided we had enough of him and would regard him as our manager no longer," he said. "For weeks, he's been handling us like a lot of cattle. We may not be the best team in the league, but we don't intend to put up with Stallings' tactics."

Cooley's revolt worked. Although a year and one-half still remained on Stallings' contract, Reach and Rogers bought it up and on June 18 sent George on his way. The reins were turned over to Billy Shettsline.

A satisfied Cooley went on to hit .312 that year while leading National League center fielders in putouts. Duff dropped to .276 in 1899, and the following winter he was traded to the Pittsburgh Pirates for pitcher Tully Sparks and second baseman Heinie Reitz.

Cooley, who had begun his big league career with St. Louis in 1893 and had hit .339 for the Cardinals in 1895, also played with the Boston Beaneaters before finishing his 13-year career in 1905 with the Detroit Tigers.

One winter, while still playing, Cooley had an off-season job tending bar in Topeka, Kansas. Hearing a lot of commotion one day, he looked up to see a band of ax-wielding women marching through the front door of the bar, screaming about the evils of demon rum. Leading the march was famous prohibitionist Carry Nation, who swung her ax as Duff ducked.

Later, as he was cleaning up the broken mirrors and bottles, Cooley may have thought to himself that getting a manager fired was a piece of cake. It's easier to lead a rebellion than to face one.

Duff Cooley

Cooley, Duff

Phillies	G	AB	H	BA	RBI	R	2B	3B	HR	SA	SB
1896	64	287	88	.307	22	63	6	4	2	.376	18
1897	133	566	186	.329	40	124	14	13	4	.420	31
1898	149	629	196	.312	55	123	24	12	4	.407	17
1899	94	406	112	.276	31	75	15	8	1	.360	15
Career	1,316	5,364	1,576	.294	557	847	180	102	26	.380	224

Corridon, Frank

Phillies: 1904–05; 1907–09
Pitcher
Nickname: Fiddler
Birthplace: Newport, Rhode Island
B: November 25, 1880
D: February 21, 1941
Batted right, threw right
Ht. 6–0; **Wt.** 170

A righthander who depended almost solely on breaking pitches, Frank won all but a dozen of his 72 lifetime major league wins with the Phillies after coming over from the Cubs halfway through his rookie season in 1904.

Perhaps Fiddler's most memorable pitching performance was opening day of the 1907 season at the Polo Grounds in New York. It had snowed the previous day, and the Giants' owner had ordered the field cleared in time for the game. Unfortunately, most of the snow was plowed in foul territory, with a little of it nudged against the outfield fences.

Corridon, who would have his best season with 18 victories that year, worked masterfully. After eight innings the Giants had only one single and the Phillies had a 3–0 lead. And the ballpark had no security. The new mayor of New York, William Gaynor, had instituted a policy whereby no city police would be dispatched to "ball parks or other private places of amusement." And Giant owner John T. Brush foolishly hadn't filled the void with private police.

Philadelphia may be remembered as the town where a stadium filled with football fans threw snowballs at Santa Claus, but New York had the snowball idea first. The bored fans, with no one to restrain them, began wandering on the field in great numbers. They also began to throw snowballs at the players, themselves, and the umpires. When one snowball whistled dangerously close to ump Bill Klem's ear, he immediately forfeited the game to the Phillies, 9–0.

Fiddler won 14 games the following season, then slipped to 11 in 1909 when his arm came up sore. After one losing year in St. Louis, he retired after the 1910 season.

Corridon, Frank

Phillies	W	L	Pct	ERA	G	CG	IP	H	BB	SO	ShO
1904	6	5	.545	2.20	12	11	94	88	28	11	1
1905	10	13	.435	3.48	35	18	212	203	57	79	1
1907	18	14	.563	2.46	37	23	274	228	89	131	3
1908	14	10	.583	2.51	27	18	208	178	48	50	2
1909	11	7	.611	2.11	27	11	171	147	61	69	3
Career	72	69	.511	2.80	180	99	1,216	1,100	375	458	10

Frank Corridon

Wes Covington lasted 11 years in the major leagues because of a bat that made a lot of noise and in spite of a mouth that did likewise.

John Wesley specialized in long home runs and long interviews that tended to get people around him a bit testy. In fact, his productive career with the Phillies, which lasted more than four seasons, was brought to a certain conclusion on the final weekend of the 1965 season. The Phillies and Mets were rained out of a game at Shea Stadium, but nobody put the tarpaulin over Covington's mouth.

"This club should have won the pennant the last couple years," Covington said. "We had the horses. I've been on a pennant winner. I would never say it unless I had been in a position to see what it takes to win a pennant.

"The club we had a year ago, one guy would break his back for the other one. Why over one year did the club become a club of guys just thinking about themselves? Why? There's a reason for this, a big reason.

"We lost 23 in a row (in 1961) and we had better spirit than we have now. What happened in the last year? If you were manager and if you had managed a club the year before with the spirit we had and something happened, would you as manager take charge then or would you turn your back? There's a good reason, a very good reason, a damn good reason why this club is in the second division."

Was Covington saying that manager Gene Mauch had lost control of the team?

"You can fill in the answer," Covington said. Three months later, the Phillies supplied their own answer. They shipped Wes to the Cubs for Doug Clemens.

From 1961 to 1965, Covington directed verbal blasts when he wasn't directing blasts from his bat over the right field wall of Connie Mack Stadium. He batted .303 in 1961 after making Philadelphia his fourth major league stop of the season, then duplicated that average in 1963 when he also smashed 17 home runs and knocked in 64 runs in just 353 at-bats. And, in his final season with the team, he had 15 homers despite only 235 at-bats.

With Wes it is best to concentrate on what he could do with a bat in his hands. A glove was an entirely different matter. Suffice it to say that Covington was born about 15 years too soon. He would have been a great designated hitter. That he stole seven bases in 1,075 major league games is all you need to know about his speed. But through his years with the Phillies, which paralleled parts of the careers of Dick Allen and John Callison, Covington was never cheated when it came to getting in his rips, either in the batter's box or in the locker room.

Covington, Wes

Phillies: 1961–65
Outfielder
Birthplace: Laurinburg, North Carolina
B: March 27, 1932
Bats left, throws right
Ht. 6–1; **Wt.** 205

Wes Covington

Covington, Wes

Phillies	G	AB	H	BA	RBI	R	2B	3B	HR	SA	SB
1961	57	165	50	.303	26	23	9	0	7	.485	0
1962	116	304	86	.283	44	36	12	1	9	.418	0
1963	119	353	107	.303	64	46	24	1	17	.521	1
1964	129	339	95	.280	58	37	18	0	13	.448	0
1965	101	235	58	.247	45	27	10	1	15	.489	0
Career	1,075	2,978	832	.279	499	355	128	17	131	.466	7

Cravath, Gavvy

Phillies: 1912–20
Outfielder
Nickname: Cactus
Birthplace: Escondido, California
B: March 23, 1881
D: May 23, 1963
Batted right, threw right
Ht. 5–10½; **Wt.** 186

Gavvy Cravath

Gavvy Cravath, the regular right fielder on the Phillies' 1915 championship team and later manager of the club for two seasons, was baseball's all-time slugger until 1921 when a fellow named Babe Ruth passed him on the all-time career home run list.

The Babe was able to take advantage of the lively ball during his career. Gavvy was not. Ruth passed Cravath in June 1921 when he hit his 120th home run on his way to 714.

It would not be totally inaccurate to describe Cravath as the Babe Ruth of his time, however. He led the National League in homers six times in a seven-season stretch beginning with the 1913 season. In 1915 he had his best power year with 24 homers during a sensational campaign in which he also led the National League in runs scored (89), RBI (115), base on balls (86), and slugging percentage (.510). That year, he also drove in eight runs in one game in a 14–6 rout of the Cincinnati Reds. He also topped the league in RBI in 1913 with a career-best 128 and had an even 100 in 1914.

Obviously, the Phillies, and no one else, knew what the team was getting when the club brought him up from Minneapolis for the 1912 season. Gavvy had kicked around the high minors for nearly a decade and had done nothing to distinguish himself while playing for three different American League teams in 1908 and 1909.

At the age of 31, Cravath was counted upon merely as a spare outfielder. But when the Phillies traded Silent John Titus to Boston, Gavvy took over the right field spot and held it much longer than anyone had a right to anticipate. And he began to flex his muscles right from the start. Although he had hit just two homers in 332 American League at-bats, he quickly began popping the ball into the left field stands with great (for that era) regularity. He smacked 11 homers in 1912, then followed with 19 the following year, his best overall (.341, league-leading figures in hits with 179 and slugging percentage with .568).

Cravath disappointed in the 1915 World Series with just a double and triple in 16 plate appearances, but maintained his popularity among the fans thereafter and was named field manager of the team during the 1919 season. By that time, the talent that had carried the Phillies to their first flag four years previously was either retired or elsewhere in the league, having been dealt by William F. Baker for large sums of money that kept the franchise barely solvent. Cravath took over for former A's pitcher star Jack Coombs with the team mired in last place with an 18–44 record. Under his direction, the Phils improved their record, but not their position. When the Phillies finished eighth and last once again in 1920, Cravath was dismissed.

He went to Salt Lake City to manage the Pacific Coast League team the following season. That team had been depleted by the PCL gambling scandal the previous year, so Gavvy was merely going from one hopeless situation to another. He resigned after one season, citing "turmoil and abuse." The following year he served as a scout for the Minneapolis team in the American Association, then was rumored returning to the Phillies in 1923 as assistant manager and pinch-hitter. In fact, Gavvy was all for it and so was manager Art Fletcher. But Minneapolis was not and refused to release Cravath from his contract.

In 1926, Cravath was elected a justice of the peace in Long Beach, California. He remained a jurist in California for the rest of his life.

Cravath, Gavvy

Phillies	G	AB	H	BA	RBI	R	2B	3B	HR	SA	SB
1912	130	436	124	.284	70	63	30	9	11	.470	15
1913	147	525	179	.341	128	78	34	14	19	.568	10
1914	149	499	149	.299	100	76	27	8	19	.499	14
1915	150	522	149	.285	115	89	31	7	24	.510	11
1916	137	448	127	.283	70	70	21	8	11	.440	9
1917	140	503	141	.280	83	70	29	16	12	.473	6
1918	121	426	99	.232	54	43	27	5	8	.376	7
1919	83	214	73	.341	45	34	18	5	12	.640	8
1920	46	45	13	.289	11	2	5	0	1	.467	0
Career	1,219	3,950	1,134	.287	719	575	232	83	119	.478	89

Even if he hadn't done another thing during his major league career, Lave Cross had one special distinction. He played for all four Philadelphia major league baseball teams.

During a career that spanned 21 years in the majors, Cross put in six seasons as a regular with the Phillies. Before that, he played for Philadelphia's teams in the American Association (1899, 1891) and the Players' League (1890), and toward the end of his career he worked for the Athletics of the American League (1901–05).

Lave, whose real name was Lafayette Napolean Cross, came to the Phillies after the American Association disbanded. Originally a catcher when he broke in with Louisville in 1887, Cross was a jack-of-all-trades. In his first two seasons with the Phillies, he not only caught, but played third, second, short, first, and the outfield. In 1892 he played in all but 14 games, although never at any position as a regular.

Cross took over the third base duties in 1894, and had his best season in the majors. He hit .386, which was only the fourth highest average on the team. That year, the entire Phillies' starting lineup hit above .300, but the team finished fourth, despite a league-leading .349 team average.

He retained his regular berth in 1895, but his average dropped 115 points to .271. After that, Lave went back to his role as a utility man.

Cross left Philadelphia after the 1897 season. He spent the next few years playing for St. Louis twice, Cleveland, and Brooklyn. He was the manager at Cleveland for part of the 1899 season.

When the American League began in 1901, Cross joined the Athletics. He was the Athletics' regular third baseman for five seasons, once hitting .342 and once .328. Lave played the final two years of his career with Washington, retiring in 1907.

Cross had two brothers, Amos and Frank, who played briefly in the majors. He was not related to Monte Cross, who followed him to the Phillies and then played with him on the Athletics.

Cross, Lave

Phillies: 1892–97
Third baseman
Birthplace: Milwaukee, Wisconsin
B: May 11, 1867
D: September 4, 1927
Batted right, threw right
Ht. 5–9½; **Wt.** 155

Lave Cross

Cross, Lave

Phillies	G	AB	H	BA	RBI	R	2B	3B	HR	SA	SB
1892	140	541	149	.275	69	84	15	10	4	.362	18
1893	96	415	124	.299	78	81	17	6	4	.398	18
1894	119	529	204	.386	125	123	34	9	7	.524	21
1895	125	535	145	.271	101	95	26	9	2	.364	21
1896	106	406	104	.256	73	63	23	5	1	.345	8
1897	88	344	89	.259	51	37	17	5	3	.363	10
Career	2,274	9,068	2,644	.292	1,345	1,332	411	135	47	.382	301

Culp, Ray

Phillies: 1963–66
Pitcher
Birthplace: Elgin, Texas
B: August 6, 1941
Bats right, throws right
Ht. 6–0; **Wt.** 200

In his first three minor league seasons, Ray Culp looked like the latest in a long line of Bob Carpenter's bonus busts. Carpenter had seen Robin Roberts develop into a Hall of Famer during the early days of his Phillies' ownership and had spent much of the rest of his active moments looking for another Roberts.

He sought Robins, he found robberies. And Culp looked like another one—$100,000 worth of potential telling Carpenter to put his hands in the air and fork over the loot.

Not that Culp's credentials as an amateur were poor. Far from it. The year before he signed his bonus contract, Ray ran off the following numbers in one stretch during the 1958 American Legion playoffs in Austin, Texas: 37 innings pitched, four hits, nine walks, 83 strikeouts. And no runs allowed. No wonder Carpenter envisioned another Roberts in the six-footer with a fastball that crackled on its way to the plate.

In his first three minor league seasons, though, he was a victim of sore arms (he had never thrown a curve ball until he turned pro), wildness, and just plain ineffectiveness. His record was 14–27, and it was difficult to differentiate between his earned run average and the Dow Jones Industrials.

In 1962, though, it all began to fall in place for Culp. He won 13 games at Williamsport (Class A), then jumped to the Phillies the following season and was named the National League Rookie Pitcher of the Year. He won 14 games, had a splendid 2.97 ERA, threw five shutouts, led the league in walks (102), struck out 176, and had an outstanding hits-to-innings-pitched ratio (148 in 203). That marked the start of a four-year roller-coaster career with the Phillies.

Culp started out nicely enough in the infamous 1964 season. In late June, he missed a no-hitter against the Cubs by one pitch, which Len Gabrielson hit for a single. But he never pitched during the 10-game losing streak in September, and manager Gene Mauch explained to anyone who'd listen: "He doesn't want the ball."

Culp defended himself on the first weekend of the season after the Phillies had blown a 6½-game lead with 12 to play.

"It wasn't that I didn't want to pitch," he said. "I don't know where anybody got that idea. I couldn't pitch. I had a sore arm. I still have it."

Culp said the arm had gone sore in a late August game against the Mets. He finished the year at 8–7, and his ERA ballooned to 4.13.

The following spring, Mauch was philosophical. "We just have to convince him that 1963 was no accident," Mauch said. And did. Culp finished with a 14–10 record and 11 complete games.

But 1966 was another downer—one complete game in a dozen starts and a 5.03 ERA despite a 7–4 record. In the off-season, Culp was traded to the Cubs for Dick Ellsworth. He lasted one so-so year in Chicago, then was dealt to the Red Sox, for whom he won 71 games in six seasons before retiring.

At least he left the game knowing that, unlike so many other young pitchers, he had returned dividends on Bob Carpenter's investment.

Ray Culp

Culp, Ray

Phillies	W	L	Pct	ERA	G	CG	IP	H	BB	SO	ShO
1963	14	11	.560	2.97	34	10	203	148	102	176	5
1964	8	7	.533	4.13	30	3	135	139	56	96	1
1965	14	10	.583	3.22	33	11	204	188	78	134	2
1966	7	4	.636	5.03	34	1	111	106	53	100	0
Career	122	101	.547	3.58	322	80	1,897	1,677	752	1,411	22

Dalrymple, Clay

Phillies: 1960–68
Catcher
Birthplace: Chico, California
B: December 3, 1936
Bats left, throws right
Ht. 6–0; **Wt.** 190

The image most people retain of Clay Dalrymple is probably negative: Connie Mack Stadium, Sandy Koufax pitching for the Dodgers, bottom of the third, the Phillies' batters are Dalrymple, Wine, and the pitcher. Time to go get a hot dog and beer. No way I'll miss anything this inning.

It's a shame because it's only a partial picture. Clay might have hit his share of two-hoppers to the second baseman, but he also threw a lot of line drives to second to thwart would-be base stealers. And, believe it or not, he wasn't always an automatic out.

In 1962, when the Phillies were turning the ashes of the previous year's 23-game losing streak into something positive, Dalrymple was one of the offensive leaders. He batted .276 with 11 home runs and 54 RBI. He also walked 70 times in 123 games. Unfortunately, they were all to be high-water figures for the prematurely bald former college heavyweight boxing champion from Chico State in California.

Dalrymple, hits or no hits, was a bargain when the Phillies drafted him from Sacramento in the Pacific Coast League for $25,000 after the 1959 season. Clay came to spring training and developed a sore arm. He fretted that Eddie Sawyer would ship him back to Sacramento, but it never happened, and he batted a healthy .272 in 82 games.

By 1961, he was Mauch's number-one catcher. For seven straight years he caught at least 101 games for Mauch. But in the seventh, his batting average dipped all the way to .172, and it improved to only .207 in 1968, his last with the Phillies. And when Mauch was dismissed that mid-season, it was only a matter of time before Dalrymple would also be gone.

He was traded after the season to the Orioles for Ron Stone and played three seasons as a deep reserve in Baltimore, playing a total of just 73 games. But in 1969, Clay had the last laugh on everybody in Philadelphia. He made it to the World Series with the Orioles and was called on to pinch-hit twice. He delivered two singles to make him a 1.000 career World Series hitter. No one has ever hit better.

Dalrymple, Clay

Phillies	G	AB	H	BA	RBI	R	2B	3B	HR	SA	SB
1960	82	158	43	.272	21	11	6	2	4	.411	0
1961	129	378	83	.220	42	23	11	1	5	.294	0
1962	123	370	102	.276	54	40	13	3	11	.416	1
1963	142	452	114	.252	40	40	15	3	10	.365	0
1964	127	382	91	.238	46	36	16	3	6	.343	0
1965	103	301	64	.213	23	14	5	5	4	.302	0
1966	114	331	81	.245	39	39	13	3	4	.338	0
1967	101	268	46	.172	21	12	7	1	3	.239	1
1968	85	241	50	.207	26	19	9	1	3	.290	1
Career	1,079	3,042	710	.233	327	243	98	23	55	.335	3

Clay Dalrymple

Davis, Curt

Phillies: 1934–36
Pitcher
Nickname: Coonskin
Birthplace: Greenfield, Missouri
B: September 7, 1903
D: October 13, 1965
Batted right, threw right
Ht. 6–2; **Wt.** 185

Curt Davis

There were several distinctive features of Curt Davis' 13-year major league career, one of which was that he was an outstanding pitcher for the Phillies during a brief stop at Baker Bowl.

In a little more than two seasons, the lanky sidearmer had a better than .500 record for the Phils, despite two seventh-place finishes.

Davis was also one of the better hitting pitchers in the National League. And he had the unusual distinction of being part of trades that involved Chuck Klein on one occasion, Dizzy Dean on another, and Joe Medwick on a third. How many players have been swapped around in that kind of company?

After he was discovered pitching for $15 a game in Oregon lumber camps, Curt toiled six years in the minors as the property of the San Francisco Seals. He spent five seasons with the Seals of the Pacific Coast League, winning 42 games his last two years there.

Eventually, Davis was bought by the Phillies for $7,500. As a 31-year-old rookie in 1934, he posted a 19–17 record, not only ranking as the ace of the Phils' staff, but leading the National League in games (51) and placing third in ERA (2.95). That was the lowest earned run average for a regular Phillies pitcher since 1920.

That year he also set a National League fielding record by participating in 12 double plays.

Davis, who had an outstanding pickoff move, was a favorite of Phillies manager Jimmie Wilson. "When you start talking about Davis," Wilson once said, "you aren't talking about a plain ace. You are talking about the ace of spades in a pinochle game when spades are trump."

In 1935, Davis was again the Phils' top hurler with a 16–14 record. He had a 2–4 log the next year when the club sent him and outfielder Ethan Allen to the Chicago Cubs for Klein and pitcher Fabian Kowalik. That summer, Davis made the All-Star team.

Curt worked through 1937 with the Bruins, then was bartered along with two other players and $150,000 to the St. Louis Cardinals for Dean.

In 1939, Davis had a 22–16 record for the Cards. He also hit .381, which was the second highest average for a pitcher in National League history. The numbers also made him one of only 14 hurlers in modern National League annals who have won 20 or more games and hit over .300 in the same season.

Davis and Medwick were traded to the Brooklyn Dodgers in 1940 for six players and cash. Curt was 13–7 for the pennant-winning Dodgers in 1941. He worked in Brooklyn until 1946 when he retired at the age of 43.

Davis, Curt

Phillies	W	L	Pct	ERA	G	CG	IP	H	BB	SO	ShO
1934	19	17	.528	2.95	51	18	274⅓	283	60	99	3
1935	16	14	.533	3.66	44	19	231	264	47	74	3
1936	2	4	.333	4.65	10	3	60	71	19	18	0
Career	158	131	.547	3.42	429	141	2,325	2,459	479	684	24

Davis, Spud

Phillies: 1928–33; 1938–39
Catcher
Birthplace: Birmingham, Alabama
B: December 20, 1904
D: August 14, 1984
Batted right, threw right
Ht. 6–1; **Wt.** 197

Spud Davis made his mark on Phillies baseball, and it wasn't just because he often gobbled meals of potatoes three times a day, which he said improved his hitting. Spud, so named by his boyhood chums for obvious reason, had the highest career batting average of all Phillies catchers.

During two terms and more than seven years in Philadelphia, Davis collected a .321 batting mark. That not only tops all Phils backstops, but is the sixth highest average on the club's all-time list.

Davis, whose lifetime average during a 16-year major league career was .308—one of the leading career marks for catchers in major league history—was also an outstanding receiver. He was an expert at handling young pitchers. His errors were infrequent, and his fielding average always ranked among the best among National League catchers.

In 1931, Spud set a Phillies record for catchers with a fielding average of .994. He made only three errors. He also led the league in assists with the resounding total of 78.

Having broken into organized ball in 1926, Davis had the distinction of being traded twice for catcher Jimmie Wilson. After he was drafted out of the minors by the St. Louis Cardinals, Spud and outfielder Homer Peel were sent to the Phillies for Wilson early in the 1928 season.

Five years later, the Phillies swapped Davis and infielder Eddie Delker back to the Cards for Wilson.

In between trades, Spud had some banner years for the Phillies. After hitting .342 on the legendary 1929 club that led the league with a .304 team batting average, he became the Phils' regular catcher in 1930.

Davis hit well over .300 the next four years, the high point of which was his .349 mark in 1933 when he finished second to teammate Chuck Klein in the race for the National League batting title. It was the third highest batting average ever for a lefthanded-hitting catcher.

After his trade back to St. Louis, Spud had .300, .317, and .273 seasons. In 1936 he was sold to the Cincinnati Reds. He stayed there until midway through the 1938 season when the Phillies got him back along with pitcher Al Hollinsworth and $55,000 in exchange for pitcher Bucky Walters.

In 1938, Davis turned the rare trick of registering an unassisted double play. Only 31 catchers in big league history have accomplished that feat.

The Phillies sold Davis to the Pittsburgh Pirates for $15,000 after the 1939 season. Spud was a reserve catcher for the Pirates in 1940 and 1941, was released, then was restored to the active list and played in 1944 and 1945. In 1946 he became a full-time coach with the Bucs and was interim manager for three games.

Davis, who played seven games in the infield when he was with St. Louis, appeared in 1,291 games as a catcher. At present, he ranks 33d in the major leagues in number of games played by a backstop.

Spud Davis

Davis, Spud (Virgil)

Phillies	G	AB	H	BA	RBI	R	2B	3B	HR	SA	SB
1928	67	163	46	.282	18	16	2	0	3	.349	0
1929	98	263	90	.342	48	31	18	0	7	.490	1
1930	106	329	103	.313	65	41	16	1	14	.495	1
1931	120	393	128	.326	51	30	32	1	4	.443	0
1932	125	402	135	.336	70	44	23	5	14	.522	1
1933	141	495	173	.349	65	51	28	3	9	.473	2
1938	70	215	53	.247	23	11	7	0	2	.307	1
1939	87	202	62	.307	23	10	8	1	0	.356	0
Career	1,458	4,255	1,312	.308	647	388	244	22	77	.430	6

It is testimony to his brilliance as a hitter that after more than nine decades, Ed Delahanty's name still stands in not only the Phillies' but also the National League's record books.

Quite simply, Delahanty was the most successful hitter of his era, and one of the finest batters ever to play the game of baseball. A strong but relatively slender man, Ed played 13 of his 16 seasons in Philadelphia. During those years, he achieved heights that have never again been approached.

His lifetime average supports the contention that Delahanty had few peers as a hitter. His .346 career mark is the fourth highest average in major league history. Only Rogers Hornsby had a higher average among righthanded hitters.

Had his life not ended suddenly and tragically less than one year after he

Delahanty, Ed

Phillies: 1888–89; 1891–1901
Outfielder, second baseman, first baseman
Nickname: Big Ed
Birthplace: Cleveland, Ohio
B: October 30, 1867
D: July 2, 1903
Batted right, threw right
Ht. 6–1; **Wt.** 170

had won a batting championship, Delahanty might have achieved even greater heights and presumably greater fame.

As it was, Big Ed's name is indelibly etched among the legends of the game. His election to the Hall of Fame occurred in 1945.

During his career, Delahanty hit above .300 for 12 straight years. Three times, he exceeded .400. He won two batting championships, one with the Phillies and one with Washington.

At one time or another, Delahanty led the National League in virtually every hitting category. Four times he was the leader in slugging average and doubles, three times he led in RBI, twice he led in total bases, and once he was first in triples, stolen bases, and home runs.

Delahanty is the Phillies' all-time leader in doubles and triples and ranks second in total bases, RBI, extra-base hits, and runs. His .348 batting average as a Phillies player ranks second to teammate Billy Hamilton, who with Ed and Sam Thompson gave the club an all–Hall of Fame outfield and probably the greatest assemblage of outfielders baseball has ever seen on one team.

Big Ed's greatest game as a hitter occurred in Chicago on July 13, 1896, when he became the second major league player (Boston's Bobby Lowe was the first) to hit four home runs in one game. He did it against the Chicago White Stockings in a game the Phillies lost, 9–8. Delahanty also had a single and six runs batted in. He is one of five National League players in history to have hit four home runs in a nine-inning game.

When Delahanty came to bat for the fifth time in the ninth inning, Chicago fans were rooting loudly for him to hit his fourth homer. He didn't disappoint them, sending the ball out of the park in left-center. The feat was so impressive that even Chicago pitcher Adonis Terry shook hands with Ed as he crossed home plate and complimented him on his achievement. After the game, the 1,100 fans who were in attendance followed Ed to the players' departing carriages.

The home run splurge helped Delahanty set a National League record that he still shares with Red Schoendienst of the St. Louis Cardinals (1948) and Joe Adcock of the Milwaukee Braves (1954). It is a record for most extra-base hits in two consecutive games. Ed's two doubles and one triple in the game after his four homers gave him a total of seven long hits in two games. Delahanty is also tied with seven others for the most consecutive hits during a season (10). He performed that feat in 1897 while collecting nine hits in a doubleheader.

In 1894, Delahanty, who once hit a ball so savagely that it broke a third baseman's ankle, went six-for-six in one game. Eleven times during his career, he laced five or more hits in one game. And in 1897 he slugged eight hits in a doubleheader.

Delahanty might have been one of the best bargains the Phillies ever got. They bought him from a minor league team in Wheeling, West Virginia, in the Tri-State League in 1888 for $1,900, a paltry sum by today's standards but a fair piece of change in the 1800s.

Ed was the oldest of five brothers, all of whom played in the big leagues. None was even close to Ed in ability, although the next-to-youngest brother, Jim, had a respectable 13-year career in the majors, playing with eight different teams.

When Ed reported to the Phillies, it was at a time when they desperately needed hitters. Manager Harry Wright had heard of Delahanty's prowess as a hitter in the minor leagues. "You better get him quick," he told club president Al Reach.

Ed reported to the Phillies in mid-season in 1888, and to the surprise of club officials, he wasn't as big a man as they had expected. He was brawny, with powerful arms and shoulders and a bull neck, but he weighed only 170 pounds.

Delahanty was said to have a two-sided personality. On the one hand, he was a fun-loving, beer-drinking, likeable guy who cared little for training and discipline. On the other, he was a moody, sometimes surly, fellow. He preferred the night life and hung out with other sports personalities of the era as well as an assortment of prostitutes in a bar at 12th and Market Streets.

After arriving in Philadelphia in 1888, Delahanty was installed at second

Ed Delahanty

base. It wasn't his regular position, but the Phillies needed him there to take the place of Charlie Ferguson who had died that spring.

Delahanty struggled in his early years with the Phillies. Although he was hitting .408 at Wheeling when the Phils bought him, his first year was especially difficult. Ed hit only .228. What's more, he had only one home run. He wasn't much better as a fielder, making 44 errors.

He did, however, steal 38 bases, which prompted this statement from manager Wright: "I thought I would get more hitting out of the big fellow. He meets the ball well, but he can't keep it away from the fielders. But he really can run. Some day, he may be a champion base-runner."

Delahanty was an outstanding base-runner throughout his career. In 16 years, he averaged nearly 30 stolen bases a season, getting as many as 58 in 1898 and leading the league in thefts in 1892.

In his second year with the Phillies, Delahanty's hitting improved, but a series of injuries limited his playing time. His average jumped to .293, although the power he would later display as a hitter was nonexistent. He hit zero home runs.

Delahanty still did not have a regular position, either. The Phillies used him at second base again, and also in the outfield and even at shortstop.

The following year, they didn't use him at all. That was 1890, the year of the Players' League raids. Delahanty signed initially with the Cleveland team in the new league. But when the Phillies offered him more money to remain with them, Ed took their contract.

There were jumpers and double-jumpers among the players. Delahanty became known as a triple-jumper when he signed a contract for the second time to play in his native Cleveland. "The scalawag," ranted Phils official John Rogers. "I thought he was a man of honor."

Evidently, cash was more important to Delahanty than honor, and he played the year in Cleveland, still not hitting .300 (he hit .298) and still not having a regular position.

When the Players' League folded at the end of the 1890 season, Delahanty and the ailing Jim Fogarty were the only two players taken back by the Phillies. Big Ed was just too good to let slip away, no matter what concessions in principle had to be made.

Upon his return, the Phillies decided to put him in left field, teaming him with Hamilton and Thompson. It turned out to be the greatest outfield in baseball history, although the Phillies continued to use Ed at first base on occasion, and once in a while at all of the other infield positions, too.

In 1891, the year of his return, Delahanty hit a meek .243. It was, however, the last poor season of his career.

The next year, Delahanty began the climb that would lead to his becoming one of the premier hitters in baseball history. He hit .306 that year, and he led the National League in games, at-bats, hits, doubles, triples, stolen bases, and slugging average.

The young slugger was even better the following year. His average soared to .368, he led the league in RBI with 146—to go along with 145 runs scored—and for the first time he established himself as a home run hitter by topping the circuit with 19. The only player who hit more home runs than that up to that point was teammate Sam Thompson, who had clubbed 20 four-baggers in 1889.

Delahanty was even better in 1894 when he crashed the .400 mark for the first time. As high as his average was, though, it was only the fourth best in the league (Hugh Duffy of Boston won the batting crown with a .438), and only the third best on the Phillies, ranking behind fellow outfielders Tuck Turner and Sam Thompson. Surprisingly, Ed failed to lead the league in a single category, and his home run total dipped to four.

Over the next four years, Delahanty continued to pummel opposing pitchers. He batted .404, .397, and .377 before slipping to .334. As soon as his average tumbled, though, Ed bounced back the following season with what was probably the most spectacular year of his career.

He hit .410 to capture his first batting championship. In addition, he was first in hits (238), doubles (55), RBI (137), slugging percentage (.582), and total bases (338). During the season, Delahanty hit safely in 31 straight games, which ranks as the second longest hitting streak in Phillies history.

Delahanty plunged to a mere .323 in 1900. By this time, his outfield sidekicks, Hamilton and Thompson, were gone, and he had a new future Hall of Famer as a running mate, second baseman Nap Lajoie.

In 1901 the newly formed American League was making raids on National League teams. In Philadelphia, a bitter war was brewing between the Phillies and the upstart Athletics under a lanky ex-catcher named Connie Mack.

The National League had passed a rule in 1893 that limited players' salaries to a maximum of $2,400. In defiance of that rule, Delahanty and Lajoie in 1900 had made a secret agreement not to sign unless they could receive more than that amount.

Eventually, Ed signed for $3,000. Nap, told he was getting the same as Delahanty, inked his contract for $2,600. When he found out otherwise, Lajoie was furious. He demanded the extra $400, but the Phillies' Rogers refused to budge.

Having thus been shafted, it was easy for Lajoie to sign the following year with Mack for $4,000. Connie offered the same salary to Delahanty, but the amount was matched by Rogers.

But Ed was to stay with the Phillies for only one more season. After hitting .354 in 1901, the Phils' great slugger jumped to the American League after all, signing with Washington. Immediately, Delahanty set about tearing apart the American League. In his first season in Washington he led the American League in batting with a .376 average, beating his old buddy Lajoie by 10 points. Ed also paced the new circuit in doubles and slugging average.

In 1903 he was off to a good start, hitting .333 by the end of June. But he was drinking heavily at this point, some said to drown the memories of a bad year he was having at the race track.

Early in July, while the team was in Detroit, Delahanty was suspended for his drinking by Washington manager Tom Loftus. Shortly afterward, Ed set out on a train, either to return to his Washington home or, as some theorists

Delahanty, Ed

Phillies	G	AB	H	BA	RBI	R	2B	3B	HR	SA	SB
1888	74	290	66	.228	31	40	12	2	1	.293	38
1889	56	246	72	.293	27	37	13	3	0	.370	19
1891	128	543	132	.243	86	92	19	9	5	.333	25
1892	123	477	146	.306	91	79	30	21	6	.495	29
1893	132	595	219	.368	146	145	35	18	19	.583	37
1894	114	489	199	.407	131	147	39	18	4	.584	21
1895	116	480	194	.404	106	149	49	10	11	.616	46
1896	123	499	198	.397	126	131	44	17	13	.631	37
1897	129	530	200	.377	96	109	40	15	5	.538	26
1898	144	548	183	.334	92	115	36	9	4	.454	58
1899	146	581	238	.410	137	135	55	9	9	.582	30
1900	131	539	174	.323	109	82	32	10	2	.430	16
1901	139	542	192	.354	108	106	39	16	8	.530	29
Career	1,835	7,505	2,597	.346	1,464	1,599	522	185	101	.505	455

conclude, to accept John McGraw's offer to join the New York Giants. He was drunk when he boarded, and got drunker as the train raced eastward. Along the way, he got into a fight and in general caused such a ruckus that, as the train was about to cross the International Bridge at Fort Erie, Ontario, the conductor stopped the train and booted Delahanty off.

Enraged, Delahanty ran up the tracks after the disappearing train, brushing aside a flagman who tried to stop him. He stumbled onto the bridge, but in the darkness, according to one account, failed to see that the span had opened for a passing boat. Ed plunged into the Niagara River and was carried over Niagara Falls.

A week later, his mangled body was found, having apparently been hit by a tourist boat at some point after the fall. His 18-year-old brother, Frank, was summoned to identify the body and Ed's luggage, which had been found along the tracks. Some $200 in cash and $1,500 in diamonds that he had with him were missing.

There was some speculation that Delahanty had met with foul play, and not fallen off the bridge on his own, after all. Whether he jumped, fell, or was pushed off of the bridge was never clearly established. The cause of his death remains a mystery to this day.

The Phillies' timing in many trades has been horrendous, but Al Demaree proved to be an exception to the rule. The man they called Steamer spent eight years in the majors, only two of them with the Phillies, but those two seasons at Baker Bowl were easily the most productive of his career.

In the first season, he helped the Phils win their first pennant. In the second, he put together a string of statistics that he would never approach again.

The Phillies obtained Demaree along with Milt Stock, who became their regular third baseman, and catcher Jack Adams from John McGraw's Giants after the 1914 season for Hans Lobert, who cracked a knee in a pre-season game and was never again the player he had been with the Phillies. On that basis alone, Demaree-for-Lobert would have been a good deal from the Philadelphia perspective.

Steamer Al won 14 games, beating the Giants six times, in the Phillies' championship season, but manager Pat Moran chose not to use him in the World Series against the Red Sox. That might have been a big mistake, as Demaree proved the following season.

In 1916, Grover Cleveland Alexander, Eppa Rixey, and Demaree made up a great three-man pitching rotation, winning 74 games among them. If Moran had been able to find any kind of consistent fourth starter, the Phillies probably would have made up the three games that separated them from the pennant-winning Dodgers.

Demaree finished at 19–14, completed 25 of 35 starts, and had an earned run average of 2.62. He struck out 130 in 285 innings. On September 20 he pitched and won both games of a doubleheader, beating the Pittsburgh Pirates, 7–0 and 13–2. But before the next season began, he was crated off to the Cubs.

Again the Phillies' timing was excellent. He lasted just half a year in Chicago and never again won more than nine games in a season. After he left the game, he stayed involved in sports but as a cartoonist rather than an active participant.

Demaree, Al

Phillies: 1915–16
Pitcher
Nickname: Steamer
Birthplace: Quincy, Illinois
B: September 8, 1886
D: April 30, 1962
Batted left, threw right
Ht. 6–0; **Wt.** 170

Al Demaree

Demaree, Al

Phillies	W	L	Pct	ERA	G	CG	IP	H	BB	SO	ShO
1915	14	11	.560	3.04	32	13	210	201	58	69	3
1916	19	14	.576	2.62	39	25	285	252	48	130	3
Career	81	72	.529	2.77	232	84	1,424	1,350	337	514	16

Demeter, Don

Phillies: 1961–63
Outfielder, third baseman, first baseman
Birthplace: Oklahoma City, Oklahoma
B: June 24, 1935
Bats right, throws right
Ht. 6–4; **Wt.** 190

Don Demeter

Don Demeter spent three of his 11 major league seasons with the Phillies. They were his best personally, and he directly and indirectly helped the Phillies go from an embarrassing 23-game losing streak in 1961 to a near pennant the year after he left them.

The lean Oklahoman came from the Los Angeles Dodgers on May 4, 1961, with third baseman Charlie Smith for pitcher Dick Farrell and infielder Joe Koppe.

In slightly less than three full years in Philadelphia, Demeter played all three outfield positions, first base, and third base. He hit .307 with 29 home runs and 107 RBI in 1962 when the team took a giant step toward respectability. And after he followed with a 22-homer, 83-RBI season in 1963, he was traded to the Detroit Tigers in the off-season for pitcher Jim Bunning and catcher Gus Triandos. Bunning won 19 games and Triandos provided several key hits in the Phillies' pennant chase in 1964. Meanwhile, Demeter played four more seasons and never came close to his 1962 numbers.

Demeter lived through the horrible 23-game losing streak in 1961. "We never thought that streak would end," he said years later. "It finally did in the second game of a doubleheader against the Braves in Milwaukee. We had a four-run lead in the ninth inning. I was playing first base and John Buzhardt was pitching. The first man up in the ninth for the Braves got a base hit. I walked over to the mound. John said to me, 'Are we going to lose it?' I said, 'Oh, no.'"

Demeter was right. His homer helped the Phillies achieve a 7–4 victory. It was the first homer of four in four games.

Later that season, he hit a homer off Sandy Koufax in a game in which he drove in seven runs against the Dodgers.

Gene Mauch convinced Demeter that he could play third base the next season, and Don responded with his best major league season. His 29 homers were the most ever hit by a Phillies third baseman in a season up to then.

When the Phillies made a trade with the Pirates for Don Hoak before the 1963 season, Demeter moved to first base and the outfield. Though his average slipped 49 points to .258, he still managed 22 homers and 83 RBI. He finished his Phillies career with 71 homers and 258 RBI in 1,447 at-bats.

Demeter, Don

Phillies	G	AB	H	BA	RBI	R	2B	3B	HR	SA	SB
1961	106	382	98	.257	68	54	18	4	20	.482	2
1962	153	550	169	.307	107	85	24	3	29	.520	2
1963	154	515	133	.258	83	63	20	2	22	.433	1
Career	1,109	3,443	912	.265	563	467	147	17	163	.459	22

Denny, John

Phillies: 1982–85
Pitcher
Birthplace: Prescott, Arizona
B: November 8, 1952
Bats right, throws right
Ht. 6–3; **Wt.** 185

John Denny came to the Phillies in September 1982 with a reputation for having much better control of his pitches than he did of his emotions. His constant battles with umpires were well documented when the Phillies acquired him from the Cleveland Indians for three minor leaguers.

It was assumed at the time that general manager Paul Owens had picked up the 29-year-old righthander in a desperate attempt to catch the St. Louis Cardinals down the stretch of the pennant race.

But Denny turned out to be a lot more than a gamble. In 1983, controlling both his pitches and his temper superbly, he became the first Phillie other than Steve Carlton to win the Cy Young Award.

The honor was richly deserved. Denny, who had never won more than 14 games in his previous seven full seasons in the majors, scored a league-leading 19 victories that season against six losses. His 2.37 earned run average was second in the league to Atlee Hammaker, and his .760 winning percentage also topped the league statistics. He walked just 53 batters in 243 innings.

The voting for the Cy Young Award was not close. Denny received 20 of 24 first-place votes and easily outdistanced Cincinnati's Mario Soto, 103 points to 61.

In the League Championship Series with the Dodgers, Denny lost Game Two. He allowed no earned runs in six innings but was beaten by three unearned tallies.

He won the only 1983 Phillies World Series victory when he defeated the Baltimore Orioles, 2–1, in the opener. He was the losing pitcher, 5–4, in Game Four.

In addition to the Cy Young Award, Denny also was named National League comeback player of the year by *The Sporting News* and was the righthanded pitcher on that publication's All-Star team.

An injury shelved him for two months in 1984 when he was 7–7 despite another fine ERA (2.45). Denny had an 11–14 record in 1985, then was traded in the off-season to the Cincinnati Reds for Gary Redus.

He played just one year with the Reds and was out of baseball at the age of 33.

Denny, John

Phillies	W	L	Pct	ERA	G	CG	IP	H	B	B SO	ShO
1982	0	2	.000	4.09	4	0	22	18	10	19	0
1983	19	6	.760	2.37	36	7	243	229	53	139	1
1984	7	7	.500	2.45	22	2	154	122	29	94	0
1985	11	14	.440	3.82	33	6	231	252	83	123	2
Career	123	108	.532	3.58	322	62	2,149	2,093	778	1,146	18

John Denny

National League batters used to look at Murry Dickson and shake their heads in amazement. How could such a slender guy, they wondered, pitch so much and still have his arm affixed to his shoulder?

Because he could throw six different pitches, Dickson was called the Thomas Edison of the mound. He epitomized the word *workhorse*. For nine straight years, he never hurled in less than 40 games, both starting and relieving, and for 10 years in a row he pitched in more than 200 innings.

Little Murry worked in all or parts of 18 big league seasons. He didn't retire until he was 43 years old. The fact of the matter was, Dickson simply loved to pitch. The curveball specialist was a tireless worker, and he would take to the mound without prodding.

His wins totaled in double figures 11 consecutive years. He was a 20-game winner once (in 1951 with the Pittsburgh Pirates) and a 20-game loser twice.

By the time Murry came to the Phillies in 1954, he had been in pro ball since 1937 and was starting to fade. The Phils landed Dickson from the Pirates for pitcher Andy Hansen, infielder Jack Lohrke, and $70,000.

In his first year with the Phillies, Dickson lost 20 games, thereby leading the league in losses for the third straight year (over that period, he was 14–21, 10–19, and 10–20). But he did have a 3.78 ERA. During the season, he lost 10 games in a row. The streak was finally snapped when Dickson, working with two days' rest, hurled a six-hit, 6–0 win over the Brooklyn Dodgers.

The following year, Dickson improved his slate to 12–11 with a 3.50 ERA. Not bad for a 39-year-old man.

After getting off to an 0–3 start in 1956, Dickson was traded along with pitcher Herm Wehmeier to the St. Louis Cardinals for pitchers Harvey Haddix, Stu Miller, and Ben Flowers.

The trade put Murry back where he had started. After two abbreviated stints with the Cardinals, he had stuck with the team in 1942. With the exception of two years in the military, Dickson toiled for the Redbirds until the end of 1948. In 1946 he led National League pitchers in won-lost percentage with a .714 on a 15–6 record.

Dickson, Murry

Phillies: 1954–56
Pitcher
Birthplace: Tracy, Missouri
B: August 21, 1916
D: September 21, 1989
Batted right, threw right
Ht. 5–10; **Wt.** 157

Murry Dickson

Murry worked five seasons for the Pirates. His days with the Phillies were followed by two years with the Cardinals and short stops with the Kansas City A's and New York Yankees.

Dickson, Murry

Phillies	W	L	Pct	ERA	G	CG	IP	H	BB	SO	ShO
1954	10	20	.333	3.78	40	12	226⅓	256	73	64	4
1955	12	11	.522	3.50	36	12	216	190	82	92	4
1956	0	3	.000	5.09	3	0	23	20	12	1	0
Career	172	181	.487	3.66	625	149	3,052⅓	3,024	1,058	1,281	27

Donahue, Frank

Phillies: 1898–1901
Pitcher
Nickname: Red
Birthplace: Waterbury, Connecticut
B: January 23, 1873
D: August 25, 1913
Batted right, threw right
Ht. and Wt. unknown

Frank Donahue

Red Donahue came to the Phillies with anything but star status, but by the time he left the team and jumped to the American League with six other teammates after the 1901 season, he had evolved into the ace of a very solid pitching staff.

A two-time 20-game winner during his four years with the Phillies, Donahue pitched the first Phillies no-hitter after the pitching mound was moved from 50 feet to 60 feet, 6 inches from the plate, beating the Boston Braves, 5–0, on July 8, 1898.

In 1897, while pitching for the St. Louis Nationals, Donahue compiled one of the shoddiest pitching lines imaginable. His record was 11 wins and a league-leading 33 losses. His earned run average was 6.13. At least he completed what he started, going the route 38 times in 42 starts. But maybe he shouldn't have, considering that in 348 innings he allowed a mind-boggling 484 hits.

So there was no parade up Broad Street when Donahue arrived. But in four years with the Phillies, he won 20 games twice and averaged more than 18 wins a season. And after 21–13 and a 2.61 ERA in 1901, he was very much in demand by the rival American League. The St. Louis Browns signed him as a charter member, and he won 22 games for them. In his next four seasons in the junior circuit, however, he failed to make the 20-win mark again. He had established his home in Philadelphia while with the Phillies and died in the city in 1913 at age 40.

Donahue, Frank

Phillies	W	L	Pct	ERA	G	CG	IP	H	BB	SO	ShO
1898	17	17	.500	3.55	35	33	284	327	80	57	1
1899	21	8	.724	3.39	35	27	279	292	63	51	4
1900	15	10	.615	3.60	32	21	240	299	50	41	2
1901	21	13	.618	2.61	35	34	304	307	60	89	1
Career	165	175	.485	4.85	368	313	2,975	3,384	690	788	25

Dooin, Red

Phillies: 1902–14
Catcher
Birthplace: Cincinnati, Ohio
B: June 12, 1879
D: May 14, 1952
Batted right, threw right
Ht. 5–9½; Wt. 165

Charlie Dooin was never a great hitter, but he lasted 13 years with the Phillies because his glove and legs made up for his bat.

A catcher with base-stealing speed is an uncommon commodity these days, but Dooin stole 20 bases in 1908. He was in double figures for seven straight years.

His lifetime average was just .240 and he topped .260 just once—that was in 1911 when he batted .328 in 74 games. He managed the team from 1910 to 1914 but was relieved of his managing duties and sold to Cincinnati in 1915, the year his successor, Pat Moran, led the Phils to their first pennant.

Dooin is recognized as the first catcher ever to wear shin guards. He popularized the use of that piece of equipment. As a catcher and manager, he was instrumental in developing the skills of future Hall of Fame pitcher Grover Cleveland Alexander after the righthander was purchased from Syracuse in 1911.

After his career ended with the Giants in 1916, he was in vaudeville as a tenor. He returned to Philadelphia in 1933 for the team's golden jubilee and teamed with former battery mate Harry Coveleski in a game between the Phillies and the old-timers.

Dooin once told this story about his days as an entertainer: "They asked me to sing at the inauguration banquet in New York City for Al Smith who had just been elected governor. There was no music. A gentleman from the audience then agreed to play the piano. Both of us got along well. When it was finished, I told him my name was Red Dooin, and in turn asked his name. He said it was Victor Herbert, and I darned near died."

Dooin, Red (Charles)

Phillies	G	AB	H	BA	RBI	R	2B	3B	HR	SA	SB
1902	94	333	77	.231	35	20	7	3	0	.270	8
1903	62	188	41	.218	14	18	5	1	0	.255	9
1904	108	355	86	.242	36	41	11	4	6	.346	15
1905	113	380	95	.250	36	45	13	5	0	.311	12
1906	113	351	86	.245	32	25	19	1	0	.305	15
1907	101	313	66	.211	14	18	8	4	0	.262	10
1908	133	435	108	.248	41	28	17	4	0	.306	20
1909	141	468	105	.225	38	42	14	1	2	.272	14
1910	103	331	80	.242	30	30	13	4	0	.305	10
1911	74	247	81	.328	16	18	15	1	1	.409	6
1912	69	184	46	.234	22	20	9	0	0	.283	8
1913	55	129	33	.256	13	6	4	1	0	.301	1
1914	53	118	21	.178	8	10	2	0	1	.220	4
Career	1,289	4,003	961	.240	344	333	139	31	10	.298	133

Red Dooin

It was only logical that Mickey Doolan should be remembered for his great hands around shortstop. Doolan, who came from the coal regions, was also a dental student when he joined the Phillies from Jersey City for the 1905 season. Later, he practiced dentistry in the off-season.

He is rated as one of the great defensive shortstops in Phillies history and was often compared with two of his contemporaries, Honus Wagner and Joe Tinker, for his fielding.

He was nowhere near those two Hall of Famers with a bat, however. His lifetime average was only .230. His high average in nine seasons with the Phillies was just .263, and he had no power with 15 home runs in 5,976 career at-bats.

But his arm was great and his range was greater, enabling him to cover up the limitations of any third baseman who played alongside him.

Doolan, who was born Michael Joseph Doolittle, jumped to the Federal League in 1914. He came back to the National League in 1916 and closed out his career in Brooklyn a year later.

Doolan, Mickey

Phillies: 1905–13
Shortstop
Birthplace: Ashland, Pennsylvania
B: May 7, 1880
D: November 1, 1951
Batted right, threw right
Ht. 5–10; **Wt.** 170

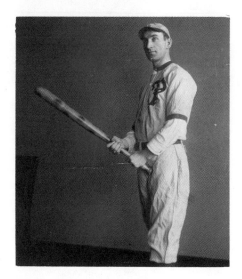

Mickey Doolan

Doolan, Mickey

Phillies	G	AB	H	BA	RBI	R	2B	3B	HR	SA	SB
1905	136	492	125	.254	48	53	27	11	1	.360	17
1906	154	535	123	.230	55	41	19	7	1	.297	16
1907	145	509	104	.204	47	33	19	7	1	.275	18
1908	129	445	104	.234	49	29	25	4	2	.321	5
1909	147	493	108	.219	35	39	12	10	1	.291	10
1910	148	536	141	.263	57	58	31	6	2	.354	16
1911	146	512	122	.238	49	51	23	6	1	.313	14
1912	146	532	137	.258	62	47	26	6	1	.335	6
1913	151	518	113	.218	43	32	12	6	1	.270	17
Career	1,727	5,976	1,376	.230	554	513	244	81	15	.306	173

Duggleby, Bill

Phillies: 1898; 1901–02; 1903–07
Pitcher
Nickname: Frosty Bill
Birthplace: Utica, New York
B: March 17, 1874
D: August 31, 1944
Threw right
Ht. and Wt. unknown

Bill Duggleby

In three separate terms with the Phillies, Bill Duggleby was a solid pitcher who more than 75 years after he played still ranks among the leaders in many of the club's all-time mound categories.

But Duggleby achieved his greatest notoriety away from the pitching rubber. He earned that prominence in two ways, once with the bat and once in the courtroom.

In 1898, in his first major league trip to the plate, Duggleby hit a grand slam home run. The blast gave him the distinction of being the first of 24 National League players to hit home runs in their first at-bats, and the first of two to do it with a grand slam.

Duggleby, who hit only six home runs in his eight-year career, also gained a measure of prominence during the American League's 1902 player raids. After jumping from the Phillies to the A's, Duggleby and his fellow club hoppers were ordered by the Pennsylvania Supreme Court to return to the Phillies. In a complex legal tussle, Duggleby and pitcher Chick Fraser were the only ones of about a dozen jumpers to obey the order.

Duggleby ranks sixth on the Phillies' all-time pitching list in complete games and hits, seventh in innings pitched, eighth in wins, and 10th in shutouts and runs allowed.

He won in double figures six times while working for the Phillies, including 1901 when he was 19–12 and 1905 when he was 18–17.

Frosty Bill first joined the Phillies in 1898. He pitched in only nine games, and didn't reappear until 1901. In 1902, Connie Mack lured Duggleby and a gang of other Phillies to the A's in the new American League. Bill pitched in two games, then followed the court order back to the Phillies.

Duggleby worked into the 1907 campaign with the Phillies. He was sold to Pittsburgh during the season, and finished his career there.

Duggleby, Bill

Phillies	W	L	Pct	ERA	G	CG	IP	H	BB	SO	ShO
1898	3	3	.500	5.50	9	4	54	70	18	12	0
1901	19	12	.613	2.87	34	25	275⅔	294	40	94	5
1902	11	17	.393	3.37	33	25	259	282	57	60	0
1903	13	18	.419	3.75	36	28	264⅓	318	79	57	3
1904	12	14	.480	3.78	32	22	223⅔	265	53	55	2
1905	18	17	.514	2.46	38	27	289	270	83	75	1
1906	13	19	.406	2.25	42	22	280⅓	241	66	83	5
1907	0	2	.000	7.45	5	2	29	43	11	8	0
Career	92	102	.474	3.19	240	158	1,732	1,836	423	452	17

Elliott, Jumbo

In 1930 the Phillies had a team batting average of .315, but they lost 102 games. The reason was obvious. The club had one of the most woeful pitching staffs ever to set foot on a big league mound. Its combined earned run average was 6.71.

Clearly, the Phils needed fresh blood on the hill, and in the winter of 1930, they got it in the person of Jumbo Elliott, a huge man who could throw hard and often.

The Phillies paid a heavy price for Elliott's services. To pry him away from the Brooklyn Dodgers, they had to give up the heavy-hitting Lefty O'Doul and infielder Fresco Thompson. The three were the key figures in the multiplayer deal.

Elliott, no relation to the famed Villanova coach of the same name, proved his worth in his first year in Philadelphia, posting a 19–14 record and tying for the league lead in wins. Appearing in 52 games, he also led the circuit in that category. Although he started 30 games, he also relieved in 22 more, registering five saves.

Jumbo's 4.27 ERA helped to lower the team's league high to a more reasonable 4.58. But 1931 was to be the only substantial season he gave the Phillies. Elliott slipped to an 11–10 record the next year and a 6–10 mark the following season.

The Phils sent him to the Boston Braves in 1933, which turned out to be his last season in the majors.

Elliott's major league career spanned 10 seasons, beginning with a brief stint with the St. Louis Browns in 1923. He worked parts of five seasons for the Dodgers, his best record being 10–7 in 1930.

Phillies: 1931–34
Pitcher
Birthplace: St. Louis, Missouri
B: October 22, 1900
D: January 7, 1970
Batted right, threw left
Ht. 6–3; Wt. 235

Jumbo Elliott

Elliott, Jumbo (James)

Phillies	W	L	Pct	ERA	G	CG	IP	H	BB	SO	ShO
1931	19	14	.576	4.27	52	12	249	288	83	99	2
1932	11	10	.524	5.42	39	8	166	210	47	62	0
1933	6	10	.375	3.84	35	6	161⅔	188	49	43	0
1934	0	1	.000	10.80	3	0	5	8	4	1	0
Career	63	74	.460	4.24	252	51	1,206⅔	1,338	414	453	8

Ennis, Del

In the days of Shibe Park, later to be known as Connie Mack Stadium, it was the mark of a true power hitter to be able to send an occasional ball to the roof of the distant bleachers in left field. It was certainly no shot that could be made by slap hitters, and even decent home run hitters usually couldn't poke a baseball that far.

It was a blast reserved solely for genuine power hitters, guys with large arms, strong wrists, and rippling muscles. The Phillies have had only a few such hitters. Del Ennis was one of the best of them.

A man of solid build, the kind that made him a perfect high school fullback who gained all-state recognition, Ennis had huge forearms and powerful shoulders. More than anything, though, it was his strong, quick wrists that were the key to his long-distance hitting. The old manager Gabby Street, who was part of the game for nearly 50 years, once said that Del had "the best-looking wrist action of any player I ever saw."

Ennis hit some vicious shots with those wrists. During a 14-year major league career, including 11 years with the Phillies, Del was never very selective. He clubbed nearly every kind of pitcher with the possible exception of Ewell Blackwell, who always gave him a hard time.

As a Phillie, Del ranks among the great hitters in club history. On the team's all-time list, he is second in home runs, third in total bases and runs batted in, fourth in hits and extra bases, fifth in doubles, eighth in runs, and 10th in triples.

Ennis hit 259 of his total of 288 home runs with the Phillies. Seven times he hit 25 or more four-baggers in one season, and eight times he led the club in

Phillies: 1946–56
Right fielder, left fielder
Birthplace: Philadelphia, Pennsylvania
B: June 8, 1925
Bats right, throws right
Ht. 6–0; Wt. 195

homers. He hit more home runs than any Phillies player at Shibe Park (133), and in both 1948 and 1952 he hit a home run in every park in the National League. He also hit five grand slam homers for the Phillies.

One of the great RBI men in club history, Del drove in 1,124 runs as a Phillie. He chased home more than 100 runs six times while a Phil. Nine times he led the club in RBI, and once he tied for the lead.

Ennis led the National League in RBI in 1950 with 126. That year, he set a club record with 41 runs batted in in one month (July). Included in that spree was a seven-RBI game in 13–3 victory over the Chicago Cubs. Del also drove in seven runs in 1955 in a game against the St. Louis Cardinals.

In addition to driving in runs, Ennis also had a penchant for coming up with a hit at the right time, even when there were no men on base. Three times during his career, he broke up no-hitters. In 1946 his two-out eighth inning single spoiled a perfect game by Red Barrett of the St. Louis Cardinals. The following year, Del snapped a hitless string by Hal Gregg of the Brooklyn Dodgers. In 1956, Del's hit broke up a no-hit bid by Ray Monzant of the New York Giants.

When he hit the ball, Del usually hit it hard. A perfect case of how hard he hit occurred in 1947 when Ennis crushed a drive against the center field wall in St. Louis's Sportsman's Park. The drive carried 442 feet on the line. The ball bounced all the way back to the infield, and Ennis had to be content with a double.

Despite his hitting heroics, Ennis was often booed by the hometown fans. Some ballyard psychologists rationalized that Ennis hit so well, the fans expected him to do something heroic every trip to the plate. Del claims he never let the booing bother him. "Maybe it bothered me a little at first," he says, "but then I got immune to it."

During most of his playing days in Philadelphia, Ennis was the team's only native son. Del grew up in the Olney section of Philadelphia, the elder of two boys. Del's father was a supervisor in the straw hat department of Stetson Hat Company.

Ennis was first spotted in 1942 by Phillies scout Jocko Collins. At the time, Ennis was a senior at Olney High School. Collins had come to an Olney game to watch a pitcher on the team. But after Del bombed two shots into the tennis courts in distant left field, Collins switched his attention to Ennis, who in high school played the outfield, first base, and catcher.

A quiet, shy teenager, Ennis paid little attention to Collins, resisting the veteran scout's advances by telling him he wasn't good enough to play pro ball. But Collins persisted in his attempts to get the Ennis name on a contract. Throughout the spring and summer, he continued to chase the youngster. Eventually, Del's father returned a signed contract.

Del was assigned the following season to the Phils' Class B team at Trenton. There, as a raw 18-year-old, Ennis hit .346 with 18 home runs and 93 RBI.

Shortly after the season ended, Ennis joined the navy, where he spent the next two years. Although he fought in the South Pacific, Del got to play a little baseball as well. In competition with players such as Johnny Vander Meer, Billy Herman, and Schoolboy Rowe, Ennis attracted a considerable amount of attention. Word of his ability circulated through the grapevine back to major league offices, and Phils general manager Herb Pennock began getting trade offers from teams interested in "the kid in the Navy."

Pennock politely declined the invitations to give up his budding star. In April 1946, Del was discharged from the Navy and joined the Phillies. The club planned to give Del another year of seasoning in the minors, but manager Ben Chapman put him in left field on the team's first western swing. In his second game as a regular, Del laced a bases-loaded double to beat the Pittsburgh Pirates. Ennis had a couple of other long hits during the trip, including two home runs in a doubleheader at Wrigley Field. His first home run was off Cubs ace Claude Passeau. After that, Del was in the lineup to stay.

At mid-season, Ennis was named to the National League All-Star team. He went on to finish the season with a .313 average, leading the Phillies or tying for the club lead in seven hitting categories. At the end of the season, Del was named Rookie of the Year by *The Sporting News*. He was also eighth in the balloting for Most Valuable Player.

Del Ennis

Throughout the season, Chapman had worked diligently with Ennis to polish his skills. Del needed to learn to bunt, and although he was a good fielder with a strong arm, he had to learn the best ways to catch and to throw. The long hours of work paid off for Ennis. While he was never a great fielder, he was more than adequate, and he always ranked among the league leaders in assists by outfielders. Del led the National League in assists in 1948 (he also led the league's outfielders in errors in 1948, 1949, and 1954).

In 1947, Ennis met up with the sophomore jinx. His average tumbled to .275 and his home run production dropped from 17 to 12. His RBI total, however, increased from 73 to 81. At one point during the season, Ennis went on a hitting rampage with safeties in 19 straight games.

Del bounced back in 1948 with a .290 average. That year, he hit 30 home runs, which would begin a streak in which he would hit 20 or more home runs in all but one season for the next 10. He tied for fifth in the league in home runs, while placing second in doubles, third in total bases, and fifth in slugging average.

The following season, Ennis continued to improve. Switching to a 42-ounce bat, his average increased to .302 and his RBI total went up to 110. Again, Del placed second in the league in doubles, and he was fourth in total bases and slugging average and fifth in RBI.

By 1949, Ennis had arrived as one of the premier power hitters in the National League. He was consistently placing among the league leaders in long-distance clouting, and pitchers considered him one of the most dangerous hitters to face.

The finest season of his career took place in 1950. Ennis reached career highs in average (.311), RBI (126), and home runs (31). Del was first in the league in RBI, fourth in average, and fifth in home runs. Throughout the season, Del's power-hitting and clutch hits provided the Phillies with the backbone of their hitting attack.

Ennis had numerous key hits. There was his grand slam home run, double, and seven RBI—all in the seventh and eighth innings—against Chicago in July. Three days later he drove in seven more runs as the Phillies beat the Pirates in a doubleheader, one of his hits being another grand slam.

He had five hits in an 8–7, 19-inning victory over the Reds in the longest game ever played at Shibe Park. And in the final week of the season, as the Phillies faltered, Del had a homer, three singles, and four RBI to help beat the Braves, 8–7.

Del also hit into 25 double plays during the season, a Phillies club record. In the World Series, he managed only two hits in 14 trips to the plate. Otherwise, though, 1950 was a marvelous season for Ennis, and he was a top contender for the league's MVP award, won by teammate Jim Konstanty.

Ennis never had another year quite like the one he had in 1950. In 1951, however, he was the starting right fielder for the National League All-Star team, although his season's average dipped to .267, and he had low home run (15) and RBI (73) totals.

Between 1952 and 1956, Ennis had home run totals of 20, 29, 25, 29, and 26, and only once did he drive in fewer than 100 runs. Del was consistently among the league leaders in RBI, ranking third in 1952, fourth in 1953, fifth in 1954, and third in 1956. His numbers put him in the company of hitters such as Stan Musial, Duke Snider, Willie Mays, Ted Kluszewski, Hank Sauer, Roy Campanella, and Gil Hodges.

In 1954, Ennis had one of the most unusual games of his career. In the second game of a doubleheader with the Cardinals, Ennis dropped a fly ball with two out and the bases loaded. All three runners scored. With the boos still ringing in his ears, Del came to bat in the bottom of the same inning with two on and two out. Ennis hit the first pitch to the left field roof. The Phils went on to win, 6–5.

Ennis was again a starter for the National League All-Stars in 1955. By this time, Del had begun wearing glasses. His .296 average with 29 homers and 120 RBI that year showed that Ennis could still swing the bat with authority.

After the 1956 season, however, the Phillies traded Ennis to St. Louis for infielder Bobby Morgan and outfielder Rip Repulski.

Ennis had an excellent year in 1957 for the Cards, hitting .286, driving in

105 runs, which ranked second in the league, and drilling 24 home runs. Del played less the following year, and his production dropped accordingly.

At the end of the season, he was traded to the Cincinnati Reds. He played there briefly before being swapped early in 1959 to the Chicago White Sox. Although he was only 34, and had plenty of baseball left, Ennis was getting bored with the game. He retired at the end of the season.

Ennis, Del

Phillies	G	AB	H	BA	RBI	R	2B	3B	HR	SA	SB
1946	141	540	169	.313	73	70	30	6	17	.485	5
1947	139	541	149	.275	81	71	25	6	12	.410	9
1948	152	589	171	.290	95	86	40	4	30	.525	2
1949	154	610	184	.302	110	92	39	11	25	.525	2
1950	153	595	185	.311	126	92	34	8	31	.551	2
1951	144	532	142	.267	73	76	20	5	15	.408	4
1952	151	592	171	.289	107	90	30	10	20	.475	6
1953	152	578	165	.285	125	79	22	3	29	.484	1
1954	145	556	145	.261	119	73	23	2	25	.444	2
1955	146	564	167	.296	120	82	24	7	29	.518	4
1956	153	630	164	.260	95	80	23	3	26	.430	7
Career	1,903	7,254	2,063	.284	1,284	985	358	69	288	.472	45

Etten, Nick

Phillies: 1941–42; 1947
First baseman
Birthplace: Spring Grove, Illinois
B: September 19, 1913
D: October 18, 1990
Batted left, threw left
Ht. 6–2; **Wt.** 198

Nick Etten

Big and strong, Nick Etten was known in his day as a solid hitter who on occasion could tear the cover off the ball.

Originally signed off the Villanova campus, Etten broke into the big leagues at the end of 1938 with the Philadelphia A's after serving nearly six years in the minors. After spending parts of two mediocre seasons as a reserve first baseman, Nick was shipped back to the minors by the A's. He had two fine seasons at Baltimore, and was bought by the Phillies.

Immediately, Etten became the Phils' regular first baseman and had one of the best records of a nine-year big league career. His .311 batting average was a career high. He also led first basemen in number of errors (23).

Etten was not much of a fielder. Once, when second baseman Danny Murtaugh suggested that Nick try for some of the balls hit between first and second instead of just running to the bag with the hope that Murtaugh would field them, the husky first sacker had this to say: "Son, they pay Ol' Nick to hit. You can't hit, so you catch all those balls, and I'll knock in the runs for both of us."

Etten slumped in 1942, and the Phillies promptly packed him off to the New York Yankees in exchange for catcher Tom Padden, pitcher Al Gerheauser, and $10,000. It was hardly one of the Phils' more astute trades.

In 1943, Nick drove in 107 runs while hitting .271 and helping the Yanks to the American League pennant. The following year he led the American League in home runs with 22 and hit .293. In 1945 he hit .285 and led the league in runs batted in with 111.

Nick dipped to .232 in 1946, which convinced the Yankees to give up on him. The Phillies grabbed him back, but Etten was never able to regain his old job, eventually losing out to a former pro basketball player named Howie Schultz, whom the Phillies had picked up from Brooklyn. Etten left baseball after the 1947 season.

He returned to the minors and hit well over three seasons, including a .313 average with 43 home runs and 155 RBI in 1948 for Casey Stengel's Oakland Oaks of the Pacific Coast League.

But he never got the call to return to the majors, and retired from baseball after the 1949 season.

Etten, Nick

Phillies	G	AB	H	BA	RBI	R	2B	3B	HR	SA	SB
1941	151	540	168	.311	79	78	27	4	14	.454	9
1942	139	459	121	.264	71	37	21	3	8	.375	3
1947	14	41	10	.244	8	5	4	0	1	.415	0
Career	937	3,320	921	.277	526	426	167	25	89	.423	22

For seven big league seasons with the Phillies, Sid Farrar existed as a baseball oddity. No one, either before or since, did what he did as a big leaguer, and probably no one ever will.

Farrar was perhaps the only first baseman in baseball who went through his career batting ninth in the order. It wasn't that the muscular New Englander couldn't hit. His lifetime average of .253 was respectable for its time.

Sid was the Phillies' first first baseman, joining the club for its initial season in the National League in 1883. At present, he is the second highest ranking Phillie of all time in games played at first base.

Farrar performed in 816 contests between his arrival and his departure in 1889. He was reputed to be a good fielder, but he usually made more than 30 and sometimes more than 40 errors each season, a high figure for a first baseman.

His best year at the plate was in 1887 when he hit .282. That year, he also had a career high 72 RBI.

In 1890, when the players' union formed its own Players' League, Sid and a number of his teammates abandoned the Phillies. Farrar's desertion was especially upsetting to Phils president Al Reach, who regarded Sid as one of his most loyal players.

When the Players' League disbanded after one season, some of the jumpers were taken back by the Phillies. But Farrar wasn't one of them. The club refused to let him back on the team, and as a result Sid's baseball career ended.

Later, Farrar became prominent again, not as a baseball player but as the father of world-famous opera star Geraldine Farrar.

Farrar, Sid

Phillies: 1883–89
First baseman
Birthplace: Paris Hill, Maine
B: August 10, 1859
D: May 7, 1935
Threw right
Ht. 5–10; **Wt. unknown**

Farrar, Sid

Phillies	G	AB	H	BA	RBI	R	2B	3B	HR	SA	SB
1883	99	377	88	.233	29	41	19	8	0	.326	
1884	111	428	105	.245	45	62	16	6	1	.318	
1885	111	420	103	.245	36	49	20	3	3	.329	
1886	118	439	109	.248	50	55	19	7	5	.358	10
1887	116	443	125	.282	72	83	20	9	4	.395	24
1888	131	508	124	.244	53	53	24	7	1	.325	21
1889	130	477	128	.268	58	70	22	2	3	.342	28
Career	943	3,573	904	.253	412	497	157	53	18	.342	82

Sid Farrar

Farrell, Dick

Phillies: 1956–61; 1967–68
Pitcher
Nickname: Turk
Birthplace: Boston, Massachusetts
B: April 8, 1934
D: June 11, 1977
Batted right, threw right
Ht. 6–4; **Wt.** 215

Dick Farrell

Dick Farrell was a strapping righthander who made his reputation with the Phillies as a pitcher who lived about as fast as he threw. And Turk had a sizzling fastball.

Despite his birthplace, the fun-loving hurler was far from being a proper Bostonian. When he became a regular member of the Phillies in 1957, Farrell soon hooked up with some of the other hard-living members of the pitching staff to form what became known as the Dalton Gang. It was a group, including Jim Owens, Jack Meyer, and a few others, who believed life should not get in the way of having a good time.

On occasion, Farrell was also an outstanding relief pitcher. As a youth, he had polio, but he overcame the illness and launched his pro career in 1953. Dick was a starting pitcher throughout his minor league days. When he joined the Phillies, he was converted to a reliever.

In his rookie year in 1957, Farrell was one of the outstanding relief hurlers in the National League. With a sharp-breaking curve and excellent control that combined with a sinking fastball to make him highly effective, Dick won 10 out of 12 games and collected 10 saves. He had the lowest earned run average in the league (2.39) and tied for fifth in saves.

Farrell continued his rookie success in the early part of 1958. During the first half of the season, Turk rang up a 6–2 record with nine saves and 1.13 ERA. He was selected for the National League All-Star team, and in the game struck out four of the seven batters he faced. But Dick slipped badly in the second half, and he finished the season with an 8–9 record, 11 saves, and a 3.35 earned run average.

He had a miserable year in 1959, and wound up going to the Phillies' Triple-A club in Buffalo. But the next year, Dick bounced back with a 10–6 mark, seemingly regaining the form that had given him the most wins for a reliever in his rookie year.

Early in 1961, however, the Phillies sent Farrell and shortstop Joe Koppe to the Los Angeles Dodgers for third baseman Charlie Smith and outfielder Don Demeter. It was a good trade for the Phillies, but a horrible one for the Dodgers, who let Farrell go that fall to the Houston Colts in the expansion draft.

Short on pitching, Houston converted Farrell back into a starter.

Dick worked for the Colts (later Astros) for a little more than five years. Despite the club's deep second-division finishes, he was its leading pitcher in four of those five years, posting 10–20, 14–13, 11–10, 11–11, and 6–10 records. Dick also hurled in the 1962 and 1964 All-Star games.

In May 1967, the Phillies, sorely in need of relief pitching, purchased Dick from the Astros. He returned to the bullpen and went 9–6 for the Phils. He dropped to 4–6 the next year, but still tied his career high of 12 saves. The Phils gave him his unconditional release at the end of the following season.

Farrell currently ranks fourth in saves on the Phillies' all-time career list.

He died in an auto accident in 1977 in England where he was living.

Farrell, Dick

Phillies	W	L	Pct	ERA	G	CG	IP	H	BB	SO	ShO
1956	0	1	.000	12.46	1	0	4⅓	6	3	0	0
1957	10	2	.833	2.39	52	0	82⅓	74	36	54	0
1958	8	9	.471	3.35	54	0	94	84	40	73	0
1959	1	6	.143	4.74	38	0	57	61	25	31	0
1960	10	6	.625	2.70	59	0	103⅓	88	29	70	0
1961	2	1	.667	6.30	5	0	10	10	6	10	0
1967	9	6	.600	2.05	50	0	92	76	15	68	0
1968	4	6	.400	3.48	54	0	82⅔	83	32	57	0
1969	3	4	.429	4.01	46	0	74	92	27	40	0
Career	106	111	.488	3.45	590	41	1,704⅓	1,628	468	1,177	5

Charlie Ferguson was the Phillies' first legitimate star and the first genuine baseball hero in the city of Philadelphia.

In an area that was a hotbed of baseball activity—at one point Philadelphia had four professional teams—Ferguson captured the fancy of baseball fans from the mayor of the city on down. He was the toast of the town, and when his career came to a tragic early ending, a whole city wept.

Had his career continued, Ferguson undoubtedly would hold a place today in the Hall of Fame. As it was, Charlie's career ended abruptly after four memorable seasons when he died of typhoid fever just after the start of his fifth campaign.

While he played, Ferguson was the Phillies' best pitcher, best hitter, and best base-runner. When he took over at second base on days he wasn't pitching, he was called the finest second sacker in the National League.

It made no difference where he was stationed, Ferguson played without flaw. What's more, he constantly outsmarted his rivals. George Reach, son of the Phillies' first president, once said, "Ferguson was really a great player, I'll go even further than that, and say he was wonderful."

John K. Tener, a major league player in the 1880s, following which he was National League president and governor of Pennsylvania, went even further. "With due respect to Wagner, Cobb, and Ruth," he once said, "I believe Ferguson would have been recognized as king of them all had he lived another 10 or 15 years."

Ferguson was just a slender 21-year-old from the hills of Virginia when he joined the Phillies in 1884. He had a 21–25 record that season for the sixth-place Phils who won only 39 games all year.

His rookie year launched Ferguson on a spree during which he was a 20-game winner in each of the four years he played. In 1885 he and Ed Daily were virtually the club's only pitchers, winning 52 games out of the Phils' total of 56. Charlie started 45 games—and completed 45 games. In fact, during his four-year career, he finished 165 of the 170 games he began.

In 1885, Ferguson also became the first Phillies pitcher to hurl a no-hitter. On August 29, he beat the Providence Grays, 1–0, striking out eight and walking two. The Phils made six errors behind him.

Ferguson wound up the year with a 26–20 record. One of his wins was a 24–0 victory over Indianapolis. By this time, Charlie had also established himself as a batting star. It was impossible to keep him out of the lineup, so when he wasn't pitching he played the outfield. He hit .306.

The year of 1886 turned out to be Ferguson's finest. On the mound, he was virtually invincible, posting a 30–9 record, leading the league with a 1.98 ERA and striking out 212 batters while pitching 395 innings, the first time he'd gone less than 400.

During the season, Charlie reeled off 12 straight wins, the second highest streak in Phillies history. On October 9 he won both games of a doubleheader with Detroit, taking the first game 5–1, and working six innings in the second to get a 6–1 triumph. He was the first pitcher in baseball history to win two games in one day.

In 1887, Ferguson didn't pitch as often as before because the Phillies were starting to use him as their regular second baseman. Still, Charlie registered a 22–10 record on the mound, and he hit .337.

By now, Ferguson was riding high as the biggest name in Philadelphia sports. It all came to an end, though, the following spring.

During spring training, Ferguson contracted typhoid fever. At first, his teammates were unconcerned. "Fergy is big and strong," they agreed. "He'll lick this and be back with us before we know it."

But Charlie's condition worsened. His fever burned deeper. Finally, on April 29, just 12 days after his 25th birthday, Ferguson succumbed to the dreaded fever.

Philadelphia baseball fans went into shock as the news of Charlie's death raced through the city. People wept unashamedly. "Charlie Ferguson is dead," they cried.

Ferguson, Charlie

Phillies: 1884–87
Pitcher, outfielder, second baseman
Birthplace: Charlottesville, Virginia
B: April 17, 1863
D: April 29, 1888
Batted both, threw right
Ht. 6–0; **Wt.** 165

Charlie Ferguson

The grief-stricken Phillies donned black arm bands. They tried to be brave, telling themselves, "We've got to win now, just for poor Charlie's sake." But it was no use. Fergy was irreplaceable, and his loss was too much of a strain on the players' emotions as well as the team's playing strength. It is hard to lose a star pitcher, hitter, fielder, and runner. The Phillies, having entered the season as the probable pennant winner, finished a distant and disappointing third.

Ferguson, Charlie

Phillies	W	L	Pct	ERA	G	CG	IP	H	BB	SO	ShO
1884	21	25	.457	3.54	50	46	416⅔	443	93	194	2
1885	26	20	.565	2.22	48	45	405	345	81	197	5
1886	30	9	.769	1.98	48	43	395⅔	317	69	212	4
1887	22	10	.688	3.00	37	31	297⅓	297	47	125	2
Career	99	64	.607	2.67	183	165	1,514⅔	1,402	290	728	13

Fernandez, Chico

Phillies: 1957–59
Shortstop
Birthplace: Havana, Cuba
B: March 2, 1932
Bats right, throws right
Ht. 6–0; Wt. 165

Chico Fernandez

When the Phillies traded seemingly half their farm system for Chico Fernandez, two things happened. The club figured it had solved its shortstop problems once and for all. And Chico became the first black player to appear for the team in a regular-season game.

The latter turned out to be a far more significant reality than the former. Although he was not the first black player to wear a Phillies uniform (John Kennedy was), Fernandez launched the team into the modern process of having blacks in the lineup, a condition the Phils had procrastinated about longer than all but the Boston Red Sox.

The Cuban-born Chico was the club's opening day shortstop in 1957. Fernandez had come to the club just a few weeks earlier in a trade with the Brooklyn Dodgers in which the Phils gave up outfielder Elmer Valo, pitchers Ron Negray and Ben Flowers, first baseman Tim Harkness, shortstop Mel Geho, and $75,000.

Since 1952, the Phillies had had a different regular shortstop every year. The strong-armed, graceful Fernandez was viewed as the ultimate successor to the aging Granny Hamner, the last Phils shortstop of any duration.

Fernandez, who played six years in the minors starting in 1951, had played four years in the International League at Montreal. He was regarded as one of the better minor league shortstops, although he was prone to making errors. His only previous major league experience was a partial season in 1956 with the Dodgers.

Chico was the Phillies' regular shortstop for two years. He hit .262 his first year. Although he had good range as a fielder, Fernandez continued to make a fair amount of errors.

In 1958 his average tumbled to .230. Chico duplicated his previous year's RBI total with 51.

The next spring the Phillies picked up shortstop Joe Koppe in a trade. Fernandez lost his starting job, and he saw action mostly in a reserve role. That winter, Chico was traded with pitcher Ray Semproch to the Detroit Tigers for infielders Alex Cosmidis and Ted Lepcio and outfielder Ken Walters.

Fernandez was the Tigers' regular shortstop for the next three seasons. His average was in the .240s each year. Detroit sent Chico to the New York Mets in 1963, his last season in the majors.

Fernandez, Chico (Humberto)

Phillies	G	AB	H	BA	RBI	R	2B	3B	HR	SA	SB
1957	149	500	131	.262	51	42	14	4	5	.336	18
1958	148	522	120	.230	51	38	18	5	6	.318	12
1959	45	123	26	.211	3	15	5	1	0	.268	2
Career	856	2,778	666	.240	259	270	91	19	40	.329	68

When Elmer Flick replaced Sam Thompson as the Phillies' right fielder for the 1898 season, it brought about a baseball rarity—a Hall of Famer taking over the position of another Hall of Famer.

Flick, a .315 lifetime hitter, had four brilliant years with the Phillies. His best was 1900 when he batted .367, collected 200 hits, stole 35 bases, drove in 110 runs, and scored 106. His lowest average with the Phils was .302 as a rookie.

Flick's 1900 season included statistics among the league leaders in nearly every category. His batting average was second in the league, just three points behind Honus Wagner. His 11 home runs trailed Boston's Herman Long by one. He led the league in RBI, was just one behind Wee Willie Keeler in hits, and was second to Wagner in doubles and slugging average (.545). He led the league in total bases with 297.

Though his numbers slipped in 1901, he was still tied for fourth in the league in home runs, fifth in slugging average (.500), tied for second in triples, and tied for fifth in total bases (270).

After the 1901 season, Elmer jumped to Connie Mack's rival Athletics as nearly every other Phillie of value signed on with the American League. After the Pennsylvania Supreme Court ruled that Flick and two other jumpers could not play for the Athletics, they were assigned to Cleveland.

With the Indians, Flick led the American League in hitting (.308) in 1905 and twice was the league's stolen-base leader.

He was named to baseball's Hall of Fame in 1963, eight years before he died in his lifelong hometown of Bedford, Ohio.

Flick, Elmer

Phillies: 1898–1901
Outfielder
Birthplace: Bedford, Ohio
B: January 11, 1876
D: January 9, 1971
Batted left, threw right
Ht. 5–9; **Wt.** 168

Elmer Flick

Flick, Elmer

Phillies	G	AB	H	BA	RBI	R	2B	3B	HR	SA	SB
1898	134	453	137	.302	81	84	16	13	18	.448	23
1899	127	485	166	.342	98	98	22	11	2	.458	31
1900	138	545	200	.367	110	106	32	16	11	.545	35
1901	138	540	180	.333	88	112	32	17	8	.500	30
Career	1,483	5,597	1,752	.313	757	948	268	164	48	.445	330

Not only was Jim Fogarty one of the first of a great line of big league players to come out of San Francisco, he was also one of the first baseball rebels.

Fogarty wasn't overendowed with talent, but he was a versatile player who spent most of his time with the Phillies as their regular right fielder. He also played second, third, and short on occasion, and even pitched in seven games (0–1 record).

After the Phillies purchased his contract from the minors in 1884, he became an extremely popular player with the fans. One of the early Californians to make it all the way to the East to play big league baseball, the handsome Fogarty, whose brother Joe had a brief stint in the majors with the St. Louis Browns, ultimately became one of the more tragic stories of his era. He died of tuberculosis in the midst of his career.

Fogarty, Jim

Phillies: 1884–89
Outfielder, infielder
Birthplace: San Francisco, California
B: February 12, 1864
D: May 20, 1891
Batted right, threw right
Ht. 5–10½; **Wt.** 180

Fogarty's best season was in 1886 when he hit .293. In 1889 he led the National League in stolen bases with 99. That year, he also threw out 42 base-runners from right field.

In the winter of 1888–89, Fogarty, teammate George Wood, and others participated in a worldwide tour in which they formed a team of National League All-Stars playing the Chicago White Stockings.

On the trip, the players discussed their perceived mistreatment by the owners. Fogarty became convinced of the need to stand up for players' rights. "We've got to get more money out of this game. We attract the fans, but the owners pocket all the profits," he said upon his return.

In 1890, Jim was one of the first of many Phillies to jump to the Baseball Brotherhood's new Players' League. Jim started off as the Philadelphia team's player-manager.

Late in the season, though, his health had started to deteriorate. Fogarty had to step down as manager.

After the league folded, Fogarty and young Ed Delahanty were the only players taken back by the Phillies. "Jim's a sick man. He's repentant, and I don't think we should dump him," said the sentimental Phillies president Al Reach.

By the start of next season, though, Fogarty was fading fast. After rejoining the Phillies, he never played a game for them. Jim died on May 20, 1891, at just 27 years of age.

Fogarty, Jim

Phillies	G	AB	H	BA	RBI	R	2B	3B	HR	SA	SB
1884	97	378	80	.212	37	42	12	6	1	.283	
1885	111	427	99	.232	39	49	13	3	0	.276	
1886	77	280	82	.293	47	54	13	5	3	.407	30
1887	126	495	129	.261	50	113	26	12	8	.410	102
1888	121	454	107	.236	35	72	14	6	1	.300	58
1889	128	499	129	.259	54	107	15	17	3	.375	99
Career	751	2,880	709	.246	320	508	110	55	20	.343	325

Jim Fogarty

Fraser, Chick

Phillies: 1899–1900, 1902–04
Pitcher
Birthplace: Chicago, Illinois
B: March 17, 1871
D: May 8, 1940
Batted right, threw right
Ht. 5–10½; **Wt.** 188

In two years with the Phillies at the turn of the century, Chick Fraser won 36 games and discovered what many players on the team learned even more vividly under the stewardships of William F. Baker and Gerald Nugent—that generosity would not be a franchise tradition.

Fraser, who pitched for 14 years and was a 212-game loser, jumped to Connie Mack's Athletics when the Phillies refused to pay him more than $2,400 after the 1901 season. After a year with the A's, Fraser returned to the Phillies in order to comply with a Pennsylvania Supreme Court order upholding the validity of the option clause in his contract.

The only pitcher ever to win 20 games in a season for both the Phillies and A's, Fraser pitched a no-hitter September 18, 1903, against the Chicago Cubs. In what has been the most one-sided no-hitter in modern Phillies history, Fraser beat the Cubs, 10–0, despite a major-league-record four errors behind him.

Overall, however, he was not nearly as effective as he had been in his first tour of duty, and by 1904 he was a 24-game loser. The Phils moved him on to Boston, where he lost 22 in 1905. Then Fraser lost 20 times for the Cubs in 1906, giving him the unique post-1900 distinction of having lost 20 games in three consecutive years with three different teams.

This is not to say that Fraser was not a pitcher of considerable talent. Chick also won 175 games in his career. But his greatest moment might have been when he explained why he jumped the Phillies to play for the A's.

"I left the Phillies because they held me too cheap," Fraser said. "I was disgusted with the treatment I received. I wrote that I could not train in Philadelphia because of the damp cement floor in the (Baker Bowl) clubhouse, which always gave me a bad cold. I wrote (William) Shettsline, asking him if he would pay my expenses if I trained in Hot Springs, Arkansas. He replied, offering me pay on the basis of $8 a week. That settled it. I went to Connie Mack."

Presumably Mr. Mack, never loose with the purse strings himself, offered at least $9 a week.

Chick Fraser

Fraser, Chick (Charles)

Phillies	W	L	Pct	ERA	G	CG	IP	H	BB	SO	ShO
1899	21	12	.636	3.35	35	29	271	278	85	68	4
1900	15	9	.625	3.15	29	22	223	250	93	58	1
1902	12	13	.480	3.42	27	24	224	238	74	97	3
1903	12	17	.414	4.50	31	26	250	260	97	104	1
1904	14	24	.368	3.25	42	32	302	287	100	127	2
Career	175	212	.452	3.68	433	342	3,356	3,460	1,332	1,098	22

Barney Friberg was the kind of guy who would play anywhere the manager asked him to play. If the team had needed somebody to take care of the bats, Barney probably would've done that, too.

During his career with the Phillies, he played all four infield positions. He also played the outfield, caught one game, and almost pitched. Friberg was the kind of unselfish player every team should have.

A scrappy hustler who could handle the bat, Friberg broke in with the Chicago Cubs in 1919 and retired after playing the 1933 campaign with the Boston Red Sox. In 1923 and 1924, he was the Cubs' regular third baseman. He hit .318 in the former.

The Phillies bought Friberg in 1925. That year and the next, he was the club's regular second baseman. A solid fielder, he led the league's second sackers in putouts in 1926, a year in which he also led National League batters in strikeouts with 77.

In 1927, Barney was moved to third base, where he led the league in turning double plays. Friberg had never hit above .270 for the Phillies, however, and in 1928 he became a utility man, playing first, second, short, third, and the outfield.

As usual, the Phillies were short on pitchers as they went to spring training in 1929. Always the team man, Barney volunteered to pitch. He had thrown in one game when he was with the Cubs, but he needed to learn the fine points of the position. He spent most of spring training learning them.

Shortly before the Phillies broke camp, shortstop Tommy Thevenow drove his car off the road one night and was badly injured. Friberg was asked to fill in at shortstop, with the result that he had to abandon his plans to pitch. Barney played that position, and when Thevenow returned to the team, he played the outfield and second. Friberg hit .301, one of eight of the team's top players who passed the .300 mark that season.

The following year, Barney was back to his role as a utility man. Nevertheless, he played in 105 games and finished the season with a .341 batting average. That was the year the club hit .315 as a team, but lost 102 games.

Friberg's average tumbled in the next two years, but he continued to play often, filling in wherever necessary. He was sold to the Red Sox at the end of the 1932 season. Barney hit .317 in his last season.

Friberg, Barney

Phillies: 1925–32
Infielder, outfielder
Birthplace: Manchester, New Hampshire
B: August 18, 1899
D: December 8, 1958
Batted right, threw right
Ht. 5–11; Wt. 178

Barney Friberg

Friberg, Barney (Gustaf)

Phillies	G	AB	H	BA	RBI	R	2B	3B	HR	SA	SB
1925	91	304	82	.270	22	41	12	1	5	.385	1
1926	144	478	128	.268	51	38	21	3	1	.331	2
1927	111	335	78	.233	28	31	8	2	1	.278	3
1928	52	94	19	.202	7	11	3	0	1	.266	0
1929	128	455	137	.301	55	74	21	10	7	.437	1
1930	105	331	113	.341	42	62	21	1	4	.447	1
1931	103	353	92	.261	26	33	19	5	1	.351	1
1932	61	154	37	.240	14	17	8	2	0	.318	0
Career	1,299	4,169	1,170	.281	471	544	181	44	38	.373	51

Fryman, Woodie

Phillies: 1968–72
Pitcher
Birthplace: Ewing, Kentucky
B: April 12, 1940
Bats right, throws left
Ht. 6–3; **Wt.** 197

Woodie Fryman

Woodie Fryman didn't start playing baseball for pay until long after most players sign their first professional contracts. But that fact certainly didn't stop him from having a long and productive career.

When he began the 1983 season in the Montreal Expos' bullpen at the age of 43, it marked his 18th season in the big leagues. He spent 4½ of them with the Phillies.

Woodie came to Philadelphia in one of the Phillies' major trades of the 1960s. On December 16, 1967, the Phillies traded their ace righthander, Jim Bunning, to the Pittsburgh Pirates for Fryman, a 12-game winner as a Pirate rookie in 1965, infielder Don Money, and two lesser players.

Fryman worked more than 200 innings and pitched 10 complete games in each of his first two seasons with the Phillies.

His career in Philadelphia followed a pattern, to say the least. A fastball pitcher, Woodie would have a good first half of the season, then trail off badly in the second half. His best year with the Phils was his first in 1968. He won a dozen games, completed 10 of them, had 151 strikeouts in 214 innings, and compiled a 2.78 earned run average. He was selected as a member of the National League All-Star team but didn't see action in the game.

The tobacco-farming gentleman from Kentucky, who didn't sign a pro contract until he was 25, reversed his pattern in 1972. He got off to a terrible start with a terrible team and was 4–10 when Paul Owens gave him the break of his life by selling him to the Detroit Tigers. There Woodie won 10 of 13 decisions and led the Tigers to the American League East championship.

Fryman, Woodie

Phillies	W	L	Pct	ERA	G	CG	IP	H	BB	SO	ShO
1968	12	14	.462	2.78	34	10	214	198	64	151	5
1969	12	15	.444	4.42	36	10	228	243	89	150	1
1970	8	6	.571	4.08	27	4	128	122	43	97	3
1971	10	7	.588	3.38	37	3	149	133	46	104	2
1972	4	10	.286	4.35	23	3	120	131	39	69	2
Career	141	155	.481	3.77	619	68	2,413	2,367	890	1,587	27

Garber, Gene

Another of the great steals of the mid-'70s by Paul Owens, Gene Garber was purchased by the Phillies' Toledo farm team from the Kansas City Royals on July 12, 1974, then was bought from Toledo by the Phillies 15 days later.

He won all four of his decisions that year and had a 2.06 earned run average and four saves. Over the next 3½ years, he won 29 more games, all in relief, and saved 47 more. In 1975 he led National League pitchers in appearances (71). His best season with the Phillies was 1977 when he won eight games and saved 19 and had a 2.36 earned run average for 103 innings.

Unfortunately, he was the losing pitcher in the game that probably caused Phillies fans more anguish than any other in their history. He was working in his third inning of the third game of the 1977 League Championship Series and had a 5–3 lead breezing into the ninth when Greg Luzinski dropped Manny Mota's fly ball at the left field fence, leading the way to a three-run Dodger rally and a 6–5 loss.

In 1982 he was one of the main forces as the Atlanta Braves shocked the baseball world by winning the National League West. He had been traded to the Braves by the Phillies on June 15, 1978, for Dick Ruthven.

His 218 career saves placed him in the all-time top 10 for a time. In 1978 when he was with the Braves, he struck out Cincinnati's Pete Rose to end his 44-game hitting streak.

He was considered extremely rude by opposing batters, not just because he turned his back on them before delivering his pitches, but also because of his nasty assortment of pitches, including one of baseball's best change-ups.

Phillies: 1974–78
Pitcher
Birthplace: Elizabethtown, Pennsylvania
B: November 13, 1947
Bats right, throws right
Ht. 5–10; **Wt.** 175

Gene Garber

Garber, Gene

Phillies	W	L	Pct	ERA	G	CG	IP	H	BB	SO	ShO
1974	4	0	1.000	2.06	34	0	48	39	31	27	0
1975	10	12	.455	3.60	71	0	110	103	27	69	0
1976	9	3	.750	2.81	59	0	93	78	30	92	0
1977	8	6	.571	2.36	64	0	103	82	23	78	0
1978	2	1	.667	1.38	22	0	39	26	11	24	0
Career	96	113	.459	3.34	931	4	1,509	1,464	445	940	0

Gleason, Kid

Kid Gleason lived a full baseball life. He started out as a pitcher and won 138 major league games. Then he switched to second base and the outfield and ended his 22-year career with 1,944 hits. He managed the White Sox, who, in his first year at the helm, became the Black Sox when they dumped the 1919 World Series to the Cincinnati Reds. And, until just before his death, he coached for Connie Mack on the great A's teams of 1929–31.

Gleason was an outstanding competitor. In fact, no less a competitor than John McGraw praised him for his fighting spirit and courage.

"Gleason was without doubt the gamest and most spirited ball player I ever saw," the great Giants manager said. "And that doesn't except Ty Cobb. He was a great influence for good on any ball club, making up for his lack of stature by his spirit and fight. He could lick his weight in wildcats and would prove it at the drop of a hat."

He was good enough to win 38 games—highest total in Phillies history—against 17 losses for the Phillies in 1890. His earned run average that year was 2.63.

He returned to the Phillies in 1903 after performing brilliantly in St. Louis, Baltimore, and New York. By that time he was 37 years old, but three years later, at 40, he was still the Phillies' regular second baseman, playing 135 games.

He voluntarily left managing after the 1923 season with the White Sox and

Phillies: 1888–1891, 1903–08
Pitcher, outfielder, second baseman
Birthplace: Camden, New Jersey
B: October 26, 1866
D: January 2, 1933
Batted left, threw right
Ht. 5–7; **Wt.** 158

denied rumors that he would go to Detroit as a coach. He said at the time that he had worked himself into a nervous wreck and that he just wanted to take some time to get back his health. He joined the A's in 1925 and was with them until the spring of 1932 when poor health forced him out of uniform. He died the following year of heart failure.

Gleason, Kid (William)

Phillies	G	AB	H	BA	RBI	R	2B	3B	HR	SA	SB
1888	24	83	17	.205	5	4	2	0	0	.229	3
1889	30	99	25	.253	8	11	5	0	0	.302	4
1890	63	224	47	.210	17	22	3	0	0	.223	10
1891	65	214	53	.248	17	31	5	2	0	.290	6
1903	106	412	117	.284	49	65	19	6	1	.368	12
1904	153	587	161	.274	42	61	23	6	0	.334	17
1905	155	608	150	.247	50	95	17	7	1	.303	16
1906	135	494	112	.227	34	47	17	2	0	.269	17
1907	36	126	18	.143	6	11	3	0	0	.167	3
1908	2	1	0	.000	0	0	0	0	0	.000	0
Career	1,966	7,452	1,944	.261	823	1,020	216	80	15	.317	328

Phillies	W	L	Pct	ERA	G	CG	IP	H	BB	SO	ShO
1888	7	16	.304	2.84	24	23	200	199	53	89	1
1889	9	15	.375	5.58	29	15	205	242	97	64	0
1890	38	17	.691	2.63	60	54	506	479	167	222	6
1891	24	22	.522	3.51	53	40	418	431	165	100	1
Career	138	131	.513	3.79	299	240	2,389	2,552	906	744	11

Kid Gleason

Goliat, Mike

Phillies: 1949–51
Second baseman
Birthplace: Yatesboro, Pennsylvania
B: November 3, 1925
Bats right, throws right
Ht. 6; Wt. 180

Of all the regulars on the 1950 Whiz Kids, none had a more curious career than Mike Goliat.

Originally a top prospect in the Phillies' farm system, Mike was the team's regular second baseman in 1950. Yet he couldn't make the starting lineup the following season, and in 1952 he was out of baseball.

It was a strange career for the nimble, young infielder with the strong arm. Goliat, the son of a coal miner and one of nine children, had worked hard to get to the majors. And, like everyone else on the 1950 team, he made a contribution to the Phillies' pennant.

Mike had come to the Phillies, not through a scout, but through his own perseverance. A good high school and sandlot player in Western Pennsylvania, Goliat joined the Army in 1945 at the age of 19. He played service ball with some professionals, whose talents did not awe him. Mike figured if they were good enough to play pro ball, so was he.

When he got out of the Army in 1946, Goliat set his course on a pro career. His first move was to take himself to the Phillies' Class D farm team in Vandergrift, Pennsylvania, and ask for a tryout. He got it, made the team, and in 1947 hit .370.

The Phils promoted Goliat to their Wilmington club in 1948. Mike hit .315 to win another promotion to the Triple-A club in Toronto.

Mike was hitting .286 for the Maple Leafs when the Phils called him to Philadelphia in the summer of 1949. Although Goliat had played first and third base throughout most of his minor league career, the Phillies needed a second baseman, and Mike was their man. At Toronto he had begun to play a little at second, but he was still learning the position when he reported to the parent club.

Goliat had to learn the position quickly. Although he joined the Phillies with a badly injured knee, which he had suffered in a collision on his last day in Toronto, Mike was inserted right away into the starting lineup.

The Phillies wanted to X-ray the knee, but Goliat refused to allow them to until they consented to let him stay in the lineup, no matter what the X-ray revealed. It was too hard getting here, Mike insisted.

The knee was not Mike's only problem. In his first 46 at-bats, he got only three hits. Goliat had a lot of confidence in his hitting, though, and he kept plugging away. Eventually, he pulled out of his slump, raising his average in 55 games to .212. It was not much of an average, but considering what he had to overcome, the Phillies were satisfied.

In 1950, Goliat was firmly entrenched as the Phillies' regular second baseman. That season he didn't hit for a high average (.234), but he came through with many clutch hits and wound up the season with 64 RBI. Mike hit 13 home runs.

Goliat's chief problem at the plate was his willingness to chase bad balls. One of his strengths was the way he handled Brooklyn Dodger pitchers. Mike jumped on the Dodgers on opening day when he rocked Don Newcombe for four hits, and he rarely let up on them thereafter.

In early August, Goliat went on a spree the day after getting married. On August 5 his two-run homer beat the St. Louis Cardinals, 2–1. Two days later he had a single, double, and triple as the Phils blanked the Cards, 9–0. The next day he had two singles and a double in a 6–5 victory over the Dodgers.

Goliat got only three hits in 14 at-bats in the World Series, but he scored the Phillies' first run of the fall classic, singling and eventually scoring on Richie Ashburn's sacrifice fly.

In 1951, Goliat inexplicably lost his touch. Fined for violations in spring training, he stopped hitting somewhere along the way, and the Phillies sent him to their Baltimore Triple-A farm club. Mike hit .282 for the Orioles. When he came back to Philadelphia at the end of the season, he was sold on waivers to the St. Louis Browns.

Mike played a little at the end of the 1951 season and the beginning of the '52 campaign with the Browns before getting his release. Goliat never played another day in the majors.

Goliat, Mike

Phillies	G	AB	H	BA	RBI	R	2B	3B	HR	SA	SB
1949	55	189	40	.212	19	24	6	3	3	.323	0
1950	145	483	113	.234	64	49	13	6	13	.366	3
1951	41	138	31	.225	15	14	2	1	4	.340	0
Career	249	825	186	.225	99	87	21	10	20	.348	3

Mike Goliat

Despite being in Philadelphia for only two less-than-memorable seasons, Chile Gomez made one extremely notable contribution to the Phillies.

He was the first Latin American ever to pull on a Phillies uniform.

Gomez was a youthful baseball standout in his native Mexico. He was discovered by major league scouts while touring the United States with a team of Mexican all-stars.

The Phillies signed Chile and brought him to the club in 1935. As a utility infielder, he hit .230 his first year.

Gomez, who went to high school in Los Angeles, became the team's regular second baseman in 1936. He hit .232.

Chile played one other year in the big leagues. That was in 1942 when he was a reserve infielder with the Washington Senators.

Gomez, Chile

Phillies: 1935–36
Second baseman, shortstop
Birthplace: Villaunion, Mexico
B: May 23, 1909
Bats right, throws right
Ht. 5–10; **Wt.** 165

Chile Gomez

Gomez, Chile (Jose)

Phillies	G	AB	H	BA	RBI	R	2B	3B	HR	SA	SB
1935	67	222	51	.230	16	24	3	0	0	.243	2
1936	108	332	77	.232	28	24	4	1	0	.250	0
Career	200	627	142	.226	50	56	9	3	0	.250	3

Gonzalez, Tony

Phillies: 1960–68
Outfielder
Birthplace: Camaguey, Cuba
B: August 28, 1936
Bats left, throws right
Ht. 5–9; **Wt.** 170

Tony Gonzalez

Tony Gonzalez made a huge impression on the Phillies on opening day 1960, when he was a 23-year-old rookie for the Reds. In fact, he made such an impression that general manager John Quinn quickly traded for him that June, and Gonzalez settled into a nine-year productive career with the team.

He and Gene Mauch arrived the same year and left the same year, and Gonzalez gave Mauch some solid defense in center field and good efforts at the plate throughout his career.

His hitting secret was relaxation.

"I don't have any tension," he said. "I don't get nervous. Each time I go up to the plate I feel I'm gonna get a hit. I say each time I go up there, 'I'm gonna hit that ball hard.' If I hit the ball hard four times, at least I got to get two or three hits."

For his career, Tony Gonzalez got 1,485 hits. His lifetime average was .286. And, although he wasn't a home run hitter as such, he had tremendous power to the opposite field.

"The year he hit 20 homers (1962), 17 of them were to the left of center, which was amazing for a guy that size," said Mauch of the 5–9, 170-pound lefty swinger.

Gonzalez hit .300 three times, including his best year, 1967, when his .339 average was second in the National League to the late Roberto Clemente.

An outstanding fielder, Tony twice led National League outfielders in fielding. In 1962, Tony handled all 276 of his chances in the outfield without an error, making him one of only four Phillies outfielders to field 1.000 in seasons in which they played in at least 100 games. His .983 also led the league in 1967.

His career .359 on-base percentage is the 10th best since the Phillies began compiling the figure in 1926. His 29 sacrifice flies tie him for ninth on the team's all-time list. He is also 10th in intentional walks (45) and strikeouts (549).

Gonzalez, Tony

Phillies	G	AB	H	BA	RBI	R	2B	3B	HR	SA	SB
1960	78	241	72	.299	33	27	17	5	6	.485	2
1961	126	426	118	.277	58	58	16	8	12	.437	15
1962	118	437	132	.302	63	76	16	4	20	.494	17
1963	155	555	170	.306	66	78	36	12	4	.436	13
1964	131	421	117	.278	40	55	25	3	4	.380	0
1965	108	370	109	.295	41	48	19	1	13	.457	3
1966	132	384	110	.286	40	53	20	4	6	.406	2
1967	149	508	172	.339	59	74	23	9	9	.472	10
1968	121	416	110	.264	38	45	13	4	3	.337	6
Career	1,559	5,195	1,485	.286	615	690	238	57	103	.413	79

Gonzalez closed out his 12-year career in 1972 as a member of the California Angels. He also played for the San Diego Padres and Atlanta Braves after leaving the Phillies.

When Billy Murray became the Phillies' manager for the 1907 season, he brought with him from Jersey City a third baseman named Ed Grant.

A curiosity of sorts since he had a degree from the oldest university in the nation, Harvard Eddie became Ironman Eddie between 1908 and 1910. In that three-year stretch, he played in 452 games. He led the league in at-bats in both 1908 (598) and 1909 (629).

Although he lacked power (five lifetime homers in 959 major league games) and even though his big league average was a point under .250, there was a monument erected in his memory at the Polo Grounds in New York in 1921. The reason: Grant, who played his last game for the Giants in 1915, was a World War I hero who lost his life as an acting major while leading his battalion to the rescue of another battalion in the Argonne Forest in France on October 5, 1918. He was 35.

Grant, Ed

Phillies	G	AB	H	BA	RBI	R	2B	3B	HR	SA	SB
1907	74	268	65	.243	19	26	4	3	0	.280	10
1908	147	598	146	.244	32	69	13	8	0	.293	27
1909	153	631	170	.269	37	75	18	4	1	.315	28
1910	153	579	155	.268	67	70	15	5	1	.316	25
Career	959	3,383	844	.249	277	399	79	30	5	.295	153

Throughout the 1980s, when future Hall of Famers and other big names dominated the Phillies' roster, one of the unsung heroes of the club was Greg Gross.

He was always ready when needed, playing left field, center field, right field, first base . . . he even pitched an inning once. For 10 seasons, Gross was the consummate professional for the Phillies, a valuable utility man who was fundamentally as sound as anyone on the team.

Gross had one other value to the club. He was an exquisite pinch-hitter. He was so good, in fact, that when he retired from baseball after the 1989 season, he ranked third on the all-time list for number of pinch-hits and had the most at-bats of any pinch-hitter in baseball history. Gross came to the plate 588 times as a pinch-hitter and belted 143 hits. Only Manny Mota with 150 and Smoky Burgess with 145 had more pinch-hits than Gross.

Greg led the Phillies in pinch-hits eight times, once getting as many as 19 in a season (1982), when he led the National League and came within one of tying the Phillies' all-time record.

Unquestionably, Gross's finest moments as a pinch-hitter came in the 1980 League Championship Series against the Houston Astros. He had three key hits in four at-bats, driving in an insurance run with a single in the first game, singling to start a three-run, eighth-inning rally that tied the score in the fourth game, and dropping a perfect bunt single to load the bases during the famous eighth-inning rally against Nolan Ryan in the deciding game.

Grant, Ed

Phillies: 1907–10
Third baseman
Nickname: Harvard Eddie
Birthplace: Franklin, Massachusetts
B: May 21, 1883
D: October 5, 1918
Batted left, threw right
Ht. 5–11½; **Wt.** 168

Ed Grant

Gross, Greg

Phillies: 1979–88
Outfielder
Birthplace: York, Pennsylvania
B: August 1, 1952
Bats left, throws left
Ht. 5–10; **Wt.** 160

Greg Gross

Gross, who was National League Rookie of the Year in 1974 while playing with the Astros, had arrived in Philadelphia in 1979 as part of an eight-player trade with the Chicago Cubs that also brought the Phils Manny Trillo. Although he never played as a regular with the Phillies, he saw a considerable amount of action each season, hitting as high as .333 in 1979 and .322 in 1984.

Greg saw his most action in 1983 when he appeared in 136 games and hit .302. He started in 52 games in the outfield, playing all three spots.

The one thing Gross didn't do was hit for power. In his entire Phillies career, he hit just two home runs. He had five others during his 17-year big league career, all coming in 1977 with the Cubs when he hit .322.

Gross's career with the Phillies came to an end after the 1988 season. He spent the following year back in Houston before retiring.

Gross, Greg

Phillies	G	AB	H	BA	RBI	R	2B	3B	HR	SA	SB
1979	111	174	58	.333	15	21	6	3	0	.349	5
1980	127	154	37	.240	12	19	7	2	0	.312	1
1981	83	102	23	.225	7	14	6	1	0	.304	2
1982	119	134	40	.299	10	14	4	0	0	.328	4
1983	136	245	74	.302	29	25	12	3	0	.376	3
1984	112	202	65	.322	16	19	9	1	0	.376	1
1985	93	169	44	.260	14	21	5	2	0	.314	1
1986	87	101	25	.248	8	11	5	0	0	.297	1
1987	114	133	38	.286	12	14	4	1	1	.353	0
1988	98	133	27	.203	5	10	1	0	0	.211	0
Career	1,749	3,670	1,058	.288	304	447	130	46	7	.354	39

Gross, Kevin

Phillies: 1983–88
Pitcher
Birthplace: Downey, California
B: June 8, 1961
Bats right, throws right
Ht. 6–5; **Wt.** 203

Kevin Gross was the Phillies' first choice in the secondary phase of the January 1981 free-agent draft and proved his value by winning 60 games in five full seasons and part of another before he was traded to the Montreal Expos.

His best season was 1985 when he became a regular part of the starting rotation and won 15 games. He also completed six starts, pitched two shutouts, and hurled 19 consecutive scoreless innings.

He reached double figures in victories twice in the next three seasons as a starting pitcher and pitched at least 200 innings each year.

In 1988 he worked 232 innings and had a 12–14 record with a 3.69 earned run average. That December he was dealt to the Expos for pitchers Floyd Youmans and Jeff Parrett. Two years later he joined the Los Angeles Dodgers.

Gross needed less than three seasons in the minors before joining the Phillies in the midst of the 1983 pennant race. He posted a 4–6 record, including the only regular-season victory the Phillies had in 12 games against the Dodgers. He did not pitch in the postseason against the Dodgers or Baltimore Orioles.

He started 14 games and made 30 relief appearances in 1984 before joining the regular rotation the following season.

Gross struck out 12 Expos in April 1988. He fanned 10 batters in three other games as a Phillie. He led the staff in victories in 1985, 1986, and 1988.

An accomplished artist, Gross sold several of his paintings while a member of the Phillies. In 1992, he painted another kind of masterpiece, pitching a no-hitter with the Dodgers.

Kevin Gross

Gross, Kevin

Phillies	W	L	Pct	ERA	G	CG	IP	H	BB	SO	ShO
1983	4	6	.400	3.56	17	1	96	100	35	66	1
1984	8	5	.615	4.12	44	1	129	140	44	84	0
1985	15	13	.536	3.41	38	6	206	194	81	151	2
1986	12	12	.500	4.02	37	7	242	240	94	154	2
1987	9	16	.360	4.35	34	3	201	205	87	110	1
1988	12	14	.462	3.69	33	5	232	209	89	162	1

Career: Active major league player

When the Phillies landed Harvey Haddix in a trade with the St. Louis Cardinals in May 1956, there were high hopes that the club had finally found that long-sought first-rate pitcher to go along with the established duo of Robin Roberts and Curt Simmons.

The Phils had paid a high price for Haddix, giving up two seasoned pitchers, Murry Dickson and Herm Wehmeier, and utility infielder Bobby Morgan. At long last, it seemed, they had a third front-line starter of proven merit.

Haddix, however, wasn't around long enough to satisfy that expectation. He played less than two seasons with the Phillies, posting 12–8 and 10–13 records. As was often the case with the club's puzzling trading program of the era, Harvey was shipped away to the Cincinnati Reds at the end of the 1957 season for outfielder Wally Post, who was banished in a short time himself.

While he was with the Phillies, though, Haddix teamed with Simmons to give the team one of the better lefthanded one-two punches in the league. The pair had simultaneous seven-game winning streaks in 1956.

Haddix, a standout fielder who later won three Golden Gloves, was used at times as a pinch-hitter and pinch-runner. In 1957 he hit a career high .309 with the Phillies.

The Kitten, so named because of his resemblance to former St. Louis Cardinal pitcher Harry (The Cat) Brecheen, had his greatest moment after leaving the Phillies. In 1959, having been dealt to the Pittsburgh Pirates, Harvey pitched a perfect game for 12 innings against the Milwaukee Braves. In the 13th inning, the Braves put men on with an error and a walk to Hank Aaron. Joe Adcock followed with a home run, but the final score was counted as 1–0 after Aaron, thinking the ball had hit the wall, touched second and then headed for the dugout and was thus passed on the bases by Adcock.

Harvey, who had a 20–9 record in his rookie year in 1953 with the Cardinals, and an 18–13 mark the next year, was a double-figure winner eight times in his 14-year career. He was chosen for the 1953, 1954, and 1955 National League All-Star teams, and won two games in the 1960 World Series for the Pirates.

In the final three years of his career, the last two of which were with the Baltimore Orioles, Haddix was an effective relief pitcher. The Kitten finished his playing career in 1965.

He has served as a pitching coach in the minors and with the New York Mets, Reds, and Pirates.

Haddix, Harvey

Phillies: 1956–57
Pitcher
Nickname: The Kitten
Birthplace: Medway, Ohio
B: September 18, 1925
Bats left, throws left
Ht. 5–9½; **Wt.** 170

Harvey Haddix

Haddix, Harvey

Phillies	W	L	Pct	ERA	G	CG	IP	H	BB	SO	ShO
1956	12	8	.600	3.48	31	11	207	196	55	154	2
1957	10	13	.435	4.06	27	8	170⅔	176	39	136	1
Career	136	113	.546	3.63	453	99	2,235	2,154	601	1,575	20

Hallman, Bill

Phillies: 1888–89, 1892–97, 1901–03
Second baseman, shortstop
Birthplace: Pittsburgh, Pennsylvania
B: March 30, 1867
D: September 11, 1920
Batted right, threw right
Ht. 5–8; Wt. unknown

During his 14-year career in the big leagues, Bill Hallman had the unusual distinction of playing for three different Philadelphia pro teams. What's more, he played with the Phillies on three different occasions.

The well-traveled Hallman was an infielder of some note when he first joined the Phillies in 1888. Before his playing days were over, Billy had played every position on the diamond, including pitcher and catcher. He played everything but pitcher and first base in his rookie year.

Hallman's primary position was second base. Only two other Phillies second basemen have played more games at that position than Bill.

His first regular position with the Phillies, though, was shortstop.

In 1889, Hallman was moved into that position early in the season as a replacement for veteran Art Irwin. The team captain, Irwin had become disenchanted with the Phillies' manager Harry Wright and had feuded with the pilot. Wright benched Irwin, then sold him in mid-season to Washington.

Hallman was the regular shortstop for only one season. The following year he jumped to the new Players' League formed by the Baseball Brotherhood, the players' union.

Bill was with the Philadelphia club for the one-year existence of the Players' League. The following year, he wound up with the Philadelphia Athletics of the American Association, the city's third big league team.

In 1892, Hallman returned to the Phillies, and for the next five years was their regular second baseman, although he did pitch two innings of relief in a game in 1896.

Hallman strung together some fine seasons for the Phillies. Beginning in 1892, he compiled batting averages of .292, .307, .309, .314, and .320. In three of those seasons he scored more than 100 runs.

In the middle of 1897 the Phillies sent Hallman to St. Louis, where he became the third of four managers that season for the 12th-place Browns. He moved to Brooklyn in 1898 and was the regular second baseman.

After being out of the majors for two years, Hallman wound up in Cleveland in 1901. Early in the season he was sent to the Phillies, and he became their regular second baseman, although he hit only .184 after rejoining the team.

Hallman was the club's starting third baseman in 1902. He concluded his career in 1903 as a reserve infielder and outfielder.

Hallman, Bill

Phillies	G	AB	H	BA	RBI	R	2B	3B	HR	SA	SB
1888	18	63	13	.206	6	5	4	1	0	.302	1
1889	119	462	117	.253	60	67	21	8	2	.346	20
1892	138	586	171	.292	84	106	27	10	2	.382	19
1893	132	596	183	.307	76	119	28	7	4	.398	22
1894	119	505	156	.309	66	107	19	7	0	.374	36
1895	124	539	169	.314	91	94	26	5	1	.386	16
1896	120	469	150	.320	83	82	21	3	2	.390	16
1897	31	126	33	.262	15	16	3	0	0	.286	1
1901	123	445	82	.184	38	46	13	5	0	.236	13
1902	73	254	63	.248	35	14	8	4	0	.311	9
1903	63	198	42	.212	17	20	11	2	0	.288	2
Career	1,503	6,012	1,634	.272	769	937	234	81	21	.348	200

Bill Hallman

Recent records notwithstanding, Billy Hamilton might have been the greatest base stealer ever to play the game of baseball.

Although he played at a time when there were substantial differences from the game as it is today, Hamilton swiped more bases than anyone in major league history, except Rickey Henderson and Lou Brock. Billy's 937 pilfers rank one behind Brock—who accumulated his total in 19 years compared to Hamilton's 14—and 45 more than Ty Cobb.

Hamilton led his league in steals seven times. Three of those times he stole more than 100 bases, and three other times his totals exceeded 90.

He was called the "human rocket," fast as a deer, yet slippery as an eel when sliding into base. In an era when famed base stealer King Kelly made famous the expression "Slide, Kelly, Slide," Hamilton far surpassed even his larceny totals.

Billy was an outstanding hitter, too. His lifetime .344 batting average is tied for sixth place with Ted Williams and Tris Speaker on the list of all-time batting leaders.

In 1961, Hamilton was elected to the Hall of Fame.

Billy broke in with Worcester of the New England League in 1888. He spent one and one-half years with Kansas City of the American Association, where he won the stolen base crown with 117 thefts. He was purchased by the Phillies in 1889 from Kansas City.

In 1890, his first year in Philadelphia, Hamilton became the Phils' leadoff batter and left fielder. His .325 average launched a six-year career as a Phillie in which he joined with Sam Thompson and Ed Delahanty to give the club three future Hall of Fame outfielders in what was probably the greatest outfield ever to perform together.

Hamilton won two batting championships, placing first in 1891 with a .340 average and leading again in 1893 with a .380 mark. His 1891 title made him the Phillies' first batting champion. While with the Phillies, he also led the league in runs three times, including 1894 when he set the still-standing major league record with 192.

A small fellow, Hamilton also holds the current major league record for most consecutive games scoring one or more runs in a season (24). He set the mark in 1894 when he scored 35 runs in those 24 games.

In addition, he holds National League marks for most years with 150 or more runs (four) and most combined hits and walks in a season (346).

Hamilton also has the longest hitting streak in Phillies history. His 36-game streak is the fifth highest in National League history.

Billy has the highest career batting average (.357) of all Phillies. He is also the club's career leader in stolen bases (508) and ranks ninth in runs.

In 1890, Hamilton won his first stolen base title with the Phillies with 102 burglaries. The following year, while playing 133 games, he swiped 111, which ranked as an all-time National League record until broken in 1974 by Lou Brock. "Billy's record," said one writer, "may last to the end of time."

While he was running opposing catchers ragged, Hamilton also won his first batting crown, led the league in walks (102), runs (141), and hits (179), and at one point performed the unusual feat of slugging three triples in one game.

In 1892, Hamilton finished second in the league batting race with a .330 average. But the next year, he was back on top with a .380 mark. That season, he and his outfield teammates Thompson and Delahanty finished first, second, and third in the batting race. The Phillies, despite a fourth-place finish, led the league in hitting with a team average of .301.

By 1893, Billy had been moved to center field, where his speed was of much more value to the team. From then on, Hamilton stayed in that position.

Hamilton's best year at the plate took place in 1894. He hit .404. Not only did he fail to win the batting title, despite having the highest average of his career, but he finished fifth in the race. And three of his outfield teammates were ahead of him (including reserve Tuck Turner).

Nevertheless, that was the year that Hamilton scored his record-breaking 192 runs. He also led the circuit in walks (102) and stolen bases (98), and for the first of two times he went over the 200-hit mark with 220.

Hamilton, Billy

Phillies: 1890–95
Center fielder
Nickname: Sliding Billy
Birthplace: Newark, New Jersey
B: February 16, 1866
D: December 15, 1940
Batted left, threw left
Ht. 5–6; **Wt.** 165

Billy Hamilton

Hamilton continued his lusty hitting in 1895, swatting the ball at a .389 clip, which didn't even make the top five. He did, however, again lead the league in runs (166), stolen bases (97), and walks (96).

Having given the Phillies six straight outstanding seasons, Hamilton figured he deserved a modest salary boost. John Rogers, the man running the club by then, took the cheap way out by trading Billy to Boston for fading third baseman Billy Nash. It was the first in a long series of bad trades made by the Phillies over the ensuing decades.

Hamilton continued to perform brilliantly in Boston, hitting well over .300 for the next five years. He won two more stolen base titles.

After he retired as a big league player after the 1901 season, Hamilton became a player-manager in the minors. He won three batting titles, including one in 1904 when he hit .412. He quit playing in 1910, but continued to manage. Later, he became a part owner of the Worcester team, then a member of the Eastern League. He also served for several years as a scout with the Boston Red Sox.

Hamilton, who had invested wisely, lived comfortably on property he had purchased in Clinton, Maryland, until his death in 1940.

Hamilton, Billy

Phillies	G	AB	H	BA	RBI	R	2B	3B	HR	SA	SB
1890	123	496	161	.325	49	133	13	9	2	.399	102
1891	133	527	179	.340	60	141	23	7	2	.421	111
1892	139	554	183	.330	53	132	21	7	3	.410	57
1893	82	355	135	.380	44	110	22	7	5	.524	43
1894	129	544	220	.404	87	192	25	15	4	.528	98
1895	123	517	201	.389	74	166	22	6	7	.495	97
Career	1,591	6,268	2,158	.344	736	1,690	242	94	40	.432	937

Hamner, Granny

Phillies: 1944–59
Shortstop, second base, pitcher
Nickname: Ham
Birthplace: Richmond, Virginia
B: April 26, 1927
Bats right, throws right
Ht. 5–10; Wt. 163

The person who originated the nickname "Fightin' Phils" must have had Granny Hamner in mind. The clutch-hitting Phillies captain was a cocky firebrand who battled and clawed every step of the way.

Ham, as his teammates called him, typified the spirit of the Fightin' Phils. He was a take-charge kind of player with a quick temper who never took any guff from anybody.

Hamner was a regular for the Phillies for 10 seasons. He also played parts of five other years in Philadelphia. Mostly he was a shortstop, but he also made his mark as a second baseman and even tried his hand at pitching in the twilight years of his career.

Signed for an $8,000 bonus in 1944 at age 17, Hamner was never a .300 hitter as a regular, but he was an extremely reliable batter with men on base, as his RBI totals each year indicated. Furthermore, Granny was an exceptionally fine fielder with a strong arm and a wide range.

Hamner was the anchorman and leader in the Phillies' infield in 1950. That year he enjoyed one of his finest seasons, hitting .270 while driving in 82 runs.

Granny, whose personality and style of play were similar to those of the other great shortstop in modern Phillies history, Larry Bowa, was a child prodigy for the Phils after the Brooklyn Dodgers had decided against claiming him. Signed right out of high school, he was inserted immediately into the starting lineup. Despite his tender age, Ham hit .247 in 21 games. At one point, however, he made six errors in one game.

His confidence somewhat shaken, Hamner was sent to Utica in 1945 where the manager, Eddie Sawyer, took special pains to get him back on track. Hamner returned to the Phillies at the end of the season, joining his older brother Garvin, also an infielder whose big league career consisted of 32 games with the '45 Phils.

Hamner was in the Army during most of the the 1946 season, then spent the bulk of 1947 back with Utica. After hitting .291 there, he came to the Phillies to stay in 1948.

With veteran Eddie Miller entrenched at shortstop, Granny played most of the '48 campaign at second base, taking the job away from Emil Verban. He hit a respectable .260. The following year he was moved to shortstop while the slower Miller was switched to second. It was the start of a long, successful tenure at that position for Hamner.

In 1949, Granny led the National League in at-bats, and the league's shortstops in assists and double plays. He also hit .263 while beginning to establish himself as a frequent doubles hitter. Four times during his career, Granny hit more than 30 doubles, including the 32 he hit in 1949 and the 39 he hit to tie for second in the league in 1954.

The 1949 season also began one other Hamner trait. He played in every game that season, as he also did in 1950 and 1953. His 157 games in 1950 tied Joe Tinker of the Cubs (in 1908) for a National League record for most games played (prior to the expanded schedule) by a shortstop.

When the 1950 season began, Granny was just 22 years old. But already, he was being placed among the elite of major league shortstops. He had all the tools for stardom, and he was as adept with the bat as he was with the arm and glove.

The season was filled with timely hits and brilliant fielding plays by Hamner. In the World Series, Granny was the only Phillie to hit for a respectable average. He had six hits in 14 at-bats for a .429 average.

Granny Hamner

Unfortunately, Hamner also made a crucial error in the Series, bobbling Bobby Brown's grounder in the eighth inning of the third game. At the time, the Phillies had their only lead of the Series, 2–1, Granny having scored the go-ahead run. But a run scored on the error, and the Yankees went on to score again in the ninth for a 3–2 victory.

The following season Hamner's average slipped to .255. In addition, his 477-game consecutive streak came to an end on September 19. In 1952, although he was removed as captain by manager Eddie Sawyer, Granny came back strongly. En route to a .275 average, he was selected the starting shortstop for the National League All-Stars.

Hamner was a member of the All-Star team again in 1953. Then in 1954, the Phillies shifted Granny to second base so they could get Ted Kazanski into the lineup at shortstop. Again, Ham was named to the All-Star team, this time as the starting second baseman. With that choice, Hamner became the first player in the history of the All-Star game to win starting berths at two different positions.

Granny had career highs in home runs (21) and RBI (92) in 1953. The next year he had a career high in average (.299).

In 1956 an injury to his left shoulder having hampered his ability to play the infield, Hamner began thinking about becoming a pitcher. The Phillies put him in three games on the mound during the season. In his first appearance, he pitched one inning and struck out two of the hard-hitting Milwaukee Braves. Later, he lost one game.

Hamner went to the Phillies' instructional school that winter and took intensive lessons in pitching. Although possessed of a strong arm that could generate a lively fastball, Granny also worked to develop a knuckleball. Throughout spring training of 1957, Ham worked hard to become a pitcher.

He hurled only one scoreless inning that season, then pretty much abandoned the idea of pitching. The Phillies still had a spot for him, though. Hamner went back to being the club's regular second baseman.

Gran didn't have much of a year at the plate in 1957. The ensuing year, he was off to a good start when bad luck arrived. Hamner hurt his knee and missed much of the season. He still hit .301 during a limited number of appearances.

Early in 1959, Hamner and the Phillies parted company when Gran was traded to the Cleveland Indians for pitcher Humberto Robinson. Granny played the rest of the season with the Indians, then went back to the minors to try to learn more about pitching. He tried to make a comeback as a pitcher in 1962 with the Kansas City Royals, but had one loss in three games. Ham retired at the end of the season.

During his career with the Phillies, Hamner etched his name among the club's all-time leaders in a number of categories. He has more home runs than any other Phillies shortstop (61).

He ranks third in games played among shortstops, and among all Phillies he is seventh in at-bats and doubles.

Hamner, Granny (Granville)

Phillies	G	AB	H	BA	RBI	R	2B	3B	HR	SA	SB
1944	21	77	19	.247	5	6	1	0	0	.260	0
1945	14	41	7	.171	6	3	2	0	0	.220	0
1946	2	7	1	.143	0	0	0	0	0	.143	0
1947	2	7	2	.286	0	1	0	0	0	.286	0
1948	129	446	116	.260	48	42	21	5	3	.350	2
1949	154	662	174	.263	53	83	32	5	6	.353	6
1950	157	637	172	.270	82	78	27	5	11	.380	2
1951	150	589	150	.255	72	61	23	7	9	.363	10
1952	151	596	164	.275	87	74	30	5	17	.428	7
1953	154	609	168	.276	92	90	30	8	21	.455	2
1954	152	596	178	.299	89	83	39	11	13	.466	1
1955	104	405	104	.257	43	57	12	4	5	.343	0
1956	122	401	90	.224	42	42	24	3	4	.329	2
1957	133	502	114	.227	62	59	19	5	10	.345	3
1958	35	133	40	.301	18	18	7	3	2	.444	0
1959	21	64	19	.297	6	10	4	0	2	.437	0
Career	1,531	5,839	1,529	.262	708	711	272	62	104	.383	35

Harper, George

Phillies: 1924–26
Outfielder
Birthplace: Arlington, Kentucky
B: June 24, 1892
D: August 18, 1978
Batted left, threw right
Ht. 5–8; **Wt.** 167

George Harper

George Harper spent only one full season of his 11 in the majors with the Phillies (an appendectomy put him on the disabled list for half of another), but it was a beauty.

Playing for Art Fletcher in 1925, Harper batted .349, sixth best in the National League, in 132 games. He smacked 18 home runs, drove in 97, and had a .558 slugging percentage, fifth best in the league.

The year before, in a season he split between the Phils and Reds (he was obtained in a trade for Curt Walker), Harper was the leading fielding outfielder in the National League with only four errors in 286 chances.

Coming off the 1925 season, Harper quite naturally thought he was worth more money. Phillies president William F. Baker, also quite naturally, pleaded abject poverty. Harper became a holdout, didn't sign until March 29, and didn't join the team until it was on its way north from its Florida spring training site.

Still he got off to a good start and was hitting .314 after 56 games when he was rushed to a Boston hospital for an appendectomy on July 4. He missed the remainder of the season.

In January 1927 the Phillies traded Harper and Butch Henline, another holdout the previous spring, to the New York Giants for minor league sensation Fresco Thompson. Harper hit .331 for the Giants, later moved on to the Cardinals and Braves, and retired after the 1929 season as a lifetime .303 hitter.

Harper was half owner of a sawmill in Magnolia, Arkansas, where he died in 1978.

Harper, George

Phillies	G	AB	H	BA	RBI	R	2B	3B	HR	SA	SB
1924	109	411	121	.294	55	68	26	6	16	.504	10
1925	132	495	173	.349	97	86	35	7	18	.558	10
1926	56	194	61	.314	38	32	6	5	7	.505	6
Career	1,073	3,398	1,030	.303	528	505	158	43	91	.455	58

Hayes, Von

Phillies: 1983–91
Outfielder, first baseman
Birthplace: Stockton, California
B: August 31, 1958
Bats left, throws right
Ht. 6–5; **Wt.** 185

Von Hayes cost the Phillies five players when they made a deal with the Cleveland Indians on December 9, 1982. They only received two for him when they sent him to the California Angels nine seasons later.

His value to Phillies fans was reflected in those numbers. The slim Californian never lived up to his "new Ted Williams" billing after he arrived at the Vet. Also, Pete Rose hung the "5-for-1" nickname on him almost as soon as he joined the team, and he carried it like an albatross around his neck for the rest of his career in Philadelphia.

Even some truly outstanding seasons never quite made him the hero people expected him to become.

His best season was in 1986 when he batted .305 with 19 home runs, 98 RBI, 186 hits, 24 stolen bases, and a league-leading 107 runs scored. At 28, he finally seemed ready to fulfill his enormous potential.

But he never quite approached that season again. His 26-homer, 28-steal, 101-walk season in 1989 was offset by a .259 batting average, second lowest in his Phillies career. It did, however, mark only the seventh time in club history that anyone had a 20–20 year.

Hindsight is always 20–20, though, and Phillies fans never focused properly on Hayes after the club gave up veteran Manny Trillo, super prospect Julio Franco, and three other players for the youngster with the sweet lefthanded swing despite a .250 rookie season with the Indians.

Hayes got off to a woeful start in the Phillies' pennant-winning season. He wound up hitting .265 in 124 games, then went hitless in just five post-season at-bats.

The following season, he rebounded to .292 with 16 homers, but the fans did not warm to him. And nothing he did from then until he was traded for Ruben Amaro, Jr., and Kyle Abbott would change their feelings. His career hit its nadir in 1991 when he failed to hit a home run in 284 at-bats during an injury-filled .225 season.

Despite the lack of respect, Hayes put up some pretty impressive numbers in his nine years with the Phillies. He ranks sixth in the modern era in career bases on balls with 619 and fourth in stolen bases with 202. His on-base percentage of .363 is ninth best since 1926. He also ranks fourth in intentional walks (74), fifth in sacrifice flies (43), and seventh in strikeouts (671).

Von Hayes

His 121 walks in 1987 are the fourth best ever for the Phillies. His 46 doubles in 1986 rank sixth.

The most memorable performance in his career happened in the first inning of a game against the New York Mets in 1985 when he hit two home runs and drove in six runs. He became the first player in major league history to hit two homers in the first inning, and he tied all-time records with two extra-base hits, two runs scored, and eight total bases in an inning.

A year later, he connected for three homers and drove in six runs in a game against the San Francisco Giants.

In 1986 he was named National League player of the week three times. Hank Aaron is the only other player so honored.

Hayes, Von

Phillies	G	AB	H	BA	RBI	R	2B	3B	HR	SA	SB
1983	124	351	93	.265	32	45	9	5	6	.370	20
1984	152	561	164	.292	67	85	27	6	16	.447	48
1985	152	570	150	.263	70	76	30	4	13	.398	21
1986	158	610	186	.305	98	107	46	2	19	.480	24
1987	158	556	154	.277	84	84	36	5	21	.473	16
1988	104	367	100	.272	45	43	28	2	6	.409	20
1989	154	540	140	.259	78	93	27	2	26	.461	28
1990	129	467	122	.261	73	70	14	3	17	.413	16
1991	77	284	64	.225	21	43	15	1	0	.306	9
Career	1,495	5,249	1,402	.267	696	767	282	36	143	.416	253

Hebner, Richie

Phillies: 1977–78
First baseman
Birthplace: Brighton, Massachusetts
B: November 26, 1947
Bats left, throws right
Ht. 6–1; **Wt.** 195

Richie Hebner

When the Andy Messersmith decision mandated free agency and the reentry draft resulted in incredibly escalating salaries, Phillies owner Ruly Carpenter vowed that he wasn't going to get involved in such foolishness. Richie Hebner changed his mind for him.

Hebner became a free agent after the 1976 season, his eighth as the Pirates' regular third baseman. His level of production with the Bucs had been consistently high, and his salary demands were reasonable. And the Phils had a gaping hole at first base since Dick Allen had written his good-bye during the 1976 division-clinching festivities in Montreal. Hebner reached for a first baseman's mitt to break in as Carpenter reached for his checkbook.

For two seasons, Hebner was a highly efficient member of the Phillies. He was the one dependable lefthanded hitter with reasonable power, he did more than an adequate job at his new position, and he kept the clubhouse loose with his friendliness and humor.

An example of the latter: one night, after Hebner had delivered the winning hit, a writer asked Richie if he still dug graves with his dad in the off-season. Hebner replied with a straight face: "Don't close your eyes too long."

Hebner also buried several of the better righthanded pitchers in the league during his two-year hitch with the Phillies. He smacked 35 homers and drove in 133 runs in 832 at-bats.

His philosophy of hitting was hardly out of the Ted Williams' happy-zone book.

"See the ball and hit it," he explained during his last season with the Phillies. "I see the ball, hit it, run, take a shower, couple of drinks and go to bed.

The more you think in this game, the more you get in trouble. Some guys explain baseball like they went through Harvard."

He played on two Eastern Division champs in two seasons, but when the Phillies signed Pete Rose prior to the 1979 campaign, Hebner didn't need a Harvard degree to realize he was odd-man-out in the lineup. He also made it known early that he wasn't planning on spending much time on the bench. Late in spring training, the Phillies, desperate for a starting pitcher, traded Hebner to the Mets for Nino Espinosa.

Hebner, Richie

Phillies	G	AB	H	BA	RBI	R	2B	3B	HR	SA	SB
1977	118	397	113	.285	62	67	17	4	18	.484	7
1978	137	435	123	.283	71	61	22	3	17	.464	4
Career	1,908	6,144	1,694	.276	890	865	273	57	203	.438	38

The name of Ken Heintzelman may not be among the first ones to surface on any list of the 1950 Whiz Kids, but the mild-mannered pitcher made a quiet but important contribution to the Phillies' second National League pennant.

Heintzelman was a stylish lefthander who had broken into pro ball in 1935 as a 19-year-old. He made it to the majors on a permanent basis in 1939 with the Pittsburgh Pirates.

With the exception of three years of military service, Kenny toiled for five uneventful seasons with the Pirates, his best record being an 11–11 mark in 1941.

Heintzelman, who had the reputation of being a "hard-luck" pitcher, battled injury and illness through much of his career. His fortunes finally began to change in May 1947, when the Pirates sold him to the Phillies.

Ken continued to post losing records for the next two years, although in 1948 he beat the New York Giants, 8–1, with a one-hitter. Then in 1949 his luck turned around. That year, Heintzelman was one of the aces of the National League, winning 17 and losing only 10, far and away his best year in the majors.

Tied for the league lead with five shutouts, Ken at one point won nine straight, the season's longest winning streak, and he hurled 32⅔ consecutive scoreless innings. Philadelphia fans voted him the team's most valuable player.

It was a season in which everything clicked for Ken. From a team standpoint, Heintzelman's success was important because it helped to pave the way for the Phillies' rise up the National League ladder.

The 1950 season proved to be a disappointment for Ken from a won-lost standpoint. He was lifted from the starting rotation after getting off to a 1–8 start. The record, however, was misleading. In eight of his 13 starts, Ken held the opposition to three runs or less.

From mid-season on, Heintzelman toiled in the bullpen. Late in the season, he won two important games, one with 6⅓ innings of relief against Cincinnati after starter Bubba Church was hit by a line drive, and one in a starting role the final week of the season against Boston.

Heintzelman started the third game of the World Series in 1950. He gave up only four hits in 7⅔ innings, but three straight walks sent him to the showers with the Phils holding their only lead of the Series, 2–1. After a Granny Hamner error allowed the Yankees to tie the score, the Phils eventually lost the game in 10 innings, 3–2.

Ken pitched two more years with the Phillies, then retired from baseball after the 1952 season. One of his finest games came in 1951 when he defeated Warren Spahn and the Boston Braves, 1–0, in 15 innings.

Heintzelman, Ken

Phillies: 1947–52
Pitcher
Birthplace: Peruque, Missouri
B: October 14, 1915
Bats right, throws left
Ht. 5–11½; **Wt.** 185

Ken Heintzelman

Heintzelman, Ken

Phillies	W	L	Pct	ERA	G	CG	IP	H	BB	SO	ShO
1947	7	10	.412	4.04	24	8	136	144	46	55	0
1948	6	11	.353	4.29	27	5	130	117	45	57	2
1949	17	10	.630	3.02	33	15	250	239	93	65	5
1950	3	9	.250	4.09	23	4	125⅓	122	54	39	1
1951	6	12	.333	4.18	35	3	118⅓	119	53	55	1
1952	1	3	.250	3.16	23	0	42⅔	41	12	20	0
Career	77	98	.440	3.93	319	66	1,501⅔	1,540	630	564	19

Henline, Walter

Phillies: 1921–26
Catcher
Nickname: Butch
Birthplace: Fort Wayne, Indiana
B: December 20, 1894
D: October 9, 1957
Batted right, threw right
Ht. 5–10; **Wt.** 175

Walter Henline

Although the Irish Meusel trade by President William F. Baker to the New York Giants in 1921 has been one of the most criticized deals in Phillies history—and rightly so, considering the devious way Baker set up the deal—it cannot be said that the Phillies came away empty-handed.

Hardly. In addition to a good hitting outfielder named Curt Walker, they also picked up catcher Butch Henline, who had all of one game's experience in the major leagues.

Henline turned out to be a diamond in the rough. Over the period from 1922 to 1926, he caught more games than any other Phillies catcher and put together a lifetime batting average of .304 with the team.

His first two full seasons with the team turned out to be his best. In 1922 he managed a career-high 14 home runs and 64 RBI and a .316 average in 125 games. That year he became the first National Leaguer in the modern era to hit three home runs in one game when his three round-trippers powered the Phillies to a 26–23 victory over the Chicago Cubs.

In 1923, though his power and appearances slackened, he put together a lifetime-topping .324 batting average.

But even a catcher who could hit could not escape the ultimate destiny of nearly everyone who played for Trader Baker. On January 7, 1927, Henline went to Brooklyn in a three-corner deal that also involved the Giants and brought Fresco Thompson to the Phillies.

Butch caught for the Dodgers for three years as a backup, then moved on to the White Sox for two brief seasons there. He later became a respected major league umpire.

Henline, Walter

Phillies	G	AB	H	BA	RBI	R	2B	3B	HR	SA	SB
1921	33	111	34	.306	8	8	2	0	0	.324	1
1922	125	430	136	.316	64	57	20	4	14	.479	2
1923	111	330	107	.324	46	45	14	3	7	.448	7
1924	115	289	82	.284	35	41	18	4	5	.426	1
1925	93	263	80	.304	48	43	12	5	8	.479	3
1926	99	283	80	.283	30	32	14	1	2	.360	1
Career	740	2,101	611	.291	268	258	96	21	40	.414	18

For reasons that had to do with his unfulfilled potential, Pancho Herrera has often been held up as the symbol of futility with regard to Phillies baseball. He was a classic case of a player who couldn't do in the major leagues what he did in the minors.

A large man who was extremely fast for a guy his size, Herrera was earmarked for stardom when he first joined the Phillies in 1958. Pancho was going to be the big power hitter who also hit for high average.

Certainly, his minor league credentials supported that expectation. The Cuban slugger hit .308 for Schenectady in his first season in pro ball in 1955. After a .286 season in the same town, he ripped off .306 and .282 marks in the next two years at Miami.

That earned Pancho a trip to the big leagues in late 1958. He went 0-for-11 initially, but then cranked out eight hits in his next 10 at-bats, and finished the season with a .270 average in 29 games.

Herrera needed a little more seasoning, so he spent the 1959 campaign with Buffalo. Pancho tore up International League pitching, leading the circuit in hitting (.329), hits (187), home runs (37), and RBI (128).

In 1960, after Ed Bouchee was traded, Pancho was the Phillies' regular first baseman. Pancho hit a highly creditable .281 with 17 home runs and 71 RBI. At one point in the season, he had a 20-game hitting streak. Unfortunately, he struck out 136 times, which stands as the National League record for most strikeouts in a 154-game season. He also led National League first basemen in assists and errors.

At times the Phillies used Herrera at second base in 1960, which surely qualified him as one of the largest second sackers ever to play the position. That venture was squelched, however, and Pancho returned full-time to first base in 1961.

His average sloughed off to .258, and his home run total dropped to 13. During the winter, the Phillies traded Herrera and another young player who never lived up to his promise, Ted Savage, to the Pittsburgh Pirates for third baseman Don Hoak. Unable to make the Pirates' roster, Pancho, as it turned out, had played his last big league game in 1961 when he was with the Phillies.

Herrera, Pancho

Phillies: 1958, 1960–61
First baseman, second baseman, third baseman
Nickname: Frank
Birthplace: Santiago, Cuba
B: June 16, 1934
Bats right, throws right
Ht. 6–3; Wt. 220

Pancho Herrera

Herrera, Pancho (Juan Francisco)

Phillies	G	AB	H	BA	RBI	R	2B	3B	HR	SA	SB
1958	29	63	17	.270	6	5	3	0	1	.365	1
1960	145	512	144	.281	71	61	26	6	17	.455	2
1961	126	400	103	.258	51	56	17	2	13	.408	5
Career	300	975	264	.271	128	122	46	8	31	.430	8

Over the years the Phillies made a habit of peddling good, young pitchers to other teams where they often became standout hurlers. Kirby Higbe was one of those pitchers.

Higbe was in Philadelphia for only a short time before going on to stardom with the Brooklyn Dodgers. He had come to the Phillies in 1939 in a trade with the Chicago Cubs in which the Phillies gave up another good, young pitcher, Claude Passeau, for Higbe, pitcher Ray Harrell, outfielder Joe Marty, and $50,000.

In slightly less than two years with the Phillies, the uninhibited hurler with a lively fastball, who had been up briefly with the Cubs in 1937 and 1938, established himself as the ace of the pitching staff. He had a 10–14 record for the Phils in 1939 and a 14–19 mark in 1940. In both years, Higbe led the league in walks, and in 1940 he led in strikeouts and was picked for the All-Star team.

That fall Higbe was sent to the Dodgers in exchange for $100,000 and three nondescript players (pitchers Vito Tamulis and Bill Crouch and catcher Mickey Livingston). He celebrated his liberation from the lowly Phils by

Higbe, Kirby

Phillies: 1939–40
Pitcher
Birthplace: Columbia, South Carolina
B: April 8, 1915
D: May 6, 1985
Batted right, threw right
Ht. 5–11; Wt. 190

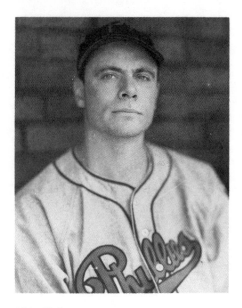

Kirby Higbe

posting a 22–8 record and pitching the Dodgers to the National League pennant.

In the next three seasons (wrapped around two years in the service), Higbe won 46 games for Brooklyn, including a record of 17–8 in 1946. Later, Kirby pitched for the Pittsburgh Pirates and New York Giants before retiring in 1950 after 12 years in the majors.

Higbe, Kirby

Phillies	W	L	Pct	ERA	G	CG	IP	H	BB	SO	ShO
1939	10	14	.416	4.86	34	14	187	208	101	79	1
1940	14	19	.424	3.72	41	20	283	242	121	137	1
Career	118	101	.539	3.69	418	98	1,952⅓	1,763	979	971	11

Hoerner, Joe

Phillies: 1970–72, 1975
Pitcher
Birthplace: Dubuque, Iowa
B: November 12, 1936
Bats right, throws left
Ht. 6–1; **Wt.** 200

Joe Hoerner

In his two tours of duty with the Phillies, Joe Hoerner, who didn't make it to the major leagues until he was 28 but stayed around until he was 40, proved himself an excellent lefthanded short reliever.

In fact, he was so terrific in 1970 that he was the Phillies' only representative at the All-Star Game. That year, he had a 9–5 record with nine saves. His nine relief victories led the National League.

He had joined the Phillies that year as part of the trade with the Cardinals that sent Dick Allen to St. Louis for Tim McCarver.

Joe had a 1.97 ERA in 46 games the following year. In 1972 he was traded to the Atlanta Braves along with a minor leaguer for a couple of busts named Jim Nash and Gary Niebauer. The minor leaguer turned out to be Andre Thornton.

Twice in the early 1970s with the Phillies, Hoerner suffered irregular heartbeats while pitching. It was not the first problem he had with his heart. In 1956 he had driven a car into a tree in his hometown of Decatur, Iowa. Three years later he began having dizzy spells. In 1970 doctors traced his problem to strain on his heart and the 1956 accident. A hometown doctor suggested that Joe switch from overhand motion to sidearm. It turned out to be great advice as Hoerner's wicked sidearm delivery drove fear into every lefthanded hitter except the Cubs' Billy Williams, whom Hoerner could hardly retire.

After the 1974 season the Kansas City Royals released Hoerner, and it looked like his career might be over at the age of 37. But Phillies GM Paul Owens envisioned Joe as the ideal man to work out of his bullpen to get one lefthanded batter out. Hoerner came back to Philadelphia and gave Danny Ozark a 2.57 ERA in 21 innings and 25 games.

Hoerner, Joe

Phillies	W	L	Pct	ERA	G	CG	IP	H	BB	SO	ShO
1970	9	5	.643	2.64	44	0	58	53	20	39	0
1971	4	5	.444	1.97	49	0	73	57	21	57	0
1972	0	2	.000	2.05	15	0	22	21	5	12	0
1975	0	0	.000	2.57	25	0	21	25	8	20	0
Career	39	34	.534	2.99	493	0	563	519	181	412	0

Switch-hitting Walt Holke, who came to the Phillies near the tag end of an 11-year big league career, was a stabilizing force around first base, something the team had been lacking ever since Fred Luderus ran out of steam in 1919.

The sack was handled by Gene Paulette in 1920 before Commissioner Kennesaw Mountain Landis barred him from the game. Ed Konetchy took over for the bulk of 1921, and Roy Leslie took a turn in 1922, but was found lacking.

Holke, who had hit as high an average as .351 with the Giants and who had also played first for the Braves on a regular basis for four years, was purchased from Boston before the 1923 season. That year he batted .311 in 147 games and led the league in double plays by a first baseman with 136, while fielding .991. The following season he played 148 games and batted an even .300.

Holke made 42 putouts at first base in a 26-inning game.

In 1925 he began the year as the regular, but lost his job to Chicken Hawks and was sold to the Cincinnati Reds on waivers in July. The Reds released him at the end of the season.

Holke, Walt

Phillies	G	AB	H	BA	RBI	R	2B	3B	HR	SA	SB
1923	147	562	175	.311	70	64	31	4	7	.418	7
1924	148	563	169	.300	64	60	23	6	6	.394	3
1925	39	86	21	.244	17	11	5	0	1	.337	0
Career	1,212	4,456	1,278	.287	487	464	153	58	24	.363	81

Holke, Walt

Phillies: 1923–25
First baseman
Birthplace: St. Louis
Nickname: Union Man
B: December 25, 1892
D: October 12, 1954
Batted both, threw left
Ht. 6–1½; Wt. 185

Walt Holke

Without the relief pitching of Al Holland, the Phillies never would have won the National League pennant in 1983.

The hard-throwing lefthander replaced an aging Tug McGraw as the club's lefthanded closer that season after the Phillies obtained him and second baseman Joe Morgan from the San Francisco Giants for pitchers Mike Krukow and Mark Davis and minor league outfielder Charles Penigar.

The North Carolina A&T graduate immediately had his finest major league season, winning eight games and saving 25 with a 2.25 earned run average in 68 appearances. In 92 innings he struck out 100 batters while walking only 30. He was named the National League relief pitcher of the year.

His season patterned the Phillies' year—okay at first, terrific after the All-Star Game, and torrid down the stretch. Holland allowed just seven earned runs in 54 innings after the All-Star Game. In his last 15 appearances, he earned seven saves and was charged with just one earned run in 19⅓ innings pitched.

He carried his excellence into the postseason. In the League Championship Series against the Los Angeles Dodgers, he struck out three in three scoreless innings over two games. In the World Series against the Baltimore Orioles, he pitched 3⅔ scoreless innings and struck out five.

He was not nearly as effective in 1984. Although he saved 29 games, he slipped to a 5–10 record, and his ERA jumped to 3.40 in 68 appearances.

On April 20, 1985, Holland was traded to the Pittsburgh Pirates for Kent Tekulve. He later pitched for the California Angels and New York Yankees before leaving the major league scene in 1987.

His 29 saves in 1984 tie for the third highest ever recorded in a season by a Phillies pitcher, and the 25 in 1983 rank seventh. His 55 saves are seventh on the team's all-time list, and his combination of 13 victories and 55 saves is the eighth highest total in the team's record book.

Holland, Al

Phillies: 1983–85
Pitcher
Birthplace: Roanoke, Virginia
B: August 16, 1952
Bats right, throws left
Ht. 5–11; Wt. 207

Al Holland

Holland, Al

Phillies	W	L	Pct	ERA	G	CG	IP	H	BB	SO	ShO
1983	8	4	.667	2.25	68	0	92	63	30	100	0
1984	5	10	.333	3.40	68	0	98	82	30	61	0
1985	0	1	.000	4.50	3	0	4	5	4	1	0
Career	34	30	.531	2.98	384	0	646	548	232	513	0

Hughes, Tommy

Phillies: 1941–42, 1946–47
Pitcher
Birthplace: Ashley, Pennsylvania
B: October 7, 1919
D: November 28, 1990
Batted right, threw right
Ht. 6–1; Wt. 190

Tommy Hughes

If World War II hadn't occurred, there's no telling how good Tommy Hughes might have been. The tall righthander was a prime example of the way players' talents were eroded by long years in the military service.

When Hughes joined the Phillies' pitching staff in 1941, he had a blazing fastball and the physical equipment to be a big winner in the major leagues.

In his first season in the minors, Tommy had posted a 9–0 record in 13 games at Dover in the Eastern Shore League. He struck out 85 batters in 80 innings. In 1940 he had a 14–11 mark at Baltimore in the International League.

Hughes rang up 9–14 and 12–18 records in his first two years with the Phillies, despite playing for teams hopelessly mired in the National League cellar. In 1941, Tommy hurled a one-hitter against the Chicago Cubs.

He joined the Army that winter and spent more than four years in the service. After his discharge in early 1946, Hughes rejoined the Phillies, but he never regained his prewar style.

Following losing seasons in 1946 and 1947, Tommy was traded to the Cincinnati Reds for outfielder-infielder Bert Haas. The veteran Haas had a good season for the Phils in 1948, but Hughes couldn't win a game for the Reds and was released.

Hughes, Tommy

Phillies	W	L	Pct	ERA	G	CG	IP	H	BB	SO	ShO
1941	9	14	.391	4.45	34	5	170	187	82	59	2
1942	12	18	.400	3.06	40	19	253	224	99	77	0
1946	6	9	.400	4.38	29	3	111	123	44	34	2
1947	4	11	.267	3.47	29	4	127	121	59	44	1
Career	31	56	.356	3.92	144	31	688	698	308	221	5

Hurst, Don

Phillies: 1928–34
First Baseman
Birthplace: Maysville, Kentucky
B: August 12, 1905
D: December 6, 1952
Batted left, threw left
Ht. 6–0; Wt. 215

Don Hurst's career was brief and brilliant. He lasted in the major leagues for only seven years, all but four months with the Phillies and, along with Lefty O'Doul and Chuck Klein, gave the Phillies an awesome middle of the batting order in 1929 and 1930.

His 19 home runs as a rookie in 1928 were a Phillies record for a first-year player until Dick Allen broke it in 1964. Hurst came to the Phillies that season from the St. Louis Cardinal farm system as the key in a deal that sent catcher Jimmie Wilson to the Cards. Wilson came back to the Phillies in 1934, and this time the Phils traded Don to the Cubs for Dolph Camilli.

In between those two trades, Hurst was a constant home run threat at Baker Bowl and everywhere else in the league. He was a big, strong guy who hit over .300 for four straight seasons from 1929 to 1932 and who led the National League in hitting for part of the 1932 season, finishing at .339.

That season, he led the National League in RBI with 143. He had 125 RBI in 1929, a year in which he hit home runs in six consecutive games.

The joke in those seasons was that all the Philadelphia newspapers had a standing headline kept in the composing room for use at least twice a week. It read: Klein Hits Two Home Runs, Hurst One but Phillies Lose.

By all logic, Hurst should have been entering his peak seasons after 1932. He was just 27 years old, and he had 102 home runs in his five big league seasons. But it didn't work out that way.

"I think maybe he was sick or something of that sort," former Phillies owner Gerald Nugent once offered. Whatever the reason, Hurst's star dipped almost as quickly as it had risen. In 1933 he figured he deserved a lot more money based on his outstanding 1932 figures. The Phillies disagreed, and Hurst held out almost until opening day. That sequence of events might explain why his average slipped to .267 and his home run output dipped from 24 to eight. But things got no better the following year. After 40 games, his average was .262 and the Phillies moved him to Chicago for Camilli in what turned out to be one of the better deals in the team's history. With the Cubs, he batted .199 in 51 games and was sent to the minors, winding up eventually in Los Angeles where he had threatened to go to become an actor during his hold out. He died on his way to a hospital in 1952 at the age of 47. One of his sons, James, made it as a Broadway actor, fulfilling his father's ambition to go on stage.

On a baseball stage for five terrific years, Don Hurst could light it up with anybody.

Hurst, Don

Phillies	G	AB	H	BA	RBI	R	2B	3B	HR	SA	SB
1928	107	396	113	.285	64	73	23	4	19	.508	3
1929	154	589	179	.304	125	100	29	4	31	.525	10
1930	119	391	128	.327	78	78	19	3	17	.522	6
1931	137	489	149	.305	91	63	37	5	11	.468	8
1932	150	579	196	.339	143	109	41	4	24	.547	10
1933	147	550	147	.267	76	58	27	8	8	.389	3
1934	40	130	34	.262	21	16	9	0	2	.377	1
Career	905	3,275	976	.298	610	510	190	28	115	.478	41

Don Hurst

Jackson, Grant

The ironic thing is that in the 11 years after he left the Phillies, Grant Jackson got 11 major league starts and became an outstanding reliever. Ironic because one of the reasons the Phillies traded him was the way he complained in his last season with the team whenever anyone suggested that a demotion to the bullpen might change his ailing fortunes.

"The bullpen, no way," Jackson would bellow. He felt he had earned his spot in the starting rotation the previous season when he won 14 games and was the only Phillie representative in the All-Star Game. But as he was unable to get hitters out in 1970, it was hinted that the solution might be a stretch of relief. He resisted and wound up with a 5–15 record, one complete game in 23 starts, and a ticket to the Baltimore Orioles.

It turned out to be the best thing that ever happened to Buck. He accepted the bullpen and became one of baseball's top relievers of the 1970s, first with the Orioles, then with the Pittsburgh Pirates.

When the Phillies signed Jackson, they had visions of a strong starter. He had a fastball that crackled. And in 1969 he fanned 180 men in 253 innings. But he seemed to lose his confidence under Frank Lucchesi in 1970, and, soon after being traded, he hinted that Lucchesi and the Phillies weren't exactly in tune with the Urban League when it came to racial matters. Jackson is black. Several other black ex-Phillies of the era supported Jackson's contention.

Phillies: 1965–70
Pitcher
Birthplace: Fostoria, Ohio
Nickname: Buck
B: September 28, 1942
Bats right, throws left
Ht. 6–0; Wt. 180

Grant Jackson

Jackson's best season as a reliever was in 1979 with the Pirates when he won eight games, saved 14, and had a 2.96 ERA in 72 appearances.

For his career, which spanned 17 major league seasons, he pitched 16 complete games and had 79 saves. Not bad for a guy who once said, "The bullpen, no way."

Jackson, Grant

Phillies	W	L	Pct	ERA	G	CG	IP	H	BB	SO	ShO
1965	1	1	.500	7.07	6	0	14	17	5	15	0
1966	0	0	.000	4.50	2	0	2	2	3	0	0
1967	2	3	.400	3.86	43	0	84	86	43	83	0
1968	1	6	.143	2.95	33	1	61	59	20	49	0
1969	14	18	.438	3.34	38	13	253	237	92	180	4
1970	5	15	.250	5.28	32	1	150	170	61	104	0
Career	86	75	.534	3.46	692	16	1,359	1,272	511	889	5

Jackson, Larry

Phillies: 1966–68
Pitcher
Birthplace: Nampa, Idaho
B: June 2, 1931
D: August 28, 1990
Batted right, threw right
Ht. 6–1½; **Wt.** 175

Larry Jackson

When the Phillies traded for Larry Jackson in April of 1966, they thought they had gone out and bought themselves a pennant.

What they really did was give away a future Hall of Famer (Ferguson Jenkins) as a throwaway in the trade. They never did win a pennant in the three years Jackson pitched for them, but it wasn't Larry's fault. He was a real professional whose mediocre record (41–45) in Philly was the result of weak hitting behind him, not poor pitching on his part.

For his career, Larry Jackson put some pretty good numbers on the board. He won 194 games and could have easily surpassed 200 if he had been willing to join Gene Mauch and the expansion Montreal Expos in 1969. The Expos drafted him, fully expecting to sign him. But Jackson had said before the draft that he would retire rather than put his 37-year-old body through a season of losses and frustration.

Jackson came to the Phillies with Bob Buhl in exchange for Adolfo Phillips, John Herrnstein, and Jenkins. His first year, he had a 15–13 record, making him the third biggest winner on the staff, a 2.99 ERA, and a league-leading five shutouts, but the Phillies finished fourth, eight games out of first place. The gamble that Mauch and John Quinn had taken proved a failure the following year when Jackson slipped to 13–15 and the Phillies slipped to fifth, 19 games out. And by 1968, Jackson's 13–17 record appeared as a positive accomplishment in what became a negative season as the Phillies slumped to eighth place.

Jackson returned to Idaho after that season and entered private business and politics. A lifelong Republican, Jackson was elected to the Idaho house of representatives and served four terms, rising to the chairmanship of the house appropriations committee. A bid to win his party's nomination as governor in 1978 proved unsuccessful. Later he became commissioner of the Idaho Industrial Commission.

Jackson, Larry

Phillies	W	L	Pct	ERA	G	CG	IP	H	BB	SO	ShO
1966	15	13	.536	2.99	35	12	247	243	58	107	5
1967	13	15	.464	3.09	40	11	262	242	54	139	4
1968	13	17	.433	2.77	34	12	244	229	60	127	2
Career	194	183	.515	3.40	558	149	3,263	3,206	824	1,709	37

Johnson, Deron

One of the best purchases the Phillies ever made took place on December 3, 1968, when they bought the contract of Deron Johnson from the Atlanta Braves for a minimal amount.

For three years, Deron gave the team maximum offensive efficiency. He was the power, the heart of the matter when it came to offense, and he delivered the way it was predicted he would in the late 1950s when he was a Yankee farmhand phenom.

He never made it with the Yankees, was a bust with the Kansas City A's, but had some big years in Cincinnati, especially 1965 when he hit 32 home runs and drove in a league-leading 130 runs. But when he arrived in Philly, he was coming off a .208 nightmare that quickly turned into fun time, thanks in no small part to Phillies hitting instructor Billy DeMars, whose spot Johnson later filled for the organization.

DeMars taught Deron that as long as he kept his front (left) shoulder down when he swung, he would achieve full power and also hit for a decent average.

Johnson listened to DeMars and read Ted Williams: "I'll never forget reading one of his books in which he wrote, 'If you want to be a good hitter, work at it extra hard.' "

Johnson told that story on July 11, 1971, a day on which he did something that no big league batter has ever exceeded. He hit three home runs against the Montreal Expos and, including a homer on his last at-bat the previous night, became the 11th major league player to power four homers in as many at-bats.

That was a year in which Deron hit 34 homers and drove in 95 runs with a team that didn't put a whole bunch of people on base ahead of him. The previous season, he had hit 27 homers and accounted for 93 RBI on an equally inept squad.

In 1973, though, he got off to a slow start and never accelerated. Early in the season, he was sold to the Oakland A's. He wound up his major league career with 245 homers.

Phillies: 1969–73
First baseman, outfielder
Birthplace: San Diego, California
B: July 17, 1938
D: April 23, 1992
Batted right, threw right
Ht. 6–2; **Wt.** 200

Deron Johnson

Johnson, Deron

Phillies	G	AB	H	BA	RBI	R	2B	3B	HR	SA	SB
1969	138	475	121	.255	80	51	19	4	17	.419	4
1970	159	574	147	.256	93	66	28	3	27	.456	0
1971	158	582	154	.265	95	74	29	0	34	.490	0
1972	96	230	49	.213	31	19	4	1	9	.357	0
1973	12	36	6	.167	5	3	2	0	1	.306	0
Career	1,765	5,940	1,447	.244	923	706	247	33	245	.420	11

Johnson, Syl

By the time he came to the Phillies, Syl Johnson was in the twilight zone of a 19-year major league career. But he had enough left to give the Phillies nearly seven more seasons.

Johnson, who began in organized ball in 1920 and who first appeared in the majors in 1922, came to the Phillies with outfielder Johnny Moore in a trade with the Cincinnati Reds. The Phils gave up pitcher Ted Kleinhans and outfielder Wes Schulmerich.

A control artist with a sharp-breaking curve, Syl was both a starter and a reliever. In 1934 he led National League firemen in games (34) pitched in relief, 32 after joining the Phillies. He also started 10 games that year.

Syl's best season for the Phils was in 1935 when he posted a 10–8 record. At one point, he won eight straight games.

In 1936 he ranked among the league leaders in saves with seven. The following season, he was listed as a coach, but he was pressed into service and wound up working in 32 games.

By 1939, Johnson was still a coach on the team, but was regularly called to the mound. That year he had an 8–8 record and led Phillies pitchers in ERA.

Phillies: 1934–40
Pitcher
Birthplace: Portland, Oregon
B: December 31, 1900
D: February 20, 1985
Batted right, threw right
Ht. 5–11½; **Wt.** 180

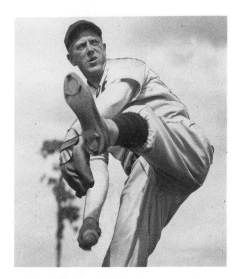

Syl Johnson

In the earlier years of his career, Johnson pitched for the Detroit Tigers, St. Louis Cardinals, and Reds. Between 1929 and 1931 during an eight-season term with the Cards, Johnson had records of 13–7, 12–10, and 11–9, the best marks of his career.

Johnson, Syl

Phillies	W	L	Pct	ERA	G	CG	IP	H	BB	SO	ShO
1934	5	9	.357	3.49	42	4	134	122	24	54	3
1935	10	8	.556	3.56	37	8	174⅔	182	31	89	1
1936	5	7	.417	4.30	39	1	111	129	29	48	0
1937	4	10	.286	5.02	32	4	138	155	22	46	0
1938	2	7	.222	4.23	22	2	83	87	11	21	0
1939	8	8	.500	3.81	22	6	111	112	15	37	0
1940	2	2	.500	4.20	17	2	40⅔	37	5	13	0
Career	112	117	.489	4.06	542	82	2,165⅔	2,290	488	920	13

Johnstone, Jay

Phillies: 1974–78
Outfielder
Birthplace: Manchester, Connecticut
B: November 20, 1945
Bats left, throws right
Ht. 6–1; Wt. 175

Jay Johnstone

It played Philadelphia for more than four years, making 462 stage appearances before live audiences and several thousand backstage. Or so it seemed.

It was the Jay and Danny Show, starring sometime starting outfielder Jay Johnstone and manager Danny Ozark. They were baseball's version of the Odd Couple, as different as Oscar Madison and Felix Unger and almost as funny.

It seemed during those years when the Phillies were finally building to the greatest era of their history that Jay Johnstone's role was easy to explain. One, hit the ball well. Two, get under Danny Ozark's skin, like a tick driving a basset hound to distraction.

"Play Jay Every Day." That was Philadelphia's mid-70s answer to "Kilroy Was Here." It was scrawled on the door to the Phillies' clubhouse. Hardly a game went by that some fan didn't hang a bedsheet over the upper deck railing with the demand—Play Jay Every Day.

The days he played, which were many, Johnstone was excellent. He had spent the early part of his career in the American League, but was dumped by Oakland in 1973 while in the midst of his second sub-.200 season. Then he was dropped by the Cardinals during spring training in 1974 and was signed by Toledo, the Phillies' Triple-A farm. In mid-season, the Phils purchased his contract in one of the greatest steals of the franchise's history.

Jay hit .295 for the rest of that season, lifted his average to .329 the following year, and maintained that level (.318) while finishing second in the league in doubles (38) in 1976. That season, he went 7-for-9 in the League Championship Series against the Reds.

The following season he slipped to .284, then was traded to the Yankees in June 1978 for Rawly Eastwick.

It was no fluke that he went from easy out to .300 hitter with the Phillies—just a lot of hard work that began after the 1972 season. Every morning at 6:15 he met with ex-Dodger player and current Chicago Cubs manager Jim Lefebvre and Lefebvre's father in order to restructure his game.

"I had decided that I had to take a better approach to the game," said Jay. "I didn't have to look at a mirror to know where I was."

And eventually Johnstone didn't need a mirror to keep his batting eye sharp. A hitting tee would do just fine. Johnstone spent endless hours in the catacombs of the Vet, working with the tee, improving his batting stroke. And afterward there was always room for a little fun, much of it at Danny Ozark's expense.

"I like to have fun, but I don't try to hurt anyone," Johnstone said. "As long as my name gets in the paper and nothing derogatory is said, it's fine with me."

Jay was more than fine with the fans of Philadelphia, who have been known to brutalize more than a few athletes in their history. They idolized Johnstone.

He left town as one of the most popular Phillies of all time, even though Ozark never did get around to playing Jay every day.

After his 20-year career ended in 1985, Johnstone became an announcer. In 1992 he was a broadcaster on the Phillies' cable network. He also has written three books.

Johnstone, Jay

Phillies	G	AB	H	BA	RBI	R	2B	3B	HR	SA	SB
1974	64	200	59	.295	30	30	10	4	6	.475	5
1975	122	350	115	.329	54	50	19	2	7	.454	7
1976	129	440	140	.318	53	62	38	4	5	.457	5
1977	112	363	103	.284	59	64	18	4	15	.479	3
1978	35	56	10	.179	4	3	2	0	0	.214	0
Career	1,748	4,703	1,254	.267	531	578	215	38	102	.394	50

Willie Jones was a typical good ole Southern boy. He came out of the Carolina hills with an easygoing manner and a drawl as thick as molasses. His feet always seemed to hurt, and the only thing slower than the way he talked was the way he walked.

Put him on a baseball field, though, and Willie was a different person. He was quick, strong, and aggressive. Once in uniform, the big, affable puppy dog of a guy was transformed into a prowling tiger who pounced on the balls hit by opposing bats as well as those thrown by opposing pitchers with equal ferocity.

Jones was a marvelous fielder with exceptional range, fast hands, and a powerful throwing arm. He could also hit.

Jones had a long and distinguished career with the Phillies, one of the best third basemen who ever played in Philadelphia. He inscribed his name in the National League record book, and he is among the leaders in numerous all-time categories for the Phillies.

Willie holds the National League record for most consecutive years as the leading fielder among third basemen. He led fellow third sackers in 1953, 1954, 1955, and 1956, as well as 1958. He also shares the National League record for third basemen for most years of leading the league in putouts (seven).

To date Jones has played the second highest number of games for third basemen in club history. On the club's all-time list, Willie ranks eighth in games and home runs, ninth in RBI and at-bats, and 10th in total bases.

When the major league scouts discovered Jones playing in a semipro league in South Carolina, they could hardly contain themselves. They called Willie another Pie Traynor. Even Pie, at the time the generally acknowledged king of third basemen, made such a comparison. "He's better than I was," Traynor said.

A first baseman in high school, Willie had spent three years in the Navy, where legend has it he hit .700 in service ball. Upon his discharge in 1946, Jones hooked up with a semipro team in a league filled with ex–Southern Association players. Jones played shortstop and third base, and hit somewhere around .500.

Willie was the talk of the Carolinas, and scouts from all over the majors flocked to see him. Eventually, Phillies head scout Johnny Nee signed Jones with the inducement of a $16,500 bonus. The following spring, Willie was considerably overweight when he reported to Clearwater. "He must have trained on corn pone and beans," sniped manager Ben Chapman, who promptly sent Willie to the minors.

Jones needed only two years in the minors to get ready for the big time. He spent 1947 at Terre Haute, where he hit .307 before coming up to the Phillies at the close of the season. Then he divided 1948 between Utica and Toronto,

Jones, Willie

Phillies: 1947–59
Third baseman
Nickname: Puddin' Head
Birthplace: Dillon, South Carolina
B: August 16, 1925
D: October 18, 1984
Batted right, threw right
Ht. 6–1; **Wt.** 188

again coming to Philadelphia late in the year. Willie hit .333 in 17 games with the Phillies.

That prompted manager Eddie Sawyer, employing a slick piece of psychology, to pronounce that the only man on the squad who was sure of a starting job in 1949 was Jones. With his confidence thus boosted, Willie went out and hit a not-so-robust .244 for the Phils.

Willie, however, did have his good moments. In the fourth game of the season, he socked four doubles against the Boston Braves, tying a major league record for most doubles in one game. Later in the season, Puddin' Head, a name he got as a boy, was part of the Phillies' five-home-run barrage in the eighth inning against the Cincinnati Reds. During that inning, Jones not only homered but tripled as well. Only five other National Leaguers have done that in one inning.

Jones also led the league's third basemen in putouts, assists, and errors. It was to be the only time in his big league career he would lead the league in miscues.

The 1950 season was a memorable one for Jones. Playing in every game, Willie hit .267 with 25 home runs, 88 RBI, and 100 runs scored. He hit two grand slams during the season, was the National League All-Star team's starting third baseman, and got into a memorable fight with the Reds' Connie Ryan after sliding hard into second base to break up a double play. The fight precipitated an all-out brawl between the teams.

Willie had gotten off to a flying start that season. His three-run, ninth-inning homer beat the Dodgers in a game in April. The next day, he hit a grand slam in his first at-bat. In early May, Jones hit two homers in one game to beat the Cubs, and a three-run circuit blast to edge the Pirates.

Toward the end of the season, Willie's hitting dropped off considerably. At one point he had one hit in 26 times up. He came out of the slump with a game-winning, ninth-inning double against the Braves.

In the World Series that fall, Jones had the team's second highest average, but it was only .286.

Unlike most of his teammates, Jones did not falter in 1951. Willie hit .285, the highest average of his career. Again, he made the All-Star team.

Although he continued to hit the long ball, Jones slumped during the next two seasons. Then over the next five years, he seemed to alternate good years and bad years at the plate. All the while, however, Willie was fielding brilliantly.

In 1957, Jones seemed to be off to his finest year. He drove in 29 runs in his first 41 games. But a tailspin at the plate dropped him to a .218 average for the season and only 47 RBI.

The following year, Jones had another memorable game. He drove in eight runs, which, nevertheless, was four short of the National League record set in 1924 by Jim Bottomley of the Cardinals.

Willie was still going strong in 1959 when the Phillies abruptly swapped

Willie Jones

him to the Cleveland Indians for outfielder Jim Bolger and cash. Less than one month later, the Indians shipped Jones to the Cincinnati Reds. Pud spent 1960 and the early part of 1961 with the Reds before calling a halt to his 15-year big league career.

Jones, Willie

Phillies	G	AB	H	BA	RBI	R	2B	3B	HR	SA	SB
1947	18	62	14	.226	10	5	0	1	0	.258	2
1948	17	60	20	.333	9	9	2	0	2	.467	0
1949	149	532	130	.244	77	71	35	1	19	.421	3
1950	157	610	163	.267	88	100	28	6	25	.456	5
1951	148	564	161	.285	81	79	28	5	22	.470	6
1952	147	541	135	.250	72	60	12	3	18	.383	5
1953	149	481	108	.225	70	61	16	2	19	.385	1
1954	142	535	145	.271	56	64	28	3	12	.402	4
1955	146	516	133	.258	81	65	20	3	16	.401	6
1956	149	520	144	.277	78	88	20	4	17	.429	5
1957	133	440	96	.218	47	58	19	2	9	.332	1
1958	118	398	108	.271	60	52	15	1	14	.420	1
1959	47	160	43	.269	24	23	9	1	7	.469	0
Career	1,691	5,826	1,502	.258	812	786	252	33	190	.410	40

Judd, Oscar

If ever there was a player who epitomized Phillies pitchers during the club's dreary years, it was Oscar Judd. The Canadian southpaw was the classic Phillie losing pitcher.

On stronger teams, Judd would have certainly fared better. But with the lowly Phillies of the mid-1940s, pitching was a constant struggle that seldom went in the unfortunate hurler's favor.

The highlight of Oscar's career with the Phils was in 1946 when he was the ranking lefthander on the staff. Judd posted an 11–12 record that season. The only time he topped that mark was with an 11–6 record in 1943 for the Boston Red Sox.

Oscar, owner of a respectable fastball and curve, tied with Schoolboy Rowe for the most wins on the team in 1946. A good hitter who was often used as a pinch-hitter, he also had the highest batting average on the team with a .316 mark. Proving he could also field, Judd went through the season without making an error.

Judd, whom the Phils had picked up on waivers from the Red Sox in 1945 (he had broken into pro ball in 1934), never had much of a record after the 1946 season. Oscar departed from the major leagues in 1948. He had spent eight years in the big time.

Phillies: 1945–48
Pitcher
Birthplace: Rebecca, Ontario
Nickname: Ossie
B: February 14, 1908
Bats left, throws left
Ht. 6–½; Wt. 180

Oscar Judd

Judd, Oscar

Phillies	W	L	Pct	ERA	G	CG	IP	H	BB	SO	ShO
1945	5	4	.556	3.80	23	3	83	80	40	36	1
1946	11	12	.478	3.53	30	12	173⅓	169	90	65	1
1947	4	15	.211	4.60	32	8	146⅔	155	69	54	1
1948	0	2	.000	6.91	4	0	14⅓	19	11	7	0
Career	40	51	.440	3.90	161	43	771⅔	744	397	304	4

Karl, Andy

Phillies: 1943–46
Pitcher
Birthplace: Mt. Vernon, New York
B: April 8, 1914
D: April 8, 1989
Batted right, threw right
Ht 6–1½; **Wt.** 175

Andy Karl

In the last 50 years the Phillies have been blessed with a long line of outstanding relief pitchers. The granddaddy of them all, however, was a slender righthander who, unlike many hurlers of his day, would rather relieve than start.

That was in the mid-1940s, back in a time when relief pitching was not a highly specialized art and saves were something that only lifeguards and firemen thought about.

Andy Karl was the first of the fine Phillies firemen. In 1945 he appeared in 67 games, which not only led the National League that year, but stood as a club record until Jim Konstanty broke it in 1950. It still ranks as the 11th highest total on the Phillies' all-time list.

Karl also had 15 saves that year, although they weren't counted as such at the time. In retrospective record searches, that mark was found to have tied an all-time National League record until broken by Hugh Casey of the Brooklyn Dodgers in 1947. (Saves were officially adopted as a pitching statistic in 1969.)

Andy, whose real name was Anton, had graduated from Mahattan College in 1935. He kicked around the minors for six years before joining the Boston Red Sox in 1943.

That July, the Bosox sold him to the Phillies, and a career in the bullpen was born.

"I had never done well as a starter, but I always seemed to have pretty good luck relieving," Karl said. "I was lucky because I could pitch a lot and not get tired. And it didn't take me long to warm up. I could get ready in a hurry."

After appearing in nine games in 1943, Karl appeared in 38 games, all out of the bullpen, in 1944. He had a 3–2 record with a 2.33 ERA.

In 1945, Karl was the premier reliever in the National League, winning nine and losing eight.

Amazingly, he didn't get his first save until June. But then he picked up steam, ending with a flurry in September when he saved seven of the entire total of nine games won that month by the Phillies.

Andy was deferred from military service because he worked during the off-season in his father's mechanical contracting business, which had a number of defense contracts.

He appeared in 39 games in 1946 with a 3–7 record and five saves. The following spring the Phillies traded him to the Boston Braves for catcher Don Padgett.

Karl spent the 1947 season with the Braves, then retired from baseball.

Karl, Andy (Anton)

Phillies	W	L	Pct	ERA	G	CG	IP	H	BB	SO	ShO
1943	1	2	.333	7.00	9	2	27	44	11	4	0
1944	3	2	.600	2.23	38	0	89	76	21	26	0
1945	9	8	.529	2.99	67	1	181	175	50	51	0
1946	3	7	.300	4.96	39	0	65	84	22	15	0
Career	19	23	.452	3.51	191	1	423	451	130	107	0

Kazanski, Ted

Phillies: 1953–58
Shortstop, second baseman, third baseman
Birthplace: Hamtramck, Michigan
B: January 25, 1934
Bats right, throws right
Ht. 6–1; **Wt.** 175

During a period in the late 1940s and early 1950s when the Phillies were handing out bonus money like it was lollipops at the candy store, Ted Kazanski received one of the highest prices in club history for his signature.

The Phillies forked over $100,000 to Kazanski only a few days after he graduated from high school. With that money, the club figured it had bought itself a shortstop for years to come.

It never happened. In six years of irregular status, Kazanski was unable to master big league pitching. He drifted out of the majors in 1958, another example of the Phillies' mostly unprofitable spending spree of the era.

Ted started off slowly in the farm system in 1951, but he improved each year and by 1953, while playing for Baltimore, was being hailed as the best shortstop in the minors. The Phillies brought him up in the middle of 1953 after he'd hit .290 for the Orioles.

Kazanski spent one and one-half years with the Phillies before he was sent down to Syracuse in 1955. He hit .307 there, earning a trip back to the big leagues the following season.

The Phillies switched Teddy to second base in 1956, and he started there most of the season. But he hit only .211, although he did hit the only inside-the-park grand slam home run in Phillies history.

The following year, Kazanski hit .265 as a reserve infielder, his highest average in the majors. In 1958, though, he slipped back to .228 and never again played in the big leagues.

Kazanski, Ted

Phillies	G	AB	H	BA	RBI	R	2B	3B	HR	SA	SB
1953	95	360	78	.217	27	39	17	5	2	.308	1
1954	39	104	14	.135	8	7	2	0	1	.183	0
1955	9	12	1	.083	1	1	0	0	1	.333	0
1956	117	379	80	.211	34	35	11	1	4	.277	0
1957	62	185	49	.265	11	15	7	1	3	.362	1
1958	95	289	66	.228	35	21	12	2	3	.315	2
Career	417	1,329	288	.217	116	118	49	9	14	.299	4

Ted Kazanski

Grover Cleveland Alexander was already with the Phillies when Bill Killefer joined the team at the tail end of the 1911 season, but most people considered the two as one. In fact, both were traded to the Cubs as a package after the 1917 season, mainly because both were about to be drafted into the U.S. Army.

Killefer is best remembered as a great handler of pitchers and an extremely accurate thrower. In addition to Alex, Reindeer Bill also caught Hall of Famer Eppa Rixey while with the Phillies.

Killefer, however, did not catch for the Phillies in the 1915 World Series, and it could have been a big reason the Red Sox were able to win in five games. His arm had gone dead on him the day after Labor Day and was not rejuvenated until the following spring.

Never a good hitter (lifetime average of .238), Killefer, nevertheless, was universally respected as the best catcher in the National League in the later stages of his seven-year career with the Phillies.

"He was an outstanding catcher, and not only when Alexander was pitching," Benny Bengough once said. "Alex was easy to catch. He was never an inch or two away from the plate. But Bill could handle the wild ones, too."

So well that he was charged with just 69 errors in 636 games with the Phillies. He accepted more than 57 chances for every error with the Phillies. His fielding average was .983.

Killefer also had two tours of duty as a big league manager, with the Cubs (1921–25) and St. Louis Browns (1930–33). He had more success behind the plate than he did in the dugout. The fourth-place finish by the Cubs in 1923 was his only season as a first-division pilot.

Killefer, Bill

Phillies: 1911–17
Catcher
Nickname: Reindeer Bill, Paw Paw
Birthplace: Bloomingdale, Michigan
B: October 10, 1887
D: July 2, 1960
Batted right, threw right
Ht. 5–10½; **Wt.** 200

Bill Killefer

Killefer, Bill

Phillies	G	AB	H	BA	RBI	R	2B	3B	HR	SA	SB
1911	6	16	3	.188	2	3	0	0	0	.188	0
1912	85	268	60	.224	21	18	6	3	1	.280	6
1913	120	360	88	.244	24	25	14	3	0	.300	2
1914	98	299	70	.234	27	27	10	1	0	.278	5
1915	105	320	76	.238	24	26	9	2	0	.278	5
1916	97	286	62	.217	27	22	5	4	3	.294	2
1917	125	409	112	.274	31	28	12	0	0	.303	4
Career	1,035	3,150	751	.238	240	237	86	21	4	.283	39

Klein, Chuck

Phillies: 1928–33; 1936–39; 1940–44
Right fielder
Birthplace: Indianapolis, Indiana
B: October 7, 1904
D: March 28, 1958
Batted left, threw right
Ht. 6–0; Wt. 185

One day in late July 1928, a big, gawky kid with a suitcase in each hand sauntered into the Phillies clubhouse, introducing himself as Chuck Klein. Manager Burt Shotton, in the midst of what would become the team's third straight year in last place, took a quick look at the young fellow. "They tell me you can hit," he said. "Goodness knows, we need hitters."

Little did Shotton know at the time that he was looking at a player who would become not only one of the Phillies' best hitters of all-time, but one of the finest batsmen in National League history.

In three separate stints with the Phillies, Klein compiled record after record and honor upon honor on his way to becoming a member of the Hall of Fame. He won a National League batting championship and was the loop's home run king four times. He won a triple crown, and he hit four home runs in one game. He was named the National League's Most Valuable Player once by the Baseball Writers' Association and twice by *The Sporting News*.

There was virtually nothing the lefthanded-hitting slugger couldn't do with the bat. And although he played only 12 full seasons in the majors as a regular, he finished his 17-year career with 300 home runs, 2,076 hits, and a lifetime batting average of .320.

Even today Chuck still holds a bushel of National League hitting records. He holds the marks for most total bases by a lefthanded hitter in one season (445), most RBI by a lefthanded batter in one season (170), most long hits by a lefthanded batter in one season (107), most consecutive years of 400 or more total bases (two), most games with one or more hits in a season (135), and most runs scored in two consecutive games (eight).

He is also tied for National League records for most consecutive years leading the league in total bases (four), most consecutive years with 200 or more hits (five), and most consecutive years leading the league in runs (three).

Altogether, Klein led or tied for the league lead four times in home runs and total bases; three times in runs scored, slugging average, and assists; twice in hits and doubles; and once in batting average and stolen bases.

The starting right fielder for the National League in the first All-Star Game in 1933, Chuck holds numerous Phillies hitting records. In addition to the aforementioned National League marks (which, of course, are Phillies records, too), he leads the club in highest slugging average for one season (.687), most doubles in one season (59), second highest number of home runs by an outfielder (241), and most home runs at Baker Bowl (156).

On the all-time Phillies career list, Klein ranks third in extra-base hits and home runs; fourth in total bases, doubles, RBIs, and runs; fifth in batting average; and sixth in hits.

In his career with the Phillies, Klein hit six grand slam home runs (tied for the team record). Twenty-eight times, he hit two or more home runs in one game, and six times he got five or more hits in one game. He hit for the cycle twice, once in 1931 and once in 1933. He had five seasons with 200 or more hits; his 250-hit season in 1930 ranks as the sixth highest total in National League history. Four times he hit more than 30 home runs.

A conscientious worker, Klein was the kind of player who hustled all the time. Even when the Phillies were trailing by eight or nine runs in the late innings, Klein played as though the game were on the line. Although he was an unpolished outfielder in the beginning, he had a strong arm and good speed, and made many outstanding plays in right field.

The only spot on his otherwise impressive record is the fact that Klein's home park was Baker Bowl, which had a right field wall only 280 feet from home plate. Over the years, Chuck's critics belittled his feats because of the wall, a point they used to deny his entry into the Hall of Fame until 1980.

Early in his career, Klein showered home runs over the wall and into Broad Street with such regularity that he was a menace to passing traffic. Many auto windshields were broken when Chuck was playing. Owner William Baker had a standing policy of paying for them. More than once Klein hit home runs that carried across Broad Street and onto the adjacent Reading Railroad track.

Before he died in 1930, Baker did what he could to lower Klein's home run totals by adding 15 feet of screen to the top of the right field wall. Baker explained his curious action by saying, "Home runs have become too cheap at the Philadelphia ballpark." Baker's detractors speculated, however, that the screen was really erected to keep Klein from equaling the home run totals of Babe Ruth and the accompanying salary level.

The wall notwithstanding, Klein's first six seasons in Philadelphia were magnificent. A rawboned fellow from Indiana, Chuck had entered the professional ranks in 1927 with Evansville of the Three I League. Originally the property of the St. Louis Cardinals, he was already 21 at that point, and was a combination outfielder–first baseman. In 14 games that year, Klein hit .327, good enough to get him promoted in 1928 to Fort Wayne of the Central League. There he hit .331 with 26 home runs.

In mid-July the Phillies paid the Fort Wayne club $5,000 for Klein. Although the New York Yankees had an option on him, they failed to exercise it, and the Phillies had themselves a slugger, instead of Ruth and Lou Gehrig having themselves a lefthanded-hitting teammate.

When he reported to the Phillies, Klein had only 102 minor league games of experience. In his first trip to the plate for the Phillies, he popped up as a pinch-hitter. The next day, though, he hit a home run and double. He finished his first season with a lofty .360 average and 11 home runs.

The following year, Klein teamed with Lefty O'Doul and Don Hurst to give the Phillies one of the hardest-hitting trios in major league history. Peppering away at the right field wall, the threesome combined for 106 home runs. Up to that point, the only better home run combination was the Ruth-Gehrig duo.

The entire Phillies outfield—Klein, O'Doul, and Denny Sothern—hit .300, a feat the Phillies' outfield of Klein, Kiddo Davis, and Hal Lee duplicated in 1932.

Klein was roundly overshadowed by O'Doul in 1929. Lefty tore apart National League pitching for a league-leading .398 average. Chuck settled for a .356, although he led the circuit in home runs with a then National League record 43 while driving the 145 runs and scoring 126.

That year Klein hit a home run in every opposing park. In July he hit 14 home runs and drove in 40 runs. His home run total of 43 stood as a Phillies record until broken by Mike Schmidt with 48 in 1980.

Klein went into the final day of the season tied with Mel Ott of the New York Giants for the home run lead with 42 each. In the second game of a doubleheader, Phillies pitchers walked Ott five times, once with the bases loaded, after Klein had hit his 43d homer to take the lead.

In 1930, Klein had his greatest season. It was a season in which the Phillies hit .315 as a team, yet finished in last place, 40 games out of first with a 52–102 record.

Chuck hit .386, drove in 170 runs, clubbed 40 homers, and had 250 hits, none of which was enough to lead the league. (That was the year the Giants'

Bill Terry hit .401 with 254 hits and the Cubs' Hack Wilson had 56 homers and 190 RBI.)

He did, however, lead the league in runs (158), doubles (59), and total bases (445), and, as the owner of a strong throwing arm, he led in outfield assists with 44, a modern National League record that still stands. He also had two 26-game hitting streaks during which he went 53-for-110 and 49-for-113.

Klein began the 1931 season with a bang. He hit two home runs in the opening game to give the Phillies a 9–5 win over the New York Giants. For the season, though, he hit a quiet .337, but led the league in runs and in RBI, in each case registering 121. His 31 homers also were high for the league, as were his total bases (347) and slugging average (.584).

Chuck's bat boomed again in 1932, a year in which he hit three grand slam homers. By the end of June, he had 24 four-baggers, the most any National Leaguer had ever hit by that date.

The 1932 Phillies wound up in fourth place, their highest finish since 1917. As usual, since the departure of O'Doul after the 1930 season, Chuck was the club's big hitter. He tied Mel Ott for the lead in home runs (38), and led in hits (226), runs (152), stolen bases (20), total bases (420), and slugging average (.646). He also led National League outfielders in assists (29) and errors (15). His final average was .348, and he collected 137 RBI. He was named MVP by the two organizations that voted on the award.

From a statistical standpoint, 1930 may have been Klein's best year, but from a standpoint of leading his peers, 1933 was Chuck's greatest year. Altogether, he led the league in eight categories. That year he won the league's triple crown, a feat only five other National Leaguers (Paul Hines, 1878; Hugh Duffy, 1894; Heinie Zimmerman, 1912; Rogers Hornsby, 1922 and 1925; and Joe Medwick, 1937) accomplished.

Klein had a .368 batting average, 28 home runs, and 120 RBI. He also led the league in hits (223), total bases (365), slugging average (.602), doubles (44), and outfield assists (21).

The 1933 season capped a five-year hitting spree for Klein that was one of the greatest statistical accumulations in major league history. Over that period, Chuck hit 180 home runs, collected 693 RBI, and batted .359.

By this time Klein's exploits had captured the fancy of Chicago Cubs president Bill Veeck, Sr. Veeck initiated trade talks with the Phillies' president, Gerald Nugent, a man who, after taking over the club following the death of William Baker, would gain a reputation for sending away his big stars.

Veeck died before the negotiations were completed, but his successors consummated the deal, and Klein went to the Cubs in November 1933. The Phillies received aging ex-Yankee shortstop Mark Koenig, pitcher Ted Kleinhans, outfielder Harvey Henrick, and $65,000.

The sale made Phillies fans irate. But by then they had a "what's the use" attitude. Furthermore, their anger was somewhat soothed by Klein's unspectacular showing in Chicago.

In his first game against the Phillies, Chuck bashed two home runs to help the Cubs to a 10–3 victory. But he hit only .301 for the season, drilling just 20 home runs and failing for the first time since 1929 to lead the league in a single department. He was, however, picked for his second and last National League All-Star team.

In 1953, Klein slipped even further down the ladder, hitting a mere .293 with 21 home runs. During the season the speedy outfielder scored eight runs in a doubleheader, including five in one game, to establish a National League record for runs scored in two straight games. That year the Cubs won the pennant. Chuck, whose two-run homer launched Chicago to a 3–1 win in the fifth game, hit .333 in the World Series, which the Detroit Tigers won, 4–2.

Klein began the 1936 season in Chicago, but in May he was traded back to the Phillies with pitcher Fabian Kowalik and $50,000 for outfielder Ethan Allen and pitcher Curt Davis.

His return to Philadelphia was, to say the least, a triumphant one. Just 50 days after taking up his old place in right field, Klein accomplished his greatest feat. He hit four home runs in one game. It happened in a 10-inning joust with the Pittsburgh Pirates at Forbes Field. Klein's fourth homer in the top of the 10th propelled the Phils to a 9–6 victory.

The total was nearly five. In the second inning, Chuck hit a drive to right field which Paul Waner pulled down with his back against the wall. As it was, Klein's total made him only the third player up to that point to hit four home runs in one game. At present, only 11 players in the major leagues have achieved that distinction.

Klein finished the season with a .306 batting average, 25 home runs, and 104 RBI. Obviously, he was happy to be back at good old Baker Bowl.

Chuck's average soared to .325 in 1937, although he was somewhat hampered by injuries. But it was to be his last season over .300. In 1938, Klein dropped to a .247 average and his home run output fell to just eight.

After getting off to an even slower start in 1939, Klein was released by the Phillies. In June, he was signed by the Pirates, and he staged a comeback, hitting .284 for the year.

The Bucs gave him his release at the end of the season, however, leaving Klein with the distinct impression that his career was over. It wasn't. The Phillies signed Chuck in the spring of 1940, bringing him to the club for the third time.

Chuck was the Phillies' regular right fielder in 1940. But he was hardly the Chuck Klein of old. Playing now in Shibe Park, the once-great slugger, although he was only 35 years old, could manage only seven home runs. Worse than that, he had an embarrassing .218 batting average.

It was an era in which the Phillies were mired in their most extended period in the National League basement. With the coming of World War II and the ensuing shortage of players, Klein stayed with the Phillies for four more years.

Used mostly as a pinch-hitter, he posted miserable averages. Over that period, he hit only one home run. Along the way the Phillies made Chuck a coach. He retired as an active player in 1944.

Klein ran a bar in Northeast Philadelphia after his playing days ended. But with financial and domestic problems, his life went downhill, and after becoming paralyzed by a stroke he moved back to his native Indianapolis. There, ravaged by cancer, he died before his 54th birthday.

Chuck Klein

Chuck Klein (right) and Cy Williams formed one of the top home run duos in Phillies history.

Klein, Chuck

Phillies	G	AB	H	BA	RBI	R	2B	3B	HR	SA	SB
1928	64	253	91	.360	34	41	14	4	11	.577	0
1929	149	616	219	.356	145	126	45	6	43	.657	5
1930	156	648	250	.386	170	158	59	8	40	.687	4
1931	148	594	200	.337	121	121	34	10	31	.584	7
1932	154	650	226	.348	137	152	50	15	38	.646	20
1933	152	606	223	.368	120	101	44	7	28	.602	15
1936	117	492	152	.309	86	83	30	7	20	.520	6
1937	115	406	132	.325	57	74	20	2	15	.495	3
1938	129	458	113	.247	61	53	22	2	8	.356	7
1939	25	47	9	.191	9	8	2	1	1	.340	1
1940	116	354	77	.218	37	39	16	2	7	.333	2
1941	50	73	9	.123	3	6	0	0	1	.164	0
1942	14	14	1	.071	0	0	0	0	0	.071	0
1943	12	20	2	.100	3	0	0	0	0	.100	1
1944	4	7	1	.143	0	1	0	0	0	.143	0
Career	1,753	6,486	2,076	.320	1,201	1,168	398	74	300	.543	79

Knabe, Otto

Phillies: 1907–13
Second baseman
Birthplace: Carrick, Pennsylvania
B: June 12, 1884
D: May 17, 1961
Batted right, threw right
Ht. 5–8; **Wt.** 175

Otto Knabe

Franz Otto Knabe joined the Phillies in 1907 and remained their regular second baseman for the next seven seasons before jumping to Baltimore of the new Federal League for the 1914 season as player-manager.

When he went to Baltimore, he took with him shortstop Mickey Doolan, thus breaking up one of the great double-play combinations in that era. In fact, many rated Knabe and Doolan as nearly the equal of Johnny Evers and Joe Tinker when it came to making the pivot at second base.

You won't find Knabe in the Hall of Fame, though, because his bat would never get him there. His career average for 1,284 games was .247, and in his career with the Phillies, his .282 in 1912 was the only time he surpassed the .263 mark. Defensively, however, he was outstanding. In 1913 he led the National League second basemen in assists with 446 (Doolan led the shortstops with 482).

Knabe replaced a legend, Kid Gleason, at second base for the Phillies. Gleason, knowing that his career was over, went out of his way to teach everything he knew to the round-faced youngster of unquestionable Germanic parentage. Knabe, like Gleason, was a fun-loving, good-natured person who quickly fit in with his teammates. He was also adept at getting on base, then stealing another one. He was the kind of player even a Philadelphia fan wouldn't boo, although the fans did manage to mangle the pronunciation of his name. They incorrectly made the *K* silent, and he became Otto Nobby.

In two years in Baltimore after leaving the Phillies, Otto managed the Feds to third place, then eighth. When the league folded, he returned to the National League for a season split between the Pirates and Cubs before retiring.

He remained a Philadelphia resident until his death in 1961. After his playing days, he had several skirmishes with local police concerning accusations of running an illegal gambling business in the Northeast section of the city.

Knabe, Otto

Phillies	G	AB	H	BA	RBI	R	2B	3B	HR	SA	SB
1907	129	444	113	.255	34	67	16	9	1	.338	18
1908	151	555	121	.218	27	63	26	8	0	.294	27
1909	113	400	94	.235	33	40	13	3	0	.283	9
1910	137	510	133	.261	44	73	18	6	0	.325	15
1911	142	528	125	.237	42	99	15	6	1	.294	23
1912	126	426	120	.282	46	56	11	4	0	.326	16
1913	148	571	150	.263	53	70	25	7	2	.342	14
Career	1,284	4,467	1,103	.247	364	572	178	48	8	.314	143

Little did the Phillies know in 1948 when they purchased the contract of Jim Konstanty from the Toronto Maple Leafs, their Triple-A farm club, that they were buying a pennant. Konstanty was an aging, paunchy, scholarly pitcher who threw an assortment of junk pitches and who had failed in previous appearances with two major league teams.

He hardly seemed a likely candidate for the big leagues, much less stardom. In fact, when Toronto manager Eddie Sawyer was promoted to the Phillies and took Konstanty along with him, Maple Leaf officials were shocked.

But Sawyer knew what he was doing, although even Eddie had no reason to visualize just how significant his selection of Konstanty would become.

It all became apparent, however, in 1950 when Big Jim turned in one of the greatest seasons in the history of relief pitchers. Appearing in a record-setting 74 games, Konstanty posted a spectacular 16–7 record. To that he added 22 saves and an earned run average of 2.66.

Konstanty was the single most important player during the Phillies' capture of the National League pennant. His performance was acknowledged by his selection as the league's Most Valuable Player, an honor never before accorded to a relief pitcher.

A few years earlier, no one would've thought it possible. Konstanty came out of upstate New York with a degree in physical education from Syracuse

Konstanty, Jim

Phillies: 1948–54
Pitcher
Birthplace: Strykersville, New York
B: March 2, 1917
D: June 11, 1976
Batted right, threw right
Ht. 6–1½; **Wt.** 202

Jim Konstanty

Whenever Jim Konstanty had a problem with his pitching mechanics he sought the advice of undertaker friend Andy Skinner.

University, where he had lettered in soccer, basketball, boxing, and baseball. Although he had pitched some in high school, Jim was strictly an infielder in college.

After graduating, Konstanty began a career as a phys-ed teacher and coach. He pitched a little in an independent league, too. That led to a minor league contract in 1941 with the Syracuse Chiefs.

At that point, and for several years to come, Konstanty was not so much a professional baseball player as he was a high school teacher who played ball in the summer. His early records did nothing to dispel that notion.

In his first pro season, the Chiefs sent him to Springfield. Jim proceeded to lead the Eastern League in losses with 19, while winning only four games.

A starter most of the time, Konstanty continued along an unspectacular course in the minors for the next 2½ seasons. Then in mid-1944, with Jim's hurling getting better, the pitching-starved Cincinnati Reds bought his contract and brought him to the big leagues. Konstanty worked in 20 games, 12 as a starter, and registered a 6–4 record.

Jim spent the next year in the service. When he returned to the Reds in 1946, they traded him to the Boston Braves for outfielder Max West. Boston manager Billy Southworth didn't think much of Jim's assortment of slow curves, sinkers, sliders, and palm balls, and quickly unloaded him on Toronto.

Konstanty's career seemed over. Jim entertained notions of quitting baseball, especially after the Philadelphia A's, who at the time had a working agreement with Toronto, brought up a handful of players but passed over the hefty pitcher.

But a 13–13 record in 1947 encouraged him to stay. When the Phillies took over the affiliation with Toronto in 1948 and sent Sawyer to manage the club, Konstanty's future looked better. After posting a 10–10 record, Jim was called to the Phillies late in the season.

In 1949, Konstanty began to prove the wisdom of Sawyer's decision. Converted by Eddie entirely into a relief artist, Jim was one of the league's top firemen, posting a 9–5 record and saving 12 more games.

Entering the 1950 season, Konstanty was at 33 one of the oldest players on the team. But Jim kept himself in excellent shape. And with a rubber arm that usually needed only about 20 pitches to get ready for a game, he was ideally suited for the job that lay ahead.

Konstanty also had the proper temperament for a reliever. He was almost devoid of emotion when he was pitching. Yet, he had supreme confidence in himself; he was totally convinced that he had pitching down to a fine science. Jim, in fact, was so sure of himself that it sometimes irritated his teammates as well as his opponents. His confidence bordered on arrogance.

Another great Konstanty asset was his superb control. He could throw all of his pitches anywhere he wanted, and seldom issued bases on balls. Jim, himself, felt his strongest point was his control.

The 1950 season wasn't very old before Konstanty began asserting himself. He wore a steady path in from the bullpen, time after time coming in to win or to save a game for one of the members of the Phillies' otherwise youthful pitching staff.

Between July 19 and August 30, Konstanty worked 38 innings in 17 games and allowed only one run. That run was a homer by Ralph Kiner, which came during one of Jim's most memorable games.

On August 25, Jim entered a game against the Pittsburgh Pirates in the seventh inning with the score tied, 6–6. Ultimately, the Phillies won the game, 9–7, in the 15th inning. Konstanty was still around at the end. He worked a full nine innings, and had allowed only one run and five hits.

Proving that was no freak, Konstanty pitched 10 innings in a game September 15 against the Cincinnati Reds. Jim also got the win in that game, a 19-inning affair.

Of course, Konstanty wasn't completely unbeatable. Sometimes he got lit up, as was the case on July 4 when he came in against the Boston Braves in the ninth inning with the Phils leading, 9–8. Jim served a grand slam homer to Sid Gordon.

Usually, when Jim was having trouble with his pitches he had an easy solution. Call the undertaker.

The undertaker in this case was Andy Skinner, a close friend and confidant of Konstanty. Skinner caught Jim during off-season workouts, and was thoroughly acquainted with the hurler's delivery and his pitches. Andy diagnosed Jim's problems with uncanny ability. In mid-July Skinner, summoned to Philadelphia by Konstanty, solved a mechanical problem Jim was having with his slider.

Konstanty finished the regular season with a direct hand in 38 of the Phillies' 91 victories. He finished 62 of the 74 games he entered while pitching 152 innings and allowing only 45 earned runs.

Jim, a member of the National League All-Star team, was named the top pitcher in the league by *The Sporting News,* which also chose him for its season-ending major league all-star team.

In the opening game of the World Series against the New York Yankees, Sawyer stunned the baseball world by naming Konstanty as his starting pitcher. Jim had not been a starter in his 133 previous appearances in a Phillies uniform, but with the rest of the pitching staff either exhausted or injured, Sawyer had little choice.

Konstanty was masterful. In eight innings of work, he gave up only four hits. One was a fourth-inning double by Bobby Brown, who came around to score on two outfield flies. It was the only run of the game, and Jim was the loser in a heartbreaking decision.

The bespectacled hurler worked two other games in the Series, relieving in the third and fourth games. He was on the mound for a total of 15 innings, allowing nine hits and four runs.

In 1951, Konstanty's effectiveness diminished, and he stumbled to a 4–11 record. He improved the following year, then in 1953 seemed to regain his old form with a 14–10 record. That year he was the starting pitcher in 19 games.

The next season the Phillies sold Konstanty to the Yankees. In 1955, at the age of 38, Jim led the Yankees in games (45) and saves (11) while going 7–2.

Konstanty toiled in New York until 1956 when the Yanks released him. He hooked on with the St. Louis Cardinals, then retired at the end of the season.

Today, Jim's name is prominent in the Phillies' record book. He is eighth on the club's all-time list in career saves (54) and 10th among pitchers in games played (314).

Konstanty, Jim

Phillies	W	L	Pct	ERA	G	CG	IP	H	BB	SO	ShO
1948	1	0	1.000	0.93	6	0	9⅔	7	2	7	0
1949	9	5	.643	3.25	53	0	97	98	29	43	0
1950	16	7	.696	2.66	74	0	152	108	50	56	0
1951	4	11	.267	4.05	58	0	115⅔	127	31	27	0
1952	5	3	.625	3.94	42	2	80	87	21	16	1
1953	14	10	.583	4.43	48	7	170⅔	198	42	45	0
1954	2	3	.400	3.78	33	0	50	52	12	11	0
Career	66	48	.579	3.46	433	14	945⅔	957	269	268	2

Lajoie, Napoleon

Phillies: 1896–1900
Infielder
Nickname: Nap, Larry
Birthplace: Woonsocket, Rhode Island
B: September 5, 1875
D: February 7, 1959
Batted right, threw right
Ht. 6–1; **Wt.** 195

Napoleon Lajoie

The Cleveland Indians were the team for which Nap Lajoie played most of his career, the Philadelphia Athletics were the club for which he compiled his highest average (.426), but the Phillies can rightfully claim this Hall of Famer as their own, also.

Larry came to Philadelphia a few months after signing his first pro contract with the Fall River, Massachusetts, team. He was a throw-in. The Phils had paid $1,500 for outfielder Phil Geier, and the manager at Fall River, Charley Marston, was so pleased with the payment that he included Lajoie in the transaction.

Geier lasted two seasons and 109 games with the Phillies. Lajoie became an immediate star.

In his five seasons with the Phils, Nap never batted less than .324. In 1897 and 1898, he had 127 RBI and more than 100 runs scored in each. His first two years with the Phillies he played first base, before swinging over to second in 1898.

In his second year with the club, he led the National League in slugging percentage. The next season, he topped the circuit in doubles and RBI.

In 1901 he jumped the Phillies and signed on with Connie Mack. When an injunction prevented him from playing in Philadelphia with anyone but the Phillies, his contract was transferred to Cleveland, a team he also managed from 1905 to 1909. Because of Lajoie's fame and popularity, the Cleveland team took on the nickname "Naps" and kept it until he returned to the Athletics in 1915. It was only then that they became the Indians.

Lajoie's .422 batting average in 1901 with the Athletics was the highest ever achieved in the American League. Larry knew the value of eyesight to good hitting. He would not read newspapers or books on trains and would not go to moving pictures for fear they would hurt his batting eyes.

A slashing hitter whom third basemen played in short left field for fear of his wicked liners, Lajoie was a great hit-and-run batter.

Nap was elected to the Hall of Fame in 1937, the second year of balloting.

Lajoie, Napoleon

Phillies	G	AB	H	BA	RBI	R	2B	3B	HR	SA	SB
1896	39	175	57	.326	42	36	12	7	4	.543	7
1897	127	545	197	.361	127	107	40	23	9	.569	20
1898	147	608	197	.324	127	113	43	11	6	.460	25
1899	77	312	118	.378	70	70	19	9	6	.554	13
1900	102	451	152	.337	92	95	33	12	7	.510	22
Career	2,480	9,589	3,242	.338	1,599	1,502	657	163	83	.467	381

Leach, Fred

Phillies: 1923–28
Outfielder
Birthplace: Springfield, Missouri
B: November 23, 1897
D: December 10, 1981
Batted left, threw right
Ht. 5–11; **Wt.** 183

When the Phillies traded Fred Leach to the Giants after the 1928 season for Lefty O'Doul, they cited the fact that Leach was coming off a disappointing season.

The "disappointing season" included a .304 average in 145 games, 179 hits, 83 runs scored, and 96 RBI. Of course, the Phillies in those days had trouble with all kinds of figures, including the ones that flowed through the box office. And, along with O'Doul, the Giants sent a $25,000 check.

When Leach was traded, he was coming off his fourth consecutive .300-plus season. He played three more years with the Giants, hitting over .300 in two of them, then held out for more money and was sold to the Boston Braves before the 1932 season.

He slipped to .247 with the Braves, then slipped out of the major leagues forever. His lifetime average for 10 seasons was .307.

Leach, Fred

Phillies	G	AB	H	BA	RBI	R	2B	3B	HR	SA	SB
1923	52	104	27	.260	16	5	4	0	1	.327	1
1924	8	28	13	.464	7	6	2	1	2	.821	0
1925	65	292	91	.312	28	47	15	4	5	.442	1
1926	129	492	162	.329	71	73	29	7	11	.484	6
1927	140	536	164	.306	83	69	30	4	12	.444	2
1928	145	588	179	.304	96	83	36	11	13	.469	4
Career	991	3,733	1,147	.307	509	543	196	53	72	.446	32

Fred Leach

Cliff Lee played 521 major league games and hit just 38 home runs. But on Memorial Day, 1922, he hit one of the most historic blasts in Philadelphia history.

Batting against the Giants' Art Nehf, Lee became the first player ever to hit a ball completely over the left field bleacher wall at Baker Bowl. The ball cleared the wall easily and landed in Lehigh Avenue.

A year before that titanic home run, Lee was strictly a backup utility man with the Pirates. The Phillies bought his contract just before the start of the 1921 season and reaped tremendous dividends. In his three full years with the team, Cliff played wherever the Phils needed him and batted over .300 each time.

Two years after The Homer, Lee was gone, having been traded to the Reds for outfielder Joe Schultz and, you guessed it again, money.

Lee will go down as the only Phillie in history to clear the left field wall at Baker Bowl, although players from other teams did it. Boston's Walter Berger picked Memorial Day of 1931 to duplicate the feat, and Ducky Medwick of the Cards took Claude Passeau over the wall in 1937.

Lee, Cliff

Phillies: 1921–24
Utility man
Birthplace: Lexington, Nebraska
B: August 4, 1896
D: August 25, 1980
Batted right, threw right
Ht. 6–1; **Wt.** 175

Lee, Cliff

Phillies	G	AB	H	BA	RBI	R	2B	3B	HR	SA	SB
1921	88	286	88	.308	29	31	14	4	4	.427	5
1922	122	422	136	.322	77	65	29	6	17	.540	8
1923	107	355	114	.321	47	54	20	4	11	.493	3
1924	21	56	14	.250	7	4	3	2	1	.429	0
Career	521	1,583	475	.300	216	216	87	28	38	.462	14

Cliff Lee

Leonard, Dutch

Phillies: 1947–48
Pitcher
Birthplace: Auburn, Illinois
B: March 25, 1909
D: April 17, 1983
Batted right, threw right
Ht. 6–0; **Wt.** 175

Dutch Leonard

By the time Dutch Leonard joined the Phillies, he had already spent 17 years in professional baseball. Although he was once one of the premier pitchers in the American League, there was some doubt as to whether the 38-year-old had much left in his aging right arm.

Leonard showed that there was. In his first season with the Phillies, Dutch posted a 17–12 record for a team that tied for seventh place, and led the staff in innings pitched, strikeouts, and earned run average. Owner of what was generally regarded as the best knuckleball in the majors at the time, Leonard had the fourth best ERA (2.68) in the league. An outstanding defensive player, Leonard also had a 1.000 fielding average for the season.

In 1948, Leonard, whom the Phillies had purchased from the Washington Senators, was again the mainstay of the pitching staff, although he reversed the numbers in his won-lost record. Again, Dutch led the staff in innings, strikeouts, and ERA. This time, his ERA (2.51) was second best in the league.

That winter, the Phillies traded Leonard and pitcher Walt Dubiel to the Chicago Cubs for pitcher Hank Borowy and first baseman Eddie Waitkus. Dutch pitched five more seasons with the Cubs before retiring in 1953.

In his earlier days, Leonard had hurled for the Brooklyn Dodgers (1933–36); before then he had served three years in the minors. He spent most of 1936 and 1937 back in the minors, then was picked up by the Senators. Leonard had nine strong years with the lowly Nats, including a 20–8 season in 1939, an 18–13 year in 1941, and a 17–7 campaign in 1945.

Leonard, Dutch (Emil)

Phillies	W	L	Pct	ERA	G	CG	IP	H	BB	SO	ShO
1947	17	12	.586	2.68	32	19	235	224	57	103	3
1948	12	17	.414	2.51	34	16	225⅔	226	54	92	1
Career	191	181	.513	3.25	640	192	3,218⅓	3,304	738	1,170	30

Litwhiler, Danny

Phillies: 1940–43
Outfielder
Birthplace: Ringtown, Pennsylvania
B: August 31, 1916
Bats right, throws right
Ht. 5–10; **Wt.** 198

In the entire history of major league baseball, only four outfielders have played 150 or more games in a season without committing an error. Danny Litwhiler was the first of the four to perform that feat.

In 1942, his third year as a Phillie left fielder, Litwhiler played in 151 games, accepted 317 chances and did not make a single error. Since then, Rocky Colavito (1965), Curt Flood (1966), and Terry Puhl (1979) have matched Litwhiler's feat, which is generally considered to be one of the most notable fielding accomplishments in baseball.

Litwhiler came up to the Phillies in 1940 and batted safely in 21 straight games. Danny, who had great hands but a weak arm, took over the starting left field post in 1941. His .305 average and 18 home runs that year were both career highs. He also placed fourth in the league in total bases with 275.

In 1942, Litwhiler led the Phillies in all major offensive categories, including at-bats, runs, hits, games, total bases, doubles, triples, home runs, RBI, and batting average. No Phillies player has done that since then.

Litwhiler, who rarely made more than a couple of errors in any of the other seasons during his 11-year career, was shipped to the St. Louis Cardinals with outfielder Earl Naylor for outfielders Buster Adams, Dain Clay, and Coaker Triplett during the 1943 season. He helped St. Louis to pennants in 1943 and 1944. He drove in 82 runs in '44.

Danny played later with the Boston Braves and Cincinnati Reds. Although he was never a full-time starter during his two years in Boston and four years in Cincinnati, he always was a respectable hitter, and, of course, an outstanding fielder.

Litwhiler, a graduate of Bloomsburg State College, was head baseball coach, first at Michigan State University for 20 years, and later at Florida State University. More than 100 of his players, including Kirk Gibson, Steve Garvey, Mike Marshall, and Dick Howser, went into professional baseball.

Litwhiler has also written five baseball books, including one that translates baseball terms into seven other languages. He has developed a number of baseball products, including the widely used Jugs Speed Gun that times the speed of a thrown baseball.

A member of six halls of fame, including the Helms Foundation, Litwhiler was international president of the United States Baseball Federation from 1978 to 1983. He was a driving force behind the inclusion of baseball in the Olympics, and was a member of the U.S. Olympics Baseball Committee from 1969 to 1983.

Danny Litwhiler

Litwhiler, Danny

Phillies	G	AB	H	BA	RBI	R	2B	3B	HR	SA	SB
1940	36	142	49	.345	17	10	2	2	5	.493	1
1941	151	590	180	.305	66	72	29	6	18	.466	1
1942	151	591	160	.271	56	59	25	9	9	.389	2
1943	36	139	36	.259	17	23	6	0	5	.410	1
Career	1,057	3,494	982	.281	451	428	162	32	107	.438	11

Lobert, Hans

Phillies: 1911–14
Third baseman
Nickname: Honus
Birthplace: Wilmington, Delaware
B: October 18, 1881
D: September 14, 1968
Batted right, threw right
Ht. 5–9; **Wt.** 170

The nickname was Honus, as in Honus Wagner, but Hans Lobert played his own game at third base and played it well.

Well enough to make Horace Fogel think that he had traded for the pennant when Lobert was included in a four-for-four package with the Cincinnati Reds. At the time, Fogel called it the biggest trade in Phillies history.

Despite badly bowed legs, which reminded people of Honus Wagner, Lobert was a great runner and base stealer as well as an outstanding defensive third baseman. In his last year in Cincinnati, he played only 90 games but stole 41 bases and batted .309.

Lobert once raced a horse around the bases. After leading part of the way, he lost by a nose. He was also clocked circling the bases in 13.8 seconds.

In his four years with the Phillies, Hans was extremely productive. Twice he batted .300 or better. In 1911 he stole 40 bases. Two years later, he had 41. But he was beginning to become injury-prone. In 1912 his activity was cut to 65 games because of a cracked rib, followed by a broken kneecap.

Lobert was one player whom owner William F. Baker paid enough to keep him from jumping to the Federal League after the 1913 season.

Giant manager John McGraw had been eyeing Lobert for some time, and Baker finally let him have Hans in a trade after the 1914 season. The price was steep—the Phillies got Al Demaree, Milt Stock, and catcher Jack Adams in return. And McGraw came out on the short end for a change when Lobert again suffered a cracked kneecap in a pre-season game. He played only 147 games at third base over the next three years and never hit higher than .251 for the Giants.

Lobert made the world tour with the Giants and Chicago White Sox in the winter of 1913–14. When the two teams went on a European tour in 1924, Lobert served as Giants manager John McGraw's secretary.

Lobert was head baseball coach at West Point from 1918 to 1925. He later was a coach with the Giants and served for nearly four years as a minor league manager before joining the Phillies in 1934 as a coach.

In a 14-year major league career, Lobert batted .274 and stole 316 bases. He later became a manager for the Phillies and handled the 1942 team that limped home in eighth place with a 42–109 record.

Hans Lobert

Lobert, Hans

Phillies	G	AB	H	BA	RBI	R	2B	3B	HR	SA	SB
1911	147	541	154	.285	72	94	20	9	9	.405	40
1912	65	257	84	.327	33	37	12	5	2	.436	13
1913	150	573	172	.300	55	98	28	11	7	.424	41
1914	135	505	139	.275	52	83	24	5	1	.349	31
Career	1,317	4,563	1,252	.274	482	640	159	82	32	.366	316

Lonborg, Jim

Phillies: 1973–79
Pitcher
Nickname: Lonnie, Gentleman Jim
Birthplace: Santa Maria, California
B: April 16, 1943
Bats right, throws right
Ht. 6–5; **Wt.** 200

One of the outstanding gentlemen ever to play the game, Jim Lonborg came to the Phillies before the 1973 season along with Kenny Brett in a trade with the Milwaukee Brewers in which Paul Owens surrendered Don Money.

In six full seasons with the Phillies, Lonnie won 75 of his 157 major league career victories. In two seasons, 1974 and 1976, he was particularly outstanding.

He had a 17–13 record and a 3.21 earned run average with 16 complete games in 1974 and was one of the primary reasons the Phillies began to shed their loser image and develop as contenders. Then, in 1976, when the team won its first division title, Gentleman Jim had an 18–10 record and a National League career-best 3.08 earned run average. He won the clinching game in the division race, beating the Montreal Expos, 4–1, on September 26. Lonborg retired 10 of the last 11 batters he faced. This was a season after shoulder problems threatened his career.

In the second game of the League Championship Series, he no-hit the Reds for five innings before giving up four runs and taking the loss in the sixth.

The following season he had an 11–4 record although he missed the first 1½ months of the season with a shoulder injury. In the second game of the LCS with the Dodgers, he was the losing pitcher after delivering a hanging slider that Dusty Baker hit out of the park for a grand slam homer.

More shoulder miseries dropped his record to 8–10 the following year. He retired after four games in 1979.

Nobody knows how great Lonnie could have been if he hadn't been injured so many times. His third year in the majors, he led the Red Sox to the World Series with a 22–9 record, won the Cy Young Award, then won two World Series games before losing the seventh game. Bosox manager Dick Williams, asked before the final game for his pitching plans, answered, "Lonborg and champagne."

It didn't work out that way, and Lonborg never had a season like that again. That winter, he tore knee ligaments while skiing and posted a losing record over the next four years before being traded to the Brewers.

After his retirement, he returned to school, got his dental degree, and since then has been a practicing dentist in Massachusetts.

Jim Lonborg

Lonborg, Jim

Phillies	W	L	Pct	ERA	G	CG	IP	H	BB	SO	ShO
1973	13	16	.448	4.88	38	6	199	218	80	106	0
1974	17	13	.567	3.21	39	16	283	280	70	121	3
1975	8	6	.571	4.13	27	6	159	161	45	72	2
1976	18	10	.643	3.08	33	8	222	210	50	118	1
1977	11	4	.733	4.10	25	4	158	157	50	76	1
1978	8	10	.444	5.21	22	1	114	132	45	48	0
1979	0	1	.000	11.57	4	0	7	14	4	7	0
Career	157	137	.534	3.86	425	90	2,465	2,400	823	1,475	15

Rogers Hornsby never put on a Phillies uniform, but he helped them win a lot of games during the 1950s. He did it merely with the power of a simple suggestion.

In 1954, Stan Lopata was a struggling young hitter who had great potential. But since joining the Phillies in late 1948, he had never lived up to the expectations the club had for him. A big, strong guy, Lopata had not been more than a second-string catcher for the Phillies, and he had not hit more than eight home runs in a season.

Hornsby advised Lopata to try a new batting stance. Bat from a crouch, the Hall of Famer suggested, because it would give Stan a better view of the ball.

Lopata gave it a try. Suddenly, he began hitting the ball like never before. When the season ended, Lopata had a .290 batting average and he'd hit 14 home runs, both personal highs.

The following year Stan continued to hit well with 22 home runs, and for the first time he became the Phillies' starting catcher. At mid-season, Lopata was selected for the National League All-Star team, an honor he was to repeat in 1956.

In 1956, Stan really came into his own, enjoying one of the finest years of any catcher in Phils history. Lopata bashed 32 home runs, 25 as a catcher, which were at the time more than any Phillies catcher had ever hit in one season and a Phillies record for righthanded batters. He also drove in 95 runs and had an average of .267.

At long last, Lopata had fulfilled the potential the Phillies originally saw for him when they paid Stan a $20,000 bonus in 1946.

At that point, Lopata was a red-hot sandlot prospect in the Detroit area. The Phils bested the Detroit Tigers for his signature on a contract and immediately sent their new catcher to their farm system.

In his second year in the minors, Lopata was the Eastern League's most valuable player while catching for Utica. He had another good season at Toronto the next year, at one point driving in eight runs in a game. Stan was promoted to the parent club at the end of the 1948 season.

Lopata was Andy Seminick's understudy over the next few years. In 1950 he hit only .209 as the Phils won the National League pennant. The following season he was sent down to the minors.

The big receiver returned to Philadelphia in 1952 only to find himself again the number-two man, this time behind the newly acquired Smoky Burgess. Eventually, the two shared duties behind the plate. When Stan wasn't catching, he played first base, a new position for him, but one that allowed the Phillies to keep his bat in the lineup.

By early 1955, with Burgess having been traded and with Lopata's batting crouch paying dividends, Stan took over as the Phils' regular catcher. In 1956 he tied for the league lead in most double plays by a catcher (10). That year he also tied for second in the league in doubles (33) and was the Phillies' co-leader with Del Ennis in RBI with 95.

Lopata worked behind the plate for the Phils through the 1958 season. During spring training in 1959, he was sent along with infielders Johnny O'Brien and Ted Kazanski to the Milwaukee Braves for pitcher Gene Conley and infielders Joe Koppe and Harry Hanebrink.

Stan fared poorly in Milwaukee, and early in the 1960 season he bowed out of baseball.

Lopata, Stan

Phillies: 1948–58
Catcher, first baseman
Nickname: Big Stash
Birthplace: Delray, Michigan
B: September 12, 1925
Bats right, throws right
Ht. 6–2; **Wt.** 210

Stan Lopata

Lopata, Stan

Phillies	G	AB	H	BA	RBI	R	2B	3B	HR	SA	SB
1948	6	15	2	.133	2	2	1	0	0	.200	0
1949	83	240	65	.271	27	31	9	2	8	.425	1
1950	58	129	27	.209	11	10	2	2	1	.279	1
1951	3	5	0	.000	0	0	0	0	0	.000	0
1952	57	179	49	.274	27	25	9	1	4	.402	1
1953	81	234	56	.239	31	34	12	3	8	.419	3
1954	86	259	75	.290	42	42	14	5	14	.544	1
1955	99	303	82	.271	58	49	9	3	22	.538	4
1956	146	535	143	.267	95	96	33	7	32	.535	5
1957	116	388	92	.237	67	50	18	2	18	.433	2
1958	86	258	64	.248	33	36	9	0	9	.388	0
Career	853	2,601	661	.254	397	375	116	25	116	.452	18

Luderus, Fred

Phillies: 1910–20
First baseman
Birthplace: Milwaukee, Wisconsin
B: September 12, 1885
D: January 4, 1961
Batted left, threw right
Ht. 5–11½; **Wt.** 185

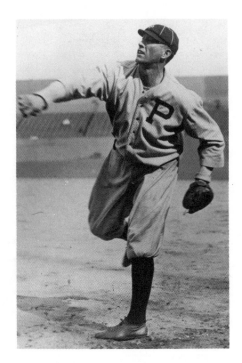

Fred Luderus

He was the opposite of his predecessor, Kitty Bransfield, on defense. Fred Luderus was a butcher. In 1911, his first season as a regular, he led National League first basemen in errors with 22. And in three of his next five seasons, he again led the NL's first sackers in miscues.

He was, however, an outstanding member of the Phillies for a decade. His bat was live, and he was a durable sort, having held the major league record for consecutive games for a time with 533. And he was the offensive star in a losing cause in the 1915 World Series.

Luderus served notice immediately after replacing Bransfield early in the 1911 season that he was going to be an offensive force with which to be reckoned. His average was .301, and he finished second in the league in home runs (16) and third in RBI (99).

His best home run season was 1913 when he slammed 18. He finished second in the league in hitting in 1915 with a .315 average, losing out by five points to the Giants' Larry Doyle in the final week of the season.

But Luderus is remembered for his inability to catch a baseball more than for his ability to hit one.

Even his manager, Pat Moran, would get on him about his fielding lapses. "Drop that board, you big Dutchman, drop that board," Moran would yell from the bench when yet another grounder would roll through Luderus's legs. In 1914 he committed an alarming 30 errors, nearly all of them on ground balls.

In the World Series, though, he hit .438 (7-for-16) and slammed a home run over the fence in the fifth game, which the Boston Red Sox won with a couple of cheap home runs into the roped-off outfield area at Baker Bowl. (By then Fred had become the Phillies' captain.)

There was nothing cheap about Luderus with a bat in his hand. He finished his 21-year major league career, in which all but 25 games were played with the Phillies, with 1,344 hits and 642 RBI. His lifetime average was .277.

In 1919, Luderus completed his 533-game consecutive streak and had a big season with a .293 average, third best of all the years in which he was a regular. In September the Phillies held a Fred Luderus Day at Baker Bowl. Their timing was terrific. Had they waited any longer, they might have been missing the guest of honor. Fred played only 16 games in 1920, was released to the Cincinnati Reds on waivers, and never played in the major leagues again.

He managed in the minor leagues for a while. The next time he saw the Phillies play in person was three decades after his release when he attended the 1950 World Series, thanks to friends at the Milwaukee Yacht Club who chipped in and bought him a round-trip airplane ticket. Luderus was a grounds supervisor at the club.

In 1957, Luderus was elected to the Wisconsin Athletic Hall of Fame. Four years later, he died in Milwaukee of a heart attack at the age of 75.

Luderus, Fred

Phillies	G	AB	H	BA	RBI	R	2B	3B	HR	SA	SB
1910	21	68	20	.294	14	10	5	4	0	.485	2
1911	146	551	166	.301	99	69	24	11	16	.472	6
1912	148	572	147	.257	69	77	31	5	10	.381	8
1913	155	588	154	.262	86	67	32	7	18	.432	5
1914	121	443	110	.248	55	55	16	5	12	.388	2
1915	141	499	157	.315	62	55	36	7	7	.457	9
1916	146	508	143	.281	53	52	26	3	5	.374	8
1917	154	522	136	.261	72	57	24	4	5	.351	5
1918	125	468	135	.288	67	54	23	2	5	.378	4
1919	138	509	149	.293	59	60	30	6	5	.405	6
1920	16	32	5	.156	4	1	2	0	0	.219	0
Career	1,346	4,851	1,344	.277	642	570	251	54	84	.403	55

This goes back to 1968 and the June free-agent draft. It was also the point at which Johnny Bench was crossing the fine line between outstanding prospect and superstar without ever stopping to be a mere star.

Everybody wanted someone like Bench—a powerful fellow who was no defensive liability behind the plate and who could hit for average.

Paul Owens, then the Phillies' farm director, thought he just might have found his man in Niles, Illinois, just outside Chicago. This kid was big and could hit the ball long and hard. And you didn't have to worry about him blocking the plate. He was a linebacker in high school who was wooed by Kansas and Notre Dame among big-time football powers.

The name was Gregory Michael Luzinski, out of Notre Dame High.

"We had him at the top of our list," Owens said the day after the draft. "We took him as a first baseman, but we also see possibilities of him as a catcher."

It was a great idea, but it was scrapped in Luzinski's first year at Huron.

"Dallas Green was his manager at Huron," Owens remembered years later. "Greg's average wasn't too high, but he was hitting home runs. Our feeling was, 'Don't mess around with switching his position because there's the chance you might lose him (mentally).' And we could see he was going to be a good hitter."

Luzinski for several years became a great hitter for average as well as power. Luzinski never caught a game in his major league career, even though he caught and played first all four years in high school. And Luzinski's first manager in the Phillies' organization was also his last manager in the Phillies' organization—Dallas Green.

By then, the man they called Bull was lost mentally at the plate. His average, which had reached .300 three straight years in the mid-1970s, dipped to .228 by 1980. He tried everything to shake out of it and made a big contribution in the League Championship Series when his two-run homer in Game One was the difference as the Phillies beat the Houston Astros. It was the only homer of the five-game series. But Bull went 0-for-9 in the World Series and, when Gary Matthews arrived, his Phillies career immediately moved into the past tense.

When it was in the present tense, it was awesome.

Greg showed a bit of what was to come in 1973 when he hit .285 with 29 home runs and 97 RBI for Danny Ozark's first team. That same year, a rookie

Luzinski, Greg

Phillies: 1970–80
Outfielder
Nickname: Bull
Birthplace: Chicago, Illinois
B: November 22, 1950
Bats right, throws right
Ht. 6–1; **Wt.** 220

Greg Luzinski

third baseman also showed some promise with 18 homers, but he hit .196. His name was Mike Schmidt.

The next year, Luzinski shattered his knee in June while trying to make a routine catch in left field, which, it turned out, became his regular spot. At the time he had only seven homers. But Schmidt busted loose with 36 homers, and Phillies fans eagerly awaited the season when the two of them would be near the top of their games. It would be Callison and Allen (1964) or Klein and Hurst (1929) all over again.

In 1975 it happened. Schmidt hit 38 home runs, and Luzinski added 34 while driving in 120 runs and batting .300. Bull's power production slipped to 21 the following year, but he hit .304. Late that season, he assessed himself.

"I've reached the point where I think I am capable of hitting .300 all the time while I'm still capable of hitting home runs," he said. "With my present stroke, I'm capable of hitting 40 home runs."

The following season was his best year—and provided his worst moment. The Phillies won 101 games. Luzinski (39) and Schmidt (38) hit 77 home runs between them, and the Bull drove in 130 runs. But in Game Three of the League Championship Series with the Dodgers, he dropped Manny Mota's fly ball against the left field fence in the ninth inning. The Phillies went from winners to losers, and Danny Ozark became a man who will be second-guessed forever for having Luzinski in the game at that point.

The following year, Luzinski still could hit home runs (35) but could no longer hit .300 (.265). And in 1979 and 1980 both his power and average deteriorated badly.

In 1981 the Phillies gave him to the White Sox for practically nothing, even though he still had four years of productive designated hitting ahead of him in the American League. Bull could no longer produce as a National Leaguer, however. His weight, always a concern, had become a liability to the point where the Phillies and every other National League team believed his knees could give anytime because of the constant pounding on the artificial grass.

He will always be remembered in Philadelphia for the good years when he could give a thrill to a full house at the Vet with one compact swing of his bat.

Luzinski, Greg

Phillies	G	AB	H	BA	RBI	R	2B	3B	HR	SA	SB
1970	8	12	2	.167	0	0	0	0	0	.167	0
1971	28	100	30	.300	15	13	8	0	3	.470	2
1972	150	563	158	.281	68	66	33	5	18	.453	0
1973	161	610	174	.285	97	76	26	4	29	.484	3
1974	85	302	82	.272	48	29	14	1	7	.394	3
1975	161	596	179	.300	120	85	35	3	34	.540	3
1976	149	533	162	.304	95	74	28	1	21	.478	1
1977	149	554	171	.309	130	99	35	3	39	.594	3
1978	155	540	143	.265	101	85	32	2	35	.526	8
1979	137	452	114	.252	81	47	23	1	18	.427	3
1980	106	368	84	.228	56	44	19	1	19	.440	3
Career	1,821	6,505	1,795	.276	1,128	880	344	24	307	.478	37

Maddox, Garry

Phillies: 1975–86
Outfielder
Birthplace: Cincinnati, Ohio
B: September 1, 1949
Bats right, throws right
Ht. 6–3; **Wt.** 175

Ralph Kiner said it best about Garry Lee Maddox.
The New York Mets announcer, in one of his most lucid moments, once declared: "Two-thirds of the earth is covered by water, the other third by Garry Maddox."

For the vast majority of his dozen seasons with the Phillies, Maddox was the best defensive center fielder in baseball. Bill Conlin, of the *Daily News*, accurately nicknamed Maddox "The Secretary of Defense." He won eight Gold Glove awards, third highest number by National League outfielders behind only Hall of Famers Roberto Clemente and Willie Mays. His career fielding average was .983.

And he was no slouch at the plate, either. In 1976, his first full year with the Phillies, he finished second in the National League in hitting with a .330 average. His lifetime average for 15 major league seasons was .285, and he finished with 1,802 hits. He hit safely in 20 straight games in 1978.

Never a real power-hitting threat, Maddox still hit double figures in home runs in four straight years from 1977 to 1980. During that same stretch, he stole 22, 33, 26, and 25 bases. And from 1976 to 1980, he drove in between 61 and 74 runs a season.

His double in the 10th inning of the fifth game of 1980 League Championship Series drove in the winning run, putting the Phillies in position to win their first World Championship. But like all players who achieve greatness in a certain area, he also is well remembered for a mistake he made in the field.

It happened in the 1978 League Championship Series against the Los Angeles Dodgers. The Phillies had lost the first two games of the best-of-five series at home, had won the third in Los Angeles, and were tied in the 10th inning in the fourth when Maddox dropped a routine fly ball in center field, allowing the winning run to score.

It was the low point in the slim, sensitive Vietnam veteran's big league career, which had begun with the San Francisco Giants in 1972. As a sophomore, he hit .319 for the second highest average of his career. But he started out slowly in 1975 and was hitting only .135 in 17 games when Phillies general manager Paul Owens made what began as an extremely unpopular trade. He sent flamboyant Willie Montanez to the Giants even-up for Maddox.

The Phillies finished second that year with Maddox playing a brilliant center field, then won the NL East title in four of the next five seasons with Maddox as a cornerstone of the team.

But in 1980, Maddox was having a subpar season at the plate going into September. Early that month, Owens called a team meeting on the West Coast and singled out Maddox and shortstop Larry Bowa for giving less than a full effort. Both players responded positively, and the Phillies rallied to win the division and eventually clinch their first world title.

Maddox drove in nine runs and batted .286 (20-for-70) in 17 LCS games.

Garry Maddox

His home run gave the Phillies their lone victory in the 1982 World Series against the Baltimore Orioles.

Maddox retired after seven at-bats in the 1986 season. He ranks third in Phillies history in sacrifice flies (51), sixth in stolen bases (189), and eighth in intentional walks (51).

A diligent worker for the Child Guidance Center during and after his career, Maddox has served in recent years as a commentator on Phillies cablecasts.

Maddox, Garry

Phillies	G	AB	H	BA	RBI	R	2B	3B	HR	SA	SB
1975	99	374	109	.291	46	50	25	8	4	.433	24
1976	146	531	175	.330	68	75	37	6	6	.456	29
1977	139	571	167	.292	74	85	27	10	14	.448	22
1978	155	598	172	.288	68	62	34	3	11	.410	33
1979	148	548	154	.281	61	70	28	6	13	.425	26
1980	143	549	142	.259	73	59	31	3	11	.386	25
1981	94	323	85	.263	40	37	7	1	5	.337	9
1982	119	412	117	.284	61	39	27	2	8	.417	7
1983	97	324	89	.275	32	27	14	2	4	.367	7
1984	77	241	68	.282	19	29	11	0	5	.390	3
1985	105	218	52	.239	23	22	8	1	4	.339	4
1986	6	7	3	.429	1	1	0	0	0	.429	0
Career	1,749	6,331	1,802	.285	754	777	337	62	117	.413	248

Magee, Sherry

Phillies: 1904–14
Outfielder
Birthplace: Claredon, Pennsylvania
B: August 6, 1884
D: March 29, 1929
Batted right, threw right
Ht. 5–11; **Wt.** 179

Sherwood Magee had talent to burn and a temper to do likewise.

One of the superstars of the early part of the 20th century, Magee has been overlooked, perhaps unfairly, by the Hall of Fame veterans' committee.

After all, in 16 stormy big league seasons, 11 with the Phillies, Sherry had 2,169 hits, 1,187 RBI, and a .291 average. In 1910 his statistics were particularly outstanding, especially when you consider he had only six home runs. In addition to topping the league in batting average (.331), he also led the NL in RBI (123) and runs scored (110). Three years earlier, he had batted .328, second in the league to Honus Wagner.

Magee, however, was better known for his conduct on the field, which was often deplorable, and his conduct in the clubhouse, which could be downright nasty. He took needling one step beyond the bounds of good judgment and actually bullied many of his younger teammates once he established himself as a star. He was especially tough on a future Hall of Famer, Eppa Rixey. And his family and the Dode Paskerts had a mutual hate going for years.

In 1914, Magee hit Rixey in the head with a paper laundry bag filled with water from the sixth floor of New York's Metropole Hotel. Real highbrow comedy!

Another story has it that one afternoon Dode Paskert hit a home run. Everybody in the ball park cheered—except Magee's two sons, who booed lustily from behind third base. Dode touched the plate, stepped into the dugout, and went to Fist City with Sherry.

Magee's worst moment, though, happened in 1911. It involved an altercation with umpire Bill Finneran in a home game against St. Louis. Here is how an unbylined story in *The Bulletin* reported the matter:

"A disgraceful scene marked the final game of the series between the Phillies and St. Louis at Broad and Huntingdon Sts. this afternoon when Sherwood Magee, the Phillies' star fielder and batsman, made an attack upon Umpire Finneran.

"The assault occurred in the Phillies' half of the third inning and created much excitement. . . .

"After Magee had struck out, he threw his bat into the air and rushed at the umpire, punching Finneran in the mouth. Finneran, who had pulled off his mask at Magee's approach, fell in a heap at the plate and the blood poured from his mouth and nose."

A touch of irony: Magee later became a National League umpire.

For his actions against Finneran, though, Magee was fined $200 and suspended for the balance of the season (the incident took place July 10). Later the suspension was cut to 36 days.

Magee also had the kind of luck that no man should endure. In 1914 he finished his 11th year with the Phillies, who finished sixth. In the off-season, he was traded to the World Champion Braves. That year, the Braves finished second—to the Phillies.

Magee played in one World Series, for the 1919 Cincinnati Reds, who beat the Black Sox. It figured.

Magee is also believed to have been the cause of the sacrifice fly rule going into effect. Lobbying strongly and successfully for the rule was manager Billy Murray, presumably because it would improve Magee's average.

Once he left Philadelphia, Magee never hit .300 again. But while he was in Philly, he was sort of an early version of Dick Allen. Controversy followed him everywhere. He had some friends. He had more enemies. The biggest one was himself.

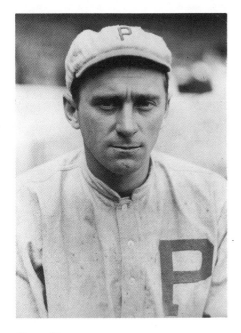

Sherry Magee

Magee, Sherry

Phillies	G	AB	H	BA	RBI	R	2B	3B	HR	SA	SB
1904	95	364	101	.277	57	51	15	12	3	.409	11
1905	155	603	180	.299	98	100	24	17	5	.420	48
1906	154	563	159	.282	67	77	36	8	6	.407	55
1907	140	503	165	.328	85	75	28	12	4	.455	46
1908	143	508	144	.283	57	79	30	16	2	.417	40
1909	143	522	141	.270	66	60	33	14	2	.398	38
1910	154	519	172	.331	123	110	39	17	6	.507	49
1911	121	445	128	.288	94	79	32	5	15	.483	22
1912	132	464	142	.306	66	79	25	9	6	.438	30
1913 ·	138	470	144	.306	70	92	36	6	11	.479	23
1914	146	544	171	.314	103	96	39	11	15	.509	25
Career	2,084	7,441	2,169	.291	1,187	1,112	425	166	83	.291	441

In 1960, Art Mahaffey was about to turn 22 years of age and was the brightest pitching prospect to come out of the Phillies' farm system since Robin Roberts and Curt Simmons. He was big and strong with a fastball that crackled.

Two years later, he already had 37 big league wins, including six shutouts, and was in the National League all-time record book for most strikeouts in a game. On April 23, 1961, he pitched a four-hit shutout against the Cubs in which he fanned 17 batters. At the time, it equaled the league record held by Dizzy Dean and was one strikeout short of the major league record held by Bob Feller.

Five years later, he had pitched his last game in the major leagues. And, in 1969, he was pitching in the semipro Pen-Del league, a bitter man at 31 with his big league career far behind him.

Before he pitched his first game Mahaffey predicted that he would pick off the first batter to reach base against him. The prediction came true when, shortly after being brought up from Buffalo, Mahaffey entered a game against

Mahaffey, Art

Phillies: 1960–65
Pitcher
Birthplace: Cincinnati, Ohio
B: June 4, 1938
Bats right, throws right
Ht. 6–1; **Wt.** 185

Art Mahaffey

the St. Louis Cardinals in the seventh inning. Bill White reached first, but Mahaffey promptly picked him off. He also picked off the next batter who got to first.

Mahaffey was the pitcher the night Chico Ruiz stole home in September 1964 to start the Phillies on their memorable 10-game losing streak that knocked them out of a pennant they had all but clinched. By that time, he was also a major league bowler, which attests to his diverse athletic skills.

But what had happened to the young man with the blazing speed who won 19 games and made the National League All-Star team in 1962?

Art always put the blame for his short career squarely on the shoulders of one man, Gene Mauch. He claims that Mauch pitched him with a sore arm and made matters even worse.

"I never should have taken all those pain pills and pain shots to keep going," he told the *Bulletin*'s Sandy Grady years after he had retired. "Other guys rested when they had arm problems."

His arm miseries began in 1963, the year after he won 19, and intensified until he was traded to the Cardinals in the Bill White–Dick Groat swap shortly after the 1965 season. This was after a season in which Mahaffey said of Mauch: "He hates my guts and I hate his guts."

His comment the morning of the trade: "Everybody knows how I feel about Mauch. But when I heard about the trade, I eliminated Mauch from my mind."

Mahaffey couldn't eliminate the pain. He worked only 35 innings with the Cardinals, had a 1–4 record, and was sent to the minor leagues. What had begun as an exceptionally promising major league career was ended at the age of 28.

Mahaffey, Art

Phillies	W	L	Pct	ERA	G	CG	IP	H	BB	SO	ShO
1960	7	3	.700	2.31	14	5	93	78	34	56	1
1961	11	19	.367	4.11	36	12	219	205	70	158	3
1962	19	14	.576	3.94	41	20	274	253	81	177	2
1963	7	10	.412	3.99	26	6	149	143	48	97	1
1964	12	9	.571	4.53	34	2	157	161	82	80	2
1965	2	5	.286	6.21	22	1	71	82	32	52	0
Career	59	64	.480	4.17	185	46	999	959	368	639	9

Martin, Hersh

Phillies: 1937–40
Center fielder
Nickname: Ray
Birthplace: Birmingham, Alabama
B: September 19, 1909
D: November 17, 1980
Batted right, threw right
Ht. 6–2; **Wt.** 190

Sometimes known as Hersh and sometimes known as Ray, Hershel Ray Martin was the Phillies' regular center fielder in the late 1930s.

Described in one baseball publication as "a sprightly fellow who on sundry occasions has scored from second on a bunt," Martin was one of the few bright spots during one of the Phillies' most miserable periods. Despite playing on three last-place teams and one that finished seventh, Hersh usually flirted with the .300 mark at the plate.

In 1938, his best year, Martin hit .298 and was picked for the National League All-Star team.

Hersh came to the Phillies in 1937 after apprenticing in the minors for five years. Before reaching the majors, he was a third baseman and a noted base stealer.

The Phillies converted Martin into an outfielder, and he patrolled center field during three seasons as a regular. In his rookie year, he led the National League in putouts.

Martin hit .283 as a freshman while coming to bat more than any other Phillie. After his fine season in 1938, he came back the next year with a .282 mark.

In 1940, Hersh lost his status as a regular, and after the season drifted out of the majors. He resurfaced in 1944 with the New York Yankees. He was the Yanks' starting left fielder in 1944 and 1945, hitting .320 and .267, respectively.

Martin, Hersh

Phillies	G	AB	H	BA	RBI	R	2B	3B	HR	SA	SB
1937	141	579	164	.283	49	102	35	7	8	.409	11
1938	120	466	139	.298	39	58	36	6	3	.421	8
1939	111	393	111	.282	22	59	28	5	1	.387	4
1940	33	83	21	.253	5	10	6	1	0	.349	1
Career	607	2,257	643	.285	215	331	135	29	28	.408	33

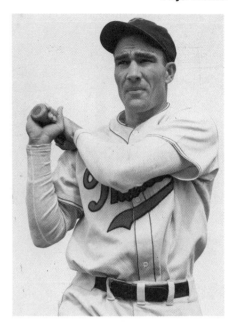

Hersh Martin

They called him Sarge. It was with good reason.

Gary Matthews was a take-charge guy, a strong force on the field and in the clubhouse, a player who with his fiery spirit and hard-driving style of play was a leader of the troops with whom he took the field of battle.

"I got the name from Pete Rose," Matthews said. "It means, take charge. Go out and hustle. That's Pete's motto, and mine, too."

Matthews' take-charge qualities were never more obvious than in the 1983 League Championship Series when he whipped the Phillies to a three-games-to-one victory over the Los Angeles Dodgers. Gary slammed six hits in 14 at-bats for a .429 average, blasting three home runs and driving in eight. He was named the Most Valuable Player of the series.

After hitting a home run and a single in a losing cause in the second game, Matthews really took over in the third game. He collected three hits and a walk, drilling a fourth-inning home run, a fifth-inning, two-run single, and another RBI single in the seventh. By the time the Phillies' 7–2 win was in the bank, Matthews had not only driven in four runs, but had also scored two more.

Gary wasn't through, though. The next day, his three-run homer in the first inning set the stage for another 7–2 victory in the pennant-clinching game.

In the World Series, Matthews had four hits, including a home run in Game Three.

Matthews, who had been benched during the year, ended the 1983 regular season with a .258 batting average. It was the lowest of his three years in Philadelphia.

After coming to the Phillies in 1981 from the Atlanta Braves in a trade for pitcher Bob Walk, Matthews had hit .301 that season, making Phillies fans at least partly forgive the club for letting Greg Luzinski get away. Gary followed that with a .281 mark in 1982 with 19 home runs and 83 RBI while playing in all 162 games.

Matthews had originally broken into the majors in 1972 with the San Francisco Giants. He hit .290 and was named Rookie of the Year. After five solid seasons on the West Coast, he signed with the Braves as a free agent, playing in Atlanta for four years until joining the Phillies.

In his first 11 seasons in the big leagues, Matthews never hit below .278, three times going over .300. Thirteen times during his career he homered in double figures, and five times he had more than 80 RBI.

During spring training in 1984 the Phillies swapped Matthews, outfielder Bob Dernier, and pitcher Porfi Altamirano to the Cubs for pitcher Bill

Matthews, Gary

Phillies: 1981–83
Left fielder
Nickname: Sarge
Birthplace: San Fernando, California
B: July 5, 1950
Bats right, throws right
Ht. 6–2; **Wt.** 185

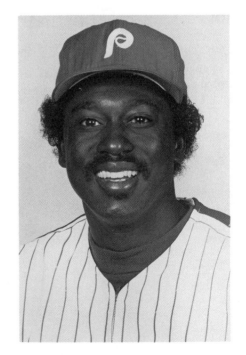

Gary Matthews

Campbell and utility man Mike Diaz—unquestionably one of the Phils' worst trades of the era. Matthews stayed with the Cubs until getting dealt to the Seattle Mariners in 1987, his last season in the big leagues.

Matthews, Gary

Phillies	G	AB	H	BA	RBI	R	2B	3B	HR	SA	SB
1981	101	359	108	.301	67	62	21	3	9	.451	15
1982	162	616	173	.281	83	89	31	1	19	.427	21
1983	132	446	115	.258	50	66	18	2	10	.374	13
Career	2,033	7,147	2,011	.281	978	1,083	319	51	234	.439	183

May, Pinky

Phillies: 1939–43
Third baseman
Birthplace: Laconia, Indiana
B: January 18, 1911
Bats right, throws right
Ht. 5–11½; Wt. 165

Pinky May

In an era when the Phillies finished last with monotonous regularity, Pinky May was one of the few bright lights on an otherwise dismal collection of clubs.

An excellent fielder and a respectable hitter, May put in five workmanlike seasons with the Phillies, who had rescued him from the minors where he had spent seven seasons as a New York Yankee farmhand.

May was drafted by the Phillies in time for the 1939 season after hitting .331 the previous year for the Newark Bears. In his rookie year, Pinky hit .287 and drove in 62 runs, although he had only two homers. He climbed to a .293 average the next year and was named to the National League All-Star team.

That was Pinky's best year at the plate. But the one-time Indiana University student was also a defensive standout. He led National League third basemen in fielding in 1939, 1941, and 1943. In 1941 he had the most putouts, assists, and double plays among third basemen while posting a fielding average of .972.

May entered the military after the 1943 season. When he was discharged, Pinky went to spring training with the Phillies but was released. Nevertheless, in his five years with the Phillies, he played more games at third base than all but four other players in club history.

After his retirement from baseball, Pinky became a highly successful minor league manager, working for 26 years, mostly in the Cleveland Indians' farm system. He won overall league championships at Keokuk (1955), Burlington (1958), and Selma (1962) before retiring from baseball in 1972.

A hot-tempered fellow, Pinky was said to have picked up his nickname because he was always angry. May was the Phillies' captain in the early 1940s. His son Milt became a respectable major league catcher, working mostly for the Pittsburgh Pirates, Detroit Tigers, and San Francisco Giants.

May, Pinky (Merrill)

Phillies	G	AB	H	BA	RBI	R	2B	3B	HR	SA	SB
1939	135	464	133	.287	62	49	27	3	2	.371	4
1940	136	501	147	.293	48	59	24	2	1	.355	2
1941	142	490	131	.267	39	46	17	4	0	.318	2
1942	115	345	82	.238	18	25	15	0	0	.281	3
1943	137	415	117	.282	48	31	19	2	1	.345	2
Career	665	2,215	610	.275	215	210	102	11	4	.337	13

The career of Erskine Mayer took off like a space capsule, made a couple of quick, impressive orbits, then crashed to the ground as rapidly as it had ascended.

Mayer was picked up in the draft before the 1912 season and showed a year later that he had fine potential when he broke even in 18 decisions with a nice 3.11 earned run average.

The following season the Phillies slumped to sixth, but nobody could blame Mayer. That was the year Tom Seaton took his 27 victories to the Federal League, but Mayer tried his best to make up for Tom's absence with a 21–19 record, 24 complete games, and a career-high 321 innings pitched.

He repeated the 21 victories (with 15 losses) in the 1915 championship season, and his earned run average dipped to 2.36, a career best. But he slipped to 20 complete games and tallied most of those before his Independence Day marriage.

Although he was slumping, Mayer got a big vote of confidence from manager Pat Moran, who started him in the second game of the World Series against the Red Sox. Erskine may have lost some of his effectiveness, but none of his gameness. His opponent, who eventually beat him with the bat, was George Foster, who pitched a three-hitter and collected three hits. The third one, a single in the ninth, was the 10th hit off Mayer and chased home Larry Gardner with the run that proved to be the game-winner.

Moran came back with Mayer in the fifth game, but Erskine was chased in the third inning. Still, people figured that Erskine would keep winning his 20 games the next several seasons.

It didn't happen that way, and many observers blamed Mayer when the Phillies finished second to the Dodgers in the 1916 National League pennant race. His record slipped to 7–7, and he completed just seven starts, although his earned run average was a credible 3.15.

Erskine closed out his Phillie career with an 11–6 record in 1917 and a 7–4 mark in 1918. He was traded to the Pirates in mid-season and played a year and one-half for the Bucs.

Still, he is in the Phillies' record book with a present Hall of Famer and a future one. Mayer, Grover Cleveland Alexander, and Steve Carlton were the only Phillies pitchers to start two World Series games in the first 100 years of the franchise.

Mayer, Erskine

Phillies: 1912–18
Pitcher
Birthplace: Atlanta, Georgia
B: January 6, 1891
D: March 10, 1957
Batted right, threw right
Ht. 6–0; **Wt.** 168

Erskine Mayer

Mayer, Erskine

Phillies	W	L	Pct	ERA	G	CG	IP	H	BB	SO	ShO
1912	0	1	.000	6.43	7	0	21	27	7	5	0
1913	9	9	.500	3.11	39	7	171	172	46	51	2
1914	21	19	.525	2.58	48	24	321	308	91	116	4
1915	21	15	.583	2.36	43	20	275	240	59	114	2
1916	7	7	.500	3.15	28	7	140	148	33	62	2
1917	11	6	.647	2.76	28	11	160	160	33	64	1
1918	7	4	.636	3.12	13	7	104	108	26	16	0
Career	91	70	.565	2.96	245	93	1,427	1,415	345	482	12

No one has ever denied that the Phillies never would have had the chance to be World Champions without Bake McBride's immense contributions in 1980.

The season was absolutely remarkable for McBride in that Dallas Green kept moving him to different spots in the lineup and McBride kept producing exactly the way that a hitter was supposed to produce. When he batted leadoff, he got on base. When he batted third, he drove in runs. When he batted cleanup, he hit home runs.

His greatest home run of the season came on the next-to-last weekend

McBride, Bake

Phillies: 1977–81
Outfielder
Birthplace: Fulton, Missouri
B: February 3, 1949
Bats left, throws right
Ht. 6–2; **Wt.** 190

against Montreal leading off the ninth inning. It gave the Phillies a 2–1 victory and a 1½-game lead over the Expos, and it earned McBride a standing ovation that wouldn't stop until he came out of the dugout and tipped his cap.

For the season, Bake had easily a career-high 87 RBI and batted .309. And even with it all, he got in trouble with some fans after the season was over for criticizing the selection of Mike Schmidt as World Series MVP.

McBride, who was Rookie of the Year with the Cardinals in 1974, came to the Phillies on June 15, 1977, for Tommy Underwood, Rick Bosetti, and Dane Iorg. He carried the Phillies to the National League East title that year by hitting .339 in 85 games and stealing 27 bases. And he hit a home run in the League Championship Series off Don Sutton in Game Two.

He also homered in the LCS the following season in the fourth and final game against the Dodgers. His most memorable post-season homer, though, was in the first game of the 1980 World Series when his three-run shot was the game-winner in a game in which the Phillies trailed, 4–0, at one point.

By the end of that 1980 season, McBride was playing on pride alone. His knees ached like crazy and had to be drained periodically. It got even worse in the strike-shortened 1981 season. And before the start of the 1982 season, McBride was traded to the Cleveland Indians for relief pitcher Sid Monge. He retired after the 1983 season with the Indians.

He will be remembered by Phillies fans as a quiet man who sometimes looked like he was loafing, when, in reality, he was hurting badly. He could be uncooperative with the media at times, extremely cooperative at other times.

But he will most be remembered as a player who helped the Phillies to their first World Championship by doing whatever was asked of him in 1980.

McBride, Bake

Phillies	G	AB	H	BA	RBI	R	2B	3B	HR	SA	SB
1977	85	280	95	.339	41	55	20	5	11	.564	27
1978	122	472	127	.269	49	68	20	4	10	.392	28
1979	151	582	163	.280	60	82	16	12	12	.411	25
1980	137	554	171	.309	87	68	33	10	9	.453	13
1981	58	221	60	.271	21	26	17	1	2	.385	5
Career	1,071	3,853	1,153	.299	430	548	167	55	63	.420	183

Bake McBride

McCarver, Tim

Phillies: 1970–72, 1975–80
Catcher
Birthplace: Memphis, Tennessee
B: October 16, 1941
Bats left, throws right
Ht. 6–0; Wt. 183

It was the middle of the 1975 season, and Tim McCarver had just been released by the Boston Red Sox. He would soon be 34 years old, and he was tired of split fingers and foul tips to the larnyx. So he came to Philadelphia looking for a job in the Phillies' broadcast booth.

Paul Owens said no, there were no openings at announcer, but he did have one at catcher. So James Timothy strapped on the chest protector, pulled down the mask, and hung around for six more years, the last making him one of a handful of major leaguers to play in four different decades.

In the late 1970s, McCarver, who caught in three World Series for the Cardinals in the 1960s, became Steve Carlton's designated catcher and designated talker. Not that Timmy didn't earn his keep in other ways, even if he did hit a grand slam single (hit the ball out of the park but passed a runner between first and second) on the day the nation was celebrating its Bicentennial.

Tim had his best season with the bat in 1977 when he batted .320. His career spanned 21 seasons and 1,909 games. He batted a lifetime .271 and will go down in history as one of the few catchers to catch Hall of Famers on two different teams (Bob Gibson in St. Louis, Carlton in Philadelphia).

He also broke his hand in a game at San Francisco in May 1970, then saw replacement Mike Ryan come into the hospital with the same injury as he was leaving.

McCarver finally got to the broadcasting booth in 1980 and was part of the Phillies' announcing team for three years before joining the Mets in 1983 and later becoming a network broadcaster.

A man who combines wit with thoughtfulness, McCarver had a high school stadium named after him in his native Memphis. Someone asked him if stadiums weren't normally named for dead people. His answer: "They named it after my arm."

McCarver, Tim

Phillies	G	AB	H	BA	RBI	R	2B	3B	HR	SA	SB
1970	44	164	47	.287	14	16	11	1	4	.439	2
1971	134	474	132	.278	46	51	20	5	8	.392	5
1972	45	152	36	.237	14	14	8	0	2	.329	1
1975	47	59	15	.254	7	6	2	0	1	.339	0
1976	90	155	43	.277	29	26	11	2	3	.432	2
1977	93	169	54	.320	30	28	13	2	6	.527	3
1978	90	146	36	.247	14	18	9	1	1	.342	2
1979	79	137	33	.241	12	13	5	1	1	.314	2
1980	6	5	1	.200	2	2	1	0	0	.400	0
Career	1,909	5,529	1,501	.271	645	590	242	57	97	.388	61

Tim McCarver

Ed McFarland was an outstanding defensive catcher who could handle pitching staffs as well as anyone in his time, which was the turn of the century when the American League was formed as real competition for the National League.

McFarland showed his true value in 1901, his last of five seasons with the Phillies. The American League, in its first big raid on the National League rosters, took pitchers Chick Fraser, Wiley Piatt, and Strawberry Bill Bernhard. The trio had accounted for 40 of the Phillies' 75 victories.

The following season, McFarland again did most of the catching, and the Phillies actually upped their victory total to 83. McFarland was given much of the credit for the upsurge.

Ed was no slouch at the plate. In his four full seasons with the Phillies, he never batted lower than .282. Twice he went over the .300 mark.

McFarland, Ed

Phillies: 1897–1901
Catcher
Birthplace: Cleveland, Ohio
B: August 3, 1874
D: November 28, 1959
Batted right, threw right
Ht. 5–10; **Wt.** 180

McFarland, Ed

Phillies	G	AB	H	BA	RBI	R	2B	3B	HR	SA	SB
1897	38	130	29	.223	16	18	3	5	1	.346	2
1898	121	429	121	.282	71	65	21	5	3	.375	4
1899	96	324	108	.333	57	59	22	10	1	.472	9
1900	94	344	105	.305	38	50	14	8	0	.392	9
1901	74	295	84	.285	32	33	14	2	1	.356	11
Career	894	3,007	826	.275	383	398	146	50	12	.368	65

Ed McFarland

His .963 fielding percentage topped all National League catchers in 1900. In 1901, working with virtually a whole new staff, he upped the figure to .970.

McFarland joined the parade after the 1901 season, leaving the Phillies for the Chicago White Stockings. He played there six seasons as a backup catcher, then spent a year with the Red Sox before he retired at the age of 34.

McGraw, Tug

Phillies: 1975–84
Pitcher
Birthplace: Martinez, California
B: August 30, 1944
Bats right, throws left
Ht. 6–0; **Wt.** 170

Tug McGraw

For nearly a decade Tug McGraw was the Phillies' top lefthanded reliever on the field and the team's court jester off it. "I could have fun in a stalled elevator," he said in 1965 after joining the New York Mets as a 20-year-old. He had a ball through a professional baseball career that covered 21 seasons, seven League Championship Series, and three World Series.

But whenever Phillies fans think about him, they will remember a scene that looked like an overcrowded elevator instead of a stalled one. On October 21, 1980, in a Veterans Stadium packed with screaming fans and police dogs and horses, McGraw struck out Willie Wilson to clinch the only World Championship in Phillies history, then threw his arms in the air and did a dance while waiting for his teammates to jump on him on the mound.

It climaxed a remarkable second half of the regular season and post-season for McGraw, who cemented his role as one of the most popular athletes in the history of Philadelphia. It also marked the second time in his career that Frank Edwin McGraw had carried a team to remarkable heights with his heroics on the mound and his words in the clubhouse. In 1973, McGraw's rallying cry, "You Gotta Believe," was the catalyst for the New York Mets' improbable drive to within a game of the World Championship.

But for Phillies fans, that was nothing compared to what he did after he came off the disabled list on July 17, 1980. For the rest of the regular season, McGraw allowed only three earned runs over 52⅓ innings and 33 games. His record was 5–1 with 13 saves during that period. And he climaxed it with a pitching performance against the Montreal Expos on the final week of the season that he called "the peak of my career."

"There is no way I can pitch any better," he told Hal Bodley in the book *The Team That Wouldn't Die.* "I flash back on that all the time. I see hitters looking at pitches and swinging and missing at pitches that were as perfect as I could throw them—location-wise, rotation-wise, mechanics-wise."

The Phillies went to Montreal for the final weekend needing to win two out of three to clinch the National League East title. In a 2–1 victory on Friday night, McGraw faced the last six Expo hitters and struck out five of them. Then he earned the clinching victory the following day when the Phillies scored a 6–4 victory in 11 innings on Mike Schmidt's two-run homer.

But that was just a preview to the LCS against the Houston Astros. The Phillies won in five pulsating games, and McGraw pitched in all five. He was the loser of Game Three, but saved the first and fourth contests.

Then, in the World Series, he pitched in four of the six games against the Kansas City Royals, winning Game Five and saving the opener and the clincher. He fanned 10 Royals in eight innings, including the strikeout of Wilson that began the celebration that wouldn't end until the next afternoon when McGraw, holding the *Philadelphia Daily News* over his head, had a message from the City of Brotherly Love to New York City.

"Take this championship and stick it," he told the Big Apple.

McGraw's use of the English language was usually more thoughtful and humorous. Like the way he named his fastballs, for instance. One was the John Jameson. "I like my Irish whiskey straight," he explained. Others were named for Peggy Lee ("Is that all there is?"), Bo Derek ("It has a nice little tail on it"), and Cutty Sark ("It sails").

And it was McGraw who kept the Phillies loose when they appeared on the brink of losing the division championship after building a huge lead in 1976, Tug's second season with the Phillies. He had pitched for the Mets from 1965 to 1974, including the Miracle Mets World Championship team in 1969 and the 1973 squad which rallied from last place early in September to the pennant while McGraw screamed, "You Gotta Believe," after every game. He saved 25 games for the Mets that year, two fewer than his career high the season before.

But after a disappointing year in 1974, the Mets traded him to the Phillies with Don Hahn and Dave Schneck for Del Unser, Mac Scarce, and outstanding catching prospect John Stearns.

McGraw paid immediate dividends, saving 14 games and winning nine while posting a 2.97 earned run average in 1975. Then he was instrumental in helping the Phillies win three straight NL East championships. During that period, he won 22 games and saved 29 while averaging 59 appearances a season.

Along with most of his teammates, he slumped in 1979. His ERA soared to 5.14, taking much of the glitter off his 14 saves. And he was still struggling in 1980 until he began his remarkable streak in mid-July.

"I don't think I have ever been more proud to be a baseball player," he said after the World Series that year. "It was a very great year."

It also was McGraw's last great year in the majors. He pitched four more seasons, saving 10 games in the abbreviated 1981 season, but when the Phillies reached the post-season again in 1983, McGraw played a vastly different role from his 1980 heroics. He was not used either against the Los Angeles Dodgers in the LCS or the Baltimore Orioles in the World Series.

He retired after the 1984 season, leaving a legacy of positive clubhouse talk and positive career statistics.

At one point in 1983, he had made the tenth highest number of pitching appearances in baseball history. His 463 games for the Phillies are the third highest total among all pitchers. He is second in saves with 94 and second in relief victories with 49. His combination of 143 victories and saves is second on the club's career list, one behind teammate Ron Reed.

McGraw remained in the Philadelphia area after his retirement. He has been a regular commentator on local television news broadcasts and is a frequent participant in old-timers' games across the country.

McGraw, Tug (Frank)

Phillies	W	L	Pct	ERA	G	CG	IP	H	BB	SO	ShO
1975	9	6	.600	2.97	56	0	103	84	36	55	0
1976	7	6	.538	2.51	58	0	97	81	42	76	0
1977	7	3	.700	2.62	45	0	79	62	24	58	0
1978	8	7	.533	3.20	55	0	90	82	23	63	0
1979	4	3	.571	5.14	65	0	84	83	29	57	0
1980	5	4	.556	1.47	57	0	92	62	23	75	0
1981	2	4	.333	2.66	34	0	44	35	14	26	0
1982	3	3	.500	4.31	34	0	40	50	12	25	0
1983	2	1	.667	3.56	34	0	56	58	19	30	0
1984	2	0	1.000	3.79	25	0	38	36	10	26	0
Career	96	92	.511	3.13	824	5	1,516	1,318	582	1,109	1

McQuillan, George

Phillies: 1907–10, 1915–16
Pitcher
Birthplace: Brooklyn, New York
B: May 1, 1885
D: March 30, 1940
Batted right, threw right
Ht. 6–0; **Wt.** 170

George McQuillan

When it comes to the great debuts in major league baseball, few rank any higher than that of George Washington McQuillan.

Certainly no pitcher ever broke in with more of a flourish. Just 22 years old, McQuillan hurled 25 consecutive scoreless innings in 1907, at the start of what would become an in-and-out 10-year big league career. It's a major league record that still stands.

McQuillan had been playing in the minors for three years when the Phillies purchased him early in 1907. On May 8 he pitched one scoreless inning, but he soon was sent to Providence for more seasoning. After compiling a 19–7 record there, he was called back to the Phillies, and on September 22 he picked up where he had left off.

George got three starts, and hurled shutouts in each of them. He wound up with a 0–0 no-decision in a nine-inning game with the St. Louis Cardinals; beat the Chicago Cubs in a six-inning game, 6–0; and blanked the Cincinnati Reds, 1–0, on a nine-inning two-hitter. The streak ended on October 2 when the Pittsburgh Pirates touched McQuillan for one run in the first inning in a 4–1 Phillies win.

McQuillan ended the season with a 4–0 record. Technically still a rookie, he continued to set the National League on its ear in 1908, setting club records for a first-year pitcher that still stand in games started (42) and completed (32) while posting a 23–17 record with a sparkling 1.52 earned run average, third best in the league. His games (48) and innings pitched (359⅔) were each second. His record would have been even better had he not lost five games by 1–0 scores.

By then, McQuillan was being hailed as the next Christy Mathewson. "He'll be Matty's successor as the No. 1 pitcher in the league," his supporters claimed.

It never happened. A guy who was strongly attracted to the bright lights, McQuillan slipped to a 13–16 mark in 1909. The following year he was 9–6 but led the league with a 1.60 ERA. Early in the season, however, manager Red Dooin suspended George for training violations. In August, McQuillan was suspended again, this time by club president Horace Fogel, for the remainder of the season.

Having had their fill of him, the Phillies sold McQuillan to the Reds, who dumped him after one year. He surfaced with the Pirates in 1913, but after nearly three uneventful seasons was sold back to the Phillies late in 1915.

George managed to win four of seven decisions to help the '15 Phils capture their first National League pennant. He did not appear, though, in the World Series.

After pitching with the Phillies in 1916, McQuillan was gone again. He appeared briefly with Cleveland in 1918 before drifting permanently out of the big leagues.

McQuillan, George

Phillies	W	L	Pct	ERA	G	CG	IP	H	BB	SO	ShO
1907	4	0	1.000	0.66	6	5	41	21	11	28	3
1908	23	17	.575	1.52	48	32	360	263	91	114	7
1909	13	16	.448	2.14	41	16	248	202	54	96	4
1910	9	6	.600	1.60	24	13	152	109	50	71	3
1915	4	3	.571	2.11	9	5	64	60	11	13	0
1916	1	7	.125	2.76	21	1	62	58	15	22	0
Career	85	89	.489	2.38	273	105	1,577	1,382	401	590	17

When Henry Lee Meadows arrived in the major leagues with the St. Louis Cardinals in 1915, he was treated as the act between the fat lady and the sword swallower.

Step right up, ladies and gents, and see the eighth wonder of the world, the baseball pitcher who wears eyeglasses while performing! He'll amaze you with his ability to throw the ball over a plate he must have trouble seeing!

After 188 major league victories in 15 years, five of them with the Phillies, there was no question that the first major leaguer to wear glasses on the field was something more than a character that fell off the back of a carnival wagon.

He won 58 games over a three-year stretch with the Pirates, including a league-leading 20 in 1926. And, although he wasn't quite as successful with the Phillies (16 wins in 1920, his best with them), he made sure the fans got home in time for supper.

Meadows was the fastest-working pitcher of his time—an early version of Jim Kaat with not quite as long a career.

Specs came to the Phillies in the middle of the 1919 season for two nondescript pitchers. Although his records in his three full years with the Phillies were less than flattering (16–14, 11–16, 12–18), so were the teams for which he played. He was first-class material, and the other teams in the league knew it. Specs was also getting mighty tired of seeing well-pitched games float down the Schuylkill because his teammates couldn't catch the ball. Baker heard about it and told reporter Fred Lieb: "I've heard reports that Meadows isn't overly happy here, but he'll pitch for the Phillies until his whiskers grow down to his knees."

Oh? Specs didn't even have to wait for the five o'clock shadow. On May 23, 1923, he was traded to the Pirates for Cotton Tierney, Whitey Glazner, and Bill Baker's favorite player—a $50,000 check.

Meadows, Lee

Phillies: 1919–23
Pitcher
Nickname: Specs
Birthplace: Oxford, North Carolina
B: July 12, 1894
D: January 23, 1963
Batted both, threw right
Ht. 5–9; Wt. 190

Lee Meadows

Meadows, Lee

Phillies	W	L	Pct	ERA	G	CG	IP	H	BB	SO	ShO
1919	8	10	.444	2.48	18	15	149	128	49	88	3
1920	16	14	.533	2.84	35	19	247	249	90	95	3
1921	11	16	.407	4.31	28	15	194	226	62	52	2
1922	12	18	.400	4.02	33	19	237	264	71	62	2
1923	1	3	.250	13.05	8	0	20	40	15	10	0
Career	188	180	.511	3.38	490	219	3,151	3,280	956	1,063	25

Irish Meusel was a classic example of the bad decisions made during the William F. Baker era. He was a lucky draft pick who improved his average each season he was with the team. He batted over .300 in three of his four seasons as a Phillie, then was traded to the Giants in a deal that Commissioner Landis later said he never would have approved had he realized the circumstances surrounding it.

The brother of Yankee outfielder Bob Meusel, Irish had only two big league at-bats (Washington in 1914) when the Phillies plucked him off the Los Angeles Pacific Coast League roster before the 1918 season.

Although he had a weak throwing arm, Meusel had speed and decent power. By 1921 he had become a threat to finish very high in the batting race, but when Baker saw a chance to make a deal with the Giants and get another fat check, he fabricated a situation. Meusel was hitting .353 with 12 homers and 51 RBI in 89 games when Baker charged him with indifference and benched him for several games in July. He then traded Irish to the Giants for $30,000, Butch Henline, Curt Walker, and Jesse Winters, explaining that the deal was made "for the team's good."

Wrote Jimmy Isaminger in *The Sporting News*: "Of course, nobody believed Mr. Baker when he said he got rid of Meusel for the team's good. If that really

Meusel, Emil

Phillies: 1918–21
Outfielder
Nickname: Irish
Birthplace: Oakland, California
B: June 9, 1893
D: March 1, 1963
Batted right, threw right
Ht. 5–11½; Wt. 178

The New Phillies Encyclopedia

Emil Meusel

was the case, he would be subject to severe censure for thus rewarding a bad actor."

There was nothing bad about Irish Meusel's act with the Giants. He tore apart the Pirates in a late-August five-game sweep in 1921 to help the Giants make the World Series, then set a record by driving in seven runs in an eight-game Series.

The following year, he established a World Series record for a four-game set by driving in seven more runs. In his five full years with New York, he topped the .300 mark three times and never dipped below .292. He drove in more than 100 runs four consecutive times, including 132 in 1922 and a league-leading 125 in 1923. Once again, the Phillies were deprived of the prime years of an outstanding player because of stupidity at the front office level.

Meusel, Emil

Phillies	G	AB	H	BA	RBI	R	2B	3B	HR	SA	SB
1918	124	473	132	.279	62	47	25	6	4	.383	18
1919	135	521	159	.305	59	65	26	7	5	.411	24
1920	138	518	160	.309	69	75	27	8	14	.473	17
1921	89	343	121	.353	51	59	21	7	12	.560	8
Career	1,294	4,900	1,521	.310	818	701	250	93	106	.464	113

Meyer, Jack

Phillies: 1955–61
Pitcher
Birthplace: Philadelphia, Pennsylvania
B: March 23, 1932
D: March 9, 1967
Batted right, threw right
Ht. 6–1; **Wt.** 175

Jack Meyer

When Jack Meyer joined the Phillies in 1955, it was the old case of local boy makes good.

Perhaps one of the finest pitchers in Philadelphia schoolboy history, Meyer had been a flame-throwing righthander at William Penn Charter School. After attending Wake Forest College and the University of Delaware, the curly-haired blond was signed by Jocko Collins and joined the Phils' farm system in 1951. He rose quickly up the ranks. In 1954 his 15 victories and league-leading strikeout total led International League champion Syracuse to the Little World Series championship over Louisville of the American Association.

The winner of the first Blue Cross pitchometer contest (in 1949), Meyer was mostly a relief pitcher during his seven years in the big leagues. His crackling fastball proved to be a successful late-inning closer for the Phillies. Jack registered nearly one strikeout per inning while hurling in 202 big league games.

Meyer's best season turned out to be his rookie campaign in 1955 when he led National League relievers with 16 saves. Jack's 6–11 record in 50 games that year was deceiving as he regularly came in from the bullpen to thwart enemy rallies.

In 1958, Meyer set a major league record for relief pitchers by striking out the first six batters he faced in a game against the Pittsburgh Pirates. Phils pitchers fanned 21 Bucs—another record—in their 3–2, 14-inning win.

A fun-loving guy who occasionally showed flashes of a hot temper, Meyer's career was shortened by a back injury, and he retired in 1961. In 1967, Jack died of a heart attack while watching a 76ers- Boston basketball playoff game on television.

Meyer, Jack

Phillies	W	L	Pct	ERA	G	CG	IP	H	BB	SO	ShO
1955	6	11	.353	3.43	50	0	110⅓	75	66	97	0
1956	7	11	.389	4.41	41	2	96	86	51	66	0
1957	0	2	.000	5.73	19	0	37⅔	44	28	34	0
1958	3	6	.333	3.59	37	1	90⅓	77	33	87	0
1959	5	3	.625	3.36	47	1	93⅔	76	53	71	0
1960	3	1	.750	4.32	7	0	25	25	11	18	0
1961	0	0	.000	9.00	1	0	2	2	2	2	0
Career	24	34	.414	3.92	202	4	455	385	244	375	0

Meyer, Russ

Phillies: 1949–52
Pitcher
Nickname: The Mad Monk
Birthplace: Peru, Illinois
B: October 25, 1923
Bats both, throws right
Ht. 6–1; **Wt.** 175

Even if he hadn't done anything else, Russ Meyer would go down as one of the most colorful players in the modern era of the Phillies.

A generous, likable fellow off the field, Meyer had a legendary temper that erupted occasionally. In addition, Russ was always capable of performing colorful antics of one kind or another.

As a pitcher, Meyer had a 13-year big league career that had some great moments. In 1949, for instance, Russ was the premier righthanded pitcher in the National League, posting a 17–8 record and a 3.08 ERA while teaming with Ken Heintzelman to give the third-place Phillies an outstanding one-two punch on the mound. At one point late in the season, Meyer won eight straight games, one of which was a one-hitter against the Boston Braves. Connie Ryan's first-inning double was the only safety in the 3–1 win.

Russ had come to the Phillies in the fall of 1948 after his contract was purchased from the Chicago Cubs. Originally signed by the Chicago White Sox in 1941, Meyer played four years of minor league ball (he was also in the Army one year) before joining the Cubs, who signed him as a free agent.

Meyer's 10–10 record in 1948 was his best in two seasons with the Cubs. At one point he came within one out of pitching a no-hitter against the St. Louis Cardinals when Whitey Kurowski bashed a ninth-inning single. He reported to the Phillies in 1949 with little fanfare, but Russ, whose bread-and-butter pitch was a screwball, proved a pleasant surprise.

Despite his big year in 1949, Meyer was not a major factor in the Phillies' 1950 pennant drive. He slipped to a 9–11 record, although he did win some key games, including a 4–3 victory over the Brooklyn Dodgers in early September.

Throughout his career, Meyer was plagued by injuries. He broke his left ankle in a collision at first base in 1947 and his right ankle in a slide at third in 1948. He suffered a severe spike injury in 1951, and had back and shoulder injuries in later seasons.

Meyer's quick temper also detracted at times from his pitching. He was injured kicking the pitching rubber in anger, once just missed the clubhouse boy when he fired a bar of soap, broke a toe kicking a steel locker, and one time was slapped with a 10-day suspension after grabbing umpire Frank Dascoli so hard while protesting a call (on a Jackie Robinson steal of home) that all the buttons popped off of the ump's jacket.

Probably Meyer's most memorable outburst occurred as he was being removed from the mound after getting hit heavily. Russ was so angry that he fired the resin bag high in the air. As Meyer stood fuming, the bag dropped squarely on his head, covering his hat with resin, bringing roars of laughter from the crowd and his ejection from the game by umpire Augie Donatelli. Once in the dugout, Meyer was caught by TV cameras making obscene gestures at the umpire, and was ultimately fined $100 and suspended for three days.

The Phillies traded Russ for first baseman Earl Torgeson in 1953 in part of a four-club deal in which Meyer wound up with Brooklyn. Over the next two

Russ Meyer

years, Russ gave the Dodgers 15–5 and 11–6 records. Meyer returned to the Cubs in 1956, then pitched for the Cincinnati Reds, Boston Red Sox, and Kansas City A's before retiring in 1959.

Meyer, Russ

Phillies	W	L	Pct	ERA	G	CG	IP	H	BB	SO	ShO
1949	17	8	.680	3.08	37	14	213	199	70	78	2
1950	9	11	.450	5.30	32	3	159⅔	193	67	74	0
1951	8	9	.471	3.48	28	7	168	172	55	65	2
1952	13	14	.481	3.14	37	14	232⅓	235	65	92	1
Career	94	73	.563	3.99	319	65	1,531⅓	1,606	541	672	13

Miller, Bob

Phillies: 1950–58
Pitcher
Birthplace: Detroit, Michigan
B: June 16, 1926
Bats right, throws right
Ht. 6–3; **Wt.** 190

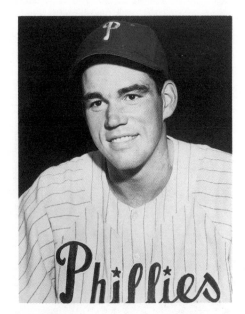

Bob Miller

Although he put in all or parts of 10 seasons with the Phillies, Bob Miller had only one year that was worth noting. But what a year that was. If it hadn't been for Miller, the Phillies never would have won the pennant in 1950.

A big, rawboned rookie that year, Miller had joined the club after signing for a $2,500 bonus. A high school sensation in Detroit, and a sandlot teammate of Stan Lopata, Miller had enlisted in the Army at age 18. After a two-year hitch in the Pacific, he enrolled as a student at the University of Detroit. Phillies scout Eddie Krajnik spotted Bob at an amateur tournament and inked him to a contract in 1947.

Miller spent the next two years at Terre Haute, then reported to the Phillies in 1950. Despite his youth, Miller won a spot in the starting rotation in spring training.

Once the regular season began, Miller was unbeatable. Combining a sizzling fastball with an excellent sinker and good control, Bob won his first eight decisions, beginning with a 2–1 victory over the Boston Braves and Vern Bickford in his first start.

During the early part of the season, Miller was one of the major reasons the Phillies were able to stay in the pennant race. With Ken Heintzelman and Russ Meyer experiencing slumps, Bob's contribution to the pitching staff was especially valuable.

In mid-season, however, the law of averages began catching up with Miller. Although he pitched some good games, he lost more than he won. Then in September, a shoulder injury sidelined him for nearly two weeks. When he came back, he had two more starts, both in the final week of the season. Each time, he was knocked out of the box.

Nevertheless, Miller finished the season with a fine 11–6 record and a 3.57 ERA. He had played a vital role in the Phillies' first pennant in 35 years.

Bob was the starting pitcher in the fourth game of the World Series. But he was knocked out after hurling one-third of an inning as the Yankees touched him for two runs en route to a 5–2 triumph and Series sweep.

Miller was troubled by a sore arm in 1951 and spent part of the year back in the minors at Wilmington. He stayed in the minors for most of 1952. After rejoining the Phillies late that year, Bob stayed with the club through the 1958 season. He never won more than eight games, and after 1955 he was used mostly as a relief pitcher.

The bushy-browed hurler was picked up by the St. Louis Cardinals in 1959, but Bob didn't make the club.

Miller, Bob

Phillies	W	L	Pct	ERA	G	CG	IP	H	BB	SO	ShO
1949	0	0	.000	0.00	3	0	2⅔	2	2	0	0
1950	11	6	.647	3.57	35	7	174	190	57	44	2
1951	2	1	.667	6.82	17	0	34⅓	47	18	10	0
1952	0	1	.000	6.00	3	0	9	13	1	2	0
1953	8	9	.471	4.00	35	8	157⅓	169	42	63	3
1954	7	9	.438	4.56	30	5	150	176	39	42	0
1955	8	4	.667	2.41	40	0	89⅔	80	28	28	0
1956	3	6	.333	3.24	49	3	122⅓	115	34	53	1
1957	2	5	.286	2.69	32	0	60⅓	61	17	12	0
1958	1	1	.500	11.69	17	0	22⅓	36	9	9	0
Career	42	42	.500	3.96	261	23	822	889	247	263	6

A scrappy little guy who had a lively bat and tremendous fielding instincts, Johnny Mokan was hardly ever mentioned during his career without the words "spark plug" or "pepper pot" next to his name. He hustled and scratched for the Phillies for 5½ years after they picked him up for next to nothing from the Pirates in July 1922.

For three years he hit .300, with his best coming in 1925 when he batted .330. In 1926 he saw his most action ever, playing in 127 games and batting 456 times.

The following year he failed to hit a home run in 213 at-bats and was traded in December to the Cardinals for Jimmy Ring. The Cardinals released him to the minor leagues before he ever had a chance to play for them.

Although he had 563 major league hits, the hit he remembered best was in 1919 when he was playing for Waco against Galveston. Tex Johnson, who had spent three previous seasons in the majors, was the Galveston pitcher. On that particular day he was throwing like a major leaguer. Through nine innings Johnson had a no-hitter, but his team hadn't scored either. Galveston went down in order in the top of the tenth, and the first two Waco hitters were retired in the bottom of the inning. Mokan was next up. He guessed fastball, and guessed right, hitting a home run for a 1–0 victory.

"If it hadn't been that we needed the game, or had I been the last man up in the bottom of the ninth and he was in the lead, I doubt if I would have spoiled his record," Mokan recalled. "But that fastball looked too good so I just let the bat rip."

Mokan, Johnny

Phillies: 1922–27
Outfielder
Birthplace: Buffalo, New York
B: September 23, 1895
D: February 10, 1985
Batted right, threw right
Ht. 5–7; Wt. 165

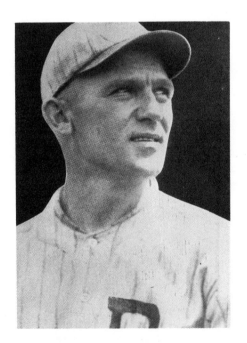

Johnny Mokan

Mokan, Johnny

Phillies	G	AB	H	BA	RBI	R	2B	3B	HR	SA	SB
1922	47	151	38	.252	27	20	7	1	3	.370	1
1923	113	400	125	.313	48	76	23	3	10	.460	6
1924	96	366	95	.260	44	50	15	1	7	.363	7
1925	75	209	69	.330	42	30	11	2	6	.488	3
1926	127	456	138	.303	62	68	23	5	6	.414	4
1927	74	213	61	.286	33	22	13	2	0	.366	5
Career	582	1,936	563	.291	273	282	98	17	32	.409	26

Money, Don

Phillies: 1968–72
Shortstop, third baseman
Birthplace: Washington, D.C.
B: June 7, 1947
Bats right, throws right
Ht. 6–1; **Wt.** 170

Don Money

It was 1968, and the Phillies' attempts to win pennants with veterans had proved disastrous. Now the team tried to build for the future. One of the big deals sent an aging but still productive Jim Bunning to Pittsburgh for Don Money.

The Phillies' rebuilding hopes were tied to Money and farm system product Larry Hisle. In fact, both came north with the big club for the 1968 season.

Don was a 20-year-old shortstop at the time. After a week, the Phillies decided it was unwise to rush Money and Hisle and sent them back to San Diego (Pacific Coast League).

After a .303 season at San Diego, Money came to the majors for good. He was the Phillies' shortstop in 1969, then played three years at third. He fulfilled his promise in 1970 when he hit .295 with 14 homers and 66 RBI, but never got out of the .220s in his other three seasons. In his big year, he missed 27 games after being hit in the eye by a bad-hop grounder.

He was traded to the Milwaukee Brewers after a 1972 season that saw him reach a personal National League high with 15 homers. He spent 11 seasons with the Brewers and was a productive member of the 1982 American League champions.

Money, Don

Phillies	G	AB	H	BA	RBI	R	2B	3B	HR	SA	SB
1968	4	13	3	.231	2	1	2	0	0	.385	0
1969	127	450	103	.229	42	41	22	2	6	.327	1
1970	120	447	132	.295	66	66	25	4	14	.463	4
1971	121	439	98	.223	38	40	22	8	7	.358	4
1972	152	536	119	.222	52	54	16	2	15	.343	5
Career	1,720	6,215	1,623	.261	729	798	302	36	176	.406	80

Montanez, Willie

Phillies: 1970–75
First baseman, outfielder
Nickname: Willie the Phillie
Birthplace: Catano, Puerto Rico
B: April 1, 1948
Bats left, throws left
Ht. 6–0; **Wt.** 170

One of the great afterthoughts in Phillies history, Willie Montanez was the player the Cardinals gave the Phils to replace Curt Flood, who refused to report.

That happened in 1970. The previous year, Montanez had torn up his leg in a sliding mishap and had missed virtually the whole season. He was a medical question mark when he arrived at Eugene, the Phillies' Triple-A farm.

The following year Willie and the opening of Veterans Stadium were the two biggest exclamation points in town. A first baseman by trade, Willie was moved to center field out of desperation. He responded as if he had been playing the position all his life, making several spectacular catches. And on offense, the Phillies got more than they expected.

Even Willie had categorized himself as a "singles and doubles hitter." But in 1971, for one unexplicable season, he became a genuine home run hitter, pounding out 30 home runs and driving in 99 runs while batting .255.

It took Montanez two more years to reach his full potential as a hitter. During that stretch, the Phillies moved him back to first base from the outfield. And the fans loved him, since he was a self-confessed "hot dog" who flipped the bat defiantly as he walked from the on-deck circle to the plate on offense and snapped at high pop flies instead of catching them normally on defense.

By 1974 his home run production had slipped to seven, but he had 79 RBI and a .304 batting average.

The Phillies became excited at the opportunity to give Dick Allen a second chance. Allen was a first baseman who couldn't play any other position on defense. Meanwhile, Garry Maddox was off to a terrible start in San Francisco. The Phillies tried to solve two problems at once by trading Willie to the Giants for Maddox in May 1975.

At first the trade was terribly unpopular among the fans, who had grown to regard Willie the Phillie as their hero. But Maddox became a Gold Glove fixture in center field and Montanez drifted from team to team, despite usually acceptable statistics, until he landed back with the Phillies late in the 1982 season from the minors.

He was overweight and out of shape, and his bat was rusty. He was released at the end of the season. At age 34, Montanez's major league career was over.

Willie Montanez

Montanez, Willie

Phillies	G	AB	H	BA	RBI	R	2B	3B	HR	SA	SB
1970	18	25	6	.240	3	3	0	0	0	.240	0
1971	158	599	153	.255	99	78	27	6	30	.471	4
1972	147	531	131	.247	64	60	39	3	13	.405	1
1973	146	552	145	.263	65	69	16	5	11	.370	2
1974	143	527	160	.304	79	55	33	1	7	.410	3
1975	21	84	24	.286	16	9	8	0	2	.452	0
1982	18	16	1	.063	1	0	0	0	0	.063	0
Career	1,632	5,843	1,604	.275	802	645	279	25	139	.402	32

The words *checkered* and *spotty* might best describe the career of Earl Moore, both with the Phillies and before.

In a seven-year career in the American League, almost all of it with the Cleveland Indians, Moore had pitched mostly around the .500 mark, although he did have an 18–9 record and a league-leading 1.77 ERA in 1903. By 1907 he had been tossed on the discard pile by the Yankees. But the Phillies rescued him at the tag end of the 1908 season, and Moore gave indications of big moments to come.

In three games and 26 innings, he didn't allow an earned run. He completed all three starts, although poor fielding cost him one of three decisions.

In 1909 he carried the pitching staff on his back, leading the way with an 18–12 record and a 2.10 ERA. He set a then-club record with 13 strikeouts in a 3–0 victory over the Brooklyn Dodgers. The following season, even though he was suspended for a period by manager Red Dooin for breaking training rules, Earl had his best year with the Phillies, going 22–15 and leading the league with 185 strikeouts. There was nothing wrong with the way he pitched in 1911 either, even though his 19 defeats in 34 decisions were tops in the league.

In 1912, Moore's career took a giant backward step when his hand was broken by a batted ball. He finished 9–14 and was sold after a dozen outings the following season to the Chicago Cubs. He played in 1914 in the Federal League, then passed from the big league scene.

Moore, Earl

Phillies: 1908–13
Pitcher
Nickname: Crossfire
Birthplace: Pickerington, Ohio
B: July 29, 1878
D: November 28, 1961
Batted right, threw right
Ht. 6–0; **Wt.** 195

Earl Moore

Moore, Earl

Phillies	W	L	Pct	ERA	G	CG	IP	H	BB	SO	ShO
1908	2	1	.667	0.00	3	3	26	20	8	16	1
1909	18	12	.600	2.10	38	24	300	238	108	173	4
1910	22	15	.595	2.58	46	19	283	228	121	185	6
1911	15	19	.441	2.63	42	21	308	265	164	174	5
1912	9	14	.391	3.31	31	10	182	186	77	79	1
1913	1	3	.250	5.02	12	0	52	50	40	24	0
Career	160	153	.511	2.78	387	230	2,767	2,467	1,102	1,397	34

Moore, Johnny

Phillies: 1934–37
Right fielder
Birthplace: Waterville, Connecticut
B: March 23, 1902
D: April 4, 1991
Batted left, threw right
Ht. 5–10½; **Wt.** 175

Johnny Moore

In the 1930s, when good hitters were rather abundant in the Phillies' lineup, Johnny Moore was one of the best of the group. Consistently among the league leaders in hitting, Moore had four seasons above .300 for the Phillies en route to a 10-year lifetime batting average in the big leagues of .307.

Moore also played with the Chicago Cubs and Cincinnati Reds during his career. His start in professional baseball had been in 1924 with Elmira. Johnny moved up the ranks through New Haven and Waterbury, and then joined the Bruins for a few games in 1928.

He spent most of that season, however, with Reading. Moore came back to the Cubs in 1929, but wound up playing most of that and the next season in the Pacific Coast League with Los Angeles.

Johnny was back in Chicago in 1931. The next year he became the Cubs' regular center fielder and hit .305 as Chicago won the National League pennant. He was the center fielder over whose head Babe Ruth's "pointed" home run flew in the 1932 World Series.

Chicago traded Moore to Cincinnati in 1933. John had a mediocre year and was sent the following season to the Phillies with pitcher Syl Johnson for pitcher Ted Kleinhans and outfielder Wes Schulmerich. He wound up the 1934 campaign with a .343 average for the Phils.

Playing right field, Moore hit over .300 for the next three seasons for the Phillies. In 1935, he hit at a .323 clip. He followed that with a .328 mark and a .319 average.

A respectable power hitter, Johnny hit 19 home runs in 1935. That year and in 1934 he led the Phillies in RBI with 93 each season. Johnny's batting averages led the team in 1934, 1935, and 1936.

In 1936, Moore hit three consecutive home runs and collected six RBI to lead the Phillies to a 16–4 victory over the Pittsburgh Pirates.

Johnny saw only part-time duty in 1937, and although he could still hit, the Phillies sold him to the Los Angeles Angels of the Pacific Coast League at the end of the season.

After winning two PCL batting titles, Moore played briefly in the big leagues again in 1945 with the Cubs. After his playing days, he became a successful scout for the Braves and later the Expos. He signed more than 200 players, including Hall of Famer Eddie Mathews.

Moore, Johnny

Phillies	G	AB	H	BA	RBI	R	2B	3B	HR	SA	SB
1934	116	458	157	.343	93	68	34	6	11	.515	7
1935	153	600	194	.323	93	84	33	3	19	.483	4
1936	124	472	155	.328	68	85	24	3	16	.494	1
1937	96	307	98	.319	59	46	16	2	9	.472	2
Career	846	3,013	926	.307	452	439	155	26	73	.449	23

Mulcahy, Hugh

Phillies: 1935–40, 1945–46
Pitcher
Nickname: Hughie, Losing Pitcher
Birthplace: Brighton, Massachusetts
B: September 9, 1913
Bats right, throws right
Ht. 6–2½; **Wt.** 190

Playing for losing teams has never been conducive to satisfactory records. Nobody proved that better than Hugh Mulcahy.

A big righthander with more than average talent, Mulcahy never had a winning season in his nine-year big league career. But he sure had some swell losing ones, which may have had something to do with the nickname hung on him.

The Phillies finished last in five of the eight seasons Hugh played for them. Twice they finished next to last. Accordingly, Mulcahy posted records such as 8–18, 10–20, 9–16, and 13–22.

Mulcahy led the National League in losses in 1938 (20) and 1940 (22). He also led the league in walks (1937) and hits allowed (1940). In 1940 he was among the league leaders in complete games with 21, but equaled an all-time

Phillies record with 12 straight losses. He was picked that year for the National League All-Star team.

Hughie was a workhorse, though, and in his four main years with the Phillies (1937–40), he pitched well over 200 innings each season. In 1937 he worked in 56 games (31 of them in relief), which at the time set a National League record for most games pitched in one season.

Mulcahy began in baseball in 1933. The Phillies bought him from Manchester (New Hampshire) in 1934. He was up briefly with the Phils in 1935 and 1936 (the year he posted a 25–14 record with Hazelton) before sticking the whole season in 1937.

He was the first major league player inducted into the service in 1941 and was not discharged until 1945. During his absence, the Phillies had three different owners.

Hugh looked on his early draft philosophically. Asked if he considered being the first major leaguer drafted as a stroke of bad luck, Mulcahy replied: "I don't know. I might have got hit with a line drive if I spent six more months with the Phillies."

Mulcahy, thought by some to have been one of the better hurlers in the National League before his Army days, spent the end of the 1945 season and the 1946 campaign with the Phillies. But by then he had lost his effectiveness. He retired after a short stint with the Pittsburgh Pirates in 1947.

Hugh Mulcahy

Mulcahy, Hugh

Phillies	W	L	Pct	ERA	G	CG	IP	H	BB	SO	ShO
1935	1	5	.167	4.78	18	0	52⅔	62	25	11	0
1936	1	1	.500	3.22	3	2	22⅓	20	12	2	0
1937	8	18	.308	5.13	56	9	215⅔	256	97	54	1
1938	10	20	.333	4.61	46	15	267⅓	294	120	90	0
1939	9	16	.360	4.99	38	14	225⅔	246	93	59	1
1940	13	22	.371	3.60	36	21	280	283	91	82	3
1945	1	3	.250	3.81	5	1	28⅓	33	9	2	0
1946	2	4	.333	4.45	16	1	62⅔	69	33	12	0
Career	45	89	.336	4.49	220	63	1,161⅓	1,271	487	314	5

One thing could always be said about Joe Mulvey. He could make an error at the crack of the bat.

Although errors were a much more frequent occurrence in his days, Mulvey went a little overboard. In 1884, for instance, he led National League third basemen in bobbles with no less than 73. The following year, he cut down to 62 boots, but still led the league. In neither year did he lead his team in errors. But in both years he topped his fellow third sackers in the league in putouts with 151 and 144, respectively, proving he could catch the ball once in a while.

Joe's errors decreased further in the ensuing years, but his fielding average never reached .900, which was not uncommon in those days, either. His name remains in the record book, not for most errors by a third baseman in a season (that distinction belongs to New York's Charles Hickman, who made 91 miscues in 1900), but for most errors in one nine-inning game. In a game in 1884, Mulvey booted six balls.

A big man with a bushy mustache, Mulvey was the Phillies' regular third baseman for six years. Originally on the Providence club, he joined the Phillies in 1883 while still a rookie. He didn't play much that first year, but in 1884 he nailed down a starting berth.

Mulvey's batting averages with the Phillies ranged from a low of .216

Mulvey, Joe

Phillies: 1883–89, 1892
Third baseman
Birthplace: Providence, Rhode Island
B: October 27, 1858
D: August 21, 1928
Batted right, threw right
Ht. 5–11½; **Wt.** 178

Joe Mulvey

(1888) to a high of .289 (1889). During his career in Philadelphia, he played enough games to rank fourth on the team's all-time list for third basemen.

In 1890, Mulvey bolted to the Players' League formed by the players' union. He played for the Philadelphia entry and hit .287. The following year, after the Players' League had disbanded, he joined the Philadelphia Athletics of the American Association.

Joe came back to the Phillies in 1892, but missed most of the season because of an illness. He played for Washington in 1893 and Brooklyn in 1894 before bowing out of the big leagues.

Mulvey, Joe

Phillies	G	AB	H	BA	RBI	R	2B	3B	HR	SA	SB
1883	3	12	6	.500	3	2	1	0	0	.583	
1884	100	401	92	.229	32	47	11	2	2	.282	
1885	107	443	119	.269	64	74	25	6	6	.393	
1886	107	430	115	.267	53	71	16	10	2	.365	27
1887	111	474	136	.287	78	93	21	6	2	.369	43
1888	100	398	86	.216	39	37	12	3	0	.261	18
1889	129	544	157	.289	77	77	21	9	6	.393	23
1892	25	98	14	.143	4	9	1	1	0	.173	2
Career	987	4,063	1,059	.261	431	598	157	70	29	.355	120

Murtaugh, Danny

Phillies: 1941–43, 1946
Infielder
Birthplace: Chester, Pennsylvania
B: October 8, 1917
D: December 2, 1976
Batted right, threw right
Ht. 5–9; **Wt.** 165

Danny Murtaugh

A scrappy Irishman who came off the sandlots of Chester, Pennsylvania, Danny Murtaugh achieved prominence mostly as the manager of the Pittsburgh Pirates.

But Danny was also a hustling infielder, the kind of player managers liked because of his determination and willingness to keep battling. Although not blessed with great talent, the aggressive Murtaugh put in nine seasons in the major leagues.

Originally signed with his buddy Mickey Vernon in 1937 by the St. Louis Browns, Danny came to the Phillies after five and one-half seasons in the minors. In his rookie year in 1941, Murtaugh led the National League in stolen bases with 18, despite playing in only 85 games.

Murtaugh played second and third base and shortstop in 1942, then settled into the keystone post for good in 1943. After two years in the service, he returned to the Phillies in 1946, but spent most of the year at Rochester, where he teamed with Eddie Joost to form the Red Wings' double-play combination.

Murtaugh played briefly the next year with the Boston Braves, then moved on to Pittsburgh where he became the Pirates' regular second sacker for the next three years. He hit .290 in 1948 and .294 in 1950. In '48 he led National League second basemen in putouts, assists, and double plays.

Murtaugh left the majors after the 1951 season to become a player-manager in the Pirates' farm system. He became the Bucs' pilot in 1957.

Danny served four different terms as the Pirates' manager, winning the World Series in 1960 and 1971.

Murtaugh, Danny

Phillies	G	AB	H	BA	RBI	R	2B	3B	HR	SA	SB
1941	85	347	76	.219	11	34	8	1	0	.248	18
1942	144	506	122	.241	27	48	16	4	0	.289	13
1943	113	451	123	.273	35	65	17	4	1	.335	0
1946	6	19	4	.211	3	1	1	0	1	.421	0
Career	767	2,599	661	.254	219	263	97	21	8	.317	49

For many years, Bill Nicholson was one of the premier power hitters in the National League. By the time he joined the Phillies, Nicholson's power had waned, but he was a valuable man to have handy as the Phillies drove toward their 1950 pennant.

A graduate of Washington College in his home town of Chestertown, Maryland, Nicholson had come off the campus to join the Philadelphia A's in 1936. He stayed only a short time, then went to the minors where he tore apart opposing pitching for the next three years.

Nicholson was purchased by the Chicago Cubs midway through the 1939 campaign. From the time he arrived in the Windy City until he left it at the end of 1948, Swish, as Brooklyn fans had tagged him because of his lusty swing, was the heavy man in the Cubs' long-ball arsenal.

A four-time National League All-Star selection, Nicholson led the circuit in home runs and RBI in 1943 and 1944. In 1943 he hit a career-high .309 while blasting 20 homers and driving in 128 runs. The next year he socked 33 four-baggers and collected 122 RBI while hitting .287 and also leading the league in runs with 116 and in total bases with 317.

That year, over a two-day period, Bill hit four home runs in four consecutive at-bats. Later, he extended that streak to six homers in four games.

Nicholson had an off-season in 1945, the year the Cubs won the pennant. But he drove in eight runs in the World Series, which at the time tied a record.

In 1948, Chicago traded Bill to the Phillies for Harry Walker. The following season, Nicholson took over as the Phillies' regular right fielder.

A shoulder injury reduced Bill's playing time, and he hit only .234 in 1949. Then a muscle ailment kept him out of action in early 1950. By the time he got back, the Phils were in the midst of a heated pennant race.

Nicholson made two major contributions during the race. In July, in a game at Shibe Park, his two-run, pinch-hit homer in the eighth inning defeated the Dodgers and Ralph Branca, 6–4. Six days later at Ebbets Field, Bill poled a ninth-inning three-run homer off Don Newcombe to break a 1–1 tie.

Late in the summer Bill began feeling ill and losing weight. His condition was diagnosed as diabetes and he was hospitalized. He did not appear in the World Series. Nicholson, however, came back in 1951, and for the next three seasons continued his pinch-hitting duties for the Phillies.

Nicholson, Bill

Phillies: 1949–53
Outfielder
Nickname: Swish
Birthplace: Chestertown, Maryland
B: December 11, 1914
Bats left, throws right
Ht. 6–0; **Wt.** 205

Bill Nicholson

Nicholson, Bill

Phillies	G	AB	H	BA	RBI	R	2B	3B	HR	SA	SB
1949	98	299	70	.234	40	42	8	3	11	.391	1
1950	41	58	13	.224	10	3	2	1	3	.448	0
1951	85	170	41	.241	30	23	9	2	8	.459	0
1952	55	88	24	.273	19	17	3	0	6	.511	0
1953	38	62	13	.210	16	12	5	1	2	.419	0
Career	1,677	5,546	1,484	.268	948	837	272	60	235	.465	27

Much was always made about the rotund shape of Ron Northey. But his size never seemed to hamper either the way he swung the bat or the way he threw the ball.

A right fielder most of his career, Northey had one of the best throwing arms of any outfielder ever to wear a Phillies uniform. It was easy for Ron to crank up a throw from deep right field to the plate, and he did it on numerous occasions.

Northey led National League outfielders in assists in 1944 when he cut down 24 base-runners. That year Ron had his finest overall season, hitting .288 with 22 home runs (third in the league) and 104 RBI. Of particular note that year was Northey's 15th-inning homer that gave the Phillies a 1–0 victory over the Boston Braves in the longest 1–0 game ever decided by a homer.

Northey, Ron

Phillies: 1942–44, 1946–47, 1957
Outfielder
Birthplace: Mahanoy City, Pennsylvania
B: April 26, 1920
D: April 16, 1971
Batted left, threw right
Ht. 5–10; **Wt.** 195

The chunky outfielder, who attended Duke University, put in three different terms with the Phillies. After entering organized ball in 1939, he joined the Phillies in 1942. He was a regular until entering the military in 1945. The next season, Northey returned to the Phils, but slumped at the plate. He was traded to the Cardinals for Harry Walker and pitcher Fred Schmidt early in the 1947 season.

Northey was traded for Walker twice during his career. In 1949 the Cardinals sent Ron and infielder Lou Klein to the Cincinnati Reds for Walker.

Ron had hit .321 as a part-timer for St. Louis in 1948. In addition to the Reds, Northey also played briefly with the Chicago Cubs and Chicago White Sox.

In the later part of his 12-year career, Northey became a superb pinch-hitter. He had nine pinch-hit home runs, including three grand slams, a National League record.

Northey came back to the Phillies after being signed as a free agent in 1957. Used exclusively as a pinch-hitter, Ron had some key hits, including his ninth career pinch-hit home run in his first appearance after rejoining the club. He retired at the end of the season.

Ron Northey

Northey, Ron

Phillies	G	AB	H	BA	RBI	R	2B	3B	HR	SA	SB
1942	127	402	101	.251	31	31	13	2	5	.331	2
1943	147	586	163	.278	68	72	31	5	16	.430	2
1944	152	570	164	.288	104	72	35	9	22	.496	1
1946	128	438	109	.249	62	55	24	6	16	.441	1
1947	13	47	12	.255	3	7	3	0	0	.319	1
1957	33	26	7	.269	5	1	0	0	1	.385	0
Career	1,084	3,172	874	.276	513	385	172	28	108	.450	7

O'Doul, Lefty

Phillies: 1929–30
Left fielder
Birthplace: San Francisco, California
B: March 4, 1897
D: December 7, 1969
Batted left, threw left
Ht. 6–0; **Wt.** 180

He only played in Philadelphia for two seasons, but in that short period Lefty O'Doul established himself as one of the leading hitters in Phillies history.

O'Doul was a muscular Californian who produced averages of .398 and .383 as a Phillie while teaming with Chuck Klein, Don Hurst, and others to give the club one of the best hitting lineups ever to play the game of baseball.

Lefty's .398 mark, which was one hit shy of being .400, led the National League in 1929. It ranks as the highest batting average in modern Phillies history.

That season, the Phillies had one of the all-time leading hitting records with six regulars batting above .300, four of them driving in more than 100 runs, and Klein, Hurst, and O'Doul each clouting more than 30 home runs. The club led the league with a .309 batting average.

O'Doul had just arrived in Philadelphia that season, having come by way of the New York Giants, who had given Lefty and $25,000 to the Phillies for outfielder Fred Leach. O'Doul had been in and out of the majors for nearly 10 years, but spent most of the decade in the minors, much of the time with the San Francisco Seals of the Pacific Coast League.

Lefty was originally a pitcher. He had brief flings as a hurler with the New York Yankees in 1919, 1920, and 1922, pitching in 11 games without a decision (he also played two games in the outfield). In 1923, O'Doul worked in 23 games as a relief pitcher with the Boston Red Sox, garnering a 1–1 record.

He returned to the minors after that season. When he resurfaced in the majors in 1928 at age 31, O'Doul had been converted to a full-time outfielder.

Lefty hit .319 for the Giants in 1928. When he arrived in Philadelphia the next season, he was immediately inserted into the lineup in left field, and played his first full season in the majors.

O'Doul's hitting exploits that year were nothing short of phenomenal. He walked away with the batting title while delivering a National League record (tied the following year by Bill Terry) of 254 hits. Lefty also set a modern National League record of reaching base the most times in one season (334).

O'Doul hit 32 home runs, fifth highest in the league; collected 122 RBI; scored 152 runs, second in the circuit; placed third in total bases with 397; and had a .622 slugging average, good for fifth place. Ironically, his longest hitting streak was only 16 games, although he also had a 15-game streak.

In 1930, O'Doul continued his torrid pace, but this time finished fourth in the batting championship behind Terry's .401. Lefty's .383 was second on the Phillies to Klein's .386.

O'Doul hit 22 home runs, drove in 97, and scored 122. At one stage of the season, he hit two pinch-hit home runs in a row (they were four days apart).

To the great disappointment of Phillies fans, the club traded O'Doul after the season to the Brooklyn Dodgers. The Phillies, according to president William Baker, were more in need of pitching than O'Doul's bat. Brooklyn also received second baseman Fresco Thompson while giving up outfielder Hal Lee and pitchers Jumbo Elliott and Clise Dudley.

Lefty hit .336 in his first year with the Dodgers. In 1932 he won his second batting title, hitting .368. For the third time in four years, O'Doul had more than 200 hits, and he had 21 homers, 120 runs, and 90 RBI. Only five players in the major leagues have won batting crowns while playing on two different teams.

O'Doul, who eight times in his career had five hits or more in a game, slipped in 1933. During the season, the Dodgers sent him back to the Giants. With eight straight hits at one point, he finished the season with a .284 average.

In 1934, at the age of 37, O'Doul was relegated to part-time duty with the Giants. It was Lefty's last year in the majors, and he went out with his batting touch still intact, hitting .316.

For many years after that, he was the popular manager of the San Francisco Seals and a highly respected authority on the art of hitting a baseball.

Lefty O'Doul

O'Doul, Lefty (Francis)

Phillies	G	AB	H	BA	RBI	R	2B	3B	HR	SA	SB
1929	154	638	254	.398	122	152	35	6	32	.622	2
1930	140	528	202	.383	97	122	37	7	22	.604	3
Career	970	3,264	1,140	.349	542	624	175	41	113	.532	36

Orth, Al

The Phillies collected their share of bargains in the 19th century, but one of the biggest had to be Al Orth.

Orth, a righthanded deliberate thrower whose nickname "The Curveless Wonder" also tells you that his pitches were straight, nonetheless made his presence felt almost immediately after his contract was purchased from Lynchburg in the Virginia League for $1,000. He continued to pitch steady baseball for the team until 1902 when he jumped to the American League.

In his first season, Orth had a similar year to the one that Whitey Ford had as a Yankee rookie in 1950. He won his first eight decisions and wasn't beaten until the last day of the season.

That was the only year with the Phillies in which Orth failed to win in double figures. His best year was his last (1901) when he finished 20–12. Two years before that his 2.49 ERA topped the league.

In 1902 he joined Hall of Famer Ed Delahanty, Harry Wolverton, and Jack Townsend in jumping to the Washington Senators for fatter contracts. He

Phillies: 1895–1901
Pitcher
Nickname: The Curveless Wonder
Birthplace: Danville, Indiana
B: September 5, 1872
D: October 8, 1948
Batted left, threw right
Ht. 6–0; **Wt.** 200

Al Orth

closed out his 15-year career with the Yankees and led the American League in victories with 27 in 1906.

Orth, Al

Phillies	W	L	Pct	ERA	G	CG	IP	H	BB	SO	ShO
1895	8	1	.889	3.89	11	9	88	103	22	25	0
1896	15	10	.600	4.41	25	19	196	244	46	23	0
1897	14	19	.424	4.63	36	29	282	349	82	64	2
1898	15	13	.536	3.02	32	25	250	290	53	52	1
1899	14	3	.824	2.49	21	13	145	149	19	35	3
1900	14	14	.500	3.78	33	24	262	302	60	68	2
1901	20	12	.625	2.27	35	30	282	250	32	92	6
Career	204	189	.519	3.37	440	324	3,355	3,564	661	948	31

Paskert, Dode

Phillies: 1911–17
Outfielder
Birthplace: Cleveland, Ohio
B: August 28, 1881
D: February 12, 1959
Batted right, threw right
Ht. 5–11; **Wt.** 165

Dode Paskert

It would not be unfair to compare Dode Paskert, center fielder for the first pennant-winning Phillies team, with Rich Ashburn, who played the same position with the 1950 champs, and Garry Maddox, who was in center when the Phillies won their first World Championship.

All three were excellent fielders. All three could bat near the top of the lineup in several spots and be a plus. All three could run the bases extremely well. And, although Ashburn became a .300 hitter in his rookie year in the majors, both Paskert and Maddox also proved later in their careers that they were capable of reaching that level of excellence themselves.

Both Maddox and Paskert came to Philadelphia in big trades, but had to wait several years to get into the World Series.

President Horace Fogel beamed when he announced the Paskert deal just before spring training in 1911. He was proud of himself for having extracted Paskert and third baseman Hans Lobert from the Cincinnati Reds. In fact, he predicted that it would lead to the Phillies' first pennant.

It did—five seasons later in 1915 when Paskert, ironically, had his weakest season of seven with the club.

Dode came to Philadelphia after a season he would top only once in his career. He batted .300 for Clark Griffith's Redlegs with 51 stolen bases.

In his second year with the Phillies, Dode stole 15 less bases but batted 15 points higher and scored 39 more runs. By 1915, though, his average slipped to .244 in only 109 games with just nine stolen bases. Still, he remained the best center fielder in the National League, and when William F. Baker traded him to the Chicago Cubs before the 1918 season, Philadelphians, already smarting over the dealing of Grover Cleveland Alexander to the Cubs, were livid. In this case, though, Baker made an outstanding trade. In exchange for the 36-year-old outfielder, he got himself a 30-year-old slender center fielder from Notre Dame named Cy Williams.

Paskert played his last game in the major leagues in 1921. In the three seasons after that, Williams slammed a total of 91 home runs.

Paskert, Dode

Phillies	G	AB	H	BA	RBI	R	2B	3B	HR	SA	SB
1911	153	560	153	.273	47	96	18	5	4	.345	28
1912	145	540	170	.315	43	102	38	5	1	.409	36
1913	124	454	119	.262	29	83	21	9	4	.374	12
1914	132	451	119	.264	44	59	25	6	3	.366	23
1915	109	328	80	.244	39	51	17	4	3	.348	9
1916	149	555	155	.279	46	82	⁻30	7	8	.402	22
1917	141	546	137	.251	43	78	27	11	4	.363	19
Career	1,715	6,017	1,613	.268	577	868	280	78	40	.360	293

Passeau, Claude

Phillies: 1936–39
Pitcher
Birthplace: Waynesboro, Mississippi
B: April 9, 1909
Bats right, throws right
Ht. 6–3; **Wt.** 198

During the decade between the mid-1930s and mid-1940s, Claude Passeau was one of the premier pitchers in the National League. He went 10 straight years with wins in double figures, even while working for the Phillies over a three-year period in which they finished last twice and seventh once.

Passeau was a big, strong-armed hurler with a degree from Millsaps (Mississippi) College and four seasons in the minors when he came to the Phillies in 1936. At one point, he had struck out 68 batters in five minor league games. The property of the Pittsburgh Pirates, Claude was landed by the Phils in a trade which sent catcher Al Todd to the Bucs for Passeau and catcher Earl Grace.

Passeau had a good rookie year (11–15) that included a three-hit, 7–0 win over the Boston Braves, stopping a 14-game losing streak, and an even better sophomore season (14–18) with the Phillies. In the latter, he led the league in innings pitched (292⅓), games started (34), and hits allowed (348), still a Phillies club record.

In 1938, Passeau got the Phillies' first win in Shibe Park after it had become the team's regular home. He beat Boston in the second game of a doubleheader, 10–8.

As they always seemed to do with good, young pitchers, the Phillies unloaded Passeau in 1939, shipping him to the Chicago Cubs for pitchers Kirby Higbe and Ray Harrell, outfielder Joe Marty, and $50,000.

Claude went on to have seven outstanding seasons with the Cubs. His best year was in 1940 when he registered a 20–13 record. He was 19–14 in 1942, and his 17–9 log in 1945 led Chicago to the National League pennant. He beat the Detroit Tigers with a one-hitter, facing only 28 batters and winning, 3–0, in the third game of the World Series.

Passeau, who led the National League in strikeouts in 1939, pitched in two All-Star games. He was the losing pitcher in 1941 when Ted Williams hit a dramatic three-run homer in the ninth.

He registered 27 shutouts during his 13-year career, which ended in 1947.

Claude Passeau

Passeau, Claude

Phillies	W	L	Pct	ERA	G	CG	IP	H	BB	SO	ShO
1936	11	15	.423	3.48	49	8	217⅓	247	55	85	2
1937	14	18	.438	4.34	50	18	292⅓	348	79	135	1
1938	11	18	.379	4.52	44	15	239	281	93	100	0
1939	2	4	.333	4.24	8	4	53	54	25	29	1
Career	162	150	.519	3.32	444	188	2,719⅔	2,856	728	1,104	27

Philley, Dave

Phillies: 1958–60
Outfielder, first baseman
Birthplace: Paris, Texas
B: May 16, 1920
Bats both, throws right
Ht. 6–0; **Wt.** 188

Dave Philley

At an age when most ball players are trying to figure out the size of their pension checks, Dave Philley was one of the premier pinch-hitters in baseball.

Philley, a rugged Texan whom the Phillies bought from the Detroit Tigers in 1957, had been a big league regular since 1946. He had logged a number of fine seasons, including three with the Philadelphia A's.

In 1958, at the age of 38, Philley lashed 18 pinch-hits, tied for the third highest number for a Phillies player.

The same year, Philley also established a major league record for consecutive pinch-hits in a season with eight. Beginning on September 9 and ending on the last day of the season, September 28, Dave poked five singles, two doubles, and one home run, while driving in six runs. In his first trip to the plate in 1959, he got another hit, thereby setting a major league mark for most consecutive pinch-hits.

During a little more than two seasons with the Phillies, Philley proved to be extremely versatile, playing the outfield and first base along with handling his pinch-hitting chores.

The switch-hitting veteran hit .309 in 1958 and .291 in 1959. He was hitting at a .333 clip when the Phils sold him to the San Francisco Giants in the spring of 1960.

Philley played 18 years in the big leagues, beginning with the Chicago White Sox. He played for the A's, Cleveland Indians, Baltimore Orioles, White Sox again, and Tigers before jumping to the National League with the Phillies. After the Giants, he went back to the American League and played with the Orioles and Boston Red Sox.

Philley was a regular center fielder in the American League for a number of years. He also played first and third base. One of his best seasons as a regular was in 1953 when he hit .303 for the A's. Dave had come to the A's in 1951 in a three-team swap that also brought to the A's outfielder Gus Zernial from the White Sox and pitcher Sam Zoldak and catcher Ray Murray from the Indians. The A's sent pitcher Lou Brissie to Cleveland and outfielder Paul Lehner to Chicago, which also landed outfielder Minnie Minoso from the Indians.

Dave holds the American League record for most hits in a season by a pinch-hitter. In 1961 he laced 24 pitch-hits for the Red Sox. His 93 career pinch-hits ranks ninth on the all-time major league career list.

Philley, Dave

Phillies	G	AB	H	BA	RBI	R	2B	3B	HR	SA	SB
1958	91	207	64	.309	31	30	11	4	3	.444	1
1959	99	254	74	.291	37	32	18	2	7	.461	0
1960	14	15	5	.333	4	2	2	0	0	.467	0
Career	1,904	6,296	1,700	.270	729	789	276	72	84	.377	102

Piatt, Wiley

Phillies: 1898–1900
Pitcher
Nickname: Iron Man
Birthplace: Blue Creek, Ohio
B: July 13, 1874
D: September 20, 1946
Batted left, threw left
Ht. 5–10; **Wt.** 175

Few rookies in Phillies history ever burst on the scene with as much success as Wiley Piatt, a slick little southpaw.

In his first season with the Phillies, Piatt posted a 24–14 record while leading the league in shutouts (six) and ranking fifth in strikeouts. Piatt pitched 306 innings, completing 33 of the 37 games he started. He also tossed a pair of four-hitters, one of them a 1–0 shutout against Cleveland.

That wasn't too shabby for a rookie. But wily Wiley had an encore. The following season he humbled the sophomore jinx by recording a 23–15 record, working in 305 innings while leading a pitching staff that also included 21-game winners Chick Fraser and Red Donahue.

The Phillies had great hopes for their young sensation. But they began to fade in 1900 when Piatt, slowed by arm problems, slipped to a meager 9–10 record in just 22 games.

Piatt was still a highly regarded moundsman, however, and with the American League about to be launched, he became a target for the raiders of the fledgling circuit. Connie Mack and the Philadelphia Athletics waved contracts at a number of the rival Phillies players. A handful of them, including Piatt, took the bait.

Piatt settled into the A's starting rotation in 1901, but after posting a 5–12 record in 18 games was sold in July to the Chicago White Sox. Piatt remained in the Windy City through the 1902 season, but drew his release after going 12–12.

He hooked on with the Boston Beaneaters in 1903 and went 8–13 in 25 games in his last big league season. Two of those losses were noteworthy. They came on the same day in a doubleheader with Pittsburgh. Piatt went the distance in both games, making him the only pitcher in the 20th century to lose two complete games in one day.

Wiley Piatt

Piatt, Wiley

Phillies	W	L	Pct	ERA	G	CG	IP	H	BB	SO	ShO
1898	24	14	.632	3.18	39	33	306	285	97	121	6
1899	23	15	.605	3.45	39	31	305	323	86	89	2
1900	9	10	.474	4.70	22	16	161	194	71	47	1
Career	86	79	.521	3.60	182	139	1,391	1,481	455	517	12

There was always something "horsey" about Charley Pittinger. Whether it was his habits on the mound or his face, Pittinger couldn't escape the connection with the noble equine.

But Pittinger was no nag when he chucked a baseball. In his most successful season with the Phillies, he won 23 games, led the National League in appearances with 46, and tossed a one-hitter.

A real workhorse, Pittinger had four straight years of working in more than 300 innings during his eight-year big league career. The year he was 23–14 with the Phillies, he toiled in 337 innings.

Charley had come to the Phils in what was a big trade at the time. In five seasons with the Boston Beaneaters, he had been a 27-game winner once and a 23-game loser another time. But the Phillies needed to bolster their sagging pitching staff, and they sent pitcher Chick Fraser and team captain and star third baseman Harry Wolverton to Boston to get the slender righthander.

After Pittinger's arrival in Philadelphia, some of the ruder fans called him "Horse Face." Philadelphia sports writer Horace Fogel once referred in print to Charley as "the horse-faced Mr. Pittinger." That prompted an angry letter from a young girl. "It was most unkind of you to write what you did about Charley Pittinger," she complained. "I think he is beautiful for a man." In his next column, Fogel said, "A beautiful pitcher, but hardly a beautiful man."

Pittinger was a mighty pretty sight on the mound in 1905 when he was the leader of the staff and helped the Phillies to a fourth-place finish.

His effectiveness greatly diminished the following year, though, and Charley's record plummeted to 8–10 in 20 games. He was 9–5 in 1907, a season that turned out to be Pittinger's last in the majors. He died just two years later.

Pittinger, Togie

Phillies: 1905–07
Pitcher
Nickname: Horse Face
Birthplace: Greencastle, Pennsylvania
B: 1871
D: January 14, 1909
Batted left, threw right
Ht. 6–2; **Wt.** 175

Togie Pittinger

Pittinger, Togie (Charles)

Phillies	W	L	Pct	ERA	G	CG	IP	H	BB	SO	ShO
1905	23	14	.622	3.10	46	29	337	311	104	136	4
1906	8	10	.444	3.39	20	9	130	128	50	43	2
1907	9	5	.643	3.00	16	8	102	101	35	37	1
Career	115	112	.507	3.10	262	187	2,040	2,017	734	832	20

Post, Wally

Phillies: 1958–60
Right fielder
Birthplace: St. Wendelin, Ohio
B: July 9, 1929
D: January 6, 1982
Batted right, threw right
Ht. 6–1; **Wt.** 190

The arrival of Wally Post in Philadelphia was the continuation of an old, familiar story. Throughout the 1950s and into the 1960s, the Phillies had made a habit of bringing in heavy-hitting outfielders who had seen better days.

Jim Greengrass, Wally Westlake, Peanuts Lowrey, and Rip Repulski had paraded through town before Post, each carrying excellent credentials and the promise of leading the Phillies to the National League's promised land. Each not only never did that, but generally produced very little in a short span with the team.

Post was another in the long line of such hitters. He came to the Phillies in 1958 as one of the premier sluggers in the league, having hit 96 home runs in the three previous years, including 40 in 1955.

He left, a little more than two seasons later, in a cloud of disappointment.

The Phillies had parted with pitcher Harvey Haddix to get Post from the Cincinnati Reds. Wally, who had been playing professionally since 1946 after being signed out of high school as a pitcher, was the Phillies' regular right fielder in 1958 and 1959.

One who struck out often, Post decided to cut down on his swing in 1958. As a result, he fanned less, and his average jumped 38 points over the previous year's mark to .282. His home run totals, however, dropped to 12, his career low as a regular.

In 1959, Wally went back to the big swing. He upped his home run production to 22, his batting average dived to .254, and for the third time in his career he led the National League in strikeouts.

During the season, Post did manage a home run in every park in the league. He also threw out two base runners in the same inning, a feat he had done once before with the Reds.

Post, who consistently ranked among the league leaders in assists by outfielders, was hitting .286 in 1960 when the Phillies peddled him, outfielder Harry Anderson, and first baseman Fred Hopke to the Reds for outfielders Lee Walls and Tony Gonzalez. Wally departed, having hit four pinch-hit home runs for the Phillies (he had 10 career pinch-hit homers).

Back with the Reds, Post somewhat resumed his heavy stick work. Although he had no seasons that quite matched his 1955 year when he blasted 40 homers, drove in 116 runs, and hit .309, he hit .282 and .294 for the Reds with 39 homers over the two years.

Post, a rookie with the Reds in 1954—although he had been up briefly as early as 1949, a year after he was switched from pitcher to full-time outfielder—played with the club until 1963 when he went to the Minnesota Twins. He finished his career the next year with the Cleveland Indians.

Post, Wally

Phillies	G	AB	H	BA	RBI	R	2B	3B	HR	SA	SB
1958	110	379	107	.282	62	51	21	3	12	.449	0
1959	132	468	119	.254	94	62	17	6	22	.457	0
1960	34	84	24	.286	12	11	6	1	2	.452	0
Career	1,204	4,007	1,064	.266	699	594	194	28	210	.485	19

Wally Post

Whoever created the phrase "hard-luck pitcher" must have had Ken Raffensberger in mind. The plucky southpaw had to be as unlucky as anybody who ever heaved a baseball from the mound.

Yet, Raffensberger was a talented pitcher who had some fine seasons in the big leagues. Unfortunately, many of his seasons were with poor teams.

In 1944, for instance, Ken posted a 13–20 record for the last-place Phillies. He led the league in losses. But he was also chosen for the National League All-Star team and emerged the winning pitcher, the only Phillies hurler ever to win the mid-summer classic.

Raffensberger lost 10 games during his career by 1–0 scores. He pitched two full seasons and parts of three others for the Phillies, during which time he was the club's main lefthander. In 1946, Ken led Phillies pitchers in strikeouts.

Ken began in organized ball in 1937. He had short stands with the St. Louis Cardinals and Chicago Cubs before coming to the Phillies in 1943. The Phils traded Raffensberger and catcher Hugh Poland to the Cincinnati Reds for catcher Al Lakeman in mid-1947.

Raffensberger blossomed with the Reds. In 1949 he was 18–17 and led the league in games started (38), hits (289), and shutouts (five). Ken's next best victory total was in 1952 when he was 17–13.

A master control pitcher, Raffensberger gave up only 449 walks in 2,152 innings during his career, a 1.88 walk-per-game ratio. His tantalizing slow curve helped him to 31 career shutouts. Ken pitched two one-hitters in 1948.

Raffensberger, Ken

Phillies: 1943–47
Pitcher
Birthplace: York, Pennsylvania
B: August 8, 1917
Bats right, throws left
Ht. 6–2; **Wt.** 185

Ken Raffensberger

Raffensberger, Ken

Phillies	W	L	Pct	ERA	G	CG	IP	H	BB	SO	ShO
1943	0	1	.000	1.13	1	1	8	7	2	3	0
1944	13	20	.394	3.06	37	18	258⅔	257	45	136	3
1945	0	3	.000	4.44	5	1	24⅓	28	14	6	0
1946	8	15	.348	3.63	39	14	196	203	39	73	2
1947	2	6	.250	5.49	10	3	41	50	8	16	1
Career	119	154	.436	3.60	396	133	2,151⅔	2,257	449	806	31

Going into the final month of the 1987 season, Shane Rawley looked as if he were going to give the Phillies back-to-back Cy Young Award winners.

Rawley, who wrote screenplays in the off-season, was putting on an Academy Award performance on the mound that season. Through August his record was 17–6.

And then he suddenly lost his effectiveness. Not just for the rest of the year—he was 0–5 in seven starts in September—but for the remainder of his career.

Rawley had joined the Phillies in June 1984 in a trade in which the New York Yankees received Marty Bystrom and Keith Hughes.

It rates as one of the best deals the Phillies made that decade. But for a while, it looked as if it were a contender for a list of the top 10 deals in the franchise's history.

Rawley, a 14-game winner for the Yankees in 1982, won 10 games in 16 decisions for the rest of the '84 season.

In 1985 he won 13 with a low 3.31 earned run average. And the following season he was 11–7 on July 29 when he was disabled for the rest of the season with a broken bone in his shoulder.

The lefthander came back strong in 1987. He was the Phillies' opening-day pitcher; he shut out the Montreal Expos in late April; and he won eight straight games between July 31 and August 21. Despite his late-season slump, Rawley

Rawley, Shane

Phillies: 1984–88
Pitcher
Birthplace: Racine, Wisconsin
B: July 27, 1955
Bats right, throws left
Ht. 6–0; **Wt.** 170

Shane Rawley

tied for the National League lead in games started (36) and was seventh in innings pitched.

Unfortunately for him, his 1988 season picked up where 1987 had left off. He won just eight of 24 decisions and was traded in the off-season to the Minnesota Twins for Tommy Herr. He pitched for a year with the Twins, was released, and failed a tryout with the Boston Red Sox in 1990.

Rawley, Shane

Phillies	W	L	Pct	ERA	G	CG	IP	H	BB	SO	ShO
1984	10	6	.625	3.83	18	3	120	117	27	58	0
1985	13	8	.619	3.31	36	6	199	188	81	106	2
1986	11	7	.611	3.53	23	7	158	166	50	73	1
1987	17	11	.607	4.38	36	4	230	250	86	123	1
1988	8	16	.333	4.18	32	4	198	220	78	87	1
Career	111	118	.485	4.02	469	41	1,871	1,934	763	1,007	7

Reed, Ron

Phillies: 1976–83
Pitcher
Birthplace: La Porte, Indiana
B: November 2, 1942
Bats right, throws right
Ht. 6–6; **Wt.** 215

Ron Reed

Ron Reed was the righthanded half of the bullpen that helped lead the Phillies to their only World Championship in 1980.

The tall former National Basketball Association player had filled a major role in the bullpen ever since the Phillies had acquired him from the St. Louis Cardinals for Mike Anderson after the 1975 season.

Reed's transfer from the starting rotation to the bullpen was a drastic change. In the five previous seasons with the Atlanta Braves and Cardinals before coming to Philadelphia, Reed had pitched in 145 games, all but two as a starter.

But, except for six emergency starts in eight full seasons with the Phillies, the LaPorte, Indiana, native and Notre Dame graduate was strictly a reliever—and an extremely effective one.

In 458 games with the Phillies, Reed saved 90 games and won 57. He ranks fifth on the club's all-time list for appearances, third in saves, first in relief victories (54), and first in relief victories plus saves (144). His 13 relief victories in 1979 was the second most ever recorded by a Phillie.

He and lefthanded Tug McGraw complemented each other perfectly. McGraw's "out pitch" was a screwball. Reed was still strictly a power pitcher at the age of 41 when he helped the Phillies win the 1983 National League pennant.

Reed had double figures in saves and an earned run average of less than 3.00 in each of his first three years with the Phillies, and the team made the NL playoffs each time. His best save total came in 1978 when he was credited with 17. His 2.23 ERA that season also was a career best. His only other double-figure save season was in 1982 when he had 14.

Reed appeared in two World Series games in 1980 and three in 1983. He was in 11 League Championship Series games with the Phillies and 12 overall.

In 1969 his 18 victories helped the Braves win the National League West title.

Reed was traded to the Chicago White Sox after the 1983 season for Jerry Koosman. He played one year and retired after 19 big league seasons.

Reed, Ron

Phillies	W	L	Pct	ERA	G	CG	IP	H	BB	SO	ShO
1976	8	7	.533	2.46	59	1	128	88	32	96	0
1977	7	5	.583	2.76	60	0	124	101	37	84	0
1978	3	4	.429	2.23	66	0	109	87	23	85	0
1979	13	8	.619	4.15	61	0	102	110	32	58	0
1980	7	5	.583	4.05	55	0	91	88	30	54	0
1981	5	3	.625	3.10	39	0	61	54	17	40	0
1982	5	5	.500	2.66	57	0	98	85	24	57	0
1983	9	1	.900	3.48	61	0	96	89	34	73	0
Career	146	140	.510	3.46	751	55	2,476	2,374	633	1,481	8

Ring, Jimmy

Phillies: 1921–25, 1928
Pitcher
Birthplace: Brooklyn, New York
B: February 15, 1895
D: July 6, 1965
Batted right, threw right
Ht. 6–1; **Wt.** 170

In one dozen big league seasons, Jimmy Ring won 118 games, including 68 in six years with the Phillies. These are impressive figures, but one can only wonder what they would have been if Ring had possessed one more quality—control.

Big Jimmy was a fastball pitcher, and when he was able to get his pitch over the plate, he was devastating. But that was hardly an every-time-out happening. Much of the time he was afflicted with the same disease that curtailed the promise, in varying degrees, of Rex Barney, Ryne Duren, Mitch Williams, and Steve Dalkowski.

In four straight seasons between 1922 and 1925, Ring led the National League in bases on balls, with totals between 103 and 119. And even when he returned to the Phils for his second tour of duty in 1928, he walked 103 in 173 innings. By that time he was 33 years old and prematurely washed up. He finished the season with a 4–17 record and never pitched in the big leagues again.

"One day he is good and another day he is not," manager Arthur Fletcher said in 1925 about the ace of his pitching staff. "Ring's control never was good. It always has been a hard matter for him to put the ball where he wants it, and in every game in which he pitched he walks several batters. But he is doing the best he can. I know it, and I would know if he was not."

Ring came to the Phillies after the 1920 season and was the only player involved in the three-man deal who did not make the Hall of Fame. He was traded by Cincinnati along with Greasy Neale, a member of the Football Hall of Fame, for Eppa Rixey, whose plaque is on the wall at Cooperstown.

Jimmy's best year with the Phils was 1923, when he finished 18–16 with a team that won only 50 of 154 games. John McGraw, the legendary Giants manager, used to pick an All-America team in those days. That season he tabbed Ring.

"It is one thing for a pitcher to win ball games with a good team, but to win just as well with a tailender is truly remarkable," McGraw wrote.

Two years later, McGraw dealt two journeyman pitchers to the Phillies for Ring, but Jimmy's career was on the downslide. He went 11–10 in New York and was dealt to the Cardinals, where he was 0–4 before coming back to the Phillies for the 1928 season, his last in the majors.

Jimmy Ring

Ring, Jimmy

Phillies	W	L	Pct	ERA	G	CG	IP	H	BB	SO	ShO
1921	10	19	.345	4.24	34	21	246	258	88	88	0
1922	12	18	.400	4.58	40	17	249	292	103	116	0
1923	18	16	.529	3.76	39	23	313	336	115	112	0
1924	10	12	.455	3.97	32	16	215	236	108	72	1
1925	14	16	.467	4.37	38	21	270	325	119	93	1
1928	4	17	.190	6.40	35	4	173	214	103	72	0
Career	118	149	.442	4.06	389	154	2,389	2,545	953	835	9

Rixey, Eppa

Phillies: 1912–20
Pitcher
Nickname: Eppa Jephtha
Birthplace: Culpepper, Virginia
B: May 3, 1891
D: February 28, 1963
Batted right, threw left
Ht. 6–5; **Wt.** 210

Eppa Rixey

For years, Eppa Rixey and Sam Rice were the Hall of Fame's forgotten men. Rice was an American League hitter whose career fell 13 hits shy of 3,000. Rixey was a National League pitcher who held the record for lefthanded wins at 266 until Warren Spahn passed him on the way to 363.

Fittingly, both Rixey and Rice were chosen by the old-timer's committee in 1963. Justice seemed to prevail. But not really. Rixey never made the ceremony. One month and one day after he was elected to the Hall of Fame, Rixey died in Cincinnati on February 28 at the age of 71.

Rixey had done his best pitching in Cincinnati after a yo-yo, up-and-down career with the Phillies. He was 10–10 as a rookie in 1912, slipped to 2–11 in 1914, then was only 11–12 despite a 2.39 earned run average for the 1915 National League champs before rising to 22–10 in 1916. But even then, his achievements in Philadelphia were dwarfed by Ol' Pete Alexander, who won his personal high 33 that season.

From there, his career with the Phillies took a real dip. Although his ERA was a healthy 2.27 the following year, he led the NL in losses with a 16–21 record. And after a poor 6–12 record in 1919, he really hit the skids with 11–22 in 1920, again topping the league in defeats.

That ran his lifetime record in Philadelphia to 87–103, which won't even buy you a ticket to the Hall of Fame as a spectator. But baseball people knew he was far better than his record showed.

Cincinnati knew it as well as anyone. William Baker swallowed the bait and the couple of fish that went with it. He swapped Rixey to the Reds for Jimmy Ring, who couldn't find home plate, and Greasy Neale, who preferred the gridiron to the diamond.

A University of Virginia alumnus, Rixey averaged 20 victories a season in his first five in Cincinnati. His best was 1922 when he won 25, tops in the league. In all, he spent 21 years in the majors. One negative stat: His 251 career losses rank him fifth in the majors.

Rixey, Eppa

Phillies	W	L	Pct	ERA	G	CG	IP	H	BB	SO	ShO
1912	10	10	.500	2.50	23	10	162	147	54	59	3
1913	9	5	.643	3.11	35	9	156	148	56	75	2
1914	2	11	.154	4.37	24	2	103	124	45	41	0
1915	11	12	.478	2.39	29	10	177	163	64	88	2
1916	22	10	.688	1.85	38	20	287	239	74	134	3
1917	16	21	.432	2.27	39	23	281	249	67	121	4
1919	6	12	.333	3.97	23	11	154	160	50	63	1
1920	11	22	.333	3.48	41	25	284	288	69	109	1
Career	266	251	.515	3.15	692	290	4,495	4,633	1,082	1,350	39

Roberts, Robin

Phillies: 1948–61
Pitcher
Nickname: Robbie
Birthplace: Springfield, Illinois
B: September 30, 1926
Bats both, throws right
Ht. 6–1; **Wt.** 190

Throughout the long history of the team, there is no name more synonymous with Phillies baseball than that of Robin Roberts.

Roberts is perhaps the most dominant name in Phillies history, and the one name that above all others is locked into a permanent position as the club's most representative symbol.

A big, easygoing guy with an extremely likable manner, Robbie was the most successful righthanded pitcher the Phillies ever had, and was one of the all-time National League greats. A Hall of Fame selection, Roberts ranks among the leaders in many career categories in the league.

Roberts had a blazing fastball and an awesome curve, both of which he threw with pinpoint control. Throughout his career, Robbie steadfastly refused to throw brush-back pitches. His critics claimed this refusal allowed hitters the opportunity to dig in because they knew the strapping hurler wouldn't throw at them.

Robbie had as fluid a motion as any righthander. While most pitchers always seemed to look like they were working hard, Roberts would wind up slowly and easily, appearing as though he was hardly laboring. It was a great piece of deception. Out of that relaxed motion would explode a sizzling fastball or a crackling curve that would burst in on a hitter, seemingly before Robbie was even done with his follow-through.

That was the way Robbie worked for 19 big league seasons. Fourteen of those campaigns were with the Phillies, during which time Roberts put together a set of statistics that was as impressive for the durability it demonstrated as for its quality.

Roberts leads the Phillies in career pitching statistics in games, losses, innings, complete games, runs allowed, hits allowed, and earned runs allowed. He ranks second in wins and strikeouts and third in shutouts and walks.

A cool pitcher under pressure, Robbie won 20 games for six straight years between 1950 and 1955. In the National League, only Christy Mathewson and Mordecai Brown also achieved that record, and they did it in the early 1900s.

At present Roberts is the 22d winningest pitcher in major league history with 286 career victories. His 609 games started place him 16th in the majors in that category, and his 4,689 innings pitched rank 18th on the all-time list.

Stemming from his willingness to challenge every hitter rather than use craft, cunning, and an occasional knock-down pitch, Roberts was hit often during his career. He was especially vulnerable to the home run. As a result, he holds a number of major league records, not all of them favorable.

He has the mark for the most years leading the league in starts (six), hits allowed (five), and home runs (five) and is tied for most years leading the league in runs (three) and batters faced (four). He also has the major league records for most home runs allowed in a season (46) and in a career (505), and most years in which he allowed 30 or more home runs (eight).

Roberts led the National League in wins four times, in complete games five times, in innings pitched five times, in shutouts twice, in strikeouts twice, and in fielding percentage once.

He was named the major league Player of the Year by *The Sporting News* in 1952. The same publication selected him as major league Pitcher of the Year in 1952, 1953, and 1955. He was picked on *The Sporting News'* major league All-Star teams in 1952, 1953, 1954, and 1955.

Roberts was named to the National League All-Star team seven times. He was the starting pitcher in an unprecedented five games (1950, 1951, 1953, 1954, 1955). He had no decisions in five actual appearances (he did not play in 1952 and 1956), and in 14 innings gave up 17 hits and 10 runs (all earned).

In 1976, Roberts became a member of the baseball Hall of Fame. He has also been inducted into the Philadelphia Baseball Hall of Fame, and is one of only four players to have had his number (36) retired by the Phillies.

Throughout his long career, Robbie never pitched a no-hitter, but he came close. Twice in 1954 he hurled one-hitters. In one game, he gave up a leadoff home run to Bobby Adams, then retired the next 27 Cincinnati Reds in order in an 8–1 victory. In the other, he beat the Milwaukee Braves, 4–0, yielding only a third inning double to Del Crandall. A third one-hitter came in 1960 when Roberts gave up a fifth-inning single to Felipe Alou en route to a 3–0 triumph over the San Francisco Giants.

An extremely durable pitcher, Roberts led the Phillies in innings pitched every year from 1950 to 1960. Six straight times he worked more than 300 innings.

During his career, Roberts also lost a number of games because of poor support, either in the field or at the plate. Forty-four of his losses came when the Phillies were shut out.

Roberts' two greatest seasons were 1950 and 1952. In the former, he led the Phillies to the World Series, posting his first 20-win season and hurling the club to victory in the famous season-ending game with the Brooklyn Dodgers. In 1952, his 28–7 record was the high point of his career, and the most wins any National League pitcher had recorded since Dizzy Dean won 28 in 1935. No one in the league has matched that figure since.

Considering the fact that the Phillies signed him for a mere $25,000 bonus, Roberts may have been one of the best bargains in baseball history, too.

One of six children of parents who had immigrated to the United States from Great Britain in 1921, Robin was known mostly for his basketball exploits in his younger days. He was a standout cager in high school, and in 1946 he was voted the top college player in the state of Michigan.

After graduating from Lanphier High School in Springfield, Illinois, where he was also an excellent football and baseball player, Roberts joined the military as an Army Air Force cadet.

He was assigned to study at Michigan State University. After the war ended and he was discharged, Robbie stayed there. He arranged to get a basketball scholarship while majoring in physical education and played baseball almost as an afterthought.

During the summers of 1946 and 1947, Roberts pitched in an independent league in New England. There he started attracting the attention of scouts, including the Phillies' Chuck Ward. After outlasting the New York Yankees and Boston Braves in particular, Ward signed Roberts to a bonus contract following his graduation from college.

Robbie went to spring training with the Phillies, then was assigned to their farm club in Wilmington, Delaware. He only stayed there for two months. In that time, Roberts fashioned a 9–1 record, striking out 121 batters in 96 innings. He fanned 18 hitters in one game and 17 in another.

That was enough to convince the Phillies that Robbie was ready for the majors. Not quite 22 years of age, Roberts joined the Phillies in June 1948.

In his first game Roberts pitched a five-hitter but lost to the Pittsburgh Pirates, 2–0. Robin, however, demonstrated the kind of poise on the mound that gave him the appearance of a veteran pitcher. By the end of the season it was evident that he was headed for stardom, despite only a 7–9 record.

The 1949 season confirmed that assumption. With the Phillies at long last inching their way up the National League ladder with a crop of young players, Roberts posted a 15–15 record. He lost several close games, and he was not yet the ace of the staff. But his turn was approaching.

It came in 1950. Roberts became the solid man on the pitching staff—the stopper, the leader, the guy who could carry the team on his back.

It was a great season for Robbie. And he pitched some memorable games. In May, he tangled with the Reds' Ewell Blackwell, who allowed the Phillies just three hits and one run. Roberts gave the Reds two hits and won, 1–0. In late July he hurled three consecutive shutouts, erasing the Reds, Cubs, and Pirates and helping the Phillies take over permanent possession of first place. A two-run homer by Enos Slaughter finally broke Roberts' scoreless streak at 32⅔ innings in a game in which Robbie bested Howie Pollet and the Cardinals, 4–2.

During his streak, Roberts won seven games in a row. On September 12 he won his 19th game of the season and seemed certain to win well in excess of 20 games. But a string of misfortunes surfaced during which he tried five times to win number 20 without succeeding. In the five attempts, Robbie was hit hard only once. He lost three of the other games by scores of 1–0, 3–2, and 3–1.

Roberts' sixth try for the elusive 20th win came on the last day of the season. With the Phillies protecting only a one-game lead over the Brooklyn Dodgers, it was left to Robbie to pitch what would become one of the most memorable games in Phillies history.

Roberts was pitching his third game in five days. He was opposed by Don Newcombe, also seeking his 20th win. Robbie issued only five hits, and the Phillies won, 4–1, on Dick Sisler's 10th-inning home run.

To get to that point, though, Roberts had to survive a hair-raising ninth inning in which he gave a magnificent exhibition of clutch pitching. With the score tied 1–1, Roberts gave up a walk to Cal Abrams and a single to Pee Wee Reese. With none out, Duke Snider singled to center, whereupon Richie Ashburn made an electrifying throw to the plate to nail Abrams. But Roberts still had to face the heart of the Dodger order. He intentionally walked Jackie Robinson to load the bases, then retired Carl Furillo on a foul pop and Gil Hodges on a fly to right to end the inning.

In the top of the 10th, it was the exhausted Roberts who started the Phillies' pennant-winning explosion. He led off the inning with a single to center. After Ed Waitkus singled, Ashburn tried to bunt but forced Roberts at third. Sisler's homer followed. After that, it was merely a matter of Robbie going to the mound and calmly retiring the Dodgers in order.

The triumph finally gave Robbie his 20-win season. With Roberts and his close friend Curt Simmons combining for 40 percent of the team's victories, the Phillies entered their first World Series in 35 years.

Roberts was too tired to pitch the opener. But he got the call in the second game, hooking up with the New York Yankees' Allie Reynolds. After nine innings, the score was tied, 1–1. In the top of the 10th, Roberts gave up a home run to Joe DiMaggio, which proved to be the difference as the Yanks won, 2–1. Robbie worked one scoreless inning in relief in the fourth game of the Series.

While many of his teammates slumped, Roberts hurled well again in 1951, posting a 21–15 record. It was a record that was peppered with a number of losses in which Phillies' bats often were silent while Robbie pitched.

That was not the case, though, in 1952. With a 28–7 record, Roberts fashioned the best mark in the league in 17 years. It was also the most wins for

Robin Roberts

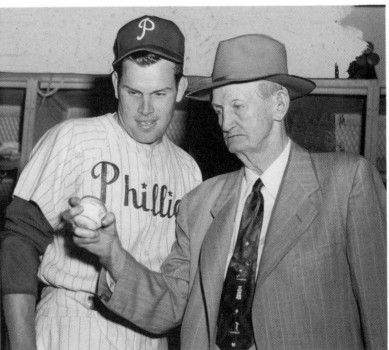

Two of baseball's all-time pitching greats, Robin Roberts (left) and Cy Young, compared grips in the early 1950s.

a Phillies pitcher since Grover Cleveland Alexander won 30 in 1917. His won-lost percentage of .800 established a Phillies record.

While registering the lowest ERA of his career (2.59), Roberts ran off winning streaks of nine, eight, and seven games during the season. He had 30 complete games. In nine of them, he allowed no walks. Roberts won 21 of his last 23 decisions, getting his 28th triumph on the final day of the season with a 7–4 victory over the Giants.

In August 1952, Roberts also started a streak of complete games that would run for nearly a year. Over that stretch, he completed 28 games in a row. Although the streak ended, Robin compiled the glowing total of 33 complete games in 1953 en route to a 23–16 season.

Roberts continued to pile up impressive statistics in 1954, the year he tossed two one-hitters. On the way to a 23–15 log, the strong-armed individualist continued his ability to mix the unusual with the commonplace. At one point during the season, he won three games in six days, two of the wins coming in relief. He also went 15 innings to register a 3–2 victory over the Cardinals.

Robbie was still rolling along in 1955. That year, he posted his sixth straight 20-win season, this time with a 23–14 mark. His streak ended the following year, however, as Robbie settled for a 19–18 record. He lost his bid for number 20 to the Giants on the final game of the season.

That year Roberts set several Phillies records of dubious note. By giving up 46 home runs, a major league record, and 147 earned runs, he set all-time Phillies marks.

In 1957, Roberts had a new experience. For the first time since joining the Phillies, he had a one-sided losing record. It was 10–22, and the losses were a league high. Many of Robbie's troubles that season stemmed from a muscle spasm in his back which affected his delivery. His fastball lacked its old zip, and some thought the great hurler was nearing the end of his career.

Roberts worked hard the following winter and spring with trainer Frank Wiechec, who developed a special set of exercises to rebuild the strength in the pitcher's arm and upper body. It worked. Roberts made a sparkling comeback, posting a 17–14 record, despite the team's last-place finish.

During the season, Roberts won his 200th game, a 3–1, three-hit victory over the Cubs. He also lost three games by 1–0 scores and three more games by one run.

The old zip was clearly back in Roberts' arm. But the Phillies finished last in the next two seasons, and with little support Roberts managed 15–17 and 12–16 records. By Roberts' standards, the records were less than acceptable, but considering what he was playing with, they weren't bad at all.

Roberts' 1961 record, however, was bad. Hampered by a knee injury and again pitching with a last-place team, Robbie pitched infrequently. His record was 1–10.

The Phillies were sure the great hurler, who played the game with such zest, even to the point of diving into bases, had come to the end of the road. In the fall of 1961 they sold him to the Yankees for $25,000.

Roberts never pitched for the Yankees because they, too, gave up on him, handing him his unconditional release at the start of the 1962 season. It was a mistake the Yanks would later regret.

Less than one month after being let go by New York, Roberts was signed by the Baltimore Orioles. Over the next three and one-half seasons, Robbie compiled records of 10–9, 14–13, 13–7, and 5–7 and helped to stabilize a young Baltimore pitching staff that in a few years would lead the Birds to the American League pennant.

In mid-season in 1965, the Orioles released Roberts. He was signed shortly thereafter by the Houston Astros. Roberts pitched the rest of that season and the first half of 1966 in Houston until he was released and signed by the Chicago Cubs. He was cut loose by the Cubs at the end of the season.

Still believing he could pitch in the big leagues, Roberts went to the Phillies' Reading farm club in 1967 to try to hurl his way back. At 41 years old, Roberts worked among players half his age. He had a 5–3 record, but there would be no return trip to the majors.

Twenty seasons after he began, Roberts' brilliant career came to a close. Robbie, however, continued his contact with baseball. In the mid-1970s, he was named head baseball coach at the University of South Florida, a position he held until the mid-'80s.

Roberts, Robin

Phillies	W	L	Pct	ERA	G	CG	IP	H	BB	SO	ShO
1948	7	9	.438	3.19	20	9	146⅔	148	61	84	0
1949	15	15	.500	3.69	43	11	226⅔	229	75	95	3
1950	20	11	.645	3.02	40	21	304⅓	282	77	146	5
1951	21	15	.583	3.03	44	22	315	284	64	127	6
1952	28	7	.800	2.59	39	30	330	292	45	148	3
1953	23	16	.590	2.75	44	33	346⅔	324	61	198	5
1954	23	15	.605	2.97	45	29	336⅔	289	56	185	4
1955	23	14	.622	3.28	41	26	305	292	53	160	1
1956	19	18	.514	4.45	43	22	297⅓	328	40	157	1
1957	10	22	.313	4.07	39	14	249⅔	246	43	128	2
1958	17	14	.548	3.24	35	21	269⅔	270	51	130	1
1959	15	17	.469	4.27	35	19	257⅓	267	35	137	2
1960	12	16	.429	4.02	35	13	237⅓	256	34	122	2
1961	1	10	.091	5.85	26	2	117	154	23	54	0
Career	286	245	.539	3.41	676	305	4,688⅔	4,582	902	2,357	45

Gene Mauch had a way with words. Like when the Phillies traded Jim Owens for Cookie Rojas after the 1962 season, Mauch took on new math.

"Sometimes you add by subtracting," he said.

What he meant was that there are times when you create a plus by getting rid of a minus, which was Mauch's opinion of Owens.

But Cookie Rojas had his own idea. He would be a positive force almost anywhere Mauch wanted to put him, which was almost anywhere.

He proved it for the first time in 1964 after sitting around collecting splinters most of the 1963 season. The native of Havana, Cuba, became Mauch's number-one utility man and hit .291 in 109 games. The following season, he batted .303, his personal high in 16 major league seasons. And in 1966, he drove in 55 runs for a Phillies career high while playing in 156 games.

By 1967 he had even pitched in one game, meaning that he had played all nine positions in his career at Connie Mack Stadium.

Also by then, his batting average was on a downward stairway. Each year it was a little lower than the one before, starting in 1966. In 1969 it dipped all the way to .228, and that's not quite enough, no matter how much utility you have.

The Phillies, figuring they had squeezed all they could out of a talent that came so cheaply, packaged him in the Dick Allen–Curt Flood–Tim McCarver deal. For a while, it looked as if the decision was right. Cookie batted .106 in 23 games with the Redbirds and was shipped off to Kansas City in the American League.

The move revitalized Rojas's career. He became the Royals' regular second baseman over that and the next five seasons. His average reached .300 in 1971 and never fell below .254.

In the process of finishing a career that produced 1,660 hits, Rojas showed the Phillies a little old math. Sometimes you don't add just by subtracting.

Rojas managed the California Angels to a 75–79 record and a fourth-place finish in the American League West in 1988.

Rojas, Cookie

Phillies: 1963–69
Utility man
Nickname: Cookie
Birthplace: Havana, Cuba
B: March 6, 1939
Bats rights, throws right
Ht. 5–10; **Wt.** 160

Cookie Rojas

Rojas, Cookie (Octavio)

Phillies	G	AB	H	BA	RBI	R	2B	3B	HR	SA	SB
1963	64	77	17	.221	2	18	0	1	1	.286	4
1964	109	340	99	.291	31	58	19	5	2	.394	1
1965	142	521	158	.303	42	78	25	3	3	.380	5
1966	156	626	168	.268	55	77	18	1	6	.329	4
1967	147	528	137	.259	45	60	21	2	4	.330	8
1968	152	621	144	.232	48	53	19	0	9	.306	4
1969	110	391	89	.228	30	35	11	1	4	.292	1
Career	1,822	6,309	1,660	.263	593	714	254	25	54	.337	74

Rose, Pete

Phillies: 1979–83
First baseman, right fielder
Nickname: Charlie Hustle
Birthplace: Cincinnati, Ohio
B: April 14, 1941
Bats both, throws right
Ht. 5–11; **Wt.** 203

As a member of the visiting team, Pete Rose always commanded respect when he came to Philadelphia. But it wasn't until he joined the Phillies and could be seen on a regular basis that he was fully appreciated.

After he became a Phillie in 1979, the full measure of the man was revealed. The sight became more awesome as time went on. Rose showed that he was truly a giant in a game in which there have been few of equal stature.

There is virtually nothing that the man couldn't do well. It was, however, the subtle phases of the game in which Rose excelled that really honed one's appreciation for the way he played baseball.

He rarely made a mistake. He made the right plays in the field, whether he was playing second, third, or first base or left or right field, all of which he did as a starter. He handled a bat as a conductor handles a baton. He did what had to be done at the plate, always willing to sacrifice himself for the benefit of the team. He had superb instincts as a base-runner. And he never stopped hustling.

"It's like he's in high gear all the time," former Phillies coach Billy DeMars once said. "The son of a gun never drops down to first gear. He's always in fourth."

To Rose, it would be unpardonable not to hustle. He played that way all his life, and even as his age dipped deeper into the 40s, he remained the one and only Charlie Hustle.

"Hustle is something that's born in you," Pete has said. "I didn't get to the majors on God-given ability. I got there on hustle, and I have had to hustle to stay."

Of course, Rose did a few things with the bat, too. In 1985 he passed Ty Cobb on the all-time hit list when he lashed out number 4,192. He finished with 4,256.

On the all-time major league list, Rose ranks second in singles and doubles, sixth in total bases, fourth in runs, and first in games and at-bats. He is the all-time National League leader in hits, singles, games, and at-bats.

Rose holds the all-time record for most hits and total bases by a switch-hitter, and the National League mark for home runs by a switch-hitter. He is also tied with Willie Keeler for the league record for hitting safely in 44 consecutive games. And his record of 10 years with 200 or more hits is a major league mark.

Rose is grouped in a class that includes names such as Cobb, Stan Musial, Hank Aaron, Honus Wagner, Babe Ruth, Willie Mays, and Tris Speaker.

How did he do it? "I'm a worker, a hard hat, a guy who isn't perfect and doesn't pretend to be," Rose said. "I've always had to push myself and set goals because I don't have a lot of talent."

Rich Ashburn, the Phillies' ex–center fielder and present broadcaster, took another approach to analyze Rose. "If you're looking for a secret to Pete Rose's success," he wrote in the *Evening Bulletin*, "it would be his ability to concentrate; the ability to shut out everything else, his personal problems, the cheers, the boos. When Rose steps into the baseball world, all the other worlds are left behind.

"It is almost impossible to play every game with intensity," Ashburn continued. "He plays every game, every time at bat, every pitch with intensity. Pete is a player for all seasons, all decades, all time."

Rose won three batting titles: 1968 (.335), 1969 (.348), and 1973 (.338). He led or tied for the lead in hits seven times, led in doubles five times, and was first in runs four times. He hit above .300 in 15 of his 24 big league seasons.

Among his hundreds of awards, Pete was the Rookie of the Year in 1963, the Most Valuable Player in 1973, the World Series MVP in 1975. In 1979 he was named by *The Sporting News* as the Baseball Player of the Decade and by sportswriters and broadcasters as the Athlete of the Decade. He was also picked on 16 All-Star teams at a record-setting five different positions—first base, second base, third base, left field and right field.

Recognized as baseball's first $100,000 singles hitter, Rose has a .381 batting average in seven League Championship Series and a .269 mark in six World Series.

The youngest player ever to pass the 2,000-hit and 3,000-hit marks, Rose was a scrappy, 150-pound, 18-year-old whose uncle, Buddy Bloebaum, a scout for the Cincinnati Reds, helped to get him a tryout. The Reds were unimpressed but grudgingly signed him to a Class D contract.

After three strong minor league seasons, Rose went to spring training in 1963 with the Reds. No one expected him to stay with the club for long, but Pete badgered Fred Hutchinson so much that the Reds' manager finally let him play. After that, Rose never left the lineup.

Rose's first major league hit was a triple off the Pittsburgh Pirates' Bob Friend. At the time, Pete was 0-for-12.

The man who many times was described as a little boy in a man's body because of his tremendous enthusiasm, went on to play 16 seasons with the Reds. Rose was the heart of some outstanding Cincinnati teams. Along the way, he got his 1,000 hit off of the New York Mets' Dick Selma (1968), his 2,000th hit off of the San Francisco Giants' Ron Bryant (1973), and his 3,000th off of the Montreal Expos' Steve Rogers (1978). Rose passed Frankie Frisch as the all-time switch-hitter with his 2,881st hit in 1977. The following year, the entire nation watched as Pete chased first Tommy Holmes, then Willie Keeler, and ultimately Joe DiMaggio's 56-game hitting streak. Pete stopped at 44.

Cincinnati's determination not to offer Rose what he considered a suitable contract resulted in Pete's entering the free-agent market after the 1978 season. Although they stepped out of the running for his services at one point, the Phillies finally signed Rose to a $3.2 million, four-year contract.

Rose immediately established his worth by pounding out a .331 batting average in 1979. He also passed Honus Wagner as the National League's all-time singles hitter with 2,427.

Pete Rose

In 1980, Rose's average slipped to .282, but he was a key figure in the Phillies' drive to their first World Championship. He started three different rallies in the division-clinching 6–4 victory over the Expos. In the League Championship Series against the Houston Astros, Rose not only hit .400, but also scored the winning run in the Phillies' 5–3 win in the fourth game when he bowled into Astro catcher Bruce Bochy, knocking him and the ball askew. The play was reminiscent of Rose's 1970 collision with Cleveland Indians catcher Ray Fosse in the All-Star Game. Pete scored the winning run in the 12th inning by charging into the catcher, Rose's dinner guest the night before.

Rose was a .261 hitter in the 1980 World Series. His most memorable contribution was with his glove. With one out and the bases loaded in the ninth inning of the sixth and final game, Pete caught Frank White's foul pop-up after it had bounced out of the mitt of catcher Bob Boone. The catch helped preserve the Phillies' 4–1 lead and Series-clinching victory.

The play was typical of the kind of heads-up performer Rose has always been. "The man," his former Reds manager Sparky Anderson told Ray Didinger, then of the *Evening Bulletin,* "is the greatest competitor I've ever seen. He's a star, yet he doesn't look down on other people. He's the only man I've ever seen who really believes in that old cliche about giving 100 percent."

Rose, usually the first man in the clubhouse before a game, hit more balls in batting practice and took more grounders in infield drills than anyone on the team. He was a superb analyst of the game and one of the sport's most accessible players to the press.

In 1981, Rose tied the National League's all-time record for most hits with a single off Houston's Nolan Ryan. The game was the last before the players' strike. Sixty days later the strike ended, and in his first game back, Rose broke Stan Musial's record when he grounded an eighth-inning single to left field on a pitch served by the St. Louis Cardinals' Mark Littell.

With 60,651 fans watching, the game was stopped. Musial stepped onto the field to congratulate the new record holder. Ironically, Pete had been a rookie second baseman in 1963 in the game in which Musial made his last appearance as a player, getting his last two hits to either side of Rose.

"He's been a credit to baseball," Musial said of the man who broke his substantial record. "He would have been a great player for the Gashouse Gang."

Rose's average dipped to .271 in 1982. A year later, with age finally starting to take its toll, Pete slipped to .245 and for the first time in his career rode the bench while others played ahead of him.

Clutch player that he always was, Pete bounced back with a .375 average in the LCS and a .313 mark in the 1983 World Series.

Shortly after the Series, though, Rose's career with the Phillies ended. The club elected not to renew his contract—in effect a release—and a memorable five-year career in Philadelphia was over.

After a brief time in Montreal with the Expos, Rose returned to Cincinnati to complete his career as a player and begin one as manager. He managed the Reds from 1984 to early in the 1988 season when he was suspended from baseball for allegedly betting on baseball games. While Rose has never admitted it, there was overwhelming evidence that he had bet on games while he was managing the Reds.

Rose served a term in federal prison for income tax evasion.

Rose, Pete

Phillies	G	AB	H	BA	RBI	R	2B	3B	HR	SA	SB
1979	163	628	208	.331	59	90	40	5	4	.430	20
1980	162	655	185	.282	64	95	42	1	1	.354	12
1981	107	431	140	.325	33	73	18	5	0	.390	4
1982	162	634	172	.271	54	80	25	4	3	.337	8
1983	151	493	121	.245	45	52	14	3	0	.286	7
Career	3,562	14,053	4,256	.303	1,314	2,165	746	135	160	.409	198

Rowe, Schoolboy

In the mid to late 1940s, Schoolboy Rowe was the mainstay of the Phillies' pitching staff. Although the best days of his career had passed by the time he arrived in Philadelphia, Rowe made a strong contribution to the post–World War II rise of the Phillies.

He toiled for the Phillies for five years, beginning in 1943 when he arrived from Brooklyn where the Dodgers had decided his pitching days were over. Rowe proceeded to post a 14–8 record in his first Philadelphia season. After two years in the military service, he returned to the Phils and gave them three more outstanding years.

A crafty veteran who relied on a variety of pitches, including a knuckleball, the big Texan gave stability to the Phillies' youthful staff in the late 1940s. He was the oldest player on the team, and had been in the big leagues since 1933.

Rowe spent only one year in the minor leagues before joining the Detroit Tigers in 1933. A year later, he led the Tigers to the American League pennant with a 24–8 record. In the process he tied a league record that still stands with 16 consecutive wins. He went 19–13 and 19–10 over the next two years before being sidetracked with an arm injury.

After a stint back in the minors in 1938, Schoolboy returned to the Tigers, and in 1940 again led them to the World Series with a 16–3 mark. Two years later, Detroit sold him to the Dodgers. After seeing only limited action, Brooklyn sent Rowe to the minors for the rest of the year. The next spring they sold him to the Phillies.

Playing for his old Tiger manager, Bucky Harris, Rowe was rejuvenated and quickly became the bellweather of the Phillies' mound corps.

Throughout his career, Rowe was also a standout batter, one of the best hitting pitchers in baseball history. In 15 big league seasons, he had a .263 lifetime average with 18 home runs, including a grand slam in each league. Rowe ranks third on the Phillies all-time list for home runs by pitchers.

Often used as a pinch-hitter, he hit .300 or better three times during his career, including once with the Phillies in 1943 when his 15 pinch-hits led the league.

Schoolboy was also a member of the 1947 National League All-Star team.

Phillies: 1943–49
Pitcher
Birthplace: Waco, Texas
B: January 11, 1910
D: January 8, 1961
Batted right, threw right
Ht. 6–4½; **Wt.** 210

Schoolboy Rowe

Rowe, Schoolboy (Linwood)

Phillies	W	L	Pct	ERA	G	CG	IP	H	BB	SO	ShO
1943	14	8	.636	2.94	27	11	199	194	29	52	3
1946	11	4	.733	2.12	17	9	136	112	21	51	2
1947	14	10	.583	4.32	31	15	195⅔	232	45	74	1
1948	10	10	.500	4.07	30	8	148	167	31	46	0
1949	3	7	.300	4.82	23	2	65⅓	68	17	22	0
Career	158	101	.610	3.87	382	137	2,219⅓	2,330	558	913	23

Ruthven, Dick

Dick Ruthven had a checkered career with the Phillies that spanned two tours of duty and a full decade of time.

Ruthven made his greatest contribution to the club in 1980 when his 17–10 record helped the Phillies to the National League East title. In the League Championship Series that year, he was the winning pitcher in the pennant-clinching fifth game with two innings of hitless relief.

Over the years, Rufus had a series of setbacks that prevented him from reaching his full potential. Injuries, particularly one that resulted in an elbow operation in 1979, the strike in 1981, and a disagreement with manager Pat Corrales in August 1982 kept him from working full seasons. Yet, in May 1983, Corrales was the one member of the Phillie brain trust who didn't want to trade the competitive righthander.

Pat was overruled, and Ruthven was dealt to the Chicago Cubs for Willie Hernandez, who helped the Phillies win the NL East title.

Phillies: 1973–75, 1978–83
Pitcher
Nickname: Rufus
Birthplace: Sacramento, California
B: March 27, 1951
Bats right, throws right
Ht. 6–3; **Wt.** 190

Dick Ruthven

Ruthven had shown up Corrales when he threw his glove into the stands after being removed from a game with the Astros in August 1982. He started one more game the rest of the season and was on the bench through the pennant race in September.

An intelligent man with a sarcastic personality, Ruthven was chosen by the Phillies in the first round of the January 1973 draft and jumped directly from Fresno State College, where he was a biology major, into the Phillies rotation without benefit of any minor league experience. He had two losing seasons, was sent to the minors in 1975, then was dealt to the Chicago White Sox after the season. His first three seasons with the Phillies featured a right arm that could throw a brilliant curve and a mind that went for strikeouts.

When he returned to the Phillies from the Atlanta Braves in exchange for Gene Garber in June 1978, he was a different athlete. Andy Messersmith had helped him make the transition from thrower to pitcher, but Ruthven had suffered a falling out with the Braves owner Ted Turner, who Ruthven claimed had made a pass at his wife.

Dick went 13–5 upon his return to Philadelphia as the Phillies won the NL East for the third straight season. General manager Paul Owens said after the season that the team never would have reached the playoffs without Ruthven.

Dick won his first six games, including a one-hitter, in 1979 before the elbow injury destroyed his season. But he came back with his best season in 1980. In the World Series, he pitched nine strong innings in Game Three, leaving with a 3–3 tie.

In 1981, he finished 12–7 and made the All-Star team for a second time (the first was with Atlanta in 1976), but the following year he made waves when he threw his glove in the stands, and his days with the Phillies were numbered.

Ruthven, Dick

Phillies	W	L	Pct	ERA	G	CG	IP	H	BB	SO	ShO
1973	6	9	.400	4.22	25	3	128	125	75	98	1
1974	9	13	.409	4.01	35	6	213	182	116	153	0
1975	2	2	.500	4.17	11	0	41	37	22	26	0
1978	13	5	.722	2.98	20	9	151	136	28	75	2
1979	7	5	.583	4.28	20	3	122	121	37	58	3
1980	17	10	.630	3.55	33	6	223	241	74	86	1
1981	12	7	.632	5.14	23	5	147	162	54	80	0
1982	11	11	.500	3.79	33	8	204	189	59	115	2
1983	1	3	.250	5.61	7	0	34	46	10	26	0
Career	123	127	.492	4.14	355	61	2,109	2,155	767	1,145	17

In his first four full seasons with the Phillies, Juan Samuel appeared to be hitting a line drive or running full speed toward a possible Hall of Fame career.

The young second baseman struggled with his defense, but he managed to average the following numbers while batting mostly leadoff from 1984 to 1987: 102 runs scored, 175 hits, 35 doubles, 15 triples, 19 home runs, 80 RBI, and 51 stolen bases.

He became the first player in major league history to reach double figures in doubles, triples, home runs, and stolen bases in each of his first four seasons. In 1987, before he had reached the age of 27, he hit 28 home runs, drove in 100 runs, stole 35 bases, and had a league-leading 15 triples. He also led the league with 19 triples in 1984. His 72 stolen bases that year were the most by a Phillie in the 20th century and represent the only single season after 1900 on the Phillies' list of the top 10 stolen base seasons in history.

And then, suddenly in 1988, he became just another player. His average, which ranged between .264 and .272 in his first four seasons, dipped to .243. His home run production dropped off to 12 and his RBI to 67.

Meanwhile, his defense showed no improvement. Although he reduced his errors to 18 in 1987 and 16 in 1988 after making 25 in 1986, he still had not mastered the footwork necessary to be a good major league second baseman. So the Phillies moved him to center field in 1989.

The experiment lasted 50 games with unhappy results. Finally, on June 15, the Phillies pulled the trigger on a trade, sending Samuel to the New York Mets for Lenny Dykstra and Roger McDowell.

Samuel's career continued to slip with the Mets, who eventually sent him to the Los Angeles Dodgers. Later he joined the Kansas City Royals, who released him after the 1992 season.

But for four seasons he was the best offensive second baseman in Phillies history after a minor league career that was spectacular enough to allow the Phillies to trade Julio Franco to the Indians before the 1983 season.

Despite his brief Phillies career, Samuel makes several appearances in the team's all-time records. His 701 at-bats in 1984 is the most ever recorded by a Phillie in one season. He also is sixth (663 in 1985) and 10th (655 in 1987) on that list. His 19 triples in 1984 ties for fifth in the single-season rankings. He is eighth in career triples (70), third in stolen bases (249), and fifth in strikeouts (824). And he is the only Phillies player ever to record at least 15 doubles, triples, and homers twice in a season (1984 and 1987).

Samuel, Juan

Phillies: 1983–89
Second baseman, outfielder
Nickname: Sammy
Birthplace: San Pedro de Macorís, Dominican Republic
B: December 9, 1960
Bats right, throws right
Ht. 5–11; Wt. 170

Juan Samuel

Samuel, Juan

Phillies	G	AB	H	BA	RBI	R	2B	3B	HR	SA	SB
1983	18	65	18	.277	5	14	1	2	2	.446	3
1984	160	701	191	.272	69	105	36	19	15	.442	72
1985	161	663	175	.264	74	101	31	13	19	.436	53
1986	145	591	157	.266	78	90	36	12	16	.448	42
1987	160	655	178	.272	100	113	37	15	28	.502	35
1988	157	629	153	.243	67	68	32	9	12	.380	33
1989	51	199	49	.246	20	32	3	1	8	.392	11
Career:	Active major league player										

Sand, Heinie

Phillies: 1923–28
Shortstop
Birthplace: San Francisco, California
B: July 3, 1897
D: November 3, 1958
Batted right, threw right
Ht. 5–9; **Wt.** 160

Heinie Sand

Heinie Sand spent six seasons with the Phillies. In four the Phillies finished dead last. Once the team was seventh. Once it reached the giddy heights of sixth.

But if one man had had his way, Sand would have had a World Series share after the 1924 season. That was the season in which Sand, then a second-year shortstop who was coming into his own as a player for the Phillies, was approached and offered a bribe from a New York Giants player before a weekend series between the two teams. At the time the Giants and Brooklyn were in a race to the wire for the National League pennant; John McGraw's Giants had a 1½-game lead on the Dodgers with three to play to Brooklyn's two.

Sand not only refused the bribe; he reported it. And shortly after the season was over, the man who had originally signed Jimmy O'Connell, the Giant player who had offered the bribe, suggested that Sand get O'Connell's World Series share.

"The World Series share which would have gone to O'Connell . . . should be given to Sand," said George Putnam, the secretary of the San Francisco Pacific Coast League team. "I believe that Judge Landis . . . should see that this is done."

The state of baseball at the time was nervous. The Black Sox scandal was only five years old when Sand reported that O'Connell had offered him $500 "to ease up" during the last weekend series. In a statement made by Sand a week after the bribe offer, he indicated that O'Connell wasn't the only Giant involved in the attempt.

"It will be worth $500 to you if you don't bear down too hard," Sand testified O'Connell told him.

"I asked him what he meant and he said, 'You know what I mean. Your club.' One word led to another and he told me that (Giant coach) Cozy Dolan was in on it. When I asked if the rest of the Giants knew about it, he said, 'Sure (Frankie) Frisch, (George) Kelly, and (Ross) Youngs understand.'

"I was startled. I always took O'Connell for a square shooter and I was surprised, and as I though it over I became enraged. I said: 'Tell your friends that there is not enough money in New York to bribe me and that they are in for a licking today.' "

The Giants won the pennant, but O'Connell was barred from baseball for life. Frisch, Kelly, and Youngs not only escaped further implication but were later voted into baseball's Hall of Fame. And Heinie Sand never got a World Series share.

In his half dozen big league seasons, no one ever accused John Henry Sand of not bearing down. His hitting skills were limited, as his .258 average attests, and he was capable of as many as 60 errors a season at shortstop. But he was a hustling subscriber to the work ethic who cost the Phillies $40,000 when they purchased his contract from Salt Lake City of the Pacific Coast League after the 1922 season. He was deemed the ideal hitter to attack the right field fence at Baker Bowl when he arrived in Philadelphia.

It never happened. He hit only 18 home runs in more than 3,000 at bats with the Phillies. In his next-to-last year with the team, his batting average reached .299. But it slipped back to .211 the following season, and Sand was out of the big leagues for good at the end of 1928.

Sand played in the minor leagues until 1934, then retired to San Francisco where he entered the plumbing business. He died in 1958, and the obituaries duly credited him as a man who "helped uncover one of the game's major scandals."

He was also the subject of one of the shortest poems in history. He struck out slightly more often than one of every ten at-bats, but the two-word rhyme was inevitable:

Sand
fanned.

Not when the integrity of baseball needed him, he didn't.

Sand, Heinie (Henry)

Phillies	G	AB	H	BA	RBI	R	2B	3B	HR	SA	SB
1923	132	470	107	.228	32	85	16	5	4	.309	7
1924	137	539	132	.245	40	79	21	6	6	.340	5
1925	148	496	138	.278	55	69	30	7	3	.385	1
1926	149	567	154	.272	37	99	30	5	4	.363	2
1927	141	535	160	.299	49	87	22	8	1	.376	5
1928	141	426	90	.211	38	38	26	1	0	.277	1
Career	848	3,033	781	.258	251	457	145	32	18	.344	21

Sanford, Jack

Phillies: 1957–58
Pitcher
Birthplace: Wellesley Hills, Massachusetts
B: May 18, 1929
Bats right, throws right
Ht. 6–0; **Wt.** 190

Years after he left the city, the memory of Jack Sanford still haunts Phillies fans. He was the big one who got away, the guy the team let go for such a small price that the trade still sticks in the craw as one of the worst the Phillies ever made.

It wouldn't have been so bad except for two things. Only two seasons earlier, Sanford had had one of the finest seasons in major league history for a rookie pitcher. And after he departed, he continued to have fine seasons during a 12-year career.

Jack was no kid when he came to the Phillies. He had labored seven years in the minors, posting records such as 15–9, 12–4, 15–11, and 16–8. After spending nearly two years in the Army, he didn't arrive in Philadelphia until late in the 1956 season at the age of 27.

Sanford hadn't even been discharged when he pitched his first game. In fact, he had been in Philadelphia only five days when he scattered four hits over seven innings to beat the Chicago Cubs, 4–1.

That game served as an indication of what was in store for National League batters. In 1957, Sanford won 19, lost 8, and led the National League in strikeouts with 188. Only Grover C. Alexander (1911), Christy Mathewson (1901), Gary Nolan (1967), Dizzy Dean (1932), and Dwight Gooden (1984) registered more strikeouts in their rookie seasons.

In one game, Jack fanned 13 Cubs in a 1–0 victory. He was a member of the National League All-Star team. And he won every complete game (there were 15) that he pitched.

At the end of the season, Sanford was named Rookie of the Year by the Baseball Writers' Association and Rookie Pitcher of the Year by *The Sporting News.*

The sophomore jinx bit Jack in 1958, and he slipped to a 10–13 record. It was at that point that the Phillies made their memorable *faux pas.* They traded Sanford to the San Francisco Giants for pitcher Ruben Gomez and catcher Valmy Thomas, neither of whom did anything whatsoever in their combined total of three seasons with the Phillies.

Meanwhile, Sanford had some outstanding years for the Giants, including records of 15–12 in 1959, 13–9 in 1961, 24–7 in 1962, and 16–13 in 1963. In 1962, Sanford won 16 straight games while leading the Giants to the National League pennant. He had a 1–2 record in the World Series.

The hard-throwing righthander, who had pitched six no-hitters in high school and five no-hitters in the service, allowed seven grand slam home runs during his career.

In late 1965 he was sold to the California Angels. The following year, he became a relief pitcher and fashioned a 13–7 record. Jack played with the Angels and Kansas City A's in 1967, his final year as a player.

Jack Sanford

Sanford, Jack

Phillies	W	L	Pct	ERA	G	CG	IP	H	BB	SO	ShO
1956	1	0	1.000	1.38	3	0	13	7	13	6	0
1957	19	8	.704	3.08	33	15	236⅔	194	94	188	3
1958	10	13	.435	4.44	38	7	186⅓	197	81	106	2
Career	137	101	.576	3.69	388	76	2,049⅓	1,907	737	1,182	14

Schmidt, Mike

Phillies: 1972–89
Third baseman, first baseman
Birthplace: Dayton, Ohio
B: September 27, 1949
Bats right, throws right
Ht. 6–2; Wt. 195

Two bad knees, the result of football injuries, kept Michael Jack Schmidt from being a first-round selection in baseball's free-agent draft in June 1971.

The rest of his body—the magnificently sculptured upper body, the blacksmith arms, the marvelously quick reflexes—is the reason he will be inducted into baseball's Hall of Fame in Cooperstown, New York, in the first round of his eligibility in 1995—only the eighth third baseman ever enshrined there.

There never has been a better one.

Only Babe Ruth led the major leagues outright in home runs for more seasons than Schmidt, who was number one seven times—in 1974, 1975, 1976, 1980, 1981, 1983, and 1986. Babe did it in nine seasons.

Schmidt's 13 seasons with 30 or more homers tied Ruth for second place on the all-time list, two behind Hank Aaron. His 11 seasons with 35 or more homers tied him for second with Aaron, one behind Ruth.

His 548 career homers are the seventh highest total in history, trailing only Aaron, Ruth, Willie Mays, Frank Robinson, Harmon Killebrew, and Reggie Jackson and placing him ahead of Hall of Famers like Mickey Mantle, Jimmie Foxx, Ted Williams, and fellow third baseman Eddie Mathews.

And he wasn't just a slugger.

Although he didn't play his first big league game until he was less than a month shy of his 24th birthday, Schmidt ranks 17th on the major league lifetime list in RBI (1,595), 13th in walks (1,507), 15th in extra-base hits (1,015), and eighth in multiple-home-run games (45).

In the National League, he ranks third in homers, sixth in RBI, sixth in walks, seventh in extra-base hits, and fifth in multiple-home-run games. He drove in 100 or more runs nine times.

And he wasn't just a hitter.

Schmidt won 10 Gold Gloves, missing only in the 1985 season in a period from 1976 to 1986. His lifetime fielding average was .955, including a .980 season in 1986. He made only six errors in 304 total chances in 124 games that year, which was part of the reason he was able to capture his third Most Valuable Player award.

Schmidt also won back-to-back MVP awards in 1980 and 1981, was the World Series MVP in 1980, and made the National League All-Star team 11 times. He was voted the All-Star starter eight times. In 10 games he batted .278 with a homer and three RBI in 18 at-bats.

He could also run early in his career before his knees became worse. He stole 29 bases in 1975, just missing membership in the 30–30 club.

And he leads the Phillies in games played (2,404), hits (2,234), homers, RBI, extra-base hits, at bats (8,352), walks, intentional walks (202), sacrifice flies (108), total bases (4,404), runs (1,506), and strikeouts. His 408 doubles are second to Ed Delahanty's 432. His .381 on-base percentage is second to Rich Ashburn's .394 since the Phillies began keeping that statistic in 1946. He is fifth in singles (1,219) and seventh in stolen bases (171).

No Phillie has ever matched his single-season records of 48 home runs (1980), 128 walks (1983), or 26 intentional walks (1986).

And he played all of his 18 seasons (16 full) in the major leagues with the Phillies.

All of which makes him arguably the greatest Phillies player in the history of a team that has featured everyday players like Chuck Klein, Delahanty, and

Billy Hamilton and pitchers like Grover Cleveland Alexander, Robin Roberts, and Steve Carlton.

About the only dubious achievement in his brilliant career happened in 1973, his first season in the majors. Although he hit 18 homers and drove in 52 runs in 367 at-bats over 132 games, he batted only .196. No Hall of Famer has ever batted below .200 in a season in which he played at least 100 games.

At that point, Schmidt was adjusting to life at a new position in the big leagues. Two years earlier, he was playing at Ohio University and terrorizing Mid-America Conference pitchers. Playing shortstop in 1971, he was named to the NCAA All-America second team after hitting .331 in 37 games with 10 homers and 35 RBI. The late Tony Lucadello, who signed more than 50 major league players, had been following him from his schoolboy days at Fairview High in Dayton.

Lucadello tried to persuade the Phillies to take Schmidt as their first-round choice, but his questionable knees dropped him into the second round. He was selected on the pick after the Kansas City Royals took George Brett. It is hard to imagine a situation ever again when two future Hall of Famers playing the same position are selected with back-to-back picks after the first round, but it happened in June 1971.

Schmidt beat Brett to the majors by one year when he debuted with the Phillies by replacing Don Money at third base in the third inning on September 12, 1972, against the New York Mets.

He had been sent to Double-A Reading as a second baseman after he signed. He struggled there, batting .211 in 74 games with eight homers and 31 RBI. Nevertheless, he was promoted to the club's Triple-A farm team in Eugene, Oregon for 1972 and was named the Triple-A All-Star second baseman after hitting .291 with 26 homers and 91 RBI in 131 games. He struck out 145 times, but he showed a good batting eye by drawing 87 bases on balls.

Eugene manager Andy Seminick, in a post-season analysis, pegged his star perfectly. "I feel he has to be a real fine player," Seminick said. "He's aggressive and will hit with power. I think third base is his best position."

The Phillies thought so, too, playing Schmidt at third in 11 of 13 appearances in a September callup.

Schmidt got his first major league hit in the bottom of the fifth inning of his first game when he singled against Jim McAndrews after striking out in his first at-bat. On September 16, he hit his first home run, a three-run shot against Montreal's Balor Moore. He finished the year with a .206 batting average and 15 strikeouts in 34 at-bats.

His alarming strikeout-to-at-bat ratio continued in his first full season, when he admitted he had problems with manager Danny Ozark.

"He called me Dutch because he figured I was a big, dumb kid," Schmidt said about the manager.

In reality, Ozark was trying to befriend the young third baseman, almost act as a father figure toward him.

Schmidt showed his power potential that year by hitting two grand slams and five three-run homers. But he struck out 136 times in 367 at-bats. Part of his problem might have been a dislocated shoulder that cost him the end of spring training and the first 10 games of the regular season. He did tie Greg Luzinski for most game-winning RBI (9).

In 1974 he suddenly blossomed into a full-blown star, and he gave a hint of the kind of season it would be when he crushed a game-winning home run off the New York Mets' Tug McGraw on opening day.

He lifted his average 86 points to .282. Although he had two more strikeouts than he did as a rookie, he batted 221 more times. He walked 106 times and hit a major-league leading 36 homers, becoming the first Phillie to lead the National League in that department since Chuck Klein (28 in 1933) and the first to top the majors since Gavvy Cravath (24 in 1915). His 116 RBI were second to Johnny Bench, who had 129. He also finished second to Bench in total bases (315 to 310). His .546 slugging percentage topped the NL, and his 108 runs scored was second to Pete Rose. He stole 23 bases. He grounded into four double plays, making him the toughest hitter in the National League to

Mike Schmidt

Mike Schmidt (right) and Eddie Mathews, two of the finest players ever to play third base, got together during an old-timers game in the 1980s.

double up. He committed 26 errors at third, but only five after the All-Star break. In the All-Star Game he walked twice in two at-bats after setting a record for write-in votes while finishing second to Ron Cey in the balloting.

His brilliant career had taken off.

In 1975 his average slipped to .249 and his RBI total to 95, and his strikeout total soared to a career-high 180, but he upped his home run total to 38 as he just missed becoming baseball's sixth 30–30 player. He finished a point behind St. Louis Cardinal Ken Reitz in the Gold Glove voting. And the Phillies finished in second place, their highest position in the standings since 1964.

The Phillies won the National League East title in each of the next three years.

In 1976, Schmidt tied a major league record when he hit four home runs in four successive at-bats at Wrigley Field against a Chicago Cubs' franchise that he bedeviled throughout his career. The Phillies had trailed early in the game, 12–1 and 13–2, but Schmidt led them to an 18–16 victory in 10 innings with eight RBI. Three days later, he hit his 100th homer at Pittsburgh off John Candelaria. His 11 home runs in April equaled the major league record. His 38 homers gave him his third straight major league HR title. He cut his strikeouts to 149 and lifted his average 13 points to .262. He also reached triple figures in walks for the third straight season with 100.

He improved most of his numbers in 1977, upping his average to .274, hitting 38 homers for the third straight year (but slipping to fourth in the NL in that category), walking 104 times, and cutting his strikeouts to 122. His RBI total slipped from 107 to 101. He had 25 home runs in the first 77 games when he broke his finger in a fight with Pittsburgh pitcher Bruce Kison on July 8. He had to wear a splint after that. He hit a career-high 11 triples and had a 13-game hitting streak. But he suffered through a miserable post-season, going 1-for-16 against the Los Angeles Dodgers as the Phillies were deprived of a World Series appearance, three games to one.

A succession of injuries led to a disappointing 1978 season. He hit just 21 homers, drove in 78 runs, and batted .251. He missed three games in early June with a strained right knee and was inactive for 20 days after he pulled the hamstring in his right leg on June 29.

Although the Phillies disappointed as a team in 1979 with a fourth-place finish, Schmidt had a tremendous season that was highlighted by a then-career-high 45 home runs, including the 200th of his career against San Francisco's

Vida Blue on May 17. Schmidt also hit four homers in four at-bats for the second time in his career on July 6 and 7 against the San Francisco Giants. He hit one on his final at-bat the first day and three in his first three at-bats the following day. He also hit two home runs, including the game winner in the 10th inning, in a 23–22 victory over the Cubs at Wrigley on May 17. He had more walks (120) than strikeouts (115) for the first time.

In 1980, Schmidt and the Phillies had their greatest season. He raised his batting average to .286 and reached a personal high of 48 homers, breaking Mathews' record for homers by a third baseman. His 17 game-winning RBI included four in the Phillies last five victories, including the pennant-clincher at Montreal on October 5. He then hit .381 with two homers and seven RBI in the World Series, adding that MVP award to the regular-season one.

His 260th homer on July 25 broke the team record previously held by Del Ennis. His 46th of the season on October 2 broke his own club record, then he hit one in each of the last two games, including the one against Stan Bahnsen in the 10th inning on October 4 that clinched the pennant and led to the club's only World Championship.

"We're the World Champions and no one will ever forget that," Schmidt said in the clubhouse after the 4–1 victory over the Kansas City Royals in game six. The next day at the Kennedy Stadium celebration, he told the fans of Philadelphia to take the championship and "savor it."

He surely did. "I feel very, very lucky to have been part of it," he said. "I hope it will happen again, but nothing will be like the first time."

It never did happen again for Schmidt, even though he played in the divisional playoff in 1981 and reached the World Series in 1983. And he never had a personal season like 1980 again—although he might have in 1981 if the strike hadn't shortened the season by 50 days.

Consider that his 31 homers in 354 at-bats in that strike-shortened season were hit at the same ratio—11.42—as his 48 in 548 at-bats in 1980. And that his 91 RBI constituted one every 3.89 at-bats compared to one per 4.53 at-bats in 1980.

Schmidt's average was a career-high .316, fourth best in the league, and he drew more walks than strikeouts (73 to 71) for only the second time in his career. He led the league in homers, RBI, runs scored (78), and walks. It was no wonder that he was named MVP, making him only the third National Leaguer to win back-to-back awards (after Ernie Banks and Joe Morgan, before Dale Murphy). His homer off Mike Scott at Shea Stadium on August 14 made him the 44th player in history to hit 300 in a career. On September 20, his 310th (off Kent Tekulve) made him the greatest home run hitter in Philadelphia history, passing the A's Jimmie Foxx. And on October 2, his came to the plate as a pinch-hitter with two on in the ninth inning against the Cubs and hit his first pinch-hit homer to win the game.

Schmidt led the NL in walks (107) in 1982, when he hit .280 with 35 home runs and 87 RBI. And in 1983 he helped the Phillies to their second NL pennant in four years when he reached the 40-homer plateau for the third time. His 40 homers and 128 walks led the league, and, although his average slipped to .255, he had 109 RBI, then hit .467 (7-for-15) as the Phillies won the League Championship Series over the Dodgers in four games. But he slipped badly in the five-game World Series loss to the Baltimore Orioles, getting one single in 20 at-bats.

On May 28, Schmidt struck out four times on a total of 12 pitches, then hit a game-winning two-run homer in his fifth at-bat against Montreal's Jeff Reardon, depriving the major league career save leader of one. He hit a Phillies-record seventh grand slam at Wrigley on August 15.

His 36 homers and 106 RBI topped the league in a .277 season in 1984 that featured his 400th home run on May 15 off Los Angeles Dodger pitcher Bob Welch.

In 1985 he had 33 homers and 93 RBI while batting .277 again. He was hitting just .189 with five home runs and 15 RBI when he was moved to first base on May 22. He batted .300 after the switch. On April 15 he played in his 1,795th game, breaking Rich Ashburn's record for most appearances as a Phillie.

The following year, Schmidt annexed his third MVP award, becoming only the seventh player in major league history to do it. The other six—Stan Musial, Roy Campanella, Joe DiMaggio, Mickey Mantle, and Foxx—all are Hall of Famers. At 37, he became the second oldest MVP ever (Willie Stargell was the oldest) after leading the league with 37 homers and 119 RBI, hitting .290, and walking 89 times against 84 strikeouts. He broke Ralph Kiner's record by leading the National League in homers for the eighth season. On April 26 he drove in his 1,287th run to break Delahanty's club record. And he moved back to third base during the season and had his best fielding year.

And he admitted that his third MVP award was "special." "This one means a little more to me than the others," he added.

Schmidt reached a great milestone at 4:53 P.M. on April 17, 1987, when he hit a three-run game-winning home run off Don Robinson in Pittsburgh to become the 14th player in major league history to hit 500 homers. On May 17 he scored his 1,366th run, breaking Delahanty's mark. On June 14 he hit three homers and drove in six runs against the Expos. On September 15 he tied Mathews' record for most seasons hitting 30 or more homers at nine. And five days later, he passed Mathews and became the all-time homer-hitting third baseman when he connected off Randy St. Clair in Montreal.

For the season, Schmidt finished with a .293 average (his second best), 35 homers, and 113 RBI.

Although he previously had said he would retire after the 1987 season, he returned for his 17th spring training in 1988. And while he reached a few career milestones, including passing Mickey Mantle for seventh place on the home run list with his 537th on July 14 and getting his 1,000th extra-base hit on August 4, it was a frustrating season for him. A shoulder injury sidelined him on August 7 for the rest of the year, in which he had 12 homers, 62 RBI, and a .249 average in 108 games.

Schmidt, Mike

Phillies	G	AB	H	BA	RBI	R	2B	3B	HR	SA	SB
1972	13	34	7	.206	3	2	0	0	1	.294	0
1973	132	367	72	.196	52	43	11	0	18	.373	8
1974	162	568	160	.282	116	108	28	7	36	.546	23
1975	158	562	140	.249	95	93	34	3	38	.523	29
1976	160	584	153	.262	107	112	31	4	38	.524	14
1977	154	544	149	.274	101	114	27	11	38	.574	15
1978	145	513	129	.251	78	93	27	2	21	.435	19
1979	160	541	137	.253	114	109	25	4	45	.564	9
1980	150	548	157	.286	121	104	25	8	48	.624	12
1981	102	354	112	.316	91	78	19	2	31	.644	12
1982	148	514	144	.280	87	108	26	3	35	.547	14
1983	154	534	136	.255	109	104	16	4	40	.524	7
1984	151	528	146	.277	106	93	23	3	36	.536	5
1985	158	549	152	.277	93	89	31	5	33	.532	1
1986	160	552	160	.290	119	97	29	1	37	.547	1
1987	147	522	153	.293	113	88	28	0	35	.548	2
1988	108	390	97	.249	62	52	21	2	12	.405	3
1989	42	148	30	.203	28	19	7	0	6	.331	0
Career	2,404	8,352	2,234	.267	1,595	1,506	408	59	548	.527	174

He tried to come back in 1989, hitting two home runs on opening day and passing Ashburn for most career hits with number 2,217 on April 20. Saddled with a .203 batting average after 42 games, though, he called it quits before a game in San Diego on May 29.

"The fire I've had in me for 17 years has gone out," he said.

Some lasts:

Home run—May 2 in the first inning at the Vet against Houston's Jim Deschaies.

Hit—A bunt single on May 25 against Tim Belcher in the eighth inning at Dodger Stadium.

At-bat—A walk against Terry Mulholland in the ninth inning in Candlestick Park on May 28.

Schmidt's number 20 was retired in a pre-game ceremony attended by 56,789 at the Vet. During a nine-minute speech, he talked about being a role model. "All kids need heroes," he said. "I hope I have touched kids in a positive way."

He also talked about the Phillies fans. "I'll always miss the goose bumps I got when you cheered me," he said.

Schmidt not only got goose bumps; he gave them—to kids and adult fans. More of them than any other player in Phillies history.

And he'll give them at least one more time—when he makes his acceptance speech at Cooperstown in 1995.

Think of Phillies pitchers and the 1910s, and your mind will undoubtedly focus on one man—Grover Cleveland Alexander. But for one year, Tom Seaton, not teammate Alex, was the top pitcher on the team.

Seaton joined the Phillies after the 1911 season when his contract was purchased from Portland in the Pacific Coast League, where he had won 24 games. A clever pitcher, he possessed a fastball that had all the deceit of a crowbar across the skull. His combination of power and finesse made him appear to be a star of the future.

He showed well as a rookie with a 16–12 record, then blossomed in 1913. He led the staff in every pitching category and topped the league with 27 wins (against 12 losses), 322⅓ innings pitched, 136 walks, and 168 strikeouts. His ERA was 2.60.

With figures like those, Tom figured he was in line for a hefty salary increase, but owner William Baker disagreed, offering instead a small raise to $3,500. When the Federal League came along and offered to double Seaton's salary, he jumped to the Brooklyn club, where he was a 25-game winner in 1914.

While the 1915 Phillies were winning the pennant, Seaton's career was beginning an alarming downward skid. He was 15–17 with Brooklyn and Newark, then returned to the National League and the Chicago Cubs when the Federal League folded after the season. His last two major league seasons saw him split 20 decisions as his once-awesome fastball appeared gone for good.

By 1920, Seaton was released by the San Francisco Seals in the PCL and blacklisted from the game for his alleged gambling activities. The official word out of San Francisco was that Seaton and teammate Casey Smith had been fired "for the good of baseball." When Little Rock tried to add them to its Southern Association roster later that year, three other league members said they would refuse to take the field as long as the pair was in uniform. Neither played organized baseball again.

Seaton, Tom

Phillies: 1912–13
Pitcher
Birthplace: Blair, Nebraska
B: August 30, 1889
D: April 10, 1940
Batted left, threw right
Ht. 6–0; **Wt.** 175

Tom Seaton

Seaton, Tom

Phillies	W	L	Pct	ERA	G	CG	IP	H	BB	SO	ShO
1912	16	12	.571	3.28	44	16	255	246	106	118	2
1913	27	12	.692	2.60	52	21	322	262	136	168	6
Career	93	64	.592	3.14	231	90	1,340	1,235	530	644	16

Seminick, Andy

Phillies: 1943–51, 1955–57
Catcher
Birthplace: Pierce, West Virginia
B: September 12, 1920
Bats right, throws right
Ht. 5–11; **Wt.** 187

To look at him was to know that Andy Seminick was a big league catcher. He was not tall, and he was not sleek. He was built low to the ground, a barrel-chested man with thick legs and arms like a blacksmith, a bald head, and chiseled features. He was the perfect image of the rough, tough men who made their living behind the plate.

For the Phillies, Seminick, personally a mild-mannered individual, was a link between the dreary days of the mid-1940s and the new era of the Whiz Kids and the years that followed. Andy had first joined the Phils in 1943. He was a grizzled 30-year-old veteran when the club won the pennant in 1950, and he was still around in the declining years of the team in the late '50s.

The young Phillies of 1950 called him Grandpa Whiz. Manager Eddie Sawyer said, "If it weren't for the way Andy handled those kids, we never would've had this great pitching staff."

Seminick had his finest season in 1950 when he hit .288 with 24 home runs. In his 15-year major league career, Andy never came close to hitting that high in any other season.

The youngest of 10 children and the son of a coal miner, Seminick grew up in Western Pennsylvania. His idol was Mickey Cochrane. At age 19, Andy was working in the mines when he hurt his back. It was then he decided to pursue a baseball career.

In 1940, Seminick attended a Pittsburgh Pirates tryout camp. He was given a Class D contract, but he hit only .156 in 19 games and was released. Undaunted, Andy saved his money and took a bus to Florida the next spring. He finally landed a job, again with a Class D team.

This time Andy didn't let the chance escape him. An infielder and outfielder as well as a catcher during his minor league days, Seminick played two more years in Class D. His .325 average in 1942 got him a promotion to Knoxville, where he hit .305 and was purchased in September 1943 by the Phillies.

For the rest of that season and part of the next, the Phillies tried Seminick at several positions. Unfortunately, he hit poorly, and Andy was sent back to the Triple-A team at Buffalo.

Seminick returned in 1945, playing catcher, third base, and the outfield. In 1946 the Phillies decided to make him exclusively a catcher.

Throughout the late 1940s, Seminick was the Phils' regular catcher. Andy didn't usually hit for a high average—he was a hard swinger and a dead pull hitter who often was an all-or-nothing batter. Nor was he flashy behind the plate. He had more than his share of dropped pop-ups, wild throws to second, and passed balls. In fact, he led National League catchers in errors five times during his career.

In the pre–Whiz Kid days, Seminick was a favorite target of the Shibe Park boobirds. In 1949, though, the fans began to get in Andy's corner.

Seminick had some great moments that year. On June 2 he hit three home runs in a game against the Cincinnati Reds. Two of the homers came in the same inning, giving Andy the distinction of being only one of 13 National League players to have performed that feat. Seminick's two homers combined with circuit blasts by Del Ennis, Willie Jones, and Schoolboy Rowe to give the Phillies five home runs in the inning.

Less than two weeks later, Seminick hit three home runs in a doubleheader against the Cardinals. The next month he hit a homer and double in the same inning.

Andy's heavy hitting won for him the starting berth at catcher in the All-Star Game. By then he was being cheered by the fans instead of being booed. Ironically, he had at the time the largest organized fan club of any Phillie player.

In 1950, Andy's take-charge attitude, his astute handling of pitchers, and his fearless ability to block the plate in the face of a charging runner combined with his batting heroics to give Seminick his greatest season.

It was a season in which he hit two grand slams (he had five in his career) and won several other key games with his big bat. On May 21, Andy's two-run, ninth-inning homer beat St. Louis, 4–2. One of his biggest blasts was a homer that beat the Cardinals, 1–0, on September 12.

In mid-August, Seminick was involved in another kind of blast. This was one of the biggest free-for-alls in Phillies' annals.

It really began the previous game when New York Giants second baseman Eddie Stanky waved his arms to distract Andy as he batted. The next day, Seminick bowled over the Giants' Hank Thompson at third base. Stanky resumed his arm-waving antics and was ejected from the game. His replacement, Bill Rigney, was attempting to force Seminick at second a few innings later when Andy came in with a high, hard slide.

The players exchanged blows. Both benches emptied onto the field, and a fist-swinging brawl transpired. It took the police to stop it.

In the final week of the 1950 season, the Giants' Monte Irvin slammed into Seminick in a play at the plate. Andy's ankle was fractured. Although barely able to walk, Seminick caught a doubleheader the next day, and he played each of the remaining games of the season and all of the World Series games.

Seminick's average slipped badly in 1951, although it is worth noting that he walked five times in one game. That winter he was traded along with outfielder Dick Sisler, infielder Eddie Pellagrini, and pitcher Niles Jordon to the Cincinnati Reds for catcher Smoky Burgess, second baseman Connie Ryan, and pitcher Howie Fox.

Andy hit .256 in his first year with the Reds, then slackened to .235 in each of the next two seasons. Early in 1955 the Reds sent him back to the Phils with outfielders Jim Greengrass and Glen Gorbous for, strangely enough, Burgess, pitcher Steve Ridzik, and outfielder Stan Palys.

The rugged catcher played through the 1956 season for the Phillies. He retired at the end of the season, although he did catch in a few games the following year after becoming a Phillies coach.

During his long years in Philadelphia, Seminick accumulated 123 home runs to rank 10th on the Phillies' all-time list. He hit more home runs than any other Phillies catcher.

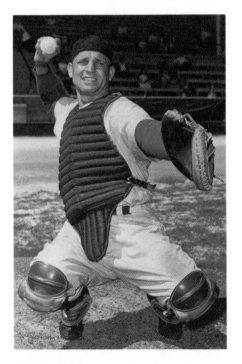

Andy Seminick

Seminick, Andy

Phillies	G	AB	H	BA	RBI	R	2B	3B	HR	SA	SB
1943	22	72	13	.181	5	9	2	0	2	.292	0
1944	22	63	14	.222	4	9	2	1	0	.286	2
1945	80	188	45	.239	26	18	7	2	6	.394	3
1946	124	406	107	.264	52	55	15	5	12	.414	2
1947	111	337	85	.252	50	48	16	2	13	.427	4
1948	125	391	88	.225	44	49	11	3	13	.368	4
1949	109	334	81	.243	68	52	11	2	24	.503	0
1950	130	393	113	.288	68	55	15	3	24	.524	0
1951	101	291	66	.227	37	42	8	1	11	.375	1
1955	93	289	71	.246	34	32	12	1	11	.408	1
1956	60	161	32	.199	23	16	3	1	7	.360	3
1957	8	11	1	.091	0	0	0	0	0	.091	0
Career	1,304	3,921	953	.243	556	495	139	26	164	.417	23

In addition to his work as a coach, Andy also served as a minor league manager and a scout for the Phillies. He was largely responsible for helping Bob Boone convert to a catcher.

Short, Chris

Phillies: 1959–72
Pitcher
Nickname: Styles
Birthplace: Milford, Delaware
B: September 19, 1937
D: August 1, 1991
Batted right, threw left
Ht. 6–4; **Wt.** 205

Chris Short

Until Steve Carlton came along, Chris Short was the greatest lefthanded pitcher in Phillies history.

In fact, his contributions are still very much in evidence in the Phillies' record book. He ranks in the top 10 in 12 categories—fourth in victories (132), third in losses (127), fourth in games (459), third in games started (301), 10th in complete games (88), fourth in shutouts (24), fourth in innings pitched (2,252), fourth in hits (2,129), third in runs (949) and earned runs (845), second in walks (762), and third in strikeouts (1,585).

He struck out 10 or more batters in a game 17 times, including 18 Mets on the final weekend of the 1986 season.

Although he was not much of a hitter, as his .126 lifetime average attests, he shocked Warren Spahn in 1962 when he went 4-for-4 against the Hall of Famer to be.

Short won the first game ever played in the Houston Astrodome when he blanked the Astros, 2–0, in the 1965 opener. It was one of the stylish lefthander's three opening-day shutouts. The other two were over the Los Angeles Dodgers, 2–0, in 1968 and the Chicago Cubs, 2–0, in 1970.

The Delaware native was probably rushed to the major leagues too early in his career. He was only 21 when the Phillies decided to bring him north with the team in 1959. Three years later, though, he began to assert himself with an 11–9 record.

In 1964 he blossomed with 17 victories and a 2.20 earned run average. By 1968 he had drawn the greatest possible praise from Gene Mauch, who earlier in Short's career had said he would trade him for "a bale of hay."

"He was the best lefthanded pitcher I ever managed," Mauch said.

Short's best season with the Phillies was 1966 when he had a 20–10 record and became the first lefty to win that many for the Phils since Hall of Famer Eppa Rixey scored 22 victories in 1916.

At the peak of his career, his earned run average was below 3.00 in five of six consecutive seasons. And three straight years, he was in double figures in complete games, topped by 19 in 1966.

Yet Short will probably be best remembered for two things. First, he was one of the two pitchers that Gene Mauch called upon constantly in the Phillies' aborted pennant drive in 1964. Second, he had the reputation of being baseball's worst dresser.

Short lost the second, fifth, and eighth games in the Phillies' 10-game losing streak near the end of the 1964 season. He also broke the losing streak with a 4–3 victory over the Cincinnati Reds in the next-to-last game of the season.

In 1969 a lower back ailment caused him to undergo surgery, and Short missed all but two games. Although he pitched as a regular the next two seasons, he was never the same. He was let go by the Phillies after the 1972 season, spent a year with Milwaukee, and retired.

The most memorable individual effort of his career came against the Mets on October 2, 1965. He pitched 15 shutout innings and struck out 18 in a game that was suspended when still scoreless after 18 innings. No other Phillies pitcher has ever struck out that many batters in a game.

Short slipped into a coma in October 1988 after collapsing in his insurance office with a brain aneurism. He never regained consciousness and died almost three years later.

Short, Chris

Phillies	W	L	Pct	ERA	G	CG	IP	H	BB	SO	ShO
1959	0	0	.000	8.36	3	0	14	19	10	8	0
1960	6	9	.400	3.95	42	2	107	101	52	54	0
1961	6	12	.333	5.95	39	1	127	157	71	80	0
1962	11	9	.550	3.42	47	4	142	149	56	91	0
1963	9	12	.429	2.95	38	6	198	185	69	160	3
1964	17	9	.654	2.20	42	12	221	174	51	181	4
1965	18	11	.621	2.82	47	15	297	260	89	237	5
1966	20	10	.667	3.54	42	19	272	257	68	177	4
1967	9	11	.450	2.40	29	8	199	163	74	142	2
1968	19	13	.594	2.93	42	9	270	236	81	202	2
1969	0	0	.000	7.20	2	0	10	11	4	5	0
1970	9	16	.360	4.30	36	7	199	211	66	133	2
1971	7	14	.333	3.85	31	5	173	182	63	95	2
1972	1	1	.500	3.91	19	0	23	24	8	20	0
Career	135	132	.506	3.43	501	88	2,325	2,215	806	1,629	24

One thing about some of those philosophical paragraphs that Gene Mauch would issue from time to time—they sure sounded good. Had a nice authoritative ring to them, too. So what if they didn't all come true.

It was early in the 1962 season, and Roy Sievers was struggling mightily to get his average above .200. He had been the key player in an off-season trade with the White Sox. To get the balding 35-year-old, the Phillies had to part with pitcher John Buzhardt, who had stopped the 23-game losing streak the previous season, and infielder Charlie Smith. The fans were impatient, booing Sievers every time he approached the plate. Mauch was philosophical.

"Roy Sievers is a .290 hitter, and .290 hitters hit .290," he said. "Think of all the fun he's going to have getting to .290."

Now the bad news. Although he recovered somewhat, Sievers never did get to .290. His average reached just .262, although he did hit 21 home runs and drove in 80 runs. And 1963 was even more disappointing as Roy's average slipped to .240. Again, his power production was adequate with 19 homers and 82 RBI.

By 1964, the Phillies were ready to contend seriously for a pennant, but Sievers wasn't ready to play as a regular. He wasn't a .290 hitter. For that matter, he wasn't even a .190 hitter when the Phillies sold him to the Washington Senators in the city in which he had his finest years. Roy was released during the 1965 season, ending a 17-year career that began in 1949 when he was named American League Rookie of the Year for the St. Louis Browns.

Sievers, Roy

Phillies: 1962–64
First baseman
Nickname: Squirrel
Birthplace: St. Louis, Missouri
B: November 18, 1926
Bats right, throws right
Ht. 6–1; **Wt.** 195

Roy Sievers

Sievers, Roy

Phillies	G	AB	H	BA	RBI	R	2B	3B	HR	SA	SB
1962	144	477	125	.262	80	61	19	5	21	.455	2
1963	138	450	108	.240	82	46	19	2	19	.418	0
1964	49	120	22	.183	16	7	3	1	4	.325	0
Career	1,887	6,387	1,703	.267	1,147	945	292	42	318	.475	14

Simmons, Curt

Phillies: 1947–50, 1952–60
Pitcher
Birthplace: Egypt, Pennsylvania
B: May 19, 1929
Bats left, throws left
Ht. 5–11; **Wt.** 175

When the Phillies signed Curt Simmons to a $65,000 bonus in 1947, it was one of the highest sums any major league team had paid up to that point to an untested player. Unlike many big bonus payments of the era, nobody ever said the Phillies didn't get their money's worth with Simmons.

Although it took him a few years to develop into a mature big league pitcher, Curt turned into one of the Phillies' top hurlers. An overpowering lefthander with a sizzling fastball and a crackling curve, Simmons ranks among the leaders in each of the 11 all-time career categories for Phils starting pitchers.

His best season was in 1950 when, despite two military interruptions, Curt chalked up a 17–8 record. In more than a decade of hurling for the Phillies, Simmons had many other fine seasons, even though he often toiled for poor teams or had his seasons broken up by unusual circumstances.

Simmons was a high school and American Legion sensation when the Phillies discovered him. Hailing from the little town of Egypt, not far from Allentown, Curt, who as a teenager once had struck out 23 batters in a game, and had pitched his team to two straight state Legion titles, was wooed by Phils scout Cy Morgan, as well as by scouts from 14 of the other 15 major league clubs.

So anxious were the Phillies to sign Simmons that they sent the entire club to Egypt for an exhibition game to face Curt and the local town team. The occasion was the dedication of a community baseball field. The Phillies figured the trip would not only be a valuable goodwill gesture, but would also help to drive down the bidding price on Curt, who they figured would get hammered by the big league batters.

At least, the latter assumption was wrong. With 4,500 townsfolk cheering wildly, Simmons struck out 11 Phils and would've beaten them if two of his out-fielders hadn't collided trying to make the final putout in the ninth inning. As a result, the game ended in a 4–4 tie. And the price for Simmons' services went up.

The Phillies were locked in a bidding war with the Detroit Tigers and Boston Red Sox, but eventually they prevailed. Curt signed, and went immediately to the Phils' farm club in Wilmington. A raw 18-year-old, Simmons won 13 of 18 games for the Blue Rocks and struck out 197 batters in 149 innings.

At the end of the season, Simmons was called up to the parent club. He drew the starting assignment on the last day of the season against the New York Giants. That year the Giants, with a powerhouse lineup featuring Johnny Mize, Willard Marshall, and Walker Cooper, had set a major league record for most home runs by a team. Curt stopped the Giants on five hits, beating them, 3–1.

Despite such an auspicious debut, Simmons still had a long way to go. Required to be on the Phillies' roster because of the bonus, Curt pitched poorly over the next two seasons. First he had control problems—he walked 12 batters in one game against the Giants—then when he decided just to put the ball over, he was pounded by opposing batters.

Suddenly, in 1950, however, all the pieces fit together. Simmons began pitching the way the Phils had predicted he would. Curt had both the stuff and the control, and he won games regularly. One of his best early-season efforts was a masterful three-hit, 6–1 win over the hard-hitting Boston Braves.

Simmons was sailing along in mid-season when the first of two military interruptions occurred. On July 29, Curt had to take two weeks off for National Guard training camp.

Curt came back from that excursion to pick up where he left off, teaming with his close friend Robin Roberts to spearhead the pitching staff as the Phillies drove for the National League pennant.

On September 3, Simmons had perhaps his finest game to date, blanking Boston, 2–0, and for the first time in his career, not walking a batter. Three days later, he held the Dodgers to one hit entering the ninth inning, but gave up a walk and a single and was replaced by Jim Konstanty, who failed to hold the Phillies' 2–0 lead.

The following week Simmons had to leave the team to join his National Guard unit again. The unit had been called into federal service. Curt's season was over. It was a heartbreaking development, one that not only deprived Simmons of a certain 20-win season, but also took him out of the World Series.

Because Curt had not pitched in nearly a month, manager Eddie Sawyer vetoed a suggestion to put him on the Series roster.

Simmons spent the next year in the service, then rejoined his team in 1952. His record was 14–8 that year. Curt tied for the league lead in shutouts with six and was the starting pitcher for the National League All-Star team.

In 1953, Curt was again a member of the All-Star team. That year, while posting a 16–13 record, he pitched the finest game of his career. It happened against the Boston Braves on May 16. Curt gave up a leadoff single to Bill Bruton, then retired the next 27 batters. Simmons struck out 10 Braves, including Bruton the next three times he batted.

Simmons might have won 20 games that year, too, except for another unusual interruption. He was pushing a power mower across his lawn when his foot accidentally got under the machine. Curt lost part of his left big toe. Had it not been for the heavy boots he was wearing, the accident could have been much worse. As it was, Simmons lost one month of the season.

After the accident, Curt had to readjust his style. He went 14–15 in 1954, and was third in the league in ERA with a 2.81 mark and third in complete games with 21.

In 1955, Curt was plagued by arm trouble, and his record slipped to 8–8. But he came back strongly the next two years, posting records of 15–10 and 12–11 for mediocre teams. In 1956, Simmons won seven straight complete games. In 1957 he was again the starting (and losing) pitcher for the National League All-Stars.

The following year Simmons' effectiveness seemingly slipped. Curt won only seven games in 1958. Then he developed a sore arm in 1959, and the Phillies sent him back to the minors to try to recover.

The Phillies, thinking Curt's career was over, gave up on him in 1960, handing him his unconditional release. The St. Louis Cardinals, however, had other ideas. Seven days after his release, they signed him.

Simmons proved he was far from done. From 1960 to 1964, his records for the Cardinals read 7–4, 9–10, 10–10, 15–9, and 18–9. In 1964 he was one of the aces of the pennant-winning St. Louis pitching staff. Moreover, he gained a measure of vindication by beating the Phillies in a crucial late-season game that helped knock his former club out of the pennant. Simmons started and lost in his only World Series appearance that year.

Curt pitched for the Cardinals until 1966, when he was sold to the Chicago Cubs. Midway through the following year, after working mostly in relief, Simmons was picked up by the California Angels. His 20-year big league career came to an end after the 1967 season.

Curt Simmons

Simmons, Curt

Phillies	W	L	Pct	ERA	G	CG	IP	H	BB	SO	ShO
1947	1	0	1.000	1.00	1	1	9	5	6	9	0
1948	7	13	.350	4.87	31	7	170	169	108	86	0
1949	4	10	.286	4.59	38	2	131⅓	133	55	83	0
1950	17	8	.680	3.40	31	11	214⅔	178	88	146	2
1952	14	8	.636	2.82	28	15	201⅓	170	70	141	6
1953	16	13	.552	3.21	32	19	238	211	82	138	4
1954	14	15	.483	2.81	34	21	253	226	98	125	3
1955	8	8	.500	4.92	25	3	130	148	50	58	0
1956	15	10	.600	3.36	33	14	198	186	65	88	0
1957	12	11	.522	3.44	32	9	212	214	50	92	2
1958	7	14	.333	4.38	29	7	168⅓	196	40	78	1
1959	0	0	.000	4.50	7	0	10	16	0	4	0
1960	0	0	.000	18.00	4	0	4	13	6	4	0
Career	193	183	.513	3.54	569	163	3,348⅓	3,313	1,063	1,697	36

Sisler, Dick

Phillies: 1948–51
Left fielder, first baseman
Birthplace: St. Louis, Missouri
B: November 2, 1920
Bats left, throws right
Ht. 6–2; **Wt.** 205

On nearly every team, there has been one memorable feat that ranks above all others as the single most significant occurrence in the team's history. Without question, Dick Sisler's dramatic home run in 1950 rates that esteemed position with the Phillies.

It was a home run that ranks in importance to the team with those of Bobby Thomson of the Giants in 1951 and Bill Mazeroski of the Pirates in 1960. From a Phillies' perspective, no one in the team's 110 years ever laced a bigger hit, or one that meant so much to the club, indeed the whole city, as Sisler's.

The story of Dick's home run has become a legend: The Phillies teeter on the brink of losing their first National League pennant in 35 years after blowing a seven and one-half game lead with 11 games left in the season. They are in Brooklyn for the final two games of the season, and the Dodgers have already won the first game of the series. Another Brooklyn win will force a playoff between two teams, a certain invitation to the Phillies' demise, if their recent performances can be used as a barometer.

On the final game Sunday, Robin Roberts and Don Newcombe lock up in a tense duel with neither pitcher yielding any ground. The score is tied 1–1 as the game enters the 10th inning.

The Phillies put two men on base, and with one out, Sisler steps to the plate. He already has three singles in the game, and he has scored the Phillies' only run. His father, George, a member of the Hall of Fame, sits in the stands behind the Dodger dugout. He is the head scout and an instructor for Brooklyn.

Newcombe works Sisler to a 1–2 count, then tries to blow a fastball on the outside corner of the plate past Dick. Sisler swings and sends a long drive deep to left field. The ball sails into the stands, and Sisler has a three-run homer. Roberts blanks the Dodgers in the bottom of the 10th, and the Phillies win, 4–1.

Pandemonium erupts in the streets of Philadelphia. The Phillies have won the pennant. And Dick Sisler is a hero for all time.

Although he had four good seasons for the Phillies, it wouldn't have mattered if Sisler never had another hit. The home run assured him a place among Phillies royalty.

The home run was the climax of an excellent year for Dick. One of the club's most popular players, the handsome Sisler had the best season of his eight-year career in 1950, hitting .296 with 13 home runs and 83 RBI.

He hit a home run in every park in the league that year, and was a member of the All-Star team.

In the early part of the year, Sisler went on a brief but torrid hitting streak. Batting around .350 at the time, Dick went five-for-five with a homer and five RBI to beat the St. Louis Cardinals, 9–6. The next day he got three more hits, extending his streak to eight consecutive safeties before it was stopped. The streak was two short of tying the National League record.

Like many of his teammates, Sisler faltered in the World Series. Dick fell harder than most of them, though, managing only one hit in 17 trips to the plate. He collected one of the Phils' three RBI in the Series.

Sisler had come to the Phillies in the spring of 1948 in a trade with the Cardinals; St. Louis received infielder Ralph LaPointe and $20,000 for Dick.

Dick was a member of a noted baseball family. In addition to his father, his older brother, George, Jr., was in the front office of the Cardinals and later became a career minor league executive, and his younger brother, Dave, later pitched for seven years in the majors, most notably with the Boston Red Sox.

Dick attended Colgate University for one year but dropped out to enter professional baseball at the age of 18. Signed in 1939 by the Cardinals, Sisler spent four years in the minors, plus three in the Navy. He was brought up by St. Louis at the start of 1946.

Although he was an outfielder throughout his minor league days, Sisler was switched to his father's old position, first base, when he got to the Cardinals. That, plus the inevitable comparison made between him and his father, worked against Dick. But he was not the kind of person to complain.

As it turned out, however, Sisler split his time between left field and first base in 1946. He hit a creditable .260 and got to play for a World Series winner.

In 1947, playing only sparingly, Dick's average tumbled to .203. But in 1948, having joined the Phillies, Sisler became a different player.

Playing regularly for the first time in his big league career, Dick hit a solid .274. He was the Phils' starting first baseman, but he was hardly a gazelle around the bag. Dick led National League first sackers in errors. The Phils wanted a better fielder at first, and in the winter of 1948 they grabbed Eddie Waitkus from the Cubs. Dick was ticketed for the bench. But when Waitkus was shot in June, Sisler moved back in at first. His fielding improved, and he hit .289 for the season.

With Waitkus recovered in 1950, it was the same story again. Only this time, the Phillies weren't going to let Dick rot on the bench. Manager Eddie Sawyer wanted Sisler in left field.

Dick worked hard in spring training to learn the position. He wasn't comfortable with it at first, but gradually his competence improved. It reached the point where Sisler's fielding was a pleasant surprise.

After his unforgettable 1950 season, Sisler played one more year in Philadelphia. He hit .287, which was the second highest average on the slump-riddled team.

That winter, in a trade that Phillies fans never accepted, the club shipped Dick, catcher Andy Seminick, pitcher Niles Jordan, and infielder Eddie Pellagrini to the Cincinnati Reds for catcher Smoky Burgess, second baseman Connie Ryan, and pitcher Howie Fox.

The swap began the breakup of the Whiz Kids. For Sisler, it launched a downward spiral in which he wound up out of the majors after 1953.

Sisler played in only 11 games with the Reds in 1952 before being sent back to the Cardinals. Dick became the Redbirds' regular first baseman that season, and hit .261 for them (.256 for both teams). In 1953, Sisler was moved off first to make way for a big youngster named Steve Bilko. Dick saw limited duty that year.

In later years, Sisler became a coach, serving for several major league teams, and a manager for one and one-half seasons with the Reds and in the minors.

Dick Sisler

Sisler, Dick

Phillies	G	AB	H	BA	RBI	R	2B	3B	HR	SA	SB
1948	121	446	122	.274	56	60	21	3	11	.408	1
1949	121	412	119	.289	50	42	19	6	7	.415	0
1950	141	523	155	.296	83	79	29	4	13	.442	1
1951	125	428	123	.287	52	46	20	5	8	.414	1
Career	799	2,606	720	.276	360	302	118	28	55	.406	6

He learned early in his athletic life that his job would be to set the table for someone else—and not to expect any tips for it.

At Pershing High School in Detroit, Ted Sizemore was one fine point guard. At most schools, he would have grabbed nearly all the headlines. At Pershing, he passed the ball to Spencer Haywood and Ralph Simpson, then dropped back and played defense.

For five seasons in his 12-year major league career, Sizemore batted behind Lou Brock in St. Louis. This meant he spent his offensive life doing two things—watching good pitches go by while Brock stole second, then giving himself up by hitting to the right side to advance Sweet Lou to third. When Brock stole his 118 bases in 1974, Sizemore got to watch most of them from the batter's box.

So he shouldn't have been surprised when he came to the Phillies for the 1977 season and found himself (a) replacing the popular Dave Cash while (b)

Sizemore, Ted

Phillies: 1977–78
Second baseman
Birthplace: Gadsden, Alabama
B: April 15, 1946
Bats right, throws right
Ht. 5–10; Wt. 165

Ted Sizemore

expected to do his job with no fanfare. The only way he could get noticed was through his absence.

In 1977, Sizemore hit .281, played 152 games, led the league's second basemen in double plays (104), and listened as Philadelphia fans discussed Bake McBride's speed, Greg Luzinski's and Mike Schmidt's power, Bob Boone's consistency, Rich Hebner's smooth batting stroke, Larry Bowa's first grand slam, Steve Carlton's Cy Young Award, and the team's 101 wins.

In 1978, Sizemore broke his hand—and people finally noticed that he wasn't around as the Phillies struggled in his absence. He returned, the team won its third straight NL East title and lost its third straight championship series, and Sizemore was moved to the Cubs in the deal that brought Manny Trillo to Philadelphia. He will go down in Phillies history as a guy who bridged the two-year gap at second base between a couple of All-Star performers. He deserved more, but, after all, that was the story of his whole athletic life.

Sizemore, Ted

Phillies	G	AB	H	BA	RBI	R	2B	3B	HR	SA	SB
1977	152	519	146	.281	47	64	20	3	4	.355	8
1978	108	351	77	.219	25	38	12	0	0	.254	8
Career	1,411	5,011	1,311	.262	430	577	188	21	23	.321	59

Smith, Lonnie

Phillies: 1978–81
Outfielder
Birthplace: Chicago, Illinois
B: December 22, 1955
Bats right, throws right
Ht. 5–9; **Wt.** 170

When the Phillies traded Lonnie Smith in a three-cornered deal that got them Bo Diaz, the sports talk shows in Philadelphia were inundated with angry callers who questioned getting rid of an exciting young performer who had hit well over .300 in both his full seasons in the majors.

Sure Lonnie fell down on the basepaths a lot, and granted he wasn't a Garry Maddox clone in the outfield, but he certainly was an offensive catalyst.

It turned out that the Phillies came out all right in the trade because Diaz gave them more than even they could have expected. But Smith went on to lead the Cardinals to the 1982 World Championship and finished near the top of the Most Valuable Player voting.

In reality, Smith was ready for the major leagues long before the majors were ready for him. He spent four full seasons at Oklahoma City in the American Association waiting for something to open up at the major league level. When the opportunity developed, he grabbed it with both hands, hitting .339 in 100 games and stealing 33 bases with the 1980 World Champions. At the end of that splendid season, he was named National League Rookie of the Year by both *The Sporting News* and *Baseball Digest*. He batted .600 (3-for-5) in

Lonnie Smith

the League Championship Series against Houston and .263 (5-for-19) in the World Series.

In the wretched split season that followed, Lonnie played in only 62 games but had three game-winning hits and batted .324. He incurred the anger of the front office during the winter of 1980, though, when he agreed to take some running lessons from a fabled Villanova track coach, the late Jumbo Elliott, then failed to show up for them.

When the Phillies decided they had to go elsewhere for a catcher who could keep them in contention, they willingly included Smith in the deal.

Lonnie played on two more World Championship teams (Cardinals in 1982, Kansas City Royals in 1985) and two pennant winners in Atlanta (1991 and 1992).

Smith, Lonnie

Phillies	G	AB	H	BA	RBI	R	2B	3B	HR	SA	SB
1978	17	4	0	.000	0	6	0	0	0	.000	4
1979	17	30	5	.167	3	4	2	0	0	.233	2
1980	100	298	101	.339	20	69	14	4	3	.443	33
1981	62	176	57	.324	11	40	14	3	2	.472	21
Career:	Active major league player										

Sparks, Tully

Tully Sparks spent most of his 120-win career with the Phillies, but for some reason his won-lost record never quite measured up to his earned run average.

For seven straight years, between 1903 and 1909, Tully's ERA was below 3.00. In three consecutive seasons beginning in 1905, it was 2.18 or below. Yet, except for 1907, his record was mostly well below .500 or slightly above that figure.

In 1907, though, he had the kind of season most pitchers never achieve. He was 22–8 for a .714 percentage with an even 2.00 ERA and had 24 complete games out of 33. At one point he won 10 games in a row.

The year before he had 29 complete games and a 2.16 ERA with a 19–16 record.

In 1908 his statistics began to dip noticeably. In 1909 he reported out of condition and stayed that way the rest of the season, finishing with just six wins in 17 decisions and only a half dozen complete games in 24 starts.

After three games of the 1910 season, his Phillies and big league career was over.

Phillies: 1897, 1903–10
Pitcher
Birthplace: Monroe, Louisiana
B: April 18, 1877
D: July 15, 1937
Batted right, threw right
Ht. and Wt. unknown

Tully Sparks

Sparks, Tully

Phillies	W	L	Pct	ERA	G	CG	IP	H	BB	SO	ShO
1897	0	1	.000	10.13	1	1	8	12	4	0	0
1903	11	15	.423	2.72	28	27	248	248	56	88	0
1904	7	16	.304	2.64	26	19	201	208	43	67	3
1905	14	11	.560	2.18	34	20	260	217	73	98	3
1906	19	16	.543	2.16	42	29	317	244	62	114	6
1907	22	8	.714	2.00	33	24	265	221	51	90	3
1908	16	15	.516	2.60	33	24	263	251	51	85	2
1909	6	11	.353	2.95	24	6	122	126	32	40	1
1910	0	2	.000	6.00	3	0	15	22	2	4	0
Career	120	138	.465	2.79	313	202	2,336	2,231	629	778	19

Stock, Milt

Phillies: 1915–18
Third baseman
Birthplace: Chicago, Illinois
B: July 11, 1893
D: July 16, 1977
Batted right, threw right
Ht. 5–8; **Wt.** 154

Milt Stock

hillies fans everywhere should occasionally hoist a tall one in the memory of Milt Stock. After all, he helped the Phillies reach two of the four World Series in which they've participated.

He also once caused 12,000 boilermakers to quit work, but then again, Stock had all kinds of unusual ways to get himself involved in stories. His daughter was the wife of Eddie Stanky.

But about those two World Series appearances . . .

The 1915 champions were winging along toward the National League title with decent-field, no-hit Bobbie Byrne at third base when Pat Moran decided he needed more punch in his lineup and went instead with Stock, beginning in August. Milt hit .260, stole six bases, got 15 RBI in 69 games, and played all five Series games against the Red Sox at third. He also fielded his position extremely well. His teammates called him "Handle Hit," because he got so many hits off the handle of his bat.

For the next three seasons, Stock was the Phillies' regular third baseman. Just before the 1919 season, Baker traded him to the St. Louis Cardinals for three mediocrities. It proved to be one of Baker's worst deals, since Stock hit .300 or better in his first four years with the Cards. He ended up with 1,806 hits and a .289 average in his 14-year active career in the majors.

Later he became a coach, which is how he helped the Phillies win their second NL championship. He was the third base coach who waved Cal Abrams home in the ninth inning on the play in which Abrams was thrown out by 15 feet at the plate by Rich Ashburn. This bonehead decision got him as well as manager Burt Shotton fired.

But what's this about getting 12,000 boilermakers to refuse to work? Seems these folks wanted Stock dismissed from his off-season job in 1918 because Milt, working in Mobile, refused to join the Boilermakers' Union.

Stock clearly knew how to get himself in the middle of things, positively or negatively.

Stock, Milt

Phillies	G	AB	H	BA	RBI	R	2B	3B	HR	SA	SB
1915	69	227	59	.260	15	37	7	3	1	.330	6
1916	132	509	143	.281	43	61	25	6	1	.360	21
1917	150	564	149	.264	53	76	27	6	3	.349	25
1918	123	481	132	.274	42	62	14	1	1	.314	20
Career	1,628	6,249	1,806	.289	696	839	270	58	22	.361	155

Taylor, Jack

Phillies: 1892–97
Pitcher
Nickname: Brewery Jack
Birthplace: Staten Island, New York
B: March 23, 1873
D: February 7, 1900
Batted right, threw right
Ht. 6–1; **Wt.** 190

hen the Phillies plucked Jack Taylor out of the New York Giants organization, they had no idea what they were getting. After all, Taylor had pitched in just one major league game and was really just another 18-year-old hotshot with what looked like a lively arm.

Little did the Phillies know that Taylor would turn into the ace of their pitching staff, a three-time 20-game winner who would win in double figures five times in five years.

Over a three-year period, Jack won 69 games for the Phillies. He was 23–13 in 1894, 26–14 the following season, and 20–21 in 1896.

All the while Brewery Jack was the heart of the Phillies' pitching staff, a workhorse who three times in Philadelphia pitched more than 300 innings in a season.

After the Phillies bought Taylor from the Giants, it took Jack a while to get started. He didn't get his act in gear until 1893, when he went 10–9 in 25 games.

The next year, though, Taylor took off, beginning his streak of 20-plus-win seasons, each time leading the Phillies in victories.

With only four pitchers carrying the brunt of the load, Taylor became the workhorse of the staff, logging 298 innings in 1894, 335 in 1895, 359 in 1896, and 317 in 1897. Annually, he started 34 or more games, and in 1897 he had the durability to finish 35 of the 37 games he started.

Taylor's one problem was control. He often walked more men than he struck out. Hardly an overpowering hurler, he also always allowed far more hits than he had innings pitched.

After he slipped to a 16–20 record in 1897, the Phillies sold Taylor to St. Louis, where the next year he had the dubious distinction of losing 29 games (winning 15). Jack led the league not only in losses, but also in games (50), starts (47), complete games (42), innings pitched (397⅓), and hits (465).

That was enough for the Cardinals. They dumped Jack on Cincinnati, where in 1899 he went 9–10.

A year later Taylor was dead of Bright's disease, a condition that affects the kidneys. He was 26 years old.

Taylor, Jack

Phillies	W	L	Pct	ERA	G	CG	IP	H	BB	SO	ShO
1892	1	0	1.000	1.13	1	1	8	4	3	3	0
1893	10	9	.526	4.24	25	14	170	189	77	41	0
1894	23	13	.639	4.08	41	31	298	347	96	76	1
1895	26	14	.650	4.49	41	33	335	403	83	93	1
1896	20	21	.488	4.79	45	35	359	459	112	97	1
1897	16	20	.444	4.23	40	35	317	376	76	88	2
Career	120	117	.506	4.23	270	208	2,078	2,468	581	528	7

Jack Taylor

Philadelphia and Tony Taylor had a 15-year love affair. The scrappy infielder from Cuba was with the Phillies for two different periods, and each time the fans loved him.

He was the best of times, and the worst, and the bitterest, and the almost-sweetest.

In 1961, his first full year with the team (he had come from the Cubs the previous year in the Don Cardwell–Ed Bouchee deal), Tony hit .250. That was the year the Phillies lived through the 23-game losing streak.

In 1964 he batted .251 and watched with his teammates as the Phillies blew a 6½-game lead with 12 to play and lost the pennant to the St. Louis Cardinals.

In 1970 he batted .301, topping that mark for the first time, but could see the Phillies deteriorating into a bad ball club once again. The following season, John Quinn did him a favor by sending him to the Detroit Tigers. Two years later, he batted .303 and helped the Tigers win the American League East.

Detroit released him after the 1973 season. Paul Owens signed him as a free agent. And from opening day, the love affair between the city and the player went from warm to torrid.

The Mets were on top by one run in the ninth inning of the opener when Taylor came up as a pinch-hitter. The crowd, which hadn't seen its adopted son in three seasons, gave him a standing ovation.

Taylor responded with a single, Mike Schmidt hit a home run, the Phillies won and the standing ovation became a tradition.

"For the next three years, I got standing ovations," he said.

He became one of the top clutch pinch-hitters in the game. In September 1975, he got his 2,000th big league hit, and he retired after the 1976 season with a career total of 2,007 and a .261 average. That was the year the Phillies finally won the National League East for their first post-season appearance in 26 years.

Taylor is in the top 10 in six categories on the Phillies' all-time list. He ranks fourth in games with 1,669, sixth in at-bats (5,799) and strikeouts (818), seventh in singles (1,178), and 10th in stolen bases (136).

Taylor, Tony

Phillies: 1960–71, 1974–76
Infielder
Birthplace: Central Alara, Cuba
B: December 19, 1935
Bats right, throws right
Ht. 5–9; Wt. 170

Tony Taylor

Taylor, who later coached the Phillies, remembered his biggest thrill. It happened in 1964 and someone else was in center stage that day.

"Jim Bunning's perfect game," he said. "I was very proud of him and I made a play (on Jesse Gonder) that made his perfect game possible."

It's almost impossible to find the perfect love affair. Tony Taylor and the fans of Philadelphia came as close as you could.

Taylor, Tony

Phillies	G	AB	H	BA	RBI	R	2B	3B	HR	SA	SB
1960	127	505	145	.287	35	66	22	4	4	.370	24
1961	106	400	100	.250	26	47	17	3	2	.323	11
1962	152	625	162	.259	43	87	21	5	7	.342	20
1963	157	640	180	.281	49	102	20	10	5	.367	23
1964	154	570	143	.251	46	62	13	6	4	.316	13
1965	106	323	74	.229	27	41	14	3	3	.319	5
1966	125	434	105	.242	40	47	14	8	5	.346	8
1967	132	462	110	.238	34	55	16	6	2	.312	10
1968	145	547	137	.250	38	59	20	2	3	.311	22
1969	138	557	147	.262	30	68	24	5	3	.339	19
1970	124	439	132	.301	55	74	26	9	9	.462	9
1971	36	107	25	.234	5	9	2	1	1	.299	2
1974	62	64	21	.328	13	5	4	0	2	.484	0
1975	79	103	25	.243	17	13	5	1	1	.340	3
1976	26	23	6	.261	3	2	1	0	0	.304	0
Career	2,195	7,680	2,007	.261	598	1,005	298	86	75	.352	234

Tekulve, Kent

Phillies: 1985–88
Pitcher
Nickname: Teke
Birthplace: Cincinnati, Ohio
B: March 5, 1947
Bats right, throws right
Ht. 6–4; **Wt.** 180

When he was with the Pittsburgh Pirates, there was always something very ominous about Kent Tekulve. That intimidating look. That menacing underhanded motion. Those unhittable pitches.

It always seemed that Tekulve was snuffing out a Phillies rally, helping those haughty and hated Pirates to another victory. He was never a very welcome visitor when Pittsburgh came to town.

Then he moved to Philadelphia. And like magic, that ominous look disappeared—except to other teams—replaced by a presence that commanded huge respect and a sigh of relief that he was now on the Phillies' side.

Tekulve pitched for three and one-half seasons in Philadelphia. During that time, his considerable skill as a relief pitcher could finally gain some appreciation from Phillies fans.

Teke was used much of the time with the Phillies as a setup man. But it was a valuable role, and he appeared in 291 games with the Phils, winning 24 and saving 25.

In 1987 he appeared in 90 games, which not only was a club record, but led the league as well. The year before he had posted an 11–5 record with a 2.54 earned run average while appearing in 73 games.

Tekulve led the Phillies' staff in saves in 1985 with 14. He had originally come to the Phils early in the 1985 season, traded by the Pirates for pitchers Al Holland and Frankie Griffin. By then, Tekulve had become one of the all-time leaders in relief pitching.

A rookie in 1974, the graduate of Marietta (Ohio) College was a late bloomer, not making the big leagues until he was 27 years old. Over the years with the Pirates, he frequently led the league in games pitched, once going as high as 94 in 1979, when he went 10–8 with 31 saves while pitching the Bucs to the World Championship. He earned a record three saves in the World Series against the Baltimore Orioles.

By the time he retired after spending one year with the Cincinnati Reds, Tekulve had appeared in the second highest total of games (1,013) for a pitcher in big league history. His 94 wins in relief ranked seventh on the all-time list, and he was also in the top 10 in saves.

Tekulve was also an excellent fielder who at one point played in 291 consecutive games without making an error. He made just 13 errors in his entire 16-year big league career.

The slender hurler played his last season in 1989. A few years later he rejoined the Phillies as a television announcer.

Tekulve, Kent

Phillies	W	L	Pct	ERA	G	CG	IP	H	BB	SO	ShO
1985	4	10	.286	2.99	58	0	72	67	25	36	0
1986	11	5	.688	2.54	73	0	110	99	25	57	0
1987	6	4	.600	3.09	90	0	105	96	29	60	0
1988	3	7	.300	3.60	70	0	80	87	22	43	0
Career	94	87	.519	2.77	1,013	0	1,384	1,249	468	748	0

Kent Tekulve

When the American League was formed, it naturally enough needed baseball players. The National League, which was approaching the end of its second decade, had baseball players. The American League dangled bigger bucks. A slew of National Leaguers jumped.

Not Roy Thomas, the gentleman from Norristown who remained a loyalist and who spent 12 years as the Phillies' center fielder. This puts him in longevity right up there with Rich Ashburn, Cy Williams, and Garry Maddox. His batting approach was much more Ashburn than it was Maddox.

Thomas, whose brother Bill played for the Phillies in 1902, was the original Walking Man. The leadoff hitter led the National League in bases on balls five straight years beginning in 1900. Then, after a 1905 season in which he slipped to third, he regained the top slot the next two years. His 946 career walks are second in Phillies history.

He could hit—1,537 safeties with a lifetime batting average of .290. He hit over .300 his first three seasons and five of his first seven.

He could also score runs. In 1899 he set the National League record for most runs (137) by a rookie. The next year, he led the circuit with 132. Twice more during his career he scored more than 100 runs, and he averaged 108 runs per season during his first seven years in the majors.

And he could field. Thomas led National League center fielders in fielding percentage five times, while leading all NL outfielders in putouts twice and assists once.

Thomas joined the Phillies directly from the University of Pennsylvania campus where he had been a star outfielder for the Quakers. He stayed with the Phillies for nine years, refusing out of loyalty to jump to the upstart American League when it was formed in 1901. Roy played with the Pittsburgh Pirates and Boston Braves before returning to the Phillies in 1910.

After his 13-year big league career, he coached at both the University of Pennsylvania and Haverford College. At the age of 46, as player-manager of Bradenton in the Florida League, Thomas batted .325. The following year, as player-manager at Oneonta of the New York–Penn League, he hit .301 in 40 games.

The following year, he retired. A decade later, he accepted a lifetime pass to all major league games. He was probably disappointed that it wasn't a contract instead.

A gentleman and scholar to the end, Thomas passed away in 1959 at his Norristown home. He was 85.

Thomas, Roy

Phillies: 1899–1908, 1910–11
Outfielder
Birthplace: Norristown, Pennsylvania
B: March 24, 1874
D: November 20, 1959
Batted left, threw left
Ht. 5–11; **Wt.** 150

Roy Thomas

Thomas, Roy

Phillies	G	AB	H	BA	RBI	R	2B	3B	HR	SA	SB
1899	150	547	178	.325	47	137	12	4	0	.362	42
1900	140	531	168	.316	33	132	4	3	0	.335	37
1901	129	479	148	.309	28	102	5	2	0	.334	27
1902	138	500	143	.286	24	89	4	7	0	.322	17
1903	130	477	156	.327	27	88	11	2	1	.365	17
1904	139	496	144	.290	29	92	6	6	3	.345	28
1905	147	562	178	.317	31	118	11	6	0	.358	23
1906	142	493	125	.254	16	81	10	7	0	.302	22
1907	121	419	102	.243	23	70	15	3	1	.301	11
1908	6	24	4	.167	0	2	0	0	0	.167	0
1910	23	71	13	.183	4	7	0	2	0	.239	4
1911	21	30	5	.167	2	5	2	0	0	.233	0
Career	1,471	5,296	1,537	.290	299	1,013	100	53	7	.333	244

Thompson, Fresco

Phillies: 1927–30
Second baseman
Birthplace: Centreville, Alabama
B: June 6, 1901
D: November 20, 1968
Batted right, threw right
Ht. 5–8; **Wt.** 150

Fresco Thompson

After hitting .324 in 1929, Fresco Thompson figured he was due for a pretty good raise. Trouble was, Phillies president William Baker didn't agree, even going so far as to produce several press clippings that suggested Thompson wasn't much of a fielder.

Always a resourceful fellow, Thompson came back the next day with an armload of scrapbooks. "If you're going to pay off on clippings, read some of these," he said.

Fresco won his point. That's something he did a lot of during his four years as the Phillies' regular second baseman. A man of small size, Thompson was extremely adept at winning points by his wits.

Using his head proved useful to Thompson following his playing days, too. Fresco became an executive with the Brooklyn and Los Angeles Dodgers, advancing to vice president in the 1950s.

While he was in Philadelphia, Thompson was a hard-hitting, speedy ball player. The Phillies landed Fresco and pitcher Jack Scott from the New York Giants as part of a three-way trade in which the Phils sent outfielder George Harper to the Giants and catcher Butch Henline to the Dodgers.

Thompson had played briefly with New York in 1925 and 1926, but his first regular duty came after he arrived at Baker Bowl. The likable keystoner hit .303 in 1927. The following year he dropped to .287, then came back with his .324, one of six Phillies starters to exceed .300. He scored 115 runs while slamming 202 hits.

In 1930, Fresco, which was his middle name (his first name was Lafayette), hit .282. As always, he was not a power hitter; in fact, he hit only 12 home runs during his four years in Philadelphia. He did hit a bushel of doubles, though, compiling between 32 and 41 in each of his four years.

As a fielder, Thompson led National League second basemen in putouts in 1927 and 1929. He ranked first in errors in 1928 and 1929.

After the 1930 season, the Phillies included Fresco in one of their less memorable trades. With outfielder Lefty O'Doul, he was sent to the Dodgers for outfielder Hal Lee, pitchers Clise Dudley and Jumbo Elliott, and $25,000.

Thompson hit .265 in a part-time role with Brooklyn in 1931. The remainder of his big league career consisted of one at-bat with the Dodgers in 1932 and one at-bat with the Giants in 1933.

Thompson, Fresco

Phillies	G	AB	H	BA	RBI	R	2B	3B	HR	SA	SB
1927	153	597	181	.303	70	78	32	14	1	.409	19
1928	152	634	182	.287	50	99	34	11	3	.390	19
1929	148	623	202	.324	53	115	41	3	4	.419	16
1930	122	478	135	.282	46	77	34	4	4	.395	7
Career	669	2,560	762	.298	249	400	149	34	13	.398	69

If there was anything Sam Thompson couldn't do on a baseball field, it was never very obvious. The big, strong outfielder from Indiana could hit, run, throw, and field.

Thompson ranks as one of the finest batters in Phillies history, a man who could hit with power as well as for high averages. He is a member of the Hall of Fame, one of the Phillies' famed outfield trio of the 1890s, all of whom won places in the baseball shrine.

Big Sam was the first National League player to hit 20 home runs in a season, the first man to get 200 hits in a season, and the first slugger to record 300 total bases in one campaign. He hit more home runs (127) during his career than any other player before the turn of the century.

In 1894, Thompson had one of the great batting sprees in big league annals. In seven trips to the plate, Sam smashed six hits, including a home run, triple, double, and three singles, thereby achieving baseball's rare cycle.

Thompson's hitting eruption came during one of the Phillies' more memorable games. They pounded 36 hits, good for 49 total bases, to gain a 29–4 victory over the Louisville Colonels. The runs, hits, and total bases were each all-time Phillies records. Remarkably, they all came off of one pitcher, an unfortunate soul named Jack Wadsworth who went the distance for the Colonels.

Thompson was already an established star when the Phillies bought him from Detroit. He had led Detroit to the National League championship in 1887, winning the batting title with a .372 mark and leading the league in RBI (166), slugging average (.571), triples (23), hits (203), and at-bats (545).

When Detroit disbanded after the 1888 season, the team astutely sold its players. Thompson, a four-year veteran, was grabbed by the Phillies.

In his first season with the Phils, Sam walloped 20 home runs, almost an unheard of total in that era. In fact, no one hit more homers than that until 1899 when Buck Freeman clubbed 25 for the Washington team.

The following year, Thompson led the National League in hits with 172. He led the circuit in hits for the third time in 1893 with 222. That year he had the league's second highest batting average with a .370.

Big Sam had his highest batting average in 1894 when he soared to a .407 mark. It was only the third highest average in the league, ranking behind Hugh Duffy's .440 and teammate Tuck Turner's .416.

In 1895, Thompson was fourth in the loop with a .392 average. But he won the RBI crown with 165 and again led the league in home runs with 18.

Thompson always ranked high in the league in assists. In 1891 he led the league with a career-high total of 32.

He also led the league's right fielders in fielding percentage in 1893 and 1896.

Sam could steal a base, too. In his first seven seasons with the Phillies, he averaged nearly 26 a year.

When the Players' League was formed in 1890, Thompson was one of the first Phillies to jump ship. But, although he signed a contract with the new

Thompson, Sam

Phillies: 1889–98
Right fielder
Birthplace: Danville, Indiana
Nickname: Big Sam
B: March 5, 1860
D: November 7, 1922
Ht. 6–2; **Wt.** 207

Sam Thompson

league, the Phillies persuaded Sam to return to them. As a result, Thompson, unlike many of his teammates, spent no playing time in the players' union league.

Altogether, Thompson played 10 seasons for the Phillies. Back problems began to slow him down in the last few years, and by 1897 he was seeing very little duty.

Thompson retired from the major leagues after the 1898 season. He returned to the Detroit area, where he played semipro baseball for several years. In 1906, with Detroit by then having a team in the American League, Sam, at age 46, came out of retirement to play for the injury riddled Tigers. He only appeared in eight games, however, before slipping back into retirement.

Big Sam had a lifetime batting average of .331, which ranks 25th on the all-time list.

Thompson has the fourth highest lifetime batting average in Phillies history. On the club's all-time list, he ranks third in triples, fifth in runs and RBI, and ninth in doubles. He stands 12th in games played by Phils outfielders.

Thompson laced five or more hits in six different games. In a double-header in 1894, he collected eight hits.

He shares a National League record for most doubles (six) in two consecutive games in 1895.

Thompson, Sam

Phillies	G	AB	H	BA	RBI	R	2B	3B	HR	SA	SB
1889	128	533	158	.296	111	103	36	4	20	.492	24
1890	132	549	172	.313	102	116	41	9	4	.443	25
1891	133	554	163	.294	90	108	23	10	7	.415	29
1892	153	609	186	.305	104	109	28	11	9	.432	28
1893	131	600	222	.370	126	130	37	13	11	.530	18
1894	99	437	178	.407	141	108	29	27	13	.686	24
1895	119	538	211	.392	165	131	45	21	18	.654	27
1896	119	517	154	.298	100	103	28	7	12	.449	12
1897	3	13	3	.231	3	2	0	1	0	.385	0
1898	14	63	22	.349	15	14	5	3	1	.571	2
Career	1,407	5,984	1,979	.331	1,299	1,256	340	160	127	.505	229

Thon, Dickie

Phillies: 1989–91
Shortstop
Birthplace: South Bend, Indiana
B: June 20, 1958
Bats right, throws right
Ht. 5–11; **Wt.** 178

He wasn't flashy. And he didn't dominate the headlines. But for three years, Dickie Thon gave the Phillies a solid, workmanlike performance at shortstop, the best the club had in nearly a decade.

A scrappy player who never backed down from a confrontation, Thon was a decent hitter with occasional power and a solid although not spectacular fielder.

In his three seasons with the Phillies, he hit .271, .255, and .252. His best year was the first; a torrid second half in which he hit .311 helped him finish with more home runs (15) than any shortstop in the National League and the most for a Phillies shortstop since Granny Hamner had 17 in 1952. Dickie also tied Shawon Dunston for the most RBI (60) for an NL shortstop that year.

In 1989, Thon broke up Tom Browning's perfect game with a double in the ninth inning. And in 1990 he ended Frank Viola's bid for a no-hitter with a sixth-inning grand slam.

In many ways, Thon was lucky to be playing. He had come back from a serious beaning that nearly cost him his sight in one eye, and could have cost him his life.

In 1984, while playing with the Houston Astros, Dickie, then one of the premier young players in the league, was hit in the head by a pitch by Mike Torrez of the New York Mets. The most critical effect of the pitch was a fractured eye socket, which seriously impaired Thon's vision.

It took Thon four years to recover. Surgery, unsuccessful attempts at comebacks, a trip to the minors, even quitting briefly, and almost constant visual problems spelled an endless litany of frustration for Thon.

But Dickie persevered. "I'll be back," he told friends. And he was right.

Let go by Houston, the player who was once considered the top offensive shortstop in the league joined the San Diego Padres. After a year as a platoon player, he was signed by the Phillies as a free agent, and he quickly took over as the club's regular shortstop.

While in Philadelphia, Thon was voted the Most Courageous Athlete by the Philadelphia Sports Writers' Association.

Dickie, who was born in Indiana while his father was a student at Notre Dame but who grew up in Puerto Rico, was also named the first-team shortstop on *The Sporting News* major league All-Star team in 1983 when he hit 29 home runs and batted .286.

Thon's career in Philadelphia came to an abrupt halt after the 1991 season when the Phillies allowed him to become a free agent. Subsequently, Dickie signed with the Texas Rangers and was their starting shortstop in 1992.

Thon, Dickie

Phillies	G	AB	H	BA	RBI	R	2B	3B	HR	SA	SB
1989	136	435	118	.271	60	45	18	4	15	.434	6
1990	149	552	141	.255	48	54	20	4	8	.350	12
1991	146	539	136	.252	44	44	18	4	9	.351	11
Career	1,302	4,204	1,110	.264	402	473	183	41	70	.377	171

Dickie Thon

They called him Silent John and Tight Pants whenever he ran out to play right field, which was for a decade at Baker Bowl. This was because no one ever knew he was around, except when his thighs rubbed together when he ran. He wore a handlebar mustache and constantly chewed at a toothpick when he played.

He might have been quiet, but he was also special. For one thing, he took over the position of a Hall of Famer, Elmer Flick, in right field in 1903 and stayed there until mid-season of 1912 when he was traded to the Braves for Doc Miller. He spoke softly ("He doesn't even make any noise when he spits," Kid Gleason once observed) and carried a pretty big stick, especially in 1905, his second full season as the darling of the right field bleacher fans.

That year he batted .308 with 99 runs scored, 89 RBI, 14 triples, and 548 at-bats—numbers he would never again match as a Phillie. But he consistently hit in the .270–.280 range.

In 1911, however, the year before he was traded, he suffered a broken leg in mid-season. John was never quite the same player after that.

He was released to the American Association Kansas City team in 1914. On opening day of 1915, Titus was beaned by Minneapolis pitcher Bill Burns, ending his active playing career.

He returned to Philadelphia for the Golden Jubilee game in 1933 and played for the old-timers against the current Phillies team. He singled in the final inning but exhausted himself getting to third. Hans Lobert, in the coaching box, appointed himself pinch-runner and scored on Stan Coveleskie's single.

It was appropriate that Lobert ran for Titus, because he had once said possibly the kindest thing anyone ever said about Silent John.

"He had the best eye of any batter I ever saw," Lobert said. "He wouldn't swing at a pitch an inch outside or an inch inside the plate."

Titus also caught just about anything hit to him. From 1909 through 1911, he led all National League right fielders in fielding.

Titus died in his hometown of St. Clair in 1943 from the effects of a stroke suffered the previous year.

Titus, John

Phillies: 1903–12
Outfielder
Nicknames: Silent John, Tight Pants
Birthplace: St. Clair, Pennsylvania
B: February 21, 1876
D: January 8, 1943
Batted left, threw left
Ht. 5–9; Wt. 165

John Titus

Titus, John

Phillies	G	AB	H	BA	RBI	R	2B	3B	HR	SA	SB
1903	72	280	80	.286	34	38	15	6	2	.404	5
1904	146	504	148	.294	55	60	25	5	4	.387	15
1905	147	548	169	.308	89	99	36	14	2	.436	11
1906	145	484	129	.267	57	67	22	5	1	.339	12
1907	145	523	144	.275	63	72	23	12	3	.382	9
1908	149	539	154	.286	48	75	24	5	2	.360	27
1909	151	540	146	.270	46	69	22	6	3	.348	23
1910	143	535	129	.241	35	91	26	5	3	.325	20
1911	76	236	67	.284	26	35	14	1	8	.453	3
1912	45	157	43	.274	22	43	9	5	3	.452	6
Career	1,401	4,958	1,400	.282	561	738	252	72	38	.385	140

Trillo, Manny

Phillies: 1979–82
Second baseman
Birthplace: Edo Mongas, Venezuela
B: December 25, 1950
Bats right, throws right
Ht. 6–1; **Wt.** 150

Manny Trillo

Manny Trillo gave the Phillies four excellent seasons at second base and established major league records for both most games (89) and most chances accepted (479) without an error in 1982.

But he will best be remembered by Phillies fans for his great play in the 1980 season, especially in the League Championship Series and the World Series.

That season he batted .292 and established personal career highs in runs scored, average, doubles, and triples. He was the Most Valuable Player in the LCS when he hit .381 and made a crucial relay throw to the plate to cut down a run in the fifth game.

In the World Series, another tremendous relay throw cut down Darrell Porter in the pivotal fifth game. Then, in the 10th inning of the same game, he singled off the glove of Dan Quisenberry to drive in what proved to be the winning run.

Trillo gave the Phillies stability at second base, something the team had lacked since Dave Cash opted for free agency after the 1976 season. The trade with the Cubs in which the Phillies gave up five players for Trillo, Greg Gross, and Dave Rader turned out to be one of the best ever made by Paul Owens.

At first, though, the fruits of the deal were not reaped. On May 3, 1979, Trillo suffered a broken arm when hit by a Rick Sutcliff pitch and missed 40 games. Even so, he won the Gold Glove that year and repeated in 1981 and 1982. He had a rifle arm (the Phillies signed him to his first professional contract as a catcher) which he used to make opposing batters "run out" grounders to second. He waited until the last possible second before sidearming the ball to the first baseman.

The Phillies became disenchanted with Manny's demands for a long-term contract for big bucks in 1982. He was going into his option year, and the Philadelphia front office decided that, since they would be unable to sign him for suitable terms, they would get what they could for him.

The result was a five-for-one trade with the Indians in which the Phillies obtained Von Hayes and the Indians got Trillo, George Vukovich, Julio Franco, Jay Baller, and Jerry Willard. Trillo later played with the Montreal Expos, San Francisco Giants, Chicago Cubs, and Cincinnati Reds before retiring after the 1989 season.

Trillo, Manny

Phillies	G	AB	H	BA	RBI	R	2B	3B	HR	SA	SB
1979	118	431	112	.260	42	40	22	1	6	.357	4
1980	141	531	155	.292	43	68	25	9	7	.412	8
1981	94	349	100	.287	36	37	14	3	6	.395	10
1982	149	549	149	.271	39	52	24	1	0	.319	8
Career	1,763	5,911	1,554	.263	571	595	239	33	61	.345	56

Turner, Tuck

Phillies: 1893–96
Outfielder
Birthplace: New Brighton, New York
B: February 13, 1873
D: July 16, 1945
Batted left
Ht. and Wt. unknown

If ever there was a player in the wrong place at the wrong time, it was Tuck Turner.

Turner compiled the highest batting average in Phillies history in 1894 when he hit a sizzling .416. Yet, not only did Tuck finish second to Hugh Duffy in the National League batting race (Duffy hit .438), but the poor fellow couldn't even crack the Phillies' starting lineup.

The year 1894 happened to be the season in which the Phillies' regular outfield trio of Sam Thompson, Ed Delahanty, and Billy Hamilton all hit over .400. Aside from that, there was no way Turner was going to break into a lineup that included three future Hall of Famers.

Turner did get to see a considerable amount of action that year as injuries to Thompson and Delahanty limited their playing times. Tuck played in 80 games as a reserve outfielder. He had 141 hits, scored 91 runs, and collected 82 RBI. He also pitched one game in relief that year, yielding nine hits in six innings of work.

A rookie the previous year, Turner had hit a mere .323 in a limited role in 1893. After his spectacular season in 1894, Tuck came back the next year with a .386 average as a part-timer.

He should have stopped then. The following year Tuck's bat mysteriously turned to lead. Hitting .219 early in the season, Turner was sold to St. Louis where his hitting improved only slightly. He hit .243 for the season.

In 1897 the Browns made Tuck their regular right fielder. He hit .291 in his first full-time post.

The next season, Turner's average plummeted an incredible 92 points to .199. That was it for Tuck in the big leagues.

Turner, Tuck (George)

Phillies	G	AB	H	BA	RBI	R	2B	3B	HR	SA	SB
1893	36	155	50	.323	13	32	4	3	1	.406	7
1894	80	339	141	.416	82	91	21	9	1	.540	11
1895	59	210	81	.386	43	51	8	6	2	.510	14
1896	13	32	7	.219	8	12	2	0	0	.281	6
Career	377	1,496	478	.320	213	294	67	38	7	.429	53

Tuck Turner

Unser, Del

Phillies: 1973–74, 1979–82
Outfielder
Birthplace: Decatur, Illinois
B: December 9, 1944
Bats left, throws left
Ht. 6–1; Wt. 180

Del Unser had two tours of duty with the Phillies. He was the team's regular center fielder in 1973 and 1974, then returned in 1979 to give the team two years of extraordinary pinch-hitting and spot play.

But he will live in Phillies fans' hearts for his heroics in post-season play in 1980.

In the deciding fifth game of the League Championship Series in Houston, he hit a two-out pinch-hit single in the eighth inning when the Phillies scored five times in a memorable come-from-behind effort, then doubled in the 11th and scored the game-winning run when Garry Maddox singled.

Unser, Del

Phillies	G	AB	H	BA	RBI	R	2B	3B	HR	SA	SB
1973	136	440	127	.289	52	64	20	4	11	.427	5
1974	142	454	120	.264	61	72	18	5	11	.399	6
1979	95	141	42	.298	29	26	8	0	6	.482	2
1980	96	110	29	.264	10	15	6	4	0	.391	0
1981	62	59	9	.153	6	5	3	0	0	.203	0
1982	19	14	0	.000	0	0	0	0	0	.000	0
Career	1,799	5,215	1,344	.258	481	617	179	42	87	.358	64

Del Unser

In the World Series, doubles in the second and fifth games keyed Phillie victories. He wound up with a .400 average (2-for-5) in the LCS and a .500 average (3-for-6) in the World Series.

In 1979 he set a major league record by hitting three consecutive pinch-hit home runs in games between June 30 and July 10. That year he batted .298, a personal high, and had an amazing 29 RBI in just 141 plate appearances.

In 1981 his offensive skills deteriorated greatly as his average slipped to .153. He was released after going hitless in 14 plate appearances in 1982.

Unser was the Phillies' hitting instructor from 1985 to 1988. In September 1989 he was named director of player development.

Verban, Emil

Phillies: 1946–48
Second baseman
Nicknames: The Antelope, Dutch
Birthplace: Lincoln, Illinois
B: August 27, 1915
Bats right, throws right
Ht. 5–11; **Wt.** 165

Although his stay in Philadelphia was relatively brief, Emil Verban was a favorite of Phillies fans in the 1940s. A graceful fielder whose smooth play at second base earned him the nickname "The Antelope," Verban was the key player in the Phillies' infield from 1946 to 1948, and probably the finest fielding second baseman outside of Manny Trillo to wear a Phillies uniform in the last 40 years.

Verban was such a good fielder that roommate Schoolboy Rowe called him the best second baseman in the majors since Charley Gehringer played the position for the Detroit Tigers in the 1930s. "In my opinion," said general manager Herb Pennock, "Verban is the best defensive second baseman in baseball." To this, Chicago Cubs manager Charley Grimm added, "Verban is the best in the National League, and there is no one even close to him."

Emil spent eight years in the minor leagues before getting to the majors with the St. Louis Cardinals in 1944. Verban led the Cards in hitting in the World Series that year with a .412 average.

In his second big league season, Verban led National League second basemen in fielding. But early in 1946, the Cardinals sent him to the Phillies for catcher Clyde Kluttz. Emil helped the Phillies that year to a third-place tie in the league in team fielding percentage.

The next season, Verban, playing in every game, enjoyed his finest big league season, hitting .285 and leading the Phils' regulars in fielding. He was the starting second baseman on the National League All-Star team. That year, Verban's salary was $12,500.

Verban also set a major league record that still stands with the fewest number of strikeouts (eight) by a righthanded batter in 150 or more games.

Emil, who had also been a reserve on the 1946 All-Star team, was sold late in the 1948 campaign to the Chicago Cubs for an estimated $10,000 after Granny Hamner emerged from the minors as the team's regular second sacker. Verban continued to play outstanding ball in the Windy City. Never a power hitter, Emil hit his first major league home run in 1948 after 2,423 trips to the plate without one.

The agile defensive ace's skills began to slip, and in 1950 he was sold in mid-season to the Boston Braves. He was used sparingly in Boston. At the end of the season, Verban was assigned to Seattle of the Pacific Coast League. After that, Emil never returned to the majors.

Emil Verban

Verban, Emil

Phillies	G	AB	H	BA	RBI	R	2B	3B	HR	SA	SB
1946	138	473	130	.275	34	44	17	5	0	.332	5
1947	155	540	154	.285	42	50	14	8	0	.341	5
1948	55	169	39	.231	11	14	5	1	0	.272	0
Career	853	2,911	793	.272	241	301	99	26	1	.325	21

Until they got Eddie Waitkus, the Phillies hardly knew what it was like to have the same first baseman for two years in a row. For a dozen years before his arrival in 1949, the Phils had had a different player at first every season with the exception of 1941 and 1942 when Nick Etten held down the bag.

Waitkus's arrival was, therefore, viewed with considerable satisfaction after the Phils nudged him and pitcher Hank Borowy away from the Chicago Cubs for pitchers Dutch Leonard and Walt Dubiel. He was, it was hoped, going to be the Phillies' first sacker for years to come.

Eddie, as stylish and as graceful a fielder as ever put on the Phillies' livery, gave the club three full seasons and parts of two others at first. A line-drive hitter with a good eye and a quick bat, Waitkus was a big part of the team's 1950 season when he hit .284 as the leadoff batter.

For Waitkus, the 1950 season was noteworthy for two other reasons, one being the mere fact that he played at all. The other had to do with Dick Sisler's pennant-winning home run. Although that hit was unforgettable, easily forgotten is the fact that it was Waitkus who scored the actual winning run, coming home on Sisler's blast with the Phils' second run. Eddie had singled to center and moved to second when Richie Ashburn's bunt forced Robin Roberts at third.

Eddie's appearance during the 1950 season was a tribute to his perseverance and willingness to work hard to overcome seemingly insurmountable odds.

Such a situation occurred on the night of June 15, 1949, when a deranged 19-year-old girl named Ruth Ann Steinhagen summoned Waitkus to her room in the Edgewater Beach Hotel in Chicago. To lure him to her room, she used the pretext that she was from Eddie's hometown and had some important news for him. When Waitkus arrived, she invited him to sit down, then calmly walked to the closet, removed a .22 rifle, and shot the first baseman in the chest.

Waitkus did not know the girl. But she had developed a crush on him, having first seen him play with the Cubs. "If I can't have him, nobody can," she said after the shooting.

The bullet passed through Eddie's chest and lung, and lodged in his back near the spine. Waitkus was seriously injured, ultimately requiring five operations.

It was a shocking event for the whole baseball world. Especially distressing was the fact that Waitkus was off to his finest year. At the time of the shooting, Eddie was hitting .306 and was doing a masterful job holding the Phils' young infield together. He was named an honorary member of the All-Star team.

Waitkus had just come to the Phillies the previous winter. His arrival was surrounded by great expectations because in Eddie the club finally had the kind of first baseman it had long been lacking.

A dapper, urbane prep school graduate who had attended Boston College for one year and who spoke three foreign languages, Eddie had been signed by the Cubs as an 18-year-old. His first year in organized ball was in 1939. Waitkus hit .326, .303, .293, and .336 as he worked his way up the minor league ladder.

After spending three years in the military, where he played no service ball, Waitkus, although he had been up briefly with the Cubs in 1941, got his first major test with Chicago in 1946. Eddie led the Cubs with a .304 batting average and was one of the top rookies in the National League.

Over the next two years, Waitkus hit .292 and .295 while fielding almost flawlessly. He was picked for the National League All-Star team in 1948. During the off-season in 1948, he was swapped to the Phillies.

After he was shot Waitkus went through a long period of rehabilitation. In November 1949 the Phillies sent him to Clearwater, Florida, for the winter. There, Waitkus worked out every day with trainer Frank Wiechec.

Eddie made it back in grand style in 1950. Although he was the club's oldest regular and often got tired during the season, Waitkus performed brilliantly. During the year he had several 5-for-5 days. He led the team in doubles with 32. And he was his old smooth, classy self around the bag at first.

As a fielder, Eddie's specialty was digging throws out of the dirt. "With Waitkus at first, you don't have to waste any time aiming the ball before you

Waitkus, Eddie

Phillies: 1949–53, 1955
First baseman
Birthplace: Cambridge, Massachusetts
B: September 4, 1919
D: September 15, 1972
Batted left, threw left
Ht. 6–0; **Wt.** 170

Eddie Waitkus

throw it," said shortstop Granny Hamner. "You just let it fly. You know that if it's in the right general direction, Eddie will come up with it."

Waitkus slumped as did most of his teammates in 1951. But he came back in 1952 to hit .289. By 1953, though, the Phils had obtained Earl Torgeson, and Eddie's days at first base were numbered.

The Phils sold him to the Baltimore Orioles in 1954. Waitkus became the regular first baseman for the first Oriole team after the club moved from St. Louis. He hit .283.

In 1955, after playing part of the season with Baltimore, Waitkus was sold back to the Phillies. He hit .280 for the Phils in a limited role. At the end of the season, after 11 years in the majors, Eddie called it quits.

Waitkus ranks sixth on the Phils' all-time list of most games played by a first baseman. The graceful lefty was stationed at first in 585 games.

Waitkus, Eddie

Phillies	G	AB	H	BA	RBI	R	2B	3B	HR	SA	SB
1949	54	209	64	.306	28	41	16	3	1	.426	3
1950	154	651	182	.284	44	102	32	5	2	.359	3
1951	145	610	157	.257	46	65	27	4	1	.320	0
1952	146	499	144	.289	49	51	29	4	2	.375	2
1953	81	247	72	.291	16	24	9	2	1	.356	1
1955	33	107	30	.280	14	10	5	0	2	.383	0
Career	1,140	4,254	1,214	.285	373	528	215	44	24	.374	28

Walker, Curt

Phillies: 1921–24
Outfielder
Birthplace: Beeville, Texas
B: July 3, 1896
D: December 9, 1955
Batted left, threw right
Ht. 5–9½; **Wt.** 170

Curt Walker

Think about lefthanded-hitting Phillies outfielders named Walker and you'll probably immediately strike on Harry, who won a batting championship with the team in 1947.

It turns out that Harry the Hat wasn't the lefthanded-hitting Phils outfielder with the highest lifetime average. Or the most career hits.

Those honors belong to Curt Walker, whose 12 years in the majors sandwiched the 1920s and whose .304 lifetime average and 1,475 career hits were lost in the fact that he never got to play in a World Series.

He didn't think it would come to that. In 1921 he was playing for the New York Giants under John McGraw, hitting the ball well and looking forward to his first of several fall classics (the Giants won the National League pennant from 1921 to 1924). Instead, he found himself in Philadelphia late that season, traded by McGraw with a fistful of players for Irish Meusel. Curt steamed over his fate for a while, but soon his good humor took over.

"I was with Augusta in the Sally League in 1919 and was goin' so good the Yankees bought me," he said. "But that was the year they got Babe Ruth. They couldn't keep us both on the same club and they had a heck of a time deciding whether to keep me or the Babe.

"Miller Huggins flipped a coin and I lost and went back to Augusta. It wasn't long before McGraw, realizing he had a chance for the pennant, began

Walker, Curt

Phillies	G	AB	H	BA	RBI	R	2B	3B	HR	SA	SB
1921	21	77	26	.338	8	11	2	1	0	.390	0
1922	148	581	196	.337	89	102	36	11	12	.499	11
1923	140	527	148	.281	66	66	26	5	5	.378	12
1924	24	71	21	.296	8	11	6	1	1	.451	0
Career	1,359	4,858	1,475	.304	688	718	235	117	64	.440	96

looking around for some good, experienced outfielders. He bought me—so he could trade me to the Phillies for Meusel."

Walker had his best year in the major with the Phillies in 1922 when he batted .337 with 102 runs scored and 89 RBI.

He was traded to Cincinnati early in the 1924 season for George Harper and batted over .300 in four of his six full seasons with the Reds. After his baseball career, he returned to his Beeville, Texas, home where he served as a local Justice of the Peace.

Walker, Harry

When the Phillies landed Harry Walker in a trade with the St. Louis Cardinals early in the 1947 season, the slender center fielder had a reputation as a good hitter who had never quite fulfilled his potential.

About the time Walker started zipping on his red, white, and blue Phillies uniform that year—for the second time in his career—he started fulfilling that promise.

That season Walker, swapped by the Cards with pitcher Fred Schmidt for outfielder Ron Northey, became the first Phillies player to win a batting championship since 1933. Harry hit .363. Hitting over .400 early in the season, Walker ran away with the crown, finishing 46 points above second-place Bob Elliott. It was the largest margin of victory in a National League batting race since 1924.

Walker, whose father Dixie had a brief big league career with the Washington Senators, was with the Phillies in spring training in 1939 but never appeared with them during the regular season. He joined the Cardinals in 1940, but did not become a regular until 1943. That year, he hit .294, made his first All-Star team, and helped St. Louis capture the National League pennant.

The next year, Walker entered the armed forces. He won the Purple Heart and Bronze Star while serving under General Patton.

Prior to his batting title, Walker's chief claim to fame was his hit that won the 1946 World Series. Harry's shot to left-center field scored Enos Slaughter from first base with the winning run in the seventh game of the Cards' 4–3 victory over the Boston Red Sox. Walker hit .412 in the Series.

After winning the batting crown, Harry never came close to another title. In 1948, the Phillies shifted him to left field to make room for a sparkling rookie center fielder named Richie Ashburn. At the end of the season, Walker was traded to the Chicago Cubs for Bill Nicholson.

During the 1949 season, the Cubs shipped Harry to the Cincinnati Reds. Walker finished the season with a .300 average. It was, however, his last big season. In 1950 he was back with the Cardinals. He played sparingly, and then retired after the 1951 season.

Walker, one of the game's most astute students of hitting, was the manager of the Cardinals in 1955. That year he unpacked his bat briefly to take a few turns as a pinch-hitter. Harry later managed the Pittsburgh Pirates and Houston Astros, altogether spending nine years as a big league pilot.

The batting title, one of nine that Phillies batters have claimed, was also significant for several other reasons. Having played his first 10 games of the season in St. Louis, Walker was the first National League player to win the title while playing for two teams. And with brother Dixie having won the batting crown in 1944 with the Brooklyn Dodgers, Harry's title gave the Walkers the National League's first batting champ brother combination.

Walker, who used a two-tone, dark-barrel bat, also won the league's triples title in 1947 with 16. That year he was the senior circuit's starting center fielder in the All-Star Game.

Nicknamed Harry the Hat because he constantly fussed with his cap while at the plate, Walker had suffered a back injury in the war. It prevented him from bending down very far. Often, he caught low liners by sliding feet first in the direction of the ball.

Phillies: 1947–48
Outfielder
Nickname: The Hat
Birthplace: Pascagoula, Mississippi
B: October 22, 1918
Bats left, throws right
Ht. 6–2; **Wt.** 175

Harry Walker

Walker, Harry

Phillies	G	AB	H	BA	RBI	R	2B	3B	HR	SA	SB
1947	130	488	181	.371	41	79	28	16	1	.500	13
1948	112	332	97	.292	23	34	11	2	2	.355	4
Career	807	2,651	786	.296	214	385	126	37	10	.383	42

Walters, Bucky

Phillies: 1934–38
Third baseman, pitcher
Birthplace: Philadelphia, Pennsylvania
B: April 19, 1909
D: April 22, 1991
Batted right, threw right
Ht. 6–1; **Wt.** 180

Bucky Walters

Baseball history is filled with examples of players who have been switched from one position to another with spectacular results. Bucky Walters was such a player.

A native of the Mt. Airy section of Philadelphia, Walters was an outstanding sandlot baseball and basketball player in various city leagues when he signed in 1929 as a pitcher-infielder with Montgomery (Alabama) of the Southeastern Association. Walters forsook the mound after his first minor league season to concentrate on becoming an infielder. After four more seasons in the minors (during which he hit .326 once and .376 another time and played two years for future West Chester State football coach Glenn Killinger) and several visits to the Boston Braves and then the Boston Red Sox, Bucky was sold to the Phillies in 1934.

He became the Phillies' regular third baseman and hit .260 in what was actually his first full season in the majors. And, although he had not pitched since 1929, Walters also worked a few games on the mound.

Those appearances convinced manager Jimmie Wilson that Walters should be a pitcher. Persuaded that he was not going to stay in the majors as a third baseman, Walters began the conversion the following spring. Bucky had a natural sinker and he threw hard. Under Wilson's tutelage, the switch was made with relative ease.

The switch may have been one of the smartest moves in Wilson's career. Not only did Walters become one of the mainstays of the Phillies' pitching staff, but he eventually turned into one of the premier hurlers in the National League after the Phils traded him to the Cincinnati Reds.

Walters was a tireless worker who lacked control in his early years as a pitcher. But he gained stature with each year, although, like his fellow moundsmen, he never had a winning record with the Phillies.

In his first spring training game as a pitcher, Walters was so wild he had to be taken out before someone got hurt. That night, Bucky was disconsolate.

The next day, he decided to try again to pitch. "You'll be one of the best in the league," Wilson told him.

After a 9–9 record in his first season as a pitcher, Walters had an 11–21 mark in 1936. That gave him the league lead in losses.

Walters teamed with Claude Passeau and Hugh Mulcahy to give the Phillies a credible mound corps, despite the team's miserable position in the standings each year. In 1937, Walters led the staff with a 14–15 record and was selected for the All-Star Game. It was to be the first of five times Bucky played in the mid-season classic.

In June 1938, the Phillies did the inevitable. They traded Bucky to the Reds for catcher Spud Davis, pitcher Al Hollingsworth, and $55,000. The following season, Walters was named the National League's Most Valuable Player while chalking up a 27–11 record and pitching the Reds to the pennant. Bucky led the league in wins, ERA (2.29), innings pitched (319), games (36), complete games (31), and strikeouts (137).

Walters again pitched the Reds to the pennant in 1940, this time with a 22–10 record. Again, he led the league in ERA (2.48), complete games (29), and innings pitched (305). He also won two World Series games (he had lost two the year before) as the Reds beat the Detroit Tigers.

Bucky went on to have four more excellent seasons for the Reds, including the 1944 campaign when he posted a 23–8 record. That year, a two-out, eighth inning single by Connie Ryan gave the Boston Braves their only base-runner, thus depriving Walters of a perfect game.

In August 1948, with his pitching career winding down, Walters was named manager of the Reds. He managed the team until late 1949. Bucky made one appearance on the mound with the Boston Braves in 1950 before ending his 16-year big league career.

In 1957, Walters was a pitching instructor with the Phillies.

Walters, Bucky (William)

Phillies	W	L	Pct	ERA	G	CG	IP	H	BB	SO	ShO
1935	9	9	.500	4.17	24	8	151	168	68	40	2
1936	11	21	.344	4.26	40	15	258	284	115	66	4
1937	14	15	.483	4.75	37	15	246⅓	292	86	87	3
1938	4	8	.333	5.20	12	9	83	91	42	28	1
Career	198	160	.553	3.30	428	242	3,104⅔	2,990	1,121	1,107	42

Wasdell, Jimmy

Phillies: 1943–46
Outfielder, first baseman
Birthplace: Cleveland, Ohio
B: May 15, 1914
D: June 6, 1983
Batted left, threw left
Ht. 5–11; **Wt.** 185

Jimmy Wasdell was one of the legions of players who performed for a variety of other teams before passing through Philadelphia in the twilight of their careers.

In Jimmy's case, he was one of the many wartime players the Phillies put on the field. A popular fellow, Wasdell had made stops at Washington, Brooklyn, and Pittsburgh before coming to Philadelphia. He played at Cleveland after leaving the Phillies.

After having been bought by the Phils in early 1943, Wasdell played at first base and in the outfield over the next three seasons. The best results were in 1945 when he hit .300. Primarily a singles hitter, he hit seven home runs that year, the most he ever hit in one season.

Wasdell was a regular throughout his three full seasons in Philadelphia, which is something he hadn't been before his arrival (except for the 1942 season with the Pirates). A rookie with the Senators in 1937, Jimmy made history in 1939 when he made four errors in one game. The multiple blunders equaled a modern major league record.

Jimmy, who began in organized ball in 1935, was peddled to the Indians by the Phillies in 1946. He retired early in 1947.

Known for his sometimes zany behavior, Wasdell was suspended by the Phillies for three days in 1945 after socking teammate Vince DiMaggio during a train trip. Jimmy claimed that Vince's singing was disturbing his card game.

While playing for Washington, Jimmy also fulfilled a lifetime ambition once by charging a bunt and getting the ball to first by hiking it through his legs like a football center. Only trouble was, the second baseman wasn't covering the bag, and the ball rolled all the way down the right field line. The next day, Wasdell was on his way back to the minors in Minneapolis.

Wasdell, Jimmy

Phillies	G	AB	H	BA	RBI	R	2B	3B	HR	SA	SB
1943	141	522	136	.261	67	54	19	6	4	.343	6
1944	133	451	125	.277	40	47	20	3	3	.355	0
1945	134	500	150	.300	60	65	19	8	7	.412	7
1946	26	51	13	.255	5	7	0	2	1	.392	0
Career	888	2,866	782	.273	341	339	109	34	29	.365	29

Jimmy Wasdell

Weyhing, Gus

Phillies: 1892–95
Pitcher
Birthplace: Louisville, Kentucky
B: September 29, 1866
D: September 3, 1955
Batted right, threw right
Ht. 5–10; **Wt.** 145

Gus Weyhing

Gus Weyhing's reputation preceded him when he made his grand entrance at Baker Bowl. The slim righthander was known as a hard-boiled moundsman who could fling the daylights out of a ball and who never backed down from an opportunity to trek to the hill to pitch.

Gus had started his big league career in the American Association with the Philadelphia Athletics, and in three years he had won 84 games while working in more than 400 innings each season. In 1890 he took up the union cause and jumped to the Players' League with Brooklyn, where he won 30 games. When that league collapsed, Weyhing returned to the Athletics and was a 32-game winner in 1891.

By the time he moved over to the Phillies in 1892, after the American Association folded, Weyhing was regarded as one of the top pitchers in professional baseball.

That reputation was not diminished in his first season with the Phillies when he registered a 32–21 mark, making it the fourth year in a row in which Gus had won 30 or more games. Weyhing's brilliant season saw him rank third in the National League in innings pitched (470) and strikeouts (202), tied for second in shutouts (six), and tied for fifth in wins.

Weyhing continued his outstanding pitching the following year by going 23–16. But the many innings he had pitched were starting to take a toll. Gus was losing his effectiveness, as demonstrated by his 16–14 mark in 1894.

By 1895, Weyhing's arm was really bothering him. After going just 0–2, Gus was unloaded by the Phillies. He found work in Pittsburgh, then finished the season in Louisville, losing 21 games overall.

Although he never regained the skills he had demonstrated early in his career, Weyhing hung around until 1901, playing with Washington, St. Louis, Brooklyn, Cleveland, and Cincinnati. In Washington he lost 26 one year and 23 another.

Gus, whose brother John pitched briefly in the American Association in the late 1880s, had won 264 games for 10 different teams when he finally bowed out of the big leagues.

Weyhing, Gus

Phillies	W	L	Pct	ERA	G	CG	IP	H	BB	SO	ShO
1892	32	21	.604	2.66	59	46	470	411	168	202	6
1893	23	16	.590	4.75	42	33	345	399	145	101	2
1894	16	14	.533	5.82	38	25	266	365	116	81	2
1895	0	2	.000	20.00	2	0	9	23	13	5	0
Career	264	232	.532	3.89	538	448	4,324	4,562	1,566	1,665	28

White, Bill

Phillies: 1966–68
First baseman
Birthplace: Lakewood, Florida
B: January 28, 1934
Bats left, throws left
Ht. 6–0; **Wt.** 185

One of baseball's all-time class acts, Bill White came to Philadelphia at the tag end of a career that produced 1,706 hits, 202 homers, and 870 RBI in just 13 seasons.

There should have been more, but White suffered an accident while playing racquetball in St. Louis after the 1966 season, his first with the Phillies. He tripped during the match and severed the Achilles tendon in his right leg.

Although he played two more seasons with the Phillies and part of another with the Cardinals, he was never the same. Thus, Philadelphians got to see him on an everyday basis only one full year when he had all his capabilities.

What they saw that year was a man who was a consummate professional. He played first base as well as anyone, hit 22 home runs, drove in 103 runs, and batted .276. It marked the fourth time in the majors that he had gone over the 100 RBI mark and his sixth consecutive season with 20 or more home runs. In addition, while a member of the St. Louis Cardinals, he had batted over .300 four times.

When White returned after the racquetball injury, he was a shell of his former self. He limped noticeably when he made his 1967 debut in late May and finished the season with only 33 RBI in 308 at-bats. In 1968 the snap in his bat was obviously gone, and his average slipped to .239.

Bill retired after that season, then changed his mind and played 49 games with the Cardinals in 1969 before calling it quits for good at the age of 35 and turning to the broadcast booth. He worked in Philadelphia television for a while and was the voice of the New York Yankees for 18 years. He was named the president of the National League in 1989.

White, Bill

Phillies	G	AB	H	BA	RBI	R	2B	3B	HR	SA	SB
1966	159	577	159	.276	103	85	23	6	22	.451	16
1967	110	308	77	.250	33	29	6	2	8	.360	6
1968	127	385	92	.239	40	34	16	2	9	.361	0
Career	1,673	5,972	1,706	.286	870	843	278	65	202	.455	103

Bill White

Any discussion of the top third basemen in Phillies history must include Pinky Whitney. A slender Texan, Whitney played in an era when the Phillies had spectacular hitters, poor pitchers, and usually a spot in the lower levels of the National League standings.

Whitney was the Phillies' captain and a good-field, good-hit player who was extremely popular during his years in Philadelphia.

In two stints with the Phillies, Whitney wound up playing more games at third base (1,076) than all but two players (Willie Jones and Mike Schmidt) in club history.

Pinky, a minor league rookie in 1925, broke into the majors with the Phillies in 1928. He hit .301 in his rookie year. But that was merely a warmup. The following season, Whitney teamed with Chuck Klein, Lefty O'Doul, and others to give the Phillies a phenomenal .309 team batting average. Seven players hit more than .300, and Pinky was one of them with a .327 mark.

Whitney was also one of four Phils to drive in more than 100 runs in 1929, which made him one of nine players in big league history to have 100 or more RBI in each of his first two seasons. That year he also hit for the cycle, something only three other Phillies in history have done.

In 1930, Pinky continued his torrid hitting, this time blasting out a .342 average. Although not a home run hitter, Whitney was consistently among the league leaders in doubles. As a result, he drove in 117 runs, his third straight year with more than 100 RBI.

Two years later, Whitney drove in 124 runs, not only his personal high but also the highest total for a third baseman in Phillies history. In July alone, Pinky drove in 38 runs. He also had a .298 average that year with a career high of 13 home runs.

Early the next season, the Phillies traded Whitney and left fielder Hal Lee to the Boston Braves for outfielder Wes Schulmerich, who was gone from the Phils less than a year later, and utility infielder Fritz Knothe, who was out of the majors at the end of the season.

Whitney, obviously disappointed at leaving Philadelphia, had three mediocre seasons with the Braves. Fortunately for him, the Phillies got him back at the beginning of the 1936 season in a trade for infielder Mickey Haslin.

Whitney responded by hitting .294 for the Phils. During the season, he was picked as the National League's starting third baseman in the All-Star Game.

Pinky swelled to the finest average of his career in 1937 when he hit .341, good for the fifth highest mark in the league. He also led National League third basemen in fielding, duplicating the title he had won in 1932. Whitney's .982 fielding average in 1937 still stands as the top mark for Phillie third sackers.

Whitney finished his 12-year big league career in 1939. By that time, his

Whitney, Pinky

Phillies: 1928–33, 1936–39
Third baseman
Birthplace: San Antonio, Texas
B: January 2, 1905
D: September 1, 1987
Batted right, threw right
Ht. 5–10; **Wt.** 165

Pinky Whitney

place at the hot corner had been taken by another Pinky (May), giving the Phillies almost a solid decade of Pinkys at third.

Whitney, who played a little second and first base in his final years, had by then etched his name in a number of places in the Phillies' record book. Today, his .307 average stands as the ninth highest batting mark among all Phillies players. His 734 runs batted in as a Phillie place him 10th on the club's all-time list.

Whitney, Pinky (Arthur)

Phillies	G	AB	H	BA	RBI	R	2B	3B	HR	SA	SB
1928	151	585	176	.301	103	73	35	4	10	.426	3
1929	154	612	200	.327	115	89	43	14	8	.482	7
1930	149	606	207	.342	117	87	41	5	8	.465	3
1931	130	501	144	.287	74	64	36	5	9	.433	6
1932	154	624	186	.298	124	93	33	11	13	.449	6
1933	31	121	32	.264	19	12	4	0	3	.372	1
1936	114	411	121	.294	59	44	17	3	6	.394	2
1937	138	487	166	.341	79	56	19	4	8	.446	6
1938	102	300	83	.277	38	27	9	1	3	.343	0
1939	34	75	14	.187	6	9	0	1	1	.253	0
Career	1,539	5,765	1,701	.295	927	696	303	56	93	.415	45

Whitted, Possum

Phillies: 1915–19
Outfielder
Birthplace: Durham, North Carolina
B: February 4, 1890
D: October 16, 1962
Batted right, threw right
Ht. 5–8½; **Wt.** 168

Possum Whitted

By the end of the 1914 season, the Phillies decided they had taken enough of Sherry Magee's talents and temper. So they traded the still-capable outfielder to the World Champion Boston Braves for Possum Whitted and utility infielder Oscar Dugey.

The deal worked out better than anyone could have anticipated. In 1915 the Phillies succeeded the Braves as National League champs, and Whitted settled in as the Philadelphia left fielder, batting .281, a point higher than Magee.

Just to show it wasn't a fluke, Whitted also batted .281 in 1916, and, to prove he wasn't in a rut, he dipped all the way down to .280 as the Phillies repeated the previous year's second-place finish in 1917.

The following year, Possum wanted more money. Club president William F. Baker said no, and Whitted said no money, no play. He finally ended his holdout just before the season began. He played just 24 games that year, then regained his old starting spot in 1919, but ran into a personality conflict with manager Gavvy Cravath, who succeeded Jack Coombs.

In August, just to show who was boss, Cravath persuaded Baker to trade Possum, and Whitted was on his way across state to Pittsburgh.

For the rest of the season, he caught fire, batting .389 in 35 games with the Bucs. He put in two more decent years in Pittsburgh, pinch-hit once for the 1922 Brooklyn Dodgers and finished his career in the minors. Later he coached baseball for many years at Duke University.

Whitted, Possum (George)

Phillies	G	AB	H	BA	RBI	R	2B	3B	HR	SA	SB
1915	128	448	126	.281	43	46	17	3	1	.339	24
1916	147	526	148	.281	68	68	20	12	6	.399	29
1917	149	553	155	.280	70	69	24	9	3	.373	10
1918	24	86	21	.244	3	7	4	0	0	.291	4
1919	78	289	72	.249	32	32	14	1	3	.336	5
Career	1,021	3,628	978	.270	451	440	145	60	23	.362	116

Williams, Cy

At times it's better to be lucky than good. Take, for instance, the Dode Paskert–for–Cy Williams trade that William F. Baker swung with the Cubs at the end of the 1917 season. Dode was nearing the end of a long, prosperous career as one of the premier center fielders in the game. Williams was coming off a poor season in which he led the league in strikeouts and batted only .241.

Williams stayed with the Phillies for 13 seasons. He was one player who Baker was willing to pay to keep. He was the Babe Ruth of the National League, leading it in homers four times, the last three as a Phillie, including 41 in 1923. No Phillies center fielder has ever had more homers or RBI (114) than Williams did that season.

Opposing players teased the Phillies by saying that Baker's monthly payroll was $250 and that Cy Williams got $200 of it. While that was understating things a bit, Williams never got nearly the money he deserved.

A lefthanded, dead pull hitter, Cy slugged vicious line drives that clanged off the tin wall in right field at Baker Bowl. While many of his home runs were the cheap type over the short, high fence, just as many that would have gone out of a more conventional ball park simply brought flakes of rust as they crashed off the tin and back to the right fielder.

Although the "Williams shift" is commonly thought to have applied to Ted Williams, a similar shift was used against Cy in the early 1920s by the Chicago Cubs. Cy was such a confirmed pull-hitter that the Cubs, and eventually other teams, stationed all three outfielders between the right field foul line and center field, and three of the four infielders between first and second bases.

The shift never bothered Williams, though. At the top of his career, he was awesome. Beginning in 1920, his third year with the Phillies, he batted between .320 and .345 in five of seven seasons. In 1927, at the age of 40, he slugged 30 homers. Used as a pinch-hitter three years later, he batted .471 (8-for-17).

Today he remains sixth on the Phillies' all-time list in total bases, fifth in home runs, seventh in extra-base hits, eighth in hits and RBI, ninth in bases on balls, and 10th in runs scored and batting average.

Although his career stats are not quite Hall of Fame caliber (.292 average, 251 home runs, 1,981 hits), much can be attributed to the fact that Cy was a late bloomer. He didn't reach the majors until he was 25 and didn't become a regular until he was 28.

Williams, a graduate of the University of Notre Dame, became a bank president after he retired from baseball.

Phillies: 1918–30
Outfielder
Birthplace: Wadena, Indiana
B: December 21, 1887
D: April 23, 1974
Batted left, threw left
Ht. 6–2; **Wt.** 180

Williams, Cy (Fred)

Phillies	G	AB	H	BA	RBI	R	2B	3B	HR	SA	SB
1918	94	351	97	.276	39	49	14	1	6	.373	10
1919	109	435	121	.278	39	54	21	1	9	.393	9
1920	148	590	192	.325	72	88	36	10	15	.497	18
1921	146	562	180	.320	75	67	26	6	18	.488	5
1922	151	584	180	.308	92	98	30	6	26	.514	11
1923	136	535	157	.293	114	98	22	3	41	.576	11
1924	148	558	183	.328	93	101	31	11	24	.552	7
1925	107	314	104	.331	60	78	11	5	13	.522	4
1926	107	336	116	.345	53	63	13	4	18	.568	2
1927	131	492	135	.274	98	86	18	2	30	.502	0
1928	99	238	61	.256	37	31	9	0	12	.445	0
1929	66	65	19	.292	21	11	2	0	5	.554	0
1930	21	17	8	.471	2	1	2	0	0	.588	1
Career	2,002	6,780	1,981	.292	1,005	1,024	306	74	251	.470	115

Cy Williams

Wilson, Glenn

Phillies: 1984–87
Right fielder, left fielder
Nickname: Willie
Birthplace: Baytown, Texas
B: December 22, 1958
Bats right, throws right
Ht. 6–1; **Wt.** 190

Glenn Wilson

A number of outstanding throwing arms have graced right field for the Phillies over the years. None was any better than Glenn Wilson's.

The flamboyant outfielder had a howitzer for an arm. It was so strong that on more than one occasion Wilson threw out runners at first base after they'd hit would-be singles to right.

Wilson, who led National League outfielders in assists in 1985, 1986, and 1987, had such a strong arm that few base-runners took chances running on it.

Glenn could also hit. After a disappointing first year with the Phillies (during which he played left field), he turned into a solid batsman who supplied occasional power. Wilson had his best year in 1985 when he hit .275 with 14 home runs and 102 RBI. He was named to the National League All-Star team. His RBI total ranked fifth best in the league, and his 39 doubles placed second.

Wilson had come to the Phillies in one of their most controversial trades of the era. During spring training in 1984 the Phillies sent relief pitcher Willie Hernandez and first baseman Dave Bergman (who had just come in a trade from the San Francisco Giants) to the Detroit Tigers for Wilson and catcher John Wockenfuss. What made the trade so controversial was that Hernandez went on to win the American League's Cy Young Award and Most Valuable Player Award in 1984 for the World Champion Tigers.

At the time, however, the Phillies were far more in need of a solid outfielder than they were of relief pitching.

The deal didn't look good the first year, especially when Wilson struggled. But in the ensuing years, as Hernandez faltered, it looked increasingly better.

A two-time collegiate All-American at Sam Houston University, Wilson had been with the Tigers since 1982. He had hit .292 and .268 with Detroit, at first playing center field, then shifting to right.

With the Phillies, Wilson became a favorite of the fans with his exciting style of play. The congenial Texan was voted the team's most valuable player in 1985, and one year later was presented the Good Guy Award by the Philadelphia Sports Writers' Association.

The Phillies sent Wilson and relief pitcher Mike Jackson to the Seattle Mariners after the 1987 season for outfielder Phil Bradley, who spent just one year in Philadelphia before moving on. It wasn't much of a trade from the Phillies' standpoint, especially after Jackson developed into a standout fireman.

Wilson spent less than one season in Seattle. He was swapped to the Pittsburgh Pirates, then in 1989 moved closer to home with the Houston Astros. He concluded his career in the farm system of the Atlanta Braves.

Wilson, Glenn

Phillies	G	AB	H	BA	RBI	R	2B	3B	HR	SA	SB
1984	132	341	82	.240	31	28	21	3	6	.372	7
1985	161	608	167	.275	102	73	39	5	14	.424	7
1986	155	584	158	.271	84	70	30	4	15	.413	5
1987	154	569	150	.264	54	55	21	2	14	.381	3
Career	1,191	4,137	1,096	.265	521	451	209	26	98	.399	27

Wilson, Jimmie

Phillies: 1923–28, 1934–38
Catcher
Nickname: Ace
Birthplace: Philadelphia, Pennsylvania
B: July 23, 1900
D: May 31, 1947
Batted right, threw right
Ht. 6–1½; **Wt.** 200

If ever there was a case to disprove the notion that you can't go home, Jimmie Wilson was it. A native Philadelphian from the Kensington section of the city, Wilson kept leaving the city, then returning to it, during a 25-year career in pro baseball.

One of the most popular Phillies of his era, Jimmie was a hefty fellow who played hard, usually hit well, and was a solid catcher. As a backstop, his forte was handling pitchers, which he did with commendable skill and which helped at the end of his career to create a demand for his services as a manager.

Wilson had two terms in Philadelphia. In the second one, he was the Phillies' player-manager.

Jimmie's first love was soccer. As a teenager, he left Philadelphia the first time to join a crack pro soccer team in Bethlehem. Eventually though, the youngster saw that baseball had the best opportunities for him, and he returned home, packed his bags, and hit the road again, this time reporting to the New Haven, Connecticut, baseball team in the Eastern League.

Wilson stayed there for three years. In 1923 he was picked up by the Phillies—who gave New Haven several players, including pitcher Stan Baumgartner—and returned home to take up residence behind the plate at Baker Bowl. At first Wilson was a backup backstop, but in 1925 he won the starting job. Jimmie expressed his gratitude by hitting .328.

Over the next two years, Wilson was the Phillies' Rock of Gibraltar, a solid performer who gave the club some much needed stability. He hit .305 in 1926 and .275 in 1927.

In early 1928 the St. Louis Cardinals talked the Phillies into trading Wilson. Jimmie was swapped for outfielder Howard Peel and catcher Spud Davis.

Jimmie, who on occasion also played the outfield, first base, and second base during his career, had six good seasons with the Cards. His best years were in 1929 and 1930 when he hit .325 and .318, respectively. Wilson was also given the assignment off the field of sticking close to a young and wild rookie pitcher named Dizzy Dean.

In the fall of 1933, the Phillies were casting about for a manager, having fired Burt Shotton. They decided Jimmie was their man. Wilson came back again, the Phillies trading infielder Eddie Delker and one of the players they had received for Wilson, catcher Spud Davis.

Wilson was player-manager of the Phillies for slightly less than five years. Although he shared duties behind the plate each season, Jimmie was named the starting National League catcher in the 1935 All-Star Game (he had previously been picked for the 1933 All-Star team).

During his second term with the Phillies, Wilson's best year behind the plate was in 1934 when he hit .292. As a manager, he didn't fare as well. His teams finished seventh three times and eighth twice.

Late in 1938, Wilson quit as manager. The following year, Jimmie joined the Cincinnati Reds as a coach. He appeared in a few games for the Reds in 1939 and 1940, then retired as a player. In 1941, Wilson was appointed the manager of the Chicago Cubs. He piloted the Cubs until 1944.

During his career, Wilson played in four World Series. He was a member of the Cards in 1928, 1930, and 1931 and the Reds in 1940. In 1928 his two errors in the sixth inning of the third game still stand as a World Series record he shares for most errors by a catcher in one inning and in one nine-inning game. In 1940 the 40-year-old Wilson stepped in for the injured Ernie Lombardi and not only caught six games for the champion Reds, but also stole the only base of the Series and hit .353.

Wilson also set a record, since broken, during the 1933 season when he made 18 putouts in one game. In 1927 he equaled a record by having zero chances in an extra-inning (13) game.

Jimmie Wilson

Wilson, Jimmie

Phillies	G	AB	H	BA	RBI	R	2B	3B	HR	SA	SB
1923	85	252	66	.262	25	27	9	0	1	.310	4
1924	95	280	78	.279	39	32	16	3	6	.421	5
1925	108	335	110	.328	54	42	19	3	3	.430	5
1926	90	279	85	.305	32	40	10	2	4	.398	3
1927	128	443	122	.275	45	50	15	2	2	.332	13
1928	21	70	21	.300	13	11	4	1	0	.386	3
1934	91	277	81	.292	35	25	11	0	3	.365	1
1935	93	290	81	.279	37	38	20	0	1	.359	4
1936	85	230	64	.278	27	25	12	0	1	.343	5
1937	39	87	24	.276	8	15	3	0	1	.345	1
1938	3	2	0	.000	0	0	0	0	0	.000	0
Career	1,525	4,778	1,358	.284	621	580	252	32	32	.370	86

Wine, Bobby

Phillies: 1960–68
Shortstop
Nickname: Wino
Birthplace: New York, New York
B: September 17, 1938
Bats right, throws right
Ht. 6–1; **Wt.** 187

Maybe Gene Mauch saw a lot of himself in Bobby Wine—a scrappy infielder who had a great glove but who never hit well at the major league level. Whatever the reason, Wine played 12 years in the major leagues, and every one of them was for Mauch, both with the Phillies and Expos.

Bobby was beaned during his minor league career, and that circumstance often was blamed for his lack of hitting at the big league level. But, although his average never went above the .244 he hit in his first full season (1962), he was always a bit of a clutch hitter, even though he was also an easy strikeout. In 1963, when he won the National League Gold Glove as a shortstop, he drove in 44 runs on just 90 hits. And in 1970, when he played a career-high 159 games, he drove in 51 runs for the Expos.

Through most of his early career with the Phillies, he was constantly battling Ruben Amaro for the regular shortstop job—and usually winning. But toward the end of his Phillies career, he was plagued with lower back problems.

He learned a lot about baseball from Mauch and was signed by the Phillies as a coach when he was released by the Expos in 1972. He was with the Phils through 1983 and was acting manager whenever Danny Ozark, Dallas Green, or Pat Corrales was thrown out of a game.

Wine had a 16–25 record as the Atlanta Braves manager in 1985. He served as a coach for the Braves from 1985 to 1988 and still scouts for the Braves. His son, Robbie, had a brief major league career.

Wine, Bobby

Phillies	G	AB	H	BA	RBI	R	2B	3B	HR	SA	SB
1960	4	14	2	.143	0	1	0	0	0	.143	0
1962	112	311	76	.244	25	30	15	0	4	.331	2
1963	142	418	90	.215	44	29	14	3	6	.306	1
1964	126	283	60	.212	34	28	8	3	4	.304	1
1965	139	394	90	.228	33	31	8	1	5	.292	0
1966	46	89	21	.236	5	8	5	0	0	.292	0
1967	135	363	69	.190	28	27	12	5	2	.267	3
1968	27	71	12	.169	7	5	3	0	2	.296	0
Career	1,164	3,172	682	.215	268	249	104	16	30	.286	7

Bobby Wine

It was early in the 1971 season, and Rick Wise was bemoaning the lack of offensive firepower in the Phillies lineup.

"It's getting so that you have to pitch a shutout and hit a home run to win around here," he muttered to no one in particular.

Pitching a shutout and hitting a home run in the same game is remarkable and unusual enough. What Wise did on June 23, 1971, was astounding. He pitched a no-hitter and hit two home runs against the Reds at Riverfront Stadium.

In fact, he came within one batter of pitching the Phillies' second perfect game in seven years (ironically, Wise was the starting pitcher in the second game of the doubleheader in which Jim Bunning pitched his perfect game in 1964). In the sixth inning, Wise walked .204-hitting Dave Concepcion on five pitches to give Cincinnati its only base-runner.

"I got a little tired and tried to overpower the ball on my throws instead of taking time," Wise admitted afterward.

His home runs, a two-run shot off Ross Grimsley in the fifth inning and a solo homer off Clay Carroll in the eighth, merely enhanced his reputation at the time as baseball's best hitting pitcher. And, after John Vukovich had picked off Pete Rose's line drive to third for the final out, Wise said he considered it his second no-hitter of his career.

In 1968 against the Dodgers, a terrible scoring decision gave Jeff Torborg a hit on a ball that Bobby Pena muffed at shortstop, costing Wise a second gem. In the game after Bunning's perfect game, Wise made the first start of his major league career and held the Mets hitless until the fifth inning.

Wise was on the Phillies in 1964 because of a rule that allowed bonus players only one year in the minors. After that, they had to stay in the majors or be subject to waivers. Wise figured he'd be going along for the ride in '64. Instead, he made a mighty contribution to the pennant the Phillies almost won, winning five of eight decisions.

Two years later, he returned to the majors to stay and, by 1969, he established himself as one of the best pitchers in the National League with a 15–13 record and 14 complete games to go along with a 3.23 earned run average.

In 1971 the no-hitter was one of his 17 victories and 17 complete games. Rick's ERA was 2.88, and there's no question his success that season helped shape the course of the Phillies' future.

Rick believed his statistics had earned him a hefty raise; general manager John Quinn thought Wise's demands were excessive. The St. Louis Cardinals were having the same kind of trouble with one of their pitchers, so Quinn and Bing Devine agreed to swap their reluctant aces.

That's how Steve Carlton became a Phillie.

Although the Phillies definitely got the best of the Carlton-Wise exchange, Rick went on to fashion good statistics of his own. By the time his 17-year career ended in 1981, he had a lifetime record of 188–181 and 1,647 career strikeouts.

He also pitched with the Boston Red Sox, Cleveland Indians, and San Diego Padres. His 19–12 record led the Red Sox to the American League pennant in 1975.

His 717 strikeouts rank him in a tie for eighth place on the all-time Phillies list. He is one of only eight big league pitchers to beat each of the 26 teams.

Wise, Rick

Phillies: 1964, 1966–71
Pitcher
Birthplace: Jackson, Michigan
B: September 13, 1945
Bats right, throws right
Ht. 6–1; **Wt.** 180

Rick Wise

Wise, Rick

Phillies	W	L	Pct	ERA	G	CG	IP	H	BB	SO	ShO
1964	5	3	.625	4.04	25	0	69	78	25	39	0
1966	5	6	.455	3.73	22	3	99	100	24	58	0
1967	11	11	.500	3.28	36	6	181	177	46	111	3
1968	9	15	.375	4.55	30	7	182	210	37	97	1
1969	15	13	.536	3.23	33	14	220	215	61	144	4
1970	13	14	.481	4.17	35	5	220	253	65	113	1
1971	17	14	.548	2.88	38	17	272	261	70	155	4
Career	188	181	.509	3.68	505	138	3,125	3,224	804	1,647	30

The New Phillies Encyclopedia

Wolverton, Harry

Phillies: 1900–04
Third baseman
Birthplace: Mt. Vernon, Ohio
B: December 6, 1873
D: February 4, 1937
Threw right
Ht. and Wt. unknown

Harry Wolverton

Wrightstone, Russ

Phillies: 1920–28
Infielder, outfielder
Birthplace: Bowmansdale, Pennsylvania
B: March 18, 1893
D: March 1, 1969
Batted left, threw right
Ht. 5–10½; Wt. 176

Russ Wrightstone

Poor Harry Wolverton will long be remembered for one thing, just as Joe Kuharich is remembered for one thing. Kuharich to date is the only Notre Dame football coach in history with a losing record. And Wolverton was the manager of the 1912 Yankees that lost 102 games, making them the worst team in the history of baseball's proudest organization.

He was also one of the few players to jump from the National League to the American League then jump back to the National League during the same season.

That happened in 1902. Harry, the Phillies' regular third baseman in 1900 and 1901, when he batted .309, was enticed to join the Washington club in the American League along with Ed Delahanty. Delahanty stayed in the American League, but Wolverton came back to the Phillies after 59 games in the nation's capital and played his final 34 games of the season for Bill Shettsline.

The following season was his best in the majors with a .308 average, 12 triples, and 72 runs scored. He played one more year with the Phillies, moved on to Boston for a season, then served as a pinch-hitter and spot player in his season as Yankee manager. He batted .300, and therefore he must have been better than many of his players, even at the age of 38.

Wolverton died in Oakland on February 4, 1937, when he was struck by an automobile as he stepped off a curb on a rainy night.

Wolverton, Harry

Phillies	G	AB	H	BA	RBI	R	2B	3B	HR	SA	SB
1900	101	383	108	.282	58	42	10	8	3	.373	4
1901	93	379	117	.309	43	42	15	4	0	.369	13
1902	34	136	40	.294	16	12	3	2	0	.346	3
1903	123	494	152	.308	53	72	13	12	0	.383	10
1904	102	398	106	.266	49	43	15	5	0	.329	18
Career	782	3,001	833	.278	352	346	95	53	7	.352	83

Russ Wrightstone, a Pennsylvania Dutchman from the central part of the state, was an extremely dangerous man with a bat in his hand. In eight full seasons with the Phillies, he batted over .300 five times, reaching a personal high of .346 in 1925.

Yet he played in just 72 games that year and only once surpassed 119 box score appearances in any season. There was an obvious reason—Wrightstone was even more dangerous with a glove in his hand.

Manager after manager tried to find a spot in the field to hide him and didn't succeed. In 1925, Wrightstone played every infield position, plus the outfield. No one ever tried him at catcher, for obvious reasons.

On June 11, 1926, Wrightstone had one of the most productive games in Phillies history. In a 13–11 Phils' victory over the Pittsburgh Pirates, Wrightstone slammed two doubles, a triple, and a home run in six at-bats. He drove in six runs and scored three more, all in the first three innings of the game when the Phillies scored 11 of their 13 runs.

Wrightstone made his most famous successful fielding play by accident. Bill Hubbell was pitching for the wretched 1921 team, and Rogers Hornsby was the batter. He hit a line drive wickedly back up the middle. It struck Hubbell on the head and bounced nicely into Wrightstone's glove for a putout. No one has ever been sure if Russ ever saw the ball before it snuggled into his glove.

The following spring the Phillies moved their spring training site to Leesburg, Florida, an inland town that was infested by mosquitoes. The Phillies had trouble catching a mosquito bite, much less a baseball. Their infield—Wrightstone included somewhere in it—became known as "The Two O'Clock Infield" because it would take to the field after the regular workout and put on a dazzling fielding exhibition. It was said that they would then go to sleep for the rest of the day. Once the regular season started, the infield was in a state of perpetual slumber.

Wrightstone played all but 30 of his 909 big league games with the Phillies. He spent the latter part of his final season with the Giants and batted just .160 for the New Yorkers. He went into his final season with a .301 lifetime average and came out at .297.

Wrightstone, Russ

Phillies	G	AB	H	BA	RBI	R	2B	3B	HR	SA	SB
1920	76	206	54	.262	17	23	6	1	3	.345	3
1921	109	372	110	.296	51	59	13	4	9	.425	4
1922	99	331	101	.305	33	56	18	6	5	.441	4
1923	119	392	107	.273	57	59	21	7	7	.416	5
1924	118	388	119	.307	58	55	24	4	7	.443	5
1925	72	286	99	.346	61	48	18	5	14	.591	0
1926	112	368	113	.307	57	55	23	1	7	.432	5
1927	141	533	163	.306	75	62	24	5	6	.403	9
1928	33	91	19	.209	11	7	5	1	1	.319	0
Career	909	2,992	889	.297	425	427	152	34	60	.431	35

If ever a name sounded like it belonged to a ballplayer, Johnny Wyrostek's was it.

Johnny Wyrostek. Shut your eyes, and the name gives you a clear image of a big, strong, good-looking, slightly weathered fellow who could hit, run, throw, and field.

And that, of course, was an image of the real Johnny Wyrostek, a favorite of Phillies fans during his two stops in Philadelphia. Wyrostek was the Phillies' regular center fielder in 1946 and the starting right fielder in 1947, following brief visits with the Pittsburgh Pirates and St. Louis Cardinals.

Breaking into organized ball when he was 18 years old, Wyrostek never quite made the grade in two trials with the Bucs, who eventually traded him to the Cards for another minor leaguer, pitcher Elwin (Preacher) Roe. Johnny led the American Association in hitting in 1944 at Columbus with a .358 average. Although he was the property of the Cards, he never played for them, spending 1945 in the Army.

The Cardinals sold Wyrostek to the Phillies for $20,000 in 1946, and the lefthanded-hitting outfielder blossomed. He hit .281 and .273 and in 1946 led National League outfielders in putouts. In one doubleheader he had eight hits. In early 1948 the Phillies traded John to the Cincinnati Reds for shortstop Eddie Miller, one of the leading men in the league at his position.

The hustling Wyrostek was stunned by the trade. "It was the saddest day of my baseball life," he said. "I never felt so low."

Johnny had four good seasons with the Reds, including a career high .311 batting average in 1951. In early 1952, however, the Reds shipped him back to Philadelphia with pitcher Kent Peterson for pitcher Bubba Church. Wyrostek played in right field for the Phillies for the next two years.

The hustling Wyrostek was not colorful, but he was highly respected by his peers as a solid performer who gave his best effort day in and day out. "Johnny is one of those fellows who goes about his job without making a big show of it," said Phillies manager Steve O'Neill.

With age creeping up on him, Wyrostek shared his right field duties in 1954 with young Mel Clark. He also took an occasional turn at first base. Johnny's career ended in spring training in 1955 when the Phillies gave him his unconditional release.

Wyrostek, Johnny

Phillies: 1946–47, 1952–54
Outfielder
Birthplace: Fairmont City, Illinois
Nickname: Barney
B: July 12, 1919
D: December 12, 1986
Batted left, threw right
Ht. 6–2; **Wt.** 180

Wyrostek, Johnny

Phillies	G	AB	H	BA	RBI	R	2B	3B	HR	SA	SB
1946	145	545	153	.281	45	73	30	4	6	.383	7
1947	128	454	124	.273	51	68	24	7	5	.390	7
1952	98	321	88	.274	37	45	16	3	1	.352	1
1953	125	409	111	.271	47	42	14	2	6	.359	0
1954	92	259	62	.239	28	28	12	4	3	.351	0
Career	1,221	4,240	1,149	.271	481	525	209	45	58	.383	33

Johnny Wyrostek

All the Team's Men

The following lists indicate the more than 1,500 players who have performed for the Phillies between 1900 and 1992 and the 211 who played in at least one game between 1883 and 1899.

Figures in parentheses indicate years played with the Phillies. All statistics refer only to the players' careers with the Phillies and do not account for service with other major league teams.

A

Abbaticchio, Ed (1897–98) infielder: 24-for-102, .235, in 28 games.

Allen, Bob (1890–94) shortstop: 492-for 2,077, .237, in 567 games.

Allen, Hezekiah (1884) catcher: 2-for-3, .667, in one game.

Anderson, Dave (1889–90) pitcher: 1–2 with 7.45 ERA in eight games.

Andrews, Ed (1884–89) second baseman–outfielder: 602-for-2,309, .261, in 536 games.

B

Bastian, Charlie (1885–88, 91) second baseman–shortstop: 246-for-1,260, .195, in 349 games.

Beam, Ernie (1895) pitcher: 0–2 with 11.52 ERA in nine games.

Becker, Bob (1897–98) pitcher: 0–2 with 6.52 ERA in six games.

Benedict, Art (1883) second baseman: 4-for-15, .267, in three games.

Bernhard, Bill (1899–1900) pitcher: 21–16 with 3.97 ERA in 53 games.

Bowman, Sumner (1890) pitcher: 0–0 with 7.88 ERA in one game.

Boyle, Jack (1893–98) first baseman–catcher: 554-for-2,019, .274, in 474 games.

Breitenstein, Alonzo (1883) pitcher: 0–1 with 9.00 ERA in one game.

Brouthers, Dan (1896) first baseman: 75-for-218, .344, in 57 games.

Brown, Willard (1891) first baseman–catcher: 107-for-441, .243, in 115 games.

Buckley, Dick (1894–95) catcher: 75-for-272, .276, in 81 games.

Buffinton, Charlie (1887–89) pitcher–outfielder: 77–50 with 2.89 ERA in 133 games; 133-for-584, .228, in 159 games.

Burke, Eddie (1890) outfielder: 113-for-430, .263, in 100 games.

Burris, Al (1894) pitcher: 0–0 with 18.00 ERA in one game.

C

Callahan, Nixey (1894) pitcher: 1–2 with 10.06 ERA in nine games.

Carsey, Kid (1892–97) pitcher: 94–71 with 4.72 ERA in 192 games.

Casey, Dan (1886–89) pitcher: 72–59 with 2.98 ERA in 142 games. Led National League pitchers with 2.86 ERA in 1887.

Cassian, Ed (1891) pitcher: 1–3 with 2.84 ERA in six games.

Childs, Cupid (1888) second baseman: 0-for-4, .000, in two games.

Chiles, Pearce (1899–1900) infielder–outfielder: 132-for-449, .294, in 130 games; nicknamed "What's the Use."

Clements, Jack (1884–97) catcher: 1,074-for-3,717, .289, 70 home runs. One of the few lefthanded catchers in major league history.

Coleman, John (1890) pitcher: 0–1 with 27.00 ERA in one game.

Coleman, John F. (1883–84) pitcher–outfielder: 18–63 with 4.88 ERA in 86 games; 125-for-525, .238, in 133 games.

Pre-1900 Players

Dan Brouthers

More than 1500 players have worn the Phillies' uniform, including Barney Friberg, sliding home in a 1929 game at Baker Bowl.

375

Monte Cross

Conn, Bert (1898–1900) pitcher: 0–3 with 7.77 ERA in five games.

Connor, Roger (1892) first baseman: 166-for-564, .294, in 155 games.

Connors, Jerry (1892) outfielder: 0-for-3, .000, in one game.

Conway, Bill (1884) catcher: 0-for-4, .000, in one game.

Cook, Paul (1884) catcher: 1-for-12, .083, in three games.

Cooley, Duff (1896–99) outfielder: 582-for-1,888, .308, in 440 games.

Croft, Henry (1899) second baseman: 1-for-7, .143, in two games.

Cross, Lave (1892–97) catcher– infielder–outfielder: 815-for- 2,770, .294, in 674 games.

Cross, Monte (1898–1901) shortstop: 467-for-2,031, .230, in 573 games.

Crowley, John (1884) catcher: 41-for-168, .244, in 48 games.

Cusick, Tony (1884–87) outfielder: 59-for-298, .198, in 84 games.

D

Daily, Ed (1885–87) pitcher: 42–36 with 2.76 ERA in 83 games.

Day, Bill (1889–90) pitcher: 1–4 with 5.04 ERA in eight games.

Decker, Harry (1889–90) catcher– infielder–outfielder: 10-for-49, .204, in 16 games.

Delahanty, Ed (1888–89, 91–1901) infielder–outfielder: 2,213-for-6,359, .348, in 1,555 games. The only player to lead both the American and National Leagues in hitting.

Delahanty, Tom (1894) second baseman: 1-for-4, .250, in one game.

Denny, Jerry (1891) infielder: 21-for-73, .288, in 19 games.

Devlin, Jim (1887) pitcher: 0–2 with 6.00 ERA in two games.

Dolan, Joe (1899–1901) infielder: 111-for-516, .215, in 145 games.

Donahue, Frank (1898–1901) pitcher: 73–48 with 3.26 ERA in 137 games. Also known as Red.

Donohue, Joe (1891) shortstop– outfielder: 7-for-22, .318, in six games.

Douglas, Klondike (1898–1904) catcher–infielder–outfielder: 518-for-1,985, .261, in 541 games.

Dowd, Tommy (1897) outfielder: 114-for-391, .292, in 91 games.

Dowse, Tom (1892) catcher–out-fielder: 10-for-54, .185, in 16 games.

Doyle, Conny (1883) outfielder: 15-for-68, .221, in 16 games.

Duggleby, Bill (1898, 1901–07) pitcher: 89–100 with 3.18 ERA in 229 games.

Dunkle, Davey (1897–98) pitcher: 6–6 with 5.33 ERA in 19 games.

Dupaugher, Mike (1884) catcher: 2-for-10, .200, in four games.

E

Elberfeld, Kid (1898) third baseman: 9-for-38, .237, in 14 games; nicknamed "The Tabasco Kid."

Ellis, Ben (1896) infielder: 1-for-16, .063, in four games.

Esper, Duke (1890–92) pitcher: 36–21 with 3.47 ERA in 65 games.

F

Fanning, Jack (1894) pitcher: 1–3 with 8.16 ERA in five games.

Farrar, Sid (1883–89) first baseman: 782-for-3,092, .253, in 816 games.

Farrell, Jack (1886) second baseman: 11-for-60, .183, in 17 games.

Ferguson, Bob (1883) second baseman–pitcher: 85-for-329, .258, in 86 games; 0–0 with 9.00 ERA in one game. Began season as manager; nicknamed "Death to Flying Things."

Ferguson, Charlie (1884–87) pitcher–infielder–outfielder: 99–64 with 2.67 ERA in 183 games; 277-for-963, .288, in 257 games.

Fields, Jocko (1891) shortstop: 7-for-30, .233, in eight games.

Fifield, Jack (1897–99) pitcher: 19–35 with 4.59 ERA in 62 games.

Figgemeier, Frank (1894) pitcher: 0–1 with 11.25 ERA in one game.

Fisher, Newt (1898) catcher–in-fielder: 3-for-26, .115, in nine games.

Flick, Elmer (1898–1901) outfielder: 683-for-2,023, .338, in 537 games.

Fogarty, Jim (1884–89) infielder– outfielder–pitcher: 626-for-2,533, .247, in 660 games; 0–1 with 4.50 ERA in seven games.

Fraser, Chick (1899–1900, 1902–04) pitcher: 75–77 with 3.53 ERA in 164 games.

Fultz, Dave (1898–99) infielder– out-fielder: 12-for-60, .200, in 21 games.

G

Gallagher, Bill (1883) outfielder: 0-for-8, .000, in two games.

1887–1890 Goodwin Old Judge
cigarettes, Ed Andrews

1895 Mayo Cut Plug,
George Haddock

1887–1890 Goodwin Old Judge
cigarettes, Dan Casey

1887–1890 Goodwin Old Judge
cigarettes, Sid Farrar

1895 Mayo Cut Plug,
Billy Hamilton

1910 T206, George McQuillen

1910 T206, Harry Coveleski

1911 T205, Dode Paskert   1911 T205, John Bates

1911 T205, Bob Ewing

1900 Phillies program

1895 Mayo Cut Plug, Ed Delahanty

T201 Mecca, John Titus

T202 Hassan, Red Dooin and Mickey Doolan

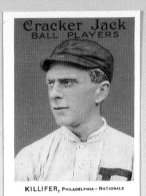

1915 Crackerjack, Gavvy Cravath

1915 Crackerjack,
Grover Cleveland Alexander

1915 Crackerjack, Bill Killifer

1915 World Series program

1911 Turkey Red, Sherry Magee

1911 Turkey Red, Kitty Bransfield

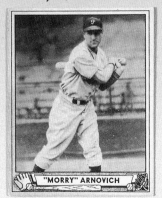

1939 Playball, Morrie Arnovich

1936 BB, Dolph Camilli

Jimmy Ring
PITCHER, PHILADELPHIA, N.L.

1922 Exhibit, Jimmy Ring

1933 Goudey, Phil Collins

1939 Playball, Chuck Klein

1933 Goudey, Spud Davis

1933 Goudey, Dick Bartell

1941 Playball, Joe Marty

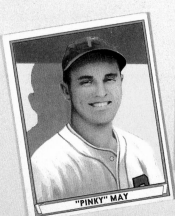

1941 Playball, Pinky May

1934–36 Diamon Stars, Joe Marty

uniform patch

1941 Phillies team photo

PHILADELPHIA PHILLIES 1941

1944 Blue Jays patch

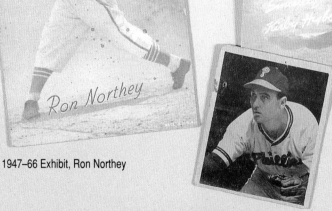

1947–66 Exhibit, Ron Northey

1939–46 Exhibit, Kirby Higbe

1948 Bowman, Dutch Leonard

1950 Bowman, Dick Sisler

1951 Berk Ross, Granny Hamner

1949 Bowman, Ken Heintzelman

1950 Phillies team photo

19 Fightin' Phillies 50

Back Row JOCKO THOMPSON, EDDIE WAITKUS, MIKE GOLIAT, KEN JOHNSON, RICHIE ASHBURN, ED WRIGHT, BLIX DONNELLY, DICK WHITMAN, BUBBA CHURCH, RUSS MEYER, BILL NICHOLSON
Second Row FRANK WEICHEC, Trainer; STAN HOLLMIG, KEN TRINKLE, STAN LOPATA, ROBIN ROBERTS, JIM KONSTANTY, CURT SIMMONS, KEN SILVESTRI, BOB MILLER, HANK BOROWY,
MILO CANDINI, FRANK POWELL, Traveling Secretary.
Seated MAJE McDONNELL, GRAN HAMNER, PUDDIN' HEAD JONES, DEL ENNIS, DUSTY COOKE, Coach; EDDIE SAWYER, Manager; BENNIE BENGOUGH, Coach; CY PERKINS, Coach; DICK SISLER,
RALPH CABALLERO, KEN HEINTZELMAN.
(Reading from left to right)   Bat Boys STEVE IWASKO, FRANK CAMPANARO, KENNY BUSH

1947 Homogenized Bond, Del Ennis

1954 Bowman, Curt Simmons

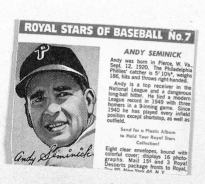

ROYAL STARS OF BASEBALL No.7

ANDY SEMINICK

Andy was born in Pierce, W. Va.,
Sept. 12, 1920. The Philadelphia
Phillies' catcher is 5' 10½", weighs
186, hits and throws right-handed.
    Andy is a top receiver in the
National League and a dangerous
long-ball hitter. He tied a modern
League record in 1949 with three
homers in a 9-inning game. Since
1940 he has played every infield
position except shortstop, as well as
outfield.

Send for a Plastic Album
to Hold Your Royal Stars
Collection!

Eight clear envelopes, bound with
colorful cover; displays 16 photo-
graphs. Mail 15¢ and 3 Royal
Desserts package fronts to Royal,
Box 90, New York 46, N. Y.

1952 Royal Pudding, Andy Seminick

1950 World Series program

1950 Phillies pin

1951 Bowman, Robin Roberts

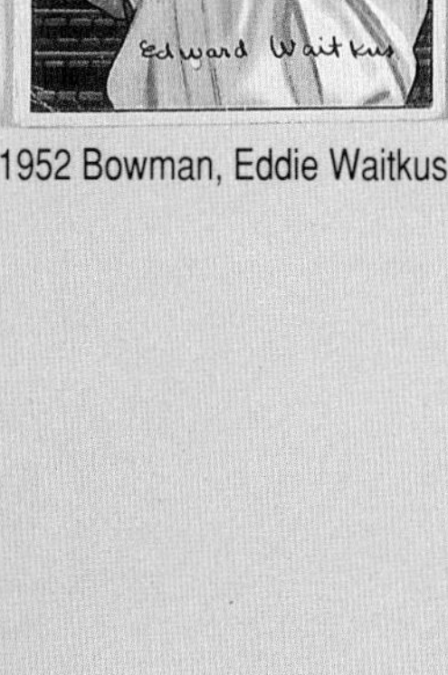

1952 Bowman, Eddie Waitkus

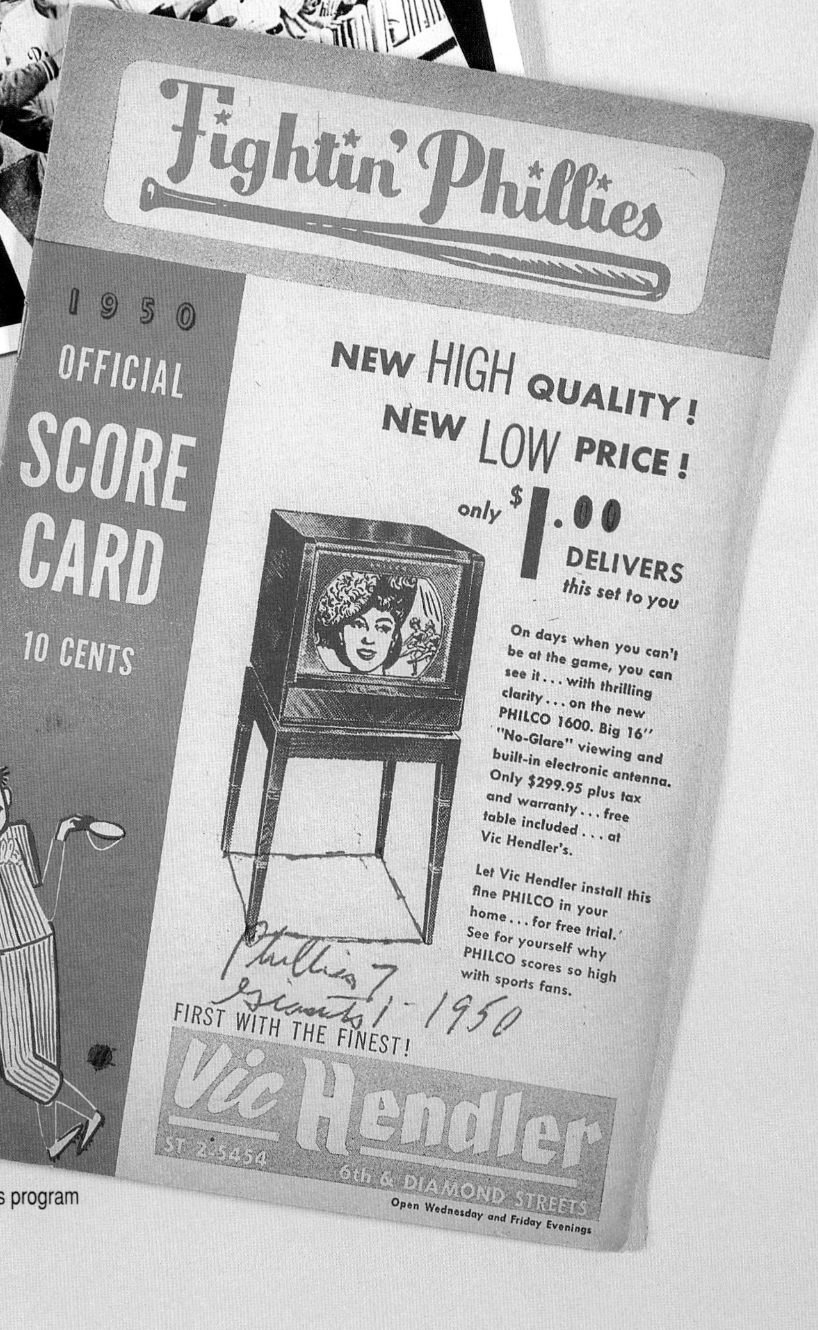

1950 Phillies program

Phillies uniforms, caps,
and pennants courtesy of
Mitchell & Ness Nostalgia Company,
Philadelphia

1953 Phillies yearbook

1953 Topps,
Smoky Burgess

1953 Bowman,
Richie Ashburn

1949 Sealtest, Russ Meyer

1953 Bowman, Jim Konstanty

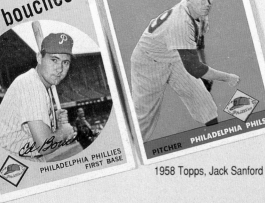

1959 Topps, Ed Bouchee

1958 Topps, Jack Sanford

1966 Topps, Gene Mauch

1962 Topps, Art Mahaffey

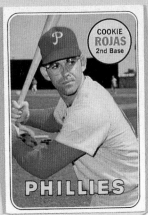

1969 Topps, Cookie Rojas

1964 Topps giants, Jim Bunning

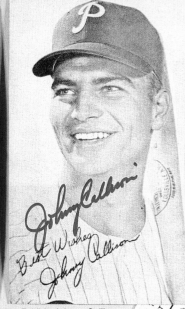

1960s Exhibit, Johnny Callison

1960s Phillies logo

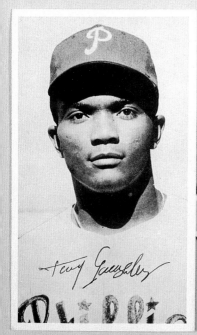

1968 Phillies photocard, Tony Gonzalez

1964 World Series tickets

1964 Phillies button, Dick Allen

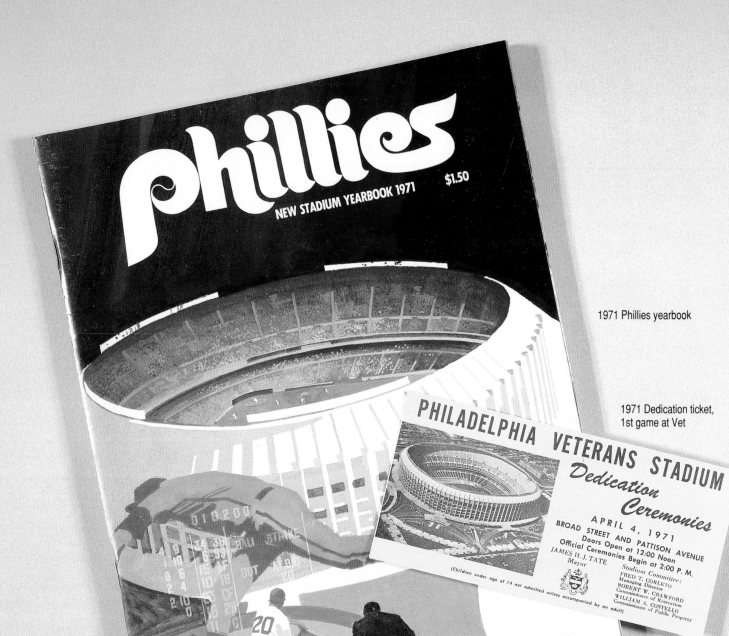

1971 Phillies yearbook

1971 Dedication ticket,
1st game at Vet

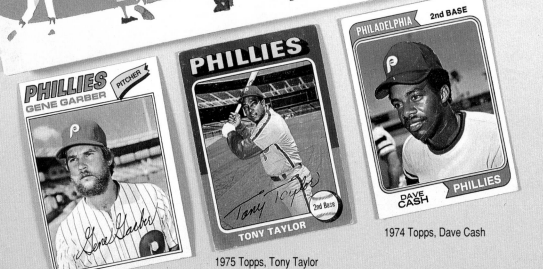

1977 Topps, Gene Garber

1975 Topps, Tony Taylor

1974 Topps, Dave Cash

1976 Tops, Bob Boone

1981 Drake, Pete Rose

1983 Topps, Mike Schmidt

1981 Topps Photo Card,
Steve Carlton

1978 Topps, Larry Bowa

1982 Topps sticker, Garry Maddox

1976 National League
Centennial patch

1980s Phillies patch

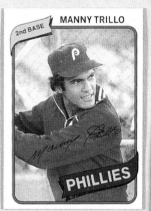

1980 Topps, Manny Trillo

1979 Topps, Larry Christenson

1971 Topps, Denny Doyle

1980 World Series program

1980 World Series tickets

1983 100th Anniversary patch

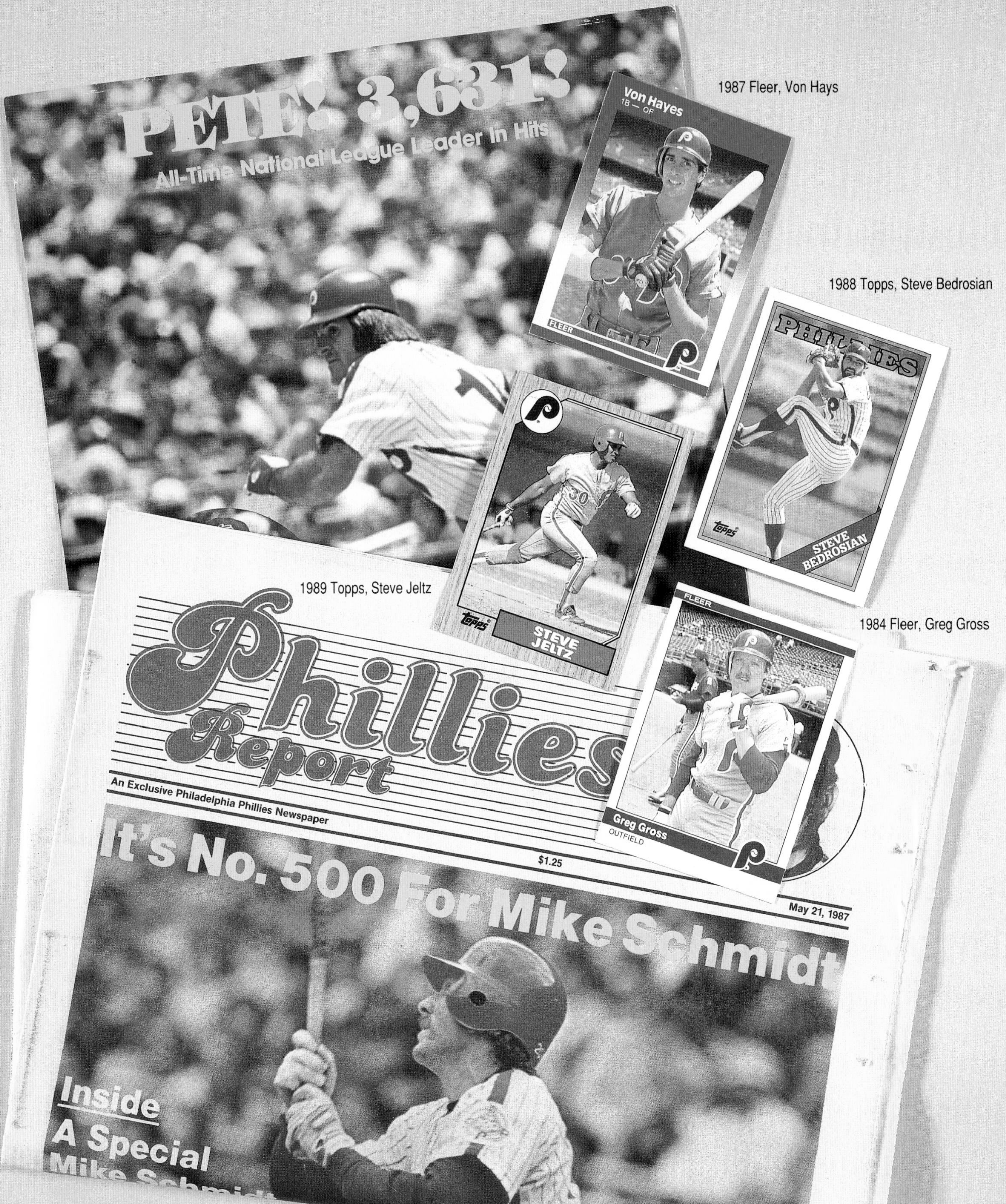

PETE! 3,631!
All-Time National League Leader In Hits

1987 Fleer, Von Hays

1988 Topps, Steve Bedrosian

1989 Topps, Steve Jeltz

1984 Fleer, Greg Gross

Phillies Report
An Exclusive Philadelphia Phillies Newspaper

$1.25

It's No. 500 For Mike Schmidt

Inside
A Special
Mike Schmidt

May 21, 1987

1987 *Phillies Report*

Gallagher, Bill (1896) shortstop: 15-for-49, .306, in 14 games.

Ganzel, Charlie (1885–86) catcher: 21-for-128, .164, in 35 games.

Gardner, Gid (1888) second baseman: 2-for-3, .667, in one game.

Garvin, Ned (1896) pitcher: 0–1 with 7.62 ERA in two games.

Geier, Phil (1896–97) infielder–outfielder: 101-for 372, .271, in 109 games.

Gillen, Sam (1897) shortstop: 70-for-270, .259, in 75 games.

Gladman, Buck (1883) third baseman: 0-for-4, .000, in one game.

Gleason, Kid (1888–91) pitcher–infielder–outfielder: 79–69 with 3.39 ERA in 166 games; 142-for-620, .229, in 182 games.

Goeckel, Bill (1899) first baseman: 37-for-141, .262, in 37 games.

Gormley, Ed (1891) pitcher: 0–1 with 5.63 ERA in one game.

Grady, Mike (1894–97) catcher– infielder: 188-for-568, .330, in 181 games.

Graulich, Lew (1891) catcher–first baseman: 8-for-26, .308, in seven games.

Grey, Bill (1890–91) catcher– infielder–outfielder: 49-for-203, .241, in 57 games.

Grim, John (1888) second baseman–outfielder: 1-for-7, .143, in two games.

Gross, Emil (1883) catcher: 71-for-231, .307, in 57 games.

Gumbert, Ad (1896) pitcher: 5–3 with 4.56 ERA in 11 games.

Gunning, Tom (1887) catcher: 27-for-104, .260, in 28 games.

H

Haddock, George (1894) pitcher: 4–3 with 5.79 ERA in 10 games.

Hagan, Art (1883) pitcher: 1–14 record with 5.45 ERA in 17 games.

Hallman, Billy (1888–89, 92–97, 1901–03) second baseman: 1,179-for-4,243, .278, in 1,065 games (also pitched in one game, 0–0, with 18.00 ERA).

Hamilton, Billy (1890–95) outfielder: 1,079-for-3,020, .357, with 508 stolen bases, in 729 games.

Harbridge, Bill (1883) infielder–outfielder–catcher: 62-for-280, .221, in 73 games.

Hardie, Lew (1884) catcher: 3-for-8, .375, in three games.

Harper, George (1894) pitcher: 6–5 with 5.34 ERA in 12 games.

Henderson, Hardie (1883) pitcher: 0–0 with 19.00 ERA in one game.

Hiland, John (1885) second baseman: 0-for-9, .000, in three games.

Hilsey, Charlie (1883) pitcher: 0–3 with 5.54 ERA in three games.

Hodson, George (1895) pitcher: 1–2 with 9.53 ERA in four games.

Hoover, Buster (1884) infielder–outfielder: 8-for-42, .190, in 10 games.

Hulen, Bill (1896) shortstop: 90-for-339, .265, in 88 games.

I

Inks, Bert (1896) pitcher: 0–1 with 8.10 ERA in three games.

Irwin, Art (1886–89, 94), shortstop: 296-for-1,268, .233, in 345 games.

J

Johnson, John (1894) pitcher: 1–1 with 6.27 ERA in four games.

Johnson, Tom (1897) pitcher: 1–2 with 4.66 ERA in five games.

Jones, Alex (1894) pitcher: 1–0 with 2.00 ERA in one game.

Jordan, Charlie (1896) pitcher: 0–0 with 9.00 ERA in two games.

K

Kappel, Joe (1884) catcher: 1-for-15, .067, in four games.

Keefe, Tim (1891–93) pitcher: 32–29 with 3.21 ERA in 72 games.

Keener, Harry (1896) pitcher: 3–11 with 5.89 ERA in 16 games.

Kelly, Charlie (1883) third baseman: 1-for-7, .143, in two games.

Kelly, Kick (1883) catcher: 0-for-3, .000, in one game.

Kilroy, Mike (1891) pitcher: 0–2 with 9.90 ERA in three games.

Kling, Bill (1891) pitcher: 4–2 with 4.32 ERA in 12 games.

Knell, Phil (1892) pitcher: 5–5 with 4.05 ERA in 11 games.

Knight, Joe (1884) pitcher: 2–4 with 5.47 ERA in six games.

L

Lajoie, Napoleon (1896–1900) infielder: 721-for-2,055, .351, in 492 games; nicknamed Larry.

Lampe, Henry (1895) pitcher: 0–2 with 7.57 ERA in seven games.

Lauder, Bill (1898–99) third baseman: 251-for-944, .266, in 248 games.

Leahy, Dan (1896) shortstop: 2-for-6, .333, in two games.

Lewis, Fred (1883) outfielder: 40-for-160, .250, in 38 games.

Lipp, Tom (1897) pitcher: 0–1 with 15.00 ERA in one game.

Lucid, Con (1895–96) pitcher: 7–7 with 6.83 ERA in 15 games.

Lukens, Al (1894) pitcher: 0–1 with 10.20 ERA in three games.

Lynch, Tom (1884–85) outfielder–catcher: 25-for-101, .248, in 26 games.

Lyons, Harry (1887) second baseman: 0-for-4, .000, in one game.

M

Madison, Art (1895) infielder: 12-for-34, .353, in 11 games.

Magee, Bill (1899–1902) pitcher: 5–9 with 4.74 ERA in 17 games.

Manning, Jack (1883–85) outfielder: 341-for-1,289, .265, in 309 games.

Maul, Al (1887, 1900) pitcher: 6–5 with 5.83 ERA in 12 games.

Mayer, Ed (1890–91) third baseman–shortstop–second baseman–outfielder: 167-for-752, .222, in 185 games.

McCarthy, Tommy (1886–87) outfielder–pitcher: 18-for-97, .186, in 26 games; 0–0 with 0.00 ERA in one game.

McCauley, Al (1890) first baseman: 102-for-418, .244, in 112 games.

McClellan, Bill (1883–84) shortstop: 191-for-776, .246, in 191 games.

McElroy, Jim (1884) pitcher: 1–12 with 4.84 ERA in 13 games.

McFarland, Ed (1897–1901) catcher: 447-for-1,522, .294, in 423 games.

McFetridge, John (1890, 1903) pitcher: 2–11 with 4.60 ERA in 15 games.

McGill, Willie (1895–96) pitcher: 15–12 with 5.46 ERA in 32 games.

McGinnis, Gus (1893) pitcher: 1–3 with 4.38 ERA in five games.

McGuire, Deacon (1886–88) catcher: 96-for-368, .261, in 103 games.

McLaughlin, Barney (1887) second baseman: 45-for-205, .220, in 50 games.

Mertes, Sandow (1896) outfielder: 34-for-143, .238, in 37 games.

Miller, Cyclone (1884) pitcher: 0–1 with 10.00 ERA in one game.

Miller, Kohly (1897) second baseman: 2-for-11, .182, in three games. Also known as Frank.

Morelock, Harry (1891–92) infielder: 1-for-17, .059, in five games.

Morton, Sparrow (1884) pitcher: 0–2 with 5.29 ERA in two games.

Motz, Frank (1890) first baseman: 0-for-2, .000, in one game.

Mulvey, Joe (1883–89, 1892) third baseman: 725-for-2,700, .269, in 682 games.

Murphy, Con (1884) pitcher: 0–3 with 6.58 ERA in three games.

Murphy, Ed (1898) pitcher: 1–3 with 5.10 ERA in seven games.

Murphy, Morgan (1898, 1900) catcher: 27-for-122, .221, in 36 games.

Murray, Tom (1894) shortstop: 0-for-2, .000, in one game.

Myers, Al (1885, 89–91) second baseman: 408-for-1,663, .245, in 420 games.

N

Nash, Billy (1896–98) third baseman: 160-for-634, .252, in 189 games.

Neagle, Jack (1883) pitcher–outfielder: 12-for-73, .164, in 18 games; 1–7 with 6.93 ERA in eight games.

Nolan, Edward (1885) pitcher: 1–5 with 4.17 ERA in seven games; nicknamed "The Only."

Nops, Jerry (1896) pitcher: 1–0 with 5.14 ERA in one game.

O

O'Connor, Frank (1893) pitcher: 0–0 with 11.25 ERA in three games.

Orth, Al (1895–1901) pitcher: 110–81 with 3.49 ERA in 193 games; nicknamed "The Curveless Wonder."

Owens, Red (1899) second baseman: 1-for-21, .048, in eight games.

P

Piatt, Wiley (1898–1900) pitcher: 56–39 with 3.59 ERA in 100 games.

Pierre, Dick (1883) shortstop: 3-for-19, .158, in five games.

Plock, Walt (1891) outfielder: 2-for-5, .400, in two games.

Purcell, Blondie (1883–84) outfielder–pitcher: 222-for-853, .260, in 200 games; 2–6 with 4.28 ERA in 12 games.

Pyle, Shadow (1884) pitcher: 0–1 with 4.00 ERA in one game.

R

Reilly, Charlie (1892–95) infielder: 255-for-1,061, .241, in 283 games.

Remsen, Jack (1884) outfielder: 9-for-43, .209, in 12 games.

Ringo, Frank (1883–84) catcher– infielder–outfielder: 54-for-312, .173, in 86 games.

S

Sanders, Ben (1888–89) pitcher– outfielder: 38–28 with 2.82 ERA in 75 games; 105-for-405, .259, in 101 games.

Saylor, Lefty (1891) pitcher: 0–0 with 6.00 ERA in one game.

Scheible, John (1894) pitcher: 0–1 with 189.00 ERA in one game.

Schriver, Pop (1888–1890) catcher– infielder: 143-for-568, .251, in 152 games.

Schultze, John (1891) pitcher: 0–1 with 6.60 ERA in six games.

Sharrott, John (1893) pitcher: 4–2 with 4.50 ERA in 12 games.

Shindle, Bill (1891) third baseman: 87-for-415, .210, in 103 games.

Shugart, Frank (1897) shortstop: 41-for-163, .252, in 40 games.

Sixsmith, Ed (1884) catcher: 0-for-2, .000, in one game.

Smith, Edgar (1883) pitcher: 0–1 with 15.43 ERA in one game.

Smith, Phenomenal (1890–91) pitcher: 9–13 with 4.28 ERA in 27 games; real name was John Francis Gammon.

Smith, Tom (1895) pitcher: 2–3 with 6.88 ERA in 11 games.

Sparks, Tully (1897, 1903–10) pitcher: 94–97, with 2.56 ERA in 224 games.

Stallings, George (1897–98) first baseman–outfielder: 2-for-9, .222, in three games; nicknamed "The Miracle Man."

Stephenson, Dummy (1892) outfielder: 10-for-37, .270, in eight games.

Strike, John (1886) pitcher: 1–1 with 4.80 ERA in two games.

Sullivan, Joe (1894–96) shortstop: 281-for-868, .324, in 217 games.

Sunday, Billy (1890) outfielder– pitcher: 31-for-119, .261, in 31 games; 0–0 with ∞ ERA in one game.

T

Taylor, Jack (1892–97) pitcher: 96–77 with 4.34 ERA in 195 games.

Thomas, Roy (1899–1908, 1910–11) outfielder: 1,364-for-4,629, .295, in 1,286 games; also pitched one game with 0–0 record and 3.00 ERA.

Thompson, Sam (1889–98) outfielder: 1,469-for-4,413, .333, in 1,031 games.

Thornton, John (1891–92) pitcher: 15–18 with 3.74 ERA in 40 games.

Titcomb, Cannonball (1886) pitcher: 0–5 with 3.73 ERA in five games.

Turner, Tuck (1893–96) outfielder– pitcher: 279-for-736, .379, in 188 games; 0–0 with 7.50 ERA in one game.

Tyng, Jim (1888) pitcher: 0–0 with 4.50 ERA in one game.

V

Vadeboncoeur, Gene (1884) catcher: 3-for-14, .214, in four games.

Vickery, Tom (1890, 1893) pitcher: 28–27 with 3.78 ERA in 59 games.

Vinton, Bill (1884–85) pitcher: 13–16 with 2.42 ERA in 30 games.

W

Wagenhorst, Woodie (1888) third baseman: 1-for-8, .125, in two games.

Waitt, Charlie (1883) outfielder: 1-for-3, .333, in one game.

Ward, Piggy (1883, 89) infielder: 4-for-30, .133, in eight games.

Warner, Fred (1883) third baseman– outfielder: 32-for-141, .227, in 39 games.

Weyhing, Gus (1892–95) pitcher: 71–53 with 4.14 ERA in 141 games.

Wheeler, George (1896–99) pitcher: 21–20 with 4.24 ERA in 50 games.

White, C. B. (1883) infielder: 0-for-1, .000, in one game.

White, Deke (1895) pitcher: 1–0 with 10.06 ERA in three games.

Whitrock, Bill (1896) pitcher: 0–1 with 3.00 ERA in two games.

Wood, George (1886–89) outfielder– pitcher: 470-for-1,796, .262, in 422 games; 0–0 with 9.00 ERA in three games.

Wood, Pete (1889) pitcher: 1–1 with 5.21 ERA in three games.

Y

Yingling, Joe (1894) shortstop: 1-for-4, .250, in one game.

Post-1900 Players

Buster Adams

A

Abbott, Fred (05) catcher–first baseman: 25-for-128, .195, in 42 games.

Abbott, Kyle (92–) pitcher: current Phillies player.

Ackerfelds, Darrel (90–91) pitcher: 7–3 with 4.31 ERA in 101 games; three saves.

Acosta, Cy (75) pitcher: 0–0 with 6.00 ERA in six games, all relief.

Adams, Bert (15–19) catcher–first baseman: 122-for-606, .201, in 240 games.

Adams, Bob (31–32) pitcher: 0–1 with 5.25 ERA in five games.

Adams, Buster (43–45, 47) outfielder: 330-for-1,240, .266, in 345 games.

Adduci, Jim (89) first baseman: 7-for-19, .368, in 13 games.

Aguayo, Luis (80–88) second baseman–shortstop–third baseman: 208-for-867, .240, in 471 games.

Albright, Jack (47) shortstop: 23-for-99, .232, in 41 games.

Alexander, Grover Cleveland (11–17, 30) pitcher: 190–91 with 2.31 ERA in 338 games; 15 saves. Elected to Hall of Fame in 1938. His overall major league record in 20 seasons was 373–208.

Allen, Bob (37) pitcher: 0–1 with 6.75 ERA in three games.

Allen, Dick (63–69, 75–76) first baseman–second baseman–shortstop–third baseman–outfielder: 1,144-for-3,935, .291, in 1,070 games; 204 home runs.

Allen, Ethan (34–36) outfielder: 427-for-1,351, .316, in 331 games.

Almon, Bill (88) first baseman–shortstop–third baseman: 3-for-26, .115, in 20 games.

Altamirano, Porfirio (82–83) pitcher: 7–4 with 3.93 ERA in 60 games; two saves.

Amaro, Ruben Sr. (60–65) first baseman–second baseman–shortstop–third baseman–outfielder: 379-for-1,571, .241, in 668 games.

Amaro, Ruben Jr. (92–) outfielder–pinch hitter: current Phillies player.

Ames, Red (19) pitcher: 0–2 with 6.19 ERA in three games; one save.

Andersen, Larry (83–86) pitcher: 7–10 with 3.20 ERA in 148 games; seven saves.

Anderson, George (59) second baseman: 104-for-477, .218, in 152 games. Also known as Sparky.

Anderson, Harry (57–60) first baseman–outfielder: 407-for-1,516, .268, in 438 games.

Anderson, John (58) pitcher: 0–0 with 7.88 ERA in five games.

Anderson, Mike (71–75, 79) pinch-hitter–first baseman–outfielder: 272-for-1,105, .246, in 488 games (included is one game as pitcher in 1979: 0–0, ERA 0.00).

Andrews, Fred (76–77) second baseman: 8-for-29, .276, in 16 games.

Andrews, Stan (45) catcher: 11-for-33, .333, in 13 games.

Andrus, Bill (37) third baseman: 0-for-2, .000, in three games.

Antolik, Joe (44) catcher: 2-for-6, .333, in four games.

Antonelli, John (45) first baseman–second baseman–shortstop–third baseman: 129-for-504, .256, in 125 games.

Arlett, Buzz (31) first baseman–outfielder: 131-for-418, .313, in 121 games.

Arnovich, Morrie (36–40) outfielder: 459-for-1,592, .288, in 442 games.

Ashburn, Richie (48–59) outfielder: 2,217-for-7,122, .311, in 1,794 games.

Ashby, Andy (91–92) pitcher: 2–8 with 6.67 ERA in 18 games.

Attreau, Dick (26–27) first baseman: 31-for-144, .215, in 61 games.

Atwood, Bill (36–40) catcher: 220-for-961, .229, in 342 games.

Averill, Earl (63) pinch-hitter–catcher–first baseman–third baseman–outfielder: 19-for-71, .268, in 47 games.

Aviles, Ramon (79–81) second baseman–shortstop–third baseman: 51-for-190, .268, in 116 games.

Ayrault, Bob (92–) pitcher: current Phillies player.

B

Backman, Wally (91–92) second baseman–third baseman–pinch-hitter: 58-for-233, .249, in 136 games.

Baecht, Ed (26–28) pitcher: 3–2 with 6.49 ERA in 38 games.

Bahnsen, Stan (82) pitcher: 0–0 with 1.35 ERA in eight games.

Bair, Doug (87) pitcher: 2–0 with 5.93 ERA in 11 games.

Baird, Doug (19) third baseman: 61-for-242, .252, in 66 games.

Baker, Floyd (54–55) second baseman–third baseman: 5-for-30, .167, in 28 games.

Baldschun, Jack (61–65) pitcher: 39–34 with 3.18 ERA in 333 games, all relief; 59 saves.

Baldwin, Henry (27) shortstop–third baseman: 5-for-16, .313, in six games.

Baller, Jay (82; 92) pitcher: 0–0 with 6.16 ERA in 12 games.

Bancroft, Dave (15–20) shortstop–second baseman–outfielder: 634-for-2,523, .251, in 681 games. Elected to Hall of Fame 1971.

Bannister, Alan (74–75) outfielder–shortstop–second baseman: 19-for-86, .221, in 50 games.

Barojas, Salome (88) pitcher: 0–0 with 8.31 ERA in six games.

Barrett, Dick (43–45) pitcher: 20–47 with 3.96 ERA in 96 games; two saves.

Barrett, Tommy (88–89) second baseman: 17-for-81, .210, in 50 games.

Barry, John (01–04) first baseman–second baseman–shortstop–third baseman–outfielder: 395-for-1,467, .269, in 378 games. Also known as Shad.

Barry, Rich (69) pinch-hitter–outfielder: 6-for-32, .188, in 20 games.

Barry, Thomas (04) pitcher: 0–1 with 40.50 ERA—one game started and pitched ⅔ inning.

Bartell, Dick (31–34) shortstop–second baseman (3 games): 695-for-2,359, .295, in 587 games.

Bashore, Walt (36) third baseman–outfielder: 2-for-10, .200, in 10 games.

Bateman, John (72) catcher: 56-for-252, .222, in 82 games.

Bates, Del (70) catcher: 8-for-60, .133, in 22 games.

Bates, Bud (39) outfielder: 15-for-58, .259, in 15 games. Also known as Hubert.

Bates, Johnny (09–10) outfielder: 224-for-766, .292, in 211 games.

Batiste, Kim (91–) shortstop: current Phillies player.

Baumgartner, Stan (14–16, 21–22) pitcher: 6–12 with 4.48 ERA in 60 games. Later covered the Phillies for the *Philadelphia Inquirer*.

Baumholtz, Frankie (56–57) outfielder–pinch-hitter: 27-for-102, .265, in 78 games. Record as pinch-hitter 14-for-54.

Beck, Boom-Boom (39–43) pitcher: 12–33 with 4.73 ERA in 127 games; three saves.

Beck, Fred (11) outfielder: 59-for-210, .281, in 66 games.

Becker, Beals (13–15) outfielder–first baseman (one game): 349-for-1,158, .301, in 338 games.

Bedell, Howie (68) pinch-hitter: 1-for-7, .143, in nine games. His lone Phillies RBI broke Don Drysdale's then-record shutout streak at 58⅔ innings.

Bedrosian, Steve (86–89) pitcher: 21–18 with 3.04 ERA in 218 games; 103 saves. Also known as Bedrock.

Beebe, Fred (11) pitcher: 3–3 with 4.47 ERA in nine games.

Behan, Petie (21–23) pitcher: 7–15 with 4.76 ERA in 40 games; two saves.

Bell, Juan (92–) shortstop: current Phillies player.

Belinsky, Bo (65–66) pitcher: 4–11 with 4.61 ERA in 39 games; one save.

Bender, Chief (16–17) pitcher: 15–9 with 2.75 ERA in 47 games; five saves. Also played one game as third baseman. Elected to Hall of Fame in 1953.

Benge, Ray (28–32, 36) pitcher: 58–82 with 4.69 ERA in 210 games: 15 saves.

Benjamin, Stan (39–42) first baseman–second baseman–third baseman–outfielder: 169-for-749, .226, in 228 games.

Bennett, Dave (64) pitcher: 0–0 with 9.00 ERA in one game.

Bennett, Dennis (62–64) pitcher: 30–28 with 3.48 ERA in 95 games; five saves.

Bennett, Joe (23) third baseman: no batting record, one game.

Bentley, Jack (26) first baseman–pitcher: 62-for-240, .258, in 75 games; 0–2 with 8.28 ERA in seven games.

Benton, Stan (22) second baseman: 4-for-19, .211, in six games.

Berger, Wally (40) outfielder–first baseman: 13-for-41, .317, in 20 games.

Berly, Jack (32–33) pitcher: 3–5

Bo Belinsky

Bill Bernhard

Huck Betts

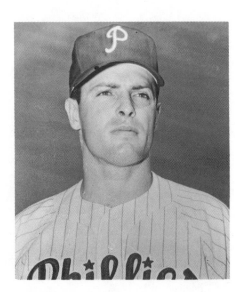

Bob Bowman

with 6.28 ERA in 34 games; two saves.

Bernhard, Bill (00) pitcher: 15–10 with 4.77 ERA in 32 games; two saves.

Berry, Joe (02) catcher: 1-for-4, .250, in one game. Also known as Hodge.

Bertrand, Lefty (36) pitcher: 0–0 with 9.00 ERA in one game.

Betts, Huck (20–25) pitcher: 18–27 with 4.40 ERA in 157 games; eight saves.

Bicknell, Charlie (48–49) pitcher: 0–1 with 6.83 ERA in 30 games.

Bird, Doug (79) pitcher: 2–0 with 5.16 ERA in 32 games.

Bishop, Jim (23–24) pitcher: 0–4 with 6.39 ERA in 22 games; one save.

Bittiger, Jeff (86) pitcher: 1–1 with 5.52 ERA in three games.

Bivin, Jim (35) pitcher: 2–9 with 5.79 ERA in 47 games; one save.

Blackburne, Lena (19) third baseman–first baseman (one game)–second baseman (one game)–shortstop (one game): 58-for-291, .199, in 72 games.

Blackwell, Tim (76–77) catcher: 2-for-8, .250, in five games.

Blake, Sheriff (31) pitcher: 4–5 with 5.58 ERA in 14 games; one save.

Blanton, Cy (40–42) pitcher: 10–20 with 4.55 ERA in 47 games.

Blatnik, Johnny (48–50) outfielder: 110-for-427, .258, in 131 games.

Blattner, Buddy (49) second baseman–shortstop–third baseman–pinch-hitter: 24-for-97, .247, in 64 games.

Blaylock, Marv (55–57) first baseman–outfielder–pinch-hitter: 175-for-745, .235, in 286 games.

Bloodworth, Jimmy (50–51) first baseman–second baseman–third baseman–pinch-hitter: 28-for-138, .203, in 75 games.

Boever, Joe (90–91) pitcher: 5–8 with 3.17 ERA in 102 games; six saves.

Boitano, Dan (78) pitcher: 0–0 with 0.00 ERA in one game.

Boland, Ed (34–35) outfielder–pinch-hitter: 19-for-77, .247, in 38 games.

Bolen, Stew (31–32) pitcher: 3–12 with 5.88 ERA in 33 games.

Bolger, Jim (59) pinch-hitter–outfielder: 4-for-48, .083, in 35 games.

Bolling, John (39) first baseman: 61-for-211, .289, in 69 games.

Booker, Rod (90–91) second baseman–shortstop–third baseman: 41-for-184, .223, in 101 games.

Boone, Bob (72–81) catcher–first baseman–third baseman–outfielder: 957-for-3,690, .259, in 1,125 games.

Boozer, John (62–64, 66–69) pitcher: 14–16 with 4.09 ERA in 171 games; 15 saves.

Borowy, Hank (49–50) pitcher: 12–12 with 4.24 ERA in 31 games.

Bosetti, Rick (76) outfielder–pinch-runner: 5-for-18, .278, in 13 games.

Bouchee, Ed (56–60) first baseman: 419-for-1,494, .280, in 410 games.

Bowa, Larry (70–81) shortstop–second baseman (one game): 1,798-for-6,815, .264, in 1,739 games.

Bowman, Bob (55–59) outfielder–pinch-hitter: 129-for-519, .249, in 256 games (included is five games as pitcher in 1959: 0–1 with 6.00 ERA).

Bowman, Joe (35–36) pitcher: 16–30 with 4.70 ERA in 73 games; two saves.

Boyle, Jack (12) third baseman–shortstop: 7-for-25, .280, in 15 games.

Brack, Gib (38–39) outfielder–first baseman–pinch-hitter: 159-for-552, .288, in 163 games. Also known as Gil.

Brackinridge, John (04) pitcher: 0–1 with 5.56 ERA in seven games.

Bradley, Phil (88) outfielder: 150-for-569, .264, in 154 games.

Brady, Charlie (05) pitcher: 1–1 with 3.46 ERA in two games (both starts and complete games).

Bragan, Bobby (40–42) catcher–second baseman–shortstop–third baseman: 318-for-1,366, .233, in 395 games.

Bramhill, Art (35) shortstop–third baseman: 0-for-1, .000, in two games.

Brandon, Darrell (71–73) pitcher: 15–17 with 4.06 ERA in 130 games; eight saves.

Brandt, Jackie (66–67) outfielder–pinch-hitter: 43-for-183, .235, in 98 games.

Bransfield, Kitty (05–11) first baseman: 801-for-2,974, .269, in 814 games.

Brantley, Cliff (91–) pitcher: current Phillies player.

Brashear, Roy (03) second baseman–first baseman: 17-for-75, .227, in 20 games.

Brennan, Ad (10–13) pitcher: 30–22 with 2.87 ERA in 91 games; three saves.

Bressler, Rube (32) outfielder: 19-for-83, .229, in 27 games.

Brett, Ken (73) pitcher: 13–9 with 3.44 ERA in 31 games.

Brewster, Charlie (43) shortstop: 35-for-159, .220, in 49 games.

Brickell, Fred (30–33) outfielder: 215-for-833, .258, in 236 games.

Briggs, John (64–71) outfielder–first baseman–pinch-hitter: 488-for-1,944, .251, in 695 games.

Brink, Brad (92–) pitcher: current Phillies player.

Brinker, Bill (12) outfielder–third baseman–pinch-hitter: 4-for-18, .222, in nine games.

Brittin, Jack (50–51) pitcher: 0–0 with 6.75 ERA in six games, all relief.

Brown, Buster (07–09) pitcher: 9–6 with 3.09 ERA in 31 games. Also known as Charles.

Brown, Lloyd (40) pitcher: 1–3 with 6.21 ERA in 18 games; three saves.

Brown, Ollie (74–77) outfielder–pinch-hitter: 138-for-523, .264, in 269 games.

Brown, Paul (61–63, 68) pitcher: 0–8 with 6.00 ERA in 36 games; one save.

Brown, Tommy (51–52) outfielder–second baseman–first baseman–third baseman–pinch-hitter: 47-for-221, .213, in 96 games.

Browne, Byron (70–72) outfielder–pinch-hitter: 85-for-359, .237, in 183 games.

Browne, Earl (37–38) outfielder–first baseman–pinch-hitter: 116-for-406, .286, in 126 games.

Browne, George (01–02, 12) outfielder: 79-for-312, .253, in 84 games.

Bruggy, Frank (21) catcher–first baseman: 86-for-277, .310, in 86 games.

Bruner, Roy (39–41) pitcher: 0–7 with 5.74 ERA in 19 games.

Brusstar, Warren (77–82) pitcher: 18–11 with 3.23 ERA in 179 games, all relief; six saves.

Buhl, Bob (66–67) pitcher: 6–8 with 4.93 ERA in 35 games; one save.

Bullock, Eric (89) outfielder: 0-for-4, .000, in six games.

Bunning, Jim (64–67, 70–71) pitcher: 89–73 with 2.93 ERA in 226 games, 208 as starter; two saves.

Burchell, Fred (03) pitcher: 0–3 with 2.86 ERA in six games.

Burdette, Lew (65) pitcher: 3–3 with 5.45 ERA in 19 games.

Burgess, Smoky (52–55) catcher–pinch-hitter: 332-for-1,049, .316, in 327 games.

Burich, Bill (42, 46) shortstop–third baseman: 23-for-81, .284, in 27 games.

Burk, Mack (56, 58) catcher–pinch-hitter–pinch-runner: 1-for-2, .500, in 16 games.

Burkart, Elmer (36–39) pitcher: 1–1 with 4.93 ERA in 16 games.

Burke, Bob (37) pitcher: 0–0 with ∞ ERA in two games.

Burns, Bill (11) pitcher: 6–10 with 3.42 ERA in 21 games; one save.

Burns, Ed (13–18) catcher–outfielder (one game)–shortstop (one game): 183-for-795, .230, in 320 games.

Burns, George (25) outfielder: 102-for-349, .292, in 88 games.

Busby, Paul (41, 43) outfielder–pinch-hitter: 15-for-56, .268, in 36 games. Also known as Red.

Buskey, Joe (26) shortstop: 0-for-8, .000, in five games.

Buskey, Mike (77) shortstop: 2-for-7, .286, in six games.

Butcher, Max (38–39) pitcher: 6–21 with 2.94 ERA in 31 games.

Butler, Charlie (33) pitcher: 0–0 with 9.00 ERA in 11 games.

Buzhardt, John (60–61) pitcher: 11–34 with 4.18 ERA in 71 games.

Byrne, Bob (13–17) second baseman–third baseman: 259-for-1,067, .243, in 311 games.

Bystrom, Marty (80–84) pitcher: 24–22 with 4.23 ERA in 69 games.

C

Caballero, Putsy (44–45, 47–52) second baseman–shortstop–third baseman–pinch-hitter–pinch-runner: 150-for-658, .228, in 322 games.

Cady, Hick (19) catcher: 21-for-98, .214, in 34 games. Also known as Forrest.

Caldwell, Earl (28) pitcher: 1–4 with 5.71 ERA in five games, all as starter.

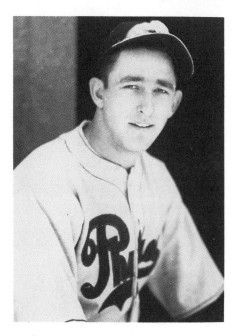

Joe Bowman

Johnny Briggs

Bobby Byrne

Putsy Caballero

Caldwell, Ralph (04–05) pitcher: 3–5 with 4.20 ERA in 13 games; one save.

Calhoun, Jeff (87–88) pitcher: 3–1 with 2.20 ERA in 45 games; one save.

Callahan, Leo (19) outfielder–pinch-hitter: 54-for-235, .230, in 81 games.

Callison, Johnny (60–69) outfielder–pinch-hitter: 1,438-for-5,306, .271, in 1,432 games; 185 home runs.

Camilli, Dolph (34–37) first baseman: 585-for-1,985, .295, in 540 games; 92 home runs.

Camnitz, Howie (13) pitcher: 3–3 with 3.67 ERA in nine games.

Campbell, Bill (84) pitcher: 6–5 with 3.43 ERA in 57 games; one save.

Campusano, Sil (90–91) outfielder: 22-for-130, .169, in 81 games.

Candini, Milo (50–51) pitcher: 2–0 with 4.35 ERA in 33 games, all relief.

Cantwell, Mike (19–20) pitcher: 1–6 with 4.76 ERA in ten games.

Capron, Ralph (13) outfielder: 0–1, .000, in two games.

Cardenal, Jose (78–79) first baseman–outfielder–pinch-hitter: 60-for-249, .241, in 116 games.

Cardwell, Don (57–60) pitcher: 17–26 with 4.47 ERA in 76 games; one save.

Carlin, Jim (41) outfielder–third baseman–pinch-hitter: 3-for-21, .143, in 16 games.

Carlson, Hal (24–27) pitcher: 42–48 with 4.13 ERA in 119 games; three saves.

Carlton, Steve (72–86) pitcher: 241–161 with 3.09 ERA in 499 games.

Carman, Don (83–90) pitcher: 53–52 with 4.05 ERA in 312 games; 10 saves.

Carreno, Amalio (91) pitcher: 0–0 with 16.20 ERA in three games.

Cash, Dave (74–76) second baseman: 608-for-2,052, .296, in 484 games.

Castillo, Braulio (92) outfielder: 24-for-128, .188, in 56 games.

Castle, John (10) outfielder: 1-for-4, .250, in three games.

Cater, Danny (64) outfielder–first baseman–third baseman–pinch-hitter: 45-for-152, .296, in 60 games.

Causey, Cecil (20–21) pitcher: 10–17 with 3.99 ERA in 42 games; three saves. Also known as Red.

Cavanaugh, Pat (19) third baseman: 0-for-1, .000, in one game.

Chalmers, George (10–16) pitcher: 29–41 with 3.41 in 121 games; six saves.

Chamberlain, Wes (90–   ) outfielder: current Phillies player.

Champion, Billy (69–72) pitcher: 12–31 with 4.99 ERA in 97 games; one save.

Chapin, Darrin (92) pitcher: 0–0 with 9.00 ERA in one game.

Chapman, Ben (45–46) outfielder–third baseman–pitcher: 16-for-52, .308, in 25 games. His record as pitcher was 0–0 with 6.75 ERA in four games. He was playing manager.

Cheek, Harry (10) catcher: 2-for-4, .500, in two games.

Cheney, Larry (19) pitcher: 2–5 with 4.58 ERA in nine games.

Chetkovich, Mitch (45) pitcher: 0–0 with 0.00 ERA in four games.

Childress, Rocky (85) pitcher: 0–1 with 6.21 ERA in 16 games. Also known as Rodney.

Childs, Pete (02) second baseman: 78-for-403, .194, in 123 games.

Chiles, Pearce (00) first baseman–second baseman–outfielder: 24-for-111, .216, in 33 games.

Chiozza, Dino (35) shortstop: 0-for-0 in two games.

Chiozza, Lou (34–36) second baseman–third baseman–outfielder: 451-for-1,528, .295, in 402 games.

Christenson, Larry (73–83) pitcher: 83–71 record with 3.79 ERA in 243 games; four saves.

Church, Bubba (50–52) pitcher: 23–17 with 3.34 ERA in 71 games; two saves.

Cieslak, Ted (44) third baseman–outfielder–pinch-hitter: 54-for-220, .245, in 85 games.

Clancy, Bud (34) first baseman–pinch-hitter: 12-for-49, .245, in 20 games.

Clark, John (38) catcher–pinch-hitter: 19-for-74, .257, in 52 games. Also known as Cap.

Clark, Mel (51–55) outfielder–pinch-hitter–third baseman (one game): 182-for-649, .280, in 210 games.

Clark, Ron (74–75) pinch-hitter: 0-for-1, .000, in one game.

Clarke, Jay (19) catcher: 15-for-62, .242, in 26 games. Also known as Nig.

Clay, Bill (02) outfielder: 2-for-8, .250, in three games.

Clay, Danny (88) pitcher: 0–1 with 6.00 ERA in 17 games.

Clemens, Doug (66–68) pinch-hitter–outfielder–first baseman (one game): 56-for-251, .223, in 177 games; record as pinch-hitter 26-for-116.

Clement, Wally (08–09) outfielder–pinch-hitter: 8-for-39, .205, in 19 games.

Coble, Dave (39) catcher: 7-for-25, .280, in 15 games.

Coffman, Dick (45) pitcher: 2–1 with 5.13 ERA in 14 games, all relief.

Cohen, Alta (33) outfielder–pinch-hitter: 6-for-32, .188, in 19 games. Also known as Al.

Coker, Jimmie (58, 60–62) catcher: 65-for-286, .227, in 99 games.

Cole, Dave (55) pitcher: 0–3 with 6.38 ERA in 7 games.

Coleman, Choo Choo (61) catcher–pinch-hitter: 6-for-47, .128, in 34 games.

Collard, Hap (30) pitcher: 6–12 with 6.80 ERA in 30 games. Also known as Earl.

Collins, Phil (29–35) pitcher: 72–79 with 4.67 ERA in 265 games; 2 saves. Also known as Fidgety Phil.

Colton, Larry (68) pitcher: 0–0 with 4.50 ERA in one game.

Combs, Pat (89–   ) pitcher: current Phillies player.

Comer, Steve (83) pitcher: 1–0 with 5.19 ERA in three games.

Command, Jim (54–55) third baseman–pinch-hitter: 4-for-23, .174, in 14 games.

Compton, Mike (70) catcher: 18-for-110, .164, in 47 games.

Conger, Dick (43) pitcher: 2–7 with 6.09 ERA in 13 games.

Conley, Bob (58) pitcher: 0–0 with 7.56 ERA in two games, both as starter.

Conley, Gene (59–60) pitcher: 20–21 with 3.35 ERA in 54 games; one save.

Conn, Bert (00–01) 1900—pitcher: 0–2 with 8.31 ERA in four games. 1901—second baseman: 4-for-18, .222, in five games.

Connell, Gene (31) catcher: 3-for-12, .250, in six games.

Consolo, Billy (62) third baseman: 2-for-5, .400, in 13 games.

Cook, Dennis (89–90) pitcher: 14–11

with 3.63 ERA in 63 games; one save.

Cooney, Jimmy (27) shortstop: 70-for-259, .270, in 76 games.

Cooper, Claude (16–17) outfielder–pinch-hitter–first baseman (one game): 23-for-133, .173, in 80 games.

Corbett, Gene (36–38) first baseman–second baseman–third baseman: 13-for-108, .120, in 37 games.

Corcoran, Tim (83–85) first baseman–pinch-hitter: 110-for-390, .282, in 208 games.

Corrales, Pat (64–65) catcher: 39-for-175, .223, in 65 games.

Corridon, Frank (04–05; 07–09) pitcher: 60–49 with 2.42 ERA in 138 games, 81 complete games; three saves.

Cotter, Dick (11) catcher: 13-for-46, .283, in 20 games.

Cotter, Ed (26) third baseman–shortstop–pinch-hitter: 8-for-26, .308, in 17 games.

Couch, John (23–25) pitcher: 11–18 with 5.08 ERA in 82 games; five saves.

Courtney, Ernie (05–08) first baseman–second baseman–shortstop–third baseman–outfielder–pinch-hitter: 395-for-1,599, .247, in 461 games.

Coveleski, Harry (07–09) pitcher: 11–12 with 2.09 ERA in 34 games; one save.

Covington, Chet (44) pitcher: 1–1 with 4.66 ERA in 19 games, all relief.

Covington, Wes (61–65) outfielder–pinch-hitter: 396-for-1,396, .284, in 522 games.

Cowan, Billy (67) outfielder–pinch-hitter–third baseman–second baseman: 9-for-59, .153, in 34 games.

Cowley, Joe (87) pitcher: 0–4 with 15.43 ERA in five games.

Cox, Danny (91–92) pitcher: 6–8 with 4.80 ERA in 32 games.

Cox, Larry (73–75) catcher: 10-for-58, .172, in 42 games.

Craig, Roger (66) pitcher: 2–1 with 5.56 ERA in 14 games, all relief; one save.

Cravath, Gavvy (12–20) outfielder–pinch-hitter: 1,054-for-3,618, .291, in 1,103 games. He was playing manager.

Crawford, Glenn (45–46) outfielder–

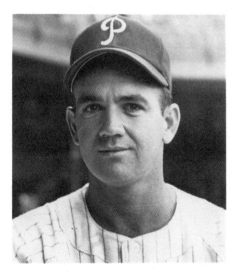

Bubba Church

shortstop–second baseman: 89-for-303, .294, in 83 games.

Crawford, Larry (37) pitcher: 0–0 with 15.00 ERA in six games, all relief.

Crist, Ches (06) catcher: 0-for-11, .000, in six games.

Cristante, Leo (51) pitcher: 1–1 with 4.91 ERA in 10 games.

Cross, Monte (00–02) shortstop: 332-for-1,446, .230, in 424 games.

Crouch, Bill (41) pitcher: 2–3 with 4.42 ERA in 20 games; one save.

Crumpler, Ray (25) pitcher: 0–0 with 7.71 ERA in three games.

Cruz, Todd (78) shortstop: 2-for-4, .500, in three games.

Culp, Benny (42–44) catcher: 5-for-26, .192, in 15 games.

Culp, Bill (10) pitcher: 0–1 with 8.10 ERA in four games, all relief; one save.

Culp, Ray (63–66) pitcher: 43–32 with 3.64 ERA in 131 games; one save.

Culver, George (73–74) pitcher: 4–1 with 5.17 ERA in 28 games. Pitched no-hitter against Phillies in 1968 while pitching for Cincinnati at Connie Mack Stadium.

Curry, Tony (60–61) outfielder–pinch-hitter: 71-for-281, .253, in 110 games.

Curtis, Cliff (11–12) pitcher: 4–6 with 2.94 ERA in 18 games.

D

Dahlgren, Babe (43) first baseman–third baseman–shortstop–catcher (one game): 146-for-508; .287, in 136 games.

Dailey, Sam (29) pitcher: 2–2 with 7.54 ERA in 20 games.

Dalrymple, Clay (60–68) catcher–

pinch-hitter: 674-for-2,881, .234, in 1,006 games.

Daniels, Fred (45) second baseman–third baseman: 46-for-230, .200, in 76 games.

Dark, Al (60) third baseman–first baseman (one game): 48-for-198, .242, in 55 games.

Darrow, George (34) pitcher: 2–6 with 5.51 ERA in 17 games; one save.

Daulton, Darren (83, 85–) catcher: current Phillies player.

Davis, Curt (34–36) pitcher: 37–35 with 3.42 ERA in 105 games; seven saves.

Davis, Dick (81–82) outfielder–pinch-hitter: 51-for-164, .311, in 73 games.

Davis, Dixie (18) pitcher: 0–2 with 3.06 ERA in 17 games.

Davis, Kiddo (32, 34) outfielder: 293-for-969, .302, in 237 games. Also known as George.

Davis, Jacke (62) outfielder–pinch-hitter: 16-for-75, .213, in 48 games.

Davis, Mark (80–81) pitcher: 1–4 with 7.02 ERA in 11 games, 10 as starting pitcher.

Davis, Spud (28–33, 38–39) catcher: 790-for-2,462, .321, in 814 games.

Dawley, Bill (88) pitcher: 0–2 with 13.50 ERA in eight games.

Dean, Wayland (26–27) pitcher: 8–17 with 6.23 ERA in 35 games.

Decatur, Art (25–27) pitcher: 7–18 with 6.19 ERA in 56 games; two saves.

Deininger, Pep (08–09) outfielder–second baseman (one game): 44-for-169, .260, in 56 games. Also known as Otto.

DeJesus, Ivan (82–84) shortstop:

Ivan DeJesus

366-for-1,468, .249, in 463
games.

DeJesus, Jose (90–) pitcher: current Phillies player.

Delahanty, Ed (00–01) outfielder–first baseman–second baseman: 366-for-1,081, .339, in 270 games. Four brothers also played in major leagues. Elected to Hall of Fame in 1945.

De Leon, Jose (92–) pitcher: current Phillies player.

Del Greco, Bobby (60–61, 65) outfielder–pinch-hitter–second baseman–third baseman: 100-for-416, .240, in 149 games.

Delker, Ed (32–33) second baseman–third baseman: 17-for-103, .165, in 55 games.

Del Savio, Garton (43) shortstop: 1-for-11, .091, in four games.

Demaree, Al (15–16) pitcher: 33–25 with 2.80 ERA in 71 games; two saves.

Demeter, Don (61–63) outfielder–first baseman–third baseman: 400-for-1,447, .276, in 413 games.

Dennehy, Tod (23) outfielder: 7-for-24, .292, in nine games. Also known as Tom.

Denny, John (82–85) pitcher: 37–29 with 2.80 ERA in 95 games.

Dernier, Bob (80–83, 88–89) outfielder: 230-for-955, .241, in 439 games.

Devine, Mickey (18) catcher: 1-for-8, .125, in four games.

Devore, Josh (13–14) outfielder–pinch-hitter: 27-for-92, .293, in 53 games.

Diaz, Bo (82–85) catcher: 294-for-1,147, .256, in 333 games.

Dickson, Murry (54–56) pitcher: 22–34 with 3.71 ERA in 79 games; three saves.

Dietrick, Bill (27–28) outfielder–shortstop–pinch-hitter: 21-for-106, .198, in 57 games.

Dietz, Dutch (43) pitcher: 1–1 with 6.50 ERA in 21 games, all relief; two saves.

Dillard, Gordon (89) pitcher: 0–0 with 6.75 ERA in five games.

Dillhoeffer, Pickles (18) catcher: 1-for-11, .091, in eight games. Also known as Bill.

DiMaggio, Vince (45–46) outfielder: 120-for-471, .255, in 133 games. Brother of Joe and Dom DiMaggio.

Dineen, Kerry (78) outfielder–pinch-hitter: 2-for-8, .250, in five games.

Dinges, Vance (45–46) outfielder–first baseman–pinch-hitter: 146-for-501, .291, in 159 games.

Diorio, Ron (73–74) pitcher: 0–0 with 3.10 ERA in 25 games, all relief; one save.

Dodge, John (12–13) third baseman–second baseman–shortstop (one game): 12-for-95, .126, in 33 games.

Dolan, Cozy (12–13) third baseman–outfielder–shortstop–pinch-hitter–first baseman (one game): 47-for-176, .267, in 66 games. Also known as Alvin.

Dolan, Joe (00–01) third baseman–second baseman–shortstop: 54-for-294, .184, in 84 games.

Donahue, She (04) shortstop–third baseman–second baseman–first baseman: 43-for-200, .215, in 58 games. Also known as Charles.

Donahue, Deacon (43–44) pitcher: 0–2 with 6.75 ERA in eight games, all relief. Also known as John.

Donahue, Frank (00–01) pitcher: 37–23 with 3.04 ERA in 67 games. Also known as Red.

Donnelly, Blix (46–50) pitcher: 16–22 with 3.70 ERA in 113 games; eight saves.

Donovan, Jerry (06) catcher–pinch-hitter–outfielder (one game)–shortstop (one game): 33-for-166, .199, in 61 games.

Dooin, Red (02–14) catcher–outfielder–first baseman–third baseman–second baseman (one game): 922-for-3,831, .241, in 1,218 games. Playing manager from 1910 to 1914. Also known as Charles.

Doolan, Mickey (05–13) shortstop–second baseman: 1,077-for-4,571, .236, in 1,301 games.

Douglas, Klondike (00–04) catcher–third baseman–first baseman–outfielder: 298-for-1,128, .264, in 318 games. Also known as Bill.

Dowell, Ken (87) shortstop: 5-for-39, .128, in 15 games.

Downey, Tom (12) third baseman–shortstop–pinch-hitter: 50-for-171, .292, in 54 games.

Downs, Dave (72) pitcher: 1–1 with 2.74 ERA in four games.

Doyle, Denny (70–73) second baseman: 376-for-1,567, .240, in 446 games.

Doyle, Jack (04) first baseman–second baseman (one game): 52-for-236, .220, in 66 games.

Bo Diaz

Vance Dinges

Denny Doyle

Drake, Solly (59) outfielder–pinch-hitter: 9-for-62, .145, in 67 games.

Drews, Karl (51–54) pitcher: 25–25 with 3.74 ERA in 93 games, 60 as starting pitcher; three saves.

Dubiel, Monk (48) pitcher: 8–10 with 3.89 ERA in 37 games; four saves. Also known as Walt.

Dudley, Clise (31–32) pitcher: 9–15 with 3.84 ERA in 43 games; one save.

Duffy, Hugh (04–06) outfielder–pinch-hitter: 25-for-87, .287, in 34 games. Playing manager 1904 to 1906. Elected to Hall of Fame in 1945.

Dugas, Gus (33) first baseman–pinch-hitter–outfielder (one game): 12-for-71, .169, in 37 games.

Dugey, Oscar (15–17) second baseman–outfielder–pinch-hitter: 31-for-161, .193, in 127 games.

Duggleby, Bill (01–07) pitcher: 86–97 with 3.18 ERA in 220 games, 181 of them as starting pitcher; four saves.

Duncan, Mariano (92–   ) second baseman–shortstop–outfielder: current Phillies player.

Duncan, Vern (13) outfielder–pinch-hitter: 5-for 12, .417, in eight games.

Dunham, Lee (26) first baseman–pinch-hitter: 1-for-4, .250, in five games.

Dunn, Jack (00–01) pitcher: 5–6 with 4.89 ERA in 12 games. During career with other teams in National League he played infield and outfield on a regular basis as well as pitched.

Duren, Ryne (63–65) pitcher: 6–2 with 3.39 ERA in 41 games; two saves.

Durning, George (25) outfielder–pinch-hitter: 5-for-14, .357, in five games.

Dykstra, Lenny (89–   ) outfielder: current Phillies player.

E

Easler, Mike (87) outfielder–pinch-hitter: 31-for-110, .282, in 33 games. Also known as Hit Man.

Easton, John (55, 59) pinch-hitter: 0-for-3, .000, in four games.

Eastwick, Rawly (78–79) pitcher: 5–7 with 4.61 ERA in 73 games, all relief; six saves.

Edwards, Doc (70) catcher: 21-for-78, .269, in 35 games.

Elliott, Ace (29–32) pitcher: 11–24 with 6.95 ERA in 120 games; four saves. Also known as Hal.

Elliott, Jumbo (31–34) pitcher: 36–35 with 4.53 ERA in 129 games; seven saves.

Ellsworth, Dick (67) pitcher: 6–7 with 4.38 ERA in 32 games.

Emery, Cal (63) pinch-hitter–first baseman: 3-for-19, .158, in 16 games.

Emery, Spoke (24) outfielder–pinch-hitter: 2-for-3, .667, in five games. Also known as Herrick.

Ennis, Del (46–56) outfielder–first baseman (one game): 1,812-for-6,327, .286, in 1,630 games. He is second on all-time list for Phillies home runs with 259.

Enzmann, Johnny (20) pitcher: 2–3 with 3.84 ERA in 16 games.

Erickson, Don (58) pitcher: 0–1 with 4.63 ERA in nine games; one save.

Erickson, Paul (48) pitcher: 2–0 with 5.29 ERA in four games.

Espinosa, Nino (79–81) pitcher: 19–22 with 4.18 ERA in 59 games.

Essegian, Chuck (58) outfielder–pinch-hitter: 28-for-114, .246, in 39 games.

Essian, Jim (73–75) catcher–pinch-hitter (one game)–third baseman (one game): 3-for-24, .125, in 21 games.

Etten, Nick (41–42, 47) first baseman: 299-for-1,040, .287, in 304 games.

Evers, Johnny (17) second baseman–third baseman: 41-for-183, .224, in 56 games. Elected to Hall of Fame in 1946. Middleman of great double-play combination Tinker to Evers to Chance.

Ewing, Long Bob (10–11) pitcher: 16–15 with 3.42 ERA in 38 games, 35 as starting pitcher.

Eyrich, George (43) pitcher: 0–0 with 3.38 ERA in nine games, all relief.

F

Faircloth, Rags (19) pitcher: 0–0 with 9.00 ERA in two games, both relief. Also known as Jim.

Fallenstin, Ed (31) pitcher: 0–0 with 7.13 ERA in 24 games, all relief.

Farmer, Ed (74, 82–83) pitcher: 4–13 with 5.91 ERA in 73 games.

Farrell, Dick (56–61, 67–69) pitcher: 47–41 with 3.26 ERA in 359 games; 65 saves.

Feinberg, Ed (38–39) shortstop–second baseman–outfielder: 7-for-38, .184, in 16 games.

Felix, Harry (02) pitcher: 1–3 with 5.60 ERA in nine games.

Ferguson, Alex (27–29) pitcher: 14–28 with 5.37 ERA in 70 games; two saves.

Fernandez, Chico (57–59) shortstop–second baseman (two games): 277-for-1,145, .242, in 342 games.

Ferrarese, Don (61–62) pitcher: 5–13 with 3.95 ERA in 47 games; one save.

Fick, John (44) pitcher: 0–0 with 3.38 ERA in four games, all relief.

File, Sam (40) shortstop–third baseman (one game): 1-for-13, .077, in seven games. Also known as Larry.

Fillingim, Dana (25) pitcher: 1–0 with 10.38 ERA in five games.

Finley, Bob (43–44) catcher–pinch-hitter: 91-for-362, .251, in 122 games.

Finn, Mickey (33) second baseman: 40-for-169, .237, in 51 games.

Finneran, Happy (12–13) pitcher: 0–2 with 2.98 ERA in 17 games; one save. Also known as Joe.

Finney, Lou (47) pinch-hitter: 0-for-4, .000, in four games.

Fireovid, Steve (84) pitcher: 0–0 with 1.59 ERA in six games.

Fittery, Paul (17) pitcher: 1–1 with 4.53 ERA in 17 games.

Fitzgerald, Mike (18) outfielder–pinch-hitter: 39-for-133, .293, in 66 games.

Flager, Wally (45) shortstop–second baseman (one game): 42-for-168, .250, in 49 games.

Flaherty, Patsy (10) outfielder (one game)–pitcher (one game): 1-for-2, .500, in two games. As pitcher in one game was 0–0 with 0.00 ERA in one-third of an inning.

Fleming, Tom (02, 04) outfielder–pinch-hitter: 6-for-22, .273, in eight games.

Fletcher, Art (20, 22) shortstop: 223-for-775, .288, in 222 games.

Fletcher, Darrin (90–91) catcher: 34-for-158, .215, in 55 games.

Flick, Elmer (00–01) outfielder: 380-for-1,085, .350, in 276 games. Elected to Hall of Fame 1963.

Flitcraft, Hilly (42) pitcher: 0–0 with 8.10 ERA in three games, all relief.

Flowers, Ben (56) pitcher: 0–2 with 5.71 ERA in 32 games.

Foley, Tom (85–86) second baseman–shortstop: 60-for-219, .274, in 85 games.

Fonseca, Lew (25) second baseman–first baseman–pinch-hitter: 149-for-467, .319, in 126 games.

Foote, Barry (77–78) catcher–pinch-hitter: 16-for-89, .180, in 57 games.

Ford, Curt (89–90) outfielder–pinch-hitter: 33-for-160, .206, in 130 games.

Ford, Hod (24) second baseman: 144-for-530, .272, in 145 games. Also known as Horace.

Fortune, Gary (16, 18) pitcher: 0–2 with 7.50 ERA in six games.

Fox, Henry (02) pitcher: 0–0 with 18.00 ERA in one game, one inning pitched; one save.

Fox, Howie (52) pitcher: 2–7 with 5.08 ERA in 13 games.

Fox, Terry (66) pitcher: 3–2 with 4.50 ERA in 36 games, all relief; four saves.

Foxen, Bill (08–10) pitcher: 16–18 with 2.45 ERA in 56 games.

Foxx, Jimmie (45) first baseman–third baseman–pinch-hitter: 60-for-224, .268, in 89 games (including nine games as pitcher: 1–0 with 1.59 ERA). Elected to Hall of Fame 1951.

Franco, Julio (82) shortstop–third baseman: 8-for-29, .276, in 16 games.

Francona, Tito (67) first baseman–outfielder (one game): 15-for-73, .205, in 27 games.

Franks, Fletcher (14) pinch-hitter: 0-for-1, .000, in one game.

Fraser, Chick (00, 02–04) pitcher: 53–63 with 3.51 ERA in 130 games, 117 games as starting pitcher; two saves. Also known as Charles.

Freed, Ed (42) outfielder–pinch-hitter: 10-for-33, .303, in 13 games.

Freed, Roger (71–72) outfielder–pinch-hitter–catcher (one game): 106-for-477, .222, in 191 games.

Freeman, Marvin (86–90) pitcher: 4–5 with 5.33 ERA in 31 games; one save. Also known as Starvin' Marvin.

Freese, Gene (59) third baseman–

Lew Fonseca

second baseman–pinch-hitter: 107-for-400, .268, in 132 games.

Friberg, Barney (25–32) second baseman–third baseman–shortstop–outfielder–first baseman–catcher (one game): 686-for-2,504, .274, in 795 games.

Frink, Fred (34) outfielder: no batting record, two games.

Fritz, Larry (75) pinch-hitter: 0-for-1, .000, in one game.

Froelich, Ben (09) catcher: 0-for-1, .000, in one game. Also known as Bill.

Frohwirth, Todd (87–90) pitcher: 3–3 with 3.94 ERA in 72 games.

Frye, Charlie (40) pitcher: 0–6 with 4.65 ERA in 15 games.

Fryman, Woodie (68–72) pitcher: 46–52 with 3.75 ERA in 157 games; three saves.

Fuchs, Charlie (43) pitcher: 2–7 with 4.27 ERA in 17 games; one save.

Fullis, Chick (33–34) outfielder–third baseman (one game): 223-for-749, .298, in 179 games.

G

Gabrielson, Len (39) first baseman: 4-for-18, .222, in five games. His son, Len, played nine years in major leagues from 1960–1970.

Gallia, Bert (20) pitcher: 2–6 with 4.50 ERA in 18 games; two saves.

Gamble, Oscar (70–72) outfielder–pinch-hitter–first baseman (one game): 166-for-690, .241, in 254 games.

Gandy, Bob (16) outfielder: 0-for-2, .000, in one game.

Garber, Gene (74–78) pitcher: 33–22 with 2.68 ERA in 250 games, all relief; 51 saves.

Garcia, Kiko (83–85) second baseman–shortstop–third baseman: 48-for-181, .265, in 145 games.

Gardiner, Art (23) pitcher: 0–0 in one game. He is not credited with any innings pitched. Only data on him show he gave up a hit and a walk.

Gerheauser, Al (43–44) pitcher: 18–35 with 4.05 ERA in 68 games, 60 games as starting pitcher.

Ghelfi, Tony (83) pitcher: 1–1 with 3.14 ERA in three games.

Gilbert, Charlie (46–47) outfielder–pinch-hitter: 99-for-412, .240, in 171 games.

Girard, Charlie (10) pitcher: 1–2 with 6.41 ERA in seven games.

Glaviano, Tommy (53) third baseman–second baseman–pinch-hitter–shortstop (one game): 15-for-74, .203, in 53 games. Also known as Rabbit.

Glazner, Whitey (23–24) pitcher: 14–30 with 5.29 ERA in 63 games, 47 as starting pitcher; one save.

Gleason, Kid (03–08) second baseman–shortstop–first baseman–outfielder–third baseman (one game): 558-for-2,228, .250, in 587 games.

Glossop, Al (42) second baseman–pinch-hitter–third baseman (one game): 102-for-454, .225 in 121 games. Also known as Alban.

Glynn, Bill (49) first baseman–pinch-hitter: 2-for-10, .200, in eight games.

Goliat, Mike (49–51) second baseman–first baseman–third baseman: 184-for-810, .227, in 241 games.

Gomez, Chile (35–36) shortstop–second baseman: 128-for-554, .231, in 175 games. Also known as Jose.

Gomez, Ruben (59–60, 67) pitcher: 3–11 with 5.63 ERA in 49 games; two saves.

Gonzalez, Orlando (78) outfielder–pinch-hitter–first baseman: 5-for-26, .192, in 26 games.

Gonzalez, Tony (60–68) outfielder–pinch-hitter: 1,110-for-3,758, .295, in 1,118 games.

Good, Wilbur (16) outfielder–pinch-hitter: 34-for-136, .250, in 75 games.

Gorbous, Glen (55–57) outfielder–pinch-hitter: 60-for-259, .232, in 109 games.

Gorman, Howie (37–38) outfielder–pinch-hitter: 4-for-20, .200, in 14 games.

Gorman, Tom (86) pitcher: 0–1 with 7.71 ERA in eight games.

Goulish, Nick (44–45) outfielder–pinch-hitter: 3-for-12, .250, in 14 games.

Grabarkewitz, Bill (73–74) second baseman–third baseman–outfielder–pinch-hitter: 23-for-96, .240.

Grabowski, Reggie (32–34) pitcher: 4–8 with 5.73 ERA in 51 games.

Grace, Earl (36–37) catcher–pinch-hitter: 102-for-444, .230, in 166 games. Also known as Bob.

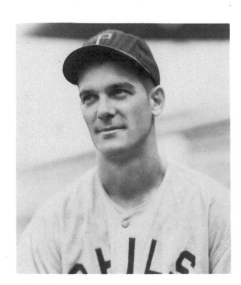

Al Glossop

Graham, George (12) catcher–pinch-hitter: 17-for-59, .288, in 24 games. Also known as Peaches.

Graham, Wayne (63) outfielder–pinch-hitter: 4-for-22, .182, in 10 games.

Grant, Ed (07–10) third baseman–shortstop: 536-for-2,074, .258, in 526 games.

Grant, Jim (23) pitcher: 0–0 with 13.50 ERA in two games, both relief.

Grasmick, Lou (48) pitcher: 0–0 with 7.20 ERA in two games, both relief.

Grate, Don (45–46) pitcher: 1–1 with 9.37 ERA in seven games.

Gray, John (58) pitcher: 0–0 with 4.15 in 15 games.

Green, Dallas (60–64, 67) pitcher: 20–22 with 4.16 ERA in 175 games; four saves.

Green, June (28–29) pitcher: 0–0 with 18.38 ERA in six games, all relief. Also used as pinch-hitter and was 5-for-20 in that role. Overall batting stats were 7-for-25, .280.

Green, Patsy (02) third baseman: 11-for-65, .169, in 19 games.

Greene, Tommy (90–) pitcher: current Phillies player.

Greengrass, Jim (55–56) outfielder–pinch-hitter–third baseman: 132- for-538, .245, in 180 games.

Greenwood, Bob (54–55) pitcher: 1–2 with 3.92 ERA in 12 games.

Grimes, Ray (26) first baseman–pinch-hitter: 30-for-101, .297, in 32 games. Also known as Oscar.

Grimsley, Jason (89–91) pitcher: 5–12 with 4.35 ERA in 27 games.

Grissom, Lee (41) pitcher: 2–13 with 3.99 ERA in 29 games.

Groat, Dick (66–67) shortstop–third baseman–first baseman (one game)–pinch-hitter: 155-for-610, .254, in 165 games.

Gross, Greg (79–88) outfielder–pinch-hitter–pitcher: 431-for-1,547, .279, in 1,080 games; 0–0 with 0.00 ERA in one game.

Gross, Kevin (83–88) pitcher: 60–66 with 3.87 ERA in 203 games; one save.

Grotewold, Jeff (92) first baseman–pinch-hitter: 13-for-65, .200, in 72 games.

Gutierrez, Jackie (88) shortstop–

third baseman: 19-for-77, .247, in 33 games.

H

Haas, Bert (48–49) third baseman–first baseman–pinch-hitter: 94-for-334, .281, in 97 games.

Hacker, Warren (57–58) pitcher: 4–5 with 5.04 ERA in 29 games.

Haddix, Harvey (56–57) pitcher: 22–21 with 3.74 ERA in 58 games, 51 games as starting pitcher; two saves. Also used as pinch-hitter. Also known as "The Kitten."

Hafey, Bud (39) outfielder–pinch-hitter: 9-for-51, .176, in 18 games. Record as pitcher 0–0 with 33.75 ERA in two games, both in relief. Also known as Dan.

Hahn, Don (75) outfielder–pinch-hitter: 0-for-5, .000, in nine games.

Haislip, Jim (13) pitcher: 0–0 with 6.00 ERA in one game.

Hall, Bert (11) pitcher: 0–1 with 4.00 ERA in seven games.

Hall, Bob (04) third baseman–shortstop–first baseman: 26-for-163, .160, in 46 games.

Hall, Dick (67–68) pitcher: 14–9 with 3.14 ERA in 80 games, all relief but one (which was complete game); eight saves.

Hallahan, Bill (38) pitcher: 1–8 with 5.46 ERA in 21 games. Also known as Wild Bill.

Hallman, Bill (01–03) second baseman–third baseman–first baseman–outfielder–shortstop–pinch-hitter: 187-for-897, .208, in 259 games.

Hamilton, Earl (24) pitcher: 0–1 with 10.50 ERA in three games, all relief.

Hamilton, Jack (62–63) pitcher: 11–13 with 5.14 ERA in 60 games; three saves.

Hamner, Garvin (45) second baseman–shortstop–third baseman: 20-for-101, .198, in 32 games. Also known as Wes.

Hamner, Granny (44–59) shortstop–second baseman–third baseman–pitcher: 1,518-for-5,772, .263, in 1,501 games; record as pitcher 0–1 with 3.89 ERA in four games, one as starting pitcher.

Hamrick, Ray (43–44) second baseman–shortstop: 92-for-452, .204, in 118 games.

Handley, Lee (47) third baseman–

Dick Hall

second baseman–pinch-hitter–shortstop (one game): 70-for-277, .253, in 101 games.

Hanebrink, Harry (59) second baseman–third baseman–pinch-hitter–outfielder (one game): 25-for-97, .258, in 57 games; record as pinch-hitter 11-for-41.

Hansen, Andy (51–53) pitcher: 8–9 with 3.34 ERA in 97 games, all but one as relief pitcher; seven saves.

Hansen, Snipe (30, 32–35) pitcher: 22–44 with 4.84 ERA in 145 games; six saves. Also known as Roy.

Harman, Bill (41) catcher–pinch-hitter–pitcher: 1-for-14, .071, in 15 games; record as pitcher 0–0 with 4.85 ERA in five games.

Harmon, Chuck (57) outfielder–third baseman–first baseman–pinch-hitter–pinch-runner: 22-for-86, .256, in 57 games.

Harmon, Terry (67, 69–77) second baseman–shortstop–third baseman–first baseman–pinch-hitter: 262-for-1,125, .233, in 547 games.

Harper, George (24–26) outfielder–pinch-hitter: 355-for-1,100, .323, in 297 games.

Harrell, Ray (39) pitcher: 3–7 with 5.40 ERA in 22 games.

Harrelson, Bud (78–79) second baseman–shortstop–third baseman–outfielder (one game)–pinch-hitter: 42-for-174, .241, in 124 games.

Harrington, Mike (63) pinch-runner: no batting record or fielding record, one game.

Harris, Greg (88–89) pitcher: 6–8 with 2.86 ERA in 110 games.

Harris, Herb (36) pitcher: 0–0 with

10.29 ERA in four games, all relief.

Hartley, Mike (91–) pitcher: current Phillies player.

Hartranft, Ray (13) pitcher: 0–0 with 9.00 ERA in one game (relief). Also known as Charles.

Hasenmayer, Don (45–46) second baseman–third baseman–pinch-hitter: 3-for-30, .100, in 11 games.

Haslin, Mickey (33–36) second baseman–shortstop–third baseman–pinch-hitter: 195-for-726, .269, in 224 games.

Hawks, Nelson (25) first baseman–pinch-hitter: 103-for-321, .322, in 105 games. Also known as Chicken.

Hayes, Charlie (89–91) third baseman: 328-for-1,320, .248, in 378 games.

Hayes, Von (83–91) first baseman–outfielder: 1,173-for-4,306, .272, in 1,208 games.

Head, Ralph (23) pitcher: 2–9 with 6.66 ERA in 35 games.

Hearn, Jim (57–59) pitcher: 10–6 with 4.04 ERA in 81 games; three saves.

Heathcote, Cliff (32) first baseman–pinch-hitter: 11-for-39, .282, in 30 games.

Hebner, Richie (77–78) first baseman–third baseman–second baseman–pinch-hitter: 236-for-832, .284, in 255 games.

Hegan, Jim (58–59) catcher: 23-for-110, .209, in 50 games.

Heintzelman, Ken (47–52) pitcher: 40–55 with 3.83 ERA in 165 games; six saves.

Heltzel, Heinie (44) shortstop: 4-for-22, .182, 11 games.

Terry Harmon

Hemingway, Ed (18) second baseman–third baseman–first baseman (one game): 23-for-108, .213,
in 33 games.

Hemsley, Rollie (46–47) catcher–
pinch-hitter: 32-for-142, .225, in
51 games.

Hemus, Solly (56–58) second baseman–third baseman–pinch-hitter:
60-for-629, .269, in 352 games.

Hendrick, Harvey (34) outfielder–
third baseman–first baseman–
pinch-hitter: 34-for-117, .293, in
59 games.

Henline, Butch (21–26) catcher–
outfielder–pinch-hitter: 519-for-
1,706, .304, in 576 games.

Hennessey, George (42) pitcher: 1–1
with 2.65 ERA in five games.

Henrich, Fritz (24) outfielder–
pinch-hitter: 19-for-90, .211, in 36
games.

Henry, Jim (39) pitcher: 0–1 with
5.09 ERA in nine games; one save.

Herbert, Ray (65–66) pitcher: 7–13
with 3.98 ERA in 48 games; three
saves.

Hernaiz, Jesus (74) pitcher: 2–3 with
5.93 ERA in 27 games, all relief;
one save.

Hernandez, Willie (83) pitcher: 8–4
with 3.29 ERA in 63 games; seven
saves.

Herr, Tommy (89–90) second baseman: 304-for-1,108, .274, in 297
games.

Herrera, Pancho (58, 60–61) first
baseman–second baseman–third
baseman–pinch-hitter: 264-for-
975, .271, in 300 games.

Herrnstein, John (62–66) outfielder–first baseman–pinch-hitter: 92-for-415, .222, in 213
games.

Heusser, Ed (38, 48) pitcher: 3–2
with 5.28 ERA in 34 games, all
relief; three saves.

Higbe, Kirby (39–40) pitcher: 24–33
with 4.17 ERA in 75 games, 62 as
starting pitcher; three saves.

High, Andy (34) third baseman–
second baseman–pinch-hitter: 14-
for-68, .206, in 47 games.

Hilgendorf, Tom (75) pitcher: 7–3
with 2.13 ERA in 53 games, all
relief.

Hiller, Chuck (67) second baseman–
pinch-hitter: 13-for-43, .302, in 31
games.

Hilly, Bill (14) outfielder–pinch- hitter: 3-for-10, .300, in eight games.

Hisle, Larry (68–71) outfielder–
pinch-hitter: 230-for-974, .236, in
314 games.

Hoak, Don (63–64) third baseman–
pinch-hitter: 87-for-381, .228, in
121 games.

Hoch, Harry (08) pitcher: 2–1 with
2.77 ERA in three games, all as
starter.

Hodge, Bert (42) third baseman–
pinch-hitter: 2-for-11, .182, in
eight games.

Hodkey, Eli (46) pitcher: 0–1 with
12.46 ERA in two games.

Hoerner, Joe (70–72, 75) pitcher:
13–12 with 2.28 ERA in 133
games, all relief; 21 saves.

Hoerst, Frank (40–42, 46–47)
pitcher: 10–33 with 5.17 ERA in
98 games; one save.

Hoffman, Bill (39) pitcher: 0–0 with
13.50 ERA in three games, all
relief.

Hogg, Brad (18–19) pitcher: 18–25
with 3.29 ERA in 51 games, 44 as
starting pitcher; one save.

Hohman, Bill (27) outfielder: 5-for-
18, .278, in seven games.

Holden, Joe (34–36) catcher–pinch-
hitter: 2-for-24, .083, in 17 games.

Holke, Walt (23–25) first baseman–
pinch-hitter: 365-for-1,211, .301,
in 334 games.

Holland, Al (83–85) pitcher: 13–15
with 2.85 ERA in 139 games; 55
saves.

Holley, Ed (32–34) pitcher: 25–37
with 4.23 ERA in 79 games, 71 as
starting pitcher.

Hollingsworth, Al (38–39) pitcher:
6–25 with 4.87 ERA in 39 games,
31 as starting pitcher.

Hollins, Dave (90–) third baseman–pinch-hitter: current Phillies
player.

Hollmig, Stan (49–51) outfielder–
pinch-hitter: 67-for-265, .253, in
94 games.

Holloway, Jim (29) pitcher: 0–0 with
13.50 ERA in three games, all
relief.

Hopkins, Marty (34) third baseman:
3-for-25, .120, in 10 games.

Houston, Harry (06) catcher: 0-for-
4, .000, in two games.

Howell, Ken (89–) pitcher: current
Phillies player.

Howley, Dan (13) catcher: 4-for-32,
.125, in 22 games.

Hubbell, Wilbert (20–25) pitcher:
36–55 with 4.77 ERA in 155

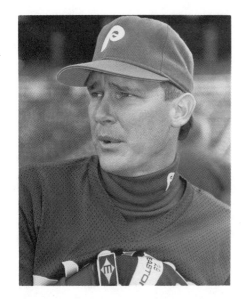

Tom Herr

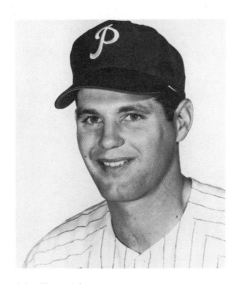

John Herrnstein

Tommy Hutton

games; seven saves. Also known as Bill.

Huber, Clarence (25–26) third baseman–pinch-hitter: 216-for-812, .266, in 242 games.

Hudson, Charles (83–86) pitcher: 32–42 with 4.02 ERA in 127 games.

Hughes, Keith (87) outfielder–pinch-hitter: 20-for-76, .263, in 37 games.

Hughes, Roy (39–40, 46) shortstop–third baseman–second baseman–first baseman (one game)–pinch-hitter: 119-for-513, .232, in 155 games.

Hughes, Tommy (41–42, 46–47) pitcher: 31–52 with 3.72 ERA in 132 games; three saves.

Hulswitt, Rudy (02–04) shortstop–third baseman (three games): 362-for-1,422, .255, in 379 games.

Hume, Tom (86–87) pitcher: 5–5 with 3.98 ERA in 86 games; four saves.

Humphries, Bert (10–11) pitcher: 4–1 with 4.23 ERA in 16 games; two saves. Also known as Albert.

Humphries, John (46) pitcher: 0–0 with 4.01 ERA in 10 games.

Hurst, Don (28–34) first baseman–outfielder–pinch-hitter: 946-for-3,124, .303, in 854 games.

Hutto, Jim (70) outfielder–first baseman–catcher–third baseman (one game)–pinch-hitter: 17-for-92, .185, in 57 games.

Hutton, Tom (72–77) first baseman–outfielder–pinch-hitter: 305-for-1,206, .253, in 651 games.

I

Iburg, Ham (02) pitcher: 11–18 with 3.89 ERA in 30 games, all as starting pitcher.

Imlay, Doc (03) pitcher: 0–0 with 7.24 ERA in nine games, all relief.

Iorg, Dane (77) first baseman–pinch-hitter: 5-for-30, .167, in 12 games.

Irelan, Hal (14) second baseman–shortstop–third baseman–pinch-hitter: 39-for-165, .236, in 67 games.

Isales, Orlando (80) outfielder: 2-for-5, .400, in three games.

J

Jacklitsch, Fred (00–02, 07–10) catcher–third baseman–outfielder–first baseman–second baseman–pinch-hitter: 137-for-616, .223, in 231 games.

Jackson, Grant (65–70) pitcher: 23–43 with 3.99 ERA in 154 games; three saves.

Jackson, John (33) pitcher: 2–2 with 6.00 ERA in 10 games.

Jackson, Ken (87) shortstop: 4-for-16, .250, in eight games.

Jackson, Larry (66–68) pitcher: 41–45 with 2.96 ERA in 109 games, 104 as starting pitcher.

Jackson, Mike (70) pitcher: 1–1 with 1.50 ERA in five games, all relief.

Jackson, Mike (86–87) pitcher: 3–10 with 4.11 ERA in 64 games; one save.

Jacobs, Elmer (14, 18–19) pitcher: 16–18 with 3.14 ERA in 49 games; one save. Also known as Bill.

Jahn, Art (28) outfielder–pinch-hitter: 21-for-94, .223, in 36 games.

James, Chris (86–89) outfielder–third baseman–pinch-hitter: 292-for-1,149, .254, in 326 games.

James, Jeff (68–69) pitcher: 6–6 with 4.51 ERA in 35 games.

Javier, Stan (92) outfielder– pinch-hitter: 72-for-276, .261, in 74 games.

Jeffries, Irv (34) second baseman–third baseman (one game)–pinch-hitter: 43-for-175, .246, in 56 games.

Jelks, Greg (87) first baseman–outfielder–pinch-hitter: 1-for-11, .091, in 10 games.

Jeltz, Steve (83–89) shortstop–second baseman–third baseman: 351-for-1,646, .213, in 653 games.

Jenkins, Ferguson (65–66) pitcher: 2–1 with 2.51 ERA in eight games; one save. Elected to Hall of Fame in 1991.

Jennings, Hughie (01–02) first baseman–shortstop–second baseman: 158-for-592, .267, in 160 games. Elected to Hall of Fame in 1945.

Johnson, Alex (64–65) outfielder–pinch-hitter: 110-for-371, .296, in 140 games.

Johnson, Charlie (08) outfielder–pinch-hitter: 4-for-16, .250, in six games.

Johnson, Darrell (61) catcher: 14-for-61, .230, in 21 games.

Johnson, Dave (77–78) first baseman–second baseman–third baseman–pinch-hitter: 67-for-245, .273, in 122 games. Hit two pinch-hit grand slam home runs during 1978 season.

Johnson, Deron (69–73) outfielder–

Chris James

third baseman–first baseman–
pinch-hitter: 477-for-1,897, .251,
in 563 games.

Johnson, Jerry (68–69) pitcher: 10–
17 with 3.91 ERA in 49 games, 32
as starting pitcher; one save.

Johnson, Ken (50–51) pitcher: 9–9
with 4.36 ERA in 34 games, 26 as
starting pitcher.

Johnson, Si (40–43, 46) pitcher: 26–
48 with 4.10 ERA in 137 games;
five saves. Also known as Silas.

Johnson, Syl (34–40) pitcher: 36–51
with 4.02 ERA in 211 games; 23
saves.

Johnstone, Jay (74–78) outfielder–
first baseman–pinch-hitter: 427-
for-1,409, .303, in 462 games.

Jok, Stan (54) pinch-hitter: 0-for-3,
.000, in three games.

Jones, Barry (92) pitcher: 5–6 with
4.64 ERA in 44 games.

Jones, Dale (41) pitcher: 0–1 with
7.56 ERA in two games.

Jones, Broadway (23) pitcher: 0–0
with 9.00 ERA in three games, all
relief. Also known as Jesse.

Jones, Nippy (52) first baseman: 5-
for-30, .167, in eight games.

Jones, Ron (88–91) outfielder–
pinch-hitter: 65-for-237, .274, in
97 games.

Jones, Willie (47–59) third baseman–first baseman (one game)–
pinch-hitter: 1,400-for-5,419,
.258, in 1,520 games. He hit 180
home runs with the club and had
two or more home runs in a game
12 times. Also known as Puddin'
Head.

Jonnard, Bubber (26–27, 35)
catcher–pinch-hitter: 46-for-178,
.258, in 73 games. Also known as
Clarence.

Jordan, Buck (38) third baseman–
first baseman–pinch-hitter: 93-
for-310, .300, in 87 games.

Jordan, Niles (51) pitcher: 2–3 with
3.19 ERA in five games, all as
starting pitcher.

Jordan, Ricky (89–   ) first baseman–
pinch-hitter: current Phillies
player.

Jorgens, Orville (35–37) pitcher:
21–27 with 4.70 ERA in 144
games; five saves.

Joseph, Rick (67–70) third baseman–
first baseman–outfielder–second
baseman (one game)–pinch-hitter: 142-for-579, .245, in 253
games.

Judd, Oscar (45–48) pitcher: 20–33
with 4.08 ERA in 89 games; four
saves; also used as pinch-hitter.

Jumonville, George (40–41) shortstop–third baseman (one game)–
second baseman (one game)–
pinch-hitter: 6-for-41, .146, in 17
games.

Jurisich, Al (46–47) pitcher: 5–10
with 4.48 ERA in 47 games; four
saves.

K

Kaat, Jim (76–79) pitcher: 27–30
with 4.23 ERA in 102 games, 87 as
starting pitcher.

Kahoe, Mike (05) catcher–pinch-hitter: 13-for-51, .255, in 16 games.

Kane, Harry (05–06) pitcher: 204
with 3.00 ERA in eight games, five
as starter.

Kantlehner, Erv (16) pitcher: 0–0
with 9.00 ERA in three games.

Karl, Andy (43–46) pitcher: 16–19
with 3.48 ERA in 153 games, all
but four as relief pitcher; 22 saves.

Kaufmann, Tony (27) pitcher: 0–3
with 10.42 ERA in five games, all
as starter.

Kazanski, Ted (53–58) second baseman–shortstop–third baseman–
pinch-hitter: 288-for-1,329, .217,
in 417 games.

Keating, Chick (26) shortstop–
second baseman–third baseman
(one game): 0-for-2, .000, in four
games.

Keegan, Ed (59, 62) pitcher: 0–3 with
10.59 ERA in 10 games.

Keenan, Jim (20–21) pitcher: 1–2
with 6.37 ERA in 16 games.

Keister, Bill (03) outfielder: 128-for-
400, .320, in 100 games.

Kelleher, Hal (35–38) pitcher: 4–9
with 5.95 ERA in 50 games.

Kelly, Bill (28) first baseman: 12-for-
71, .169, in 23 games.

Kelly, Mike (26) pitcher: 0–0 with
9.45 ERA in four games, all relief.

Kenders, Al (61) catcher: 4-for-23,
.174, in 10 games.

Kennedy, John (57) third baseman:
0-for-2, .000, in five games.

Kennedy, Vern (44–45) pitcher: 1–8
with 4.75 ERA in 24 games.

Kern, Jim (84) pitcher: 0–1 with
10.13 ERA in eight games.

Kerksieck, Bill (39) pitcher: 0–2 with
7.18 ERA in 23 games. Also
known as Wayman.

Killefer, Bill (11–17) catcher–first

Alex Johnson

Si Johnson

Ricky Jordan

baseman (one game)–pinch-hitter: 471-for-1,958, .241, in 636 games.

Kimball, Newt (43) pitcher: 1–6 with 4.10 ERA in 34 games; two saves.

Kimmick, Wally (25–26) first baseman–second baseman–shortstop–third baseman–pinch-hitter: 49-for-169, .290, in 90 games.

King, Lee (21–22) outfielder–pinch-hitter: 70-for-269, .260, in 83 games.

Kipper, Thornton (53–55) pitcher: 3–4 with 5.27 ERA in 55 games, all but three as relief pitcher; one save.

Klaus, Billy (62–63) third baseman–shortstop–second baseman–pinch-hitter: 52-for-266, .195, in 113 games.

Klein, Chuck (28–33, 36–44) outfielder–first baseman (one game)–pinch-hitter: 1,705-for-5,238, .326, in 1,405 games. He hit 300 home runs in major league career of which 243 were for the Phillies. Elected to Hall of Fame in 1980.

Kleinhans, Ted (34) pitcher: 0–0 with 9.00 ERA in five games, all relief.

Kleinow, Red (11) catcher: 1-for-8, .125, in four games.

Klippstein, Johnny (63–64) pitcher: 7–7 with 2.28 ERA in 60 games, all but one game as relief pitcher; nine saves.

Knabe, Otto (07–13) second baseman–outfielder (six games)–pinch-hitter: 856-for-3,434, .249, in 946 games. Also known as Franz.

Knicely, Alan (85) catcher–pinch-hitter: 0-for-7, .000, in seven games.

Knight, Jack (25–26) pitcher: 10–18 with 6.71 ERA in 68 games; five saves.

Knothe, Fritz (33) third baseman–second baseman–pinch-hitter: 17-for-113, .150, in 41 games.

Knothe, George (32) second baseman: 1-for-12, .083, in six games.

Knowles, Darold (66) pitcher: 6–5 with 3.05 ERA in 69 games, all relief; 13 saves.

Koecher, Dick (46–48) pitcher: 0–4 with 4.91 ERA in seven games.

Koegel, Pete (71–72) first baseman–catcher–third baseman–outfielder–pinch-hitter: 13-for-75, .173, in 53 games.

Konetchy, Ed (21) first baseman–pinch-hitter (one game): 86-for-268, .321, in 72 games.

Konstanty, Jim (48–54) pitcher: 51–39 with 3.63 ERA in 314 games, all but 23 as relief pitcher; 54 saves. Voted 1950 National League MVP.

Koosman, Jerry (84–85) pitcher: 20–19 with 3.67 ERA in 55 games.

Koppe, Joe (59–61) shortstop–second baseman–third baseman–pinch-hitter (one game): 139-for-595, .234, in 190 games.

Koster, Fred (31) outfielder–pinch-hitter: 34-for-151, .225, in 76 games.

Koupal, Lou (29–30) pitcher: 5–9 with 5.89 ERA in 28 games, 16 games as starting pitcher; two saves.

Kowalik, Fabian (36) pitcher: 1–5 with 5.38 ERA in 22 games.

Koy, Ernie (42) outfielder–pinch-hitter: 63-for-258, .244, in 91 games.

Kracher, Joe (39) catcher–pinch-hitter: 1-for-5, .200, in five games.

Kraus, Tex (43, 45) pitcher: 13–24 with 3.81 ERA in 53 games, 38 as starting pitcher; two saves.

Kroll, Gary (64) pitcher: 0–0 with 3.00 ERA in two games, all relief.

Krueger, Otto (05) shortstop–outfielder–third baseman (one game)–pinch-hitter: 21-for-114, .184, in 46 games.

Krug, Henry (02) outfielder–second baseman–shortstop–third baseman: 45-for-198, .227, in 53 games.

Kruk, John (89–) first baseman–outfielder–pinch-hitter: current Phillies player.

Krukow, Mike (82) pitcher: 13–11 with 3.12 ERA in 33 games, all as starting pitcher.

Kucek, Jack (79) pitcher: 1–0 with 9.00 ERA in four games, all relief.

Kuenn, Harvey (66) outfielder–first baseman–third baseman–pinch-hitter: 47-for-159, .296, in 86 games.

Kuzava, Bob (55) pitcher: 1–0 with 7.31 ERA in 17 games. He pitched with eight different teams in 10-year major league career.

L

LaGrow, Lerrin (80) pitcher: 0–2 with 4.15 ERA in 25 games, all relief; three saves.

Lajoie, Napolean (00) second baseman–third baseman (one game):
152-for-451, .337, in 102 games.
Also known as Larry. Elected to
the Hall of Fame in 1937.

Lake, Steve (89–) catcher–pinch-
hitter: current Phillies player.

Lakeman, Al (47–48) first baseman–
catcher–pinch-hitter: 40-for-
250, .160, in 87 games (included is one game as pitcher in
1948; ⅔ inning, 0–0 with 13.50
ERA).

LaMaster, Wayne (37–38) pitcher:
19–26 with 5.86 ERA in 68 games,
42 games as starting pitcher; four
saves.

Lambert, Gene (41–42) pitcher: 0–1
with 2.70 ERA in three games.

Landrum, Don (57) outfielder: 1-for-
7, .143, in 2 games.

Lanning, Tom (38) pitcher: 0–1 with
6.43 ERA in three games.

Lapihuska, Andy (42–43) pitcher:
0–2 with 7.04 ERA in four games.

LaPointe, Dave (91) pitcher: 0–1
with 16.20 ERA in two games.

LaPointe, Ralph (47) shortstop–
pinch-hitter: 65-for-211, .308, in
56 games.

Larson, Dan (78–81) pitcher: 4–6
with 3.73 ERA in 21 games, 14 as
starting pitcher.

Lavalliere, Mike (84) catcher: 0-for-
7, .000, in six games.

Lavender, Jim (17) pitcher: 5–8 with
3.55 ERA in 28 games; one save.

Laxton, Bill (70) pitcher: 0–0 with
13.50 ERA in two games, all relief.

Leach, Fred (23–28) outfielder–first
baseman–pinch-hitter: 636-for-
2,040, .312, in 539 games.

LeBourveau, Bevo (19–22) outfielder–pinch-hitter: 212-for-772,
.275, in 268 games.

Lee, Bill (43–45) pitcher: 14–22 with
3.48 ERA in 57 games, 48 as
starting pitcher; four saves.

Lee, Cliff (21–24) first baseman–
outfielder–catcher (two games)–
third baseman (one game)–pinch-
hitter: 325-for-1,119, .315, in 338
games.

Lee, Hal (31–33) outfielder–pinch-
hitter: 257-for-893, .288, in 239
games.

Lefebvre, Joe (83–86) outfielder–
first baseman–third baseman–
pinch-hitter: 122-for-436, .280, in
167 games.

Legg, Greg (86–87) second base-

man–pinch-hitter: 9-for-22, .409,
in 14 games.

Lehman, Ken (61) pitcher: 1–1 with
4.26 ERA in 41 games, all but two
as relief pitcher; one save.

Lehr, Clarence (11) outfielder–
shortstop–second baseman–
pinch-hitter: 4-for-27, .148, in 23
games.

Lemon, Jim (63) outfielder–pinch-
hitter: 16-for-59, .271, in 31
games.

Lennon, Ed (28) pitcher: 0–0 with
8.76 ERA in five games, all relief.

Leon, Isidore (45) pitcher: 0–4 with
5.35 ERA in 14 games.

Leonard, Dutch (47–48) pitcher: 29–
29 with 2.60 ERA in 66 games, 60
as a starting pitcher. Also known
as Emil.

Lepcio, Ted (60) third baseman–
shortstop–second baseman–
pinch-hitter: 32-for-141, .227, in
69 games.

Lerch, Randy (75–80) pitcher: 35–41
with 4.42 ERA in 136 games, 113
as starting pitcher; one save.

Lerian, Walt (28–29) catcher–pinch-
hitter: 126-for-512, .246, in 201
games. Also known as Peck.

Lersch, Barry (69–73) pitcher: 18–
32 with 3.73 ERA in 168 games;
six saves.

Leslie, Roy (22) first baseman–
pinch-hitter (two games): 139-for-
513, .271, in 141 games.

Letchas, Charlie (39, 44, 46) second
baseman–third baseman–short-
stop–pinch-hitter: 107-for-453,
.236, in 134 games.

Levan, Jesse (47) outfielder: 4-for-9,
.444, in two games.

Levy, Ed (40) pinch-hitter: 0-for-1,
.000, in one game.

Lewis, Bert (24) pitcher: 0–0 with
6.00 ERA in 12 games, all relief.

Lezcano, Sixto (83–84) outfielder–
pinch-hitter: 82-for-295, .278, in
127 games.

Lindell, Johnny (53–54) outfielder–
pinch-hitter: 8-for-23, .348, in 18
games (including five games as
pitcher in 1953, three as starting
pitcher: 1–1 with 4.30 ERA).

Lindeman, Jim (91–92) outfielder–
first baseman–pinch-hitter: 42-
for-134, .313, in 94 games.

Lindsay, Doug (91–) catcher: current Phillies player.

Linz, Phil (66–67) third baseman–
shortstop–second baseman–

Hal Lee

Ad Liska

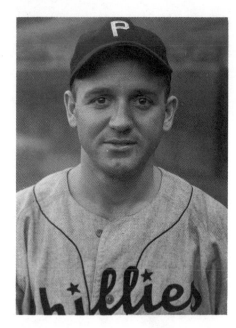

Tony Lupien

Sparky Lyle

pinch-hitter: 18-for-88, .205, in 63 games.

Linzy, Frank (74) pitcher: 3–2 with 3.24 ERA in 22 games, all relief.

LiPetri, Angelo (56, 58) pitcher: 0–0 with 5.40 ERA in 10 games, all relief.

Lis, Joe (70–72) outfielder–first baseman–pinch-hitter: 67-for-300, .223, in 134 games.

Liska, Ad (32–33) pitcher: 5–1 with 3.78 ERA in 53 games, all but one as relief pitcher; two saves.

Litwhiler, Danny (40–43) outfielder–pinch-hitter: 425-for-1,462, .291, in 374 games.

Livingston, Mickey (41–43) catcher–first baseman–pinch-hitter: 157-for-711, .221, in 268 games.

Loan, Bill (12) catcher: 1-for-2, .500, in one game. Also known as Mike.

Lobert, Hans (11–14) third baseman–shortstop–second baseman (one game)–pinch-hitter: 549-for-1,876, .292, in 497 games.

Lock, Don (67–69) outfielder–pinch-hitter: 131-for-565, .232, in 215 games.

Locke, Bobby (62–64) pitcher: 1–0 with 4.50 ERA in 22 games, all relief. Also known as Larry.

Lohrke, Lucky (52–53) shortstop–third baseman–second baseman–pinch-hitter: 8-for-42, .190, in 37 games. Also known as Jack.

Lohrman, Bill (34) pitcher: 0–1 with 4.50 ERA in four games; one save.

Lonborg, Jim (73–79) pitcher: 75–60 with 3.98 ERA in 188 games, 175 games as starting pitcher; one save.

Long, Herman (04) second baseman: 1-for-4, .250, in one game.

Lonnett, Joe (56–59) catcher–pinch-hitter: 54-for-325, .166, in 143 games.

Lopata, Stan (48–58) catcher–first baseman–pinch-hitter: 655-for-2,545, .257, in 821 games.

Lopatka, Art (46) pitcher: 0–1 with 16.88 ERA in four games.

Lopez, Marcelino (63) pitcher: 1–0 with 6.00 ERA in four games, two of them as starting pitcher.

Lord, Carl (23) third baseman–pinch-hitter: 11-for-47, .234, in 17 games. Also known as Carleton.

Loughlin, Larry (67) pitcher: 0–0 with 15.19 ERA in three games.

Lovenguth, Lynn (55) pitcher: 0–1

with 4.50 ERA in 14 games, all relief.

Loviglio, Jay (80) second baseman (one game)–pinch-runner: 0-for-5, .000, in 16 games.

Lowrey, Peanuts (55) outfielder–second baseman–first baseman (one game)–pinch-hitter: 20-for-106, .189, in 54 games. Also known as Harry.

Lucas, Fred (35) outfielder–pinch-hitter: 9-for-34, .265, in 20 games.

Lucier, Lou (44–45) pitcher: 0–1 with 3.23 ERA in 14 games, all relief; one save.

Luderus, Fred (10–20) first baseman–pinch-hitter: 1,313-for-4,746, .277, in 1,311 games.

Lupien, Tony (44–45) first baseman–pinch-hitter: 186-for-651, .286, in 168 games.

Lush, John (04–07) first baseman–outfielder–pitcher–pinch-hitter: 171-for-637, .268, in 205 games; record as a pitcher is 23–26 with 2.58 ERA in 54 games, 51 as starting pitcher.

Luzinski, Greg (70–80) outfielder–first baseman–pinch-hitter: 1,299-for-4,630, .281, in 1,289 games; 223 home runs.

Lyle, Sparky (80–82) pitcher: 12–9 with 4.37 ERA in 92 games, all relief; six saves.

Lyons, Terry (29) first baseman: no record as batter, one game.

M

MacDonald, Harvey (28) outfielder–pinch-hitter: 4-for-16, .250, in 13 games.

Mackanin, Pete (78–79) third baseman–shortstop–second baseman–first baseman (one game): 3-for-17, .176, in 18 games.

Madden, Tom (11) catcher: 21-for-76, .276, in 28 games.

Maddox, Garry (75–86) outfielder–pinch-hitter: 1,333-for-4,698, .284, in 1,330 games.

Maddux, Mike (86–89) pitcher: 10–13 with 5.03 ERA in 64 games; one save.

Madrid, Alex (88) pitcher: 1–1 with 2.76 ERA in five games.

Magee, Bill (02) pitcher: 2–4 with 3.67 ERA in eight games, six of them as starting pitcher.

Magee, Sherry (04–14) outfielder–first baseman–shortstop–second baseman–pinch-hitter: 1,647-

for-5,505, .299, in 1,520 games.

Mahaffey, Art (60–65) pitcher: 58–60 with 4.09 ERA in 173 games, 143 of them as starting pitcher.

Mahan, Art (40) first baseman: 133-for-544, .244, in 146 games (including one game as pitcher: 0–0 with 0.00 ERA, one inning pitched).

Maher, Frank (02) pinch-hitter: 0-for-1, .000, in one game.

Maher, Tom (02) outfielder: no batting record, one game.

Maharg, Bill (16) outfielder: 0-for-1, .000, in one game.

Main, Alex (18) pitcher: 2–2 with 4.63 ERA in eight games. Also known as Miles.

Malis, Cy (34) pitcher: 0–0 with 4.91 ERA in one game.

Malkmus, Bobby (60–62) shortstop–second baseman–third baseman–pinch-hitter: 108-for-480, .255, in 208 games.

Mallon, Les (31–32) first baseman–second baseman–shortstop–third baseman–pinch-hitter: 206-for-722, .285, in 225 games.

Malone, Chuck (90) pitcher: 1–0 with 3.68 ERA in seven games.

Mancuso, Gus (45) catcher: 35-for-176, .199 in 70 games.

Mangus, George (12) outfielder–pinch-hitter: 5-for-25, .200, in 10 games.

Marnie, Hal (40–42) second baseman–shortstop–third baseman–pinch-hitter: 49-for-222, .221, in 96 games. Also known as Harry.

Maroney, Jim (10) pitcher: 1–2 with 2.14 ERA in 12 games; one save.

Marsh, Tom (92) outfielder–pinch-hitter: 25-for-125, .200, in 42 games.

Marshall, Doc (04) catcher–pinch-hitter: 2-for-20, .100, in eight games.

Marshall, Rube (12–14) pitcher: 5–9 with 4.24 ERA in 43 games; two saves.

Martel, Marty (09) catcher–pinch-hitter: 11-for-41, .268, in 24 games. Also known as Leon.

Martin, Hersh (37–40) outfielder–pinch-hitter: 435-for-1,521, .286, in 405 games.

Martin, Jack (14) shortstop: 74-for-292, .253, in 83 games. Also known as John.

Martin, Jerry (74–78) outfielder–

pinch-runner–pinch-hitter–first baseman: 185-for-729, .254, in 444 games.

Martin, Renee (84) pitcher: 0–2 with 4.60 ERA in nine games.

Martinez, Carmelo (90) first baseman–outfielder–pinch-hitter: 48-for-198, .242, in 71 games.

Marty, Joe (39–41) outfielder–pinch-hitter: 327-for-1,231, .266, in 351 games (including one game as pitcher in 1939: 0–0 with 4.50 ERA in four innings pitched).

Mason, Hank (58, 60) pitcher: 0–0 with 10.13 ERA in four games, all relief.

Masters, Walt (37) pitcher: 0–0 with 36.00 ERA in one game, in relief.

Masterson, Paul (40–42) pitcher: 1–0 with 5.84 ERA in eight games.

Mathews, Greg (92) pitcher: 2–3 with 5.16 ERA in 14 games.

Matteson, Henry (14) pitcher: 3–2 with 3.10 ERA in 15 games.

Matthews, Gary (81–83) outfielder: 396-for-1,421, .279, in 395 games.

Matthewson, Dale (43–44) pitcher: 0–3 with 4.34 ERA in 28 games, all but two in relief.

Matuszek, Len (81–84) first baseman–pinch-hitter: 93-for-392, .237, in 167 games.

Maul, Al (00) pitcher: 2–3 with 6.16 ERA in five games, four of them as starting pitcher.

Maun, Ernie (26) pitcher: 1–4 with 6.45 ERA in 14 games.

Mauney, Dick (45–47) pitcher: 12–14 with 2.99 ERA in 53 games; four saves.

Mauser, Tim (91) pitcher: 0–0 with 7.59 ERA in three games.

May, Pinky (39–43) third baseman–shortstop (one game)–pinch-hitter: 610-for-2,215, .275, in 665 games.

Mayer, Erskine (12–18) pitcher: 76–61 with 2.81 ERA in 206 games, 140 as starting pitcher; five saves.

Mayes, Paddy (11) outfielder–pinch-hitter: 0-for-5, .000, in five games.

Mayo, Jackie (48–53) outfielder–first baseman–pinch-hitter: 51-for-240, .213, in 139 games.

Mazzera, Mel (40) outfielder–first baseman–pinch-hitter: 37-for-156, .237, in 69 games. Also known as Mike.

McAvoy, George (14) pinch-hitter: 0-for-1, .000, in one game.

McBride, Bake (77–81) outfielder–

Joe Marty

Harry McCurdy

pinch-hitter: 616-for-2,109, .292, in 553 games.

McCarver, Tim (70–72, 75–80) catcher–first baseman (one game)–pinch-hitter: 397-for-1,461, .272, in 628 games.

McCloskey, John (06–07) pitcher: 3–2 with 3.60 ERA in 12 games.

McCormack, Don (80–81) catcher: 2-for-5, .400, in five games.

McCormick, Frank (46–47) first baseman–pinch-hitter: 152-for-544, .279, in 150 games.

McCormick, Moose (08) outfielder–pinch-hitter: 2-for-22, .091, in 11 games.

McCurdy, Harry (30–33) catcher–pinch-hitter: 139-for-488, .285, in 281 games.

McDonough, Ed (09–10) catcher–pinch-hitter (one game): 1-for-10, .100, in six games.

McDowell, Roger (89–91) pitcher: 12–17 with 2.90 ERA in 154 games; 44 saves.

McElroy, Chuck (89–90) pitcher: 0–1 with 5.18 ERA in 27 games.

McFadden, Barney (02) pitcher: 0–1 with 8.00 ERA in one game started and completed.

McFarland, Ed (00–01) catcher–third baseman (one game)–pinch-hitter (one game): 189-for-639, .296, in 168 games.

McFetridge, John (03) pitcher: 1–11 with 4.91 ERA in 14 games, 13 as starting pitcher.

McGaffigan, Patsy (17–18) second baseman–shortstop–outfielder (one game): 49-for-252, .194, in 73 games.

McGraw, Bob (28–29) pitcher: 12–13 with 5.97 ERA in 80 games, all but seven as relief pitcher; five saves.

McGraw, Tug (75–84) pitcher: 49–37 with 3.10 ERA in 473 games; 94 saves.

McInnis, Stuffy (27) first baseman: no record as batter—playing manager, one game. Also known as John.

McKee, Rogers (43–44) pitcher: 1–0 with 5.87 ERA in five games.

McLaughlin, Warren (00, 03) pitcher: 0–2 with 6.52 ERA in four games, two of them as starting pitcher.

McLeod, Jim (33) third baseman–shortstop (one game): 45-for-232, .194, in 67 games. Also known as Soule.

McLish, Cal (62–64) pitcher: 24–17 with 3.68 ERA in 66 games, 57 of them as starting pitcher; one save.

McPherson, John (04) pitcher: 1–10 with 3.66 ERA in 15 games, 12 of them as starting pitcher.

McQuillan, George (07–10, 15–16) pitcher: 54–49 with 1.79 ERA in 149 games; seven saves.

McWilliams, Larry (89) pitcher: 2–11 with 4.10 ERA in 40 games.

Meadows, Lee (19–23) pitcher: 48–61 with 3.69 ERA in 122 games, 115 of them as starting pitcher; one save. Also known as Henry.

Meadows, Louie (90) outfielder–pinch-hitter: 1-for-14, .071, in 15 games.

Melendez, Francisco (84–86) first baseman–pinch-hitter: 5-for-31, .161, in 30 games.

Melton, Rube (41–42) pitcher: 10–25 with 3.99 ERA in 67 games, 34 of them as starting pitcher; four saves.

Meoli, Rudi (79) shortstop–second baseman–third baseman (one game)–pinch-hitter: 13-for-73, .178, in 30 games.

Metz, Len (23–25) shortstop–second baseman: 10-for-58, .172, in 30 games.

Meusel, Emil (18–21) outfielder–second baseman–first baseman–pinch-hitter: 572-for-1,855, .308, in 486 games. Also known as Irish.

Meyer, Benny (25) second baseman: 1-for-1, 1.000, in one game. His one hit was a double giving him slugging average of 2.000.

Meyer, Jack (55–61) pitcher: 24–34 with 3.92 ERA in 202 games, all but 24 as relief; 21 saves.

Meyer, Russ (49–52) pitcher: 47–52 with 3.64 ERA in 134 games, 109 games as starting pitcher; three saves. Also known as "The Mad Monk."

Micelotta, Bob (54–55) shortstop–pinch-hitter–pinch-runner: 0-for-7, .000, in 17 games. Also known as Mickey.

Milbourne, Larry (83) infielder: 16-for-66, .242, in 41 games.

Miller, Bob (42–58) pitcher: 42–42 with 3.96 ERA in 261 games; 15 saves.

Miller, Doc (12–13) outfielder–pinch-hitter: 81-for-264, .307, in 136 games. Also known as Roy.

Miller, Dots (20–21) second baseman–third baseman–shortstop–first baseman–outfielder (one game)–pinch-hitter: 182-for-663, .274, in 182 games. Also known as John.

Miller, Eddie (48–49) shortstop–second baseman–pinch-hitter: 170-for-734, .232, in 215 games.

Miller, Elmer (29) pitcher–outfielder–pinch-hitter: 9-for-38, .237, in 31 games; his record as a pitcher is 0–1 with 11.12 ERA in eight games.

Miller, Hugh (11) pinch-hitter: no record as batter, one game.

Miller, Keith (88–89) outfielder–third baseman–pinch-hitter: 11-for-58, .190, in 55 games.

Miller, Ralph (20–21) third baseman–shortstop–first baseman–outfielder (one game)–pinch-hitter: 136-for-542, .251, in 154 games.

Miller, Red (23) pitcher: 0–0 with 32.40 ERA in one game, relief. Also known as Leo.

Miller, Russ (27–28) pitcher: 1–13 with 5.40 ERA in 35 games; one save.

Miller, Stu (56) pitcher: 5–8 with 4.46 ERA in 24 games, 15 of them as starting pitcher.

Millette, Joe (92) shortstop: 16-for-78, .205, in 33 games.

Millies, Wally (39–41) catcher–pinch-hitter: 51-for-250, .204, in 111 games.

Milligan, John (28–31) pitcher: 3–8 with 5.05 ERA in 33 games.

Milnar, Al (46) pitcher: 0–0 with 108.00 ERA in one game.

Mitchell, Clarence (23–28) pitcher: 40–57 with 4.98 ERA in 135 games, 108 of them as starting pitcher; three saves.

Mitchell, Fred (03–04) pitcher: 14–22 with 4.13 ERA in 41 games, all as starting pitcher.

Mokan, Johnny (22–27) outfielder–third baseman–pinch-hitter: 526-for-1,795, .293, in 532 games.

Molinaro, Bob (82–83) outfielder–pinch-hitter: 6-for-32, .188, in 38 games.

Mollenkamp, Fred (14) first baseman: 1-for-8, .125, in three games.

Monchak, Al (40) shortstop–second baseman (one game)–pinch-hitter: 2-for-14, .143, in 19 games.

Money, Don (68–72) shortstop–third baseman–outfielder–second baseman: 455-for-1,885, .241, in 524 games.

Monge, Sid (82–83) pitcher: 10–1 with 4.18 ERA in 61 games.

Monroe, John (21) second baseman–third baseman: 38-for-133, .286, in 41 games.

Montague, John (75) pitcher: 0–0 with 9.00 ERA in three games, all relief.

Montanez, Willie (70–75, 82) first baseman–outfielder–pinch-hitter: 620-for-2,334, .266, in 651 games.

Monteagudo, Rene (45) outfielder–pinch-hitter–pitcher: 58-for-193, .301, in 114 games; he had 18 pinch-hits during season in 52 pinch-hit appearances for a .346 average; his record as pitcher, 0–0 with 7.49 ERA in 14 games, all relief.

Moore, Brad (88–90) pitcher: 0–0 with 1.08 ERA in eight games.

Moore, Chief (34–35, 36) pitcher: 8–16 with 5.48 ERA in 55 games; three saves. Also known as Euel.

Moore, Cy (33–34) pitcher: 12–18 with 4.94 ERA in 71 games; one save.

Moore, Dee (43, 46) catcher–outfielder–third baseman–first baseman–pinch-hitter: 28-for-126, .222, in 48 games.

Moore, Earl (08–13) pitcher: 67–64 with 2.64 ERA in 172 games; two saves.

Moore, Johnny (34–37) outfielder–pinch-hitter: 604-for-1,837, .329, in 489 games.

Moran, Pat (10–14) catcher–pinch-hitter: 69-for-329, .210, in 117 games.

Morandini, Mickey (90–   ) second baseman–pinch-hitter: current Phillies player.

Morehead, Seth (57–59) pitcher: 2–9 with 5.31 ERA in 64 games, all but 12 in relief; one save.

Moreland, Keith (78–81) catcher–third baseman–outfielder–first baseman–pinch-hitter: 118-for-405, .291, in 138 games.

Moren, Lew (07–10) pitcher: 48–56 with 2.88 ERA in 139 games, 104 of them as starting pitcher; three saves.

Morgan, Bobby (54–56, 57) shortstop–third baseman–second baseman–pinch-hitter: 236-for-963, .245, in 281 games.

Morgan, Joe (60) third baseman–

Eddie Miller

Bert Niehoff

Joe Oeschger

pinch-hitter: 11-for-83, .133, in 26 games.

Morgan, Joe (83) second baseman: 93-for-404, .230, in 123 games. Elected to Hall of Fame in 1990.

Morris, John (66) pitcher: 1–1 with 5.27 ERA in 13 games, all relief.

Morris, John (91) outfielder–pinch-hitter: 28-for-127, .220, in 85 games.

Morrison, Jim (77–78) second baseman–third baseman–outfielder (one game)–pinch-hitter: 20-for-115, .174, in 58 games.

Moser, Walt (06) pitcher: 0–4 with 3.59 ERA in six games, four of them as starting pitcher.

Mott, Bitsy (45) shortstop–second baseman–third baseman: 64-for-289, .221, in 90 games.

Mrozinski, Ron (54–55) pitcher: 1–3 with 5.36 ERA in 37 games, all but five in relief; one save.

Mueller, Emmett (38–41) second baseman–third baseman–outfielder–first baseman (two games)–shortstop (one game)–pinch-hitter: 324-for-1,281, .253, in 441 games.

Mulcahy, Hugh (35–40, 45–46) pitcher: 45–89 with 4.49 ERA in 218 games; nine saves. Also known as Losing Pitcher.

Mulholland, Terry (89–   ) pitcher: current Phillies player.

Mullen, Moon (44) second baseman–third baseman (one game)–catcher (one game)–pinch-hitter: 124-for- 464, .267, in 118 games. Also known as Ford.

Mulligan, Dick (46) pitcher: 2–2 with 4.75 ERA in 19 games; one save.

Muniz, Manny (71) pitcher: 0–1 with 7.20 ERA in five games; all relief.

Munninghoff, Scott (80) pitcher: 0–0 with 4.50 ERA in four games, all relief.

Munson, Red (05) catcher–pinch-hitter (one game): 3-for-26, .115, in nine games.

Murphy, Dale (90–   ) outfielder–pinch-hitter: current Phillies player.

Murphy, Dwayne (89) outfielder–pinch-hitter: 34-for-156, .218, in 98 games.

Murphy, Ed (42) first baseman–pinch-hitter: 7-for-28, .250, in 13 games.

Murphy, Herb (14) shortstop: 4-for-26, .154, in nine games. Also known as Dummy.

Murphy, Morgan (00) catcher: 10-for-36, .278, in 11 games.

Murray, Pat (19) pitcher: 0–2 with 6.29 ERA in eight games.

Murtaugh, Danny (41–43, 46) second baseman–shortstop–third baseman: 325-for-1,323, .246, in 348 games.

Mussill, Barney (44) pitcher: 0–1 with 6.05 ERA in 16 games, all relief.

Myers, Bert (00) third baseman: 5-for-28, .179, in seven games.

N

Nagel, Bill (41) second baseman–outfielder–third baseman (one game)–pinch-hitter: 8-for-56, .143, in 17 games.

Nahem, Sam (42, 48) pitcher: 4–6 with 5.86 ERA in 63 games.

Nahorodny, Bill (76) catcher–pinch-hitter: 1-for-5, .200, in three games.

Nash, Jim (72) pitcher: 0–8 with 6.32 ERA in nine games, eight as starting pitcher.

Naylor, Earl (42–43) outfielder–pitcher–first baseman (one game)–pinch-hitter: 54-for-288, .188, in 109 games; in 1942 he appeared in 20 games as a pitcher, 0–5 with 6.12 ERA, four games as a starting pitcher.

Neale, Greasy (21) outfielder: 12-for-57, .211, in 22 games. He was coach of Philadelphia Eagles from 1941 to 1950 and was elected to Pro Football Hall of Fame in 1969.

Neeman, Cal (60–61) catcher–pinch-hitter: 36-for-191, .188, in 78 games.

Negray, Ron (55–56) pitcher: 6–6 with 3.84 ERA in 58 games; three saves.

Neibauer, Gary (72) pitcher: 0–2 with 5.21 ERA in nine games.

Neiger, Al (60) pitcher: 0–0 with 5.68 ERA in six games, all relief.

Nelson, Red (12–13) pitcher: 2–0 with 3.33 ERA in six games.

Newell, Tom (87) pitcher: 0–0 with 36.00 ERA in two games.

Newsome, Skeeter (46–47) shortstop–second baseman–third baseman–pinch-hitter: 158-for-685, .231, in 207 games.

Niarhos, Gus (54–55) catcher: 2-for-14, .143, in 10 games.

Nichols, Chet (30–32) pitcher: 1–5 with 7.01 ERA in 30 games; one save. His son had nine-year major league career in 1950s and 1960s.

Nichols, Kid (05–06) pitcher: 10–7 with 2.82 ERA in 21 games, 18 of them as starting pitcher. Elected to Hall of Fame in 1949. Also known as Charles.

Nicholson, Bill (49–53) outfielder–pinch-hitter: 161-for-677, .238, in 317 games. Also known as "Swish."

Nicholson, Frank (12) pitcher: 0–0 with 6.75 ERA in two games, both relief.

Niehoff, Bert (15–17) second baseman–first baseman–third baseman–pinch-hitter: 351-for-1,438, .244, in 408 games.

Nieto, Tom (89–90) catcher–pinch-hitter: 8-for-50, .160, in 28 games.

Nixon, Al (26–28) outfielder–pinch-hitter: 154-for-529, .291, in 172 games.

Noles, Dickie (79–81, 90) pitcher: 6–10 with 4.01 ERA in 76 games; six saves.

Norris, Leo (36–37) shortstop–second baseman–third baseman–pinch-hitter: 252-for-962, .262, in 270 games.

Northey, Ron (42–44, 46–47, 57) outfielder–pinch-hitter: 556-for-2,069, .269, in 600 games.

Novikoff, Lou (46) outfielder–pinch-hitter: 7-for-23, .304, in 17 games.

O

Oana, Prince (34) outfielder–pinch-hitter: 5-for-21, .238, in six games.

Oates, John (75–76) catcher–pinch-hitter: 102-for-368, .277, in 127 games.

O'Brien, Mickey (23) catcher–pinch-hitter: 7-for-21, .333, in 15 games. Also known as Frank.

O'Donnell, Harry (27) catcher–pinch-hitter: 1-for-16, .063, in 16 games.

O'Doul, Lefty (29–30) outfielder–pinch-hitter: 456-for-1,166, .391, in 294 games; hit .398 in 1929 and .383 in 1930.

Oeschger, Joe (14–19, 24) pitcher: 30–48 with 3.21 ERA in 148 games, 76 of them as starting pitcher; four saves.

Oldis, Bob (62–63) catcher–pinch-hitter: 40-for-165, .242, in 85 games.

Oliver, Al (84) first baseman–outfielder–pinch-hitter: 29-for-93, .312, in 28 games.

Oliver, Gene (67) catcher–first baseman–pinch-hitter: 59-for-263, .224, in 85 games.

O'Neal, Skinny (25, 27) pitcher: 0–0 with 9.24 ERA in 13 games. Also known as Oran.

O'Neal, Randy (89) pitcher: 0–1 with 6.23 ERA in 20 games.

O'Neil, John (46) shortstop–pinch-hitter: 25-for-94, .266, in 46 games.

O'Rourke, Joe (29) pinch-hitter: 0-for-3, .000, in three games.

Orth, Al (00–01) pitcher–outfielder (seven games)–pinch-hitter (five official at-bats): record as pitcher 32–35 with 2.97 ERA in 68 games, 63 of them as starting pitcher, one save; record as hitter 76-for-257, .296, in 80 games.

Osborn, Fred (07–09) outfielder–first baseman (one game)–pinch-hitter: 228-for-907, .251, in 266 games. Also known as Wilfred.

Owens, Jim (55–56, 58–62) pitcher: 24–46 with 4.54 ERA in 119 games, 89 of them as starting pitcher; one save.

P

Packard, Gene (19) pitcher: 6–8 with 4.15 ERA in 21 games, 16 of them as starting pitcher; one save.

Padden, Tom (43) catcher–pinch-hitter (one game): 12-for-41, .293, in 17 games.

Padgett, Don (47–48) catcher–pinch-hitter: 67-for-232, .289, in 111 games.

Pagan, Jose (73) third baseman–first baseman–outfielder–second baseman (one game)–pinch-hitter: 16-for-78, .205, in 46 games.

Palmer, Dave (88) pitcher: 7–9 with 4.47 ERA in 22 games.

Palmer, Lowell (69–71) pitcher: 3–10 with 5.39 ERA in 67 games.

Palys, Stan (53–55) outfielder–pinch-hitter: 6-for-58, .276, in 19 games.

Pardo, Al (88–89) catcher: 0-for-3, .000, in three games.

Parker, Dixie (23) catcher: 1-for-5, .200, in four games.

Parkinson, Frank (21–24) second baseman–shortstop–third baseman–pinch-hitter: 335-for-1,311, .256, in 378 games.

Jim Owens

Frank Parkinson

Johnny Podgajny

Parrett, Jeff (89–90) pitcher: 16–15 with 3.94 ERA in 119 games; seven saves.

Parrilla, Sam (70) outfielder–pinch-hitter: 2-for-16, .125, in 11 games.

Parrish, Lance (87–88) catcher–pinch-hitter: 205-for-890, .230, in 253 games.

Paskert, Dode (11–17) outfielder–shortstop–second baseman–first baseman–third baseman (one game)–pinch-hitter: 933-for-3,434, .272, in 953 games. Also known as George.

Pasquariello, Mike (19) first baseman: 1-for-1, 1.000, in one game.

Passeau, Claude (36–39) pitcher: 38–55 with 4.13 ERA in 151 games, 96 of them as starting pitcher; six saves.

Paulette, Gene (19–20) second baseman–outfielder–first baseman–shortstop–pinch-hitter: 225-for-805, .279, in 210 games.

Peacock, Johnny (44–45) catcher–first baseman (one game)–pinch-hitter: 72-for-327, .220, in 116 games.

Pearce, Frank (33–35) pitcher: 5–6 with 4.77 ERA in 32 games.

Pearce, Harry (17–19) second baseman–shortstop–third baseman–first baseman (one game)–pinch-hitter: 88-for-424, .208, in 135 games.

Pearson, Ike (39–42, 46) pitcher: 11–47 with 4.82 ERA in 141 games; seven saves.

Peel, Homer (29) outfielder–first baseman (one game)–pinch-hitter: 42-for-156, .269, in 53 games.

Peguero, Julio (92) outfielder: 2-for-9, .222, in 14 games.

Pellagrini, Eddie (51) second baseman–shortstop–third baseman–pinch-hitter: 46-for-197, .234, in 86 games.

Pena, Roberto (68) shortstop–pinch-hitter: 130-for-500, .260, in 138 games.

Penson, Paul (54) pitcher: 1–1 with 4.50 ERA in five games, three of them as starting pitcher.

Peraza, Luis (69) pitcher: 0–0 with 6.00 ERA in eight games, all in relief.

Perez, Tony (83) first baseman–pinch-hitter: 61-for-253, .241, in 91 games.

Peterman, Bill (42) catcher: 1-for-1, 1.000, in one game.

Peters, John (21–22) catcher–pinch-hitter: 80-for-298, .268, in 110 games.

Peterson, Kent (52–53) pitcher: 0–1 with 5.29 ERA in 18 games; two saves.

Pettit, Lefty (37) pitcher: 0–1 with 11.25 ERA in three games. Also known as Leon.

Pezzullo, John (35–36) pitcher: 3–5 with 6.36 ERA in 42 games; one save. Also known as Pretzels.

Pfeil, Bobby (71) catcher–outfielder–pinch-hitter–shortstop (one game)–second baseman (one game)–first baseman (one game): 19-for-70, .271, in 44 games.

Philley, Dave (58–60) outfielder–first baseman–pinch-hitter: 143-for-476, .300, in 204 games.

Phillips, Adolfo (64–66) outfielder–pinch-hitter: 23-for-103, .223, in 56 games.

Phillips, Buz (30) pitcher: 0–0 with 5.61 ERA in 14 games, all but one as relief pitcher.

Phillips, Taylor (59–60) pitcher: 1–5 with 5.61 ERA in 42 games, all but four as relief pitcher; one save.

Piatt, Wiley (00) pitcher: 9–10 with 4.65 ERA in 22 games, 20 of them as starting pitcher.

Picciuto, Nick (45) third baseman–second baseman–pinch-hitter: 12-for-89, .135, in 36 games.

Pickrel, Clarence (33) pitcher: 1–0 with 3.95 ERA in nine games, all relief.

Pickup, Ty (18) outfielder: 1-for-1, 1.000, in one game. Also known as Clarence.

Pierce, Ray (25–26) pitcher: 7–11 with 5.56 ERA in 60 games.

Pillette, Duane (56) pitcher: 0–0 with 6.56 ERA in 20 games, all relief. His father had four-year major league career as pitcher.

Pina, Horacio (78) pitcher: 0–0 with 0.00 ERA in two games, both in relief.

Pinto, Lerton (22, 24) pitcher: 0–1 with 5.65 ERA in 12 games, all relief. Also known as Bill.

Pitko, Alex (38) outfielder: 6-for-19, .316, in seven games.

Pittinger, Togie (05–07) pitcher: 40–29 with 3.15 ERA in 82 games, 65 of them as starting pitcher; two saves. Also known as Charlie.

Podgajny, Johnny (40–43) pitcher:

20–33 with 3.91 ERA in 94 games, 56 of them as starting pitcher.

Poff, John (79) outfielder–first baseman (one game)–pinch-hitter: 2-for-19, .105, in 12 games.

Poindexter, Jennings (39) pitcher: 0–0 with 4.15 ERA in 11 games, all but one as relief pitcher. Also known as Chester.

Poland, Hugh (47) catcher–pinch-hitter: 0-for-8, .000, in four games.

Porto, Al (48) pitcher: 0–0 with 0.00 ERA in three games, all relief.

Possehl, Lou (46–48, 51–52) pitcher: 2–5 with 5.26 ERA in 15 games, eight of them as starting pitcher.

Post, Wally (58–60) outfielder–pinch-hitter: 250-for-931, .269, in 276 games.

Powell, Jake (45) outfielder–pinch-hitter: 40-for-173, .231, in 48 games.

Power, Vic (64) first baseman–pinch-hitter: 10-for-48, .208, in 18 games.

Powers, Les (39) pinch-hitter: 0-for-3, .000, in three games.

Pratt, Todd (92–   ) catcher–pinch-hitter: current Phillies player.

Prendergast, Mike (18–19) pitcher: 13–15 with 3.20 ERA in 38 games, 30 of them as starting pitcher; one save.

Prim, Ray (35) pitcher: 3–4 with 5.77 ERA in 29 games.

Proly, Mike (81) pitcher: 2–1 with 3.86 ERA in 35 games, all but two in relief; two saves.

Pruett, Hubert (27–28) pitcher: 9–21 with 5.63 ERA in 44 games, 37 of them as starting pitcher; one save.

Puckett, Troy (11) pitcher: 0–0 with 13.50 ERA in one game, in relief.

Purnell, Jesse (04) third baseman: 2-for-19, .105, in seven games.

Q

Qualters, Tom (53, 57–58) pitcher: 0–0 with 14.00 ERA in eight games, all relief.

Quinn, John (11) catcher: 0-for-2, .000, in one game.

R

Rader, Dave (79) catcher–pinch-hitter: 11-for-54, .204, in 31 games.

Rader, Don (21) shortstop: 9-for-32, .281, in nine games.

Raffensberger, Ken (43–47) pitcher: 23–45 with 3.49 ERA in 92 games, 66 of them as starting pitcher; six saves.

Raffo, Al (69) pitcher: 1–3 with 4.13 ERA in 45 games, all relief.

Ragan, Pat (23) pitcher: 0–0 with 6.00 ERA in one game, all relief.

Ragland, Frank (33) pitcher: 0–4 with 6.81 ERA in 11 games.

Rambo, Pete (26) pitcher: 0–0 with 14.73 ERA in one game, in relief. Also known as Warren.

Ramos, Pedro (67) pitcher: 0–0 with 9.00 ERA in six games, all relief.

Rapp, Goldie (21–23) third baseman–shortstop–second baseman (one game)–pinch-hitter: 230-for-883, .260, in 218 games. Also known as Joseph.

Rawley, Shane (84–88) pitcher: 59–48 with 3.88 ERA in 145 games.

Rawlings, Red (20–21) second baseman–pinch-hitter (one game): 164-for-638, .257, in 158 games. Also known as Johnny.

Raymond, Lou (19) second baseman: 1-for-2, .500, in one game.

Ready, Randy (89–91) second baseman–third baseman–outfielder: 154-for-609, .253, in 249 games.

Reams, Leroy (69) pinch-hitter: 0-for-1, .000, in one game.

Rebel, Art (38) outfielder–pinch-hitter: 2-for-9, .222, in seven games.

Redus, Gary (86) outfielder–pinch-hitter: 84-for-340, .247, in 90 games.

Reed, Jerry (81–82) pitcher: 1–1 with 5.91 ERA in 11 games, all relief.

Reed, Milt (13–14) shortstop–second baseman–third baseman (one game)–pinch-hitter: 28-for-131, .214, in 57 games.

Reed, Ron (76–83) pitcher: 57–38 with 3.06 ERA in 458 games.

Reid, Scott (69–70) outfielder–pinch-hitter: 10-for-68, .147, in 38 games.

Reis, Tommy (38) pitcher: 0–1 with 18.00 ERA in four games, all relief.

Rementer, Butch (04) catcher: 0-for-2, .000, in one game. Also known as Willis.

Rensa, Tony (30–31) catcher–pinch-hitter: 52-for-201, .259, in 73 games.

Repulski, Rip (57–58) outfielder–pinch-hitter: 192-for-754, .255, in 219 games.

Reynolds, Ken (70–72) pitcher: 7–24 with 4.35 ERA in 72 games, 48 of them as starting pitcher.

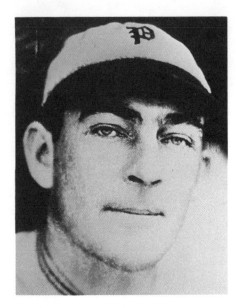

Flint Rhem

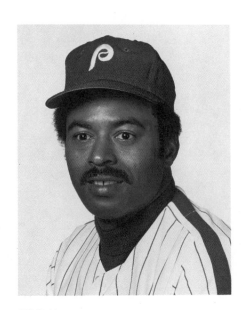

Bill Robinson

Reynolds, Ronn (86) catcher–pinch-hitter: 27-for-126, .214, in 43 games.

Rhem, Flint (32–33) pitcher: 16–21 with 4.94 ERA in 54 games, 39 of them as starting pitcher; three saves.

Rice, Bob (26) third baseman–shortstop–second baseman: 8-for-54, .148, in 19 games.

Richardson, Ken (46) second baseman: 3-for-20, .150, in six games.

Richbourg, Lance (21) second baseman–pinch-hitter: 1-for-5, .200, in 10 games.

Richert, Pete (74) pitcher: 2–1 with 2.25 ERA in 21 games, all relief.

Richie, Lew (06–09) pitcher: 22–28 with 2.05 ERA in 94 games, 50 of them as a starting pitcher; two saves.

Ridzik, Steve (50, 52–55, 66) pitcher: 17–14 with 3.64 ERA in 107 games.

Riley, Lee (44) outfielder–pinch-hitter (one game): 1-for-12, .083, in four games.

Ring, Jimmy (21–25, 28) pitcher: 68–98 with 4.43 ERA in 218 games, 192 of them as starting pitcher; three saves.

Ripple, Charlie (44–46) pitcher: 1–1 with 9.45 ERA in 11 games, all but one in relief.

Ritchie, Wally (87–89, 91–   ) pitcher: current Phillies player.

Ritter, Hank (12) pitcher: 0–0 with 4.50 ERA in three games, all relief.

Rivera, Ben (92–   ) pitcher: current Phillies player.

Rixey, Eppa (12–17, 19–20) pitcher: 87–103 wih 2.83 ERA in 252 games, 196 of them as starting pitcher; six saves. Elected to Hall of Fame in 1963.

Rizzo, Johnny (40–41) outfielder–third baseman–pinch-hitter: 158-for-602, .262, in 202 games.

Roach, Mel (62) third baseman–second baseman–first baseman–outfielder–pinch-hitter: 20-for-105, .190, in 65 games.

Roberts, Dave (82) catcher–second baseman–third baseman: 6-for-33, .182, in 33 games.

Roberts, Robin (48–61) pitcher: 234–199 with 3.46 ERA in 529 games, 472 of them as starting pitcher; 24 saves. Elected to Hall of Fame in 1976.

Robinson, Bill (72–74, 82–83) out-

fielder: 260-for-996, .261, in 351 games.

Robinson, Craig (72–73) shortstop–second baseman–pinch-hitter: 36-for-161, .224, in 51 games.

Robinson, Don (92) pitcher–pinch-hitter: 1–4 with 6.18 ERA in eight games as pitcher; 0-for-2 as pinch-hitter.

Robinson, Humberto (59–60) pitcher: 2–8 with 3.37 ERA in 64 games, all but five as relief pitcher; one save.

Rodriguez, Pedro (59) pitcher: 0–0 with 13.50 ERA in one game, in relief. Also known as Freddy.

Roebuck, Ed (64–66) pitcher: 10–8 with 2.84 ERA in 110 games, all in relief; 15 saves.

Roenicke, Ron (86–87) outfielder–pinch-hitter: 81-for-353, .229, in 165 games.

Rogodzinski, Mike (73–75) outfielder–pinch-hitter: 25-for-114, .219, in 99 games; record as pinch-hitter was 21-for-73.

Rogovin, Saul (55–57) pitcher: 12–9 with 4.41 ERA in 38 games, 29 of them as starting pitcher.

Rojas, Cookie (63–69) second baseman–outfielder–shortstop–third baseman–catcher–first baseman (one game)–pitcher (one game)–pinch-hitter: 812-for-3,104, .262, in 880 games; pitched one game in 1967, 0–0 with 0.00 ERA.

Rose, Pete (79–83) first baseman–outfielder: 826-for-2,841, .291, in 745 games.

Ross, Bob (56) pitcher: 0–0 with 8.10 ERA in three games, all relief.

Roth, Frank (03–04) catcher–pinch-hitter–third baseman (one game)–second baseman (one game)–first baseman (one game): 119-for-449, .265, in 149 games.

Rowan, Jack (11) pitcher: 3–4 with 4.70 ERA in 12 games, six of them as starting pitcher.

Rowe, Schoolboy (43, 46–49) pitcher: 52–39 with 3.12 ERA in 128 games, 95 of them as starting pitcher; four saves; pinch-hitter record 19-for-74, .257.

Rowell, Bama (48) third baseman–outfielder–second baseman–pinch-hitter: 47-for-196, .240, in 77 games.

Roy, Charlie (06) pitcher: 0–1 with 4.91 ERA in seven games, all but one as relief pitcher.

Roy, Luther (29) pitcher: 3–6 with 8.39 ERA in 21 games, 12 of them as starting pitcher.

Roznovsky, Vic (69) catcher–pinch-hitter: 3-for-13, .231, in 13 games.

Ruble, Art (34) outfielder–pinch-hitter: 15-for-54, .278, in 19 games. Also known as Bill.

Rucker, Dave (85–86) pitcher: 3–4 with 4.50 ERA in 58 games; one save.

Rudolph, Dutch (03) pinch-hitter: 0-for-1, .000, in one game. Also known as John.

Ruffin, Bruce (86–91) pitcher: 42–59 with 4.16 ERA in 198 games; three saves.

Russell, John (83–88) catcher–outfielder–pinch-hitter: 172-for-741, .232, in 259 games.

Ruthven, Dick (73–75, 78–83) pitcher: 78–65 with 4.00 ERA in 207 games.

Ryal, Mark (89) outfielder–pinch-hitter: 8-for-33, .242, in 29 games.

Ryan, Blondy (35) shortstop–second baseman (one game)–third baseman (one game)–pinch-hitter: 34-for-129, .264, in 39 games. Also known as John.

Ryan, Connie (52–53) second baseman–first baseman–pinch-hitter: 212-for-824, .257, in 244 games.

Ryan, Mike (68–73) catcher–pinch-hitter: 225-for-1,185, .190, in 392 games.

S

Sadowski, Bob (61) third baseman–pinch-hitter: 7-for-54, .130, in 16 games.

Salisbury, Bill (02) pitcher: 0–0 with 13.50 ERA in two games.

Salvo, Manny (43) pitcher: 0–0 with 27.00 ERA in one game, in relief.

Samuel, Juan (83–89) second baseman–outfielder–pinch-hitter: 921-for-3,503, .263, in 852 games.

Sanchez, Alejandro (82–83) outfielder–pinch-hitter: 6-for-21, .286, in 15 games.

Sand, Heinie (23–28) shortstop–third baseman–pinch-hitter: 781-for-3,033, .258, in 848 games.

Sandberg, Ryne (81) shortstop– second baseman (one game): 1-for-6, .167, in 13 games.

Sanford, Jack (56–58) pitcher: 30–21 with 3.61 ERA in 74 games, 61 of them as starting pitcher.

Sanicki, Ed (49, 51) outfielder–

pinch-hitter: 5-for-17, .294, in 20 games.

Saucier, Kevin (78–80) pitcher: 8–8 with 4.11 ERA in 70 games, all but two in relief; one save.

Savage, Hal (12) second baseman: 0-for-3, .000, in two games.

Savage, Ted (62) outfielder–pinch-hitter: 89-for-335, .266, in 127 games.

Sawatski, Carl (58–59) catcher–pinch-hitter: 100-for-381, .262, in 134 games.

Scanlan, Frank (09) pitcher: 0–0 with 1.64 ERA in six games, all relief; one save.

Scarce, Mac (72–74) pitcher: 5–18 with 3.65 ERA in 141 games, all relief; 21 saves.

Scarritt, Russ (32) outfielder–pinch-hitter: 2-for-11, .182, in 11 games.

Scarsone, Steve (92) second baseman: 2-for-13, .154, in seven games.

Schaffer, Jimmy (66–67) catcher–pinch-hitter: 2-for-17, .118, in 20 games.

Schanz, Charley (44–47) pitcher: 25–41 with 4.19 ERA in 141 games, 72 of them as starting pitcher; 14 saves.

Scharein, George (37–40) shortstop–second baseman–third baseman (one game)–pinch-hitter: 316-for-1,317, .240, in 388 games.

Schatzeder, Dan (86–87) pitcher: 6–4 with 3.76 ERA in 51 games; two saves.

Schell, Danny (54–55) outfielder–pinch-hitter: 77-for-274, .281, in 94 games.

Scherrer, Bill (88) pitcher: 0–0 with 5.40 ERA in eight games.

Schesler, Dutch (31) pitcher: 0–0 with 7.28 ERA in 17 games, all relief.

Schettler, Lou (10) pitcher: 2–6 with 3.20 ERA in 27 games; one save.

Schilling, Curt (92–   ) pitcher: current Phillies player.

Schmidt, Freddy (47) pitcher: 5–8 with 4.68 ERA in 29 games.

Schmidt, Mike (72–89) third baseman–first baseman–second baseman–shortstop–pinch-hitter: 2,234-for-8,352, .267, in 2,404 games. National League MVP 1980, 1981, 1986.

Schott, Gene (39) pitcher: 0–1 with 4.91 ERA in four games, all relief.

Schroll, Al (59) pitcher: 1–1 with

Mike Ryan

Dick Selma

Ray Semproch

9.00 ERA in three games, all relief.

Schu, Rick (84–87, 91) third baseman–first baseman–pinch-hitter: 212-for-871, .243, in 330 games.

Schueler, Ron (74–76) pitcher: 16–20 with 4.01 ERA in 125 games; four saves.

Schulmerich, Wes (33–34) outfielder–pinch-hitter: 135-for-417, .324, in 112 games.

Schulte, Wildfire (17) outfielder–pinch-hitter: 32-for-149, .215, in 64 games. Also known as Frank.

Schulte, Ham (40) second baseman–shortstop (one game)–pinch-hitter (one game): 103-for-436, .236, in 120 games. Also known as Herman.

Schulte, John (28) catcher–pinch-hitter: 28-for-113, .248, in 65 games.

Schultz, Howie (47–48) first baseman–pinch-hitter: 91-for-416, .219, in 120 games.

Schultz, Joe (24–25) outfielder–pinch-hitter: 102-for-348, .293, in 112 games.

Scott, Jack (27) pitcher–pinch-hitter: 9–21 with 5.09 ERA in 48 games, 25 of them as starting pitcher; one save; record as pinch-hitter was 7-for-28, .250.

Scott, Lefty (45) pitcher: 0–2 with 4.43 ERA in eight games, all but two relief. Also known as Marshall.

Scott, LeGrant (39) outfielder–pinch-hitter: 65-for-232, .280, in 76 games.

Searcy, Steve (91–92) pitcher: 2–1 with 4.65 ERA in 28 games.

Seaton, Tom (12–13) pitcher: 43–24 with 2.90 ERA in 96 games, 62 of them as starting pitcher; three saves.

Sebra, Bob (88–89) pitcher: 3–5 with 5.32 ERA in nine games.

Sedgwick, Duke (21) pitcher: 1–3 with 4.92 ERA in 16 games.

Selma, Dick (70–73) pitcher: 11–21 with 3.93 ERA in 142 games, all but 10 in relief; 26 saves.

Seminick, Andy (43–51, 55–57) catcher–outfielder–third baseman–pinch-hitter: 716-for-2,936, .244, in 985 games.

Semproch, Ray (58–59) pitcher: 16–21 with 4.44 ERA in 66 games, 48 of them as starting pitcher; three saves.

Sentelle, Paul (06–07) third base-

man–second baseman–outfielder–shortstop–pinch-hitter: 44-for-195, .226, in 66 games.

Seoane, Manny (77) pitcher: 0–0 with 6.00 ERA in two games, one as starting pitcher.

Service, Scott (88) pitcher: 0–0 with 1.69 ERA in five games.

Shantz, Bobby (64) pitcher: 1–1 with 2.25 ERA in 14 games, all relief.

Shea, Merv (44) catcher–pinch-hitter (one game): 4-for-15, .267 in seven games.

Shea, Nap (02) catcher: 1-for-8, .125, in three games.

Shean, Dave (08–09) shortstop–second baseman–first baseman–outfielder–pinch-hitter: 33-for-160, .206, in 50 games.

Sheerin, Charley (36) second baseman–third baseman–shortstop–pinch-hitter: 19-for-72, .264, in 39 games.

Shepherd, Keith (92) pitcher: 1–1 with 3.27 ERA in 12 games; two saves.

Sherlock, Monk (30) first baseman–second baseman–outfielder–pinch-hitter: 97-for-299, .324, in 92 games. Also known as John.

Shields, Ben (31) pitcher: 1–0 with 15.19 ERA in four games, all relief.

Shilling, Jim (39) second baseman–shortstop–third baseman: 10-for-33, .303, in 11 games.

Shipanoff, Dave (85) pitcher: 1–2 with 3.22 in 26 games; three saves.

Shockley, Costen (64) first baseman–pinch-hitter: 8-for-35, .229, in 11 games.

Short, Chris (59–72) pitcher: 132–127 with 3.38 ERA in 459 games, 301 as starting pitcher; 16 saves.

Shultz, Wallace (11–12) pitcher: 1–7 with 6.00 ERA in 27 games, all but seven in relief; one save.

Shuman, Harry (44) pitcher: 0–0 with 4.05 ERA in 18 games, all relief.

Sicking, Eddie (19) shortstop–second baseman–pinch-hitter: 40-for-185, .216, in 61 games.

Sievers, Roy (62–64) first baseman–outfielder–pinch-hitter: 255-for-1,047, .244, in 331 games.

Sigman, Tripp (29–30) outfielder–pinch-hitter: 42-for-129, .326, in 62 games.

Silvestri, Ken (49–51) catcher–shortstop (one game)–second baseman (one game)–pinch-hitter: 7-for-33, .212, in 19 games. Also known as Hawk.

Simmons, Curt (47–50, 52–60) pitcher: 115–110 with 3.66 ERA in 325 games, 262 of them as starting pitcher; four saves.

Simpson, Wayne (75) pitcher: 1–0 with 3.19 ERA in seven games, five as starting pitcher.

Singleton, John (22) pitcher: 1–10 with 5.90 ERA in 22 games. Also known as Sheriff.

Sisler, Dick (48–51) first baseman–outfielder–pinch-hitter: 519-for-1,809, .287, in 508 games. His father George Sisler is in Hall of Fame, and his brother Dave had seven-year career in major leagues as pitcher.

Sivess, Pete (36–38) pitcher: 7–11 with 5.46 ERA in 62 games; three saves.

Sizemore, Ted (77–78) second baseman–pinch-hitter: 223-for-870, .256, in 260 games.

Slagle, Jimmy (00–01) outfielder: 202-for-757, .267, in 189 games. Also known as Rabbit.

Slaughter, Barney (10) pitcher: 0–0 with 5.50 ERA in eight games, all but one as relief pitcher; one save.

Smalley, Roy (55–58) shortstop–third baseman (one game)–second baseman (one game)–pinch-hitter: 94-for-461, .204, in 186 games. Father of former major league player of same name.

Smith, Al (38–39) pitcher: 1–4 with 6.06 ERA in 42 games, all but one as relief pitcher; one save.

Smith, Bill (62) pitcher: 1–5 with 4.29 ERA in 24 games.

Smith, Bobby Gene (60–61) outfielder–third baseman (one game)–pinch-hitter: 106-for-391, .271, in 177 games. Also known as B.G.

Smith, Charley (61) third baseman–shortstop–pinch-hitter: 102-for-411, .248, in 112 games.

Smith, George (19–22) pitcher: 27–63 with 4.04 ERA in 155 games, 94 of them as starting pitcher; three saves.

Smith, Jake (11) pitcher: 0–0 with 0.00 ERA in two games, both in relief.

Smith, Jimmy (21–22) second baseman–shortstop–third baseman

(one game)–pinch-hitter: 82-for-361, .227, in 105 games.

Smith, Lonnie (78–81) outfielder–pinch-runner–pinch-hitter: 163-for-508, .321, in 196 games.

Smoll, Lefty (40) pitcher: 2–8 with 5.37 ERA in 33 games. Also known as Clyde.

Smythe, Harry (29–30) pitcher: 4–9 with 6.31 ERA in 44 games, all but 10 in relief; three saves. Also known as Bill.

Sorrell, Bill (65) third baseman–pinch-hitter: 5-for-13, .385, in 10 games.

Sothern, Denny (26, 28–30) outfielder–pinch-hitter: 365-for-1,273, .287, in 321 games.

Spalding, Dick (27) outfielder–pinch-hitter: 131-for-442, .296, in 115 games.

Sparks, Tully (03–10) pitcher: 94–96 with 2.44 ERA in 223 games, 197 of them as starting pitcher; seven saves.

Speece, Byron (30) pitcher: 0–0 with 13.27 ERA in 11 games, all relief.

Spencer, Tubby (11) catcher: 5-for-32, .156, in 11 games. Also known as Ed.

Sperry, Stan (36) second baseman–pinch-hitter: 5-for-37, .135, in 20 games.

Spindel, Hal (45–46) catcher–pinch-hitter: 21-for-90, .233, in 37 games.

Spotts, Jim (30) catcher–pinch-hitter (one game): 0-for-2, .000, in three games.

Spragins, Homer (47) pitcher: 0–0 with 6.75 ERA in four games, all relief.

Spring, Jack (55) pitcher: 0–1 with 6.75 ERA in two games, both relief.

Sproull, Charlie (45) pitcher: 4–10 with 5.94 ERA in 34 games, 19 of them as starting pitcher; one save.

Stack, Eddie (10–11) pitcher: 11–12 with 3.84 ERA in 33 games, 26 of them as starting pitcher.

Stainback, Tuck (38) outfielder–pinch-hitter: 21-for-81, .259, in 30 games. Also known as George.

Stanceu, Charley (46) pitcher: 2–4 with 4.24 ERA in 14 games, 11 of them as starting pitcher.

Stanicek, Steve (89) pinch-hitter: 1-for-9, .111, in nine games.

Stanley, Buck (11) pitcher: 0–0 with

6.35 ERA in four games, all relief. Also known as John.

Starr, Charlie (09) pinch-hitter: 0-for-3, .000, in three games.

Stearns, John (74) catcher: 1-for-2, .500, in one game.

Steevens, Morrie (64–65) pitcher: 0–1 with 10.13 ERA in 10 games, all relief.

Stein, Justin (38) third baseman–second baseman–pinch-hitter: 10-for-39, .256, in 11 games.

Steinbrenner, Gene (12) second baseman: 2-for-9, .222, in three games.

Steineder, Ray (24) pitcher: 1–1 with 4.34 ERA in nine games, all relief.

Stengel, Casey (20–21) outfielder–pinch-hitter: 148-for-504, .294, in 153 games. He managed in major leagues for 24½ years and was in World Series 10 times, winning seven times. He was elected to Hall of Fame in 1966.

Stephenson, Walt (37) catcher–pinch-hitter: 6-for-23, .261, in 10 games.

Stevens, Bobby (31) shortstop–pinch-hitter: 12-for-35, .343, in 12 games.

Stewart, Dave (85–86) pitcher: 0–0 with 6.48 ERA in 12 games.

Stewart, Glen (43–44) shortstop–third baseman–second baseman–first baseman–catcher (one game)–pinch-hitter: 154-for-713, .216, in 228 games.

Stewart, Walt (40) outfielder: 4-for-31, .129, in 10 games. Also known as Neb.

Stock, Milt (15–18) third baseman–shortstop–pinch-hitter: 483-for-1,781, .271, in 474 games.

Stone, Gene (69) first baseman–pinch-hitter: 6-for-28, .214, in 18 games.

Stone, Jeff (83–87) outfielder–pinch-hitter: 241-for-827, .291, in 296 games.

Stone, Ron (69–72) outfielder–first baseman–pinch-hitter: 188-for-782, .240, in 362 games. Also known as Palm Tree.

Stoner, Lil (31) pitcher: 0–0 with 6.59 ERA in seven games, all but one in relief.

Stoviak, Ray (38) outfielder–pinch-hitter: 0-for-10, .000, in 10 games.

Strincevich, Nick (48) pitcher: 0–1 with 9.00 ERA in six games, all but one in relief.

Stuart, Dick (65) first baseman–third baseman (one game)–pinch-hitter: 126-for-538, .234, in 149 games. Also known as Dr. Strangeglove.

Stuffel, Paul (50, 52–53) pitcher: 1–0 with 5.73 ERA in seven games, all but one in relief.

Stutz, George (26) shortstop–pinch-hitter (one game): 0-for-9, .000, in six games.

Suhr, Gus (39–40) first baseman–pinch-hitter: 67-for-223, .300, in 70 games.

Sulik, Ernie (36) outfielder–pinch-hitter: 116-for-404, .287, in 122 games.

Sullivan, Frank (61–62) pitcher: 3–18 with 4.54 ERA in 68 games; six saves.

Sullivan, John (68) catcher–pinch-hitter: 4-for-18, .222, in 12 games.

Sullivan, Tom (22) pitcher: 0–0 with 11.25 ERA in three games, all relief.

Surhoff, Rich (85) pitcher: 1–0 with 0.00 ERA in two games.

Susce, George (29) catcher–pinch-hitter: 5-for-17, .294, in 17 games. Father of player of same name who had five-year major league career as pitcher.

Sutherland, Gary (66–68) shortstop–outfielder–second baseman–third baseman–pinch-hitter: 95-for-372, .255, in 173 games.

Sutthoff, Jack (04–05) pitcher: 9–17 with 3.72 ERA in 32 games, 24 of them as starting pitcher.

Sveum, Dale (92) infielder–pinch-hitter: 24-for-135 .178, in 54 games.

Sweetland, Les (27–30) pitcher: 25–51 with 6.32 ERA in 135 games, 81 of them as starting pitcher; four saves.

T

Taber, Ed (26–27) pitcher: 0–1 with 10.80 ERA in nine games, all but one in relief. Also known as Lefty.

Tabor, Jim (46–47) third baseman–pinch-hitter: 183-for-714, .256, in 199 games.

Taitt, Doug (31–32) outfielder–pinch-hitter: 34-for-153, .222, in 42 games. Also known as Poco.

Tamulis, Vito (41) pitcher: 0–1 with 9.00 ERA in six games, all but one in relief.

Jim Tabor

Tauby, Fred (37) outfielder–pinch-hitter: 0-for-20, .000, in 11 games.

Taylor, Tony (60–71, 74–76) second baseman–third baseman–shortstop–first baseman–outfielder–pinch-hitter: 1,511-for-5,799, .261, in 1,669 games.

Tekulve, Kent (85–88) pitcher: 24–26 with 3.01 ERA in 291 games; 25 saves.

Terlecki, Bob (72) pitcher: 0–0 with 4.73 ERA in nine games, all relief.

Thevenow, Tommy (29–30) shortstop: 236-for-890, .265, in 256 games.

Thoenen, Dick (67) pitcher: 0–0 with 9.00 ERA in one game, in relief.

Thomas, Bill (02) outfielder–second baseman (one game)–first baseman (one game)–pinch-hitter (one game): 2-for-17, .118, in six games.

Thomas, Derrel (85) second baseman–shortstop–third baseman–outfielder–catcher–pinch-hitter: 19-for-92, .207, in 63 games.

Thomas, Frank (64–65) first baseman–outfielder–third baseman (one game)–pinch-hitter: 62-for-220, .282, in 74 games.

Thomas, Roy (00–08, 10–11) outfielder–pitcher (one game)–pinch-hitter (one game): 1,186-for-4,082, .291, in 1,136 games; record as pitcher is one game pitched in relief in 1900, 0–0 with 3.38 ERA.

Thomas, Tommy (35) pitcher: 0–1 with 5.25 ERA in four games, all but one in relief.

Thomas, Valmy (59) catcher–third baseman (one game): 28-for-140, .200, in 66 games.

Thomason, Erskine (74) pitcher: 0–0 with 0.00 ERA in one game, in relief.

Thompson, Fresco (27–30) second baseman–pinch-hitter: 700-for-2,332, .300, in 575 games.

Thompson, Jocko (48–51) pitcher: 6–11 with 4.24 ERA in 41 games, 21 of them as starting pitcher; one save.

Thompson, Milt (86–88) outfielder–pinch-hitter: 343-for-1,204, .285, in 368 games.

Thon, Dickie (89–91) shortstop–pinch-hitter: 395-for-1,526, .259, in 431 games.

Tierney, Cotton (23) second baseman–outfielder–third baseman: 152-for-480, .317, in 121 games.

Tincup, Ben (14–15, 18) pitcher: 8–11 with 2.93 ERA in 46 games; one save.

Titus, John (03–12) outfielder–pinch-hitter: 1,208-for-4,344, .278, in 1,218 games. Also known as Silent John.

Todd, Al (32–35) catcher–outfielder–pinch-hitter: 235-for-836, .281, in 304 games.

Tolan, Bobby (76–77) first baseman–outfielder–pinch-hitter: 73-for-288, .253, in 125 games.

Toliver, Fred (85–87) pitcher: 1–7 with 4.67 ERA in 26 games, one save.

Torgeson, Earl (53–55) first baseman–pinch-hitter: 277-for-1,019, .272, in 293 games.

Torre, Frank (62–63) first baseman–pinch-hitter: 80-for-280, .286, in 200 games.

Tovar, Cesar (73) third baseman–outfielder–second baseman–pinch-hitter: 88-for-328, .268, in 97 games.

Townsend, Jack (01) pitcher: 10–6 with 3.45 ERA in 19 games, 16 of them as starting pitcher.

Tragesser, Walt (19–20) catcher–pinch-hitter: 64-for-290, .221, in 97 games.

Triandos, Gus (64–65) catcher–first baseman (one game)–pinch-hitter: 61-for-270, .226, in 103 games.

Trillo, Manny (79–82) second baseman: 516-for-1,860, .277, in 502 games.

Trinkle, Ken (49) pitcher: 1–1 with 4.00 ERA in 42 games; two saves.

Triplett, Coaker (43–45) outfielder–pinch-hitter: 228-for-907, .251, in 309 games.

Turner, Shane (88) third baseman–shortstop–pinch-hitter: 6-for-35, .171, in 18 games.

Twitchell, Wayne (71–77) pitcher: 33–43 with 3.57 ERA in 188 games, 92 of them as starting pitcher; two saves.

Tyson, Turkey (44) pinch-hitter: 0–1, .000, in one game.

U

Uecker, Bob (66–67) catcher–pinch-hitter: 49-for-242, .202, in 96 games.

Ulrich, Dutch (25–27) pitcher: 19–

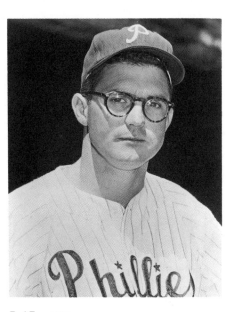

Earl Torgeson

The New Phillies Encyclopedia

Johnny Vergez

Ozzie Virgil

27 with 3.48 ERA in 98 games; two saves.

Underwood, Tom (74–77) pitcher: 28–20 with 4.02 ERA in 89 games, 60 of them as starting pitcher; three saves.

Unser, Del (73–74, 79–82) outfielder–first baseman–pinch-hitter: 327-for-1,218, .268, in 550 games.

V

Vatcher, Jim (90) outfielder–pinch-hitter: 12-for-46, .261, in 36 games.

Valo, Elmer (56, 61) outfielder–pinch-hitter: 92-for-334, .275, in 148 games.

Van Buren, Deacon (04) outfielder: 10-for-43, .233, in 12 games.

Van Dusen, Fred (55) pinch-runner: no batting record, one game.

Van Dyke, Ben (09) pitcher: 0–0 with 3.68 ERA in two games, both relief.

Verban, Emil (46–48) second baseman–pinch-hitter (one game): 323-for-1,182, .273, in 348 games.

Verbanic, Joe (66) pitcher: 1–1 with 5.14 ERA in 17 games, all relief.

Verdel, Al (44) pitcher: 0–0 with 0.00 ERA in one game, in relief.

Vergez, Johnny (35–36) third baseman–shortstop–pinch-hitter: 147-for-586, .251, in 163 games.

Vines, Bob (25) pitcher: 0–0 with 11.25 ERA in three games, all relief.

Virgil, Ozzie, Jr. (80–85) catcher–pinch-hitter: 279-for-1,134, .246, in 383 games.

Vorhees, Cy (02) pitcher: 3–3 with 3.83 ERA in 10 games, four of them as starting pitcher.

Vukovich, George (80–82) outfielder–pinch-hitter: 114-for-419, .272, in 221 games.

Vukovich, John (70–71, 76–77, 79–81) first baseman–second baseman–shortstop–third baseman–pinch-hitter: 51-for-313, .163, in 153 games.

W

Wagner, Gary (65–69) pitcher: 11–15 with 3.59 ERA in 118 games, all but three in relief; 15 saves.

Wagner, Hal (48–49) catcher–pinch-hitter: 0-for-8, .000, in four games.

Waitkus, Eddie (49–53, 55) first

baseman–pinch-hitter: 649-for-2,313, .281, in 613 games.

Walczak, Ed (45) second baseman–shortstop: 12-for-57, .211, in 20 games.

Walk, Bob (80) pitcher: 11–7 with 4.56 ERA in 27 games, all as starting pitcher.

Walker, Curt (21–24) outfielder–first baseman (one game)–pinch-hitter: 391-for-1,256, .311, in 333 games.

Walker, Harry (47–48) outfielder–first baseman–third baseman (one game)–pinch-hitter: 278-for-820, .339, in 242 games. Also known as "The Hat." Had brother and father both named Dixie who played in major leagues.

Walker, Martin (28) pitcher: 0–1 with 0.00 ERA in one game, as starting pitcher.

Wallace, Dave (73–74) pitcher: 0–1 with 16.12 ERA in seven games, all relief.

Wallace, Doc (19) shortstop: 1-for-4, .250, in two games.

Wallace, Huck (12) pitcher: 0–0 with 0.00 ERA in four games, all relief. Also known as Harry.

Wallace, Mike (73–74) pitcher: 2–1 with 4.14 ERA in 28 games, all but three in relief; one save.

Walls, Lee (60–61) first baseman–third baseman–outfielder–pinch-hitter: 109-for-442, .247, in 156 games.

Walsh, Augie (27–28) pitcher: 4–10 with 6.05 ERA in 39 games; two saves. Also known as August.

Walsh, Jimmy (10–13) outfielder–second baseman–shortstop–third baseman–catcher–first baseman (one game)–pitcher (one game)–pinch-hitter: 188-for-711, .264, in 259 games. His record as pitcher in 1911 is 0–1 with 12.00 ERA in one game.

Walsh, John (03) third baseman: 0-for-3, .000, in one game.

Walsh, Walt (20) pinch-hitter: no batting record, two games.

Walters, Bucky (34–38) third baseman–second baseman–pitcher–outfielder–pinch-hitter: 169-for-654, .258, in 267 games (does not include hitting record in 15 games in 1938—exact hitting figures unavailable; batting average was .286); record as pitcher 38–53 with 4.51 ERA in

115 games, 102 of them as starting pitcher.

Walters, Ken (60–61) outfielder–first baseman–third baseman (one game)–pinch-hitter: 143-for-606, .236, in 210 games.

Waner, Lloyd (42) outfielder–pinch-hitter: 75-for-287, .261, in 100 games. He was elected to Hall of Fame in 1967. Also known as Little Poison. His brother Paul, known as Big Poison, also member of Hall of Fame.

Ward, Joe (06, 09–10) first baseman–second baseman–shortstop–third baseman–outfielder–pinch-hitter: 105-for-437, .240, in 157 games.

Warner, Jack (33) second baseman–third baseman–shortstop–pinch-hitter: 76-for-340, .224, in 107 games.

Warren, Bennie (39–42) catcher–first baseman–pinch-hitter: 205-for-915, .224, in 335 games.

Warthen, Dan (77) pitcher: 0–1 with 0.00 ERA in three games, all relief.

Wasdell, Jimmy (43–46) outfielder–first baseman–pinch-hitter: 424-for-1,524, .278, in 434 games.

Washburn, Libe (03) pitcher–outfielder–pinch-hitter: 3-for-18, .167, in eight games; record as pitcher is 0–4 with 4.37 ERA in four games, all starts and complete games.

Washer, Buck (05) pitcher: 0–0 with 6.00 ERA in one game, in relief.

Watkins, Dave (69) catcher–outfielder–third baseman (one game)–pinch-hitter: 26-for-168, .176, in 69 games.

Watkins, Ed (02) outfielder: 0-for-3, .000, in one game.

Watkins, George (35–36) outfielder–first baseman: 179-for-670, .267, in 169 games.

Watson, Milt (18–19) pitcher: 7–11 with 3.94 ERA in 31 games, 15 of them as starting pitcher.

Watt, Eddie (74) pitcher: 1–1 with 4.03 ERA in 42 games, all relief; six saves.

Watt, Frank (31) pitcher: 5–5 with 4.84 ERA in 38 games; two saves.

Watwood, Cliff (39) first baseman: 1-for-6, .167, in two games. Also known as John.

Webb, Bill (43) pitcher: 0–0 with 9.00 ERA in one game, in relief.

Wehmeier, Herm (54–56) pitcher: 20–22 with 4.17 ERA in 59 games, 49 of them as starting pitcher.

Wehrmeister, Dave (84) pitcher: 0–0 with 7.20 ERA in seven games.

Weinert, Lefty (19–24) pitcher: 14–30 with 4.43 ERA in 99 games, 45 of them as starting pitcher; two saves. Also known as Phil.

Weintraub, Phil (38) first baseman: 109-for-351, .311, in 100 games.

Weiser, Bud (15–16) outfielder–pinch-hitter: 12-for-74, .162, in 41 games.

Welchonce, Harry (11) outfielder–pinch-hitter: 14-for-66, .212, in 26 games.

Wendell, Lew (24–26) catcher–pinch-hitter: 10-for-62, .161, in 40 games.

Wenz, Fred (70) pitcher: 2–0 with 4.50 ERA in 22 games, all relief; one save.

Westlake, Jim (55) pinch-hitter: 0-for-1, .000, in one game.

Westlake, Wally (56) pinch-hitter: 0-for-4, .000, in five games.

Weston, Mickey (92) pitcher: 0–1 with 12.27 ERA in one game.

Wheat, Mack (20–21) pinch-hitter: 57-for-257, .222, in 88 games.

White, Bill (66–68) first baseman–pinch-hitter: 328-for-1,270, .258, in 396 games.

White, Doc (01–02) pitcher–outfielder–pinch-hitter: 74-for-277, .267, in 92 games; record as pitcher is 30–33 with 2.82 ERA in 67 games, 62 of them as starting pitcher; one save.

White, Sammy (62) catcher–pinch-hitter: 21-for-97, .216, in 41 games.

Whiting, Jesse (02) pitcher: 0–1 with 5.00 ERA in one game as starter and pitched complete game.

Whitman, Dick (50–51) outfielder–pinch-hitter: 35-for-149, .235, in 94 games.

Whitney, Pinky (28–33, 36–39) third baseman–first baseman–second baseman–pinch-hitter: 1,329-for-4,322, .307, in 1,157 games.

Whitted, Possum (15–19) outfielder–first baseman–third baseman–second baseman–pinch-hitter: 522-for-1,902, .274, in 523 games. Also known as George.

Wilber, Del (51–52) catcher–pinch-hitter: 68-for-247, .275, in 86 games.

Wilhelm, Kaiser (21) pitcher: 0–0

Lloyd Waner

Phil Weintraub

with 3.38 ERA in four games, all relief. Also known as Irving.

Williams, Cy (18–30) outfielder–pinch-hitter: 1,553-for-5,077, .306, in 1,463 games.

Williams, George (61) second baseman–pinch-hitter: 9-for-36, .250, in 17 games.

Williams, Mike (92–) pitcher: current Phillies player.

Williams, Mitch (91–) pitcher: current Phillies player.

Williams, Walt (03) pitcher: 1–1 with 3.00 ERA in two games, both as starting pitcher and both complete games. Also known as Pop.

Willingham, Hugh (31–33) shortstop–third baseman–outfielder (one game)–pinch-hitter: 9-for-38, .237, in 28 games. Also known as Tom.

Willoughby, Claude (25–30) pitcher: 38–56 with 5.83 ERA in 210 games; nine saves.

Wilson, Billy (69–73) pitcher: 9–15 with 4.23 ERA in 179 games, all relief; 17 saves.

Wilson, Glenn (84–87) outfielder–pinch-hitter–pitcher: 557-for-2,099, .265, in 562 games; 0–0 with 0.00 ERA in one game.

Wilson, Hack (34) outfielder–pinch-hitter: 2-for-20, .100, in seven games. Elected to Hall of Fame in 1979. He played in major league just 12 seasons, hit 244 home runs, and had slugging average of .545.

Wilson, Jimmie (23–28, 34–38) catcher–outfielder–first baseman–second baseman–pinch-hitter: 732-for-2,545, .288, in 838 games. He was playing manager from 1934 to 1938.

Wilson, Maxie (40) pitcher: 0–0 with 12.86 ERA in three games, all relief.

Wiltsie, Hal (31) pitcher: 0–0 with 9.00 ERA in one game, in relief. Also known as Whitey.

Wine, Bobby (60, 62–68) shortstop–third baseman–first baseman– outfielder–pinch-hitter: 420-for-1,943, .216, in 731 games.

Winters, Jesse (21–23) pitcher: 12–22 with 5.13 ERA in 73 games; three saves.

Wise, Rick (64–71) pitcher: 75–76 with 3.60 ERA in 219 games, 178 of them as starting pitcher. He pitched no-hit game at Cincinnati June 23, 1971.

Withrow, Frank (20, 22) catcher–pinch-hitter: 31-for-153, .203, in 58 games.

Wockenfuss, John (84–85) catcher–pinch-hitter: 58-for-217, .267, in 118 games.

Woehr, Andy (23–24) third baseman–second baseman (one game)–pinch-hitter: 47-for-193, .244, in 63 games.

Wolfe, Bill (02) pitcher: 0–1 with 4.00 ERA in one game, as starter and completed game.

Wolverton, Harry (00–01, 02–04) third baseman: 523-for-1,790, .292, in 453 games.

Woods, Jim (60–61) third baseman–pinch-hitter: 17-for-82, .207, in 34 games.

Woodward, Frank (18–19) pitcher: 6–9 with 4.79 ERA in 19 games, 12 of them as starting pitcher.

Wrightstone, Russ (20–28) third baseman–first baseman–outfielder–shortstop–second baseman–pinch-hitter: 885-for-2,967, .298, in 879 games.

Wyatt, Whit (45) pitcher: 0–7 with 5.26 ERA in 10 games, all as starting pitcher.

Wyrostek, Johnny (46–47, 52–54) outfielder–first baseman–pinch-hitter: 538-for-1,996, .270, in 588 games.

Y

Yarnell, Rusty (26) 0–1 with 18.00 ERA in one game, in relief.

Yeabsley, Bert (19) pinch-hitter: no batting record, three games.

Young, Bobby (58) second baseman–pinch-hitter: 14-for-60, .233, in 32 games.

Young, Del (37–40) shortstop–second baseman–pinch-hitter: 213-for-950, .224, in 309 games.

Young, Dick (51–52) second baseman–pinch-hitter: 18-for-77, .234, in 20 games.

Young, Mike (88) outfielder–pinch-hitter: 33-for-146, .226, in 75 games.

Youmans, Floyd (89) pitcher: 1–5 with 5.70 ERA in 10 games.

Z

Zachry, Pat (85) pitcher: 0–0 with 4.26 ERA in 10 games.

Zachary, Tom (36) pitcher: 0–3 with 8.10 ERA in seven games; one save. Made a place in history for himself in 1927 while pitching for Washington by serving up pitch that Babe Ruth hit for his 60th home run of the season.

Ziegler, Charlie (00) third baseman: 3-for-11, .273, in three games.

Zimmer, Chief (03) catcher–pinch-hitter: 26-for-118, .220, in 37 games.

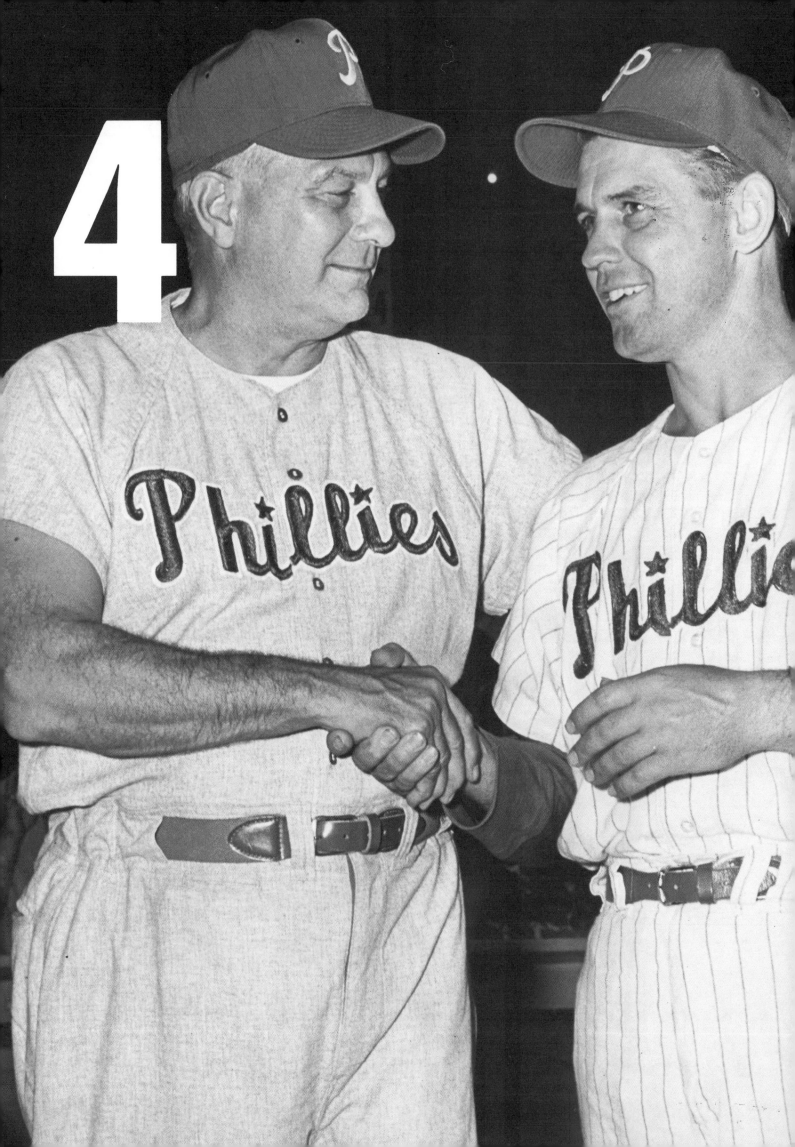

The Strategists

Forty-seven different men have managed the Phillies since they began playing in 1883. No two were ever alike.

Over the years, the team has been run by virtually every kind of individual. Among the men who have made out lineup cards, there was a former medical school student, an ex-Phillies ticket taker, an alleged bigamist, a former college professor, a dentist, three future umpires, the owner of baseball's highest single-season batting average, and the man known as the Father of Professional Baseball.

This odd assortment has gone by names such as Blondie, Chief, Stuffy, Wild Bill, Whiskey Face, Stud, and countless other names that best go unmentioned.

There are three Hall of Famers among the ranks, two of whom earned their credentials as managers.

Pat Moran, Eddie Sawyer, Dallas Green, and Paul Owens led the Phillies to pennants. Sawyer, Owens, Hans Lobert, and George Myatt each managed the team twice.

The average tenure for a Phillies manager (not counting interim pilots) has been 2.4 years. Only 10 skippers held the managerial post with the Phillies for four or more years.

Despite all of their differences, Phillies managers share many similarities. Thirty-seven of them came to the Phils with no prior managerial experience, and 34 of them never managed another big league club after leaving the Phillies. Twenty-eight Phils leaders never managed in the big leagues either before coming to the Phillies or after leaving them.

Just 10 Phillies managers could be considered men who came up through the team's farm system, either as players or minor league managers. Thirty-seven Phils managers played in the big leagues, but only a handful of them could be considered star players. Eighteen Phillies leaders played for the Phillies at some point during their careers.

The winningest manager in Phillies history is also the losingest pilot the Phils ever had. In a nine-year career with the Phillies, Gene Mauch won 645 and lost 684. Mauch also worked in the most games (1,331).

Harry Wright, a Hall of Fame member who is often referred to as the Father of Professional Baseball, used to be considered the winningest manager of the Phillies. But Wright was recently discovered to have managed only part of the 1890 season, instead of the whole season. This discovery reduced his overall Phillies record to 636–566 over a 10-year period between 1884 and 1893.

Among managers who sat in the dugout for more than a few games, Arthur Irwin has the best percentage (.574), and Lobert has the worst (.275).

The oldest man ever to manage the Phillies was Steve O'Neill, who was 63 when he guided the club in 1954. The youngest were Blondie Purcell (1883) and George Stallings (1897), both 29.

No Phillies manager has ever lost an All-Star Game. Sawyer was the winning pilot in the National League's 8–3 triumph in Detroit in 1951, Green was a 5–4 winner in 1981 in Cleveland, and Owens recorded a 3–1 victory in San Francisco in 1984.

These managers and all the others during the Phillies' 110 years are the subjects of the following pages.

Two of the finest managers in Phillies' history have been Eddie Sawyer (left) and Gene Mauch.

Manager Profiles

1883

Ferguson, Bob

Record: 4–13 (.235)
Birthplace: Brooklyn, New York
B: January 31, 1845; **D:** May 3, 1894

Bob Ferguson

Bob Ferguson had extensive managerial experience when he became the first pilot of the Phillies. Unfortunately, credentials don't score runs.

Ferguson, despite having been largely responsible for assembling the first Phillies team from scratch, lasted just 17 games. His demise had a direct connection with his ability as a judge of talent.

For reasons that allow the imagination to wander, but most likely because he caught everything hit in the air to him, Ferguson carried the nickname "Death to Flying Things." DTFT had been a teammate of Al Reach in Brooklyn in the 1860s, and was later player-manager for Hartford in the first National League season in 1876.

After two third-place finishes at Hartford, Fergy moved to Chicago, where he spent one season, then became the skipper of the Troy (New York) team.

At one point, Ferguson was also president of the league, which required that a player serve as the chief executive.

He piloted Troy for four seasons. When the National League decided to install franchises in New York and Philadelphia, Troy was shipped to Manhattan, and Worcester became the Phillies.

Reach hired his old friend to run his new club in Philadelphia. Because all of the Worcester players had been sold before the franchise folded, it was necessary to find a whole new roster.

The owner and the manager dug up players mostly from assorted minor league teams. One of the best players on the team was none other than Ferguson himself. Bob was the regular second baseman.

After getting off to a respectable start, losing just 4–3 to the Providence Grays in their first National League game, the Phillies went into a tailspin and were hopelessly outclassed by the rest of the league.

Reach removed Ferguson after the Phillies' record reached 4–13. Bob continued to play second for the rest of the season, hitting .258. He led National League second basemen in errors with 88.

Ferguson left the Phillies at the end of the season. In 1884 he jumped to the American Association, where he managed the Pittsburgh Alleghenies for one season and the New York Metropolitans for nearly two.

Throughout his career, Ferguson was a player-manager. He wound up a nine-year playing career with a .271 batting average. Ferguson's lifetime record as a manager was 416–515 (.447). His teams never finished above third place.

Bob wound up his career in baseball as an umpire.

Ferguson, Bob

	W	L	T	Pct
1883	4	13	0	.235
Phillies	4	13	0	.235
Career	416	515	0	.447

1883

Purcell, Bill (Blondie)

Record: 13–68 (.160)
Birthplace: Paterson, New Jersey
B: March 16, 1854; **D:** February 20, 1912

The Phillies didn't have to go to much trouble to find their second manager. President Al Reach merely summoned his left fielder.

Blondie Purcell, a veteran player, was the club's regular left fielder when Bob Ferguson became the club's first managerial casualty after 17 games of the 1883 season. Although he had no previous experience running a big league team, Purcell was awarded the hopeless job of trying to splice a loose band of nondescripts into a team.

Like his predecessor, he failed. Blondie's squad played even worse than it had before he became the boss. At the end of the season, the Phillies were so deeply entrenched in last place that they were 23 games behind the seventh-place Detroit Wolverines.

Purcell, who hit .268 that season, tossed in his scorecard at the end of the year. Perhaps because the experience left some deep scars, Blondie never again ventured into managerial waters.

He did play the following year for the Phillies, hitting .252. Purcell's playing career spanned 12 years, beginning in 1879 and ending in 1890. Before coming to the Phillies, he played for Syracuse, Cincinnati, Cleveland, and Buffalo in the National League. Later, he saw action with Philadelphia and Baltimore of the American Association and Boston of the National League.

Purcell was primarily an outfielder. His lifetime batting average was .267. He also had a 15–43 record in 79 games as a pitcher, including a 2–6 mark for the Phillies in 1883.

Purcell, Blondie

	W	L	T	Pct
1883	13	68	1	.160
Phillies	13	68	1	.160
Career	13	68	1	.160

Blondie Purcell

The tombstone that sits above the remains of Harry Wright in Philadelphia's West Laurel Hill Cemetary bears the inscription "The Father of Baseball."

While that bold contention may be disputed by the descendents of Abner Doubleday and Alexander Cartwright, it is not as far removed from the truth as some of baseball's more familiar folklore would make it seem. Wright, it could be argued, was at the very least the father of professional baseball.

He was, after all, the man who put together the first professional team. In 1869, Harry was the player-manager of the Cincinnati Redlegs, a touring team that traveled the country playing anybody who wanted a game. The club paid its players salaries ranging from $800 to $1,400 for the season. In 1869 and 1870 it won 87 consecutive games.

The pioneering Hall of Famer was also the man who gave flannel uniforms to the game of baseball. Harry's creation was particularly noteworthy because he was the first one to cut away the pantlegs, producing knickers.

"What I had in mind," Wright said later, "was fewer clothes. You couldn't play ball well with inches of flannel flapping around your ankles. This was a special misfortune to the infielders who were likely to gather in their trouser bottoms when they reached for the ball."

To dress up his creation, Wright also introduced colored stockings. A version of the red stockings in which he outfitted his first team in Cincinnati are still worn by that club.

A native of England and son of a famous cricket player, Wright came to the United States as a small boy. He was raised in New York City, where his first love was also cricket.

Harry joined the Cincinnati team in 1867. He was the club's center fielder and an outstanding hitter. That year he cracked seven home runs in one game in Newport, Kentucky.

Wright, who also played shortstop, pitcher, and catcher on occasion, was a fine player, but he wasn't in a class with his brother George. Generally regarded as the best player of his era, George was a hard-hitting shortstop. He was inducted into the Hall of Fame in 1942, the earliest player taken into the shrine.

Harry continued to play, but in 1869 he became a manager and organized the Redlegs into a professional team. He was the first man to recruit players from outside the team's residential area. The highest salary went to brother George. He was paid $1,400, while Harry received $200 less.

The club didn't lose a game for one and one-half years. It traveled 12,000 miles with nine men. During that period, Wright gained a considerable reputation as an astute manager. The Cincinnati *Enquirer* called him a "baseball Edison."

1884–93

Wright, Harry

Record: 636–566–24 (.530)
Birthplace: Sheffield, England
B: January 10, 1835; **D:** October 3, 1895

Harry Wright

In 1871, Harry was lured to Boston where he managed and played for the city's National Association team. In 1875 the team had a 71–8 record. When the Red Stockings, as the Boston club was known, became one of the original members of the National League in 1876, Wright continued as manager. He piloted the Boston team until 1881, winning a total of six pennants in his 11 seasons there.

Wright, who played until he was in his early 40s, had crossed paths many times with Al Reach, the first professional player. A year after Reach was awarded a franchise in Philadelphia, he hired Wright to be his manager.

In their first year in the National League, the Phillies had established a record for ineptitude that would never again be approached in the annals of baseball. "We need a real manager," Reach had confided to his co-owner John Rogers.

Wright was given the job of building the flimsy franchise into one that was competitive. It wasn't easy. Harry began by fielding an almost entirely new team in 1884. The club improved substantially, moving from eighth to sixth in the standings. In his 10 years as the Phillies' manager, that would be Wright's only second-division team.

Harry was a dignified fellow, recognized by friends and foes as a fine gentleman. Possessing the era's characteristic handlebar mustache and a flowing beard, his usual attire on the bench included a tophat, coat, and tie.

His skills as a manager were quite advanced for his day. Unlike many skippers of the late 1800s, Wright was a thinking manager who relied more on strategy than brute force.

No less an authority than Hughie Jennings, a Hall of Fame member and early adversary of Wright's when Jennings was with the Baltimore Orioles, realized Harry's genius. "He could look further into a ball game than any man I ever met," said Jennings, who became a manager himself after his playing days ended. "Before the game started, he had every inning figured out and he expected the play to go precisely along the lines he planned."

Characteristic of Wright's style was an incident that occurred with the great hitter Ed Delahanty. Harry signaled for a bunt, but Delahanty swung away and socked a double. After the inning was over, Wright chastized his hitter for ignoring his sign. Delahanty shot back that a double was better than a bunt. "But you changed the entire course of the game," Wright argued.

Harry may have been rigid, but he always knew what he was doing and why he was doing it. His Phillies teams reflected that philosophy. The clubs played smartly and, being well grounded in the fundamentals of the game, made few mental errors.

During Wright's tenure, the team was always among the leading contenders for the National League pennant. Although the Phillies never finished first, much to the chagrin of Reach and Rogers, the team was second once, third three times, and fifth four times after Harry's initial season.

The result of all the Phillies' high finishes was that Wright won the second highest number of games of all managers in the club's history.

It was while Wright piloted the club that the Phillies bought the raw, young Delahanty for the then-high sum of $1,900. Delahanty and Billy Hamilton, another youngster whom Wright helped to develop, wound up in the Hall of Fame.

Wright was inducted into the Hall in 1953.

The fact that Harry never won the pennant eventually led to his demise as the Phillies' manager.

Tired of the team's being a bridesmaid nearly every year, Rogers urged the removal of Wright after the 1893 season. He claimed that Harry had been in the game too long, and that his tactics were becoming obsolete.

At first Reach balked at the suggestion. But eventually he agreed. Wright's contract was not renewed for the 1894 season.

The dismissal stunned the old pioneer. The Phillies tried to soothe his disappointment by persuading the National League to create a special office for him as chief of umpires. But Wright died at age 60, less than a year after the Phillies had let him go. There were some who said that the loss of his job hastened Harry's death.

Wright, Harry

	W	L	T	Pct
1884	39	73	1	.348
1885	56	54	1	.509
1886	71	43	5	.623
1887	75	48	5	.610
1888	69	61	1	.531
1889	63	64	3	.496
1890	36	31	1	.537
1891	68	69	1	.496
1892	87	66	2	.569
1893	72	57	4	.558
Phillies	636	566	24	.530
Career	1,225	885	26	.581

When Harry Wright came down with a case of temporary blindness early in the 1890 season, the Phillies were not only left without a manager, but in those days when no coaches existed they had nobody ready to take over.

The most logical place to find someone was behind the plate. There, Jack Clements had emerged as a team leader, and, therefore, seemed as good a choice as anybody to pilot the team.

The lefthanded Clements took the reins in April when the Phillies were in first place in the National League. It was a season in which Ed Delahanty had jumped to the Players' League, but the Phillies still had a formidable lineup that included future Hall of Famers Billy Hamilton and Sam Thompson and eventual 38-game winner Kid Gleason.

Clements drove the Phillies to 13 wins in 19 games, but the club fell into second place. Apparently, that was enough to get Jack replaced. He never ventured into the skipper's chair again.

Clements, Jack

	W	L	T	Pct
1890	13	6	0	.684
Phillies	13	6	0	.684
Career	13	6	0	.684

During his long career in baseball, Al Reach performed several duties successfully. He was the first professional player and a prominent team owner.

But when he tried managing, Reach was pretty much of a bust.

Al led the club he owned for 11 games in 1890. He had taken over after dumping Jack Clements, who had replaced the ailing Harry Wright.

Reach who had no managerial experience thought he could do a better job than Clements. Instead he took over a second place club and drove it into third where it stayed most of the season.

Reach had the good sense to give up the reins after guiding the Phillies to a 4–7 record. Rookie shortstop Bob Allen replaced him, and held the fort until Wright returned later in the season.

Reach, Al

	W	L	T	Pct
1890	4	7	0	.364
Phillies	4	7	0	.364
Career	4	7	0	.364

1890

Clements, Jack

Record: 13–6 (.684)
Birthplace: Philadelphia, Pennsylvania
B: June 24, 1864; **D:** May 23, 1941

1890

Reach, Al

Record: 4–7 (.364)
Birthplace: London, England
B: May 25, 1840; **D:** January 14, 1928

1890

Allen, Bob

Record: 25–10 (.714)
Birthplace: Marion, Ohio
B: July 10, 1867; **D:** May 4, 1943

Bob Allen

Although his name is not among the most familiar managers in Phillies history Bob Allen has one credit that he shares with no other Phils skipper.

Allen is the only man in club history to serve as manager in his rookie year as a player.

Allen was a first-year player and the club's starting shortstop in 1890. Early in the season, regular manager Harry Wright developed a serious eye problem and was forced to spend the next few months of the season at home in bed.

After catcher Jack Clements and then owner-president Al Reach had managed in Wright's place, Allen got his chance. Allen took over in late May and led the Phillies for the next 35 games, a total that was more than either Clements or Reach managed. Bob took over a club that was in third place and got it into second.

Wright returned for the last 55 games of the season, and the Phillies finished third, 9½ games behind front-running Brooklyn.

After Wright's arrival, Allen went back to being just a player. He hit .226 for the season.

Allen was the Phillies' regular shortstop through the 1893 season. Then after spending the next season as a reserve, he went back to the minors. He resurfaced in the big leagues in 1897 with the Boston Beaneaters.

Allen's stint as Phillies manager served as training for the 1900 season. That year, Bob skippered the Cincinnati Reds. The Reds had a 62–77 record, finishing seventh in the National League.

Allen never managed in the big leagues after that season.

Allen, Bob

	W	L	T	Pct
1890	25	10	0	.714
Phillies	25	10	0	.714
Career	87	87	0	.500

1894–95

Irwin, Arthur

Record: 149–110–4 (.574)
Birthplace: Toronto, Ontario
B: February 14, 1858; **D:** July 16, 1921

Art Irwin

Like anybody who follows a legend, Arthur Irwin was faced with a difficult task as soon as he accepted the job as Phillies manager.

Irwin replaced Harry Wright, the baseball pioneer who ran the Phillies for 10 seasons. Ironically, it had been Wright who had bounced Irwin from the team when Arthur was the Phillies' shortstop a few years earlier.

Arthur had been the Phillies' captain, playing with the club from 1886 to 1889. Although he never hit higher than .254 for the Phillies, he was a wily player with a reputation for having a thorough knowledge of the game. He was also one of the first players to wear a fielder's mitt.

In 1889, however, Irwin grew unhappy with Wright's tactics as a manager. The two feuded openly. At first, Wright benched his shortstop. Then, in mid-season he banished him to Washington.

It was a good break for Irwin. Arthur was named manager of the Washington team for the rest of the season. Although the club finished last, Irwin's career as a manager had been launched.

Irwin jumped to the Players' League in 1890, but the following year he resumed his managerial duties, leading Boston to the American Association pennant. He returned to Washington in mid-season in 1892 and was the middle of three managers. The Phillies hired him the next season.

Irwin, who spent 13 seasons as a player, finishing with a career average of .241, was expected to win the pennant for the Phillies in 1894. With a future Hall of Fame outfield of Ed Delahanty, Billy Hamilton, and Sam Thompson, the Phillies were the team to beat for the National League title.

But despite a team batting average of .349, which included four players hitting .400 or above, the Phillies finished a disappointing fourth with a 71–57 record.

The team was nearly as devastating at the plate the following season, but again the pennant eluded them. They did, however, move up to third place, improving their record to 78–53.

Irwin, who had predicted a pennant before the 1895 season, suddenly found himself expendable. He argued with co-owner John Rogers. When the New York Giants offered him a job as manager, the Phillies let him go without resistance.

Arthur lasted a little more than half the season in New York before being fired. He returned to Washington late in the 1898 season as the club's fourth manager that year, then managed the Senators in 1899. The club finished in 11th place both years.

Irwin's lifetime record as a manager was 416–427. By the time he stopped managing, Arthur was on his way to becoming moderately wealthy. Years earlier, he had secured a patent on his fielder's glove, and Phillies president Al Reach had been producing the piece of equipment as fast as the machines at his sporting goods company could crank them out.

Irwin died at the age of 63 under somewhat mysterious circumstances. His body was found in the Atlantic Ocean. Arthur was believed to have jumped from a steamship he was riding from New York to Boston. Newspaper reports at the time attributed his apparent suicide to family problems. Irwin was alleged to have led a dual life with wives and families in both New York and Boston.

Irwin, Art

	W	L	T	Pct
1894	71	57	1	.555
1895	78	53	2	.595
Phillies	149	110	3	.574
Career	416	427	15	.493

In his brief stint as manager of the Phillies, Billy Nash provided two good reasons to rank among the club's most forgettable pilots.

First, he found a way to finish in eighth place during his only managerial season, despite the presence on his roster of four future Hall of Fame players. Second, he was the player the Phillies received in one of the worst trades the club ever made.

Nash was a decent player with a lifetime average of .275 during his 15 years in the big leagues. He had spent most of his career with the Boston Beaneaters, and was the third baseman, captain, and sparkplug on the club's three pennant-winning teams of the early 1890s.

Nash was hardly in a class with the Phillies' center fielder Billy Hamilton, a future Hall of Famer. But when Hamilton asked for a small salary increase, John Rogers, who was running the Phillies, promptly shipped him to Boston for Nash.

By that time Nash, who broke into the majors in 1884 with Richmond of the American Association, was sliding rapidly over the hill. Rogers, though, was more interested in Billy's assumed managerial qualities, despite the absence of any experience.

Billy was handed the reins after the Phillies let Arthur Irwin drift quietly off to New York. The club placed eighth in a 12-team league, finishing 23½ games out of first. It was a disappointing season, considering that the club had Ed Delahanty, Sam Thompson, Dan Brouthers, and, after mid-season, Nap Lajoie. All four eventually joined the Hall of Fame.

Nash joined the hall of retreat. The Phillies dismissed him after the season. Billy played two more years with the club, but he made no future attempts to manage in the big leagues. Instead, Nash became an umpire. He worked in the National League for many years.

Nash, Billy

	W	L	T	Pct
1896	62	68	1	.477
Phillies	62	68	1	.477
Career	62	68	1	.477

1896

Nash, Billy

Record: 62–68–1 (.477)
Birthplace: Richmond, Virginia
B: June 24, 1865; **D:** November 16, 1929

Billy Nash

The New Phillies Encyclopedia

1897–98

Stallings, George

Record: 74–104–2 (.417)
Birthplace: Augusta, Georgia
B: November 17, 1867; **D:** May 13, 1929

George Stallings

In the late 1800s baseball players were generally a rough bunch—crude, semi-literate, hard-drinking types whose idea of fun was a brawl outside the local saloon.

Even these early paragons of machoism, however, were no match for George Tweedy Stallings, whom the Phillies hired as their manager in 1897. An abusive tyrant, Stallings made his mark in Philadelphia by becoming the first manager to be overthrown by the players.

The son of a Confederate general, a graduate of Virginia Military Institute, and a two-year student of medicine at the College of Physicians and Surgeons in Baltimore, Stallings was a polished, mannerly gentleman off the field. But on the field, he was a slave-driving, superstitious demon whose profanity, derisive treatment of his players, and conniving schemes produced nothing but contempt and hatred among his athletes.

Hired to replace the complacent Billy Nash, Stallings had little previous big league experience. While in college, he had been given a tryout as a catcher by the Phillies and Harry Wright in 1887. The Phillies didn't sign him, but Wright talked Stallings into giving up medicine for baseball.

Stallings played in four games with Brooklyn in the National League in 1890. Otherwise, with the exception of a few games with the Phillies while he was manager, his playing career was spent entirely in the minors. He also managed, and in 1896 he attracted attention as the fighting pilot of Detroit in the Western League.

George became the Phillies' manager at age 29. Immediately, he alienated his team by his tantrums and showers of abuse. The Phillies' performance slipped in concert with their morale, and the team finished a disappointing 10th in the 12-team league.

The situation worsened the following season. Stallings' tirades became more frequent, and the players' discontent with their manager became more obvious. The players' hatred reached the point of no return in mid-June. A committee led by outfielder Duff Cooley informed Phillies owners Al Reach and John Rogers that it would no longer play for Stallings.

The threatened strike never materialized. Stallings was fired and paid off for the remainder of his three-year contract. At the time, the Phillies were in eighth place with a 19–27 record.

About the only useful accomplishment of Stallings during his short stay in Philadelphia was his conversion of Nap Lajoie from first to second base. Lajoie became a Hall of Famer at that position.

Stallings went on to bigger and better things, too, but didn't tone down his act. George spent the 1901 season as manager of his old Detroit club, which had entered the new American League. He finished third, but was let go and wound up back in the minors.

George piloted Buffalo to the Junior World Series championship in 1904. He returned to the majors in 1909 to head the New York Yankees for two years. In 1913 Stallings began an eight-year stint as skipper of the Boston Braves.

Stallings' 1914 team achieved fame as the "Miracle Braves." In last place on July 4, 15 games out of first, the Braves caught fire in the second half of the season and won the National League pennant by 10½ games. The Braves followed their astonishing league title with a four-game sweep of the Philadelphia Athletics in the World Series.

Even then, Stallings was still playing the role of wild man. He "could fly into a schizophrenic rage at the drop of a pop fly," sportswriter Tom Meany wrote.

Stallings ended his managerial career in 1920. In 13 seasons in the majors, his teams compiled an 879–898 record.

Stallings, George

	W	L	T	Pct
1897	55	77	2	.417
1898	19	27	0	.413
Phillies	74	104	2	.416
Career	879	898	35	.495

No one ever took over the job of Phillies manager with less credentials than Billy Shettsline. Yet in his five years in the driver's seat, the rotund localite compiled one of the club's more successful managerial records.

Shettsline worked for four decades with the Phillies, rising from a handyman and ticket taker to club president. He knew baseball thoroughly from an administrative standpoint. But he had never gone past the sandlot level as a player, and he had no experience running a team on the field.

In 1898, however, following the players' rebellion against manager George Stallings, Shettsline was summoned to replace the deposed pilot. At the time, Billy was working in the Phillies' front office.

When Shettsline took over, the Phillies were a dispirited group, mired in eighth place with a 19–27 record. Billy not only pulled the club back together, but he produced more wins than losses (59–44) and edged the club to a sixth-place finish.

That earned Shettsline the job for the following year. The 1899 club turned out to be one of the best all-around teams in Phillies history.

With three 20-game winners, Wiley Piatt, Red Donahue, and Chick Fraser; the league ERA leader, Al Orth; the batting champion, Ed Delahanty; and two other future Hall of Famers, Nap Lajoie and Elmer Flick, the Phillies won 94 games—more than any Phillies team until 1976. Although the team finished third, it was in the pennant race most of the season.

The talent-laden Phillies continued to play well during the next two years, finishing third in 1900 and second in 1901. Never noted for his agility, the corpulent Shettsline set a new level of gracelessness during spring training in 1900 following an 11–6 victory over St. Mary's College in a game at Charlotte, North Carolina. "Manager Shettsline was so pleased at the playing of his regulars," said a report in the *Evening Bulletin*, "that he fell out of the carriage and got a mud bath."

The 1901 team was riddled with defections to the new American League, including Lajoie and pitchers Fraser, Piatt, and Bill Bernhard to the Philadelphia Athletics. Its second-place finish, seven and one-half games behind the front-running Pittsburgh Pirates, and its 83–57 record were accomplished against a considerable handicap.

The handicap became more of a burden in 1902 when virtually all the prominent Phillies bolted to the American League. The only player of substance who remained loyal to the team was Roy Thomas. Although the rest of the teams in the National League were affected by the new circuit's player raids, the Phillies were hit particularly hard. As a result, Shettsline's club tumbled to seventh place.

The club's heavy losses to the American League and its resultant impotence on the field led to a 50 percent reduction in attendance in 1902. That created financial problems for owners Al Reach and John Rogers, and soon forced them to sell the team.

Under the new ownership of James Potter and his syndicate, Shettsline was lifted from the dugout and sent back to the front office. Although he became the Phillies' president a few years later, the most successful stage of his lengthy career would remain his five years as manager.

1898–1902

Shettsline, Billy

Record: 367–303–7 (.548)
Birthplace: Philadelphia, Pennsylvania
B: October 25, 1863; **D:** February 22, 1933

Billy Shettsline

Shettsline, Billy

	W	L	T	Pct
1898	59	44	1	.573
1899	94	58	2	.618
1900	75	63	3	.543
1901	83	57	0	.593
1902	56	81	1	.409
Phillies	367	303	7	.548
Career	367	303	7	.548

1903

Zimmer, Chief

Record: 49–86–4 (.363)
Birthplace: Marietta, Ohio
B: November 23, 1860; **D:** August 22, 1949

Chief Zimmer

Charles Louis Zimmer had a 19-year career as a catcher for seven different teams from 1884 to 1903. As a player, he is best remembered as one of Cy Young's favorite catchers. His last team was the Phillies where he was the player-manager for one season. The previous two seasons, he had been the Pirates' catcher. With Zimmer reaching the age of 43, it was time for Bucs owner Barney Dreyfuss to find another job for his backstop.

So when Dreyfuss orchestrated the sale of the Phillies to Philadelphia socialite Jimmy Potter, it almost appeared that Zimmer came with the package, like a previously arranged marriage.

The divorce was quick. The marriage lasted just one year, a poor one at that. The Phillies finished seventh, 39½ games behind the Pirates, winning only 49 games. For a man accustomed to working with pitchers for all those years, Zimmer obviously had trouble putting together a decent pitching staff.

At the end of the season, Zimmer was fired as manager and went back behind the plate. He joined the National League umpiring staff.

Zimmer, Chief

	W	L	T	Pct
1903	49	86	4	.363
Phillies	49	86	4	.363
Career	49	86	4	.363

1904–06

Duffy, Hugh

Record: 206–251–7 (.451)
Birthplace: Cranston, Rhode Island
B: November 26, 1866; **D:** October 19, 1954

Hugh Duffy

Hugh Duffy is a genuine Hall of Fame member, elected for his feats as a player. A 17-year outfielder, mostly with the pre-1900 Boston Beaneaters, he collected 2,282 hits, and in 1894 he recorded the highest National League average ever (.440).

His lifetime average was a splendid .324. In his three years as Phillie manager, he was also forced to be the spare outfielder because of a lack of funds in the ball team's bank account. He was 25-for-87 with the Phillies.

The Phillies were the second of four teams that he managed. Were he to be judged on his managerial abilities alone, they would be getting the ladder out of the closet in Cooperstown today, getting ready to remove his plaque.

He finished eighth in the new American League with the Milwaukee entry in 1901 and was one of the top raiders of National League talent.

With the Phillies, he finished eighth, then fourth twice. He moved on to the White Sox for two seasons beginning in 1910 and wound up sixth and fourth. And he got a two-year shot with the Red Sox in 1921 and 1922, finishing fifth and eighth. Thus, in eight years, he never finished higher than fourth. Only two of his teams won more than they lost.

His first Phillies team lost 100 of 152 games, but it also added a player, Sherry Magee, who would become a cornerstone of the franchise for the next decade.

It was rebuilding time for the team that had been decimated by the American League raids, but now Duffy was on the other side. The fact that the Phillies hired him said volumes about the realization by the National League that it had to accept the new league.

Duffy got a break when Jimmy Potter decided baseball was not his game and resigned as president. The title was given to Bill Shettsline, a man who had worn almost all the hats one could in baseball. He was a baseball man through and through, and he and Duffy worked hard to rebuild the team through deals and signings.

One good deal before the 1905 season began brought first baseman Kitty Bransfield from the Pirates. Togie Pittinger came over from Boston for Harry Wolverton and went 23–14 in 1905. And Frank Corridon was picked up from the Cubs.

A mainstay who arrived in 1905 was shortstop Mickey Doolan, who never hit much for average but was an outstanding fielder with an outstanding throwing arm. Duffy mixed and matched this group with his veterans and helped the team improve by 31 wins. The fourth-place finish was laudable, but it might have been too much too soon. In 1906 the Phils held on to fourth, but dropped 12 games off their 1905 pace, and Hugh Duffy moved on to Providence in the International League. Twice more he would return to the major leagues as a manager. He would never be more successful than he was in Philadelphia, where he turned the franchise around from terrible to decent in just three seasons.

Duffy, Hugh

	W	L	T	Pct
1904	52	100	3	.342
1905	83	69	3	.546
1906	71	82	1	.464
Phillies	206	251	7	.451
Career	535	671	15	.444

William Jeremiah Murray, like his predecessor, was an Irishman who was born in New England. There the similarities ended. While Hugh Duffy made the Hall of Fame with his bat, Billy Murray never played a game of baseball at the major league level.

He arrived in Philadelphia from the International League's Jersey City franchise, where he had a reputation as a good developer of talent and an awfully nice guy to be around as long as his Irish temper was kept below the boiling point.

Under most circumstances, Billy's Irish wit came to the forefront. An example: Murray's 1907 team finished third and won 83 games. When two tremendous pitching prospects arrived at the tail end of the season, the city became excited, just as it did in the middle year of Duffy's managing troika. With pitchers like George McQuillan and Harry Coveleskie ready to join a team that was able to win 83 games the season before, the Phillies might be real contenders.

Coveleskie, however, put his foot in his mouth and became a piece of Murray's blarney. In one of Harry's first appearances, a runner reached base on him. On the next pitch, the runner took a tremendous lead, but Harry paid no attention, and second was stolen without a throw.

At the end of the inning, Murray demanded to know why Harry had ignored the runner. In an answer that might have inspired the first Polish joke, Covie said, "I didn't know he was there."

After the game, Murray had a clubhouse meeting with his catcher, Red Dooin, and his infield, in addition to Coveleskie.

First he demanded angrily of first baseman Kitty Bransfield, "Did you know there was a runner on first and not tell Covie?"

Bransfield confessed.

Otto Knabe, the second baseman, was next on the firing line.

"Otto, is it also true that there was a runner on base and you didn't tell Harry?" Murray asked.

The same question was put to shortstop Mickey Doolin, third baseman Ed Grant and catcher Red Dooin. All pleaded guilty.

Murray banged his fist and announced: "From now on, we'll have no further secrets on this club. Whenever a runner gets to base on Harry, I want you men to tell him. Do you understand?"

They understood. The word motivation wasn't popularized then, but they understood that normally Billy Murray tried to motivate them with a feather

1907–09

Murray, Billy

Record: 240–214–4 (.529)
Birthplace: Peabody, Massachusetts
B: April 13, 1864; **D:** March 25, 1937

instead of an icepick. Billy Martin, Billy Murray wasn't. Which probably brought about his downfall.

The following year, Harry Coveleskie transcended from the Polish Joke to the Giant Killer, a nickname that forever will bring memories of his feat of knocking off the Giants three times in a week in the heat of a torrid pennant race that wound up with the Cubs winning the first playoff.

But the Phillies slipped back to fourth. The victory count was the same as the previous season (83). Yet the Phillies lost seven more than they had in 1908.

In 1909 the Phillies suffered another setback. Their position dropped to fifth, their 74–79 record represented a drop of nine games in the win column and an addition of eight in the loss ledger. Since the personnel were basically the same as the previous two years, the age-old theory about baseball might have been invented right here: You can't fire the players, so you fire the manager. Especially if you're Horace Fogel, former sports writer and forerunner to Bill Veeck as a showman and promoter.

Soon after taking over the presidency of the Phillies, Fogel called a press conference. He must have loved making the calls instead of taking them. It was his show to orchestrate, rather than review, for a change. Murray was the victim.

"We're going to be a live wire ball club, so we need a live wire organization from top to bottom," said Fogel, who was determined to change the nickname of the team from the Phillies to the Live Wires. "Billy Murray is a nice fellow. I like him. But he didn't put enough fight into his club. His contract will not be renewed."

Murray, Billy

	W	L	T	Pct
1907	83	64	2	.565
1908	83	71	1	.539
1909	74	79	1	.484
Phillies	240	214	4	.529
Career	240	214	4	.529

1910–14

Dooin, Charlie (Red)

Record: 392–370–13 (.514)
Birthplace: Cincinnati, Ohio
B: June 12, 1879; **D:** May 14, 1952

To date only 10 Phillies managers with a year or more service have been able to break the .500 career record. One of them was Red Dooin, who took the Phillies to the brink of their first National League pennant, but was fired at the end of the 1914 season.

He was appointed manager of the Phillies before the 1910 season in a decision that seemed popular with everyone, although most people had soft spots in their hearts for Billy Murray, who was fired by team president Horace Fogel.

Dooin was quite familiar with the Phillies, having been their catcher since 1902. And when he wasn't catching, he was singing. A fine Irish tenor, he could be heard both at Sunday Mass and on the vaudeville stages in the off-season.

But Red wasn't singing sweet ditties early in his first year at the helm. A couple of his promising pitchers, Earl Moore and George McQuillan, were suspended for breaking training rules early in the season. Moore got the message and wound up winning 22 games, but McQuillan didn't shape up and was given an indefinite suspension in mid-season by Fogel.

Dooin's first team was led by Sherry Magee, whose .331 average gave him the batting title. And managing seemed to inspire Dooin the catcher, who raised his own batting average, which never dazzled anyone anyway, 17 points to .242.

The 1910 Phillies improved their record by four games over the previous year, finishing in fourth place with a 78–75 record.

Although Dooin had a big season (for him) with the bat, he also helped shape the destiny of himself and his team. He came up with a lame shoulder early in the season, which forced Fogel to find himself a good backup catcher. The choice was Pat Moran.

Before the 1911 season could even begin, the Phillies were talking proud. A four-for-four trade with the Reds netted Hans Lobert, Dode Paskert, and two pitchers. Fogel was overjoyed. "I think (it) will give the Phillies their first pennant," Horace announced, then added, "Isn't that right, Charlie?"

Red Dooin nodded yes.

Then the season started, and the Giants, Cubs, and Pirates shook their heads no. The Phillies made only a one-game improvement in their overall record. And this despite the fact that Grover Cleveland Alexander burst on the scene. Almost released in spring training by Dooin, who was talked out of it by Moran, Alex proceeded to win 28 games and fashion an earned run average of 2.14.

But during the season Magee was suspended for punching umpire Bill Finneran, John Titus broke a leg sliding into home, and Dooin's own leg was also broken in a play at the plate.

Despite their problems, the Phillies were still in first place as late as August 3. But they faded badly, and finally finished 19½ games out of first.

Everyone was excited as 1912 approached. After all, hadn't the Phillies suffered some incredible bad luck down the stretch in 1911? Surely it couldn't happen again.

It did, only worse, in 1912.

Magee broke his wrist during the pre-season City Series with the Athletics, missed a month, came back to the lineup and went right back out again after an outfield collision. Hans Lobert broke a kneecap, Otto Knabe broke a hand, and Dooin himself was knocked to the sidelines with an intestinal illness. Three pitchers missed parts of the season because of ailments or injuries. And the Phils limped home fifth.

The next season was Dooin's best as a manager. The team finished a distant second to the Giants, but built hope because of the pitching (Tom Seaton 27 wins, Alexander 22) and the best one-two home run hitting tandem in the league in Gavvy Cravath (19) and Fred Luderus (18). The seeds were surely planted for the 1915 pennant, but Red was denied the privilege of directing that team.

Owner William F. Baker's reluctance to bid against the Federal League cost him talent. Suddenly the Phillies were without their keystone combination of many years—Knabe and Mickey Doolin. Young pitchers Seaton and Ad Brennan also joined the new league, and the Phils dipped to sixth, 20½ games behind.

After the season, Baker gave a press dinner at which he accused Dooin of losing control of the team (this after Baker had lost half the team to the Feds) and announced that he was being replaced by Pat Moran.

Dooin never managed at the major league level again. He played and coached with the New York Giants through 1917, that year picking up his only World Series paycheck. He played in Rochester in 1918 and managed at Reading in 1919 before retiring from baseball.

Having starred for years in a vaudeville Irish comedy act called "His Last Night Out" and having invested heavily in real estate, he was financially independent.

After Dooin left baseball he lived in Atlantic City. But when the banks collapsed in 1929, he lost much of his holdings.

Dooin returned to vaudeville, did some gigs on radio, and moved to Rochester, New York. He died there on May 14, 1952, at the age of 71.

Red Dooin

Dooin, Charlie (Red)

	W	L	T	Pct
1910	78	75	4	.510
1911	79	73	1	.520
1912	73	79	0	.480
1913	88	63	8	.583
1914	74	80	0	.481
Phillies	392	370	13	.514
Career	392	370	13	.514

1915–18

Moran, Pat

Record: 323–257–6 (.556)
Birthplace: Fitchburg, Massachusetts
B: February 7, 1876; **D:** March 7, 1924

Pat Moran

Pat Moran's record as a manager does its own talking. He only had two big league managing jobs in his life—with the Phillies and the Cincinnati Reds. Each time he won a pennant in his first year at the helm.

He lost the 1915 World Series and won the 1919 one with the Reds. His career as a manager spanned nine seasons, seven of them winners. And it is only speculation as to what he might have done if his life hadn't suddenly ended in spring training in 1924, a month after his 48th birthday.

A backup catcher with a .235 career batting average through his 14-year playing career, which included stints with the Chicago Cubs' championship teams of 1906, 1907, and 1909, Moran learned the game and its strategies and fine points from behind the plate and on the bench. And when William F. Baker named him to succeed Red Dooin after the 1914 season, Moran wasted no time in putting everything he had learned into the team he inherited.

"This is not a sixth-place team," he hammered into the Phillies from day one of spring training at St. Petersburg's Coffee Pot Park. A man who instinctively could pick out the phony from the genuine product, Moran weeded out the potential troublemakers in spring training and got rid of anyone who couldn't make the basic plays. He worked out an intricate system of signs that were virtually theft-proof. He made the players walk to and from their headquarters hotel, about three miles from the park. And he drilled his team on fundamentals and discipline.

"Moran was an inspiring leader," said infielder Bobby Byrne. "He had the knack of building a player up. Pat would make a fellow think he was better than he really was, and first thing you know, the player would be doing better than he knew how."

But the main thing that made Moran different from his fellow managers of the era was his ability to handle a pitching staff. Much of it came from his own days as a catcher, but the instruction went much deeper than that. Moran would catch batting practice and hit the pitcher with situations. "Man on first, none out, a ball and a strike on the batter," he would say to the pitcher. "Where are you going to throw the ball?" he would ask. If the pitcher didn't have the right answer—inside because of the possibility of a hit-and-run in this case—Moran would bawl him out in front of the entire team. And it didn't matter if the pitcher was Bareback Joe Oeschger or Grover Cleveland Alexander. By the time the Phillies broke camp and headed north, the pitchers knew the right pitch in every conceivable situation.

Moran also put a severe curb on gambling after several players got involved in a big-league crap game on the first trip of the season. Pat knew he had a good club and he was determined to keep a strong hand on it.

No question he got results. The Phillies never dropped below second and led the National League most of the way. The team won its first eight games and won the race easily, but suffered a terrific blow when star catcher Bill Killefer came up with a dead arm in the last month of the season.

Killefer was unable to catch in any of the World Series games, and the Boston Red Sox won, four games to one. But Moran had accomplished something that no other Phillies manager had done before, or would do for the next 35 years. A year after turning down an invitation to become a National League umpire, Moran was manager of a pennant winner.

Moran guided the Phillies to second place in 1916, winning one more game than the pennant winners, then repeated the position in 1917. But, while the 1916 team was in the pennant race until the last week of the season, the 1917 team faded in July and wound up 10 full games behind. And less than three months after that season, Baker traded Alexander to the Chicago Cubs. The deal left Moran hopping mad. He didn't try to hide his opinions, either, and when the Phillies dropped to sixth in 1918, Baker concluded the season by calling a dinner at which he announced: "I've let Pat Moran go." In effect, the announcement was the gateway to three decades in which mediocrity became a reason for applause.

Moran didn't stay unemployed very long. The Cincinnati Reds offered a contract; Pat accepted and won the World Championship in his first year when the Reds beat the Chicago Black Sox, five games to three. Cincinnati finished second twice and third once over the next four seasons and was looking for another pennant when the squad arrived in Orlando, Florida, for spring training in 1924.

But, on March 6, Moran was admitted to a local hospital, suffering from kidney and heart trouble. At first the hospital reports were encouraging: no danger of pneumonia, a likely stay of about 10 days. But the next morning, the news was grim. Moran was sinking toward a coma fast, and death was a possibility. By afternoon the reports were worse: "The attending physicians hold virtually no hope for his recovery . . . he cannot last for more than an hour or so."

With his wife and two children at his side, Moran died that evening.

Moran, Pat

	W	L	T	Pct
1915	90	62	1	.592
1916	91	62	1	.595
1917	87	65	2	.572
1918	55	68	2	.447
Phillies	323	257	6	.556
Career	748	586	9	.561

Jack Coombs had a successful career as a pitcher with Connie Mack's A's before he took over as Phillies manager and a happy lifetime coaching baseball at four colleges after he left the employ of William F. Baker.

His managing career in the major leagues lasted 62 games and was unpleasant, to say the least. First of all, local hero Jack was replacing Pat Moran, who had been fired by Baker despite the fact that he had been one of baseball's most successful managers during his tenure.

For another, Baker interfered with anything that Coombs tried to accomplish. The Phillies managed to stay close to .500, but in June lost 13 in a row. That stretch was soon followed by a five-game losing streak. Baker became impatient, and on July 9, 1919, announced he was firing Coombs in favor of outfielder Gavvy Cravath.

When the news reached the clubhouse, chaos broke out. Nearly every player vowed that he would not play that day, claiming the firing was wholly unjustified. It took pleas from Cravath and Coombs to get them to take the field for a game against the Chicago Cubs.

Before the game, though, one pitcher fungoed 19 balls over the right field fence at Baker Bowl. Another threw at least one dozen balls into the stands. Struggling hard to get control, Cravath finally got all but five players in line. Those five went to the clubhouse and continued the drinking spree that most of the players had started that morning. Dressed in street clothes, the five then went to the center field stands where they started a tirade against Baker. Many of the bleacherites joined in, and the noise was heard throughout the ballpark.

Eventually, the game was played, the Phillies losing, 5–4. The next day several players were fined; one (catcher Hick Cady, a close friend of Coombs) was released, and another (pitcher Frank Woodward) was traded.

Coombs and Baker then got into a dispute over whether the manager was fired or resigned. When Coombs said he was fired, an angry Baker vowed to withhold his pay. Later Baker accused Coombs of "going on a jamboree" with his players the day he was fired.

In his playing days, Coombs won 31 games for the Athletics in 1910 and had a career record of 159–110. He won all five World Series decisions in which he was involved.

After leaving the Phillies, Coombs, a graduate of Colby College, coached four years at Williams, four years at Princeton, three years at Rice, and 24 years at Duke. Among his stars at Duke was Dick Groat.

Coombs retired after the 1952 season to Palestine, Texas, where he died five years later at the age of 74.

1919

Coombs, Jack

Record: 18–44–1 (.290)
Birthplace: LeGrande, Iowa
B: November 18, 1882; **D:** April 15, 1957

Jack Coombs

Coombs, Jack

	W	L	T	Pct
1919	18	44	1	.290
Phillies	18	44	1	.290
Career	18	44	1	.290

1919–20

Cravath, Gavvy

Record: 91–137–0 (.399)
Birthplace: Escondido, California
B: March 23, 1881; **D:** May 23, 1963

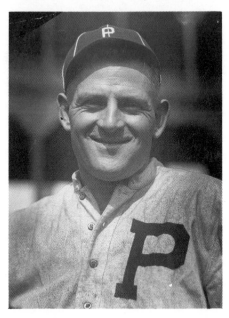

Gavvy Cravath

Gavvy Cravath, who joined the Phillies at the age of 31 and became a power-hitting star, was not nearly as fortunate when he took over the managerial reins in 1919, replacing Jack Coombs in mid-season.

However, managing seemed to do wonders for Cactus Cravath's ability to hit a baseball, even if it didn't rub off on his players. He lifted his average 109 points to .341 from the previous season and led the National League in home runs with 12.

A month after he took over as manager, the rumors were running strong that the Cubs were going to dump a game to the Phillies. Cravath, reached in his hotel room after the Phillies won the game, 3–0, was asked to comment.

"I certainly don't know anything about it," Cravath said. "Jeez, I don't know why they gotta bring a thing like this up just because we win one. Gee, we're likely to win a game most any time."

In 1920, Baker traded baseball's best shortstop, Dave Bancroft, from under Cravath and the team finished eighth again with a 62–91 record, which was a notable improvement over the previous season's 47–90. It was not, however, enough to save Cravath's job as manager or player. At the age of 40, his days in the major leagues were over.

After sitting for many years as a justice of the peace, Cravath died in 1963 in Laguna Beach, California.

Cravath, Gavvy

	W	L	T	Pct
1919	29	46	0	.387
1920	62	91	0	.405
Phillies	91	137	0	.399
Career	91	137	0	.399

1921

Donovan, Wild Bill

Record: 25–62 (.287)
Birthplace: Lawrence, Massachusetts
B: October 13, 1876; **D:** December 9, 1923

They called him Wild Bill because he couldn't find the plate with any regularity as a youngster growing up in Philadelphia. Later, he developed into a fine big league pitcher. Twice in his career, which spanned 18 years, he won 25 games in a season, and he wound up with 187 victories.

As he had done when he signed Jack Coombs, Phillies president William F. Baker picked a familiar face from the Philadelphia scene when he chose Wild Bill Donovan to succeed Gavvy Cravath as Phillies manager for the 1921 season. Unlike Coombs, however, Donovan had managing experience at the major league level. He guided the New York Yankees for three seasons from 1915 to 1917, getting them home fourth in 1916, when he had his only winning season as a manager.

The best base-stealing pitcher in baseball history (36, plus the only stolen base ever recorded by a pitcher in World Series history), Donovan began his managing career with Providence in the International League in 1913. One of his best players in his two seasons there was Babe Ruth, a pitcher at the time. Donovan has been given some credit for The Babe's maturation as a ball player.

Based on his success at Providence, Donovan was hired by Jacob Ruppert to guide the Yankees in 1915. The impatient Ruppert fired him after the 1917 season, much to the dismay of everyone connected with the club, because Donovan was an extremely popular figure.

Wild Bill's popularity followed him to Philadelphia. Alas, good fortune did not. He lost two of his starting infielders before the season even started. Judge Landis threw first baseman Gene Paulette out of baseball for previous associations with gamblers, and shortstop Art Fletcher sat out the season mourning the death within a month's time of his father and brother.

Donovan was greeted by a stable of sore-armed pitchers, a group of regulars who were less than thrilled playing for what Baker was paying them, and an owner who constantly meddled in the manager's territory.

In July Baker's meddling hit a peak. First he suspended outfielder Irish Meusel, saying he was guilty of indifference. Then he peddled him along with Casey Stengel and Johnny Rawlings to the New York Giants, claiming he was forced to get rid of Meusel for the good of the team.

Donovan, who had not been consulted on the deal, was irate. A war of words erupted between the owner and the manager. Meanwhile, the commissioner, Judge Landis, got into the act and summoned Meusel to his office, whereupon he learned that it was not Donovan but Baker who had suspended the outfielder.

About this time, Donovan mysteriously left the team, going on a scouting trip and leaving Kaiser Wilhelm in charge. In Buffalo, Donovan disclosed that Baker had fired him on the grounds that he had been summoned to testify in the Black Sox trial in Chicago (in 1920), and therefore must have close ties with gamblers.

The reference incensed Donovan, who, in fact, had not testified at the trial. Donovan appealed to Landis to enforce his contract with the Phillies. Eventually, after a barrage of statements and telegrams, Landis ordered Baker to pay Donovan's salary in full.

Wild Bill managed in the minor leagues in New England for the next two years before dying suddenly on December 9, 1923, at the age of 47 in Forsyth, New York.

Donovan, Wild Bill

	W	L	T	Pct
1921	25	62	0	.287
Phillies	25	62	0	.287
Career	245	301	6	.449

Bill Donovan

Irving (Kaiser) Wilhelm was William F. Baker's next victim. "Kize," as he became known in Philadelphia, had quit baseball during World War I to become a government inspector of motors. He had been a so-so pitcher for nine years in the major leagues, including a stint in the Federal League, and nine more in the minors with moderate to poor success. His lifetime major league record was 57–105 and it included three 20-loss campaigns, one when he was 4–23.

After the war, he went into private business in Buffalo, but he couldn't get baseball out of his life. So, in 1920 he joined Wild Bill Donovan as a coach for Jersey City in the International League. The following season, Donovan signed with the Phillies and brought Wilhelm along with him. When Baker fired Donovan, he promoted Wilhelm to the head spot.

Wilhelm was Baker's kind of manager, which meant he came cheaply. But his tenure was doomed from the start. Baker somehow combined the get-rid-of-all-stars (except Cy Williams) philosophy with a win-now ethic. Obviously, the two didn't mix.

Wilhelm was expected to be an interim manager. "It is difficult to believe that any baseball man of reputation would come here under present conditions," wrote Jimmie Isaminger in *The Sporting News*. But after winning 26 of 67 decisions at the end of the 1921 season, Wilhelm was signed for 1922.

He was hailed as somewhat of a miracle worker after driving the Phillies to seventh place and a 57–96 record. With Cy Williams' 26 home runs leading the way, the Phils smashed a record 116 balls out of Baker Bowl and the other

1921–22

Wilhelm, Irving (Kaiser)

Record: 83–137–1 (.377)
Birthplace: Wooster, Ohio
B: January 26, 1874; **D:** May 21, 1936

Kaiser Wilhelm

National League parks, earning the nickname "Kize Wilhelm's Home Run Congress."

"No manager could have done better with the collection of rots and spots that represented the Phils this year," wrote Isaminger.

Nevertheless, Baker ditched his manager, even though he had produced a hustling, fighting team that was warmly appreciated by the fans, replacing him with aging shortstop Art Fletcher.

Kize floated through the minor league scene for eight years after leaving the Phillies. He managed at Bridgeport in 1925 and part of the 1929 season at Rochester, and also did some scouting for the Chicago Cubs and Rochester. In 1930 he took the head coaching job at the University of Rochester, but quit after one year. He died in 1936 in Rochester at the age of 52.

Wilhelm, Irving (Kaiser)

	W	L	T	Pct
1921	26	41	0	.388
1922	57	96	1	.373
Phillies	83	137	1	.377
Career	83	137	1	.377

1923–26

Fletcher, Art

Record: 231–378–3 (.380)
Birthplace: Collinsville, Illinois
B: January 5, 1885; **D:** February 6, 1950

Art Fletcher

Art Fletcher was a paradox.

A polite, well-mannered gentleman off the field, Art was a bulldog once the game started. He would argue, taunt, snarl, even bite if it meant winning a game. He was acknowledged as one of baseball's greatest sign stealers as manager of the Phillies, interim manager of the Yankees after Miller Huggins' sudden death, and long-time Yankee coach.

He lasted four full years with William F. Baker, even though he fought the Phillies' owner tooth and nail on just about everything. From those statistics, it would have appeared that Fletcher wanted to manage more than anything. Yet, when he was offered the job of Yankee manager, most prestigious in baseball, after the 1929 season, he respectfully declined.

"I thank you, Colonel, for offering me the job," Fletcher told Yankees owner Jake Ruppert. "But I'd rather stay with you as coach."

Ruppert was dumbfounded. "Just because you had that trouble with Baker and he sold your players? We've got lots of players, and money, in this organization."

Fletcher, though, was adamant. "Just the same, I'd rather you gave the managerial job to someone else and that I could stay on with the team as coach."

He stayed on until 1945 when he retired after suffering a heart attack. Five years later, another attack in Los Angeles ended his life at age 65.

Fletcher's four years as Phillies manager, aside from the constant arguments with the owner, saw the team rise as high as sixth in 1925. By that time, he had already drawn numerous suspensions and fines for his conduct on the field. As a manager, he was very much the same high-strung person he had been as a shortstop in a 13-year big league career. And, in 1926, when the team slid back to eighth place, Fletcher became involved in the famous Bill Klem incident. Klem, an umpire of considerable note, always claimed that he had never made a wrong call in his life. This day, Jimmie Wilson, the catcher, disagreed with a Klem call and was sent to the center field clubhouse.

Fletcher tried to protect his player but was threatened by the same fate if he didn't return to the dugout. A few minutes later, he came out again and was banished by Klem. Art went to the clubhouse and, minutes later, a blackboard appeared with the message "Catfish Klem," a nickname the ump detested.

Klem and the National League umpiring chief, John Heydler, suspended Fletcher indefinitely. It turned out they had punished an innocent man. It was Wilson, not Fletcher, who had arranged for the chalkboard.

While he was under suspension, Fletcher was fired by Baker. It would be his first and last managing job, except for the 6–5 record he posted as Yankee skipper in 1929 as Huggins was dying of blood poisoning in a New York hospital.

Fletcher, Art

	W	L	T	Pct
1923	50	104	1	.325
1924	55	96	1	.364
1925	68	85	0	.444
1926	58	93	1	.384
Phillies	231	378	3	.380
Career	237	383	3	.382

No one ever confused the 1927 Phillies with the 1927 Yankees. The only similarity was that some people considered Cy Williams to be the Babe Ruth of the National League. The '27 Yankees had their Murderers' Row. The '27 Phillies had their Murdered Row, the pitching staff. No pitcher came close to breaking the .500 level. The team finished 51–103, nine games out of seventh place.

A Philadelphia legend, Athletics first baseman Stuffy McInnis, was the unfortunate who got to manage this collection of misfits and ragtag talents. The manager might have been different, but it was business as usual in the front office for the Phillies. A $50,000 check was the sweetest thing William F. Baker got back for trading spitballer Hal Carlson to the Cubs. Carlson had been named to the National League All-Star team the season before.

McInnis wasn't used to such blundering. In his 19-year career as a first baseman, he had played in five World Series, collected 2,406 hits, and compiled a .308 lifetime average. His 1927 Phillies barely outplayed what their manager had hit. Their 51–103 record worked out to .331.

Working under a one-year contract, McInnis was unceremoniously dumped by Baker after the unsuccessful season.

McInnis, Stuffy

	W	L	T	Pct
1927	51	103	1	.331
Phillies	51	103	1	.331
Career	51	103	1	.331

While he was with the Phillies, Burt Shotton had the somewhat dubious distinction of managing the losingest team in the club's first half century as well as the winningest team between 1917 and 1949.

All that was in the period of six seasons. They were seasons in which the Phillies generally combined a furious hitting attack with pitching that was just a shade above forlorn.

Shotton, who as a swift outfielder was also given the nickname of Barney (after race-car driver Barney Oldfield), had a long and sometimes unconventional career in baseball. The most prominent part occurred late in his career when twice he piloted the Brooklyn Dodgers to the National League pennant, only to be fired after losing the 1950 flag to—of all teams—the Phillies.

Burt broke into organized baseball in 1903. Six years later he advanced to

1927

McInnis, Stuffy

Record: 51–103–1 (.331)
Birthplace: Gloucester, Massachusetts
B: September 19, 1890; **D:** February 16, 1960

Stuffy McInnis

1928–33

Shotton, Burt

Record: 370–549–4 (.403)
Birthplace: Brownhelm, Ohio
B: October 18, 1884; **D:** July 29, 1962

the St. Louis Browns and became the club's regular center fielder. While in St. Louis, he also became the protégé of Branch Rickey. When he was manager, Rickey refused to work on Sundays. Shotton was the club's Sunday manager, a practice that continued when the two joined forces later with the St. Louis Cardinals.

Shotton played in 14 seasons, including one with the Washington Senators. He finished with a .270 career batting mark.

After piloting Syracuse in the International League for two seasons, Burt was summoned to the Phillies. His first club in 1928 lost 109 games, the most for any Phillies team until 1941.

By then, though, Chuck Klein had joined the Phillies, and with Lefty O'Doul and others, he gave the club a blistering batting attack. The 1929 team hit .309 but finished only fifth as its pitching staff combined for a 6.13 earned run average. The situation was even more ridiculous the next year when the Phillies hit .315 as a team, yet finished eighth with 102 losses. The moundsmen that year gave up 6.71 earned runs per game.

Through all of this, Shotton remained a sometimes gentle, sometimes austere leader who could be caustic and tough. As was the case later in his managerial career, too, Burt was never terribly popular with his players or the writers, largely because of his aloofness. But he did have a creative streak.

That was demonstrated during one spring training when Shotton discovered that his athletes were sneaking out of the hotel after hours to visit the local dance halls. Concluding that the players were leaving by a fire escape, one night Burt painted the railing green. The next morning, an inspection at breakfast revealed five Phillies with green hands. Their dancing nights came to a screeching halt.

Burt Shotton

Shotton's team improved to the point that in 1932 it finished a rousing fourth. No Phillies team had placed in the first division since 1917, and none would again until 1949.

It was a one-shot venture, however. The Phillies slipped back to seventh the following year, and Shotton was dismissed. "I did the best job I could," he said.

Shotton spent 1934 as a coach with the Cincinnati Reds, then managed in the International League until joining the Cleveland Indians as a coach in 1942, serving as a kind of elderly adviser to youthful manager, Lou Boudreau. After four seasons with the Indians, he became a scout for Rickey and the Dodgers.

In 1947 commissioner Happy Chandler suspended Dodger manager Leo Durocher for the season for "conduct detrimental to baseball." Shotton was named the team's manager, and Brooklyn won the pennant. That season the Dodgers' Jackie Robinson also became the first black player in the major leagues. Shotton strongly supported Robinson and the cause for which he stood.

Durocher resumed his duties in 1948, and Shotton was sent to supervise the Dodgers' farm clubs. Midway through the season, Durocher quit abruptly to become manager of the New York Giants, and Shotton was recalled to pilot the team.

He finished third that year, then won the flag again in 1949. As they did in 1947 when ex-Phillies pilots Shotton and Bucky Harris were opponents, the Dodgers lost in the World Series to the New York Yankees.

As Brooklyn's manager, Shotton worked in street clothes, a cap and windbreaker being his only baseball clothing (he wore a uniform as the Phillies' pilot). Although his image was one of a kindly, grandfatherly fellow, it was a false portrayal. Burt was not easy to get along with. As Dick Young wrote in the New York *Daily News,* "He makes more mistakes in his relations with people than he does on the ballfield. He will do anything to win."

Shotton didn't win the 1950 pennant; the Phillies beat his Dodgers on the final day of the season. Burt came under heavy fire for that failure, and he was fired after the season.

Burt never forgave Brooklyn for the way the affair was handled and in the ensuing years turned bitter about the game of baseball.

Shotton, Burt

	W	L	T	Pct
1928	43	109	0	.283
1929	71	82	1	.464
1930	52	102	2	.338
1931	66	88	1	.429
1932	78	76	0	.506
1933	60	92	0	.395
Phillies	370	549	4	.403
Career	697	764	8	.477

Jimmie Wilson had the misfortune to be the Phillies manager at a time when the team had some of its most serious financial problems. Wilson's teams bore the consequences of those problems.

In the slightly less than five years that Jimmie managed, the Phillies alternated between bad and awful, finishing seventh three times and eighth twice. Wilson's five-season record is the worst of those who piloted the Phillies in more than 300 games.

The record was in no way an achievement singularly attributable to Wilson. While Jimmie managed, Phillies president Gerry Nugent, in an attempt to pay the bills, dealt away such stars as Dick Bartell, Dolph Camilli, and Bucky Walters, plus a gang of lesser players. The players on the team changed so often that it was a chore for Wilson just to keep track of his latest roster.

Jimmie rarely complained. He took what Nugent gave him and struggled each year to make his team presentable. It seldom worked, though.

A popular Philadelphia native, Wilson had been an outstanding National League catcher during his playing days. He broke in with the Phillies in 1923 after starting in the minors in 1920. The Phillies traded Wilson to the St. Louis Cardinals in 1928. Jimmie helped the Cards to three National League pennants.

After the Phillies unloaded Burt Shotton at the conclusion of the 1933 season, Wilson became Nugent's leading candidate as a replacement. Jimmie had always had managerial aspirations, and he was a special favorite of the Phillies' president.

Wilson was obtained in a trade, and in 1934 he became player-manager of the Phillies. Jimmie continued to play throughout his days as the team's skipper, although it was in a part-time role.

His teams, however, were a sad bunch. Although usually stacked with good hitters, the Phillies' pitching was poor. Ironically, as a catcher, Wilson had always enjoyed a reputation as a superb handler of pitchers.

Wilson's first team finished seventh with a 56–93 record. The next year the club improved its numbers to 64–89, but remained in seventh. In 1936, having lost 14 games in a row at one point, the Phillies plunged to eighth with a 54–100 mark. They bobbed up to seventh with a 61–92 mark in 1937, then fell back to eighth with a 45–105 log in 1938.

"Managing the Phillies was no different from managing anywhere else," Wilson once said, "except that you didn't have the players. You'd expect to win every day, and then you'd get your brains beaten out."

Despite the records, Wilson was regarded as an astute manager. His battles with St. Louis Cardinals manager Frankie Frisch, a former roommate who had a falling out with Wilson, were particularly memorable. Writer John Lardner called the clashes of the two pilots "a collision of runaway razor blades."

Jimmie quit the team in disgust with two games left in the 1938 season. "Even Connie Mack finishes last when he has no players," Wilson grumbled.

Although Wilson's teams never amounted to much, the manager was successful in at least one area. Jimmie was the one who converted Bucky Walters into a pitcher.

1934–38

Wilson, Jimmie

Record: 280–477–6 (.371)
Birthplace: Philadelphia, Pennsylvania
B: July 23, 1900; **D:** May 31, 1947

Jimmie Wilson

Originally a third baseman, Walters had a strong arm, which Wilson correctly surmised could produce some effective hurling. Although Walters had control problems at first and occasionally became discouraged, Wilson offered him a case of champagne if he'd stick with it. Eventually Bucky collected.

After he left the Phillies, Wilson landed with the Cincinnati Reds as a player-coach. In Cincinnati, he was reunited with Walters, who by then had been traded by the Phillies after becoming a successful pitcher.

In 1940, Wilson and Walters helped the Reds to the World Championship. The two Philadelphia natives were given a rousing welcome when they returned to their homes in the city.

Wilson was named manager of the Chicago Cubs in 1941. He headed the Cubs until early in the 1944 season. Although the Cubs won the National League pennant in 1945, Wilson's teams leading up to that triumph finished sixth twice and fifth once, and were in eighth when he departed.

He was fired in May 1944. Shortly thereafter he landed a job as a coach with the Reds, a post he held through the 1946 season.

"Coaching is a better job, anyway," he said. "It's the best job in baseball."

After leaving the Reds, Wilson moved to Florida where he bought into a fruit business. He wasn't interested in baseball anymore, he said. He was an orange grower now.

Nearly three decades of baseball had taken its toll on Jimmie. But so had the loss of his only son in World War II. Wilson never recovered from that.

On May 31, 1947, while eating with friends in a restaurant in Florida, he died suddenly of a heart attack.

Wilson, Jimmie

	W	L	T	Pct
1934	56	93	0	.376
1935	64	89	3	.418
1936	54	100	0	.351
1937	61	92	2	.399
1938	45	103	1	.304
Phillies	280	477	6	.371
Career	493	735	9	.401

1939–41

Prothro, Doc (James)

Record: 138–320–2 (.302)
Birthplace: Memphis, Tennessee
B: July 16, 1893; **D:** October 14, 1971

Unfortunately for him, Doc Prothro exemplifies the classic case of a man who was at the wrong place at the wrong time.

Prothro had the misfortune to manage three of the worst teams in Phillies history, a circumstance that cast more shadows on Doc's image as a manager than perhaps it should have.

The fact that Prothro has the losingest record of anyone who led the Phillies for more than one season was not a record that was all Doc's fault. Known as a knowledgeable baseball man, Prothro happened to be in Philadelphia when the team's roster was nearly devoid of talent.

Prothro, a graduate of the University of Tennessee dental school, had been a highly successful minor league manager when he came to the Phillies. In 11 seasons in the Southern Association with the Memphis Chicks and Little Rock Travelers, he had won three pennants, finished second twice, and ended up in third three times.

He is "smart, resourceful, a never-say-die type," said *Inquirer* sportswriter Stan Baumgartner, a Pacific Coast league teammate of Prothro's in 1926. "He played baseball to the hilt, fought to the last ditch, and was always an inspiration to players associated with him."

Doc had begun in baseball in 1920 when Clark Griffith plucked him off a Memphis semipro team and brought him to the Washington Senators. At the time, Prothro had been a practicing dentist for three years.

Prothro was up and down with the Senators over the next four years as a reserve third baseman. In 1925 he went to the Boston Red Sox, where he started for the only time in his career and hit .313. Doc left the big leagues as a player after a brief visit with the Cincinnati Reds in 1926. He bowed out with a .318 average in 180 games.

Although he continued to practice dentistry during the off-season, Prothro gained a reputation as one of the smartest managers in the South. He had vetoed several big league jobs by the time he accepted Gerry Nugent's offer to succeed Jimmie Wilson.

When he joined the Phillies, Prothro was blindly optimistic. "They'll give me every opportunity to do something with the club. I hope I can do them justice," he said.

Instead, Doc's first team in 1939 waltzed out and lost 106 games, to that point the second highest number of losses in club history. The manager, however, maintained his courage. "I didn't come here to manage a last-place club," he said. "I intend to get out of the cellar next year."

In 1940 the Phillies lost three fewer games but remained in eighth place. The following year the club lost 111 games, the most in team history, and finished last for the third time under Prothro and the fifth time in the last six years.

Although it hadn't helped Prothro's cause when Nugent traded three of the team's best players, first Claude Passeau, then Morrie Arnovich, and finally Kirby Higbe, Doc bore the blame for the Phillies' horrendous performances, and was let go.

The deposed manager took his dismissal like a true soldier.

"There is nothing I'd like better than to manage the Phillies," he said. "But he (Nugent) can't be blamed for making a change."

Prothro, whose son Tommy was a highly successful college and pro football coach, most recently with the Los Angeles Rams and San Diego Chargers, returned to Memphis where he became manager again and part-owner of the Chicks. Eventually, he retired to his sizable farm in nearby Arkansas.

Doc Prothro

Prothro, Doc

	W	L	T	Pct
1939	45	106	1	.298
1940	50	103	0	.327
1941	43	111	1	.279
Phillies	138	320	2	.302
Career	138	320	2	.302

1938, 1942

Lobert, Hans (John)

Record: 42–111 (.275)
Birthplace: Wilmington, Delaware
B: October 18, 1881; **D:** September 14, 1968

During a career that spanned more than 40 years in organized baseball, there were few jobs that escaped Hans Lobert. Player, coach, manager, scout, he was the epitome of a career baseball man.

He served twice as manager of the Phillies, a team for whom he also played and worked as a coach. Although his managerial activities were unsuccessful, he had a reputation as a skillful and knowledgeable pilot.

No less an authority than Danny Murtaugh attested to that. The Phillies' second baseman in 1942 (Lobert's only full year at the helm), the future four-time manager of the Pittsburgh Pirates often praised his former boss.

"After spending about two weeks with Lobert, I was amazed at his knowledge of baseball and his ability to teach it," Murtaugh said in the book *Teenagers, Graybeards and 4-Fs.* "When I became a manager, I used a lot of the things Hans talked to me about, such as how to teach base-running."

In his playing days, Lobert had been a spectacular base-runner, one of the best of his era. In 1904 he was said to have run the 100-yard dash in 9.5 seconds. A year later he was timed going to first base on a bunt in 3.4 seconds and circling the bases in 13.8 seconds, both swift times even by present standards.

Lobert broke into the big leagues with the Pirates in 1903. At the time, Pittsburgh writers thought he so closely resembled Honus Wagner that they gave Lobert the same nickname as the future Hall of Fame shortstop.

During his 14-year big league playing career, Lobert performed briefly for the Pirates and Chicago Cubs. He played five seasons with the Cincinnati Reds, four with the Phillies, and three with the New York Giants. While with the Reds, he became one of the league's best base-stealers and top third basemen.

After hitting .309 in 1910 for the Reds, Lobert was traded to the Phillies where he hit .285, 327, .300, and .275. The Phillies traded him to the Giants before the 1915 season. Hans finished his major league career in 1917 with a .281 lifetime batting average.

From 1918 to 1925, Lobert was the head baseball coach at West Point. He was a coach with the Giants in 1928, and a minor league manager from 1929 to 1932.

In 1934 new Phillies manager Jimmie Wilson hired Hans as his first lieutenant. When Wilson quit in 1938 with two games left in the season, Lobert managed the team, losing both games.

Lobert was given a crack at being the club's full-time manager in 1942 following the dismissal of Doc Prothro. The team was one of the Phillies' worst, losing 109 games.

It had little talent, and for the fifth straight year the Phillies finished in eighth place. The club was also last in the National League in batting average, fielding percentage, and earned run average, and it had the second most losses in Phillies history.

With the arrival of new president William Cox, Lobert was dumped unceremoniously by the Phillies, despite his long affiliation with the team. His abrupt dismissal was for Lobert an unhappy end for such a loyal employee.

Hans spent the next two seasons as a coach with the Reds. He relinquished his full-time status after 1944.

Lobert, Hans

	W	L	T	Pct
1938	0	2	0	.000
1942	42	109	0	.278
Phillies	42	111	0	.275
Career	42	111	0	.275

Hans Lobert

1943

Harris, Bucky (Stanley)

Record: 38–52–2 (.422)
Birthplace: Port Jervis, New York
B: November 8, 1896; **D:** November 8, 1977

The reign of Bucky Harris was one of the shortest but most controversial of all Phillies managers.

Harris was the most successful and most experienced pilot ever to wear a Phillies uniform. Unfortunately for the Phillies, he accumulated neither much success nor much experience during his brief stay in Philadelphia. But he did figure in one of the club's most bizarre events.

Elected to the Hall of Fame in 1975, Harris was a big league manager for 29 years. Only two other managers (Connie Mack and John McGraw) managed in more games than Bucky's 4,406 or won more games than his 2,157.

By the time he came to the Phillies in 1943, Harris had been heading teams since 1924. That year, at the age of 27, Bucky won fame as the "Boy Manager" when he led the Washington Senators to the American League pennant and World Series crown against the New York Giants. He won the league flag again the following year, but was beaten in the Series by the Pittsburgh Pirates.

Harris skippered the Senators for five years, the Detroit Tigers for another five, the Boston Red Sox for one, and Washington again for eight seasons. Other than the two pennant winners, only five of those teams finished in the first division. But Harris was regarded as one of baseball's premier managers when William Cox signed him to a Phillies contract in 1943.

"Harris is the man I wanted from the beginning," said the Phillies' new owner.

Only 14 Phillies reported to spring training at Hershey, Pennsylvania, but with his many contacts Harris soon started bringing players to Philadelphia. Schoolboy Rowe, Babe Dahlgren, Jimmy Wasdell, Al Gerheauser, and Dick Barrett joined the Phillies through various deals.

Soon Harris had his collection of misfits and castoffs playing so well that they were within striking distance of the first division, a rarity for Phillie teams. All the while, though, animosity was developing between Harris and Cox.

Bucky disliked the owner's constant intrusions in the clubhouse and his increasingly frequent attempts to tell the players how to play. Cox, who originally had made Harris a member of the club's board of directors, blamed Bucky for the club's losses. He was also unhappy that Harris wasn't a 24-hour-a-day yes-man.

In late July, although the Phillies were in fifth place, Cox leaked the story that Harris was being dismissed. Bucky learned of his firing after being contacted for his comments while with the club in St. Louis.

The players exploded when the news of the firing reached them. After a two-hour meeting in Harris' hotel room, 24 of them signed a petition that said they would strike unless Cox reinstated Harris and gave him a chance to resign. "We feel that because of his background and experience, he is entitled to that decency," the petition said. Later in the day, Cox, who had flown to St. Louis, confronted the team while Harris and his successor Fred Fitzsimmons talked outside the clubhouse. The rebellion, highlighted by the tongue lashing given Cox by captain Pinky May, raged until Cox finally called Harris into the clubhouse and apologized to him for the way he handled the affair. "The ouster," Cox said, "is not intended in any way to reflect on your ability as a baseball manager." Harris accepted the apology, telling the players, "The stand you have taken on my behalf flatters me no little." Bucky urged the players to drop their plans to strike and to give their best for Fitzsimmons.

A few days later, however, the feud between Harris and Cox spilled over into the newspapers. Charges and countercharges flew back and forth. "He's an All-American jerk," Harris said of Cox. To that Cox replied, "He calls me an All-American jerk. Doesn't he know what league he's in?"

Each side accused the other of distorting the truth. When Harris gave his side of the story, he casually mentioned Cox's taste for betting on Phillies games. The remark eventually led to an investigation that resulted in Cox being banned from baseball.

Harris, on the other hand, continued in baseball, first going to Buffalo in the International League as manager–general manager. In 1947 he returned to the majors and managed the New York Yankees to a World Series victory over the Brooklyn Dodgers, managed by another ex-Phillies pilot, Burt Shotton. Bucky went to Washington in 1950 for his third term with the Senators. He stayed there for five seasons, then joined the Tigers for the second time. He wound up his managerial career in Detroit in 1956.

Harris's final record as a manager was 2,157–2,218 (.493). During 12 seasons as a player, extending from 1919 to 1931, which included nine seasons as the starting second baseman for the Senators, Harris had a lifetime batting average of .274.

Bucky Harris

Harris, Bucky

	W	L	T	Pct
1943	38	52	2	.422
Phillies	38	52	2	.422
Career	2,157	2,218	31	.493

When Freddie Fitzsimmons was hired to manage the Phillies, club president William Cox called him "the greatest living disciple of John McGraw." The statement was a clear indication of Cox's knowledge of baseball.

Fitzsimmons, or Fat Freddie as he was called, had played for seven years under McGraw. The experience did little for Freddie in his only stint as a major league manager.

Fitzsimmons managed the Phillies during their ragamuffin days. A fierce competitor who hated to lose, Freddie piloted some of the worst teams in

1943–45

Fitzsimmons, Fred

Record: 105–181–2 (.367)
Birthplace: Mishawaka, Indiana
B: July 28, 1901; **D:** November 18, 1979

Phillies history. If nothing else, the club's constant losses gave Fitz numerous opportunities to fly into his familiar post-game rages. Trunk throwing and bat breaking were two of his specialties.

As a player, Fat Freddie had been unaccustomed to losing. After breaking into the pro ranks in 1920, he had joined the New York Giants late in the 1925 season. Fitzsimmons had some outstanding years with the Giants, including a 20–9 season in 1928 and a 19–7 record in 1930. Before leaving New York in 1937, Fitz pitched for two pennant winners.

A superb fielding pitcher, Fitzsimmons had some fine years with the Brooklyn Dodgers, too. At the age of 39 in 1940, he posted a 16–2 record. By the time he hurled his last game in 1943, Freddie had a lifetime record of 217–146.

Fitzsimmons was a player-coach with the Dodgers when Cox hired him to replace Bucky Harris. Earlier that season, Freddie had refused a Dodger assignment to manage their Montreal farm club. But he came to the Phillies highly recommended by his boss, Branch Rickey, a friend of Cox.

Freddie took over the team in the midst of one of its more turbulent periods. The controversial firing of Harris and the threatened players' strike that followed barely preceded his assuming the reins. Morale on the team was at a low ebb.

"I've been around major league baseball a long time, and I think I know how to handle men," Fitzsimmons said. "I'll get a chance to try."

In Freddie's debut, the Phillies went out and thrashed the World Champion St. Louis Cardinals shortly after a stormy clubhouse meeting in which Cox had apologized to Harris for the way he was dismissed. Altogether, the Phillies won 16 of their first 20 games under Fitzsimmons.

But the club soon went into a tailspin. Second baseman Danny Murtaugh, one of the key players, was drafted. By the end of the season, the Phillies had tumbled from fifth, the spot they were in when Freddie arrived, to seventh.

A no-nonsense pilot, who was easygoing off the field but extremely nervous during a game, Fitzsimmons was signed by Cox for the 1944 season. Although the Phillies' president was banned from baseball before the season began, Freddie stayed, riding the club home to an eighth-place finish. It wasn't entirely Freddie's fault. After a strong start, the team faded in mid-season as World War II continued to drain the Blue Jays' roster.

By 1945 few players of major league caliber were left on the squad. The Phillies were a band of misfits, and players joined and left the team in droves. No less than 19 pitchers worked for the team that year.

The Phillies lost 51 of their first 69 games and were buried deep in the National League basement. The beleaguered Fitzsimmons could take losing no longer. He resigned in late June.

In accepting his resignation, general manager Herb Pennock said, "I realize that we have been unable to supply Fitzsimmons with adequate material because of the scarcity of good players. But I want to say that no man has ever worked harder or cooperated better than he has."

After leaving the Phillies, Fitzsimmons was out of baseball until 1948 when he joined the Boston Braves as pitching coach. The next year he was appointed to the same position with the Giants. He remained there until 1955. Later he spent three seasons with the Chicago Cubs and one with the Kansas City A's.

Freddie Fitzsimmons

Fitzsimmons, Fred

	W	L	T	Pct
1943	26	38	1	.406
1944	61	92	1	.399
1945	18	51	0	.261
Phillies	105	181	2	.367
Career	105	181	2	.367

The managerial career of Ben Chapman may have been short, but it was never dull. The man who was born on Christmas day was one of the liveliest personalities of his or any other era.

Chapman was a high-strung guy who was as controversial as he was colorful. He was also aggressive, volatile, and demanding, traits which sometimes got him into trouble as both a player and a manager.

Except for 1946 when he herded the Phillies into fifth place, Chappie had little success as a skipper from a won-lost standpoint. But he did lay much of the groundwork that led to the team's pennant in 1950.

Ben played a part in the development of players such as Del Ennis, Andy Seminick, Willie Jones, Granny Hamner, Curt Simmons, and Richie Ashburn. He gave his okay to the signing of Robin Roberts, and inked Bubba Church himself. He had also recommended Hamner to the Phillies after the Brooklyn Dodgers had turned the teenage infielder away.

Raised in Alabama, Ben, a confirmed southerner with a touch of Indian blood, had briefly attended Purdue University on a football scholarship. He dropped out after two months to sign a New York Yankee contract with scout Johnny Nee, later a Phillies' bird dog.

One of the fastest players of his era, Chapman joined the Yankees in 1930 and became the club's regular right fielder. He led the American League in stolen bases four times while usually hitting over .300.

After leaving the Yankees in 1936, Chapman played twice with the Washington Senators, as well as the Boston Red Sox, Cleveland Indians, and Chicago White Sox. Branded as a clubhouse lawyer and unmanageable, Chapman was involved in one scrape after another. In New York he feuded with Babe Ruth and once prompted 15,000 people to sign a petition urging his banishment after he made remarks that were construed as anti-Semitic. In Boston he had a fist fight with manager Joe Cronin. And in Cleveland, he was part of the "Cry Baby" players' rebellion that attempted to oust manager Ossie Vitt.

Chapman went back to the minors in 1942 to start two new careers: pitching and managing. Ben piloted Richmond of the Piedmont League into the playoffs, but he was suspended from baseball for the 1943 season for punching an umpire. He returned to Richmond in 1944 and had a 13–6 record and a .320 batting average when he was bought by the Brooklyn Dodgers, whose war-time pitching staff was desperately in need of arms.

Ben, who had a lifetime batting average of .302, was 5–3 as a hurler in Brooklyn. In 1945 he was traded to the Phillies for catcher Johnny Peacock. Ten days after the swap, he was named to replace Freddie Fitzsimmons as manager.

Claiming that it "was the greatest thing that ever happened to me," Chappie, a former New York and Boston teammate and best friend of Phils general manager Herb Pennock, quickly set up guidelines for his new club. There was to be no card playing or drinking in the clubhouse, and all conversation in the dugout had to be about baseball.

Chapman succeeded in getting his players hustling, but the club still finished eighth. The next year, following a rigorous spring training in which Ben introduced evening blackboard sessions, sliding pits, and a football camp atmosphere, the Blue Jays jumped to fifth place with a lineup put together mostly by the acquisition of veteran players plus a handful of youngsters.

Chapman's emotions were often in evidence. A screamer and complainer, he battled frequently and vehemently with umpires, occasionally sounded off in the press, and sometimes rode his players heavily as he tried to extract hustling habits from them. Infielders, and particularly their shins, were especially vulnerable because of Ben's practice of lashing the hardest grounders he could hit during infield drills.

In 1947 another side of Chapman surfaced. Ben and some of the other Phillies were especially vicious with their dugout needling of Jackie Robinson.

1945–48

Chapman, Ben

Record: 196–276–4 (.415)
Birthplace: Nashville, Tennessee
B: December 25, 1908

Ben Chapman

Although Chapman later claimed he was merely trying to determine the inner strength of the major league's first black player, his racial remarks were sufficiently severe to draw a reprimand from National League president Ford Frick.

Chapman fined his players fifty cents for the first half hour they were late for practice or a game, and ten cents each minute thereafter. It didn't help, and in 1947 the Phillies tumbled to a seventh-place tie. They were in sixth place when owner Bob Carpenter fired Chapman in the middle of the 1948 season. At the time, Chapman was one of the highest paid skippers in the majors with a bonus clause for attendance in his contract.

The firing, which resulted from an accumulation of complaints against Chapman and reached a head with Ben's constant complaining to and about Carpenter and the way he ran the team, was, nevertheless, a shock to the deposed manager. After emerging from a clubhouse meeting with his players, he said: "I feel that I received my reward when a majority of the players left the room with tears rolling down their cheeks. That convinced me that I was not a complete flop as a manager."

Carpenter shed little light on the subject. "I'd like to make it clear that there is a difference between firing a man and concluding business with him," he said.

Chapman returned to the minors to coach and manage. He spent one year in 1952 as a coach with the Cincinnati Reds, but was otherwise unable to land another big league post.

After leaving professional baseball, Chapman sold insurance and coached Babe Ruth and American Legion baseball teams for a number of years in Birmingham, Alabama.

Chapman, Ben

	W	L	T	Pct
1945	28	57	2	.329
1946	69	85	1	.448
1947	62	92	1	.403
1948	37	42	0	.468
Phillies	196	276	4	.415
Career	196	276	4	.415

1948

Cooke, Dusty (Allen)

Record: 6–6–1 (.500)
Birthplace: Swepsonville, North Carolina
B: June 23, 1907; **D:** November 21, 1987

After Ben Chapman was fired and before Eddie Sawyer took over, Dusty Cooke served as interim manager of the Phillies. It was one of many jobs he performed with the club during his seven years in Philadelphia.

Cooke was originally part of the New York Yankee contingent that followed Herb Pennock to the Phillies after he became general manager. A reserve outfielder during eight years in the major leagues, Cooke had been a teammate of Pennock's with Yankee teams in the early 1930s.

Dusty and Ben Chapman, also a Yankee outfielder then, were close friends. When Pennock hired Chapman to manage the Phillies, Ben asked Cooke to join him. Dusty was hired as a trainer, a position he held with the Phillies until being named a coach in 1948.

After his transfer to the coaching lines, Cooke worked with the hitters, as well as with the outfielders and infielders. Dusty, who played three seasons with New York, four with the Boston Red Sox, and his final year in 1938 with the Cincinnati Reds, had been a respectable hitter in his day. His lifetime average was .280, and in 1935 he hit .306 in 100 games for the Bosox.

When Chapman was fired during the All-Star break in 1948, president Bob Carpenter put Cooke in charge of the team. Dusty ran the club for 10 days. After Sawyer's arrival, Cooke went back to coaching.

In an unusual move, Sawyer retained all of his predecessor's coaches. Throughout Eddie's reign, Cooke was the team's first-base coach.

Dusty's career with the Phillies reached its apex when the club won the pennant in 1950. Cooke was probably the most visible member of that team's coaching staff.

He stayed with the club through the 1952 season, departing after Sawyer was dismissed.

Cooke, Dusty

	W	L	T	Pct
1948	6	6	1	.500
Phillies	6	6	1	.500
Career	6	6	1	.500

Dusty Cooke

Of the 47 men who have managed the Phillies, the name probably most commonly associated with the team is Eddie Sawyer. Mention the phrase "Phillies manager," and he is usually the first who comes to mind.

There are numerous reasons for that, not the least of which is that Sawyer is one of only four pilots who led the Phillies to a National League pennant. He did it at a time when the club—and the city—were as starved for a pennant as they've ever been.

Sawyer is the only regular manager ever to have piloted the Phillies twice. Altogether, he led the team for four full seasons and parts of four others. He ranks fifth among Phillies leaders in games played (817) and games won, and sixth in most losses.

Ironically, despite the warmth Philadelphians have always had for Eddie, his Phillies really had only two good seasons, 1949 and 1950. The rest of the time the Phillies had mediocre to poor seasons, particularly during Sawyer's second term when the club never escaped from eighth place.

That may not have been as much a reflection on Sawyer as it was on the caliber of teams he had. Eddie was a sound baseball man whose knowledge of the game was impeccable.

"If we didn't have Sawyer as a manager, we'd be in the second division," said pitcher Jim Konstanty in 1950. "He gets 20 percent more out of a team than any man I ever saw."

It was true. Sawyer had a special knack for getting extra mileage out of his players, especially the younger ones. That was one of the main reasons the Phillies hired Eddie in the first place.

A dignified, scholarly gentleman with a good wit, Sawyer had established a reputation as being a skillful manager during his minor league days. He was tolerant and unflappable, and he used a fatherly approach with his young players. Yet Eddie could be tough as nails, and when the situation dictated, he could crack down on players with loose ideas.

Sawyer was a bit of a contradiction: an intellectual in the sometimes seamy world of baseball. Eddie was a Phi Beta Kappa graduate of Ithaca College where he played halfback on the football team, was a pitcher and outfielder on the baseball squad, and majored in physical education. He also had a master's degree from Cornell, where he studied biology and physiology.

Signed in 1934 to a contract with the New York Yankees, Sawyer was a fleet, hard-hitting outfielder who rose quickly through the farm system. In his first four years, he hit above .300 each season and appeared headed for stardom with the Yankees, or so they thought.

1948–52, 1958–60

Sawyer, Eddie

Record: 390–423–4 (.479)
Birthplace: Westerly, Rhode Island
B: September 10, 1910

Eddie Sawyer

But in 1937, while playing for Oakland in the Pacific Coast League, Eddie suffered a severe shoulder injury diving for a catch. The injury was so severe and so painful and responded so poorly to treatment that Sawyer quit baseball at the end of the season, returning to Ithaca to teach at the college.

The following year, however, the Yankees, short on outfielders at their Binghamton farm team, asked Sawyer to help them out. He reentered the game, then signed the next year as player-manager for New York's Amsterdam team in the Canadian-American League.

Sawyer led the league in hitting in 1939 with a .369 average, and his team won the league pennant. The next year Amsterdam finished third, but won the league playoffs. Sawyer won a promotion to Norfolk in the Piedmont League for the 1941 season. His team finished fourth. He then went to Binghamton in the Eastern League, where his team's placed third and sixth.

In his early days of managing, Sawyer was playing, too, although he stopped performing as a regular after 1941. He was also teaching biology at Ithaca and working as assistant director of athletics during the off-season. While in Binghamton, he also coached the local high school football team.

In 1944, with the Phillies embarking on a move to bolster their farm system, Sawyer was hired by general manager Herb Pennock to run the club's Eastern League team at Utica. Eddie was one of the members of the Phillies' Yankee connection, a network that included Pennock, Ben Chapman, head scout Johnny Nee, and coaches Benny Bengough, Dusty Cooke, and Cy Perkins.

At Utica, Sawyer's teams won two pennants and finished third, and he had a leading role in the development of the Phillies' young players. That role continued when he was moved to Toronto of the International League in 1948. By that time players such as Richie Ashburn, Granny Hamner, Willie Jones, and Stan Lopata had come under Sawyer's guidance.

Despite Eddie's growing reputation for developing young players, some baseball people were surprised when on July 26, 1948, the Phillies selected a man who had never played in the big leagues to be their manager. But Sawyer's decisive, self-assured, straightforward style was appealing to the Phillies, and it soon became apparent why.

Sawyer, aged 38 when he was hired, spent the remainder of the 1948 season learning to know his players and the National League. The team finished sixth, the same place it was when Eddie took over.

By 1949, Sawyer's patient methods began reaping rewards. His eager young team leaped to third place, despite the loss of first baseman Eddie Waitkus in a shooting incident. It was the Phillies' highest finish since 1917.

To get there, though, Sawyer had to shed temporarily his mild demeanor and unleash a tirade that nearly sent his players running for cover. The incident occurred in mid-August while the Phils were in New York for a series with the Giants.

The club was in fifth place at the time. Sawyer, furious with his players' lackadaisical attitude, blasted them at a fiery team meeting in his hotel suite. The explosion worked. The Phillies played well the rest of the season and won 16 of their last 26 games.

In 1950, with the Phillies primed to become pennant contenders, one of Sawyer's main jobs was to keep the club on an even keel, all the while making sure that the players didn't get overconfident. A master psychologist, Eddie did a brilliant job, not only balancing the egos of his young and his veteran players, but also in keeping the team pumped up throughout the season, even when it went into a late-September tailspin that almost cost it the pennant.

"I try to treat my players like I wanted to be treated when I was a player and seldom was," Sawyer philosophized.

After the Phillies had finally clinched the flag, much of the credit went to their noble skipper. "He is the man chiefly responsible for our winning," said Del Ennis. "He really knows how to manage men, and how to get the best play from them."

It was, of course, Sawyer who had rescued Konstanty from the minors and converted him to a relief pitcher. And it was Eddie who brought players such as Robin Roberts, Curt Simmons, Ashburn, Ennis, Jones, and Hamner to the brink of stardom.

If there was any criticism of Sawyer, it was that he failed to use his entire team. In 1950, in particular, at least a half-dozen players seldom saw action. When they were needed, they tended to be rusty.

"I had brought it out to our kids when I had them in the minor leagues," explained Eddie. "Once you have a job, keep it by being domineering. I think every one of them would resent being taken out of the lineup. They didn't need rest. They needed a job more."

Although he was never noted as a particularly daring manager, Sawyer shocked the baseball world with his bold selection of Konstanty to start the 1950 World Series. It was one of the few moves Eddie was able to make that attracted much attention during the Yankees' sweep.

The 1950 season turned out to be the Phillies' lone year of glory under Sawyer. In 1951 the egos that Eddie had so diligently protected the year before got away from him. Swelled heads developed, and with them came a building resentment of the man the players used to affectionately call "Skip."

In addition, Sawyer was beginning to be criticized for his lack of aggressiveness and resourcefulness and for some of his strategy. In an effort to get his team under control, Eddie initiated rules for his players that served only to alienate them further.

The 1951 season was a disaster, the Phillies collapsing all the way to fifth place. In 1952 there were more rules, and more failure. On June 26, with the team stuck in sixth place, Sawyer was dismissed. It was a difficult move for owner Bob Carpenter, but one that was necessary for the salvation of the dissension-riddled team.

In the years that followed, Sawyer rejected a number of offers to manage other teams, claiming he was through with baseball. He worked for a Philadelphia-area company that manufactured golf balls, advancing from salesman to vice president in charge of sales.

In 1958, however, the Phillies beckoned again. Although Sawyer had been out of touch with baseball for six years, the Phillies wanted him back as a replacement for Mayo Smith. Eddie took the reins on July 22.

"We recalled him not only because he did such a good job before," said general manager Roy Hamey, another ex-Yankee, "but because I didn't want the team to work under an unknown in the middle of the season."

When Sawyer entered the clubhouse to manage again, it was like a family reunion. The players, including the remaining Whiz Kids, welcomed him back warmly. Even Roberts, who had earlier gone nearly an entire season during which Sawyer's only words to him were "hello," "good-bye," and "you're pitching tomorrow," was happy to see Eddie.

The club was in seventh place when Sawyer arrived. It wound up eighth. The Phillies had deteriorated badly from the mid-1950s on, and by the latter part of the decade it was one of the worst teams in baseball. Even Sawyer's presence had no effect. The team finished eighth again in 1959.

After losing the first game of the 1960 season, Sawyer abruptly quit, much

Sawyer, Eddie

	W	L	T	Pct
1948	23	40	0	.365
1949	81	73	0	.526
1950	91	63	3	.591
1951	73	81	0	.474
1952	28	35	0	.444
1958	30	40	0	.429
1959	64	90	1	.416
1960	0	1	0	.000
Phillies	390	423	4	.480
Career	390	423	4	.480

to the shock of the Phillies as well as everybody else. "I'm 49 years old, and I want to live to be 50," said Sawyer, who didn't see eye-to-eye with new general manager John Quinn.

He returned to his old job at the golf ball company. In 1963 he came back once again to the Phillies as a special scout, and in the early 1970s Sawyer worked as a scout for the Kansas City Royals.

1952–54

O'Neill, Steve

Record: 182–140–2 (.565)
Birthplace: Minooka, Pennsylvania
B: July 6, 1891; **D:** January 26, 1962

Steve O'Neill

The Phillies had a habit of hiring inexperienced managers, but that practice was hardly the case with Steve O'Neill. Stout Steve had run clubs during 11 different seasons when the Phillies gave him a job in 1952.

O'Neill was the surprise choice of the Phillies to replace Eddie Sawyer after his mid-season firing. Although he managed only one full season, Steve worked during three years in Philadelphia, and he had some of the best clubs between the Whiz Kids and the 1970s.

His .565 won-lost percentage is the highest among all Phillies managers who stuck around for more than 300 games.

O'Neill joined the Phillies when the club was in a state of upheaval. Many of the players had ceased to get along with Eddie Sawyer, at least in part because of Sawyer's efforts to impose a number of restrictions on the team.

When O'Neill took over, he immediately lifted the rules. He permitted wives to go on road trips and ultimately to spring training, rescinded rules against card playing, and ended curfews. The result was an abrupt surge upward in team morale, and a quick turnaround on the field.

In O'Neill's first game, the Phillies beat the New York Giants, 7–2. The team went on to win four of six games against the Giants and Brooklyn Dodgers. The club was in sixth place with a 28–35 record when O'Neill arrived, but it closed the season as the hottest team in the major leagues. The Phillies won 59 of 91 games while finishing in fourth place, one game out of third.

The Phillies had great expectations for the following season. They got off to a magnificent start, winning nine of their first 11 games. But in May, Curt Simmons cut off part of a toe in a lawn mower accident, and he missed part of the season. The team fell back and eventually wound up tied for third place with the St. Louis Cardinals, 22 games out of first place.

In 1954, O'Neill again had the club in third place when on July 15, without prior warning, he was relieved of his duties. At the time the Phillies had a 40–37 record.

Steve's departure had been rumored off and on since the arrival of new general manager Roy Hamey, who repeatedly denied the stories. When he did ax the easygoing, popular O'Neill, Hamey performed the second biggest surprise of the season. (The first was his subsequent appointment of Terry Moore as manager.)

Hamey tried to make his decision look good. "The decision to fire O'Neill came within the last 48 hours," he said at a press conference attended by both O'Neill and Moore. "This is no criticism of O'Neill."

It was uncertain, however, what it was. Nevertheless, O'Neill retreated from the game, ending a long career in baseball that dated back to 1910 when he broke in as a minor league player.

The son of Irish immigrants, O'Neill had worked as a coal miner as a boy in upstate Pennsylvania. Although Steve had three other brothers—Jim, Jack, and Mike—who played major league baseball, he was by far the best of the quartet.

As a catcher, O'Neill was given a tryout early in his career with the Philadelphia Athletics. Connie Mack rejected the youngster, saying he didn't think he could hit major league pitching. Later Connie admitted his mistake.

O'Neill spent 17 seasons in the majors, including 13 with the Cleveland Indians. A standout catcher for the Indians, he hit .321 while helping the Tribe to the 1920 World Championship. Steve played later for the Boston Red Sox,

New York Yankees, and St. Louis Browns before concluding his career in 1928 with a .263 average.

For the next six years, O'Neill caught in the minors. During five of those seasons, he was also a manager, first at Toronto, then at Toledo. In 1935 he replaced Walter Johnson in mid-season as the manager of the Indians.

O'Neill piloted Cleveland for two and one-half seasons. Over the next five years, he spent four managing in the minors and one (1941) as a coach with the Detroit Tigers. Steve began a six-year spell as skipper of the Tigers in 1943.

While with Detroit, O'Neill is credited by Hal Newhouser as the man who developed him into one of the league's finest pitchers. The Tigers won the World Series in 1945 and finished second three other times.

The Tigers dumped O'Neill after the 1948 season, and after a year as a coach with the Indians, he replaced the ailing Joe McCarthy on June 23, 1950, as manager of the Red Sox. Despite an abundance of talent, Steve's teams finished only third in each of two seasons. After the 1951 season, the Red Sox made him a scout, the position he held just before his appointment with the Phillies.

O'Neill concluded his managerial career with a 1,040–821–17 (.559) regular season record. During his 14 years as a big league pilot, none of his teams finished below fifth place. Eleven teams finished in the first division.

O'Neill, Steve

	W	L	T	Pct
1952	59	32	0	.648
1953	83	71	2	.539
1954	40	37	0	.519
Phillies	182	140	2	.565
Career	1,040	821	17	.559

1954

Moore, Terry

Record: 35–42 (.455)
Birthplace: Vernon, Alabama
B: May 27, 1912

Although he had a successful career as a player, Terry Moore's term as a manager was strictly a bust.

Moore managed the Phillies for slightly less than three months. Rather than advancing during that time, the club slid backward.

A star center fielder for the St. Louis Cardinals, Moore had no experience as a manager when he came to the Phillies. After retiring as a player at the end of the 1948 season, he spent the next four years with the Cards as a coach. In 1953, Moore was hired by the Phillies as a scout, a position he was holding when he became manager.

Terry was appointed to the post following the sudden dismissal of Steve O'Neill. At the time, the Phillies were in third place with a 40–37 record. O'Neill's firing on July 15 by new general manager Roy Hamey came as a complete surprise. But it wasn't as surprising as Hamey's appointment of Moore.

"The appointment of Moore is a shot in the dark," Hamey admitted. "He's always been an alert, hard-working, hustling ball player. It's the kind of spirit Terry showed as a ball player that I want instilled in our team."

The untested Moore, who had no apparent managerial ambitions, was given a contract only until the end of the season. "I hadn't even thought about managing," he said years later. "But I thought I'd give it a try. I had played under a lot of great managers, and I had some ideas."

Moore immediately moved Richie Ashburn out of the number-two spot in the batting order and into the leadoff position. He also switched Del Ennis from left field to right field.

But the Phillies lost two straight doubleheaders in Cincinnati at the start of Moore's term and slumped badly after that, falling to sixth place, then moving

Terry Moore

briefly up to fourth. A season-ending spurt pushed the Phils from fifth place back up to fourth, where they ended the season, despite a record (75–79) that was under .500. At that, the Phils barely made the first division, finishing just three games ahead of the sixth-place Cardinals and 22 games behind the pennant-winning New York Giants.

Moore was released at the end of the season. Hamey said he was too inexperienced. "I wasn't a Roy Hamey man," Moore said, understating the case.

Terry returned to St. Louis in 1956, coaching with the Cardinals until 1958. After that, Moore operated a bowling business in the St. Louis area for many years.

Terry had spent all his playing career with the Cardinals. Breaking into the major leagues in 1935, he played 11 seasons in St. Louis, most of the time as the club's regular center fielder. Moore, who spent three years in the military service, was the Cards' captain.

Moore was one of the top defensive center fielders of his era. He was a sparkling fielder, the possessor of a strong throwing arm, and he regularly ranked among the league's defensive leaders.

He was also a respectable hitter. His best year was 1940 when he hit .304. He had a lifetime average of .280.

Moore played in four All-Star games and two World Series.

Moore, Terry

	W	L	T	Pct
1954	35	42	0	.455
Phillies	35	42	0	.455
Career	35	42	0	.455

1955–58

Smith, Mayo

Record: 264–282–2 (.484)
Birthplace: New London, Missouri
B: January 17, 1915; **D:** November 24, 1977

Mayo Smith

When the Phillies announced the signing of Mayo Smith as the manager of the 1955 team, players, fans and press had an identical reaction. "Mayo who?"

Of all the figures the Phillies have unearthed to run the club over the years, none was more unknown than Smith. Mayo came from the deepest recesses of obscurity.

"I'm sorry to say, I've never heard of the man," said Terry Moore when told who was replacing him. Terry was part of a majority. The new pilot was so unfamiliar to localites that when reporting his appointment, the *Evening Bulletin* labeled him Ed Mayo Smith in the headline.

Edward Mayo Smith was his full name. But hardly anybody knew he was called Mayo, except, perhaps, Roy Hamey, the Phillies' general manager and the man who signed Smith. To add to the confusion, one of the Phillies' coaches at the time was named Ed Mayo.

Hamey, however, had been a big fan of Smith's. "During the four years I was with the Yankees, I observed Smith's work closely, and we believe his accomplishments have earned him the opportunity to manage in the majors," Hamey said. "We wanted a young, alert manager, and Smith seems to fill the bill."

Only the most astute trivia buff could have recalled that Smith had actually passed through Philadelphia once before. In his only year as a major league player in 1945, Mayo had been a reserve outfielder for the Philadelphia Athletics. In 73 games he hit a less than robust .212.

Prior to that, Smith had been kicking around the minor leagues since 1933. A respectable hitter, he spent much of that time in the International League, playing for Toronto and Buffalo. In 1944 he led the league in hitting with a .340 average.

That got him drafted by the A's. But Smith's big league career ended after he came down with rheumatic fever. After being in bed for two months, he went to Portland in the Pacific Coast League where he spent the next three seasons.

In 1949, Smith joined the Yankee's system as player-manager at Amsterdam (New York) in the Canadian-American League. Ironically, that was the same team on which Eddie Sawyer got his start in managing 10 years earlier.

Smith moved up to Norfolk (Virginia) in the Piedmont League in 1951. He finished first in each of the next two years, earning a promotion to Birmingham (Alabama) in the Southern Association. Smith's teams there placed fourth and third.

The following year Smith, at the age of 39, was hired by the Phillies after they obtained his release from New York. At his first press conference, Mayo admitted, "I know nothing about the Phils."

The feeling was mutual. After they got to know each other, though, Smith and his players seemed to get along well at first, and there was a genuine feeling that the new skipper could steer the club back up the National League ladder.

In his first year on the job, Smith led the Phillies to fourth place. Although the team lost 13 games in a row in early May, it finished the season strongly with 40 wins in the last 70 games. Smith finished second to Walter Alston of the Brooklyn Dodgers in the balloting for National League Manager of the Year.

"To say that his players respect Smith is the understatement of the year," *Sport Magazine* chortled. "They respect him as a manager, gentleman and a man with a tremendous desire to win."

Perhaps they did respect him, but in the ensuing years few of Smith's players liked him. He was too mild for some, too aloof for others. Although he was an innovative manager at times, he had increasingly less talent with which to work as the years went by.

Smith presided over the demise and breakup of the aging Whiz Kids. At first, their places were filled from the ranks of other aging players and from the products of an assortment of ill-advised trades.

The Phillies slipped to fifth in 1956. The switch to a youth movement in 1957 resulted in another fifth-place finish, although the club reached first place on July 15, the first time the Phillies had been that high that late in the season since 1950.

By 1958, though, the team's shortcomings were becoming obvious. The Phillies had failed to keep pace with the rest of the league in signing black players; they had concentrated too heavily on signing pitchers at the expense of other players; and they were poorly prepared to replace the fading Whiz Kids adequately.

Nevertheless, the 1958 team was in the thick of the pennant race during the first half of the season. Just before the All-Star break, the club won seven straight games to vault to within two and one-half games of first. But shortly after the break the Phillies lost seven straight, and they soon found themselves eight and one-half games back.

On July 22, returning from a road trip, Smith was fired with the Phillies in seventh place. He was replaced by Sawyer, under whom the Phillies dropped to the cellar in what was the first of four straight last-place finishes.

In late September, Smith signed to manage the Cincinnati Reds in 1959. But he lasted only until the following July before being replaced by Fred Hutchinson with the team in seventh place.

Mayo spent the next seven years as a scout for the Yankees. He returned to managing in 1967 with the Detroit Tigers. After finishing second that year,

Smith, Mayo

	W	L	T	Pct
1955	77	77	0	.500
1956	71	83	0	.461
1957	77	77	2	.500
1958	39	45	0	.464
Phillies	264	282	2	.484
Career	662	612	5	.520

Smith led the Tigers the next season to the American League pennant and the World Championship.

The Tigers finished second and fourth in the succeeding years under Smith. Mayo retired after the 1970 season.

1960

Cohen, Andy

Record: 1–0 (1.000)
Birthplace: Baltimore, Maryland
B: October 25, 1904; **D:** October 29, 1988

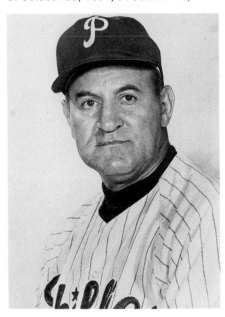

Andy Cohen

When Eddie Sawyer dropped his bombshell on the Philadelphia sports scene by resigning after the first game of the 1960 season, the Phillies wasted no time hiring Gene Mauch. But Mauch was in Minneapolis, and it would take him a day to reach Philadelphia. Someone had to manage the second game of the season.

The someone was coach Andy Cohen. The Phillies beat the Reds, and Cohen became the only unbeaten manager in Philadelphia Phillies history.

Cohen had a three-year career as a New York Giants infielder in the late 1920s. He batted .281 in a total of 262 games. His brother Sid had a 3–7 record in parts of three seasons with the Washington Senators in the mid-1930s.

Cohen, Andy

	W	L	T	Pct
1960	1	0	0	1.000
Phillies	1	0	0	1.000
Career	1	0	0	1.000

1960–68

Mauch, Gene

Record: 645–684–2 (.485)
Birthplace: Salina, Kansas
B: November 18, 1925

They called the man a lot of things in his often brilliant, often hectic nine years in Philadelphia.

They called him Number Four. The Little General. Skipper. The Genius. Several phrases that we feel compelled to keep out of a book of this sort.

Gene Mauch won more games than any other Phillies manager, but they never called him the one thing he wanted more than anything. They never called him Champ.

In 1964 they almost did, but something terrible happened in the last 12 games of the season, which is why we can't reprint what a lot of Philadelphians still call the man whom others insist was easily the greatest manager in the franchise's history.

One thing no one will dispute—Mauch had the temperament to be a manager. He backed down from no one. He had a sharp wit and a temper to match. On his best days, he managed to steal a victory by manipulating his roster one move beyond the opposition, then walked into his office and wrote all the writers' stories for them, figuratively, by splashing the post-game press conference with some of the greatest quotes you could imagine. On his worst days, he would overmanage the team into a loss and conduct a surly, snarling post-game interview.

And he had a steel trap of a memory. Two examples:

His Connie Mack Stadium office, 1966. The discussion came around to an obscure shortstop in the lowest of the minor leagues. Did Mauch know anything about him?

"Sure do," Mauch said. "He's hitting .289."

"No he's not," someone countered. "He's hitting .306."

Mauch got a confused look on his face, then explained: "Must've had a helluva lot of hits since the last time the *Sporting News* came out."

Naturally, everyone checked out the most recent *Sporting News.* Naturally the obscure shortstop was hitting .289.

Shea Stadium, September 1973. Willie Mays night. The Mets were playing the Expos, and every microphone attached to a hand was following Mays wherever he went. Expo manager Mauch sat alone in the third base dugout. Co-author Bilovsky approached him.

"Gene, what's the greatest play you ever saw Willie Mays make?" he asked.

Mauch stared through his questioner, as always, thinking out his answer before he began to give it, which might explain why Mauch is one of the few Phillies managers of recent vintage who didn't lead the league in malaprops. Finally he spoke.

"Well, you ought to know," he said. "You were there that night."

Bilovsky had covered about two dozen games in 1964, but when Mauch described the play, the writer realized that he indeed had been there to see it.

It was hard to sneak anything past Mauch. He could handle almost anything. Except, his detractors will point out, a 6½-game lead with 12 left and a panic button to push. Or a 2–1 lead in the American League playoffs and a chance to try to force a victory in Game Four when it's Game Five he *has* to win.

The big victory always seemed to escape the Little General. And, for a guy who started the 1944 season under Leo Durocher, a guy who would get his most at-bats in a major league season 13 years later, a guy who got the most out of his limited playing talent and had no patience with anyone who didn't do likewise, it hurt badly.

He has been described as the best third-place manager in baseball history. Give him a team of less than average talent, the reasoning went, and he'd find a way to get it to play third-place baseball. Give him a team of superior abilities, and he'd turn it into a third-place outfit by overmanaging, injecting himself into games in which his skills are not needed.

Gene Mauch

When Mauch was tabbed to replace Eddie Sawyer as Phillies manager one game into the 1960 season, there was some question whether the Almighty could have turned the Phillies into a third-place team. To ask the 34-year-old Mauch, youngest manager in the majors, to do it would have been unfair. After all, hadn't Sawyer resigned with the statement that he was 49 years old and wanted to live to be 50?

Mauch tried. He barked at umpires, encouraged some players, booted others in the pants. He insulted aging Hall of Famer-to-be Robin Roberts ("He throws like Betsy Ross"), tarnishing the last remaining hero Philadelphia baseball fans had. He had a first baseman (Pancho Herrera) about to eat his way out of the majors, an outfielder (Tony Curry) who couldn't catch a baseball, and a pitching staff that couldn't pitch.

In 1961 things got worse. The team lost 107 games, including 23 in a row, a modern record. Mauch later said that the success the team would enjoy in 1963 and 1964 was built during the losing streak.

Beginning in 1962, the Phillies—and Mauch's mystique—began to take off. The team finished one game over .500. Mauch sat Johnny Callison on the last day of the season to insure a .300 average for his rising star. He made a third baseman out of power-hitting Don Demeter and a great defensive catcher out of Clay Dalrymple. In 1963 the Phillies were the hottest team in the league for the last two months and finished fourth, 12 games behind the Dodgers.

Even so, nobody was ready for what would happen in the first 150 games of 1964.

Everything broke right. Jim Bunning, tossed on a scrap heap by the Detroit Tigers, pitched like a man possessed. Chris Short suddenly matured into a great lefthander. Dick Allen, playing a new position (third base), hit home runs the likes of which hadn't been seen in Philadelphia since the glory days of Jimmie Foxx. Callison hit 31 homers and drove in 104 runs. And, with just 12 games to go, the Phillies had a 6½-game lead on both the Cincinnati Reds and the St. Louis Cardinals.

It was right there that someone gave Mauch a panic button, and the manager didn't hesitate before pushing it. Three times each he used Bunning and Short with just two days rest. He kept calling on relievers who had spent most of the year at Little Rock. He used Little Rock's Adolfo Philips as an occasional starter in center. And the whole magic ball unwound before his eyes. Needing to win only four of the last 12 games to give the Phillies their first pennant since 1950, he won the last two. The Phils finished in a tie for second, one game back.

Phillies fans, long-sufferers that they are, were willing to forgive. Just give us a pennant in 1965 or 1966, they pleaded, and no one will talk about 1964 again.

It wasn't to happen. Mauch and Allen, the best pure talent he ever managed anywhere, including Reggie Jackson, began to slide apart philosophically. Mauch's philosophy was that a player should be on time and sober; Dick's differed occasionally. Mauch at times was tempted to look the other way, especially when Allen arrived at the ballpark glassy-eyed one night, then hit two of the longest home runs Gene had ever seen. But as the rift between Mauch and Allen widened after 1965, when Gene foolishly threatened to fine Dick if he told his side of the Frank Thomas fight, the manager tried to win pennant after pennant with proven veterans from other teams for which he traded the Phillies' future.

When the vets didn't produce the pennant, the team—and Mauch—had troubles. Gene was fired in mid-season 1968 when it became apparent that either he or Allen had to leave.

He had no trouble getting a job. In 1969 he was named the first manager of the expansion Montreal Expos, where he stayed for seven years, building the franchise to a competitive edge. The next five years were in Minnesota, where he had been in the American Association when the Phillies signed him. Despite Calvin Griffith's tight-fisted policy, he was able to produce three winning seasons.

And in 1982, his second year with the California Angels, it appeared Gene had finally reached the top. He won the American League West, then won the first two games of the best-of-five league championship series against the Milwaukee Brewers. He still had a one-game lead going into Game Four, but chose to pitch Tommy John with one day's rest less than normal. John was beaten, the Angels lost Game Five, and Mauch was eased out of his job in his 23d year of managing. He returned as Angels pilot in 1985. On year later he came within one strike of his first World Series, but Dave Henderson of the Boston Red Sox hit a home run and once again Mauch was an also-ran. He managed one more year, then retired.

Mauch, Gene

	W	L	T	Pct
1960	58	94	0	.382
1961	47	107	1	.305
1962	81	80	0	.503
1963	87	75	0	.537
1964	92	70	0	.568
1965	85	76	1	.528
1966	87	75	0	.537
1967	82	80	0	.506
1968	26	27	0	.491
Phillies	645	684	2	.485
Career	1,902	2,037	3	.483

The short, unhappy managerial career of Bob Skinner with the Phillies lasted 215 games and was doomed almost from the first day he took the job, succeeding Gene Mauch on June 15, 1968, after it became obvious that Mauch and slugger Dick Allen could not coexist under the same roof. Skinner very quickly found himself working under the same circumstances. It happened in spring training of 1969 after Skinner and Allen spent a relatively peaceful last 107 games of the 1968 season together.

Skinner, a friendly, soft-spoken sort whose appearance belied his Marine training, tried to stroke Allen. But in early May, Dick missed a flight to St. Louis one morning, then missed the same flight the next morning. As a result, he missed one complete game and part of another against the Cardinals. Skinner, furious, fined Allen $1,000.

In late June, Skinner suspended Allen for missing a twi-nighter at Shea Stadium. Allen then moved into a storage area between the regular clubhouse and the manager's office on the third base side of Connie Mack Stadium. And, in early August, after Allen failed to show for an exhibition game at Reading, Skinner handed in his resignation.

It was probably the only choice Bob had. Other than Allen, his 1969 team had little talent. The Phillies, who had gone 48–59 under Skinner in 1968, were 20 games under .500 (44–64) when he resigned. It was obvious that the front office was going to give him little support in his bouts with Allen. And the rest of the lineup, with the exception of prospects like center fielder Larry Hisle and pitcher Rick Wise, was a collection of journeymen playing the game, basically, for one more paycheck.

Skinner, who later coached in the National League for 10 years with the Pittsburgh Pirates and Atlanta Braves, spent 12 years in the major leagues as a player, the bulk of them with the Pirates, and had a lifetime average of .277. Three times, he batted over .300.

In 1977 he was interim manager for one game with the San Diego Padres, winning it. In recent years, he has served as a Triple-A manager at Tucson for the Houston Astros.

1968–69

Skinner, Bob

Record: 92–123 (.428)
Birthplace: LaJolla, California
B: October 3, 1931

Bob Skinner

Skinner, Bob

	W	L	T	Pct
1968	48	59	0	.449
1969	44	64	0	.407
Phillies	92	123	0	.428
Career	93	123	0	.431

His nickname was Stud. What else? George Myatt called everybody Stud. He had a foghorn voice that rattled windows when he said, "How ya doin', Stud," to everyone from owner Bob Carpenter to the kid he paid for parking his car.

His function with the Phillies, in addition to being the third base coach, was to fill those gaps after Dick Allen would drive one manager crazy and wait for the next one to arrive. He filled in for two games after Gene Mauch was fired and before Bob Skinner arrived in 1968, winning them both. And he took over in August 1969 after Skinner resigned and managed an awful Phillies team to a 19–35 record the rest of the way.

While others made noises about "handling" Allen, Myatt would have no part of the idle chatter. "God Almighty Hisself couldn't handle the man," he said.

When Myatt was named manager, he called Allen up to his hotel room and told him, "I'm going to lay my cards on the table. I won't have any rules. Just do it on the field. If you can get drunk and play, that's okay."

Allen liked what he heard. "Skip," he said, "nobody's ever talked to me like that before. I believe I can play for you."

1968, 1969

Myatt, George

Record: 21–35 (.375)
Birthplace: Denver, Colorado
B: June 14, 1914

George Myatt

Myatt, who was a coach with the Phillies from 1964 to 1972, thought he would get the manager's job in 1970 and was disappointed when the Phillies gave it to Frank Lucchesi. Still, he remained loyal to the Phillies and returned to his familiar post in the third base coaching box.

George had played for seven years in the major leagues, two as the regular second baseman for the Washington Senators during World War II. He hit .283 in 407 games, once lashing six straight hits in a game in 1944.

After his playing days he managed in the minor leagues, and then was a coach with the Senators, Chicago White Sox, Chicago Cubs, Milwaukee Braves, and Detroit Tigers before joining the Phillies.

Myatt, George

	W	L	T	Pct
1968	2	0	0	1.000
1969	19	35	0	.352
Phillies	21	35	0	.375
Career	21	35	0	.375

1970–72

Lucchesi, Frank

Record: 166–233 (.416)
Birthplace: San Francisco, California
B: April 24, 1927

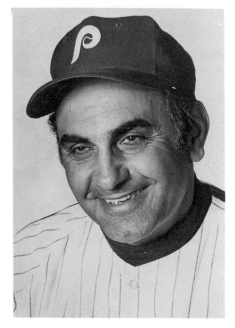

Frank Lucchesi

It reads like the itinerary of a bus bound for nowhere—Medford, Thomasville, Pine Bluff, Pocatello, Salt Lake City, High Point–Thomasville, Williamsport, Chattanooga, Little Rock, San Diego, Reading, Eugene.

Finally, after 19 years, the bus pulled into Philadelphia on September 26, 1969. Frank Lucchesi got off and walked into the only job he ever wanted, manager of the Phillies. He was an absolute loyalist to the organization and reminded everyone, "I don't bleed blood. I bleed Phillie red."

Lucchesi was a nice man with a heart of gold who bled a lot during his 2½-year stint as Phillies manager. He wept on opening day in 1970 when he was given a standing ovation during introductions. He wept in July 1972 at a press conference at which his firing was announced. "It's the old story," he said. "You can't fire the troops, so you have to fire the general."

Somebody should have fired the troops. The three teams that Lucchesi managed for the Phillies were basically bad. That he got the 1970 club home 73–88 was, in many ways, remarkable. That was the last team to play at Connie Mack Stadium.

The following April, Lucchesi and troops opened the Vet. They won a opening day, then only 66 more times the rest of the season, one a no-hitter by Rick Wise. And in 1972, Skipper Lucchesi had Steve Carlton and little else. The Phillies were 26–50 when his buddy Paul Owens dropped the knife on his neck and took over the team himself.

Lucchesi's stint with the Phillies was not without its off-the-field problems. The black players on the team felt that the organization, including Frank, was not sensitive to their needs. But Lucchesi could be credited with turning Larry Bowa from a slumping youngster into a major league shortstop, and eventually Bowa evolved into an All-Star. The wolves were howling for Bowa's scalp after two months of his rookie season. Lucchesi preached patience instead, and it paid off.

Patience was Lucchesi's trademark. Unfortunately for him, Job couldn't have won with the talent Lucchesi was given. But he did clean up the Phillies' image with the fans, with whom he was immensely popular, and he did bridge the gap between the troubled Dick Allen years and the building back to respectability of the franchise.

He tried to be fair to his players, but he could also be tough. "There's only 18 inches between a pat on the back and a kick in the butt," he loved to say.

He was also cooperative to a fault with the press. Substituting the word "bleeping" for obscenities had become the vogue with the newspaper people.

Lucchesi took it one step beyond that. Noticing it in the papers, he began to talk that way in his post-game interviews. "I can't understand how we lost that bleeping game," he would say with a straight face.

He had a radio pre-game show, that he did by himself. It was so bad, it was good. The fans loved it, just as they loved him.

Managing the Phillies was the first time in 25 years as a player and manager that he ever wore a big league uniform. He would later manage the Texas Rangers for one full year and parts of two others before taking a job with the Cleveland Indians, where he coached, managed in the minor leagues, and served as chief of scouting.

He returned to managing in 1987 as interim pilot of the Chicago Cubs after the firing of Gene Michael. In 25 games, Lucchesi's Bruins went 8–17.

Lucchesi, Frank

	W	L	T	Pct
1970	73	88	0	.453
1971	67	95	0	.414
1972	26	50	0	.342
Phillies	166	233	0	.416
Career	316	399	0	.442

Paul Owens was never your stuffed-shirt, country-club-set general manager or farm director for the Phillies. His philosophy was simple: "The closer I get to the subject, the more I'll know about it." He rolled up his sleeves and got down with the common folk.

In 1972, after years as a successful farm director and minor league player and manager, Owens succeeded John Quinn as general manager on June 3. He inherited an organization in which most of the talent was in the minor leagues. The big team had Steve Carlton setting records and little else.

Owens believed the only way to find out what he had at the big league level was to observe it from the manager's bench. So, on July 10, in what he called the toughest decision of his life, he fired Frank Lucchesi and took over as Phillies manager.

Under Owens, the Phillies finished 33–47. After the season, Paul returned to the front office and entrusted the field manager's job to Danny Ozark.

Eleven years later, Owens made a return trip to the dugout. On July 18, 1983, Owens fired manager Pat Corrales and put himself in the position of field manager for a second time. At the time, the Phillies were in first place in the NL East, but were playing only one game over .500 (43–42). Under Owens, they caught fire in September and pranced to the NL East crown. Despite the usual bickering, the Phillies won 47 times and lost just 30 the rest of the way, then buried the Dodgers in four in the League Championship Series.

After losing the World Series to the Baltimore Orioles, four games to one, Owens announced that he was relinquishing the general manager's job to remain as field manager for 1984.

It did not turn out to be a very satisfying year. The Phillies had been picked by many to repeat as National League champions, and they challenged for the league lead for several months, but then their performance fell off, and they finished a disappointing fourth.

With characteristic candor Owens said after one particularly tough loss, "It was just one of those games where you're going to have to go home and cry about it."

Owens was re-signed for the following season. But after the Phillies lost 14 of their last 16 games, he decided that he had had enough of the managing game. The Pope returned to the front office where he became assistant to president Bill Giles, a position he has held ever since.

1972, 1983–84

Owens, Paul

Record: 161–158 (.505)
Birthplace: Salamanca, New York
B: February 7, 1924

Paul Owens

Owens, Paul

	W	L	T	Pct
1972	33	47	0	.413
1983	47	30	0	.610
1984	81	81	0	.500
Phillies	161	158	0	.505
Career	161	158	0	.505

1973–79

Ozark, Danny

Record: 594–510–1 (.538)
Birthplace: Buffalo, New York
B: November 26, 1923

Danny Ozark

Danny Ozark probably will never get the credit he deserves for his role in lifting the Phillies from National League East tailenders into three straight division titles.

There are reasons.

He will be remembered instead as the manager who didn't realize his team had been eliminated from the division race in 1975. Also, as the manager who didn't substitute Jerry Martin for Greg Luzinski in left field in the ninth inning of the third game of the 1977 League Championship Series against the Dodgers.

Those are the negatives for the man who was born Daniel Leonard Orzechowski in Buffalo in 1923. There are also many positives.

His 594 victories in less than seven seasons place him third in the list of Phillie managers. It took Harry Wright 10 seasons before the turn of the century to win 636 and Gene Mauch almost nine to win 645. Ozark's .538 winning percentage is topped only by Dallas Green, Bill Shettsline, Pat Moran, and Steve O'Neill—among managers with 100 or more victories.

In 1976, when the Phillies won their first NL East title, Ozark was named major league manager of the year by *Sporting News* and National League manager of the year by *Associated Press* and *United Press International.*

Ozark was well qualified to become a major league manager when he succeeded Paul Owens on November 1, 1972. Unfortunately for him, he arrived with a couple of media strikes against him. The *Associated Press* had reported earlier that Dave Bristol had gotton the job. Other sources indicated that former pitching great Jim Bunning was the front-runner. When Ozark was named, it was a complete surprise.

He had spent the previous eight seasons as manager Walt Alston's third base coach in Los Angeles after playing and managing in the Dodger system for more than two decades. It had always been assumed that he would be Alston's successor when the Dodger pilot retired. But when the Phillies, at the suggestion of vice president Bill Giles, contacted Ozark about the possibility of coming to Philadelphia, he reacted favorably.

Once he arrived in spring training in 1973, Ozark did much of what Pat Moran had done when he took over the Phillies in 1915. Danny spent the entire spring working on fundamentals, an area in which the young squad was found sorely lacking. His first team improved by 12 victories over the previous squad and was in the tight National League East race until early September, fading to last place in the end.

Ozark's 1974 team continued the improvement by going 80–82 as Mike Schmidt blossomed as a hitter. Schmidt had resented Ozark in his rookie year. "He called me Dutch," Schmidt remembered, "because he thought I was dumb."

In 1975 the Phillies improved to 86–76 and finished second to the Pirates. But it was Danny who came off sounding dumb late in the season when he insisted the Phillies still had a chance for the division title on the night they were eliminated.

There was no eliminating the 1976 team, which saw a 15½-game lead over Pittsburgh shrink to three before the Phillies pulled away for their first title in 26 years. But the playoff-wise Cincinnati Reds beat the Phillies three straight in the LCS.

The following season, the Phillies won 101 regular season games for the second straight time and had a 1–1 record in the LCS and a two-run lead going into the ninth inning of Game Three. All season long, Ozark had used Jerry Martin as a left field defensive replacement for Greg Luzinski in that situation. This game he didn't; Luzinski dropped Manny Mota's fly ball at the wall, and three runs later the Dodgers had the win. The next night, Los Angeles clinched in a downpour at the Vet, and Phillies fans never forgave Ozark.

Ozark led the Phillies to their third straight NL East title in 1978, but again the team lost in four to the Dodgers. In 1979 the Phillies started great, but slumped badly in June and July as Ozark joked about getting fired. The ax finally fell on August 31 in Atlanta.

Danny took the change almost philosophically. He went to the broadcast booth and said good-bye to Philadelphia by offering the greatest analysis of a baseball game the city had ever heard.

Danny returned to his old job as Dodger third base coach for 1980. Two years later, he joined Frank Robinson with the San Francisco Giants. After the 1984 season, he retired from baseball.

Ozark, Danny

	W	L	T	Pct
1973	71	91	0	.438
1974	80	82	0	.494
1975	86	76	0	.531
1976	101	61	0	.623
1977	101	61	0	.623
1978	90	72	0	.556
1979	65	67	1	.492
Phillies	594	510	1	.538
Career	618	542	1	.533

If the knock against Danny Ozark was that he was too easygoing to get the most out of the Phillies, the team certainly picked the right kind of replacement. Dallas Green, who took over on September 1, 1979, and led the Phillies to their first World Championship the following year, managed with a sledgehammer approach. He was as subtle as a crowbar.

He screamed at his players when they did wrong but seldom patted their backs for doing something right. That, he reasoned, was their job. Some of the more sensitive Phillies, especially Garry Maddox, had trouble with the Dallas Green approach. Others, like Larry Bowa, yelled right back and engaged in shouting matches with the manager. But in the end, Green won.

When he took over for Ozark, the idea was much the same as when Paul Owens went to the dugout in July 1972. Farm director Green, who was being groomed as Owens' successor as general manager, was to get a first-hand idea of what the team needed. Except that Dallas enjoyed the job so much, he decided to stay on in 1980.

No one could ever accuse Green of managing by the book down the stretch in 1980. He chewed out the team unmercifully in Pittsburgh in August. He benched Garry Maddox, Bob Boone, and Greg Luzinski for a spell. And through it all, he was amazingly blunt.

"I get a feeling we're not all in this thing together," he said with incredible candor six games before the end of the regular season. "I wouldn't be surprised if there aren't a few guys out there in that clubhouse who are rooting against us to win this thing. The last two weeks I've been checking up on some things. I've watched these guys very closely. I've watched how they attend to their business and it's almost back to the same old thing. The we're-gonna-do-it-our-way thing . . .

"It's all the little things they continue to do, things they know tick me off.

1979–81

Green, Dallas

Record: 169–130–2 (.565)
Birthplace: Newport, Delaware
B: August 4, 1934

We're fighting for a pennant. This is a time when you have to put everything aside. I don't care if it's at home, if it's in the clubhouse, if it's the manager. You just gotta put it all aside and say, 'It's we, not I.' "

We, not I. Dallas Green had that message pasted on his office wall. Some players considered it a bit hypocritical. After all, wasn't Green constantly complaining to the press about them instead of confronting them directly?

Nevertheless, Dallas succeeded as the Phillies won their first National League pennant in 30 years and their first World Series ever.

Green came back as manager again in 1981. The Phillies were just beginning to roll toward what Dallas thought would be a second World Championship when the strike stopped the season. When the season restarted, Green seemed somewhat uninterested. He wanted to get back into the front office, to assume the role of general manager, but Owens was showing no interest in retiring.

The Cubs came along, offering the GM's job there. Green accepted it verbally during the mini-playoff, a result of the split season. When the Phillies were eliminated by the Expos in the fifth game, he packed and headed for another great challenge, finding a championship for the Cubs, who hadn't seen post-season action since 1945.

As vice president and general manager in Chicago, Green got his Cubs to the National League playoffs in 1984. But the NL East winners lost to the San Diego Padres in the LCS. They never got to the playoffs again, and following a fiery tenure, Green left after the 1987 season.

He was appointed manager of the New York Yankees in 1989, but he was fired after posting a 56–65 record in 121 games. Since then, he has served as a major league scout for the New York Mets.

Dallas Green

Green, Dallas

	W	L	T	Pct
1979	19	11	0	.633
1980	91	71	0	.562
1981	59	48	2	.551
Phillies	169	130	2	.565
Career	225	195	2	.536

1982–83

Corrales, Pat

Record: 132–115–1 (.532)
Birthplace: Los Angeles, California
B: March 20, 1941

Pat Corrales was a manager of few rules, but he had one that would certainly insure that a player like Dick Allen wouldn't be in his lineup very long.

"Be on time," Pat said his number-one rule was upon being named Dallas Green's successor on November 4, 1981.

In his first year at the helm, the Phillies were almost on time. In fact, when Steve Carlton hypnotized the Cardinals in the opener of a key three-game series at the Vet on September 13, it put the Phillies up on the Cards, and it looked like they were on their way to their fifth National League East championship since 1976. But Mike Krukow lost a heartbreaker the following night, and, in the pivotal third game, Corrales called on recently purchased John Denny, who was chased early. The Phillies never led the league again.

Almost overlooked in the late-season problems (in August, Dick Ruthven, taken out of a game after an infield error, elected to throw his glove into the stands and was soon out of the starting rotation) was the job that Corrales had done keeping the team in the race all the way.

A quiet man, although a stern disciplinarian, Corrales had grown up in the Phillies' farm system. His first minor league manager was Paul Owens—after an amateur career in Fresno, California, in which he starred in the same American Legion program that produced Dick Selma, Jim Maloney, and Dick Ellsworth.

He reached the majors with the Phillies in 1964, then moved to the Cardinals in 1966 and to Cincinnati in 1968. He backed up Johnny Bench for four seasons and played in his only World Series in 1970 before closing out his career with the San Diego Padres in 1973.

Five years later, he was named manager of the Texas Rangers, succeeding Billy Hunter on the last day of the season.

In 1979 he got the Rangers home in third place with an 83–79 record but was fired the following season after the Rangers slipped to fourth. In 1981 he assisted Texas general manager Eddie Robinson and helped set up a scouting system in the Latin American nations. He was still engaged in this project when the Phillies called him.

Eighty-five decisions into the 1983 season, with the team in first place, the Phillies made an unprecedented move and relieved Corrales of his managerial duties.

Two weeks later, he was back in the dugout as manager of the Cleveland Indians, becoming only the fourth manager in major league history to pilot teams in both the National and American Leagues in the same season.

Corrales managed the Indians until 1987. His 1986 Indians were the 10th big league team ever to lose 100 games the previous year and come back to finish .500 or better the next.

In recent years he has been a coach with the New York Yankees and most recently the Atlanta Braves.

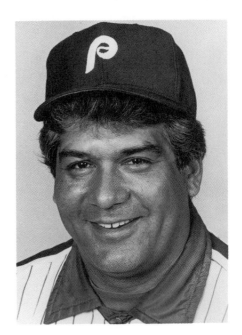

Pat Corrales

Corrales, Pat

	W	L	T	Pct
1982	89	73	0	.549
1983	43	42	1	.508
Phillies	132	115	1	.532
Career	572	634	5	.474

In 1983 the Phillies weren't the only team in the organization to go to the World Series. Down on the farm, the Portland Beavers, the Phils' Triple-A affiliate, won the Pacific Coast League championship and advanced to the Little World Series.

That event hardly went unnoticed in the Phillies' front office. John Felske, the man who managed that team, had become the heir apparent to the skipper's post with the parent club.

Thus, it was no big surprise when Felske was appointed Phillies manager after the 1984 season had ended, taking over for Paul Owens. Felske had been groomed for the position for several years.

A former catcher who had spent 12 seasons as a player, all in the minor leagues except for brief stops with the Chicago Cubs and Milwaukee Brewers, for whom he played in a total of 54 big league games and hit .135, Felske was a well-traveled fellow. After retiring as a player, he had managed six seasons in the Brewers' system and had put in two years as a bullpen coach with the Toronto Blue Jays.

Felske was lured to the Phillies' organization in 1982 as manager of the Double-A Reading club. After finishing third there, he was promoted to Portland, and his team went all the way to the last Triple-A round before losing in a five-game series with Tidewater of the International League.

The following year, Felske was brought up to the Phillies to work as a coach under Owens. The idea was for him to watch, to listen, and to learn the subtleties of managing in the big leagues.

Felske took these lessons with him into the 1985 season, but the year did not pan out the way either he or anyone else on the team hoped it would. Saddled with a ton of mediocre performances and a weak pitching staff, the Phillies finished in fifth place with a paltry 75–87 record.

A likable chap who was nearly always accommodating, Felske was extremely patient with his team, although on more than one occasion it could have used a swift boot to the seat of the pants.

In 1986 the Phillies moved up to second place with an 86–75 record, but finished a distant 21½ games behind the front-running Mets. Felske was often

1985–87

Felske, John

Record: 190–194 (.495)
Birthplace: Chicago, Illinois
B: May 30, 1942

John Felske

the subject of criticism in some segments of the local press, much of it focusing on his laid-back demeanor.

In 1987 the criticism increased. Felske was accused of losing control of the team and of being insensitive to his black players. Although he denied the charges, Felske was piloting a sinking ship.

The end came in mid-June with the Phillies buried in fifth place and the season rapidly disintegrating. Felske was fired after managing the Phils for two and one-half years. He had one-half year left on his contract.

Felske returned to his home in suburban Chicago, where he ran several successful oil and lube operations. Although offered managerial jobs at the minor league level, he steadfastly refused to return to baseball.

Felske, John

	W	L	T	Pct
1985	75	87	0	.463
1986	86	75	0	.534
1987	29	32	0	.475
Phillies	190	194	0	.495
Career	190	194	0	.495

1987–88

Elia, Lee

Record: 111–142–1 (.439)
Birthplace: Philadelphia, Pennsylvania
B: July 16, 1937

Lee Elia

Rare is the player who gets to perform for his hometown team. Even rarer is the manager who is able to pilot the team of his native city.

Lee Elia was one, and almost the other. A native of the Olney section of Philadelphia, he managed the Phillies for parts of two seasons.

Inglorious as those seasons were, Elia was only the third manager in Phillies history to run his hometown team. The others were Billy Shettsline and Jimmie Wilson.

Elia enjoyed a long and varied connection with the Phillies. A former All–Public League selection in football, baseball, and basketball at Olney High School, the one-time star quarterback was signed by the Phillies after one year at the University of Delaware. Elia spent six years as a player in the Phillies' organization but never made it to the big leagues. The Phils traded him to the Chicago White Sox in 1965, and Elia played briefly in the majors in 1966 and 1968.

After his playing career ended in 1973, Elia began a long climb through the Phillies' farm system as a manager. He spent five seasons in the minors, then became a coach with the Phillies for two years, including the World Championship 1980 team.

Elia managed the Chicago Cubs in 1982 and 1983. It was in the Windy City that Elia unleashed his famous tirade about Cubs fans: "Eighty-five percent of the world's workin', the other 15 come out here (to Wrigley Field)," he roared after one particularly galling Chicago loss.

After that explosion helped to get him fired late in the 1983 season, Elia returned to the Phillies to manage the Triple-A club at Portland. He became a coach with the Phillies in 1985 and was serving in that capacity when John Felske was fired in mid-1987.

"I've got Phillies blood," Elia said at the time. "All I want to do is work for the Phillies."

After taking over a team that was in fifth place and in the midst of a six-game losing streak, Elia got the Phillies to play more aggressively and whipped the club home to a fourth-place finish, going 51–50 after the managerial switch.

The 1988 season proved far less successful. Despite Elia's efforts, the Phils played horribly. A rash of injuries to key players didn't help. Suddenly, with just nine games left in the season and the Phils having lost 28 of their last 38 games, new general manager Lee Thomas dismissed Elia. At the time, the club had a 60–92 record and was headed for its worst season since 1972.

"The Phillies have to get rid of a few people (players) before they can start to move up," Elia said in what would become a telling prophecy.

Elia, the one-time shortstop, remained in baseball after his axing. He spent the 1989 season as a coach with the New York Yankees under Dallas Green. Then he returned to the Phillies and managed the Class A Clearwater Phillies for the next two years. In 1991, Clearwater had its best season in club history.

Elia moved up to the Triple-A level in 1992 to become manager of the Phillies' Triple-A team at Scranton/Wilkes-Barre. He piloted the Red Barons to a division title and into the finals of the International League playoffs, where they lost to Colombus in the last inning of the final game. After the season, he left the Phillies' organization, and later became bench coach of the Seattle Mariners.

Elia, Lee

	W	L	T	Pct
1987	51	50	0	.505
1988	60	92	1	.395
Phillies	111	142	1	.439
Career	238	300	1	.442

For some time, John Vukovich had wanted to manage a big league team. But he didn't expect his one chance so far to happen the way it did.

Vukovich was named interim manager of the Phillies after Lee Elia was fired near the end of the 1988 season. The former Phillies infielder led the Phils for nine games, posting a 5–4 record.

Vukovich was a remote candidate for the Phils' job the next season when Nick Leyva got the position. He was also a candidate for the skipper's job with the Chicago White Sox for 1992, and in the late 1980s he had come close to managing the Chicago Cubs.

Though managing on a full-time basis has yet to become part of Vukovich's résumé, he has served many years in the big leagues. He played in 10 big league seasons, spending 1970–71 and 1976–81 as a utility infielder with the Phillies. He served six years as a coach with the Cubs, and since 1988 has been a coach with the Phillies.

Vukovich also played with the Milwaukee Brewers and Cincinnati Reds. He was a member of World Championship teams in 1976 with the Reds and 1980 with the Phillies.

Vukovich, John

	W	L	T	Pct
1988	5	4	0	.556
Phillies	5	4	0	.556
Career	6	5	0	.545

1988

Vukovich, John

Record: 5–4 (.556)
Birthplace: Sacramento, California
B: July 31, 1947

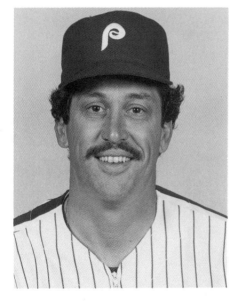

John Vukovich

1989–91

Leyva, Nick

Record: 148–189–1 (.438)
Birthplace: Ontario, California
B: August 16, 1953

Like those of so many of his predecessors, Nick Leyva's term as manager of the Phillies was short, not so sweet, and a little bit like a car trying to run without the use of all its cylinders.

Leyva was an unknown when he came to the Phillies. At 35, he was also the team's youngest manager since Gene Mauch grabbed the reins at 34 in 1960. And he came without much experience but with the sturdy backing of general manager Lee Thomas, his long-time friend, one-time boss, and close associate when the two were with the St. Louis Cardinals.

Leyva had never managed in the big leagues before. He had never even played in the big leagues before. His only big league contact had been as a coach for five years with the Cardinals.

The first Phillies manager who didn't come out of the organization in more than a decade, Leyva promised an aggressive, exciting team. He said when he was hired that he'd be tough, that he'd demand hustle, and that he wasn't going to be fazed by the big salaries of many of his players.

"I'm dealing with grown men," he said. "I'm not a baby-sitter. As long as they give 100 percent and don't embarrass me or the organization, we'll be all right."

Unfortunately, the Phillies weren't all right. There always seemed to be some problems. Players hurt. Players pouting. Players failing to hustle. The Phils bumped along on a long, uphill climb with little speed.

In Leyva's first year the club was 67–95, a one-game improvement over the previous year but still bad enough to corral a spot in last place.

There was hope the second year as the dealings of Thomas began taking effect. The Phillies pulled up to fourth place, their 77 victories being the highest total in three years.

Leyva, whose background consisted largely of three years as a player and six years as a manager in the St. Louis farm system, seemed to be gaining in managerial skill and experience. Occasionally a move would backfire, and Leyva would be singed by the heat of the fans and the press, but he appeared to have the Phillies on the right track.

That all came bursting apart, however, early in the 1991 season. After a spring training that was rampant with rumors of Leyva's imminent demise, the season was only 13 games old when Thomas fired his friend Leyva. "I didn't like the way the club was going, and I thought we had to make a change," Thomas said.

At the time, the Phillies' record was 4–9. Not good, to be sure, but not nearly so much Leyva's fault as it was the fault of the shoddy performance of many of the team's players.

Leyva's dismissal was the earliest a manager was ever fired by the Phillies. He had also served the longest stint since Dallas Green.

When he was fired, Leyva still had nearly two years left on his contract. He sat out the rest of the 1991 season, then took a job for '92 as manager of the Syracuse Chiefs, the top farm team of the Toronto Blue Jays. Ironically, in his first game as pilot of the Chiefs, he faced his Phillies predecessor, Lee Elia, the skipper of Scranton/Wilkes-Barre.

Leyva, Nick

	W	L	T	Pct
1989	67	95	1	.414
1990	77	85	0	.475
1991	4	9	0	.308
Phillies	148	189	1	.438
Career	148	189	1	.438

Nick Leyva

When the Phillies hired Jim Fregosi, they broke a long-standing tradition. Fregosi was the first Phils leader in many years who had previously been an outstanding player.

The last successful player to become manager of the Phillies had been Bob Skinner in 1968. Before that, few prominent players held the reins of the Phils.

Fregosi had been a six-time All-Star, a premier shortstop who had played 18 seasons in the big leagues, most notably with the California Angels, but also with the New York Mets, Texas Rangers, and Pittsburgh Pirates.

Fregosi had a lifetime batting average of .265. He hit .278 with 22 home runs and 82 RBI in 1968, his best all-around year in the majors. Three years later he was traded to the Mets for Nolan Ryan and three minor leaguers.

After his playing career ended, Fregosi became a manager. He piloted the Angels for three and one-half seasons, leading his club to the West Division title in the American League in 1979 and posting an overall record of 237–249. He was replaced in mid-1981 by Gene Mauch.

Fregosi managed at Louisville from 1983 to 1986, winning two division championships. He joined the Chicago White Sox as manager in late June 1986 and held that position through 1988, compiling a record of 193–226.

The ex-infielder joined the Phillies in 1989, originally serving as a special assignments man for his former Angels teammate, Lee Thomas.

The next season he was named a minor league pitching instructor, a position he held until summoned to manage the Phillies on April 23, 1991.

In his first season at the helm of the Phillies, Fregosi had to contend with numerous injuries to key players, including outfielder Len Dykstra and catcher Darren Daulton, who were hurt in an auto accident. Although the pitching staff also underwent a major upheaval and there was little offense, the Phillies still managed to finish in third place, their highest finish since 1986. Fregosi's record after taking over for Nick Leyva was 74–75.

In 1992, however, Fregosi's Phillies tumbled into last place early in the season, and stayed there for the duration of the campaign. Once again, injuries to key players such as Dykstra, Dale Murphy, Tommy Greene, and Jose DeJesus took a heavy toll, but that was only part of the problem. For much of the season, the Phillies simply played bad baseball, and with a patched-together lineup that often more closely resembled a Triple-A squad, they were wholly outclassed by the rest of the division.

1991–

Fregosi, Jim

Record: 144–167 (.463)
Birthplace: San Francisco, California
B: April 4, 1942

Jim Fregosi

Fregosi, Jim

	W	L	T	Pct
1991	74	75	0	.497
1992	70	92	0	.432
Phillies	144	167	0	.463
Career	574	642	0	.472

The Front Office

After the first season when the Phillies won only 17 of 98 games, friends of club president Al Reach tried to convince him that owning a professional baseball team was a bad idea. The Phillies, they argued, should be disbanded, and Reach should concentrate on less futile ways of spending his money.

Because Reach refused to wither under such pressure, the Phillies survived their first major crisis. There have been a few more crises since then, but 110 years after that first pathetic season, the club that Reach built is one of the pillars of the National League.

Getting to that point hasn't been easy. The franchise has struggled much of the time, several times even staggering to the brink of collapse.

To some extent, the Phillies' troubles were helped along by the people who ran the team. Among the club's long line of presidents and other front office personnel, there have been some marvelous cases in which the ability to run a baseball team was not a requirement of the job.

Conversely, the Phillies have been endowed with other executives who were as capable as anyone who ever ran a baseball team. Operating a strong franchise was their primary objective, and although their teams were not always winners, they maintained a position as a respectable member of the league.

The winners and the losers should be obvious as you read the following chapter on presidents, general managers, and other front office people.

The Presidents

Al Reach was the classic American success story, an immigrant who rose from the streets of New York City to become a millionaire.

Whether it was selling newspapers as a boy on Broadway, blazing a trail as a baseball pioneer, or building a mammoth sporting goods company, practically everything that Reach did was done well and with good results.

Reach was the first president of the Phillies. A strong case could be made that during the club's first 90 years he was also the most successful.

During his reign, Reach not only created a new professional team, he developed it into one of the cornerstones of the National League. In his 20 years as president, he built two ball parks, the Phillies finished in the first division 14 times, and the club posted a winning record of 1,339–1,260 for the best percentage (.515) under any club president until Ruly Carpenter.

Reach was an innovator who achieved several significant milestones in his life. As a player, he is usually considered to have been the first professional. As a businessman, he was one of the first to manufacture baseball bats, balls, and gloves.

Born in 1840 in London, England, Reach came to the United States at the age of one. He was raised in Brooklyn where his industrious nature surfaced early.

As a boy, Reach sold newspapers, but as soon as he was big enough, he took

1883–1902

Alfred J. Reach

Ruly Carpenter (with manager Danny Ozark) presided over the most successful era in Phillies history.

a job in an iron foundry. Toiling as an iron molder with heavy tools and near the hot furnaces, he worked 12-hour days. Some of his work went into the construction of New York's finest hotels of the day along Fifth Avenue.

When he wasn't working, Reach played baseball, first on vacant lots and then with some of the local teams in the Brooklyn area. Although a lefthander, he was originally a catcher.

In his early twenties, Reach played for the Brooklyn Eckfords, a prominent club in the New York area. During a series in Philadelphia, Al attracted the attention of Colonel Thomas Fitzgerald, manager of the Philadelphia Athletics, a team that traveled the country to play.

Fitzgerald enticed Reach to join the Athletics by offering the young player a contract and a full-time salary. Reach accepted the offer and, although he continued to live in Brooklyn, he joined the Athletics in 1863.

In those days, some teams paid a few of their players under the table, but Reach was the first man to accept pay openly. And he soon justified his salary. Installed as a lefthanded second baseman, young Al quickly became the team's leading hitter.

In 1868 he was named first-team All-American by the New York *Clipper*. Baseball was not quite the same in those days; in fact, in 1869 a team called the Brooklyn Atlantics defeated the Athletics, 51–48. But the 5–6, 155-pound Reach was usually good for three or four hits a game, and he earned a reputation as the home run king of the era. Moreover, he developed a big local following.

A new professional league, the National Association, forerunner of the National League, was formed in 1871. The Athletics not only joined it, they captured the pennant, winning 22 of 29 games. Reach, by then a resident of Frankford, led the team in hitting with a .348 average. He never hit that high again, but he became the team's manager for the 1874 and 1875 seasons.

By this time, Al's entrepreneurial instincts had been activated. Reach opened a cigar store at 404½ Chestnut Street. He ran the store before and after the games, and it became a local hangout for sporting types.

About this time, Reach also noticed the increasing demand for baseballs, bats, and other sporting goods, and the corresponding absence of any stores that supplied such items. The observation prompted him to open a sporting goods store at 6 South Eighth Street in 1874, one year before his playing days ended.

The store thrived and by 1881 Reach moved to a larger store at 23 South Eighth Street. Simultaneously, he took in a partner, Benjamin J. Shibe, an expert on leather and a manufacturer of whips. The partnership was formed to launch a business to manufacture sporting goods. Soon the men opened a plant at Palmer and Tulip Streets in North Philadelphia.

Although he had become a full-time businessman, Reach retained his contacts in baseball. In late 1882, he was approached by an old friend, Colonel A. G. Mills, about starting a baseball franchise in Philadelphia.

Mills, a former player, had become the president of the National League, which had been formed in 1876. He wondered if Reach would be interested in running a club. If so, Mills would move the ailing Worcester, Massachusetts, franchise to Philadelphia.

Reach jumped at the chance. He enlisted the aid of Colonel John I. Rogers, a lawyer and member of the governor's staff. The two became equal partners in the new team.

There were no players involved in the transaction—they had been gobbled up by other teams as soon as it became apparent that the failing Worcester Brown Stockings would be folded. Thus Reach and Rogers had to start from scratch, recruiting players and even constructing a ballpark.

The players came from an assortment of directions, some locally and some from minor professional teams elsewhere. A ballfield, called Recreation Park, was refurbished in the block surrounded by Ridge and Columbia Avenues, and 24th and 25th Streets. And the team was named Phillies, which served the purpose of identifying the team's geographic roots.

The first team in 1883 was a dismal failure. It won only 17 of 98 games. But Reach was not discouraged. The following season he brought in new players, and most importantly, turned the managerial reins over to Harry Wright, a baseball pioneer himself and one of the game's premier managers.

Under Wright, the Phillies improved tremendously. In the ensuing years, the club moved into a new showplace stadium, Philadelphia Base Ball Park,

Al Reach

where it became a regular pennant contender. The club became the residence of a number of future Hall of Fame players, including Ed Delahanty, Nap Lajoie, and Elmer Flick, who got their starts in Phillies uniforms.

It was Reach who gambled on spending $1,900, a staggering figure in those days, for Delahanty, at the time a raw young hitter in the minors. And it was Reach who, seeing the enormous commercial possibilities of baseball, promoted his team until it became the most popular one in the city, despite competition off and on from three other professional clubs.

Under Reach, the Phillies finished second twice, third six times, fourth six times, sixth twice, seventh once, eighth twice, and tenth once. Although the club never won a pennant, the Philadelphia franchise developed a reputation as one of the most solid in the National League.

There were, of course, disappointments and problems during Reach's administration. The club engaged in bitter battles over players in 1890 with the Players' League and in 1901 with the American League. The losses of players to those leagues, especially Delahanty, Lajoie, and Flick, the sudden death of star pitcher Charlie Ferguson, the devastating fire at Philadelphia Park, and the players' mutiny over the tactics of manager George Stallings all contributed to a less-than-smooth tenure for Reach.

By the early 1890s, Reach was spending more time with his sporting goods business and less time with the Phillies. The militant and often stubborn Rogers took a larger hand in the operation of the team.

Meanwhile, the A. J. Reach Company was flourishing. The company opened another plant in Brantford, Ontario, and moved its store to a large building at 1820 Chestnut Street.

The relationship between Reach and Shibe couldn't have been better. Reach's son George married Shibe's daughter. And when the American League began, Reach recommended his partner for a franchise in Philadelphia.

The ensuing sequence was laced with irony. Shibe became the first owner of the American League's Philadelphia Athletics. And the Reach ball became the official ball of the new league. Yet the presence of the young circuit and its player raids on the Phillies were probably the deciding factors in Reach's decision to end his ownership in the National League.

Financially crippled by the raids, Reach and Rogers had to secure a loan from Pittsburgh Pirates owner Barney Dreyfus. Soon afterward the Phillies were sold to a syndicate headed by James Potter. The selling price was $170,000. Reach and Rogers retained the title to Philadelphia Park, leasing it back to the new owners.

Eventually, Reach sold his sporting goods store, too. But his manufacturing company continued to crank out new baseballs, using a special winding machine that Reach invented. The company also produced a huge assortment of other sporting goods, and for a number of decades it published the official American League *Reach Baseball Guide*.

The Philadelphia *Ledger* in 1915 described Reach's operation in glowing terms. "The establishment of Mr. Reach has grown to larger proportions, and the name is synonymous with baseball," it said.

The Reach Company, along with the A. G. Spalding Company, founded by another old baseball-playing pioneer, were the dominant firms in the sporting goods field in the country.

Before retiring, Reach sold his company to the rival Spalding firm. He lived his final years in Atlantic City. Reach died on January 14, 1928. He left an estate valued at $1,017,868.

1903–04

James Potter

If Jimmy Potter had bought, say, a polo franchise instead of the Phillies in March 1903, maybe it would have all worked out for the best. Or if Potter had been able to find a professional squash league, he might have been comfortable.

As it turned out, baseball was not Potter's game. It belonged to red-blooded American males. Potter's blood had a bluish tint to it.

He bought the team from its original owner, Alfred J. Reach, via syndicate for $170,000. Not that the new ownership was in favor of moving the team from Broad and Huntingdon to the Main Line. Potter, a socialite with heavy

University of Pennsylvania connections, was also a broker whose clients had not necessarily achieved the social status to which he was accustomed. He had many of them join in his investment in the sport of "base ball."

Here's everything you need to know about Potter's tenure as president: the bleachers collapsed. So did the team.

On August 6, 1903, the fans were attracted to a disturbance behind the left field bleachers. They ran to the top of the stands to see what the commotion was about. A balcony fell under the weight, a score of fans were killed, and more than 200 others were hospitalized.

The Phillies finished seventh that year. In 1904 they dropped to eighth and last for the first time since 1883. After the season, Potter realized that baseball wasn't his game. He got out. The stockholders held a reorganization meeting and the presidency of the team was passed to Bill Shettsline.

1905–08

William J. Shettsline

Bill Shettsline

Bill Shettsline had already been involved in the operation of a baseball team at many levels when he succeeded Jimmy Potter as club president in 1905.

He had been field manager of the team from 1898 to 1902 and was acting as business manager when he was asked to fill the top spot.

He served through the 1908 season, during which time the Phillies finished third once and fourth three times.

During his tenure the Phillies changed managers once, hiring Bill Murray to replace Hugh Duffy after the 1906 season.

But, in his most important move, Shettsline signed a semipro outfielder shortly after he was named president. His name was Sherry Magee, a free spirit off the field and a tremendous talent on it. Shetts also made the trade that brought Kitty Bransfield from Pittsburgh, and he sent Harry Wolverton to Boston for pitcher Togie Pittinger, who went 23–17 in his first year with the Phillies. He also signed Hall of Famer Kid Nichols after the Cardinals had released him, but Nichols was washed up.

Under Shettsline's leadership, the 1908 Phillies drew 420,660, a club record to that point.

1909

Israel W. Durham

Israel Durham

Izz Durham served as president of the team for only a few months in 1909 before his death in June 28 of that year.

Durham and James P. McNichol were the city's two top political bosses. Along with banker Clarence Wolf, they formed a syndicate and bought the club from the group that James Potter had originally headed.

Bill Shettsline, who had served as president after Potter stepped down, was returned to the position of business manager.

Durham had high hopes for the team. "We will save neither money nor effort to bring a first National League championship to Philadelphia," he announced.

Even as he took over the presidency, however, Durham was a sick man. After his death, neither McNichol nor Wolf decided they had any real interest in running the team. They sold it on November 26, and the new buyer was a surprise to everyone.

1909–12

Horace S. Fogel

Horace Fogel was a sportswriter, a good one at that, but everyone knows even the best sportswriters don't make the kind of money it takes to buy a baseball team. But when the Phillies were sold, Fogel was installed as president and insisted that he was running the whole show. He also tried to insinuate that he was the only owner of a $350,000 property.

Actually, the money came from the Taft family in Cincinnati, originally the largest shareholders in Bill Giles' syndicate, through Charles Murphy, the Chicago Cubs' president.

Things were never dull around Broad and Huntingdon with Fogel, who had managed Indianapolis in 1887 and the New York Giants in 1902 (combined 38–72–2 record), at the controls. He even tried to change the team's nickname from Phillies to Live Wires. His sportswriting buddies ignored the idea. He tried to have a wedding staged inside a lion's cage at the pitcher's mound—with the lion acting as one of the witnesses.

Soon after he took over the presidency, he fired manager Bill Murray and replaced him with catcher Red Dooin, who made the club better and more exciting.

In 1911, Fogel swung the biggest trade the Phillies had ever made to that point. He sent pitchers George McQuillan and Lew Moren, third baseman Ed Grant, and outfielder John Bates to the Reds for third baseman Hans Lobert, center fielder Dode Paskert, and pitchers Jack Rowan and Fred Beebe.

In 1912, though, Horace overstepped his bounds. Out with his writer friends drinking one night during the frenetic Giants-Cubs pennant race (Fogel was very much pro-Cub because of his affiliation with Murphy), the Phillies' president made the following charges:

- The 1912 pennant race was fixed.
- The National League umpires favored the Giants.
- Roger Bresnahan, the Cardinal manager, played his weakest lineup against his old team, the Giants.

Unfortunately for Fogel, the writers printed his words, chapter and verse. League president Tom Lynch was livid and filed charges against Fogel, who tried to laugh them off.

But it was no laughing matter when Lynch convened a meeting of the owners at New York's Waldorf Astoria Hotel shortly after the season ended. Former Cincinnati mayor Julius Fleischmann, a minority stockholder in the Reds, acted as presiding judge as the owners sat as a court. Lynch listed seven charges against Fogel, whose peers found him guilty on five counts. Lynch ordered Fogel "barred forever from the councils of the National League."

Fogel was crushed. He made an unsuccessful run at Congress as a Democrat and died on November 15, 1928, a broken man.

Horace Fogel

1912–13

Albert D. Wiler

Albert D. Wiler's role as Phillies president lasted less than three months and could be labeled that of caretaker.

After Horace Fogel was expelled from the game, the Cincinnati group that had backed Fogel decided that it wanted to get rid of the Phillies. While it sought a buyer, the franchise was in a state of limbo. During that period, Wiler became the stopgap president of the team. He left the position when a syndicate headed by William H. Locke purchased the team on January 15, 1913.

1913

William H. Locke

William H. Locke's lifetime desire was to own and operate a major league baseball team. In many ways, he was like current Phillies owner Bill Giles, a man without the wealth it took to achieve his burning ambition, but one who would find a way to do it.

When Horace Fogel was tossed out of baseball by National League President Tom Lynch, it opened up the opportunity for Locke to try to put together a group to take over what, at the time, was a very healthy franchise. The ballpark was still in relatively decent condition, and the roster was downright appealing.

Locke grabbed the opportunity by the throat and didn't let go. He was the biggest investor in his group, which included a cousin, William F. Baker, who was a former New York City police commissioner and a man of considerable means. Baker became the second biggest investor in the syndicate. Locke made his bid, which was accepted by Fogel's backers. On January 15, 1913, Locke's dream became reality.

Sadly, it ended quickly. Six months to the day after he assumed control of the team, Locke was dead. His demise probably changed the course of the franchise's history, since he was regarded as an astute baseball man from his days as Barney Dreyfuss' number-one assistant with the Pittsburgh Pirates.

During his brief tenure with the Phillies, Locke had worked hard. He held daily conferences with manager Red Dooin on ways to improve the team. He tried to buy up all outstanding stock so that his interests would be solely in command.

His death led to the tenure of William F. Baker. Two years later, Baker got what Locke had wanted so badly—the Phillies won the National League pennant.

1913–30

William F. Baker

In his 18 years as president of the Phillies, former New York City police commissioner William F. Baker took the franchise from good days to bad days. He made some of the worst trades in major league history, allowed his ballpark to deteriorate so badly that it became hazardous, won one pennant, and finished last eight times.

He ran his operation on a financial shoestring, even when things were going well in the mid-teens. During the latter years of his ownership, he was constantly trading whatever talent he had to get cash to meet the payroll.

Baker died in Montreal on December 4, 1930, a controversial figure in Philadelphia to the end. The big complaint about him was that he never dipped into his own pocket to finance the team. Although he was a man of considerable means, he chose instead to let the team pay for itself. In addition, some Philadelphians resented the fact that he spent most of his years as team president commuting back and forth from New York City, instead of establishing a permanent residence in Philadelphia.

It can also be soundly argued that the Phillies won the 1915 pennant in spite of him, not because of him. Their chances of winning the World Series that year were hindered badly by his desire to generate more revenue by roping off some areas in left and center field, resulting in three cheap Boston home runs.

He also failed to endear himself to the loyal Phillies fans in 1925 when, in Common Pleas Court testifying in a suit contesting the ownership of shares of Phillies stock, Baker admitted that he was hoping to sell the team eventually.

"We (Baker and his partners) thought that when I could get the club up to the first division, we could get a good price for it," he said.

In reality, Baker was never a baseball man before he took over the presidency of the Phillies after the death of William H. Locke. He assumed leadership only to protect his investment.

William Baker

But once he got his feet wet, Baker became a mover and shaker. He fired eight different managers during his tenure, including Pat Moran, who had led the team to the 1915 pennant.

Baker showed a total lack of understanding for the game after the 1913 season when the Federal League was formed and offered many baseball stars much larger contracts. Instead of fighting back, Baker offered those Phillies who were approached small salary increases, if any at all. As a result, he lost his second base–shortstop combination of Otto Knabe and Mickey Doolan, utility man Runt Walsh, and pitchers Tom Seaton and Ad Brennan.

But after the 1914 season, Baker did something right. He changed managers after the team finished a disappointing sixth, replacing Red Dooin with Moran.

"I didn't have to go far to find a successor," Baker told guests at an annual off-season dinner he sponsored. "I found him right on the ball club in Coach Pat Moran. I've watched Pat and like the way he goes about his work. He knows a lot of baseball. I think he'll make us a fine manager."

Baker was right. The first year under Moran, the Phillies won the pennant. They might have done better in the World Series if part of the outfield hadn't been roped off. In the fifth and final game of the Series, Harry Hooper, who had hit two home runs all season, hit two into the roped-off area and Duffy Lewis hit one. Baker took a terrible beating in the national press, which called him the goat of the Series.

After the 1917 season, Baker made one of the worst trades in the history of the franchise. He moved Grover Cleveland Alexander and Bill Killefer to the Cubs for $60,000, pitcher Mike Pendergast, and catcher Pickles Dillhoefer. Baker insisted at the time of the deal that it was made strictly because Alexander was going to be drafted for service in World War I and there was no way he was going to gamble on Ol' Pete's safe return. But when pressed on the issue several years later, Baker told the real reason for the trade.

"Because I needed the money," he admitted.

One of the biggest critics of the Alexander trade was manager Moran, who let it be known that he and the boss did not see eye to eye on it. Baker's response was to fire Moran at the end of the 1918 season.

In 1920, Baker made another awful trade. He shipped future Hall of Fame shortstop Davey Bancroft to the Giants for shortstop Art Fletcher, pitcher Bill Hubbell, and $100,000. The money was the key, although Baker tried to justify the deal by saying that Fletcher would do just as well as Bancroft. At the time, Bancroft was 28 and Fletcher was 35.

The Roaring Twenties were not accompanied by roaring crowds at Baker Bowl. Only once in the decade did attendance surpass 300,000. Baker incurred the wrath of Phillies fans by continuing to trade stars for lesser players and large sums of cash.

He dealt Casey Stengel and Irish Meusel to the Giants in 1921. Three years later, even Giant manager John McGraw, who had been the beneficiary of Baker's trades, tired of it. He ripped Baker for his manner of conducting business. He said that he, along with other owners, would run Baker out of baseball.

The Phillies president fought back. He accused McGraw of tampering with players on other teams, making them dissatisfied with playing anywhere but for the Giants.

McGraw never got Baker out of baseball, and Baker continued to sell whatever good players he had until his death. He never got around to selling Chuck Klein (another owner would do that) but he did put a 12-foot screen atop the right field fence in order to cut down on Chuck's home runs. The belief was that he did so to keep Klein from approaching Babe Ruth's record and then approaching the owner for a healthy raise in salary.

A month before he died, Baker made his last trade, sending Lefty O'Doul, who had hit .398 and .383 in his two seasons with the Phillies, and Fresco Thompson to Brooklyn. In exchange, he received three lesser players and $25,000 in cash.

At his funeral in New York, baseball commissioner Judge Kenesaw Mountain Landis praised Baker as "a pillar of the baseball community." In reality, his policies were a bitter pill for Phillies fans to swallow. And because of the sad state of finances on the team, the policy of trading stars for cash continued for more than a decade.

1931–32

Lewis C. Ruch

To be president of the Phillies was a position Lewis C. Ruch neither sought nor wanted. But once named, Ruch proved to be a capable and effective administrator who worked extremely hard to make the club respectable.

Ruch's appointment was strictly a matter of fate, as was his original involvement with the Phillies. He was elected to the club presidency after the sudden death of William Baker.

The genial, easygoing native of Canal Fulton, Ohio, had been connected with the Phillies as a stockholder since 1913. Although he rarely took an active part in the club's operation, he served for many years as the team's vice president.

Ruch became president on January 5, 1931, at the age of 69. At the time, he had been retired from private business for 10 years because of ill health. He had no plans to run the club, but when the board of directors passed him the reins, Ruch plunged enthusiastically into the job.

"Naturally, we are going to try and improve the Phillies," said Ruch upon his appointment. The club had finished eighth in four out of the previous five seasons.

Urging everyone to call him Charlie, the popular Ruch added, "From what I understand, it takes a healthy and active man to run the Phillies. I'll do everything possible to bring about a winning club."

Ruch vowed to spend every day from the start of spring training until the end of the season with the club. And he did, moving from his home in Brooklyn to Philadelphia, pumping his energy into the operation.

Ruch attended nearly every home game, sitting in a box behind home plate. "By watching his expressions," said Bill Dooly in the Philadelphia *Record,* "we could tell how the Phillies were doing as surely as a glance at the scoreboard."

Under his administration, Ruch saw the Phillies progress to sixth place in 1931 and to fourth in 1932. It was the only time the club finished in the first division between 1918 and 1949.

Charlie also engineered the end of a long contract dispute with slugger Chuck Klein, who staged a holdout that lasted through all of spring training in 1931. Ruch signed Klein to a three-year contract for $45,000, a heavy sum for the Phillies at the time but far short of what many of Klein's followers thought he was worth.

Ed Pollock in the *Public Ledger* praised Ruch as a sportsman and a "business man of proven acumen. He came into baseball as the president of a major league club at a time when finances were more important than pennants. The golden era had ended. He knew it. The players didn't. He had to cut overhead expenses and at the same time satisfy the stars. He came out of his temporary retirement and did a great job through two tough years."

Ruch had come by his status honestly. Born on a farm in 1862, Charlie, whose father died in the Civil War, was raised in poverty. He had little formal education. Even as a youth he worked full-time as a farmhand. At the age of 21 he was earning $15 a month on a farm, plus fifty cents for each cord of wood he cut.

Lewis Ruch

Finding farm life unfulfilling, Ruch moved to Ravenna, Ohio, where he got a job in a hardware and farm implement store, earning $25 a month. After six months he had saved his entire earnings of $150 and, upon the urging of the store owner, enrolled in a six-week business course in a school in Poughkeepsie, New York.

After returning once more to Ravenna to work briefly in the store, Ruch landed a position as a salesman with a milling company selling oats; his territory was New York and New England.

Ruch remained a feed salesman for 10 years. During that period he met and became close friends with Will Locke and Will and James Baker. At the Baker brothers' insistence, Ruch joined their freight transportation company in New York, but after four years there, he left to accept a position with a nationwide outdoor advertising company. Ruch worked for the company for 15 years, rising to company secretary before declining health forced him to retire in 1920.

Over the years Ruch had stayed close to Locke and the Bakers. One day, while he was still an advertising executive, he received an urgent call from Will Baker. Locke was attempting to pick up an option he had to buy the Phillies, but several of his financial supporters had backed out at the last minute, and the deal was on the verge of collapsing. Locke and the Bakers were making a final attempt to arrange the sale. Could Ruch help out?

Charlie agreed, and later that day he was on a train from Brooklyn to Philadelphia to sign the papers. The year was 1913, and although it wasn't his intent, Ruch had become part-owner of the Phillies.

One month after the transaction was completed, Locke died, and Will Baker was elevated to the club presidency. Ruch was named vice president, a position he would hold until Baker's death in 1930 cast him into the role of president.

At the time of Baker's death, he and Ruch owned the controlling interest in the Phillies. There was speculation that the club would be sold; a group headed by Ty Cobb was anxious to purchase it, as were several others.

But Baker's will stipulated that the club could not be sold. Ruch was hauled reluctantly out of retirement to direct it.

After two seasons, Ruch, his health again failing, tendered his resignation as president on the advice of his physician. Charlie was then 71.

Soon after he left the club, Ruch moved permanently to his winter home in Miami. An avid gardener, he spent the remaining years tending his showplace garden.

Ruch died in Miami at the age of 75 on August 30, 1937.

1932–43

Gerald P. Nugent

On the day he was elected president of the Phillies, Gerald P. Nugent made an announcement to the press. "I will not trade or sell any of my key men, Bartell, Whitney or Klein, no matter how attractive the figure or how promising the material offered. They are the nucleus of our club, the foundation from which we must build."

Less than two years after making that statement, Nugent had not only traded that trio, but he'd swapped or sold an army of others. It was not so much a commentary on a man going back on his word as it was a statement on the dire straits to which the team could drive him.

In his 10 seasons at the helm of the Phillies, Nugent ruled over the sorriest period in the club's history. It was an era of terrible teams, playing much of the time in a miserable stadium with little success and equally little support from the fans. The combination of these formed a perpetually bleak financial picture in which Nugent struggled valiantly to make ends meet.

Gerry, it was said, was always just one step ahead of the sheriff. The team's debts almost always exceeded its income. In the end that dilemma forced the beleaguered Nugent to relinquish control of his team.

Probably no one tried harder in the face of such overwhelming odds to make a go of it. Nugent was an astute businessman with an extremely thorough knowledge of baseball. "But no matter how good an operator you are," he once said, "you have to have some luck."

Nugent had none, and neither did his hapless charges. The Phillies never got above seventh place during Gerry's presidency, finishing eighth six times and seventh four. The club seldom drew many more than 200,000 fans for the season, falling below that mark twice and only going above 250,000 once. Sometimes they attracted no more than 200 or 300 for a game.

It usually cost about $350,000 a year to operate the team, $250,000 of that going for payroll. Nugent figured that each paid admission brought in $1, which gave the club an annual income normally in the $200,000 range. That left an annual deficit of about $150,000.

Nugent's method for balancing the budget was simple. Nearly every year he sold off one or two of his best players.

Over the years, Nugent sold and traded away a virtual All-Star team. Bucky Walters, Dolph Camilli, Claude Passeau, Kirby Higbe, Curt Davis, Morrie Arnovich, Spud Davis, Klein, Bartell, and Whitney; as soon as a player showed more than average ability, he was gone.

Gerry Nugent

During one six-year stretch, Nugent virtually assured other teams of winning the National League pennant five different times with his trades of key players. Walters with the Cincinnati Reds in 1939 and Camilli with the Brooklyn Dodgers in 1941 even became National League Most Valuable Players.

"Nugent makes pennants in Philadelphia, but he doesn't fly them here," wrote Harold Parrott in *This Week* magazine.

Nugent even traded one player, outfielder Kiddo Davis, twice in two years. On December 12, 1932, he swapped Davis to the New York Giants for Chick Fullis and Gus Dugas. Later, the Giants sent Davis to the St. Louis Cardinals. Then on June 15, 1934, Nugent got Davis back in a trade for—would you believe—Chick Fullis. On December 13, 1934, the much-traveled Davis was again peddled back to the Giants for pitcher Joe Bowman.

No one ever claimed Nugent didn't know what he was doing. Gerry was regarded as one of the shrewdest traders in baseball. "If I had been able to keep our topnotch players," he said, "we would have been a pennant threat every year."

But the bill collectors always beckoned. And Nugent had to peddle his stars to raise cash. Most of the time, he did rather well.

When Gerry sent Klein to the Chicago Cubs in 1933, he received three players and $65,000. Three years later, he got Klein back, along with $50,000.

Nugent parlayed the trade of catcher Al Todd in 1935 into an even bigger payoff. Upon sending Todd to the Pittsburgh Pirates, Nugent demanded to have in exchange that "fat kid you have pitching in the minors." Thus Passeau came to the Phillies as a throw-in. Three and one-half years later, the Cubs gave Nugent $50,000 and three players for Passeau. One of the players was Higbe, whom Nugent sent to the Dodgers in 1940, for three players and $100,000. Although he gave up some heavy talent, the Phillies president realized $150,000 from his original trade of Todd.

Nugent rated his smartest trade as the one in which he lifted young shortstop Bartell from the Pirates. Always the possessor of a good underground network, Gerry learned that Bartell had argued with Pittsburgh owner Barney Dreyfus. Nugent persuaded Dreyfus to unload Bartell for Tommy Thevenow and Claude Willoughby, two average players. Dick became one of the league's premier shortstops for the Phillies. Eventually, Nugent sent him to the Giants for four players and $70,000.

The Phils president inspired a lot of emotion with his wheeling and dealing. He was panned and pitied; admired and ridiculed. His constant trades were frustrating to the fans, who watched their heroes parade in and out of Philadelphia with sickening regularity.

"We'll trade anyone provided we can improve the club," Nugent once said. His trades rarely helped the club, except at the bank.

Nugent had the uncanny knack, though, of spotting obscure talent. He usually demanded such talent as throw-ins in trades. In several years when that player developed into a major league star, Nugent would have the material for another trade.

Gerry's ability to dig up unknown minor leaguers was a tribute to his vast knowledge of the game and all its parts. It was this familiarity that helped Nugent earn a job with the Phillies in the first place.

Born October 25, 1892, in Philadelphia, Nugent was a football and baseball star at Northeast High School. After graduating, he took a job with a leather business and worked there until joining the Army in 1917. Nugent served in Europe in World War I, earning two citations for bravery.

After returning home, Nugent worked as a purchasing agent for a hook and eye firm. In the early 1920s, he met Mae Mallon, a secretary to and close friend of Phillies president William Baker and his wife. The two dated, and eventually Mallon introduced Nugent to her boss. Baker was so impressed with Nugent's knowledge of baseball that he offered him a job as his assistant.

Nugent began work for the Phillies in 1925. Soon afterward, he and Mae were married. A year later he was named business manager, and in 1928 he joined the club's board of directors. Having long been a baseball fanatic who devoured everything he could read on the subject, Nugent played a valuable role as Baker's righthand man. One of his moves was to purchase the contract of Klein for $7,500 from a minor league team.

When Baker died in 1930, he willed 500 shares of Phillies stock to Mae and 700 shares to his wife. Two years later, at the age of 40, Nugent was elected president of the club when Charlie Ruch retired. Then, in 1934, Mrs. Baker died, leaving her 700 shares to Mrs. Nugent and the Nugents' son, Gerald.

With the 1,200 shares that his wife and son now owned plus some stock he had previously bought himself, Nugent now controlled 51 percent of the Phillies stock.

Mae, who had served under Ruch as treasurer and assistant secretary of the club, was added to the board of directors and named a vice president, the first woman to hold a position that high in the National League. Despite her lofty appointment, she refused to discuss it with the press. "Gerry does all the talking for this family," she said.

Gerry did more than talk. He bought, he sold, he traded, he cajoled. No matter what he did, though, financial problems always seemed to intrude. At one point, Nugent had to put his stock as collateral to keep the team afloat. On at least one other occasion, he used his own salary to pay a debt, although he and Mae reportedly drew a combined salary of only $20,000. He even had to borrow sometimes so that he could send the team to spring training.

In the early years, the Phillies were hampered by the absence of Sunday baseball. The only times the team could expect to attract much of a crowd were Saturday afternoons and holidays. But in 1934, Sunday baseball was legalized. The attendance, 156,421 in 1933, jumped to 169,885 in 1934 and then to 205,470 the following year.

Nugent also managed to escape, at long last, from the motley problems of Baker Bowl. The $25,000 rent, plus $15,000 in taxes and $500 in upkeep that he paid each year were not insurmountable. What was, though, was the miserable condition of the obsolete structure.

Although he had tried many times to break the 99-year lease signed long ago by his predecessors, Nugent finally succeeded in 1938 after threatening court action. The estate of Charles Murphy, former owner of the Chicago Cubs and the owners of Baker Bowl, relented after Nugent agreed to make $25,000 payments over the next six years.

Nugent tried to set up a farm system, too, naming Swarthmore College graduate Johnny Ogden, a former pitcher and minor league executive, as the team's first farm director. Ogden had one scout, Patsy O'Rourke.

The Phillies' president had a reputation as an innovator. He was a strong supporter of interleague games. He introduced the knothole gang and Ladies' Day to Philadelphia. And he proposed a Shaughnessey playoff plan in which the top four teams in each league would oppose each other over a two-week period to determine the pennant winners. Nugent thought this plan, used in the minor leagues, would generate a considerable amount of fan interest. Few others at the time agreed.

Following a hunting accident in which Chicago White Sox pitcher Monte Stratton extinguished a budding career by shooting himself in the foot (ultimately resulting in the amputation of his leg), Nugent advocated placing a clause in contracts that would ban players from hunting. This idea also had little support.

While Nugent's mind worked overtime, his players did little else but lose. Gerry, though, was the eternal optimist. "We're on the upgrade and will have to be figured as a pennant factor this year," he said in 1941. That year the club lost the most games of any Phillies team in history.

In fact, during Nugent's ownership, the club had four of the Phillies' seven losingest seasons.

There was always some group or individual trying to buy the Phillies. Chocolate manufacturer Milton Hershey once offered $6 million with the idea of moving the club to Hershey, Pennsylvania. A California group wanted to buy the club for $5 million and move it to Los Angeles. Hall of Famer Bill Terry, then the Giants manager, and Philadelphia Eagles owner Alexis Thompson tried to put together a group to purchase the club. And there were other attempts by such potential buyers as Bill Veeck, Branch Rickey, Dan Topping, John B. Kelly, Sr., Moe Annenberg, and the Philadelphia Chamber of Commerce.

In 1940 a group of the Phillies' minority stockholders tried to oust Nugent and take control of the club. After a well-publicized battle that culminated in a stormy meeting of the team's owners, the group lost its cause because of insufficient support.

In his Thanksgiving Day column in the Philadelphia *Record* the next day, Red Smith wrote: "Because holders of at least 51 percent of the Phillies' stock agree he is a peachy fellow, turkey will grace the Nugent board this gladsome day, even though crow may be the *pièce de résistance* for some minority stockholders."

By this time, though, Nugent's back was inching closer to the wall. The Phillies' debts were mounting. And Gerry had new adversaries. National League president Ford Frick and the four owners comprising the league's board of directors were closing in for the kill.

In late 1942 it was becoming increasingly obvious that the National League wanted Nugent out and that Gerry had run out of options. The war having decimated his team, he had no players left to sell. Reportedly, he owed the league $150,000 and was two years behind in rent at Shibe Park.

Frick moved swiftly, appointing a group from his office to run the Phillies while a new owner was sought. The new owner appeared almost immediately. Waiting in the wings to take over the club was William D. Cox, a friend of Rickey's and the man Frick apparently wanted to own the Phillies.

Meanwhile, Nugent sadly closed his office at Phillies headquarters in the Packard Building. "The scene," wrote Ed Pollock in the *Evening Bulletin,* "was what you would expect at a funeral. Club employees looked like red-eyed mourners."

Nugent bowed out gracefully. Later, he was named president of the Inter-State League, a minor league in the Middle Atlantic area. He served in that position until 1952, then took a post as a stockbroker for a prestigious Philadelphia firm.

1943

William D. Cox

In just one short year as president of the Phillies, William D. Cox showed that he was a master at capturing headlines and creating turmoil.

Probably no chief executive in the history of the franchise was ever as successful at turning the spotlight away from his team and onto himself. Cox, once described as "impatient, impetuous, and inexperienced," was embroiled in one fracas after another.

A glib, convincing talker, Cox had the promotional instincts of a circus barker and a head substantially less knowledgeable than he thought it was for running a baseball team. Cox was an astute businessman. The trouble was he insisted on operating the Phillies with the same strict regimen with which he ran his lumber company.

He arrived on the scene with a considerable amount of fanfare in early 1943 after the National League had relieved Gerry Nugent of the franchise. Heading a 30-man syndicate, 20 of whose members were from Philadelphia, including one of the Phillies' present stockholders, F. Eugene Dixon, Jr., as well as his father, Cox outbid another syndicate led by John B. Kelly, Sr., for ownership of the team. The group put up $190,000 in cash, plus a $50,000 note for 4,950 of the team's 5,000 shares.

Officially, the new group took title on March 15, 1943. At a press conference, Cox declared, "The Phillies will not want for an all-out show of energy, alertness and winning spirit." He also said, "Whoever the manager is, there will never be an attempt on my part to interfere." The statement would sound hollow a few months later.

Cox was 33 when he became president, the youngest man in that position in the major leagues. A native New Yorker, he was born November 14, 1909, and grew up on swanky Riverside Drive, graduating from high school at the age of 15 and attending New York and Yale Universities. Cox played a little baseball in college, but he was mostly known athletically for his success as an amateur track man.

Leaving Yale in his senior year, Cox worked for a New York bank, an investment firm, and finally a lumber company, which named him its president in 1936. Later, he founded his own lumber firm.

His first involvement with professional sports occurred in 1941 when he became part-owner of the New York Americans, a football team in the American League. Cox established a reputation for himself by running onto the field during one game to protest a referee's call. His action earned his team a 15-yard penalty.

When Cox took control of the Phillies, he promised a fighting club. It was—even fighting at one point with its president. But the team that Cox inherited had only two bona fide major league players. And when spring training began at Hershey, Pennsylvania, there were only 14 players in camp.

Cox's first move had been the appointment of Bucky Harris as the team's new manager. A veteran major league pilot, Harris made some immediate improvements in the Phillies, and in the early part of the season the club even flirted with the first division.

The new president, who delighted in suiting up and practicing with the team, worked diligently to build the club into a winner. He acquired a number of respectable players, most notably Schoolboy Rowe, Babe Dahlgren, and

Jimmy Wasdell. He bought a farm team at Utica, increasing the club's minor league holdings to two.

Overall, the Phillies of 1943 were vastly improved from the previous five years of eighth-place finishers. They wound up in seventh place with more wins than any team since 1935. The fans responded eagerly. Attendance in 1943 not only was more than double that of 1942, but also was the highest for a Phillies team since 1916.

"Some of Cox's maneuvers and statements were given a poor press and the public reacted unfavorably," said Ed Pollock in the *Evening Bulletin*. "But at least he kept the fans talking about him and his ball club."

Cox tried a lot of schemes to generate interest. On opening day, for instance, he set up a footrace before the game between the Brooklyn Dodgers and the Phillies. The Phillies won when Dodger manager Leo Durocher ordered his players to jog and "save your running for the ball game."

The new owner was convinced that track and baseball had a lot in common. In pursuit of that notion, he hired a veteran track coach, Harold Anson Bruce, as the team's trainer and physical fitness director. Neither Harris nor the players were particularly thrilled by the intrusion.

But intrusions were part of Cox's style. He often gave instructions to players, usually in conflict with Harris' strategy. Cox made a habit of barging into the locker room before and after games, a practice generally frowned on. He was shocked when some of the writers advised him to stay out of the clubhouse.

During his reign, Cox feuded with National League president Ford Frick, with some of the other owners in the league, and even with officials of his farm team at Trenton, who protested to Commissioner Landis that he was raiding the club of its players.

Cox also aroused the ire of the fans when he traded popular and talented outfielder Danny Litwhiler. But that was nothing compared to the furor he created with his mid-season firing of Harris.

Climaxing a long and widening rift between the president and the manager, Cox leaked the firing of Harris to the press while the club was in St. Louis. Bitter exchanges between the two men followed. At one point, almost as an aside, Harris told reporters that Cox had a habit of betting on the Phillies. The remark landed like an exploded bomb.

Through a letter written to him by a Philadelphia sports editor, Judge Landis, who had strict rules against gambling, learned what Harris had said. Quickly, the commissioner launched an investigation. It dragged on for months amid rumors, innuendoes, and speculation.

Finally, on November 23, 1943, the commissioner announced that he was banning Cox from organized baseball for life. Despite a hearing on December 3 where Cox defended himself, Landis' original verdict stood.

Although banned from baseball, Cox continued to participate in sports. In 1945 he became part-owner with Branch Rickey of the Brooklyn Dodgers of the All-America Pro Football Conference. The team later merged with the New York Yanks and entered the National Football League.

In 1956, Cox proposed to set up and finance a three-month summer training camp for Olympic prospects. His intention—"to save America from defeat by Russia"—was well-received but never accepted.

A year later he turned his interests to soccer, vainly attempting to form a 10-nation league. In 1966 he headed the New York entry in the North American Professional Soccer League. In the late 1960s he became general manager of that league's San Diego Toros, and then executive vice president of the St. Louis Stars.

He died in Mount Kisco, New York, on March 28, 1989.

William Cox

In an era when most baseball teams were the part-time toys of owners whose main interests and occupations were elsewhere, Bob Carpenter was a rarity. His only job was running the Phillies.

He did it for 29 years, pouring his energy and his family's fortune into a team that most of the time lost money and finished in the second division.

1943–72

Robert R. M. Carpenter, Jr.

Despite his team's sometimes shoddy performances, Carpenter was a major power in the National League and the biggest name among Philadelphia sports executives. While owners of other teams in the city came and went with regularity, Carpenter was a pillar of consistency.

For nearly four decades—counting Bob's years as well as those of his son, Ruly—the Carpenter name was synonymous with the Phillies. During those years, the Phillies were a franchise that rose and fell and rose again.

The highlight of Bob's regime was the club's 1950 National League pennant. He also presided over the signing of Hall of Famer Robin Roberts as well as such stars as Richie Ashburn, Dick Allen, and Mike Schmidt. And he championed the city's construction of Veterans Stadium.

Perhaps Carpenter's chief contribution to the Phillies, though, was the dignity he gave to a flimsy franchise. Bob changed the image of the club, giving it the respectability it had for so long been lacking.

Carpenter teams finished over .500 twelve times, placing in the first division nine times in his 29 years. The club either finished in or tied for first one time, second once, third twice, fourth five times, fifth seven times, sixth four times, seventh three times, and eighth six times. Over this period, Carpenter had 12 managers.

Bob never took a salary, and he never expected to show heaping profits from the Phillies. "If anybody goes into this business for money," he once said, "he should have his head examined."

But Carpenter wasn't anxious to lose money, either. He was a tough-minded businessman who described himself as "an awful skinflint" and who worked hard to achieve success with the Phillies. "I always wanted to make money," he admitted, "because there's no satisfaction in doing something if you don't make a success of it."

When Carpenter took over the Phillies, they were anything but a success. The franchise was in ashes, the result of the previous Nugent and Cox regimes. "All we had to start with," said Bob, "was 25 second-division players and one minor leaguer named Turkey Tyson."

The Phillies had a working agreement with one minor league team (Trenton) and one scout. There was only one player on the roster who would be with the club three years later, young catcher Andy Seminick.

Although he was only 28 years old, the youngest club president in National League history when he took the reins of the Phillies, Carpenter did not come to Philadelphia as a babe in the woods.

Bob's father, Robert R. M. Carpenter, Sr., was a vice president of the mammoth Du Pont Company and a noted sportsman and naturalist. His mother was a member of the du Pont family, and an uncle, Walter S. Carpenter, had been president of the giant chemical company.

Born August 31, 1915, the year of the Phillies' first pennant, Bob had been a football, basketball, and baseball star at Tower Hill School in Wilmington. Although more interested in sports than in academics, he attended Duke University, where he earned a varsity letter as an end on the football team.

Carpenter quit college before his senior year to get married. He took a job in the public relations department of Du Pont. But Bob was unhappy in the position and left it after spending two years there.

By this time, he had become involved in sports activities in Wilmington, Delaware, near his home. He promoted boxing shows and owned several fighters. He raised champion Chesapeake Bay retrievers. And in 1937 he won the Delaware state badminton championship.

In the late 1930s, Bob convinced Connie Mack of the need for a minor league team in Wilmington. The two became partners in the Blue Rocks of the Inter-State League. Carpenter was president, and Mack agreed to use the club as a farm team for the A's.

The future Phillie president also became the owner of the Wilmington Blue Bombers, a professional basketball team then in the American League, and he was the driving force behind the construction of a new stadium in the city.

The senior Carpenter, meanwhile, had made it known that if the Phillies ever came up again for sale, he would be interested in buying the team. R. Sturgis Ingersoll, a director of the club, recalled hearing that, and when the Phillies lost their second owner in less than one year, Carpenter was contacted.

After what the Phillies had been through—Gerry Nugent having to relinquish possession of the team and Bill Cox being kicked out of baseball—Commissioner Kenesaw M. Landis was in no mood to play games with the floundering franchise. But Connie Mack went to bat for the Carpenters, assuring Landis that they would be good for baseball. Others gave similar recommendations.

On November 23, 1943, the franchise was officially awarded to the Carpenters. The price tag was an estimated $400,000, with the Delaware family getting 80 percent of the stock at the time. The senior Carpenter put up the money, and the junior Carpenter was installed as president.

With World War II at its height, Bob faced being drafted. So he would have someone to run the club when that happened, his first move was to hire an old friend, Herb Pennock, as general manager.

Pennock, known as the Squire of Kennett Square, was a former pitcher and most recently had been the farm director of the Boston Red Sox. He had been friendly with the Carpenters for many years, even to the point of taking Bob as a youngster on a road trip with him when he played for the New York Yankees.

In 1943, the Phillies had finished seventh, but they had been eighth in the five previous seasons. Pennock and Carpenter formulated a plan to pull the club out of the National League dungeon. It would be a slow process, but the basic idea was to build a strong farm system.

"The first thing I want to do is build up the farm system," said Carpenter at his first Phillies press conference. "We're not going to beat anybody's brains out by trying to get a good club right off the bat. But we are going to start working for one systematically."

With Pennock teaching the young owner the facts of life about big league baseball, the two put their plan into action. Eventually, it became known as "the five-year plan." Carpenter was drafted into the Army in March 1944 and served until January 1946, leaving Pennock to carry out the plan alone.

Herb, however, had the Carpenter fortune behind him. Within four years, the Phillies had doled out bonuses amounting to $1,250,000. And the farm system was built up to a level where the club soon had nine scouts and working agreements with 11 minor league teams.

Bob Carpenter

During the early days of Carpenter's presidency, the Phillies languished in eighth place. But after two years there, they climbed to fifth in 1946. The team that year was made up mostly of veteran players picked up from other teams. Their function was to make the club respectable until the youngsters arrived from the farms.

Meanwhile, Carpenter lavished huge sums on young players. A bonus of $65,000 went to Curt Simmons, $25,000 to Robin Roberts, and lesser amounts to players such as Richie Ashburn, Granny Hamner, Willie Jones, Stan Lopata, Bob Miller, Bubba Church, and others. Bob would stop at nothing to sign a player he thought would help the Phillies, often outbidding some of the wealthier teams, such as the Yankees, Red Sox and Cardinals. To get Simmons, he even sent the entire Phillies squad to Curt's hometown of Egypt, Pennsylvania, to face the lefthander's local team. Simmons put on a dazzling show, nearly beating the Phillies. After the game, Carpenter treated all comers to a chicken dinner at the local fire hall.

There was nothing bashful about Carpenter when it came to opening his checkbook. As he later would demonstrate, that went for established players, too. Bob once offered the St. Louis Cardinals $500,000 for Stan Musial. And he handed Brooklyn Dodger owner Walter O'Malley a signed blank check for Duke Snider and Gil Hodges.

Of course, Carpenter's big bucks didn't always produce dividends for the Phillies. The club had some notorious flops such as Tom Qualters, Tom Casagrande, Steve Arlin, Stan Hollmig, and Ted Kazanski, to name a few recipients of big bonuses.

"We've had some mighty distressing experiences," Carpenter said in a sizable understatement.

The scion of the wealthy Delaware family was, however, always attempting some positive change. He even tried to improve the club's image by changing its nickname. In 1944, Carpenter held a contest to pick a new name. The winner was Blue Jays. However, the name never gained much acceptance, and in 1949 it was officially dropped.

Carpenter in 1946 hired a woman scout, Edith Houghton. A former softball star, she is believed to have been the first female scout in baseball.

Pennock died suddenly in 1948, leaving Carpenter to run the club. When the senior Carpenter died a year later, Bob was strictly on his own.

He acted as the club's general manager for six years, until signing Roy Hamey in 1954. As GM, Bob traded away Harry Walker, who had won the batting championship just one year earlier. But he made the deals that gave the Phillies such key members of the 1950 team as Dick Sisler and Eddie Waitkus. And he swung the trades that dealt away Sisler, Seminick, Church, and Russ Meyer.

The high point of Carpenter's administration came in 1950 when the players whom he and Pennock had planted on the farms ripened to produce a National League pennant. Bob had not expected the players to win the flag until 1951 or 1952. Winning it earlier, with a team that averaged just 26 years of age, justified the $2 million that Bob by then had pumped into a long-range development plan.

Although the Phillies lost the 1950 World Series, it was assumed that the club would avenge that defeat many times over in future years. But to Carpenter's great disappointment, that team never again came close to a flag.

In the years that followed the pennant, some of the stars of the Whiz Kids never approximated their 1950 performances again. Eddie Sawyer, the manager who had been so popular a few years earlier, fell out of favor in 1952 and was fired. And the team in general did a downhill slide from which it never recovered.

One of the main criticisms of the team's inability to recover was its reluctance to sign black players. While most of the other major league teams, but particularly those in the National League, were scouting and signing black as well as Latin American players, the Phillies steadfastly refused to disrupt their waspish image. The team was the last in the National League to sign black players, waiting until 1956, some 10 years after Jackie Robinson joined the Dodgers.

"I'm not opposed to Negro players," Carpenter said at the time. "But I'm not going to hire a player of any color or nationality just to have him on the team."

It was sometimes said that Roy Campanella, a Philadelphia native, would have preferred to have played with the Phillies instead of the Dodgers. But he wasn't the only great star the Phils could have but didn't sign. Al Kaline and Carl Yastrzemski could have worn Phillies uniforms, but got away. So did Hank Aaron.

Carpenter, by his own admission, was always somewhat preoccupied with big, strapping pitchers who could throw hard. In that regard, he packed his major and minor league rosters with such fellows: Bob Miller, Steve Ridzik, Jack Meyer, Jim Owens, Don Cardwell, Dick Farrell, Jack Sanford, Dallas Green, Art Mahaffey, Jack Hamilton, Chris Short, Ray Culp, Dennis Bennett, Rick Wise. Some had it, some didn't, but all were raised through the Phillies' farm chain.

One such pitcher the Phillies developed but let go in an ill-advised trade was Ferguson Jenkins, who became one of the outstanding hurlers in the major leagues. It was just the reverse situation with Robin Roberts. The great righthander, often rated by Carpenter as his number-one player, performed brilliantly year after year in Philadelphia. Repeatedly Carpenter turned down trade offers for Roberts. When he finally did move him, reluctantly and only after it had become apparent that Robbie and new manager Gene Mauch couldn't get along, he refused $75,000 from one club, instead accepting $20,000 from the Yankees so that the future Hall of Famer could play for a pennant contender.

Carpenter was like that. A generous man, he loaned money to many of his players who wanted to buy businesses or homes or who were simply short of cash. And he often took care of their expenses when they were ill or had problems. When Eddie Waitkus was shot, Bob ordered the best available medical care. Then he paid for a winter of rehabilitation in Florida for Waitkus and trainer Frank Wiechec.

Carpenter could be a strict president. He was opposed to his players enjoying too much nightlife. When the post-game habits of some of the Phillies seemed to become a problem in 1954, Bob and GM Hamey hired detectives to follow them. The tactic backfired when infielder Granny Hamner discovered that he was being trailed home after a game. Hamner called police who arrested the detective. Hamner exploded in a well-publicized tirade, demanding and subsequently getting an apology from Carpenter.

Bob could get pretty mad himself. One famous outbreak occurred at spring training in 1949. The Boston Red Sox were visiting Clearwater for an exhibition game. Expecting to see the mighty Red Sox sluggers, a large crowd poured into the stadium. Boston manager Joe McCarthy, however, had left Ted Williams and Vern Stephens home.

When Carpenter learned this, he was irate. Bob grabbed a microphone and announced to the fans that they could have their ticket money refunded. The well-intended gesture merely served to infuriate the Red Sox, especially McCarthy. A near brawl followed in which several Red Sox and Phillies officials almost engaged in a fistfight.

Carpenter could throw his weight around when necessary. When A. B. (Happy) Chandler's contract as baseball commissioner came up for renewal, Bob led the fight to oust him. He also led the drive to install National League president Ford Frick as commissioner. Carpenter's side won both battles.

A devoted follower of football, Carpenter showed an interest on several occasions in owning a pro franchise. As early as 1944 he tried to convince his fellow baseball owners to buy pro football teams because it would be good business. Bob saw the proliferation of pro football on the horizon. In 1959 he briefly considered buying a team in the new American Football League.

Carpenter was heavily involved in the demise of Connie Mack Stadium as a major league park and the emergence of Veterans Stadium. In 1954, although he wasn't anxious to do so, Bob bought Connie Mack Stadium when the A's left for Kansas City. Even then, though, he realized the faults of the old park.

Soon afterward, Carpenter began a campaign for a new stadium. Originally, Bob favored a site in Fairmount Park at 33rd Street and Columbia Avenue. In the ensuing years possible sites were suggested almost as regularly as feasibility studies appeared. The effort to build a new stadium dragged on, enmeshed in problems and red tape. At one point Carpenter bought land in New Jersey with the idea of erecting his own stadium.

Carpenter sold Connie Mack Stadium in 1961 to a developer. The Phillies continued to play there, while the new stadium campaign staggered along. Finally, with Carpenter, the owners of the Philadelphia Eagles, and others prodding the city, a new stadium site was selected in South Philadelphia. It opened as Veterans Stadium in 1971.

By then the Phillies had run the gamut from pennant winner to doormat to

Phillies president Bob Carpenter has 3-year-old future president Ruly on his lap in this 1943 photo.

pennant contender to mediocrity. Carpenter's team had been on a frustrating roller coaster.

On November 22, 1972, Bob announced that he was stepping out as president. His son, Ruly, became the chief executive, and Bob took the position of chairman of the board.

Carpenter died at his home outside of Wilmington on July 8, 1990. He was 74.

1972–81

Ruly Carpenter

In his nine years as president of the Phillies, Ruly Carpenter watched his team and the sport it played change completely.

The Phillies were, in a word, wretched when Ruly assumed control of the team from his father, Bob, on November 22, 1972, 29 years after Bob's father had bought the franchise and given it to his son to run. Ruly was three at the time his father took over the team.

He was 10 when the team won its second National League championship, but by the time he got to Yale, the team had reached bottom.

At Yale, Ruly was a two-way end on the football team and captained the baseball team on which he pitched and batted .350. He was also teased constantly by his classmates and friends about how bad his father's baseball team was.

Ruly had gone to New Haven with the idea of pursuing a career in law, but he changed his mind while at school.

"The teasing and criticism from my teammates and classmates in college convinced me that I wanted to do something about the Phillies. It was kind of a challenge," he said.

That's putting it mildly. In Carpenter's junior year in college, the team lost 23 straight games.

After Carpenter graduated from Yale, he took some graduate courses in business administration at the University of Delaware and served as the Blue Hens' assistant baseball coach. In 1963, he joined the Phillies in the accounting department. By the spring of 1964, he and Paul Owens worked together for the first time, evaluating the talent on the lowest minor league teams in the Phillies' chain. To this day, Carpenter says that he enjoyed player development more than anything else in baseball.

Perhaps that is because player development is about the only phase of baseball that has remained constant. Meanwhile, Owens liked what he saw of the young man who would someday become his boss.

"His dedication and intensity were so great, I was certain once he got experience, he would make a fine baseball executive," Owens said. "It was never said, but I figured sooner or later that Bob Carpenter would turn the Phillies over to him and wanted him to gain experience in all areas."

Both Owens and Ruly could see something was wrong with the Phillies' farm system. In 1965, at Ruly's urging, Owens was named farm director. Ruly became Paul's assistant. The roots had been planted to turn the team around by developing players instead of trying to trade for them.

Ironically, though, the Phillies were still a horrible team when Ruly assumed the presidency after the 1972 season. About the only thing they had going for them was the result of a trade. In John Quinn's last major deal, he talked the Cardinals into giving him Steve Carlton for Rick Wise.

In June 1972, Owens replaced Quinn as general manager. A month later he fired Frank Lucchesi and named himself field manager, explaining that he had to see firsthand what his team was all about. Ruly agreed totally with that philosophy.

In November, Bob Carpenter called a press conference to announce that he was stepping down as president of the team and turning the reins over to Ruly, who, at 32, would become the youngest president in the major leagues at that time.

The Phillies had won only 59 games that season. Four years later, they won their first of three straight National League East titles.

On all three occasions, they lost in the playoffs. A storm of controversy was brewing about manager Danny Ozark, but Carpenter defended the only manager he had ever hired to that point.

There were other problems, too. Baseball had changed completely. A decade earlier, management held a hammer over the players. Then Curt Flood challenged the reserve clause, which bound a player to a club as long as the club wanted him, taking the case all the way to the Supreme Court. Eventually, free agency was born. With it came bidding wars for players who had exercised their options, and salaries escalated as agents arrived en masse to do the players' bidding.

Ruly hated it all. He admitted that things had not been right in the past, but that now they had swung the other way. At first he refused to get into any auctions for players, preferring instead to sign his own stars like Mike Schmidt and Greg Luzinski to lucrative, long-term contracts. His philosophy hadn't really changed. He believed the Phillies had developed the players and that they should enjoy the fruits of their labor.

Finally, in 1980, they did. The Phillies won the division, won the League Championship Series, won the World Series. The town went crazy. Ruly remembers the parade down Broad Street, the endless masses of humanity smiling and cheering.

"It was the greatest day of my life, more awesome, more emotional than I ever dreamed it would be," he said.

But that was one day of happiness. There were too many other days of misery. "It isn't fun anymore," Ruly told his close friends almost from day one of the salary escalations and the arrival of the agents. He blamed the spiraling salaries on "the stupidity of certain owners."

In the off-season after the 1980 World Series, Atlanta Braves owner Ted Turner gave a $3.5 million, five-year contract to Claudell Washington, a former prospect who had become a journeyman outfielder. For the Carpenter family, it was the last straw.

On March 6, 1981, Ruly Carpenter made the announcement that stunned the baseball world. The Phillies, he said, were up for sale. He urged Bill Giles, the team's executive vice president, to try to put together a partnership and assume command, something Giles was able to do after the 1981 World Series.

"It was one of the most difficult decisions my family has ever had to make, especially in light of the recent successes the team has had," Carpenter said in announcing the team was on the block. "The primary reason for this decision to sell is that it has become very apparent to me that some deeply ingrained philosophical differences exist between the Carpenter family and some of the other owners as to how the baseball business should be conducted. It's just impossible to continue with our philosophy. So, rather than continue to beat our heads against the wall, we have decided to sell."

During the 1981 season—the year of the strike—Carpenter amplified on his philosophical differences with some other owners.

"I have to make adjustments for what my peers have done," he said. "That's why I'm getting out—because of what my peers have done. We've paid top dollar and we've paid more money than we should have in certain situations. The players have been treated fairly. Some of them have been treated more fairly than they deserved."

That was one reason. Here was another.

"In the past five years, 90 percent of my time has been directed toward things not directly related to what happens on the field in a ball game. Labor negotiations, negotiations on contracts, constant hassles with agents—the sideshows which have become more important than what's happening on the field. And there have been so many sideshows the last couple of years."

So many that Ruly Carpenter finally decided to leave the carnival.

Ruly Carpenter

Bill Giles has lived baseball since the day he was born. And he achieved his lifelong dream on October 29, 1981, when a partnership he headed purchased the Phillies from the Carpenter family, ending almost four decades of ownership by the Du Pont heirs.

The son of former National League President Warren Giles, Bill was born in Rochester, New York, in 1934 while his father was a minor league executive.

1981–

William Y. Giles

He got his first job in baseball as a summer employee of the Reds in the mid-1950s while he was still in college. Shortly afterward, he joined the Reds' front office on a full-time basis. In 1962, he joined the new Houston franchise as traveling secretary and publicity director. By 1967 he was a vice president of the Astros.

On October 10, 1969, Giles joined the Phillies as vice president, business operations, as the Phillies prepared to move from Connie Mack Stadium to Veterans Stadium. Giles had helped open the Astrodome in Houston.

Three years and several promotional ventures later, Giles was elevated to executive vice president. He is universally recognized as one of the main reasons the Phillies changed their image from shabby losers to progressive winners through the 1970s.

When Ruly Carpenter shocked the baseball world by announcing during spring training in 1981 that he was putting his World Championship team up for sale, he encouraged Giles to try to put together a group to buy the team. The sale was finalized shortly after the World Series. The price tag was about $30 million.

Giles' partners included Taft Broadcasting Company, which owned Channel 29 in Philadelphia and which was granted rights to the Phillies games for 10 years beginning in 1982, J. D. B. Associates (John Drew Betz and Robert Hedbert), Tri-Play Associates (brothers Alexander K., James Mahlon, and William Clifton Buck), former 76er owner Fitz Eugene Dixon and Mrs. Rochelle Levy. None of the partners held as much as a 50 percent share of the partnership.

The first two years of Giles' stewardship were highly successful from an on-the-field standpoint. His first team finished second to the World Champion St. Louis Cardinals in the National League East and his second won the NL East and the League Championship Series before losing to the Baltimore Orioles in the World Series.

The team was not nearly as successful at the turnstile, however. Giles said shortly after assuming command of the team that his group's objective was not to make a lot of money but not to lose money, either. However, the Phillies' attendance slipped badly in 1983, and the group was generally acknowledged to have slipped into red ink for the second straight season.

The key to all of baseball's future, however, is something in which Giles has a keen interest and stake. He is one of the members of baseball's television committee, which has entrusted to it the matter of the distribution of potential cable monies and, ultimately, the shape of the game for years to come.

Bill Giles

Giles is also a member of the rules committee and the National League executive committee.

In 1986, Taft Broadcasting sold its 47 percent share in the Phillies to Giles, Dixon, and the other stockholders. Giles became the largest single stockholder in the club.

Since 1983 the Phillies have not fared well under Giles' reign, their highest finish being second place in 1986. The team that Giles predicted would be the "team of the '80s" ended the decade with an overall record of 783–780–3, two pennants, and one World Series championship.

After Paul Owens gave up his job as general manager to become manager of the team in 1983, Giles assumed the role of directing the Phils' on-field fortunes. For five years, he and other members of the front office ran the baseball operation.

"The Gang of Six," as it came to be called, was often criticized in the press and by fans for some of the moves it made. One of the trades that backfired sent relief pitcher Willie Hernandez to the Detroit Tigers, and he became the American League's Cy Young Award winner as well as the Most Valuable Player.

Phillies fans also always seemed to hold Giles responsible for trading away future Hall of Famer Ryne Sandberg and for breaking up the 1980 championship team, perhaps prematurely and with little in return.

On the plus side, Giles was the man chiefly responsible for bringing the signing of Pete Rose to fruition. A man who always treated his players and other employees fairly, Giles also brought in general manager Lee Thomas in a move of considerable foresight.

Giles made perhaps one of his boldest moves when he signed catcher Lance Parrish to a Phillies contract in 1987. At the time, major league owners, who would eventually be found guilty of collusion, were adamantly refusing to sign free agents. Giles broke the logjam by signing Parrish, who had become a free agent after playing with the Detroit Tigers.

Since Giles became president, the Phillies have had seven managers. Under Giles, the team has staged emotional retirement nights for soon-to-be Hall of Famers Steve Carlton and Mike Schmidt, as well as numerous special events that have been geared to building fan interest and making a Phillies game an entertaining event for fans.

No one, of course, has had more to do with turning the Phillies into one of the major league's most lucrative franchises than Giles. His promotional skills and his ability to market a team and keep it popular, despite less than satisfactory records on the field, are virtually unchallenged in major league circles.

The General Managers

The unenviable task of rebuilding a franchise that was in ruins confronted Herb Pennock when he was hired as the Phillies' general manager.

A former big league pitcher who would be named to the Hall of Fame in 1948, Pennock was the first real general manager the Phillies ever had. Prior to his arrival, most of the GM duties had been handled by the club's presidents.

But Bob Carpenter, facing a call to the Army, named his long-time friend to the post shortly after taking over the team in 1943. "Pennock is now in charge of the operation of the entire club," Carpenter said. It was the most power held by anyone up to that point other than the president.

Probably no one ever faced a more difficult job. As a result of the previous two regimes, the Phillies were in shambles. The team had few players of substance and no farm system to speak of. In addition, the club had to compete with World War II for what few players it could get its hands on.

Pennock did have one valuable asset: Carpenter money. That was a vital commodity in reconstructing a franchise, and Pennock used it freely. He and Carpenter devised a five-year plan, which included hiring nine scouts and a farm system director, establishing a chain of minor league teams, and signing good, young players.

Pennock said he wanted big, rawboned pitchers who could "zip that apple over the plate" and batters "who pack a punch when it is needed and are no powder puffs at the plate."

Between 1944 and 1948, the Phillies handed out $1,250,000 in bonus money to young players, including such future stars as Robin Roberts, Richie Ashburn, Curt Simmons, Granny Hamner, Willie Jones, and a handful of others who would form the nucleus of the 1950 pennant winners. Some of the money, of course, went for clunkers, too.

Pennock made few trades of substance, two noteworthy exceptions being his acquisitions of Emil Verban and Harry Walker. He also bought a number of veteran players with the intention of using them to hold the fort until the youngsters matured. Frank McCormick, Jim Tabor, Johnny Wyrostek, and Dutch Leonard were a few of his acquisitions.

Herb did amazingly well, considering he had no prior experience as a wheeler-dealer. Before coming to the Phillies, the Kennett Square, Pennsylvania, native had been farm director for the Boston Red Sox, working under general manager Eddie Collins.

A southpaw pitcher during his playing days, Pennock broke into the majors in 1912 with the Philadelphia Athletics. Subsequently, he worked for

1943–48

Herb Pennock

Herb Pennock

Present and future Phillies connections were in abundance at this 1947 meeting of (from left) National League president Warren Giles, whose son Bill became the Phils president, Phillies general manager Herb Pennock, St. Louis Cardinals owner Sam Breadon, and future Phils general manager Roy Hamey, then with the Pittsburgh Pirates.

the Red Sox and New York Yankees before ending his career in 1934 back with Boston.

During his 22 years, Pennock had a 241–162 record, including a 21–9 log in 1924 and a 23–11 mark in 1926, both with the Yankees. Herb also won five World Series games without suffering a loss.

After Pennock joined the Phillies, a steady trickle of ex-Yanks and Bosox followed him. From Boston, he brought Joe Reardon to serve as farm director, and Jimmie Foxx, Skeeter Newsome, Oscar Judd, and Tabor were plucked off the Red Sox roster. Former Yankees included Johnny Nee, who came as head scout, minor league manager Eddie Sawyer, and ex-teammates Ben Chapman to manage and Benny Bengough, Cy Perkins, and Dusty Cooke to coach.

Originally, Pennock signed a five-year contract with the Phillies at an estimated annual salary of $15,000. The Wenonah Military Academy graduate quickly established farm teams in cities such as Carbondale, Pennsylvania, Dover, Delaware, and Schenectady and Utica, New York.

The farm system began to flourish. Meanwhile, with the newly acquired veterans, plus some already arrived young players such as Del Ennis and Andy Seminick, the Phillies finally made it all the way to fifth place in 1946.

In 1947, Pennock tried to buy Enos Slaughter, offering the St. Louis Cardinals a reported $150,000. St. Louis owner Sam Breadon flatly refused the offer, scoffing, "I thought you wanted to buy him, not rent him for a month."

Pennock, who once tried to ban the press from the clubhouse, never saw the fruits of his labors. While attending the major league winter meetings in New York, he died January 30, 1948, of a cerebral hemorrhage. He was just short of his 54th birthday.

Three seasons after he died, Pennock's hard work materialized in a Phillies pennant.

1954–59

Roy Hamey

After going six years without a full-time general manager, the Phillies appointed Roy Hamey to the top post in 1954. The selection was made with the expectation that Hamey, a veteran baseball executive, would rebuild the fading Whiz Kids into a pennant contender.

It never happened. The year before Hamey arrived, the Phillies had finished in a third-place tie. When Roy departed after five years, the Phillies were in last place, having slipped steadily during that period.

It wasn't as though Hamey didn't try. The affable, unruffled general manager was a prolific trader, making 19 major swaps during his time as Phils general manager. But few of his trades worked out.

Hamey was the man who brought us Valmy Thomas, Sparky Anderson, Glen Gorbous, and Ruben Gomez, to name a few of the less than glittering lights that he acquired in trades. He also brought to town a steady stream of once-good but over-the-hill veterans such as Bob Kuzava, Saul Rogovin, Warren Hacker, Roy Smalley, Frankie Baumholtz, and Peanuts Lowrey.

"We've all got ideas about trades, but some of the ideas are the kind that can't be imposed on the other fellow without using an anesthetic," Hamey once told the *Evening Bulletin*'s Frank Yeutter.

Roy, born in 1902 in Valley City, Illinois, had his first job in baseball in 1925 as a ticket taker for the nearby Springfield team of the Three-I League. Soon afterward, he became secretary of the team.

In 1934, Hamey joined the New York Yankees' system as general manager of the Binghamton (New York) farm team. He became GM for the Kansas City Blues in 1937, his team winning the Junior World Series the following year. Roy spent nine years in Kansas City, then was hired as president of the American Association in 1946. He stayed 10 months on the job before taking over as general manager of the Pittsburgh Pirates, a position he held until 1950. That year he returned to the Yankees as assistant general manager of the parent club.

Hamey came to Philadelphia in April 1954. His first deal was two months later when he bought pitcher Herm Wehmeier from the Cincinnati Reds. Part of the arrangement gave the Reds permission to buy pitcher Karl Drews from the Phillies a few days later.

That same year Hamey vetoed the chance to get slugger Ralph Kiner. Roy didn't think the future Hall of Famer would help the Phillies.

Over the next five years, Hamey traded for players such as Harvey Haddix, Wally Post, Stu Miller, and Solly Hemus—and then swapped them away later. He also presided over the breakup of the Whiz Kids, as well as the fruition of the Phillies' farm system, which produced seven players on the 1957 roster.

During Hamey's regime, the Phillies finished fourth twice, fifth twice and eighth once. The club had four managers in that time.

What happened? "The young fellows didn't develop as fast as we thought they would, and the older players didn't hold up as long as we believed they would," Hamey tried to explain.

Roy considered his best trade to be the one he made for Chico Fernandez in 1957. The Phillies gave the Brooklyn Dodgers Elmer Valo, Mel Geho, Tim Harkness, Ben Flowers, Ron Negray, and $75,000 for the Cuban shortstop.

His worst, he said, was the one in which the Phillies got Jim Greengrass, Gorbous, and Andy Seminick from the Reds for Smoky Burgess, Steve Ridzik, and Stan Palys. "The man had phlebitis and we didn't know it," said Hamey of Greengrass, the key figure in the swap.

Hamey was also not terribly proud of his trade that sent Del Ennis to the St.

Roy Hamey

Louis Cardinals for Rip Repulski and Bobby Morgan. And who can forget his swapping Jack Sanford to the San Francisco Giants for Thomas and Gomez?

"I made some good trades, and some ones that didn't work out so good," Roy said.

Hamey resigned from the Phillies as general manager. He became general manager of the Yankees in 1961, and his clubs won three straight pennants and two World Series before his retirement at the end of the 1963 season.

1959–72

John Quinn

Like current Phillies president Bill Giles and former president Ruly Carpenter, baseball encased John Quinn's entire lifetime.

He was almost destined to become a general manager because his father, Bob, served in that capacity with the St. Louis Browns before becoming president of the Boston Red Sox and the Boston Braves.

Quinn, who consummated 51 deals when he was with the Phillies, was part of a family legacy in baseball that continues to this day. His son Bob is currently the general manager of the San Francisco Giants, and his son-in-law, Roland Hemond, is the GM of the Baltimore Orioles.

John Quinn, who was born in Columbus, Ohio, on April 1, 1908, while his father was the general manager of the minor league team there, attended Boston College, getting his degree in 1929. He joined the Red Sox immediately after college and, when his father became president of the Braves in 1936, John followed him across town as the team's secretary.

After nine years he was named general manager of the Braves in 1945. At that point, the club had almost as pathetic a past performance chart as the Phillies, not having won a pennant since 1914.

Quinn set out to fill that void and succeeded in three years when his 1948 Braves reached the World Series. He quickly proved himself a master trader. He coaxed the Dodgers out of Eddie Stanky for Ray Sanders and Bama Rowell. He talked the Browns into giving him aging veteran Jeff Heath. And, in the real biggie, he sent Billy Herman and a fistful of nonentities to the Pirates for Bob Elliott before the 1947 season.

In 1947, Elliott was the National League MVP for the Braves. He drove in 100 runs, hit 23 home runs, scored 99 times, and led the league with a whopping 131 bases on balls.

Eddie Dyer, the Cardinals manager, called Elliott-for-Herman "the greatest trade ever made."

That's debatable, but what isn't is that Quinn had made his mark as one of the top general managers in baseball. And when the Braves moved on to Milwaukee, Quinn had a few more tricks to pull.

The first came before the move was enacted. The Yankees, looking for their annual pennant insurance, decided that Johnny Sain, a 1948 Braves pitching hero, was the policy that fit their needs. Quinn said that was fine with him, but the premium would be $50,000 cash plus a minor leaguer named Lew Burdette. All Lew did was deny that he threw a spitball, win 20 games two straight years, take four of six World Series decisions in 1957 and 1958, and capture 203 victories in an 18-year major league career.

The trade that solidified the 1957–58 successes was the one that brought an aging Red Schoendienst from the Cardinals. Schoendienst was the catalyst that carried the 1957 Braves to the World Championship and the 1958 team to the National League pennant.

After that season, Bob Carpenter, who normally opened his checkbook wide only for tall, strong pitching prospects, broke out the ballpoint and signed Quinn as the Phillies' vice president and general manager.

When asked why he picked Quinn, Carpenter replied simply, "I wanted to get the best."

John Quinn arrived in Philadelphia at a time when the franchise was in disarray. Carpenter had fallen in love with the Whiz Kids (who won the pennant for him in 1950) so thoroughly that he kept many of them around too long.

Quinn immediately set out to change the image of the team. His first trade was one of his best. He shipped Gene Freese to the White Sox for Johnny Callison, who had been brought up too soon and put under too much pressure in Chicago. In 1961, Don Demeter came from the Dodgers, gave the Phillies 2½ good seasons, then was sent to the Tigers in the deal that netted Jim Bunning.

Nobody knew it at the time, but Quinn's swap of Jim Owens to the Reds for Cookie Rojas paid immense dividends. Quinn stole Tony Gonzalez from the Reds and took Wes Covington off baseball's scrap heap. The team was rebuilt, and in 1964 it almost won a pennant it never should have been in a position to win, then found a way to lose it after it appeared to have it won.

Manager Gene Mauch decided after the season that all he needed to win the 1965 pennant were a few key veterans. Quinn got him Dick Stuart and Ray Herbert, along with Bo Belinsky.

The next season, Mauch wanted more veterans, so Quinn swung a couple of blockbuster deals that netted Bill White, Dick Groat, Larry Jackson, and Bob Buhl. Unfortunately, he threw a young Canadian pitcher into the Jackson-Buhl deal. His name was Ferguson Jenkins, and it is now on a plaque in Cooperstown.

In 1967, Mauch said he needed a lefthanded starter, so Quinn sent Ray Culp to the Cubs for Dick Ellsworth. But all the trades led nowhere. That season the Phillies finished 82–80 for their sixth straight year over .500, at the time a team record. It was also their last positive season until 1974.

Meanwhile, Quinn traded on. Dick Allen had become a problem. He missed flights, missed games, and verbally fought with Mauch and successor Bob Skinner. After the 1969 season, Quinn engineered a deal that changed the course of baseball history. He packaged four players, including Allen, for three Cardinals, including brilliant center fielder Curt Flood. Flood refused to report, then challenged baseball's reserve clause in the courts, opening the door for free agency and the re-entry draft.

But Quinn saved his best trade for last. In spring training of 1972, Rick Wise was a holdout. So was Steve Carlton in St. Louis. Quinn suggested a swap of the two reluctant pitchers, and got it. The rest is history. Wise, a better than average pitcher, remained a better than average pitcher. Carlton became an instant superstar, winning 27 games with a dreadful team his first season on the way to 300-plus victories and the Hall of Fame. He won four Cy Young Awards and was a 20-game winner five times.

On June 3, 1972, four months after the Carlton deal, John Quinn "retired." That was the word used by the Phillies in the first press conference on one of the most bizarre weekends in the history of team-media relations.

It was the ninth inning of a tie game between the Phillies and the Reds when Larry Shenk summoned everyone into Bob Carpenter's office for a major announcement. After a brief protest, the press and electronic media retreated to Carpenter's office. They were greeted at the door by Quinn, hand outstretched to everyone. Then Carpenter made his announcement that John had "retired" and that Paul Owens would be the new general manager. Meanwhile, the Reds were scoring the winning run, which no newsman saw.

Quinn will go down in Phillies history in a positive light. He won three pennants in Boston and Milwaukee and almost won one in Philadelphia. No one can really say which was the more impressive feat.

He was always a gentleman, a man who dressed extremely well and whose starched white collar became his symbol. There were those who said the game had passed him by, that he was from the old school. After all, hadn't he signed Tony Curry to a minor league contract after a year in the majors so that he didn't have to guarantee him the major league minimum? The age of neck chains and open collars and agents and free agency had arrived, but Quinn was never seen without his tie firmly knotted about his neck.

Maybe some of it was true. Maybe certain parts of the game had passed John Quinn. But when he died, he did leave an enormous legacy. His last big trade will someday be recorded positively in the Hall of Fame.

John Quinn

Paul Owens paid to play in his first professional baseball game. Baseball has been returning compound interest ever since.

Especially in 1980 when the Phillies won their first World Series ever. Except for the pitching staff, this was Paul Owens' team, one way or another.

1972–83

Paul Owens

Paul Owens

Consider:

- First baseman Pete Rose—signed as a free agent when Owens was general manager.
- Second baseman Manny Trillo—signed his first contract with the Phillies as a catcher in 1968 when Owens was farm director.
- Shortstop Larry Bowa—then–farm director Owens agreed to a small signing bonus to Bowa, who had not been drafted, after watching films of Bowa playing shortstop and hitting.
- Third baseman Mike Schmidt—drafted and signed while Owens was farm director.
- Left fielder Greg Luzinski—drafted and signed while Owens was farm director.
- Center fielder Garry Maddox—arrived after a trade engineered by general manager Owens.
- Right fielder Bake McBride—arrived after general manager Owens battled the trading deadline in round-the-clock dealings.
- Catcher Bob Boone—drafted and signed by Phillies while Owens was farm director.

Clearly, the World Champions were, above all, the Pope's team. He had signed some of them, traded for others, managed some of them, haggled contracts with all of them, and, most of all, loved them all.

And because he loved them, he chewed them out occasionally. Like in June 1979 in Montreal when the Phillies were on their way to a fourth-place finish and playing like they were perfectly satisfied with it. He screamed and yelled and told them that they were letting Danny Ozark down after Danny had stuck up for them. That time, they didn't get the message, and Ozark was fired two months later.

The following season, the Phillies lost back-to-back games to the then-woeful San Diego Padres on August 30 and 31 and headed for San Francisco, seemingly content to let another pennant slip away. Only Owens wouldn't let them do it.

The next afternoon, before the Phillies took the field to play the Giants, Owens called a clubhouse meeting.

"I was as mad as I've ever been," Owens said. "I was screaming and my hands were trembling. I said, 'You guys played the first five months for yourselves. You've gone your own different ways. (Dallas Green) has been trying to get things across to you and now I'm telling you, and I know I'm also speaking for Ruly Carpenter, the man's right and you better stop your goddam pouting. The last month is Ruly Carpenter's and mine.'

"I told them I stuck my neck out after 1979 by not making any moves because I wanted to give them another chance. I told them I felt they had all the ability they needed. After that Pittsburgh fiasco (a series sweep by the Pirates earlier in August), I watched them battle back and get in the thick of the race again. Then, I felt they were slipping. I put it a little more strongly than that."

In fact, what Owens did was invite any Phillie who disagreed with him to fight it out. None of them did. Instead they went about the business of winning their first World Championship ever. And in the locker room afterward, there was Paul Owens on the platform, holding the trophy that symbolized it all, as tears of joy streamed down his cheeks.

Joy because three decades of learning the game of baseball at every level had finally paid the ultimate reward.

It all began in 1951 in Olean, New York. Owens had just graduated from St. Bonaventure and was set to teach school. At the age of 27 with a three-year service hitch during World War II in his past, baseball seemed the least logical path. But when the general manager at Olean invited him for a tryout, he accepted. The GM said he would leave Paul a ticket, but Paul didn't even ask for it, paying his way into the ballpark instead.

He ended up playing that night. Olean's regular first baseman had broken his jaw. Pope collected a single and double and was on his way to a .407 average and PONY League rookie of the year honors.

He quit the game two years later, returning to Olean as player-manager two years after that, and has been with the Phillies' organization ever since.

He managed for four years at the minor league level, served as the Phillies' West Coast scout for five seasons, then was named farm director in 1965. He was joined in that office by a young man out of Yale named Ruly Carpenter. The rest is history.

On June 3, 1972, the Phillies called a press conference during the ninth inning of a baseball game to announce that John Quinn was retiring as general manager and that his position would be filled by Paul Owens. When the media people filed out of Bob Carpenter's private box, the game was over. So was the image of the Phillies as a stingy, backward organization. The forward move had been firmly established by the opening of Veterans Stadium and the hiring of Bill Giles as executive vice president.

Little more than a month after Owens was named general manager, he took one more drastic step. He fired popular Frank Lucchesi and installed himself as field manager.

"There were serious problems," Owens said. "I felt I knew what we had in the way of talent. Since I've always considered myself a good evaluator, I figured if I lived, ate, and slept with the players, I would know just what I had. I had confidence I could turn the thing around. I could have buried myself, but I had to do it."

After that season, Owens had seen what he wanted to see. He knew he had a great pitcher in Steve Carlton, a fine shortstop in Larry Bowa, a good first baseman in Willie Montanez, a super prospect in Greg Luzinski and precious little else. So he hired Danny Ozark, who probably has never been given the proper credit for what he accomplished as a manager, moved himself back upstairs and watched it happen. He knew he had kids in his farm system who were almost ready—Schmidt, Boone, Larry Christenson, Dick Ruthven—and what he didn't have, he knew how to get in trades that netted Maddox, McBride, Trillo, Tug McGraw, and Ron Reed.

He also either got terribly lucky or was incredibly smart in picking up the likes of Gene Garber, Jay Johnstone, and Ollie Brown for next to nothing.

From 1976 to 1978, the Phillies won the National League East, and Owens figured his dream of making the World Series had finally arrived. But the team was swept in '76 by the Reds and taken out, three games to one, by the Dodgers in 1977 and 1978.

The following year, despite the signing of Pete Rose, the team stumbled home fourth and, during the last month, was managed by Dallas Green, who like Owens had been the farm director and, like the Pope, had an angry streak that surfaced just often enough to let the players know he meant what he said.

And now, more than four decades after paying his way into his first game, Owens is still in baseball and loving almost every minute of it.

Owens, who would swing 46 trades in his tenure as the Phillies' GM, had yet another streak of anger when the Phillies were moving along at a win-one, lose-one pace in July 1983. He fired manager Pat Corrales and took over the job himself.

This movement from the front office to the dugout was far more successful than the one in 1972. Under Owens, the Phillies complained about platooning—and won while they moaned. Owens led the team to the NL East title, to the National League pennant, and into the World Series, which the Baltimore Orioles won by a 4–1 count.

At the end of the season, Owens relinquished his general manager's seat to stay in the dugout and attempt to win a World Series championship in 1984. It meant more headaches than he could ever endure as GM, but, then again, Paul Owens always paid the price—from his first pro game on.

The Phils didn't win the pennant in 1984, and at the end of the season Owens stepped down. The Pope returned to the front office to work as an assistant to club president Bill Giles. Much of his work has involved evaluating minor league talent and advising other members of the baseball staff.

1987–88

Woody Woodward

For five years the duties of general manager of the Phillies were handled by a committee called the Gang of Six that was headed by club president Bill Giles.

But the Gang of Six made too many moves that turned into a gang of sticks.

Eventually, it became apparent even to them that what this team really needed, aside from a healthy influx of solid players, was a suitable general manager, a baseball man who could make the decisions and run the field operation the way it should be.

Enter Woody Woodward.

A first cousin of actress Joanne Woodward, Woody had been a journeyman major league infielder for eight years, playing with the Milwaukee and Atlanta Braves and the Cincinnati Reds. Seldom a starter, except in the 1966 and 1967 seasons with Atlanta, Woodward was a good-field, no-hit type who carried a lifetime .236 batting average into retirement.

A graduate of Florida State University, where he not only was an All-American shortstop playing under ex-Phillies outfielder Danny Litwhiler, but also earned bachelor's and master's degrees, Woodward had dabbled in business, broadcasting, and coaching baseball at Florida State after retiring as a big league player.

Eventually he wound up with the Reds, first as minor league coordinator, then as assistant general manager. After four years in that job, he joined the New York Yankees as vice president of baseball administration. "General manager" was added to his title in 1986. One year later, though, he quit the Yankees and on October 28, 1987, moved to the Phillies to serve in the same position.

Woodward wasted little time making his presence felt. He signed free agents Bob Dernier and David Palmer, and in a big trade shipped popular outfielder Glenn Wilson and up-and-coming reliever Mike Jackson to the Seattle Mariners for outfielder Phil Bradley.

It was not a deal that panned out well for the Phillies. Bradley was a big disappointment, and Jackson went on to become a top reliever.

The soft-spoken and generally colorless Woodward made one other trade of note, sending one-time phenom Jeff Stone, Rick Schu, and Keith Hughes to the Baltimore Orioles for Mike Young and Frank Bellino. That, too, wasn't much of a deal.

That season the Phillies were horrible. The 1988 Phils were headed toward their worst record since 1972. And, unbeknownest to all but the Phillies' inner sanctum, Woodward was headed for the out box.

On June 8, Giles made the stunning announcement that Woodward had been fired and farm director Jim Baumer had been demoted. The move shocked Woodward as well as nearly everybody else.

"It just didn't work out," said Giles. "Sometimes when you live with people for six months, you get to learn things. I'd rather not say, other than it's best for the organization to get somebody different in that role."

What was left unsaid was that Woodward had failed to get along with most of the Phillies' front office. He had particularly alienated the minor league staff, as well as some long-term Phillies employees, who resented what were said to be his autocratic and often secretive methods.

Veteran scout Ray Shore was named to fill Woodward's spot on an interim basis.

Although he struck out with the Phillies, Woodward landed on his feet just six weeks later when he was named vice president of baseball operations for the Mariners, a job he still holds.

Woody Woodward

1988–

Lee Thomas

Around the Phillies' offices at Veterans Stadium, Lee Thomas is the picture of corporate success. Impeccably groomed, usually wearing a proper business suit and tie, Thomas could easily pass as a banking executive or some other corporate dandy.

But it's all a ruse.

Thomas is no button-down dullard waiting for the next cotillion. Not a chance. This is a guy who has the guts of a bank robber, the nerve of a steeplejack, and the courage of an NFL quarterback all rolled into one. He's a closet daredevil. He's a riverboat gambler in Brooks Brothers clothes; a secret agent without a gun; an airplane test pilot driving a four-door sedan. Thomas probably could have earned a living as a window washer on skyscrapers.

Lee Thomas has ably demonstrated these tendencies and more since becoming vice president and general manager of the Phillies on June 21, 1988.

When Thomas barreled into Philadelphia to take charge of a comatose team, it was obvious that massive changes were needed. He readily complied. He held the team up by its ankles and shook it until every loose filling dropped to the floor.

Thomas not only dismantled the Phillies with fearless resolve. He also gave new meaning to the word *change.* He revamped the minor league department, altered the scouting system, hired not one but two new managers, and turned the roster into something that has changed about as often as a railroad schedule.

As a wheeler-dealer, Thomas has been virtually incomparable in Phillies annals. In his first three and one-half years on the job he made 24 trades and 14 free-agent signings. No past Phillies GM ever made that many deals in the same period: not Paul Owens, not John Quinn, not anybody.

Thomas is well on his way to ranking as the Phillies' king of barter. As a result, only one player—Darren Daulton—who had been with the Phillies when Thomas arrived was still with the club in 1992.

Lee Thomas

Many of Thomas's deals have been blockbusters. He sent Chris James to the San Diego Padres for John Kruk and Randy Ready. He pried Terry Mulholland, Dennis Cook, and Charlie Hayes away from the San Francisco Giants for Steve Bedrosian and a minor leaguer. He coaxed Len Dykstra and Roger McDowell away from the New York Mets for Juan Samuel. He gave up Jeff Parrett and two minor leaguers to the Atlanta Braves for Dale Murphy and Tommy Greene. And he snatched Mitch Williams away from the Chicago Cubs in exchange for Chuck McElroy and Bob Scanlan.

All have been highly successful trades. "There are some things we've lucked out on," Thomas says. "I like the Lenny Dykstra deal. Nobody ever thought they could get him away from the Mets, and I never thought we could either, right up until the last two or three hours the day we did it. You've got to like the Kruk trade and the one that got us Mulholland," he adds.

When Thomas joined the Phillies, he preached patience, saying he needed to learn the organization before making any moves. He warned fans not to assume he would make the club an instant success.

"I don't walk on water. So don't look for me as a savior," he said.

Thomas had come from the St. Louis Cardinals where for 18 years he had worked his way up through the ranks after his playing days ended. With the Redbirds, he was a minor league coach and manager, a bullpen coach with the parent club, an assistant in the sales and promotions department, a traveling secretary, and finally director of player development, a position he held for seven years and until he was hired by the Phillies.

As a player, Thomas had been an outfielder and first baseman. Originally signed by the New York Yankees, he spent seven years in the minors before landing with the Yanks in 1961. Instead of enjoying the spoils that went with being on what is generally regarded as one of the great teams in baseball history, Thomas was traded early in the season to the California Angels. There, he blossomed into a power-hitter, slugging 50 home runs over the 1961 and 1962 seasons and hitting .285 and .290, respectively.

Thomas tailed off in 1963 and was eventually traded to the Boston Red Sox. Later, he played with the Atlanta Braves, Chicago Cubs, and Houston Astros before finishing his big league playing career after the 1968 season. In eight years, he had a career batting average of .255 with 106 home runs and 428 RBI.

Having held so many different positions in baseball, Thomas was well prepared for the job that awaited him in Philadelphia. But not even he realized how tough the job was going to be.

The Phillies were coming off a 1987 season in which they had finished a disappointing fourth. By the time Thomas got to Philadelphia in 1988, the club was not only floundering on the field, but it had also just undergone a startling front-office shake-up, and its minor league and scouting systems were in disarray.

By the end of the 1988 season, the Phillies had careened to their worst record since 1972. The team had played atrociously in spots and poorly throughout the season, its mixture of declining stars, unproductive veterans, and fill-ins having played neither well nor with much enthusiasm.

Thomas showed little patience with his team. Before the season ended, he fired manager Lee Elia. A few weeks later he named an old St. Louis Cardinals associate, Nick Leyva, to take Elia's place.

Thomas also began changing the roster. He jettisoned disappointing catcher Lance Parrish, Bradley, and pitchers Shane Rawley and Kevin Gross before the year was over. And he started bringing in replacements who he thought could perk up this unlively team.

In the ensuing years, the trades continued. Thomas also bolstered the minor league system, bringing in Lance Nichols as farm director, firing him, then naming Del Unser to the post. Thomas also dismissed Leyva and brought in Jim Fregosi as manager.

Slowly, the Phillies began improving on the field. After finishing sixth again in 1989, they moved up to a fourth-place tie in 1990 and third place in 1991.

The Phillies climb was far from over. In 1992, the team tumbled back into the cellar, leaving Thomas with the need to make additional changes before the Phillies could become a legitimate contender.

The Support Staff

In the early days of the Phillies, the team had few full-time employees who didn't wear baseball uniforms. The nonplaying staff was as minimal as the sparse offices from which the club operated.

Usually, the team's president handled the business side of the operation, along with a few key people. These people performed a variety of duties, unlike the specialists of today.

One such person was Jimmy Hagen, a former newspaper copy boy from South Philadelphia. Hagen joined the Phillies in 1904. He worked for more than 40 years, serving 10 different presidents and handling an assortment of jobs.

The position with which Jimmy was most closely associated was traveling secretary. Hagen served in that capacity from the 1920s until his retirement in the mid-1940s. But he was really a jack-of-all-trades, and he did a lot of things for the team, including acting as its publicity man.

Billy Shettsline was another long-time club employee who served in a variety of assignments. Shetts was most noted as a Phillies manager and president. But he also did bookkeeping and ticket sales, and served as business manager during his four-decade career with the Phillies.

Over the years, numerous other people spent long years of service with the Phillies. Most of the time, they worked out of the spotlight, toiling quietly behind the scenes to keep the club functioning.

Among those having the longest connections with the Phillies was George Harrison, who joined the team as its treasurer in 1943. Harrison became executive vice president and later vice president and director of finance during an association that lasted until 1981.

At the same time, R. Sturgis Ingersoll was counsel and a director, Art Fletcher was public relations director and later secretary, and Frank Powell advanced from traveling secretary to director of sales. All joined the Phillies in the mid-1940s and served the club for more than 25 years.

Another long-time employee of the club was Mae Nugent. A secretary to president William Baker in the early 1920s, she remained with the team after her marriage to Gerry Nugent and eventually rose to vice president, treasurer, and director before leaving the team in 1942.

During their 110 years the Phillies have had offices at a variety of spots.

Through its early years at Baker Bowl, the club was headquartered at the stadium, its offices housed behind the center field bleachers.

The team also had offices in the Packard Building, the Fidelity-Philadelphia Building, and the Bellvue-Stratford Hotel, all in center city, before it purchased Connie Mack Stadium and moved its business operation there.

Many long-term staffers got their start at Connie Mack Stadium. Included were Joe Reardon, the club's first farm system director who held that post from 1943 to 1954, and Gene Martin, another minor league director and later a player personnel advisor.

Andy Clarke spent nearly 30 years with the Phillies, starting in ticket sales and then becoming park superintendent in 1955. Ray Krise, Tom Hudson, and Frank Sullivan also began in ticket sales in the mid-1950s and stayed with the club for many years. Krise retired in the 1980s as ticket manager. Hudson, for many years the director of advertising, and Sullivan, the director of promotions, were still with the Phillies in the 1990s in key front-office capacities.

Another present employee who has been with the club for many years is Larry Shenk. He joined the Phillies in 1964 as publicity director, and he is now vice president and director of public relations.

Dave Montgomery joined the Phillies in 1971 after earning an MBA degree from Penn's Wharton School. He progressed to director of marketing and ticket sales before succeeding Bill Giles as executive vice president in October 1981, after Giles ascended to the presidency. In 1992, Montgomery added the title of chief operating officer.

Another veteran of the front office is Pat Cassidy, who began with the club as an usher and has spent some 40 years with the team, including long stints as director of stadium operations and most recently as director of office operations.

There have also been a number of long-time Phillies working at the field level. Kenny Bush began with the team in 1949 as a batboy and worked his way up to become the home team's clubhouse and equipment manager, a position he held until 1990. Before Bush, Unk Russell ran the Phillies' clubhouse for many years, and Ace Kessler operated the visitors' locker room for more than 40 years. He was succeeded by his son, Ted Kessler, who had the same post for another 30 years.

The trainers with the most longevity were Leo (Red) Miller and Frank Wiechec. Miller, who started with the Phillies as a batboy, treated players for 23 years until 1943. Wiechec, one of the nation's leading athletic trainers of his era, worked for the club from 1948 until the mid-1960s. Strength and flexibility coach Gus Hoefling served with the Phillies for 17 years.

Two others who put in many years with the Phillies include Benny Bengough and Maje McDonnell. Bengough spent 14 years as a coach and many more years after that as the team's goodwill ambassador. Beginning in the late 1940s, McDonnell served as batting practice pitcher and coach, and he is still working in the club's community relations department.

The Phillies have had a number of prominent scouts over the years, starting with Joe (Patsy) O'Rourke, a virtual one-man scouting bureau for more than three decades. O'Rourke, who also doubled on occasion as the team's public address announcer, had a part in both Grover Cleveland Alexander and Chuck Klein joining the Phillies. As a minor league manager, O'Rourke saw Alexander playing in the minors and convinced the Phillies that they should sign him. Later, as a scout, it was O'Rourke who signed Klein to his first Phillies contract.

Another scout of considerable note was Tony Lucadello, who signed 51 players who reached the major leagues, including Mike Schmidt and Ferguson Jenkins. Lucadello joined the Phillies in 1957 after working for the Chicago Cubs. He remained with the club until taking his life in 1989.

Other prominent Phillies scouts include Jocko Collins (signer of Del Ennis), Chuck Ward (Robin Roberts), Eddie Bockman (Larry Bowa and Dick Ruthven), Eddie Krajnik (Richie Ashburn and Stan Lopata), Cy Morgan (Curt Simmons), Johnny Ogden (Dick Allen), and Johnny Nee (Willie Jones), who was head scout and later director of player personnel.

The Ballparks

During a period that has progressed from the horse and buggy to the space shuttle, the Phillies have gone from playing their home games on an odd-shaped lot in North Philadelphia to a multimillion-dollar sports complex in South Philadelphia.

In 110 years the Phillies have had four home fields: Recreation Park, Philadelphia Park/Baker Bowl, Shibe Park/Connie Mack Stadium, and Veterans Stadium. Each had its own special set of characteristics, and each was substantially better than the one before it.

Until the last two dozen years, the focal point of professional baseball in the city was always North Philadelphia. At least 10 ballparks have adorned the streets of North Philly and been used by professional baseball teams. In 1890 there were three major league teams in Philadelphia playing on separate fields within a few blocks of each other.

The city's first professional team, the Athletics, played in the 1860s at a park at 15th Street and Columbia Avenue. In 1866 the Athletics—with future Phillies owner Al Reach playing second base—defeated the Atlantic Club of Brooklyn for the league championship before a paid crowd of 3,000. Newspaper accounts claimed that 20,000 fans actually saw the game, most of them from trees, from rooftops, or through windows of surrounding buildings.

Philadelphia's first bona fide enclosed park was Jefferson Park, also known as Athletic Park. The Athletics played there as members of the National Association from 1871 to 1875 and again in 1876 in the newly formed National League. Although the club failed to complete that season, the field at 25th and Jefferson Streets remained intact, and it was used again by the Athletics when they joined the American Association in 1882. The field remained in the team's hands until the AA went out of existence in 1891.

By then, other teams and other parks had surfaced in North Philadelphia. The Philadelphia Centennials of the National Association played on a field appropriately called Centennial Park in 1875; the American Association Athletics briefly used Oakdale Park in 1882; Keystone Park was the home field of the Philadelphia Keystones of the Union Association in 1884; and Forepaugh Park, named because it had been the site of the Forepaugh Circus, was used as a baseball field in 1890 by the Philadelphia Quakers of the Players' League and by the Athletics in 1891. On April 30, 1890, a crowd of 17,182 packed the Forepaugh Park grounds to watch the Quakers in a game with the Boston Reds.

When the Phillies came to town in 1883, they immediately took up residence at Recreation Park. They stayed there until moving in 1887 to the Philadelphia Base Ball Park, later to be called Baker Bowl.

In 1890 the Phillies were playing at Philadelphia Park at Broad Street and Lehigh Avenue, the Athletics were doing battle at Jefferson Park, and the Quakers were holding forth at Forepaugh Park at Broad and Dauphin Streets—three big league teams, all playing within a short distance of each other.

When they became members of the new American League in 1901, the Athletics played at a new, 11,000-seat field called Columbia Park at 29th Street and Columbia Avenue. Connie Mack and his Athletics opened Shibe Park in 1909.

To most Phillies fans, no ball park was more popular than Shibe Park/Connie Mack Stadium, home of the Phillies from 1938 to 1970.

The Phillies played briefly at Columbia Park in 1903 while awaiting repairs to Baker Bowl. In 1894 the Phillies had also spent time at the University of Pennsylvania's baseball field after Baker Bowl had been destroyed by a fire.

Recreation Park

In the early years of baseball, it wasn't difficult to create a playing field. The days of huge steel and concrete complexes, or even wooden ones, were still far in the future.

It was a simple matter to find a lot, clear it, cut out a diamond, and hire a local carpenter to build some stands. A couple of rooms on the sides of the stands where the players could change clothes were a nice addition, but not totally necessary. If need be, the players could always come to the park dressed to play.

When the Phillies were formed in the spring of 1883, their home park was such a field. Recreation Park was a tiny ball field that provided little more than a place for a handful of grown men in funny-looking costumes to play an increasingly popular game called baseball before a small crowd of spectators.

Recreation Park was not new to the game of baseball. It had been used for that purpose as early as 1860 when it was one of a number of ballparks located in the same area of North Philadelphia.

Teams known as Winona, Equity and Pennsylvania competed at Recreation Park, which bordered on the terminal for a horse trolley traction company. On June 26, 1860, Equity defeated Pennsylvania, 65–52.

During the Civil War, Recreation Park was occupied by a cavalry of the Union Army. The site became a ballfield once again after the War, but with the focus on several other nearby fields, it was used by many amateur teams and a prominent black team called the Philadelphia Pythians.

In 1866, the grounds, then going under the name of Columbia Park, were enclosed with a nine-foot fence. Amateur teams continued to play there until 1875 when the Philadelphia Centennials of the newly formed National Association made the park their home.

The Centennials resodded and leveled the field, built a 10-foot fence, a clubhouse and added a grandstand pavilion. According to ballpark researcher Jerrold Casway, "the most distinctive feature of the new ballpark was a mammoth sign advertising the *Sunday Item* newspaper. It could be seen throughout the city."

Crowds of up to 5,000 attended Centennials' games. The National Association, however, folded after the 1875 season. The park became the home field for a couple of semiprofessional teams, the Whitestockings and the Athletics, who had not survived their first season in the National Association.

Even those teams stopped playing at the park by the late 1870s, however, as neglect turned it into a rundown dump with overgrown weeds and deteriorating grandstands blighting the landscape. The only activity at the park was a horsemarket.

In 1882 Al Reach, hoping to attract a National League franchise to Philadelphia, formed a team called "Fillies" and located it at the old ballpark, which he called Recreation Park.

Reach cleared the grounds, resodded and leveled the field and built a three-section wooden grandstand. The main section contained folding chairs and private boxes in the rear. Benches lined the outfield. Dressing rooms and offices were built along the sides of the grandstand, and a press box sat atop it.

The park was on an irregularly shaped plot bordered by Columbia and Ridge Avenues and 24th and 25th Streets. The main entrance of the field was where Ridge, Columbia, and 24th nearly met.

The playing field, located in what was then the outer region of North Philadelphia, was a tiny area. Today, even some Little League fields take up more space.

It was 300 feet down the left field line from home plate to the stands. Center field was 331 feet away, but then the park jutted out into Ridge Avenue, reaching 369 feet before receding to 247 feet down the right field line. Home plate was 79 feet from the grandstand behind it.

Jammed to capacity the stands could accommodate 1,500 people. But the

A partial view of Recreation Park with the 1884 Phillies in the foreground.

bleachers could seat another 2,000, and with standing room crowds packed into the open areas, the park could hold 6,500 comfortably and up to 10,000 if necessary.

When Reach secured the Phillies' franchise from Worcester, Massachusetts, he had no players. But at least he had a field on which to play, and in 1883 Recreation Park became the first home of the Phillies.

The Phillies conducted their spring training at Recreation Park and thus were no strangers to the old but refurbished venue. Their first game at the park was on April 2 when they met the Ashland Club, a semipro team from Manayunk. Phillies pitcher John Coleman hurled a no-hitter.

Later in the month the Phillies played the American Association Athletics in what would be the first City Series game. A crowd of 10,000 squeezed into every available space on the lot to see the game.

For opening day the seats were painted red and the outfield walls were painted white. Not only did the white fences prove to be bothersome to batters. So, too, did the sun because home plate faced the setting sun, making it hard for batters to see incoming pitches.

Nevertheless, the Phillies made their National League debut on May 1, 1883, at Recreation Park in a game against the Providence Grays. The Phillies gave their fans a good show, but lost, 4–3. Winning pitcher Charles (Old Hoss) Radbourne and loser Coleman each yielded six hits as the Grays overcame a 3–0 Phillies lead with four runs in the eighth inning.

The loss set the tone for the season. The Phillies managed just 17 wins in 98 games, and fans began to lose interest. Many started to switch allegiance to the Athletics, who had won the American Association championship in 1883 and resided just a few blocks away at Oakdale Park at 12th and Huntingdon Streets.

Although the National League required an admission price of 50 cents, Reach got permission to reduce it to 25 cents. He also tried giving away trolley tickets to fans to get to the park. To generate extra income he even rented the park for other sporting events such as bicycle racing and college football.

Recreation Park, or the Horse Market as the grounds had sometimes been called before the Phillies' arrival, was the club's home field for four years. During that period, the park was the scene of the team's first no-hitter, hurled in 1885 by Charlie Ferguson.

By the mid-1880s, the Phillies were outdrawing the Athletics, their rivals a few blocks away. So packed was Recreation Park for each game that in 1886 Reach was getting anxious to find another field.

"We are having difficulty finding space for all the people who want to pay to see us play," he said. "Our Ridge Avenue park isn't big enough to handle our crowds. We've got a real team now, and we've got to get a park worthy of our team."

The next year, the Phillies deserted Recreation Park, moving farther uptown to a new stadium.

Recreation Park was left to local sandlotters. Eventually, the site was covered with houses and forgotten. Today, there is no evidence of its place in Phillies history. The irregular plot sits in the midst of a rundown section of the city. Except for a few homes and a storefront church, the site of the old park contains mostly a decaying collection of abandoned houses and businesses.

Philadelphia Park– Baker Bowl

When it was built at a cost of $101,000, Baker Bowl was hailed as the finest baseball stadium in the nation, a magnificent showplace that was the pride of Philadelphia and the envy of other cities. When the Phillies moved out of the stadium after 51½ years there, Baker Bowl was the laughingstock of baseball, damned and discredited, an obsolete relic that was derisively called a "cigar box."

Originally known as the Philadelphia Base Ball Park, or Huntington Park, the ball yard had a long and colorful history, despite its eventual shortcomings. It was the scene of high humor and of awful tragedy, of both brilliant and wretched play, of drama, deceit, death, and destruction.

It was the playground of Grover Cleveland Alexander and Chuck Klein; of the Hall of Fame outfield of Ed Delahanty, Billy Hamilton, and Sam Thompson; and of Roy Thomas, Cy Williams, and Sherry Magee.

The Phillies played in their first World Series at the stadium. Gavvy Cravath and Kitty Bransfield each drove in eight runs in single games there. Red Donahue pitched the club's second no-hitter at the park. And the Phillies won games of 24–0 and 29–4 and lost games of 28–6 and 20–16. In one 20–14 Phillies win over the St. Louis Cardinals, the teams combined to hit 10 home runs.

While there was sometimes comedy on the field, there was occasionally catastrophe in the stands. The stadium was struck by three major disasters and an assortment of smaller ones.

The site of the stadium was originally a dumplike area bordered by Broad Street, Lehigh Avenue, 15th Street, and Huntington Avenue. The Cohosksink Creek ran through the site, which was lower than street level, forming a pond along the way.

When the stadium was built, it took an estimated 100,000 wagon loads of dirt to fill the gullies on the field and another 20,000 loads to bring it even with the adjacent streets.

The master plan for the park, devised by Reach, was unlike that of any other stadium of the era. The outside of the stadium was brick. Paneled brick

The uneven dimensions of Baker Bowl are evident from the air. Broad Street runs across the center of the picture, and Lehigh Avenue is on the left.

Inside Baker Bowl: the starting batteries for this 1916 game were announced by a man with a megaphone.

with ornamental mouldings also enclosed the playing field. A pavilion rising 23 rows on one side of home plate and 16 rows on the other, seating 5,000, and grandstands down the right and left field lines, accommodating another 7,500, gave the park a total seating capacity of 12,500.

Each end of the pavilion was topped by two 75-foot-high turrets. Another turret over the main entrance rose 165 feet and was 39 feet in diameter. Sheds for 55 carriages were located beneath the stands.

Reading Railroad tracks ran along Broad Street next to the park. At times, locomotives would billow smoke or spray sparks toward the grandstands.

The main entrance of the stadium was at 15th and Huntington. Although there were seven entrances altogether, three remained closed except for emergencies. The club's offices and the clubhouse were in the center field stands at Broad and Lehigh.

Like its predecessor, Recreation Park, Philadelphia Park had unusual dimensions. Although the distance down the left field line eventually became 335 feet after bleachers were installed in 1910, the original distance was more than 400 feet. It was 408 feet to straightaway center. The field presented an especially inviting target to lefthanded hitters with its short right field, which at first was a scant 272 feet from home plate.

Later that distance, as well as the other dimensions, would change several times. Eventually the right field wall would be located 280.5 feet from the plate, and the left field fence would shrink, too.

The height of the various walls also changed. Of particular note, the right field fence was originally 40 feet high. Later, it was raised to 60 feet with the addition of a 12-foot double screen. Despite that height, pop flies were often converted to hits, and balls rained down on Broad Street with monotonous regularity.

Philadelphia Park opened on April 30, 1887. It was a festive occasion, which began when the Phillies and the opposing New York Giants were paraded up Broad Street in open carriages.

A crowd estimated to be nearly 20,000, the largest gathering ever known to have attended a baseball game, packed the stadium far beyond its capacity. The crowd was so large that the outfield had to be roped off and standing room provided on the field.

Spectators were about evenly divided between men and women, although baseball crowds of the era usually consisted almost entirely of men and boys. Also in attendance were Mayor Edwin Fitler and his directors, the receiver of taxes, and nearly all prominent city officials, as well as a large contingent from high society.

The opening was such a major event on the city's calendar that the Athletics, playing Brooklyn in an American Association game the same day at 25th and Jefferson Streets, moved their starting time up several hours so their fans could see both games.

Beck's Military Band gave a concert before the game. That was followed by the official opening of the park. Here's how the *Evening Bulletin* described it: "The formal ceremony of raising the club's flag was a picturesque scene, all of the players of the visiting and home teams participating, and as manager Harry Wright raised the big flag to the breeze, three mighty cheers that must have been heard for miles rent the air."

The game itself gave the Phillies' fans further reason to cheer. In the bottom of the first inning, the first nine Phillies to bat all hit safely, and nine runs crossed the plate.

During the game, the crowd, herded behind the ropes in the outfield, occasionally surged forward. As a result, a number of hits went among the spectators and were declared ground-rule doubles. It was a hitters' game throughout, the Phillies coasting to a 19–10 victory.

For the rest of the season, the Phillies celebrated the opening of their new park in grand style, engaging in a hotly contested pennant race with the Detroit Wolverines and Chicago White Stockings, eventually finishing in second place. Fans flocked to the park in great numbers. The new stadium received endless testimonials to its beauty and modern design.

In the ensuing years, the Phillies, with their snappy stadium, heavily outdrew the rival Athletics. But owners Reach and Colonel John Rogers were always on the lookout for ways to help pay for their new ball yard. At the time, bicycle races were popular. To capitalize on that popularity, the owners built a quarter-mile racing track around the edge of the field. The track was 15 feet wide and had banked turns. For years afterward, outfielders had to run up the banks to catch fly balls.

On the morning of August 6, 1894, the Phillies were working out at the park, preparing for an afternoon game with the Baltimore Orioles. At 10:40 A.M., one of the players noticed a fire in the grandstand. The players raced to the fire and tried to put it out. But it was hopeless. The fire spread through the wooden structure too fast for them.

"Run for your clothes," someone yelled. The players raced to the clubhouse and tried quickly to change into their regular attire. By then, much of the stadium was ablaze. The players had to fight their way to the street through smoke and flames. The shirt of third baseman Tricky Charley Reilly, a player who once blew a bunt foul, caught fire. Worse yet, pitcher George Harper, the last player to leave, was temporarily trapped inside the stadium. After vainly attempting several exits, he finally escaped the burning park by jumping through a window.

All the players eventually reached the street unharmed. As they did, the first of the city's fire apparatus was arriving. Soon every available department in the city had rushed men and equipment to the scene as the blaze roared out of control.

In a short time, the nearby Omnibus Company, with stables for 350 horses, caught fire. Then several stores and three or four houses began to burn. The fire spread quickly, creating a general panic in the neighborhood.

It took several hours to extinguish the blaze. The damage was estimated to be $250,000. Subsequent investigations never uncovered the cause of the holocaust. One possibility was sparks from a locomotive. Another was suggested by the *Evening Bulletin:* "It is by no means impossible that the notion of incendiorism may have been put in the head of some malicious scamp by the reports of a like occurrence in Chicago on the previous day." The report added, "The fire is a misfortune which will be regretted by many lovers of that wholesome sport." The most likely version, which became the accepted explanation for the fire, was that the calamity was caused by a torch being used by a plumber to make repairs.

After the fire, the Phillies played six games at the University of Pennsylvania's University Field at 37th and Spruce Streets, winning five of

The main entrance to Baker Bowl at 15th and Huntingdon Streets often drew a crowd at game-time.

them. Essentially a football field at the time, the site is now the location of dormitories. The Phillies returned to Philadelphia Park on August 18, spectators sitting in temporary stands.

Reach was determined to have no more fires at the stadium. During the off-season, Philadelphia Park was rebuilt using mostly steel and brick. Designed by a builder who had experience constructing bridges, the park featured a cantilever pavilion, a radical new architectural technique in stadium construction.

The stadium was the most modern in baseball and the pride of Philadelphia. Tourists made special trips up Broad Street to view the ornate structure. It was a showplace, the most magnificent baseball park of its day.

The rebuilt park, which had a swimming pool in the clubhouse, was completed in 1895. By the time the building was finished, it had a seating capacity of almost 18,800.

The stadium that was being called the finest in the world was especially tailored to hitters, but there was always a measure of curiosity over why the Phillies played so much better at home than they did on the road. Some light was shed on that one afternoon in 1898 in a game with the Cincinnati Reds.

Reds infielder Tommy Corcoran was coaching third base and kicking dirt around when his spikes caught on something in the ground. At first, Corcoran thought it was a vine. Upon closer inspection, he realized it was a wire. Corcoran tugged on the wire, and several feet of it came out of the ground.

Tommy halted the game, and tugged some more. The more he yanked, the more wire emerged from the ground. As both teams followed him, Corcoran kept pulling wire out of the ground all the way across center field. The wire led up a brick wall and into the Phillies' clubhouse where the curious party found reserve catcher Morgan Murphy sitting with a telegraph instrument beside an open window through which the wire passed.

The surprised Murphy tried to hide the device, as well as a pair of opera glasses. But it was too late. Murphy's game was over. The other side now knew that he was picking up opposing catchers' signs through his glasses, then relaying a signal to the third base coach. A buzzer was buried beneath the dirt. One buzz was a fastball, two a curve. By keeping his foot on the buzzer, the coach knew the pitch that was coming, and could signal the information to the batter.

No one revealed how long the Phillies had been stealing the signs. Some felt the trick was the work of the club's devious manager, George Stallings. Regardless of who the culprit was, the Phillies' batting averages dropped off after Corcoran's expose.

The Phillies' batting averages didn't stay down very long at Philadelphia

Park. But in 1903 something else went down: an overhanging balcony with nearly 400 spectators on it.

The Phillies had been sold for $180,000 the previous winter by the Reach-Rogers duo to a group headed by Philadelphia socialite James Potter. The former owners, however, retained possession of Philadelphia Park, renting it to the new owners (operating under the name of Philadelphia Base Ball and Amusement Company) for $10,000 a season.

On August 8, with 10,000 in attendance, the Phillies squared off in a doubleheader with the Boston Braves. The Braves won an exciting first game, 5–4.

The fans were anxious for another close game in the nightcap, and they got it. The score was 3–3 in the fourth inning. With two outs, the Braves' Joe Stanley was at the plate when the accident occurred.

Although the cause of the accident has been erroneously reported over the years, accounts at the time clearly indicate that what happened was actually initiated by two drunks and a group of young girls. As the drunks staggered along 15th Street, they were followed by the girls, who were taking great pleasure in teasing them. Suddenly, the drunks had enough of the youngsters' fun. One of the men lurched after the girls, and grabbed one of them by the hair. The girl fell. When she did, the drunk tumbled on top of her.

Shrieks of "help" and "murder" from the other girls filled the air. The cries attracted the attention of some fans in the bleachers down the left field line. They ran to an overhanging balcony to see what was happening.

When the first group ran to the balcony, which protruded 30 feet above 15th Street, it caught the attention of others. More people raced to the balcony. They, in turn, lured even more curiosity seekers to the small wooden deck, which measured 23 feet wide and 100 feet long.

Suddenly, the balcony broke loose under all the weight, and with a roar followed by the screams of the people on it, crashed heavily to the cement pavement below. It was 5:40 P.M. "In the twinkling of an eye," said a report in the *Philadelphia Inquirer,* "the street was piled four deep with bleeding, injured, shrieking humanity struggling amid the piling debris."

After the first wave of bodies fell, others behind them panicked and forced those now in the front off the broken deck and into the street. Others tried to hold on to broken timbers and pieces of the balcony, but eventually lost their grips and also plunged into the sea of bodies and debris.

Spectators in the rest of the stadium witnessed the tragedy in stunned horror. Then, fearing that the whole park might collapse, people began scrambling to escape. Panic set in. Some people jumped 20 feet onto the playing field. About the only cool heads in the park belonged to the players. "For God's sake, keep these people back," someone yelled from the stands. The men of both teams raced to the edges of the stands and pleaded with the spectators to stay calm. In the aftermath, the players were given much of the credit for averting further disaster.

Out on 15th Street, though, it was another story. "I never saw such a sight," said policeman Charles Muskert, one of the first to arrive on the scene. "People were lying everywhere, some jammed in the debris, some cut and bleeding, some struggling and kicking the others."

A policeman named Robinson remembered an even ghastlier scene. "Some of (the people) had their clothing almost torn from their bodies while others were so besplattered with blood and mud as to be almost unrecognizable," he said.

The rescue effort mobilized quickly. Since there weren't enough ambulances in the city to transport all of the dying and injured, police commandeered everything on wheels—private automobiles driving along Broad Street, trolley cars, even trolley repair wagons. Nine area hospitals received victims. "I remember nothing until I found myself in a grocer's wagon coming to the hospital," one injured man said.

As the people lay on the street, their broken bodies entangled, pickpockets and looters arrived. Police were too busy aiding the victims to bother with the hoodlums.

The game, of course, was not completed. Phillies management was distraught. "Business manager Billy Shettsline," said the *Inquirer,* "was so badly prostrated by the shock that he could scarcely tell a coherent story."

In the early moments after the accident, three known deaths had occurred. But the death toll rose as the debris and the injured were peeled from the pile. The battering some of the men had taken was immense.

"In the fall of the overhanging balcony," said an *Inquirer* account citing the death of Nicholas Moser, a local politician, "Mr Moser was terribly injured. Nearly every bone in his face and body was broken, but though the bodies of others fell upon him, he never lost consciousness."

The accident received page-one coverage for days in all the Philadelphia newspapers. Ultimately, the number of deaths reached 12. The injured totaled 232.

An investigation was launched by the city to determine the reason the balcony collapsed. It was discovered that the timbers supporting the balcony were rotted and gave way with the weight of nearly 400 people.

Numerous lawsuits were filed. Both the Phillies and the park's owners tried to absolve themselves of the blame. Meanwhile, everyone searched for the drunks and the girls. None of them was ever located.

The Phillies were scheduled to move to Columbia Park, the Athletics' field at 29th and Columbia, while Philadelphia Park was repaired. But nine consecutive rainouts kept the Phils from making their Columbia Park debut. Finally, they played their first game there on August 20. Between then and September 10 the Phillies played 16 games at Columbia Park, winning six, losing nine, and tying one.

Afterward the Phillies went on a road trip. When they returned home, the park had been fixed. New wooden bleachers had been installed down the left field line. Also, a 40-foot tin fence was erected in right.

Unusual incidents, however, continued. In 1905, the park played host to one of the two longest games in Phillies history, a 20-inning, 2–1 loss to the Chicago Cubs. A year later, fans attacked the New York Giants as they were leaving the park.

The fracas occurred after a fight between Giants manager John McGraw and Phillies third baseman Paul Sentelle had evolved into a full-scale riot between the teams. After the two battlers were ejected, they fought again under the stands.

In those days, the visiting team dressed in its hotel, there being no clubhouse for it at Philadelphia Park. The game was hotly contested, and the teams nearly came to blows again after the final out. When the Giants left the

With the short right field wall in the background, Baker Bowl was frequently used as parade grounds for police and firemen's bands, as was the case here in 1913.

park to ride to their hotel in open carriages drawn by big, black horses wearing blankets marked, "New York Giants, World's Champions," a group of angry fans tried to snatch the blankets. Players grabbed the coachmen's whips and swung at the crowd.

Nearby, street vendors were selling lemonade. The fans plucked lemon halves out of trash cans and threw them at the Giants. As this was going on, New York catcher Roger Bresnahan stood in the rear carriage, kicking at the fans. As the carriage lurched forward, Bresnahan lost his balance and tumbled into the unruly mob.

The caravan moved on, apparently with no one realizing Bresnahan's predicament. Surrounded by hundreds of fans, the catcher kicked with his spikes and fought his way into a corner grocery store where he barricaded himself until rescued a half hour later by police. Roger was fined $10 for disturbing the peace.

In the ensuing years at Philadelphia Park, a lady had a baby in the bathroom. A couple was married in a lion's cage on the pitcher's mound. Promotion-minded owner Horace Fogel once released 100 pigeons with free tickets strapped to their legs in an effort to generate interest among the fans. And in 1912, the Giants' Jeff Tesreau became the only visiting player ever to hurl a no-hitter at Baker Bowl.

By the end of the first decade of the 20th century, however, the stadium had begun to show its age. The once-magnificent edifice was antiquated and suffered by comparison to the new parks being built, especially the one a few blocks down Lehigh Avenue called Shibe Park.

Major renovations were in order and in 1910 the park got a facelift. Bleachers were installed in the outfield, extending from the left field foul line to the clubhouse in center field. The grandstands beyond the third and first bases were also extended, and the original bleachers along the left field foul line were curled to meet the new bleachers in the outfield. The curved bleachers had a special name. They were called field seats.

With the renovations, the playing dimensions were changed. The left field line was no longer 415 feet; it was shortened to 335. The right field line became one foot longer at 273.

The old park had something else new, too. In 1913, William F. Baker became the Phillies' president. Soon afterward, the stadium was renamed Baker Bowl.

The same year Baker arrived, the fans demonstrated once again their dislike for the Giants. This time a group of them clustered in the center field bleachers. Every time the Giants came to bat, the group waved its hats and coats, and, using mirrors, deflected the sun's rays into the faces of the batters.

Umpire Brennan asked the fans to stop. When they wouldn't, he asked Phillies manager Red Dooin to make the same request. It was suspected, but never proved, that the bleacherites were Dooin's friends, planted in center field specifically to distract the Giants. Dooin meandered out to the bleachers, and not too forcefully suggested that the fans behave.

They complied briefly, but the next inning began flashing mirrors again. This time, Brennan sent the police to center field. As the fans were being ejected, others got into the act by hurling bricks at the Giants. Brennan forfeited the game to New York.

Afterward, Giant manager McGraw told a sportswriter, "I have seen a great many bonehead plays, but why Red Dooin should have pulled that one is beyond me."

The Phillies, through president Baker, filed a protest of the forfeit. The protest was upheld, and the game was ordered resumed the next time New York came to town. The Giants won anyway.

The Phillies in 1913 finished second to the Giants, drawing more fans for the season than in any year since the club began. Some 470,000 people entered Baker Bowl. It was the second largest season attendance in the park's history, exceeded only by the 1916 attendance of 515,365, a figure that was by far the Phillies' highest total until 1946.

From the outside, viewed down the third-base line along 15th Street Baker Bowl hardly looked like a baseball park.

A view of the left field stands shows a rare packed house at Baker Bowl. The clubhouse appears in center field (right).

The third largest attendance in Baker Bowl history was in 1915 when 449,898 people passed through the gates. That was the year the Phillies won their first pennant and met the Boston Red Sox in the World Series.

Although it was in a state of decline, Baker Bowl was spruced up for the occasion. It turned out to be the site of the Phillies' only World Series victory prior to 1980 when Grover Alexander beat the Red Sox in the opener, 3–1.

The second game was significant, too, although the Phillies lost. It was the first Series game attended by a United States President. Woodrow Wilson, watching the game with his fiance, Mrs. Edith Galt, threw out the first ball and got it back as a souvenir after umpire Charlie Rigler recovered it.

Two of the three Series games in Philadelphia drew crowds of 20,306, a huge turnout by Baker Bowl standards. The large crowds were attributable to team president Baker's adding extra seats in front of the left field stands and right field wall. The new seats reduced the size of the playing field, and Baker

Baker Bowl was showing signs of disrepair in the 1920s.

was roundly criticized for adding them after three Boston home runs went into the area in the Red Sox's 5–4 victory in the clinching game.

After the Series, the park continued on its steady decline. By now, the swimming pool inside the clubhouse, where Alexander and Mike Doolin had engaged in frequent underwater "rassling" bouts, was dry. And the pool table, situated in the outer room of the clubhouse, was being used mostly for craps and poker.

In the 1920s, "The Hump," as the park came to be known because it sat at the top of a hill along Broad Street, had turned into an eccentric antique that was a joke. Spectators sitting in the pavilion were often showered with rust sprays when foul balls landed on the decaying tin roof. Other times, they were scorched by cigarette butts flipped indiscriminantly out of the press box.

For a number of years, groundskeeper Sam Payne kept two ewes and a ram under the stands. The sheep kept the grass trimmed, which for the penny-pinching Phillies saved the expense of a maintenance crew and equipment. Baker Bowl housed the livestock until 1925 when the ram charged Billy Shettsline, a club official. The ponderous Shettsline escaped the ram's wrath, but soon afterward the sheep received their outright releases.

The crowds in center field continued to be one of the Phillies' secret weapons. On warm summer days, they were especially effective in their white shirts, providing a difficult background for the hitters.

In 1925 home plate was moved back seven feet so that the right field wall became 280 feet away. "I'm tired of hearing the fans talk about pop-fly homers," said manager Art Fletcher, who had ordered the change.

The stadium was sometimes described by fans as "the most abominable" park in the country. Sportswriter Red Smith in the Philadelphia *Record* called it "a cobwebby House of Horrors." But the stadium was also intimate. Fans in the front rows sat so close to the playing field that they were almost part of the game.

In 1927, Baker Bowl was struck by another disaster. The Phillies had just scored eight runs in the sixth inning of a game against the World Champion St. Louis Cardinals when rain began falling. It was a Saturday afternoon game, the date was May 14.

As the rain got heavier, hundreds of fans from the bleachers ran for cover to the lower deck side of first base. Without warning, two sections of the stands,

One of many mishaps at Baker Bowl occurred in 1927 when stands behind first base collapsed, resulting in several injuries.

containing about 300 spectators, suddenly collapsed into a heap. Each section was 20 feet wide and contained seven rows of seats.

Fifty people were injured and one man died, although it was later determined that he had suffered a heart attack. Baker, rushing back from a meeting in New York, was astounded at the extent of the damage. The Phillies, he claimed, had made $30,000 worth of repairs to the stands at the beginning of the season.

City officials were unimpressed. "Baker Bowl is the worst constructed place I ever saw," barked coroner Fred Schwartz, Jr. "It should be closed until thoroughly reconstructed to make it safer for a gathering of large crowds."

Like the collapse of the balcony in 1903, the 1927 accident was attributed to the park's old age. A main girder had developed wet rot and was too weak to support the added weight in the stands.

Once again, the Phillies were obligated to move their show elsewhere. This time, they slipped down the street to Shibe Park, where they played the last 12 games of their home stand. When they returned from the ensuing road trip, the club resumed its games at Baker Bowl, where repairs had been made at a cost of $40,000.

Although it had always been a hitter's paradise, especially if the hitter was lefthanded, Baker Bowl was a place in the 1920s and 1930s in which no respectable pitcher ever liked to set foot. It was almost impossible to pitch a low-scoring game, much less a shutout.

No hitter inflicted more damage on opposing pitchers than the Phillies' Chuck Klein. The powerful lefthanded slugger rattled one hit after another off and over the right field fence. Once, he even blasted a ball through the fence—rusted as it was.

When Klein batted, kids in the upper stands rushed to the corner to peer out over the fence so they could be in a position to watch if Chuck clouted a ball onto Broad Street. Numerous windshields of passing autos were shattered that way. Baker paid for the damage.

So frequent were Klein's blasts over the right field wall that in 1929 Baker added 12 feet of screen to the tin barrier. "Home runs have become too cheap at the Philadelphia ball park," Baker explained. Few believed the explanation. It was, even the mildest cynics felt, the cheap owner's way of keeping Klein from hitting so many home runs that he would demand a higher salary.

Chuck still managed 43 homers that year. It was a year in which the Phils hit .309 as a team. At one point, they scored 88 runs in 12 games. The following year, they had a combined average of .315 but finished in last place, losing 102 games. The Phillies' pitching staff had a team earned run average of 6.71.

That season, no pitcher hurled a shutout at Baker Bowl. There were 71 home runs hit in the first 41 games. Over the 77-game home season, the average score was 8–7 in favor of the visitors.

Such heavy hitting was hardly confined to 1929 or 1930. In 1934, for instance, during a six-game stretch with the Brooklyn Dodgers and Boston Braves, the Phillies outscored their opponents, 63–55.

That same year, the first legal Sunday game in Philadelphia was played at Baker Bowl. The Dodgers beat the Phillies, 8–7.

A year later, on May 30, 1935, the park that was mockingly called a cigar box had another milestone. Babe Ruth played his last big league game. The once mighty slugger was then with the Boston club, which was known from the mid-1930s to early 1940s as the Bees. In the first game of a doubleheader, Ruth opened in left field. He went hitless in his first trip to the plate. Barely able to move, the aging home run king took himself out of the game after the first inning. It was, according to accounts of the day, a wise move that saved the Babe from potential embarrassment.

Although lefthanded batters hit balls out of the park with ease, few balls ever came off the bats of righthanders to clear the left field barrier. Only five righthanders ever hit balls out of the stadium in left field. The first was the Phillies' Cliff Lee, who clubbed a shot over the stands in 1922 off Giants pitcher Art Nehf. In later years, Jimmie Foxx during a City Series game, and Hal Lee, Joe Medwick, and Wally Berger during the regular season, duplicated the feat.

The Lifebuoy sign on the right-center field wall was one of Baker Bowl's most prominent landmarks.

Rogers Hornsby once slammed a ball through a window and into the Phillies' clubhouse in center field.

At its best, Baker Bowl was a park in which the fans sat so close to the field that they could hear what the players said to each other. "And as players, we could sit in the dugout and smell the peanuts in the stands," remembered pitcher Bucky Walters.

"It was a real hitters' paradise," Walters added. "The hitters always fattened up their averages at Baker Bowl. When visiting teams came in, all their pitchers would always come up with lame arms."

Outfielder Johnny Moore once recalled how he used to play the tricky right field fence: "Sometimes, batters would hit bullets to the right field wall, and the balls would drop straight down," he said. "But sometimes a ball would hit off the telephone poles holding up the fence. If you weren't careful, the ball would bounce all the way back to the infield."

Because the clubhouse was in center field, players had to walk across the diamond to get there. If taken out during a game, that meant a player would wait in the dugout until the end of the inning before taking the long walk to the locker room.

Bullpens were located along the edges of the playing field. "One day," remembered outfielder Ethan Allen, "one of our pitchers, Snipe Hansen, had been sent down to the bullpen just before the game was to begin, and had just gotten himself settled on the bench when he saw a ball rolling toward him. He reached down, casually picked it up, and threw it back toward the infield. Unfortunately, the game had begun, and what Hansen retrieved was an overthrow at first base."

Gamblers always populated the stands. Small-time gamblers sat along the left field line and would bet 50 to 75 cents on every pitch. "Two to one it's a strike," someone would shout. A symphony of takers would yell their responses.

The big-time gamblers sat behind first base. Often, this group included local mobsters who attended games accompanied by a bevy of chorus girls. The gamblers usually managed to sneak a few of the neighborhood kids in with them.

The press box was a section of the stands behind home plate. Only some chicken wire separated it from the regular stands.

The stadium's clubhouse had one shower room that could accommodate just four players at a time. Windows in the home clubhouse looked out over the playing field. On their way into the room, players, many of whom lived in the neighborhood in rooming houses or hotels, always stopped to chat with the neighborhood kids and sign autographs.

One of the enduring characters at Baker Bowl was an energetic fan named "Ball Hawk" George. Present at every game, George stood outside the stadium behind home plate at 15th and Huntington and tracked down foul balls, which he would then return to the club for fifty cents. George was notorious for using whatever means he could to beat kids to the balls.

In the 1930s the decrepit Hump, its seats grimy from the coal dust billowing from passing locomotives, its flagpole struck by lightning, was being used for boxing and wrestling matches, for donkey baseball games, midget auto racing, fire department parades and crusades, and high school was well as professional football games. The stadium had for many years been an important site in the city for outdoor boxing matches. In 1919, Benny Leonard fought Patsy Kline there. Primo Carnera met George Godfrey in 1930, drawing a gate of $180,000, the city's second largest at the time. Luis Firpo, Mickey Walker, Tommy Loughran, and numerous others had fights at Baker Bowl.

The Philadelphia Eagles used the stadium as their home field from 1933, their first year in the National Football League, to 1935. The Eagles' first NFL home game was played against the Portsmouth Spartans at night. It was one of two night games played by the Eagles at Baker Bowl in 1933, using rented, portable lights strung on poles.

Jokes ran rampant about the stadium. A Chicago writer called it the toilet bowl. Another comic said that nothing was alive at the park except the ivy on the clubhouse wall.

The stadium's press box was a case for hilarity itself. Always the scene of pranks among the writers, it was unlike any of the facilities to which present scribes are accustomed.

"In most ball parks," said the syndicated columnist Red Smith who covered the Phillies in his early years as a sportswriter, "the press is segregated in a detention pen tucked away up under the roof. In Baker Bowl, however, the press box was a section about 10 rows deep in the second deck of the grandstand directly behind home plate.

"There, enclosed by a fence of tall iron palings, the flowers of Philadelphia letters drowsed over scorebooks and whiled away the afternoon throwing peanuts at the head of Stan Baumgartner of the *Philadelphia Inquirer*, who sat in the front row."

The Phillies' manager in the late 1930s, Jimmie Wilson, often complained that the old stadium played havoc with his pitching staff. "A pitcher goes along well for four or five innings, and then a couple of pop flies which would be easy outs in other parks hit that wall for doubles or triples," he said. "I have to yank my pitcher and use maybe a couple more during a game. After one home stand, the staff is coming apart at every seam."

For the Phillies, the end of a long but storied residence in the old park came on June 30, 1938. Appropriately, the opponent was the Giants, the same team the Phillies faced when the stadium opened 51½ years earlier. Just as appropriately, the Phillies lost, 14–1.

"Baker Bowl passed out of existence as the home of the Phillies yesterday afternoon," Bill Dooly wrote in the lead of his game story in the Philadelphia *Record*. "Equal to the occasion, the Phillies almost passed out with it by providing one of their inimitable travesties, a delineation in which they drolly absorbed a 14 to 1 pasting."

The last out at Baker Bowl was made by Bill Atwood. The Phillies' Phil Weintraub hit the last single, and the Giants' Hank Leiber hit the last home run. The last run was scored by New York's Mel Ott. The last winning pitcher was Slick Castleman, and the last losing pitcher was Claude Passeau. Phillies

The end of Baker Bowl was near in 1950 when a section of the wall along 15th Street collapsed during a wind storm.

manager Wilson was the last to leave the stadium. The Phillies, of course, left in last place.

The end came swiftly and without much fanfare. For the most part, the players were glad to be moving to a new home at Shibe Park. A typical reaction was that of left fielder Morrie Arnovich, who had swallowed a beetle the previous week at Baker Bowl just as he caught a fly ball. "Phooey," said Morrie. "Are there any beetles in Shibe Park?"

The Phillies' final record at Baker Bowl was 1,957 wins, 1,778 losses, and 29 ties.

After the Phillies' departure, Baker Bowl was used for an assortment of events. Boxing matches and football games continued to be held there. An ice-skating rink was built, as was a midget auto racetrack. A rodeo came to the park once.

Father Divine and his followers held a rally in the stadium in 1939. Several times there were plans to convert it to a sports center. One of those times, the plan was to set up a new franchise in the National Hockey League there. The Philadelphia Board of Education wanted the property on several occasions, once to build a new Central High School and once to make an athletic field. And the Lutheran Church considered building an office on the site. The property was also used as a parking lot and a used car lot, and at one point there was a taproom in what had been the clubhouse.

Three times parts of the stadium were destroyed by fire—in 1939, 1943, and 1950.

Ownership of the stadium changed hands several times. Finally, the park was torn down in the early 1950s.

There is no hint today that the site has such a colorful history. A gas station minimarket, a car wash, and a fast food establishment have taken the place of the stadium that began as the best in baseball—and ended as the worst.

Shibe Park—Connie Mack Stadium

"I'm sure the Phillies will play better at Shibe Park, and I look for a real spurt once they have gotten to know the field."

The statement was made by Connie Mack in 1938 as he welcomed his new tenants to the Athletics' stadium at 21st Street and Lehigh Avenue.

Mack wasn't much of a prophet. After their arrival at Shibe Park, the Phillies went on a spurt that produced five straight eighth-place finishes and

Shibe Park was considered the nation's finest stadium when it was opened in 1909.

seven trips to the cellar in eight years. Included in that masterful demonstration of consistency were five of the seven losingest teams in Phillies history.

The Phillies were not exactly strangers to Shibe Park, either. They had played 12 games there in 1927 after one of Baker Bowl's several catastrophes. And they were frequent visitors in the City Series skirmishes that preceded the regular season.

By the time the Phillies arrived at Shibe Park, the stadium had been in use for 29 years. Ground had been broken for the stadium at the 5.75 acre site, which was originally farmland, on April 13, 1908. The stadium was named for Benjamin Shibe, the owner of the A's and not so coincidentally a partner of the Phillies' first president, Al Reach, in the sporting goods business and the father-in-law of Reach's son, George.

It took two months to grade the land with 40 workers and 50 teams of horses carrying away 15,000 wagonloads of dirt. Much of the sod covering the field was imported from Columbia Park. More than 500 tons of steel were used in the structural work during construction of the stadium, the first to use such material. Completed in less than one year, Shibe Park cost $500,000.

The facade of the pavilion had a French Renaissance motif. The pavilion seated 8,000 spectators between first and third bases. Seating for an additional 12,000 was provided in two uncovered concrete bleachers that extended to the left and right field corners. The seating capacity was 20,000, but some 10,000 more people could stand behind ropes in the outfield on banked terraces.

The seats in the grandstands were steel folding chairs, an innovation of the park. Also, there were garages for up to 200 cars beneath the left field and right field bleachers.

"Shibe Park," said the Philadelphia *Evening Telegraph* when the stadium opened, "is an enduring monument to the national past-time: baseball—the greatest game ever intended for all classes of people, for all ages and for women as well as men."

The park opened for business on April 12, 1909, when the Athletics met the Boston Red Sox in the season's opener. A line of spectators began forming to enter the stadium at 7 A.M., five hours before the gates opened and eight hours before the game started.

It was the largest gathering ever to see a baseball game up to that point. A paid attendance of 30,162 entered the stadium, but the total crowd was closer to 35,000 because of the number of free tickets issued. Thousands of others were turned away, and still thousands more crowded onto rooftops of houses along 20th Street.

A number of Phillies players were on hand for the opener, along with Mayor John Reburn, other city officials, and assorted celebrities and baseball dignitaries. Words such as "magnificent" and "immense" were used over and over to describe the new structure. "Shibe Park is the greatest place of its character in the world," gushed Ban Johnson, the American League president.

In its early days, Shibe Park had a seating capacity of 20,000 with an upper deck only behind home plate.

The playing field, unlike its predecessors, had adequate space. Fans were not seated on top of the players. And the dimensions were spacious—378 feet down the left field line, 340 to right, and a huge 515 to center.

In the first game, the A's, behind the six-hit pitching of Eddie Plank, walloped the Red Sox, 8–1. The victory, however, was marred by the death of starting catcher Mike (Doc) Powers. The A's backstop had eaten a cheese sandwich before the game. It failed to digest properly, although Powers caught the entire game. In the clubhouse afterward, he was striken and rushed to a hospital. He died of intestinal complications two weeks later.

Shibe Park was the first of a long line of stadiums to be built. In the years immediately following its construction, Forbes Field went up in Pittsburgh, Comisky Park in Chicago, Ebbets Field in Brooklyn, League Park in Cleveland, and Fenway Park in Boston.

During the A's occupancy and before the Phillies moved in, Shibe Park was the scene of some of baseball's greatest events. In fact, probably more baseball lore unfolded at Shibe Park in its early decades than in any other ballpark in the country, with the possible exception of Yankee Stadium.

The A's won seven pennants (1910, 1911, 1913, 1914, 1929, 1930, 1931) and five World Series (1910, 1911, 1913, 1929, 1930) while playing at Shibe Park. They also finished in eighth place seven straight times—from 1915 to 1921.

Shibe Park was the place where the A's staged their famous 10-run seventh inning in the fourth game of the 1929 World Series against the Chicago Cubs, overcoming an 8–0 deficit to win, 10–8.

It was also the place where in 1912 the Detroit Tigers refused to play a game in protest of the suspension of Ty Cobb. An odd assortment of local college and sandlot players were rounded up to play that day as the Tigers. They lost to the A's, 24–2.

Lou Gehrig hit four home runs in one nine-inning game at Shibe Park in 1932. Pat Seerey did likewise for the Chicago White Sox in an 11-inning game in 1948. Ted Williams went 6-for-8 in a doubleheader on the last day of the 1941 season at Shibe Park to finish with a .406 batting average. Babe Ruth hit a home run over the rooftops on 20th Street. And Tony Lazzeri drove in 11 runs in one game, a 25–2 New York Yankees rout of the A's in 1936.

Jimmie Foxx, who hit 28 balls during his career over the left field roof, slammed his record 58 home runs in 1932 and won the batting crown in 1933 while playing at Shibe Park. Al Simmons and Ferris Fain each won two batting titles there. Lefty Grove won 31 while losing only four in 1931. From these legends along with other Hall of Famers Eddie Collins, Mickey Cochrane,

Chief Bender, Home Run Baker, and Rube Waddell to Bing Miller, Jimmy Dykes, and latter-day giants such as Sam Chapman, Eddie Joost, Gus Zernial, and Bobby Shantz, Shibe Park was the home park for an endless parade of baseball greats and near-greats playing in the flannels of the Philadelphia Athletics.

In its first decade, the stadium underwent frequent changes. Bleachers were added in left field early in the park's life. Then in 1925 an upper deck was installed atop the bleacher sections that ran from third base to left field, first base to right field, and left field to center field.

A mezzanine seating 2,500 people was added in 1929, and the following year, 3,500 more seats were tacked on to the main grandstand. In those days, the right field wall was only 12 feet high. Residents on 20th Street could watch games from their upstairs windows and rooftops. Most of the homes had rows of bleachers on their roofs, and the residents not only sold seats for 25 cents to World Series and other big games, they even hawked hot dogs and drinks. The practice was eliminated in 1935 when 22 feet were added to the existing 12-foot high wall.

Lights were installed at the stadium in 1939, despite the protests of 20th Street residents. The lights and the crowd noises, they said, would disturb their sleep. Moreover, the possibility of getting plunked with a home run ball would prevent them from using their porches at night. Worse yet, fans from the upper deck would be able to look directly into their bedrooms, an invasion of privacy the residents found intolerable.

Twenty-five residents appeared at City Hall to protest the planned installation. But the lights went up anyway. The park was the first in the American League and the third in baseball with lights.

It cost $115,000 to bring night baseball to Shibe Park. The original installation included two free-standing towers, each 147 feet high, and six towers on the pavilion roofs. Each tower had eight banks of lights. The eight towers contained 780 lights altogether, each light giving off 1,500 watts. That gave the stadium some 1.2 million watts of electricity and more than 2 billion

During the 1920s, roof-top viewing was popular at Shibe Park along 20th Street. It was easy to see over the low right field wall.

candlepower, enough to light a highway running from Philadelphia to Cleveland.

The A's first night game was played May 16, 1939. Although the home team lost to the Cleveland Indians, 8–3, in 10 innings, it was a festive event, attended by numerous dignitaries. Said Will Harridge, president of the American League, "The lights at Shibe Park are wonderful. I could see details of a baseball game as well as I could if it had been daylight."

An employee of the stadium reported that his family saw the lights from their front porch in Clementon, New Jersey. He was one of 450 extra employees, including 56 ushers and 150 vendors, hired for the occasion. Ten additional mounted police were also on duty.

Although there were only seven night games played at Shibe Park the first year, baseball under the lights would become a regular fixture in all home schedules in future years. It would also provide some comic relief. Once a player whose name has been lost in the ages, thinking he was chasing a baseball, made a spectacular catch of an oversized moth. The Indians' Al Rosen suffered a broken nose when smacked by a pop fly he had lost in the lights.

The lights would also play a historical role in the All-Star Game. In 1943 the game was played at night at Shibe Park, the first time the contest was held under the lights. With 31,938 in attendance, Bobby Doerr's three-run homer carried the American League to a 5–3 victory. Vince DiMaggio had a single, triple, and homer for the National League, and Johnny Vander Meer struck out six batters. The game was delayed at one point for 65 minutes as city officials practiced a blackout.

Shibe Park was the scene of one other All-Star Game, a memorable five-inning contest in 1952. With the Phillies' Curt Simmons starting on the mound, the National League won, 3–2, before a crowd of 32,785. The game was halted because of rain, but not before A's pitcher Bobby Shantz etched his name in All-Star immortality. Shantz, who went on to win 24 games and the American League's MVP award that year, struck out Whitey Lockman, Jackie Robinson, and Stan Musial in order in the fifth inning. The feat prompted years of speculation as to what Shantz might have done had the contest not been halted.

The Shibe Park in which Shantz registered his amazing strikeout streak was not much different from the stadium the Phillies moved into in 1938. It was in both eras an attractive stadium, a good place to watch a ball game, and a vast improvement over old Baker Bowl.

The Phillies had been considering the move to Shibe Park for a long time. At one point, several years before their arrival, Connie Mack was so sure they were coming that he had an office and a clubhouse built for the Phillies on the ground floor. They sat empty for several years because the Phillies could not break their 99-year lease at Baker Bowl.

When they finally did arrive, the Phillies came with high expectations. The calamities that had plagued them throughout their years at Baker Bowl could be consigned to history. It was the dawning of a new era for the Phillies—or so they thought.

The club made its debut at Shibe Park in a Fourth of July doubleheader against the Boston Bees. A crowd of about 12,000 showed up. Before the game, Phillies president Gerry Nugent, no longer saddled with the outlandish $50,000 a year rental payments he had been forced to make at Baker Bowl, and his wife were presented a bouquet of flowers by the A's. A band played before the game and between innings.

In the absence of any further ceremony, the Phillies went out and lost the first game, 10–5. They came back to win the nightcap, 10–2, with Claude Passeau getting the win.

Passeau had lost the last game at Baker Bowl. He was delighted with the new stadium, which contrasted sharply with the old one. "It's a swell place to pitch," he said. "Jimmie Wilson told me to use a knee-high fast one as much as I wanted to. In Baker Bowl, that toss was usually good for a smack against the right field wall by lefthanded hitters. Today, when I let the number one go, I had no fear."

The hitters were just as happy. "The park was made for me," chortled

In the late 1940s, Shibe Park often drew large crowds for both the Phillies and Athletics.

Morrie Arnovich, who had stroked three hits in the second game and who no longer had to worry about swallowing beetles while playing on defense.

There was mixed reaction, though, among the fielders. "I felt five years younger and 100 percent safer," said third baseman Pinky Whitney. "I never knew when a ground ball was going to bounce off a pebble and go for a hit or hit me in the chin at Baker Bowl."

On the other hand, right fielder Tuck Stainback lost two fly balls in the sun. And center fielder Hersh Martin played a scoreboard carom so badly that Arnovich had to race over from left field to get the ball in right-center.

But nobody regretted the departure from Baker Bowl, even when the Phillies' batting averages began to dip. The Phillies' new-found luxury was a strong tonic for morale, even though it had no effect on the team's place in the standings.

When the park got lights in 1939, the Phillies participated in the evening outings. The team's first night game occurred on June 2 against the Pittsburgh Pirates. Kirby Higbe, acquired a few days earlier in a trade for Passeau, arrived in town just in time to pitch. Before a crowd limited to 9,858 by a driving rain, Higbe walked eight, and the Phillies lost, 5–2.

In the years that followed, there were more changes at the park. It was the first stadium to use a public address system, and the first to post the lineups of both teams on the scoreboard.

The Eagles, having left Baker Bowl for a four-year spell at Municipal Stadium in South Philadelphia, began playing at Shibe Park in 1940. They continued to play there until the 1958 season. The NFL All-Star Game was played at Shibe Park in 1942.

In the early 1940s, there was an unsuccessful drive to erect neon foul poles. Phillies players came and went with astonishing regularity as World War II took its toll on major league rosters. And outdoor prize fights and concerts were added to the park's repertoire of events. About the only thing that remained constant was Connie Mack's electrically heated dugout seat.

To youngsters, Shibe Park had a special charm. Kids could pay their 75-cent general admission fee and roam the park free of crowds and restrictions. The ritual for a kid was to go to the park early and see both teams take batting practice, sit back and watch the game, then collect autographs as the players left the main gate at 21st and Lehigh. The home team players usually parked their cars in the tiny lot across 21st Street. Visiting players piled into buses at the same corner. Autographs were easy to get in both cases. If a young hound was especially diligent, and it was getaway day for one of the teams, he could sprint the six blocks to North Philadelphia Station where the departing team could usually be found idling on the platform, awaiting its train.

The end of World War II brought about a surge in fan interest in baseball everywhere. Crowds began turning out for ball games in large numbers, and in 1946, the Phillies for the first time passed the one million mark in attendance. They attracted 1,045,247 fans. Although the A's had attracted a number of large crowds to Shibe Park, including a turnout of 38,800 for a July 13, 1931, game against the Washington Senators, the Phillies set their club record on May 11, 1947, when 41,660 (40,952 paid) crammed every available space in the park to see the Phillies and Brooklyn Dodgers in a Sunday doubleheader. At the time, Shibe Park's capacity was 33,000.

The Phillies were in fifth place, and the Dodgers, on their way to a National League pennant, were in third. But the pennant race wasn't the big attraction. After two previous games had been played in unfavorable weather, Philadelphia fans were flocking to the stadium to get a glimpse of a new phenomenon in baseball: a black major league player.

Jackie Robinson was in his first year in the big leagues, having been signed a year earlier by the Dodgers' Branch Rickey. In his first encounter with the Phillies earlier in the season at Ebbets Field, Robinson had been unmercifully harassed by Blue Jays' manager Ben Chapman, a southerner, and some of his players and coaches. Chapman had promised to continue his barrage when Robinson came to Philadelphia, but calmer heads had prevailed by game time on Sunday.

Spectators, many of them blacks attending their first major league game, began arriving at the stadium at 5 A.M., six and one-half hours before the gates opened. By game time, not only was every seat taken, but all standing room and aisle spaces were filled as well.

The fans certainly got their money's worth. Behind the pitching of Dutch Leonard and Schoolboy Rowe, the Phillies captured both games, 7–3 and 5–4. Phillies manager Chapman was ejected from the second game by umpire George Barr after protesting too strenuously that Brooklyn's Robinson had stepped into a pitch while trying to bunt, and should not be awarded first as a hit batter.

The final out of the game came when Phils center fielder Harry Walker made a diving catch of Pee Wee Reese's line drive. As Walker, stunned by his tumble, rolled over on his face, 1,000 fans poured onto the field to help him up.

The crowd was only the third largest in baseball that day. The Boston Braves and New York Giants performed before 51,840 at the Polo Grounds, and the Detroit Tigers and Chicago White Sox were watched by 45,755 at Comiskey Park.

A panoramic view across the outfield at Connie Mack Shibe Park in the early 1950s.

The main entrance of Shibe Park was at 21st Street and Lehigh Avenue.

But it was the largest crowd during the Phillies' tenure at Shibe Park. The A's drew a comparable gathering in 1934 when some 42,000 turned out to watch the Mackmen stop Schoolboy Rowe's 16-game winning streak with a 13–5 victory over the Tigers. Another large group appeared on July 16, 1948, for a doubleheader between the A's and the Cleveland Indians. Although an estimated 60,000 tried to enter the park for that game, 37,684 actually made it through the gates to see the Indians knock the A's out of first place with 6–1 and 8–5 wins.

In that same year, the right field wall came close to being removed. Connie Mack, wanting to build bleachers that would hold 18,000 additional spectators where the wall stood, petitioned the city to allow him to make the changes. His request was denied. As an alternative, Mack added box seats in left and right fields and turned all sideline seats in the park so they pointed toward home plate. The additions increased the seating capacity to 33,223.

Capacity was rarely approached, but the park was the site of some historic moments nonetheless. On June 18, 1948, a young bonus pitcher named Robin Roberts made his major league debut, pitching a five-hitter, but losing to the Pirates, 2–0. On June 2, nearly a year later, the Phillies hit five home runs, two by Andy Seminick, in a 10-run eighth inning to beat the Cincinnati Reds, 12–3.

The fans took a game into their own hands later in 1949. Although the Phillies had been involved in other forfeits, one that occurred on August 21 resulted from one of the ugliest events in which the club was involved.

The incident took place in the ninth inning of the second game of a doubleheader between the Phils and the Giants. The Phillies had won the first game, 4–0, but were losing the second game, 3–2, when New York's Joe Lafata slammed a low liner to center field. Richie Ashburn made what appeared to be a fine running catch, but second base umpire George Barr ruled that he had trapped the ball.

Ashburn charged to the infield to protest, claiming he had caught the ball eight inches off the ground. He was quickly joined in the argument by Del Ennis, Granny Hamner, and some others. Manager Eddie Sawyer called Barr's ruling "the most stupid decision I have ever seen."

The fans agreed. For the next 15 minutes, the crowd of 19,742 booed and hissed, and when the Phillies began to return to their positions after losing the argument with Barr, they threw bottles, cans, papers, and whatever else they could find onto the field. Both Ashburn and Ennis were nearly hit by flying objects.

Shibe Park was renamed Connie Mack Stadium in 1953. On some nights, huge crowds came to watch the Phillies.

Sawyer pulled his team from the field while public address announcer Dave Zinkoff urged the crowd to end the barrage. Despite his booming voice, the Zink's pleas were drowned out by the booing mob, a number of whom even jumped onto the field.

Another attempt was made at resuming play, but this time a tomato came crashing into umpire Al Barlick, and a bottle hit another official, Lee Ballanfant. That did it. The umpires awarded the Giants a 9–0 forfeit victory.

More pleasant events, though, were soon to follow for the Phillies. In 1950, Shibe Park finally had itself another pennant winner as the Whiz Kids captured the National League flag. It had been 19 years since a pennant flew at the stadium.

During that exhilarating season, the park was the scene of numerous special performances. The Phillies went into first place for good on July 25 with a doubleheader sweep of the Chicago Cubs, 7–0 and 1–0. Del Ennis drove in seven runs in the seventh and eighth innings of a 13–3 win over the Cubs. Jim

A scoreboard was purchased from the Yankees in 1956 and relocated to Connie Mack Stadium.

In the early 1960s, the Phillies often attracted scant crowds to Connie Mack Stadium, a sign of the club's losing teams.

Konstanty saved or won 38 games en route to an MVP award, Roberts had his first 20-win season, Eddie Waitkus came back from his gunshot wound, and the Whiz Kids attracted the attention of the whole nation.

On September 15 that year, the Phillies beat the Reds, 8–7, in 19 innings in the longest game ever played at Shibe Park. Ennis and Waitkus had five hits apiece.

The first and second games of the World Series were played at the stadium. There were 30,746 in attendance for the opener when Konstanty, a surprise starter, lost a heartbreaker to the New York Yankees, 1–0. The next afternoon, the crowd increased to 32,660 as Roberts had another close loss, 2–1.

In subsequent years, the stadium would have no events that matched the 1950 season. But the park continued to undergo changes. In 1953 its name was changed to Connie Mack Stadium in honor of the venerable A's owner. A year later, the A's headed west to Kansas City, and the Phillies were left as the sole baseball occupants.

Bob Carpenter bought the park from the A's for $1,657,000. He did so with some reluctance. "We need a ballpark as much as we need a hole in the head," he said.

Nevertheless, with the park in the Phillies' possession, the center field wall was shortened in 1955 from 468 to 447 feet. It was moved in again in 1968 to 410 feet.

As it always had been, the pregame batting cage was stored behind the fence in center field. Before each game, after batting practice was over, groundskeepers would dutifully wheel the metal cage across the diamond to its storage space. It was a ritual that Philadelphia baseball fans not only expected, but could almost visualize in their sleep.

After the 1955 season, the Phillies bought a new scoreboard. At least, it was new for them. Actually, it was the scoreboard from Yankee Stadium, the Phillies having purchased it from the New York Yankees. It replaced the one that had been installed by the A's in 1941. The new scoreboard went into use at Connie Mack Stadium in time for the 1956 season. Later, a clock was installed atop the scoreboard, some 75 feet high. Balls that hit it were considered home runs.

Carpenter, who by now was visualizing a Phillies stadium on a more grand scale elsewhere in the city, sold Connie Mack Stadium to a real estate developer for $600,000 in 1961. The park was sold again in 1964, this time to the owner of the Philadelphia Eagles, Jerry Wolman. The Phillies leased the stadium from its new owners.

While all of this was happening off the field, the Phillies were mixing the

Players run for cover and fans get set to charge the field after the last out of the final game in 1970.

good with the bad on the field. Roberts gave up a leadoff home run to Bobby Adams, then pitched a perfect game the rest of the way against the Reds in 1954. Ashburn won batting titles in 1955 and 1958. Willie Jones drove in eight runs in a 1958 game with the Cardinals. And Art Mahaffey struck out 17 Cubs in 1961.

That was also the year of the Phillies' infamous 23-game losing streak, a modern National League record.

The Dodgers' Sandy Koufax pitched a no-hitter against the Phillies in 1964 at Connie Mack Stadium. He also pitched the final regular season game of his career at the park in 1966.

Cincinnati's George Culver in 1968 and Montreal's Bill Stoneman in 1969 also hurled no-hitters at the stadium.

Groundskeeper John Godfrey removed home plate from Connie Mack Stadium the day after the last game in 1970.

A major fire struck Connie Mack Stadium in 1971, ruining what was left of the old ball park.

And in 1964, Chico Ruiz stole home to give the Reds a 1–0 triumph which started the Phillies on a 10-game losing streak that cost them the pennant.

In the 1960s the stadium was the scene of some prodigious home run hitting by the Phillies' Dick Allen. Three clouts in particular stand out. One was a 529-foot drive in 1965 that cleared the roof in left-center field. Another came in 1967 and cleared the center field wall between the flagpole and the stands, the only ball ever to leave the park at that point. A third slam of Allen's cleared the top of the scoreboard, which was 50 feet high, in right-center field.

In all, Allen hit 15 balls over the left field roof and another eight that crashed against the billboards *atop* the roof. He and Foxx reign as the champions of long-distance clouting at Shibe/Connie Mack, while visiting players such as Ruth, Williams, who put a ball into a backyard on 20th Street, Mickey Mantle, Willie Mays, Frank Howard, and Willie McCovey also swatted memorable tape-measure home runs there.

Connie Mack Stadium was always regarded as a hitters' park, but it was also a good park in which to see a game. Despite some obstructed seats, most fans got good views of the proceedings, especially because seats were generally close to the field.

The clubhouses were small, and players had to walk across a corridor beneath the stands to get to them. Bullpens were located at the far end of each foul line. The Phillies had always used the left field bullpen until Gene Mauch took over the team. Mauch switched the Phils' pen to right field so that he could watch his relievers from the dugout along the third base line.

The Phillies passed the one million mark in attendance six times (1946, 1950, 1957, 1964, 1965, 1966) while playing at the stadium. The largest single-season attendance was 1,425,891 in 1964.

In its final years, the stadium deteriorated badly, as did the neighborhood around it. Vandalism was on the rise, parking was scarce, and the facilities had become obsolete. Largely because of the stadium's location, the Phillies drew only 519,414 in 1969, despite having a decent fifth-place club.

The end of the aging stadium was approaching. By 1970 it was the oldest major league baseball park in the country. A new field was being readied for the Phillies in South Philadelphia. On October 1, 1970, the stadium played host to its last of more than 6,000 baseball games.

The Phillies were pitted against the Montreal Expos in a game that would decide last place. But 31,822 fans showed up. And the Phillies brought back Claude Passeau, who won the first game for the team when it became a regular tenant at Shibe Park in 1938.

"I remember all the good things that happened here," said Mauch, the Expos' manager and former Phillies pilot. "I don't remember the bad things."

From the sixth inning on, the steady sound of hammering could be heard in the stands as fans prospected for souvenirs. Others used wrenches, screwdrivers, and whatever else they had brought to tear away seats and other memorabilia.

The game was delayed frequently by spectators running onto the field to scoop up dirt or into the dugouts to grab bats, balls, or gloves or to shake hands with the players. Public address announcer Art Wolfe's repeated requests for order were ignored.

After the game, the Phillies planned to have a helicopter swoop down and lift away home plate, carting it off to its new home in South Philadelphia. The team also planned to give away parts of the stadium as souvenirs. But the chaos was so great that the plans were abandoned.

The contest was over in the bottom of the 10th inning when Oscar Gamble singled home Tim McCarver to give the Phillies a 2–1 victory. As soon as McCarver crossed the plate, thousands of fans poured onto the field in further search of trophies. So, too, did Phils manager Frank Lucchesi. His mission was to give Gamble a victory hug.

By the time Lucchesi caught up with Gamble, the two were surrounded by frenzied fans. Gamble brushed off Lucchesi's attempted celebration. "Run, man, run like hell," Oscar yelled. "We'll be happy later."

The last winning pitcher at Connie Mack Stadium was Dick Selma. The last loser was Howie Reed. The last word on the park was delivered by Bob Carpenter. "Progress," he said, "I guess that's what you'd have to call it. But damn, I hate to leave this place."

The Phillies left having won 1,205 and lost 1,340 in their 32½ years at the park.

A year after the team vacated the stadium, much of it was destroyed by fire. The financially troubled Wolman continued to own the park, but liens and back taxes mounted, plunging the site into heavy debt. Ultimately, the park was sold to a developer, and the remains of the building were demolished in 1976.

There were plans to use the site for a hospital, for an industrial park, and for a supermarket. None materialized. The site existed as a weed and rat-infested lot filled with debris until residents successfully persuaded the city to clean it up.

The lot sat vacant until 1990 when a church was built there. The Deliverance Evangelistic Church, with a sanctuary that seats 5,100, takes up much of the plot that was once a ballfield. It was a field that in its day played a major role in the history of big league baseball.

Veterans Stadium

On the day that Veterans Stadium opened in 1971, a whole city breathed a collective sigh of relief. The opening of the stadium marked the conclusion of a long and often acrimonious struggle that dated back to the mid-1950s.

At least it could be said that the park's opening was better late than never. But getting to that point was a tedious and frustrating process, not to mention costly.

As early as 1953, Mayor Richardson Dilworth was anxious to have a new stadium erected in Philadelphia. He had strong support, particularly from Judge Raymond Pace Alexander, then a member of City Council, millionaire builder John B. Kelly, Sr., and Phillies owner Bob Carpenter.

Dilworth envisioned a stadium that he figured would cost about $11 million. Over the next few years, several committees were appointed, one to determine whether a new stadium was feasible and another to select a site.

In the ensuing years, disagreements far outnumbered agreements. About the only certainty was that the Phillies, as well as the Eagles, were more than ready to abandon Connie Mack Stadium. Both Carpenter and Eagles president Frank McNamee went before the City Planning Commission to urge construction of a new municipal stadium as soon as possible.

Although it had originally been intended to have the stadium ready by 1959 or 1960, those years came and went. In 1961, Dilworth warned, "If we don't get a stadium, we'll lose major league sports, and people will think Philadelphia is a creepy city."

Finally, in 1964, a referendum was placed on the ballot giving voters the chance to approve the city's taking a $25 million loan with which to build the stadium. The measure passed by nearly 41,000 votes.

Meanwhile, the arguments raged on. Should the stadium be domed or undomed? Should it be round or square? Scores of questions were raised, none with answers. Even the Phillies and the Eagles bickered over the shape of the stadium.

Of even greater disagreement was the location of the park. From the time the stadium was first proposed until it was finally opened, at least nine different sites were recommended. Carpenter originally favored a field at 33rd Street and Columbia Avenue in Fairmount Park. A developer proposed a site in Cherry Hill, New Jersey. City officials suggested a park at 30th Street Station over the railroad tracks. A spot in Torresdale along the Delaware River, Roosevelt Park at Broad and Pattison, Eighth and Race, and 11th and Vine were also recommended. There was also consideration given to developing a sports complex with a stadium and an indoor arena that would make Philadelphia "the sports capital of the world." The notion was rejected because of the $75 million price tag.

Eventually, the present location was chosen. By then, though, the $25 million cost the voters had approved had become obsolete. So in 1967, voters were asked to grant the city power to make an extra $13 million loan. Again, the electorate voted to increase its own taxes.

Finally, on October 2, 1967, a ground-breaking ceremony was held at the Broad Street and Pattison Avenue site. "Today," said Mayor James Tate as he stuck a spade in the ground, "we, the city officials, are demonstrating that we are prudently spending the $38 million which has been allocated by the voters of Philadelphia to afford them the prestige of having the greatest sports stadium in the nation."

Tate's wielding a shovel did not, however, resolve the existing disputes, one of which had become the matter of selecting a name for the stadium. Furthermore, the opening of the stadium, originally intended to happen eight

In 1976, the wrecking ball did what the baseball could never do—it turned Connie Mack Stadium into rubble.

years earlier, was obviously going to miss its target date of 1967, not to mention 1968, 1969, and 1970.

There was one delay after another. A squabble persisted over the certification of funds. Bickering continued over the stadium's design. There was a fight over the scoreboard. And a major snowstorm, a strike, a fire, heavy rain, accidents, high winds, and even a grand jury probe over the misuse of funds and materials contributed to further setbacks in the construction schedule.

At least, a name was finally picked. Despite newspaper polls that indicated a preference for names such as Philadelphia Stadium or the Philadium, City Council president Paul D'Ortona pushed through a bill to have the complex called Philadelphia Veterans Stadium in honor of the city's war veterans.

Veterans Stadium was at long last finished in 1971. Built on a 74-acre site that was formerly marshland, the park was made in the shape of an octorad, an architect's word that comes from the Latin words for eight and radius, or eight points on eight radii.

The stadium was constructed with 87,000 cubic yards of concrete, 7,600 tons of reinforced steel, and 1,440 tons of structural steel. An Astro turf floor covered the entire playing surface of 146,000 square feet. From ground level, the park rose 160 feet high. It was 840 feet in diameter. The left and right field lines were 330 feet, and it was 408 feet to dead center field.

Seating capacity for baseball was originally 56,371. The stadium had parking for 12,000 cars. There were 13 escalators, two miles of ramps, only two sets of stairs, 62 rest rooms, and 60 concession stands. An animated, $3 million scoreboard was operated by a computer.

The multicolored, multipurpose stadium, the largest in the National League and the third largest in the major leagues, was completed at a final cost of about $52 million.

The Phillies made their long-awaited debut at Veterans Stadium on April 10. As was the case when they closed Connie Mack Stadium the previous year, the opponent was again the Montreal Expos. "It's got to be the best new park in baseball," said Montreal manager Gene Mauch. "It looks like they've taken the good things from all the other new parks, added some things of their own, and whipped them into a pretty good place."

The game was preceded by the usual hoopla that accompanies occasions such as the opening of new stadiums. The city gave out more than 100,000 free tickets to assure a full house. Mayor Tate and baseball commissioner Bowie Kuhn were in attendance. Four F-106 Air Force jets flew over the stadium; TV

With the Navy Yard, JFK Stadium, and the Spectrum in the background, Veterans Stadium rises from the ground during the early stages of construction in 1969.

host Mike Douglas sang the National Anthem; 1,000 balloons were released; Expos' owner Jean Trapeau rode onto the field in a dog sled; and Phils catcher Mike Ryan caught a ball that was dropped 150 feet from a helicopter.

After struggling with wind currents to make the catch, Ryan presented the ball to Marine Corporal Frank Mastrogiovanni, a Vietnam veteran who had lost both legs in combat. He threw out the first pitch.

The largest baseball crowd at the time in the history of Pennsylvania, 55,352, packed the stadium, despite temperatures in the low 40s. Although the atmosphere was full of gaiety, there were some problems with the new park, including a broken water pipe on the first level and long waiting lines at the concession stands. "Forty-five million bucks and you can't even get a hot dog," one fan grumbled.

Jim Bunning was the starting pitcher for the Phillies. On his first pitch, Montreal's Boots Day sent a grounder to the mound, and Bunning threw to first baseman Deron Johnson to record the stadium's first out.

Although the Expos' Ron Hunt scored the first run on Bob Bailey's double, the Phillies went on to win, 4–1. It was Mauch's first opening day loss in Philadelphia.

Larry Bowa got the park's first hit, a triple, and Don Money clubbed the first home run. Bunning got the first win with Joe Hoerner getting a save and Bill Stoneman taking the loss. "Getting to pitch the first game here meant a lot to me," said Bunning, working his 17th and final big league season. "I was pretty keyed up."

For the rest of the year, Veterans Stadium proved to be just the right tonic to revive fan interest. Some 1,511,223 spectators flocked to the park, more than double the number the previous year and a temporary Phillies record.

Starting with 1971, the Phillies have attracted more than one million fans every year. In 1976 the club cracked the two million barrier, drawing 2,480,150. Since then, the attendance has exceeded two million nine more times, reaching a high in 1979 with 2,775,011.

During those years, the Phillies have added to the entertainment package, although it is not hard to find baseball purists who object to the intrusion of "gimmicks" at the games. Each opening day game has been a special attraction, with former executive vice president and current president Bill Giles masterminding an assortment of ways to deliver the first ball.

Among the various attempts—some successful, some not—have been

The completed Vet opened for business in 1971 at Broad Street and Pattison Avenue.

people flying out of chutes on kites, two of whom crashed into center field, a man parachuting from an airplane, another blasting out of a cannon, a stunt artist dangling from a trapeze suspended from a helicopter, and a horseman from Boston, naturally, for the Bicentennial year. Kite Man I, II, and III, Cannon Man, Cycle Man, Parachute Man, and others have all come in the name of delivering the first ball.

One of the most spectacular stunts at the stadium took place in 1972 when high wire artist Karl Wallenda walked across the top of the Vet, from one side to the other. Wallenda did a handstand in the middle of his walk. Considering the wind currents that exist at the stadium, it was an astonishing accomplishment.

In recent years, the Vet has also been the residence of an odd-looking creature who cavorts around the field and in the stands, teasing players, umpires, and fans alike, dancing feverishly, and careening about on a three-wheeled cycle of some kind. He is the Phillie Phanatic, in real life Dave Raymond, and his good humor and excellent sense of timing have made him far and away the most entertaining mascot in the major leagues.

Veterans Stadium has also been the scene of some of the crowning achievements in Phillies history. Some of the longest hits at the park came off the bat of Greg Luzinski. One of his drives was particularly memorable. It was a 500-foot belt that struck the Liberty Bell in center field in 1972.

Also in 1972, the Phillies scored 11 runs in the seventh inning of an 11–4 win over the San Francisco Giants at Veterans Stadium. It was the biggest inning for the club in 38 years.

The Vet has been the site of a number of outstanding accomplishments by pitcher Steve Carlton. In 1972, Carlton beat the Cincinnati Reds for his 15th consecutive win, the longest win streak in Phillies history. Carlton also registered his 200th career victory at the Vet, a 13–2 decision over the Houston Astros in 1978. Carlton pitched three one-hitters at the Vet—in 1975 against the New York Mets, in 1979 against the Mets again, and in 1980 against the St. Louis Cardinals. And in 1981, he recorded his 3,000th strikeout at the park.

The longest game at Veterans was a 20-inning affair in which the Phillies

One of the most memorable events ever to occur at Veterans Stadium came on Memorial Day, 1976, when high-wire artist Karl Wallenda walked across the top of the stadium on a tightrope is what was probably the Phillies' most dazzling promotion.

defeated the Atlanta Braves, 5–4, in 1973. Two days after that battle, the Braves and Phillies played before a crowd of 60,120, then the second largest one-game attendance in National League history. A throng of 63,346 attending a twin bill in 1978 between the Phillies and Pittsburgh Pirates was then the second highest total at a National League doubleheader.

Ironically, the Phillies have never clinched a division title in Philadelphia. But the Phillies have participated in five league championship series at the Vet.

The first was in 1976. That was also the year the Phillies played host to the All-Star Game, which was won, 7–1, by the National League before a crowd of 63,974. Five Phillies, Luzinski, Bob Boone, Mike Schmidt, Larry Bowa, and Dave Cash, played in the game.

In their first three years in the playoffs, the Phillies failed to win a single game at the Vet. In 1976, the club bowed to the Reds in Games One and Two at home. The Dodgers captured the third and fourth games of the 1977 series at the Vet. And the Phillies lost the first and second games of the 1978 playoffs to Los Angeles. The second loss of the 1977 series was especially grating. Playing in a game-long downpour while officials steadfastly refused to halt the action, the Phillies lost a controversial 4–1 decision to Tommy John.

The Phillies' losing playoff jinx was finally broken in 1980. After dropping six straight playoff games at home, the Phillies defeated Houston, 3–1, behind the pitching of Carlton and a two-run homer by Luzinski in the first game of the championship series.

The long drought was at last over, but even better days lay just ahead. By 1980 the capacity of Veterans Stadium had been pushed upward until it reached 65,000. In the second game of the playoffs, 65,476 herded into the park. But the Phillies lost to the Astros, 7–4, in 10 innings.

Nevertheless, the next time the Phillies appeared at the Vet was in the World Series. Having clinched the pennant in Houston, the team entered its first Series in 30 years, and only its third in the club's history. In each Series up to this point, the Phillies had a different home field.

The crowds kept getting bigger. In the opener, 65,791 jammed the stadium to watch the Phillies gain their first Series victory since 1915 with a 7–6 triumph over the Kansas City Royals. The next day the Phillies won again, 6–4.

After winning one and losing two in Kansas City, the Phillies returned to the Vet for the sixth game of the Series. On the night of October 21, with 65,838 shrieking fans rocking its foundations, Veterans Stadium was the site of the greatest event in Phillies history.

The Phillies defeated the Royals, 4–1, to win the World Series.

When Tug McGraw struck out the Royals' Willie Wilson to end the game, it was as though all the ghosts of the Phillies' past had finally been exorcised. The miserable teams, the near-misses, the frustration, and the bad jokes that had trailed the Phillies from Recreation Park to Baker Bowl to Shibe Park were at long last overcome.

Since that glorious moment in Phillies history, Veterans Stadium has been the home of additional milestones.

In 1981, Pete Rose tied the National League record for most hits in a career when on June 10 he singled off the Astros' Nolan Ryan for his 3,630th safety. It was that last game before the season was interrupted by a players' strike. When play resumed two months later, Rose broke the record on August 10 with a single off Mark Littell of the Cardinals. Stan Musial, the man whose record Rose broke, was at the Vet for the event.

Later that same year, Schmidt reached another pinnacle in his career. The soon-to-be two-time MVP and five-time home run king slammed another of his numerous blasts out of the park in a game on September 10 against the Pirates' Kent Tekulve. It was Schmidt's 310th career home run, a record for a Philadelphia baseball player. The mark had been held by the A's Jimmie Foxx.

At the end of 1981 the Phillies were back in the playoffs. But this time it was in a series pitting the first- and second-half winners of the division, a system devised because of the players' strike.

After falling behind at Montreal, the second-half winners, two games to none, the Phillies came back at the Vet to win, 6–2 and 6–5. But a 3–0 Expo

Through its two decades, Veterans Stadium has featured all the gimmicks of a modern, promotion-oriented ballpark.

victory in the fifth game ended the Phillies' season and their Veterans Stadium streak of five straight post-season wins.

Veterans Stadium was again the site of playoffs and a World Series in 1983. In the LCS the Phillies defeated the Los Angeles Dodgers in four games, the last two wins coming at the Vet. The clincher, the first Phillies pennant won at the Vet, came on October 8 when the Phillies rode the home runs of Gary Matthews and Sixto Lezcano to a 7–2 victory.

In the World Series that followed, the Phillies returned home after splitting a pair of games in Baltimore against the Orioles and lost all three games at the Vet. In the final game, a 5–0 defeat, 67,064 fans packed the Vet to watch the Phillies' futility.

Since then, there have been no more playoff or World Series events at the Vet. For the next decade the Phillies settled into a routine of mediocrity, all the while, however, putting approximately two million fans in the seats each season.

In their first 21 seasons at the Vet, the Phillies averaged 2,057,298 fans per year. The team drew as many as 63,816 for a night game with Cincinnati in 1984.

Milestone events continued to happen at the Vet, even though the team had little success in the standings. Emotional farewell nights were held for Steve Carlton and Mike Schmidt. On August 15, 1990, Terry Mulholland pitched the first nine-inning no-hitter at the Vet. In beating the San Francisco Giants, 6–0, Mulholland also gave the Phillies their first no-hitter at home in the 20th century. On April 28, 1991, the Phillies added another distinction, recording their first triple play at the Vet and the club's first tri-killing since 1968. Randy Ready snared Tony Gwynn's line drive, stepped on second base, and threw to Ricky Jordan at first.

In recent years, the stadium has undergone a change in playing surface while adding new luxury sky boxes at the roof level of the park and a new electronic message board in center field. A considerable amount of repair work has also been done to the Vet, but in places the stadium has been a victim of the aging process, eroding and falling into a state of disrepair that its owners, the city of Philadelphia, could not afford to fix.

The Phillies have dug deep into their own pockets to maintain the stadium. Occasionally, thought has been given to the possibility of the team building a baseball-only park. Because of a lack of money and appropriate space, however, such an idea has never materialized, and the Vet continues to be the home of the Phillies. It is a home that has carved a memorable niche in the history of Phillies baseball.

PHILLIES HOME RECORDS AT EACH STADIUM

Park	Years	W	L	T	Pct
Recreation Park	1883–86	102	117	5	.466
Baker Bowl	1887–1938	1,957	1,778	29	.524
University of Pennsylvania	1894	5	1	0	.833
Columbia Park	1903	6	9	1	.400
Shibe Park/Connie Mack Stadium	1927,1938–70	1,205	1,340	13	.473
Veterans Stadium	1971–92	929	744	2	.555

7

The Hall of Famers

There are 30 plaques hanging on the walls of the baseball Hall of Fame at Cooperstown, New York, that acknowledge the superior performances of men who have been connected in one way or another with the Phillies.

Although some of those affiliations with the Phillies are tenuous, the group of Hall of Famers includes some of the most illustrious names in baseball history. Ten of the players won a combined total of 18 batting championships (not all while playing with the Phillies). Nine hitters won 21 home run crowns. Nine pitchers won 20 games or more 56 times. And three men elected to the Hall as managers won 15 pennants.

Most of the 30 men earned their Hall of Fame credentials with teams other than the Phillies. Many either started their careers in Philadelphia, then went on to reach greater heights elsewhere, or ended their careers with the Phillies after performing brilliantly for other teams.

Only four players—Pete Alexander, Ed Delahanty, Chuck Klein, and Robin Roberts—won entry into the baseball shrine mainly because of their records with the Phillies. Two others, Billy Hamilton and Sam Thompson, had their best years in Philadelphia, but gave superb accounts of themselves with other teams, too. And five players—Dave Bancroft, Elmer Flick, Ferguson Jenkins, Nap Lajoie, and Eppa Rixey—broke in with the Phillies, but essentially merited Hall of Fame induction for their work after departing from Philadelphia. Others—Roger Connor, Tom McCarthy, and Casey Stengel—made brief stops on the way from and to other places.

By far the largest group consists of players who came to the Phillies in the twilights of their careers: Chief Bender, Dan Brouthers, Hugh Duffy, Johnny Evers, Jimmie Foxx, Hughie Jennings, Tim Keefe, Joe Morgan, Kid Nichols, Paul Waner, and Hack Wilson. Most played only a year or two in Philadelphia.

Bucky Harris, Harry Wright, and Stengel were elected to the Hall as managers. Three others—Earle Combs, Bob Lemon, and Herb Pennock—were inducted as players, but performed other duties for the Phillies, the first two as coaches and the latter as a general manager.

Power-hitting Jimmie Foxx (left) posted Hall of Famer numbers in the American League before being welcomed in 1945 by the Phillies and manager Ben Chapman.

Grover Cleveland Alexander

Pitcher
Phillies: 1911–17, 1930
Major leagues: 1911–30
Elected: 1938
Birthplace: Elba, Nebraska
B: February 26, 1887
D: November 4, 1950
Batted right; threw right

A member of the third group of players inducted into the Hall of Fame, Grover Alexander was the second Phillies player selected for the baseball shrine. One of the great pitchers in the history of the game, Alexander is tied with Christy Mathewson as the third winningest pitcher in the major leagues. He ranks second in career shutouts and ninth in innings pitched. A 28-game winner in his rookie season in 1911, Alex never won less than 19 games in his first seven years with the Phillies. He won more than 30 games three times, including 1915 when his 31–10 mark led the Phillies to the National League pennant. That year Alex tossed four one-hitters and three two-hitters. His fourth one-hitter clinched the pennant for the Phillies. Subsequently, his 3–1 win over the Boston Red Sox in the first game of the World Series was the only Phillies Series win until 1980. After he was traded from the Phillies in 1918, Alexander was a 20-game winner twice for the Chicago Cubs and once for the St. Louis Cardinals, the latter in 1927 when he was 40 years old.

	W	L	Pct	ERA	G	CG	IP	H	BB	SO	ShO
Phillies	190	91	.676	2.31	338	220	2,514	2,131	561	1,409	61
Career	373	208	.642	2.56	696	439	5,189	4,868	953	2,199	90

David James Bancroft

Shortstop
Phillies: 1915–20
Major leagues: 1915–30
Elected: 1971
Birthplace: Sioux City, Iowa
B: April 20, 1891
D: October 9, 1972
Batted left and right; threw right

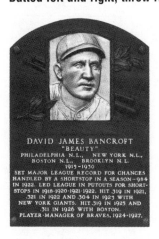

The first outstanding shortstop of the Phillies and certainly one of the best the club ever had at that position, Dave Bancroft was a fiery switch-hitter with a strong arm who got his nickname—Beauty—from his smooth fielding. As a rookie, he was the spark plug on the Phillies' 1915 pennant-winning team. Bancroft had come to the club following his discovery as a cross-handed batter in the Pacific Coast League. He gave the Phillies nearly five and one-half seasons of brilliant play at shortstop. After the Phillies traded him in 1920, Bancroft became even better. His hitting improved to the point that he had three straight .300 seasons for the New York Giants. He hit above .300 twice more during a four-year stint as playing-manager for the Boston Braves. Dave played two seasons with the Brooklyn Dodgers before finishing his 16-year career with the Giants.

	G	AB	H	BA	RBI	R	2B	3B	HR	SA	SB
Phillies	670	2,523	634	.251	162	331	89	20	14	.319	64
Career	1,913	7,182	2,004	.279	591	1,048	320	77	32	.358	145

The pitching exploits of Chief Bender were essentially associated with the Philadelphia Athletics, a team for which the one-quarter Chippewa Indian toiled for 12 seasons from 1903 through 1914. During that period, Bender helped the A's win five American League pennants and three World Championships. Connie Mack called Bender his "greatest clutch pitcher." Chief was a 20-game winner only twice, but his outstanding control, whistling fastball, and superb intelligence made him one of the top pitchers of his era. He pitched a no-hitter in 1910. After playing the 1915 season in the Federal League, he joined the Phillies, and for two years split his time between starting and relieving. Bender had some standout games with the Phillies, particularly in 1917 when he posted an 8–2 record and beat the pennant-winning New York Giants several times.

Charles Albert Bender

Pitcher
Phillies: 1916–17
Major leagues: 1903–17, 1925
Elected: 1953
Birthplace: Brainerd, Minnesota
B: May 5, 1883
D: May 22, 1954
Batted right; threw right

	W	L	Pct	ERA	G	CG	IP	H	BB	SO	ShO
Phillies	15	9	.625	2.75	47	12	236	221	60	86	4
Career	210	128	.621	2.45	459	261	3,028	2,645	712	1,711	41

When he came to the Phillies, Dan Brouthers was 38 years old and in his 18th season in the big leagues. He could still hit, but his career was behind him, and his contribution to the Phillies was relatively small. In earlier years, though, Brouthers was one of·the premier hitters in the game. Owner of the ninth highest lifetime batting average in big league history, Dan won five batting championships, four in the National League and one in the American Association. His highest average was .374 in 1883. He was the home run king in 1881 and 1886, and six years in a row he led the league in slugging average. Brouthers played for 11 teams during his career, his longest term coming with Buffalo, a National League club with whom he played from 1881 to 1885. Dan hit over .300 for 16 consecutive years.

Dennis Joseph Brouthers

First baseman
Phillies: 1896
Major leagues: 1879–96, 1904
Elected: 1945
Birthplace: Sylvan Lake, New York
B: May 8, 1858
D: August 2, 1932
Batted left; threw left

	G	AB	H	BA	RBI	R	2B	3B	HR	SA	SB
Phillies	57	218	75	.344	41	42	13	3	1	.445	7
Career	1,673	6,711	2,296	.342	1,295	1,523	460	205	106	.520	256

Earle Bryan Combs

Coach
Phillies: 1954
Major leagues: 1924–35 (player)
Elected: 1970
Birthplace: Pebworth, Kentucky
B: May 14, 1899
D: July 21, 1976
Batted left; threw right

Although he was not among the most prominent names on the mighty New York Yankees teams of his era, Earle Combs was one of the club's steadiest hitters. Eight times he hit above .300 during a career that spanned just 12 seasons in the major leagues. Earle hit .356 on the great Yankee team of 1927. That year, he led the American League in hits with 231 and in triples, one of three times he paced the circuit in three-baggers. Combs hit .350 in four World Series, the 10th best mark in the majors. Earle was also an outstanding center fielder, who covered a considerable amount of ground while playing between Babe Ruth and various other New York outfielders. After retiring as a player, Combs spent 10 years as a coach with the Yankees, then coached with the St. Louis Browns and Boston Red Sox before coming to the Phillies in 1954. Earle was in the dugout for the Phillies for just one year.

	G	AB	H	BA	RBI	R	2B	3B	HR	SA	SB
Career	1,454	5,748	1,866	.325	629	1,186	309	154	58	.462	96

Roger Connor

First baseman
Phillies: 1892
Major leagues: 1880–97
Elected: 1976
Birthplace: Waterbury, Connecticut
B: July 1, 1857
D: January 4, 1931
Batted left; threw left

As one of the leading first basemen of his era, Roger Connor established his reputation mostly while playing for the New York Giants. A 6–3, 220-pounder, Connor spent nine seasons with the Giants and three with their predecessors in Troy. Roger played only one season with the Phillies, who got him from the Giants and then traded him back to New York. His year in Philadelphia was not one of his better seasons, although he led the National League in doubles. During 17 years as a regular, Connor hit over .300 11 times. He led the league with a .371 mark, his career high, in 1885. One of the league's first power-hitters, Roger was also a good triples hitter. He ranks fifth in the majors in career triples. Connor wound up his 18 big league years with the St. Louis Cardinals.

	G	AB	H	BA	RBI	R	2B	3B	HR	SA	SB
Phillies	155	564	166	.294	73	123	37	11	12	.463	22
Career	1,997	7,794	2,467	.317	1,322	1,620	441	233	137	.486	244

Not only was Ed Delahanty probably the finest all-around hitter ever to wear a Phillies uniform, he was one of the greatest hitters in the major leagues. Ed's lifetime batting average is fourth highest on the all-time list. In a career spent mostly with the Phillies, except for one season in Cleveland with the Players' League and one and one-half years at the end of his life with the Washington Senators, Delahanty led the National League at one time or another in virtually every batting category. He hit over .300 12 different times, going over .400 three times. His .410 in 1899 won the National League batting championship, his first of two hitting crowns. He also won one home run title and three RBI championships. Delahanty, the Phillies' all-time leader in two hitting categories and second in six more, was the second major league player and the first Phillie to hit four home runs in one game.

Edward James Delahanty

Outfielder
Phillies: 1888–89, 1891–1901
Major leagues: 1888–1903
Elected: 1945
Birthplace: Cleveland, Ohio
B: October 30, 1867
D: July 2, 1903
Batted right; threw right

	G	AB	H	BA	RBI	R	2B	3B	HR	SA	SB
Phillies	1,555	6,359	2,213	.348	1,286	1,367	442	157	87	.508	411
Career	1,835	7,505	2,597	.346	1,464	1,599	522	185	101	.505	455

By the time he came to Philadelphia, Hugh Duffy's days as a player were essentially over. Duffy's primary role with the Phillies was as manager. Hugh piloted the club for three seasons, finishing eighth once and fourth twice. His eighth-place club was the first Phillies squad to lose 100 games. Duffy filled in once in a while in the outfield. His last season as a regular had been in 1899. Before that, Duffy had established himself as one of the top hitters in baseball, and his .438 average in 1894 ranks as the highest of all time. That year, his third of nine with the Boston Beaneaters, Duffy won the triple crown, leading in home runs (18) and RBI (145). Beginning in 1889 with the Chicago White Stockings, Duffy hit over .300 in 10 straight seasons. He was also the National League's home run king in 1897 and drove in more than 100 runs eight times.

Hugh Duffy

Outfielder-manager
Phillies: 1904–06
Major leagues: 1888–1901, 1904–06
Elected: 1945
Birthplace: Cranston, Rhode Island
B: November 26, 1866
D: October 19, 1954
Batted right; threw right

	G	AB	H	BA	RBI	R	2B	3B	HR	SA	SB
Phillies	34	87	25	.287	8	17	3	2	0	.368	3
Career	1,737	7,042	2,282	.324	1,299	1,553	325	118	105	.448	574

John Joseph Evers

Second baseman
Phillies: 1917
Major leagues: 1902–17, 1922, 1929
Elected: 1946
Birthplace: Troy, New York
B: July 21, 1881
D: March 28, 1947
Batted left; threw right

The middle of the famed Tinker to Evers to Chance double-play combination of the Chicago Cubs, Johnny Evers was a flashy fielder who played with such intensity that he was nicknamed "The Human Crab." Although not as spectacular as legend has made him out to be, Evers was a pioneer at perfecting the double-play pivot at second base. He spent 12 seasons in Chicago, anchoring a defense that helped the Cubs to four pennants in the early 1900s. Johnny was not an outstanding hitter; he hit .300 only twice in his career, including .341 in 1912. He was the league's MVP in 1914 with the pennant-winning Boston Braves. When he came to the Phillies, after three and one-half seasons with the Braves, Johnny was used strictly in a reserve capacity. It was the end of a long career for Evers, although he made brief appearances in the majors later, once at the age of 48. Evers managed the Cubs in 1913 and 1921 and the Chicago White Sox in 1923.

	G	AB	H	BA	RBI	R	2B	3B	HR	SA	SB
Phillies	56	183	41	.224	12	20	5	1	1	.279	8
Career	1,783	6,134	1,658	.270	538	919	216	70	12	.334	324

Elmer Harrison Flick

Right fielder
Phillies: 1898–1902
Major leagues: 1898–1910
Elected: 1963
Birthplace: Bedford, Ohio
B: January 11, 1876
D: January 9, 1971
Batted left; threw right

Of all the players who have slipped away from the Phillies, Elmer Flick was one of the most critical losses. Had he stayed in Philadelphia, with the friendly right field wall at Baker Bowl beckoning, Flick might have rated among the club's all-time hitting leaders. As it was, in just four seasons with the Phillies, Elmer still earned a special place in the club records. His .345 career average as a Phillie ranks as the third highest among all players. Elmer hit above .300 all four years in Philadelphia, reaching the apex in 1900 when he hit .378 and led the league in RBI with 110. After jumping to the Philadelphia Athletics in 1902 during the American League player raids, Flick was soon sold to the Cleveland Indians, with whom he spent the next nine seasons. Elmer led the American League in hitting with a .306 average in 1905. He hit above .300 four times in Cleveland, leading the league in triples three times and in stolen bases twice.

	G	AB	H	BA	RBI	R	2B	3B	HR	SA	SB
Phillies	537	2,023	683	.338	377	400	102	60	29	.490	119
Career	1,483	5,597	1,752	.313	757	948	268	164	48	.448	330

One of the great power-hitters in baseball history, Jimmie Foxx began and ended his 20-year career in Philadelphia. In between, he hit the ninth highest number of home runs in major league annals, including 58 in 1932, which tied for the most ever hit by a righthanded batter. Foxx ranks fourth on the all-time list in slugging percentage and sixth in RBI. In eight years as a regular with the Philadelphia Athletics and six more with the Boston Red Sox, Jimmie had 10 seasons of 35 or more home runs. He drove in 100 or more runs 13 times, and hit above .300 11 times. Foxx won four home run titles, two batting championships, three RBI crowns, and three MVP awards. He captured the triple crown in 1933. At the end of his career, Foxx played one season with the Phillies, seeing action as a reserve on a team whose roster was devastated by World War II. Jimmie played first and third base and pitched for the 1945 Phillies.

James Emory Foxx

First baseman
Phillies: 1945
Major leagues: 1925–42, 1944–45
Elected: 1951
Birthplace: Sudlersville, Maryland
B: October 22, 1907
D: July 21, 1967
Batted right; threw right

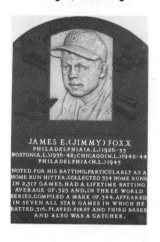

	G	AB	H	BA	RBI	R	2B	3B	HR	SA	SB
Phillies	89	224	60	.268	38	30	11	1	7	.420	0
Career	2,317	8,134	2,646	.325	1,921	1,751	458	125	534	.609	88

His name might not be a household word when it comes to Phillies baseball, but Billy Hamilton was one of the team's most stellar outfielders. Not only does Hamilton have the highest career batting average of any Phillie, he is also the team's all-time stolen base king. One of the swiftest players ever to step onto the diamond, Billy led his league in stolen bases seven times. Only Rickey Henderson and Lou Brock had more steals during their careers. Hamilton won two batting championships during his six years with the Phillies. His highest averages were .400 and .389, neither of which won batting crowns. Hamilton's lifetime average is the eighth highest in major league history. A leadoff batter who led the league in walks five times and who hit over .300 12 times, Billy was always among the league leaders in runs scored. In 1894 he scored 192 runs, a major league record that still stands. Billy was also an outstanding defensive player. The final six years of his career were spent with the Boston Beaneaters.

William Robert Hamilton

Center fielder
Phillies: 1890–95
Major leagues: 1888–1901
Elected: 1961
Birthplace: Newark, New Jersey
B: February 16, 1866
D: December 15, 1940
Batted left; threw left

	G	AB	H	BA	RBI	R	2B	3B	HR	SA	SB
Phillies	729	3,020	1,079	.357	367	874	126	51	23	.456	508
Career	1,591	6,268	2,158	.344	736	1,690	242	94	40	.432	937

Stanley Raymond Harris

Manager
Phillies: 1943
Major leagues: 1924–43, 1947–48, 1950–56
Elected: 1975
Birthplace: Port Jervis, New York
B: November 8, 1896
D: November 8, 1977
Batted right; threw right

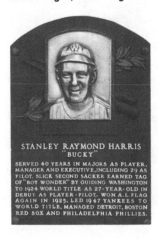

Bucky Harris had one of the longest managerial careers in major league history. It spanned 29 seasons. In that time, Harris worked in more games and captured more victories than any manager except Connie Mack and John McGraw. Only Mack lost more games than Bucky. Harris's stint with the Phillies was the low point of his career; he was fired midway through his first season following a series of acrimonious tussles with club president William Cox. Harris later helped to get Cox banned from baseball for betting on games. Over the rest of his career, Bucky managed three different times with the Washington Senators, twice with the Detroit Tigers, and once each with the Boston Red Sox and New York Yankees. As the "Boy Manager" in 1924 and 1925, Harris led the Senators to American League pennants and one World Series title. He led the Yankees to the World Championship in 1947.

	G	W	L	Pct
Phillies	90	38	52	.422
Career	4,407	2,157	2,218	.493

Ferguson Arthur Jenkins

Pitcher
Phillies: 1965–66
Major leagues: 1965–83
Elected: 1991
Birthplace: Chatham, Ontario
B: December 13, 1943
Bats right; throws right

One of the worst trades in Phillies history sent throw-in Ferguson Jenkins to the Chicago Cubs in 1966 along with Adolfo Phillips and John Herrnstein for Larry Jackson and Bob Buhl. The club believed that Jenkins did not possess a major league fastball. Fellow Hall of Famer Robin Roberts, then with the Cubs, quickly discovered otherwise, and Jenkins became one of the dominant pitchers of his era. The National League Cy Young Award winner in 1971, Jenkins won 20 or more games for six straight years with the Cubs beginning in 1967, including 24 in 1971. Traded to the Texas Rangers in 1974, he won a career-high 25 games in his first American League season. He is the only pitcher in major league history to strike out more than 3,000 batters while walking less than 1,000. He was a league leader in complete games four times, including 30 in 1971 when he led the National League in innings pitched with 325. He ranks ninth in major league history in strikeouts, 21st in shutouts, 24th in victories, and 17th in games started (594).

	W	L	Pct	ERA	G	CG	IP	H	BB	SO	ShO
Phillies	2	1	.667	2.57	8	0	14	10	3	12	0
Career	284	226	.557	3.34	664	267	4,498	4,142	997	3,192	49

The great teams in baseball have always had great shortstops. The Baltimore Orioles of the 1890s were no exception. On a team featuring players such as Willie Keeler, John McGraw, Wilbert Robinson, and Joe Kelley, Hughie Jennings was a hard-hitting, brilliant-fielding, base-running demon who helped spark the Orioles to three straight National League pennants. Over a five-year period, Jennings never hit less than .328, and once hit .398. He was equally adept on defense; he was usually among the league leaders in fielding. Jennings came to the Phillies from the Brooklyn Dodgers, who had picked him up from Baltimore as his career began to wind down. By that time, Jennings had moved to first base. The Phillies paid the lofty sum of $3,000 for him, but Hughie played only part-time in his two seasons in Philadelphia. Soon after leaving the Phillies, Jennings became a manager. He piloted the Detroit Tigers for 14 years, winning pennants in his first three years. After his playing days, he also attended law school at Cornell and became a practicing attorney in Scranton, Pennsylvania.

Hugh Ambrose Jennings

Shortstop–first baseman
Phillies: 1901–02
Major leagues: 1891–1903, 1907, 1909, 1912, 1918
Elected: 1945
Birthplace: Pittston, Pennsylvania
B: April 2, 1869
D: February 1, 1928
Batted right; threw right

	G	AB	H	BA	RBI	R	2B	3B	HR	SA	SB
Phillies	160	592	158	.267	71	70	34	6	2	.355	21
Career	1,285	4,903	1,527	.311	840	994	232	88	18	.406	359

Although he was in the twilight of his career when he came to the Phillies, Tim Keefe could still throw well enough to post a 19–16 record in 1892, his next-to-last year in baseball. Keefe pitched in the big leagues for 14 seasons, the last two and one-half with the Phillies. The eighth-winningest pitcher in major league history, Keefe ranks 12th in the majors in innings pitched and third in complete games. His best years were spent in New York, where he played for teams in the American Association, National League, and Players' League. He had a 41–27 record in 1883 and a 42–20 mark in 1886. Four other times, he won more than 30 games. Keefe broke into the majors in 1880 with Troy. Between 1885 and 1889, he was the mainstay of the New York Giants, winner of two National League pennants. During those five years, Keefe won 172 games, usually starting more than 50 and sometimes more than 60 times per season. He won 19 straight games in 1888 during a six-week period.

Timothy John Keefe

Pitcher
Phillies: 1891–93
Major leagues: 1880–93
Elected: 1964
Birthplace: Cambridge, Massachusetts
B: January 1, 1856
D: April 23, 1933
Batted right; threw right

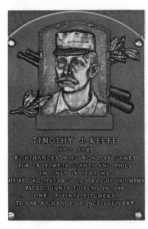

	W	L	Pct	ERA	G	CG	IP	H	BB	SO	ShO
Phillies	32	29	.532	3.21	72	57	569	550	207	215	3
Career	342	225	.603	2.62	600	557	5,061	4,452	1,224	2,527	39

Charles Herbert Klein

Right fielder
Phillies: 1928–33, 1936–39, 1940–44
Major leagues: 1928–44
Elected: 1980
Birthplace: Indianapolis, Indiana
B: October 7, 1904
D: March 28, 1958
Batted left; threw right

Although his entry into the Hall of Fame came much later than it should have, Chuck Klein demonstrated during a 17-year career that he was one of the outstanding lefthanded hitters in National League annals. He won four home run titles and one batting championship, and he led the league in slugging average three times, in RBI twice, in hits twice, and in runs three times. In 1933 he won the triple crown with a .368 batting average, 44 homers, and 120 RBI. Twice chosen as the League's Most Valuable Player, Chuck hit over .300 nine times, once reaching .386. He's among the Phillies' leaders in nearly every hitting category. Klein hit four home runs in one game. He was also a good base-runner, once leading the league in stolen bases, and a hustling outfielder with a strong throwing arm. He holds the modern major league one-season record among outfielders with 44 assists. The Phillies shipped Klein away twice, once to the Chicago Cubs and once to the Pittsburgh Pirates. They got him back each time. In his later years with the Phillies, Klein served as a coach, playing only occasionally.

	G	AB	H	BA	RBI	R	2B	3B	HR	SA	SB
Phillies	1,405	5,238	1,705	.326	983	963	336	64	243	.553	71
Career	1,753	6,486	2,076	.320	1,201	1,168	398	74	300	.543	79

Napolean Lajoie

Second baseman
Phillies: 1896–1900
Major leagues: 1896–1916
Elected: 1937
Birthplace: Woonsocket, Rhode Island
B: September 5, 1875
D: February 7, 1959
Batted right; threw right

Generally hailed as the finest second baseman the game of baseball has ever known, Nap Lajoie was the first Phillies player elected to the Hall of Fame. He entered the shrine in its second year of elections. Originally a first baseman, he was shifted to second in his third season with the Phillies. In five years with the Phillies, Nap's batting averages ranged from .324 to .378. A magnificent fielder as well as a brilliant hitter, Lajoie jumped to the Philadelphia Athletics of the American League in 1901, and led the league in batting with a .422 average, a league record that still exists. That year, he also led in home runs, RBI, hits, runs, and slugging average. After moving to the Cleveland Indians, Lajoie won two more batting crowns. He hit over .300 sixteen times during his 21-year career, which ended back with the A's. Nap is fifth in doubles and 10th in hits on the all-time career list. He managed the Indians from 1905 to 1909.

	G	AB	H	BA	RBI	R	2B	3B	HR	SA	SB
Phillies	492	2,055	721	.351	458	421	147	62	32	.529	87
Career	2,480	9,589	3,242	.338	1,599	1,502	657	163	83	.467	381

His connection with the Phillies was limited, but Bob Lemon was the team's pitching coach in 1961. That was the year the team lost 23 in a row and 107 during the season. As a pitcher for the Cleveland Indians, Lemon lost only a few more games than that in his whole career. Switched from third base to the mound in 1946, Bob became one of the American League's best hurlers, was a 20-game winner seven times, and was named three times as the league's outstanding pitcher. Lemon led the league in complete games five times. He pitched a no-hitter in 1948, one of two years in which he helped the Indians win the American League pennant. In the other pennant-winning year, 1954, he had his best record at 23–7. Lemon managed the Kansas City Royals, Chicago White Sox, and New York Yankees. His New York teams won two league pennants and the World Series in 1978.

Robert Granville Lemon

Coach
Phillies: 1961
Major leagues: 1946–58 (player)
Elected: 1976
Birthplace: San Bernardino, California
B: September 22, 1920
Bats left; throws right

	W	L	Pct	ERA	G	CG	IP	H	BB	SO	ShO
Career	207	128	.618	3.23	460	188	2,850	2,559	1,251	1,277	31

Undistinguished as his two years with the Phillies were as a reserve outfielder, Tommy McCarthy went on to enjoy a celebrated career with the St. Louis Browns of the American Association and then with the Boston Beaneaters in the National League. In Boston he and Hugh Duffy were inseparable, becoming known as "The Heavenly Twins." Duffy called McCarthy "the smartest ballplayer I ever saw." Tom's statistics weren't particularly glowing; he hit over .300 only four times in his 13 years in the majors. His best year was in 1890 when he hit .350 and led the league with 83 stolen bases. McCarthy patroled the outfield on Boston's pennant-winning clubs of the early 1890s. He wound up his career with the Brooklyn Dodgers. Owner of a rifle arm, McCarthy in 1888 gunned down 44 base-runners from his spot in right field.

Thomas Francis Michael McCarthy

Outfielder
Phillies: 1886–87
Major leagues: 1884–96
Elected: 1946
Birthplace: Boston, Massachusetts
B: July 24, 1864
D: August 5, 1922
Batted right; threw right

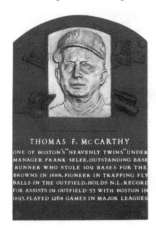

	G	AB	H	BA	RBI	R	2B	3B	HR	SA	SB
Phillies	26	97	18	.186	9	13	6	1	0	.268	16
Career	1,275	5,128	1,496	.292	666	1,069	192	53	44	.376	468

Joe Leonard Morgan

Second baseman
Phillies: 1983
Major leagues: 1963–84
Elected: 1990
Birthplace: Bonham, Texas
B: September 19, 1943
Bats left; throws right

Joe Morgan played only one year with the Phillies and played well for only one month. But the month was September, the year was 1983, and Morgan's hot bat was a major factor in the team's winning the National League pennant and reaching the World Series for the second time in four seasons. After struggling under .200 for most of the season, Morgan finished with a .230 average, his worst in 20 full seasons in the major leagues. He is best remembered as a strong hitter for Cincinnati's "Big Red Machine" that captured three National League championships and two World Series titles in the 1970s. He was one of nine players in major league history to win back-to-back Most Valuable Player awards (in 1975 and 1976 for the World Champions). In addition to his 2,517 hits, he drew 1,865 walks, leading the NL four times and reaching the century mark eight times, including six seasons in a row (1972–77). He broke into the majors with Houston in 1963 and got the game-winning hit against the Phillies that precipitated Gene Mauch's famous post-game destruction of the clubhouse food spread. He retired after the 1984 season, which he spent with the Oakland Athletics, his fifth major league team.

	G	AB	H	BA	RBI	R	2B	3B	HR	SA	SB
Phillies	123	404	93	.230	59	72	20	1	16	.403	18
Career	2,649	9,277	2,517	.271	1,113	1,650	449	96	268	.427	689

Charles Augustus Nichols

Pitcher
Phillies: 1905–06
Major leagues: 1890–1901, 1904–06
Elected: 1949
Birthplace: Madison, Wisconsin
B: September 14, 1869
D: April 11, 1953
Batted right; threw right

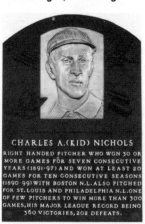

In the 1890s, Kid Nichols and Cy Young were the two best pitchers in the major leagues. Nichols, who hurled from 1890 to 1901 for the Boston Beaneaters, won 30 games or more in seven consecutive seasons. He won 20 or more four other times, finishing his 15-year career tied for sixth place in all-time career wins. He's fourth in complete games and 11th in innings pitched. Nichols won 35 games in 1892. After being out of the big leagues for two seasons, he returned in 1904 as player-manager of the St. Louis Cardinals, and at the age of 35 posted a 21–13 record. He came to the Phillies in mid-1905 after being dismissed by the Cardinals. He won 10 games in three months for the Phillies. In 1906, Nichols pitched in four games, but with little left in his arm, called a halt to his long and distinguished career.

	W	L	Pct	ERA	G	CG	IP	H	BB	SO	ShO
Phillies	10	7	.588	2.82	21	16	150	146	41	51	1
Career	362	207	.636	2.95	621	533	5,086	4,912	1,268	1,868	48

Elected to the Hall of Fame as a pitcher, Herb Pennock's affiliation with the Phillies was as the club's general manager after the team was purchased by Bob Carpenter. While serving in that capacity, Pennock was the architect of the Phillies' farm system, which in subsequent years produced the bulk of the 1950 pennant-winning team. Herb's career as a player spanned 22 seasons. He broke in with the Philadelphia Athletics in 1912 but didn't become successful until joining the Boston Red Sox in 1915. Pennock's best years were spent with the New York Yankees, for whom he pitched from 1923 to 1933. His top years were in 1924 (21–9) and 1926 (23–11), his only 20-win seasons. Pennock finished his career with the Red Sox. He also had a 5–0 record in five World Series.

Herbert Jeffries Pennock

General manager
Phillies: 1943–48
Major leagues: 1912–34
Elected: 1948
Birthplace: Kennett Square, Pennsylvania
B: February 10, 1894
D: January 30, 1948
Batted left and right; threw left

	W	L	Pct	ERA	G	CG	IP	H	BB	SO	ShO
Career	241	162	.598	3.61	617	248	3,558	3,900	916	1,227	35

Despite his eight seasons with the Phillies at the start of his major league career, Eppa Rixey was not elected to the Hall of Fame on the strength of his performances in Philadelphia. The University of Virginia graduate had only mediocre success with the Phillies, only once winning more than 20 games and twice losing more than 20. He had an 11–12 record on the 1915 pennant-winning team, and lost the final game of the World Series. The following year his 22–10 mark was by far his best as a Phillie. After being traded to the Cincinnati Reds, however, Rixey, who stood a towering 6–5, blossomed into a consistent pitcher. He was a three-time 20-game winner, his top effort being 25–13 in 1922. Generally regarded as the best lefthanded pitcher in Cincinnati history, Rixey hurled for the Reds until he was 42. Altogether, he spent 21 seasons in the major leagues.

Eppa Rixey

Pitcher
Phillies: 1912–17, 1919–20
Major leagues: 1912–17, 1919–33
Elected: 1963
Birthplace: Culpepper, Virginia
B: May 3, 1891
D: February 28, 1963
Batted right; threw left

	W	L	Pct	ERA	G	CG	IP	H	BB	SO	ShO
Phillies	87	103	.458	2.83	252	100	1,604	1,518	479	690	16
Career	266	251	.515	3.15	692	290	4,495	4,633	1,082	1,350	39

Robin Evan Roberts

Pitcher
Phillies: 1948–61
Major leagues: 1948–66
Elected: 1976
Birthplace: Springfield, Illinois
B: September 30, 1926
Bats left and right; throws right

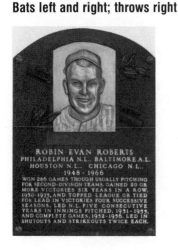

The all-time leader in most of the Phillies' pitching categories, Robin Roberts was one of the premier pitchers in the National League during the early 1950s when he won 20 or more games six years in a row. In 1950 he pitched the Phillies to the National League pennant, winning his 20th game to clinch the flag on the last day of the season. Voted once as the Major League Player of the Year and three times as the major league's outstanding pitcher, his best season was in 1952 when he posted a 28–7 record. He was the starting pitcher in five consecutive All-Star Games, led the league in complete games five times, and pitched three one-hitters. After a 14-year career with the Phillies, he divided the final five years of his major league career between the Baltimore Orioles, Houston Astros, and Chicago Cubs. Robbie won 37 games in his first three years with Baltimore. His career total of wins ranks 22d on the all-time major league list.

	W	L	Pct	ERA	G	CG	IP	H	BB	SO	ShO
Phillies	234	197	.543	3.45	529	272	3,740	3,661	718	1,871	35
Career	286	245	.539	3.41	676	305	4,689	4,582	902	2,357	45

Charles Dillon Stengel

Outfielder
Phillies: 1920–21
Major leagues: 1912–25 (player)
Elected: 1966
Birthplace: Kansas City, Missouri
B: July 30, 1890;
D: September 29, 1975
Batted left; threw left

Casey Stengel gained admittance into the Hall of Fame as a manager, although his connection with the Phillies was as a fun-loving outfielder. Stengel hit .292 as the club's regular right fielder in 1920, and was hitting .305 after 24 games when he was traded in 1921. His managerial career covered 25 seasons during which Casey won 10 pennants and seven World Series titles with the New York Yankees. Stengel piloted the Brooklyn Dodgers (1934–36), Boston Bees (1938–43), Yankees (1949–60), and New York Mets (1962–65). He ranks fifth on the all-time list of managers in games, seventh in wins, fifth in losses, first in World Series games (63) and wins (37), and second in Series losses (26) and percentage (.587). Stengel won an unprecedented five straight flags with the Yankees, and finished 10th four times in a row with the Mets. As a player, he saw action over 14 seasons, mostly with the Dodgers, but also with the Pittsburgh Pirates, New York Giants, and Boston Braves. His lifetime average was .284.

	G	W	L	Pct
Career	3,812	1,926	1,867	.508

A member of the Phillies' all–Hall of Fame outfield of the early 1890s, Sam Thompson was one of the first true home run hitters in baseball. He was the first player to hit 20 homers in a season, and at the turn of the century had hit more four-baggers than any other player. Thompson was also the first player to get 200 hits in a season. Sam won two home run crowns and two RBI titles during his 15-year career. In 1887, during a four-year stint with the Detroit Wolverines, he led the league in batting with a .372 average. Sam hit .407 for the Phillies in 1894. He hit over .300 seven times as a regular. His 222 hits in 1893 were at the time a National League record. In 10 seasons with the Phillies, Thompson carved his name in the books as one of the club's all-time hitting leaders. He has the fourth highest batting average in team history. He was also an outstanding defensive player with a strong throwing arm. In 1891 he threw out 32 base-runners.

	G	AB	H	BA	RBI	R	2B	3B	HR	SA	SB
Phillies	1,031	4,413	1,469	.333	957	925	272	106	95	.507	189
Career	1,407	5,984	1,979	.331	1,299	1,256	340	160	127	.505	229

Samuel L. Thompson

Right fielder
Phillies: 1889–98
Major leagues: 1885–98, 1906
Elected: 1974
Birthplace: Danville, Indiana
B: March 5, 1860
D: November 7, 1922
Batted left; threw left

One of the finest singles hitters of all time, Lloyd Waner was an exceptional leadoff batter during an 18-year career, mostly noted for his 14 sterling seasons with the Pittsburgh Pirates. Lloyd teamed with his Hall of Fame brother Paul to form the best-hitting brother combination ever to play the game. Lloyd, known as Little Poison, had 198 singles in his rookie year in 1927, a modern record that still stands. He hit over .300 ten times as a regular. In 7,772 trips to the plate, Waner struck out just 173 times. Lloyd had brief flings in the early 1940s with the Boston Braves, Cincinnati Reds, Phillies, and Brooklyn Dodgers before ending his career back in Pittsburgh. He was signed by the Phillies as a free agent, and spent the 1942 season with the club as a part-time center fielder and pinch-hitter. Although he'd slowed down considerably by then, Waner was still one of the better hitters on the war-torn Phillies roster.

	G	AB	H	BA	RBI	R	2B	3B	HR	SA	SB
Phillies	100	287	75	.261	10	23	7	3	0	.307	1
Career	1,992	7,772	2,459	.316	598	1,201	281	118	28	.394	67

Lloyd James Waner

Center fielder
Phillies: 1942
Major leagues: 1927–42, 1944–45
Elected: 1967
Birthplace: Harrah, Oklahoma
B: March 16, 1906
D: July 22, 1982
Batted left; threw right

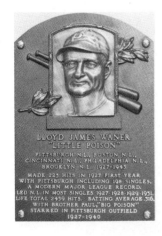

Lewis Robert Wilson

Right fielder
Phillies: 1934
Major leagues: 1923–34
Elected: 1979
Birthplace: Elwood City, Pennsylvania
B: April 26, 1900
D: November 23, 1948
Batted right; threw right

At 5–6 and 190 pounds, Hack Wilson didn't look much like a slugger. But he was one of the most successful home run hitters in National League history. He still holds the league record for most homers in a season, having hit 56 in 1930. That was one of four times Wilson led the circuit in four-base hits. Originally with the New York Giants, Hack joined the Chicago Cubs in 1926, and in six years in the Windy City posted an assortment of glittering hitting statistics. In 1930 he also drove in 190 runs, a single season record that still stands. Hack hit .356 that year, his highest of five seasons over .300. He hit .345 with 39 homers and 159 RBI in 1929. A fun-loving, free spirit, Wilson played only 12 seasons in the majors. He played for two and one-half seasons with the Brooklyn Dodgers before joining the Phillies late in 1934. Hack had little to contribute to the Phillies during his brief time with the club. His career ended at the close of the season.

	G	AB	H	BA	RBI	R	2B	3B	HR	SA	SB
Phillies	7	20	2	.100	3	0	0	0	0	.100	0
Career	1,348	4,760	1,461	.307	1,062	884	266	67	244	.545	52

William Henry Wright

Manager
Phillies: 1884–93
Major leagues: 1876–93
Elected: 1953
Birthplace: Sheffield, England
B: January 10, 1835
D: October 3, 1895
Batted right; threw right

Sometimes referred to as "The Father of Baseball," Harry Wright assembled the first professional team in 1869. A traveling team, it was called the Cincinnati Red Stockings, and Wright led it to 87 straight victories over a one and one-half year period. During that time, he also designed the first true baseball uniforms. The pioneering Wright became manager of the Boston Red Stockings in 1876 when the National League began. He worked there for six years, winning pennants in 1877 and 1878. Harry also piloted the Providence Grays for two years before joining the Phillies for their second season in the National League. In 10 seasons with the Phillies, Wright's teams never finished out of the first division after his first year in Philadelphia. Harry's 636 wins rank second among Phillies managers. His highest finish was in 1887 when the Phillies finished second. The Phillies also placed third three times under Wright.

	G	W	L	Pct
Phillies	1,292	636	566	.530
Career	2,110	1,225	885	.581

Media in the Hall of Fame

There are three other members of the Hall of Fame who were connected with the Phillies. They were people who were part of the media.

Allen Lewis and Ray Kelly covered the Phillies for many years for local newspapers. As recipients of the J. Taylor Spink Award, they are members of the writers' wing of the Hall of Fame.

By Saam, a Phillies broadcaster for many years, was the winner of the Ford Frick Award, which also earned him a spot in the Hall.

Lewis was the first one of the group inducted, entering the Hall of Fame on August 1, 1982. A baseball writer with the *Philadelphia Inquirer* from 1946 to 1979, he first covered the Phillies in 1949. He became the newspaper's beat writer in 1957. Lewis was a member of major league baseball's rules committee from 1958 to 1972 and served as its chairman from 1960 to 1972. He has also served for more than a decade on the Hall of Fame's veterans committee, a post he still holds. A baseball historian of considerable note, Lewis has authored several baseball books and for the last 10 years has written a column on Phillies history for the newspaper *Phillies Report*. He is a graduate of Haverford College.

Kelly entered the Hall of Fame posthumously on July 23, 1989, after working some 50 years for the Philadelphia *Evening Bulletin*. A star soccer player as a youngster, Kelly began at the *Bulletin* at the age of 16 as a copy boy. He worked his way up the sports staff, and in the 1940s became the beat writer for the Philadelphia A's. Kelly was the beat writer for the Phillies from 1956 to 1979. During much of that time, he was also a correspondent for *The Sporting News*.

Saam, a graduate of Texas Christian University, was inducted at Cooperstown on August 5, 1990. During a career in Philadelphia that went from 1937 to 1975, he broadcast more than 8,000 games, starting with the A's in 1938. Saam did both A's and Phillies games from 1939 to 1949, then just A's from 1950 to 1954. When the A's left town, he rejoined the Phillies on a full-time basis and handled their games from 1955 until his retirement in 1975.

Great Moments

The Phillies have had many memorable moments during the long history of the franchise. Heroic victories, spectacularly pitched games, and brilliant hitting performances have all, on occasion, been part of the Phillies' long and sometimes glorious history.

Three particular events rank at the pinnacle of Phillies successes. Dick Sisler's pennant-winning home run in 1950, the perfect game by Jim Bunning in 1964, and the sixth and deciding game of the 1980 World Series hold special places of distinction.

No other games, events, or performances equal this magnificent trio. Truly, they represent the apex of Phillies seasons, and they comprise the major part of the following chapter.

Of course, these are not the only great moments in Phillies history. There have been others, such as the eight no-hitters tossed by Phils pitchers; four-home-run games by Ed Delahanty, Chuck Klein, and Mike Schmidt; eight-RBI games by Kitty Bransfield, Gavvy Cravath, Willie Jones, and Schmidt; and the high strikeout games of Chris Short and Art Mahaffey.

Other great moments include Pete Rose's record-setting 3,631st hit, Steve Carlton's 3,118th strikeout and his 15th straight win, the five-home-run inning in 1949, which included two by Andy Seminick, the "shootout in Chicago" when the Phillies topped the Cubs, 23–22, and Mickey Morandini's unassisted triple play in 1992.

The heroics of Sisler, Bunning, and the 1980 Phillies, as well as brief looks at some of the other top moments, make up this chapter.

Dick Sisler's Home-Run— The Biggest Hit in Phillies History

One day when Robin Roberts was in eighth grade in Springfield, Illinois, his two-room schoolhouse was visited by a famous former big league baseball player.

Grover Cleveland Alexander stood at the front of one of the rooms and offered his young listeners some words of encouragement. "You don't know," said the old pitcher, "maybe some of you youngsters will be pitching in a World Series in a few years."

It was the only time that Roberts and Alexander, future and former Phillies pitching greats and Hall of Famers, ever met. Although it took more than a few years to materialize, Alexander's remark did come true. Getting that to happen, though, took one of the most memorable games in Phillies history.

The date was October 1, 1950. The setting was Ebbets Field in Brooklyn. It was the final game of the season, and it matched the first-place Phillies against the second-place Brooklyn Dodgers. The Phillies had a one-game lead and needed a victory to clinch the pennant. A loss would put the teams in a tie, requiring a best-of-three playoff series.

The playoff was unnecessary. The Phillies triumphed, 4–1, in 10 innings to qualify for their first World Series in 35 years.

It was a game in which Dick Sisler hit the most memorable home run in Phillies history. Richie Ashburn made the most memorable throw in Phillies history. And Roberts pitched one of the grittiest games in Phillies history.

Played before a standing-room-only crowd of 35,073 with an estimated 30,000 more fans turned away at the gate, the contest was decided in the top of the 10th when Sisler laced a three-run homer.

"I've hit some better, but none ever meant so much," Sisler said. "It's the biggest hit I ever got. How I love this park."

Ecstatic Phillies greet Dick Sisler (8) at home plate after his three-run home run beat the Brooklyn Dodgers and gave the Whiz Kids the pennant in 1950.

Stan Lopata puts the tag on runner Cal Abrams to keep the Brooklyn Dodgers from forcing playoff in 1950.

To reach that point, Roberts and the Dodgers' Don Newcombe had engaged in a brilliant pitching duel. Both pitchers sought their 20th wins. Roberts, making his sixth attempt to win number 20, was starting for the third time in the last five days.

The Dodgers fielded a lineup that was among the most powerful in baseball. Gil Hodges, Duke Snider, and Roy Campanella each hit more than 30 home runs in 1950, and Snider, Jackie Robinson, and Carl Furillo all hit above .300.

But Brooklyn found Roberts' pitches a mystery. The Dodgers failed to get a hit until Pee Wee Reese's leadoff double in the fourth inning. Reese, however, was stranded at second as Roberts retired Snider, Robinson, and Furillo.

Meanwhile, the Phillies pecked away at Newcombe. They put runners on base in the third, fourth, and fifth innings. But the runners got no farther than first base each time.

Philadelphia finally cracked into the scoring column in the sixth inning. After Eddie Waitkus and Ashburn grounded out, Sisler slammed a ground single to right. Del Ennis followed with a bloop single to center. Then Willie Jones drilled a single to left, and Sisler came scampering home. The inning ended when Furillo raced to deep right-center to haul in Granny Hamner's drive.

The Dodgers retaliated in the bottom of the sixth on a freak hit. With two outs, Reese lofted a fly to right-center that hit a wire screen above the wall. The ball came to rest on a ledge above the wall, and was ruled a ground-rule home run.

"When the ball came down the screen, it had back English on it, and it just balanced on the ledge," said Phillies right fielder Ennis. "I could've thrown my glove up and hit it, it was just laying there."

The score remained tied, despite additional threats by the Phillies. The team had men on again in the seventh, eighth, and ninth innings but couldn't score. After eight innings, Brooklyn's only other hit was a single by Campanella.

The Dodgers, however, finally got a solid threat going in the bottom of the ninth. Cal Abrams opened with a walk and moved to second on Reese's single, his third hit of the game. Then Snider drilled a single to center.

Dodger third base coach Milt Stock, ironically a third baseman on the Phillies' pennant-winning team in 1915, imprudently and with little respect for Ashburn's arm, waved Abrams home as Cal rounded third. But Ashburn, playing a few feet shallow in center, fielded the ball on one hop, and rifled a perfect throw to the plate. Catcher Stan Lopata fielded the peg and moved up the line to nail Abrams by 15 feet.

The throw saved the pennant for the Phillies. "I was in perfect position for that kind of play," said Ashburn. "Maybe it wasn't the best throw I made all year, but I don't know of one that came at a better time."

Stock, who was fired along with Dodger manager Burt Shotton, a former Phillies pilot, after the season ended, defended himself. "I'd do it again if I had to call it again," he said.

Despite the play, the Phillies were still in big trouble in the inning with Reese on third and Snider on second and only one out. Robinson was given an intentional walk. Then Roberts retired Furillo on a foul pop and Hodges on a fly to right.

As the game moved into extra innings, the Phillies pounced on the tiring Newcombe. Roberts led off with a single up the middle. Waitkus followed with a bloop single to center. Ashburn bunted, but Newcombe fielded the ball and forced Roberts out at third. Roberts, sliding head first into the bag, got a painful eye full of lime.

Sisler was the next batter. Dick already had three singles in the game, despite a badly sprained wrist that had kept him out of action three weeks earlier and that he aggravated sliding into second in the fourth inning. The wrist was heavily taped. As Sisler stepped to the plate, he was watched closely by a man seated behind the Dodgers' dugout, Dick's father George, a Hall of Famer and now a scout for Brooklyn.

Newcombe worked to a 1–2 count, then tried to blow a fastball by on the outside of the plate. Sisler swung and the ball sailed to deep left.

Gene Kelly, the Phillies' play-by-play announcer, was calling the action: "Newcombe is set . . . And the stretch . . . Delivery . . . Swing . . . A fly . . . Very, very deep toward left field . . . Getting back, Abrams . . . Way, way back . . . He can't get it . . . It's a home run . . . Grrreat. A home run for Dick Sisler, and the Phillies lead, 4–1 . . . One out and Sisler gets a left field home run . . . His 13th of the season . . . It just cleared the barrier in left field, 350 feet away from home plate."

The Phillies mobbed Sisler as he crossed the plate. But the game was not over yet. Roberts still needed to retire the Dodgers in the bottom of the 10th as the Ebbets Field lights came on.

"We only needed three more outs, and I just kept bearing down," Roberts said. "After all the pressure, I was kind of relaxed in the bottom of the 10th. After you had been through what we went through, and you had a three-run lead, three outs didn't seem that tough."

Robbie got the first batter, Campanella, to line out to Jackie Mayo, a defensive replacement for Sisler in left. Next, pinch-hitter Jim Russell, batting for Billy Cox, struck out. The final hitter was Tommy Brown, pinch-hitting for Newcombe. Roberts got him to loft a high pop on the first base side. Waitkus grabbed it in foul territory, and at long last the grueling pennant race was over.

Shortstop Hamner described his feelings. "I started to the mound to congratulate Robbie. As I did, tears started running out of my eyes. I couldn't stop them."

The wild scene that erupted on the pitcher's mound carried over into the clubhouse. It was a deliriously happy band of Phillies. "It's a dream," Sisler kept repeating.

Back in Philadelphia, instant celebrations arose. Sirens screamed, tugboats tooted, horns honked, and joyful fans spilled into the streets in a victory party that extended through the night. Connie Mack was elated. "They truly lived up to their name, the Fightin' Phils," he said.

Although the Phillies had started the season as an 8–1 shot to win the pennant, manager Eddie Sawyer revealed a prediction he had made. "Nobody ever heard me pick the Phils to win," he said. "But I did. I wrote it on a sealed envelope dated April 18. It's in my desk at Shibe Park. I picked the Phils by 10 games. I never doubted that we would win. If we hadn't lost Simmons, Miller, and Church, we would have won by 10, too."

Meanwhile, a weary Roberts slumped on a stool in the clubhouse, reddened and stinging from the lime. Robbie had given up only five hits, struck out two, and walked three. The Phillies' outfield had made just five putouts. "The only time I felt tired was when I sat down in front of the locker," he said.

When asked for a reaction to his son's home run, George Sisler had an honest answer. "I don't know exactly how I felt," said the former American

Richie Ashburn's throw nailed Cal Abrams at the plate, and Robin Roberts got the win in the Phillies' 4–1 victory over the Dodgers.

League great. "Here I am working for one ball club, and my son wins the pennant for the other one. I felt awful and terrific at the same time."

As the Phillies' clubhouse rocked in celebration, some of the Dodgers began visiting to extend their congratulations. Jackie Robinson was the first to arrive. The great Dodger star entered the Phillies' locker room smiling broadly, and proceeded around the room, shaking hands with the winners.

Pee Wee Reese came next, followed by Gil Hodges, manager Shotton, Preacher Roe, and some of the other Dodgers. "It took a great team to beat us," said Shotton, who skippered the Phillies to their only first division finish (in 1932) between 1917 and 1949.

"How could Ashburn dare to play so close?" Shotton wondered. "Milt (Stock) played it right. In a 1–1 game with no outs, you send in the lead run. We still had men on second and third with our big hitters coming up."

Such trivia no longer mattered as the bedlam continued in the clubhouse. After celebrating for an hour, the Phillies piled onto the team bus that would take them to the train station for the trip home. As the bus wound through the Brooklyn streets, some of the players yelled at pedestrians, "How did the Dodgers do today?"

The train ride back to Philadelphia seemed to take almost no time. When the train pulled into North Philadelphia Station, Sisler, Jones, and Jim Konstanty got off to get their cars. Some 5,000 fans, however, had jammed into and around the ancient station. The players were mobbed, particularly Sisler, who had to dash into a grocery store to escape the well-wishers.

The situation was nothing compared to the one at the 30th Street Station where the rest of the Phillies arrived. More than 30,000 jubilant fans had packed the station to greet the new pennant winners.

The Phillies could hardly get off the train. Finally, behind police escorts, the players inched through the clawing, screaming crowd.

Ennis, his shirt ripped by the crowd, surveyed the madhouse. "I never guessed it would be anything like this," he said.

Of course, there never was a game like that, either.

For one magic moment, Dick Sisler surpassed all the baseball accomplishments of George, his Hall of Fame father.

Phillies' heroes on October 1, 1950, in Brooklyn were (from left) Robin Roberts, Eddie Sawyer, and Dick Sisler.

October 1, 1950

Phillies	AB	R	H	O	A
Waitkus, 1b	5	1	1	18	0
Ashburn, cf	5	1	0	2	1
Sisler, lf	5	2	4	0	0
Mayo, lf	0	0	0	1	0
Ennis, rf	5	0	2	2	0
Jones, 3b	5	0	1	0	3
Hamner, ss	4	0	0	1	2
Seminick, c	3	0	1	2	1
a-Caballero	0	0	0	0	0
Lopata, c	0	0	0	2	0
Goliat, 2b	4	0	1	1	3
Roberts, p	2	0	1	1	6
Totals	**38**	**4**	**11**	**30**	**16**

Brooklyn	AB	R	H	O	A
Abrams, lf	2	0	0	2	0
Reese, ss	4	1	3	3	3
Snider, cf	4	0	1	3	0
Robinson, 2b	3	0	0	4	3
Furillo, rf	4	0	0	3	0
Hodges, 1b	4	0	0	9	3
Campanella, c	4	0	1	2	4
Cox, 3b	3	0	0	1	2
b-Russell	1	0	0	0	0
Newcombe, p	3	0	0	3	2
c-Brown	1	0	0	0	0
Totals	**33**	**1**	**5**	**30**	**17**

a-Ran for Seminick in 9th.
b-Struck out for Cox in 10th.
c-Fouled out for Newcombe in 10th.

Phillies   0 0 0 0 0 1 0 0 0 3 — 4
Brooklyn 0 0 0 0 0 1 0 0 0 0 — 1

Errors: none. Runs batted in: Jones, Reese, Sisler 3. Two-base hits: Reese. Home runs: Reese, Sisler. Sacrifice: Roberts. Double plays: Reese, Robinson, and Hodges; Roberts and Waitkus. Left on base: Philadelphia 7, Brooklyn 5. Bases on balls: Roberts 3, Newcombe 2. Struck out: Roberts 2, Newcombe 3. Umpires: Goetz, Dascoli, Jorda, and Donatelli. Time, 2:35. Attendance, 35,073.

Whiz Kids let loose after harrowing journey to 1950 National League pennant.

It hadn't been done in a regular season game in the major leagues in 42 years. Don Larsen had pitched a perfect game in the 1956 World Series, but the last major leaguer to pitch an entire game during the regular season without allowing a runner to reach base had been Charles Robertson of the Chicago White Sox, who did it against the Detroit Tigers in 1922.

And as far as the National League was concerned, it had never been done, period. It's true that Harvey Haddix pitched 12 perfect innings against the Milwaukee Braves in 1959, but The Kitten gave up base-runners and actually lost the game in the 13th.

But this was a special day in a special year for a special pitcher. It was Father's Day, and Jim Bunning was the father of seven children. The year was

Jim Bunning's Perfect Game

Jim Bunning became the Phillies' only perfect pitcher on June 21, 1964.

1964, and it looked like the Phillies were going to breeze to their first pennant in 14 years and only the third in their history. Gus Triandos, who had come to the Phillies with Bunning in a trade with the Tigers before the season, was the catcher that day. Triandos would later call 1964 the Year of the Blue Snow.

On this particular day, the snow would have melted before anyone could have verified its color. New York City was sweltering. The temperature would top 90 degrees before the afternoon ended.

The day started the way every Sunday had for Bunning since he could remember. Mass and Communion. A devout Catholic, Bunning hit the church pew and the Communion rail every Sunday, whether the baseball team was home or on the road.

After church, the pattern changed a bit. Bunning had a meeting with a lawyer in the hotel lobby. He was also concerned about leaving tickets for wife Mary, daughter Barbara, and the wife of Danny Cater, all of whom were driving to New York from Cherry Hill, New Jersey, to watch the doubleheader.

Little did Bunning realize it at the time, but his day would end with an appearance on the Ed Sullivan Show. With him would be Ken Venturi, who won the U.S. Open that day. "I win the U.S. Open and I end up playing second fiddle," Venturi grumped playfully at Bunning backstage.

There is no question that Bunning had nary a glimpse into what was about to happen when he went out to warm up before the doubleheader opener. He admitted it himself in the book *The Story of Jim Bunning*, told to *Associated Press* sportswriter Ralph Bernstein.

"I felt nothing spectacular warming up before the game," Jim said, "felt no different from any other day. Actually, I don't place much stock in the fact that you have or don't have good stuff when warming up. It's not important. It only means something when you're out on the mound and throwing. I can recall many days where I felt great warming up, had great stuff and went out and got clobbered. And I can remember days when I didn't think I had a prayer while warming up and went out and won a ball game."

For Bunning, pre-game was mundane. For others, it was exciting.

Like for Gene Mauch, the manager who three months later would turn from genius to goat.

"We knew when he was warming up that this was something special," Mauch said. "The way he was throwing, so live and as high as he was. Not high with his pitches. High himself."

Others noticed. One teammate commented that Bunning was throwing as if he had "popped a greenie." Bunning's explanation was that he loosened up quickly in the Shea Stadium heat.

And then the game started, for what it was worth. Seemingly-pennant-bound Philadelphia versus cellar-bound New York. A mismatch made in Expansion Heaven. Jim Bunning versus Tracy Stallard—living history versus living history. Perfection versus imperfection. After all, Stallard did give up Roger Maris's 61st home run in 1961.

If Bunning had warmed up especially well, he started the game just as much out of character. The New York leadoff hitter was Jim Hickman. Bunning hung two sliders to him, and Hickman fouled them back into the screen.

Bunning was a consummate professional. It wasn't his style to yell things at the opposing batter. Normally, he let his pitches make his statements. Not this day.

"I shouted to Hickman, 'You had your chance, you won't get any more like that,'" Bunning related through Bernstein in the book. "That was the last pitch he got to hit all day. I don't usually holler at hitters. It's rare. But Hickman hits me pretty good and I figured if he didn't hit those high sliders, I was in pretty good shape. I struck him out three times that day.

"Well, things went along smoothly through the first four innings. Nobody reached base. My defense didn't have a hard chance."

In the fifth, Jesse Gonder gave the Phillies' defense a chance to be heroic, and Tony Taylor answered the challenge splendidly. Gonder lined a ball between first and second. The Elias Sports Bureau was already recording it as a base hit when Taylor somehow knocked the ball down, scrambled after it and threw out the slow-moving catcher by a step.

At that point, Bunning joined the group that had looked upon the day as special. He began to think no-hitter. Not perfect game, but no-hitter.

Worse than that, he began to talk no-hitter. One of the great superstitions of baseball is that a no-hitter is never discussed when the pitcher is working on one. It's an unwritten rule that everyone follows.

Bunning chose to break the rule.

"I'm just not superstitious," Bunning wrote in his book. "I don't believe in this kind of thing. Sure I talked about it incessantly. I was a one-man cheerleader. Just as I was in my first no-hitter against Boston in 1958, I urged my fielders to dive for the ball, do anything to get them out.

"I started to think in terms of a perfect game after the sixth inning. After all, it meant getting only nine straight batters out."

By the top of the ninth, Bunning needed only three straight outs.

Charlie Smith, an ex-Phillie, was first. He was retired on a foul pop.

George Altman was next. He got in front of a pitch and knocked it out of the park but way foul. Then Altman fanned.

John Stephenson was batter number 27. Rich Ashburn was the announcer, and if Jim Bunning wasn't afraid to challenge superstitions, neither was Ashburn.

Here is the way Ashburn called history:

"One out away from a perfect game for Jim Bunning. Johnny Stephenson coming on. He stands between Jim Bunning and 27 straight outs . . . I don't know how Bunning feels down there, but I'll tell you one thing. This is about as nervous as I've ever been involved in any kind of a baseball game.

"Stephenson up there. He's hitting .274. Curve ball, swung on and missed. Strike one. Mets fans cheering Jim on every pitch now. We have a lot of Phillies fans here also.

"One strike on Johnny Stephenson. Phillies playing him as a pull hitter. Strike one the count. Bunning getting the sign from Triandos. And here's the windup . . . the pitch . . . Stephenson takes it outside, ball two. Just missing with

Shea Stadium scoreboard told the story as Mets pinch-hitter John Stephenson struck out to become 27th straight victim of Jim Bunning.

that breaking ball again. Looks like Bunning is going with all breaking stuff to Stephenson . . .

"Two and two the count. Ball two, strike two, one strike away.

"Here's the pitch.

"Strike three! He gets him! A perfect game for Jim Bunning! Twenty-seven straight men for Jim Bunning!"

Ashburn's calling of the final out was as perfect as Bunning's performance. Rich was excited and he let his listening audience know it. If you heard it, you'll never forget it.

Mary Bunning described the feat perfectly.

"I'd compare it to something I hope to do someday," she said. "Give a sitdown dinner for 20 people and have everything turn out perfect."

Jim, Mary, and Barbara Bunning wanted to spend the time between the end of the doubleheader and the start of the Ed Sullivan Show celebrating the events of the day. They went to Toots Shor's, but it was closed. So was just about every other club.

So the Bunnings wound up toasting the perfect game with sandwiches at a Howard Johnson's. Such an ordinary way to celebrate one of the extraordinary feats in baseball history.

June 21, 1964

Phillies	AB	R	H	O	A
Briggs, cf	4	1	0	2	0
Herrnstein, 1b	4	0	0	7	0
Callison, rf	4	1	2	1	0
Allen, 3b	3	0	1	0	2
Covington, lf	2	0	0	1	0
a-Wine, ss	1	1	0	2	1
T. Taylor, 2b	3	2	1	0	3
Rojas, ss-lf	3	0	1	3	0
Triandos, c	4	1	2	11	1
Bunning, p	4	0	1	0	0
Totals	32	6	8	27	7

New York	AB	R	H	O	A
Hickman, cf	3	0	0	2	0
Hunt, 2b	3	0	0	3	2
Kranepool, 1b	3	0	0	8	1
Christopher, rf	3	0	0	4	0
Gonder, c	3	0	0	6	2
R. Taylor, lf	3	0	0	1	0
C. Smith, ss	3	0	0	2	1
Samuel, 3b	2	0	0	0	1
c-Altman	1	0	0	0	0
Stallard, p	1	0	0	0	2
Wakefield, p	0	0	0	0	0
b-Kanehl	1	0	0	0	0
Sturdivant, p	0	0	0	1	0
d-Stephenson	1	0	0	0	0
Totals	27	0	0	27	9

a-Ran for Covington in 6th.
b-Grounded out for Wakefield in 6th.
c-Struck out for Samuel in 9th.
d-Struck out for Sturdivant in 9th.

| Phillies | 1 | 1 | 0 | 0 | 0 | 4 | 0 | 0 | 0 | —6 |
| New York | 0 | 0 | 0 | 0 | 0 | 0 | 0 | 0 | 0 | —0 |

Errors: none. Runs batted in: Callison, Allen, Triandos 2, Bunning 2. Two-base hits: Triandos, Bunning. Home run: Callison. Sacrifices: Herrnstein, Rojas. Left on bases: Philadelphia 5, New York 0. Bases on balls: Off Stallard 4 (Briggs, T. Taylor, Allen, Covington). Strikeouts: By Bunning 10 (Hickman 3, C. Smith, Hunt, Kranepool, Christopher, R. Taylor, Altman, Stephenson), by Stallard 3 (Callison, Herrnstein, Allen), by Sturdivant 3 (Rojas, Triandos, Briggs). Runs and earned runs: Stallard 6–6. Hits: Off Stallard 7 in 5⅔ innings, off Wakefield 0 in ⅓ inning, off Sturdivant 1 in 3 innings. Wild pitch: Stallard. Winning pitcher: Bunning (7–2). Losing pitcher: Stallard (4–3). Umpires: Sudol, Pryor, Secory, and Burkhart. Time, 2:19. Attendance, 32,026.

Free, at Last—The Phillies Win the World Series

It was, without doubt, the single most memorable moment in Philadelphia sports history. Bigger than any championship the Athletics ever won. Bigger than the Whiz Kids.

Certainly bigger than the back-to-back Stanley Cups the Flyers annexed in the mid-1970s, or the 69–13 championship season of the 76ers a decade before.

The Eagles, in all their glory years, had never matched it. Neither had Dempsey-Tunney at Municipal Stadium.

Those were events. This was The Event.

It happened at 11:29 on a coolish night in South Philadelphia. October 21, 1980. Tying runs on base, winning run at the plate in the presence of Willie Wilson.

And the man who could make the ordinary dramatic was on the mound. Tug McGraw . . . The Tugger . . . Scroogie. Seven years earlier, he had led the Mets to the National League pennant with his left arm and his mouth.

"You gotta believe," he yelled one day in early September when the Mets seemed hopelessly out of it in the National League East. It became the rallying call. You Gotta Believe.

Seven years later, on October 21, 1980, Philadelphia wanted to believe that the evil spirits that had plagued the franchise almost from its inception had finally been exorcised. And there were some positive signs that the demons had been chased.

Mike Schmidt's two-run homer in the 11th inning at Montreal that clinched the National League East title on the last day of the season was one.

So was the incredible League Championship Series with the Houston Astros. A routine Steve Carlton victory in the opener of the best-of-five set, then four straight extra-inning games. Down two-to-one after three games with the last two in the Dome. Pete Rose running over Bruce Bochy at the plate in Game Four. Del Unser picking up Schmidt in Game Five. Garry Maddox, out of the doghouse and on his teammates' shoulders.

Bob Walk winning Game One. Rose letting a Dennis Leonard pitch hit him on the knee. Larry Bowa stealing second with the team four runs down.

Carlton winning Game Two, And, after the Kansas City Royals came back to tie it, the Phillies coming from behind to take Game Five.

Dickie Noles knocking down George Brett in Game Four and Brett never again finding his batting eye. Manny Trillo's great relay throw that cut down Darrell Porter in Game Five, then Manny getting the winning hit off Dan Quisenberry in the ninth inning.

And then, on the second putout of the ninth inning of the sixth game, the message came across more clearly than ever. The demons were gone, hopefully forever.

McGraw had acquired a new nickname down the stretch and through the postseason when he was on the mound virtually every day. Tylenol Tug. Every morning, McGraw explained, he got up and popped six Tylenol, then sat back and waited for his left arm to stop aching. Tug took Tylenol; the rest of the City of Brotherly Love needed Valium.

The score was 4–1, Phillies, entering the ninth inning of Game Six. McGraw struck out Amos Otis leading off the inning, then gave up a walk and two singles to load the bases. By this time the field was encircled by police horses and dogs, a sure-fire way to control the 65,839 fans in the Vet. There would be no way to control the millions watching on television in the Delaware Valley, though, especially if the Phillies found a way to lose the game and, the following night, the World Series.

Frank White hit a routine pop foul near the Phillies' dugout. Catcher Bob

On the morning after, general manager Paul Owens and field manager Dallas Green rode down Broad St. in the victory parade.

Bob Boone loses ninth inning pop fly in Game Six but Pete Rose alertly made the catch, leaving the Phillies one out away from the World Championship.

Boone made the call, then saw the ball pop out of his glove. But first baseman Pete Rose was alert as ever. He picked off the ball before it hit the ground for the second out . . . and chased the evil spirits.

Willie Wilson was next. Willie was coming off an outstanding season—and a wretched World Series. He had already established a record with 11 strikeouts. The count reached one-and-two. Then McGraw reached back and threw the last fastball he had in him. Wilson swung and missed. The magic moment had arrived.

The streets of Philadelphia came alive. Phillies fans came out of their living rooms and celebrated something that had taken 97 years to accomplish—a World Championship.

McGraw leaped in the air as the final pitch stuck in Boone's glove. Then he glanced toward third where Series MVP Mike Schmidt played. He waited for Schmidt, who leaped into the suddenly developing pile of Phillies humanity at the mound.

Outside the Vet, the sounds were like V-J Day revisited. People drove through the streets of the city hanging out of cars with horns blaring. Folks danced in the streets in South Philly and West Philly and the Northeast and the suburbs.

The parade the next day down Broad Street was a mass of humanity, bleary-eyed, teary-eyed, cheering their heroes. The mob at Kennedy Stadium went crazy, especially when Schmidt told them to take the championship "and savor it" and when McGraw thrust the *Philadelphia Daily News* with the "We Win!" headline on it and told New York City to "stick it." McGraw raised the newspaper with his left hand. It was an effort. The night before he might not have been able to do it.

"I don't know what Dallas Green had in mind, but if I didn't get Wilson, I was calling him to the mound," Tug said. "I had nothing left. Nothing."

Nothing but the greatest sports moment in Philadelphia history.

(See box score with other 1980 World Series games.)

Strikeout of Willie Wilson for final out had Tug McGraw jumping for joy.

World Series MVP Mike Schmidt leaps onto Tug McGraw at mound after final out of Game Six.

The 1979 Shootout in Chicago

Of the thousands of games the Phillies have played, none was ever as wild and woolly as the famous "shootout in Chicago," played at Wrigley Field on May 17, 1979.

It was a game in which the two teams combined not only for 45 runs, but also for 49 hits, including 11 home runs, 10 doubles, and two triples. Eleven pitchers worked in the four-hour, three-minute marathon. The Phillies had a 21–9 lead and blew it before finally winning in the 10th inning, 23–22, on Mike Schmidt's second home run of the day.

In 1922 the Phillies had lost a 26–23 game to the Cubs. And in 1981 they would win an 18–16 battle with Chicago. But the 1979 skirmish—second only to the '22 game in combined runs by two teams—was truly the weirdest of them all.

It was the highest-scoring one-run game and the highest-scoring extra-inning game in the 20th century.

The Phillies had defeated the Cubs, 13–0, the previous day. "Don't forget to get me some runs," Phils starter Randy Lerch implored his teammates as he left the clubhouse to warm up.

A wind of 20 to 30 miles per hour roared toward left field throughout the game. Surprisingly, only 14,952 spectators were in the stands to watch the slugfest unfold.

What they saw, though, was nothing short of unbelievable. Dave Kingman hit three home runs and drove in six. Larry Bowa had five hits, all by the sixth inning. And the Phillies batted around in three different innings while using 17 players to the Cubs' 19.

In the first inning Schmidt and Bob Boone each hit three-run home runs, and Lerch also homered, to vault the Phils to a 7–0 lead. That should have been enough for Lerch in any normal game, but this wasn't a normal game. Randy gave up six runs in the bottom of the first, including a three-run homer to Kingman.

Amazingly, the second inning was scoreless, but the Phillies came back with eight runs in the third with the help of a three-run homer by Garry Maddox.

After two more runs in the fourth and four in the fifth, the Phillies coasted

Only relief pitcher Rawly Eastwick was able to tame the hitters in 1979 Shootout in Chicago.

into the bottom of the fifth with a 21–9 lead. But the Cubs, who had scored three times in the fourth with the help of a wind-aided two-run Kingman home run, were poised for a comeback.

With Bill Buckner lashing a grand slam home run and Jerry Martin a two-run homer—both off Tug McGraw—the Cubs exploded for seven runs, then added three more in the sixth and three in the eighth, all six runs coming off Ron Reed, who had entered the game with a scoreless streak of 21⅓ consecutive innings.

As the game entered the ninth inning, the score was miraculously tied, 22–22.

In the bottom of the ninth, Rawly Eastwick, one of only two Phils pitchers left, became the first hurler of the day to set the opposing side down in order. Eastwick's 1–2–3 inning sent the game into extra innings and set the stage for Schmidt.

With Chicago's crack reliever Bruce Sutter on the mound, Schmidt drilled a titanic shot over the left field bleachers to give the Phillies a one-run lead. It was the 14th home run of the season and 10th in the month of May for Schmidt, who was on his way to a 45-home-run season.

"I hit the same pitch of Sutter's, the split-fingered fastball, that I swing and miss at all year," Schmidt said.

In the bottom of the 10th, Eastwick again retired the side in order, including a strikeout of Kingman on an 0–2 change-up.

The victory, at long last, belonged to the Phillies. It was the climax of a 10–4 road trip for the Phils, who returned home in first place.

It was a spot they would not hold much longer. The shootout turned out to be the high point of the club's season. But what a high point it was!

Phillies 23, Cubs 22
May 17, 1979

Phillies	AB	R	H	RBI
McBride, rf	8	2	3	1
Bowa, ss	8	4	5	1
Rose, 1b	7	4	3	4
Schmidt, 3b	4	3	2	4
Unser, lf	7	1	1	2
Maddox, cf	4	3	4	4
Gross, cf	2	1	1	1
Boone, c	4	2	3	5
Meoli, 2b	5	0	1	0
Lerch, p	1	1	1	1
Bird, p	1	1	0	0
Luzinski, ph	0	0	0	0
Espiñosa, pr	1	1	0	0
McGraw, p	0	0	0	0
Reed, p	0	0	0	0
McCarver, ph	1	0	0	0
Eastwick, p	0	0	0	0
Totals	**53**	**23**	**24**	**23**

Chicago	AB	R	H	RBI
DeJesus, ss	6	4	3	1
Vail, rf	5	2	3	1
Burris, p	0	0	0	0
Thompson, cf	2	1	1	0
Buckner, 1b	7	3	4	7
Kingman, 1b	6	4	3	6
Ontiveros, 3b	7	1	1	1
Martin, cf	6	2	3	3
Sutter, p	0	0	0	0
Foote, c	6	1	3	1
Sizemore, 2b	4	2	2	1
Caudill, p	0	0	0	0
Murcer, rf	2	0	1	0
Lamp, p	0	0	0	0
Moore, p	1	0	1	1
Hernandez, p	1	0	0	0
Dillard, 2b	1	2	1	0
Biitner, ph	1	0	0	0
Kelleher, 2b	1	0	0	0
Totals	**56**	**22**	**26**	**22**

```
Phillies   7  0  8  2  4  0  1  0  0  1 — 23
Chicago    6  0  0  3  7  3  0  3  0  0 — 22
```

Errors: Schmidt 2, Kingman, DeJesus. Double play: Philadelphia 2. Left on base: Philadelphia 15, Chicago 7. Two-base hits: Bowa 2, G. Maddox 2, Rose 2, Foote, Martin, DeJesus, Boone. Three-base hits: Moore, Gross. Home runs: Kingman 3 (12), Schmidt 2 (14), Boone (2), Lerch (1), G. Maddox (6), Ontiveros (1), Buckner (4), Martin (3). Stolen bases: Bowa, Meoli. Sacrifice flies: Unser, Gross.

Phillies	IP	H	R	ER	BB	SO
Lerch	⅓	5	5	5	0	0
Bird	3⅔	8	4	4	0	2
McGraw	⅔	4	7	4	3	1
Reed	3⅓	9	6	6	0	0
Eastwick W, 1–0	2	0	0	0	0	1

Chicago	IP	H	R	ER	BB	SO
Lamp	⅓	6	6	6	0	0
Moore	2	6	7	7	2	1
Hernandez	2⅔	7	8	6	7	1
Caudill	1⅓	3	1	1	2	3
Burris	1⅔	1	0	0	0	1
Sutter L, 1–1	2	1	1	1	1	0

Hit by pitcher: By Hernandez (Boone). Time, 4:03. Attendance, 14,952.

It was a storybook setting that no one would have dared to predict.

On April 18, 1987, at 4:51 P.M. at Pittsburgh's Three Rivers Stadium, Mike Schmidt became the first Phillies player to hit 500 home runs. The blow propelled Schmidt into the realm of home run immortals, putting him in a select group in which only 13 players in all of baseball preceded him.

Schmidt's blast came on a 3–0 pitch with two on and two outs in the top of the ninth inning. At the time, the Phillies, having blown a 5–0 lead earlier in the game, trailed, 6–5.

The home run, coming off of the Pirates' Don Robinson, gave the Phillies an improbable 8–6 victory.

"The only thing missing was that I would have liked to have hit it at Veterans Stadium," Schmidt said afterward.

Robinson had retired the Phillies' slugger 50 times in the 57 previous times he had faced him, although four of Schmidt's hits off the Pittsburgh relief ace had been home runs.

Pitching carefully, Robinson threw three straight balls. Then he grooved a fastball on the lower part of the plate. With that classic swing, Schmidt swung, and there was never a doubt where the ball was headed. Traveling on a low line, it flew over the fence, cleared the Phillies' bullpen, and landed against a backdrop.

Schmidt knew immediately that it was gone. Within a few steps of home plate, he did a little dance. Halfway between first and second, he clapped his hands. He jumped on second base, then clapped his hands again between second and third.

After getting a jubilant handshake from third base coach Jim Davenport, Schmidt approached home plate where the entire Phillies team had poured out of the dugout to await him. Schmidt was engulfed by his teammates, and in the stands Pittsburgh fans erupted with a standing ovation.

"I knew if I got a pitch to hit, I was going to drive it," Schmidt said. "It was the greatest thrill of my lifetime."

Schmidt, who had hit his 499th home run a night earlier, had gone hitless in seven at-bats leading up to number 500.

Of the 14 players who have hit 500 homers, nine were younger than Schmidt when they did it. Seven needed more than Schmidt's 16 seasons to reach 500.

Mike Schmidt Hits His 500th Home Run

Phillies 8, Pirates 6
April 18, 1987

Phillies	AB	R	H	RBI
Thompson, cf	5	1	2	0
Samuel, 2b	4	1	0	0
Hayes, 1b	2	2	1	0
Schmidt, 3b, ss	4	2	1	3
Easler, lf	4	1	2	1
James, lf	0	0	0	0
Tekulve, p	0	0	0	0
Parrish, c	5	1	1	3
Wilson, rf	4	0	1	0
Aguayo, ss	4	0	1	0
Bedrosian, p	0	0	0	0
Schu, 3b	0	0	0	0
Carman, p	3	0	0	0
Jeltz, ph	0	0	0	0
G. Gross, lf	1	0	0	0
Totals	36	8	9	7

Pittsburgh	AB	R	H	RBI
Cangelosi, cf	3	1	0	0
Belliard, ss	0	0	0	0
Van Slyke, rf	3	0	1	1
Ray, 2b	4	1	1	3
Morrison, 3b	3	1	0	0
Diaz, 1b	4	1	1	1
Robinson, p	0	0	0	0
Bonilla, lf	4	0	1	0
Ortiz, c	3	0	0	0
LaValliere, ph	1	0	1	0
Almon, ss	2	0	0	0
Bonds, cf	1	1	0	0
Walk, p	0	0	0	0
Gonzalez, ph	1	0	0	0
Easley, p	0	0	0	0
Reynolds, ph	1	0	1	0
Fisher, p	0	0	0	0
Bream, 1b	2	1	1	0
Totals	32	6	7	5

```
Phillies    1 0 4 0 0 0 0 0 3 — 8
Pittsburgh  0 0 0 0 1 0 1 4 0 — 6
```

Game-winning RBI: Schmidt (1). Error: Ortiz, Aguayo. Double play: Phillies 1. Left on base: Philles 7, Pittsburgh 3. Home runs: Parrish (1), Diaz (2), Ray (1), Schmidt (5). Stolen bases: Thompson (2), Samuel 2 (3), Hayes 2 (2), Morrison (1). Sacrifice fly: Van Slyke.

Phillies	IP	H	R	ER	BB	SO
Carman	7	4	2	1	1	2
Bedrosian	1	2	4	4	2	0
Tekulve (W, 1–0)	1	1	0	0	0	0

Pittsburgh	IP	H	R	ER	BB	SO
Walk	3	5	5	4	3	4
Easley	3	1	0	0	0	4
Fisher	2	1	0	0	1	1
Robinson (L, 2–1)	1	2	3	3	2	0

Wild pitch: Walk, Robinson. Balk: Walk. Time, 2:47.
Attendance, 19,361.

Carlton Wins 15th Straight Game

Of all the outstanding games hurled by Phillies pitchers, one of the most exciting was surely the August 17, 1972, contest when Steve Carlton won his 15th game in a row.

The game had all the trimmings of a World Series.

Although the Phillies that year were buried deep in last place in the National League East, Carlton was in the midst of one of the greatest seasons any pitcher ever had. When the season ended, he would have 27 of the team's 59 victories and would win his first of four Cy Young Awards.

No Phillies pitcher had ever won 15 in a row when Carlton took the mound against the Cincinnati Reds. In fact, no one in the National League had won that many games since 1962 when Jack Sanford collected 16 straight decisions for the San Francisco Giants.

It was Carlton's wife Betty's birthday, and a crowd of 53,377 thundered into Veterans Stadium to watch Steve go for his 15th straight and 20th win of the season. Even before the game started, the fans were on their feet, stomping and cheering for Carlton. From the moment he first set foot on the field, the Vet rocked with the clamor of the fans.

Carlton was facing a team that within a few years would be the powerhouse of the National League. The soon-to-be Big Red Machine's lineup boasted the likes of Pete Rose, Joe Morgan, Johnny Bench, and George Foster; the Phillies at the time were 27½ games out of first place with a 42–69 record, 10 games behind the fifth-place Montreal Expos.

The Phillies jumped out to a 2–0 lead in the second, but key hits by Rose and Morgan gave Cincinnati a 3–2 edge in the third. Eventually, however, the Phillies rode two-run homers by Deron Johnson and Willie Montanez to a 9–4 victory. Carlton finished with two strikeouts and four walks while allowing seven hits. It was his first victory over the Reds since 1967.

Although he admitted he had trouble with his curve ball and was not at his sharpest, Carlton had his 15th straight win and was assured a spot in the Phillies' record book.

"I guess I was excited," he said afterward. "We all were excited."

Carlton was back in the clubhouse when the fans started chanting his name. Interim manager Paul Owens approached Steve at his locker and urged him to go back to the playing field.

"To be called back that way by the crowd, I've never seen anything like that in my life," Owens said as he stood in the dugout watching Carlton accept the applause of the fans.

Steve Carlton acknowledges ovation from fans after 15th straight victory in 1972.

It would be another 15 minutes before Carlton left the field. He shook hands and signed autographs, and seemed reluctant to leave. When he finally did, he returned to another hero's welcome in the clubhouse.

"This is the greatest thing that's ever happened to me in the big leagues," he said.

At least up to that point, he was right.

Phillies 9, Reds 4
August 17, 1972

Cincinnati	AB	R	H	BI	O	A
Rose, lf	5	1	1	1	4	0
Morgan, 2b	3	0	1	1	2	4
Tolan, cf	3	1	0	0	3	0
Bench, 1b	3	0	1	1	9	0
Menke, 3b	4	0	0	0	2	2
Foster, rf	4	0	0	0	1	0
Concepcion, ss	3	1	2	0	4	4
Plummer, c	4	1	2	1	2	3
Grimsley, p	0	0	0	0	0	0
Sprague, p	0	0	0	0	0	0
a-Javier	1	0	0	0	0	0
Carroll, p	0	0	0	0	0	0
b-McCrae	1	0	0	0	0	0
Totals	**31**	**4**	**7**	**4**	**27**	**13**

Phillies	AB	R	H	BI	O	A
Harmon, 2b	3	2	2	0	2	2
Bowa, ss	4	1	2	1	1	3
Money, 3b	4	0	0	1	1	2
Montanez, cf	4	2	2	2	4	0
Luzinski, lf	4	2	3	1	2	0
Johnson, 1b	4	1	2	2	10	0
Hutton	0	0	0	0	1	0
Robinson, rf	3	0	3	1	3	0
Bateman, c	3	1	2	0	3	1
Carlton, p	4	0	0	0	0	4
Totals	**33**	**9**	**16**	**8**	**27**	**12**

a-Flied to Robinson for Sprague in 7th.
b-Flied to Luzinski for Carroll in 9th.

Cincinnati	0	0	3	0	0	0	1	0	0	— 4
Phillies	0	2	0	0	3	2	2	0	x	— 9

	IP	H	R	ER	BB	SO
Carlton	9	7	4	4	4	2
Grimsley	4⅓	9	5	5	1	2
Sprague	1⅔	4	2	1	1	0
Carroll	2	3	2	2	1	1

Errors: Bench. Double play: 1 Cincinnati, Concepcion to Bench. Left on base: Phillies 4, Cincinnati 5. Two-base hits: Robinson, 2, Plummer, Morgan. Three-base hit: Montanez. Home runs: Johnson (7), Montanez (12), Rose. Stolen bases: Harmon, Tolan (2), Rose. Sacrifices: Bowa, Grimsley (2). Sacrifice flies: Money, Robinson.

Wild pitch: Carroll 7th. Umpires: Froemming, Landes, Davidson, Donatelli. Time, 2:04. Attendance, 42,635.

Mickey Morandini Makes an Unassisted Triple Play

It took fewer than 10 seconds. But in that short span, Mickey Morandini inscribed his name in the record book, achieving one of the rarest feats in baseball.

By snaring a line drive off the bat of the Pittsburgh Pirates' Jeff King, touching second base to retire Andy Van Slyke and tagging Barry Bonds who stood a few feet away, Morandini became only the ninth player in big league history and the first in the National League in 65 years to pull off an unassisted triple play.

It happened in the sixth inning of a Phillies 3–2 loss September 20, 1992, at Three Rivers Stadium. Curt Schilling was on the mound for the Phillies.

Leading off the sixth, Van Slyke poked a single to right. Bonds followed by beating out an infield hit to shortstop. Then up stepped King, who slashed a low line drive.

"Catching his ball was probably the hardest thing about the whole play," Morandini said. "I had to go to my right and dive for the ball. After that, it was take two steps, tag the bag, and tag the runner.

"As soon as I caught it," Morandini added, "I knew we had a triple play. A lot of things have to go right. You have to have no outs. You have to have the guys running. You have to have a line drive to a middle infielder. In this case, it all happened."

Morandini was the first second baseman ever to record an unassisted triple play during the regular season. The only other time a second sacker did it was the celebrated triple play of the Cleveland Indians' Bill Wambsganss in the 1920 World Series. Ironically, the player who hit the ball, pitcher Clarence Mitchell of the Brooklyn Dodgers, later played with the Phillies.

Directly or indirectly, the Phillies have been involved in several other major league unassisted triple plays.

The first unassisted triple play in the National League was registered in 1923 by Boston Braves shortstop Ernie Padgett against the Phillies. In 1927,

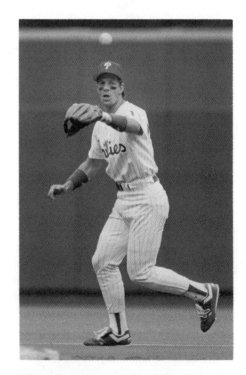

Mickey Morandini made the Phillies first unassisted triple play.

Jimmy Cooney got a triple play for the Chicago Cubs. One week later, he was traded to the Phillies. Cooney was also a base-runner in a triple play scored by the Pirates' Glenn Wright in 1925.

The Phillies had 25 previous triple plays, none of them unassisted.

Morandini, who said he had never seen an unassisted triple play before at any level of baseball, was thrilled with his accomplishment, once it sank in.

"I'm lucky to be part of history," he said. "It's something I'll never forget."

Pirates 3, Phillies 2 (13)
September 20, 1992

Phillies	AB	R	H	RBI
Javier, cf	5	0	1	0
Morandini, 2b	6	0	2	0
Kruk, 1b	4	0	1	0
Hollins, 3b	6	1	2	1
Pratt, c	6	0	1	0
Duncan, lf	5	1	1	1
Castillo, rf	3	0	1	0
Amaro, rf	2	0	0	0
Ju. Bell, ss	4	0	0	0
Grotewold, ph	1	0	0	0
Millette, ss	0	0	0	0
Schilling, p	3	0	1	0
Jordan, ph	1	0	0	0
Williams, p	0	0	0	0
Daulton, ph	1	0	0	0
Shepherd, p	0	0	0	0
Totals	47	2	10	2

Pittsburgh	AB	R	H	RBI
Espy, rf	4	1	2	0
Ja. Bell, ss	5	0	1	0
VanSlyke, cf	6	0	1	0
Bonds, lf	5	1	2	0
King, 3b	5	0	1	2
Merced, 1b	5	1	1	0
LaValliere, c	4	0	2	0
Young, pr	0	0	0	0
Patterson, p	0	0	0	0
Belinda, p	0	0	0	0
Cole, ph	1	0	0	0
Mason, p	0	0	0	0
Lind, 2b	2	0	0	0
Clark, ph	0	0	0	0
Pennyfeather, pr	0	0	0	0
Neagle, p	0	0	0	0
Cox, p	0	0	0	0
Martin, ph	1	0	0	0
Prince, c	1	0	0	0
Tomlin, p	2	0	0	0
Varsho, ph	0	0	0	1
Garcia, 2b	0	0	0	0
Redus, ph	1	0	0	0
Wehner, 3b	1	0	0	0
Totals	43	3	10	3

Phillies	0 1 0 0 0 0 0 1 0 0 0 0 0 — 2	
Pittsburgh	0 0 0 1 0 0 1 0 0 0 0 0 1 — 3	

Two outs when winning run scored. Errors: Castillo (2). Double play: Pittsburgh 2. Triple play: Phillies 1. Left on base: Phillies 9, Pittsburgh 9. Two-base hits: Espy (7), Merced (27). Three-base hits: Javier (1), Bonds (5). Home runs: Hollins (25), Duncan (8). Stolen bases: Javier (15), Morandini (7). Sacrifices: Ja. Bell. Sacrifice flies: King, Varsho.

Phillies	IP	H	R	ER	BB	SO
Schilling	9	9	2	1	1	3
Williams	2	0	0	0	1	3
Shepherd (L, 1–1)	1⅔	1	1	1	2	1

Wild pitch: Schilling. Time, 3:46. Attendance, 21,652.

Pittsburgh	IP	H	R	ER	BB	SO
Tomlin	7	8	1	1	1	5
Neagle	1	1	1	1	0	2
Cox	1	0	0	0	0	0
Patterson	⅔	1	0	0	1	1
Belinda	2⅓	0	0	0	1	1
Mason (W, 5–6)	1	0	0	0	0	1

Phillies Hit Five Home Runs in One Inning

As hitting explosions go, the Phillies' salvo in 1949 in the eighth inning of a game at Shibe Park is unparalleled in club history.

The Phillies were in the midst of a three-week batting slump when they tangled June 2 with the Cincinnati Reds. As the Phils entered the bottom of the eighth, trailing, 3–2, there were no signs that the slump was ending.

Former Phillies pitcher Ken Raffensberger was working on a four-hitter when Del Ennis stepped to the plate to lead off the inning. Ennis promptly belted Raffensberger's first pitch into the upper deck in left field, and what would become a 10-run inning with five home runs had begun.

On the very next pitch, Andy Seminick slammed his second home run of the game over the left field roof. The blow finished Raffensberger, who was replaced by Jess Dobernic.

After Stan Hollmig lined out to shortstop, Willie Jones homered into the lower left field stands. Eddie Miller followed by popping out for the second out, but Schoolboy Rowe, a fine hitting pitcher, hammered the fourth home run of the inning into the upper deck in left.

Reds manager Bucky Walters, another former Phillies pitcher, summoned Kent Peterson from the bullpen, but the onslaught continued. Richie Ashburn walked, and Granny Hamner doubled off the left field wall, just missing a home run by a foot. Eddie Waitkus reached first on an error by the Reds' Ted Kluszewski with Ashburn scoring. Then Ennis doubled to drive in Hamner.

Seminick then drilled a pitch into the left field lower deck for his second home run of the inning and third of the game. Hollmig was hit by a pitch and scored on a triple by Jones before Miller struck out to end the inning.

By then, the Phillies had taken a 12–3 lead, scoring 10 runs on eight hits, one walk, one hit batter, and one error. The Phillies went on to win by that score with Rowe getting the next-to-last win of his 15-year big league career.

No other Phillies team ever hit five home runs in one inning, either before or since. And only two other teams in big league history have done it—the New York Giants in a 17–3 win over the Reds in 1939 and the San Francisco Giants in a 14–0 victory over the Reds in 1961.

Phillies 12, Reds 3
June 2, 1949

Cincinnati	AB	R	H	RBI
Adams, 3b	4	0	1	0
Baumholtz, rf	4	0	1	1
Stallcup, ss	4	0	0	0
Bloodworth, 2b	4	0	1	0
Kluszewski, 1b	4	0	0	0
Litwhiler, lf	3	1	1	0
Mueller, c	4	1	2	0
Wyrostek, cf	4	1	1	1
Raffensberger, p	3	0	1	1
Dobernic, p	0	0	0	0
Peterson, p	0	0	0	0
Kress, ph	1	0	0	0
Totals	**35**	**3**	**8**	**3**

Phillies	AB	R	H	RBI
Ashburn, cf	3	1	0	0
Hamner, ss	5	2	3	0
Waitkus, 1b	5	1	0	0
Ennis, lf	4	2	2	2
Seminick, c	4	3	3	5
Hollmig, rf	4	1	1	1
Mayo, rf	0	0	0	0
Jones, 3b	5	1	2	2
Miller, 2b	5	0	0	0
Simmons, p	2	0	0	0
Lopata, ph	0	0	0	0
Rowe, p	1	1	1	1
Totals	**38**	**12**	**12**	**11**

```
Cincinnati   0  0  0  0  2  0  1  0  0 — 3
Phillies     0  1  0  0  0  1  0  10 x — 12
```

Errors: Adams, Kluszewski 2, Ennis. Two-base hits: Bloodworth, Adams, Mueller, Raffensberger, Hamner. Three-base hit: Jones. Home runs: Seminick 3, Ennis, Jones, Rowe. Left on base: Cincinnati 6, Phillies 8. Bases on balls: Raffensberger 4, Peterson 1, Rowe 1. Strikeouts: Simmons 6, Raffensberger 4, Peterson 1, Rowe 1. Hits: off Simmons 8 in 7 innings; Rowe 0 in 2; Raffensberger 6 in 7; Dobernic 2 in ⅔; Peterson 4 in ⅓. Hit by pitcher: by Peterson (Hollmig). Winning pitcher: Rowe (2–3). Losing pitcher: Raffensberger (6–4). Umpires: Barr, Ballanfant, and Barlick. Time, 2:39. Attendance, 10,549.

Phillies who hit five home runs in one inning in 1949 game were (from left) Schoolboy Rowe, Del Ennis, Andy Seminick, and Willie Jones. Seminick homered twice.

The New Phillies Encyclopedia

Phillies No-Hitters

Terry Mulholland pitched the first Phillies' home no-hitter in the 20th century.

Phillies pitchers have not exactly turned in a bushel of no-hitters. In fact, only eight Phils have pitched such games. At one point, the club went 58 years between no-hitters.

The first Phillies no-hitter was pitched by Charlie Ferguson. On August 29, 1885, he blanked the Providence Grays, 1–0. Ferguson struck out eight and walked two.

Red Donahue became the next Phillies no-hit pitcher, whitewashing the Boston Braves, 5–0, on July 8, 1898, at Baker Bowl. Donahue struck out one and walked two.

On September 18, 1903, Chick Fraser no-hit the Chicago Cubs, 10–0, in Chicago. Four Cubs fanned, and five got bases on balls.

The first lefthander to pitch a no-hitter for the Phillies was John Lush. On May 1, 1906, he beat the Brooklyn Dodgers, 6–0, striking out 11 and walking three in a game at Brooklyn.

No other Phillies pitcher recorded a no-hitter until June 21, 1964, when Jim Bunning pitched a perfect game against the New York Mets at Shea Stadium. Bunning struck out 10 en route to a 6–0 victory in what was the major leagues' first regular season perfect game in 42 years.

Seven years later, Rick Wise fired a no-hitter at the Cincinnati Reds at Crosley Field. The Phillies won the June 23, 1971, game, 4–0, with Wise not only striking out three and walking one, but also delivering two home runs and collecting three RBI.

Another long no-hit drought followed. The next Phillies no-hitter came August 15, 1990, when Terry Mulholland beat the San Francisco Giants, 6–0, at Veterans Stadium in the first home no-hitter by a Phils pitcher in the 20th century. Mulholland struck out eight, walked none, and came within one batter of hurling a perfect game.

Tommy Greene added the eighth no-hitter to the Phillies' list on May 23, 1991, when he beat the Montreal Expos, 2–0, at Olympic Stadium. Greene struck out 10 and walked seven.

Phillies pitchers have tossed 49 one-hitters, including five each by Grover Cleveland Alexander and Steve Carlton, three by Robin Roberts, and two each by Frank Corridon and Tully Sparks.

NO-HIT GAMES BY PHILLIES

Red Donahue, July 8, 1898, Boston at Philadelphia

Boston	AB	R	H	O	A
Long, ss	3	0	0	3	2
Tenney, 1b	4	0	0	6	0
Duffy, cf	4	0	0	2	0
Collins, 3b	4	0	0	2	0
Stahl, lf	3	0	0	1	0
Stivetts, rf	3	0	0	0	0
Lowe, 2b	3	0	0	3	1
Bergen, c	3	0	0	7	2
Willis, p	2	0	0	0	2
Totals	29	0	0	24	7

Phillies	AB	R	H	O	A
Cooley, cf	4	0	0	5	0
Douglas, 1b	3	2	2	8	0
Delahanty, lf	4	1	3	5	0
Lajoie, 2b	4	0	0	2	4
Flick, rf	2	1	0	4	0
McFarland, c	2	0	1	1	0
Lauder, 3b	4	0	0	0	1
Cross, ss	2	1	1	2	3
Donahue, p	2	0	1	0	0
Totals	27	5	7	27	8

Boston   0 0 0 0 0 0 0 0 0 — 0
Phillies   1 1 0 0 3 0 0 0 x — 5

Errors: Cross, Stahl, Lauder. Two-base hit: McFarland. Stolen bases: Long, Douglas, Delahanty 2. Sacrifices: Donahue, Cooley. Left on base: Boston 4, Philadelphia 10. Bases on balls; Donahue 2, Willis 8. Strikeouts: Donahue 1, Willis 7. Hit by pitcher: by Willis (Douglas, Cross). Passed ball: Bergen. Umpires: Gaffney and Brown. Time, 1:50.

Chick Fraser, September 18, 1903, Philadelphia at Chicago

Phillies	AB	R	H	O	A
Thomas, cf	3	0	1	4	0
Hallman, 2b	5	2	1	2	3
Wolverton, 3b	4	2	2	1	2
Barry, lf	5	3	3	1	0
Titus, rf	4	2	2	1	0
Douglas, 1b	5	1	3	13	0
Hulswitt, ss	4	0	1	1	5
Zimmer, c	4	0	1	4	1
Fraser, p	3	0	0	0	2
Totals	37	10	14	27	13

Chicago	AB	R	H	O	A
Slagle, cf	3	0	0	0	0
McCarthy, lf	4	0	0	1	0
Chance, 1b	2	0	0	12	0
Jones, rf	4	0	0	0	0
Tinker, ss	4	0	0	2	5
Kling, c	4	0	0	5	5
Evers, 2b	3	0	0	5	5
Casey, 3b	2	0	0	2	3
Graham, p	2	0	0	0	3
Currie, p	1	0	0	0	1
Totals	29	0	0	27	22

Errors: Hulswitt 3, Hallman, Slagle, McCarthy, Kling. Left on base: Chicago 7, Philadelphia 7. Two-base hits: Zimmer, Barry. Double plays: Kling, Casey; Zimmer, Wolverton; Fraser, Hulswitt, Douglas. Sacrifice hit: Titus. Stolen bases: Chance 2. Struck out: by Graham 4, Fraser 4. First base on balls: off Graham 3, Fraser 5. Hit by pitcher: Wolverton. Umpires: Emslie and Moran. Time, 1:40. Attendance, 2,000.

Phillies   4 0 0 0 2 0 1 0 3 — 10
Chicago   0 0 0 0 0 0 0 0 0 — 0

John Lush, May 1, 1906, Philadelphia at Brooklyn

Phillies	AB	R	H	O	A
Thomas, cf	4	2	2	1	0
Ward, 3b	5	2	4	0	2
Magee, rf	4	1	1	0	0
Titus, lf	4	1	2	2	0
Bransfield, 1b	4	0	1	7	1
Doolin, ss	2	0	0	1	3
Gleason, 2b	4	0	1	2	2
Dooin, c	4	0	0	11	0
Lush, p	4	0	0	3	1
Totals	35	6	11	27	9

Brooklyn	AB	R	H	O	A
Lumley, rf	4	0	0	3	0
Maloney, cf	3	0	0	3	0
Casey, 3b	4	0	0	2	3
Jordan, 1b	4	0	0	6	1
Batch, lf	2	0	0	1	0
Lewis, ss	2	0	0	1	0
Hummel, 2b	3	0	0	4	2
Bergen, c	3	0	0	6	3
Eason, p	2	0	0	1	2
a-McIntyre	1	0	0	0	0
Knolls, p	0	0	0	0	0
Totals	28	0	0	27	11

a-Batted for Eason in 8th.

```
Phillies   2 0 0 1 0 0 0 2 1—6
Brooklyn   0 0 0 0 0 0 0 0 0—0
```

Errors: Casey 2, Doolin, Bergen, Eason. Three-base hit: Ward. Hits: off Eason 9, in eight innings; off Knolls 2, in one inning. Sacrifice hits: Doolin, Casey. Stolen base: Titus. Left on base: Philadelphia 6, Brooklyn 4. First base on balls: off Eason 3, off Knolls 1, off Lush 3. First base on errors: Philadelphia 2, Brooklyn 1. Struck out: by Eason 1, by Knolls, 1, by Lush 11. Umpire: O'Day. Time, 1:45.

See page 560 for Jim Bunning's perfect game.

Rick Wise, June 23, 1971, Philadelphia at Cincinnati

Phillies	AB	R	H	RBI
Harmon, 2b	4	0	0	0
Bowa, ss	4	0	0	0
McCarver, c	3	0	2	0
Johnson, 1b	2	0	0	0
Lis, lf	2	1	0	0
Stone, lf	1	0	0	0
Montanez, cf	4	0	1	0
Freed, rf	4	1	1	1
Vukovich, 3b	4	0	1	0
Wise, p	4	2	2	3
Totals	32	4	7	4

Cincinnati	AB	R	H	RBI
Rose, rf	4	0	0	0
Foster, cf	3	0	0	0
May 1b	3	0	0	0
Bench, c	3	0	0	0
Perez, 3b	3	0	0	0
McRae, lf	3	0	0	0
Granger, p	0	0	0	0
Helms, 2b	3	0	0	0
Concepcion, ss	1	0	0	0
Stewart, ph	1	0	0	0
Grimsley, p	1	0	0	0
Carbo, ph	1	0	0	0
Carroll, p	0	0	0	0
Cline, lf	1	0	0	0
Totals	27	0	0	0

```
Phillies    0 1 0 0 2 0 0 1 0—4
Cincinnati  0 0 0 0 0 0 0 0 0—0
```

Phillies	IP	H	R	ER	BB	SO
Wise W, (8–4)	9	0	0	0	1	3

Cincinnati	IP	H	R	ER	BB	SO
Grimsley (L, 4–3)	6	4	3	3	2	1
Carroll	2	2	1	1	1	1
Granger	1	1	0	0	0	1

Double plays: Cincinnati 2. Left on base: Philadelphia 5, Cincinnati 1. Two-base hits: Montanez, Freed. Home runs: Wise 2 (4). Hit by pitch: by Grimsley (Lis). Umpires: Dale, Gorman, Pelekoudas, and Harvey. Time, 1:53. Attendance, 13,329.

Terry Mulholland, August 15, 1990, San Francisco at Philadelphia

San Francisco	AB	R	H	RBI
Parker, cf	3	0	0	0
Anderson, 2b	3	0	0	0
Downs, p	0	0	0	0
Clark, 1b	3	0	0	0
Mitchell, lf	3	0	0	0
Williams, 3b	3	0	0	0
Litton, rf	3	0	0	0
Kennedy, c	2	0	0	0
Bathe, ph	1	0	0	0
Uribe, ss	3	0	0	0
Robinson, p	2	0	0	0
Kingery, cf	0	0	0	0
Carter, ph	1	0	0	0
Totals	27	0	0	0

Phillies	AB	R	H	RBI
Dykstra, cf	4	1	1	1
Daulton, c	3	2	1	2
V. Hayes, lf	2	0	0	0
Murphy, rf	4	0	0	0
Kruk, 1b	4	1	2	1
Herr, 2b	3	1	1	0
C. Hayes, 3b	4	0	1	1
Thon, ss	4	1	1	0
Mulholland, p	3	0	1	1
Totals	31	6	8	6

```
San Francisco  0 0 0 0 0 0 0 0 0 — 0
Phillies       1 0 0 0 3 2 0 0 x — 6
```

Error: C. Hayes. Double play: Phillies 1 (Thon, Herr, and Kruk). Left on base: Phillies 5. Two-base hits: Dykstra, Kruk. Home runs: Daulton (10).

San Francisco	IP	H	R	ER	BB	SO
Robinson (L, 8–4)	6	7	6	6	4	3
Downs	2	1	0	0	0	0

Phillies	IP	H	R	ER	BB	SO
Mulholland (W, 7–6)	9	0	0	0	0	8

Time, 2:09. Attendance, 32,156.

Tommy Greene fired the Phillies' last no-hitter in 1991.

**Tommy Greene, May 23, 1991,
Philadelphia at Montreal**

Phillies	AB	R	H	RBI
Backman, 2b	4	0	1	0
Booker, 3b	4	0	1	0
Kruk, lf	3	1	1	0
Jordan, 1b	4	0	2	1
V. Hayes, c	4	1	1	0
Fletcher, c	4	0	1	1
Thon, ss	4	0	0	0
Morris, rf	3	0	1	0
Greene, p	4	0	0	0
Totals	**34**	**2**	**8**	**2**

Montreal	AB	R	H	RBI
DeShields, 2b	2	0	0	0
Grissom, cf	4	0	0	0
Calderon, lf	2	0	0	0
Galarraga, 1b	4	0	0	0
Walker, rf	4	0	0	0
Wallach, 3b	2	0	0	0
Hassey, c	2	0	0	0
Owen, ss	3	0	0	0
Boyd, p	2	0	0	0
Bullock, ph	0	0	0	0
Ruskin, p	0	0	0	0
Jones, p	0	0	0	0
Totals	**25**	**0**	**0**	**0**

Phillies	1	0	0	0	0	0	0	0	1	—2
Montreal	0	0	0	0	0	0	0	0	0	—0

Left on base: Phillies 7, Montreal 6. Two-base hits: Kruk (6), V. Hayes (9), Fletcher (4). Three-base hits: Jordan (2). Stolen bases: Backman (1), DeShields (18), Calderon (11). CS: DeShields (6). Sacrifice: DeShields.

Phillies	IP	H	R	ER	BB	SO
Greene (W, 3–0)	9	0	0	0	7	10

Montreal	IP	H	R	ER	BB	SO
Boyd (L, 2–5)	8	6	1	1	1	6
Ruskin	0	2	1	1	0	0
Jones	1	0	0	0	1	0

Ruskin pitched to 2 batters in the 9th. Wild pitch: Boyd. Time, 2:25. Attendance, 8,833.

Pete Rose Sets Record for Hits

Few games at Veterans Stadium were more memorable than the one in which Pete Rose set the National League record for most career hits. It was a night that none of the 60,561 fans who were there will likely ever forget.

Some 60 days earlier, on June 10, 1981, Rose had tied Stan Musial's National League record with a first-inning single off Nolan Ryan of the Houston Astros. The hit, coming off a fastball on a 2–1 count, in Rose's first trip to the plate in the first inning, dropped into left-center field and gave Pete 3,630 career hits.

A crowd of 57,386 was on hand to see Rose break the record. But Ryan struck him out the next three times before leaving in the eighth inning when he developed stiffness in his back. Ryan had allowed just two hits and had a 4–0 lead at the time. The Phillies went on to score five runs in the eighth to win, 5–4, with Steve Carlton gaining his ninth win in 10 decisions.

Right after the game, major league players went on strike. They did not return to action until August 10. That afternoon, Rose drove to the Vet from his home in Ohio, where he had gone for the duration of the strike. Rose was anxious to break the record, and so were the fans who jammed Veterans Stadium.

Musial was on hand, seated in a box seat near the Phillies' dugout. When Rose came to bat in the first inning, everyone in the stadium stood and cheered. Pete sent a grounder to shortstop Garry Templeton, who booted the ball and was charged with an error.

Batting against Bob Forsch of the St. Louis Cardinals, Rose grounded out the next two times up. Then in the eighth, after changing to a lighter bat, and facing reliever Mark Littell, Rose hit a 0–1 fastball between short and third. The ball hopped into left field, and Rose had his record 3,631st hit.

Fireworks exploded. Musial jumped the fence to congratulate Rose. And the fans stood and cheered for minutes on end.

"I wouldn't classify it (the hit) as a bleeder," Rose said. "Pete Rose gets a lot of hits like that. You didn't think I was going to hit a home run, did you?"

It mattered little that the Phillies lost, 7–3. Rose had his record. Ironically, it broke the mark held by a man who played his last year the year Pete broke in as a rookie.

First Game after Strike—Pete Rose's 3,631st Hit
August 10, 1981

St. Louis	AB	R	H	RBI
Templeton, ss	4	0	2	1
Herr, 2b	5	0	1	0
Hernandez, 1b	5	2	2	1
Hendrick, cf	4	1	1	1
Iorg, lf	3	1	3	0
Littell, p	1	0	0	0
Sutter, p	0	0	0	0
Oberkfell, 3b	3	0	2	2
S Lezcano, rf	4	1	1	1
Tenace, c	4	1	1	1
Brummer, c	0	0	0	0
Forsch, p	2	0	0	0
Landrum, lf	2	1	2	0
Totals	**37**	**7**	**15**	**7**

Phillies	AB	R	H	RBI
Rose, 1b	5	2	1	0
Trillo, 2b	4	0	1	0
McBride, rf	3	0	0	0
L Smith, rf	1	1	1	0
Schmdt, 3b	4	0	2	2
Matthews, lf	4	0	0	1
Maddox, cf	3	0	0	0
Moreland, c	1	0	0	0
Bowa, ss	3	0	1	0
Aguayo, ss	1	0	0	0
B Boone, c	2	0	0	0
Proly, p	0	0	0	0
D Davis, ph	1	0	1	0
Christenson, p	1	0	0	0
Gross, ph	1	0	0	0
Lyle, p	0	0	0	0
Unser, cf	2	0	0	0
Totals	**36**	**3**	**7**	**3**

St. Louis   1 0 0 2 0 1 1 0 2 — 7
Phillies   1 0 0 0 0 0 0 2 0 — 3

Error: Templeton 2. Left on base: St. Louis 5, Phillies 7. Two-base hits: Schmidt, Oberkfell, Landrum, Bowa, D. Davis. Home runs: Hernandez (5), Hendrick (11), S. Lezcano (3), Tenace (2). Stolen base: Oberkfell. Sacrifice: Templeton.

St. Louis	IP	H	R	ER	BB	SO
Forsch (W, 7–2)	5	1	1	0	1	0
Littell	2⅓	5	2	2	0	2
Sutter S, 12	1⅔	1	0	0	0	0

Phillies	IP	H	R	ER	BB	SO
Christenson (L, 2–6)	5	8	3	3	0	4
Lyle	2	4	2	2	1	1
Proly	2	3	2	2	0	1

Wild pitch: Forsch. Time, 2:26. Attendance, 60,561.

Stan Musial joined Pete Rose after Phillies' first baseman broke Musial's National League record for career hits in 1981.

Two of the finest pitchers for the Phillies in the 1960s were lefthander Chris Short and righthander Art Mahaffey. Both were tall, slender hurlers who had crackling fastballs. For much of their stay with the Phillies, they were also roommates.

Short and Mahaffey also had one other thing in common. They had the two highest strikeout games in Phillies history.

Short set the club record on October 2, 1965, when he fanned 18 New York Mets in 15 innings at Shea Stadium in the second game of a doubleheader. The game eventually lasted 18 innings before it was halted by a New York curfew with the score tied at 0–0.

Short, Mahaffey Set Strikeout Records

Chris Short struck out 18 Mets in a 15-inning game in 1965.

Art Mahaffey established Phillies record for strikeouts in a nine inning game when he fanned 17 Cubs in 1961.

Mahaffey struck out 17 Chicago Cubs in a 6–0 victory at Connie Mack Stadium on April 23, 1961, in the second game of a doubleheader. At the time, the feat tied Dizzy Dean of the St. Louis Cardinals for the National League record.

Short didn't get his first strikeout of the game in until he fanned Bud Harrelson to end the second inning. He struck out the side only twice (in the third and seventh innings) and three times failed in an inning to strike out anybody.

The Phils' southpaw was in trouble several times during the game, including in the third inning when he had to pitch out of a bases-loaded jam. The Mets had runners on first and second in the bottom of the ninth.

During his 15 innings of work, Short gave up nine hits and walked three. The Phillies managed just five hits off Mets starter Rob Gardner, who also pitched 15 innings, struck out seven, and walked two.

Short was lifted for a pinch-hitter in the 16th inning. The game continued on through 18 innings before being halted by a 1 A.M. curfew.

Mahaffey's masterpiece had a more suitable ending. Making his second start of the season, the righthander scattered four hits and walked just one while setting a Phillies record for most strikeouts in a regulation game.

Mahaffey fanned two Cubs in the first inning, then struck out Ron Santo, Ernie Banks, and Frank Thomas in the second. He struck out the side in the sixth. Art gave up his first hit of the game in the third to former Phillie Ed Bouchee. The Cubs put two men on base only once—in the fifth.

The Phils' victory was aided by John Callison, who drove in four runs with a sacrifice fly and a three-run homer.

Art Mahaffey Fans 17
April 23, 1961

Chicago	AB	R	H	RBI	O	A
Heist, cf	4	0	0	0	0	0
Zimmer, 2b	4	0	1	0	2	8
Will, rf	4	0	1	0	1	0
Santo, 3b	4	0	0	0	0	0
Banks, ss	4	0	0	0	4	4
Thomas, lf	3	0	0	0	0	0
Bouchee, 1b	2	0	1	0	12	2
S. Taylor, c	2	0	0	0	2	0
Thacker, c	0	0	0	0	1	0
a-Ashburn	1	0	0	0	0	0
Bartell, c	0	0	0	0	1	1
Anderson, p	2	0	1	0	1	3
b-Drake	1	0	0	0	0	0
Drott, p	0	0	0	0	0	0
Totals	30	0	4	0	24	18

Phillies	AB	R	H	RBI	O	A
Sadowski, 3b	4	1	0	0	0	0
T. Taylor, 2b	2	2	1	0	2	1
Callison, rf	2	1	1	4	3	0
Smith, lf	4	0	0	0	1	0
Gonzalez, cf	4	0	2	2	1	0
Herrera, 1b	2	1	1	0	4	0
Dalrymple, c	3	0	0	0	16	1
Amaro, ss	3	1	2	0	0	1
Mahaffey, p	2	0	0	0	0	1
Totals	26	6	7	c-5	27	4

	IP	H	R	ER	BB	SO
Mahaffey	9	4	0	0	1	17
Anderson (6)	7	5	5	3	3	3
Drott	1	2	1	1	0	1

a-Lined out for Thacker in 8th.
b-Struck out for Anderson in 8th.
c-Herrera scored on Santo's error in 2nd.

Errors: Santo 2, Herrera. Two-base hits: Herrera, Bouchee. Three-base hit: Amaro. Home run: Callison. Sacrifices: T. Taylor, Mahaffey. Double plays: Zimmer, Banks, and Bouchee; Banks, Zimmer, and Bouchee; Zimmer and Banks. Left on base: Chicago 5, Phillies 2.

Umpires: Dascoli, Secory, Venzon, Sudol. Time, 2:16. Attendance, 16,027.

Chicago	0	0	0	0	0	0	0	0	0—0
Phillies	1	1	0	0	3	0	0	1	x—6

Chris Short Fans 18
October 2, 1965

Phillies	AB	R	H	RBI	O	A
Phillips, cf	6	0	1	0	5	0
e-Callison, rf	1	0	0	0	0	0
Rojas, 2b	6	0	1	0	2	3
Allen, 3b	7	0	2	0	2	2
Stuart, 1b	7	0	1	0	16	1
Amaro, ss	0	0	0	0	0	0
Johnson, lf	6	0	0	0	2	0
g-Briggs, cf	1	0	0	0	1	0
Gonzalez, rf, cf, lf	5	0	1	0	2	0
Wine, ss	5	0	0	0	1	8
Hernnstein, 1b	1	0	0	0	2	0
Corrales, c	6	0	0	0	19	1
k-Dalrymple, c	1	0	0	0	2	0
Short, p	5	0	0	0	0	1
d-Covington	1	0	0	0	0	0
j-Sorrell	1	0	0	0	0	0
Baldschun, p	0	0	0	0	0	1
Wagner, p	0	0	0	0	0	0
Totals	**59**	**0**	**6**	**0**	**54**	**17**

New York	AB	R	H	RBI	O	A
Hunt, 2b	8	0	2	0	6	5
Christopher, rf, lf	7	0	2	0	2	0
Smith, 3b	8	0	1	0	0	4
Hickman, 1b	6	0	2	0	20	1
Swoboda, lf	1	0	0	0	1	0
Napoleon, lf	5	0	0	0	6	0
Gossen, c	4	0	1	0	8	0
Klaus, ss	1	0	0	0	2	5
Jones, cf	7	0	1	0	5	0
Harrelson, ss	3	0	0	0	1	3
Cannizzaro, c	2	0	0	0	2	1
Gardner, p	5	0	0	0	0	3
a-Selma	0	0	0	0	0	0
b-McMillan	1	0	0	0	0	0
c-Shaffer	1	0	0	0	0	0
f-Lewis, rf	0	0	0	0	0	0
h-Stephenson, c	1	0	0	0	1	0
i-Kranepool	1	0	0	0	0	0
Sutherland, p	0	0	0	0	0	0
Ribant, p	0	0	0	0	0	0
Totals	**61**	**0**	**9**	**0**	**54**	**22**

a-Ran for Goosen in 9th.
b-Struck out for Harrelson in 9th.
c-Struck out for Gardner in 15th.
d-Flied out for Short in 16th.
e-Popped out for Phillips in 16th.
f-Hit by pitch for Napoleon in 16th.
g-Grounded out for Johnson in 17th.
h-Flied out for Canizzaro in 17th.
i-Struck out for Sutherland in 17th.
j-Popped out for Corrales in 18th.
k-Fouled out for Wagner in 18th.

Errors: Harrelson, Goosen. Double play: Rojas, Wine, Stuart. Left on base: Phillies 9, New York 12. Two-base hits: Hunt, Christopher, Hickman, Gonzalez. Stolen bases: Rojas, Hickman, Hunt. Sacrifice: Wine.

	IP	H	R	ER	BB	SO
Short	15	9	0	0	3	18
Wagner	2	0	0	0	1	1
Baldschun	1	0	0	0	0	2
Gardner	15	5	0	0	2	7
Sutherland	2	1	0	0	1	0
Ribant	1	0	0	0	0	0

Hit by pitcher: by Wagner, Lewis. Umpires: Weyer, Kibler, Secory, Burkhart. Time, 4:29. Attendance, 10,371.

Phillies	0 0 0 0 0 0 0 0 0 0 0 0 0 0 0 0 0 0
New York	0 0 0 0 0 0 0 0 0 0 0 0 0 0 0 0 0 0

Phillies with Hot Bats

The Phillies have had some memorable individual offensive performances over the years. Here are the best of them:

Ed Delahanty, Chuck Klein, and Mike Schmidt each hit four home runs in one game. Delahanty's four homers came July 13, 1896, in Chicago in a 9–8 loss to the Chicago White Stockings. Klein hit his four out of the park July 10, 1936, in a 9–6 victory over the Pittsburgh Pirates in 10 innings at Forbes Field. Schmidt slammed four home runs April 17, 1976, at Wrigley Field while the Phillies were beating the Chicago Cubs, 18–16.

Four Phillies—Kitty Bransfield, Gavvy Cravath, Willie Jones, and Mike Schmidt—each drove in eight runs in a single game.

Bransfield did it July 11, 1910, at Forbes Field, drilling two triples and three singles to lead the Phillies to an 18–0 win over the Pirates. Cravath hammered four doubles and drove in eight runs on August 8, 1915, in a 14–6 Phillies win over the Cincinnati Reds at Redland Field. Jones hit two home runs, a double, and a single as the Phillies downed the St. Louis Cardinals, 12–2, August 20, 1958, at Sportsman Park. Schmidt collected eight RBI when he socked four home runs and a single in a 1976 game against the Cubs.

Delahanty in 1894 and Connie Ryan in 1953 each had six hits in one game.

The New Phillies Encyclopedia

Ed Delahanty's Four Homers
July 13, 1896

Phillies	AB	R	H	O	A
Cooley, lf	3	1	1	1	0
Hulen, ss	4	1	1	1	4
Mertes, cf	5	1	0	1	0
Delahanty, 1b	5	4	5	9	0
Thompson, rf	5	0	1	2	0
Hallman, 2b	4	1	1	5	3
Clements, c	2	0	0	5	3
Nash, 3b	4	0	0	0	3
Garvin, p	4	0	0	0	1
Totals	**36**	**8**	**9**	**24**	**14**

Chicago	AB	R	H	O	A
Everett, 3b	3	1	2	1	3
Dahlen, ss	2	2	0	0	0
Lange, cf	4	2	2	4	0
Anson, 1b	3	0	1	12	2
Ryan, rf	4	1	1	2	0
Decker, lf	4	1	1	0	0
Pfeffer, 2b	4	0	2	1	4
Terry, p	4	1	2	2	3
Donohue, c	3	1	0	5	0
Totals	**31**	**9**	**11**	**27**	**12**

```
Phillies   2  0  0  1  3  0  1  0  1 — 8
Chicago    1  0  4  0  1  0  0  3  x — 9
```

Errors: Nash, Ryan, Decker. Two-base hits: Thompson, Lange, Decker, Terry. Three-base hits: Lange, Pfeffer. Home runs: Delahanty 4. Left on base: Philadelphia 6, Chicago 4. Bases on balls: off Terry 3, Garver 4. Struck out: by Terry 5, Garver 4. Double plays: Hulen, Hall, and Delahanty. Wild pitch: Garvin. Umpire: Emslie. Time, 2:15. Attendance, 1,100.

Chuck Klein's Four Homers
July 10, 1936

Phillies	AB	R	H
Sulik, cf	5	1	1
J. Moore, lf	5	1	1
Klein, rf	5	4	4
Camilli, 1b	4	2	1
Atwood, c	4	0	1
Wilson, c	0	1	0
Chiozza, 3b	5	0	2
Norris, ss	4	0	1
Gomez, 2b	5	0	0
Passeau, p	4	0	1
Walters, p	0	0	0
Totals	**41**	**9**	**12**

Pittsburgh	AB	R	H
Jensen, lf	4	1	1
L. Waner, cf	4	1	1
P. Waner, rf	4	2	2
Vaughan, ss	5	0	1
Suhr, 1b	4	0	2
Brubaker, 3b	5	0	0
Young, 2b	3	0	1
Lavagetto, 2b	1	1	0
Todd, c	2	0	0
Padden, c	2	1	0
Weaver, p	1	0	0
Lucas, ph	1	0	0
Brown, p	1	0	0
Schulte, ph	1	0	1
Finney, pr	0	0	0
Swift, p	0	0	0
Totals	**38**	**6**	**9**

```
Phillies   4  0  0  0  1  0  1  0  0  3 — 9
Pittsburgh 0  0  0  1  0  3  0  0  2  0 — 6
```

Errors: Norris 2, L. Waner, Vaughan 2, Young. Runs batted in: Klein 6, Norris 2, Suhr, P. Waner, Vaughan, Schulte, L. Waner, Chiozza. Two-base hit: Camilli. Three-base hit: Suhr. Home runs: Klein 4. Sacrifices: Atwood, Norris. Double plays: Chiozza, Gomez, and Camilli; Norris and Camilli; Vaughan, Lavagetto, and Suhr; Walters, Gomez, and Camilli. Left on base: Phillies 5, Pittsburgh 7. Bases on balls: off Weaver 1; off Passeau 1; off Brown 1. Hits: off Weaver 6 in 5 innings; off Passeau, 8 in 8⅔ innings; off Swift 4 in 1 inning; off Brown 2 in 4 innings; off Walters 1 in 1⅓ innings. Winning pitcher: Walters. Losing pitcher: Swift. Umpires: Sears, Klem, and Ballanfant. Time, 2:15.

Chuck Klein was one of three Phillies to hit four home runs in one game.

Mike Schmidt's Four Homers
April 17, 1976

Phillies	AB	R	H	RBI	O	A
Cash, 2b	6	1	2	2	4	3
Bowa, ss	6	3	3	1	2	0
Johnstone, rf	5	2	4	2	5	0
Luzinski, lf	5	0	1	1	0	0
Brown, lf	0	0	0	0	0	0
Allen, 1b	5	2	1	2	5	0
Schmidt, 3b	6	4	5	8	2	3
Maddox, cf	5	2	2	1	4	0
McGraw, p	0	0	0	0	0	0
e-McCarver, ph	1	1	1	0	0	0
Underwood, p	0	0	0	0	0	0
Lonborg, p	0	0	0	0	0	0
Boone, c	6	1	3	1	8	0
Carlton, p	1	0	0	0	0	0
Schueler, p	0	0	0	0	0	0
Garber, p	0	0	0	0	0	0
a-Hutton, ph	0	0	0	0	0	0
Reed, p	0	0	0	0	0	0
b-Martin, ph	1	0	0	0	0	0
Twitchell, p	0	0	0	0	0	0
c-Tolan, ph, cf	3	2	2	0	0	0
Totals	50	18	24	18	30	6

Chicago	AB	R	H	RBI	O	A
Monday, cf	6	3	4	4	4	0
Cardenal, lf	5	1	1	0	0	0
Summers, lf	0	0	0	0	3	0
d-Mitterwald, ph	1	0	0	0	0	0
Wallis, lf	1	0	0	0	0	0
Madlock, 3b	7	2	3	3	0	0
Morales, rf	5	2	1	0	1	0
Thornton, 1b	4	3	1	1	9	2
Trillo, 2b	5	0	2	3	3	4
Swisher, c	6	1	3	4	5	0
Rosello, ss	4	1	2	1	2	3
Kelleher, ss	2	0	1	0	2	1
R. Reuschel, p	1	2	0	0	1	3
Garman, p	0	0	0	0	0	0
Knowles, p	0	0	0	0	0	0
P. Reuschel, p	0	0	0	0	0	0
Schultz, p	0	0	0	0	0	1
f-Adams, ph	1	1	1	0	0	0
Totals	48	16	19	16	30	14

a-Walked for Garber in 4th.
b-Grounded out for Reed in 6th.
c-Singled for Twitchell in 8th.
d-Struck out for Summers in 8th.
e-Singled for McGraw in 10th.
f-Doubled for Schultz in 10th.

Phillies	0	1	0	1	2	0	3	5	3	3	—18
Chicago	0	7	5	1	0	0	0	0	2	1	—16

Errors: None. Double plays: Trillo, Rosello, and Thornton; Schmidt, Cash, and Allen. Left on base: Phillies 8, Chicago 12. Two-base hits: Cardenal, Madlock 2, Thornton, Boone, Adams. Three-base hits: Johnstone, Bowa. Home runs: Maddox (1), Swisher (1), Monday 2 (3), Schmidt 4 (5), Boone (1). Sacrifice: R. Reuschel, Johnstone. Sacrifice flies: Luzinski, Cash.

	IP	H	R	ER	BB	SO
Carlton	1⅔	7	7	7	2	1
Schueler	⅔	3	3	3	0	0
Garber	⅔	2	2	2	1	1
Reed	2	1	1	1	1	1
Twitchell	2	0	0	0	1	1
McGraw (W, 1–1)	2	4	2	2	1	2
Underwood	⅔	2	1	1	0	1
Lonborg	⅓	0	0	0	0	0
R. Reuschel	7	14	7	7	1	4
Garman	⅔	4	5	5	1	1
Knowles (L, 1–1)	1⅓	3	4	4	1	0
P. Reuschel	0	3	2	2	0	0
Schultz	1	0	0	0	0	0

Save: Lonborg (1). Hit by pitch: by Schueler (R. Reuschel), by Garber (Thornton), by Twitchell (Monday). Balk: Schultz. Umpires: Olsen, Davidson, Rennert, Vargo. Time, 3:42. Attendance, 28,287.

OTHER PENNANT OR DIVISION CLINCHERS

Phillies 5, Braves 0
September 29, 1915

Phillies	AB	R	H	O	A
Stock, 3b	4	0	0	2	4
Bancroft, ss	5	2	2	2	2
Paskert, cf	4	1	1	6	0
Cravath, rf	4	2	2	0	1
Luderus, 1b	4	0	1	11	0
Whitted, lf	4	0	1	1	0
Niehoff, 2b	4	0	1	1	2
Burns, c	4	0	0	4	0
Alexander, p	4	0	2	0	2
Totals	37	5	10	27	11

Boston	AB	R	H	O	A
Moran, rf	3	0	0	1	0
Evers, 2b	4	0	0	4	3
Compton, cf	4	0	0	3	0
Magee, 1b	3	0	1	9	1
Smith, 3b	3	0	0	0	3
Connally, lf	3	0	0	2	1
Maranville, ss	3	0	0	0	3
Gowdy, c	3	0	0	7	0
Rudolph, p	3	0	1	1	2
Totals	29	0	1	27	13

Phillies	3	0	0	1	0	0	1	0	0	—5
Boston	0	0	0	0	0	0	0	0	0	—0

Errors: Smith 2, Cravath. Two-base hits: Alexander, Cravath. Three-base hit: Paskert. Home run: Cravath. Left on base: Phils 7, Boston 3. First base on errors: Phils 2, Boston 1. Bases on balls: Alexander 1, Rudolph 1. Strikeouts: Alexander 4, Rudolph 6. Umpires: Rigler and O'Day. Time, 1:28.

Box Scores of Other Noteworthy Games

Phillies 4, Expos 1
September 26, 1976 (First Game)

Phillies	AB	R	H	RBI
Cash, 2b	3	1	2	0
Martin, rf, lf	4	1	1	0
Schmidt, 3b	4	0	2	0
Luzinski, lf	3	1	1	3
b-Tolan, 1b	0	0	0	0
Allen, 1b	4	0	0	0
Brown, rf	0	0	0	0
Maddox, cf	4	1	2	0
Boone, c	4	0	0	0
Bowa, ss	4	0	1	0
Lonborg, p	4	0	1	1
Totals	**34**	**4**	**10**	**4**

Montreal	AB	R	H	RBI
Unser, 1f	4	0	1	0
Garrett, 2b	3	1	0	0
Dawson, cf	4	0	1	1
Valentine, rf	4	0	0	0
Williams, 1b	4	0	0	0
Parrish, 3b	3	0	0	0
Foli, ss	3	0	2	0
Foote, c	3	0	0	0
Warthen, p	1	0	0	0
a-Cromartie	1	0	0	0
Kerrigan, p	0	0	0	0
c-Jorgenson	1	0	0	0
Murray, p	0	0	0	0
Totals	**31**	**1**	**4**	**1**

a-Grounded out for Warthen in 6th.
b-Ran for Luzinski in 8th.
c-Grounded out for Kerrigan in 8th.

Phillies   0 0 0 0 0 3 1 0 0 — 4
Montreal   0 0 0 0 0 1 0 0 0 — 1

Error: Dawson. Left on base: Phillies 5, Montreal 4.
Two-base hit: Dawson. Three-base hit: Bowa. Home run:
Luzinski (21). Stolen bases: Cash, Maddox.

	IP	H	R	ER	BB	SO
Lonborg (W, 17–10)	9	4	1	1	1	5
Warthen (L, 2–9)	6	4	3	3	1	6
Kerrigan	2	5	1	1	0	0
Murray	1	1	0	0	0	0

Hit by pitch: by Kerrigan (Luzinski). Wild pitch: Warthen.
Umpires: Tata, Gorman, B. Williams, McSherry. Time, 2:00.

Phillies 15, Cubs 9
September 27, 1977

Phillies	AB	R	H	RBI	O	A
McBride, rf	6	1	2	0	5	0
Bowa, ss	6	3	4	0	1	3
Schmidt, 3b	5	3	2	2	1	1
Luzinski, lf	4	1	1	1	3	0
Martin, 1b	1	0	1	2	0	0
Hebner, 1b	1	1	0	0	7	0
b-Brown	1	0	0	0	0	0
Hutton, 1b	2	0	1	0	2	0
Maddox, cf	4	1	1	2	3	0
Boone, c	5	2	2	3	5	0
Sizemore, 2b	3	1	1	0	0	1
Christenson, p	3	1	1	5	0	1
McGraw, p	0	1	0	0	0	1
Totals	**41**	**15**	**16**	**15**	**27**	**7**

Chicago	AB	R	H	RBI	O	A
DeJesus, ss	5	2	4	1	3	4
Gross, cf	5	2	2	2	1	0
Biittner, 1b	4	1	1	1	14	0
Murcer, rf	4	0	1	1	2	0
Ontiveros, 3b	5	1	3	2	1	5
Clines, lf	5	1	2	1	1	0
Trillo, 2b	4	1	2	0	1	3
Gordon, c	5	0	0	0	4	1
Bonham, p	2	1	1	0	0	0
a-Cardenal	1	0	0	0	0	0
P. Reuschel, p	0	0	0	0	0	0
Roberts, p	0	0	0	0	0	0
Lamp, p	0	0	0	0	0	0
c-Wallis	1	0	0	0	0	0
Giusti, p	0	0	0	0	0	0
Moore, p	0	0	0	0	0	1
d-Rosello	1	0	0	0	0	0
Totals	**42**	**9**	**16**	**8**	**27**	**15**

a-Fouled out for Bonham in 6th.
b-Struck out for Hebner in 7th.
c-Struck out for Lamp in 8th.
d-Hit into double play for Moore in 9th.

Phillies   0 2 0 0 0 2 7 1 3 — 15
Chicago   0 0 1 0 0 1 2 5 0 — 9

Errors: McBride, Luzinski, Trillo. Double plays: Moore,
DeJesus, and Biittner, McGraw, Bowa, and Hutton. Left on
base: Phillies 8, Chicago 9. Two-base hits: Bonham,
Ontiveros, Clines, Trillo. Three-base hit: Gross. Home runs:
Christenson (3), Schmidt (38). Stolen bases: DeJesus 2.
Sacrifices: Christenson, Hebner. Sacrifice fly: Murcer.

	IP	H	R	ER	BB	SO
Christenson (W, 18–6)	7	10	6	5	2	3
McGraw	2	6	3	3	0	2
Bonham (L, 10–13)	6	5	4	4	3	3
P. Reuschel	1/3	2	2	2	0	1
Roberts	1/3	0	1	1	1	0
Lamp	1 1/3	5	5	5	1	0
Giusti	1/3	4	3	3	1	0
Moore	2/3	0	0	0	0	0

Hit by pitch: by Bonham (Schmidt). Wild pitch: P. Reuschel.
Umpires: Olsen, Harvey, Rennert, Colosi. Time, 2:42.
Attendance, 4,606.

Phillies 10, Pirates 8
September 30, 1978

Phillies	AB	R	H	RBI
McBride, rf	6	2	3	0
Bowa, ss	6	1	1	0
Maddox, cf	4	2	3	0
Luzinski, lf	4	1	3	3
J Martin, lf	0	1	0	0
Hebner, 1b	4	1	2	4
Schmdt, 3b	3	0	0	1
Boone, c	5	0	2	0
Sizemore, 2b	2	0	0	0
Morrison, ph	1	0	0	0
Harrison, 2b	0	0	0	0
Lerch, p	2	2	2	2
Cardenal, ph	1	0	0	0
Brusstar, p	0	0	0	0
McCarver, ph	1	0	0	0
McGraw, p	0	0	0	0
Reed, p	0	0	0	0
Totals	**39**	**10**	**16**	**10**

Pittsburgh	AB	R	H	RBI
Taveras, ss	5	0	1	0
Moreno, cf	4	2	0	1
Parker, rf	5	2	2	2
B Robinson, 3b	5	1	3	1
Stargell, 1b	5	1	1	4
Garner, 2b	4	0	1	0
Berra, 3b	2	0	1	0
Milner, lf	2	0	0	0
Ott, c	3	1	2	0
D Robinson, p	2	0	1	0
G Jackson, p	0	0	0	0
D May ph	1	0	0	0
Whitson, p	0	0	0	0
Tekulve, p	0	0	0	0
Bibby, p	0	0	0	0
Gaston, ph	1	1	1	0
Totals	**39**	**8**	**13**	**8**

Philadelphia	1	1	0	1	0	3	0	4	0 — 10
Pittsburgh	4	0	0	0	0	0	0	0	4 — 8

Errors: Taveras, G. Jackson, Bowa. Double play: Pittsburgh 1. Left on base: Philadelphia 10, Pittsburgh 7. Two-base hits: Hebner 2, Luzinski, B. Robinson. Home runs: Lerch 2 (3), Stargel (28), Luzinski (35). Stolen base: Garner. Sacrifices: Harrelson, G. Maddox, McGraw. Sacrifice fly: Schmidt.

Phillies	IP	H	R	ER	BB	SO
Lerch (W, 11–8)	5	5	4	4	3	4
Brusstar	1	2	0	0	0	1
McGraw	2⅓	5	4	3	0	2
Reed	⅔	1	0	0	0	1

Pittsburgh	IP	H	R	ER	BB	SO
D. Robinson	4	9	3	3	0	1
G. Jackson (L, 7–5)	2	3	3	3	1	2
Whitson	1	3	2	2	0	1
Tekulve	1	1	2	2	0	0
Bibby	1	0	0	0	1	0

Hit by pitch: Hebner (by D. Robinson), Luzinski (by Tekulve). Time, 3:00. Attendance, 28,905.

Phillies 6, Expos 4
October 4, 1980

Phillies	AB	R	H	RBI
Rose, 1b	5	2	3	1
McBride, rf	5	2	3	0
Schmidt, 3b	5	1	3	2
Luzinski, lf	4	0	2	2
Reed, p	0	0	0	0
Lyle, p	0	0	0	0
Boone, ph	1	0	1	1
Dernier, pr	0	0	0	0
McCormack, c	1	0	1	0
Unser, cf, lf	4	0	1	0
Smith, lf	1	0	0	0
Moreland, c	4	0	0	0
Loviglio, pr	0	0	0	0
Brusstar, p	0	0	0	0
Aviles, ph	1	0	0	0
McGraw, p	1	0	0	0
Trillo, 2b	5	0	1	0
Bowa, ss	4	1	1	0
Christenson, p	2	0	1	0
Gross, ph, lf	1	0	0	0
Maddox, ph, cf	2	0	0	0
Totals	**46**	**6**	**17**	**6**

Montreal	AB	R	H	RBI
White, lf	3	1	2	3
Scott, 2b	4	0	3	1
Office, rf	5	0	1	0
Dawson, cf	5	0	1	0
Carter, c	4	0	0	0
Cromartie, 1b	5	0	0	0
Parrish, 3b	5	0	1	0
Speier, ss	3	0	0	0
LeFlore, pr	0	1	0	0
Manuel, ss	1	0	0	0
Rogers, p	1	1	0	0
Montanez, ph	0	0	0	0
Tamargo, ph	0	0	0	0
Raines, pr	0	1	0	0
Sosa, p	0	0	0	0
Fryman, p	0	0	0	0
Wallace, ph	1	0	0	0
Bahnsen, p	0	0	0	0
Totals	**37**	**4**	**8**	**4**

Phillies	0	0	0	0	1	0	2	0	1	0	2 — 6
Montreal	0	0	2	0	0	0	2	0	0	0	0 — 4

Game-winning RBI: Schmidt. Errors: Trillo 2, Christenson 2, Parrish, White, Moreland. Double plays: Phillies 3, Montreal 3. Left on base: Phillies 12, Montreal 6. Two-base hits: Schmidt, Scott. Home runs: White (6), Schmidt (48). Stolen bases: Dawson, LeFlore, Raines, Sacrifice hit: Scott. Sacrifice fly: White. Wild pitch: Rogers. Time, 3:51, Attendance, 50,794.

Phillies	IP	H	R	ER	BB	SO
Christenson	6	6	2	2	3	3
Reed	⅓	0	1	0	0	1
Lyle	⅔	1	1	1	1	1
Brusstar	1	0	0	0	0	1
McGraw (W, 5–4)	3	1	0	0	0	4

Montreal	IP	H	R	ER	BB	SO
Rogers	7	11	3	3	3	4
Sosa	⅔	2	0	0	0	0
Fryman	1⅓	1	1	1	2	2
Bahnsen (L, 7–6)	2	3	2	2	0	0

Phillies 13, Cubs 6
September 28, 1983

Phillies	AB	R	H	RBI
Morgan, 2b	4	2	4	3
Matuszek, 1b	6	0	2	2
Schmidt, 3b	5	2	2	2
Lefebvre, rf	5	0	1	2
Matthews, lf	3	1	0	0
Anderson, p	1	0	0	0
Holland, p	1	0	0	0
Gross, cf, lf	5	1	1	0
B. Diaz, c	5	4	5	3
DeJesus, ss	4	2	3	1
Hudson, p	2	0	0	0
Hernandez, p	1	0	0	0
Dernier, cf	2	1	1	0
Totals	44	13	19	13

Chicago	AB	R	H	RBI
Sandberg, 2b	3	1	0	0
Buckner, 1b	3	2	2	1
Hall, cf	4	0	1	1
f-Morales	1	0	0	0
Cey, 3b	4	0	0	1
Moreland, rf	4	1	2	0
Davis, c	4	2	1	0
Carter, lf	2	0	0	0
Brusstar, p	0	0	0	0
b-Grant	0	0	0	0
c-Woods, lf	1	0	0	0
Owen, ss	1	0	0	2
d-M. Diaz	1	0	0	0
Hargesheimer, p	0	0	0	0
Noles, p	0	0	0	0
Ruthven, p	1	0	0	0
Proly, p	0	0	0	0
Lefferts, p	0	0	0	0
a-Rohn	1	0	1	0
Johnson, p	0	0	0	0
Campbell, p	0	0	0	0
Bosley, lf	1	0	0	0
Veryzer, ss	0	0	0	0
e-Martinez	1	0	1	0
Totals	32	6	8	5

a-Doubled for Lefferts in 4th.
b-Announced for Brusstar in 8th.
c-Struck for Grant in 8th.
d-Grounded out for Owen in 8th.
e-Doubled for Veryzer in 9th.
f-Lined out for Hall in 9th.

```
Phillies   1  2  3  0  2  2  0  0  3 — 13
Chicago    2  1  0  2  0  0  1  0  0 — 6
```

Phillies	IP	H	R	ER	BB	SO
Hudson	3⅔	4	5	2	2	1
Hernandez (W, 9–4)	1⅓	0	0	0	1	2
Andersen	2⅓	3	1	1	0	1
Holland	1⅔	1	0	0	1	1

Wild pitch: Hernandez. Time, 3:20. Attendance, 7,680.

Game-winning RBI: Schmidt (12). Double play: DeJesus, Morgan and Matuszek, Left on base: Phillies 10, Chicago 7. Two-base hits: Morgan, Buckner 2, Davis, Moreland 2, Rohn, Lefebvre, Martinez. Three-base hits: DeJesus, Schmidt. Home runs: B. Diaz 2 (15), Schmidt (40). Stolen base: Morgan (18). Sacrifices: Carter, Owen, DeJesus. Sacrifice flies: Cey, Owen, Lefebvre.

Chicago	IP	H	R	ER	BB	SO
Ruthven (L, 13–12)	2⅔	7	6	4	0	1
Proly	⅓	0	0	0	0	0
Lefferts	1	1	0	0	1	0
Johnson	⅓	3	2	2	0	0
Campbell	1⅔	4	2	2	1	1
Brusstar	2	0	0	0	1	1
Hargeshemier	⅓	2	3	3	1	0
Noles	⅔	2	0	0	0	2

ADDITIONAL BOX SCORES

Phillies' First Game
May 1, 1883

Providence	AB	R	H	O	A	E
Paul Hines, cf	4	1	1	3	0	0
Joe Start, 1b	4	0	0	10	0	1
John Farrell, 2b	4	0	2	3	5	1
Arthur Irwin, ss	3	0	0	1	4	0
John Cassidy, rf	4	0	0	2	0	0
Cliff Carroll, lf	4	0	0	2	0	0
Chas. Radbourne, p	3	1	1	1	1	0
Jerry Denny, 3b	3	1	1	2	1	2
Bernie Gilligan, c	3	1	1	3	1	1
Totals	32	4	6	27	12	5

Phillies	AB	R	H	O	A	E
Bill Purcell, lf	4	1	2	2	0	0
Bill McClellan, ss	4	1	1	1	2	0
John Manning, rf	4	0	1	1	0	1
Bob Ferguson, 2b	4	0	0	1	3	1
Ferd Lewis, cf	4	0	0	0	0	0
Will Harbridge, 3b	4	1	1	0	5	0
John Coleman, p	4	0	0	0	6	1
Frank Ringo, c	3	0	1	5	2	0
Sid Farrar, 1b	3	0	0	17	0	0
Totals	34	3	6	27	18	3

```
Providence   0  0  0  0  0  0  0  4  0 — 4
Phillies     2  0  0  0  0  0  1  0  0 — 3
```

Two-base hits: Manning, Ringo, Radbourne, Hines. Bases on balls: off Coleman, 2. Struck out: by Coleman, 2; by Radbourne, 1. Double plays: Denny and Start; Coleman, Ringo, and Ferguson. Left on base: Providence, 4; Philadelphia, 4. Umpire: Odlin. Time, 1:30. Attendance, 1,200.

Most Hits in One Game (Major League Record)
August 17, 1894

Phillies	AB	R	H	O	A
Hamilton, cf	7	3	5	1	0
Boyle, 1b	8	3	3	9	2
Cross, 3b	8	1	1	2	5
Delahanty, lf, 2b	7	5	4	4	3
Thompson, rf	7	4	6	0	0
Hallman, 2b	1	2	1	1	2
Buckley, c	1	1	1	0	0
Sullivan, ss	7	4	5	3	0
Carsey, p	7	3	4	3	0
Grady, c	6	3	5	3	0
Turner, lf	5	0	1	1	0
Totals	**64**	**29**	**36**	**27**	**12**

Louisville	AB	R	H	O	A
Brown, cf	4	1	1	3	0
Clarke, lf	3	2	2	3	0
Grim, 2b	4	1	1	4	4
Flaherty, 3b	4	0	1	1	4
Smith, rf	4	0	1	4	1
Lutenberg, 1b	4	0	0	9	4
Richardson, ss	4	0	1	1	3
Weaver, c	1	0	0	1	0
Wadsworth, p	4	0	1	1	1
Zahner, c	2	0	0	0	0
Totals	**34**	**4**	**8**	**27**	**17**

Errors: Phillies 1 (Cross). Louisville 4 (Grimm 2, Clarke, Weaver).

```
Phillies    6  0  6  2  3  1  5  2  4 — 29
Louisville  0  0  0  2  0  2  0  0  0 —  4
```

Two-base hits: Carsey, Boyle, Thompson, Grady, Sullivan, Brown. Three-base hit: Thompson. Home runs: Thompson, Cross, Grim. Stolen bases: Boyle 3, Hamilton, Delahanty. Double plays: Cross, Hallman, to Boyle; Grim to Lutenberg. Bases on balls: off Carsey 3, off Wadsworth 2. Struck out: by Carsey 1, by Wadsworth 1. Wild pitch: Wadsworth. Passed balls: Weaver 2. Umpire: Keefe. Time of game, 2:05.

The Fastest Major League Game (51 Minutes)
September 28, 1919 (First Game)

Phillies	AB	R	H	RBI
LeBourveau, lf	4	0	0	0
Blackburne, 3b	4	1	1	0
Williams, cf	4	0	0	0
Meusel, rf	4	0	0	1
Luderus, 1b	4	0	2	0
Bancroft, ss	4	0	1	0
Paulette, 2b	3	0	0	0
Adams, c	3	0	0	0
Meadows, p	3	0	1	0
Totals	**33**	**1**	**5**	**1**

New York Giants	AB	R	H	RBI
Burns, lf	2	1	1	1
Youngs, rf	3	1	1	0
Kauff, cf	4	1	1	2
Doyle, 2b	4	1	2	0
Fletcher, ss	4	0	2	0
Frisch, 3b	4	0	1	1
Kelly, 1b	4	1	3	1
Smith, c	3	0	1	1
J. Barnes, p	4	1	1	0
Totals	**32**	**6**	**13**	**6**

```
Phillies          1  0  0  0  0  0  0  0  0  — 1
New York Giants   0  1  3  0  0  2  0  0  x  — 6
```

Error: Fletcher. Double plays: Philadelphia 2. Left on base: Philadelphia 6, New York 7. Two-base hits: Blackburne, Burns, Youngs, Fletcher, Kelly, J. Barnes. Stolen base: Burns. Sacrifice hit: Barnes. Sacrifice fly: Burns.

	IP	H	R	ER	BB	SO
Meadows (L, 12–20)	8	13	6	6	3	1
J. Barnes (W, 25–9)	9	5	1	1	0	2

Time, 0:51

Most Runs For Two Teams (Major League Record)
August 25, 1922

Chicago	AB	R	H	O	A
Heathcote, cf	5	5	5	4	0
Hollochor, ss	5	2	3	5	2
Kelleher, ss	1	0	0	0	0
Terry, 2b	5	2	2	2	2
Friberg, 2b	1	0	1	0	0
Grimes, 1b	4	2	2	7	1
Callahan, rf	7	3	2	2	0
Miller, lf	5	3	4	1	0
Krug, 3b	5	4	4	1	1
O'Farrell, c	3	3	2	1	1
Hartnett, c	0	0	0	4	0
Kaufmann, p	2	0	0	0	1
Stueland, p	1	0	0	0	0
Eubanks, p	0	0	0	0	1
Morris, p	0	0	0	0	0
Osborne, p	0	0	0	0	0
a-Barber	1	2	0	0	0
b-Maisel	1	0	0	0	0
Totals	**46**	**26**	**25**	**27**	**9**

Phillies	AB	R	H	O	A
Wrightstone, 3b	7	3	4	0	2
Parkinson, 2b	4	1	2	4	6
Williams, cf	3	1	0	2	0
Lebourveau, cf	4	2	3	0	0
Walker, rf	6	2	4	2	0
Mokan, lf	4	2	3	1	0
Fletcher, ss	3	1	0	0	2
Smith, ss	4	2	1	1	3
Leslie, 1b	2	1	0	4	0
Lee, 1b	4	4	3	6	0
Henline, c	2	1	2	4	0
Withrow, c	4	1	2	0	1
Ring, p	2	0	1	0	1
Weinert, p	4	2	1	0	0
c-Rapp	0	0	0	0	0
Totals	**53**	**23**	**26**	**24**	**14**

a-Batted for Kaufmann in 4th.
b-Batted for Steuland in 7th.
c-Batted for Weinert in 9th.

```
Phillies  0  3  2  1  3  0  0  8  6 — 23
Chicago   1 10  0 14  0  1  0  0  x — 26
```

Errors: Chicago 5 (Heathcote, Hollocher, Callahan, Krug, Hartnett), Philadelphia 5 (Wrightstone, Parkinson, Walker, Williams, Lee). Two-base hits: Terry, Krug 2, Mokan, Hollocher, Heathcote 2, Grimes, Parkinson, Withrow, Friberg, Walker. Three-base hits: Walker, Wrightstone. Home runs: Miller 2, O'Farrell. Stolen bases: Hollocher, Weinert. Sacrifice hits: Leslie, O'Farrell, Hollocher, Walker. Bases on balls: off Kaufmann 3, off Ring 5, off Weinert 5, off Stueland 2, off Eubanks 3, off Morris 1, off Osborne 2. Struck out: by Ring 2, by Weinert 2, by Stueland 1, by Morris 1, by Osborne 2. Hit by pitched ball: Grimes (by Weinert). Wild pitch: Stueland. Double plays: Smith to Parkinson to Lee 2; Wrightstone to Parkinson to Lee. Left on base: Chicago 9, Phillies 16. Umpires: Hart and Rigler. Time, 3:01.

Ten Home Runs in One Game
May 11, 1923

Phillies	AB	R	H	O	A
Mokan, lf	4	3	3	2	0
Sand, 3b	5	2	1	0	1
Williams, cf	5	4	3	5	0
Walker, rf	4	2	1	0	1
Holke, 1b	4	1	1	8	1
Parkinson, 2b	5	1	3	4	7
Wrightstone, ss	4	3	2	5	2
Henline, c	3	3	2	2	1
Behan, p	1	1	1	1	0
Weinert, p	1	0	0	0	1
Meadows, p	1	0	1	0	0
Totals	**37**	**20**	**18**	**27**	**14**

St. Louis	AB	R	H	O	A
Smith, cf	6	3	3	2	0
Dyer, lf	3	2	2	1	0
Mann, lf	3	2	2	0	0
Toporcer, 2b	5	1	1	3	1
Bottomley, 1b	6	1	4	7	2
Stock, 3b	6	1	3	1	1
Myers, cf	5	0	1	2	0
Freigau, ss	3	0	1	3	3
Ainsmith, c	3	1	1	4	1
McCurdy, c	1	0	0	0	1
Haines, p	1	0	1	1	0
Sherdel, p	1	1	1	0	2
Barfoot, p	0	0	0	0	0
a-Flack	1	1	1	0	0
Stuart, p	0	0	0	0	0
North, p	1	0	0	0	0
b-Blades	1	1	1	0	0
Totals	**46**	**14**	**22**	**24**	**12**

a-Batted for Barfoot in the 5th.
b-Batted for North in the 9th.

Phillies	0	0	5	3	4	2	3	3	x — 20	
St.Louis	1	1	1	3	0	3	0	3	2 — 14	

Errors: Freigau, Myers. Two-base hits: Bottomley, Sand, Stock, Mokan, Blades, Smith, Flack. Three-base hit: Stock. Home runs: Mokan 2, Williams 3, Sherdel, Dyer, Parkinson, Mann 2. Stolen bases: Smith, Dyer, Wrightstone, Mokan. Sacrifice hits: Freigau, Holke, Behan 2. Double play: Wrightstone, Parkinson, and Holke. Left on base: St. Louis 9, Philadelphia 5. Bases on balls: off Haines 2, off Sherdel 1, off Stuart 2, off North 4, off Behan 3. Struck out: by Sherdel 1, by North 1, by Meadows 2. Hits: off Haines, 3 in 2⅓ innings; off Sherdel, 7 in 2 innings; off Barfoot 2 in ⅔ inning; off Stuart, none in no innings (none out in sixth); off Behan, 11 in 5 innings; off Weinert, 7 in 2⅓ innings; off Meadows, 4 in 1⅔ innings; off North, 6 in 3 innings. Wild pitch: Behan. Winning pitcher: Behan. Losing pitcher: Sherdel. Umpires: Klem and Hart. Time, 2:20.

First Night Game in Major Leagues
May 24, 1935

Phillies	AB	R	H	O	A
Chiozza, 2b	4	0	0	1	3
Allen, cf	4	0	1	0	0
Moore, rf	4	0	1	0	0
Camilli, 1b	4	0	1	15	0
Vergez, 3b	4	0	1	0	4
Todd, c	3	1	1	3	0
Watkins, lf	3	0	0	5	0
Haslin, ss	3	0	1	0	5
Bowman, p	2	0	0	0	2
a-Wilson	1	0	0	0	0
Bivin, p	0	0	0	0	0
Totals	**32**	**1**	**6**	**24**	**14**

Cincinnati	AB	R	H	O	A
Myers, ss	3	1	1	2	3
Riggs, 3b	4	0	0	0	2
Goodman, rf	3	0	0	3	0
Sullivan, 1b	3	1	2	8	2
Pool, lf	3	0	1	0	0
Campbell, c	3	0	0	5	0
Byrd, cf	3	0	0	4	0
Kampouris, 2b	3	0	0	4	3
Derringer, p	3	0	0	1	2
Totals	**28**	**2**	**4**	**27**	**12**

Errors: none. Runs batted in: Sullivan, Campbell, Haslin. Two-base hit: Myers. Stolen bases: Vergez, Myers, Bowman. Left on base: Philadelphia 4, Cincinnati 3. Double play: Riggs, Kampouris, and Sullivan. Bases on balls: Bowman 1. Struck out: Derringer 3, Bowman 1, Bivin 1. Hits off: Bowman 4 in 7; Bivin 0 in 1. Winner: Derringer. Loser: Bowman. Umpires: Klem, Sears, and Pinelli. Time, 1:55. Attendance, 20,422.

First Home Night Game for Phillies
June 1, 1939

Pittsburgh	AB	R	H	RBI
P. Waner, rf	3	2	0	0
Vaughan, ss	4	2	1	0
Rizzo, lf	5	0	2	1
Bell, cf	3	0	1	1
Brubaker, 2b	5	1	1	1
Suhr, 1b	4	0	1	0
Handley, 3b	5	0	1	0
Berres, c	2	0	0	0
Sewell, p	3	0	0	0
Totals	**34**	**5**	**7**	**3**

Phillies	AB	R	H	RBI
Martin, cf	4	0	2	0
Mueller, 2b	4	0	0	0
Brack, 1b	4	1	1	1
Arnovich, lf	4	1	2	0
May, 3b	3	0	1	0
Scott, rf	4	0	1	0
Young, ss	3	0	1	1
Milles, c	3	0	2	0
Higbe, p	2	0	0	0
Powers, ph	1	0	0	0
Totals	**32**	**2**	**10**	**2**

Pittsburgh	2	0	0	0	0	0	0	1	2 — 5	
Phillies	0	1	0	0	0	1	0	0	0 — 2	

Errors: Scott, May. Two-base hit: Vaughan. Home runs: Brack, Brubaker. Stolen base: Handley. Sacrifices: Young, May, Higbe. Double play: Vaughan to Suhr. Left on base: Pittsburgh 11, Phillies 6. Bases on balls: off Higbe 6. Struck out: by Higbe 8, Sewell 3. Hit by pitch: by Higbe (Berres). Wild pitch: Higbe. Winning pitcher: Sewell 6–3. Losing pitcher: Higbe 2–2. Umpires: Stark, Magerkurth, and Stewart. Time, 1:55.

Babe Ruth's Last Game
May 30, 1935 (First game)

Boston	AB	R	H
Urbanski, ss	4	0	2
Thompson, rf	4	1	0
Ruth, lf	1	0	0
Lee, lf	4	1	3
Berger, cf	5	1	1
R. Moore, 1b	4	2	2
Mallon, 2b	3	1	2
Mowry, ph	1	0	0
Whitney, 3b	5	0	3
Spohrer, c	5	0	0
Frankhouse, p	4	0	1
Cantwell, p	0	0	0
Totals	**40**	**6**	**14**

Phillies	AB	R	H
Allen, cf	4	1	0
Watkins, lf	5	1	1
J. Moore, rf	3	2	1
Camilli, 1b	3	3	2
Haslin, ss	4	2	3
Chiozza, 2b	4	0	3
Todd, c	5	1	1
Vergez, 3b	3	1	0
Bivin, p	2	0	0
Boland, ph	1	0	0
Jorgens, p	0	0	0
Wilson, ph	1	0	1
C. Davis, p	0	0	0
Totals	**35**	**11**	**12**

```
Boston     0  1  1  0  2  1  1  0  0 — 6
Phillies   3  0  0  1  0  0  0  7  0 — 11
```

Errors: Urbanski, Berger, Mallon, Chiozza, Todd. Runs batted in: Berger, 1, R. Moore 2, Whitney 1, Haslin 3, Chiozza 4, Wilson 1, Watkins 1, Camilli 1. Two-base hits: Urbanski, Whitney, Lee, Haslin 2, Watkins. Three-base hits: Chiozza, R. Moore. Home runs: Berger, R. Moore. Sacrifices: Haslin, Mallon. Left on base: Boston 11, Phillies 8. Bases on balls: off Bivin 2, Jorgens 1, Frankhouse 6, Cantwell 1. Struck out: by Bivin 3, Frankhouse 1. Hits: off Bivin 10 in 6 innings; off Jorgens 3 in 2 innings; off C. Davis 1 in 1 inning; off Frankhouse 11 in 7⅔ innings; off Cantwell 1 in ⅓ inning. Winning pitcher: Jorgens. Losing pitcher: Cantwell. Umpires: Quigley, Pfirman, and Moran. Time, 2:25.

The Last Game at Baker Bowl
June 30, 1938

New York	AB	R	H
Seeds, lf	6	1	1
Danning, c	6	2	3
Ripple, rf	6	1	2
Ott, 3b	3	3	2
Leiber, cf	6	3	4
Leslie, 1b	6	2	5
Bartell, ss	4	2	2
Kampouris, 2b	5	0	0
Castleman, p	4	0	0
Totals	**46**	**14**	**19**

Phillies	AB	R	H
Mueller, 2b	2	0	0
Martin, cf	3	1	1
Klein, rf	2	0	1
Stainback, rf	2	0	0
Weintraub, 1b	3	0	1
Arnovich, lf	4	0	0
Whitney, 3b	4	0	3
Scharein, ss	4	0	0
Atwood, c	2	0	0
Clark, c	2	0	0
Passeau, p	1	0	0
Smith, p	0	0	0
Hallahan, p	2	0	1
Totals	**31**	**1**	**7**

```
New York   0  3  9  0  1  0  1  0  0  — 14
Phillies   0  0  0  1  0  0  0  0  0  — 1
```

Errors: Phillies 2 (Weintraub, Scharein). Runs batted in: Bartell 1, Leiber 5, Leslie 2, Seeds 1, Danning 1, Ripple 1, Ott 1, Klein 1. Two-base hits: Ripple, Leiber 2, Leslie 3, Danning, Bartell, Martin, Klein, Whitney. Home run: Leiber. Sacrifice: Martin. Double plays: Leiber to Bartell; Bartell to Kampouris to Leslie. Left on base: Phillies 7, New York 10. Bases on balls: off Castleman 3, off Passeau 2, off Hallahan 3. Struck out: by Passeau 2, by Smith 1, by Castleman 3. Hits: off Passeau 7 in 2 innings; off Smith 3 in ⅔ inning; off Hallahan, 9 in 6⅓ innings. Winning pitcher: Castleman. Losing pitcher: Passeau. Umpires: Klem, Sears, and Ballanfant. Time of game, 2:17.

Last Game at Connie Mack Stadium
October 1, 1970

Montreal	AB	R	H	RBI
Gosger, lf	5	0	0	0
Sutherland, 2b	4	0	0	0
Staub, rf	3	0	0	0
Fairly, 1b	5	0	1	0
Bailey, 3b	4	0	0	0
Day, cf	4	0	1	0
Bateman, c	4	0	1	0
Philips, pr	0	1	0	0
Brand, c	0	0	0	0
Wine, ss	4	0	2	1
Morton, p	2	0	0	0
Jones, ph	0	0	0	0
Marshall, p	0	0	0	0
Fairey, ph	1	0	0	0
Reed, p	0	0	0	0
Totals	**36**	**1**	**5**	**1**

Phillies	AB	R	H	RBI
Taylor, 2b	5	1	0	0
McCarver, c	5	1	3	1
Gamble, rf	4	0	2	1
Johnson, 1b	3	0	0	0
Stone, lf	4	0	1	0
Money, 3b	4	0	1	0
Browne, cf	4	0	1	0
Bowa, ss	4	0	0	0
Lersch, p	3	0	1	0
Selma, p	1	0	0	0
Totals	**37**	**2**	**9**	**2**

Montreal	0	0	0	0	0	0	0	1	0 — 1
Phillies	0	0	1	0	0	0	0	0	1 — 2

	IP	H	R	ER	BB	SO
Morton	7	7	1	1	1	3
Marshall	1	0	0	0	1	0
Reed (L, 6–5)	1⅓	2	1	1	0	1
Lersch	8⅓	5	1	1	3	7
Selma (W, 8–9)	1⅔	0	0	0	0	1

Errors: Money, Bailey, Taylor. Left on base: Montreal 9, Philadelphia 8. Two-base hit: Wine. Three-base hit: McCarver. Stolen bases: Bateman, McCarver. Sacrifice: Sutherland.

Time, 2:46. Attendance, 31,822.

First Game at Veterans Stadium
April 10, 1971

Montreal	AB	R	H	RBI
Day, cf	4	0	0	0
Raymond, p	0	0	0	0
Reed, p	0	0	0	0
Brand, ph	1	0	0	0
Hunt, 2b	3	1	1	0
Staub, rf	4	0	1	0
Bailey, 3b	4	0	1	1
Fairly, lf	2	0	1	0
Jones, lf	4	0	0	0
Bateman, c	4	0	2	0
Wine, ss	1	0	0	0
Fairey, ph	1	0	0	0
Laboy, ph	1	0	0	0
Stoneman, p	2	0	0	0
O'Donoghue, p	0	0	0	0
Marshall, p	0	0	0	0
Sutherland, ph	0	0	0	0
Totals	**31**	**1**	**6**	**1**

Phillies	AB	R	H	RBI
Bowa, ss	4	1	2	0
Money, 3b	3	1	1	2
Montanez, cf	2	1	1	0
Johnson, 1b	3	1	1	0
Briggs, lf	3	0	0	0
Freed, rf	3	0	2	1
McCarver, c	3	0	1	1
Doyle, 2b	2	0	0	0
Taylor, ph, 2b	2	0	0	0
Bunning, p	2	0	0	0
Hoerner, p	0	0	0	0
Totals	**27**	**4**	**8**	**4**

Montreal	0	0	0	0	0	1	0	0	0 — 1
Phillies	0	0	0	0	0	3	1	0	x — 6

	IP	H	R	ER	BB	SO
Stoneman (L, 0–1)	5	7	3	3	3	1
O'Donoghue	⅓	0	0	0	0	0
Marshall	⅓	0	0	0	0	0
Raymond	⅔	1	1	1	2	1
Reed	1⅓	0	0	0	0	1
Bunning (W, 1–0)	7⅓	6	1	1	3	4
Hoerner	1⅔	0	0	0	1	2

Save: Hoerner (1). Hit by pitch: by Bunning (Hunt). Time, 2:43. Attendance, 55,352.

Errors: Jones, Money. Double plays: Bunning, Bowa, and Johnson; Wine and Fairly. Left on base: Montreal 10, Phillies 7. Two-base hits: Hunt, Bailey. Three-base hit: Bowa. Home run: Money. Stolen bases: Hunt, Bowa. Sacrifice: Bunning. Sacrifice flies: McCarver, Money.

Longest Home Game
May 4, 1973

Atlanta	AB	R	H	RBI
Garr, rf	11	0	1	0
Jackson, ss	3	1	1	0
Perez, ss	4	0	0	0
Aaron, lf	3	0	1	0
Brown, lf	4	1	2	0
Evans, 3b	9	1	3	4
Lum, 1b	8	0	3	0
Baker, cf	8	0	1	0
Da. Johnson, 2b	8	0	2	0
Oates, c	8	0	1	0
Reed, p	4	1	0	0
Frisella, p	0	0	0	0
Gilbreath, ph	1	0	0	0
P. Niekro, p	0	0	0	0
Dietz, ph	0	0	0	0
Pierce, ph	1	0	0	0
House, p	0	0	0	0
Schueler, p	2	0	1	0
Blanks, ph	1	0	1	0
T. Kelley, p	1	0	0	0
Totals	**76**	**4**	**17**	**4**

Phillies	AB	R	H	RBI
Bowa, ss	8	0	1	0
Tovar, lf	6	0	1	0
Lersch, p	0	0	0	0
Robinson, ph	1	0	0	0
Lonborg, p	0	0	0	0
Pagan, ph	0	0	0	1
Unser, cf	7	0	0	1
Montanez, 1b	6	0	0	0
Boone, c	8	0	2	0
Schmidt, 3b	7	0	0	0
Anderson, rf	8	2	2	0
Doyle, 2b	7	2	2	1
Ruthven, p	2	0	0	0
Rgdznski, ph	0	0	0	0
Scarce, p	1	0	0	0
B. Wilson, p	0	0	0	0
Hutton, ph	1	0	1	0
Harmon, pr	0	1	0	0
Twitchell, p	0	0	0	0
Luzinski, lf	2	0	0	0
Totals	**64**	**5**	**9**	**3**

One out when winning run scored.

Atlanta 0 0 2 0 0 0 0 0 0 0 0 0 2 0 0 0 0 0 0 —4
Phillies 0 0 0 0 0 0 0 2 0 0 0 0 2 0 0 0 0 0 1 —5

Errors: Schmidt, Doyle 2, Baker, Lonborg. Double play: Atlanta 1. Left on base: Atlanta 27, Philadelphia 11. Two-base hits: Evans, Tovar, DaJohnson, Anderson, Lum, Boone. Three-base hit: Doyle. Home run: Evans (7). Sacrifices: Rogodzinski, Lum, OsBrown. Sacrifice flies: Unser, Pagan.

Atlanta	IP	H	R	ER	BB	SO
Ruthven	8	6	2	0	3	6
Scarce	3⅔	2	0	0	3	4
B. Wilson	1⅓	3	2	2	0	2
Twitchell	2	1	0	0	2	3
Lersch	3	4	0	0	1	0
Lonborg (W, 2–4)	2	1	0	0	1	0

Phillies	IP	H	R	ER	BB	SO
Reed	7	3	2	1	2	2
Frisella	3	0	0	0	0	3
P. Niekro	1	0	0	0	0	0
House	1	1	1	1	0	1
Schueler	5	3	1	1	3	4
T. Kelley (L, 0–1)	2⅓	2	1	1	2	2

Hit by pitch: by Ruthven (S. Jackson), by Scarce (Lum), by Twitchell (Da. Johnson). Wild pitch: Schueler. Balk: Ruthven. Passed Ball: Oates. Time, 5:16. Attendance, 10,158.

Most Runs, Hits in the 20th Century
June 11, 1985

New York	AB	R	H	RBI	O	A
Backman, 2b	4	1	3	1	3	3
Johnson, 3b	5	0	2	1	1	2
Hernandez, 1b	2	0	1	0	3	0
Christensen, rf	2	0	0	0	1	0
Carter, c	2	0	1	1	1	0
Reynolds, c	3	1	1	0	3	0
Heep, cf	5	1	1	0	6	1
Foster, lf	3	1	1	1	3	0
Hurdle, rf	4	1	1	0	1	0
Santana, ss	2	1	2	2	1	5
Gorman, p	0	0	0	0	0	0
Schiraldi, p	0	0	0	0	0	1
Sisk, p	2	1	0	1	0	1
Staub, ph	1	0	0	0	0	0
Sambito, p	0	0	0	0	1	0
Knight, ph	1	0	0	0	0	0
Orosco, p	0	0	0	0	0	0
Totals	**36**	**7**	**13**	**7**	**24**	**13**

Phillies	AB	R	H	RBI	O	A
Hayes, lf	6	4	3	6	3	0
Schu, 3b	7	2	4	2	0	2
Samuel, 2b	7	3	5	2	4	1
Schmidt, 3b	2	2	2	2	1	0
Jeltz, ss	4	1	1	1	1	2
Wilson, rf	6	4	3	3	0	0
Diaz, c	4	3	3	3	3	1
Rucker, p	2	1	2	0	1	0
Andersen, p	0	0	0	0	0	0
Maddox, cf	4	3	2	2	4	0
Thomas, cf	1	0	0	0	0	0
Aguayo, ss	1	1	0	1	0	0
G. Gross, 1b	2	1	1	2	6	2
Hudson, p	3	1	1	1	1	1
Wockenfuss, ph, c	1	0	0	0	3	0
Totals	**50**	**26**	**27**	**25**	**27**	**9**

Game-winning RBI: Hayes (4). Errors: Santana, Hayes, Johnson. Double plays: New York 2, Phillies 1. Left on base: New York 7, Phillies 9. Two-base hits: Diaz 3, Wilson 2, Schmidt, Santana, Foster, Johnson, Samuel, Schu, Rucker, Jeltz. Three-base hits: Schu, Maddox. Home runs: Hayes 2 (5). Stolen bases: Samuel 2 (17). Sacrifice flies: Santana, Foster, G. Gross.

New York 0 0 3 2 2 0 0 0 0 — 7
Phillies 9 7 0 0 5 1 4 0 x — 26

New York	IP	H	R	ER	BB	SO
Gorman (L, 3–3)	⅓	4	6	6	2	0
Schiraldi	1⅓	10	10	10	0	1
Sisk	2⅓	2	0	0	0	1
Sambito	3	9	10	8	5	0
Orosco	1	2	0	0	0	1

Phillies	IP	H	R	ER	BB	SO
Hudson (W, 2–6)	5	13	7	6	0	3
Rucker	3	0	0	0	2	2
Andersen	1	0	0	0	1	1

Hit by pitcher: Aguayo by Schiraldi. Wild pitch: Schiraldi, Rucker. Balk: Hudson. Time, 3:21. Attendance, 22,591.

9

The Postseason

Phillies versus Boston Red Sox
World Series

The name would come back to haunt them in post-season play in 1976. But the George Foster who helped ruin the Phillies in the 1915 World Series was a pitcher, not a power hitter.

This George Foster, nicknamed Rube, won the second game and the deciding fifth game of the 1915 World Series. His first victory started the Phillies on an incredible streak of 62 seasons and 11 games before they would win a post-season game again. His second victory, by a 5–4 count in Philadelphia, was gained by a couple of cheap ground rule home runs that brought the wrath of the national press down on the shoulders of stingy Philadelphia president William F. Baker.

Foster's first victory was also the first of seven consecutive one-run defeats for the Phillies in the World Series. It would be 1980 before the Phillies won a World Series game again after Grover Cleveland Alexander won the 1915 opener by a 3–1 score and touched off the most premature celebration in Philadelphia sports history. After Alex won the opener, the fans hoisted him and his teammates on their shoulders and paraded them around the home field as if the next three victories were as certain as sunrise and U.S. involvement in World War I.

The sun came up in the east, as usual; the World War sucked the United States into its bitter grasp in 1917; and the Boston Red Sox won four games in a row.

The Red Sox had gone into the Series as overwhelming favorites. Their 101–50 record had given them a 2½-game margin over second-place Detroit.

The Sox took the flag with a great second half. They were as low as fifth place in early May and were third on July 4. But they took first place from the Chicago White Sox on July 17 and stayed in front the rest of the way.

Boston's pitching was the key to the championship. Smoky Joe Wood led the league with a 1.49 earned run average, and Ernie Shore wasn't far behind at 1.64. Boston had the top four pitchers in the league in winning percentages in Wood (15–5) at .750, Foster and Shore (19–8) each at .704, and Babe Ruth (18–8) at .692.

On offense, the Red Sox were paced by Hall of Fame outfielder Tris Speaker, who batter .322 for manager Bill Carrigan.

Game One

The Phillies didn't exactly terrorize Red Sox starter Ernie Shore in the first post-season game in their history. In fact, under normal circumstances, the Boston pitcher might have pitched a one-hitter. But a soggy, rain-soaked field provided the Phillies just enough offense to hand Alexander the 3–1 victory.

The Red Sox had an 8–5 hitting advantage, and only one hit by a Phillie

To the Phillies, the 1980 World Series trophy symbolizes the club's most successful achievement.

The 1915 National League champions.

Grover Cleveland Alexander was the only Phillies World Series winning pitcher until 1980.

reached the outfield. But that was a bloop single by Dode Paskert in the fourth inning that led to the first run of a game in which the Phillies never trailed.

Paskert's single fell in front of right fielder Harry Hooper, who later would become the Series hero. Gavvy Cravath then bunted toward the mound. Shore had a chance for a force play at second, but chose to take the sure out at first. The decision cost him when Paskert took third on Fred Luderus' infield out and scored as Possum Whitted beat out a bouncer to second.

Alexander blanked the Red Sox through seven innings to the delight of the overflow crowd of 19,343. But after retiring the first batter in the eighth inning, he intentionally walked future Hall of Famer Tris Speaker.

The next hitter, Doc Hoblitzell, hit a potential double-play ball to third, but Milt Stock bobbled it. Stock recovered to get Hoblitzell at first, but Speaker took second. Duffy Lewis followed with a single to left, scoring Speaker, and took second on Whitted's throw to the plate.

Paskert then saved the day for the Phillies with a marvelous running catch on Larry Gardner's drive to deep center.

The Phillies won the game with a two-run rally in the bottom of the eighth even though they were unable to produce an outfield hit.

With one out, Stock worked Shore for a walk. Davey Bancroft hit a ball up the middle that looked as if it might reach the outfield, but second baseman Jack Barry, who had started the season with the Philadelphia Athletics, made a great stop behind the bag. Shortstop Everett Scott was late covering at second, however, and everybody was safe.

The play so unsettled Shore that he walked Paskert, loading the bases. Cravath then hit a bouncer to Scott, who might have had a play at the plate, but elected to take the out at first as Stock scored the winning run. When Shore failed to handle Luderus' bouncer in front of the plate, it was ruled an infield hit as Bancroft scored an insurance run.

The Red Sox brought the tying run to the plate with one out in the top of the ninth. But Babe Ruth, pinch-hitting for Shore, was retired on a sharp liner to Luderus at first, and Hooper popped to Luderus to touch off a celebration that would not be able to be repeated until the 1977 National League championship series.

Alexander walked two and struck out six in going the distance.

Game Two

Woodrow Wilson became the first United States President to witness a World Series game when he traveled from Washington to North Broad Street to watch a pitching duel between Foster and Erskine Mayer.

The Red Sox evened the series with a 2–1 victory, scoring the winning run in the ninth inning, then barely escaping in the bottom half of the inning.

The Phillies were held to three hits by Foster, while the Red Sox managed 10 hits off Mayer. But it was Foster's third hit of the game that enabled the Red Sox to take a tied-up Series back to Boston.

The Red Sox put runners on base in every inning against Mayer, but were shut out from the second to the ninth after scoring in the first. The Phillies, meanwhile, sent only 30 batters to the plate against Foster, who struck out eight while failing to issue a walk.

Hooper led off the game with a base on balls. After Scott failed to bunt him to second, Speaker sent him to third with a single to right. Then came a bizarre play on an attempted double steal. Ed Burns, who caught the entire series because first-string catcher Bill Killefer was sidelined with a dead arm, nailed Speaker at second with a perfect throw to Bancroft. The shortstop's return throw to the plate was in time to retire Hooper, but Burns dropped the ball, and the Red Sox had the lead.

It lasted until the fifth inning. Foster went into the inning with a no-hitter and came out of it in a tie.

Cravath led off with a double to deep left and scored on Luderus' double to right. With none out, the crowd of 20,306 anticipated their Phillies taking a lead, but Foster retired the next three batters, stranding Luderus at third.

Bancroft's sixth-inning single was the Phillies' only other hit off Foster.

The Red Sox scored the game winner in the top of the ninth. Gardner led off with a sharp single to left and took second when Mayer threw to first base to retire Hal Janvrin. Foster, who had doubled and singled in three previous at-bats, then slashed a ball to center for a single, scoring Gardner.

Stock led off the bottom of the inning and apparently was hit by a pitched ball. But the home plate umpire, Charles Rigler, ruled otherwise, and Stock was not awarded first base. He then hit a screaming liner to Lewis in left field. After Bancroft struck out, Paskert hit a ball deep toward the temporary center field bleachers.

Off the bat, the ball appeared to be a certain game-tying home run, but the wind held it up, and Speaker leaned into the bleachers to make the catch and end the game.

Erskine Mayer (on mound) pitched in two World Series games in 1915.

Game Three

A crowd of 42,300, which topped the previous World Series record by more than 10,000, showed up at Braves Field to see Alexander and Dutch Leonard hook up in yet another tremendous pitching duel.

For the second straight game the Phillies were held to three hits and no walks. Alexander, meanwhile, allowed just six hits, but couldn't hold on to a 1–0 lead and took a 2–1 loss.

The Phillies, who missed an opportunity to score in the first inning when they failed to get Stock in from third base with one out, took the lead in the third.

Burns started it with a single to right-center and moved to second when first baseman Hoblitzell dropped Gardner's throw on Alexander's infield chopper for an error.

Stock bunted both runners along, and Bancroft drove in Burns with a single to center, Alexander stopping at third. Barry made a marvelous catch on Paskert's fly to short right field for the second out and held Alexander at third. Cravath then hit a ball to left that would have been a three-run homer at Baker Bowl. Lewis, however, caught the ball in front of the fence, and the Phillies had squandered an opportunity to break the game open.

Leonard didn't allow a hit the rest of the way. (Stock had led off the game with the only other Philadelphia hit.)

The Red Sox tied the game in the fourth inning when Speaker tripled to the wall in right and scored on Hoblitzell's sacrifice fly.

Boston won the game in the bottom of the ninth, marking the second straight game that the Phillies lost in the last inning.

Hooper singled to right with two strikes on him. Scott failed to get down the sacrifice bunt twice, then dropped one down with two strikes on him and advanced Hooper to second. After Alexander walked Speaker intentionally, both runners moved up on an infield out.

The strategy seemed to favor walking Lewis to load the bases and pitching to Gardner, but Alexander chose to pitch to Lewis, who hit the first pitch to center field for a game-winning single.

Game Four

George (Dut) Chalmers and his famous spitball got the call for the Phillies against Shore. A third consecutive 2–1 defeat left Philadelphia needing three straight victories to capture the World Championship.

The Scotland-born Chalmers, the first European-born pitcher to start a World Series game, was the victim both of an error of omission by Bert Niehoff that led to the first run by the Red Sox and of untimely bat work by the Phillies, who had seven hits but were held scoreless until the eighth inning. By then, Boston had scored both its runs.

The Phillies were prevented from deadlocking the series by Lewis, who was the defensive star, twice robbing Cravath of apparent home runs with spectacular catches.

The Red Sox got on the board in the third inning after Lewis took away Cravath's first potential homer. Barry drew a walk, and catcher Hick Cady attempted to sacrifice the runner to second. He bunted the ball past Chalmers. Luderus made the pickup, but second baseman Niehoff failed to cover first base, and Boston had two men on.

Shore bunted them up a base, and Hooper drove in the run with an infield single toward Niehoff. Chalmers retired Scott and Speaker to avoid more trouble, but surrendered what proved to be the winning run in the sixth after Lewis robbed Cravath for a second time in the top of the inning. After Speaker was retired on a grounder to second, Hoblitzell singled to center and scored on Lewis' double down the left field line.

Cravath finally got a break in the eighth by hitting the ball to center instead of left. When the ball bounced over Speaker's head and rolled all the way to the wall, Gavvy wound up at third base with two outs. Luderus drove him in with a single to center.

Shore retired the Phillies in order in the ninth to send the crowd of 41,096 home happy.

Game Five

As if the situation weren't desperate enough, Phillies manager Pat Moran ran into one more unexpected problem when he returned to Philadelphia.

Alexander, who had pitched brilliantly in the first and third games, came up with a sore arm and was unable to take the mound. Erskine Mayer drew the assignment against second-game hero Foster.

This time, it looked as if the Phillies had finally solved Foster when they took a 2–0 lead in the first. It could have been more, but Moran employed some questionable strategy in the first inning when he had Cravath attempt a squeeze bunt with a full count, the bases loaded, and no one out.

Stock had led off the inning by being hit by a pitch. Bancroft singled him to second. When Paskert beat out a bunt toward shortstop, the Phillies had the bases loaded with none out to the delight of the crowd of 20,306.

Cravath then bunted the ball to Foster, who threw to the plate for the force out. Catcher Cady's throw to first doubled up Cravath. When Luderus doubled to left to score the two runners, the fans could do nothing except wonder what might have been had Cravath been allowed to swing away.

The Red Sox forged a tie with single runs in the second and third off Mayer. Gardner's triple and Barry's single accounted for the run in the second; Hooper's home run to the temporary seats in center (first of the series by either team) tied it in the third, and Eppa Rixey replaced Mayer on the mound.

The Phillies regained the lead with a two-run fourth. Luderus electrified the crowd with a solo homer, and the second run scored on a wild throw by Hooper that allowed Niehoff to score. He had singled and was advancing to third on Burns' single when Hooper's attempt to get him wound up in the stands behind third.

Rixey put the Red Sox down in the fifth, sixth, and seventh innings without a run. But in the eighth, Gardner scratched out a single to third, and Lewis jumped all over a "grooved" fastball from Rixey and knocked it into the stands in left.

The Red Sox scored the winning run in the ninth. With one out, Hooper again bounced a ball into the temporary center field bleachers for his second homer of the game. He became the first player in Series history to hit multiple homers in a game.

Foster, who had struggled, reached back for something extra in the bottom of the ninth, retiring the Phillies in order.

The Phillies had no one to blame but their offense for the Series loss. They hit just .182 as a team with one home run.

A Phillies run scores during an infield grounder at Baker Bowl.

The Phillies players each received a losers' share of $2,520, at the time the second highest amount for a defeated team. The winning Red Sox collected $3,780 apiece.

Phillies fans figured it would not be long before their team would be back in the Series—this time as a winner. It took 35 years, however, for the Phillies to make it back. And 65 years to win it all.

Game 1
Friday, October 8, at Philadelphia

Boston	AB	R	H	RBI	PO	A
Hooper, rf	5	0	1	0	0	0
Scott, ss	3	0	1	0	2	2
Speaker, cf	2	1	0	0	1	0
Hoblitzell, 1b	4	0	1	0	12	0
Lewis, lf	4	0	2	1	2	0
Gardner, 3b	3	0	1	0	0	1
Barry, 2b	4	0	1	0	4	4
Cady, c	2	0	0	0	3	2
a-Henriksen	1	0	0	0	0	0
Shore, p	3	0	1	0	0	4
b-Ruth	1	0	0	0	0	0
Totals	32	1	8	1	24	13

Phillies	AB	R	H	RBI	PO	A
Stock, 3b	3	1	0	0	0	2
Bancroft, ss	4	1	1	0	4	1
Paskert, cf	3	1	1	0	1	0
Cravath, rf	2	0	0	1	1	0
Luderus, 1b	4	0	1	1	10	0
Whitted, lf	2	0	1	1	3	0
Niehoff, 2b	3	0	0	0	1	4
Burns, c	3	0	0	0	7	0
Alexander, p	3	0	1	0	0	5
Totals	27	3	5	3	27	12

a-Reached first on error for Cady in 9th.
b-Grounded out for Shore in 9th.

```
Boston     0  0  0  0  0  0  0  1  0 — 1
Phillies   0  0  0  1  0  0  0  2  x — 3
```

Errors: Shore, Luderus. Left on base: Boston 9, Philadelphia 5. Stolen bases: Whitted, Hoblitzell. Sacrifice hits: Scott, Gardner, Cady, Cravath. Umpires: Klem (N.L.), O'Loughlin (A.L.), Evans (A.L.) and Rigler (N.L.). Time, 1:58. Attendance, 19,343.

Boston	IP	H	R	ER	BB	SO
Shore (L)	8	5	3	3	4	2

Phillies	IP	H	R	ER	BB	SO
Alexander (W)	9	8	1	1	2	6

Game 2
Saturday, October 9, at Philadelphia

Boston	AB	R	H	RBI	PO	A
Hooper, rf	3	1	1	0	2	0
Scott, ss	3	0	0	0	0	3
a-Henriksen	1	0	0	0	0	0
Cady, c	0	0	0	0	3	0
Speaker, cf	4	0	1	0	3	0
Hoblitzell, 1b	4	0	1	0	8	3
Lewis, lf	4	0	1	0	1	0
Gardner, 3b	4	1	2	0	0	2
Barry, 2b	4	0	1	0	0	3
Thomas, c	3	0	0	0	6	0
Janvrin, ss	1	0	0	0	1	0
Foster, p	4	0	3	1	3	0
Totals	35	2	10	1	27	11

Phillies	AB	R	H	RBI	PO	A
Stock, 3b	4	0	0	0	0	2
Bancroft, ss	4	0	1	0	2	2
Paskert, cf	4	0	0	0	1	0
Cravath, rf	3	1	1	0	1	0
Luderus, 1b	3	0	1	1	9	1
Whitted, lf	3	0	0	0	3	0
Niehoff, 2b	3	0	0	0	4	1
Burns, c	3	0	0	0	6	3
Mayer, p	3	0	0	0	1	3
Totals	30	1	3	1	27	12

```
Boston     1  0  0  0  0  0  0  0  1 — 2
Phillies   0  0  0  0  1  0  0  0  0 — 1
```

a-Popped out for Scott in 7th.

Error: Burns. Left on base: Boston 8, Philadelphia 2. Two-base hits: Foster, Cravath, Luderus. Umpires: Rigler (N.L.), Evans (A.L.), O'Loughlin (A.L.) and Klem (N.L.). Time, 2:05. Attendance, 20,306.

Boston	IP	H	R	ER	BB	SO
Foster (W)	9	3	1	1	0	8

Phillies	IP	H	R	ER	BB	SO
Mayer (L)	9	10	2	1	2	7

Game 3
Monday, October 11, at Boston

Phillies	AB	R	H	RBI	PO	A
Stock, 3b	3	0	1	0	1	0
Bancroft, ss	3	0	1	1	4	1
Paskert, cf	4	0	0	0	7	0
Cravath, rf	4	0	0	0	2	0
Luderus, 1b	3	0	0	0	3	1
Whitted, lf	3	0	0	0	2	0
Niehoff, 2b	3	0	0	0	0	2
Burns, c	3	1	1	0	5	2
Alexander, p	2	0	0	0	2	0
Totals	28	1	3	1	26	6

Boston	AB	R	H	RBI	PO	A
Hooper, rf	4	1	1	0	2	0
Scott, ss	3	0	0	0	2	1
Speaker, cf	3	1	2	0	2	0
Hoblitzell, 1b	3	0	0	1	9	0
Lewis, lf	4	0	3	1	1	0
Gardner, 3b	3	0	0	0	1	6
Barry, 2b	3	0	0	0	2	1
Carrigan, c	2	0	0	0	8	0
Leonard, p	3	0	0	0	0	2
Totals	28	2	6	2	27	10

```
Phillies   0  0  1  0  0  0  0  0  0 — 1
Boston     0  0  1  0  0  0  0  1 — 2
```

Two out when winning run scored.

Error: Hoblitzell. Double play: Philadelphia 1. Left on base: Philadelphia 3, Boston 4. Two-base hit: Stock. Three-base hit: Speaker. Sacrifice hits: Bancroft, Alexander, Stock, Scott. Sacrifice fly: Hoblitzell. Umpires: O'Loughlin (A.L.), Klem (N.L.), Rigler (N.L.) and Evans (A.L.). Time, 1:48. Attendance, 42,300.

Phillies	IP	H	R	ER	BB	SO
Alexander (L)	9	6	2	2	2	4

Boston	IP	H	R	ER	BB	SO
Leonard (W)	9	3	1	1	0	6

Game 4
Tuesday, October 12, at Boston

Phillies	AB	R	H	RBI	PO	A
Stock, 3b	4	0	1	0	0	3
Bancroft, ss	2	0	0	0	0	0
Paskert, cf	4	0	0	0	5	0
Cravath, rf	4	1	1	0	0	0
Luderus, 1b	4	0	3	1	5	0
aDugey	0	0	0	0	0	0
Becker, lf	0	0	0	0	0	0
Whitted, lf-1b	3	0	0	0	4	0
Niehoff, 2b	3	0	0	0	3	1
Burns, c	3	0	1	0	7	2
Chalmers, p	3	0	1	0	0	4
bByrne	1	0	0	0	0	0
Totals	31	1	7	1	24	10

Boston	AB	R	H	RBI	PO	A
Hooper, rf	4	0	1	1	2	0
Scott, ss	4	0	0	0	2	4
Speaker, cf	3	0	1	0	1	0
Hoblitzell, 1b	4	1	3	0	5	2
Lewis, lf	2	0	1	1	6	1
Gardner, 3b	4	0	0	0	2	2
Barry, 2b	2	1	0	0	3	1
Cady, c	3	0	2	0	6	1
Shore, p	2	0	0	0	0	1
Totals	28	2	8	2	27	12

a-Ran for Luderus in 8th.
b-Flied out for Chalmers in 9th.

Phillies	0	0	0	0	0	0	0	1	0 — 1
Boston	0	0	1	0	0	1	0	0	x — 2

Error: Barry. Double plays: Philadelphia 1, Boston 1. Left on base: Philadelphia 8, Boston 7. Two-base hit: Lewis. Three-base hit: Cravath. Stolen base: Dugey. Sacrifice hits: Whitted, Shore, Lewis. Umpires: Evans (A.L.), Rigler (N.L.), O'Loughlin (A.L.) and Klem (N.L.). Time, 2:05. Attendance, 41,096.

Phillies	IP	H	R	ER	BB	SO
Chalmers (L)	8	8	2	2	3	6

Boston	IP	H	R	ER	BB	SO
Shore (W)	9	7	1	1	4	4

Game 5
Wednesday, October 13, at Philadelphia

Boston	AB	R	H	RBI	PO	A
Hooper, rf	4	2	3	2	2	0
Scott, ss	5	0	0	0	2	2
Speaker, cf	5	0	1	0	3	0
Hoblitzell, 1b	1	0	0	0	1	0
a-Gainor, 1b	3	1	1	0	9	0
Lewis, lf	4	1	1	2	0	0
Gardner, 3b	3	1	1	0	2	3
Barry, 2b	4	0	1	1	1	0
Thomas, c	2	0	1	0	4	3
Cady, c	1	0	0	0	2	1
Foster, p	4	0	1	0	1	3
Totals	36	5	10	5	27	12

Phillies	AB	R	H	RBI	PO	A
Stock, 3b	3	0	0	0	1	1
Bancroft, ss	4	1	2	0	3	6
Paskert, cf	4	1	2	0	3	0
Cravath, rf	3	0	0	0	1	0
b-Dugey	0	0	0	0	0	0
Becker, rf	0	0	0	0	0	0
Luderus, 1b	2	1	2	3	13	2
Whitted, lf	4	0	0	0	2	0
Niehoff, 2b	4	1	1	0	1	2
Burns, c	4	0	1	0	2	2
Mayer, p	1	0	0	0	1	0
Rixey, p	2	0	1	0	0	1
c-Killefer	1	0	0	0	0	0
Totals	32	4	9	3	27	14

a-Hit into double play for Hoblitzell in 3rd.
b-Ran for Cravath in 8th.
c-Grounded out for Rixey in 9th.

Boston	0	1	1	0	0	0	0	2	1 — 5
Phillies	2	0	0	2	0	0	0	0	0 — 4

Errors: Hooper, Bancroft. Double plays: Boston 1, Philadelphia 1. Left on base: Boston 7, Philadelphia 5. Two-base hit: Luderus. Three-base hit: Gardner. Home runs: Hooper 2, Lewis, Luderus. Hit by pitcher: By Foster (Stock, Luderus), by Rixey (Hooper). Umpires: Klem (N.L.), O'Loughlin (A.L.), Evans (A.L.) and Rigler (N.L.). Time, 2:15. Attendance, 20,306.

Boston	IP	H	R	ER	BB	SO
Foster (W)	9	9	4	3	2	5

Phillies	IP	H	R	ER	BB	SO
Mayer	2⅓	6	2	2	0	0
Rixey (L)	6⅔	4	3	3	2	2

COMPOSITE BATTING AVERAGES

Boston Red Sox

Player-Position	G	AB	R	H	2B	3B	HR	RBI	BA
Foster, p	2	8	0	4	1	0	0	1	.500
Lewis, lf	5	18	1	8	1	0	1	5	.444
Hooper, rf	5	20	4	7	0	0	2	3	.350
Cady, c	4	6	0	2	0	0	0	0	.333
Gainor, 1b	1	3	1	1	0	0	0	0	.333
Hoblitzell, 1b	5	16	1	5	0	0	0	1	.313
Speaker, cf	5	17	2	5	0	1	0	0	.294
Gardner, 3b	5	17	2	4	0	1	0	0	.235
Shore, p	2	5	0	1	0	0	0	0	.200
Thomas, c	2	5	0	1	0	0	0	0	.200
Barry, 2b	5	17	1	3	0	0	0	1	.176
Scott, ss	5	18	0	1	0	0	0	0	.056
Janvrin, ss	1	1	0	0	0	0	0	0	.000
Carrigan, c	1	2	0	0	0	0	0	0	.000
Henriksen, ph	2	2	0	0	0	0	0	0	.000
Ruth, ph	1	1	0	0	0	0	0	0	.000
Leonard, p	1	3	0	0	0	0	0	0	.000
Totals	5	159	12	42	2	2	3	11	.264

Philadelphia Phillies

Player-Position	G	AB	R	H	2B	3B	HR	RBI	BA
Rixey, p	1	2	0	1	0	0	0	0	.500
Luderus, 1b	5	16	1	7	2	0	1	6	.438
Chalmers, p	1	3	0	1	0	0	0	0	.333
Bancroft, ss	5	17	2	5	0	0	0	1	.294
Alexander, p	2	5	0	1	0	0	0	0	.200
Burns, c	5	16	1	3	0	0	0	0	.188
Paskert, cf	5	19	2	3	0	0	0	0	.158
Cravath, rf	5	16	2	2	1	1	0	1	.125
Stock, 3b	5	17	1	2	1	0	0	0	.118
Whitted, lf-1b	5	15	0	1	0	0	0	1	.067
Niehoff, 2b	5	16	1	1	0	0	0	0	.063
Mayer, p	2	4	0	0	0	0	0	0	.000
Dugey, pr	2	0	0	0	0	0	0	0	.000
Becker, lf	2	0	0	0	0	0	0	0	.000
Byrne, ph	1	1	0	0	0	0	0	0	.000
Killefer, ph	1	1	0	0	0	0	0	0	.000
Totals	5	148	10	27	4	1	1	9	.182

COMPOSITE PITCHING AVERAGES

Boston Red Sox

Pitcher	G	IP	H	R	ER	BB	SO	W	L	ERA
Leonard	1	9	3	1	1	0	6	1	0	1.00
Foster	2	18	12	5	4	2	13	2	0	2.00
Shore	2	17	12	4	4	8	6	1	1	2.12
Totals	**5**	**44**	**27**	**10**	**9**	**10**	**25**	**4**	**1**	**1.84**

Philadelphia Phillies

Pitcher	G	IP	H	R	ER	BB	SO	W	L	ERA
Alexander	2	17⅔	14	3	3	4	10	1	1	1.53
Chalmers	1	8	8	2	2	3	6	0	1	2.25
Mayer	2	11⅓	16	4	3	2	7	0	1	2.38
Rixey	1	6⅔	4	3	2	2	2	0	1	2.70
Totals	**5**	**43⅔**	**42**	**12**	**10**	**11**	**25**	**1**	**4**	**2.06**

Phillies versus New York Yankees World Series

1950

It's doubtful if any city was ever more excited about a World Series than Philadelphia in 1950.

The excitement was to be expected. There hadn't been a World Series in Philadelphia since 1931, and the Phillies hadn't played in the fall classic since 1915.

Moreover, the 1950 Phillies were a team that generated excitement with their hustling, spirited play. Although the team did not have the overall talent of some of the other clubs in the National League, it was, with its assortment of youth and veterans, an interesting and colorful team that was easily likable.

And the citizens of Philadelphia sure liked the Phillies. The week of the Series, the city was awash with banners, pennants, and pictures of the players. Many downtown store windows celebrated the team with displays. Local newspapers were crammed with advertisements saluting the club. And people everywhere talked about little else but the Whiz Kids, a name originally given to the team by syndicated sportswriter Harry Grayson.

The Series shaped up as a particularly interesting one: the young and innocent Whiz Kids against the grizzled and mighty New York Yankees. It was the 17th World Series appearance in the last 30 years for the Yankees. In sharp contrast, the Phillies over the years had been the epitome of futility, having

The 1950 National League champions.

finished in the first division only once between 1917 and 1949 while placing last 16 times.

The Yankees of 1950 were a powerful team led by the aging but still dynamic Joe DiMaggio. Although DiMag hit 32 homers, drove in 122 runs, and batted .301 in 1950, he would retire from baseball after the following season.

The Bronx Bombers also featured a young catcher named Yogi Berra, who had 28 homers, a .322 average, and 124 RBI; a slick little shortstop, Phil Rizzuto, who hit .324; and former National League home run king Johnny Mize, who had 25 homers. The Yanks' starting lineup, some of whose members were platooned, also included Gene Woodling, Hank Bauer, and Jerry Coleman. It was solid from top to bottom. And its pitching staff, led by 21-game winner Vic Raschi, Allie Reynolds, and Ed Lopat, was exceptionally strong, too.

The Yankees posted a 98–56 (.636) record in 1950, emerging with the pennant after a season-long, four-team race. The Detroit Tigers finished in second three games back, followed by the Boston Red Sox four games behind and the Cleveland Indians six games off.

With such strength, the Yanks were favored to win the Series by odds ranging from 2–1 to 13–5. Neither side, however, gave the odds much credibility.

"Those betting people know from nothing," snorted Yankee manager Casey Stengel. "That's a good ball club over there in Philadelphia."

Although exhausted from their grueling pennant race, the Phillies agreed with the rival manager. In fact, to a man, the club was confident that it could win the Series. Right fielder Del Ennis put the team's feelings in perspective when he said, "We can beat 'em in five games if we get off to a good start. They still play with the same baseball and bats we do." Pitcher Jim Konstanty added: "Maybe it's corny or foolish, but I don't think the Yankees can match our spirit or will to win."

Offsetting the Phillies' optimism, however, were some cold realities. The team was minus pitcher Curt Simmons, who said he was too far out of shape to pitch and would use his 10-day pass from the Army to attend the games as a spectator. Andy Seminick, Bob Miller, and Bubba Church were still nursing injuries. And power-hitting reserve outfielder Bill Nicholson was out of the Series, having been hospitalized for nearly one month with diabetes.

The Phillies received permission to add pitcher Jocko Thompson to the roster in place of Simmons and outfielder Jackie Mayo in place of Nicholson. New York was allowed to substitute Johnny Hopp for Tommy Henrich, who was idled with an injured knee.

By the time the Series opener approached, Philadelphia was bubbling with baseball fever. All rooms in the center city hotels were taken. So, too, were the best seats at Shibe Park. Scalpers were asking $125 to $150 for tickets. There were more than 2,000 applications for press credentials, but because of space limitations, only 570 were awarded.

The day before the opener, the Yankees slipped into town, arriving unnoticed, despite the busy 6 P.M. hour, at the 30th Street Station. The team had decided against a pre-Series workout at Shibe Park, since it had just played there the previous week, and went straight to its quarters at the Warwick Hotel.

Meanwhile, the Phillies did work out at the stadium. But the workouts were secondary to the guessing game the press was playing, trying to learn the name of the Phillies' opening-day pitcher.

Manager Eddie Sawyer kept it a secret. For two days, the press played a wild game of speculation. Robin Roberts was the logical choice, but he had pitched in four of the last eight games of the season, including the physically and mentally draining pennant clincher in Brooklyn. He was exhausted. If not Roberts, how about Ken Heintzelman? A dark horse to be sure, the media figured, but he was certainly rested and might throw the Yanks off balance with his off-speed pitches.

Finally, on the day before the game, Sawyer revealed his choice. The Phillies' starter would be Konstanty.

Joe DiMaggio (right) leads the New York Yankees down the steps of 30th Street Station prior to 1950 Series opener.

The selection was a complete surprise. Konstanty, the ace reliever of the Phils' staff, had worked in 74 games in 1950, winning 16 and saving 22 en route to winning the MVP award. But he hadn't started a game in the big leagues since 1946, and he had pitched 133 consecutive games in relief. Jim had, however, pitched nine innings in relief in late August in a 15-inning, 8–7 win over the Pittsburgh Pirates. He gave up only five hits.

"The Skipper thinks I'm the pitcher to do it, so I guess that's it," Konstanty told the press.

Skipper Sawyer had sound reasons for his choice. Roberts needed another day's rest. "The Yanks," he added, "are a free-swinging team. Konstanty throws the kind of stuff that will stop a free-swinging team."

Game One

South Korea was invading North Korea as the first game of the 1950 World Series arrived. Although the newspapers proclaimed the invasion with front-page banner headlines, Philadelphians were more concerned about the imminent conflict at Shibe Park.

The first game was scheduled to begin at 1 P.M., Wednesday, October 4. All of the grandstand seats that had been on sale were purchased, but 3,000 general admission bleacher seats were to be disposed of that day. By 7 A.M., the line to purchase those one dollar seats was six blocks long.

Shibe Park was decorated with red, white, and blue bunting. As game time approached, a crowd of 30,746, including governors James Duff of Pennsylvania and Alfred Driscoll of New Jersey and Mayor Bernard Samuel of Philadelphia, had settled into their seats. Because of a mixup in the arrangements for tickets for baseball dignitaries, some 2,000 seats were unused.

In a surprise announcement, Phillies manager Eddie Sawyer had nominated relief pitcher Jim Konstanty for the opening-game starting assignment. The selection was reminiscent of Connie Mack's unexpected choice of Howard Ehmke to start the 1929 World Series for the Philadelphia A's.

Konstanty's opponent was righthander Vic Raschi, owner of a 21–8 record in 1950. Ironically, Sawyer had been Raschi's first manager in professional baseball in 1941 on the Yankees' Amsterdam (New York) farm team in the Canadian-American League. The two had remained good friends.

Commissioner Albert (Happy) Chandler threw out the first ball. After a 30-second prayer for peace, the game got under way.

Both Konstanty and Raschi were brilliant. Sawyer was right, the free-swinging Yankees found Konstanty's offerings virtually unhittable. The same was true of the Phillies' attempts to solve the deliveries of Raschi. As a result, the Yankees won behind Raschi's two-hitter, 1–0.

The Yankees threatened in the third inning when Raschi led off with a single. Gene Woodling walked, and Phil Rizzuto moved the runners up with a sacrifice bunt. Then Yogi Berra hit a short fly to left for the second out. Konstanty intentionally walked Joe DiMaggio to load the bases, but Johnny Mize, after blasting a long foul ball to deep right field, popped out to third to end the inning.

New York scored its lone run an inning later. Bobby Brown, a recent medical school graduate from Tulane, sliced a leadoff double down the left field line. He moved to third on Hank Bauer's 400-foot fly to deep center and came home on Jerry Coleman's long fly to left.

"Brown hit a bad ball," Konstanty said later. "I threw him a slider that was at least half a foot outside. But he fell away and just managed to slice it down the left field line."

The Phillies' only threat occurred in the fifth inning when Willie Jones singled and went to second on Andy Seminick's single. The hits were the Phils' only safeties of the game, and Jones was the only man to reach second.

Raschi was simply too much. And in the locker room afterward, the Yankee pitcher was a happy man. "It's wonderful to win a ball game like that," he said. "Such a victory does something for you." Little did Vic know at the time that while he pitched, his hotel room was looted.

As for Konstanty, who allowed just five hits in eight innings of work, Mize summed up the feelings of his teammates. "He didn't throw anything fast or straight," said Johnny, "except between innings."

The final score was the third straight 1–0 World Series opener. Raschi's two-hitter was the 12th in Series history.

Mike Goliat scores first Phillies run of Series as Dick Sisler gives him the stay-up sign.

Game Two

In his first six trips to the plate in the 1950 World Series, Joe DiMaggio didn't hit a ball out of the infield. On the seventh trip, the Yankee Clipper made up for his puniness.

Leading off in the top of the 10th inning, DiMag belted a Robin Roberts pitch 400 feet into the upper deck in left-center field to give the Yankees a 2–1 victory in the second game of the Series.

DiMaggio and Roberts disagreed on a description of the pitch. "It was a tight slider, and I think I caught it before it broke," said Joe. "It was a fastball," declared Robbie.

Regardless, the blast put the New Yorkers two up in the Series in a game that was watched by a capacity crowd of 32,660 at Shibe Park. It was DiMaggio's seventh World Series home run.

The blast wrecked what had been another outstanding pitching effort by a Phillies' starter. Before the game, former Yankee great Bill Dickey, a coach with the '50 club, called Roberts "the greatest young righthander I have ever seen." Robbie, pitching with only three days rest, did justice to the Hall of Famer's praise.

Although touched for 10 hits, Roberts hurled well enough to win most games, and he would've won this one had the Phillies gotten a couple of timely hits. Other than the 10th, the only time that Robbie was in trouble was in the second inning. Jerry Coleman walked, Allie Reynolds singled, and Gene Woodling hit a high bouncer off Willie Jones' glove at third. The ball caromed over to Granny Hamner, but the shortstop's only play was at second where his throw was too late to catch Reynolds. Coleman scored on the play.

The Phillies' only score came in the fifth inning. Mike Goliat got an infield hit on a ball on which Coleman made a fine stop deep in the hole at second.

Robin Roberts was a masterful losing pitcher in second game of 1950 Series.

One out later, Eddie Waitkus bounced a grounder that hopped over Coleman's head for another single. Goliat went to third on the hit and came home with the Phillies' first run of the Series on Richie Ashburn's sacrifice fly.

The Phillies muffed numerous other opportunities to score. Hamner poled a one-out triple in the second. Then Andy Seminick slammed a 3–2 pitch over the wall but foul before bouncing out to Coleman. Goliat flied to center to end the inning.

The Whiz Kids also had men in scoring position in the seventh, eighth, ninth, and tenth innings. In the ninth, with men on first and second and one out, Goliat hit a neck-high 3–1 pitch to Phil Rizzuto for the start of a double play. In the 10th, pinch-hitter Jackie Mayo walked and took second on a sacrifice by Waitkus, but was stranded as Ashburn fouled out and Dick Sisler took a called third strike to end the game.

"You still can't win without hits and runs," manager Eddie Sawyer pontificated afterward.

Yankee pitcher Reynolds gave up only seven hits, two each by Hamner, Waitkus, and Ashburn. But it was DiMaggio who ruled the spotlight. Joe also made a sparkling catch of a long drive to right-center by Del Ennis in the sixth.

"I never felt so good about anything in my life," said Reynolds. "God bless Joe DiMaggio."

Game Three

Ken Heintzelman won only three games all season for the Phillies in 1950, but he came close to being a World Series hero in the third game.

With the Phillies' pitching staff badly depleted, manager Eddie Sawyer selected the veteran lefthander to start against New York as the Series moved to Yankee Stadium. Sawyer figured that Heintzelman's off-speed pitches might have the same tantalizing effect on the Yankees' bats as did Jim Konstanty's in the first game.

Sawyer was nearly right again. For 7⅔ innings, Heintzelman pitched brilliantly, allowing only four hits. Meanwhile, the Phillies took their first lead of the Series.

But the prosperity for the Phillies and Heintzelman was brief. With single runs in the eighth and ninth innings, the Yankees rallied to capture a 3–2 victory, the third consecutive one-run game in the Series. It was also the Phillies' seventh straight one-run World Series loss.

It was a game the Phillies should have won. It was a game that left room for

Eddie Sawyer (left) and Casey Stengel matched managerial wits in 1950.

a considerable amount of second-guessing. And it was a game that Granny Hamner and Jimmy Bloodworth would just as soon forget.

The Phillies outhit the Yankees, 10–7. Once again, though, they failed to capitalize on several scoring opportunities.

New York jumped out to a 1–0 lead in the third inning. With two outs, Phil Rizzuto walked, stole second, went to third as Andy Seminick's throw skipped into center field, and rode home on Jerry Coleman's single to left.

The Phillies tied the game in the sixth with a run off Yankee starter Eddie Lopat.

In the seventh inning, the Phillies took their first lead of the Series. Hamner singled and was sacrificed to second by Seminick. When Mike Goliat laced a single to center, Hamner raced home ahead of Joe DiMaggio's throw, and the Phillies were ahead, 2–1.

Heintzelman, meanwhile, was cruising along, his slants baffling the Yankees. In the eighth inning, Ken retired the first two batters. Then, suddenly, the southpaw's control deserted him. He walked Coleman, Yogi Berra, and DiMaggio to load the bases.

Sawyer brought in Konstanty. It appeared as though the Phillies would escape the jam when Jim got pinch-hitter Bobby Brown to hit an easy grounder to Hamner. But the shortstop dropped the ball, and Coleman raced across the plate with the tying run.

Hamner tried to make amends in the ninth with a leadoff double off New York reliever Tom Ferrick. Granny moved to third on Seminick's sacrifice, after which Goliat walked. Mike was lifted for pinch-runner Putsy Caballero. Dick Whitman was sent to the plate to pinch-hit for Konstanty. Whitman shot a grounder to first, but as Hamner tried to score, Yankee first baseman Joe Collins fired to the plate to nail the sliding Granny.

With Goliat and Konstanty out of the game, Bloodworth, a seldom-used reserve, was inserted at second, and Russ Meyer, normally a starter, was brought in to relieve. The moves soon backfired.

Meyer retired the first two Yankees in the bottom of the ninth. But Gene Woodling grounded to Bloodworth who bobbled the ball, then made a wide throw to first, and the batter was safe. The next hitter, Rizzuto, smashed a shot toward the hole at second. Bloodworth managed to knock the ball down, but couldn't recover to make the throw. Rizzuto was safe at first, while Woodling raced to third.

That brought up Jerry Coleman. The Yankees second baseman lofted a fly

Military man Curt Simmons (second from left) joins Phillies Richie Ashburn, Eddie Sawyer, and Willie Jones in dugout for World Series game.

to left-center, but neither Richie Ashburn nor Jackie Mayo, playing shallow to cut off a possible run at the plate, could get back in time, and the ball dropped over their heads for the game-winning hit.

The Phillies were now behind in the Series, 3–0. But Sawyer wasn't giving up yet. "If we can win tomorrow," he said, "our chances still won't be bad."

Game Four

As the fourth game of the Series unfolded, the Phillies' chances weren't bad. They were hopeless.

The club that had played such sparkling baseball all season, coming up repeatedly with big plays, had not only stopped hitting in the World Series, but it had also lost its sharpness. Only the pitching was keeping the Phillies in contention in each contest, but by the fourth game, that had deteriorated, too.

Forced to start the still-ailing rookie Bob Miller, the Phillies went down to a 5–2 defeat, thereby becoming the first team since the 1939 Cincinnati Reds to get swept in the Series. That sweep was administered by the Yankees, too.

The largest crowd of the Series, 68,098, saw the Yankees deliver the coup de grace. It was the New Yorkers' 13th World Championship in 17 Series and the 30th American League victory in 47 fall classics.

The Yankees got strong pitching for the fourth straight game, this time from a 21-year-old lefthander who had just reported to the club on July 1. Ed (Whitey) Ford won nine straight decisions for the Yankees during the regular season before finally losing in relief to the A's on a Sam Chapman home run.

The Phillies were no match for the young southpaw. Conversely, the Yankees jumped on Miller in the first inning, kayoing Bob after he had retired just one batter. Gene Woodling opened with a roller that Mike Goliat booted. He went to second on Phil Rizzuto's ground out, and scored on Yogi Berra's single to right. After a wild pitch, Joe DiMaggio laced a double to right-center to chase home Berra and send Miller to the showers.

The Yankees added to their 2–0 lead with three more runs in the sixth. With Jim Konstanty on the mound for the Phillies, Berra homered for the third run. After DiMaggio was hit by a pitch, Johnny Mize poked a grounder that rolled through Eddie Waitkus's legs at first. But Goliat, backing up on the play,

Johnny Mize's long stretch nips Richie Ashburn at first base after infield grounder.

made a spectacular stop and threw to Waitkus scurrying back to first to get the out. Bobby Brown, however, drilled a triple to center field scoring DiMaggio, then crossed the plate himself on Hank Bauer's fly to left.

A shutout was averted by the Phillies in the ninth. Willie Jones led off with a single. Del Ennis was hit by a pitch, but was forced at second by Dick Sisler. Then with two outs, Seminick lofted a fly ball to deep left. Woodling made a long run to reach the ball, but dropped it for a two-base error. Two runs scored, and Yank manager Casey Stengel replaced Ford with Allie Reynolds. New York fans booed Stengel's switch, but Reynolds struck out pinch-hitter Stan Lopata, and the Series was over.

For the Phillies, it was the end of four frustrating days. The team hit only .203, its big hitters having contributed little. Granny Hamner was the only consistent hitter in the Series, collecting a .429 average.

"We played only fair baseball," manager Eddie Sawyer said. "Every mistake we made hurt us. If we had played like this all season, we never would have been in the Series."

Grover Cleveland Alexander, brought to the final two games of the Series by a radio station in Omaha, Nebraska, where he lived, saw similarities between the 1950 and 1915 Phillies. "They didn't hit any better (in 1950) than they did in 1915," said the ex-Phillies pitching great.

The Yankees didn't hit well, either. New York managed only a .222 average. Through the first three games, the fearsome trio of DiMaggio, Berra, and Mize put together only four hits. As a result of the Yanks' and Phils' weak hitting, it was the lowest-scoring four-game Series in history.

"The Phillies," said Stengel, "have a fine ball club. I was surprised they gave us such a hard battle all the way."

Although disappointed, the Phillies were far from despondent. Just winning the pennant had been a major accomplishment for the young team, and the Series was somewhat anticlimactic. Besides, the players would have a losers' share of $4,081.34 (each Yankee got $5,737) to carry them over the winter, and there was a feeling that the 1950 pennant was only the first of many flags.

In contrast to the Phillies' arrival in Philadelphia after the pennant clincher, their return after the Series attracted hardly any attention. Only a couple of hundred people turned out to greet the team when it arrived at North Philadelphia Station.

Yogi Berra starts victory dance as Stan Lopata finishes futile swing that became final out of the 1950 Series.

Richie Ashburn (left) and Andy Seminick arrive in Philadelphia after train ride from New York City after sweep.

Game 1
Wednesday, October 4, at Philadelphia

New York	AB	R	H	RBI	PO	A
Woodling, lf	3	0	1	0	1	0
Rizzuto, ss	3	0	1	0	0	2
Berra, c	4	0	0	0	7	0
DiMaggio, cf	2	0	0	0	3	0
Mize, 1b	4	0	0	0	7	0
Hopp, 1b	0	0	0	0	3	0
Brown, 3b	4	1	1	1	0	0
Johnson, 3b	0	0	0	0	0	0
Bauer, rf	4	0	1	0	5	0
Coleman, 2b	4	0	0	1	1	2
Raschi, p	3	0	1	0	0	3
Totals, p	**31**	**1**	**5**	**1**	**27**	**7**

Phillies	AB	R	H	RBI	PO	A
Waitkus, 1b	3	0	0	0	9	2
Ashburn, cf	4	0	0	0	2	0
Sisler, lf	4	0	0	0	3	0
Ennis, rf	3	0	0	0	4	0
Jones, 3b	3	0	1	0	4	3
Hamner, ss	3	0	0	0	0	1
Seminick, c	3	0	1	0	1	1
Goliat, 2b	3	0	0	0	3	2
Konstanty, p	2	0	0	0	1	0
a-Whitman	1	0	0	0	0	0
Meyer, p	0	0	0	0	0	1
Totals	**29**	**0**	**2**	**0**	**27**	**10**

a-Flied out for Konstanty in 8th.

New York	0	0	0	1	0	0	0	0	0 — 1
Phillies	0	0	0	0	0	0	0	0	0 — 0

Error: Jones. Left on base: New York 9, Philadelphia 3. Two-base hit: Brown. Sacrifice hits: Rizzuto, Raschi. Umpires: Conlan (N.L.), McGowan (A.L.), Boggess (N.L.), Berry (A.L.), Barlick (N.L.) and McKinley (A.L.). Time, 2:17. Attendance, 30,746.

New York	IP	H	R	ER	BB	SO
Raschi (W)	9	2	0	0	1	5

Phillies	IP	H	R	ER	BB	SO
Konstanty (L)	8	4	1	1	4	0
Meyer	1	1	0	0	0	0

Game 2
Thursday, October 5, at Philadelphia

New York	AB	R	H	RBI	PO	A
Woodling, lf	5	0	2	1	2	0
Rizzuto, ss	4	0	0	0	2	1
Berra, c	5	0	1	0	7	0
DiMaggio, cf	5	1	1	1	3	0
Mize, 1b	4	0	1	0	6	0
Johnson, 3b	1	0	0	0	0	2
Brown, 3b	4	0	2	0	0	0
b-Hopp, 1b	1	0	0	0	3	0
Bauer, rf	5	0	1	0	1	0
Coleman, 2b	3	1	1	0	5	6
Reynolds, p	3	0	1	0	1	2
Totals	**40**	**2**	**10**	**2**	**30**	**11**

Phillies	AB	R	H	RBI	PO	A
Waitkus, 1b	4	0	2	0	8	0
Ashburn, cf	5	0	2	1	4	0
Sisler, lf	5	0	0	0	3	0
Ennis, rf	4	0	0	0	1	0
Jones, 3b	4	0	0	0	3	0
Hamner, ss	3	0	2	0	2	2
Seminick, c	2	0	0	0	5	0
a-Caballero	0	0	0	0	0	0
Silvestri, c	0	0	0	0	1	0
c-Whitman	0	0	0	0	0	0
Lopata, c	0	0	0	0	1	0
Goliat, 2b	4	1	1	0	2	2
Roberts, p	2	0	0	0	0	0
d-Mayo	0	0	0	0	0	0
Totals	**33**	**1**	**7**	**1**	**30**	**4**

a-Ran for Seminick in 7th.
b-Ran for Brown in 8th.
c-Intentionally walked for Silvestri in 9th.
d-Walked for Roberts in 10th.

New York	0	1	0	0	0	0	0	0	0	1	—2
Phillies	0	0	0	0	1	0	0	0	0	0	—1

Double plays: New York 2. Left on base: New York 11, Philadelphia 8. Two-base hits: Ashburn, Waitkus, Coleman, Hamner. Three-base hit: Hamner. Home run: DiMaggio. Stolen base: Hamner. Sacrifice hits: Roberts, Waitkus. Umpires: McGowan (A.L.), Boggess (N.L.), Berry (A.L.), Conlan (N.L.), McKinley (A.L.) and Barlick (N.L.). Time, 3:06. Attendance, 32,660.

New York	IP	H	R	ER	BB	SO
Reynolds (W)	10	7	1	1	4	6

Phillies	IP	H	R	ER	BB	SO
Roberts (L)	10	10	2	2	3	5

Game 3
Friday, October 6, at New York

Phillies	AB	R	H	RBI	PO	A
Waitkus, 1b	5	0	1	0	8	0
Ashburn, cf	4	0	1	0	0	0
Jones, 3b	3	0	1	0	1	2
Ennis, rf	4	1	1	0	3	0
Sisler, lf	4	0	1	1	2	1
Mayo, lf	0	0	0	0	1	0
Hamner, ss	4	1	3	0	2	2
Seminick, c	2	0	1	0	5	0
Goliat, 2b	3	0	1	1	4	1
d-Caballero	0	0	0	0	0	0
Bloodworth, 2b	0	0	0	0	0	0
Heintzelman, p	2	0	0	0	0	2
Konstanty, p	0	0	0	0	0	0
e-Whitman	1	0	0	0	0	0
Meyer, p	0	0	0	0	0	0
Totals	**32**	**2**	**10**	**2**	**26**	**8**

New York	AB	R	H	RBI	PO	A
Rizzuto, ss	3	1	1	0	1	1
Coleman, 2b	4	1	3	2	3	1
Berra, c	2	0	0	0	6	1
DiMaggio, cf	3	0	1	0	1	0
Bauer, lf	3	0	0	0	1	0
b-Brown	1	0	0	0	0	0
c-Jensen	0	0	0	0	0	0
Ferrick, p	0	0	0	0	0	0
Mize, 1b	4	0	0	0	9	2
Collins, 1b	0	0	0	0	1	1
Johnson, 3b	4	0	0	0	1	3
Mapes, rf	4	0	0	0	3	0
Lopat, p	2	0	1	0	1	4
a-Woodling, lf	2	1	1	0	0	0
Totals	**32**	**3**	**7**	**2**	**27**	**13**

a-Popped out for Lopat in 8th.
b-Reached first on error for Bauer in 8th.
c-Ran for Brown in 8th.
d-Ran for Goliat in 9th.
e-Reached on fielder's choice for Konstanty in 9th.

Phillies	0	0	0	0	0	1	1	0	0	—2
New York	0	0	1	0	0	0	0	1	1	—3

Errors: Hamner, Seminick. Double play: Philadelphia 1. Left on base: Philadelphia 8, New York 9. Two-base hits: Ennis, Hamner. Stolen base: Rizzuto. Sacrifice hits: Seminick 2, Heintzelman, Jones. Umpires: Boggess (N.L.), Berry (A.L.), Conlan (N.L.), McGowan (A.L.), Barlick (N.L.) and McKinley (A.L.). Time, 2:35. Attendance, 64,505.

Phillies	IP	H	R	ER	BB	SO
Heintzelman	7⅔	4	2	1	6	3
Konstanty	⅓	0	0	0	0	0
Meyer (L)	⅔	3	1	1	0	1

New York	IP	H	R	ER	BB	SO
Lopat	8	9	2	2	0	5
Ferrick (W)	1	1	0	0	1	0

Game 4
Saturday, October 7, at New York

Phillies	AB	R	H	RBI	PO	A
Waitkus, 1b	3	0	1	0	9	1
Ashburn, cf	4	0	0	0	3	0
Jones, 3b	4	1	2	0	0	4
Ennis, rf	3	0	1	0	1	0
Sisler, lf	4	0	0	0	2	0
b-K. Johnson	0	1	0	0	0	0
Hamner, ss	4	0	1	0	2	2
Seminick, c	4	0	0	0	3	1
c-Mayo	0	0	0	0	0	0
Goliat, 2b	4	0	1	0	4	4
Miller, p	0	0	0	0	0	0
Konstanty, p	2	0	1	0	0	1
a-Caballero	1	0	0	0	0	0
Roberts, p	0	0	0	0	0	0
d-Lopata	1	0	0	0	0	0
Totals	34	2	7	0	24	13

New York	AB	R	H	RBI	PO	A
Woodling, lf	4	1	2	0	4	0
Rizzuto, ss	4	0	0	0	2	4
Berra, c	4	2	2	2	10	0
DiMaggio, cf	3	1	2	1	1	0
Mize, 1b	3	0	1	0	5	1
Hopp, 1b	1	0	0	0	1	1
Brown, 3b	3	1	1	1	0	1
W. Johnson, 3b	1	0	0	0	0	0
Bauer, rf	3	0	0	1	1	0
Coleman, 2b	3	0	0	0	2	3
Ford, p	3	0	0	0	1	0
Reynolds, p	0	0	0	0	0	0
Totals	32	5	8	5	27	10

a-Struck out for Konstanty in 8th.
b-Ran for Sisler in 9th.
c-Ran for Seminick in 9th.
d-Struck out for Roberts in 9th.

Phillies	0	0	0	0	0	0	0	0	2 — 2
New York	2	0	0	0	0	3	0	0	x — 5

Errors: Goliat, Woodling, Brown. Double plays: New York 2. Left on base: Philadelphia 7, New York 4. Two-base hits: Jones, DiMaggio. Three-base hit: Brown. Home run: Berra. Hit by pitcher: By Konstanty (DiMaggio), by Ford (Ennis). Wild pitch: Miller. Umpires: Berry (A.L.), Conlan (N.L.), McGowan (A.L.), Boggess (N.L.), McKinley (A.L.) and Barlick (N.L.). Time, 2:05. Attendance, 68,098.

Phillies	IP	H	R	ER	BB	SO
Miller (L)	⅓	2	2	1	0	0
Konstanty	6⅔	5	3	3	0	3
Roberts	1	1	0	0	0	0

New York	IP	H	R	ER	BB	SO
Ford (W)	8⅔	7	2	0	1	7
Reynolds	⅓	0	0	0	0	1

COMPOSITE BATTING AVERAGES

New York Yankees

Player-Position	G	AB	R	H	2B	3B	HR	RBI	BA
Lopat, p	1	2	0	1	0	0	0	0	.500
Woodling, lf-ph	4	14	2	6	0	0	0	1	.429
Brown, 3b-ph	4	12	2	4	1	1	0	1	.333
Raschi, p	1	3	0	1	0	0	0	0	.333
Reynolds, p	2	3	0	1	0	0	0	0	.333
DiMaggio, cf	4	13	2	4	1	0	1	2	.308
Coleman, 2b	4	14	2	4	1	0	0	3	.286
Berra, c	4	15	2	3	0	0	1	2	.200
Rizzuto, ss	4	14	1	2	0	0	0	0	.143
Mize, 1b	4	15	0	2	0	0	0	0	.133
Bauer, rf-lf	4	15	0	2	0	0	0	1	.133
Collins, 1b	1	0	0	0	0	0	0	0	.000
Mapes, rf	1	4	0	0	0	0	0	0	.000
Hopp, 1b-pr	3	2	0	0	0	0	0	0	.000
W. Johnson, 3b	4	6	0	0	0	0	0	0	.000
Ferrick, p	1	0	0	0	0	0	0	0	.000
Ford, p	1	3	0	0	0	0	0	0	.000
Jensen, pr	1	0	0	0	0	0	0	0	.000
Totals	4	135	11	30	3	1	2	10	.222

Philadelphia Phillies

Player-Position	G	AB	R	H	2B	3B	HR	RBI	BA
Hamner, ss	4	14	1	6	2	1	0	0	.429
Jones, 3b	4	14	1	4	1	0	0	0	.286
Waitkus, 1b	4	15	0	4	1	0	0	0	.267
Konstanty, p	3	4	0	1	0	0	0	0	.250
Goliat, 2b	4	14	1	3	0	0	0	1	.214
Seminick, c	4	11	0	2	0	0	0	0	.182
Ashburn, cf	4	17	0	3	1	0	0	1	.176
Ennis, rf	4	14	1	2	1	0	0	0	.143
Sisler, lf	4	17	0	1	0	0	0	1	.059
Silvestri, c	1	0	0	0	0	0	0	0	.000
Lopata, c-ph	2	1	0	0	0	0	0	0	.000
Bloodworth, 2b	1	0	0	0	0	0	0	0	.000
Mayo, ph-lf-pr	3	0	0	0	0	0	0	0	.000
Meyer, p	2	0	0	0	0	0	0	0	.000
Roberts, p	2	2	0	0	0	0	0	0	.000
Heintzelman, p	1	2	0	0	0	0	0	0	.000
Miller, p	1	0	0	0	0	0	0	0	.000
Whitman, ph	3	2	0	0	0	0	0	0	.000
K. Johnson, pr	1	0	1	0	0	0	0	0	.000
Caballero, pr-ph	3	1	0	0	0	0	0	0	.000
Totals	4	128	5	26	6	1	0	3	.203

COMPOSITE PITCHING AVERAGES

New York Yankees

Pitcher	G	IP	H	R	ER	BB	SO	W	L	ERA
Raschi	1	9	2	0	0	1	5	1	0	0.00
Ford	1	8⅔	7	2	0	1	7	1	0	0.00
Ferrick	1	1	1	0	0	1	0	1	0	0.00
Reynolds	2	10⅓	7	1	1	4	7	1	0	0.87
Lopat	1	8	9	2	2	0	5	0	0	2.25
Totals	4	37	26	5	3	7	24	4	0	0.73

Philadelphia Phillies

Pitcher	G	IP	H	R	ER	BB	SO	W	L	ERA
Heintzelman	1	7⅔	4	2	1	6	3	0	0	1.17
Roberts	2	11	11	2	2	3	5	0	1	1.64
Konstanty	3	15	9	4	4	4	3	0	1	2.40
Meyer	2	1⅔	4	1	1	0	1	0	1	5.40
Miller	1	⅓	2	2	1	0	0	0	1	27.00
Totals	4	35⅔	30	11	9	13	12	0	4	2.27

Phillies versus Cincinnati Reds
National League Championship Series

1976

Never before in their lives had Phillies fans been as optimistic as they were before the start of the 1976 LCS. And it was hard to blame them for their almost cocky approach to the best-of-five series. They had won 101 games during the regular season, easily the most victories in the franchise's history. It was true that the Reds had won 102, but the Phillies had handled Cincinnati by an 8–4 spread in head-to-head action. The Phillies felt they had the bats, the arms, and the depth to take care of the Rhinelanders, especially with the first two games at the Vet.

Everybody forgot one thing: The Reds had the experience. They had been in post-season action in three of the previous four years and were the defending World Champions after beating the Red Sox in seven games in a 1975 Series that was one of the greatest ever played.

And if the Phillies' fans were cocky, the Reds players and manager weren't trying to fool anybody. Pete Rose wouldn't be complacent if the idea were to hit a target and drop some poor guy in a tank of water at the local school carnival. He didn't even need a World Series to get his competitive juices flowing. And the others—Tony Perez, Johnny Bench, Ken Griffey, Joe Morgan, George Foster, Don Gullett, Dave Concepcion—were total professionals.

Then there was Sparky Anderson, whose entire major league career as a player had been one season with the Phillies. Sparky, a wonderfully honest and square-shooting man, would talk volumes on most subjects. Sometimes he even got the subject and verb to agree. It was Monday morning after the regular season and Riverfront Stadium in Cincinnati was nearly empty. Sparky had sent out for a small pizza for lunch and was reviewing films when a visitor popped his head in the office. Would Sparky share his ideas with the Philadelphia people through the visitor's paper?

Sparky was more than willing to be interviewed. The Phillies, he said, were one fine baseball team, one of the best to come along in the National League in some time. But, Anderson cautioned, his Reds *were* the best until someone proved otherwise. He said, win or lose, the World Series was fun. National hype. Getting to the World Series, he said, was another matter. It was the worst kind of hell. "And," Sparky said, "we've gone through it. The Phillies haven't."

Hell Night I arrived in Philadelphia on Saturday, October 9. The Phillies took a 1–0 lead on Greg Luzinski's sacrifice fly, and the crowd of 62,640 felt good with Steve Carlton on the mound. But Carlton faltered and gave up a home run to George Foster. Reds starter Don Gullett had two hits and three RBI off Carlton and successor Tug McGraw, Pete Rose added three hits, and the Reds triumphed, 6–3.

Hell Night II followed. This time, Phillies manager Danny Ozark gave the ball to Jim Lonborg, and for five innings, it was 1967 and Boston's Impossible Dream once again as Lonnie took a no-hitter and a 2–0 lead into the sixth. He came out of the inning the losing pitcher after an error by Dick Allen helped open the gates to a four-run Cincinnati inning. The Reds added another two runs in the seventh inning against Tug McGraw, and what had been such a happy Philadelphia scene 48 hours earlier now had the stench of desperation with the team needing a three-game sweep in Cincinnati to live to play the World Series.

The team had its best chance of all to win a game Tuesday, October 12, in Cincinnati. Danny Ozark rolled the dice and sent Jim Kaat, who had won only two of his last dozen decisions in the regular season, figuring a veteran with World Series experience might withstand the pressure more readily than his two young starters, Larry Christenson and Tommy Underwood.

Danny was right. Kaat pitched brilliantly, taking a shutout and a 3–0 lead into the seventh inning. He was pulled in favor of Ron Reed after allowing the first two runners to reach base, and when the inning ended the Reds were on top by 4–3. But the Phillies battled back gamely, scoring twice in the eighth and once in the ninth for a 6–4 lead. With Reed throwing smoke, the Phillies looked as if they were finally going to win their first post-season game in 61 years. Then lightning struck.

George Foster picked on a Reed fastball and drilled it over the fence to close the gap to one. On the next pitch, Johnny Bench did likewise to tie the game.

At this point, Danny Ozark lifted Reed in favor of Gene Garber, who gave Dave Concepcion a single and was lifted for Tommy Underwood.

Underwood loaded the bases on two walks around a sacrifice bunt. Ken Griffey, who had sat out the final game of the regular season and cost himself a possible National League batting title in the process, hit a high chopper to the infield. It bounced off first baseman Bobby Tolan's glove, and Concepcion crossed the plate with the run that swept the Phillies.

Game 1
Saturday, October 9, at Philadelphia

Cincinnati	AB	R	H	RBI	PO	A
Rose, 3b	5	1	3	1	1	2
Griffey, rf	4	0	1	0	5	0
Morgan, 2b	2	0	0	0	1	1
Eastwick, p	0	0	0	0	0	1
Perez, 1b	3	0	0	1	8	0
Foster, lf	5	1	1	1	4	0
Bench, c	5	1	2	0	4	2
Concepcion, ss	3	2	1	0	0	2
Geronimo, cf	4	0	0	0	4	0
Gullett, p	4	1	2	3	0	0
Flynn, 2b	0	0	0	0	0	0
Totals	35	6	10	6	27	8

Phillies	AB	R	H	RBI	PO	A
Cash, 2b	4	1	1	0	2	0
Maddox, cf	4	1	2	0	2	0
Schmidt, 3b	3	0	0	1	3	3
Luzinski, lf	3	1	1	1	2	0
Allen, 1b	3	0	1	0	5	0
Brown, rf	2	0	0	0	2	0
Johnstone, ph	1	0	1	1	0	0
McCarver, c	3	0	0	0	6	0
McGraw, p	0	0	0	0	0	0
Tolan, ph	1	0	0	0	0	0
Bowa, ss	3	0	0	0	1	4
Hutton, ph	1	0	0	0	0	0
Carlton, p	2	0	0	0	0	0
Boone, c	1	0	0	0	4	0
Totals	31	3	6	3	27	7

```
Cincinnati  0 0 1 0 0 2 0 3 0 — 6
Phillies    1 0 0 0 0 0 0 0 2 — 3
```

Error: Schmidt. Double plays: Philadelphia 2. Left on base: Cincinnati 9, Philadelphia 5. Two-base hits: Rose 2, Concepcion, Bench, Gullett, Cash, Luzinski. Three-base hits: Rose, Griffey. Home run: Foster. Stolen bases: Griffey, Bench, Morgan 2. Sacrifice flies: Schmidt, Perez. Wild pitches: McGraw, Eastwick. Umpires: Sudol, Dale, Stello, Vargo, Harvey, and Tata. Time, 2:39. Attendance, 62,640.

Cincinnati	IP	H	R	ER	BB	SO
Gullett (W)	8	2	1	1	3	4
Eastwick	1	4	2	2	0	0

Phillies	IP	H	R	ER	BB	SO
Carlton (L)	7*	8	5	4	5	6
McGraw	2	2	1	1	1	4

*Pitched to two batters in 8th.

Game 2
Sunday, October 10, at Philadelphia

Cincinnati	AB	R	H	RBI	PO	A
Rose, 3b	5	2	2	1	1	2
Griffey, rf	4	1	2	1	4	0
Morgan, 2b	2	1	0	0	5	1
Perez, 1b	3	0	0	1	10	1
Foster, lf	4	0	0	1	0	0
Bench, c	4	0	1	0	4	1
Geronimo, cf	4	0	1	0	1	0
Concepcion, ss	3	1	0	0	1	5
Zachry, p	1	0	0	0	1	3
Driessen, ph	1	0	0	0	0	0
Borbon, p	2	1	0	0	0	0
Totals	33	6	6	4	27	13

Phillies	AB	R	H	RBI	PO	A
Cash, 2b	5	0	2	0	0	3
Maddox, cf	4	0	0	0	6	0
Schmidt, 3b	5	0	1	0	0	2
Luzinski, lf	4	1	1	1	4	0
Allen, 1b	3	1	1	0	12	0
Johnstone, rf	4	0	3	0	1	0
Boone, c	3	0	2	1	3	2
Bowa, ss	2	0	0	0	1	4
Lonborg, p	1	0	0	0	0	2
Garber, p	0	0	0	0	0	0
Tolan, ph	1	0	0	0	0	0
McGraw, p	0	0	0	0	0	1
Reed, p	0	0	0	0	0	0
McCarver, ph	1	0	0	0	0	0
Totals	33	2	10	2	27	14

```
Cincinnati  0 0 0 0 4 2 0 0 0 — 6
Phillies    0 1 0 0 1 0 0 0 0 — 2
```

Error: Allen. Double plays: Cincinnati 2. Left on base: Cincinnati 5, Philadelphia 10. Home run: Luzinski, Stolen base: Griffey. Sacrifice hits: Boone, Lonborg. Sacrifice fly: Perez. Wild pitch: McGraw. Umpires: Dale, Stello, Vargo, Harvey, Tata, and Sudol. Time, 2:24. Attendance, 62,651.

Cincinnati	IP	H	R	ER	BB	SO
Zachry (W)	5	6	2	2	3	3
Borbon (S)	4	4	0	0	1	0

Phillies	IP	H	R	ER	BB	SO
Lonborg (L)	5⅓	2	3	1	2	2
Garber	⅔	1	1	0	1	0
McGraw	⅓	2	2	2	0	1
Reed	2⅔	1	0	0	1	1

Game 3
Tuesday, October 12, at Cincinnati

Phillies	AB	R	H	RBI	PO	A
Cash, 2b	4	0	1	1	6	5
Maddox, cf	5	1	1	1	1	0
Schmidt, 3b	5	1	3	1	1	4
Luzinski, lf	4	0	1	1	0	0
Reed, p	1	0	0	0	0	0
Garber, p	0	0	0	0	0	0
Underwood, p	0	0	0	0	0	0
Allen, 1b	3	0	0	0	11	0
Martin, lf	1	1	0	0	1	0
Johnstone, rf	4	1	3	1	2	0
Boone, c	3	0	0	0	1	0
Harmon, pr	0	1	0	0	0	0
Oates, c	1	0	0	0	1	0
Bowa, ss	3	1	1	1	0	3
Kaat, p	2	0	1	0	0	1
Tolan, lf-1b	0	0	0	0	1	0
Totals	36	6	11	6	25	13

Cincinnati	AB	R	H	RBI	PO	A
Rose, 3b	4	0	1	0	0	1
Griffey, rf	5	1	2	1	2	0
Morgan, 2b	3	1	0	0	3	3
Perez, 1b	4	1	2	1	9	1
Foster, lf	3	1	1	2	3	0
Bench, c	3	2	1	1	3	1
Concepcion, ss	4	1	1	0	1	5
Geronimo, cf	3	0	1	2	5	0
Nolan, p	0	0	0	0	1	0
Sarmiento, p	1	0	0	0	0	0
Borbon, p	0	0	0	0	0	0
Lum, ph	1	0	0	0	0	0
Eastwick, p	0	0	0	0	0	0
Armbrister, ph	0	0	0	0	0	0
Totals	31	7	9	7	27	11

```
Phillies    0 0 0  1 0 0  2 2 1 — 6
Cincinnati  0 0 0  0 0 0  4 0 3 — 7
```

One out when winning run scored.

Errors: Rose, Perez. Double plays: Philadelphia 1, Cincinnati 1. Left on base: Philadelphia 10, Cincinnati 6. Two-base hits: Maddox, Schmidt 2, Luzinski, Johnstone, Bowa. Three-base hits: Johnstone, Geronimo. Home runs: Foster, Bench. Sacrifice hits: Kaat, Armbrister. Sacrifice flies: Cash, Foster. Wild pitch: Eastwick. Umpires: Stello, Vargo, Harvey, Tata, Sudol, and Dale. Time, 2:43. Attendance, 55,047.

Phillies	IP	H	R	ER	BB	SO
Kaat	6*	2	2	2	2	1
Reed	2†	5	4	4	1	1
Garber (L)	0‡	1	1	1	0	0
Underwood	⅓	1	0	0	2	0

Cincinnati	IP	H	R	ER	BB	SO
Nolan	5⅔	6	1	1	2	1
Sarmiento	1	2	2	2	1	0
Borbon	⅓	0	0	0	0	0
Eastwick (W)	2	3	3	2	2	1

*Pitched to two batters in 7th.
†Pitched to two batters in 9th.
‡Pitched to one batter in 9th.

Phillies versus Los Angeles Dodgers
National League Championship Series

If the Phillies were confident going into the 1976 League Championship Series, it was nothing like the positive feelings they had going into the 1977 matchup with the Los Angeles Dodgers.

The general feeling around the ball club was that the 1977 team was the best in the history of the franchise up to that point. It had won 101 games for the second year in a row. It had the league's Cy Young Award winner in Steve Carlton (23–10), a 19-game winner in Larry Christenson, and a great bullpen quartet in Tug McGraw, Ron Reed, Gene Garber, and Warren Brusstar.

It had Greg Luzinski with his 39 home runs, 130 RBI, and .309 batting average looking at a possible MVP trophy. It had Mike Schmidt and his 38 homers at third base. It had Bob Boone's with his .284 average behind the plate, and, when Carlton pitched, Tim McCarver offered his .320 bat to the lineup.

And, since it had been in the playoffs the previous season, it finally had experience.

But, as any Phillies fan had learned over the years, it also had Murphy's Law following, almost stalking, it. If something could go wrong, it would.

After the first game of the LCS, though, it looked as if even Murphy had taken the side door out. Steve Carlton blew a 5–1 lead in the seventh inning when he gave up a grand slam home run to Ron Cey. But the Phillies bounced back to win the game and silence the crowd at Dodger Stadium, 7–5, when Bake McBride, Larry Bowa, and Mike Schmidt all produced ninth-inning singles.

1977

The lessons of 1915 about premature celebration hadn't yet been learned, however. The Phillies clutched the win as if it were a guaranteed ticket to the World Series.

"All we needed in Los Angeles was a split," crowed Luzinski, who had hit a two-run homer into dead center field to start the ball rolling against Tommy John in the first inning. "We're practically unbeatable at home. I can't see any way we'll lose two out of three at the Vet."

Stick around, Greg. There are ways, one in which you would play a very large part.

It looked as if the Phillies might even get more than a split in LA when McBride hit a solo homer in the third to give the Phillies a 1–0 lead. But the Dodgers came back and tied it in the third, then made Jim Lonborg a loser in the fourth when Lonnie hung a slider that Dusty Baker hit out of the park for a grand slam homer on the way to a 7–1 Don Sutton victory.

But the Phillies were coming home to the Vet, where they had won 60 of 81 games during the regular season. Nobody expected them to finish the year 60–23 in their home park. But that's what happened in two of the most bizarre games in National League playoff history.

Game Three matched Larry Christenson and Burt Hooton. The Dodgers touched Christenson for two runs in the top of the second inning, but the crowd of 63,719 got them back, plus one more, in the bottom of the inning. Hooton became wild, and the fans began hooting at the pitcher. The louder they hooted, the more obviously unnerved Burt became. So much so that he walked, in order, Christenson, McBride, and Larry Bowa to force three runs across the plate.

The Dodgers tied the score in the top of the fourth, but the Phillies came back with two in the eighth and appeared to have everything well in hand when Gene Garber retired the first two Dodgers in the ninth.

Hello, Murphy!

Vic Davallilo, who it seemed was almost old enough to remember the 1915 Phillies, beat out a bunt. Then Manny Mota hit an 0–2 pitch high and deep to left field. Normally during the season, Danny Ozark would have had Jerry Martin in for Luzinski for defensive purposes. This day, with the most pivotal game of the year at hand, Ozark stayed with Luzinski, offering afterward the lame excuse that he wanted Luzinski's bat in the lineup in case the Dodgers tied it.

Luzinski backed up to the wall, got his glove on the ball, and couldn't hold it. Davillilo scored, and when Ted Sizemore botched the relay throw, Mota took third.

The nation had hardly recovered from the sudden turn of events when Dave Lopes hit a shot at Mike Schmidt. The ball bounced off Schmidt and was picked off alertly by Larry Bowa, who threw to first. It was a bang-bang play, but umpire Bruce Froemming ruled Lopes safe as the tying run crossed the plate.

The argument that followed was lengthy but brought no change. "He (Froemming) didn't think I could throw it over there," screamed Bowa. "I couldn't believe it, he didn't beat the throw to first," agonized Rich Hebner.

Nevertheless, Lopes moved to second when Garber's pickoff throw got away from Hebner and scored the winning run on Bill Russell's single up the middle.

The next night was simply a fitting climax to the series. It rained . . . and rained . . . and rained. Not just drizzle, either, but a steady downpour. But television, bless its dictating heart, had a time slot to fill and sponsors to please, so the game went on with National League president Chub Feeney approving and sitting in the rain as if to prove that a little bit of water never hurt anyone.

The first-game matchup was repeated—Steve Carlton versus Tommy John. This time, John's sinker, combined with the heavy, wet air, was unbeatable. Dusty Baker hit his second home run of the LCS, a two-run shot in the second inning, for the runs the Dodgers needed in a 4–1 victory.

To the Phillies' credit, they refused to complain about the rain.

"We're too dedicated and too professional to make remarks about the conditions tonight or the umpires' decisions last night," said McCarver. "The Dodgers were playing in the same conditions. The luster of their winning shouldn't be defaced by our making remarks to the contrary."

That was for the public record. Privately, of course, the Phillies were convinced even afterward that they were the better team. They hoped to get another poke at the Dodgers the following post-season. And they did.

Game 1
Tuesday, October 4, at Los Angeles

Phillies	AB	R	H	RBI	PO	A
McBride, cf	5	1	2	0	3	0
Bowa, ss	5	2	1	0	0	5
Schmidt, 3b	5	2	1	1	1	5
Luzinski, lf	3	1	1	2	1	0
Johnson, 1b	4	0	1	2	8	0
Hutton, 1b	1	0	0	0	5	0
Martin, rf	3	0	0	0	1	0
Johnstone, ph-rf	1	0	0	0	0	0
McCarver, c	3	1	1	0	4	0
Boone, c	0	0	0	0	1	0
Sizemore, 2b	3	0	0	0	3	2
Carlton, p	2	0	2	1	0	0
Garber, p	0	0	0	0	0	1
Hebner, ph	1	0	0	0	0	0
McGraw, p	0	0	0	0	0	0
Totals	36	7	9	6	27	13

Los Angeles	AB	R	H	RBI	PO	A
Lopes, 2b	5	1	2	1	3	3
Russell, ss	5	1	0	0	2	3
Smith, rf	4	1	0	0	1	0
Cey, 3b	4	1	2	4	2	4
Garvey, 1b	4	0	3	0	12	0
Baker, lf	3	0	1	0	0	0
Burke, cf	3	0	0	0	1	0
Monday, ph-cf	1	0	0	0	0	0
Yeager, c	4	0	0	0	6	1
John, p	1	0	0	0	0	1
Garman, p	0	0	0	0	0	0
Lacy, ph	1	1	1	0	0	0
Hough, p	0	0	0	0	0	1
Grote, ph	0	0	0	0	0	0
Sosa, p	1	0	0	0	0	0
Totals	36	5	9	5	27	13

Phillies	2	0	0	0	2	1	0	0	2 — 7
Los Angeles	0	0	0	0	1	0	4	0	0 — 5

Errors: Russell 2. Double play: Los Angeles 1. Left on base: Philadelphia 7, Los Angeles 7. Home runs: Luzinski, Cey. Stolen bases: Luzinski, Garvey. Sacrifice hit: Sizemore. Hit by pitch: by John (Carlton). Balks: Carlton, Sosa. Umpires: Pryor, Engel, Wendelstedt, Froemming, Rennert, and Runge. Time, 2:35. Attendance, 55,968.

Phillies	IP	H	R	ER	BB	SO
Carlton	6⅔	9	5	5	3	3
Garber (W)	1⅓	0	0	0	0	2
McGraw (S)	1	0	0	0	0	0

Los Angeles	IP	H	R	ER	BB	SO
John	4⅔	4	4	0	3	3
Garman	⅓	0	0	0	0	1
Hough	2	2	1	1	0	3
Sosa (L)	2	3	2	2	0	0

Game 2
Wednesday, October 5, at Los Angeles

Phillies	AB	R	H	RBI	PO	A
McBride, cf	4	1	2	1	0	1
Bowa, ss	4	0	1	0	0	5
Schmidt, 3b	4	0	0	0	1	1
Luzinski, lf	4	0	1	0	0	0
Hebner, 1b	4	0	2	0	11	0
Johnstone, rf	4	0	1	0	4	0
Boone, c	4	0	1	0	6	1
Sizemore, 2b	4	0	1	0	2	1
Lonborg, p	1	0	0	0	0	2
Hutton, ph	1	0	0	0	0	0
Reed, p	0	0	0	0	0	0
Brown, ph	1	0	0	0	0	0
Brusstar, p	0	0	0	0	0	0
Totals	35	1	9	1	24	11

Los Angeles	AB	R	H	RBI	PO	A
Lopes, 2b	4	0	1	1	2	1
Russell, ss	4	2	2	0	3	2
Smith, rf	4	1	2	1	2	0
Cey, 3b	3	1	1	0	2	1
Garvey, 1b	3	1	0	0	7	1
Baker, lf	4	1	1	4	3	0
Monday, cf	3	1	1	0	3	0
Burke, cf	0	0	0	0	0	0
Yeager, c	3	0	1	1	5	0
Sutton, p	3	0	0	0	0	2
Totals	31	7	9	7	27	7

Phillies	0	0	1	0	0	0	0	0	0 — 1
Los Angeles	0	0	1	4	0	1	1	0	x — 7

Errors: Sizemore, Lopes. Double play: Los Angeles 2. Left on base: Philadelphia 7, Los Angeles 3. Two-base hits: Luzinski, Monday. Three-base hit: Smith. Home runs: McBride, Baker. Stolen base: Cey. Sacrifice hit: Cey. Umpires: Engel, Wendelstedt, Froemming, Rennert, Runge, and Pryor. Time, 2:14. Attendance, 55,973.

Phillies	IP	H	R	ER	BB	SO
Lonborg (L)	4	5	5	5	1	1
Reed	2	2	1	1	1	2
Brusstar	2	2	1	1	0	2

Los Angeles	IP	H	R	ER	BB	SO
Sutton (W)	9	9	1	1	0	4

Game 3
Friday, October 7, at Philadelphia

Los Angeles	AB	R	H	RBI	PO	A
Lopes, 2b	5	1	1	1	3	3
Russell, ss	5	0	2	1	5	2
Smith, rf	5	0	0	0	2	0
Cey, 3b	4	1	1	0	1	4
Garvey, 1b	4	1	1	0	9	0
Baker, lf	4	1	2	2	0	0
Monday, cf	3	0	1	0	3	0
Grote, c	0	0	0	0	0	0
Yeager, c	2	0	1	1	3	0
Davalillo, ph	1	1	1	0	0	0
Burke, cf	0	0	0	0	1	0
Hooton, p	1	0	1	0	0	1
Rhoden, p	1	0	0	0	0	0
Goodson, ph	1	0	0	0	0	0
Rau, p	0	0	0	0	0	0
Sosa, p	0	0	0	0	0	1
Rautzhan, p	0	0	0	0	0	0
Mota, ph	1	1	1	0	0	0
Garman, p	0	0	0	0	0	0
Totals	37	6	12	5	27	11

Phillies	AB	R	H	RBI	PO	A
McBride, rf	4	0	0	1	1	1
Bowa, ss	4	0	0	1	0	5
Schmidt, 3b	4	0	0	0	1	6
Luzinski, lf	3	0	1	0	0	1
Martin, pr	0	0	0	0	0	0
Hebner, 1b	5	2	1	0	14	0
Maddox, cf	4	1	1	1	3	0
Boone, c	4	1	2	0	6	0
Sizemore, 2b	3	1	1	0	2	3
Christenson, p	0	0	0	1	0	0
Brusstar, p	0	0	0	0	0	0
Hutton, ph	1	0	0	0	0	0
Reed, p	0	0	0	0	0	0
McCarver, ph	1	0	0	0	0	0
Garber, p	0	0	0	0	0	1
Totals	33	5	6	4	27	17

Los Angeles										
Los Angeles	0	2	0	1	0	0	0	0	3 — 6
Phillies	0	3	0	0	0	0	0	2	0 — 5

Errors: Cey, Sizemore, Garber, Smith. Double play: Philadelphia 1. Left on base: Los Angeles 6, Philadelphia 9. Two-base hits: Baker, Hooton, Cey, Russell, Hebner, Mota. Sacrifice hit: Garber. Hit by pitch: by Garman (Luzinski). Passed ball: Boone. Umpires: Wendelstedt, Froemming, Rennert, Runge, Pryor, and Engel. Time, 2:51. Attendance, 63,719.

Los Angeles	IP	H	R	ER	BB	SO
Hooton	1⅔	2	3	3	4	1
Rhoden	4⅓	2	0	0	2	0
Rau	1	0	0	0	0	1
Sosa	⅔	2	2	1	0	0
Rautzhan (W)	⅓	0	0	0	0	0
Garman (S)	1	0	0	0	0	0

Phillies	IP	H	R	ER	BB	SO
Christenson	3⅓	7	3	3	0	2
Brusstar	⅔	0	0	0	1	0
Reed	2	1	0	0	1	2
Garber (L)	3	4	3	2	0	0

Game 4
Saturday, October 8, at Philadelphia

Los Angeles	AB	R	H	RBI	PO	A
Lopes, 2b	3	0	0	0	1	3
Russell, ss	4	0	1	1	1	5
Smith, rf	3	0	1	0	2	0
Cey, 3b	2	1	0	0	2	5
Garvey, 1b	2	0	0	0	12	0
Baker, lf	3	2	1	2	0	0
Burke, cf	4	0	0	0	1	0
Yeager, c	4	1	1	0	8	0
John, p	4	0	1	0	0	0
Totals	29	4	5	3	27	13

Phillies	AB	R	H	RBI	PO	A
McBride, rf	5	0	0	0	2	0
Bowa, ss	4	0	0	0	0	2
Schmidt, 3b	3	0	0	0	1	3
Luzinski, lf	4	1	1	0	3	0
Hebner, 1b	4	0	2	0	7	0
Maddox, cf	3	0	2	1	3	0
McCarver, c	2	0	0	0	3	0
Reed, p	0	0	0	0	0	0
Brown, ph	1	0	0	0	0	0
McGraw, p	0	0	0	0	0	0
Martin, ph	1	0	0	0	0	0
Garber, p	0	0	0	0	0	0
Sizemore, 2b	3	0	1	0	3	2
Carlton, p	2	0	0	0	0	0
Boone, c	2	0	1	0	5	1
Totals	34	1	7	1	27	8

Los Angeles										
Los Angeles	0	2	0	0	2	0	0	0	0 — 4
Phillies	0	0	0	1	0	0	0	0	0 — 1

Errors: None. Double plays: Philadelphia 2. Left on base: Los Angeles 6, Philadelphia 9. Two-base hit: Hebner. Home run: Baker. Stolen base: Smith. Sacrifice hit: Garvey. Hit by pitch: by John (Maddox). Wild pitch: Carlton. Umpires: Froemming, Rennert, Runge, Pryor, Engel, and Wendelstedt. Time, 2:39. Attendance, 64,924.

Los Angeles	IP	H	R	ER	BB	SO
John (W)	9	7	1	1	2	8

Phillies	IP	H	R	ER	BB	SO
Carlton (L)	5*	4	4	4	5	3
Reed	1	0	0	0	0	1
McGraw	2	1	0	0	2	3
Garber	1	0	0	0	0	1

*Pitched to one batter in 6th.

Phillies versus Los Angeles Dodgers National League Championship Series

1978

The regular season had been a real struggle for the first time in three years. The Pittsburgh Pirates, under eternal optimist Chuck Tanner, made the Phillies work for their post-season berth. It took until the next-to-last-day of the season at Three Rivers Stadium before the Phillies were able to put the Bucs away when Randy Lerch hit two home runs and got the victory in a wild 10–8 game.

One prevailing local theory was that the regular season had just been an exhibition season for the Phillies, 162 games they had to get out of the way before they could get to the real task at hand, showing the Dodgers who really had the stronger team.

The Phillies to a man felt they had been treated unjustly the previous LCS. They wanted revenge, and they felt they had the tools to get it. They had two exceptional pitchers in Steve Carlton and Dick Ruthven, who came to the Phillies on the June 15 deadline in a trade with Atlanta and won 13 of 18 decisions the rest of the way.

And they had the first two games at home.

Never before in Phillies history did such promising circumstances turn to dust so quickly. The 124,000-plus fans who showed up at the Vet for the first two games came to the park anticipating victory and left it booing. In the opener, with Larry Christenson on the mound, the Phillies fell behind by 7–1 and lost, 9–5, as Bob Welch threw his mighty fastball past them over the last $4\frac{1}{3}$ innings, striking out five. Steve Garvey's three-run homer was the big blow for the winners.

In Game Two, Danny Ozark went to Ruthven, who had won him the pennant with his great pitching down the stretch. And, through the first three innings, Dick pitched perfect baseball. The first batter in the fourth, however, was Davey Lopes, and he homered. That was more than enough for Tommy John, whose sinker pitch was working as well as it ever had, getting 18 ground ball outs. The fans had begun booing about the sixth inning and left South Philadelphia in a sour mood after the Dodgers' 4–0 victory.

It was the Phillies who were in a sour mood before Game Three. Jim Murray, the *Los Angeles Times* columnist and humorist, had written a story about Philadelphia, casting the city, its residents, and its baseball team in the worst possible light. The Phillies responded angrily with their bats, beating the Dodgers, 9–4, as Greg Luzinski and Steve Carlton both hit home runs. Carlton went the distance for his first post-season victory with the Phillies.

Saturday afternoon's Game Four was a signal for Murphy's Law to take over once again. The Phillies and Dodgers were locked in a 3–3 tie after nine innings. The Phils failed to score in the top of the 10th, and Tug McGraw retired the first two Dodgers in the bottom of the inning. But, as the Phillies had learned a year earlier, strange things can happen after you retire the first two Dodgers in an inning. This time, the evil spirits took up residence in Garry Maddox's glove. It was the best center field glove in the game; the softest hands in baseball surrounded it. But, with two outs and none on in the 10th inning, Maddox moved in on a soft line drive by Dusty Baker—and flat-out dropped it. Soon after that, the Dodgers scored the winning run off McGraw and became the National League champs for the second year in a row.

In the losing clubhouse, Maddox refused to alibi for his error, showing himself once again to be a man of class under extremely trying circumstances.

"The ball was right in my glove," Garry said. "It was not a tough play, just a routine line drive. It's something I'll never forget the rest of my life."

Maddox's best buddy, Mike Schmidt, put the situation in its proper perspective, however.

"The Phillies did not lose this series because Garry Maddox did not catch Baker's ball," Schmidt said. "The Phillies lost it because we put ourselves in a vulnerable position from the outset."

For poor Danny Ozark, it was a case of putting his foot in his mouth once again. The manager proclaimed before the start of the series that the Phillies would win it by sweeping three games. Before Game Four, he changed his tune a bit. "I didn't say which three," he said.

After Game Four, there was nothing left to say.

Game 1
Wednesday, October 4, at Philadelphia

Los Angeles	AB	R	H	RBI	PO	A
Lopes, 2b	5	2	3	2	2	3
Russell, ss	5	1	1	0	2	2
Smith, rf	3	1	1	1	1	0
North, cf	1	0	0	0	0	0
Garvey, 1b	5	3	3	4	6	1
Cey, 3b	5	0	2	1	0	1
Baker, lf	3	0	1	0	1	0
Monday, cf,rf	4	1	1	0	4	0
Yeager, c	4	1	1	1	10	0
Hooton, p	2	0	0	0	1	0
Welch, p	2	0	0	0	0	1
Totals	38	9	13	9	27	8

Phillies	AB	R	H	RBI	PO	A
McBride, rf	5	1	1	0	1	0
Bowa, ss	5	1	3	0	0	4
Maddox, cf	5	0	2	2	4	0
Luzinski, lf	4	1	1	0	1	1
Hebner, 1b	4	0	1	1	11	0
Schmidt, 3b	3	0	0	1	2	4
Boone, c	4	0	1	0	6	1
Sizemore, 2b	4	1	2	0	2	3
Christenson, p	1	0	0	0	0	0
Brusstar, p	0	0	0	0	0	0
a-Gonzalez	1	0	0	0	0	0
Eastwick, p	0	0	0	0	0	0
b-McCarver	1	0	0	0	0	0
McGraw, p	0	0	0	0	0	0
c-Martin	1	1	1	1	0	0
Totals	38	5	12	5	27	13

a-Struck out for Brusstar in 5th.
b-Flied out for Eastwick in 6th.
c-Hit home run for McGraw in 9th.

Los Angeles	0	0	4	2	1	1	0	0	1	—9
Phillies	0	1	0	0	3	0	0	0	1	—5

Errors: Lopes, Schmidt. Double plays: Russell and Garvey; Bowa, Sizemore, and Hebner. Left on base: Los Angeles 8, Phillies 7. Two-base hit: Lopes. Three-base hits: Luzinski, Monday, Garvey. Home runs: Garvey 2 (2), Lopes (1), Yeager (1), Martin (1). Sacrifice fly: Schmidt. Hit by pitcher: Smith (by Eastwick). Umpires: Weyer, Colosi, Olsen, Davidson, Williams, McSherry. Time, 2:27. Attendance, 63,460.

Los Angeles	IP	H	R	ER	BB	SO
Hooton	4⅔	10	4	4	0	5
Welch (W)	4⅓	2	1	1	0	5

Phillies	IP	H	R	ER	BB	SO
Christenson (L)	4⅓	7	7	6	1	3
Brusstar	⅔	1	0	0	0	0
Eastwick	1	3	1	1	0	1
McGraw	3	2	1	1	3	3

Game 2
Thursday, October 5, at Philadelphia

Los Angeles	AB	R	H	RBI	PO	A
Lopes, 2b	4	1	3	3	4	4
Russell, ss	4	0	1	0	1	9
Smith, rf	4	0	1	0	0	0
North, cf	0	0	0	0	0	0
Garvey, 1b	4	0	0	0	16	0
Cey, 3b	4	0	0	0	0	7
Baker, lf	4	1	1	0	0	0
Monday, cf, rf	4	1	1	0	2	0
Yeager, c	3	1	1	1	4	1
John, p	3	0	0	0	0	0
Totals	34	4	8	4	27	21

Phillies	AB	R	H	RBI	PO	A
Schmidt, 3b	4	0	1	0	0	4
Bowa, ss	4	0	0	0	1	4
Maddox, cf	4	0	1	0	5	0
Luzinski, lf	3	0	1	0	2	0
Cardenal, 1b	2	0	0	0	10	0
Boone, c	3	0	1	0	5	0
Martin, rf	2	0	0	0	1	0
Sizemore, 2b	3	0	0	0	3	1
Ruthven, p	1	0	0	0	0	0
Brusstar, p	0	0	0	0	0	0
a-Morrison	1	0	0	0	0	0
Reed, p	0	0	0	0	0	0
b-Foote	1	0	0	0	0	0
McGraw, p	0	0	0	0	0	0
Totals	28	0	4	0	27	9

a-Struck out for Brusstar in 6th.
b-Struck out for Reed in 8th.

Los Angeles	0	0	0	1	2	0	1	0	0	—4
Phillies	0	0	0	0	0	0	0	0	0	—0

Double plays: Russell-Lopes-Garvey; Lopes-Russell-Garvey; Cey-Lopes-Garvey. Left on base: Los Angeles 5, Phillies 3. Two-base hits: Smith, Baker. Three-base hit: Lopes. Home run: Lopes (2). Stolen base: Yeager. Sacrifice: John. Umpires: Colosi, Olsen, Davidson, Williams, McSherry, Weyer. Time, 2:06. Attendance, 60,643.

Los Angeles	IP	H	R	ER	BB	SO
John (W)	9	4	0	0	2	4

Phillies	IP	H	R	ER	BB	SO
Ruthven (L)	4⅔	6	3	3	0	3
Brusstar	1⅓	0	0	0	0	0
Reed	2	2	1	1	0	0
McGraw	1	0	0	0	1	0

Game 3
Friday, October 5, at Los Angeles

Phillies	AB	R	H	RBI	PO	A
McBride, rf	3	0	0	0	0	0
a-Martin, rf	2	0	1	1	1	0
Bowa, ss	5	0	1	0	2	5
Maddox, cf	5	1	1	0	3	0
Luzinski, lf	5	1	3	1	1	0
Hebner, 1b	4	0	0	0	10	0
Schmidt, 3b	4	1	1	0	1	5
McCarver, c	3	2	0	1	8	0
Sizemore, 2b	2	2	2	1	1	2
Carlton, p	4	2	2	4	0	0
Totals	37	9	11	8	27	12

Los Angeles	AB	R	H	RBI	PO	A
Lopes, 2b	4	0	0	0	2	2
North, cf	4	0	0	0	2	0
Smith, rf	4	1	1	0	2	0
Garvey, 1b	4	2	2	2	16	2
Cey, 3b	3	1	1	1	2	3
Baker, lf	3	0	1	0	0	0
Russell, s	4	0	2	1	0	2
Yeager, c	3	0	0	0	2	0
c-Lacy	1	0	0	0	0	0
Sutton, p	2	0	0	0	0	1
Rautzhan, p	0	0	0	0	0	1
b-Mota	1	0	1	0	0	0
Hough, p	0	0	0	0	1	1
d-Ferguson	1	0	0	0	0	0
Totals	34	4	8	4	27	12

a-Doubled for McBride in 6th.
b-Doubled for Rautzhan in 7th.
c-Flied out for Yeager in 9th.
d-Grounded into double play for Hough in 9th.

Phillies										
Phillies	0	4	0	0	0	3	1	0	1—9
Los Angeles	0	1	2	0	0	0	0	1	0—4

Errors: Schmidt, Lopes, Smith. Double plays: Sizemore-Bowa-Hebner (2). Left on base: Phillies 7, Los Angeles 5. Two-base hits: Schmidt, Russell, Garvey, Martin, Mota. Home runs: Carlton (1), Garvey (3), Luzinski (1). Sacrifices: Sizemore, Hebner. Umpires: Olsen, Davidson, Williams, McSherry, Colosi, Wever. Time, 2:18. Attendance, 55,043.

Phillies	IP	H	R	ER	BB	SO
Carlton (W)	9	8	4	4	2	8

Los Angeles	IP	H	R	ER	BB	SO
Sutton (L)	5⅔	7	7	4	2	0
Rautzhan	1⅓	3	1	1	2	0
Hough	2	1	1	1	0	1

Game 4
Saturday, October 6, at Los Angeles

Phillies	AB	R	H	RBI	PO	A
Schmidt, 3b	4	0	1	0	0	5
Bowa, ss	4	1	2	0	2	3
Maddox, cf	5	0	1	0	4	0
Luzinski, lf	4	1	1	2	1	0
Cardenal, 1b	4	0	1	0	11	0
Martin, rf	4	0	0	0	5	0
Boone, c	4	0	0	0	5	1
Sizemore, 2b	4	0	1	0	1	2
Lerch, p	2	0	0	0	0	1
Brusstar, p	0	0	0	0	0	0
b-McBride	1	1	1	1	0	0
Reed, p	0	0	0	0	0	0
e-Hebner	1	0	0	0	0	0
McGraw, p	0	0	0	0	0	0
Totals	37	3	8	3	29	12

Los Angeles	AB	R	H	RBI	PO	A
Lopes, 2b	5	0	1	0	1	1
North, cf	3	0	0	0	7	0
c-Monday, cf	2	0	0	0	0	0
Smith, rf	5	0	0	0	2	0
Garvey, 1b	5	1	2	1	6	2
Cey, 3b	4	3	2	1	0	2
Baker, lf	5	0	4	1	4	0
Russell, ss	4	0	3	1	2	1
Yeager, c	3	0	1	0	5	1
d-Lacy	1	0	0	0	0	0
Grote, c	0	0	0	0	2	0
Rau, p	1	0	0	0	1	0
a-Mota	0	0	0	0	0	0
Rhoden, p	1	0	0	0	0	2
f-Ferguson	1	0	0	0	0	0
Forster, p	0	0	0	0	0	0
Totals	40	4	13	4	30	9

a-Hit sacrifice bunt for Rau in 5th.
b-Hit home run for Brusstar in 7th.
c-Struck out for North in 7th.
d-Fouled out for Yeager in 8th.
e-Fouled out for Reed in 9th.
f-Struck out for Rhoden in 9th.
(Two out when winning run scored)

Phillies										
Phillies	0	0	2	0	0	0	1	0	0	0—3
Los Angeles	0	1	0	1	0	1	0	0	0	1—4

Errors: Boone, Maddox. Double play: Sizemore, Bowa, and Cardenal. Left on base: Philadelphia 7, Los Angeles 10. Two-base hits: Smith, Cey, Baker. Three-base hit: Sizemore. Home runs: Luzinski, Cey, Garvey, McBride. Stolen base: Lopes. Sacrifice hit: Mota. Umpires: Davidson, Williams, McSherry, Weyer, Colosi, Olsen. Time, 2:53. Attendance, 55,124.

Phillies	IP	H	R	ER	BB	SO
Lerch	5⅓	7	3	3	0	0
Brusstar	⅔	1	0	0	1	0
Reed	2	4	0	0	0	1
McGraw (L)	1⅔	1	1	0	1	2

Los Angeles	IP	H	R	ER	BB	SO
Rau	5	5	2	2	2	1
Rhoden	4	2	1	1	1	3
Forster (W)	1	1	0	0	0	2

Phillies versus Houston Astros
National League Championship Series

1980

At 11:29 P.M. on October 21, 1980, the first 97 years were forgotten. Or, if not forgotten, at least forgiven.

The Whiz Kids were forgiven their four straight losses to the Yankees in 1950. The 1915 Phillies were forgiven for losing four in a row to the Boston Red Sox. Danny Ozark was forgiven. Gene Mauch was forgiven. William F. Baker was forgiven. All those seasons with twice as many losses as victories were forgotten. Garry Maddox hadn't really dropped a line drive in 1978. Greg Luzinski hadn't really dropped a fly ball in 1977, and Bruce Froemming hadn't made the wrong call, either. Granny Hamner's error in 1950 wasn't that costly. And so what if Baker's greed had cost the Phillies a few cheap homers in 1915?

This was 11:29 P.M. on October 21, 1980. The dogs . . . the horses . . . Tug McGraw's pitch . . . Willie Wilson's empty swing . . . the Phillies, World Champions.

The most incredible four-week stretch in the franchise's history was over. The team that had disappointed so many times in the past pushed its fans to the brink of disappointment in 1980, yet managed to stay alive until the end.

The nucleus of the team had suffered through the bitter postseasons of 1976, 1977, and 1978. Forgotten were the proud boasts of needing just a split in Dodger Stadium to assure a trip to the World Series or promising a sweep. Experience had taught its bitter lesson. Now the Phillies stood to the side and let the Astros bury themselves with a quote. It came after the Astros won the second game of the League Championship Series to take a 1–1 record back to the Astrodome in the best-of-five playoff.

"It's ours," one voice shouted in the visiting locker room after the second game. "Nobody beats us in the Dome."

Game One had been pretty much what you could expect. The Phillies won, 3–1. Steve Carlton got the victory after working the first seven innings. Tug McGraw got the save. Greg Luzinski got the winning RBI when his two-run homer in the sixth inning erased a 1–0 Astro lead. The game would be unique

The 1980 World Champions.

in the best-ever LCS. It would be the only game among the five to end in regulation.

The Phillies should have won Game Two in regulation. Instead they lost in overtime, thanks to a poor decision at third base by Lee Elia in the bottom of the ninth inning with a score tied at 3–3.

Bake McBride led off the inning with a single to right and took second on Mike Schmidt's single to center. Lonnie Smith ran a full count, fouled off several pitches, then hit a soft line drive to right that dropped in front of Terry Puhl. McBride was held up at third by Elia, which shocked the 65,476 fans and pitcher Frank LaCorte.

"When he hit the ball, I figured the game was over," said LaCorte. "I was already started off the mound."

There was LaCorte, head down, dejectedly heading toward the visiting dugout when he spotted something out of the corner of his eye. It was McBride standing on third base.

"As soon as the ball was hit, I took off because I didn't think Puhl was going to catch it," said McBride. "I got a step from third base and Lee told me to stop. I stopped and then he said, 'Go.' You know, by the time he says go, it's too late. It's just one of those things."

"It was no fault of Bake's that he didn't score," Elia admitted. "My hands went up as if to say stop, and at the same time I said, 'No, come on.' He saw my hands go up and stopped."

When Manny Trillo fanned and Garry Maddox fouled out, the inning was over. When the Astros scored four runs in the top of the 10th, the game, in effect, was over, too.

The Astros were overjoyed in their dressing room. The Phillies put on a determined look in theirs. But things looked bleak indeed when the Phillies lost Game Three, 1–0, in 11 innings when Joe Morgan tripled to lead off the inning and pinch-runner Rafael Landestoy eventually scored on Dennis Walling's sacrifice fly.

Carlton was ineffective in Game Four, and the Phillies fell behind by a 2–0 count after seven innings to Vern Ruhle. In the fourth inning, the Phillies had a rally snuffed by what was first called a triple play, then changed to a double play on a ball Garry Maddox hit back to the mound. And the Astros could have had a 3–0 lead if Gary Woods hadn't been ruled out for leaving third base too soon on a fly ball in the sixth inning.

The Phillies took a 3–2 lead in the top of the eighth inning, but the Astros tied it in the bottom of the ninth.

Garry Maddox gets a ride from his teammates after driving in the winning run and catching the final out in the thrilling 1980 National League Championship Series with the Houston Astros.

The Phillies won it in the 10th. With Pete Rose on first, pinch-hitter Greg Luzinski blasted a double to left. Rose never broke stride and gave Astro catcher Bruce Bochy a forearm to the face before crossing the plate. Manny Trillo singled home an insurance run, and the Phillies had a 2–2 tie. Mike Schmidt reminded everyone that there would be champagne in both locker rooms before Sunday night's game, but only one team would open it afterward.

After seven innings, it looked like it would be the Astros who would do the celebrating. They had a 5–2 lead and Nolan Ryan on the mound. But the Phillies scored five in the eighth, saw the Astros tie it with two in the bottom half of the inning, then won it in the 10th when Garry Maddox chased Del Unser home from third with a double. Dick Ruthven retired six straight hitters to get the victory, and Dallas Green could be heard above everyone else (no news there) in the noisy locker room.

"How's that for team character," Green screamed. "This is the character I've been preaching about ever since spring training. Tonight there was so much character on the field, I couldn't believe it. I love it!"

Finally, after 30 years, the Phillies were in a World Series. The opposition was a team that had been the focus of baseball all season long because of one man.

Although the Kansas City Royals were an outstanding team that had won their division by 14 games over the Oakland Athletics, then in the League Championship Series had swept a New York Yankee squad that had recorded 103 wins during the regular season, this was not a team with a bunch of household names.

One, however, had captured the nation's attention. Third baseman George Brett had flirted with a .400 batting average all season before finishing at .390. He also had 24 home runs and 118 RBI, then won Game Three of the LCS with a three-run homer in the seventh inning at Yankee Stadium.

The Royals, though, were anything but a one-man team. Willie Wilson was a splendid leadoff man, Willie Aikens was a power-hitting first baseman, Dan Quisenberry was the American League save leader with 33, and Dennis Leonard was a 20-game winner.

Against a team of this magnitude, the Phillies faced several problems. But one loomed larger than any. Who would pitch the Series opener from a staff that had been stretched to the limit during the Astros series?

Game 1
Tuesday, October 1, at Philadelphia

Houston	AB	R	H	RBI
Landestoy, 2b	5	0	0	0
Cabell, 3b	4	0	1	0
Cruz, lf	3	1	1	0
Cedeno, cf	3	0	1	0
Howe, 1b	4	0	0	0
Woods, rf	4	0	2	1
Pujols, c	3	0	0	0
Bergman, pr	0	0	0	0
Reynolds, ss	2	0	0	0
Puhl, ph	1	0	0	0
Forsch, p	2	0	2	0
Leonard, ph	1	0	0	0
Totals	32	1	7	1

Phillies	AB	R	H	RBI
Rose, 1b	4	1	2	0
McBride, rf	4	0	1	0
Schmidt, 3b	3	0	0	0
Luzinski, lf	4	1	1	2
Unser, lf	0	0	0	0
Trillo, 2b	4	0	0	0
Maddox, cf	3	1	1	0
Bowa, ss	2	0	1	0
Boone, c	3	0	1	0
Carlton, p	2	0	0	0
Gross, ph	1	0	1	1
McGraw, p	0	0	0	0
Totals	30	3	8	3

Houston 0 0 1 0 0 0 0 0 0 — 1
Phillies   0 0 0 0 0 2 1 0 x — 3

Game-winning RBI: Luzinski. Error: Bowa. Double play: Philadelphia 1. Left on base: Houston 9, Philadelphia 5. Home run: Luzinski. Stolen bases: McBride, Maddox. Sacrifice hits: Forsch, Bowa. Umpires: Engel, Tata, Froemming, Harvey, Vargo, and Crawford. Time, 2:35. Attendance, 65,277.

Houston	IP	H	R	ER	BB	SO
Forsch	8	8	3	3	1	5

Phillies	IP	H	R	ER	BB	SO
Carlton (W)	7	7	1	1	3	3
McGraw (S)	2	0	0	0	1	1

Game 2
Wednesday, October 8, at Philadelphia

Houston	AB	R	H	RBI
Puhl, rf	5	1	3	2
Cabell, 3b	4	0	0	0
Morgan, 2b	2	1	1	0
Landestoy, pr, 2b	0	1	0	0
Cruz, lf	4	1	2	2
Cedeno, cf	5	1	1	1
Howe, 1b	4	0	0	0
Bergman, 1b	1	0	1	2
Ashby, c	5	0	0	0
Reynolds, ss	3	1	0	0
Ryan, p	1	1	0	0
Sambito, p	0	0	0	0
D. Smith, p	0	0	0	0
Leonard, ph	1	0	0	0
LaCorte, p	1	0	0	0
Andujar, p	0	0	0	0
Totals	36	7	8	7

Phillies	AB	R	H	RBI
Rose, 1b	4	0	2	0
McBride, rf	5	0	1	0
Schmidt, 3b	6	1	2	0
Luzinski, lf	4	1	2	1
L. Smith, pr-lf	1	1	1	0
Trillo, 2b	3	0	1	0
Maddox, cf	5	0	2	2
Bowa, ss	4	1	2	0
Boone, c	4	0	1	0
Ruthven, p	2	0	0	0
Gross, ph	0	0	0	0
McGraw, p	0	0	0	0
Unser, ph	1	0	0	0
Reed, p	0	0	0	0
Saucier, p	0	0	0	0
G. Vukovich, ph	1	0	0	0
Totals	40	4	14	3

```
Houston    0 0 1 0 0 0 1 1 0 4 — 7
Phillies   0 0 0 2 0 0 0 1 0 1 — 4
```

Game-winning RBI: Cruz. Error: Schmidt, McBride, Reynolds. Double play: Philadelphia 1. Left on base: Houston 8, Philadelphia 14. Two-base hits: Puhl, Morgan, Schmidt, Luzinski. Three-base hit: Bergman. Sacrifice hits: Ryan, Trillo 2, Gross, Cabell. Umpires: Tata, Froemming, Harvey, Vargo, Crawford, and Engel. Time, 3:34. Attendance, 65,476.

Houston	IP	H	R	ER	BB	SO
Ryan	6⅓	8	2	2	1	6
Sambito	⅓	0	0	0	1	1
D. Smith	1⅓	2	1	1	1	2
LaCorte (W)	1*	4	1	0	1	1
Andujar (S)	1	0	0	0	1	0

Phillies	IP	H	R	ER	BB	SO
Ruthven	7	3	2	2	5	4
McGraw	1	2	1	1	0	0
Reed (L)	1⅓	2	4	4	1	1
Saucier	⅔	1	0	0	1	0

*Pitched to two batters in 10th.

Game 3
Friday, October 10, at Houston

Phillies	AB	R	H	RBI
Rose, 1b	5	0	1	0
McBride, rf	5	0	1	0
Schmidt, 3b	5	0	1	0
Luzinski, lf	5	0	0	0
Trillo, 2b	5	0	2	0
Maddox, cf	4	0	2	0
Bowa, ss	3	0	0	0
Boone, c	4	0	0	0
Unser, ph	1	0	0	0
Moreland, c	0	0	0	0
Christenson, p	2	0	0	0
G. Vukovich, ph	1	0	0	0
Noles, p	0	0	0	0
McGraw, p	1	0	0	0
Totals	41	0	7	0

Houston	AB	R	H	RBI
Puhl, rf, cf	4	0	2	0
Cabell, 3b	4	0	2	0
Morgan, 2b	4	0	1	0
Landestoy, pr	0	1	0	0
Cruz, lf	2	0	1	0
Cedeno, cf	3	0	0	0
Bergman, 1b	1	0	0	0
Howe, ph	0	0	0	0
Walling, lb, rf	3	0	0	1
Pujols, c	3	0	0	0
Reynolds, ss	3	0	0	0
Niekro, p	3	0	0	0
Woods, ph	1	0	0	0
Smith, p	0	0	0	0
Totals	31	1	6	1

```
Phillies   0 0 0 0 0 0 0 0 0 0 0 — 0
Houston    0 0 0 0 0 0 0 0 0 0 1 — 1
```

One out when winning run scored.

Game-winning RBI: Walling. Errors: Christenson, Bergman. Double plays: Philadelphia 2. Left on base: Philadelphia 11, Houston 10. Two-base hits: Puhl, Maddox, Trillo. Three-base hits: Cruz, Morgan. Stolen bases: Schmidt, Maddox. Sacrifice hits: Reynolds, Cabell. Sacrifice fly: Walling. Hit by pitcher: By Niekro (Maddox). Passed ball: Pujols. Umpires: Froemming, Vargo, Harvey, Crawford, Engel, and Tata. Time, 3:22. Attendance, 44,443.

Phillies	IP	H	R	ER	BB	SO
Christenson	6	3	0	0	4	2
Noles	1⅓	1	0	0	1	0
McGraw (L)	3	2	1	1	3	1

Houston	IP	H	R	ER	BB	SO
Niekro	10	6	0	0	1	2
Smith (W)	1	1	0	0	1	2

Game 4
Saturday, October 11, at Houston

Phillies	AB	R	H	RBI
L Smith, lf	4	1	2	0
Unser, lf, rf	1	0	0	0
Rose, 1b	4	2	2	1
Schmidt, 3b	5	0	2	1
McBride, rf	4	0	2	0
Luzinski, ph	1	1	1	1
G. Vukovich, lf	0	0	0	0
Trillo, 2b	4	0	2	2
Maddox, cf	4	0	0	0
Bowa, ss	5	0	1	0
Boone, c	4	0	0	0
Carlton, p	2	0	0	0
Noles, p	0	0	0	0
Saucier, p	0	0	0	0
Reed, p	0	0	0	0
Gross, ph	1	1	1	0
Brusstar, p	1	0	0	0
McGraw, p	0	0	0	0
Totals	**40**	**5**	**13**	**5**

Houston	AB	R	H	RBI
Puhl, rf, cf	3	0	1	1
Cabell, 3b	4	1	1	0
Morgan, 2b	3	0	0	0
Woods, rf	2	0	0	0
Walling, ph	1	0	0	0
Leonard, rf	1	0	0	0
Howe, 1b	3	0	1	1
Cruz, lf	3	0	0	0
Pujols, c	3	1	1	0
Bochy, c	1	0	0	0
Landestoy, ss	3	1	1	1
Ruhle, p	3	0	0	0
D. Smith, p	0	0	0	0
Sambito, p	0	0	0	0
Totals	**30**	**3**	**5**	**3**

Phillies	0	0	0	0	0	0	0	3	0	2	— 5
Houston	0	0	0	1	1	0	0	0	1	0	— 3

Phillies	IP	H	R	ER	BB	SO
Carlton	5⅓	4	2	2	5	3
Noles	1⅓	0	0	0	2	0
Saucier	0*	0	0	0	1	0
Reed	⅓	0	0	0	0	0
Brusstar (W)	2	1	1	1	1	0
McGraw (S)	1	0	0	0	0	1

Houston	IP	H	R	ER	BB	SO
Ruhle	7†	8	3	3	1	3
D. Smith	0‡	1	0	0	0	0
Sambito (L)	3	4	2	2	1	5

Game-winning RBI: Luzinski. Error: Landestoy. Double plays: Philadelphia 3, Houston 2. Left on base: Philadelphia 8, Houston 8. Two-base hits: Howe, Cabell, Luzinski, Trillo. Three-base hit: Pujols. Stolen bases: McBride, L. Smith, Landestoy, Woods, Puhl, Bowa. Sacrifice hit: Sambito. Sacrifice flies: Howe, Trillo. Umpires: Harvey, Vargo, Crawford, Engel, Tata, and Froemming. Time, 3:55. Attendance, 44,952.

*Pitched to one batter in 7th.
†Pitched to three batters in 8th.
‡Pitched to one batter in 8th.

Game 5
Sunday, October 12, at Houston

Phillies	AB	R	H	RBI
Rose, 1b	3	0	1	1
McBride, rf	3	0	0	0
Moreland, ph	1	0	0	1
Aviles, pr	0	1	0	0
McGraw, p	0	0	0	0
G. Vukovich, ph	1	0	0	0
Ruthven, p	0	0	0	0
Schmidt, 3b	5	0	0	0
Luzinski, lf	3	0	1	0
Smith, pr	0	0	0	0
Christenson, p	0	0	0	0
Reed, p	0	0	0	0
Unser, ph-rf	2	2	2	1
Trillo, 2b	5	1	3	2
Maddox, cf	4	1	1	1
Bowa, ss	5	1	2	0
Boone, c	3	1	2	2
Bystrom, p	2	0	0	0
Brusstar, p	0	0	0	0
Gross, lf	2	1	1	0
Totals	**39**	**8**	**13**	**8**

Houston	AB	R	H	RBI
Puhl, cf	6	3	4	0
Cabell, 3b	5	1	1	0
Morgan, 2b	4	0	0	0
Landestoy, 2b	1	0	1	1
Cruz, lf	3	0	2	2
Walling, rf	5	2	1	1
LaCorte, p	0	0	0	0
Howe, 1b	4	0	2	1
Bergman, pr, 1b	1	0	0	0
Pujols, c	1	0	0	0
Ashby, ph, c	3	0	1	1
Reynolds, ss	5	1	2	0
Ryan, p	3	0	0	0
Sambito, p	0	0	0	0
Forsch, p	0	0	0	0
Woods, ph,rf	1	0	0	0
Heep, ph	1	0	0	0
Totals	**43**	**7**	**14**	**6**

Phillies	0	2	0	0	0	0	0	5	0	1	— 8
Houston	1	0	0	0	0	1	3	2	0	0	— 7

Phillies	IP	H	R	ER	BB	SO
Bystrom	5⅓	7	2	1	2	1
Brusstar	⅔	0	0	0	0	0
Christenson	⅔	2	3	3	1	0
Reed	⅓	1	0	0	0	0
McGraw	1	4	2	2	0	2
Ruthven (W)	2	0	0	0	0	0

Houston	IP	H	R	ER	BB	SO
Ryan	7*	8	6	6	2	8
Sambito	⅓	0	0	0	0	0
Forsch	⅔	2	1	1	0	1
LaCorte (L)	2	3	1	1	1	1

Game-winning RBI: Maddox. Errors: Trillo, Luzinski. Double plays: Houston 2. Left on base: Philadelphia 5, Houston 10. Two-base hits: Cruz, Reynolds, Unser, Maddox. Three-base hits: Howe, Trillo. Stolen base: Puhl. Sacrifice hits: Cabell, Boone. Wild pitch: Christenson. Umpires: Vargo, Crawford, Engel, Tata, Froemming, and Harvey. Time, 3:38. Attendance, 44,802.

*Pitched to four batters in 8th.

Phillies versus Kansas City Royals World Series

Actually, the choice to pitch the opener wasn't really a choice at all. Green had nowhere to go on a pitching staff that was overworked in the Astros series except to Bob (Whirlybird) Walk, a rookie who had won 11 games since coming to the Phillies from Oklahoma City in mid-May.

"I have no qualms about using Walk," Green said. "He did the job when we needed him. He had a little slip for awhile with his control and poise, but he's okay now."

Walk's season looked very much like another rookie's, Bob Miller, had in 1950. Miller started out quickly with eight straight victories, finished with 11 wins, tailed off badly toward the end of the season, then was hit hard in his only World Series start.

Walk had opened 6–0, but had slipped to 11–7 by season's end. And in his only World Series start, he looked like he might be headed for an early shower as well.

The first rookie to start a World Series opener since Joe Black got the call for the Brooklyn Dodgers in 1952, Walk gave up a two-run home run to Amos Otis in the second inning and another two-run shot to Willie Aikens in the third, putting the Phillies four runs down.

But as they had all through September and October, the Phillies came roaring back in their half of the third.

Larry Bowa hit a one-out single, then defied all logic by successfully stealing second with a four-run deficit.

Bob Boone's single scored Bowa, making it 4–1. Lonnie Smith singled Boone home, but was caught in a rundown between first and second and tagged out. It looked as if the Phillies might have to settle for a two-run inning against Kansas City ace Dennis Leonard.

But Pete Rose let a pitch hit him, Schmidt walked, and Bake McBride came to the plate.

"I just wanted to put the ball in play," McBride said afterward.

What he did was put the ball where no one could make a play on it, drilling a three-run homer over the right field wall and giving the Phillies a 5–4 lead as the Vet crowd of 65,791 went wild.

The score became 7–4 after the Phillies scored single runs in the fourth and fifth. Boone's double drove in the sixth run, and Garry Maddox delivered a sacrifice fly to bring in what proved to be the game winner.

Walk took the three-run lead into the eighth, retiring nine batters in a row at one point, but George Brett led off with a double, Aikens hit a two-run homer, and Tug McGraw got the call in relief.

McGraw allowed a harmless hit and struck out two in two innings to earn the save and give the Phillies their first World Series victory in 65 years, breaking an eight-game losing streak.

Another game, another come-from-behind victory for the Cardiac Kids, who rode a four-run rally in the eighth inning to a 6–4 victory, giving them a two-games-to-none lead going to Kansas City for Games Three, Four, and Five.

Meanwhile, the victory was only worth second place in the headlines the next day. The top of the page belonged to George Brett, who had flirted with a .400 average all season before finishing at .390.

Bake McBride scores winning run of second game after scoring from first on Mike Schmidt's double.

Ron Reed celebrates after saving Game Two against the Kansas City Royals for Steve Carlton.

On this night, Brett had to leave the game after the sixth inning. When the game was over, it was announced that Brett had been forced to the locker room by painful hemorrhoids.

For four innings, though, the Phillies had their own pain in the posterior—Royals pitcher Larry Gura. Steve Carlton was equal to the task, however, blanking Kansas City through the first five.

The Phillies took a 2–0 lead in the fifth on Maddox's second sacrifice fly of the Series and Bowa's RBI single. But the Royals came back with a run off Carlton in the sixth, then scored three in the seventh as wildness beset the great Lefty (he walked six while striking out 10) and Otis delivered a two-run double.

The Royals entrusted the two-run lead to Dan Quisenberry, their outstanding closer. He shut down the Phillies in the seventh.

But in the eighth the Phillies came alive. Bob Boone walked to lead off the inning and came all the way around to score as Del Unser delivered yet another clutch pinch-hit, a double.

McBride tied the game with a single. Schmidt untied it with a booming double and took third on the throw to the plate. When designated hitter Keith Moreland, playing because Greg Luzinski was suffering from the flu, singled him home, the Phillies had a two-run lead that Ron Reed protected in the ninth, striking out two batters.

But the big question on everyone's mind when the game was over was not whether the Royals could rally once they returned home. It was whether Brett would be able to participate when play resumed two nights later.

Game Three

Not only could Brett play, he could still hit like baseball's best batsman. Before the game, he joked about his hemorrhoids and the surgery he had undergone on the off-day. "My problems are all behind me," he said. Then he gave the Phillies a major problem by crunching a home run in the first inning off Dick Ruthven.

The Phillies answered with a run in the second, and the Royals went up by a run in the fourth, but Schmidt homered in the fifth to tie it again.

Kansas City took a 3–2 lead in the seventh on a homer by Otis, but Rose's single off reliever Renie Martin in the eighth scored Bowa to tie it at 3–3.

The Phillies looked as if they might break the game open and give Ruthven a well-deserved victory in the 10th. With Boone on second and Rose on first with one out, Schmidt hit a screaming shot that looked as if it would get past Frank White. But the second baseman made a brilliant play and started a double play to end the inning.

"That was the ball game right there," Green said. "If that ball goes through, it might have rolled to the wall. We got plenty of hits (14) to win most games. We just couldn't come up with the big one."

Aikens supplied the big one for the Royals in a bizarre bottom of the 10th against McGraw. U. L. Washington had started the inning with a single to left, and McGraw walked Wilson on four pitches. White attempted a bunt, but missed. Boone faked a throw to second, and Washington took off for third where Boone retired him with a throw to Schmidt. White then fanned, and McGraw could see his way out of the inning.

But Wilson stole second, Brett was walked intentionally, and Aiken ripped a pitch past Maddox in center to score the winning run.

Game Four

On a gorgeous Saturday afternoon the Phillies lost a game—and probably won the World Series.

The way they did it was ugly.

The way the game began was equally ugly from the Phillies' point of view. Larry Christenson started on the mound and retired only one batter. By the time the inning was over, the Royals had four runs, thanks to a triple by Brett and a two-run homer by Aikens.

Dickie Noles relieved Christenson, and Aikens took him over the fence for his fourth homer of the Series and a 5–1 Royal lead in the second. Meanwhile, first-game loser Leonard had things well in hand.

In the fourth inning, though, the Series took an ugly turn in the Phillies' favor.

Noles threw his hardest fastball at Brett's head on an 0–2 pitch. The third baseman went sprawling in the dirt. Before he could pick himself up, Royals manager Jimmy Frey was out of the dugout, screaming for the umpires to put a stop to this potential beanball war. Within seconds, Frey and first baseman Rose were screaming at each other. After the game, Noles insisted he wasn't throwing at Brett. "I have to use both sides of the plate," he said, but you couldn't miss the smirk on his face as he said it.

Whether Noles was throwing at Brett or not doesn't matter. The fact is that the pitch woke up the Phillies and put the Royals' bats to sleep. And, although Kansas City hung on for a 5–3 victory, it would be their last in this Fall Classic.

The Phillies served notice that they would not go down without a fight when they scored single runs in the seventh and eighth innings before Quisenberry came on to pick up the save and even the Series.

When Dickie Noles floored George Brett with a knockdown pitch in the fourth game, the Series tilted in the Phillies' favor.

Game Five

If Noles' pitch to Brett was the pivotal play of the Series, the fifth was the pivotal game.

Had the Royals been able to win it, they would have taken all the momentum back to Philadelphia, needing just one victory there to clinch the title. A victory by the Phillies would mean that just one victory before the home fans would give them their first title.

Green called on Marty Bystrom, the pitcher whose five victories in September after his call-up from the minors had been instrumental in getting the Phillies to this point. Frey countered with Gura, who had pitched well in Game Two.

Gura pitched even better on this glorious Sunday afternoon. Except for a two-run homer by Schmidt in the fourth inning, he was terrific through six, allowing just four hits and one walk.

Bystrom wasn't nearly as effective, allowing 10 hits in five-plus innings.

After blanking the Royals through four innings, he was touched for a run in the fifth and two more in the sixth before Ron Reed replaced him and allowed the lead run on Washington's sacrifice fly.

The situation looked bleak going into the ninth with the sidearming Quisenberry on the mound for the Royals. But Brett and Frey gave the Phillies a small window of opportunity. Before the inning was over, the Phillies had turned it into a picture window. If you looked through it, you could see a World Championship on the horizon.

Schmidt was the first man up. Brett and Frey discussed the situation as the Royals took the field. Brett asked Frey if he should watch for the bunt, something Schmidt tried often when his team needed base-runners late in a game. Frey's reply: "Don't give it to him."

So Brett played even with the bag at third, and Schmidt ripped a line drive that bounced off his glove for a single. Had Brett been playing normally, Schmidt's ball would have most likely been caught.

"Bunting was low on my list of priorities," said Schmidt after the game. "All I was trying to do was get a pitch I could drive."

Unser, pinch-hitting for Lonnie Smith, got a pitch he could drive and lined it to left for a double that scored Schmidt with the tying run. Moreland moved Unser to third with an infield out, but Del had to stay there when Maddox grounded out. Then Manny Trillo, whose great relay throw had cut down a run at the plate earlier in the game, became the hero when he ripped a line drive off Quisenberry's glove and beat the play at first as Unser scored.

The Phillies had the lead, but there was still a bottom of the ninth, and McGraw used it to nearly stop a lot of hearts, including his own.

Not only did McGraw walk the bases loaded, but with two on and one out, he threw a pitch that McRae hit out of the park—and barely foul. Tug patted his heart with his left hand, then got McRae to hit into a force play.

With two outs and the bases loaded, McRae struck out former Phillie Jose Cardenal. Frey was left to answer the second-guessers who wondered about Brett's positioning on Schmidt. The Phillies left for the airport and a flight back to Philadelphia, knowing they were within a game of the title with well-rested Carlton and Ruthven ready to pitch.

Game Six

K-9 Corps dogs were among the peace-keepers in late stages of Series-clinching sixth game at the Vet.

There were 65,838 fans in the Veterans Stadium stands that Tuesday night, and they wanted to party on Wednesday. Forget Game Seven, they said, we want to win this right now. Then let the parade begin!

And for seven innings, Steve Carlton gave them exactly what they wanted. He allowed just three singles. He struck out seven. He walked only two.

The Phillies built a 4–0 lead. They touched Rich Gale for two runs in the third on RBI singles by Rose and Schmidt and added single runs off Martin in the fifth and Paul Splittorf in the sixth.

Recalling how the New York fans had ripped Yankee Stadium apart following a pennant-clinching home run by Chris Chambliss a few years earlier, the Philadelphia Police Department ringed the field with horses and guard dogs late in the game to prevent the same kind of outburst.

And the Royals didn't make things easy in the final two innings.

Carlton allowed the first two runners to reach base in the eighth and was replaced by McGraw, who had earned the nickname Tylenol Tug when he revealed during the Series that he was making it a habit to take six painkillers when he got up in the morning to deaden the aches that were a result of his almost daily trips to the mound.

He loaded the bases in the eighth by walking Willie Wilson and gave up the first run as Washington delivered a sacrifice fly. And after Brett beat out an infield hit to reload the bases, he threw three straight balls to McRae before getting the slugger on a ground ball to Trillo.

In the ninth, he struck out Otis looking, but loaded the bases on a walk to Aikens and singles by John Wathan and Cardenal.

It brought Frank White to the plate and Dallas Green to the mound with a quick message.

Commissioner Bowie Kuhn (center) presents the championship trophy to Paul Owens (left), Dallas Green, and Ruly Carpenter in joyful Phillies locker room.

"I said, 'Hey, Tug, let's not make this son of a bitch as overly exciting as you're trying here.' "

Bob Boone sure tried, though. White lifted a pop fly in front of the Phillies' dugout. Boone and Rose both converged on the ball, Boone called the first baseman off—and dropped the ball.

But Rose was right there to make the catch before the ball hit the ground, and the Phillies were one out away.

It came at 11:29 P.M. With a 1–2 count on Wilson, McGraw reached back for the last fastball in his arm. He blew it by Wilson for the strikeout.

After nearly a century's worth of baseball mortal sins, the franchise finally had been given absolution. And Phillies fans everywhere had discovered what heaven could be like.

Victory parade wound through Center City Philadelphia the morning after the World Series victory.

The New Phillies Encyclopedia

Game 1
Tuesday, October 14, at Philadelphia

Kansas City	AB	R	H	RBI	PO	A
Wilson, lf	5	0	0	0	2	1
McRae, dh	3	1	1	0	0	0
G. Brett, 3b	4	1	1	0	0	2
Aikens, 1b	4	2	2	4	13	0
Porter, c	2	1	0	0	5	1
Otis, cf	4	1	3	2	1	0
Hurdle, rf	3	0	1	0	1	0
a-Wathan, rf	1	0	0	0	1	0
White, 2b	4	0	1	0	0	5
Washington, ss	4	0	0	0	1	6
Leonard, p	0	0	0	0	0	0
Martin, p	0	0	0	0	0	0
Quisenberry, p	0	0	0	0	0	0
Totals	34	6	9	6	24	15

a-Grounded into double play for Hurdle in 8th.

Kansas City	0	2	2	0	0	0	0	2	0	—	6
Phillies	0	0	5	1	1	0	0	0	x	—	7

Kansas City	IP	H	R	ER	BB	SO
Leonard (L)	3⅔	6	6	6	1	3
Martin	4	5	1	1	1	1
Quisenberry	⅓	0	0	0	0	0

Phillies	AB	R	H	RBI	PO	A
Smith, lf	4	0	2	0	3	1
Gross, lf	1	0	0	0	1	0
Rose, 1b	3	1	0	0	7	2
Schmidt, 3b	2	2	1	0	2	3
McBride, rf	4	1	3	3	3	0
Luzinski, dh	3	0	0	0	0	0
Maddox, cf	3	0	0	1	2	0
Trillo, 2b	4	1	1	0	1	2
Bowa, ss	4	1	1	0	0	3
Boone, c	4	1	3	2	6	0
Walk, p	0	0	0	0	2	0
McGraw, p	0	0	0	0	0	0
Totals	32	7	11	6	27	11

Bases on balls: Off Leonard 1 (Schmidt), off Martin 1 (Schmidt), off Walk 3 (McRae, Porter 2). Strikeouts: By Leonard 3 (Schmidt, Luzinski, Maddox), by Martin 1 (Luzinski), by Walk 3 (Wilson, G. Brett, Aikens), by McGraw 2 (Washington, Wilson). Error: Leonard. Two-base hits: Boone 2, G. Brett. Home runs: Otis, Aikens 2, McBride. Stolen bases: Bowa, White. Caught stealing: Smith. Sacrifice fly: Maddox. Hit by pitcher: By Leonard (Rose), by Martin (Luzinski). Wild pitch: Walk. Double play: Bowa, Trillo and Rose. Left on base: Kansas City 4, Philadelphia 6. Umpires: Wendelstedt, Kunkel, Pryor, Denkinger, Rennert, Bremigan. Time, 3:01. Attendance, 65,791.

Phillies	IP	H	R	ER	BB	SO
Walk (W)	7†	8	6	6	3	3
McGraw (S)	2	1	0	0	0	2

†Pitched to two batters in 8th.

Game 2
Wednesday, October 15, at Philadelphia

Kansas City	AB	R	H	RBI	PO	A
Wilson, lf	4	1	1	0	1	0
Washington, ss	4	0	1	0	0	3
G. Brett, 3b	2	0	2	0	2	2
Chalk, 3b	0	1	0	0	0	1
c-Porter	1	0	0	0	0	0
McRae, dh	4	1	3	0	0	0
Otis, cf	5	1	2	2	5	0
Wathan, c	3	0	0	1	2	0
Aikens, 1b	3	0	1	0	6	0
LaCock, 1b	0	0	0	0	2	0
Cardenal, rf	4	0	0	0	3	0
White, 2b	4	0	1	0	3	3
Gura, p	0	0	0	0	0	0
Quisenberry, p	0	0	0	0	0	0
Totals	34	4	11	3	24	9

a-Doubled in one run for Smith in 8th.
b-Grounded into double play for Maddox in 8th.
c-Called out on strikes for Chalk in 9th.

Kansas City	0	0	0	0	0	1	3	0	0	—	4
Phillies	0	0	0	0	2	0	0	4	x	—	6

Kansas City	IP	H	R	ER	BB	SO
Gura	6	4	2	2	2	2
Quisenberry (L)	2	4	4	4	1	0

Phillies	AB	R	H	RBI	PO	A
Smith, lf	3	0	0	0	0	0
a-Unser, cf	1	1	1	1	0	0
Rose, 1b	4	0	0	0	7	1
McBride, rf	3	1	1	1	2	0
Schmidt, 3b	4	1	2	1	1	1
Moreland, dh	4	1	2	1	0	0
Maddox, cf	3	1	1	0	1	1
b-Gross, lf	1	0	0	0	0	0
Trillo, 2b	2	0	0	1	6	3
Bowa, ss	3	0	1	1	0	6
Boone, c	1	1	0	0	10	1
Carlton, p	0	0	0	0	0	1
Reed, p	0	0	0	0	0	0
Totals	29	6	8	6	27	14

Bases on balls: Off Gura 2 (Boone, McBride), off Quisenberry 1 (Boone), off Carlton 6 (Aikens, G. Brett, Wathan, Wilson, Chalk, McRae). Strikeouts: By Gura 2 (Maddox, Smith), by Carlton 10 (Wilson 3, Cardenal 2, White, Washington 2, McRae, Aikens), by Reed 2 (Porter, Wathan). Error: Trillo. Two-base hits: Maddox, Otis, Unser, Schmidt. Stolen bases: Wilson, Chalk. Sacrifice hit: Washington. Sacrifice flies: Trillo, Wathan. Wild pitch: Carlton. Double plays: Bowa, Trillo, and Rose 3; Washington, White, and Aikens; Maddox, Rose, and Schmidt; Washington, White, and LaCock. Left on base: Kansas City 11, Philadelphia 3. Umpires: Kunkel, Pryor, Denkinger, Rennert, Bremigan, Wendelstedt. Time, 3:01. Attendance, 65,775.

Phillies	IP	H	R	ER	BB	SO
Carlton (W)	8	10	4	3	6	10
Reed (S)	1	1	0	0	0	2

Tug McGraw has a victory celebration message for New Yorkers and the rest of the baseball world.

Game 3
Friday, October 17, at Kansas City

Phillies	AB	R	H	RBI	PO	A
Smith, lf	4	0	2	1	0	0
b-Gross, lf	0	0	0	0	0	0
Rose, 1b	4	0	1	1	11	0
Schmidt, 3b	5	1	1	1	3	3
McBride, rf	5	0	2	0	1	0
Moreland, dh	5	0	1	0	0	0
Maddox, cf	4	0	1	0	3	0
Trillo, 2b	5	1	2	0	2	6
Bowa, ss	5	1	3	0	1	3
Boone, c	4	0	1	0	8	1
Ruthven, p	0	0	0	0	0	0
McGraw, p	0	0	0	0	0	0
Totals	**41**	**3**	**14**	**3**	**29**	**13**

Kansas City	AB	R	H	RBI	PO	A
Wilson, lf	4	1	0	0	3	0
White, 2b	5	0	0	0	4	2
G. Brett, 3b	4	1	2	1	0	3
Aikens, 1b	5	1	2	1	7	1
McRae, dh	4	0	2	1	0	0
Otis, cf	4	1	2	1	9	0
Hurdle, rf	4	0	2	0	1	0
a-Concepcion	0	0	0	0	0	0
Cardenal, rf	0	0	0	0	0	0
Porter, c	4	0	0	0	4	0
Washington, ss	4	0	1	0	1	2
Gale, p	0	0	0	0	0	1
Martin, p	0	0	0	0	0	0
Quisenberry, p	0	0	0	0	1	1
Totals	**38**	**4**	**11**	**4**	**30**	**10**

a-Ran for Hurdle in 9th.
b-Sacrificed for Smith in 10th.

Two out when winning run scored.

Phillies	0	1	0	0	1	0	0	1	0	0 — 3
Kansas City	1	0	0	1	0	0	1	0	0	1 — 4

Bases on balls: Off McGraw 2 (Wilson, G. Brett), off Gale 3 (Schmidt, Boone, Rose), off Martin 1 (Smith), off Quisenberry 2 (Maddox, Rose). Strikeouts: by Ruthven 7 (Wilson 2, White 2, Aikens 2, Porter), by McGraw 1 (White), by Gale 3 (Rose, Moreland, McBride), by Martin 1 (Rose). Two-base hits: Trillo, G. Brett. Three-base hit: Aikens. Home runs: G. Brett, Schmidt, Otis. Stolen bases: Hurdle, Bowa, Wilson. Caught stealing: Washington. Sacrifice hit: Gross. Double plays: White, Washington, and Aikens; Bowa, Trillo, and Rose; White unassisted. Left on base: Philadelphia 15, Kansas City 7. Umpires: Pryor, Denkinger, Rennert, Bremigan, Wendelstedt, Kunkel. Time, 3:19. Attendance, 42,380.

Phillies	IP	H	R	ER	BB	SO
Ruthven	9	9	3	3	0	7
McGraw (L)	⅔	2	1	1	2	1

Kansas City	IP	H	R	ER	BB	SO
Gale	4⅓	7	2	2	3	3
Martin	3⅓	5	1	1	1	1
Quisenberry (W)	2⅓	2	0	0	2	0

Game 4
Saturday, October 18, at Kansas City

Phillies	AB	R	H	RBI	PO	A
Smith, dh	4	0	0	0	0	0
Rose, 1b	4	1	2	0	8	2
McBride, rf	3	0	1	0	3	0
Schmidt, 3b	3	0	1	1	2	0
Unser, lf	4	0	1	0	1	0
Maddox, cf	4	0	1	0	2	0
Trillo, 2b	4	2	1	0	0	6
Bowa, ss	4	0	2	1	1	1
Boone, c	3	0	1	1	6	0
Christenson, p	0	0	0	0	0	0
Noles, p	0	0	0	0	1	0
Saucier, p	0	0	0	0	0	0
Brusstar, p	0	0	0	0	0	0
Totals	**33**	**3**	**10**	**3**	**24**	**9**

Kansas City	AB	R	H	RBI	PO	A
Wilson, lf	4	1	1	0	4	0
White, 2b	5	0	0	0	2	4
G. Brett, 3b	5	1	1	1	0	7
Aikens, 1b	3	2	2	3	13	0
McRae, dh	4	1	2	0	0	0
Otis, cf	4	0	2	1	1	0
Hurdle, rf	2	0	1	0	3	0
Porter, c	3	0	0	0	2	1
Washington, ss	4	0	1	0	2	3
Leonard, p	0	0	0	0	0	0
Quisenberry, p	0	0	0	0	0	0
Totals	**34**	**5**	**10**	**5**	**27**	**15**

Phillies	0	1	0	0	0	0	1	1	0 — 3
Kansas City	4	1	0	0	0	0	0	0	x — 5

Bases on balls: Off Noles 2 (Hurdle 2), off Saucier 2 (Wilson, Aikens), off Brusstar 1 (Porter), off Leonard 1 (McBride). Strikeouts: By Noles 6 (Porter 2, Wilson, G. Brett, Aikens, McRae), by Leonard 2 (Schmidt, Unser). Errors: White, Christenson, Washington. Two-base hits: McRae 2, Otis, Hurdle, McBride, Trillo, Rose. Three-base hit: G. Brett. Home runs: Aikens 2. Stolen base: Bowa. Caught stealing: McBride. Sacrifice flies: Boone, Schmidt. Wild pitches: Leonard, Saucier. Double play: G. Brett, White, and Aikens. Left on base: Philadelphia 6, Kansas City 10. Umpires: Denkinger, Rennert, Bremigan, Wendelstedt, Kunkel, Pryor. Time, 2:37. Attendance, 42,363.

Phillies	IP	H	R	ER	BB	SO
Christenson (L)	⅓	5	4	4	0	0
Noles	4⅔	5	1	1	2	6
Saucier	⅔	0	0	0	2	0
Brusstar	2⅓	0	0	0	1	0

Kansas City	IP	H	R	ER	BB	SO
Leonard (W)	7†	9	3	2	1	2
Quisenberry (S)	2	1	0	0	0	0

†Pitched to one batter in 8th.

Game 5
Sunday, October 19, at Kansas City

Phillies	AB	R	H	RBI	PO	A
Rose, 1b	4	0	0	0	7	1
McBride, rf	4	1	0	0	2	1
Schmidt, 3b	4	2	2	2	1	1
Luzinski, lf	2	0	0	0	1	0
a-Smith, lf	0	0	0	0	0	0
c-Unser, lf	1	1	1	1	0	0
Moreland, dh	3	0	1	0	0	0
Maddox, cf	4	0	0	0	2	0
Trillo, 2b	4	0	1	1	3	5
Bowa, ss	4	0	1	0	0	2
Boone, c	3	0	1	0	10	0
Bystrom, p	0	0	0	0	1	1
Reed, p	0	0	0	0	0	0
McGraw, p	0	0	0	0	0	1
Totals	33	4	7	4	27	12

Kansas City	AB	R	H	RBI	PO	A
Wilson, lf	5	0	2	0	2	0
White, 2b	3	0	0	0	2	6
G. Brett, 3b	5	0	1	1	1	2
Aikens, 1b	3	0	1	0	10	1
d-Concepcion	0	0	0	0	0	0
McRae, dh	5	0	1	0	0	0
Otis, cf	3	1	2	1	3	0
Hurdle, rf	3	1	1	0	3	0
b-Cardenal, rf	2	0	0	0	0	0
Porter, c	4	0	2	0	2	0
Washington, ss	3	1	2	1	2	2
Gura, p	0	0	0	0	2	4
Quisenberry, p	0	0	0	0	0	0
Totals	36	3	12	3	27	15

a-Ran for Luzinski in 7th.
b-Flied out for Hurdle in 7th.
c-Doubled in one run for Smith in 9th.
d-Ran for Aikens in 9th.

Phillies										
Phillies	0	0	0	2	0	0	0	0	2	— 4
Kansas City	0	0	0	0	1	2	0	0	0	— 3

Bases on balls: Off Bystrom 1 (Aikens), off McGraw 4 (Otis 2, White, Aikens), off Gura 1 (Luzinski). Strikeouts: By Bystrom 4 (Wilson, Aikens, Otis, Hurdle), by McGraw 5 (G. Brett 2, Aikens, Washington, Cardenal), by Gura 2 (Luzinski, Maddox). Errors: Aikens, G. Brett. Two-base hits: Wilson, McRae, Unser. Home runs: Schmidt, Otis. Stolen base: G. Brett. Sacrifice hits: White, Moreland. Sacrifice fly: Washington. Double plays: White, Aikens, and Gura; Gura and Aikens. Left on base: Philadelphia 4, Kansas City 13. Umpires: Rennert, Bremigan, Wendelstedt, Kunkel, Pryor, Denkinger. Time, 2:51. Attendance, 42,369.

Phillies	IP	H	R	ER	BB	SO
Bystrom	5†	10	3	3	1	4
Reed	1	1	0	0	0	0
McGraw (W)	3	1	0	0	4	5

Kansas City	IP	H	R	ER	BB	SO
Gura	6⅓	4	2	1	1	2
Quisenberry (L)	2⅔	3	2	2	0	0

†Pitched to three batters in 6th.

Game 6
Tuesday, October 21, at Philadelphia

Kansas City	AB	R	H	RBI	PO	A
Wilson, lf	4	0	0	0	3	0
Washington, ss	3	0	1	1	2	4
G. Brett, 3b	4	0	2	0	1	1
McRae, dh	4	0	0	0	0	0
Otis, cf	3	0	0	0	2	0
Aikens, 1b	2	0	0	0	6	0
aConcepcion	0	0	0	0	0	0
Wathan, c	3	1	2	0	4	1
Cardenal, rf	4	0	2	0	4	0
White, 2b	4	0	0	0	2	1
Gale, p	0	0	0	0	0	0
Martin, p	0	0	0	0	0	0
Splittorff, p	0	0	0	0	0	1
Pattin, p	0	0	0	0	0	0
Quisenberry, p	0	0	0	0	0	0
Totals	31	1	7	1	24	8

Phillies	AB	R	H	RBI	PO	A
Smith, lf	4	2	1	0	1	0
Gross, lf	0	0	0	0	0	0
Rose, 1b	4	0	3	0	9	0
Schmidt, 3b	3	0	1	2	0	0
McBride, rf	4	0	1	1	2	0
Luzinski, dh	4	0	0	0	0	0
Maddox, cf	4	0	2	0	1	0
Trillo, 2b	4	0	0	0	2	3
Bowa, ss	4	1	1	0	3	3
Boone, c	2	1	1	1	9	1
Carlton, p	0	0	0	0	0	2
McGraw, p	0	0	0	0	0	0
Totals	33	4	9	4	27	9

a-Ran for Aikens in 9th.

Kansas City	0	0	0	0	0	0	0	1	0	— 1
Phillies	0	0	2	0	1	1	0	0	x	— 4

Bases on balls: Off Gale 1 (Boone), off Martin 1 (Schmidt), off Carlton 3 (Otis, Aikens, Wathan), off McGraw 2 (Wilson, Aikens). Strikeouts: By Gale 1 (Luzinski), by Pattin 2 (Schmidt, Luzinski), by Carlton 7 (Wilson 2, Washington 2, White, Otis, Aikens), by McGraw 2 (Otis, Wilson). Errors: White, Aikens. Two-base hits: Maddox, Smith, Bowa. Caught stealing: Rose. Sacrifice fly: Washington. Double plays: Bowa, Trillo, and Rose; Bowa and Rose; Splittorff, Washington, and Aikens. Left on base: Kansas City 9, Philadelphia 7. Umpires: Bremigan, Wendelstedt, Kunkel, Pryor, Denkinger, Rennert. Time, 3:00. Attendance, 65,838.

Kansas City	IP	H	R	ER	BB	SO
Gale (L)	2	4	2	1	1	1
Martin	2⅓	1	1	1	1	0
Splittorff	1⅔†	4	1	1	0	0
Pattin	1	0	0	0	0	2
Quisenberry	1	0	0	0	0	0

Phillies	IP	H	R	ER	BB	SO
Carlton (W)	7‡	4	1	1	3	7
McGraw (S)	2	3	0	0	2	2

†Pitched to one batter in 7th.
‡Pitched to two batters in 8th.

Owner Ruly Carpenter, general manager Paul Owens, and manager Dallas Green unfurl the championship banner before 1981 game.

COMPOSITE BATTING AVERAGES

Philadelphia Phillies

Player-Position	G	AB	R	H	2B	3B	HR	RBI	BA
Unser, ph, cf, lf	3	6	2	3	2	0	0	2	.500
Boone, c	6	17	3	7	2	0	0	4	.412
Schmidt, 3b	6	21	6	8	1	0	2	7	.381
Bowa, ss	6	24	3	9	1	0	0	2	.375
Moreland, dh	3	12	1	4	0	0	0	1	.333
McBride, rf	6	23	3	7	1	0	1	5	.304
Smith, pr, lf, dh	6	19	2	5	1	0	0	1	.263
Rose, 1b	6	23	2	6	1	0	0	1	.261
Maddox, cf	6	22	1	5	2	0	0	1	.227
Trillo, 2b	6	23	4	5	2	0	0	2	.217
Brusstar, p	1	0	0	0	0	0	0	0	.000
Bystrom, p	1	0	0	0	0	0	0	0	.000
Carlton, p	2	0	0	0	0	0	0	0	.000
Christenson, p	1	0	0	0	0	0	0	0	.000
McGraw, p	4	0	0	0	0	0	0	0	.000
Noles, p	1	0	0	0	0	0	0	0	.000
Reed, p	2	0	0	0	0	0	0	0	.000
Ruthven, p	1	0	0	0	0	0	0	0	.000
Saucier, p	1	0	0	0	0	0	0	0	.000
Walk, p	1	0	0	0	0	0	0	0	.000
Gross, ph, lf	4	2	0	0	0	0	0	0	.000
Luzinski, dh, lf	3	9	0	0	0	0	0	0	.000
Totals	**6**	**201**	**27**	**59**	**13**	**0**	**3**	**26**	**.294**

Kansas City Royals

Player-Position	G	AB	R	H	2B	3B	HR	RBI	BA
Otis, cf	6	23	4	11	2	0	3	7	.478
Hurdle, rf	4	12	1	5	1	0	0	0	.417
Aikens, 1b	6	20	5	8	0	1	4	8	.400
G. Brett, 3b	6	24	3	9	2	1	1	3	.375
McRae, dh	6	24	3	9	3	0	0	1	.375
Wathan, ph, rf, c	3	7	1	2	0	0	0	1	.286
Washington, ss	6	22	1	6	0	0	0	2	.273
Cardenal, ph, rf	4	10	0	2	0	0	0	0	.200
Wilson, lf	6	26	3	4	1	0	0	0	.154
Porter, ph, c	5	14	1	2	0	0	0	0	.143
White, 2b	6	25	0	2	0	0	0	0	.080
Chalk, 3b	1	0	1	0	0	0	0	0	.000
Concepcion, pr	3	0	0	0	0	0	0	0	.000
Gale, p	2	0	0	0	0	0	0	0	.000
Gura, p	2	0	0	0	0	0	0	0	.000
LaCock, 1b	1	0	0	0	0	0	0	0	.000
Leonard, p	2	0	0	0	0	0	0	0	.000
Martin, p	3	0	0	0	0	0	0	0	.000
Pattin, p	1	0	0	0	0	0	0	0	.000
Quisenberry, p	6	0	0	0	0	0	0	0	.000
Splittorff, p	1	0	0	0	0	0	0	0	.000
Totals	**6**	**207**	**23**	**60**	**9**	**2**	**8**	**22**	**.290**

COMPOSITE PITCHING AVERAGES

Philadelphia Phillies

Pitcher	G	IP	H	R	ER	BB	SO	W	L	ERA
Brusstar	1	2⅓	0	0	0	1	0	0	0	0.00
Reed	2	2	2	0	0	0	2	0	0	0.00
Saucier	1	⅔	0	0	0	2	0	0	0	0.00
McGraw	4	7⅔	7	1	1	8	10	1	1	1.17
Noles	1	4⅔	5	1	1	2	6	0	0	1.93
Carlton	2	15	14	5	4	9	17	2	0	2.40
Ruthven	1	9	9	3	3	0	7	0	0	3.00
Bystrom	1	5	10	3	3	1	4	0	0	5.40
Walk	1	7	8	6	6	3	3	1	0	7.71
Christenson	1	⅓	5	4	4	0	0	0	1	108.00
Totals	**6**	**53⅔**	**60**	**23**	**22**	**26**	**49**	**4**	**2**	**3.69**

Kansas City Royals

Pitcher	G	IP	H	R	ER	BB	SO	W	L	ERA
Pattin	1	1	0	0	0	0	2	0	0	0.00
Gura	2	12⅓	8	4	3	3	4	0	0	2.19
Martin	3	9⅔	11	3	3	3	2	0	0	2.79
Gale	2	6⅓	11	4	3	4	4	0	1	4.26
Quisenberry	6	10⅓	10	6	6	3	0	1	2	5.23
Splittorff	1	1⅔	4	1	1	0	0	0	0	5.40
Leonard	2	10⅔	15	9	8	2	5	1	1	6.75
Totals	**6**	**52**	**59**	**27**	**24**	**15**	**17**	**2**	**4**	**4.15**

Phillies versus Montreal Expos
Split-Season Playoff

1981

It was a sorry end to a sorry season. When the players struck management—in a strike that management wanted—in early June and the strike dragged on through July, both sides had to agree on a playoff format for season's end.

The plan went like this: The first-half winners of baseball's first split-season would be the teams on top of the major league's four divisions at the time the strike suspended play. When the season resumed, everyone would be 0–0. The winner of the second half would then play the winner of the first half to determine the division winner. If a team won both divisions, it would draw a bye into the LCS.

Neat, huh?

Then the season ended, and the teams with the best record in the NL East (St. Louis) and the NL West (Cincinnati) went home while the Phillies met the Expos and the Dodgers met the Astros.

Terrific, huh?

In Philadelphia, about the only thing missing was George Kiseda, who wrote about the 76ers brilliantly in two tours with *The Bulletin*, to make a play on his favorite comment. George could have written, "*Not* only in the NBA." Baseball had dipped to that level. The regular season was meaningless.

Judging from the crowds that showed up for Games Three, Four, and Five at the Vet, so were the Division Championship Series games. Philadelphia, which had expressed so much joy the previous season and which took its post-season baseball to its heart, was especially apathetic. Part of the problem might have been that the Phillies came home from a Thursday night game in Montreal to a Friday afternoon game in Philadelphia (with the Wilmington newspaper breaking a story in the meantime that Dallas Green was definitely on his way to Chicago as general manager) behind the Expos, two games to none. But even after the Phillies won on Friday and Saturday to go to sudden death with Steve Carlton facing Steve Rogers, there were 18,000 empty seats when the game began.

Rogers had won the DCS opener over Carlton, 3–1, before a slim Canadian crowd of 34,237. In the second game, Gary Carter had homered, and Bill Gullickson bested Dick Ruthven, again by a 3–1 count.

Larry Christenson, with help from Sparky Lyle and Ron Reed, won Game Three by a 6–2 score, then in a wild fourth game, Tug McGraw brought back visions of 1980 when he won in relief as George Vukovich slammed a home run into the left field bullpen in the bottom of the ninth for the difference in a 6–5 game in which Mike Schmidt and Gary Matthews also homered.

That left it to Sunday afternoon and Carlton versus Rogers. The Expos pitcher got the key hit, a two-run single, while blanking Lefty and the Phils, 3–0, giving the Expos their first real post-season action.

Montreal lost the LCS to the Dodgers, who beat the Yankees in six games to bring to an end baseball's most embarrassing season since 1919.

Game 1
Wednesday, October 7, at Montreal

Phillies	AB	R	H	RBI
Smith, cf	4	0	2	0
Rose, 1b	4	0	2	0
Matthews, lf	4	0	1	0
Schmidt, 3b	3	0	0	0
McBride, rf	4	0	0	0
Moreland, c	4	1	3	1
c-Aguayo	0	0	0	0
Bowa, ss	3	0	0	0
d-G. Vukovich	1	0	1	0
Trillo, 2b	3	0	0	0
Carlton, p	2	0	1	0
a-Gross	1	0	0	0
Reed, p	0	0	0	0
Totals	33	1	10	1

Montreal	AB	R	H	RBI
Cromartie, 1b	5	0	2	1
White, lf, rf	4	1	1	0
Dawson, cf	4	0	2	0
Carter, c	3	0	1	1
Parrish, 3b	3	0	0	0
Wallach, rf	2	1	1	0
b-Francona, lf	0	0	0	0
Manuel, 2b	4	0	0	0
Speier, ss	1	1	1	1
Rogers, p	2	0	0	0
Reardon, p	0	0	0	0
Totals	28	3	8	3

a-flied out for Carlton in 7th.
b-walked for Wallach in 7th.
c-ran for Moreland in 9th.
d-singled for Bowa in 9th.

Phillies   0 1 0 0 0 0 0 0 0 — 1
Montreal   1 1 0 1 0 0 0 0 x — 3

Error: Moreland. Double play: Manuel-Speier-Cromartie, Speier-Manuel-Cromartie. Left on base: Phillies 7, Montreal 10. Two-base hits: Carter, Wallach, Rose, Speier, Cromartie. Three-base hits: Matthews, Dawson. Home run: Moreland (1). Stolen bases: White 2, Dawson, Francona. Sacrifices: Rogers 2. Save: Reardon (1). Game winning RBI: Speier. Wild pitch: Carlton, Reed. Umpires: Tata, Pulli, Froemming, Williams, Kibler, Crawford. Time, 2:30. Attendance, 34,327.

Phillies	IP	H	R	ER	BB	SO
Carlton (L)	6	7	3	3	5	6
Reed	2	1	0	0	2	3

Montreal	IP	H	R	ER	BB	SO
Rogers (W)	8⅔	10	1	1	2	3
Reardon (S)	⅓	0	0	0	0	0

Game 2
Thursday, October 8, at Montreal

Phillies	AB	R	H	RBI
Smith, cf	4	1	2	0
Rose, 1b	4	0	1	1
McBride, rf	4	0	2	0
Schmidt, 3b	3	0	0	0
Matthews, lf	4	0	1	0
McGraw, p	0	0	0	0
Moreland, c	3	0	0	0
Bowa, ss	4	0	0	0
Trillo, 2b	4	0	0	0
Ruthven, p	1	0	0	0
Gross, ph	1	0	0	0
Brusstar, p	0	0	0	0
Lyle, p	0	0	0	0
G. Vukovich, lf	1	0	0	0
Totals	33	1	6	1

Montreal	AB	R	H	RBI
Cromartie, 1b	4	1	2	0
White, rf	3	0	0	0
Dawson, cf	4	0	1	0
Carter, c	4	1	1	2
Parrish, 3b	4	1	0	0
Francona, lf	3	0	2	0
Speier, ss	2	0	1	1
Manuel, 2b	3	0	0	0
Gullickson, p	3	0	0	0
Reardon, p	0	0	0	0
Totals	30	3	7	3

Phillies   0 0 0 0 0 0 0 1 0 — 1
Montreal   0 1 2 0 0 0 0 0 x — 3

Errors: Schmidt, Bowa. Left on base: Philadelphia 7, Montreal 6. Two-base hits: Cromartie, LoSmith, McBride. Home run: Carter (1). Stolen bases: White, Francona. Time, 2:31. Attendance, 45,896.

Phillies	IP	H	R	ER	BB	SO
Ruthven (L)	4	3	3	2	1	0
Brusstar	2	2	0	0	1	2
Lyle	1	1	0	0	1	0
McGraw	1	1	0	0	0	0

Montreal	IP	H	R	ER	BB	SO
Gullickson (W)	7⅔	6	1	1	1	3
Reardon (S)	1⅓	0	0	0	1	1

Game 3
Friday, October 9, at Philadelphia

Montreal	AB	R	H	RBI
Cromartie, 1b	4	0	1	0
White, rf	4	1	1	0
Dawson, cf	3	0	1	0
Carter, c	3	1	2	1
Parrish, 3b	4	0	0	0
Francona, lf	4	0	1	0
Speier, ss	4	0	2	1
Manuel, 2b	3	0	0	0
W. Johnson, ph	1	0	0	0
Burris, p	2	0	0	0
Lee, p	0	0	0	0
Wallach, ph	0	0	0	0
Sosa, p	0	0	0	0
Milner, ph	1	0	0	0
Totals	**33**	**2**	**8**	**2**

Phillies	AB	R	H	RBI
Smith, cf	4	0	0	0
Boone, c	1	0	0	0
Rose, 1b	4	0	1	1
McBride, rf	4	0	0	0
Lyle, p	0	0	0	0
Gross, lf	1	0	0	0
Schmidt, 3b	3	1	2	0
Matthews, lf	4	2	3	0
Reed, p	0	0	0	0
Moreland, c	3	1	2	0
Aguayo, pr	0	1	0	0
Maddox,. cf	1	0	0	0
Bowa, ss	3	0	2	1
Trillo, 2b	2	1	1	1
Christenson, p	2	0	0	0
G. Vukovich, rf	2	0	2	1
Totals	**34**	**6**	**13**	**4**

Montreal 0 1 0 0 0 0 0 1 0 — 2
Phillies 0 2 0 0 0 2 2 0 x — 6

Errors: Dawson, Sosa, Cromartie, Manuel. Double plays: Montreal 2, Philadelphia 1. Left on base: Montreal 7, Philadelphia 9. Two-base hits: Carter, Bowa, Schmidt, White. Sacrifice: Bowa. Sacrifice fly: Carter. Time, 2:45. Attendance, 36,835.

Montreal	IP	H	R	ER	BB	SO
Burris (L)	5⅓	7	4	3	4	4
Lee	⅔	2	0	0	0	1
Sosa	2	4	2	1	0	0

Phillies	IP	H	R	ER	BB	SO
Christenson (W)	6	4	1	1	1	8
Lyle	1	2	0	0	1	0
Reed	2	2	1	1	0	0

Game 4
Saturday, October 10, at Philadelphia

Montreal	AB	R	H	RBI
Cromartie, 1b	5	0	0	0
White, rf	3	1	0	1
Dawson, cf	5	0	1	0
Carter, c	5	1	3	2
Parrish, 3b	5	1	1	0
Francona, lf	4	0	0	0
Reardon, p	1	0	0	0
Speier, ss	4	2	2	0
Manuel, 2b	1	0	1	0
Milner, ph	1	0	1	1
Phillips, 2b	1	0	0	0
Sanderson, p	1	0	0	0
Behnsen, p	0	0	0	0
Mills, ph	0	0	0	0
Sosa, p	0	0	0	0
Johnson, ph	1	0	1	1
Fryman, p	0	0	0	0
Wallach, rf	1	0	0	0
Totals	**36**	**5**	**10**	**5**

Phillies	AB	R	H	RBI
L. Smith, cf	3	0	0	0
Maddox, cf	2	0	1	0
Rose, 1b	5	1	1	0
McBride, rf	3	1	1	0
Reed, p	0	0	0	0
Aviles, ph	0	0	0	0
McGraw, p	0	0	0	0
G. Vukovich, ph	1	1	1	1
Schmidt, 3b	3	2	1	2
Matthews, lf	4	1	2	1
Moreland, c	3	0	1	2
Boone, c	1	0	0	0
Bowa, ss	4	0	1	0
Trillo, 2b	3	0	0	0
Noles, p	0	0	0	0
Brusstar, p	0	0	0	0
Lyle, p	0	0	0	0
D Davis, rf	2	0	0	0
Totals	**34**	**6**	**9**	**6**

None out when winning run scored.

Montreal 0 0 0 1 1 2 1 0 0 0 — 5
Phillies 2 0 2 0 0 1 0 0 0 1 — 6

Error: Manuel. Double play: Philadelphia 1. Left on base: Montreal 7, Philadelphia 6. Two-base hits: Speier, Carter, Maddox. Home runs: Schmidt (1), Carter (2), Matthews (1), Vukovich (1). Stolen base: Dawson. Sacrifice: Noles. Sacrifice fly: White. Time, 2:40. Attendance, 38,818.

Montreal	IP	H	R	ER	BB	SO
Sanderson	2⅔	4	4	2	2	2
Behnsen	1⅓	1	0	0	1	1
Sosa	1	0	0	0	0	1
Fryman	1⅓	3	1	1	1	0
Reardon (L)†	2⅔	1	1	1	0	1

Phillies	IP	H	R	ER	BB	SO
Noles	4*	4	2	2	2	5
Brusstar	1⅔	3	2	2	0	1
Lyle	⅓	1	0	0	0	1
Reed	1	1	1	1	1	0
McGraw (W)	3	1	0	0	0	2

*Noles pitched to three batters in 5th.
†Reardon pitched to one batter in 10th.

Game 5
Sunday, October 11, at Philadelphia

Montreal	AB	R	H	RBI
Cromartie, 1b	4	0	0	0
White, lf, rf	4	0	1	0
Dawson, cf	4	1	1	0
Carter, c	4	0	1	0
Parrish, 3b	4	1	2	1
Wallach, rf	1	0	0	0
Francona, lf	1	0	1	0
Speier, ss	4	1	0	0
Manuel, 2b	3	0	0	0
Rogers, p	3	0	2	2
Totals	**32**	**3**	**8**	**3**

Phillies	AB	R	H	RBI
Smith, cf	4	0	1	0
Rose, 1b	3	0	1	0
G. Vukovich, rf	4	0	0	0
Reed, p	0	0	0	0
Schmidt, 3b	4	0	1	0
Matthews, lf	4	0	1	0
Trillo, 2b	4	0	2	0
Bowa, ss	3	0	0	0
Boone, c	3	0	0	0
Carlton, p	2	0	0	0
a-Gross, rf	1	0	0	0
Totals	**32**	**0**	**6**	**0**

a-Flied out for Carlton in the 8th.

Montreal	0	0	0	0	2	1	0	0	0	— 3
Phillies	0	0	0	0	0	0	0	0	0	— 0

Error: Rogers. Double play: Manuel-Speier-Cromartie. Left on base: Montreal 5, Phillies 6. Two-base hit: Parrish. Game winning RBI: Rogers. Umpires: Kibler, Crawford, Tata, Pulli, Froemming, Williams. Time, 2:15. Attendance, 47,384.

Montreal	IP	H	R	ER	BB	SO
Rogers (W)	9	6	0	0	1	2

Phillies	IP	H	R	ER	BB	SO
Carlton (L)	8	7	3	3	3	7
Reed	1	1	0	0	0	1

Phillies versus Los Angeles Dodgers
National League Championship Series

1983

The road to the I-95 World Series was paved with redemption.

For the Phillies, it was a matter of redeeming themselves for their sorry performances in the LCS against the Dodgers in 1977 and 1978, not to mention 11 of 12 losses during the 1983 regular season.

For Pete Rose, it was one last glorious fling with the Phillies and an opportunity to redeem himself for a dismal regular season.

But more than anything, it was redemption for Gary Matthews.

The man they called Sarge had been busted all the way back to Private First Class in easily his worst season in the major leagues. He wasn't even an offensive specialist. The regular-season figures were downright pathetic by his standards: A .258 average with just 10 homers and 50 RBI in 446 at-bats.

In the LCS, though, the Sarge struck back. After hitting a home run in Game Two and providing the Phillies with their only run in their only loss, he erupted in Games Three and Four at the Vet to put away the Most Valuable Player award.

In Game Three, Matthews hit his second homer and drove in four runs as the Phillies assumed command with a 7–2 victory. And in Game Four, he buried the Dodgers with a three-run home run in the first inning as the Phils prevailed once again by a 7–2 count. For the LCS, he batted .429 with three homers and a record-tying eight RBI.

"I've been in some hotter streaks," Matthews said, "but this couldn't come at a better time. It really makes me feel good."

It made the Philadelphia fans feel good all over. After his fourth RBI in the seventh inning of Game Three, he was rewarded with a standing ovation as he took his position in left field. And his three-run homer in Game Four was rewarded with what some people called the loudest ovation in the history of the Vet.

"Gary's a typical member of the Phillies," said Mike Schmidt, whose solo homer provided the only run scored in Game One. "He's a man with a professional attitude. He realizes what's important is the team."

In a series that was covered with enough glory to spread it around, the pitchers also had their moments.

Gary Matthews was the big hero of the League Championship Series.

The 1983 National League champions.

Steve Carlton, whose 1977 loss to the Dodgers in the rain was one of the most memorable games in the history of the franchise, turned positive with a couple of wins. John Denny pitched splendidly and allowed no earned runs in the only Philadelphia loss. And Charles Hudson showed no fear in going the route in Game Three.

In the opener, Los Angeles hard-luck pitcher Jerry Reuss faced Carlton, who had won his 300th game in September and who had won two of his three decisions against the Dodgers in the two previous post-season matchups.

The game was decided with one mighty swing of the bat. Schmidt, coming off his third season in which he hit 40 or more home runs, ripped a Reuss pitch into the stands in dead center field in the first inning. Somehow the run stood up for the game.

It did because Carlton pitched masterfully for 7⅔ innings, allowing seven scattered hits. The Dodgers put together their biggest threat in the eighth when singles by Steve Sax and Dusty Baker and a walk to Pedro Guerrero loaded the bases with two outs. At this point, manager Paul Owens replaced the tiring Carlton with Al Holland, and Mr. T put out the fire as he had done so many times down the stretch. He got Mike Marshall on a fly ball to right, then retired LA in the ninth.

The second game was a matter of the Phillies coming apart uncharacteristically enough in the field. And it brought back painful memories of the 1978 LCS when Garry Maddox, the Phillies' Gold Glove center fielder, dropped a ball that cost the team Game Four.

This night, Maddox again dropped a ball that was catchable. It happened in the fifth inning of a 1–1 pitching duel between Denny and Fernando Valenzuela.

The Dodgers had scored a first-inning run on an error by Ivan DeJesus, and the Phillies had come back to tie on Matthews' solo homer in the second.

In the bottom of the fifth, Valenzuela led off with a line drive to the warning track in deep right-center. Maddox got to the ball but dropped it for a three-base error. After a walk, Guerrero pounded a two-run triple with two outs to make it a 3–1 game. The Dodgers added a run off Ron Reed in the eighth to even the series and headed for the Vet knowing they had to win two out of three.

They never even came close to winning one.

Owens gave the ball to Hudson, who was pitching in Peninsula in the low minors the season before and who had won eight of 16 decisions after joining the club. Charles admitted that he hadn't been able to sleep the night before. In the game, with the exception of a two-run homer by Marshall, he put the

Dodger bats to sleep, allowing just three other hits and striking out nine as he became the only pitcher to work a complete game in the series.

The Phillies scored two runs without getting a hit in the second inning, then made it 3–0 on Joe Lefebvre's sacrifice fly in the third. Marshall took Hudson downtown in the fourth with a mate aboard to make it a one-run game, and the stage was set for the Sarge.

Matthews clubbed a solo homer in the bottom of the fourth inning, smacked a two-run single in the fifth, and chased home Pete Rose (three hits) with a single in the seventh. It was the first four-RBI game in the LCS since Steve Carlton did it in Game Three in 1978.

Carlton worked the first six innings of the pennant clincher before leaving with a sore back. By that time, the Phillies had a 7–1 lead, and some people in the crowd of 64,494 had left their seats in order to stand in line to buy World Series tickets. Those who stayed cheered to the end of the 7–2 victory that marked the first time the Phillies had ever won a National League pennant at home.

Their biggest cheer, though, came in the first inning when Matthews ripped his three-run homer into the seats in left.

In the fifth, the Phillies chased Reuss, whose post-season record dipped to 0–7, with a two-run outburst. Sixto Lezcano chipped in a two-run homer to left in the sixth, and Holland retired five of the six batters he faced to put the game and the Dodgers away.

In the joyous locker room scene that followed, Manager Owens put everything in perspective.

"Nobody gave up," he said. "Even after all the baloney we went through, everybody kept at it. To me, this is a season I will never forget."

The Phillies had scored 14 runs in their last 15 innings. They were swinging their bats exceptionally well. Even though the Baltimore Orioles were a pitching-rich team, nobody expected a hitting slump in the World Series. But that's exactly what happened.

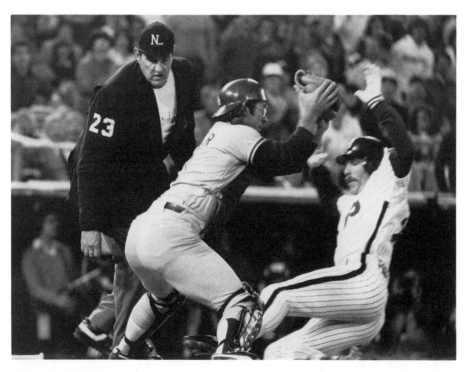

Mike Schmidt slides home safely in fourth LCS game as Steve Yeager awaits throw.

Game 1
Tuesday, October 4, at Los Angeles

Phillies	AB	R	H	RBI	PO	A
Morgan, 2b	4	0	0	0	3	1
Rose, 1b	4	0	1	0	8	1
Schmidt, 3b	3	1	2	1	0	2
Lezcano, rf	3	0	1	0	2	0
Matthews, lf	4	0	0	0	2	0
Holland, p	0	0	0	0	0	0
Maddox, cf	4	0	1	0	4	0
Diaz, c	3	0	0	0	6	0
DeJesus, ss	3	0	0	0	1	2
Carlton, p	3	0	0	0	1	3
Gross, lf	1	0	0	0	0	0
Totals	**32**	**1**	**5**	**1**	**27**	**9**

Los Angeles	AB	R	H	RBI	PO	A
Sax, 2b	4	0	3	0	1	5
Russell, ss	3	0	1	0	0	3
Baker, lf	4	0	1	0	3	0
Guerrero, 3b	2	0	0	0	0	1
Marshall, 1b	4	0	0	0	11	0
Niedenfuer, p	0	0	0	0	0	1
Yeager, c	4	0	0	0	4	0
Landreaux, cf	3	0	0	0	3	0
b-Morales	1	0	0	0	0	0
Thomas, rf	4	0	2	0	4	0
Reuss, p	1	0	0	0	0	1
a-Maldonado	1	0	0	0	0	0
Brock, 1b	1	0	0	0	1	0
Totals	**32**	**0**	**7**	**0**	**27**	**11**

a-Flied out for Reuss in 8th.
b-Fouled out for Landreaux in 9th.

Phillies										
Phillies	1	0	0	0	0	0	0	0	0	—1
Los Angeles	0	0	0	0	0	0	0	0	0	—0

Error: Schmidt. Left on base: Phillies 8, Los Angeles 9.
Home run: Schmidt (1). Stolen base: Thomas (1). Sacrifices:
Reuss, Russell. Wild pitch: Carlton, Reuss. Time, 2:17.
Attendance, 49,963.

Phillies	IP	H	R	ER	BB	SO
Carlton (W)	7⅔	7	0	0	2	6
Holland (S)	1⅓	0	0	0	0	0

Los Angeles	IP	H	R	ER	BB	SO
Reuss (L)	8	5	1	1	3	3
Niedenfuer	1	0	0	0	1	1

Game 2
Wednesday, October 5, at Los Angeles

Phillies	AB	R	H	RBI	PO	A
Morgan, 2b	3	0	0	0	4	3
Rose, 1b	3	0	0	0	7	0
Schmidt, 3b	4	0	1	0	1	3
Lezcano, rf	4	0	0	0	1	0
Matthews, lf	4	1	2	1	1	0
Maddox, cf	3	0	2	0	4	0
c-G. Gross	0	0	0	0	0	0
Diaz, c	3	0	0	0	5	1
d-Lefebvre	1	0	0	0	0	0
DeJesus, ss	2	0	1	0	1	3
e-Hayes	1	0	0	0	0	0
Denny, p	1	0	0	0	0	0
a-Perez	1	0	1	0	0	0
b-Samuel	0	0	0	0	0	0
Reed, p	1	0	0	0	0	1
f-Virgil	1	0	0	0	0	0
Totals	**32**	**1**	**7**	**1**	**24**	**11**

Los Angeles	AB	R	H	RBI	PO	A
Sax, 2b	4	0	0	0	4	4
Brock, 1b	4	1	0	0	7	0
Thomas, rf	0	0	0	0	0	0
Baker, lf	3	2	0	0	3	0
Guerrero, 3b	3	0	1	2	0	2
Landreaux, cf	3	0	2	1	3	0
Marshall, rf, 1b	4	0	0	0	2	0
Russell, ss	3	1	2	0	1	5
Fimple, c	4	0	1	1	6	1
Valenzuela, p	3	0	0	0	1	0
Niedenfuer, p	0	0	0	0	0	0
Totals	**31**	**4**	**6**	**4**	**27**	**12**

a-Singled for Denny in 7th.
b-Ran for Perez in 7th.
c-Walked for Maddox in 9th.
d-Struck out for Diaz in 9th.
e-Flied out for DeJesus in 9th.
f-Struck out for Reed in 9th.

Phillies	0	1	0	0	0	0	0	0	0	—1
Los Angeles	1	0	0	0	2	0	0	1	x	—4

Errors: Maddox, DeJesus, Russell. Double plays: Russell,
Sax, and Brock 2. Russell, Sax, and Marshall. Left on base:
Phillies 8, Los Angeles 8. Two-base hit: Maddox. Three-base
hit: Guerrero. Home run: Matthews (1). Stolen bases: Rose
(1), Russell (1). Sacrifice: Denny. Hit by pitcher: By Denny
(Guerrero). Wild pitch: Valenzuela. Time, 2:44. Attendance,
55,967.

Phillies	IP	H	R	ER	BB	SO
Denny (L)	6	5	3	0	3	3
Reed	2	1	1	1	1	1

Los Angeles	IP	H	R	ER	BB	SO
Valenzuela (W)	8*	7	1	1	4	5
Niedenfuer (S)	1	0	0	0	0	2

*Faced two batters in 9th.

General manager Paul Owens and wife Marcella
enjoy the moment of triumph over Los Angeles
after two prior failures.

Game 3
Friday, October 7, at Philadelphia

Los Angeles	AB	R	H	RBI	PO	A
Sax, 2b	3	0	0	0	1	0
Brock, 1b	4	0	0	0	5	0
Baker, lf	4	1	2	0	2	0
Guerrero, 3b	4	0	0	0	0	4
Landreaux, cf	4	0	0	0	5	0
Marshall, rf	3	1	1	2	4	0
Russell, ss	4	0	0	0	0	0
Fimple, c	3	0	0	0	7	1
Welch, p	0	0	0	0	0	0
Pena, p	1	0	1	0	0	0
a-Landestoy	1	0	0	0	0	0
Honeycutt, p	0	0	0	0	0	0
Beckwith, p	0	0	0	0	0	0
c-Thomas	1	0	0	0	0	0
Zachary, p	0	0	0	0	0	0
Totals	32	2	4	2	24	5

Phillies	AB	R	H	RBI	PO	A
Morgan, 2b	4	1	1	0	0	2
Rose, 1b	4	2	3	0	7	0
Schmidt, 3b	3	1	1	0	3	1
Lefebvre, rf	1	0	0	1	2	0
b-Lezcano, rf	2	0	0	0	0	0
Matthews, lf	3	2	3	4	2	0
Dernier, cf	0	0	0	0	0	0
G. Gross, cf, lf	3	1	0	0	4	0
Diaz, c	0	0	0	0	9	0
DeJesus, ss	4	0	1	1	0	2
Hudson, p	4	0	0	0	0	0
Totals	31	7	9	6	27	5

a-Grounded out for Pena in the 5th.
b-Struck out for Lefebvre in the 5th.
c-Struck out for Beckwith in the 7th.

Los Angeles	0	0	0	2	0	0	0	0	0 — 2
Phillies	0	2	1	1	2	0	1	0	x — 7

Error: DeJesus. Left on base: Los Angeles 5, Phillies 5. Two-base hits: Baker, Schmidt. Home runs: Marshall (1), Matthews (2). Stolen bases: Sax (1), Matthews (1). Sacrifice fly: Lefebvre. Wild pitch: Pena 2. Passed ball: Fimple. Time, 2:51. Attendance, 53,490.

Los Angeles	IP	H	R	ER	BB	SO
Welch (L)	1⅓	0	2	1	2	0
Pena	2⅔	4	2	2	1	3
Honeycutt	⅓	2	2	2	0	0
Beckwith	1⅔	1	0	0	0	3
Zachary	2	2	1	1	1	1

Phillies	IP	H	R	ER	BB	SO
Hudson (W)	9	4	2	2	2	9

Game 4
Saturday, October 8, at Philadelphia

Los Angeles	AB	R	H	RBI	PO	A
Sax, 2b	5	0	1	0	5	3
Russell, ss	4	0	1	0	3	2
Guerrero, 3b	3	1	2	0	0	2
Baker, lf	3	1	2	1	1	0
Marshall, 1b	4	0	1	0	5	2
Yeager, c	2	0	1	0	3	1
b-Monday	0	0	0	0	0	0
c-Morales	1	0	0	0	0	0
Fimple, c	0	0	0	0	1	0
Landreaux, cf	4	0	0	0	1	0
Thomas, rf	4	0	2	0	3	0
Reuss, p	2	0	0	0	0	0
Beckwith, p	0	0	0	0	0	0
Honeycutt, p	0	0	0	0	1	0
a-Landestoy	1	0	0	0	0	0
Zachary, p	0	0	0	0	1	0
d-Maldonado	1	0	0	0	0	0
Totals	34	2	10	1	24	10

Phillies	AB	R	H	RBI	PO	A
Morgan, 2b	4	0	0	0	1	1
Rose, 1b	5	1	2	0	7	1
Schmidt, 3b	5	3	3	1	2	1
Lezcano, rf, lf	4	2	3	2	2	1
Matthews, lf	3	1	1	3	1	0
Reed, p	0	0	0	0	0	0
Hayes, rf	1	0	0	0	0	0
Maddox, cf	4	0	0	1	0	0
Diaz, c	4	0	2	0	12	1
DeJesus, ss	3	0	1	0	2	4
Carlton, p	2	0	1	0	0	2
G. Gross, lf	1	0	0	0	0	0
Holland, p	0	0	0	0	0	0
Totals	36	7	13	7	27	11

a-Struck out for Honeycutt in the 7th.
b-Announced for Yeager in the 8th.
c-Struck out for Monday in the 8th.
d-Struck out for Zachary in the 9th.

Los Angeles	0	0	0	1	0	0	0	1	0 — 2
Phillies	3	0	0	0	2	2	0	0	x — 7

Error: Lezcano. Left on base: Los Angeles 9, Phillies 10. Two-base hits: Guerrero, Marshall, Schmidt, Yeager, Diaz, Thomas. Home runs: Matthews (3), Baker (1), Lezcano (1). Sacrifices: Carlton, Lezcano. Hit by pitcher: By Carlton (Yeager). Wild pitch: Carlton. Time, 2:50. Attendance, 64,494.

Los Angeles	IP	H	R	ER	BB	SO
Reuss (L)	4*	9	5	5	0	1
Beckwith	⅔	0	0	0	2	0
Honeycutt	1⅓	2	2	2	0	2
Zachary	2	2	0	0	1	1

Phillies	IP	H	R	ER	BB	SO
Carlton (W)	6	6	1	1	3	7
Reed	1⅓	3	1	0	0	2
Holland	1⅔	1	0	0	0	3

*Reuss pitched to two batters in the 5th.

Phillies versus Baltimore Orioles World Series

1983

In mid-summer 1983, if anyone had dared hazard the view that the Phillies would be in the World Series that fall, it would have been a sure sign to summon the boys in the white jackets.

There was no way the Phillies were going to the Fall Classic that year. At best, the club was playing uninspired, mediocre ball, floundering much of the summer below the .500 mark and in the middle of the pack in what was generally regarded as a weak Eastern Division.

Yet, in the second week of October, there were the Phillies, perched confidently on the highest pedestal of American sports. They had, indeed, made it to the World Series, having ridden the crest of a spectacular September drive in which they stormed to the division title and then the National League pennant.

It was the Phillies' second trip to the World Series in the last four years. But, unlike 1980 when Philadelphia was agog with Phillies fever, the 1983 Series seemed to generate considerably less enthusiasm.

Philadelphians, in fact, were almost blasé about their Series entry. Some said it was because the fans could not get excited about a team that had spent so much of the summer playing dull, uninteresting, and poor baseball. Others theorized that the Series had sneaked up so fast that fans, without the benefit of a long, furious pennant race, were simply unprepared for the Phillies' sudden emergence in the Series.

Whatever the reason, the Phillies entered the Series with something less than a resounding cheer from the fans, but with high hopes, nonetheless, of bringing the city its second major championship of the year (the pro basketball Philadelphia 76ers had won the National Basketball Association championships in the spring).

The Phillies' opponents were the Baltimore Orioles, the closest major league team to Philadelphia. Some pundits billed the games as the I-95 Series, a reference to the highway connecting the two cities.

A Philadelphia-Baltimore confrontation had enormous appeal. For one thing, such a Series matched two old but vibrant Eastern cities, both with storied baseball traditions. For years, many people in each city had longed for the time when the Phillies and the Orioles would meet in the Fall Classic. There was joy on both sides now that the time had finally arrived.

The Orioles, winners of four American League pennants since 1969, the last one in 1979, were established as slight favorites to win the Series. Baltimore had won the Eastern Division crown in the American League by a comfortable margin of six games, then had quickly disposed of the Chicago White Sox in the League Championship Series, three games to one.

The Birds featured an outstanding pitching staff led by veteran lefthanders Scott McGregor (18–7) and Mike Flanagan (12–4), rookie righthanders Mike Boddicker (16–8) and Storm Davis (13–7), and a strong bullpen led by southpaw Tippy Martinez (9–3, 21 saves) and Sammy Stewart (9–4). Future Hall of Famer Jim Palmer was also a member of the staff, although an assortment of injuries had substantially reduced his playing time.

Baltimore's offense centered on the American League's Most Valuable Player, 23-year-old Cal Ripken, Jr., a potential superstar and son of the team's third base coach, and Eddie Murray, a veteran, hard-hitting first baseman. Ripken hit .318 with 27 home runs and 102 RBI during the season. Murray registered a .306 average with 33 homers and 111 RBI.

Under first-year manager Joe Altobelli, who replaced the highly successful Earl Weaver, the Orioles relied on a platoon system in which the three outfield spots were shared by six players who could all hit well. In addition, the Birds had an outstanding defensive catcher in Rick Dempsey. Designated hitter Ken Singleton (.276, 18, 85) was also a top-flight hitter, but would ride the bench because of the elimination of his batting position for the '83 Series.

The Phillies were also without the use of one of their main players. Len Matuszek had taken over at first base during the September stretch drive and had been a big factor as the team won the division flag. But he had joined the club too late to be eligible for the Series.

Still, the Phillies did not need to yield ground to the Orioles. Their pitching staff included a 300-game winner in Steve Carlton (15–16), the National League's Cy Young Award winner in John Denny (19–6), and the league's Fireman of the Year in Al Holland (8–4, 25 saves).

The squad also had the NL's home run king in Mike Schmidt (40), the LCS MVP in Gary Matthews, and seasoned Series veterans in Pete Rose, Joe Morgan, Tony Perez, and Garry Maddox.

With interim manager Paul Owens at the helm, the Phillies were confident, as the Series began, that a repeat of 1980 was on the way.

Game One

It had been a difficult season for Garry Maddox. The man who had often been called the finest defensive center fielder in the game at the time, and one of the best of all time, languished on the Phillies' bench for long periods. He was the subject of repeated trade rumors. And he did not perform at the plate as he had in past years.

But some of the sting of that disappointing season was removed in the first game of the World Series. Maddox's eighth-inning home run provided the winning margin as the Phillies defeated the Orioles, 2–1, in Baltimore.

It was a game in which all the runs came on homers. And it was a game in which the Phils' John Denny and Birds' Scott McGregor hooked up in a magnificent pitching duel that offered World Series baseball at its best.

Played in rain throughout, the game was reminiscent of another Phillies post-season outing in 1977, in which they lost to the Dodgers in a game-long monsoon. Only this time, the bats of Maddox and Joe Morgan, who also homered, and the arms of Denny and Al Holland, who once again shut down the opposition in the late innings, supplied a far different result.

The win gave the Phillies a 1–0 lead in the Series.

Garry Maddox talks about game-winning home run in opener against Baltimore Orioles with Rich Ashburn.

With President Ronald Reagan in the stands, each team managed only five hits as Denny and McGregor matched slants. After Morgan led off by reaching first when former Phillie Todd Cruz dropped a pop-up, McGregor, a high school teammate of George Brett, retired the next nine batters in a row (Morgan was thrown out trying to steal second).

Meanwhile, Denny gave up a run to the Orioles when Jim Dwyer became the 18th batter in history to hit a home run in his first World Series trip to the plate. Dwyer, batting second in the order, drilled a 3–2 Denny pitch over the 376-foot sign in right-center.

Baltimore's 1–0 lead held up for what seemed an eternity. Morgan's leadoff single in the fourth broke McGregor's hitless pitching, but that, as well as Gary Matthews' leadoff single in the fifth, proved harmless.

All the while, Denny was kayoing the Orioles, too. After Dwyer's home run and a two-out single by Eddie Murray in the same inning, John retired 17 of the next 18 batters. In fact, the only Orioles to reach first between the first and the eighth innings were Cal Ripken, who singled in the fourth, and John Lowenstein, who singled in the seventh.

The Phillies' scoring drought ended in the top of the sixth. Morgan, one of the heroes of the Phillies' stretch drive in September, blasted a 1–2 McGregor curve over the right field wall just behind the 376-foot mark. "If he throws the curve ball to me again," Morgan had told Pete Rose on the bench before the inning began, "I'm going to hit it out."

Little Joe's boomer pulled the Phillies into a 1–1 tie, but it was left for Maddox to put it away. Leading off the eighth, Garry drilled McGregor's first pitch deep into the seats in left field. It was Maddox's first home run since August 16, and only his fifth four-bagger all season.

The next Phils batter, Bo Diaz, also bid for a homer. But left fielder Lowenstein made a leaping, backhanded catch with his glove extended over the wall on Diaz's towering fly.

The rest of the game came down to Holland. Denny was lifted after serving Al Bumbry a two-out double in the eighth. Mr. T came on to retire four of the Orioles' toughest hitters (Dan Ford, Ripken, Murray, and Gary Roenicke).

In an unusual footnote to the contest, neither team allowed a walk, despite the rain. There were only four previous Series games played without a walk. The last one was in 1967.

Game Two

In recent years, one of the Phillies' chief nemeses has been pitchers who throw just about fast enough to break a pane of glass, and who rely mostly on an assortment of pitches that do baffling things at slow speeds.

The second game of the World Series introduced the Phillies to another in the long line of pitchers who over the years have usually beaten them. His name was Mike Boddicker, an Iowa farmboy, and, worse, a rookie.

Combining with another guy from somewhere out in the hinterlands, Montana's John Lowenstein, Boddicker's baffling assortment of junk balls and pinpoint control held the Phillies to a mere three hits. The seemingly predictable result was a 4–1 victory for the Orioles to even the Series at one win apiece.

Lowenstein, Brother Lo to close friends, racked Phillie pitchers for three hits, including a titanic home run that cleared the center field fence.

The brunt of Baltimore's barrage was borne by Phils' rookie Charles Hudson. The slim righthander hurled well until a fifth-inning Oriole uprising sent three runs across the plate.

That was all Boddicker needed. After striking out three of the first four Phillies he faced, the Birds' righthander went on to retire the first nine batters in order.

In the fourth, the Phillies took a brief lead as Joe Morgan opened with an infield single. After stealing second, Morgan moved to third when Mike Schmidt reached first on Eddie Murray's error. Morgan scored on Joe Lefebvre's fly to deep center.

The lead didn't last long. Lowenstein led off the bottom of the fifth with his home run. The blow seemed to rattle Hudson, and Charles surrendered a line single to Rich Dauer, a bunt single to Todd Cruz, and a double to Rick Dempsey, which plated Dauer. Cruz scooted home on Boddicker's sacrifice fly.

Willie Hernandez replaced Hudson on the mound. After striking out John Shelby, he beaned Dan Ford and walked Cal Ripken to load the bases before retiring the Orioles' ninth batter of the inning, Murray.

The Orioles added their fourth run off Phils reliever Larry Andersen in the seventh inning on successive singles by Shelby, Ford, and Ripken.

Meanwhile, the Phillies put only two runners on base during the last five innings. Gary Matthews singled in the seventh, and Bo Diaz singled in the eighth.

For the second night in a row, no Phillies batter drew a walk as Boddicker added to the previous night's string to give Baltimore 18 straight passless innings.

Game Three

The World Series has always been an event in which the unexpected happens. The third game of the 1983 Series fit the pattern perfectly.

The Phillies failed to hold a lead with Steve Carlton on the mound; the Orioles' Jim Palmer won a game in relief; Pete Rose was benched for the first time in his World Series career; and the Phils' reliable shortstop Ivan DeJesus committed a most untimely error.

As a result of the whole, strange sequence, the Phillies frittered away a game they should have won, bowing to Baltimore, 3–2, as the Series moved to Veterans Stadium in Philadelphia.

Although they outhit the Orioles, 8–6, the Phillies were unable to come up with the hits when they needed them. Solo home runs by Gary Matthews and Joe Morgan provided the team's only scoring, but a number of other scoring opportunities fell by the wayside.

Compounding the misery was DeJesus's error. Probably the season's most unheralded Phillies player, Ivan—who made several outstanding plays earlier in the game—had performed all year with rock-solid, although quiet, efficiency, both at the plate and in the field. But his seventh-inning boot of Dan Ford's grounder let in the winning run for the Orioles.

The error gave the decision to veteran Bird hurler Jim Palmer, pitching in relief of starter Mike Flanagan. "I told the guys on the bench I hadn't won a Series game since 1971, so how about getting me some runs," the future Hall of Famer said.

Palmer, who became the first pitcher to win a Series game in each of three decades, and fellow relievers Sammy Stewart and Tippy Martinez completely shut down the Phillies. Over the final five innings, they allowed a combined total of just two hits.

Before the game began, the big news was manager Paul Owens' decision to bench Rose in favor of Tony Perez. "I'm not satisfied with my offense," Owens explained. Rose did not take the benching too well, saying he was "upset and embarrassed."

With Pete on the bench, the Phillies jumped away to a second inning 1–0 lead on Matthews' towering fly that cleared the fence in deep left-center. The next inning Morgan lined a drive over the right field barrier for a 2–0 lead.

The Phillies had men on again in each of the next three innings, but couldn't come up with a timely hit to break it open. Meanwhile, though, Carlton mowed down the Orioles. He yielded no hits over the first three innings, and only three hits through the sixth. One of those was a sixth-inning home run by Ford.

In the seventh, Carlton's nagging back injury began to affect him. Rick Dempsey hit a two-out double to left-center, went to third on a wild pitch and scored on pinch-hitter Benny Ayala's single to left. Al Holland replaced Carlton and promptly gave up a single to John Shelby.

With men on first and third, Ford smacked a grounder at DeJesus, but the ball bounced off of Ivan's glove for an error while Ayala scored with the eventual winning run.

"I just didn't catch it," said DeJesus, who claimed the ball hit a wet spot in the infield. "When the ball hit the ground, it just kept going. It skidded. I tried to knock it down, but it hit off of my glove. But I should have had it."

To his credit, DeJesus both shouldered the blame for the bobble and refused to hide from the hordes of writers after the game.

Holland, who fanned four Orioles in the last two innings, defended the shortstop. "He didn't lose it (the game)," he said. "Carlton didn't lose it; I didn't lose it. We lost it. The team lost the game. We all had a part in it."

Game Four

The bottom part of their batting order was supposed to be a weakness in the Baltimore Orioles lineup. The last four hitters, including the pitcher, were regarded as nearly automatic outs who would crumble at the hands of Phillies pitching.

It didn't work out that way, though. While the Birds' key hitters struggled at the plate, the Orioles' supposedly weak hitters carried the attack. In the fourth and probably most interesting game of the Series, number-six hitter Rich Dauer drilled three hits, drove in three runs, and scored another as Baltimore defeated the Phillies, 5–4.

It was a game in which the Phillies again kicked away scoring opportunities. Making the loss even tougher to swallow was the demise of John Denny, the second Phillies pitching ace in a row to get roughed up.

The sixth, seventh, and eighth hitters in the Orioles lineup went by the name of the Three Stooges. Dauer was anything but a stooge as he became the latest Baltimore player to assume the hero's mantle.

"The whole Series has become a prime example of Orioles baseball," Dauer said in a statement that overlooked the Phillies' merits.

Altogether the two teams pounded 20 hits, 10 by each club in by far the lustiest hitting exhibition of the Series. A real disappointment for the Phillies was the continued failure of Mike Schmidt to hit. Schmidt's broken-bat single in the third broke an 0-for-13 drought.

"I'm certainly not happy with my hitting," Schmidt said after ending the game with a 1-for-16 mark in the Series. "Either the Orioles have great pitching or I'm doing something wrong."

"They definitely have good pitching," added Pete Rose who had two hits. "Trying to figure out a pattern is tough. They all change speeds so much."

Trying to figure out Oriole starter Storm Davis was especially tough in the beginning. The Bird rookie struck out the side in the first inning. He went on to retire the first 10 batters he faced.

Denny was also going along smoothly until the fourth when he loaded the bases on consecutive singles by Jim Dwyer, Cal Ripken, and Eddie Murray. Dauer followed with a single to score Dwyer and Ripken.

The Phillies retaliated in the bottom of the fourth. Rose and Schmidt singled with the former crossing on Joe Lefebvre's double down the right field line. Gary Matthews followed with a walk to load the bases, but Greg Gross grounded into a double play to end the rally.

An inning later, though, the Phillies took the lead. Bo Diaz doubled, went to third on a wild pitch, and scored on Denny's single, the first hit by a pitcher in the Series since 1979. John came home a few minutes later on Rose's two-out double.

The Orioles came right back to regain the lead in the sixth, knocking out Denny in the process. John Lowenstein singled, Dauer doubled, and pinch-hitter Joe Nolan was intentionally walked to load the bases. Denny then walked pinch-hitter Ken Singleton to force in a run. John Shelby followed with a long fly off Phils reliever Willie Hernandez on which Matthews made a spectacular leaping catch against the wall. Dauer scored on the fly.

Baltimore added another run in the seventh off Ron Reed. Dwyer doubled and scored on Dauer's third hit, a single.

The Phillies, meanwhile, couldn't do anything with Oriole reliever Sammy Stewart, who eventually got the win. But they did get to Tippy Martinez in the ninth.

Martinez, who had taken the Phils out of an eighth-inning rally by serving a double-play grounder to Matthews, was touched for a single by Diaz. With two outs, pinch-runner Bob Dernier raced home from second on Ozzie Virgil's pinch-hit single.

But the Phils could score no more. "We finally got some hits," Matthews summarized. "But they weren't really timely hits. We're a better ball club than we've shown."

Game Five

In the first four games of the 1983 World Series, Baltimore's Eddie Murray was one of the least effective Orioles at the plate. Mired in a 2-for-16 slump, Murray hadn't played a significant role in any of the previous three Oriole victories.

In the fifth game, that role changed. Murray's two home runs combined with the five-hit pitching of Scott McGregor to lead the Orioles to a 5–0 victory and the World Championship, four games to one.

Thus ended the Phillies' late-season flurry that had carried them to division and league titles. It was a disappointing way to finish, especially because the Phillies lost four straight games, including three at home.

But the Orioles simply had too much pitching and, at the right times, too much hitting. The Phillies, on the other hand, managed only nine runs and a .195 team batting average over the five-game Series.

"There are a lot of ways to look at it, but the bottom line is, they were better than us," said Mike Schmidt, who produced only one hit in 20 at-bats.

Schmidt explained his slump by saying he could not get "comfortable" at the plate. "I was constantly trying to adjust," he said, "and it almost seemed like they knew what I was thinking. I tried as hard as I could, but it just didn't work out. I apologize for my performance, but not for my effort."

Schmidt wasn't the only nonhitting Phillie, of course. In the final game, Pete Rose and Garry Maddox each had two hits, and the only other man to get a hit and the only one to get as far as third base was Joe Morgan with an eighth-inning triple. And he fell down attempting to come home on a Rose fly ball in the Phillies' closest scoring opportunity.

The Orioles didn't exactly tear apart Phillies pitching, either. The Birds matched the Phillies' hit total, but three of their safeties were home runs. The third was by Rick Dempsey, whose .385 batting average earned him the Series Most Valuable Player award.

Murray, however, was clearly the man of the hour. His leadoff home run in the second got the Orioles out to an early lead. After Dempsey led off with a homer in the third, Eddie came back in the fourth with a titanic blast against the Vet scoreboard in right-center field following a walk to Cal Ripken.

All three homers came against the Phillies' Charles Hudson. "I made some bad pitches, and they took advantage of my mistakes," said the crestfallen rookie hurler afterward.

Ironically, Murray with three hits and Dempsey with two were the only Orioles to get hits. After Dempsey doubled and scored on John Shelby's sacrifice fly in the fifth, Marty Bystrom (three) and Willie Hernandez (nine) retired 12 straight Baltimore batters.

The Phillies turned in some outstanding fielding plays, particularly a backhanded, running catch by Gary Matthews in left and a long, running grab against the wall by Garry Maddox.

"But we just didn't get the key hits," said manager Paul Owens. "Baltimore came up with the key hits when they needed them.

"They are a fine organization," he added. "I'm proud of them. If we couldn't win, I was pleased that they could.

"I'm proud of my ball club, too. We may not be the best team that ever played the game, but we're better than the way we played."

The largest crowd in Philadelphia baseball history—67,064—and the biggest World Series gathering (excluding the previous game) since a 1964 game at Yankee Stadium attended the finale. Net receipts were a record $7,652,103.89.

Game 1
Tuesday, October 11, at Baltimore

Phillies	AB	R	H	RBI	PO	A
Morgan, 2b	4	1	2	1	1	5
Rose, 1b	4	0	1	0	11	0
Schmidt, 3b	4	0	0	0	0	1
Lezcano, rf	3	0	0	0	0	0
d-Hayes, rf	1	0	0	0	0	0
Matthews, lf	3	0	1	0	4	0
Maddox, cf	3	1	1	1	3	0
Diaz, c	3	0	0	0	7	0
DeJesus, ss	3	0	0	0	1	5
Denny, p	3	0	0	0	0	0
Holland, p	0	0	0	0	0	0
Totals	31	2	5	2	27	11

Baltimore	AB	R	H	RBI	PO	A
Bumbry, cf	4	0	1	0	4	0
Stewart, p	0	0	0	0	0	0
T. Martinez, p	0	0	0	0	0	0
Dwyer, rf	3	1	1	1	2	0
c-Ford, rf	1	0	0	0	0	0
Ripken, ss	4	0	1	0	1	4
Murray, 1b	4	0	1	0	8	0
Lowenstein, lf	3	0	1	0	2	0
e-Roenicke	1	0	0	0	0	0
Dauer, 2b	3	0	0	0	3	1
Cruz, 3b	3	0	0	0	0	3
Dempsey, c	2	0	0	0	6	1
a-Shelby, cf	1	0	0	0	0	0
McGregor, p	2	0	0	0	0	0
b-Nolan, c	1	0	0	0	1	0
Totals	32	1	5	1	27	9

a-struck out for Dempsey in 8th.
b-grounded out for McGregor in 8th.
c-flied out for Dwyer in 8th.
d-grounded out for Lezcano in 9th.
e-flied out for Lowenstein in 9th.

Error: Cruz. Double play: Ripken, Dauer, and Murray. Left on base: Phillies 2, Baltimore 4. Two-base hit: Bumbry. Home runs: Dwyer (1), Morgan (1), Maddox (1). Time, 2:22. Attendance, 52,204.

```
Phillies     0  0  0  0  0  1  0  1  0 — 2
Baltimore    1  0  0  0  0  0  0  0  0 — 1
```

Phillies	IP	H	R	ER	BB	SO
Denny (W)	7⅔	5	1	1	0	5
Holland (S)	1⅓	0	0	0	0	1

Baltimore	IP	H	R	ER	BB	SO
McGregor (L)	8	4	2	2	0	6
Stewart	⅔	1	0	0	0	1
T. Martinez	⅓	0	0	0	0	0

Game 2
Wednesday, October 12, at Baltimore

Phillies	AB	R	H	RBI	PO	A
Morgan, 2b	4	1	1	0	1	1
Rose, 1b	4	0	0	0	7	1
Schmidt, 3b	4	0	0	0	0	3
Lefebvre, rf	2	0	0	1	1	0
Matthews, lf	3	0	1	0	2	0
Gross, cf	3	0	0	0	5	0
Diaz, c	3	0	1	0	5	1
c-Samuel	0	0	0	0	0	0
Virgil, c	0	0	0	0	1	0
DeJesus, ss	3	0	0	0	1	1
Hudson, p	1	0	0	0	0	0
Hernandez, p	0	0	0	0	0	0
b-Hayes	1	0	0	0	0	0
Andersen, p	0	0	0	0	1	0
d-Perez	1	0	0	0	0	0
Reed, p	0	0	0	0	0	0
Totals	29	1	3	1	24	7

Baltimore	AB	R	H	RBI	PO	A
Bumbry, cf	2	0	0	0	2	0
a-Shelby, cf	2	1	1	0	1	0
Ford, rf	3	0	1	0	1	0
Ripken, ss	3	0	1	1	1	6
Murray, 1b	4	0	0	0	13	1
Lowenstein, lf	4	1	3	1	0	0
e-Landrum, lf	0	0	0	0	0	0
Dauer, 2b	4	1	1	0	2	2
Cruz, 3b	4	1	1	0	0	3
Dempsey, c	3	0	1	1	6	1
Boddicker, p	3	0	0	1	1	2
Totals	32	4	9	4	27	15

a-struck out for Bumbry in 5th.
b-struck out for Hernandez in 5th.
c-ran for Diaz in 8th.
d-hit into double play for Andersen in 8th.
e-ran for Lowenstein in 8th.

Error: Murray. Double play: Dauer, Ripken, and Murray. Left on base: Phillies 2, Baltimore 8. Two-base hits: Lowenstein, Dempsey. Home run: Lowenstein (1). Stolen bases: Morgan (1), Landrum (1). Sacrifice flies: Lefebvre, Boddicker. Time, 2:27. Attendance, 52,132.

```
Phillies     0  0  0  1  0  0  0  0  0 — 1
Baltimore    0  0  0  0  3  0  1  0  x — 4
```

Phillies	IP	H	R	ER	BB	SO
Hudson (L)	4⅓	5	3	3	0	3
Hernandez	⅔	0	0	0	1	1
Andersen	2	3	1	1	0	1
Reed	1	1	0	0	1	1

Baltimore	IP	H	R	ER	BB	SO
Boddicker (W)	9	3	1	0	0	6

Game 3
Friday, October 14, at Philadelphia

Baltimore	AB	R	H	RBI	PO	A
Shelby, cf	4	0	2	0	5	0
Ford, rf	3	1	1	1	1	1
Ripken, ss	3	0	0	0	1	3
Murray, 1b	4	0	0	0	10	0
Roenicke, lf	4	0	0	0	1	1
Dauer, 2b	4	0	0	0	4	2
Cruz, 3b	3	0	0	0	0	4
Dempsey, c	4	1	2	0	5	2
Flanagan, p	1	0	0	0	0	0
a-Singleton	1	0	0	0	0	0
Palmer, p	0	0	0	0	0	0
b-Ayala	1	1	1	1	0	0
Stewart, p	1	0	0	0	0	0
T. Martinez p	0	0	0	0	0	0
Totals	33	3	6	2	27	13

Phillies	AB	R	H	RBI	PO	A
Morgan, 2b	3	1	1	1	5	2
Lezcano, rf	4	0	1	0	1	0
Hayes, rf	0	0	0	0	1	0
Schmidt, 3b	4	0	0	0	0	4
Matthews, lf	3	1	1	1	0	0
Perez, 1b	4	0	1	0	8	0
Maddox, cf	4	0	0	0	1	0
Diaz, c	3	0	2	0	11	0
c-Lefebvre	0	0	0	0	0	0
d-Rose	1	0	0	0	0	0
DeJesus, ss	3	0	2	0	0	5
Carlton, p	3	0	0	0	0	0
e-Virgil	1	0	0	0	0	0
Holland, p	0	0	0	0	0	0
Totals	33	2	8	2	27	11

a-Struck out for Flanagan in the 5th.
b-Singled for Palmer in the 7th.
c-Announced for Diaz in the 9th.
d-Grounded out for Lefebvre in the 9th.
e-Grounded out for Holland in the 9th.

Errors: Cruz, Schmidt, DeJesus. Double plays: DeJesus, Morgan, Perez; Schmidt, Morgan, Perez. Left on base: Baltimore 6, Phillies 7. Two-base hits: Dempsey 2. Home runs: Matthews (1), Morgan (2), Ford (1). Wild pitch: Palmer, Carlton. Time, 2:35. Attendance, 65,792.

```
Baltimore   0 0 0 0 0 1 2 0 0—3
Phillies    0 1 1 0 0 0 0 0 0—2
```

Baltimore	IP	H	R	ER	BB	SO
Flanagan	4	6	2	2	1	1
Palmer (W)	2	2	0	0	1	1
Stewart	2	0	0	0	1	3
T. Martinez (S)	1	0	0	0	0	0

Phillies	IP	H	R	ER	BB	SO
Carlton (L)	6⅔	5	3	2	3	7
Holland	2⅓	1	0	0	0	4

Game 4
Saturday, October 15, at Philadelphia

Baltimore	AB	R	H	RBI	PO	A
Bumbry, cf	3	0	0	0	3	0
e-Ford	1	0	0	0	0	0
Stewart, p	1	0	0	0	0	0
T. Martinez, p	0	0	0	0	0	0
Dwyer, rf	5	2	2	0	0	0
Landrum, rf	0	0	0	0	0	0
Ripken, ss	5	1	1	0	0	1
Murray, 1b	4	0	1	0	9	0
Lowenstein, lf	4	1	1	0	2	0
Dauer, 2b, 3b	4	1	3	3	3	2
Cruz, 3b	2	0	1	0	0	1
a-Nolan, c	1	0	0	0	2	0
Dempsey, c	1	0	0	0	3	0
b-Singleton	0	0	0	1	0	0
c-Sakata, 2b	1	0	0	0	2	2
Davis, p	2	0	0	0	0	1
d-Shelby, cf	1	0	1	1	3	0
Totals	35	5	10	5	27	7

Phillies	AB	R	H	RBI	PO	A
Morgan, 2b	5	0	0	0	1	1
Rose, 1b	3	1	2	1	5	3
Schmidt, 3b	4	0	1	0	0	0
Lefebvre, rf	3	0	1	1	2	0
g-Perez	1	0	1	0	0	0
h-Samuel	0	0	0	0	0	0
Lezcano, rf	0	0	0	0	1	0
Matthews, lf	3	0	1	0	3	0
G. Gross, cf	3	0	0	0	3	0
i-Maddox	1	0	0	0	0	0
Diaz, c	4	1	2	0	7	0
j-Dernier	0	1	0	0	0	0
DeJesus, ss	4	0	0	0	2	1
Denny, p	2	1	1	1	3	1
Hernandez, p	0	0	0	0	0	0
Reed, p	0	0	0	0	0	0
f-Hayes	1	0	0	0	0	0
Andersen, p	0	0	0	0	0	1
k-Virgil, c	1	0	1	1	0	0
Totals	35	4	10	4	27	7

a-Intentionally walked for Cruz in the 6th.
b-Walked for Dempsey in the 6th.
c-Ran for Singleton in the 6th.
d-Hit a sacrifice fly for Davis in the 6th.
e-Struck out for Bumbry in the 6th.
f-Grounded out for Reed in the 7th.
g-Singled for Lefebvre in the 8th.
h-Ran for Perez in the 8th.
i-Grounded out for G. Gross in the 9th.
j-Ran for Diaz in the 9th.
k-Singled for Andersen in the 9th.

Error: Lowenstein. Double plays: Dauer, Murray, Andersen; DeJesus, Morgan, Ripken, Sakata, Murray. Left on base: Baltimore 8, Phillies 6. Two-base hits: Lefebvre, Diaz, Rose, Dauer, Dwyer. Sacrifice fly: Shelby. Wild pitch: Davis. Balk: Stewart. Time, 2:50. Attendance, 66,947.

```
Baltimore   0 0 0 2 0 2 1 0 0—5
Phillies    0 0 0 1 2 0 0 0 1—4
```

Baltimore	IP	H	R	ER	BB	SO
Davis (W)	5	6	3	3	1	3
Stewart	2⅓	1	0	0	1	2
T. Martinez (S)	1⅔	3	1	1	0	0

Phillies	IP	H	R	ER	BB	SO
Denny (L)	5⅓	7	4	4	3	4
Hernandez	⅓	0	0	0	0	0
Reed	1⅓	2	1	1	1	3
Andersen	2	1	0	0	0	0

Game 5
Sunday, October 16, at Philadelphia

Baltimore	AB	R	H	RBI	PO	A
Bumbry, cf	2	0	0	1	3	0
c-Shelby, cf	1	0	0	0	1	0
Ford, rf	4	0	0	0	3	0
Landrum, rf	0	0	0	0	1	0
Ripken, ss	3	1	0	0	3	0
Murray, 1b	4	2	3	3	6	0
Lowenstein, lf	2	0	0	0	0	0
b-Roenicke, lf	2	0	0	0	1	0
Dauer, 2b	4	0	0	0	2	1
Cruz, 3b	4	0	0	0	0	6
Dempsey, c	3	2	2	1	7	0
McGregor, p	3	0	0	0	0	0
Totals	**32**	**5**	**5**	**5**	**27**	**7**

Phillies	AB	R	H	RBI	PO	A
Morgan, 2b	3	0	1	0	0	1
Rose, rf	4	0	2	0	3	0
Schmidt, 3b	4	0	0	0	1	2
Matthews, lf	4	0	0	0	6	0
Perez, 1b	4	0	0	0	5	1
Maddox, cf	4	0	2	0	3	0
Diaz, c	2	0	0	0	7	0
DeJesus, ss	3	0	0	0	1	2
Hudson, p	1	0	0	0	0	0
Bystrom, p	0	0	0	0	0	0
a-Samuel	1	0	0	0	0	0
Hernandez, p	0	0	0	0	1	0
d-Lezcano	1	0	0	0	0	0
Reed, p	0	0	0	0	0	0
Totals	**31**	**0**	**5**	**0**	**27**	**6**

a-Flied out for Bystrom in the 5th.
b-Struck out for Lowenstein in the 6th.
c-Flied out for Bumbry in the 8th.
d-Grounded out for Hernandez in the 8th.

Baltimore 0 1 1 2 1 0 0 0 0 — 5
Phillies   0 0 0 0 0 0 0 0 0 — 0

Error: Diaz. Double plays: Cruz, Dauer, Murray. Left on base: Baltimore 2, Phillies 6. Two-base hits: Dempsey, Maddox. Three-base hit: Morgan. Home runs: Murray 2 (2), Dempsey (1). Sacrifice fly: Bumbry. Wild pitch: Bystrom. Time, 2:21. Attendance, 67,064.

Baltimore	IP	H	R	ER	BB	SO
McGregor (W)	9	5	0	0	2	6

Phillies	IP	H	R	ER	BB	SO
Hudson (L)	4*	4	5	5	1	3
Bystrom	1	0	0	0	0	1
Hernandez	3	0	0	0	0	3
Reed	1	1	0	0	0	0

*Hudson pitched to one batter in the 5th.

COMPOSITE BATTING AVERAGES

Baltimore Orioles

Player	G	AB	R	H	2B	3B	HR	RBI	BB	SO	E	BA
Ayala	1	1	1	1	0	0	0	1	0	0	0	1.000
Bumbry	4	11	0	1	1	0	0	1	0	1	0	.091
Cruz	5	16	1	2	0	0	0	1	3	2	.125
Dauer	5	19	2	4	1	0	0	3	0	3	0	.211
Dempsey	5	13	3	5	4	0	1	2	2	2	0	.385
Dwyer	2	8	3	3	1	0	1	1	0	0	0	.375
Ford	5	12	1	2	0	0	1	1	1	5	0	.167
Landrum	3	0	0	0	0	0	0	0	0	0	0	—
Lowenstein	4	13	2	5	1	0	1	1	0	3	1	.385
Murray	5	20	2	5	0	0	2	3	1	4	1	.250
Nolan	2	2	0	0	0	0	0	0	1	0	0	.000
Ripken	5	18	2	3	0	0	0	1	3	4	0	.167
Roenicke	3	7	0	0	0	0	0	0	0	2	0	.000
Sakata	1	1	0	0	0	0	0	0	0	0	0	.000
Shelby	5	9	1	4	0	0	0	1	0	4	0	.444
Singleton	2	1	0	0	0	0	0	1	1	1	0	.000
Boddicker	1	3	0	0	0	0	0	1	0	1	0	.000
Davis	1	2	0	0	0	0	0	0	0	2	0	.000
Flanagan	1	1	0	0	0	0	0	0	0	1	0	.000
T. Martinez	3	0	0	0	0	0	0	0	0	0	0	—
McGregor	2	5	0	0	0	0	0	0	0	0	0	.000
Palmer	1	0	0	0	0	0	0	0	0	0	0	—
Stewart	3	2	0	0	0	0	0	0	0	1	0	.000
Totals	**5**	**164**	**18**	**35**	**8**	**0**	**6**	**17**	**10**	**37**	**4**	**.213**

Philadelphia Phillies

Player	G	AB	R	H	2B	3B	HR	RBI	BB	SO	E	BA
DeJesus	5	16	0	2	0	0	0	0	1	2	1	.125
Dernier	1	0	1	0	0	0	0	0	0	0	0	—
Diaz	5	15	1	5	1	0	0	0	1	2	1	.333
G. Gross	2	6	0	0	0	0	0	0	0	0	0	.000
Hayes	4	3	0	0	0	0	0	0	0	1	0	.000
Lefebvre	3	5	0	1	1	0	0	2	0	1	0	.200
Lezcano	4	8	0	1	0	0	0	0	0	2	0	.125
Maddox	4	12	1	3	1	0	1	1	0	2	0	.250
Matthews	5	16	1	4	0	0	1	1	2	2	0	.250
Morgan	5	19	3	5	0	1	2	2	2	3	0	.263
Perez	4	10	0	2	0	0	0	0	0	2	0	.200
Rose	5	16	1	5	1	0	0	1	1	3	0	.313
Samuel	3	1	0	0	0	0	0	0	0	0	0	.000
Schmidt	5	20	0	1	0	0	0	0	6	1	.050
Virgil	3	2	0	1	0	0	0	1	0	0	0	.500
Andersen	2	0	0	0	0	0	0	0	0	0	0	—
Bystrom	1	0	0	0	0	0	0	0	0	0	0	—
Carlton	1	3	0	0	0	0	0	0	0	1	0	.000
Denny	2	5	1	1	0	0	0	1	0	1	0	.200
Hernandez	3	0	0	0	0	0	0	0	0	0	0	—
Holland	2	0	0	0	0	0	0	0	0	0	0	—
Hudson	2	2	0	0	0	0	0	0	0	1	0	.000
Reed	3	0	0	0	0	0	0	0	0	0	0	—
Totals	**5**	**159**	**9**	**31**	**4**	**1**	**4**	**9**	**7**	**29**	**3**	**.195**

COMPOSITE PITCHING AVERAGES

Baltimore Orioles

Pitcher	W	L	ERA	G	SV	IP	H	R	ER	BB	SO
Boddicker	1	0	0.00	1	0	9.0	3	1	0	0	6
Davis	1	0	5.40	1	0	5.0	6	3	3	1	3
Flanagan	0	0	4.50	1	0	4.0	6	2	2	1	1
T. Martinez	0	0	3.00	3	2	3.0	3	1	1	0	0
McGregor	1	1	1.06	2	0	17.0	9	2	2	2	12
Palmer	1	0	0.00	1	0	2.0	2	0	0	1	1
Stewart	0	0	0.00	3	0	5.0	2	0	0	2	6
Totals	**4**	**1**	**1.60**	**5**	**2**	**45.0**	**31**	**9**	**8**	**7**	**29**

Philadelphia Phillies

Pitcher	W	L	ERA	G	SV	IP	H	R	ER	BB	SO
Andersen	0	0	2.25	2	0	4.0	4	1	1	0	1
Bystrom	0	0	0.00	1	0	1.0	0	0	0	0	1
Carlton	0	1	2.70	1	0	6.2	5	3	2	3	7
Denny	1	1	3.46	2	0	13.0	12	5	5	3	9
Hernandez	0	0	0.00	3	0	4.0	0	0	0	1	4
Holland	0	0	0.00	2	1	3.2	1	0	0	0	5
Hudson	0	2	8.64	2	0	8.1	9	8	8	1	6
Reed	0	0	2.70	3	0	3.1	4	1	1	2	4
Totals	**1**	**4**	**3.48**	**5**	**1**	**44.0**	**35**	**18**	**17**	**10**	**37**

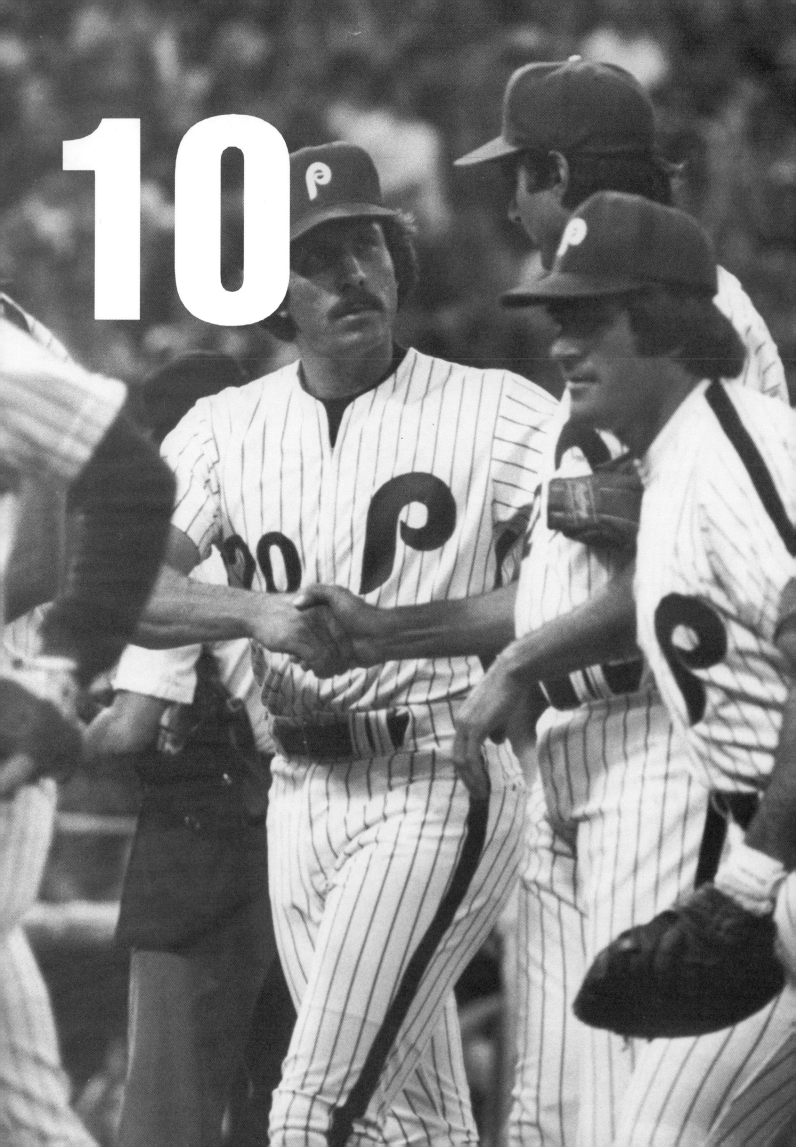

The Golden Era

Most of the history of the Philadelphia Phillies was written at the bottom of a mine shaft.

This, however, was not a franchise searching for the Hope Diamond. This was a franchise seeking hope on the diamond—and not finding much. Between 1917 and 1949, happiness was a fourth-place finish in 1932—and a lot of last-place finishes before and after.

The period between Grover Cleveland Alexander and Robin Roberts was typified by a couple of pitchers nicknamed "Boom-Boom" and "Losing Pitcher." Even great hitters like Cy Williams, Chuck Klein, and Dolph Camilli couldn't overcome pitching like that.

Ernest Hemingway should have covered the Phillies during that period. He already had the perfect title—*A Farewell to Arms.*

The glory of the 1950 Whiz Kids was supposed to last a decade. It didn't even make it into 1951. Nine years after that, Eddie Sawyer, the Whiz Kids' manager, didn't make it into Game Two. And a year after that, the Phillies went 23 games without winning one.

They teased us in 1964, then Gene Mauch and John Quinn wheezed us. Young guys left, old guys came. And by 1969 they were being propped up by an expansion team. Two years later the expansion Expos passed them.

In 1972, Steve Carlton won 27 games. The days the Phillies played without him, they were 32–87. You want to know how bad that is? A percentage of .269 is how bad. The awful 1961 team had a percentage of .305.

And then, two years later, it began to happen. You spend most of your life in a mine shaft, and you are bound to strike gold at some point.

For a decade, this franchise glittered.

The miser's touch of William F. Baker was replaced by the Midas touch.

Mike Schmidt and Steve Carlton rode the Golden Decade to the Hall of Fame.

Pete Rose jumped on for the ride at the midway point. Eventually, he may deplane at Cooperstown, too, but for now all bets are off.

Garry Maddox was the best center fielder in baseball in the Golden Decade. Dave Cash was as good a second baseman as there was at the start of it, then Manny Trillo was splendid in the middle, and Hall of Famer Joe Morgan had one helluva month at the end.

Greg Luzinski was the player for whom the Liberty Bell tolled. Luzinski hit the center field replica at the Vet on a fly one night on his way to many other gargantuan homers.

Dick Allen came back for awhile, and Jay Johnstone took part of the trip just for laughs. Bob Boone caught more games than anyone during the Golden Decade on his way to catching more games than anyone in major league history ever had. Bake McBride gave it everything he had on knees that belonged in a junkyard.

Richie Hebner saw the ball and hit it. Larry Bowa saw the ball and caught it, maybe better than any other shortstop ever has. Dick Ruthven left and came back better than ever. Larry Christenson kept getting better until injuries got the better of him. John Denny put the demon inside him on the unemployment line for one glorious year.

Gene Garber turned his back on the hitters, Tug McGraw turned the screwball on them, and Ron Reed had a fastball in his late 30s that would make a first-round draft choice green with envy.

The Phillie Phanatic made his first appearance during the club's Golden Era.

Mike Schmidt, Steve Carlton, and Pete Rose led the Phillies in their most glorious era.

The power of Dick Allen and Greg Luzinski in 1976 helped the Phillies launch a series of four divisional titles in five years.

The Golden Decade (1974–83) was a special time to be a Phillies fan. The only World Championship in 110 years came during this time. So did as many World Series appearances as in the other 100 years combined. Not even counting the split-season playoff games in 1981, the Phillies played 31 post-season games during that period. For the rest of their history, they've played nine.

The stadium was new. So were the uniforms. So were the attitudes. And the perception. The Phillies no longer were looked upon as an organization bumbling its way through life with stale leadership, a rundown stadium in a more rundown part of town, and a farm system that hadn't produced a bumper crop of legitimate major leaguers since the Whiz Kids.

There had been some exceptions. Dick Allen had as much talent as anyone who ever played the game. Ferguson Jenkins became a Hall of Fame pitcher. Chris Short developed into a lefthanded pitcher second only to Sandy Koufax for a period in the mid-1960s.

But mostly, it had been an organization limping through life on the legs of an owner who had gotten off the bus in the early 1950s and never reboarded and a general manager who was more interested in saving a dollar than doing what it took to build a winner.

Under president Bob Carpenter, general manager John Quinn, and youthful manager Gene Mauch, the Phillies had almost stolen a pennant in 1964. They came thisclose, and Mauch then persuaded the other two that the way to overcome the final obstacle was to add veteran players. As a result, the precious little that the farm system had produced was traded away.

The veterans never got the job done. And when their careers were over, the cupboard was bare.

But it was being restocked, thanks to two men who would become the cornerstones around which the Golden Decade was constructed.

One was Ruly Carpenter, son of the owner and a football player at Yale, from which he was graduated in 1962. Bob Carpenter had been thrown into baseball without any formal education in the nuances of the sport when he returned from World War II and was thrust into the position of president of the team his father had bought in 1943.

Bob Carpenter's money had put the Whiz Kids together; his lack of knowledge about the "inside" of the game and his lack of insight in recognizing the impact that black athletes would have on the sport led to the team's demise in the late 1950s and 1960s.

General manager John Quinn inspects construction of Veterans Stadium in 1969 with Ruly Carpenter, then the son of Phillies owner Bob Carpenter but soon to be club president.

The other cornerstone was Paul Owens, a former minor league player with a keen understanding of scouting and player development and a physical resemblance to Pope Paul. Dick Allen nicknamed Owens "the Pope" in 1963, and the name stuck.

As much as anything else, the Golden Era was the result of the combination of Ruly and the Pope.

They were thrown together in May 1965. They would stay together until Ruly, disgusted with the direction in which free agency was pushing baseball, would sell the team during the 1981 World Series. And their legacy would live through the 1983 World Series, which marked the end of 10 glorious years in which the Phillies won two pennants, were involved in post-season play six times, had seasons that averaged 87 victories and 17 games over .500, won .557 percent of their games, and drew an average of more than 2.3 million fans.

The Phillies had winning records nine of those 10 seasons, missing by just two games in the other. To put these feats in their proper perspective, the franchise had just 12 winning records between 1918 and 1973. Since 1983, it has had one.

And the Golden Decade happened in large part because Ruly and the Pope were teamed in a development that caused hardly a ripple when it happened—and for good reason.

Phillies fans were excited in May 1965. Not that it took much for that to happen. Chico Fernandez had them on their feet screaming in 1957, for crying out loud.

But at this point, the excitement was justified. The team had nearly won the pennant the year before. There were legitimate stars—Allen, Johnny Callison, Jim Bunning, Short—who were worth watching. Mauch was a brilliant young manager, an innovator who loved to outguess his opponent.

But the future was shaky. The farm system was not producing replacement talent. Nobody knew it better than Owens when he became farm director on May 22, succeeding Clay Dennis.

"When I took over in 1965, we were really bad," Owens said during a long interview in May 1992. "If they think we were bad in 1989 and 1990, I think we were just about as bad then."

Not only that, but Owens had an immediate problem staring at him.

"I took over 10 days before the first June draft," he said. "No one knew how the hell that was going to work. That first draft I couldn't figure anything out. I was reading reports during those 10 days, and I was getting more confused. I knew the West Coast pretty well because I had just come out of there. So I just went with the scouts who through my managing years always seemed to sign guys who at least could play."

Considering the time and scouting constraints they faced, the Phillies did reasonably well in the first draft, which was held in early June. They drafted seven players who made major league appearances, including second choice Larry Hisle, third selection Billy Champion, and fifth choice Terry Harmon.

No sooner was the draft over, though, than Owens began to learn other facts about his new role.

"We had a helluva rebuilding year to do," he remembered. "For the rest of 1965, I had to borrow six catchers. Harry Dalton had a good organization in Baltimore and he was good enough to loan me players to get through the summer. That was a good lesson right there. I said I'll never get short of catchers again.

"I've always felt that the strength of any organization is your scouting and your development at the lower level. Even today with people moving around, a good farm system is still the basis for continuity."

Owens was given some immediate help to try to straighten out the organizational mess—the owner's kid.

Ruly Carpenter had joined the front office in 1963, working under vice president George Harrison to learn the financial end of the operation. Now it was time for him to learn all about player personnel. Nobody knew the value of that knowledge—and the problems created by a lack of it—better than Bob Carpenter.

"When I took over," Owens remembered, "Ruly's dad said, 'I want Ruly to work under you and learn the business. I came out of the service and didn't have that opportunity. My dad said here's the club, you know. I want Ruly to have a background. Teach him everything you can, good and bad.'

"Ruly worked with me for seven years. The first job I gave him that first summer, we dug into the archives and went back for six years on all our scouts we had at the time. Some had been there 10–12 years. I had Ruly work on that for about two months—who they had signed, how much money they had spent, how far those players had gone, blah, blah, blah.

"I knew there was something wrong. The only knowledge I had from

Steve Carlton was still entertaining post-game interviews with the press in 1972 when he won 27 games for a last place team.

scouting on the West Coast in 1962, '63, and '64 was that Gene Martin, who was the farm director then, would bring me back for a month to run the Leesburg camp."

In 1964, Owens met Ruly for the first time when both were assigned to the Leesburg camp, which was where the lower minor league players worked out in spring training. A meeting with Martin there that spring shocked Owens.

"I sat in at that meeting and you'd have thought we had 100 prospects to hear the farm director tell it," he said. "Ruly and I talked about it. I said in my opinion—and Ruly agreed with me—that two of the 100 kids at the lower level had a chance to make the big leagues."

Neither one made it. But Owens and Carpenter both recognized that a lot of work had to be done to get the organization back to a competitive state. And a year later, they found themselves trying to eradicate the problem together.

"A month after I got the job, I said, 'Cripes, it's worse than I thought,'" Owens said. "Meanwhile, Ruly spent two months going through all that stuff in the archives. In August I went in and had a meeting with (Bob) Carpenter and Quinn. I said, 'Look, any donkey can keep this farm director's job for four years. But I'm not interested in it unless I can make the changes I want to make.'

"I said all I wanted was a two-hour meeting without any interruptions. And just to show I wasn't being partial, I said I was going to go down the scouts' list alphabetically. I said I wanted to do it right away because if you waste a year in this game, you are four years away from making it up. I told them I wanted it, otherwise I'd go back to the Coast and be as good a scout as I can be. But, I said, 'I can't do this job unless you guys okay this plan.'"

Bob Carpenter and John Quinn told Owens he could have his way. And Owens sharpened the hatchet that eventually put the Phillies on the cutting edge of player development.

"I had 20 scouts and I let eight of them go," Owens said. "I hired eight new people and put two of the others on probation. That's how we started, and four years later, in 1969, we won the Topps award for best minor leagues system. We started getting the Luzinskis and Bowas and players like that. So a lot of what we did in the early '70s was based on what we did in the farm system when we took over."

Just putting a top-notch scouting team together took time. The 1966 draft yielding only weak-hitting infielder John Vukovich, flaky pitcher Lowell Palmer, lefty pitcher Ken Reynolds, and Steve Arlin, the righthanded pitcher from Ohio State who collected a big bonus from the Phillies but never pitched for the team.

A year later, the Phillies drafted—but did not sign—Darrell Evans in January. Their first picks in the regular and secondary phases of the June draft—outfielder Pat Skrable and pitcher Doug Sandstedt—were washouts. But in 1968 they began putting the pieces of the Golden Decade puzzle together when they made Greg Luzinski, a first baseman from the Chicago suburbs, their number-one choice.

In 1969 they reached into the sixth round to grab a slow-footed third baseman from Stanford University named Bob Boone. And two years later, they ignored superscout Tony Lucadello's pleas to take a shortstop with questionable knees out of Ohio University and drafted pitcher Roy Thomas in the first round. When the shortstop was still available in the second round, they grabbed him.

That's how Mike Schmidt became a Phillie. Meanwhile, Boone was making the transition to catcher, a position he had hardly ever played before.

"People forget we drafted him as a third baseman," Owens said. "I can remember the year I sent him down (to the Florida Instructional League) at the end of 1970. I told him that his dad had started out as a catcher and switched to the infield. I asked him, 'Would you mind going down there and give it a try at catcher?' I told him he didn't run that well but he had a good arm and he was smart.

"I asked him, 'Have you ever done any catching?' He said, no, not much. But I had Andy Seminick and Lou Kahn both down there to work with him. A

Paul Owens' first major trade as general manager brought pitchers Jim Lonborg (above) and Ken Brett from the Milwaukee Brewers for infielder Don Money.

Yes, Dave Cash could turn the double play just as well as he could give the Phillies a slogan while teaching them to be winners.

week later, they called me and said, 'Pope, you won't believe it! This guy's a natural. Everything you tell him, he automatically picks it up.'

"That was the start of Bobby Boone being a catcher, and now he's caught more games than anyone who has ever played the game. And he didn't start until he was what? Twenty-four years old?"

While the seeds were being planted at the developmental level, the parent club seemed 24 years behind the times. Gene Mauch had left the scene in 1968 after battling with Dick Allen, who in turn was traded to the St. Louis Cardinals in 1970. The deal originally brought Curt Flood and Tim McCarver to the team. When Flood refused to report, the Cardinals substituted a gimpy first baseman named Willie Montanez. Willie the Phillie became a star, then was dealt straight up to the San Francisco Giants for Garry Maddox early in the 1975 season.

Frank Lucchesi became the manager in 1970 and instilled some spark in the big club, but he had nowhere near enough talent to compete.

In 1971, Veterans Stadium finally opened. Jim Bunning pitched the first game, Don Money hit a home run, and the Phillies beat the Montreal Expos, 4–1. For the rest of the season, they won 66 games, lost 95 and set an all-time attendance record. On the field, about the only thing worth cheering happened on the road when Rick Wise pitched a no-hitter and hit two home runs in a game against the Cincinnati Reds. Wise, Montanez (30 home runs), and an aging Deron Johnson (34 homers) were the only heros the fans had.

Then, early in the 1972 spring training, in John Quinn's last major trade, the Phillies sent Wise to the Cardinals in a deal that was ripped by the fans and the media. It turned out to be one of the best in the team's history. It yielded a Hall of Fame–quality pitcher named Steve Carlton.

"It was a trade we made with three five-minute phone calls," Owens remembered. "I got to Florida late in February. John got there a couple days ahead of me. We always took each other out to dinner on our anniversary. Ours happened to be February 23. We went to eat where John always ate, a restaurant behind the hotel.

"John was always gentlemanly when he was around women. He wouldn't talk business around them. He didn't think it was polite. Marci and I picked John and his wife up at the hotel, sat down to have a drink. John leaned over to me and whispered in my ear, 'Wise for Carlton.' I straightened up and leaned over to him and said, 'Even up?' He nodded. I said, 'Go,' because I had scouted Carlton. 'Go in a minute.' "

Owens said that the trade was made for financial, not talent reasons. The Phillies were having trouble signing Wise, a 17-game winner. St. Louis was having the same problem with Carlton, who had won 20.

"Both owners were saying to get the best thing you can for him," Owens said. Still Quinn was shocked at how quickly his farm director had agreed the trade was a good one for the Phillies.

"John said, 'Don't you want to check with your scouts?' I said, 'No, I know him well. The guy's going to be a great one, I just love him.' He said, 'We'll talk (to Cardinal general manager Bing Devine) when we get back to the hotel.' When we got back, we went to the bedroom so we didn't have to conduct the business in front of the wives. John called Bing back at 9 o'clock and said we'd make the deal. Bing said he wanted to run it by (manager Red) Schoendienst. He said he'd call back at 9 A.M., but as far as he was concerned, we had a deal."

The deal was announced on February 25, 1972. Without it, the Phillies would have been dismal that season. Come to think of it, even with it, they were dismal. Carlton had arguably the greatest season a pitcher has ever had, winning 27 games, completing 30 of 41 starts, striking out 310 in 341 innings, and putting together an earned run average of 1.98. The rest of the team went 32–87. The Phillies finished sixth, 11 games out of fifth.

But there were major moves being made that would redirect the team's future. Quinn was replaced as general manager by Owens. Shortly after that, Lucchesi was fired, and Owens went from the front office to the dugout for the rest of the season because he wanted to see what he had to work with. In November, Ruly Carpenter replaced his dad as club president.

A trade in May 1975 brought Dick Allen (right) back to Philadelphia, where he went to work for a second generation of Carpenter owners in Ruly.

What Owens had learned from his stint as manager was that what he appeared to have was Carlton and little else. But even in that dismal season, many of the building blocks were in order. Larry Bowa was the shortstop. Luzinski was in left field. Boone and Schmidt were completing their minor-league apprenticeships. And that winter, Owens made a key trade, sending Money to the Milwaukee Brewers for pitchers Jim Lonborg and Ken Brett. Lonborg became an important member of the 1976 and 1977 NL East championship teams; Brett won 13 games in 1973 and was traded for second baseman Dave Cash before the 1974 campaign.

"I loved Don Money, and he was a helluva ball player," Owens said, "but I knew I had Mike Schmidt coming. I was probably the only one who knew at that time that he was going to be a good ball player. But that's how I was able to make the trade with Milwaukee to get Lonborg and Brett, which gave us some stability with the pitching."

The Phillies also hired Danny Ozark as manager for the 1973 season. They finished last again in Ozark's first season, but they were actually in the race until September. In fact, they were only 4½ games out of first place on August 21. But Tug McGraw kept screaming "You Gotta Believe" in the New York Mets' clubhouse. The Mets believed. The Phillies wound up 11½ games behind the Mets in a year when Carlton slipped to 13–20.

"Turn Carlton's record around and we have a shot at winning the pennant," Owens said at the time. "We're only one or two players away from the glory seat."

The Golden Decade was about to begin, but the Phillies still had to learn how to win. Owens made an off-season deal to get Dave Cash, who taught them how.

"You'd have thought I got a second-line player for Brett," Owens said. "All the guy did was get over 200 hits for two straight years. He helped make Bowa a much better player. Dave Cash knew how to play; he knew how to win. I liked Kenny Brett. He was probably one of the best athletes I ever had. He probably could have been like his brother (future Hall of Fame third baseman George) if he had played every day. But it was one of those things I had to do. This was one of those trades where you had to believe in yourself."

The 1974 Phillies were like the cast of *Saturday Night Live*—not quite ready for prime time, but budding superstars. Schmidt went from a struggling freshman to a star sophomore, leading the major leagues in home runs. Cash contributed 206 hits, turned a league-leading 141 double plays, and gave the team the leadoff hitter it needed. Owens bought relief pitcher Gene Garber from the Royals in mid-season and added right fielder Ollie Brown in a cash deal with the Houston Astros. He also signed free agent Jay Johnstone, completing the right field combination that would help the team win the division in 1976.

"I remember when we picked up Jay Johnstone and Ollie Brown," Owens said. "Both those guys had little reputations picked up in baseball, some right and some wrong. Jay's was being so flaky. I knew Danny didn't like him at all going back to their Dodger days. Ollie Brown was supposed to be surly.

"But when I got those guys, I brought them in before Danny even talked to them. I told them, 'I know your background, know what people think, but I scouted both of you in high school, and I saw you early in your career.'

"I told each one of them, 'All I'm telling you is I've got a helluva ball club down there. I've got great guys that want to win and play. I'm wiping the sheet clean as far as I'm concerned. If you don't want to play with these guys and get enthused with the way these guys play, then your ass'll be gone as quick as I got you.'

"Jay got another 11 years in the big leagues, and Ollie Brown was the most popular player we had on the club. And they didn't cost me anything. Sometimes you got to have a feel and go with your own conviction."

The 1974 Phillies were tied for first place as late as August 2 before they faded and finished third, eight games behind the Pirates. Then Owens pulled the trigger on one major trade in the off-season and two more within a three-day period in May 1975.

The off-season deal landed McGraw and two minor league types for catching prospect John Stearns, who had been a top draft pick in 1973, center fielder Del Unser, and relief pitcher Mac Scarce. Garber and McGraw gave the team a potent righty-lefty bullpen combination.

On May 4, 1975, Owens moved the immensely popular Montanez to the Giants for Maddox, who was struggling with the bat but was the kind of defensive center fielder that comes along once a generation.

"I caught hell from the fans for the Maddox deal," Owens said. "But those are things you just have to do, and you say if I'm going to fail, I'm going to fail my way and not somebody else's way.

"When I traded for Garry, I knew I had to have that gazelle, especially with

In the late 1970s, champagne parties celebrating divisional championships became commonplace with the Phillies, but it wasn't until 1980 that they were able to toast a World Series title.

Bull on one side and I didn't know who on the other. I think for eight or nine years, Maddox was the best center fielder in baseball. He hit .330 for me one year, and he was consistent. He could play shallow and still catch balls over his head with that long, tall gait of his."

Three days after he got Maddox, Owens brought Dick Allen back to Philadelphia, getting the slugger from the Atlanta Braves, where he had refused to sign, along with catcher Johnny Oates for prospects Jim Essian and Barry Bonnell. And two months later he signed McCarver, who had been released by the Boston Red Sox.

"A lot of the talk at the time was that all Tim did was catch Carlton every fourth day," Owens said. "But it was more than that. I told Boonie it was a break for him because all he had to do was catch the other three days and take a day of rest. I told him it would keep him strong."

The 1975 Phillies made a good run at the Pirates. They were tied for first on August 18 but played two games below .500 the rest of the season and finished second, 6½ games behind. But Larry Christenson, the first-round draft choice in 1971, had developed into an 11-game winner, and Tommy Underwood, the second selection in 1972, was even better, winning 14. Bowa blossomed into a .305 hitter. Cash also hit .305. It was the first time in 26 years that each member of a major league keystone combination had batted over .300.

That winter Owens made two trades. Former phenom outfielder Mike Anderson was moved to the Cardinals for pitcher Ron Reed. Dick Ruthven, infielder Alan Bannister, and pitcher Roy Thomas were packaged to the Chicago White Sox for pitcher Jim Kaat.

The Phillies were ready to show the rest of the NL East just how good they were.

Here's how good: They took first place in the division on May 9 and never gave it up. By June 29, they were 50–20, and fans were wondering if they might break the 1954 Cleveland Indians' record of 111 victories. In late July they won four of five games from the Pirates to open a 13-game lead. On August 26, they beat NL West leader Cincinnati, 5–4, in 13 innings and were 15 in front.

Then they lost eight in a row, won one, and were swept by the Pirates in a three-game series, including a Labor Day doubleheader. After the twin-bill defeat, Larry Bowa was asked a question by a reporter. He opened his mouth but could not speak. Talk of a repeat of the Great Choke of 1964 was everywhere. Only McGraw seemed unaffected by the slide.

Paul Owens says the Phillies wouldn't have won in 1977 without Bake McBride (right), being congratulated by Tommy Hutton after hitting a home run.

On September 17 the Phillies lost to the Cubs and saw their lead over Pittsburgh trimmed to three games. But this time they didn't fold. Instead they won 13 of their last 16 games for a final nine-game margin and a franchise-best 101 victories. Nevertheless, they weren't quite a match yet for the Reds, who swept the playoffs in three games, then beat the Yankees in four in a row in the World Series.

There were some cracks to spackle in the off-season. Allen was released, and the Phillies signed Richie Hebner as their first entry into the free-agent market. They refused to sign Cash to a multiyear contract, but Owens was able to plug that gap by trading Oates to the Dodgers for Ted Sizemore. Davey Johnson, an infielder who once had hit 43 home runs in a season with the Atlanta Braves, returned from a stint in Japan and was signed by Owens "before anybody knew he was back in the States."

Then, on June 15, with the 1977 club in fourth place, just three games over .500 and eight games behind the Chicago Cubs, Owens made another major trade. He sent Underwood, Dane Iorg, and Rick Bosetti to the Cardinals for right fielder Bake McBride.

"We wouldn't have won in 1977 or the next year if I don't make the McBride deal, but in 1977 we had a lot of controversy about it," Owens said. "I knew he was dissatisfied over in St. Louis, and I knew he had some knee problems. But I also knew we just had to have a good lefthanded hitter. And all he did was hit about .340 with 11 homers and steal 20-some bases."

With McBride in the lineup, the 1977 Phillies were dynamite. They passed the Chicago Cubs in early August, wound up with their second straight 101-victory season and a five-game margin over an excellent Pirates team. They were 70–33 with McBride on the roster.

"That might have been our best ball club," Owens said. "We had a helluva bench. We could get to the 11th, 12th inning and never get set up. That roster went along with what I always believed. You need a good front eight, but you really win pennants with nine to 15, guys who can step in and do the job for 10 days. We could go into extra innings, and Danny always had moves left. Those were solid ball clubs."

It was a bench move that Ozark failed to make in the third game of the League Championship Series with the Dodgers that might have cost the Phillies their first trip to the World Series in 27 years. The Phillies and Dodgers

Manager Danny Ozark (left), unfurling division title banner with Paul Owens, was criticized for failure to make defensive substitution in Game Three of NL Championship Series that year.

had split the first two games in Los Angeles, and the Phillies had a 5–3 lead going into the ninth inning. Gene Garber retired the first two Dodgers before Vic Davilillo bunted his way on. But the game appeared over when Manny Mota lifted a deep but catchable fly to left.

Ozark, however, had not replaced Luzinski with Jerry Martin for defensive purposes as he had all season. Luzinski took a false step, then drifted back to the wall. The ball glanced off his glove for a double, scoring a run. While umpire Bruce Froemming blew a call at first base later in the inning that would have preserved the victory, the Phillies wound up losing, 6–5, then timidly lost deciding Game Four in the rain the next night.

The moment Ozark failed to replace Luzinski with Martin was the point at which his eventual firing a year and a half later became inevitable. It also was the darkest moment of the Golden Decade.

But Ozark's job was never in trouble in 1978 as the Phillies made it three straight divisional titles. This time, they slipped to 90 victories but led from early May to the end, although the Pirates made it close at the end before Randy Lerch clinched it on the next-to-last day of the season by hitting two home runs and pitching well after giving up a grand slam to Willie Stargell in the first inning.

The Phillies probably wouldn't have made it three in a row, however, if Owens hadn't traded Garber to the Braves for Dick Ruthven, a day after he dealt Johnstone to the Yankees for reliever Rawly Eastwick.

But it was the same old story in the postseason. Bob Welch blew the ball past the Phillies at the Vet in Game One, Tommy John threw ground balls in Game Two, and, after a victory in Los Angeles, the Phillies lost in Game Four when Maddox dropped an easy line drive.

It was time for Owens to make some moves in preparation for the 1979 season.

First the Phillies signed Pete Rose as a free agent in December 1978. Then Owens sent Martin, Sizemore, and three others to the Cubs for second baseman Manny Trillo, outfielder–pinch-hitter Greg Gross, and catcher Dave

Awarding of 1978 Gold Gloves to (from left) Garry Maddox, Mike Schmidt, Larry Bowa, and Bob Boone was one of few highlights of dismal 1979 season.

Owens traded Dick Ruthven, then got him back in time to win 17 games for the 1980 World Champs.

Dallas Green's mood might have occasionally matched his friend on his office wall, but he drove the Phillies to their only World Championship.

Rader in February. Finally, he moved Hebner, who had lost his first base job to Rose, to the Mets for Nino Espinosa in May.

It appeared the Phillies once again were the strongest team in the NL East, but they never recovered from a 23–22 shootout victory over the Cubs at Wrigley Field on May 17. The victory made them 24–10. They led the division by four games. The rest of the way, they were 60–68. They finished fourth, 14 games behind the World Champion Pirates. Ozark was fired in late August and replaced by Dallas Green.

Under Green, the Phillies won 19 of their last 30, giving a hint that they would be back in 1980. Owens spent an uneventful off-season, then didn't make a player move during the season until mid-September when he picked up relief pitcher Sparky Lyle from the Texas Rangers. He believed the pieces for a World Championship were all in place—and he was right.

But it took the Phillies a long time to shift into overdrive in That Championship Season. In fact, the best move that Owens might have made was into the clubhouse in early September. In a profanity-laced, screaming speech, he lashed into the underachieving team. He singled out Bowa and Maddox as two players who were especially lackadaisical. He told them that they had played the first part of the season for themselves. They were going to play the last month for Carpenter and Green.

The players responded. Down by six games in mid-August, they closed out with 32 wins and 19 losses for a 91–71 record, beating the Montreal Expos on the road in their 160th and 161st games to clinch it. Then they beat the Houston Astros in an incredible League Championship Series and the Kansas City Royals in the World Series—both of which are thoroughly documented in Chapter 9—for their first World Championship.

Carlton, Schmidt, and Rose were hailed as three of the finest players in the game—sure Hall of Famers all (though Rose's gambling activities cost him, at least temporarily, a place in Cooperstown). Boone was a marginal candidate for the Hall. Bowa arguably deserved his place among the greatest shortstops who ever played the game. Trillo was brilliant at second. McBride was a legitimate MVP candidate in right. Maddox was Maddox in center, and Luzinski, who was suffering through a terrible season, was still dangerous with the bat. Ruthven was outstanding, and McGraw was unhittable for the second half of the season coming out of the bullpen.

"We seldom beat ourselves," Owens said, remembering the 1980 team. "And you had the two big bombers (Schmidt and Luzinski) there. And Bake. I think people started to realize just how good that club was when we had the reunion here a couple years ago. Over 10 years, they forgot just how good that ball club was."

The 1981 club had the potential to be just as good. But that was the strike season. Although the Phillies won the first half, they never were the same after the strike was over. In the divisional playoff after the season, they lost to the Expos in five games.

Still, it was a memorable campaign. Rose broke Stan Musial's major league record for hits, tying the mark the day before the strike, then having to wait 60 days to break it. Schmidt had his second straight MVP year. Carlton had Cy Young–type numbers.

But the real jolts were to come off the field. A year after the World Championship had been won, the Phillies were in transition once again.

Ruly Carpenter, unhappy with the financial direction baseball was taking, announced in spring training that the family was putting the franchise on the auction block. During the World Series, it was announced that a group led by vice president Bill Giles would buy the team for $30 million. Meanwhile, Green announced that he was leaving the organization to run the operations of the Chicago Cubs.

The only constant left from the Golden Decade was Owens.

Luzinski, who was best suited to finish his career as a designated hitter, had been sold to the Chicago White Sox before the 1981 season. Bob Walk had been dealt to the Braves for Gary Matthews.

Three of the greatest players in baseball history converge near the mound when Mike Schmidt congratulates Steve Carlton for another outstanding pitching performance as Pete Rose runs past them.

Owens began making moves again in earnest in the 1981 off-season. Bob Boone was sold to the California Angels, shortly after the Phillies had traded Lonnie Smith to the Cleveland Indians for catcher Bo Diaz. Two quick trades with the Chicago Cubs—one that became the worst of Owens' life—yielded pitcher Mike Krukow and shortstop Ivan DeJesus. Gone were Bowa, Keith Moreland, Dickie Noles, and Ryne Sandberg.

The Bowa-and-Sandberg-for-DeJesus deal gave the Phillies a shortstop who would help them win the 1983 pennant at the cost of a young infielder who eventually would become an MVP and the highest paid player in baseball.

Owens said that circumstances beyond his control dictated the deal.

"Bowa and Giles had been fighting in the papers," he recalled. "Bowa called him a liar. Bill didn't want Bowa around. The Cubs were willing to talk about DeJesus, but they wanted a throw-in.

"Our people didn't know what position Sandberg was going to play. In fact, Dallas was going to put him in center field and at third base until he made the deal for Penguin (Roy Cey). Everybody knew Sandberg was going to play in the big leagues, but nobody knew he was going to be this good.

"What I'm saying is that this wasn't just a field decision. I held out for two, three weeks, I kept saying, 'Dallas, I'm not going to give you Sandberg.' But he wouldn't budge without him."

And the Phillies knew they needed DeJesus to make another run at a pennant. So Owens finally relented.

The new manager was Pat Corrales. Owens remained the general manager, but not because he wanted to.

"If Dallas hadn't gone to Chicago, my plans were to step down and let him take over, and I would work for him," he said. "I was ready to slow down. Dallas and I had more or less hired Pat in the fall of '81 before we even knew he was going to go to the Cubs."

Carlton won his fourth Cy Young Award in 1982 with 23 victories as the Phillies and Cardinals battled each other down the stretch. But it was the eventual World Champion Cards who prevailed as the Phillies finished three games behind despite 89 victories.

Late in that season, Owens picked up a righthander with a nasty assortment of pitches and a nastier disposition when he obtained John Denny from the Indians. And during the off-season, he unloaded Trillo, who was

A 1983 ceremony reunited the Big Red Machine as Reds catcher Johnny Bench (right) enjoys a moment with Phillies Pete Rose, Tony Perez, and Joe Morgan.

having contractual problems, prospect Julio Franco, and three other players to the Indians for young Von Hayes, five days after trading Krukow to the Giants for second baseman Joe Morgan and relief pitcher Al Holland.

Hayes was no factor in 1983, but Denny was. He won the Cy Young Award with a 19–6 season. Corrales was fired in July with the Phillies in first place but only a game over .500. For the second time in his career, Owens moved from the front office to the dugout.

"In 1983 nobody wanted the pennant in the East. Everybody is playing horsepoop. Bill wanted to get rid of Pat in June. I talked him out of it. I said, 'He's right there, you've got to give him a chance.'

"That was a tough team to manage—four or five potential Hall of Famers on it. Rose and Carlton and Schmitty and Morgan and Perez. Bill made the move on Pat in July and asked me to take over. An interim manager wouldn't have had any impact.

"So many times in my career, I've asked guys to do something for the good of the club. You can't turn people down. All the guys said, 'Pope, if anybody can handle 'em, you can.' "

Not only did Owens handle them, but he drove the Phillies to their second pennant in four years and their fourth in history as they went 23–8 in September to win it by six games. Then they beat the Dodgers, who had an 11–1 edge on them in the regular season, in a four-game LCS.

Although they were beaten by the Baltimore Orioles in five games in the World Series, they never would have gotten that far if general manager Owens hadn't made the trades for Holland and Denny.

"Denny's past bothered me at first, but I liked his ability," Owens said about the trade. "I got him in with (strength and conditioning coach) Gus Hoefling and got him over that hump of arguing with umpires. The guy made a complete turnaround. He got along with our guys. He just loved it. And the rest is history.

"For awhile, we had John Denny in the right frame of mind. I thought the deal was a steal at the time."

Was Owens having fun? So much so that he decided to return as manager for the 1984 season.

"People said, 'Pope, you are 60 years old. It's going to be too much for you,' " Owens said. "Shoot, that was the best year and a half I had in 10 years. Every day I knew where I was and where I had to be. I was sick and tired of the agents. I didn't miss that one bit.

"I just got enthused about it in '83, and then Bill asked me to stay in '84 until we got John Felske ready. Looking back, that was the happiest year and a half I had in a long while."

Looking back, it also was to be the end of the happiest decade in Phillies history. Owens managed the Phillies to an 81–81 record in 1984, then turned the reins over to Felske.

It wasn't just on the field that Owens was being phased out. Decisions on players were being handled by committee, not by Owens himself. His opinions more and more were being ignored.

In effect, the Phillies and Paul Owens were going their separate ways after the most glorious period in the team's history.

The Pope went riding off into the sunset, like the hero does at the end of a Western movie.

The Phillies headed back to the mine shaft.

John Denny controlled his temper and won the Cy Young Award in 1983.

11

Off the Wall

The Phillies, God love 'em, may not have been good for many seasons, but they have been interesting. Their history is more than a century of anecdotes and stories that, although not significant enough to earn a place elsewhere in this book, still need to be repeated.

Some will make you laugh; others may bring tears to your eyes. Some had a profound effect upon the shape and direction of baseball; others are nothing more than throwaway lines that were too good to really throw away.

We felt that *The New Phillies Encyclopedia* wouldn't be complete without them.

Opening the Floodgates

An innocent trade made by the Phillies in 1969 paved the way for what became one of baseball's greatest upheavals.

On October 7, general manager John Quinn sent infielders Dick Allen and Cookie Rojas and pitcher Jerry Johnson to the St. Louis Cardinals for catcher Tim McCarver, pitcher Joe Hoerner, and outfielders Byron Browne and Curt Flood.

Flood, a 12-year major league veteran with a .293 lifetime batting average, refused to report to the Phillies. Instead, he filed a suit against major league baseball in which he contested the reserve clause, which gave teams the right to determine where and for whom a player performed.

Flood called the system, which had existed in baseball since the major leagues began, one "that indentured one man to another" and an "affront to human dignity." He contended that "the inevitable consequence of this system is that baseball players perform for lower salaries than they could negotiate for themselves in an open market. Whether viewed individually or as a group," he said, "baseball players do not get their fair share of the industry's receipts."

With former Supreme Court Justice Arthur Goldberg as his attorney and with the backing of the Major League Players' Association, Flood filed suit in federal court. Although he had called Philadelphia "the nation's northernmost southern city," he claimed that the issue was not himself or the reality of playing for the Phillies—who had offered him a contract in excess of $100,000—but the reserve clause and baseball's "right to treat human beings like used cars."

The case advanced all the way to the U.S. Supreme Court, which in a 4–3 vote refused to concur with Flood's contention. Although the case was lost, it made its point: Baseball's reserve clause had to go.

Soon afterward, it did. With public sentiment coming down strongly on the side of the players, pitchers Andy Messersmith and Dave McNally were declared free agents by a lower court. In effect, the reserve clause was overturned.

Flood's test case had opened the doors for the current free agent system and the right of certain players to negotiate for themselves in an open market.

No longer would baseball owners be able to manipulate major league players, tying them with lifetime contractual obligations to the teams for which they played. Baseball would never be the same.

Flood's place in the trade to the Phillies was taken by first baseman Willie Montanez.

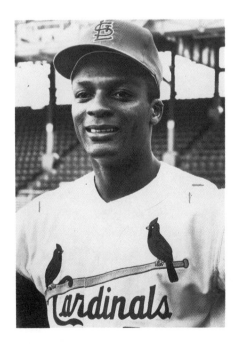

Curt Flood wore his St. Louis Cardinal uniform with distinction, but changed baseball forever when he said he wouldn't wear Phillies' doubleknits.

Quite appropriately for this chapter, Lee Meadows not only took his wife for a ride on a tire swing, he pitched in the shortest game in baseball history.

What an Outfield

Pitcher Tom Qualters was chosen by the Phillies instead of outfielder Al Kaline.

With future Hall of Famers Ed Delahanty, Sam Thompson, and Billy Hamilton playing together in the 1890s, the Phillies had what has often been called the greatest outfield in baseball history.

The Phillies could have just about matched that group a half century later.

In the 1960s and early 1970s the Phils could have lined up with an outfield of Hank Aaron, Al Kaline, and Carl Yastrzemski had it not been for a lack of foresight on the part of club management.

All three had opportunities to sign with the Phils. Yastrzemski had a tryout with the club and was set to sign if the Phillies would just add $10,000 to the $90,000 bonus they were offering. The Phillies refused, and Yastrzemski signed with the Boston Red Sox instead.

With Kaline, the Phillies were also suitably impressed after a tryout, and the choice came down to the Phillies signing either the young outfielder from Baltimore or a hard-throwing righthanded pitcher. The Phils chose the pitcher, giving him a $100,000 bonus. Tom Qualters, however, never won a game for the Phils and appeared in only seven games over a six-year period.

In Aaron's case, the future all-time home run leader also tried out with the Phillies, as did Roy Campanella and a number of other top young players from the Negro League. Aaron was told, "Don't call us; we'll call you." He never heard from the Phillies again.

Aaron, Kaline, and Yastrzemski, of course, went on to Hall of Fame careers for the Braves, Tigers, and Red Sox, respectively.

Stars of the All-Stars

Although Phillies have appeared nearly every year in the All-Star Game, the club has supplied few heroes to the mid-summer classic.

Unquestionably, the finest moment for a Phillie in an All-Star Game occurred in 1964 when Johnny Callison drilled a three-run home run with two outs in the bottom of the ninth inning to give the National League a 7–4 victory over the American League at Shea Stadium. The blow, coming off

Happy National League teammates greet John Callison after his home run won 1964 All-Star game at Shea Stadium.

Boston's Dick Radatz, earned Callison honors as the game's most valuable player.

The only Phillies pitcher ever to record a win in an All-Star Game was Ken Raffensberger, who notched the decision in 1944. Raffensberger pitched the fourth and fifth innings, allowing one hit and striking out two. His team was behind, 1–0, when he entered the game, but a four-run uprising in the fifth launched the Nationals to a 7–1 victory.

Between 1950 and 1957, a Phillies pitcher started every All-Star Game except one. Robin Roberts set a record (since tied) with five starts, and Curt Simmons got the nod twice. In the 1950 game third baseman Willie Jones played the entire 14 innings in a 4–3 National League triumph.

Besides Callison, three other Phillies have homered. Dick Allen did it in 1967 in the second inning of the National's 2–1 win in 15 innings at Anaheim. Greg Luzinski hit one in 1977 at Yankee Stadium in a 7–5 National League win. And Mike Schmidt's two-run homer in the eighth inning at Cleveland's Municipal Stadium in 1981 gave the Nationals a 5–4 victory.

The Phillies had two starters in the first All-Star Game in 1933 at Chicago's Comiskey Park. Dick Bartell was the shortstop and Chuck Klein the right fielder. The American League won that game, 4–2.

The Phillies' player with the most All-Star Game appearances is Schmidt, who played in 11 of the contests, starting eight of them.

Four Phillies managers have led All-Star teams, and each is undefeated. Eddie Sawyer (1951), Gene Mauch (1965), Dallas Green (1981), and Paul Owens (1984) all got winning verdicts.

Hoop, Grid Groups

Since the end of World War II, the Phillies have had a number of players who were outstanding athletes in other sports. The team has been especially heavily endowed with basketball stars.

Five players who graced Phillies rosters played professional basketball. Outfielder Frankie Baumholtz performed for Youngstown of the National Basketball League and Cleveland in the Basketball Association of America after playing his college ball at Ohio University, where in 1941 he was the most valuable player and led the National Invitation Tournament in scoring.

First baseman Howie Schultz (Hamline College) played for Anderson of the National League and Fort Wayne and Minneapolis of the National Basketball Association; pitcher Gene Conley (Washington State) was a member

Howie Schultz, a first baseman for the Phillies in 1947, and Gene Conley, a pitcher in 1959–60, played pro basketball.

Alvin Dark and Chuck Essegian were star football players in college before turning to baseball.

of the Boston Celtics and New York Knicks of the NBA; shortstop Dick Groat (Duke) performed for the Detroit Pistons; and pitcher Ron Reed (Notre Dame) also played for the Pistons. Groat was a two-time All-American and a national scoring champion at Duke.

The Phillies had two other players who had outstanding basketball careers. Minor league pitcher Neil Johnston was an NBA scoring champion and one of the great players in Philadelphia Warriors history. Infielder Johnny O'Brien was an All-American at Seattle University. Neither, however, played in the big leagues with the Phillies.

Other talented basketball-playing Phillies included pitcher Robin Roberts, who attended college on a basketball scholarship and was a Big Ten standout at Michigan State; pitcher Dallas Green, an All-Middle Atlantic Conference selection at the University of Delaware; pitcher Dick Hall, a top scorer and rebounder at Swarthmore College; pitcher Frank Hoerst, an outstanding player and a pro prospect at La Salle College; and infielder Dick Allen, an All-State cager in Pennsylvania at Wampum High School.

The Phillies also had several football players of note. Infielder Alvin Dark was an All-American halfback at Louisiana State University. Outfielder Chuck Essigian was a star running back for Stanford University's 1952 Rose Bowl team. Catcher Bob Finley not only played with Southern Methodist in the 1935 Rose Bowl, but he also became a prominent referee and officiated in the 1973 Super Bowl. Still another ex-Phillie, pitcher Walt Masters, was an All-American tailback at the University of Pennsylvania and later played briefly with the Philadelphia Eagles, where another ex-Phil, outfielder Earle (Greasy) Neale, was head coach for many years and later a member of the Football Hall of Fame. He also coached Washington and Jefferson College in the 1922 Rose Bowl. In addition, first baseman John Herrnstein was captain and fullback at the University of Michigan, first baseman Ed Bouchee was a fullback at the University of Washington, catcher John Stearns was a defensive back at the University of Colorado, catcher Harry McCurdy was a football and basketball standout at the University of Illinois, outfielder Phil Bradley was a quarterback at the University of Missouri, and infielder Mel Roach played quarterback at the University of Virginia.

Emancipating the Phillies

The Phillies were the next-to-last team to bring a black player to their major league roster. But it could have been the other way around. The Phils could have been the first team in the big leagues to sign black players.

It almost happened. And if Bill Veeck had had his way, not only the 1943 Phillies, but the team's whole future would have been vastly different.

Josh Gibson, Satchell Paige, Judy Johnson, Roy Campanella, Monte Irvin, and numerous other stars of the Negro League would have been Phillies, and major league baseball would have been integrated four years before Jackie Robinson came along to join the Brooklyn Dodgers.

The story unfolded during the winter of 1942–43, when Phillies owner Gerry Nugent was sinking rapidly in a sea of red ink and was looking desperately for a buyer. Veeck made him an offer.

Veeck, then an energetic young baseball executive who had spent his early years working for his father's Chicago Cubs, planned to buy the Phillies and stock the team with players from the Negro League. Phillies Cigars was going to be one of his financial backers, and Abe Saperstein was going to help him assemble a team with the best black players in the nation.

"I had not the slightest doubt that the Phillies would have leaped from seventh place to the pennant," Veeck said years later.

Veeck, however, made one crucial mistake. He told commissioner Kenesaw Mountain Landis of his plan. Landis was a hard sell, but Veeck thought he could get him to agree to the plan.

"I could not see how he could stop me," he said. "The only way the commissioner could bar me from using Negroes would be to rule officially and publicly that they were detrimental to baseball."

But Veeck was wrong. Landis, who during his 24-year reign as commissioner had worked diligently to prevent blacks from entering the major leagues, moved quickly into action in concert with National League president Ford Frick.

First, they persuaded Nugent to turn over his hapless team to the league for $500,000. Then, with Frick doing the legwork and the two keeping their actions secret, they quickly located another buyer, William Cox, a New York lumber broker.

The way was paved for Cox to purchase the Phillies, and Veeck's plan was thwarted. (Later in 1943, Cox was barred from baseball for life by Landis for betting on the Phillies.)

Had Veeck's plan succeeded, the Phillies might have had one of the great teams in baseball history. Moreover, they might have been able to corner the market on the many young black players of the future.

And who knows where that would have taken the Phillies over the years?

Who's Running This Team?

On the surface the 1890 Phillies were not a terribly noteworthy team. They finished in third place in the National League. But the 1890 Phillies share an unusual distinction with only a handful of other teams in baseball.

The 1890 Phils had four managers.

Harry Wright was the pilot for the first 22 and the last 45 games of the season. In between, the club was led by catcher Jack Clements for 19 games, owner Al Reach for 11 games, and shortstop Bob Allen for 35 games.

What happened to Wright?

A notation that appeared in the *Evening Bulletin* just after Clements took the reins sheds some light on the subject. "Manager Wright has a severe cold in his eyes, and his physician will not allow him to leave his house at present," the article said.

The 1891 *Reach Baseball Guide* went a step further. It said that Wright "went blind" during the season and was forced to the sidelines.

The Reach book further states that on the day Wright returned he was ushered into Baker Bowl riding a chariot. Each of the 4,322 fans in attendance was given a rose to wave at the returning manager.

With four managers in one season, the Phillies share the National League record with Washington in both 1892 and 1898 and St. Louis in 1895, 1896, and 1897. The American League record is also four, set by the Texas Rangers in 1977.

The World's Fastest Game

Lee Meadows was the losing pitcher in a Phillies' 6–1 loss to the Giants in a game played in 51 minutes.

As hard as it may be to believe with today's three-hour marathons, the Phillies once played a game that took exactly 51 minutes.

It happened on September 28, 1919, on the last day of the season, with the Phillies facing the New York Giants in a doubleheader at the Polo Grounds.

The swiftly completed contest is an all-time major league record.

With Lee Meadows pitching for the Phillies and Jesse Barnes on the mound for the Giants, and with 20,000 people in the stands, the Giants ran off a 6–1 victory, getting 13 hits to the Phillies' five. Both pitchers went the distance, with Barnes striking out two and Meadows fanning one.

Neither team had a record in mind during most of the game. But as the Phils came to bat in the top of the ninth, the players realized that something special was happening.

With two outs, the Phillies' Fred Luderus singled to center field. The next batter, Dave Bancroft, took a half-hearted swing, and sent an easy roller to second for the last out. Bancroft's action was the only example of a less than full effort during the entire game.

Ironically, the same two teams had once played a nine-inning exhibition game in just 31 minutes. Also played at the Polo Grounds, the 1913 contest wound up with the Phillies losing, 4–1, before a crowd of 500.

In that game, however, both teams had agreed before the game to speed up play. The batters swung mostly at the first pitch, and in many cases ran the bases at will. Both teams raced to and from the field after the innings were completed.

Quotables

Nothing on the sports pages is more pleasurable to read than a good, entertaining quote. Over the years, the Phillies have had a healthy share of lively comments, many inspired by the team's seemingly unending assortment of colorful characters.

Here are some of the more memorable lines that escaped the mouths of men who wore the uniform of the Phillies:

Infielder and horse fancier Dick Allen, when asked in the 1970s to comment on artificial playing surfaces, "If a horse can't eat it, I don't want to play on it."

Relief pitcher Tug McGraw a few years later was asked if he preferred grass or Astroturf. "I don't know," McGraw answered with a straight face. "I've never smoked Astroturf."

Having ended a 23-game losing streak as well as a 10-game winning streak of the Milwaukee Braves, the Phillies returned from a road trip in 1961 to find several hundred fans waiting for them at Philadelphia Airport. "Get off in twos and threes so they can't get us with one burst," said pitcher Frank Sullivan, peering out the windows of the airplane.

Mike Schmidt revealed to a group of sportswriters what it's like for an athlete to read the local newspapers. "Philadelphia is the only city where you can experience the thrill of victory and the agony of reading about it the next morning."

Another classic line was uttered by center fielder Len Dykstra. When asked what he thought of the trade that sent Von Hayes to the California Angels, Dykstra had a quick response. "Great trade," he said. "Who'd we get for him?"

Then there was bespectacled pitcher Johnny Podgajny. While he was pitching a game for the Phillies in 1941, his manager, Doc Prothro, was shocked to find that his hurler was peering *over* his glasses to read the catcher's signs. When Prothro urged him to get new bifocals, Podgajny shot back, "Buy focals, nothing. I just bought these." Later, it turned out the Podgajny had bought the glasses he was wearing because he "liked the feel of them."

How's That Again?

For about a 20-year period, Philadelphia was the malaprop center of the sports world. Eagles coach Joe Kuharich could dangle a participle with the best of them, and Villanova basketball coach Jack Kraft, who once called a play "the nail that broke the coffin's back," could fracture the language as well as anyone you've ever been around.

Naturally, the Phillies weren't about to take a back seat in this department. In the National League standings, yes, but not in the malaprop standings. They came up with a troika of managers—Frank Lucchesi, Paul Owens, Danny Ozark—who could get out of bed on a cold winter night and send you, head spinning, to your dictionary.

Lucchesi was a soft-hearted man, the kind who loved to spend his off-hours visiting sick kids in hospitals. He was warm and friendly and emotional, and he surely deserved something better with which to work when the Phillies promoted him in 1970 after 19 years in their minor league system.

He was also the main star, make that the only star, of the Skipper Lucchesi Show, which came on the air five minutes before every Phillies game, home and away. "Hi, fans, Skipper Lucchesi from Vets Stadium (or Wrigley Field or Riverfront Stadium) . . ." was the way every broadcast began. Lucchesi would then talk nonstop for five minutes, punctuating almost every comment with "so I just wanted to bring that out to you fans." He also managed to strangle the English language most of the time. The show was local radio's answer to national television's Batman. It was so bad that it was good.

Skipper Lucchesi (everybody called him Skipper, not Frank, because that's what he called himself) was also terrific with the press in post-game situations. Some of his stories were priceless, like the one about the time he got ejected from a game in the minor leagues because he happened to disagree with an umpire's decision.

"I didn't say a word when I went out to him," Lucchesi said. "I just kept clapping my hands together. And the closer I got to him, the harder I clapped my hands. Now he asks me what I'm doin. 'Killin' the flies and gnats,' I tell him. 'What are you talking about?' he asks. 'There's no flies and gnats around here.' 'Yes there are,' I tell him. 'There's always flies and gnats around a horse's ass.' "

Skipper Lucchesi could also spray the post-game malaprops to all fields. A couple of examples:

"Now I don't want you guys to think I'm going off on a transom . . ."

"Nobody's gonna make a scrapgoat out of me."

They didn't, of course, but they did manage to make a scapegoat out of Skipper Lucchesi. General Manager Paul (Pope) Owens took over as field manager. Owens has as sharp a baseball mind as you'll ever meet. Unfortunately, his tongue isn't quite as sharp. For instance, he once told the team official who met him at the airport, "I feel great. Why don't you turn the music on the (car) radio up a few disciples?"

Naturally the story spread, so Owens tried to cover his mistake, and compounded the felony instead. "Aw, I knew what I was saying," he told people. "I was just kidding. I knew it wasn't disciples. I knew it was decimals."

No question about it, when this Pope sat in his post-game chair, he was speaking ex catheter.

Nineteen games into his field stewardship, Owens, pumped up from yet another victory, met the press with a pounding of his fist on his desk.

"I've been saying it all along," he announced with authority. "This is a .500 club. That's why we had to make the change (in managers). And now they're proving what I said all along by playing .500 ball since I took over."

At the time, the Phillies were 8–11 under Owens.

A week earlier, someone had asked Owens to evaluate his pitching staff. He replied that so-and-so was strictly a starter and what's-his-name would be used only in relief. Then he came to Woodie Fryman. "Woodie can go either way, he's that kind of fellow," Owens said.

Next was Danny Ozark, one of the nicest people you would ever want to meet. Loved his wife and family, went to church every Sunday, didn't know the meaning of the word meanness. But did he have a way with words!

One day Ozark and Associated Press writer Ralph Bernstein were having a pre-game conversation. Danny said something, then reminded Bernstein, "But, of course, you know I'm a fascist."

"You're a what?" Bernstein said.

"No, not the Italian kind, the other kind," Danny shot back.

"What other kind?"

"You know, somebody who says one thing and means something else."

We're not being facetious in relating this story to you.

Nobody, not even an umpire, was going to make a "scrapgoat" out of Phillies manager Frank Lucchesi.

Even Phillies manager Danny Ozark had his "Watergate" in 1979.

Other prose from the Oze:

"Even Napoleon had his Watergate."

"The morality on this team is no problem."

Ozark's worst moment, though, was when the Pirates clinched the pennant in Pittsburgh by beating the Phillies to go up by seven games with six left in 1975. Everyone but Danny knew the Phillies had been eliminated.

"If we win all our games and they lose all of theirs, we're still alive," Ozark insisted loudly enough to be heard above the popping of champagne corks down the hall.

In August 1979, the Phillies fired Ozark and replaced him with Dallas Green, whose voice was several "disciples" louder and who often spoke in four-letter language that could not be quoted in print or on the electronic media.

After close to a decade, covering the Phillies wasn't nearly as much fun.

What's in a Name?

Ed Heusser's nickname was "The Wild Elk of the Wasatch."

Pitcher Hub Pruett must have muttered his nickname—"Shucks"—a lot in 1927 when he lost 17 of 24 decisions. He later became a physician.

Every team in baseball has had players with colorful and unusual nicknames. But the Phillies seem to rank among the all-time leaders in that category.

One of the strangest was the name given to the team's first manager, Bob Ferguson, who was called Death to Flying Things, presumably because he never missed a ball hit to him in the air.

Ranking just slightly behind this one were such treasures as the Wild Elk of the Wasatch (Ed Heusser), Earache (Benny Meyer), Shucks (Hub Pruett), What's the Use (Pearce Chiles), Weeping Willie (Claude Willoughby), Ed (The Only) Nolan, and Losing Pitcher (Hugh Mulcahy).

Other gems included She (Charles Donahue), Sleuth (Tom Fleming), Nibbler (Jim Hearn), Horse Face (Togie Pittinger), Handle Hit (Milt Stock), Putt-Putt (Richie Ashburn), Dirty Jack (John Doyle), Fiddler (Frank Corridon), and The Tabasco Kid (Norm Elberfeld).

The Phillies showed a partiality to food. They had Peaches (George Graham), Apples (Andy Lapihuska), Candy (John Callison), Cookie (Octavio Rojas), Peanuts (Harry Lowrey), Pretzels (John Pezzullo), Pickles (Bill Dillhoefer), Beans (Harry Keener), and Spud (Virgil Davis). There was Cod (Al Myers) and Shad (Flint Rhem and John Barry). And to wash it down, they had Brewery Jack (John Taylor), Whiskey Face (Pat Moran), and Buttermilk Tommy (Tom Dowd).

The animal kingdom was also well represented. Delegates ranged from Possum (George Whitted), Bear (Jim Owens), Tiger (Don Hoak), Chicken (Nelson Hawks), and Bull (Greg Luzinski) to Squirrel (Roy Sievers), Turkey (Cecil Tyson), Donkey (Frank Thomas), Rabbit (Tom Glaviano and Jimmy Slagle), Hawk (Ken Silvestri), and Mighty Mouse (Solly Hemus).

The Phillies got some of their nicknames from their sartorial habits. The entries included Tight Pants (John Titus), Bareback (Joe Oeschger), Highpockets (Dick Koecher), and Styles (Chris Short). Other names originated from on-field performances, such as the Curveless Wonder (Al Orth), Fidgety Phil (Phil Collins), and Boom-Boom (Walter Beck), all pitchers. And others developed off the field such as the Charmer (George Zettlein) and Cupid (Clarence Childs).

There were geographic references such as Bama (Carvel Rowell), Greek (Bobby DelGreco), and Tioga (George Burns). There were some trees such as Cactus (Gavvy Cravath) and Palm Tree (Ron Stone). And there was Fireball (Fred Wenz), Cannonball (Ledell Titcomb), and Buckshot (Tommy Brown).

Over the years, the Phillies have had at least 15 Leftys, a dozen or so Reds, and assorted Docs, Chiefs, Dutches, and Cys. They've had a number of Kids, plus Kiddo (George Davis), Kitten (Harvey Haddix), and Kitty (Bill Bransfield and Jim Kaat).

They've also had Lucky (Jack Lohrke) and Jinx (Jennings Poindexter), Coonskin (Curt Davis) and Rawhide (Jim Tabor), Stretch (Howie Schultz) and Stumpy (Al Verdel), Iron Hands (Chuck Hiller) and Stone Hands (Dick Stuart), and Swats (Carl Sawatski) and Swish (Bill Nicholson). In addition, appearances have been made by Jumbo (Jim Elliott) and Midget (Don Ferrarese), not to mention Bitsy (Elisha Mott), Runt (Jimmy Walsh), and Shorty (Glenn Crawford).

The Phillies have been blessed with Smiling Al (Al Maul) and Mad Monk (Russ Meyer), Sleepy (Bill Burns) and Nap (John Shea), Iron Man (Wiley Piatt) and Rusty (Waldo Yarnall), and Cap (John Clark), and the Hat (Harry Walker). To add to these, there's also been Beauty (Dave Bancroft), Wagon Tongue (Bill Keister), Crash (Dick Allen), Klondike (Bill Douglas), Frosty Bill (Bill Duggleby), Phenomenal (John Smith), Nails, (Len Dykstra), and, of course, the unforgettable Squack (Chester Crist).

Years Too Late

Reluctance on the part of the Phillies to sign black players as quickly as other National League teams has long been held as a reason the club slipped from its pennant-winning perch in 1950.

When the Whiz Kids won the pennant, they were the last all-white team to win a National League flag. The Phils were also the last team in the league to sign black players, waiting until 1956 to do so. That was 10 years after Jackie Robinson broke professional baseball's color barrier.

"We didn't win after 1950, but I think there's a reason," Richie Ashburn once said. "We were the last team to get any black ball players. The Giants, the Dodgers, the Braves were getting the good black ball players. We were still pretty good, but they were just getting better.

"I also know," Ashburn confided, "that (Roy) Campanella always said he wanted to play with the Phillies. He didn't want to play with the Dodgers."

Campy, a Hall of Fame catcher, was a Philadelphia native.

The Phillies' early attitude toward black players had been stamped before Campanella's arrival in the majors. In 1947, as the Dodgers with Robinson on the team prepared to make their first trip of the season to Philadelphia, Phillies general manager Herb Pennock phoned Brooklyn's Branch Rickey with some advice.

"You just can't bring the nigger here with the rest of your team, Branch," Pennock said. "We're just not ready for that sort of thing yet. We won't be able to take the field against your Brooklyn team if that boy Robinson is in uniform."

Assuring Pennock that he would be delighted to accept a forfeit victory should the Phillies decline to take the field, Rickey sent his team on to Philadelphia anyway. Upon their arrival in Philadelphia, the Dodgers found themselves being turned away at their regular quarters at the Ben Franklin Hotel. They finally found lodging in the Warwick Hotel.

The ensuing weekend series was a tense affair. The Phillies, led by manager Ben Chapman, viciously needled Robinson, at one point even releasing a black cat onto the field. As a result, and also because of previous attacks on the young

His career lasted just five games in 1957, but John Kennedy was the first black Phillie.

Hank Mason became the first black pitcher for the Phillies in 1958.

black player in an earlier series in Brooklyn, National League president Ford Frick was obliged to issue a warning to Chapman to desist.

"Of all the league's parks in those difficult first few seasons," Robinson would say years later, "that one (Shibe Park) was the lion's den."

The Phillies waited until 1956 to sign their first black players. Finally, with instructions to scour the sandlots for young blacks, Phillies scouts quickly inked 20 players to contracts. That year the club had promising blacks such as Eddie Logan, a hard-hitting outfielder from Ridley Township in suburban Philadelphia, infielders John Kennedy and Francisco Herrera, and pitcher Henry Mason in their minor league system.

The next year Kennedy, who had been a shortstop with the Kansas City Monarchs before signing with the Phillies at the age of 22, emerged as the top black prospect from a February baseball school the Phillies had conducted. Driving a battered old Ford and forced to live with a black family in the poor section of town, rather than in the swanky hotel with the white players, Kennedy spent spring training in Clearwater with the Phillies. That made him the first black player ever to zip on Phillies flannels.

Kennedy appeared in five games at the start of the regular season as a late-inning replacement at third base. He had just two at-bats. Early in the season the Phillies sent him back to the minors, and he never made it back to the big club.

Although Kennedy was the Phillies' first black player, the first black player to appear in a regulation game with the Phillies was shortstop Chico Fernandez. Obtained in late spring training in a trade with the Brooklyn Dodgers, he took the field in 1957 as the Phils' opening-day shortstop.

In 1958, Mason became the first black pitcher to appear with the Phillies.

Even after these breakthroughs, however, the Phillies were still extremely slow in the 1960s and 1970s in signing black players. As late as 1980, the World Championship club had only three blacks (Garry Maddox, Bake McBride, and Lonnie Smith) on its roster for most of the season.

Live Wires, Blue Jays, Etc.

The name Phillies is the oldest continuous nickname in baseball, dating back to the formation of the team in 1883.

All other teams of that era have either vanished or changed names, although the New York club adopted the name Giants soon after the Phillies landed in Philadelphia as the defunct Worcester Brown Stockings.

Over the years there have been several attempts to change the name of the Phillies. But all failed. One of the earliest attempts occurred shortly after Horace Fogel became president of the Phillies in 1909. Fogel wanted to change the team's name to Live Wires to signify the spirit he hoped to instill in his players. Fans and sportswriters refused to accept the name, and it died a quiet death.

In 1942 manager Hans Lobert persuaded club officials to call the team the Phils. It was Lobert's way of shedding the loser image previous teams had given the name Phillies. But that name didn't stick, either, although it has long been the club's secondary nickname.

After he became president, Bob Carpenter ran a contest in 1944 to find a new name for the team. The winning entry was Blue Jays. The club changed its logo and stationery, but hardly anyone accepted the new name. The team continued to be called Phillies, and the alternate nickname was officially dropped in 1949.

The 1950 team was popularly known as the Whiz Kids, a name given to it by sportswriter Harry Grayson. The official name of the club remained, however, the Phillies.

Second Time Around for Taft

When the Taft Broadcasting Company became one of the owners of the Phillies in 1981, it was the second time that the Taft name had been connected with the team.

In 1910, Mrs. William Howard Taft, wife of the president of the United States, bought Baker Bowl and leased it back to the Phillies for 99 years.

Two years later, Charles P. Taft, the president's brother, supplied funds that enabled Horace Fogel to put together a syndicate to buy the Phillies. At the time, Taft was the owner of the Chicago Cubs.

Taft Broadcasting, a Cincinnati-based communications conglomerate, is associated with the prominent Ohio Taft family, which also included long-time Senator and former presidential candidate Robert Taft, and his son, former Congressman Robert Taft.

Taft sold its most recent interest of 47 percent of the Phillies in 1986.

Home Sweet Home?

Of the seven divisional and league championships won by the Phillies, not a single one was clinched at home until the 1983 victory in the LCS against the Dodgers.

In 1915 the Phillies gained the National League pennant in Boston (September 29), and in 1950 they won the flag in Brooklyn (October 1).

Divisional crowns were captured in 1976 in Montreal (September 26), in 1977 in Chicago (September 27), in 1978 in Pittsburgh (September 30), and in 1980 in Montreal (October 4).

The 1980 National League crown was won in Houston (October 12).

Grounders Are Easy, But . . .

During his nine years in the big leagues, Russ Wrightstone played every position in the infield as well as the outfield. Such an assortment of duties was not so much a testimony to Wrightstone's versatility as it was to his inability to perform with much skill with a glove on his hand.

Russ was an excellent hitter and, because of that, it was imperative that the Phillies find him a spot in the lineup. After all, Wrightstone hit over .300 in five of his eight and one-half seasons with the club, and his lifetime batting average was a commendable .297.

Hitting a baseball was one thing. But when it came to fielding it, Wrightstone was strictly in foreign territory. And that was why he played so many different positions. He was a liability wherever he played in the field, and the Phillies kept shifting him around, hoping that sooner or later he would stumble into a spot where he would inflict the least amount of damage.

In 1926, Phillies manager Art Fletcher installed Russ in the outfield. Wrightstone was patrolling left field one day as the Phillies entered the ninth inning with a one-run lead over the Chicago Cubs. With two outs, the Cubs had the bases loaded and Charlie Grimm at bat.

Grimm lofted an easy fly to left in what appeared to be the game-ending out. Wrightstone gazed up at the missile and reached for it. The ball plunked into his glove and dropped right out. Two runs scored, and the Phillies once again looked up from the underside of the final score.

It was such an embarrassing muff that after the game no one mentioned it. Of course, Wrightstone felt terrible, and left the ball park in silence.

Long after dinner and well into the night, neither Wrightstone nor his teammates had yet said anything about the bobble. Finally, late that night over a cup of coffee, Russ could stand the silence no longer.

"You know what was the matter?" he blurted. "I'll tell you. It was just too goddamn high."

Please Do Not Disturb

Over the years, Baker Bowl had its share of high comedy. One particular incident that produced gales of laughter involved the great slugging outfielder Hack Wilson.

Wilson was known in his day as one who occasionally reported to the ballpark in less than playing condition, having spent the previous evening on more frivolous matters.

Such was the case one hot summer afternoon in the early 1930s in a game between the Phillies and Brooklyn Dodgers.

It was one of those games that dragged on and on as the teams took turns

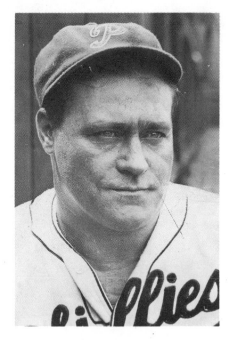

Hack Wilson (left) had a pleasant nap disrupted by an angry heave by Walter (Boom Boom) Beck.

rattling hits around Baker Bowl. Dodger manager Casey Stengel made numerous trips to the mound to confer with his struggling pitcher, a big righthander named Walter (Boom-Boom) Beck.

Finally, Stengel had tolerated Beck's generosity to Phillies hitters long enough. Casey strolled to the mound to tell Beck, later a Phillies pitcher, that he was through for the day.

Wilson, worn out from chasing line drives, decided to take advantage of the break in the action and leaned against the right field wall to rest. Soon Hack was fast asleep.

Beck, meanwhile, was not taking too kindly to Stengel's decision to lift him. In a fit of anger, Boom-Boom turned and hurled the ball as hard as he could at the right field fence. The throw clattered against the fence, just a few feet from Wilson's head.

Suddenly awakened, the startled Wilson jumped, stared wildly around, then tore after the ball, fielded it, and fired a perfect peg to second base.

The Family Feud

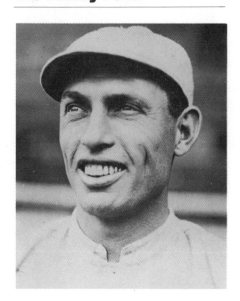

Feuds between players are as much a part of baseball as minor league phenoms who can't make the majors. Few players, though, disliked each other as passionately as Phillies outfielders Sherry Magee and Dode Paskert.

Left fielder Magee and center fielder Paskert, both Phillies standouts in the years just prior to the club's 1915 championship season, waged a bitter feud for several years. Adding spice to the antagonism, their wives and children took part in the battle, too.

The feud reached a climax one afternoon after Paskert homered into the left field bleachers. As Paskert rounded third base, Magee's two sons booed as loud as they could.

When Dode reached the Phillies' dugout, he went straight for Magee, and a brawl erupted. For several minutes, the two hammered away at each other before they were separated by teammates.

Dode Paskert brawled with Sherry Magee in the dugout after hitting a home run.

A Lucky Break

The St. Louis Browns once thought they had pulled a fast one by drafting a Phillies minor leaguer listed as G. Hamner. But the joke was on the Brownies.

The G. Hamner lifted from the draft list in 1947 was not the Granny Hamner the Browns thought they were getting. It was Garvin Hamner, Granny's older brother.

At the time, Granny was a promising young shortstop for the Phillies' Utica farm team. The Browns' management believed it had pulled off a great coup by selecting a player they figured to be Granny.

Garvin, who was three years older than Granny, never made it with the Browns, nor any other team, for that matter. Granny, who once had to borrow money from coach Jake Pitler so he could get home to Richmond, Virginia, after an unsuccessful tryout in Brooklyn with the Dodgers, was a regular for the Phillies for 10 years.

Casey Celebrates Trade

After playing with the Phillies in the 1920s, anybody who was traded had to feel as though he'd just escaped from purgatory. Outfielder Casey Stengel was a good case in point. After laboring for the Phillies for one and one-half seasons, the future Hall of Fame manager was swapped in mid-1921 to the New York Giants.

Stengel got the news while the Phillies were idling in the Baker Bowl clubhouse during a rain-delayed game. Although it was pouring rain and the field was nothing but mud, Casey, upon learning he'd been traded, raced half-dressed out of the locker room and onto the diamond.

There, he circled the bases, sliding into each bag. By the time he reached the plate, Stengel was covered with mud. And he was grinning from ear to ear. It was, he explained, his way of celebrating his liberation from the cellar-dwelling Phillies.

Here Today, Gone Today

What player had the shortest career with the Phillies? The winner in a runaway is Clyde Kluttz, a nine-year veteran who spent most of his big league career as a reserve catcher.

Clyde's career with the Phillies was so short that he never even got to put on a uniform. He came to the team in the morning and was gone in the afternoon.

The unusual sequence took place on May 1, 1946. It began when the Phillies sent center fielder Vince DiMaggio to the New York Giants in exchange for Kluttz. Several hours later, Kluttz was shipped to the St. Louis Cardinals for second baseman Emil Verban.

The exchanges gave Clyde the distinction—although hardly unique—of having been on three teams in one day.

Not counting the Phillies, Kluttz played for six major league teams during his career.

Unassisted Triple Play

The first unassisted triple play in the National League was registered against the Phillies. It was executed by Boston Braves shortstop Ernie Padgett.

It came on October 6, 1923, in a game in Boston. The Phillies had Cotton Tierney on second base and Cliff Lee at first. The batter was Walter Holke.

Holke drilled a pitch by Joe Batchelder, and the line drive was caught by Padgett. The shortstop touched second to retire Tierney, then tagged out Lee between second and first.

During the regular season, there have been only three other unassisted triple plays in the National League. (See Chapter 8 for the story of Mickey Morandini's unassisted triple play.) The American League has had four.

Padgett's play helped the Braves to a 4–1 victory in a game called after four and one-half innings because of darkness.

You Wanna Bet?

The Phillies have had more than their share of scrapes with the wheels of justice. Some have resulted in lifetime suspensions from baseball.

Two Phillies owners have been banned for life from the game. Horace Fogel and William Cox (see Chapter 5) both took their leave of the game with the compliments of the major league baseball hierarchy. Fogel was banished for a series of indiscreet comments; Cox took the plunge after it was revealed that he bet on Phillies games.

Some other Phillies or ex-Phillies have also had problems with gambling, the most recent of whom was Pete Rose, who in 1989 was suspended from baseball while a manager of the Cincinnati Reds.

After the 1920 season, a year in which baseball was embroiled in the Black Sox Scandal of 1919, Phillies first baseman Gene Paulette was kicked out of baseball by Commissioner Kenesaw Mountain Landis because of an alleged association with gamblers.

Paulette, who had been in and out of the big leagues since 1911, had come to the Phillies from the St. Louis Cardinals midway through the 1919 season. After hitting .259 for the Phils that year, he took over at first base in 1920 and hit .288 in 143 games.

After the season Landis charged that Paulette had received money from some St. Louis gamblers, who had wanted him to throw games. Paulette, insisting that he did no such thing, said he took the money as a loan. After conferring with other players, however, Landis banned Paulette for life.

In 1924 another Phillies player had a brush with gamblers but rejected their overtures. Shortstop Heinie Sand was offered a bribe by New York Giants outfielder Jimmy O'Connell to go easy on the Giants during a weekend series. Sand refused and reported the incident to his manager, Art Fletcher. Eventually, Landis found out about it, and O'Connell and a coach, Cozy Dolan, were banned for life.

Several other ex-Phillies were banned from baseball because of their gambling activities after leaving the team. Pitcher Tom Seaton while pitching in the Pacific Coast League in 1920 was blacklisted from baseball for consorting with gamblers. Another ex-Phil, infielder Jesse Levan, was permanently barred from baseball in 1959 after he was charged with being in cahoots with gamblers. Levan, then playing with Chattanooga, was accused of tipping off gamblers by fouling off a set number of pitches. Gamblers would then arrange bets based on the number of pitches fouled. Former Philadelphia A's catcher Joe Tipton, at the time playing with Memphis, was banned for participating in the same scheme.

Back in the Bushes

In the last three decades the Phillies have had a rather elaborate—albeit not always productive—farm system. It wasn't always that way, though.

In their first half century of existence the Phillies had no farm teams. Young players were either signed directly by the club and sent to independent minor league teams for seasoning, or they were purchased from minor league teams that owned them.

The Phillies had no organized scouting system and would often send injured players out to look at young prospects. The only scout the club had for many years was Joe (Patsy) O'Rourke. Later, Johnny Ogden scouted and handled the few minor league details that needed attention.

In the early 1940s, Jocko Collins began to scout for the Phillies. He would handle that post, while refereeing NBA games in the winter, for more than three decades. Cy Morgan took over ostensibly as the club's farm director.

When Bob Carpenter purchased the Phillies in 1943, the team had no farm teams and a working agreement with just one—Trenton. Carpenter hired Herb Pennock to serve as general manager, and Pennock quickly began building a farm system.

He hired scouts, including Johnny Nee, Chuck Ward, and Eddie Krajnik. In 1944 he added Utica and Bradford to the system, which by then also included Wilmington, already owned by Carpenter.

Eventually, the Phillies had working agreements with or owned 15 minor league teams at once. In 1947, five of the Phils' clubs (Utica, Wilmington, Schenectady, Carbondale, and Vandergrift) won league championships. And the Phillies' farm system had among its managers Eddie Sawyer; Lee Riley, whose son Pat is the coach of the New York Knicks and former Los Angeles

Lakers coach; Dick Carnevale, who won four straight minor league championships; and Skeeter Newsome, a former Phils shortstop who also won four titles and was the team's first pilot to win a Triple-A crown when he did it with Syracuse in 1954.

Joe Reardon was Pennock's first farm director, a post he held from 1944 to 1954. Morgan came back for two years, then was followed by Gene Martin (1957–64), Clay Dennis (1964–65), Paul Owens (1965–72), Dallas Green (1972–79), Howie Bedell (1979), Jim Baumer (1980–88), Lance Nichols (1989), and Del Unser (1989 to the present).

In the 1950s and 1960s the Phillies' farm system flourished. In 1954 the Phillies' Syracuse club went to the finals of the Junior World Series before losing to Louisville. Finally, in 1961, a Phils' club won the JWS when Buffalo swept Louisville in four straight games.

The Phillies' minor league organization was particularly productive under Owens. Much of the 1980 World Championship team, including Mike Schmidt, Greg Luzinski, Larry Bowa, and Bob Boone, came out of the Phils' farm chain of the late 1960s and early 1970s.

The system fell on hard times in the 1980s, as draft picks fizzled and the organization fell into general disarray. Through much of the mid- to late '80s, the Phillies' chain was rated the worst in all of baseball, and few players made it successfully through the system to the big leagues.

In the early 1990s, however, under Unser, the system started to turn around. In 1992 the Scranton/Wilkes Barre Red Barons went all the way to the last game of the International League (Triple-A) playoffs before losing in a best-of-five series to Columbus. The Red Barons had captured the league's regular season East Division title under manager Lee Elia, who had guided the Clearwater Phillies to the Class A Florida State League's Western Division championship in 1991.

Dallas Green was farm director of the Phillies before managing the team to the World Championship.

The Phillies have had some outstanding pitching performances in their 110 years. And they've had some awful ones, too.

The choice for worst pitching performance in Phillies history might be tough to pick. That's because there are four leading candidates, and each one is as bad as the next.

What could be a more thorough pummeling than that given to righthander Charlie Bicknell in 1948 by the St. Louis Cardinals? Bicknell gave up four home runs and hits amounting to 18 total bases in the second game of a June 6 doubleheader at Sportsmans Park.

What could be worse you say? How about this? On May 5, 1938, righthander Hal Kelleher gave up 12 runs in the eighth inning of a 21–2 loss to the Chicago Cubs at Wrigley Field.

Or how about this? In a game played August 4, 1934, at Baker Bowl, beleaguered righthander Reggie Grabowski was battered by the New York Giants for 11 hits, 10 of them singles, in the ninth inning.

A final indignity to Phillies pitchers might be the job done on righthander Bill Kerksieck on August 13, 1939, at the Polo Grounds. In that unfortunate outing, the New York Giants slugged Kerksieck offerings for six home runs, including four in one inning.

Honorable mention candidates are Dutch Schesler, who was pounded for 22 hits in a game July 11, 1931, against the Giants, and Erskine Mayer who surrendered nine consecutive hits in the ninth inning of a game on August 18, 1913.

No Relief in Sight

Bonus baby Charlie Bicknell was touched for four home runs, 18 total bases in one inning by the St. Louis Cardinals in 1948.

Who Needs a Catcher Anyway?

Almost anything that could happen did happen at Baker Bowl. Once, a pitcher even walked a batter by throwing to first base.

The unusual incident occurred in 1925 during a game between the Phillies and the Cincinnati Reds. The pitcher was the Phillies' Wilbur Hubbell, and the batter was two-time National League batting champion Edd Roush.

According to John Kieran of the *New York Times,* Hubbell, no relation to Carl, had lost a game the previous day when a batter slugged a game-winning hit while he was being intentionally walked.

"The next day," Kieran wrote, "Hubbell was pitching again, and the same situation arose—men on second and third." The strategy called for an intentional walk. Hubbell was determined not to repeat the previous day's experience.

On the instructions of manager Art Fletcher, Hubbell threw four straight pitches to first baseman Walter Holke. As soon as the fourth pitch was thrown, according to Kieran, "Out came Fletch from the dugout waving the rule book to prove that his pitcher had committed a violation which entitled the batter to take first base. He won the argument."

The rule at the time stated that a ball had to be called anytime a pitcher threw to any player other than the catcher, except in an attempt to retire a runner. Such throws were not considered balks.

Fletcher was advised to discontinue the practice in a telegram the next day from National League headquarters. The following year the rule was changed. It provided for a warning from the umpire on the first throw to any player other than the catcher. If a pitcher made a second such throw, he was ejected from the game.

You Mean with Real Money?

It was a regular practice of out-of-town sportswriters to make fun of the Phillies when they visited either Baker Bowl or Shibe Park.

One of the leading comedians was always Warren Brown, a scribe from Chicago. Brown, along with some of the New York writers, usually had something uncomplimentary to say, but on one afternoon during a game in the mid-1930s, he outdid even himself.

Brown was busy rolling a heavy metal pipe up and down the press box floor at Baker Bowl. The pipe would clank down a flight of steps, then Brown would retrieve it and start the practice again.

Phillies president Gerry Nugent, seeing what was happening, rushed from his box to the press box and demanded that Brown cease. "You fellows must remember that we have patrons and you're annoying them," said the annoyed owner. Then he added pointedly, "Patrons who *paid* to get in."

"By gosh," roared Brown, rushing to his typewriter. "What a story! The Phillies have *paying* patrons."

Doc Was Tops in a Pinch

Who holds the single season pinch-hit record for the Phillies? Greg Gross, you say?

Wrong. It's not Gross. Nor is it Dave Philley or Rene Monteaugudo.

The real record holder is a seldom-used outfielder named Roy (Doc) Miller who played for the Phillies in 1912 and 1913.

In 1913, while making 56 trips to the plate as a pinch-hitter, Miller cracked 20 hits. That's one more than Gross had in 1982, and two more than hit by Philley in 1958 and Monteaugudo in 1945.

Miller finished the 1913 season with a .345 batting average. Altogether, he had 30 hits during the season. The lefthanded hitter, who in the early part of his five-year career had been a regular with the Chicago Cubs and Boston Braves, was the National League's leading pinch-hitter in 1913.

While with the Braves in 1911, Miller had lost the batting championship to Honus Wagner by one point. Miller hit .333 that year.

Knot-Hole Gangs

The phrase "knot-hole gang" was popular throughout the country in the 1930s and 1940s. But it had its origin in Philadelphia at Baker Bowl.

In the early 1930s fans used to drill holes in a gate on 15th Street. The gate led to an alleyway, that opened onto the playing field.

A kid peering through one of the holes could only see the scoreboard and center field. But that was enough to give a knowledgeable fan enough information to tell what was happening in the game.

During Phillies games, the holes would normally attract large crowds of fans. The group became known as the knot-hole gang, a description that later spread to other cities.

Better Than Honus

If it hadn't been for the errant judgement of a second-line pitcher, the Phillies could have had a double-play combination of Honus Wagner and Nap Lajoie.

In 1897, the Phillies heard glowing reports about a slugging young infielder named Wagner who played for Paterson (New Jersey) in the Atlantic League. Because Paterson was just a short hop away from Philadelphia, the Phillies dispatched Con Lucid, a pitcher who was disabled, to check out the youthful shortstop.

Lucid saw Wagner in a game against Richmond. "Wagner can hit, but he's too clumsy for the National League," Lucid reported. "But Richmond has a shortstop, Norman Elberfeld, that caught my eye. He fields like a demon. I believe that boy will go far. You can't go wrong in investing some money in him."

Using Lucid's report as a basis, the Phillies ignored Wagner and bought Elberfeld. A few weeks later, the Pittsburgh Pirates bought Wagner for $2,100, and he went on to become the greatest shortstop in the history of baseball. Elberfeld, nicknamed Kid, had a respectable 14-year career in the major leagues, hitting .271, but he played in only 14 games for the Phillies before being traded. Unlike Wagner, he did not earn a berth in the Hall of Fame.

Cobb Almost Bought 'Em

Ty Cobb nearly became the manager and co-owner of the Phillies in 1929. Having ended his playing career the year before with the Philadelphia Athletics, Cobb was anxious to get back into baseball. He joined forces with Philadelphia real estate man Reynold H. Greenberg, and the two negotiated a deal with Phillies owner William Baker.

Greenberg wasn't interested in the team. He wanted Baker Bowl, which he planned to knock down so that he could use the space to erect an office building. Although the Phillies leased the park, they had an option to buy it at a low price.

Greenberg's plan was to buy the team and the stadium for about $900,000, paying about $200,000 for the Phillies and the rest for the real estate. He had arranged with the Athletics to move the Phillies to Shibe Park.

Cobb was to be the manager and would put up some of his own money toward the purchase price. Ty had spent 1921 through 1926 as the manager of the Detroit Tigers, and the idea of returning to the dugout was quite appealing to him.

The future Hall of Famer spent two weeks in Philadelphia getting ready for his new job. Meanwhile, the Phillies went on a road trip, won eight games in a row, and returned home having jumped from eighth to sixth place in the standings.

The club's new-found prosperity convinced Baker that his asking price was too low. He increased the price tag another $100,000. Cobb got mad, packed his bags, and went home to Georgia. The deal died, and with it went what would certainly have been an interesting era in Phillies history.

Firsts and Lasts

Along with the "firsts" they've accomplished at home, the Phillies have also taken part in a number of original experiences on the road.

The Phillies participated in the first National League game played at Ebbets Field. On April 9, 1913, they beat the Brooklyn Dodgers, 1–0, with Tom Seaton beating Nap Rucker.

On May 4, 1919, the Phillies defeated the New York Giants, 4–3, at the Polo Grounds. It was the first legal Sunday game played in New York.

The first night game in the major leagues involved the Phillies and the Cincinnati Reds. The Phils lost to the Reds, 2–1, on May 24, 1935 under the lights at Crosley Field.

The Phillies played in the first game at the Astrodome on April 12, 1965. They beat the Houston Astros, 2–0, on a four-hitter by Chris Short.

A significant "last" also involved the Phillies. On September 18, 1963, the team played in the last game at the Polo Grounds. Short beat the Mets, 5–1.

Equal Rights

The Phillies were one of the first major league teams to hire women in responsible jobs.

Mae M. Nugent, the wife of Gerry Nugent, the Phillies' president from 1932 to 1943, was the club's vice president and treasurer and a member of the board of directors from 1935 until the Phillies were taken over by the National League. Previously, she had served as secretary to William Baker and then the club's treasurer and assistant secretary under Charley Ruch.

The Phillies also hired the first female scout. In 1946, Edith Houghton, a 33-year-old ex-Wave and former softball player, joined the team. She stayed only briefly with the club.

The Grim Reaper

Catcher Walter (Peck) Lerian's life ended on a Baltimore street in 1929 when he was struck by a vehicle.

Infielder Mickey Finn died in mid-season 1933 after undergoing ulcer surgery in Allentown.

For a four-year period beginning in 1929, death stalked the Phillies in an incredibly abnormal manner.

Three active Phillies players died prematurely, as did another active ex-Phillie.

The first to pass away was a pitcher named Dutch Ulrich. He had made the Phillies as a 25-year-old rookie in 1925. By 1927 he had completed 14 of 18 starts, had an 8–11 record, and possessed a low 3.17 earned run average. The Phillies were counting on him to become the ace of the staff. However, he developed severe pneumonia and was forced to miss the entire 1928 season. Two weeks before spring training in 1929, he called Burt Shotton, told the manager that he was feeling great, and was almost ready to make his comeback.

The day before the Phillies' training camp opened, Ulrich died in Baltimore.

In the year Ulrich missed, Walter (Peck) Lerian became the Phillies' catcher. He was terrific defensively and showed signs of becoming a power hitter. After the 1929 season, great things were predicted for him. But he was killed in Baltimore on October 22. He was standing on a sidewalk when a vehicle, trying to avoid another vehicle, hopped the curb and pinned him against a building, causing the fatality.

One of the big players in a deal the Phillies made with the Dodgers before the 1933 season was Neil (Mickey) Finn, a second baseman. Finn was given the regular job by the Phillies and played 51 games before entering Sacred Heart Hospital in Allentown to undergo surgery for an ulcer. The operation, performed by club president Gerry Nugent's brother-in-law, was deemed successful. Finn had high hopes of returning to the Phillies before the season ended. On July 2, he died of complications.

Death also claimed Hal Carlson, the old spitballer whom the Phillies had traded to the Cubs. Carlson, who pitched for the Phillies from 1924 to 1927, died from severe indigestion in his Chicago hotel room in May 1930.

The Babe Goes Quietly

It would have been fitting if the career of Babe Ruth had ended with the legendary slugger hammering one of his high, majestic blasts into the distant bleachers with a huge sellout crowd standing as one to cheer him into retirement.

It would have been fitting, but it didn't happen that way. Far from it.

The Babe's glorious career ended abruptly and without fanfare in dingy Baker Bowl in a game between the lowly Phillies and the equally lowly Boston Braves.

Ruth had joined the Braves for the 1935 season after getting his release from the New York Yankees. Rebuffed in his attempts to land a job as manager of the Yankees, Ruth had signed with Boston as a player, assistant manager, and vice president with the unwritten promise that he would eventually manage the team.

Ruth struggled during the early part of the season. Overweight, injured, and in a batting slump, the 40-year-old slugger could neither hit nor field, and by mid-May his relations with Braves management had deteriorated to the point that the Bambino realized that he had made a mistake joining the Boston club.

Ruth considered quitting, but he decided to complete one last road trip with the Braves. With his average hovering around .150, he came alive briefly in Pittsburgh with three home runs, a single, and six RBI at Forbes Field. But the next day in Cincinnati, he struck out three times while going 0-for-4.

On May 29–designated Babe Ruth Day—the Braves played at Philadelphia, and with Ruth walking with the bases loaded and making a pair of running catches in left field, Boston defeated the Phillies, 8–6.

The following day was Memorial Day, and a crowd of 18,000 packed Baker Bowl for a doubleheader. Ruth was in left field for the opener, and Phils pitcher Jim Bivin got him to ground out in the top of the first inning.

In the bottom of the first with two runs already in for the Phillies, the great slugger missed an attempted shoestring catch on Lou Chiozza's looper to left. Another run scored as the ball rolled all the way to the wall where it was retrieved by shortstop Bill Urbanski, whose throw was relayed to the plate in time to catch the sliding Chiozza for the third out of the inning.

As his teammates headed for their dugout, Ruth tucked his glove into his back pocket, turned, and jogged to the clubhouse in center field.

Bert Kuczynski, then a 15-year-old spectator sitting in the left field stands and later a professional athlete with both the Philadelphia A's and Eagles, remembered the situation clearly. "He just turned, and ran right off the field," Kuczynski recalled. "He was crying like a baby, wiping the tears away. Everybody stood up. They sensed that this was it, and gave him a tremendous ovation."

Phillies backup catcher Joe Holden was in the clubhouse at the time. "The Braves' clubhouse was on the bottom floor; the Phillies on the top floor," he said. "He came up the iron steps to ours. Red (trainer Red Miller) asked him, 'Is there anything I can do, Babe?' Babe said, 'No. No. There's nothing you can do for old age.' Then I saw Red shake hands with Babe. It didn't register at the time that Babe's career was over."

But over it was. After 22 seasons, the career of the boisterous Ruth ended with a wimper in, of all places, the decrepit old bandbox known as Baker Bowl.

The Arms Race: Who Was Best?

Who had the best throwing arm among Phillies outfielders? Over the years, the team has had a number of players with strong arms. But a handful of them stand out above the rest.

The best arms probably belonged to Chuck Klein, Ron Northey, Glen Gorbous, Bob Bowman, Ken Walters, Johnny Callison, Ollie Brown, Mike Anderson, Joe Lefebvre, and Glenn Wilson.

You could take your pick of who had the best arm. Klein led the National League in assists three times and set an all-time record with 44 assists. Callison led the league four times in assists. And Gorbous made what was described as

It's impossible to discuss the strongest outfield throwing arms in Phillies' history without mentioning Glen Gorbous.

the world's longest throw when he uncorked a toss of 445 feet, 10 inches while playing in the minor leagues at Omaha.

"The strongest arm I have ever seen anywhere belonged to Gorbous," said Rich Ashburn, himself a three-time assist leader and owner of the single greatest throw in Phillies history. Ashburn nailed the Brooklyn Dodgers' Cal Abrams at home in the ninth inning of the last game of the 1950 season, helping preserve a tie score and setting the stage for Dick Sisler's three-run, game-winning homer in the 10th.

"I would go with Bowman for second best," Ashburn adds.

Long-time Phillies coach, batting practice pitcher, and front-office man Maje McDonnell rates Gorbous number one, followed by Northey and Klein.

Former Phillies scout Jocko Collins picked Northey. "He had the best arm I ever saw," Collins said. "Second best was Gorbous and then Bowman."

Said former manager Eddie Sawyer: "Northey had an excellent arm. Next would be Bowman. Walters also had a good arm, and so did Klein."

Of a more recent vintage, the arms seen by former general manager and manager Paul Owens would be ranked Callison first, Lefebvre second, then Gorbous and Bowman. "Brown also had one of the better arms I ever saw," Owens said. "Lefebvre had as good an arm as anybody, too."

Not a Bad Return

Frank (Rube) Melton gave the Phillies a worthwhile return on their investment.

During their lean years from the 1920s to the 1940s the Phillies would do almost anything for a buck. Sometimes, they were pretty creative.

Such was the case in 1940. At the minor league draft, the St. Louis Cardinals neglected to protect pitcher Rube Melton, and the ever-alert Phillies quickly claimed him for $7,500. No sooner had they claimed him, though, than Phils president Gerry Nugent sold Melton to the Brooklyn Dodgers for $15,000—a quick and tidy 100 percent profit.

Commissioner Kenesaw Mountain Landis suspected collusion and nullified the deal, ruling that the Phillies had to keep Melton for two years.

Dutifully, the Phils followed orders. After the erratic Melton, who in 1941 briefly disappeared from the Phillies because he was upset about not going to the Dodgers, posted a 10–25 record in two years, Nugent peddled him at the end of the 1942 season to the Dodgers. The price tag was a cool $30,000.

That was a 300 percent profit. And a pretty good return on his investment for the money-conscious Nugent.

Life after Baseball

To most Phillies, there has been more to life than just baseball.

Many Phils became highly successful after their playing careers ended. Some became successful businessmen. Others became good farmers. Many remained in baseball as managers, coaches, or scouts. And still others tended bar, worked in stores, or handled jobs in factories.

A number of them had occupations that were a little out of the ordinary for baseball players. Hugh Jennings and Chuck Essegian, for instance, became lawyers. Jim Lonborg and Mickey Doolan became dentists. Cy Williams became a bank president as well as an architect. And Hub (Shucks) Pruett became a physician.

Billy Sunday switched from baseball to the pulpit, becoming a world-famous evangelist. Bill White became the president of the National League. Greasy Neale became a Hall of Fame coach of the Philadelphia Eagles, leading them to championships in 1948 and 1949. Stan Baumgartner became a sports-writer with the *Philadelphia Inquirer,* covering the Phillies. Carl Sawatski became president of the Texas League.

A number of ex-Phils went into broadcasting. Bob Uecker, Buddy Blattner, Tim McCarver, Jim Kaat, Tommy Hutton, Jay Johnstone, Kent Tekulve, and Rich Ashburn were among the more prominent ones. Al Demaree turned his talents into sports cartooning. Charlie Dooin became a prominent vaudeville singer.

Many ex-Phils got into politics. Of the more successful ones, Jim Bunning, became a U.S. congressman from Kentucky after running unsuccessfully for governor. Larry Jackson was a four-term member of the Idaho house of representatives and also ran for governor.

Bill Atwood, a much-decorated pilot in World War II, started an airline with Eddie Ricenbacker and flew commercial planes for nearly 30 years.

Perhaps one of the most interesting jobs held by an ex-Phil was that of Pete Sivess. After serving as a Naval officer in World War II, he joined the Central Intelligence Agency and worked for the CIA for 25 years.

Numerous ex-Phillies became college baseball coaches. Among them were Ethan Allen, who coached at Yale, where one of his players was a first baseman named George Bush. Hans Lobert coached at West Point, Dode Paskert at Duke, Roy Thomas at Penn and Haverford, and Tony Lupien at Dartmouth. Danny Litwhiler was the coach at Michigan State and Florida State, Robin Roberts at South Florida, and Bob Miller at Detroit U. Art Mahan was baseball coach and athletic director at Villanova.

Umpiring also had its appeal. Bob Ferguson, Billy Nash, Chief Zimmer, Sherry Magee, Kitty Bransfield, and Butch Henline all became major league umpires for varying lengths of time.

Billy Sunday switched from the Phillies dugout to the pulpit.

Earl (Greasy) Neale, played for the Phillies, coached the Eagles and made the pro football Hall of Fame.

Stan Baumgartner played for the first Phillies championship team in 1915 and wrote about the second one for the *Philadelphia Inquirer* in 1950.

Mostly Odds and Ends

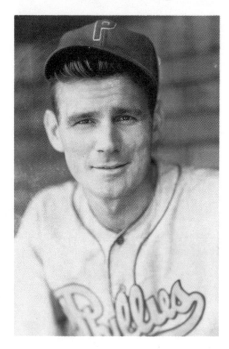

Pete Sivess had a much more successful career with the Central Intelligence Agency than as a Phillies' pitcher in the '30s.

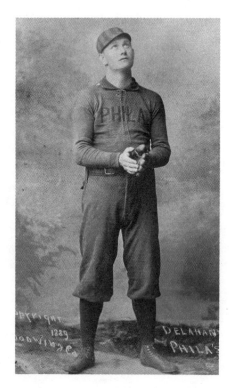

Ed Delahanty went from stardom with the Phillies to the 1902 American League batting title.

Some additional items that have not found homes elsewhere in this book are all very much a part of Phillies history, and the book would not be complete without them. Here they are in no particular order:

- The first five batting champions of the American League were all former Phillies. The group included Nap Lajoie (1901, 1903, 1904), Ed Delahanty (1902), and Elmer Flick (1905).
- In 1896, Billy Hulen played 73 games at shortstop for the Phillies. Nothing unusual about that. Except that Hulen was lefthanded all the way. Hulen played more games at shortstop (including 19 with the Washington Nationals in 1899) than any other lefthander.
- The Phillies of 1942 were so bad that they made two errors on one throw, and three errors on the same play. In a game July 28 against the Cincinnati Reds, Phils second baseman Albie Glossop fielded Gee Walker's grounder but threw wildly to first. First sacker Nick Etten retrieved the ball and fired to third trying to catch the speedy Walker. But third baseman Pinky May wasn't there, and the ball rolled down the left field line with Walker scoring. Glossop was charged with an error on his throw. And May got nailed with an error for failing to cover the base, while Etten got an error for his wild throw.
- Between 1920 and 1944 the Phillies averaged 97 losses per season. They lost 100 or more games 11 times and finished in last place 13 times.
- Pitcher Jocko Thompson was one of the major league's most decorated war heroes during World War II. He won silver and bronze stars and a purple heart. Thompson began as a paratrooper and came out a captain. He led a platoon at Anzio Beach and was a company commander during the Battle of the Bulge.
- The last major league pitcher to hurl two complete games in a doubleheader was the Phillies' Jack Scott, who beat the Cincinnati Reds, 3–1 and 3–0, on June 19, 1927.
- The youngest player ever to appear with the Phillies was 16-year-old Putsy Caballero in 1944. Tom Brown, later a Phillie, holds the major league record for most hits (24) by a 16-year-old, set in 1944 with the Brooklyn Dodgers.
- Not only did Clarence Mitchell hit into the only unassisted triple play in World Series history in 1920 while he was playing with the Brooklyn Dodgers against the Cleveland Indians, but he was also the last legal spitballer to win a game for the Phillies. Mitchell, one of 18 pitchers allowed to continue throwing the spitter after it was banned in 1920, won six games for the 1927 Phillies.
- Before he became a Phillies pitcher in 1940, Lloyd Brown gave up more home runs (15) to Lou Gehrig than any other hurler. Two of the 15 were grand slams. After playing in 2,130 consecutive games, Gehrig was replaced in 1939 by Babe Dahlgren, a Phillie in 1943.
- Either the turf was awfully slow that day, or the Phillies were sleepwalking. Whatever the case, no less than four Phils were thrown out at first base by Cincinnati right fielder Dusty Miller during a game May 30, 1895, at Baker Bowl.
- Shutouts were rare at Baker Bowl. But in 1933, Cy Moore accomplished the almost unimaginable feat of tossing three shutouts there.
- Shortstop Tommy Thevenow holds the major league record for most consecutive at-bats (3,347) without a home run.
- Shortstop Rudy Hulswitt holds the National League record for most errors in one season. In 1903 he booted 81 balls.
- When Joe DiMaggio's hitting streak was stopped at 56 straight in 1941, the last pitcher he faced was Al Smith of the Cleveland Indians. Stopper Smith hurled in 1938 and 1939 with the Phillies.
- The best switch-hitter in minor league history was outfielder Buzz Arlett, a ferocious slugger who in a 20-year career in the bushes slammed 432 home runs while batting .341. Once he hit 54 in one season, and twice he hit four in one game. Arlett played only one year in the majors—with the Phillies in 1931 when he hit .313 with 18 home runs and 72 RBI. Arlett, however, was a notoriously poor fielder and felt much more comfortable away from the spotlight. After one season the Phillies put him on waivers. There were no takers, and he returned to the minors where he played until 1937.

- Stew Bolen served the first professional home run to Ted Williams while both were playing in the Pacific Coast League. Tom Zachary gave up the 60th home run to Babe Ruth in 1927. Both moundsmen later worked for the Phillies.

- The most innings in one game ever pitched by a Phillies hurler was 21 by Mule Watson on July 17, 1918. Watson, who allowed 18 singles and one double, gave up one run in the first inning and one in the 21st in a 2–1 loss to the Chicago Cubs.

- The Phillies might have been last in the National League in many of their years, but they were sometimes first in war. Such was the case in 1942 when manager Hans Lobert, Chuck Klein, catcher Mickey Livingston, and reserve first baseman Eddie Murphy charged into the stands and stormed up to the upper deck at Shibe Park to confront a fan who was heckling the team. When they found him, the pugnacious quartet did some loud bellowing at the guy, then slammed him back into his seat, sparing him not only a few black eyes, but what could have been a flight over the upper deck railing.

- Vance Dinges is the only player ever to hit a pinch-hit, inside-the-park home run for the Phillies. He did it in 1945.

- How's this for a couple of creative trades? On December 12, 1932, the Phillies swapped Kiddo Davis to the New York Giants for Chick Fullis and Gus Dugas. So far, so good. Then on June 15, 1934, the Phillies dealt Fullis to the St. Louis Cardinals. Who do you think they got for him? Kiddo Davis, of course.

- In 1937, in his only full season with the Phillies, pitcher Wayne LaMaster had this dubious distinction. He led the Phillies in wins with 15. And he led the National League in losses with 19.

- What do Phillies pitchers Dick Ellsworth and Dick Selma and hurlers Tom Seaver and Jim Maloney have in common? All went to the same high school in Fresno, California. Lee Thomas, Roy Sievers, and Earl Weaver went to the same high school in St. Louis.

- The youngest Phillies player ever to appear in a World Series was Marty Bystrom in 1980. He was 22.

- When Don Drysdale's 58⅔ innings of scoreless pitching was finally snapped in 1968, the Phillies were the team that did it. The guy who drove in the run with a hit that broke the streak was outfielder Howie Bedell.

- John Lush in 1906 became the first lefthanded pitcher to toss a no-hitter for the Phillies. Lush had broken into the majors as a first baseman and outfielder in 1904. That year, Lush played in 95 games as a position player, hitting .276. He did not become a regular pitcher until 1906, and even that year performed in 22 games in the outfield and two at first base while pitching in 37.

- The only grand slam, inside-the-park home run for the Phillies was hit in 1956 by Ted Kazanski.

- Three Phillies have hit home runs in their first big league at-bats. Bill Duggleby did it in 1898 with a grand slam. Emmett Mueller hit one out in 1938, and Eddie Sanicki did likewise in 1949. Sanicki had three hits that year—all were home runs. When Mueller hit his homer, the Brooklyn Dodgers' Ernie Koy also hit a home run in the same game in his first big league at-bat.

- Who is the only major league player ever to appear in 150 or more games as a rookie and never appear in the big leagues again? Answer: Sparky Anderson, who played second base for the 1959 Phillies.

- Barry Lersch was an alternate member of the 1964 Olympic diving team. He also gave up the first two home runs hit into the upper deck at Veterans Stadium.

Infielder Tommy Thevenow holds the major league record for most at-bats without hitting a home run.

Trades, Acquisitions, and Sales

In 1972 the Phillies obtained Steve Carlton in a trade for Rick Wise. Carlton, of course, went on to a storybook career that included four Cy Young awards and 329 wins. Wise, on the other hand, concluded a good but not great career in 1982 with 141 fewer wins than Carlton's ultimate total.

Was that the greatest trade in Phillies history?

One of the many endearing aspects of baseball is that the sport perpetually provides topics for discussion. Whether you're debating a manager's strategy, comparing players, or rating one team against another, baseball offers material that can be endlessly argued, second-guessed, or analyzed.

Probably nothing in the sport is more widely discussed than trades. Trades provide a source of yearlong conversation. And in the case of the Phillies, some trades that were made years ago are still being talked about.

Throughout their history, the Phillies have been active traders. Many of the club's deals, especially the ones years ago that were often prompted by the need for working capital, were downright awful. But in recent decades, particularly in trades engineered by Paul Owens, the club has made an abundance of swaps that have been highly successful.

So, what are the best and the worst of the trades that the Phillies have made in their 110 years?

Such choices probably wouldn't get the same answers from any two people. They're rather arbitrary decisions.

Producing a list of bad trades is much easier than compiling the 10 best trades, simply because the Phillies have made far more of the former than they have of the latter.

Consideration in each selection was given only to those trades that had a lasting effect on the club. In other words, the trades had to be beneficial or harmful to the team over a long period. Trades such as those in which the Phillies landed a star player who moved on after a relatively short time in Philadelphia generally were ignored.

The most important measurement was what the player(s) accomplished *after* the trade. Here are the selections:

10 Best Trades

1.

February 25, 1972

Pitcher Rick Wise to St. Louis Cardinals for pitcher Steve Carlton.

Has to be the best swap in Phillies history. It was the last trade made by John Quinn. Carlton has a guaranteed spot in the Hall of Fame. Wise had a 188–181 career record and never won 20 before retiring in 1982. After the trade, Carlton's record with the Phillies was 234–161, while Wise was 113–105 with the Cardinals, Boston Red Sox, Cleveland Indians, and San Diego Padres.

2.

December 26, 1917

Outfielder Dode Paskert to Chicago Cubs for outfielder Cy Williams.

After the trade, Williams blossomed as one of the top sluggers in the National League, leading the loop in home runs three times and hitting

One of the best trades the Phillies ever made was getting Cy Williams, who won three home run crowns after joining the Phils from the Chicago Cubs.

over .300 six times in 13 years with the Phillies. Paskert, a fine player, was nearing the end of his career and played just four more years, none of them spectacular.

3.

December 4, 1963

Outfielder Don Demeter and pitcher Jack Hamilton to Detroit Tigers for pitcher Jim Bunning and catcher Gus Triandos.

Bunning became the Phillies' ace hurler of the mid-1960s, winning 74 games in four seasons, pitching a perfect game, and nearly hurling the club to a pennant in 1964. Demeter hit respectably for three more years, but retired in 1967. The other two contributed little to their new teams, although Triandos did catch Bunning's perfect game.

4.

April 7, 1948

Infielder Ralph LaPointe and $20,000 to St. Louis Cardinals for first baseman–outfielder Dick Sisler.

Where would the Phillies have been in 1950 without Sisler? Dick's homer in the last game of the regular season gave the club its first pennant in 35 years. Altogether, Sisler gave the Phils four solid years as a starter. LaPointe never played in the majors after 1948.

5.

May 4, 1975

First baseman Willie Montanez to San Francisco Giants for outfielder Garry Maddox.

It's immaterial that Montanez had a decent career as a flamboyant performer for nine teams. Maddox was simply the best defensive center fielder of his era, winning eight Gold Gloves. And he gave the Phillies 12 solid seasons at the plate, including the game-winning hit that gave the Phils the 1980 pennant.

6.

December 8, 1958

Infielder Gene Freese to Chicago White Sox for outfielder Johnny Callison.

Callison went on to enjoy a solid

10-year career with the Phillies during which he was the club's only member of the starting lineup throughout the period and one of its best hitters and defensive players. Freese, a journeyman, played only two more years as a regular, and left the big leagues in 1966.

7.

May 13, 1960

First baseman Ed Bouchee and pitcher Don Cardwell to Chicago Cubs for second baseman Tony Taylor and catcher Cal Neeman.

Two days after he was traded, Cardwell pitched a no-hitter. But he never reached the great heights expected of him. Neither did Bouchee, whose best years were already behind him. You could make a case, though, that Taylor became one of the finest second basemen in Phillies history and one of the city's most popular players during his 11 years as a regular.

8.

December 3, 1974

Outfielder Del Unser, catcher John Stearns, and pitcher Mac Scarce to New York Mets for pitcher Tug McGraw and outfielders Don Hahn and Dave Schneck.

For the better part of nine years with the Phillies McGraw was one of the major league's premier relievers. His 1980 performance alone makes the trade successful. Stearns had an up-and-down career, Unser returned five years later to the Phillies, and the others were never heard from again.

9.

February 23, 1979

Outfielder Jerry Martin, catcher Barry Foote, second baseman Ted Sizemore, and pitchers Henry Mack and Derek Botelho to Chicago Cubs for second baseman Manny Trillo, outfielder Greg Gross, and catcher Dave Rader.

He wasn't with the Phillies that long, but Trillo made a lasting impression while he was, as one of the slickest-fielding second basemen ever to play the game and as the 1980 LCS MVP.

What's more, the Phils got a valuable utility man in Gross. The price was five players who hardly made a dent in the big leagues.

10
October 18, 1973
Pitcher Ken Brett to Pittsburgh Pirates for second baseman Dave Cash.

When the Phillies traded for Cash, they were in desperate need of two things: a spark plug and a second baseman. Cash gave them both. He instilled a winning attitude in the club with his "Yes We Can" spirit. And he gave them three solid seasons on the field, leading the league in hits once and hitting .300 or more twice. Cash was the guy who whipped the Phillies into being a contender. Although he gave the Phils one good season, Brett was hardly in the same class.

10 Worst Trades

1.
November 11, 1917
Pitcher Grover Cleveland Alexander and catcher Bill Killefer to Chicago Cubs for pitcher Mike Prendergast, catcher Pickles Dillhoefer, and $60,000.

Giving up a pitcher of Alexander's stature was unforgivable, no matter what the reason (the Phillies feared he would be drafted into World War I). Alex worked 13 more years and won 183 more games, three times winning more than 20 games, en route to the Hall of Fame. Dillhoefer appeared in only eight games for the Phillies before moving on, and Prendergast left the majors in 1919.

2.
April 21, 1966
Pitcher Ferguson Jenkins, outfielder Adolfo Phillips, and outfielder–first baseman John Herrnstein to Chicago Cubs for pitchers Bob Buhl and Larry Jackson.

The Phillies didn't think the rookie Jenkins was worth saving, but Fergy sure fooled them. He ranked as one of the premier pitchers of his era and was inducted into the Hall of Fame with 284 wins. Jackson won 41 games for the Phils before retiring at the end of 1968, and Buhl gave the Phillies exactly six wins.

3.
January 27, 1982
Shortstop Larry Bowa and shortstop–second baseman Ryne Sandberg to Chicago Cubs for shortstop Ivan DeJesus.

It was bad enough that the Phillies traded one of baseball's greatest defensive shortstops—Bowa—for at best a mediocre shortstop—DeJesus. But, at the insistence of Dallas Green, by then the Cubs' general manager, the Phillies also threw in Sandberg. All he has done since then is become one of baseball's finest players, a certain Hall of Famer, an eight-time All-Star, winner of eight Gold Gloves and one home run crown, and one of the best-hitting second basemen ever to play the game.

4.
November 21, 1933
Right fielder Chuck Klein to Chicago Cubs for pitcher Ted Kleinhans, infielder Mark Koenig, outfielder Harvey Hendrick, and $65,000.

Coming off one of the greatest five-year performances in baseball history in which he didn't hit below .337, Klein was at the peak of his game, having just won the triple crown. Although he later returned to the Phillies, this trade was still one of the most lopsided. The aging Koenig never played an inning for the Phils, Hendrick played one season and retired, and Kleinhans had a 0–0 record and left before the end of the season.

5.
December 1895
Outfielder Billy Hamilton to Boston Beaneaters for third baseman Billy Nash.

A simple salary dispute resulted in Hamilton's departure, after which he had five straight .300-plus years en route to the Hall of Fame. Nash, obtained primarily to become playing-manager, drove the club home eighth in his one year as pilot and gave the Phillies three mediocre seasons as a part-time third baseman.

6.
November 22, 1920
Pitcher Eppa Rixey to Cincinnati Reds for pitcher Jimmy Ring and outfielder Greasy Neale.

Rixey left Philadelphia with average credentials to become a Hall of Famer, working 13 more big league seasons. He won 100 games in his first five years after the trade. Meanwhile, Ring was the Phils' top hurler for the next five years, but he wasn't of Rixey's caliber. Neale never amounted to much in baseball. His sport, of course, was football.

7.
June 8, 1920
Shortstop Dave Bancroft to New York Giants for shortstop Art Fletcher, pitcher Bill Hubbell, and $100,000.

Trading away future Hall of Famers in this era was a favorite trick of the Phillies. Bancroft earned his Cooperstown credentials with nine seasons (five over .300) with New York, Boston, and Brooklyn. Fletcher had two good years before retiring to give four lackluster years as the Phils' manager. Hubbell never won more than 10 games in a season as a Phillie.

8.
June 13, 1938
Pitcher Bucky Walters to Cincinnati Reds for catcher Spud Davis, pitcher Al Hollingsworth, and $55,000.

Poor trades in this era were regular occurrences for the Phillies. Walters went on to become one of the top National League pitchers, an MVP, and three-time 20-game winner. And it was the Phillies who had converted him to pitcher. Hollingsworth produced a 6–25 record in less than two seasons, while Davis, a former Phil, played less than two years as a sub.

9.
March 6, 1938
First baseman Dolph Camilli to Brooklyn Dodgers for outfielder Ed Morgan and $50,000.

Score another for the 1930s Phillies. The club always got the cash to survive for a few more months in deals like this, but it lost a ton of good players. Camilli went on to a glittering career with the Dodgers, averaging 27 homers a year for the next six seasons and leading the league once in homers and RBI. As a Phil, Morgan never made the club.

10.
December 3, 1958
Pitcher Jack Sanford to San Francisco Giants for pitcher Ruben Gomez and catcher Valmy Thomas.

Two seasons after he was named Rookie Pitcher of the Year, Sanford departed in exchange for a pitcher who gave the Phillies three wins and a catcher who gave them nothing. Sanford had nine more years in the majors, five of them as a big winner with the Giants, including a 24–7 mark in 1962.

Major Trades and Acquisitions

The preceding lists stand as arbitrary choices of the best and worst in Phillies history, but the club has made numerous other swaps over the years. It has also bought and sold players with unbending determination.

What follows is a complete list of all the significant trades, purchases, and sales the Phillies have made during their 110 years.

1892, Dec.
First baseman Roger Connor to New York Giants for catcher–first baseman Jack Boyle.

1895, Dec.
Center fielder Billy Hamilton to Boston Beaneaters for third baseman Billy Nash.

1900, Feb.
Outfielder Duff Cooley to Pittsburgh Pirates for pitcher Tully Sparks and second baseman Heinie Reitz.

1901, June
Outfielder Jimmy Slagle to Boston Braves for outfielder–infielder Shad Barry.

1904, June 20
Outfielder-infielder Shad Barry to Chicago Cubs for pitchers Frank Corridon and Jack Sutthoff.

1904, Dec. 20
Infielder Del Howard to Pittsburgh Pirates for first baseman Kitty Bransfield, infielder Otto Krueger, and outfielder Harry McCormick

1904, Dec. 20
Third baseman Harry Wolverton and pitcher Chick Fraser to Boston Braves for pitcher Togie Pittinger.

1907, June 10
Pitcher–outfielder Johnny Lush to St. Louis Cardinals for pitcher Charlie Brown.

1910, Jan. 20
Pitcher Harry Coveleski to Cincinnati Reds for pitcher Ad Brennan.

1910, Jan. 20
Pitcher Frank Corridon to Cincinnati Reds for pitcher Bob Ewing.

1910, July
Pitcher Bill Foxen to Chicago Cubs for first baseman Fred Luderus.

1911, Feb.
Pitchers George McQuillan and Lew Moren, third baseman Eddie Grant, and outfielder John Bates to Cincinnati Reds for third baseman Hans Lobert, outfielder George Paskert, and pitchers Fred Beebe and John Rowan.

1911, July 15
Pitcher Bert Humphries to Cincinnati Reds for outfielder Fred Beck and pitcher Bill Burns.

1911, Aug.
Pitcher Jack Rowan to Chicago Cubs for pitcher Cliff Curtis.

1912, July 1
Outfielder John Titus to Boston Braves for outfielder Doc Miller.

1913, June 5
Infielder John Dodge and pitcher Red Nelson to Cincinnati Reds for outfielders Beals Becker and Josh Devore.

1913, Aug. 20
Infielder–outfielder Cozy Dolan to Pittsburgh Pirates for pitcher Howie Camnitz and third baseman Bobby Byrne.

1915, Jan.
Third baseman Hans Lobert to New York Giants for pitcher Al Demaree, third baseman Milt Stock, and catcher Bert Adams.

1915, Jan.
Catcher Red Dooin to Cincinnati Reds for infielder Bert Niehoff.

1915, Feb. 10
Outfielder Sherry Magee to Boston Braves for outfielder George Whitted and infielder Oscar Dugey.

1917, Jan. 16
Pitcher Al Demaree to Chicago Cubs for pitcher Jimmie Lavender and $5,000.

1917, Nov. 11
Pitcher Grover Cleveland Alexander and catcher Bill Killefer to Chicago Cubs for pitcher Mike Prendergast, catcher Pickles Dillhoefer, and $60,000.

1917, Dec. 26
Outfielder George Paskert to Chicago Cubs for outfielder Cy Williams.

1918, Apr. 3
Infielder Bert Niehoff and cash to St. Louis Cardinals for pitcher Mule Watson.

1918, July 1
Pitcher Erskine Mayer to Pittsburgh Pirates for pitcher Elmer Jacobs.

1919, Jan. 21
Third baseman Milt Stock, catcher Pickles Dillhoefer, and pitcher Frank Davis to St. Louis Cardinals for infielders Doug Baird and Stuffy Stewart, pitcher Gene Packard, and cash.

1919, May 27
Pitcher Joe Oeschger to New York Giants for pitcher George Smith and infielder Ed Sicking.

1919, July 14
Pitchers Elmer Jacobs and Frank Woodward and third baseman Doug Baird to St. Louis Cardinals for pitcher Lee Meadows and infielder Gene Paulette.

1919, Sept.
Outfielder George Whitted to Pittsburgh Pirates for outfielder Casey Stengel.

1920, June 8
Shortstop Dave Bancroft to New York Giants for shortstop Art

Grover Cleveland Alexander was drafted shortly after the Phillies traded him to the Cubs.

Cy Williams won three home run crowns after the Phillies got him in a trade.

The Phillies got a Hubbell in 1920, but it was only Bill.

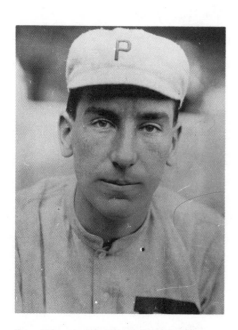

Eppa Rixey went on to a Hall of Fame career after the Phillies traded him to the Reds.

Fletcher, pitcher Bill Hubbell, and $100,000.

1920, Nov. 22
Pitcher Eppa Rixey to Cincinnati Reds for pitcher Jimmy Ring and outfielder Greasy Neale.

1921, June 30
Second baseman Johnny Rawlings and outfielder Casey Stengel to New York Giants for infielder Joe Rapp and outfielders Lee King and Curt Walker.

1921, July 10
Pitcher Cecil Causey to New York Giants for pitcher Jesse Winters and outfielder John Monroe.

1921, July 25
Outfielder Irish Meusel to New York Giants for catcher Butch Henline.

1923, Feb. 11
Pitcher George Smith to Brooklyn Dodgers for pitcher Clarence Mitchell.

1923, May 23
Pitcher Lee Meadows and second baseman Johnny Rawlings to Pittsburgh Pirates for pitcher Whitey Glazner and second baseman Cotton Tierney.

1923, Dec. 10
Second baseman Cotton Tierney to Boston Braves for infielder Hod Ford and outfielder Ray Powell.

1924, May 30
Outfielder Curt Walker to Cincinnati Reds for outfielder George Harper.

1925, May 1
Pitcher Bill Hubbell to Brooklyn Dodgers for pitcher Art Decatur.

1925, Dec. 30
Pitcher Jimmy Ring to New York Giants for pitchers Jack Bentley and Wayland Dean.

1927, Jan. 9
Outfielder George Harper to New York Giants and catcher Butch Henline to Brooklyn Dodgers in three-team deal for second baseman Fresco Thompson and pitcher Jack Scott.

1927, June 7
Pitcher Hal Carlson to Chicago Cubs for pitcher Tony Kaufmann and shortstop Jimmy Cooney.

1927, Dec. 13
Outfielder Johnny Mokan, infielder Jimmy Cooney, and catcher Bubber

Jonnard to St. Louis Cardinals for pitcher Jimmy Ring and catcher John Schulte.

1928, May 11
Catcher Jimmie Wilson to St. Louis Cardinals for catcher Spud Davis and outfielder Howard Peel.

1928, May 29
Outfielder Russ Wrightstone to New York Giants for outfielder Art Jahn.

1928, Oct. 13
Shortstop Heinie Sand and cash to St. Louis Cardinals for shortstop Tommy Thevenow.

1928, Oct. 29
Outfielder Fred Leach to New York Giants for outfielder Lefty O'Doul and $25,000.

1929, July 24
Pitcher Luther Roy to Brooklyn Dodgers for pitcher Lou Koupal.

1929, Dec. 11
Outfielder Howard Peel and pitcher Bob McGraw to St. Louis Cardinals for pitcher Grover Cleveland Alexander and catcher Harry McCurdy.

1930, Aug. 7
Outfielder Denny Sothern to Pittsburgh Pirates for outfielder Fred Brickell.

1930, Oct. 14
Outfielder Lefty O'Doul and second baseman Fresco Thompson to Brooklyn Dodgers for outfielder Hal Lee, pitchers Clise Dudley and Jumbo Elliott, and $25,000.

1930, Nov. 6
Shortstop Tommy Thevenow and pitcher Claude Willoughby to Pittsburgh Pirates for shortstop Dick Bartell.

1932, Dec. 12
Outfielder Kiddo Davis to New York Giants for outfielder Chick Fullis, first baseman Gus Dugas, and cash.

1932, Dec. 15
Pitcher Ray Benge to Brooklyn Dodgers for pitcher Austin Moore, second baseman Mickey Finn, and third baseman Jack Warner.

1933, June 17
Third baseman Pinky Whitney and outfielder Hal Lee to Boston Braves for outfielder Wes Schulmerich, infielder Fritz Knothe, and cash.

1933, Nov. 15
Infielder Eddie Delker and catcher Spud Davis to St. Louis Cardinals for catcher Jimmie Wilson.

1933, Nov. 21
Right fielder Chuck Klein to Chicago Cubs for pitcher Ted Kleinhans, infielder Mark Koenig, outfielder Harvey Hendrick, and $65,000.

1933, Dec. 20
Infielder Mark Koenig to Cincinnati Reds for infielders Irv Jeffries and Otto Bluege.

1934, May 8
Pitcher Ted Kleinhans and outfielder Wes Schulmerich to Cincinnati Reds for pitcher Syl Johnson and outfielder Johnny Moore.

1934, June 11
First baseman Don Hurst to Chicago Cubs for first baseman Dolph Camilli.

1934, June 15
Outfielder Chick Fullis to St. Louis Cardinals for outfielder Kiddo Davis.

1934, Nov. 1
Shortstop Dick Bartell to New York Giants for shortstop Blondy Ryan, third baseman Johnny Vergez, outfielder George Watkins, pitcher Pretzels Pezzullo, and cash.

1934, Dec. 13
Outfielder Kiddo Davis to New York Giants for pitcher Joe Bowman.

1935, Nov. 21
Catcher Al Todd to Pittsburgh Pirates for catcher Earl Grace and pitcher Claude Passeau.

1936, Apr. 30
Infielder Mickey Haslin to Boston Bees for third baseman Pinky Whitney.

1936, May 21
Outfielder Ethan Allen and pitcher Curt Davis to Chicago Cubs for outfielder Chuck Klein, pitcher Fabian Kowalik, and $50,000.

1936, Aug. 4
Pitcher Fabian Kowalik to Boston Bees for pitcher Ray Benge.

1936, Dec. 8
Second baseman Lou Chiozza to New York Giants for infielder George Scharein and cash.

1937, Apr. 16
Pitcher Joe Bowman to Pittsburgh

Pirates for first baseman Earl Browne.

1937, Dec. 8
Catcher Earl Grace to St. Louis Browns for catcher Cap Clark.

1938, Mar. 6
First baseman Dolph Camilli to Brooklyn Dodgers for outfielder Ed Morgan and $50,000.

1938, June 10
Infielder Justin Stein to Cincinnati Reds for infielder Buck Jordan.

1938, June 13
Pitcher Bucky Walters to Cincinnati Reds for catcher Spud Davis, pitcher Al Hollingsworth, and $50,000.

1938, July 11
Outfielder Gib Brack to Brooklyn Dodgers for outfielder Tuck Stainback.

1938, Aug. 8
Pitcher Wayne LaMaster to Brooklyn Dodgers for pitcher Max Butcher.

1939, May 29
Pitcher Claude Passeau to Chicago Cubs for outfielder Joe Marty, pitchers Kirby Higbe and Ray Harrell, and $50,000.

1939, July 13
Pitcher Al Hollingsworth to New York Yankees for infielder Roy Hughes.

1939, July 28
Pitcher Max Butcher to Pittsburgh Pirates for first baseman Gus Suhr.

1940, June 15
Outfielder Morrie Arnovich to Cincinnati Reds for outfielder Johnny Rizzo.

1940, Nov. 11
Pitcher Kirby Higbe to Brooklyn Dodgers for pitchers Vito Tamulis and Bill Crouch, catcher Mickey Livingston, and $100,000.

1941, May 8
Pitcher Vito Tamulis to Brooklyn Dodgers for pitcher Lee Grissom.

1942, Apr. 22
Pitcher Johnny Allen to Brooklyn Dodgers for pitcher George Washburn.

1942, Dec. 12
Pitcher Rube Melton to Brooklyn Dodgers for pitcher Johnny Allen and $30,000.

Clise Dudley came in the trade for Lefty O'Doul.

The Phillies traded Kiddo Davis to the Giants for Chick Fullis, then got him back two years later in a trade with the Cardinals for Chick Fullis.

Blondy Ryan, Johnny Vergez, George Watkins, and Joe Bowman (from left) came to the Phillies from the Giants in 1934.

The Phillies used Mickey Haslin as bait for a trade that returned Pinky Whitney.

1943, Jan. 22
First baseman Nick Etten to New York Yankees for catcher Tom Padden, pitcher Al Gerheauser, first baseman Ed Levy, and $10,000.

1943, Mar. 8
Outfielder Lloyd Waner and infielder Al Glossop to Brooklyn Dodgers for first baseman Babe Dahlgren.

1943, Mar. 24
Catcher-infielder Bobby Bragan to Brooklyn Dodgers for pitcher Jack Kraus and cash.

1943, June 1
Outfielders Danny Litwhiler and Earl Naylor to St. Louis Cardinals for outfielders Buster Adams, Dain Clay, and Coaker Triplett.

1943, June 6
Outfielder Dain Clay to Cincinnati Reds for infielder Charlie Brewster.

1943, June 15
Pitcher Johnny Podgajny to Pittsburgh Pirates for pitcher Dutch Dietz.

1943, Aug. 5
Catcher Mickey Livingston to Chicago Cubs for pitcher Bill Lee.

1943, Dec. 30
First baseman Babe Dahlgren to Pittsburgh Pirates for catcher Babe Phelps.

1945, Mar. 31
Pitcher Al Gerheauser to Pittsburgh Pirates for center fielder Vince DiMaggio.

1945, May 8
Outfielder Buster Adams to St. Louis Cardinals for infielders John Antonelli and Glen Crawford.

1945, June 15
Catcher Johnny Peacock to Brooklyn Dodgers for outfielder Ben Chapman.

1946, May 1
Center fielder Vince DiMaggio to New York Giants for catcher Clyde Kluttz, who was then traded to St. Louis Cardinals for second baseman Emil Verban.

1947, Mar. 27
Pitcher Andy Karl to Boston Braves for catcher Don Padgett.

Mickey Livingston came to the Phillies for one pitcher, and went for another hurler.

1947, May 2
Outfielder Ron Northey and $50,000 to St. Louis Cardinals for outfielder Harry Walker and pitcher Fred Schmidt.

1947, June 14
Pitcher Ken Raffensberger and catcher Hugh Poland to Cincinnati Reds for catcher Al Lakeman.

1947, Dec. 11
Pitcher Tommy Hughes to Cincinnati Reds for infielder–outfielder Bert Haas.

1948, Feb. 7
Outfielder Johnny Wyrostek to Cincinnati Reds for shortstop Eddie Miller.

1948, Apr. 7
Infielder Ralph LaPointe and $20,000 to St. Louis Cardinals for first baseman–outfielder Dick Sisler.

1948, Oct. 4
Outfielder Harry Walker to Chicago Cubs for outfielder Bill Nicholson.

1948, Dec. 14
Pitchers Dutch Leonard and Walt Dubiel to Chicago Cubs for pitcher Hank Borowy and first baseman Eddie Waitkus.

Veterans Roy Cullenbine, Eddie Miller, and Bert Haas (from left) joined the Phillies in 1948.

In one of their best swaps, the Phillies shipped Ralph LaPointe to the Cardinals for Dick Sisler.

1950, Apr. 27
Outfielder Johnny Blatnik to St. Louis Cardinals for pitcher Ken Johnson.

1951, June 8
Outfielder Dick Whitman and cash to Brooklyn Dodgers for infielder-outfielder Tommy Brown.

1951, Dec. 10
Catcher Andy Seminick, infielder Eddie Pellagrini, outfielder Dick Sisler, and pitcher Niles Jordan to Cincinnati Reds for catcher Smoky Burgess, second baseman Connie Ryan, and pitcher Howie Fox.

1951, Dec. 13
Catcher Jake Schmitt to New York Giants for infielder Jack Lohrke.

1952, May 23
Pitcher Bubba Church to Cincinnati Reds for outfielder Johnny Wyrostek and pitcher Kent Peterson.

1953, Feb. 16
Pitcher Russ Meyer to Boston Braves for first baseman Earl Torgeson.

1954, Jan. 13
Pitcher Andy Hansen, outfielder Jack Lohrke, and $70,000 to Pittsburgh Pirates for pitcher Murry Dickson.

1954, Mar. 28
Infielder Dick Young and $50,000 to Brooklyn Dodgers for infielder Bobby Morgan.

1955, Apr. 30
Catcher Smoky Burgess, pitcher Steve Ridzik, and outfielder Stan Palys to Cincinnati Reds for catcher Andy Seminick and outfielders Jim Greengrass and Glen Gorbous.

1956, May 11
Pitchers Murry Dickson and Herm Wehmeier to St. Louis Cardinals for pitchers Stu Miller, Ben Flowers, and Harvey Haddix.

1956, May 14
Infielder Bobby Morgan to St. Louis Cardinals for infielder Solly Hemus.

1956, Oct. 11
Pitcher Stu Miller to New York Giants for pitcher Jim Hearn.

Eddie Waitkus, Dick Sisler, and Hank Borowy (from left) were greeted by Bob Carpenter at spring training in 1949.

Coach Benny Bengough got together with Del Ennis (left) and Rip Repulski after the two were traded for each other in 1956.

1956, Nov. 19
Outfielder Del Ennis to St. Louis Cardinals for outfielder Rip Repulski and infielder Bobby Morgan.

1957, Apr. 5
Outfielder Elmer Valo, shortstop Mel Geho, first baseman Tim Harkness, pitchers Ben Flowers and Ron Negray, and $75,000 to Brooklyn Dodgers for shortstop Chico Fernandez.

1957, May 10
Outfielder Glen Gorbous to St. Louis Cardinals for outfielder Chuck Harmon.

1957, Dec. 6
Pitcher Harvey Haddix to Cincinnati Reds for outfielder Wally Post.

1958, June 13
Catcher Joe Lonnett to Milwaukee Braves for catcher Carl Sawatski.

1958, July 27
Catcher John Turk and cash to Detroit Tigers for catcher Jim Hegan.

1958, Sept. 29
Infielder Solly Hemus to St. Louis Cardinals for infielder Gene Freese.

1958, Dec. 3
Outfielder Chuck Essegian to St. Louis Cardinals for shortstop Ruben Amaro.

1958, Dec. 3
Pitcher Jack Sanford to San Francisco Giants for pitcher Ruben Gomez and catcher Valmy Thomas.

1958, Dec. 23
Pitchers Jim Golden and Gene Snyder and outfielder Rip Repulski to Los Angeles Dodgers for second baseman Sparky Anderson.

1959, Mar. 31
Catcher Stan Lopata and infielders Johnny O'Brien and Ted Kazanski to Milwaukee Braves for pitcher Gene Conley, infielder Joe Koppe, and infielder-outfielder Harry Hanebrink.

1959, May 10
Infielder Granny Hamner to Cleveland Indians for pitcher Humberto Robinson.

1959, May 12
Pitcher Seth Morehead to Chicago Cubs for pitcher Taylor Phillips.

1959, June 5
Third baseman Willie Jones to Cleveland Indians for outfielder Jim Bolger.

1959, Dec. 4
Catcher Carl Sawatski to St. Louis Cardinals for outfielder Bobby Gene Smith and pitcher Billy Smith.

1959, Dec. 5
Pitcher Ray Semproch and shortstop Chico Fernandez to Detroit Tigers for outfielder Ken Walters and infielders Ted Lepcio and Alex Cosmidis.

1959, Dec. 8
Infielder Gene Freese to Chicago

Bobby Morgan came to the Phillies twice in trades.

The Phillies acquired Ruben Gomez in one of their worst trades in 1958.

White Sox for outfielder Johnny Callison.

1960, May 13
First baseman Ed Bouchee and pitcher Don Cardwell to Chicago Cubs for second baseman Tony Taylor and catcher Cal Neeman.

1960, June 15
Outfielders Harry Anderson and Wally Post and first baseman Fred Hopke to Cincinnati Reds for outfielders Tony Gonzalez and Lee Walls.

1960, June 23
Infielder Al Dark to Milwaukee Braves for third baseman Joe Morgan.

1960, Dec. 15
Pitcher Gene Conley to Boston Red Sox for pitcher Frank Sullivan.

1960, Jan. 11
Center fielder Richie Ashburn to Chicago Cubs for infielders Alvin Dark and Jim Woods and pitcher John Buzhardt.

1961, May 4
Pitcher Dick Farrell and shortstop Joe Koppe to Los Angeles Dodgers for third baseman Charley Smith and outfielder Don Demeter.

1961, July 2
Outfielder Bobby Del Greco to Kansas City A's for outfielder Wes Covington.

1961, Nov. 28
Pitcher John Buzhardt and third baseman Charley Smith to Chicago White Sox for first baseman Roy Sievers.

1961, Dec. 15
Pitcher Taylor Phillips and infielder Bob Sadowski to Chicago White Sox for third baseman Andy Carey and pitcher Frank Barnes. When Carey refused to report, his place was taken by pitcher Cal McLish.

1962, Mar. 2
Outfielder Tony Curry and pitcher Ken Lehman to Cleveland Indians for infielder Mel Roach.

1962, Apr. 28
Pitcher Don Ferrarese to St. Louis Cardinals for pitcher Bobby Locke.

1962, Nov. 27
Pitcher Jim Owens to Cincinnati Reds for infielder Cookie Rojas.

1962, Nov. 28
Outfielder Ted Savage and first baseman Pancho Herrera to Pittsburgh Pirates for third baseman Don Hoak.

1962, Dec. 11
Outfielder Jacke Davis to Los Angeles Dodgers for catcher Earl Averill.

1963, Dec. 4
Outfielder Don Demeter and pitcher Jack Hamilton to Detroit Tigers for pitcher Jim Bunning and catcher Gus Triandos.

1964, Aug. 7
Pitcher Gary Kroll, outfielder Wayne Graham, and cash to New York Mets for outfielder Frank Thomas.

1964, Sept. 9
Pitcher Marcelino Lopez and player to be named later to Los Angeles Angels for first baseman Vic Power. Player to be named later became Vic Power.

1964, Oct. 15
Catcher Bill Heath and pitcher Joel Gibson to Chicago White Sox for pitcher Rudy May.

1964, Nov. 29
Pitcher Dennis Bennett to Boston Red Sox for first baseman Dick Stuart.

1964, Dec. 1
Outfielder-infielder Danny Cater and shortstop Lee Elia to Chicago White Sox for pitcher Ray Herbert and infielder Jeoff Long.

1964, Dec. 3
Pitcher Rudy May and first baseman Costen Shockley to Los Angeles Angels for pitcher Bo Belinsky.

1965, Oct. 27
Outfielder Alex Johnson, pitcher Art Mahaffey, and catcher Pat Corrales to St. Louis Cardinals for shortstop Dick Groat, first baseman Bill White, and catcher Bob Uecker.

1965, Nov. 29
Shortstop Ruben Amaro to New York Yankees for shortstop Phil Linz.

1965, Dec. 6
Pitcher Jack Baldschun to Baltimore Orioles for pitcher Darold Knowles and outfielder Jackie Brandt.

1966, Jan. 10
Outfielder Wes Covington to Chicago Cubs for outfielder Doug Clemens.

1966, Feb. 22
First baseman Dick Stuart to New York Mets for catcher Jim Schaffer and infielders Bobby Klaus and Wayne Graham.

1966, Apr. 21
Pitcher Ferguson Jenkins, outfielder Adolfo Phillips, and outfielder–first baseman John Herrnstein to Chicago Cubs for pitchers Bob Buhl and Larry Jackson.

1966, Nov. 30
Pitcher Darold Knowles and cash to Washington Senators for outfielder Don Lock.

1966, Oct. 7
Pitcher Ray Culp and cash to Chicago Cubs for pitcher Dick Ellsworth.

1966, Dec. 10
Pitcher Joe Verbanic and cash to New York Yankees for pitcher Pedro Ramos.

1966, Dec. 15
Pitcher John Morris to Baltimore Orioles for pitcher Dick Hall.

1967, June 6
Catcher Bob Uecker to Atlanta Braves for catcher Gene Oliver.

1967, July 11
Infielder Phil Linz to New York Mets for infielder Chuck Hiller.

1967, Dec. 15
Pitcher Dick Ellsworth and catcher–first baseman Gene Oliver to Boston Red Sox for catcher Mike Ryan.

1967, Dec. 16
Pitcher Jim Bunning to Pittsburgh Pirates for pitchers Woodie Fryman, Harold Clem, and Bill Laxton and infielder Don Money.

1969, Jan. 20
Catcher Clay Dalrymple to Baltimore Orioles for outfielder Ron Stone.

1969, Apr. 3
First baseman Bill White to St. Louis Cardinals for infielder Jerry Buchek and infielder–catcher Jim Hutto.

1969, May 5
Outfielder Don Lock to Boston Red Sox for outfielder Bill Schlesinger.

1969, Sept. 6
Pitcher Gary Wagner to Boston Red Sox for pitcher Mike Jackson.

1969, Oct. 7
First baseman Dick Allen, infielder Cookie Rojas, and pitcher Jerry Johnson to St. Louis Cardinals for catcher Tim McCarver, outfielders Curt Flood and Byron Browne, and pitcher Joe Hoerner. When Flood refused to report, he was replaced by first baseman Willie Montanez.

1969, Nov. 17
Outfielder Johnny Callison to Chicago Cubs for outfielder Oscar Gamble and pitcher Dick Selma.

1970, Nov. 3
Outfielder Curt Flood to Washington Senators for catcher–first baseman Greg Goosen, pitcher Jeff Terpko, and outfielder Gene Martin.

1970, Dec. 16
Pitcher Grant Jackson, infielder Jim Hutto, and outfielder Sam Parilla to Baltimore Orioles for outfielder Roger Freed.

1971, Apr. 22
Outfielder Johnny Briggs to Milwaukee Brewers for pitcher Ray Peters and catcher–outfielder Pete Koegel.

1971, June 12
Infielder Tony Taylor to Detroit Tigers for pitchers Carl Cavanaugh and Mike Fremuth.

1971, Oct. 22
Outfielder Larry Hisle to Los Angeles Dodgers for first baseman Tommy Hutton.

1971, Dec. 3
Catcher Jerry Rodriquez to Chicago White Sox for outfielder Bill Robinson.

1972, Feb. 25
Pitcher Rick Wise to St. Louis Cardinals for pitcher Steve Carlton.

1972, June 14
Catcher Tim McCarver to Montreal Expos for catcher John Bateman.

1972, June 15
First baseman Andre Thornton and pitcher Joe Hoerner to Atlanta

In a huge deal in 1960, the Phillies got 6–7 Frank Sullivan in a swap for 6–8 Gene Conley.

Keith Moreland went on to a fine career with the Cubs after the Phillies traded him in 1981.

Braves for pitchers Jim Nash and Gary Neibauer.

1972, Oct. 31
Infielders Don Money and John Vukovich and pitcher Bill Champion to Milwaukee Brewers for pitchers Jim Lonborg, Ken Brett, Ken Sanders, and Earl Stephenson.

1972, Nov. 30
Pitchers Ken Sanders and Ken Reynolds and infielder Joe Lis to Minnesota Twins for outfielder Cesar Tovar.

1972, Dec. 1
Outfielders Oscar Gamble and Roger Freed to Cleveland Indians for outfielders Del Unser and Terry Wedgewood.

1973, May 2
First baseman Deron Johnson to Oakland A's for catcher-outfielder Jack Bastable.

1973, May 7
Pitcher Billy Wilson to Milwaukee Brewers for pitcher Fred Linzy.

1973, Oct. 18
Pitcher Ken Brett to Pittsburgh Pirates for second baseman Dave Cash.

1973, Dec. 3
Pitcher Barry Lersch and infielder Craig Robinson to Atlanta Braves for pitcher Ron Schueler.

1973, Dec. 6
Infielder Denny Doyle to California Angels for infielder Billy Grabarkewitz, pitcher Auerelio Monteagudo, and outfielder Chris Coletta in completion of deal begun Aug. 18, 1973.

1974, Jan. 31
Catcher Mike Ryan to Pittsburgh Pirates for pitcher Jackie Hernandez.

1974, Dec. 3
Outfielder Del Unser, catcher John Stearns, and pitcher Mac Scarce to New York Mets for pitcher Tug McGraw and outfielders Don Hahn and Dave Schneck.

1974, Dec. 9
Outfielder Mike Anderson to St. Louis Cardinals for pitcher Ron Reed.

1975, Mar. 6
Outfielder Nelson Garcia to Cleveland Indians for pitcher Tom Hilgendorf.

1975, Apr. 5
Outfielder Bill Robinson to Pittsburgh Pirates for pitcher Wayne Simpson.

1975, May 4
First baseman Willie Montanez to San Francisco Giants for outfielder Garry Maddox.

1975, May 7
Catcher Jim Essian and outfielder Barry Bonnell to Atlanta Braves for infielder Dick Allen and catcher Johnny Oates.

1975, Dec. 10
Pitchers Dick Ruthven and Roy Thomas and infielder Alan Bannister to Chicago White Sox for pitcher Jim Kaat and infielder Mike Buskey.

1976, Dec. 20
Catcher Johnny Oates and pitcher Quency Hill to Los Angeles Dodgers for second baseman Ted Sizemore.

1977, June 15
Pitcher Tommy Underwood and outfielders Dane Iorg and Rick Bosetti to St. Louis Cardinals for outfielder Bake McBride and pitcher Steven Waterbury.

1977, Oct. 25
Pitcher Manny Seone to Chicago Cubs for outfielder Jose Cardenal.

1977, June 15
Pitcher Wayne Twitchell and catcher Tim Blackwell to Montreal Expos for catcher Barry Foote and pitcher Dan Warthen.

1978, Mar. 24
Infielder Fred Andrews to New York Mets for infielder Bud Harrelson.

1978, June 14
Outfielders Jay Johnstone and Bobby Browne to New York Yankees for pitcher Rawly Eastwick.

1978, June 15
Pitcher Gene Garber to Atlanta Braves for pitcher Dick Ruthven.

1978, Aug. 6
Infielder Dave Johnson to Chicago Cubs for pitcher Larry Anderson.

1979, Feb. 23
Outfielder Jerry Martin, catcher Barry Foote, second baseman Ted Sizemore, and pitchers Henry Mack and Derek Botelho to Chicago Cubs for second baseman Manny Trillo, outfielder Greg Gross, and catcher Dave Rader.

1979, Mar. 27
First baseman Richie Hebner and outfielder Jose Moreno to New York Mets for pitcher Nino Espinosa.

1979, Apr. 13
Infielder Jim Morrison to Chicago White Sox for pitcher Jack Kucek.

1979, Aug. 3
Infielder Todd Cruz to Kansas City Royals for pitcher Doug Bird.

1979, Dec. 7
Infielder Pete Mackanin to Minnesota Twins for pitcher Paul Thormodsgard.

1980, Sept. 13
Pitcher Kevin Saucier to Texas Rangers for pitcher Sparky Lyle.

1981, Mar. 1
Pitcher Randy Lerch to Milwaukee Brewers for outfielder Dick Davis.

1981, Mar. 25
Pitcher Bob Walk to Atlanta Braves for outfielder Gary Matthews.

1981, Apr. 1
Infielder Jay Loviglio to Chicago Cubs for pitcher Mike Proly.

1981, Oct. 20
Infielder Ramon Aviles to Texas Rangers for pitcher Dave Rajsich.

1981, Nov. 20
Outfielder Lonnie Smith and pitcher Scott Munninghoff to Cleveland Indians for catcher Bo Diaz.

1981, Dec. 8
Catcher Keith Moreland and pitchers Dan Larson and Dickie Noles to Chicago Cubs for pitcher Mike Krukow and cash.

1982, Jan. 27
Shortstop Larry Bowa and infielder Ryne Sandberg to Chicago Cubs for shortstop Ivan DeJesus.

1982, Feb. 16
Outfielder Bake McBride to Cleveland Indians for pitcher Sid Monge.

1982, June 15
Outfielder Wayne Nordhagen to Pittsburgh Pirates for outfielder Bill Robinson.

1982, Sept. 12
Pitchers Jerry Reed and Leroy Smith and outfielder Wil Culmer to Cleveland Indians for pitcher John Denny.

1982, Dec. 9
Second baseman Manny Trillo, shortstop Julio Franco, outfielder George Vukovich, pitcher Jay Baller, and catcher Jerry Willard to Cleveland Indians for outfielder Von Hayes.

1982, Dec. 14
Pitchers Mike Krukow and Mark Davis and outfielder C. J. Penigar to San Francisco Giants for second baseman Joe Morgan and pitcher Al Holland.

1983, May 22
Pitcher Sid Monge to San Diego Padres for outfielder Joe Lefebvre.

1983, May 22
Pitchers Dick Ruthven and Bill Johnson to Chicago Cubs for pitcher Willie Hernandez.

1983, Aug. 31
Pitchers Ed Wojna, Marty Decker, Darren Burroughs, and Lance McCullers to San Diego Padres for outfielder Sixto Lezcano and pitcher Steve Fireovid.

1983, Dec. 5
Pitcher Ron Reed to Chicago White Sox for pitcher Jerry Koosman.

1984, Mar. 24
Outfielder Alejandro Sanchez to San Francisco Giants for infielder Dave Bergman.

1984, Mar. 24
Pitcher Willie Hernandez and infielder Dave Bergman to Detroit Tigers for outfielder Glenn Wilson and catcher John Wockenfuss.

1984, Mar. 26
Outfielders Gary Matthews and Bob Dernier and pitcher Porfi Altamirano to Chicago Cubs for pitcher Bill Campbell and outfielder– first baseman Mike Diaz.

1984, June 30
Pitcher Marty Bystrom and outfielder Keith Hughes to New York Yankees for pitcher Shane Rawley.

1984, Aug. 20
Pitchers Kelly Downs and George Riley to San Francisco Giants for first baseman Al Oliver and pitcher Renie Martin.

1985, Feb. 4
First baseman Al Oliver to Los

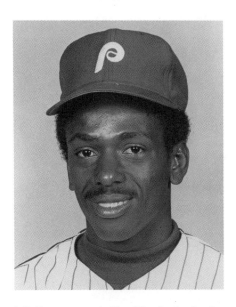

Julio Franco won a batting title after leaving the Phillies in the Von Hayes trade.

The Phillies traded themselves into a pennant when they sent Mike Krukow to the Giants and got back Joe Morgan and Al Holland.

Milt Thompson was a valuable addition to the Phillies after coming from the Braves.

Angeles Dodgers for pitcher Pat Zachry.

1985, Apr. 1
First baseman Len Matuszek to Toronto Blue Jays for pitcher Dave Shipanoff and outfielder Dave Kinnard.

1985, Apr. 6
Pitcher Bill Campbell and shortstop Ivan DeJesus to St. Louis Cardinals for pitcher Dave Rucker.

1985, Apr. 20
Pitchers Al Holland and Frankie Griffin to Pittsburgh Pirates for pitcher Kent Tekulve.

1985, Aug. 8
Catcher Bo Diaz and pitcher Greg Simpson to Cincinnati Reds for infielder Tom Foley, catcher Alan Knicely, and pitcher Fred Toliver.

1985, Sept. 13
Pitcher Rick Surhoff to Texas Rangers for pitcher Dave Stewart.

1985, Dec. 10
Catcher Ozzie Virgil and pitcher Pete Smith to Atlanta Braves for pitcher Steve Bedrosian and outfielder Milt Thompson.

1985, Dec. 11
Pitchers John Denny and Jeff Gray to Cincinnati Reds for outfielder Gary Redus and pitcher Tom Hume.

1986, Jan. 16
Pitcher Roger Cole and first baseman Ron Gideon to New York Mets for catcher Ronn Reynolds and pitcher Jeff Bittiger.

1986, June 24
Infielder Tom Foley and pitcher Lary Sorenson to Montreal Expos for pitcher Dan Schatzeder and infielder Skeeter Barnes.

1986, Dec. 11
Pitchers Charles Hudson and Jeff Knox to New York Yankees for outfielder Mike Easler and second baseman Tommy Barrett.

1987, Mar. 27
Outfielder Gary Redus to Chicago White Sox for pitcher Joe Cowley.

1987, Apr. 2
Catcher Ronn Reynolds to Houston Astros for pitcher Jeff Calhoun.

1987, June 10
Outfielder Mike Easler to New York Yankees for outfielder Keith Hughes and infielder Shane Turner.

1987, June 23
Pitcher Dan Schatzeder to Minnesota Twins for pitcher Danny Clay and third baseman Tom Schwartz.

1987, Dec. 9
Outfielder Glenn Wilson and pitcher Mike Jackson to Seattle Mariners for outfielder Phil Bradley.

1988, Mar. 21
Outfielders Jeff Stone and Keith Hughes and infielder Rick Schu to Baltimore Orioles for outfielders Mike Young and Frank Bellino.

1988, July 15
Infielder Luis Aguayo to New York Yankees for pitcher Amalio Carreno.

Jeff Parrett had a fine season in 1989 after the Phils got him from the Expos.

1988, Aug. 24
Outfielder Mike Young to Milwaukee Brewers for pitcher Alex Madrid.

1988, Oct. 3
Catcher Lance Parrish to California Angels for pitcher David Holdridge.

1988, Oct. 24
Pitcher Shane Rawley to Minnesota Twins for second baseman Tom Herr, outfielder Eric Bullock, and catcher Tom Nieto.

1988, Dec. 6
Pitcher Kevin Gross to Montreal Expos for pitchers Jeff Parrett and Floyd Youmans.

1988, Dec. 8
Outfielder Phil Bradley to Baltimore Orioles for pitchers Ken Howell and Gordon Dillard.

1988, Dec. 16
Outfielder Milt Thompson to St. Louis Cardinals for catcher Steve Lake and outfielder Curt Ford.

1989, June 2
Outfielder Chris James to San Diego Padres for outfielder John Kruk and infielder–outfielder Randy Ready.

1989, June 18
Pitcher Steve Bedrosian and infielder Rick Parker to San Francisco Giants for pitchers Terry Mulholland and Dennis Cook and third baseman Charlie Hayes.

1989, June 18
Second baseman Juan Samuel to New York Mets for outfielder Len Dykstra and pitcher Roger McDowell.

1989, July 13
Pitcher Jeff Gray to Cincinnati Reds for pitcher Bob Sebra.

1989, Sept. 2
Pitcher Larry McWilliams to Kansas City Royals for catcher Jeff Hulse.

1990, Mar. 31
Shortstop Steve Jeltz to Kansas City Royals for pitcher Jose DeJesus.

1990, July 23
Pitcher Marvin Freeman to Atlanta Braves for pitcher Joe Boever.

1990, Aug. 3
Pitcher Jeff Parrett, outfielder Jim Vatcher, and infielder Victor Rosario to Atlanta Braves for outfielder Dale Murphy and pitcher Tommy Greene.

1990, Aug. 30
Outfielder Carmelo Martinez to Pittsburgh Pirates for outfielders Wes Chamberlain, Tony Longmire, and Julio Peguero.

1990, Aug. 31
Second baseman Tom Herr to New York Mets for infielder Nikco Riesgo and pitcher Rocky Eli.

1991, Apr. 7
Pitchers Chuck McElroy and Bob Scanlan to Chicago Cubs for pitcher Mitch Williams.

1991, Dec. 8
Outfielder Von Hayes to California Angels for pitcher Kyle Abbott and outfielder Ruben Amaro.

1991, Dec. 9
Catcher Darrin Fletcher to Montreal Expos for pitcher Barry Jones.

1991, Dec. 11
Pitcher Bruce Ruffin to Milwaukee Brewers for infielder Dale Sveum.

1992, Jan. 8
Third baseman Charlie Hayes to New York Yankees for pitcher Darrin Chapin.

1992, Apr. 2
Pitcher Jason Grimsley to Houston Astros for pitcher Curt Schilling.

1992, May 28
Pitcher Donnie Elliott to Atlanta Braves for pitcher Ben Rivera.

1992, July 2
Outfielder Julio Peguero and pitcher

Steve Searcy to Los Angeles Dodgers for outfielder Stan Javier.

1992, Aug. 10
Infielder Dale Sveum to Chicago White Sox for pitcher Keith Shepherd.

1992, Aug. 11
Second baseman Steve Scarsone to Baltimore Orioles for shortstop Juan Bell.

1992, Nov. 17
Pitchers Joel Adamson and Matt Whisenant to Florida Marlins for pitcher Danny Jackson.

1992, Nov. 28
Pitcher Mike Hartley to Minnesota Twins for pitcher David West.

Major Purchases and Other Acquisitions

1900, Jan.
Outfielder Jimmy Slagle from Washington Nationals.

1900, Feb.
Pitcher Al Maul from Brooklyn Dodgers.

1900, Apr. 28
Third baseman Harry Wolverton from Chicago Cubs.

1900, June
Pitcher Jack Dunn from Brooklyn Dodgers.

1901, June 24
First baseman Hugh Jennings from Brooklyn Dodgers.

1903, Jan.
Catcher Chief Zimmer from Pittsburgh Pirates.

1904, Aug. 30
Infielder Jack Doyle from Brooklyn Dodgers.

1905, July 16
Pitcher Kid Nichols from St. Louis Cardinals.

1907, Oct.
Pitcher Earl Moore from New York Yankees.

1911, May
Catcher Tom Madden from Boston Red Sox.

1912, May
Infielder Cozy Dolan from New York Yankees.

1915, Feb. 14
Pitcher George McQuillan from Pittsburgh Pirates.

1915, Aug. 8
Pitcher Bert Humphries from Chicago White Sox.

1917, Aug. 12
Infielder Johnny Evers from Boston Braves.

1918, Dec.
Pitcher Johnny Enzmann from Cleveland Indians.

1919, July 9
Infielder Lena Blackburne from Boston Braves.

1920, Jan.
Infielder Dots Miller from St. Louis Cardinals.

1920, June
Second baseman Johnny Rawlings from Boston Braves.

1921, May
Outfielder Cliff Lee from Pittsburgh Pirates.

1921, June 28
Infielder Jimmy Smith from Cincinnati Reds.

1921, July 4
First baseman Ed Konetchy from Brooklyn Dodgers.

1922, July 14
Outfielder Johnny Mokan from
Pittsburgh Pirates.

1922, Dec. 12
First baseman Walter Holke from
Boston Braves.

1923, May 11
Second baseman Johnny Rawlings
from New York Giants.

1923, Dec.
Pitcher Earl Hamilton from
Pittsburgh Pirates.

1924, July 1
Pitcher Joe Oeschger from New York
Giants.

1925, Mar. 30
Infielder Lew Fonseca from
Cincinnati Reds.

1925, Apr. 2
Outfielder George Burns from
Cincinnati Reds.

1925, June 15
Infielder Barney Friberg from
Chicago Cubs.

1928, Oct.
Pitcher Alex Ferguson from
Washington Senators.

1930, June
Catcher Tony Rensa from Detroit
Tigers.

1931, July 27
Pitcher Sheriff Blake from Chicago
Cubs.

1932, June 4
Pitcher Flint Rhem from St. Louis
Cardinals.

1932, June 25
Outfielder Cliff Heathcote from
Cincinnati Reds.

1934, Jan.
Outfielder Ethan Allen from St.
Louis Cardinals.

1934, June 14
Third baseman Bucky Walters from
Boston Red Sox.

1935, May 20
Pitcher Tommy Thomas from
Washington Senators.

1937, Dec. 20
Pitcher Al Smith from St. Louis
Cardinals.

1938, June
Outfielder Tuck Stainback from St.
Louis Cardinals.

1939, Aug. 5
Infielder Bud Hafey from Cincinnati
Reds.

1940, Mar. 26
Outfielder Chuck Klein signed as a
free agent.

1941, Dec. 4
Outfielder Lloyd Waner signed as a
free agent.

1942, May 2
Outfielder Ernie Koy from
Cincinnati Reds.

1943, Mar. 24
Pitcher Schoolboy Rowe from
Brooklyn Dodgers.

1943, Apr. 16
Pitcher George Washburn from
Chicago Clubs.

1943, Apr. 30
First baseman–outfielder Jimmy
Wasdell from Pittsburgh Pirates.

1943, May 20
Pitcher Newt Kimball from Brooklyn
Dodgers.

1943, July
Pitcher Dick Barrett from Chicago
Cubs.

1944, Apr. 13
First baseman Tony Lupien from
Boston Red Sox.

1944, June 11
Catcher Johnny Peacock from
Boston Red Sox.

1944, July 28
Pitcher Vern Kennedy from
Cleveland Indians.

1945, Feb. 10
First baseman Jimmie Foxx signed as
a free agent.

1945, Mar. 28
Pitcher Whit Wyatt from Brooklyn
Dodgers.

1945, May 31
Pitcher Oscar Judd from Boston Red
Sox.

1945, Dec. 7
Pitcher John Humphries from
Chicago White Sox.

1945, Dec. 10
First baseman Frank McCormick
from Cincinnati Reds.

1945, Dec. 12
Shortstop Skeeter Newsome from
Boston Red Sox.

1946, Jan. 21
Infielder Roy Hughes from Chicago
Cubs.

1946, Jan. 22
Third baseman Jim Tabor from
Boston Red Sox.

1946, Feb. 5
Pitcher Al Jurisich from St. Louis
Cardinals.

1946, Feb. 5
Outfielder Johnny Wyrostek from St.
Louis Cardinals.

1946, Mar. 25
Catcher Rollie Hemsley from New
York Yankees.

1946, July 8
Pitcher Blix Donnelly from St. Louis
Cardinals.

1946, Dec. 9
Pitcher Dutch Leonard from
Washington Senators.

1947, Mar. 21
Outfielder Buster Adams from St.
Louis Cardinals.

1947, May 9
Pitcher Ken Heintzelman from
Pittsburgh Pirates.

1947, May 10
First baseman Howie Schultz from
Brooklyn Dodgers.

1948, Apr. 15
Outfielder Bama Rowell from
Brooklyn Dodgers.

1948, May 15
Pitcher Nick Strincevich from
Pittsburgh Pirates.

1948, Sept. 13
Catcher Hal Wagner from Detroit
Tigers.

1948, Oct. 11
Pitcher Russ Meyer from Chicago
Cubs.

1948, Dec. 14
Pitcher Ken Trinkle from New York
Giants.

1949, Nov. 14
Outfielder Dick Whitman from
Brooklyn Dodgers.

1950, May 9
Infielder Jimmy Bloodworth from
Cincinnati Reds.

1952, Sept. 30
Infielder Tom Glaviano from St.
Louis Cardinals.

1953, Aug. 31
Pitcher Johnny Lindell from
Pittsburgh Pirates.

1954, June 12
Pitcher Herm Wehmeier from
Cincinnati Reds.

1954, July 18
Infielder Floyd Baker from Boston
Red Sox.

1955, Feb. 10
Outfielder Peanuts Lowrey signed as
a free agent.

1955, Mar. 19
Pitcher Dave Cole from Chicago
Cubs.

1955, Apr. 30
Infielder Roy Smalley from
Milwaukee Braves.

1955, May 23
Pitcher Bob Kuzava from Baltimore
Orioles.

1955, July 9
Pitcher Saul Rogovin signed as a free
agent.

1955, Dec. 9
Outfielder Frankie Baumholtz from
Chicago Cubs.

1956, May 22
Outfielder Elmer Valo signed as a
free agent.

1957, June 26
Pitcher Warren Hacker from
Cincinnati Reds.

1957, July 30
Outfielder Ron Northey signed as a
free agent.

1957, Dec. 11
Outfielder Dave Philley from Detroit
Tigers.

1959, June 9
Outfielder Solly Drake from Los
Angeles Dodgers.

1961, June 17
Outfielder Elmer Valo signed as a
free agent.

1961, July 9
Catcher Darrell Johnson signed as a
free agent.

1962, Mar. 7
Catcher Sammy White signed as a
free agent.

1962, Apr. 5
Infielder Billy Klaus from
Washington Senators.

1963, Mar. 14
Pitcher Ryne Duren from Los Angeles Angels.

1963, Mar. 25
Pitcher Johnny Klippstein from Cincinnati Reds.

1963, May 4
Outfielder Jim Lemon from Minnesota Twins.

1964, Apr. 21
Pitcher Ed Roebuck from Washington Senators.

1964, Aug. 15
Pitcher Bobby Shantz from Chicago Cubs.

1965, Apr. 13
Pitcher Ryne Duren signed as a free agent.

1965, May 30
Pitcher Lew Burdette from Chicago Cubs.

1966, Apr. 11
Pitcher Roger Craig signed as a free agent.

1966, Apr. 13
Pitcher Steve Ridzik from Washington Senators.

1966, Apr. 23
Infielder–outfielder Harvey Kuenn from Chicago Cubs.

1967, Apr. 10
Outfielder–first baseman Tito Francona from St. Louis Cardinals.

1967, May 8
Pitcher Dick Farrell from Houston Astros.

1968, Dec. 3
First baseman Deron Johnson from Atlanta Braves.

1969, Oct. 29
Pitcher Jim Bunning signed as a free agent.

1969, Nov. 25
Pitcher Fred Wenz from Boston Red Sox.

1972, Nov. 13
Infielder Jose Pagan signed as a free agent.

1973, Aug. 10
Pitcher George Culver from Los Angeles Dodgers.

1973, Dec. 7
Pitcher Eddie Watt from Baltimore Orioles.

1973, Dec. 19
Infielder Tony Taylor signed as a free agent.

1974, June 21
Pitcher Pete Richert from St. Louis Cardinals.

1974, June 23
Outfielder Ollie Brown from Houston Astros.

1974, July 12
Pitcher Gene Garber from Kansas City Royals.

1975, Jan. 9
Pitcher Joe Hoerner signed as a free agent.

1975, July 1
Catcher Tim McCarver signed as a free agent.

1976, Mar. 22
Outfielder Bobby Tolan signed as a free agent.

1976, Apr. 19
Catcher Tim Blackwell from Boston Red Sox.

1976, Dec. 6
Infielder Richie Hebner signed as a free agent.

1977, Feb. 4
Infielder Dave Johnson signed as a free agent.

1978, Apr. 5
Infielder Ramon Aviles from Boston Red Sox.

1978, Sept. 5
Infielder Pete Mackanin from Montreal Expos.

1978, Dec. 5
Infielder Pete Rose signed as a free agent.

1979, Mar. 29
Outfielder Del Unser signed as a free agent.

1980, Jan. 31
Pitcher Lerrin LaGrow signed as a free agent.

1982, Sept. 1
Outfielder Bobby Molinaro from Chicago Cubs.

1982, Dec. 9
Infielder Larry Milbourne from Cleveland Indians.

1983, Jan. 28
Outfielder Bill Robinson signed as a free agent.

1983, Jan. 31
First baseman Tony Perez signed as a free agent.

1982, Apr. 13
Outfielder–first baseman Tim Corcoran signed as a free agent.

1983, Mar. 1
Infielder Kiko Garcia signed as a free agent.

1983, July 29
Pitcher Larry Andersen from Seattle Mariners.

1986, May 9
Outfielder Ron Roenicke from Oakland A's.

1987, Mar. 15
Catcher Lance Parrish signed as a free agent.

1987, Dec. 18
Pitcher Dave Palmer signed as a free agent.

1989, Jan. 27
Shortstop Dickie Thon from San Diego Padres.

1989, Feb. 16
Pitcher Steve Ontiveros signed as a free agent.

1989, Apr. 3
Outfielder Dwayne Murphy signed as a free agent.

1989, Dec. 1
Outfielder Carmelo Martinez signed as a free agent.

1990, Mar. 31
Pitcher Darrel Akerfelds from Texas Rangers.

1990, Apr. 8
Infielder Rod Booker signed as a free agent.

1990, Dec. 17
Pitcher Danny Cox signed as a free agent.

1991, Jan 10
Infielder Wally Backman signed as a free agent.

1991, Jan. 11
Outfielder Jim Lindeman signed as a free agent.

1991, Apr. 6
Pitcher Dave LaPoint signed as a free agent.

1991, July 15
Pitcher Steve Searcy signed as a free agent.

1991, Dec. 9
Catcher Todd Pratt signed as a free agent.

1991, Dec. 10
Infielder Mariano Duncan signed as a free agent.

1992, Feb. 4
Pitcher Greg Mathews signed as a free agent.

1992, Sept. 8
Pitcher Jose DeLeon signed as a free agent.

1992, Dec. 8
Outfielder Pete Incaviglia signed as free agent.

1992, Dec. 9
Outfielder Milt Thompson signed as a free agent.

1992, Dec. 18
Pitcher Larry Andersen signed as a free agent.

Major Sales

1901, May
Infielder Joe Dolan to Philadelphia A's.

1903, Feb.
Catcher–infielder Fred Jacklitsch to Brooklyn Dodgers.

1907, June 15
Pitcher Bill Duggleby to Pittsburgh Pirates.

1911, Aug. 9
First baseman Kitty Bransfield to Chicago Cubs.

1912, Aug.
Infielder Tom Downey to Chicago Cubs.

1913, July
Pitcher Earl Moore to Chicago Cubs.

1913, Dec.
Outfielder Doc Miller to Cincinnati Reds.

1915, Dec.
Pitcher Elmer Jacobs to Pittsburgh Pirates.

1917, Sept.
Infielder Bobby Byrne to Chicago White Sox.

1921, June 2
Outfielder Greasy Neale to Cincinnati Reds.

1923, Feb. 8
Outfielder Bevo LeBourveau to Philadelphia A's.

1924, June 20
Outfielder Cliff Lee to Cincinnati Reds.

1925, April 20
Pitcher Joe Oeschger to Brooklyn Dodgers.

1925, May 16
Infielder Hod Ford to Brooklyn Dodgers.

1925, July 9
First baseman Walt Holke to Cincinnati Reds.

1927, June 14
Pitcher Wayland Dean to Chicago Cubs.

1927, Sept. 10
Pitcher Tony Kaufmann to St. Louis Cardinals.

1929, Apr.
Catcher John Schulte to Chicago Cubs.

1929, May 14
Pitcher Alex Ferguson to Brooklyn Dodgers.

1930, Oct. 13
Pitcher Les Sweetland to Chicago Cubs.

1933, Jan. 7
Infielder Barney Friberg to Boston Red Sox.

1933, Nov.
Catcher Harry McCurdy to Cincinnati Reds.

1934, Feb. 11
Pitcher Flint Rhem to St. Louis Cardinals.

1934, May 16
Pitcher Jumbo Elliott to Boston Bees.

1934, June 27
Infielder Marty Hopkins to Chicago White Sox.

1934, July 12
Pitcher Ed Holley to Pittsburgh Pirates.

1935, May 18
Pitcher Phil Collins to St. Louis Cardinals.

1935, Aug. 2
Pitcher Euel Moore to Chicago Cubs.

1935, Aug. 8
Infielder Blondy Ryan to New York Yankees.

1936, Jan.
Pitcher Tommy Thomas to St. Louis Browns.

1936, May
Outfielder George Watkins to Brooklyn Dodgers.

1936, July
Third baseman Johnny Vergez to St. Louis Cardinals.

1938, June 22
Pitcher Snipe Hansen to St. Louis Browns.

1939, June 15
Pitcher Bill Kerksieck to Boston Bees.

1939, Oct. 27
Catcher Spud Davis to Pittsburgh Pirates.

1941, Dec. 10
Outfielder Johnny Rizzo to Brooklyn Dodgers.

1942, Sept. 9
Catcher Benny Warren to Pittsburgh Pirates.

1945, July 14
Pitcher Bill Lee to Boston Braves.

1946, Apr. 24
Pitcher Si Johnson to Boston Braves.

1948, Aug. 3
Second baseman Emil Verban to Chicago Cubs.

1950, Apr. 3
Infielder Eddie Miller to St. Louis Cardinals.

1950, June 12
Pitcher Hank Borowy to Pittsburgh Pirates.

1951, Apr. 18
Pitcher Blix Donnelly to Boston Braves.

1951, Sept. 12
Second baseman Mike Goliat to St. Louis Browns.

1952, Mar. 21
Pitcher Ken Johnson to Detroit Tigers.

1952, May 12
Catcher Del Wilber to Boston Red Sox.

1953, Aug. 25
Second baseman Connie Ryan to Chicago White Sox.

1954, Mar. 16
First baseman Eddie Waitkus to Baltimore Orioles.

1954, June 15
Pitcher Karl Drews to Cincinnati Reds.

1954, Aug. 22
Pitcher Jim Konstanty to New York Yankees.

1955, June 15
First baseman Earl Torgeson to Detroit Tigers.

1957, May 13
Infielder Bobby Morgan to Chicago Cubs.

1958, Apr. 30
Pitcher Tom Qualters to Chicago White Sox.

1959, June 14
Catcher Jim Hegan to San Francisco Giants.

1960, May 12
Outfielder Dave Philley to San Francisco Giants.

1960, May 9
Third baseman Joe Morgan to Cleveland Indians.

1961, Apr. 3
Infielder Ted Lepcio to Chicago White Sox.

1961, Aug. 4
Catcher Darrell Johnson to Cincinnati Reds.

1961, Oct. 16
Pitcher Robin Roberts to Baltimore Orioles.

1962, May 8
Infielder Billy Consolo to Los Angeles Dodgers.

1962, May 21
Catcher Jim Cooker to Baltimore Orioles.

1963, June 28
Outfielder Jim Lemon to Chicago White Sox.

1964, May 13
Pitcher Ryne Duren to Cincinnati Reds.

1964, June 29
Pitcher Johnny Klippstein to Minnesota Twins.

1964, July 16
First baseman Roy Sievers to Washington Senators.

1964, Nov. 30
First baseman Vic Power to Los Angeles Angels.

1965, June 14
Catcher Gus Triandos to Houston Colt 45s.

1965, July 10
First baseman Frank Thomas to Houston Colt 45s.

1967, June 3
Outfielder Jackie Brandt to Houston Astros.

1967, June 12
Outfielder Tito Francona to Atlanta Braves.

1967, June 22
Infielder Dick Groat to San Francisco Giants.

1972, Aug. 2
Pitcher Woodie Fryman to Detroit Tigers.

1973, Dec. 7
Outfielder Cesar Tovar to Texas Rangers.

1974, July 10
Infielder Billy Grabarkewitz to Chicago Cubs.

1977, Mar. 31
Pitcher Ron Schueler to Minnesota Twins.

1977, Dec. 8
Infielder Tommy Hutton to Toronto Blue Jays.

1978, Aug. 6
Infielder Dave Johnson to Chicago Cubs.

1979, May 11
Pitcher Jim Kaat to New York Yankees.

1979, Aug. 2
Outfielder Jose Cardenal to New York Mets.

1981, Mar. 30
Outfielder Greg Luzinski to Chicago White Sox.

1981, Dec. 6
Catcher Bob Boone to California Angels.

1982, Aug. 21
Pitcher Sparky Lyle to Chicago White Sox.

1982, Aug. 30
Pitcher Warren Brusstar to Chicago White Sox.

1983, Dec. 5
First baseman Tony Perez to Cincinnati Reds.

1989, Aug. 7
Pitcher Greg Harris to Boston Red Sox.

Milestones, Honors, and Other Facts

In many respects the lifeblood of baseball is the game's records and statistics. No sport relies more heavily on figures or has any greater quantity of them than baseball, and these are the sources on which endless comparisons have been made down through the years.

Was Ed Delahanty a better hitter than Mike Schmidt? Was Grover Cleveland Alexander a better pitcher than Robin Roberts? The only way we can really make these judgments is by comparing the records of one against the other.

Baseball thrives on such comparisons. And by making them, the game has provided not only a continuity throughout its history, but also a measurement for all future performances.

This chapter is intended to provide the readers with some of the most important statistical information regarding the Phillies, as well as many other significant aspects of the team's history.

This is really a chapter of lists. Many are statistical. Many are not. Collectively, however, they offer another dimension of the 110-year history of the Phillies.

Special thanks go to Skip Clayton for compiling many of the lists that comprise this chapter.

Phillies in Hall of Fame

Name	Years with Phillies	Year Selected	Name	Years with Phillies	Year Selected
Players					
Dave Bancroft	1915–20	1971	Sam Thompson	1889–98	1974
Dan Brouthers	1896	1945	Lloyd Waner	1942	1967
Roger Connor	1892	1976	Hack Wilson	1934	1979
Ed Delahanty	1888–89, 1891–1901	1945	**Pitchers**		
			Grover Alexander	1911–17, 1930	1938
Hugh Duffy*	1904–06	1945	Chief Bender	1916–17	1953
Johnny Evers	1917	1946	Ferguson Jenkins	1965–66	1991
Elmer Flick	1898–1902	1963	Tim Keefe	1891–93	1964
Jimmie Foxx	1945	1951	Kid Nichols	1905–06	1949
Billy Hamilton	1890–95	1961	Eppa Rixey	1912–17, 1919–20	1963
Hughie Jennings	1901–02	1945			
Chuck Klein	1928–33, 1936–39, 1940–44	1980	Robin Roberts	1948–61	1976
			Managers		
			Bucky Harris	1943	1975
Nap Lajoie	1896–1900	1937	Harry Wright	1884–93	1953
Tommy McCarthy	1886–87	1946	**General Manager**		
			Herb Pennock	1943–48	1948
Joe Morgan	1983	1990	**Coaches**		
Casey Stengel	1920–21	1966	Earle Coombs	1954	1970
*Player-manager			Bob Lemon	1961	1976

Philadelphian Jimmie Wilson (left) played with and managed the Phillies, while Casey Stengel played with the Phils before going on to a legendary managerial career.

Major Phillies Award Winners

MOST VALUABLE PLAYER, NL *(BBWAA):* Chuck Klein (1932), Jim Konstanty (1950), Mike Schmidt (1980, 1981, 1986).

CY YOUNG AWARD, NL *(BBWAA):* Steve Carlton (1972, 1977, 1980, 1982), John Denny (1983), Steve Bedrosian (1987).

ROOKIE OF THE YEAR, NL *(BWAA):* Jack Sanford, p (1957); Dick Allen, 3b (1964).

MAJOR LEAGUE EXECUTIVE OF THE YEAR *(The Sporting News):* Bob Carpenter (1950).

MOST VALUABLE PLAYER AWARD *(The Sporting News):* Chuck Klein, 1931, 1932.

MAJOR LEAGUE PLAYER OF THE YEAR *(The Sporting News):* Robin Roberts, p (1952); Mike Schmidt, 3b (1980, 1986).

MAJOR LEAGUE PITCHER OF THE YEAR *(The Sporting News):* Jim Konstanty (1950), Robin Roberts (1952, 1953, 1955), Steve Carlton (1972, 1977, 1980, 1982).

NATIONAL LEAGUE PITCHER OF THE YEAR: Jim Konstanty (1950), Robin Roberts (1952, 1955), Steve Carlton (1972, 1977, 1980, 1982), John Denny (1983).

ROOKIE OF THE YEAR *(The Sporting News):* Del Ennis, of (1946), Richie Ashburn, of (1948), Ed Bouchee, 1b (1957), Dick Allen, 3b (1964), Lonnie Smith, of (1980), Juan Samuel, 2b (1984).

ROOKIE PITCHER OF THE YEAR *(The Sporting News):* Jack Sanford (1957), Ray Culp (1963).

MAJOR LEAGUE MANAGER OF THE YEAR *(The Sporting News):* Danny Ozark (1976), Gene Mauch (1962).

ROBERTO CLEMENTE AWARD *(Commissioner's Office):* Presented annually to player "Who best typifies the game of baseball, both on and off the field."—Greg Luzinski (1978), Garry Maddox (1986).

NATIONAL LEAGUE MANAGER OF THE YEAR *(Associated Press):* Eddie Sawyer (1950), Danny Ozark (1976), Gene Mauch (1962, 1964).

NATIONAL LEAGUE MANAGER OF THE YEAR *(United Press International):* Danny Ozark (1976).

MOST VALUABLE PLAYER, LEAGUE CHAMPIONSHIP SERIES *(National League and Baseball Magazine):* Manny Trillo (1980), Gary Matthews (1983).

MOST VALUABLE PLAYER, WORLD SERIES *(Major League Baseball and SPORT Magazine):* Mike Schmidt (1980).

ROLAIDS RELIEF MAN: Al Holland (1983), Steve Bedrosian (1987).

FIREMAN OF THE YEAR: Al Holland (1983), Steve Bedrosian (1987).

COMEBACK PLAYER OF THE YEAR *(The Sporting News and UPI):* John Denny (1983).

MOST VALUABLE PLAYER, ALL-STAR GAME: Johnny Callison (1964).

MALE ATHLETE OF THE YEAR: Jim Konstanty (1950).

Garry Maddox, Mike Schmidt, and Steve Carlton (from left) collected many trophies over the years, including these Gold Glove and Cy Young awards for the 1982 season.

All-Star Game Selections

1933	Dick Bartell, ss*	1954	Smoky Burgess, c
	Chuck Klein, of*		Granny Hamner, 2b*
1935	Jimmie Wilson, c*		Robin Roberts, RHP*
1936	Pinky Whitney, 3b*	1955	Del Ennis, of*
1937	Bucky Walters, RHP		Stan Lopata, c
1938	Hershel Martin, of		Robin Roberts, RHP*
1939	Morrie Arnovich, of	1956	Stan Lopata, c
1940	Kirby Higbe, RHP		Robin Roberts, RHP
	Pinky May, 3b	1957	Jack Sanford, RHP
	Hugh Mulcahy, RHP		Curt Simmons, LHP*
1941	Cy Blanton, RHP	1958	Richie Ashburn, of
1942	Danny Litwhiler, of		Dick Farrell, RHP
1943	Babe Dahlgren, 1b	1959	Gene Conley, RHP
1944	Ken Raffensberger, LHP	1960	Tony Taylor, 2b
1946	Del Ennis, of	1961	Art Mahaffey, RHP
	Frank McCormick, 1b	1962	Art Mahaffey, RHP
	Emil Verban, 2b		Johnny Callison, of
1947	Schoolboy Rowe, RHP	1963	Ray Culp, RHP
	Emil Verban, 2b*	1964	Jim Bunning, RHP
	Harry Walker, of*		Chris Short, LHP
1948	Richie Ashburn, of*		Johnny Callison, of
1949	Andy Seminick, c*	1965	Dick Allen, 3b*
	Eddie Waitkus, 1b		Cookie Rojas, 2b
1950	Willie Jones, 3b*		Johnny Callison, of
	Jim Konstanty, RHP	1966	Dick Allen, 3b
	Robin Roberts, RHP*		Jim Bunning, RHP
	Dick Sisler, of	1967	Dick Allen, 3b*
1951	Richie Ashburn, of*		Chris Short, LHP
	Del Ennis, of*	1968	Woodie Fryman, LHP
	Willie Jones, 3b	1969	Grant Jackson, LHP
	Robin Roberts, RHP*	1970	Joe Hoerner, LHP
1952	Granny Hamner, ss*	1971	Rick Wise, RHP
	Robin Roberts, RHP	1972	Steve Carlton, LHP
	Curt Simmons, LHP*	1973	Wayne Twitchell, RHP
1953	Richie Ashburn, of	1974	Larry Bowa, ss*
	Granny Hamner, ss		Dave Cash, 2b
	Robin Roberts, RHP*		Mike Schmidt, 3b
	Curt Simmons, LHP		Steve Carlton, p

Curt Simmons was a three-time member of the National League All-Star team, while Schoolboy Rowe (kneeling) made the squad in 1947.

1975	Larry Bowa, ss
	Dave Cash, 2b
	Greg Luzinski, of
	Tug McGraw, p
1976	Greg Luzinski, of*
	Larry Bowa, ss
	Bob Boone, c
	Dave Cash, 2b
	Mike Schmidt, 3b
1977	Greg Luzinski, of*
	Mike Schmidt, 3b
	Steve Carlton, p
1978	Greg Luzinski, of*
	Larry Bowa, ss*
	Bob Boone, c
1979	Mike Schmidt, 3b*
	Larry Bowa, ss*
	Steve Carlton, p*
	Bob Boone, c†
	Pete Rose, 1b
1980	Mike Schmidt, 3b*‡
	Steve Carlton, p
	Pete Rose, 1b
1981	Mike Schmidt, 3b*
	Pete Rose, 1b
	Manny Trillo, 2b
	Steve Carlton, p
	Dick Ruthven, p
1982	Mike Schmidt, 3b*
	Manny Trillo, 2b*
	Steve Carlton, p
	Pete Rose, 1b
1983	Mike Schmidt, 3b*
1984	Mike Schmidt, 3b*
	Juan Samuel, 2b
	Al Holland, p

1985	Ozzie Virgil, c
	Glenn Wilson, of
1986	Mike Schmidt, 3b*
	Shane Rawley, p
1987	Mike Schmidt, 3b*
	Juan Samuel, 2b
	Steve Bedrosian, p
1988	Lance Parrish, c
	Kevin Gross, p
1989	Mike Schmidt, 3b*
	Von Hayes, of
1990	Len Dykstra, of*
1991	John Kruk, 1b
1992	Darren Daulton, c
	John Kruk, 1b

*Starters
†Started because of injury to Ted Simmons
‡Couldn't start because of injury
Winning pitcher: Ken Raffenberger (1944)

Home runs:	1964	Johnny Callison (Shea Stadium)
	1967	Dick Allen (Anaheim Stadium)
	1977	Greg Luzinski (Yankee Stadium)
	1981	Mike Schmidt (Cleveland Stadium)

Local Boys Who Made Good (Phillies born in the Philadelphia area)

Ruben Amaro, Jr., 1992—Philadelphia
Dave Anderson, 1889–90—Chester, Pa.
Henry Baldwin, 1927—Chadds Ford, Pa.
Charlie Bastian, 1885–88, 1891—Philadelphia
Lena Blackburne, 1919—Clifton Heights, Pa.
Charlie Brady, 1905—Clayton, N.J.
Elmer Burkart, 1936–39—Philadelphia
Ralph Caldwell, 1904–05—Philadelphia
John Castle, 1910—Honeybrook, Pa.
Pete Childs, 1902—Philadelphia
Jack Clements, 1884–97—Philadelphia
John Coleman, 1890—Bristol, Pa.
Bert Conn, 1898, 1900—Philadelphia
Jerry Connors, 1892—Philadelphia

Monte Cross, 1900–01—Philadelphia
Bill Crouch, 1941—Wilmington, Del.
Benny Culp, 1942–44—Philadelphia
Bill Day, 1889–90—Wilmington, Del.
Tod Dennehy, 1923—Philadelphia
George Durning, 1925—Philadelphia
Rawley Eastwick, 1978–79—Camden, N.J.
Del Ennis, 1946–56—Philadelphia
Charley Esper, 1890–92—Salem, N.J.
Eddie Feinberg, 1938–39—Philadelphia
Larry File, 1940—Chester, Pa.
Tom Fleming, 1902, 1904—Philadelphia
Hilly Flitcraft, 1942—Woodstown, N.J.
Billy Gallagher, 1883—Philadelphia
Kid Gleason, 1888–91, 1903–08—Camden, N.J.

Mike Grady, 1894–97—Kennett Square, Pa.

Lew Graulich, 1891—Camden, N.J.

Bill Grey, 1890–91—Philadelphia

Bill Harbidge, 1883—Philadelphia

Don Hasenmayer, 1945–46—Rosyln, Pa.

Hardie Henderson, 1883—Philadelphia

John Hiland, 1885—Philadelphia

Charlie Hilsey, 1883—Philadelphia

Frank Hoerst, 1940–42, 1946–47—Philadelphia

Bill Hoffman, 1939—Philadelphia

Buster Hoover, 1884—Philadelphia

Keith Hughes, 1987—Paoli, Pa.

Joe Kappel, 1884—Philadelphia

Chick Keating, 1926—Philadelphia

Ed Keegan, 1959, 1962—Camden, N.J.

Hal Kelleher, 1935–38—Philadelphia

Mike Kilroy, 1891—Philadelphia

Dick Koecher, 1946–48—Philadelphia

Joe Kracher, 1939—Philadelphia

Andy Lapihuska, 1942–43—Delmont, N.J.

Ed Lennon, 1928—Philadelphia

Mike Loan, 1912—Philadelphia

Hans Lobert, 1911–14—Wilmington, Del.

Carl Lord, 1923—Philadelphia

Fred Lucas, 1935—Vineland, N.J.

Al Lukens, 1894—Vineland, N.J.

Harry Lyons, 1887—Chester, Pa.

Billy Maharg, 1916—Philadelphia

Frank Maher, 1902—Philadelphia

Tom Maher, 1902—Philadelphia

Cy Malis, 1934—Philadelphia

Hal Marnie, 1940–42—Philadelphia

Al Maul, 1887, 1900—Philadelphia

Moose McCormick, 1908—Philadelphia

John McFetridge, 1890, 1903—Philadelphia

Jack Meyer, 1955–61—Philadelphia

Red Miller, 1923—Philadelphia

Harry Morelock, 1891–92—Philadelphia

Danny Murtaugh, 1941–43, 1946—Chester, Pa.

Al Neiger, 1960—Wilmington, Del.

Harry O'Donnell, 1927—Philadelphia

Joe O'Rourke, 1929—Philadelphia

Mike Pasquariello, 1919—Philadelphia

Harry Pearce, 1917–19—Philadelphia

Bill Peterman, 1942—Philadelphia

Ty Pickup, 1918—Philadelphia

Alex Pitko, 1938—Burlington, N.J.

Walt Plock, 1891—Philadelphia

John Podgajny, 1940–43—Chester, Pa.

Jesse Purnell, 1904—Glenside, Pa.

Pete Rambo, 1926—Thoroughfare, N.J.

Butch Rementer, 1904—Philadelphia

Bob Rice, 1926—Philadelphia

Lew Richie, 1906–09—Ambler, Pa.

Craig Robinson, 1972–73—Abington, Pa.

Rick Schu, 1984–87, 1991—Philadelphia

John Schultze, 1891—Burlington, N.J.

Bob Sebra, 1988–89—Gloucester, N.J.

Bobby Shantz, 1964—Pottstown, Pa.

Bill Shindle, 1891—Gloucester, N.J.

Harry Shuman, 1944—Philadelphia

Ed Sixsmith, 1884—Philadelphia

Phenomenal Smith, 1890–91—Philadelphia

Dick Spalding, 1927—Philadelphia

Jim Spotts, 1930—Honeybrook, Pa.

Ray Steinder, 1924—Salem, N.J.

John Strike, 1886—Philadelphia

George Stutz, 1926—Philadelphia

Bill Thomas, 1902—Norristown, Pa.

Roy Thomas, 1899–1908, 1910–11—Norristown, Pa.

Jim Tyng, 1888—Philadelphia

Hal Wagner, 1948–49—Riverton, N.J.

Martin Walker, 1928—Philadelphia

Augie Walsh, 1927–28—Wilmington, Del.

Bucky Walters, 1934–38—Philadelphia

Joe Ward, 1906, 1909–10—Philadelphia

Fred Warner, 1883—Philadelphia

Lefty Weinert, 1919–24—Philadelphia

Jimmie Wilson, 1923–28, 1934–38—Philadelphia

Bert Yeabsley, 1919—Philadelphia

Frank Hoerst was a Philadelphia native.

Pottstown's Bobby Shantz ended his career with the Phillies.

Players Who Played with the Phillies and the Philadelphia A's

Player	Phillies	A's
Dick Barrett	1943–45	1933
Stan Baumgartner	1914–16, 1921–22	1924–26
Chief Bender	1916–17	1903–14
Bill Bernhard	1899–1900	1901–02
Joe Bowman	1935–36	1932
Rube Bressler	1932	1914–16
Frank Bruggy	1921	1922–24
Lave Cross	1892–97	1901–05
Monte Cross	1898–1901	1902–07
Joe Dolan	1899–1901	1901
Bill Duggleby	1898–1901, 1902–07	1902
Nick Etten	1941–42, 1947	1938–39
Dana Fillingim	1925	1915
Lou Finney	1947	1931, 1933–39
Elmer Flick	1898–1901	1902
Jimmie Foxx	1945	1925–35
Chick Fraser	1899–1900, 1902–04	1901
Dave Fultz	1898–99	1901–02

Chief Bender, Jimmie Foxx (top row from left), Skeeter Newsome, and Elmer Valo (bottom row from left) all began their careers with the Athletics and later played with the Phillies.

Player	Phillies	A's
Phil Geier	1896–97	1901
John Gray	1958	1954
Ed Heusser	1938	1940
Bill Kelly	1928	1920
Nap Lajoie	1896–1900	1901–02, 1915–16
Bill Lauder	1898–99	1901
Bevo LeBourveau	1919–22	1929
Walt Masters	1937	1939
Stuffy McInnis	1927	1909–17
John McPherson	1904	1901
Fred Mitchell	1903–04	1902
Morgan Murphy	1898, 1900	1901
Bill Nagel	1941	1939
Skeeter Newsome	1946–47	1935–39
Bill Nicholson	1949–53	1936
Dave Philley	1958–60	1951–53
Wiley Piatt	1898–1900	1901
Vic Power	1964	1954
Ken Richardson	1946	1942
Bobby Shantz	1964	1949–54
Dave Shean	1908–09	1906
Stan Sperry	1936	1938
Tuck Stainback	1938	1946
Elmer Valo	1956, 1961	1940–43, 1946–54
Hal Wagner	1948–49	1937–44
Tom Zachary	1936	1918

Most Career Games with Phillies

First Base
1. Fred Luderus	1910–20	1,298
2. Sid Farrar	1883–89	816
3. Don Hurst	1928–34	815
4. Kitty Bransfield	1905–11	781
5. Pete Rose	1979–83	702

Second Base
1. Tony Taylor	1960–71, 1974–76	1,003
2. Otto Knabe	1907–13	931
3. Juan Samuel	1983–89	798
4. Bill Hallman	1888–89, 1892–97, 1901–03	779
5. Cookie Rojas	1963–69	617

Shortstop
1. Larry Bowa	1970–81	1,667
2. Mickey Doolan	1905–13	1,297
3. Granny Hamner	1944–59	924
4. Heinie Sand	1923–28	772
5. Dave Bancroft	1915–20	670

Third Base
1. Mike Schmidt	1972–89	2,212
2. Willie Jones	1947–59	1,495
3. Pinky Whitney	1928–33, 1936–39	1,076
4. Joe Mulvey	1883–89, 1892	682
5. Pinky May	1939–43	646

Outfield
1. Richie Ashburn	1948–59	1,785
2. Del Ennis	1946–56	1,610
3. Sherry Magee	1904–14	1,415
4. Johnny Callison	1960–69	1,379

5. Cy Williams	1918–30		1,324
6. Chuck Klein	1928–33, 1936–39, 1940–44		1,284
7. Garry Maddox	1975–86		1,277
8. Roy Thomas	1899–1908, 1910–11		1,257
9. Greg Luzinski	1970–80		1,221
10. John Titus	1903–12		1,185
11. Ed Delahanty	1888–89, 1891–1901		1,175
12. Tony Gonzalez	1960–68		1,054
13. Sam Thompson	1889–98		1,033
14. Gavvy Gravath	1889–98		995

Catcher

1. Red Dooin	1902–14	1,124
2. Bob Boone	1972–81	1,095
3. Jack Clements	1884–97	953
4. Clay Dalrymple	1960–68	944
5. Andy Seminick	1943–51, 1955–57	917

Most Years as a Regular Starter by Position

Position	Player	Years	
RHP	Robin Roberts	14	(1948–61)
LHP	Steve Carlton	15	(1972–86)
c	Jack Clements	10	(1885, 1887–95)
1b	Fred Luderus	9	(1911–19)
2b	Otto Knabe	7	(1907–13)
3b	Mike Schmidt	15	(1973–84, 1986–88)
ss	Larry Bowa	12	(1970–81)
lf	Sherry Magee	9	(1905–13)
	Greg Luzinski	9	(1972–80)
cf	Richie Ashburn	12	(1948–59)
rf	Chuck Klein	9	(1928–30, 1932–33, 1936–38, 1940)

Most Years with Phillies

18	Mike Schmidt	1972–89			Larry Bowa	1970–81
16	Granny Hamner	1944–59			Garry Maddox	1975–86
15	Chuck Klein	1928–33, 1936–39, 1940–44		11	Bill Hallman	1888–89, 1892–97, 1901–03
	Tony Taylor	1960–71, 1974–76			Sherry Magee	1904–14
	Steve Carlton	1972–86			Fred Luderus	1910–20
14	Jack Clements	1884–97			Jimmie Wilson	1923–28, 1934–38
	Robin Roberts	1948–61			Del Ennis	1946–56
	Chris Short	1959–72			Stan Lopata	1948–58
13	Ed Delahanty	1888–89, 1891–1901			Greg Luzinski	1970–80
					Larry Christenson	1973–83
	Red Dooin	1902–14		10	Kid Gleason	1888–91, 1903–08
	Cy Williams	1918–30				
	Willie Jones	1947–59			Sam Thompson	1889–98
	Curt Simmons	1947–50, 1952–60			John Titus	1903–12
					Pinky Whitney	1928–33, 1936–39
12	Roy Thomas	1899–1908, 1910–11			Bob Miller	1949–58
					Johnny Callison	1960–69
	Andy Seminick	1943–51, 1955–57			Terry Harmon	1967, 1969–77
	Richie Ashburn	1948–59			Bob Boone	1972–81
					Tug McGraw	1975–84

Players with Phillies Three Times

Player	First Time	Second Time	Third Time
Bill Duggleby	1898	1901	1902–07
Bill Hallman	1888–89	1892–97	1901–03
Chuck Klein	1928–33	1936–39	1940–44

Players with Phillies Two Times

Player	First Time	Second Time
Buster Adams	1943–45	1947
Grover Alexander	1911–17	1930
Dick Allen	1963–69	1975–76
Mike Anderson	1971–75	1979
Jay Baller	1982	1992
Charlie Bastian	1885–88	1891
Ray Benge	1928–32	1936
George Browne	1901–02	1912
Jim Bunning	1964–67	1970–71
Kiddo Davis	1932	1934
Spud Davis	1928–33	1938–39
Ed Delahanty	1888–89	1891–1901
Bobby Del Greco	1960–61	1965
Bob Dernier	1980–83	1988–89
Ryne Duren	1963–64	1965
Nick Etten	1941–42	1947
Ed Farmer	1974	1982–83
Dick Farrell	1956–61	1967–69
Chick Fraser	1899–1900	1902–04
Kid Gleason	1888–91	1903–08
Ruben Gomez	1959–60	1967
Dallas Green	1960–64	1967
Ed Heusser	1938	1948
Joe Hoerner	1970–72	1975
Roy Hughes	1939–40	1946
Arthur Irwin	1886–89	1894
Fred Jacklitsch	1900–02	1907–10
Elmer Jacobs	1914	1918–19
Bubber Jonnard	1926–27	1935
Ed Keegan	1959	1962
Randy Lerch	1975–80	1986
Charlie Letchas	1939	1944, 1946
Bill Magee	1899	1902
Al Maul	1887	1900
Tim McCarver	1970–72	1975–80
Warren McLaughlin	1900	1903
George McQuillan	1907–10	1915–16
Willie Montanez	1970–75	1982
Euel Moore	1934–35	1936
Bobby Morgan	1954–56	1957
Joe Mulvey	1883–89	1892
Al Myers	1885	1889–91
Dickie Noles	1979–81	1990
Ron Northey	1942–44, 1946–47	1957
Joe Oeschger	1914–19	1924
Steve Ridzik	1950, 1952–55	1966
Jimmy Ring	1921–25	1928
Bill Robinson	1972–74	1982–83
Dick Ruthven	1973–75	1978–83
Rick Schu	1984–87	1991
Andy Seminick	1943–51	1955–57
Phenomenal Smith	1890	1891
Tully Sparks	1897	1903–10

Player	First Time	Second Time
Tony Taylor	1960–71	1974–76
Ron Thomas	1899–1908	1910–11
Del Unser	1973–74	1979–82
Elmer Valo	1956	1961
Tom Vickery	1890	1893
John Vukovich	1970–71	1976–77, 1979–81
Eddie Waitkus	1949–53	1955
Joe Ward	1906	1909–10
Pinky Whitney	1928–33	1936–39
Jimmie Wilson	1923–28	1934–38
Harry Wolverton	1900–01	1902–04
Johnny Wyrostek	1946–47	1952–54

Brothers Who Played with the Phillies

Dave (1964) and Dennis (1962–64) Bennett
Dino (1935) and Lou (1934–36) Chiozza
Ed (1888–89, 1891–1901) and Tom (1894) Delahanty
Garvin (1945) and Granny (1944–59) Hamner
Fritz (1933) and George (1932) Knothe
Frank (1902) and Tom (1902) Maher
Charlie (1906) and Luther (1929) Roy
Bill (1902) and Roy (1899–1908, 1910–11) Thomas
Jim (1955) and Wally (1956) Westlake

Granny (left) and Garvin Hamner were one of nine brother combinations who played with the Phillies.

Fathers and Sons Who Played with the Phillies

Ruben Amaro, Sr., (1960–65) and Ruben Amaro, Jr. (1992)

Phillies with Shortest Careers

Hitters	Position	Year	Average	
1 game, 0 at bats:				
Bennett, Joe	3b	1923	.000	
Harrington, Mickey	pr	1963	.000	
Lyons, Terry	1b	1929	.000	
Maher, Tom	—	1902	.000	
Pfyl, Monte	1b	1907	.000	
Van Dusen, Fred	of	1955	.000	
1 game, 1 at bat, 1 hit:				
Peterman, Bill	c	1942	1.000	(single)
Pickup, Ty	of	1918	1.000	(single)

Hitters	Position	Year	Average
1 game, 1 at bat, 0 hits:			
Cavanaugh, Pat	3b	1919	.000
Fritz, Larry	1b	1975	.000
Froelich, Ben	c	1909	.000
Maher, Frank	ph	1902	.000
McAvoy, George	ph	1914	.000
Reams, Leroy	of	1969	.000
Tyson, Cecil	ph	1944	.000
Westlake, Jim	ph	1955	.000
White, C. B.	ss	1883	.000

Pitchers	L/R	Year	G	W–L	IP	H	BB	SO	ERA
Less than 1 inning:									
Gardiner, Art	R	1923	1	0–0	0	1	1	0	0.00
Walker, Marty	L	1928	1	0–1	0	2	3	0	∞
Barry, Tom	R	1904	1	0–1	⅔	6	1	1	40.50
1 inning:									
Bennett, Dave	R	1964	1	0–0	1	2	0	1	9.00
Butler, Charles	L	1933	1	0–0	1	1	2	0	9.00
Fox, Henry		1902	1	0–0	1	2	1	1	18.00
Hartranft, Ray	L	1913	1	0–0	1	3	1	1	9.00
Thoenen, Dick	R	1967	1	0–0	1	2	0	0	9.00
Thomason, Erskine	R	1974	1	0–0	1	0	0	1	0.00
Verdel, Al	R	1944	1	0–0	1	0	0	0	0.00
Webb, Bill	R	1943	1	0–0	1	1	1	0	9.00
Yarnall, Rusty	R	1926	1	0–0	1	3	1	0	18.00

Hitting

36—Billy Hamilton, 1894
31—Ed Delahanty, 1899*
26—Chuck Klein, 1930*
26—Chuck Klein, 1930*
24—Willie Montanez, 1974*
23—Goldie Rapp, 1921†
23—Johnny Moore, 1934
23—Richie Ashburn, 1948†
23—Pete Rose, 1979*
23—Lonnie Smith, 1981†
23—Len Dykstra, 1990
22—Chuck Klein, 1931*
22—Chick Fullis, 1933
22—Willie Jones, 1949 (6), 1950 (16)
21—Bob Meusel, 1921
21—Danny Litwhiler, 1940†
21—Pete Rose, 1982
20—Chuck Kelin, 1932
20—Richie Ashburn, 1951
20—Pancho Herrera, 1960†
20—Garry Maddox, 1978
19—Gavvy Cravath, 1917*
19—Pinky Whitney, 1928
19—Pinky Whitney, 1935
19—Del Ennis, 1947
19—John Kruk, 1989
18—Gene Paulette, 1920
18—Bob Meusel, 1921
18—Pinky Whitney, 1931
18—Richie Ashburn, 1955
18—Willie Jones, 1956
18—Larry Bowa, 1970

18—Larry Bowa, 1981
18—Ricky Jordan, 1988
17—Pinky Whitney, 1930
17—Chuck Klein, 1931
17—Richie Ashburn, 1950
17—Mel Clark, 1952
17—Del Ennis, 1955
17—Stan Lopata, 1956
17—Tony Gonzalez, 1962
17—Mike Schmidt, 1979
17—Pete Rose, 1981
17—Juan Samuel, 1988
16—Gavvy Cravath, 1913*
16—Lefty O'Doul, 1929
16—Del Ennis, 1946†
16—Richie Ashburn, 1953
16—Solly Hemus, 1958
16—Rick Joseph, 1969
16—Larry Bowa, 1975
15—Lefty O'Doul, 1929
15—Richie Ashburn, 1949
15—Granny Hamner, 1954
15—Richie Ashburn, 1958
15—Lee Walls, 1961
15—Dick Allen, 1969
15—Greg Luzinski, 1973
15—Garry Maddox, 1975
15—Jay Johnstone, 1976
15—Garry Maddox, 1976
15—John Kruk, 1991
*Led league
†Tied for league lead

Streaks

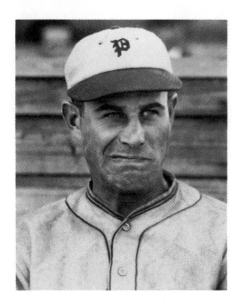

Russ Miller is co-holder of the Phillies record for most consecutive losses with 12.

Pitching, Wins

15—Steve Carlton, 1972
12—Charlie Ferguson, 1886
10—Togie Pittinger, 1905
10—Earl Moore, 1910
10—Grover Alexander, 1914
9—Tully Sparks, 1907
9—Grover Alexander, 1915
9—Ken Heintzelman, 1949
9—Robin Roberts, 1952
8—Togie Pittinger, 1905
8—Grover Alexander, 1913
8—Syl Johnson, 1935
8—Russ Meyer, 1949
8—Bob Miller, 1950
8—Robin Roberts, 1952
8—Jim Bunning, 1964
8—Jim Bunning, 1966
8—Chris Short, 1968
8—Jim Lonborg, 1976
8—Larry Christenson, 1977

8—Jim Lonborg, 1977
8—Steve Carlton, 1980
8—Ron Reed, 1983
8—Shane Rawley, 1987

Pitching, Losses

12—John Coleman, 1883
12—Russ Miller, 1928
12—Hugh Mulcahy, 1940
12—Ken Reynolds, 1972
11—Lee Grissom, 1941
11—John Buzhardt, 1960
11—Barry Lersch, 1971
11—Billy Champion, 1972
11—Kyle Abbott, 1992
10—John McFetridge, 1903
10—Tully Sparks, 1904
10—John Singleton, 1922
10—Max Butcher, 1939
10—Murry Dickson, 1954
10—Art Mahaffey, 1961

Phillies in Pro Basketball

Howie Schultz, 1b, 1947–48—Anderson, 1946–50; Ft. Wayne, 1950; Minneapolis, 1951–53.
Frankie Baumholtz, of, 1956–57—Youngstown, 1945–46; Cleveland, 1946–47.
Gene Conley, p, 1959–60—Boston, 1952–53, 1958–61; New York 1962–64.
Dick Groat, ss, 1966–67—Detroit, 1952–53.
Ron Reed, p, 1976—Detroit, 1965–67.

Frankie Baumholtz played two seasons of pro basketball.

Dick Groat was an All-American hoopster at Duke.

Team Records

COMPOSITE FINISHES
(OVER 110 YEARS)

Position	Number of Finishes	Position	Number of Finishes
First	7	Sixth	14
Second	9	Seventh	12
Third	12	Eighth	23
Fourth	21	Tenth	1
Fifth	11		

YEAR BY YEAR

Year	Manager	Finish	Won	Lost	Pct.	Attendance
1883	Bob Ferguson & Blondie Purcell	8	17	81	.173	—
1884	Harry Wright	6	39	73	.348	—
1885	Harry Wright	3	56	54	.509	—
1886	Harry Wright	4	71	43	.623	—
1887	Harry Wright	2	75	48	.610	—
1888	Harry Wright	3	69	61	.531	—
1889	Harry Wright	4	63	64	.496	—
1890	Harry Wright	3	78	54	.591	—
1891	Harry Wright	4	68	69	.496	—
1892	Harry Wright	4	87	66	.569	—
1893	Harry Wright	4	72	57	.558	—
1894	Arthur Irwin	4	71	57	.555	—
1895	Arthur Irwin	3	78	53	.595	—
1896	Billy Nash	8	62	68	.477	—
1897	George Stallings	10	55	77	.417	—
1898	George Stallings & Bill Shettsline	6	78	71	.523	—
1899	Bill Shettsline	3	94	58	.618	—
1900	Bill Shettsline	3	75	63	.543	—
1901	Bill Shettsline	2	83	57	.593	234,937
1902	Bill Shettsline	7	56	81	.409	112,066
1903	Chief Zimmer	7	49	86	.353	151,729
1904	Hugh Duffy	8	52	100	.342	140,771
1905	Hugh Duffy	4	83	69	.546	317,932
1906	Hugh Duffy	4	71	82	.464	294,680
1907	Bill Murray	3	83	64	.565	341,216
1908	Bill Murray	4	83	71	.539	420,660
1909	Bill Murray	5	74	49	.484	303,177
1910	Charlie Dooin	4	78	75	.510	296,597
1911	Charlie Dooin	4	79	73	.520	416,000
1912	Charlie Dooin	5	73	79	.480	250,000
1913	Charlie Dooin	2	88	63	.583	470,000
1914	Charlie Dooin	6	74	80	.481	138,474
1915	Pat Moran	1	90	62	.592	449,898
1916	Pat Moran	2	91	62	.595	515,365
1917	Pat Moran	2	87	63	.572	354,428
1918	Pat Moran	6	55	68	.447	122,266
1919	Jack Coombs & Gavvy Cravath	8	47	90	.343	240,424
1920	Gavvy Cravath	8	62	91	.405	330,998
1921	Bill Donovan & Irvin Wilhelm	8	51	103	.331	273,961
1922	Irvin Wilhelm	7	57	96	.373	232,471
1923	Art Fletcher	8	50	104	.325	228,168
1924	Art Fletcher	7	55	96	.364	299,818
1925	Art Fletcher	6	68	85	.444	304,905
1926	Art Fletcher	8	58	93	.384	240,600
1927	Stuffy McInnis	8	51	103	.331	305,120
1928	Burt Shotton	8	43	109	.283	182,168
1929	Burt Shotton	5	71	82	.464	281,200

Year	Manager	Finish	Won	Lost	Pct.	Attendance
1930	Burt Shotton	8	52	102	.338	299,007
1931	Burt Shotton	6	66	88	.429	284,849
1932	Burt Shotton	4	78	76	.506	268,914
1933	Burt Shotton	7	60	92	.395	156,421
1934	Jimmie Wilson	7	56	93	.376	169,885
1935	Jimmie Wilson	7	64	89	.418	205,470
1936	Jimmie Wilson	8	54	100	.351	249,219
1937	Jimmie Wilson	7	61	92	.399	212,790
1928	Jimmie Wilson & Hans Lobert	8	45	105	.300	249,219
1939	Doc Prothro	8	45	106	.298	277,973
1940	Doc Prothro	8	50	103	.327	207,177
1941	Doc Prothro	8	43	111	.279	231,401
1942	Hans Lobert	8	42	109	.278	230,183
1943	Bucky Harris & Fred Fitzsimmons	7	64	90	.416	466,975
1944	Fred Fitzsimmons	8	61	92	.399	369,586
1945	Fred Fitzsimmons & Ben Chapman	8	46	108	.299	310,389
1946	Ben Chapman	5	69	85	.448	1,045,247
1947	Ben Chapman	7*	62	92	.403	907,332
1948	Ben Chapman & Eddie Sawyer	6	66	88	.429	767,429
1949	Eddie Sawyer	3	81	73	.526	819,698
1950	Eddie Sawyer	1	91	63	.591	1,217,035
1951	Eddie Sawyer	5	73	81	.474	937,658
1952	Eddie Sawyer & Steve O'Neill	4	87	67	.565	755,417
1953	Steve O'Neill	3*	83	71	.539	853,644
1954	Steve O'Neill & Terry Moore	4	75	79	.487	738,991
1955	Mayo Smith	4	77	77	.500	922,886
1956	Mayo Smith	5	71	83	.461	934,798
1957	Mayo Smith	5	77	77	.500	1,146,230
1958	Mayo Smith & Eddie Sawyer	8	69	85	.448	931,110
1959	Eddie Sawyer	8	64	90	.416	802,815
1960	Eddie Sawyer & Gene Mauch	8	59	94	.383	862,205
1961	Gene Mauch	8	47	107	.305	590,205
1962	Gene Mauch	7	81	80	.503	762,034
1963	Gene Mauch	4	87	75	.537	907,141
1964	Gene Mauch	2*	92	70	.568	1,425,891
1965	Gene Mauch	6	85	76	.528	1,166,376
1966	Gene Mauch	4	87	75	.537	1,108,201
1967	Gene Mauch	5	82	80	.506	828,888
1968	Gene Mauch & Bob Skinner	7*	76	86	.469	664,546
1969	Bob Skinner & George Myatt	5	63	99	.389	519,414
1970	Frank Lucchesi	5	73	88	.453	708,247
1971	Frank Lucchesi	6	67	95	.414	1,511,223
1972	Frank Lucchesi & Paul Owens	6	59	97	.378	1,343,329
1973	Danny Ozark	6	71	91	.438	1,475,934
1974	Danny Ozark	3	80	82	.494	1,808,648
1975	Danny Ozark	2	86	76	.531	1,909,233
1976	Danny Ozark	1†	101	61	.623	2,480,150
1977	Danny Ozark	1†	101	61	.623	2,700,007
1978	Danny Ozark	1†	90	72	.556	2,583,389
1979	Danny Ozark & Dallas Green	4	84	78	.519	2,775,011
1980	Dallas Green	1†	91	71	.562	2,651,650
1981	Dallas Green	3‡	59	48	.551	1,638,932
1982	Pat Corrales	2	89	73	.549	2,376,394
1983	Pat Corrales & Paul Owens	1†	90	72	.556	2,128,339
1984	Paul Owens	4	81	81	.500	2,062,696
1985	John Felske	5	75	87	.463	1,830,350
1986	John Felske	2	86	75	.534	1,933,355
1987	John Felske & Lee Elia	4	80	82	.494	2,100,110

Year	Manager	Finish	Won	Lost	Pct.	Attendance
1988	Lee Elia & John Vukovich	6	65	96	.404	1,990,041
1989	Nick Leyva	6	67	95	.411	1,861,985
1990	Nick Leyva	4*	77	85	.475	1,992,484
1991	Nick Leyva & Jim Fregosi	3	78	84	.481	2,050,012
1992	Jim Fregosi	6	70	92	.432	1,927,448
						79,893,645

*Tied
†NL Eastern Division Champions
‡Won 1st half (34–24, 1½ ahead); third in 2nd half

Most Days in First Place

Year	Days	Last Day in First	Season Ended	Finish	Clinching Date
1976	156	Oct. 3	Oct. 3	1	Sept. 25
1915	135	Oct. 7	Oct. 7	1	Sept. 29
1964	133	Sept. 26	Oct. 4	2	
1978	131	Oct. 1	Oct. 1	1	Sept. 30
1950	104	Oct. 1	Oct. 1	1	Oct. 1
1983	68	Oct. 2	Oct. 2	1	Sept. 28
1913	63	June 29	Oct. 5	2	
1900	61	June 20	Oct. 14	3	
1974	61	Aug. 2	Oct. 2	3	
1977	59	Oct. 2	Oct. 2	1	Sept. 27
1911	51	July 21	Oct. 12	4	
1982	41	Sept. 13	Oct. 3	2	
1979	32	May 27	Sept. 30	4	
1953	27	May 22	Sept. 27	3(T)	
1984	26	June 30	Sept. 30	4	
1917	23	June 26	Oct. 4	2	
1954	19	May 18	Sept. 26	4	
1980	19	Oct. 5	Oct. 5	1	Oct. 4

Starting Pitchers in Phillies 10-Game Losing Streak in 1964

Date	Opponent	Pitcher	Rest	Score
Sept. 21	vs. Cincinnati	Art Mahaffey	9 days	0–1
Sept. 22	vs. Cincinnati	Chris Short	3 days	2–9
Sept. 23	vs. Cincinnati	Dennis Bennett	3 days	4–6
Sept. 24	vs. Milwaukee	Jim Bunning	3 days	3–5
Sept. 25	vs. Milwaukee	Chris Short	2 days	5–7 (12)
Sept. 26	vs. Milwaukee	Art Mahaffey	4 days	4–6
Sept. 27	vs. Milwaukee	Jim Bunning	2 days	8–14
Sept. 28	at St. Louis	Chris Short	2 days	1–5
Sept. 29	at St. Louis	Dennis Bennett	5 days	2–4
Sept. 30	at St. Louis	Jim Bunning	2 days	5–8
Oct. 1	Off. Phillies won their final two games.			
Oct. 2	at Cincinnati	Chris Short	3 days	4–3
Oct. 3	Off			
Oct. 4	at Cincinnati	Jim Bunning	3 days	10–0

Dennis Bennett had two starts during the Phillies' 10-game collapse in 1964.

Biggest Innings

BY PHILLIES

Inning	Runs	Date	Opponent
1st	10	Aug. 13, 1948	vs. New York
	10	Aug. 5, 1975	vs. Chicago
2d	11	July 14, 1934	vs. Cincinnati (1st game)
3d	11	Sept. 24, 1981	at St. Louis
4th	9	July 14, 1990	at Houston
5th	10	July 20, 1938	at Pittsburgh (1st game)
6th	12	July 21, 1923	vs. Chicago (1st game)
7th	11	July 15, 1972	at San Francisco
8th	10	Sept. 4, 1944	vs. New York
	10	June 2, 1949	vs. Cincinnati
	10	Aug. 21, 1984	at San Francisco
9th	9	July 5, 1918	vs. Cincinnati
	9	Aug. 21, 1990	at Los Angeles
10th	5	May 6, 1960	at Los Angeles
11th	5	May 6, 1966	vs. Pittsburgh
	5	May 1, 1968	at New York
	5	May 20, 1978	at New York
12th	4	Sept. 17, 1989	vs. St. Louis (1st game)
13th	3	May 7, 1977	at Los Angeles
14th	5	Aug. 9, 1916	at Cincinnati
15th	3	July 21, 1956	at Milwaukee
	3	June 30, 1961	vs. San Francisco
17th	1	Sept. 6, 1952	vs. Boston
18th	2	Sept. 15, 1950	vs. Cincinnati
19th	3	Apr. 30, 1919	vs. Brooklyn

BY OPPONENT

Inning	Runs	Date	Opponent
1st	10	July 6, 1929	vs. St. Louis
	10	May 22, 1934	vs. Pittsburgh
	10	June 8, 1989	vs. Pittsburgh
2d	10	Aug. 25, 1922	at Chicago
3d	12	Sept. 16, 1926	vs. St. Louis (1st game)
4th	14	Aug. 25, 1922	at Chicago
5th	10	July 6, 1929	vs. St. Louis
	10	June 13, 1937	vs. Chicago (1st game)
	10	Aug. 3, 1969	vs. Cincinnati
6th	12	Aug. 21, 1935	vs. Chicago (2d game)
7th	11	May 5, 1946	at Chicago
8th	12	May 5, 1938	at Chicago
	12	May 24, 1953	vs. Brooklyn (none out)
	12	May 31, 1975	vs. Houston
9th	11	Aug. 4, 1934	vs. New York (2d game)
10th	9	Aug. 24, 1947	vs. Cincinnati
11th	7	June 10, 1984	vs. Pittsburgh
12th	7	May 8, 1949	vs. Cincinnati
13th	3	May 15, 1946	vs. Chicago
14th	5	May 9, 1970	vs. Los Angeles
15th	5	Aug. 26, 1919	vs. Cincinnati (2d game)
17th	5	Sept. 13, 1974	vs. St. Louis
19th	3	Apr. 30, 1919	vs. Brooklyn

Longest Extra-Inning Games

Innings	Date	Clubs/Score				Site
21	July 17, 1918	Chicago	2	Phillies	1	Road
20	Aug. 24, 1905	Chicago	2	Phillies	1	Baker Bowl
20	Apr. 30, 1919	Phillies	9	Brooklyn	9	Baker Bowl
20	May 4, 1973	Phillies	5	Atlanta	4	Veterans Stadium

Innings	Date	Clubs/Score				Site
19	June 13, 1918	Phillies	8	St. Louis	8	Baker Bowl
19	Sept. 15, 1950	Phillies	8	Cincinnati	7	Shibe Park
18	June 1, 1919	Phillies	10	Brooklyn	9	Road
18	June 9, 1949	Phillies	4	Pittsburgh	3	Shibe Park
18	Oct. 2, 1965	Phillies	0	New York	0	Road
18	May 21, 1967	Phillies	2	Cincinnati	1	Connie Mack Stadium
18	Aug. 1, 1972	New York	3	Phillies	2	Road
17	Sept. 2, 1908	Phillies	3	Brooklyn	2	Baker Bowl
17	Sept. 6, 1952	Phillies	7	Boston	6	Shibe Park
17	June 2, 1962	Cincinnati	6	Phillies	3	Connie Mack Stadium
17	Sept. 13, 1974	St. Louis	7	Phillies	3	Veterans Stadium
17	Sept. 21, 1981	Montreal	1	Phillies	0	Road
17	June 27, 1986	Phillies	2	St. Louis	1	Road
17	June 2, 1972	Cincinnati	6	Phillies	3	Veterans Stadium
17	Aug. 21, 1980	Phillies	9	San Diego	8	Veterans Stadium

Best, Worst Season Starts

BEST		WORST	
Year	W–L	Year	W–L
1911	13–3, 14–4	1928	4–19, 5–23
1915	8–0	1930	6–15, 11–22
1964	10–2	1934	0–7, 2–8, 4–13, 6–14
1976	22–8, 26–9	1938	1–10, 2–11, 3–13, 4–15
1979	12–4, 14–5, 21–7	1941	2–9, 3–10
1981	11–5	1942	2–7, 3–12, 5–15, 6–17, 8–22
		1945	2–7, 3–13
		1946	0–6, 2–11
		1982	2–8, 3–11
		1985	1–8

Record Against Opponents (1883–99)

Franchise	Years	W–L	Pct
Baltimore	1892–99	37–61	.378
Boston	1883–89	107–148	.420
Brooklyn	1890–99	62–75	.453
Buffalo	1883–85	21–25	.457
Chicago	1883–99	119–138	.463
Cincinnati	1890–99	79–60	.568
Cleveland	1883–84	12–18	.400
Cleveland	1889–99	84–76	.525
Detroit	1883–88	45–54	.455
Kansas City	1886	14–2	.875
Indianapolis	1887–89	43–9	.827
Louisville	1892–99	66–34	.666
New York	1883–99	122–130	.484
Pittsburgh	1887–99	118–79	.599
Providence	1883–85	14–31	.311
St. Louis	1885–86	21–12	.636
St. Louis	1892–99	55–46	.545
Washington	1886–89	45–23	.662
Washington	1892–99	69–33	.676

Records Against Opponents (1900–92)

Franchise	W–L–T	Pct
Boston/Milwaukee/Atlanta	852–898–14	.487
Brooklyn/Los Angeles	755–987–10	.433
Chicago	887–1007–14	.468
Cincinnati	777–973–9	.444
Houston	225–187–0	.546
Montreal	214–209–2	.506
New York/San Francisco	721–1120–11	.392
New York Mets	301–253–1	.543
Pittsburgh	846–1044–8	.448
St. Louis	813–1081–8	.429
San Diego	157–124–0	.559

Phillies 23-Game Losing Streak (1961)

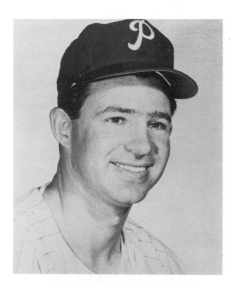

Don Ferrarese lost three games during the Phillies' 23-game losing streak.

Game	Date	Opponent	Score	Losing Pitcher
1	July 29	vs. San Francisco	4–3	Ferrarese
2	July 30	vs. San Francisco	5–2	Owens
3	Aug. 2 (G1)	at Cincinnati	4–2	Mahaffey
4	Aug. 2 (G2)	at Cincinnati	3–2	Short
5	Aug. 3	at Cincinnati	7–1	Buzhardt
6	Aug. 4	at St. Louis	9–8	Ferrarese
7	Aug. 5	at St. Louis	7–0	Brown
8	Aug. 6 (G1)	at St. Louis	3–1	Sullivan
9	Aug. 6 (G2)	at St. Louis	3–2	Owens
10	Aug. 7	vs. Pittsburgh	3–1	Buzhardt
11	Aug. 8 (G1)	vs. Pittsburgh	10–2	Mahaffey
12	Aug. 8 (G2)	vs. Pittsburgh	3–2	Short
13	Aug. 9	vs. Cincinnati	5–0	Ferrarese
14	Aug. 11	at Pittsburgh	6–0 (6)	Roberts
15	Aug. 12	at Pittsburgh	4–0	Owens
16	Aug. 13	at Pittsburgh	13–4	Buzhardt
17	Aug. 14	at Chicago	9–2	Sullivan
18	Aug. 15	at Chicago	6–5	Mahaffey
19	Aug. 16	at Chicago	9–5	Short
20	Aug. 17	at Milwaukee	7–6 (11)	Baldschun
21	Aug. 18	at Milwaukee	4–1	Owens
22	Aug. 19	at Milwaukee	4–3	Sullivan
23	Aug. 20 (G1)	at Milwaukee	5–2	Short

Some other facts:

The last win before the 23-game losing began was July 28 when John Buzhardt beat San Francisco in game two of a doubleheader at Connie Mack Stadium, 4–3.

The losing streak was snapped on August 20 when John Buzhardt beat the Braves in Milwaukee, 7–4, in the second game of a doubleheader.

After the 23-game losing streak, the Phillies won four in a row and five of seven. Their record after the losing streak was 17–20 over the final 37 games.

During the losing streak, the starting pitcher was the losing pitcher in 22 of the 23 games. Only Robin Roberts, who started the 20th game, was not the loser. Not one Phillies pitcher pitched a complete game during the losing streak.

The Phillies lost eight games by one run and three by two runs.

Baker Bowl Firsts

Game: Phillies 19, New York Giants 10 (8 innings)
Date: April 30, 1887
Winning pitcher: Charlie Ferguson, Phillies
Losing pitcher: Tim Keefe, Giants
Batter: Jim Fogarty, Phillies
Hit: Ed Andrews, Phillies

Run: Jim Fogarty, Phillies
Single: Ed Daily, Phillies
Double: Ed Andrews, Phillies
Triple: Charley Buffinton, Phillies
Home run: George Wood, Phillies
RBI: Ed Daily, Phillies
Walk: Charley Buffinton, Phillies
Stolen base: Monte Ward, Giants

Game: Phillies 2, Montreal Expos 1
  (10 innings)
Date: October 1, 1970
Winning pitcher: Dick Selma,
  Phillies
Losing pitcher: Howie Reed, Expos
Batter: Oscar Gamble, Phillies
Hit: Oscar Gamble, Phillies

Run: Tim McCarver, Phillies
Single: Oscar Gamble, Phillies
Double: Bobby Wine, Expos
Home run: John Bateman, Expos
RBI: Oscar Gamble, Phillies
Walk: Oscar Gamble, Phillies
Stolen base: Tim McCarver, Phillies

Connie Mack Stadium Lasts

Oscar Gamble had the last hit at Connie Mack Stadium.

Game: Phillies 4, Montreal Expos 1
Date: April 10, 1971
Winning pitcher: Jim Bunning,
  Phillies
Losing pitcher: Bill Stoneman,
  Expos
Batter: Boots Day, Expos
Hit: Larry Bowa, Phillies
Run: Ron Hunt, Expos
Double: Ron Hunt, Expos

Triple: Larry Bowa, Phillies
Home run: Don Money, Phillies
RBI: Bob Bailey, Expos
Walk: Ron Hunt, Expos
Stolen base: Ron Hunt, Expos
Putout: Deron Johnson, Phillies
Assist: Jim Bunning, Phillies
Error: Mack Jones, Expos
Save: Joe Hoerner, Phillies

Veterans Stadium Firsts

Spring Training Sites

1883–1900	Philadelphia	1915–18	St. Petersburg, Florida
1901	Charlotte, North Carolina	1919	Charlotte, North Carolina
1902	Washington, North Carolina	1920	Birmingham, Alabama
1903	Richmond, Virginia	1921	Gainesville, Florida
1904	Savannah, Georgia	1922–24	Leesburg, Florida
1905	Augusta, Georgia	1925–27	Bradenton, Florida
1906–08	Savannah, Georgia	1928–37	Winter Haven, Florida
1909–10	Southern Pines, North Carolina	1938	Biloxi, Mississippi
1911	Birmingham, Alabama	1939	New Braunfels, Texas
1912	Hot Springs, Arkansas	1940–42	Miami Beach, Florida
1913	Southern Pines, North Carolina	1943	Hershey, Pennsylvania
1914	Wilmington, North Carolina	1944–45	Wilmington, Delaware
		1946	Miami Beach, Florida
		1947–92	Clearwater, Florida

Jack Russell Stadium has been the Phillies' spring training home since 1955 when it was built.

Phillies-Athletics City Series Results

Year	Champion	W–L–T	All Games
1903	Phillies	4–1	4–1
1903*	A's	4–3	4–3
1904	A's	5–3	5–3
1905	Tie	4–4	4–4
1906	A's	4–1	5–1
1907	Phillies	4–0	4–0
1908	A's	3–1	3–1
1909	Phillies	5–1	5–1
1910	Tie	3–3	3–3
1911	A's	3–2	3–2
1912	Phillies	4–2	4–2
1912*	A's	4–1	5–1
1913	A's	5–0–1	5–0–1
1914	A's	4–3	4–3
1915	Tie	3–3–1	3–3–1
1918	A's	1–0	1–0
1919	Tie	2–2	2–2
1921	A's	3–2	3–2
1922	A's	1–0	1–0
1923	Phillies	2–1	2–1
1924	Phillies	3–2	3–2
1925	Phillies	5–2	5–2
1926	A's	4–2	4–2
1927	A's	4–1	5–3
1928	A's	5–1	7–2
1929	Tie	2–2	4–2
1930	Phillies	3–2	4–2
1931	Phillies	3–2	4–2

Year	Champion	W–L–T	All Games
1932	Phillies	4–1	5–2
1933	Tie	2–2	3–3
1934	A's	3–1	3–1
1935	Phillies	3–1	3–1
1936	A's	1–0	1–1
1937	A's	4–1	4–1
1938	Phillies	3–1	3–1
1939	A's	2–0	2–0
1940	Tie	1–1	1–1
1943	Tie	2–2	2–2
1945	Phillies	2–1	2–1
1946	A's	2–0	4–2
1947	Tie	2–2	2–2
1948	A's	3–2	3–2
1949	A's	2–1	2–2
1950	Phillies	2–1	2–1
1951	A's	2–1	2–2
1952	Phillies	2–1	3–1
1953	Tie	1–1	4–2
1954	Phillies	2–1	2–1

*Postseason City Series

Managers and Their Records

Years	Name	Games	W	L	T	Pct.
1883	Bob Ferguson	17	4	13	0	.235
1883	Bill Purcell	82	13	68	1	.160
1884–93	Harry Wright	1,227	636	566	24	.530
1890	Al Reach	11	4	7	0	.364
1890	Jack Clements	19	13	6	0	.634
1890	Bob Allen	35	25	10	0	.714
1894–95	Arthur Irwin	263	149	110	4	.574
1896	Bill Nash	131	62	68	1	.477
1897–98	George Stallings	180	74	104	2	.417
1898–1902	Bill Shettsline	677	367	303	7	.548
1903	Chief Zimmer	139	49	86	4	.363
1904–06	Hugh Duffy	464	206	251	7	.451
1907–09	Bill Murray	458	240	214	4	.529
1910–14	Red Dooin	775	392	370	13	.514
1915–18	Pat Moran	586	323	257	6	.556
1919	Jack Coombs	62	18	44	0	.290
1919–20	Gavvy Cravath	229	91	137	0	.399
1921	Wild Bill Donovan	87	25	62	0	.287
1921–22	Kaiser Wilhelm	221	83	137	1	.377
1923–26	Art Fletcher	612	231	378	3	.380
1927	Stuffy McInnis	155	51	103	1	.331
1928–33	Burt Shotton	923	370	549	4	.403
1934–38	Jimmie Wilson	763	280	477	6	.371
1938	Hans Lobert	2	0	2	0	.000
1939–41	Doc Prothro	460	138	320	2	.302
1942	Hans Lobert	151	42	109	0	.278
1943	Bucky Harris	92	38	52	2	.422
1943–45	Freddy Fitzsimmons	288	105	181	2	.367
1945–48	Ben Chapman	476	196	276	4	.415
1948	Dusty Cooke	13	6	6	1	.500
1948–52	Eddie Sawyer	591	296	292	3	.503
1952–54	Steve O'Neill	324	182	140	2	.565
1954	Terry Moore	77	35	42	0	.455
1955–58	Mayo Smith	548	264	282	2	.484
1958–60	Eddie Sawyer	226	94	131	1	.417

Years	Name	Games	W	L	T	Pct.
1960	Andy Cohen	1	1	0	0	1.000
1960–68	Gene Mauch	1,332	645	684	2	.485
1968	George Myatt	2	2	0	0	1.000
1968–69	Bob Skinner	215	92	123	0	.428
1969	George Myatt	54	19	35	0	.352
1970–72	Frank Lucchesi	399	166	233	0	.416
1972	Paul Owens	80	33	47	0	.413
1973–79	Danny Ozark	1,105	594	510	1	.538
1979–81	Dallas Green	301	169	130	2	.565
1982–83	Pat Corrales	248	132	115	1	.532
1983–84	Paul Owens	239	128	111	0	.536
1985–87	John Felske	384	190	194	0	.495
1987–88	Lee Elia	254	111	142	1	.439
1988	John Vukovich	9	5	4	0	.556
1989–91	Nick Leyva	338	148	189	1	.438
1991–92	Jim Fregosi	311	144	167	0	.463

Phillies Playing Managers

	Years Manager	Years Playing Manager	Positions
Bob Ferguson	1883	1883	p-2b
Blondie Purcell	1883	1883	p-3b-of
Jack Clements	1890	1890	c
Bob Allen	1890	1890	ss
Arthur Irwin	1894–95	1894	ss
Billy Nash	1896	1896	3b
George Stallings	1897–98	1897–98	1b-of
Chief Zimmer	1903	1903	c
Hugh Duffy	1904–06	1904–06	of
Red Dooin	1910–14	1910–14	c-of
Gavvy Cravath	1919–20	1919–20	of
Kaiser Wilhelm	1921–22	1921–22	p
Stuffy McInnis	1927	1927	1b
Jimmie Wilson	1934–38	1934–38	c-1b-2b
Ben Chapman	1945–48	1945–46	p-3b-of

Phillies Who Managed in the Major Leagues

	Games	Team (League),* Year
Bob Allen	179	Philadelphia (N), 1890; Cincinnati (N) 1900
Sparky Anderson	3,445	Cincinnati (N), 1970–78; Detroit (A), 1979–92
Dave Bancroft	577	Boston (N), 1924–27
Lena Blackburne	232	Chicago (A), 1928–29
Larry Bowa	208	San Diego (N), 1987–88
Bobby Bragan	927	Pittsburgh (N), 1956–57; Cleveland (A), 1958; Milwaukee (N), 1963–65; Atlanta (N), 1966
Charlie Buffinton	116	Philadelphia (P), 1890
Ben Chapman	476	Philadelphia (N), 1945–48
Jack Clements	19	Philadelphia (N), 1890
Roger Connor	46	St. Louis (N), 1896
Pat Corrales	1,211	Texas (A), 1978–80; Philadelphia (N), 1982–83; Cleveland (A), 1983–87
Roger Craig	1,449	San Diego (N), 1978–79; San Francisco (N), 1985–92
Gavvy Cravath	229	Philadelphia (N), 1919–20
Lave Cross	38	Cleveland (N), 1899
Al Dark	1,950	San Francisco (N), 1961–64; Kansas City (A), 1966–67; Cleveland (A), 1968–71; Oakland (A), 1974–75; San Diego (N), 1977
Spud Davis	3	Pittsburgh (N), 1946

	Games	Team (League),* Year
Red Dooin	775	Philadelphia (N), 1910–14
Hugh Duffy	1,221	Milwaukee (A), 1901; Philadelphia (N), 1904–06; Chicago (A), 1910–11; Boston (A), 1921–22
Doc Edwards	380	Cleveland (A), 1987–89
Kid Elberfeld	98	New York (A), 1908
Jim Essian	122	Chicago (N), 1991
Johnny Evers	375	Chicago (N), 1913, 1921; Chicago (A), 1924
Bob Ferguson	682	Hartford (N), 1876–77; Chicago (N), 1878; Troy (N), 1879–82; Philadelphia (N), 1883; Pittsburgh (AA), 1884; New York (AA), 1886–87
Art Fletcher	623	Philadelphia (N), 1923–26; New York (A), 1929
Jim Fogarty	16	Philadelphia (P), 1890
Lew Fonseca	318	Chicago (A), 1932–34
Kid Gleason	759	Chicago (A), 1919–23
Dallas Green	422	Philadelphia (N), 1979–81; New York (A), 1989
Bill Hallman	50	St. Louis (N), 1897
Bud Harrelson	284	New York (N), 1990–91
Solly Hemus	384	St. Louis (N), 1959–61

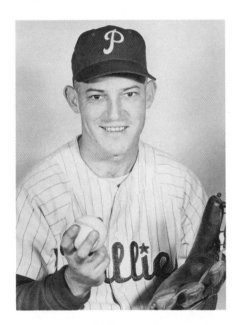

The Phillies have sent numerous players into major league managerial posts, including (top row from left) Sparky Anderson, Bobby Bragan; (bottom row from left) Davey Johnson, Solly Hemus, and Casey Stengel.

	Games	Team (League),* Year
Arthur Irwin	861	Washington (N), 1889; Boston (AA), 1891, Washington (N), 1892; Philadelphia (N), 1894–95; New York (N), 1896; Washington (N), 1898–99.
Hugh Jennings	2,171	Detroit (A), 1907–20; New York (N), 1924
Darrell Johnson	1,063	Boston (A), 1974–76; Seattle (A), 1977–80; Texas (A), 1982
Dave Johnson	1,012	New York (N), 1984–90
Bill Killefer	1,149	Chicago (N), 1921–25; St. Louis (A), 1930–33
Otto Knabe	315	Baltimore (F), 1914–15
Harvey Kuenn	279	Milwaukee (A), 1975, 1981–83
Nap Lajoie	702	Cleveland (A), 1905–09
Jim Lemon	161	Washington (A), 1968
Hans Lobert	153	Philadelphia (N), 1938, 1942
Tom McCarthy	22	St. Louis (AA), 1893
Stuffy McInnis	155	Philadelphia (N), 1927
Fred Mitchell	1,044	Chicago (N), 1917–20; Boston (N), 1921–23
Pat Moran	1,344	Philadelphia (N), 1915–18; Cincinnati (N), 1919–23
Joe Morgan	563	Boston (A) 1988–91
Danny Murtaugh	2,068	Pittsburgh (N), 1957–64, 1967, 1970–71, 1973–76
Johnny Oates	287	Baltimore (A), 1991–92
Billy Nash	131	Philadelphia (N), 1896
Kid Nichols	169	St. Louis (N), 1904–05
Blondie Purcell	82	Philadelphia (N), 1883
Cookie Rojas	154	California (A), 1988
Pete Rose	814	Cincinnati (N), 1984–89
Connie Ryan	33	Atlanta (N), 1975; Texas (A), 1977
Ken Silvestri	3	Atlanta (N), 1967
Dick Sisler	215	Cincinnati (N), 1964–65
George Stallings	1,815	Philadelphia (N), 1897–98; Detroit (A), 1901; New York (A), 1909–10; Boston (N), 1913–20
Casey Stengel	3,766	Brooklyn (N), 1934–36; Boston (N), 1938–43; New York (A), 1949–60; New York (N), 1962–65
John Vukovich	11	Chicago (N), 1986; Philadelphia (N), 1988
Harry Walker	1,235	St. Louis (N), 1955; Pittsburgh (N), 1965–67; Houston (N), 1968–72
Bucky Walters	206	Cincinnati (N), 1948–49
Del Wilbur	1	Texas (A), 1973
Kaiser Wilhelm	221	Philadelphia (N), 1921–22
Jimmie Wilson	1,237	Philadelphia (N), 1934–38; Chicago (N), 1941–44
Bobby Wine	41	Atlanta (N), 1985
Harry Wolverton	153	New York (A), 1912

*Leagues: A—American; AA—American Association; F—Federal; N—National; P—Players'

Phillies Presidents

1883–1902	Alfred J. Reach	1913–30	William F. Baker
1903–04	James Potter	1931–32	L. Charles Ruch
1905–08	William J. Shettsline	1932–42	Gerald P. Nugent
1909	Israel W. Durham	1943	William D. Cox
1909–12	Horace S. Fogel	1943–72	R.R.M. Carpenter, Jr.
1912	Alfred D. Wiler	1972–81	R.R.M. Carpenter, 3rd
1913	William H. Locke	1982–	William Y. Giles

General Managers

1943–48	Herb Pennock	1972–83	Paul Owens
1954–59	Roy Hamey	1987–88	Woody Woodward
1959–72	John Quinn	1988–	Lee Thomas

Minor League Directors

1943–54	Joseph Reardon	1972–79	Dallas Green
1955–56	William (Cy) Morgan	1980	Howie Bedell
1957–64	Eugene Martin	1981–88	Jim Baumer
1964–65	Clay Dennis	1988–89	Lance Nichols
1965–72	Paul Owens	1989–	Del Unser

Coaches

Ruben Amaro, Sr.	1980–81	Tom Ferrick	1959
Benny Bengough	1946–59	Don Hoak	1967
Carroll Beringer	1973–78	Fred Hunter	1928–31, 1933
Larry Bowa	1988–	Deron Johnson	1982–84
Dave Bristol	1982–85, 1988	Syl Johnson	1937–41
Dick Carter	1959–60	Bubber Jonnard	1935
Andy Cohen	1960	Bill Killefer	1942
Earle Combs	1954	Chuck Klein	1942–45
Bill Conroy	1922	Darold Knowles	1989–90
Dusty Cooke	1948–52	Hal Lanier	1990–91
Gavvy Cravath	1923	Bob Lemon	1961
Benny Culp	1946–47	Hans Lobert	1934–41
Jim Davenport	1986–87	Peanuts Lowrey	1960–66
Brandy Davis	1972	Eddie Mayo	1952–54
Billy DeMars	1969–81	Maje McDonnell	1951, 1954–57
George Earnshaw	1949–50	Cal McLish	1965–66
Doc Edwards	1970–72	Denis Menke	1989–
Lee Elia	1980–81, 1985–87	Ben Meyer	1925–26
		Wally Moses	1955–58
John Felske	1984	Dan Murphy	1927

In the early 1970s, the Phillies' crack coaching staff was made up of (from left) George Myatt, Billy DeMars, Ray Ripplemeyer, and Doc Edwards.

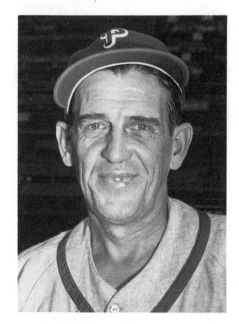

George Myatt	1964–72	Ken Silvestri	1959–60
Bob Oldis	1965–66	John Snyder	1926–27
John Onslow	1931–32	Dick Spalding	1934–36
Claude Osteen	1982–88	Herm Starrette	1979–81
Cy Perkins	1946–54	John Sugden	1926–27
Johnny Podres	1991–	Jesse Tannehill	1920
Bill Posedel	1958	Tony Taylor	1977–79,
Pat Ragan	1924		1988–89
Johnny Riddle	1959	Bob Tiefenauer	1979
Ray Ripplemeyer	1970–78	Al Vincent	1961–63
Mel Roberts	1992–	Earl Whitehill	1943
Mike Ryan	1980–	Al Widmar	1962–64,
Andy Seminick	1957–58,		1968–69
	1967–69	Bobby Wine	1972–83
Merv Shea	1944–45	Whit Wyatt	1955–57
Larry Shepard	1967		

Cy Perkins spent nine seasons as a coach with the Phillies.

Scouts (1944–92)

One of the most familiar names in Phillies' scouting was long-time bird-dog Jocko Collins, who also doubled as a prominent basketball referee.

Francisco Acevedo	1983–84	Bing Devine	1989–92
Bill Adair	1987–89	Joe DiCarlo	1972–74
Sam Albano	1946	Charles	
Hugh Alexander	1971–86	Dunkelberger	1946
Andres Alomso	1963–64	Paul Duval	1957–59,
Ruben Amaro, Sr.	1972–79, 1982		1962–80
Herb Anderson	1975–77	George Earnshaw	1948
Jim Baumer	1979–80,	Charles Eckman	1957–59
	1989–92	Ken Elam	1979
Emil Belich	1960–61,	Glenn Elliott	1960–69
	1967–71,	George Farson	1981–89
	1991–92	Tommy Ferguson	1985–92
Oliver Bidwell	1983–92	Thomas Fisher	1954–55
Jim Bierman	1990–92	Thomas Fleming	1950–56
Joe Bird	1961	Jim Fregosi, Jr.	1992
Eddie Bockman	1960–91	Grover Froese	1964–65
George Bradley	1973–80	Doug Gassaway	1975–86
Lloyd Brown	1957–58,	Charles Gault	1978–85
	1970–71	John Gillespie	1948
David Calaway	1979	Gordon Goldsberry	1974–81
Wilfredo Calvino	1987–91	Fred Goodman	1976–79
Dolph Camilli	1958–59	Eddie Goostree	1947–48
Joe Caputo	1967	Eli Grba	1992
Keith Carpenter	1977–81	Carl Green	1975–80
Patrick Colgan	1951–57	Dewey Griggs	1960–66
Jocko Collins	1944–66	Heinie Groh	1946–53
Bob Coltrim	1944–45	Warren Halverson	1968–71
Merrill Combs	1965–73	Ted Hamilton	1950–51
Bruce Connatser	1953–71	Bill Harper	1971–92
John Cottrell	1966–68	Babe Herman	1956–59
Carlos Cuervo	1983–92	Karl Heron	1984
Edward Dancisak	1960–62	Earl Hite	1951–57, 1959
Jim Davenport	1988	Henry Hodge	1948
Brandy Davis	1970–81	Edith Houghton	1946–50
Henry Dawson	1957–59	Ken Hultzapple	1988–92
Joe DeLucca	1967–69	Fred Hunter	1950–51
Thomas Denmark	1958–72	Charlie Johnson	1961

Wilbur Johnson	1966–84	Gary Nickels	1976–81
Dale Jones	1950–70	Ted Norbert	1962–63
Jerry Jordan	1985–92	Cotton Nye	1988–92
Spider Jorgensen	1975–82	Jack O'Connor	1959
Lou Kahn	1966–81	John Ogden	1960–71
Thomas Kain	1956–59	Warren Ogden	1952–55
Dave Kelley	1960–62	Bob Oldis	1967
Bill Kelly	1959–61	Luis Olmo	1964–69
Bill Kelso	1977	Mike O'Neill	1948–51
John Kennedy	1991–92	George Owens	1957
James Keown	1948, 1950–53	Paul Owens	1960–65, 1987
Tim Kibler	1959	Ken Parker	1981–82
Ralph Kimmel	1951–52	Arthur Parrack	1989–92
Hank King	1987–92	Jack Pastore	1991–92
Ron King	1989–91	Floyd Patterson	1950–55
Joseph Kozik	1950–51	Luis Peraza	1983–85
Eddie Krajnik	1944–56	Frank Perez	1988
Lewis Krause	1952–54	Jose Perez	1987
Marty Krug	1946–48	Bob Poole	1982–92
Joe Labate	1945–72	Guds Poulus	1967–76
Jerry Lafferty	1987–92	Danny Reagan	1950–61, 1964
Jesse Landrum	1964–70	Bobby Reasonover	1981–92
Walter Laskowski	1957–61	Larry Reasonover	1983–92
George Lauzerique	1992	Scott Reid	1977–83
Billy Laval	1946	Joe Reilly	1972–90
Dick Lawlor	1979–92	Guy Rhein	1950–54
Dick LeMay	1975–76	Paul Richards	1966
Art Lilly	1966–69	Bob Riley	1966–73
Don Lindberg	1972	Jay Robertson	1984–88
Wes Livengood	1954–82	Tony Roig	1981–92
Terry Logan	1990–92	Larry Rojas	1989–92
Joe Lonnett	1964–70	Edward Ruzicka	1955–56
Carl Lowenstein	1978–80	Gerald Sanders	1991–92
Tony Lucadello	1957–89	Jack Sanford	1951–55
James Mackey	1959	Eddie Sawyer	1963–66
Noe Maduro	1984	LeGrant Scott	1949–52
Eddie Malone	1965–67	Ernie Schuerman	1975–77
Ben Marmo	1957–74, 1979–81	Emil Schwob	1946
		Andy Seminick	1973–74, 1977–85
Gene Martin	1973–84		
Hershel Martin	1955–56	Ray Shore	1984–92
Fred Mathews	1946, 1949–54	Gerry Smith	1972–74
Larry Maxie	1977–78	Larry Smith	1976
Fred Mazuca	1984–92	Roy Smith	1962–63
Michael McCulley	1951–56	Ron Squire	1970–76
Joe McDonald	1986	Jimmy Stewart	1992
Maje McDonnell	1958–61	A. C. Swails	1959–80
Ted McGrew	1944–45	Roy Tanner	1991–92
Cal McLish	1967–68	Eddie Taylor	1957–58
Don McShane	1946–64	Dick Teed	1968–77
Pete Mihalic	1954–59	Rudy Terrasas	1984–87
Edward Miller	1955–56	Ben Tincup	1956
Phil Minicola	1966–69	Gilberto Torres	1962
Willie Montanez	1992	Scott Trcka	1989–92
Terry Moore	1953–54	Bill Tracey	1980–82
Cy Morgan	1944–58	Elmer Valo	1968–82
Julian Morgan	1960–61	Russ Van Atta	1947
Hap Morse	1946–65	Randy Waddill	1978–92
Ray Mueller	1971–73	Edwin Walls	1948–52
Johnny Nee	1946–56	Chuck Ward	1944–55
Lance Nichols	1990	Winfield Welch	1959–61

Tony Lucadello signed more than 50 players who made the major leagues.

Clare Whelpley	1952–57		Bill Yancey	1955–60,
Walter Widmayer	1960–63			1969–70
Carlton Willey	1971–77		Al Zarilla	1973–75
Don Williams	1977–89		Bob Zuk	1983
Robert Williams	1950–51			

Phillies Minor League Teams (1944–92)

Team	Years	Classification
Americus, Ga.	1946–50	D
Appleton, Wis.	1946–49	D
Asheville, N.C.	1959–60	A
Auburn, N.Y.	1972–77	R
Bakersfield, Calif.	1956, 1958–67	A/C
Baltimore, Md.	1951–53	AAA
Batavia, N.Y.	1967, 1988–92	A/R
Baton Rouge, La.	1948	D
Bend, Oreg.	1979–87	R
Bradford, Pa.	1944–55	D
Brunswick, Ga.	1957–58	D
Buffalo, N.Y.	1959–62	AAA
Burlington, Vt.	1972	A
Carbondale, Pa.	1946–50	D
Clearwater, Fla.	1986–92	A
Chattanooga, Tenn.	1960–61, 1963–65	AA
Concord, N.C.	1945	D
Dallas–Fort Worth, Tex.	1962	AAA
Des Moines, Iowa	1959–61	B
Dothan, Ala.	1961–62	D
Dover, Del.	1946–48	D
Elizabethtown, N.C.	1951	D
Elmira, N.Y.	1959–61	D
Eugene, Oreg.	1969–73	AAA
Eugene, Oreg.	1964–68	A
Granby, Ont.	1952–53	C
Grand Forks, N.D.	1951–52	C
Helena, Mont.	1978–83	R
High Point–Thomasville, N.C.	1957–58	B
Huron, N.D.	1965–68	A
Indianapolis, Ind.	1960	AAA
Johnson City, Tenn.	1957–60	D
Klamath Falls, Oreg.	1948–51	D
Lewiston, Mont.	1957	B
Lima, Ohio	1950–51	D
Little Rock, Ark.	1963–65	AAA
Mattoon, Ill.	1953–56	D
Macon, Ga.	1966	AA
Magic Valley, Idaho	1961–63	A/C
Martinsville, Va.	1988–92	R
Miami, Fla.	1956–58	AAA
Miami, Fla.	1962–65	A/D
Miami, Okla.	1952	D
Moultrie, Ga.	1957	D
Oklahoma City, Okla.	1976–82	AAA
Olean, N.Y.	1956–58	D
Peninsula, Va.	1970–71, 1976–85	A
Pittsfield, Mass.	1951	C
Portland, Oreg.	1983–86	AAA
Portland, Maine	1948–49	B
Portland, Maine	1987–88	AAA
Princeton, W.Va.	1990	R

Team	Years	Classification
Pulaski, Va.	1952–55	D
Pulaski, Va.	1969–75	R
Raleigh–Durham, N.C.	1969	A
Reading, Pa.	1967–92	AA
Reidsville, N.C.	1955	B
Rocky Mount, N.C.	1973–75	A
Salina, Kans.	1947–52	C
Salt Lake City, Utah	1951–57	C
San Diego, Calif.	1966–68	AAA
Sarasota, Fla.	1984	R
Schenectady, N.Y.	1946–50	C
Schenectady, N.Y.	1951–57	A
Scranton/Wilkes-Barre, Pa.	1989–92	AAA
Seaford, Del.	1949	D
Spartanburg, S.C.	1963–92	A
Spokane, Wash.	1953–54	A
Syracuse, N.Y.	1954–55	AAA
Tampa, Fla.	1957–60	D
Terre Haute, Ind.	1946–54	B
Three Rivers, Que.	1954–55	C
Tidewater, Va.	1966–68	A
Tifton, Ga.	1956	D
Toledo, Ohio	1974–75	AAA
Toronto, Ont.	1948–50	AAA
Tri City, Wash.	1952	A
Tulsa, Okla.	1957	AA
Utica, N.Y.	1944–50	A
Utica, N.Y.	1986–87	R
Vandergrift, Pa.	1947–50	C
Wala Wala, Wash.	1969–71	A
Williamsport, Pa.	1958–62	A
Wilmington, Del.	1944–52	B
Wilson, N.C.	1956	B

Phillies Minor League Champions

Year	Team/League	Manager
1947	Utica, Eastern League—Class A	Eddie Sawyer
	Wilmington, Inter-State League—Class B	Jack Saltzgaver
	Vandergrift, Middle-Atlantic League—Class C	Floyd Patterson
	Schenectady, Canadian-American League—Class C	Lee Riley
	Carbondale, North Atlantic League—Class D	Pat Colgan
1948	Carbondale, North Atlantic League—Class D	Danny Carnevale
1949	Portland, New England League—Class B	Skeeter Newsome
	Bradford, Pony League—Class D	Danny Carnevale
1950	Wilmington, Inter-State League—Class B	Skeeter Newsome
	Terre Haute, I-I-I League—Class B	Danny Carnevale
1951	Wilmington, Inter-State League—Class B	Danny Carnevale
	Grand Forks, Northern League—Class C	
	Klamath Falls, Far West League—Class D	Edward Murphy
		William DeCarlo
1952	Terre Haute, I-I-I League—Class B	Skeeter Newsome
	Miami, K-O-M League—Class D	John Davenport
1953	Spokane, Western International League—Class A	Donald Osborn
	Salt Lake City, Pioneer League—Class C	Edward Murphy
1954	Syracuse, International League—Class AAA	Skeeter Newsome
1956	Schenectady, Eastern League—Class A	Dick Carter
1957	Tampa, Florida State League—Class D	Charles Gassaway

Year	Team/League	Manager
1958	Johnson City, Appalachian League—Class D	Edmund Lyons
1960	Williamsport, Eastern League (cochampions)—Class A	Frank Lucchesi
1961	Buffalo, International League—Class AAA (Won Junior World Series)	Kerby Farrell
	Chattanooga, Southern Association—Class AA	Frank Lucchesi
1966	Spartanburg, Western Carolinas League—Class A	Bob Wellman
1967	San Diego, Pacific Coast League—Class AAA	Bob Skinner
	Spartanburg, Western Carolinas League—Class A	Dick Teed
1968	Reading, Eastern League—Class AA	Frank Lucchesi
1969	Raleigh-Durham, Carolina League—Class A	Nolan Campbell
	Pulaski, Appalachian League—Rookie	Dallas Green
1971	Peninsula, Carolina League—Class A	Howie Bedell
1972	Spartanburg, Western Carolinas League—Class A	Bob Wellman
1973	Reading, Eastern League—Class AA	Cal Emery
	Auburn, New York–Pennsylvania League—Class A	Harry Lloyd
	Spartanburg, Western Carolinas League—Class A	Howie Bedell
1975	Rocky Mount, Carolina League—Class A	Cal Emery
	Spartanburg, Western Carolinas League—Class A	Lee Elia
1977	Peninsula, Carolina League—Class A	Jim Snyder
1979	Central Oregon, Northwest League—Class A	Tom Harmon
1980	Peninsula, Carolina League—Class A	Bill Dancy
1983	Portland, Pacific Coast League—Class AAA	John Felske
1988	Spartanburg, South Atlantic League—Class A	Mel Roberts

Minor League Managers

Ruben Amaro, Sr.	1977	Brandy Davis	1970
Ramon Aviles	1984–85, 1987, 1990–92	Cot Deal	1982
		Roly DeArmas	1979–92
Al Barillari	1952–55	William DeCarlo	1951
Ted Beard	1960	James Deery	1953–54
Howie Bedell	1969–71, 1973–74	Vance Dinges	1948
		Lee Elia	1975–79, 1984, 1990–92
Del Bissonette	1948–49		
Jim Bunning	1972–76	Cal Emery	1973–77
Carl Bush	1954	Kerby Farrell	1958–62
Nolan Campbell	1967–72	John Felske	1982–83
Paul Carey	1980–83, 1985	Frank Gable	1972
Danny Carnevale	1948–52	Joseph Gantenbein	1948–49
Dick Carter	1948–52, 1956–58	Al Gardella	1952–53
		Charlie Gassaway	1952–59
Dave Cash	1990	Paul Gaulin	1949
Ron Clark	1978–82, 1984–86	Guy Glaser	1948
		Joseph Glenn	1950
Frederick Clemence	1949	Whitey Gluchoski	1948
Patrick Colgan	1947–49, 1955	Dallas Green	1968–69
Mike Compton	1976–77	Westel Griffin	1956
Billy Connors	1977	Glenn Gulliver	1989
Nick Cullop	1951	Granny Hamner	1976–77, 1988
George Culver	1986–88	Tom Harmon	1979–81
Bill Dancy	1979–92	Mike Hart	1989
Clifford Dapper	1957	Donald Hassenmayer	1950
John Davenport	1950–53	Donald Heffner	1952–53

Carl Hoverton	1958	Pat Patterson	1947–48,
John Hutchings	1960		1951–52
Spook Jacobs	1960	Ed Pebly	1986
Red Jessen	1955	Jack Phillips	1960–63
Wilbur Johnson	1960–65	Dick Porter	1948
Dale Jones	1948	Garry Powell	1970–71
Louis Kahn	1960–61, 1963,	June Raines	1975
	1966, 1970	Lee Riley	1947–52
Hub Kittle	1949–54	Mel Roberts	1988–91
Bobby Klaus	1968	Larry Rojas	1974, 1978
Lewis Krause	1948, 1954–55	Mike Ryan	1977–78
Charles Kress	1959–61	Jack Saltzgaver	1947
Max Lanier	1967	Jack Sanford	1948–50
Hillis Layne	1957	George Savino	1948–49
Arthur Lilly	1956	Eddie Sawyer	1944–48
Richard Littlefield	1962	LeGrant Scott	1948
Harry Lloyd	1971–73	Andy Seminick	1959–66,
Joe Lonnett	1965–67		1970–72
Hugh Luby	1966	Bob Skinner	1967–68
Frank Lucchesi	1956–69	Ronald Smith	1982
Bernard Lutz	1949–51	Jim Snyder	1977–81
Edmund Lyons	1958–59	Snuffy Stirnweiss	1954
Roy Majtyka	1992	Burl Storie	1955
Bobby Malkmus	1967–69	Robert Sturgeon	1955
Donald Marshall	1951	Benjamin Taylor	1957
Art Mazmanian	1976	Tony Taylor	1982–83,
Don McCormack	1988–92		1985–87
Frank McCormick	1950–51	Dick Teed	1964–67
Clyde McCullough	1959	Ben Tompkins	1960
Eddie Miller	1956	George Triandos	1954
Bobby Morgan	1964–66	Jay Ward	1983–84
Edward Murphy	1948–53, 1955	Grover Wearshing	1948
Raymond Murray	1962	Bob Wellman	1961–76
Skeeter Newsome	1949–55	Al Widmar	1957
Donald Osborn	1953–57	Richard Wilson	1956
Paul Owens	1956–59	Bob Wren	1973–75
		Bennie Zientara	1956–58

Triple-A Farm Teams and Managers

Years	Team	League	Manager
1948	Toronto	International League	Eddie Sawyer*
1949	Toronto	International League	Del Bissonette
1950	Toronto	International League	Jack Sanford
1951	Baltimore	International League	Henry (Nick) Cullop
1952–53	Baltimore	International League	Donald Heffner
1954–55	Syracuse	International League	Skeeter Newsome
1956–57	Miami	International League	Donald Osborn
1958	Miami	International League	Kerby Farrell
1959–62	Buffalo	International League	Kerby Farrell
1960	Indianapolis	American Association	John Hutchings, Ted Beard
1963	Little Rock	International League	Frank Lucchesi
1964–65	Little Rock	Pacific Coast League	Frank Lucchesi
1966	San Diego	Pacific Coast League	Frank Lucchesi
1967	San Diego	Pacific Coast League	Bob Skinner
1968	San Diego	Pacific Coast League	Bob Skinner†
1969	Eugene	Pacific Coast League	Frank Lucchesi
1970	Eugene	Pacific Coast League	Bob Wellman
1971–72	Eugene	Pacific Coast League	Andy Seminick
1973	Eugene	Pacific Coast League	Jim Bunning

Years	Team	League	Manager
1974–75	Toledo	International League	Jim Bunning
1976	Oklahoma City	American Association	Jim Bunning
1977	Oklahoma City	American Association	Cal Emery, Billy Connors, Mike Ryan
1978	Oklahoma City	American Association	Mike Ryan
1979	Oklahoma City	American Association	Lee Elia
1980–81	Oklahoma City	American Association	Jim Snyder
1982	Oklahoma City	American Association	Ron Clark, Ellis Deal, Tony Taylor
1983	Portland	Pacific Coast League	John Felske
1984	Portland	Pacific Coast League	Lee Elia
1985–86	Portland	Pacific Coast League	Bill Dancy
1987	Maine	International League	Bill Dancy
1988	Maine	International League	George Culver
1989–91	Scranton/ Wilkes-Barre	International League	Bill Dancy
1992	Scranton/ Wilkes-Barre	International League	Lee Elia

*Dick Porter took over when Eddie Sawyer moved to the Phillies.
†Bobby Klaus took over when Bob Skinner moved to the Phillies.

Team Hitting, Pitching, Fielding

	HITTING			PITCHING			FIELDING		
Year	R	HR	BA/Rank	CG	ERA/ Rank	E	DP	FA/Rank
1883	437	4	.240–8	91	5.33–8	639	62	.858–8
1884	549	14	.234–7	106	3.93–8	536	67	.888–6
1885	513	20	.229–6	108	2.39–3	447	66	.925–3
1886	621	26	.240–5	110	2.45–1	393	46	.920–3
1887	901	47	.274–4	119	3.47–2	471	76	.912–5
1888	535	16	.225–7	125	2.38–3	424	70	.923–3
1889	742	44	.266–4	106	4.00–5	466	92	.915–7
1890	827	25	.269–1	122	3.32–6	398	122*	.928–5
1891	756	21	.252.6	105	3.73–7	443	108	.925–5
1892	860	50	.262–1†	131	2.93–3	393	128	.939–1†
1893	1,011*	79*	.301–1	107	4.68–7	318	121	.943–1
1894	1,143	40	.349–1	102	5.63–10	338	111	.935–2†
1895	1,068*	61*	.330–1	106	5.47–7	369	93	.933–5
1896	890	49*	.295–5	107	5.20–11	313	112	.940–6
1897	752	40	.293–6	115	5.60–9†	296	72	.944–5
1898	823	33	.280–3	129	3.72–8	379	102	.937–9
1899	916*	30	.301–1	129	3.48–7	379	110	.940–6
1900	810	29	.290–3	116	4.12–8	330	125*	.945–3
1901	668	23	.266–4	125	2.87–2	262*	65	.954–1
1902	484	4	.247–7	118	3.50–8	305	81	.946–4†
1903	618	12	.268–5	126**	3.97–8	300	76	.947–2†
1904	571	23	.248–5†	131	3.40–7	403	93*	.936–8
1905	708	16	.260–4	119	2.81–3	275	99	.956–4†
1906	532	13	.241–4	108	2.58–3	271	83	.955–6
1907	514	12	.236–6	110	2.43–5	256	104	.957–6
1908	503	11	.244–4	116	2.11–1	238	75	.963–3
1909	514	12	.244–5	88	2.44–4	240	97	.960–2†
1910	655	33	.266–3	73	2.83–3	245	102	.960–3†
1911	658	60*	.259–5	90	3.30–5	231*	113	.962–1
1912	670	42	.267–7	82	3.25–3	231	98	.962–2

| Year | HITTING | | | PITCHING | | FIELDING | | |
	R	HR	BA/Rank	CG	ERA/Rank	E	DP	FA/Rank
1913	693	73*	.265–3	77	3.15–6	214*	112	.967–1
1914	652	63*	.263–3	85	3.06–8	324	81	.949–8
1915	589	58*	.247–5	98*	2.17–1	216	99	.965–2†
1916	581	42	.250–4	97*	2.36–3	234	119	.963–5
1917	578	38	.248–4	103	2.46–2	212	112	.967–2
1918	431	26	.244–6†	85	3.15–8	211	91	.960–8
1919	510	42*	.251–7	93	4.17–8	219	112†	.962–7†
1920	565	64*	.263–6	77	3.63–8	232	135	.964–6
1921	617	88*	.284–6	82	4.48–8	295	127	.954–8
1922	738	116*	.282–7	73	4.64–8	225	152	.965–6†
1923	748	112*	.278–7	68	5.30–8	217	172*	.965–5†
1924	676	94	.275–7	59	4.87–8	175	168*	.972–2
1925	812	100	.295–4	69	5.02–8	211	147	.965–5†
1926	687	75	.281–4	68	5.19–8	224	153	.964–7
1927	678	57	.280–4	81	5.35–8	169	152	.972–2
1928	660	85	.267–7	42	5.52–8	181	171	.970–5
1929	897	153*	.309–1	45	6.13–8	191	153	.969–6
1930	944	126	.315–2	54	6.71–8	239	169	.962–8
1931	684	81	.279–4	60	4.58–8	210	149	.965–8
1932	844*	122*	.292–1	59	4.47–8	194	133	.968–7†
1933	607	60	.274–3	52	4.34–8	183	156	.969–8
1934	675	56	.284–3	52	4.76–8	197	140	.965–8
1935	685	92	.269–6	53	4.76–7	228	145	.962–8
1936	726	103*	.281–2†	51	4.64–8	252	144	.959–8
1937	724	103	.273–5	59	5.06–8	184	157*	.970–5†
1938	550	40	.254–7	68	4.93–8	201	135	.965–8
1939	553	49	.261–8	67	5.17–8	171	133	.970–5†
1940	494	75	.238–8	66	4.40–8	181	136	.970–4†
1941	501	64	.244–8	35	4.50–8	187	147	.969–6†
1942	394	44	.232–7	51	4.12–8	194	147	.967–8
1943	571	66	.249–6	66	3.79–6	189	143	.969–8
1944	539	55	.251–7	66	3.64–5	177	138	.971–3
1945	548	56	.246–8	31	4.64–8	234	150	.961–8
1946	552	60	.250–7	61	3.72–6	184	127	.969–8
1947	589	60	.258–8	70	3.96–4	152	140	.974–5†
1948	591	91	.259–6	61	4.08–6	210	126	.964–8
1949	662	122	.254–8	58	3.89–4	156	141	.973–6
1950	722	125	.265–2	57	3.50–1	151	155	.975–5†
1951	648	108	.260–4†	57	3.81–3	138	146	.976–3†
1952	657	93	.260–4	80*	3.07–1	150	145	.975–4†
1953	716	115	.265–5	76*	3.80–2	147	161	.974–5†
1954	659	102	.267–3	78*	3.59–3	145	133	.975–5
1955	675	132	.255–6	58	3.93–4	110*	117	.980–1
1956	668	121	.252–6	57	4.20–8	144	140	.974–7
1957	623	117	.250–7	54	3.80–4	136	117	.976–5
1958	664	124	.266–1†	51	4.32–7	129	136	.977–3†
1959	599	113	.242–8	54	4.27–6	154	132	.973–8
1960	546	99	.239–8	45	4.01–7	155	129	.973–7
1961	584	103	.243–8	29	4.61–8	146	179	.976–4
1962	705	142	.260–6	43	4.28–8	138	167	.977–3†
1963	642	126	.252–3	45	3.09–3	142	147	.977–2†
1964	693	130	.258–4	37	3.36–4	157	150	.974–4†
1965	654	144	.250–6	50	3.53–5	157	153	.975–7
1966	696	117	.258–4	52**	3.57–4	113*	147	.982–1
1967	612	103	.242–7	46	3.10–4	137	174	.978–2
1968	543	100	.233–7	42	3.36–8	127	163*	.979–3†
1969	645	137	.241–9	47	4.14–10	137	157	.977–5†
1970	594	101	.238–11	24	4.17–7	114*	134	.981–1

Year	HITTING			PITCHING			FIELDING		
	R	HR	BA/Rank	CG	ERA/Rank	E	DP	FA/Rank	
1971	558	123	.233–11†	31	3.71–9	122	158	.981–3†
1972	503	98	.236–9	43	3.66–8	116	142	.981–2
1973	642	134	.249–9	49*	3.99–10	134	179*	.979–5
1974	676	95	.261–5	46	3.91–10	148	168	.976–5†
1975	735	125	.269–3	33	3.82–9	152	156	.976–4†
1976	770	110	.272–2	34	3.08–3	115	148	.981–2
1977	847*	186	.279–1	31	3.71–4	120	168	.981–2†
1978	708	133	.258–3†	38	3.33–4	104*	155	.983–1
1979	683	119	.266–4	33	4.16–10†	106*	148	.963–1
1980	728	117	.270–2	25	3.43–3	136	136	.979–5
1981	491*	169	.273–1	19	4.05–12	86	90	.980–3†
1982	664	112	.260–5	38*	3.61–6	121	138	.981–1†
1983	696	125	.249–9	20	3.34–2	152	117	.976–9
1984	720	147*	.266–1	11	3.62–9	161	112	.975–11†
1985	667	141	.245–11	24	3.68–8	139	142	.978–8
1986	739	154	.253–7†	22	3.85–7	137	157	.978–5†
1987	702	169	.254–10	13	4.18–7	121	137	.980–4†
1988	597	106	.240–12	16	4.14–12	145	139	.976–11†
1989	629	123	.243–8	10	4.04–12	133	136	.979–6†
1990	646	103	.255–9	18	4.07–9	117	150	.981–4
1991	629	111	.241–11	16	3.86–9	119	111	.981–5†
1992	686	118	.253–7	27	4.11–12	131	128	.978–11

*Led league
†Tied

League Leaders in Hitting

Billy Hamilton set the major league record for runs scored with 192 in 1894.

Average

1891	Hamilton	.340
1893	Hamilton	.380
1899	Delahanty	.410
1910	Magee	.331
1929	O'Doul	.398
1933	Klein	.368
1947	Walker	.363
1955	Ashburn	.338
1958	Ashburn	.350

Runs

1891	Hamilton	141
1894	Hamilton	192
1895	Hamilton	166
1900	Thomas	132
1910	Magee	110
1915	Cravath	89
1930	Klein	158
1931	Klein	121*
1932	Klein	152
1964	Allen	125
1981	Schmidt	78
1986	V. Hayes	107*

Hits

1890	Thompson	172*
1891	Hamilton	179
1893	Thompson	222
1899	Delahanty	238
1913	Cravath	179
1914	Magee	171
1929	O'Doul	254
1932	Klein	226
1933	Klein	223
1951	Ashburn	221
1953	Ashburn	205
1958	Ashburn	215
1975	Cash	213
1981	Rose	140
1990	Dykstra	192*

Doubles

1890	Thompson	41
1892	Connor	37
1893	Thompson	37
1895	Delahanty	49
1896	Delahanty	44
1898	Lajoie	43
1899	Delahanty	55
1901	Delahanty	39*
1914	Magee	39
1916	Niehoff	42
1930	Klein	59
1933	Klein	44
1934	E. Allen	42*
1966	Callison	40
1972	Montanez	39*
1980	Rose	42
1986	V. Hayes	46*

Triples

1892	Delahanty	21
1947	Walker	16
1950	Ashburn	14
1958	Ashburn	13

Year	Player	
1962	Callison	10*
1964	D. Allen	13*
1965	Callison	16
1972	Bowa	13
1976	Cash	12
1984	Samuel	19*
1987	Samuel	15

Home Runs

1889	Thompson	20
1893	Delahanty	19
1895	Thompson	18
1913	Cravath	19
1914	Cravath	19
1915	Cravath	24
1917	Cravath	12*
1918	Cravath	8
1919	Cravath	12
1920	Williams	15
1923	Williams	41
1927	Williams	30*
1929	Klein	43
1931	Klein	31
1932	Klein	38
1933	Klein	28
1974	Schmidt	36
1975	Schmidt	38
1976	Schmidt	38
1980	Schmidt	48
1981	Schmidt	31
1983	Schmidt	40
1984	Schmidt	36*
1986	Schmidt	37

Runs batted in

1893	Delahanty	146
1895	Thompson	165
1896	Delahanty	126
1898	Lajoie	127
1899	Delahanty	137
1900	Flick	110
1907	Magee	85
1910	Magee	123
1913	Cravath	128
1914	Magee	103
1915	Cravath	115
1931	Klein	121
1932	Hurst	143
1933	Klein	120
1950	Ennis	126
1975	Luzinski	120
1980	Schmidt	121
1981	Schmidt	91
1984	Schmidt	106*

1986	Schmidt	119
1992	Daulton	109

Stolen Bases

1889	Fogarty	99
1890	Hamilton	102
1891	Hamilton	111
1894	Hamilton	98
1895	Hamilton	97
1932	Klein	20
1941	Murtaugh	18
1948	Ashburn	32

Total Bases

1893	Delahanty	347
1895	Thompson	352
1897	Lajoie	315
1899	Delahanty	338
1900	Flick	305
1910	Magee	263
1913	Cravath	298
1914	Magee	277
1915	Cravath	266
1930	Klein	445
1931	Klein	347
1932	Klein	420
1933	Klein	365
1964	Allen	352
1975	Luzinski	322
1976	Schmidt	306
1980	Schmidt	342
1981	Schmidt	228

Slugging Average

1892	Delahanty	.495
1893	Delahanty	.583
1895	Thompson	.654
1896	Delahanty	.631
1897	Lajoie	.578
1899	Delahanty	.582
1910	Magee	.507
1913	Cravath	.568
1914	Magee	.509
1915	Cravath	.510
1926	Williams	.568
1931	Klein	.584
1932	Klein	.646
1933	Klein	.602
1966	Allen	.632
1974	Schmidt	.624
1981	Schmidt	.644
1982	Schmidt	.547
1986	Schmidt	.547

*Tied for the league lead

Nap Lajoie was one of the Phillies' premier hitters at the turn of the century.

All-Time Hitting Leaders

Games

Schmidt	2,404
Ashburn	1,794
Bowa	1,739
Taylor	1,669
Ennis	1,630
Delahanty	1,544
Magee	1,521
W. Jones	1,520
Hamner	1,501
C. Williams	1,463
Callison	1,432

Klein	1,405

Hits

Schmidt	2,234
Ashburn	2,217
Delahanty	2,211
Ennis	1,812
Bowa	1,798
Klein	1,705
Magee	1,647
C. Williams	1,553
Hamner	1,518
Taylor	1,511
S. Thompson	1,475
Callison	1,438

Home runs

Schmidt	548
Ennis	259
Klein	243
Luzinski	223
C. Williams	217
D. Allen	204
Callison	185
W. Jones	180
V. Hayes	124
Seminick	123
Cravath	117

Extra-Base Hits

Schmidt	1,015
Delahanty	667
Klein	643
Ennis	634
Magee	539
Callison	534
C. Williams	503
Luzinski	497
Allen	472
S. Thompson	456
W. Jones	444
Hamner	435

At-Bats

Schmidt	8,352
Ashburn	7,122
Bowa	6,815
Delahanty	6,352
Ennis	6,327
Taylor	5,799
Hamner	5,772
Magee	5,505
W. Jones	5,419
Callison	5,306
Klein	5,238

Doubles

Delahanty	432
Schmidt	408
Magee	337
Klein	336
Ennis	310
Ashburn	287
Hamner	271
Callison	265

S. Thompson	258
Luzinski	253
Luderus	249
Whitney	237
C. Williams	237
Maddox	230
Bowa	206

Total Bases

Schmidt	4,404
Delahanty	3,197
Ennis	3,029
Klein	2,898
Ashburn	2,764
C. Williams	2,557
Magee	2,463
Callison	2,426
Luzinski	2,263
W. Jones	2,236
S. Thompson	2,224
Hamner	2,220
Bowa	2,205

Batting Percent

Hamilton	.362
Delahanty	.348
Flick	.345
S. Thompson	.335
Klein	.326
V. Davis	.321
Leach	.312
Ashburn	.311
Whitney	.307
C. Williams	.306

Runs

Schmidt	1,506
Delahanty	1,365
Ashburn	1,114
Klein	963
S. Thompson	928
R. Thomas	916
Magee	898
Ennis	891
Hamilton	877
C. Williams	825
Bowa	816
Callison	774
Luzinski	618

Triples

Delahanty	151
Magee	127
S. Thompson	103
Ashburn	97
Callison	84
Bowa	81
Cravath	72
Samuel	70
Ennis	65
Allen	64
Klein	64
Titus	64
Lajoie	64

Runs Batted In

Schmidt	1,533	Magee	387
Delahanty	1,286	Bowa	288
Ennis	1,124	Samuel	249
Klein	983	V. Hayes	202
S. Thompson	958	Ashburn	199
Magee	889	Maddox	182
Luzinski	811	Schmidt	174
C. Williams	796	R. Thomas	164
W. Jones	753	Paskert	149
Whitney	734	Taylor	136
Hamner	705	Dooin	132
Cravath	686	Lobert	125
		Knabe	122
Stolen Bases		Titus	120
Hamilton	508		

Player	Year	Average	Home Runs	RBI
Sam Thompson	1889	.296	20 (1)	111
Sam Thompson	1894	.407 (3)	13	141 (2)
Ed Delahanty	1896	.397 (3)	13 (2)	126 (1)
Ed Delahanty	1899	.410 (1)	9 (T3)	137 (1)
Elmer Flick	1900	.367 (2)	11 (2)	110 (1)
Ed Delahanty	1901	.354 (2)	8	108 (2)
Shad Barry	1902	.287	3	57
Sherry Magee	1906	.282	6	67
Sherry Magee	1907	.328 (2)	4	85 (1)
Kitty Bransfield	1908	.304	3	71
Sherry Magee	1910	.331 (1)	6	123 (1)
Fred Luderus	1911	.301	16 (2)	99 (3)
Gavvy Cravath	1913	.341 (2)	19 (1)	128 (1)
Gavvy Cravath	1916	.283	11 (3)	70
Gavvy Cravath	1917	.280	12 (T1)	83 (3)
Cy Williams	1920	.325	15 (1)	72
Cy Williams	1921	.320	18 (3)	75
Cy Williams	1924	.328	24 (3)	93
George Harper	1925	.349	18	97
Chuck Klein	1930	.386 (3)	40 (2)	170 (2)
Chuck Klein	1931	.337	31 (1)	121 (1)
Chuck Klein	1933	.368 (1)	28 (1)	120 (1)
Danny Litwhiler	1942	.271	9	56
Ron Northey	1944	.288	22 (3)	104 (3)
Del Ennis	1946	.313	17	73
Del Ennis	1949	.302	25	110
Del Ennis	1950	.311	31	126 (1)
Del Ennis	1952	.289	20	107 (3)
Don Demeter	1962	.307	29	107
Dick Allen	1966	.317	40 (2)	110 (3)
Dick Allen	1969	.288	32	89
Greg Luzinski	1972	.281	18	68
Greg Luzinski	1977	.309	39 (3)	130 (2)
John Kruk	1991	.294	21	92

( ) = Ranking in league

Phillies Triple-Crown Leaders

Elmer Flick was one of the Phillies' best hitters at the turn of the century.

Top 10 in Lifetime Slugging Percentage

Chuck Klein	.553	Elmer Flick	.497
Dick Allen	.530	Sam Thompson	.497
Mike Schmidt	.527	Gavvy Cravath	.489
Ed Delahanty	.504	Don Hurst	.489
Cy Williams	.500	Greg Luzinski	.489

Season Batting Leaders by Position

1883–1899*

1b—Nap Lajoie	.361—1897
2b—Nap Lajoie	.378—1899
3b—Lave Cross	.386—1894
ss—Joe Sullivan	.352—1894
lf—Ed Delahanty	.410—1899
cf—Billy Hamilton	.404—1894
rf—Sam Thompson*	.407—1894
c—Jack Clements	.394—1895

*Outfielder Tuck Turner batted .416 in 339 ABs in 1894

1900–92

1b—Dolph Camilli	.339—1937
2b—Nap Lajoie	.337—1900
3b—Pinky Whitney	.342—1930
ss—Dick Bartell	.310—1934
lf—Lefty O'Doul	.398—1929
cf—Harry Walker†	.363—1947
rf—Chuck Klein	.386—1930
c—Smoky Burgess	.368—1954

†Also played 10 games with St. Louis, hit .371 with Phils, .363 overall

.300 Hitters in Season

Lefthanded catcher Jack Clements was one of the Phillies' early .300 hitters.

(Minimum 400 at bats)

Year	Player	AVG
1887	Ed Andrews	.325
1890	Billy Hamilton	.325
	Sam Thompson	.313
1891	Billy Hamilton	.340
	Jack Clements	.310
1892	Billy Hamilton	.330
	Ed Delahanty	.306
	Sam Thompson	.305
1893	Billy Hamilton	.380
	Sam Thompson	.370
	Ed Delahanty	.368
	Bill Hallman	.307
1894	Sam Thompson	.407
	Ed Delahanty	.407
	Billy Hamilton	.404
	Lave Cross	.386
	Bill Hallman	.309
	Jack Boyle	.301
1895	Ed Delahanty	.404
	Sam Thompson	.392
	Billy Hamilton	.389
	Bill Hallman	.314
1896	Ed Delahanty	.397
	Bill Hallman	.320
1897	Ed Delahanty	.377
	Nap Lajoie	.361
	Duff Cooley	.329
1898	Ed Delahanty	.334
	Nap Lajoie	.324
	Elmer Flick	.302
	Duff Cooley	.312
1899	Ed Delahanty	.410
	Elmer Flick	.342
	Roy Thomas	.325
1900	Elmer Flick	.367
	Nap Lajoie	.337
	Ed Delahanty	.323
	Roy Thomas	.316
1901	Ed Delahanty	.354
	Elmer Flick	.336
	Roy Thomas	.309
1903	Roy Thomas	.327
	Bill Keister	.320
	Harry Wolverton	.308

Year	Player	AVG
1905	Roy Thomas	.317
	John Titus	.308
1907	Sherry Magee	.328
1908	Kitty Bransfield	.304
1910	Sherry Magee	.331
	Johnny Bates	.305
1911	Fred Luderus	.301
1912	Dode Paskert	.315
	Sherry Magee	.306
1913	Gavvy Cravath	.341
	Sherry Magee	.306
	Hans Lobert	.300
1914	Beals Becker	.325
	Sherry Magee	.314
1915	Fred Luderus	.315
1919	Irish Meusel	.305
1920	Cy Williams	.325
	Irish Meusel	.309
1921	Cy Williams	.320
1922	Curt Walker	.337
	Cliff Lee	.322
	Butch Henline	.316
	Cy Williams	.308
1923	Cotton Tierney	.317
	Johnny Mokan	.313
	Walter Holke	.311
1924	Cy Williams	.328
	Walter Holke	.300
1925	George Harper	.349
	Lew Fonseca	.319
1926	Freddy Leach	.329
	Johnny Mokan	.303
1927	Freddy Leach	.306
	Russ Wrightstone	.306
	Fresco Thompson	.303
1928	Freddy Leach	.304
	Pinky Whitney	.301
1929	Lefty O'Doul	.398
	Chuck Klein	.356
	Pinky Whitney	.327
	Fresco Thompson	.324
	Don Hurst	.304
	Barney Friberg	.301
1930	Chuck Klein	.386
	Lefty O'Doul	.383
	Pinky Whitney	.342

1931	Chuck Klein	.337
	Buzz Arlett	.313
	Don Hurst	.305
1932	Chuck Klein	.348
	Don Hurst	.339
	Spud Davis	.336
	Kiddo Davis	.309
	Dick Bartell	.308
	Hal Lee	.303
1933	Chuck Klein	.368
	Spud Davis	.349
	Chick Fullis	.309
1934	Johnny Moore	.343
	Ethan Allen	.330
	Dick Bartell	.310
	Lou Chiozza	.304
1935	Johnny Moore	.323
	Ethan Allen	.307
1936	Johnny Moore	.328
	Dolph Camilli	.315
	Chuck Klein	.309
1937	Pinky Whitney	.341
	Dolph Camilli	.339
	Chuck Klein	.325
1939	Morrie Arnovich	.324
1941	Nick Etten	.311
	Danny Litwhiler	.305
1945	Jimmy Wasdell	.300
1946	Del Ennis	.313
1947	Harry Walker	.363
1948	Richie Ashburn	.333
1949	Del Ennis	.302
1950	Del Ennis	.311
	Richie Ashburn	.303
1951	Richie Ashburn	.344
1953	Richie Ashburn	.330

1954	Richie Ashburn	.313
1955	Richie Ashburn	.338
1956	Richie Ashburn	.303
1958	Richie Ashburn	.350
	Harry Anderson	.301
1962	Don Demeter	.307
	Tony Gonzalez	.302
	Johnny Callison	.300
1963	Tony Gonzalez	.306
1964	Dick Allen	.318
1965	Cookie Rojas	.303
	Dick Allen	.302
1966	Dick Allen	.317
1967	Tony Gonzalez	.339
	Dick Allen	.307
1970	Tony Taylor	.301
1974	Willie Montanez	.304
	Dave Cash	.300
1975	Larry Bowa	.305
	Dave Cash	.305
	Greg Luzinski	.300
1976	Garry Maddox	.330
	Jay Johnstone	.318
	Greg Luzinski	.304
1977	Bake McBride	.316
	Greg Luzinski	.309
1979	Pete Rose	.331
1980	Bake McBride	.309
1980	Pete Rose	.325
	Mike Schmidt	.316
	Gary Matthews	.301
1986	Von Hayes	.305
1987	Milt Thompson	.302
1990	Len Dykstra	.325
1992	John Kruk	.323

Johnny Moore hit over .300 in four straight seasons with the Phillies.

30 or More Home Runs in One Season

HR	Player	Year
48	Mike Schmidt	1980
45	Mike Schmidt	1979
43	Chuck Klein	1929
41	Cy Williams	1923
40	Chuck Klein	1930
40	Dick Allen	1966
40	Mike Schmidt	1983
39	Mike Schmidt	1983
38	Chuck Klein	1932
38	Mike Schmidt	1975
38	Mike Schmidt	1976
38	Mike Schmidt	1977
37	Mike Schmidt	1986
36	Mike Schmidt	1974
36	Mike Schmidt	1984
35	Greg Luzinski	1978
35	Mike Schmidt	1982

HR	Player	Year
35	Mike Schmidt	1987
34	Deron Johnson	1971
34	Greg Luzinski	1975
33	Dick Allen	1968
33	Mike Schmidt	1985
32	Lefty O'Doul	1929
32	Stan Lopata	1956
32	John Callison	1965
32	Dick Allen	1969
31	Don Hurst	1929
31	Chuck Klein	1931
31	Del Ennis	1950
31	John Callison	1964
31	Mike Schmidt	1981
30	Cy Williams	1927
30	Del Ennis	1948
30	Willie Montanez	1971

10 or More Home Runs in One Month

HR	Player	Month	Year
15	Cy Williams	May	1923
14	Chuck Klein	July	1929
	Mike Schmidt	June	1977
13	Deron Johnson	July	1971
	Mike Schmidt	July	1979
12	Chuck Klein	June	1932
	Dick Allen	June	1966
	Mike Schmidt	August	1975
	Mike Schmidt	May	1980
	Mike Schmidt	July	1982
11	Chuck Klein	May	1929
	Del Ennis	July	1953
	Greg Luzinksi	June	1975
	Mike Schmidt	April	1976
	Mike Schmidt	May	1979
10	Cy Williams	July	1927
	Chuck Klein	July	1930
	Chuck Klein	May	1932
	Willie Jones	July	1950
	Bill Robinson	August	1973
	Mike Schmidt	June	1974
	Greg Luzinski	July	1977

Most Home Runs by Position in One Season

	Player	HR	Year		Player	HR	Year
c	Darren Daulton	27	1992	3b	Mike Schmidt	48	1980
1b	Deron Johnson	34	1971	lf	Greg Luzinski	39	1977
2b	Juan Samuel	28	1987	cf	Cy Williams	41	1923
ss	Granny Hamner	17	1952	rf	Chuck Klein	43	1929

Most Home Runs by Position (Career)

	Player	HR		Player	HR
p	Rick Wise, Larry Christenson	11	3b	Mike Schmidt	509
			ss	Granny Hamner	61
c	Andy Seminick	121	of	Del Ennis	257
1b	Don Hurst	111	of	Chuck Klein	241
2b	Juan Samuel	91	of	Greg Luzinski	219

Two Home Runs or More in One Game

Number of Times	Player
44	Mike Schmidt
23	Chuck Klein
20	Dick Allen
17	Greg Luzinski
14	Cy Williams
12	Willie Jones
11	Dolph Camilli, Von Hayes
10	Johnny Callison
9	Del Ennis
8	Don Hurst
7	Don Demeter, Andy Seminick
6	Gavvy Cravath, Stan Lopata, Fred Luderus, Don Money, Sam Thompson
5	Cliff Lee, Johnny Moore
4	Luis Aguayo, John Briggs, Jack Clements, Wes Covington, Spud Davis, Ed Delahanty, Bo Diaz, Deron Johnson, Juan Samuel, Ozzie Virgil

Number of Times	Player
3	Darren Daulton, Richie Hebner, Jay Johnstone, Sherry Magee, Willie Montanez, Joe Morgan, Ron Northey, Lefty O'Doul, Johnny Rizzo, Bill Robinson, Dickie Thon, George Wood
2	Harry Anderson, Richie Ashburn, Vince DiMaggio, Elmer Flick, Pancho Herrera, Larry Hisle, Tommy Hutton, Ricky Jordan, John Kruk, Nap Lajoie, Freddy Leach, Hal Lee, Sixto Lezcano, Joe Marty, Johnny Mokan, Keith Moreland, Wally Post, Gary Redus, Roy Sievers, Dick Sisler, Coaker Triplett, Bennie Warren, George Watkins, Rick Wise
1	Buster Adams, Mike Anderson, Buzz Arlett, Charlie Bastian, Beals Becker, Bobby Bragan, Wes Chamberlain, Larry Christenson, Phil Collins, Roger Connor, Monte Cross, Tony Curry, Mariano Duncan, Art Fletcher, Tommy Glaviano, Mike Goliat, Bill Hallman, Billy Hamilton, Granny Hamner, George Harper, Butch Henline, Walter Holke, Dave Hollins, Chris James, Irv Jeffries, Steve Jeltz, Dave Johnson, Ron Jones, Lee King, Jack Knight, Bevo LeBourveau, Randy Lerch, Danny Litwhiler, Hans Lobert, Jack Manning, Gary Matthews, Bake McBride, Tim McCarver, Irish Meusel, Eddie Miller, Bobby Morgan, Joe Mulvey, Al Nixon, Frank Parkinson, John Peters, Bobby Pfeil, Adolfo Phillips, Cookie Rojas, Carl Sawatski, Rick Schu, Joe Schultz, Denny Sothern, Casey Stengel, Glen Stewart, Jeff Stone, Dick Stuart, Tony Taylor, Gus Triandos, Elmer Valo, Johnny Vergez, Lee Walls, Ken Walters, Bill White, Pinky Whitney, Del Wilber, Glenn Wilson, John Wockenfuss, Russ Wrightstone

Grand Slam Home Runs in Career

7	Mike Schmidt
6	Willie Jones, Chuck Klein, Cy Williams
5	Dick Allen, Del Ennis, Greg Luzinski, Andy Seminick
4	Vince DiMaggio, Russ Wrightstone
3	Lave Cross, Darren Daulton, Don Demeter, Gene Freese, Granny Hamner, George Harper, Fred Luderus, Garry Maddox, Sam Thompson
2	Bob Allen, Kitty Bransfield, Ed Bouchee, Johnny Callison, Dolph Camilli, Spud Davis, Von Hayes, Don Hurst, Chris James, Dave Johnson, Ricky Jordan, John Kruk, Freddy Leach, Danny Litwhiler, Ron Northey, Bill Robinson, Juan Samuel, Roy Sievers, Dick Stuart, Tony Taylor, Pinky Whitney
1	Harry Anderson, Bob Boone, Larry Bowa, Jack Boyle, Bobby Bragan, John Briggs, Ollie Brown, Tommy Brown, Byron Browne, Steve Carlton, Larry Christenson, Mel Clark, Jack Clements, Jimmie Coker, Phil Collins, Jim Command, Gavvy Cravath, Ed Daily, Ed Delahanty, Bo Diaz, Red Dooin, Bill Duggleby, Sid Farrar, Elmer Flick, Lew Fonseca, Jimmie Foxx, Roger Freed, Al Glossop, Tony Gonzalez, Billy Hamilton, Chicken Hawks, Charlie Hayes, Richie Hebner, Solly Hemus, Dave Hollins, Jim Hutto, Deron Johnson, Rick Joseph, Ted Kazanski, Joe Lefebvre, Don Lock, Jim Lonborg, Stan Lopata, Sherry Magee, Art Mahaffey, Bobby Malkmus, Tom Marsh, Jerry Martin, Carmelo Martinez, Bake McBride, Tim McCarver, Frank McCormick, Lee Meadows, Irish Meusel, Eddie Miller, Ralph Miller, Johnny Mokan, Willie Montanez, Keith Moreland, Bobby Morgan, Emmett Mueller, Dale Murphy, Al Myers, Skeeter Newsome, Lance Parrish, Gene Paulette, Wally Post, Tony Rensa, Rip Repulski, Jimmy Ring, Cookie Rojas, Schoolboy Rowe, Connie Ryan, Mike Ryan, John Russell, Howie Schultz, Joe Schultz, Charley Smith, Denny Sothern, Jim Tabor, Dickie Thon, Bobby Tolan, Gus Triandos, Johnny Vergez, Ozzie Virgil, Bucky Walters, Bill White, Glenn Wilson, Jimmie Wilson, Rick Wise

Four Home Runs in One Game

July 13, 1896, Ed Delahanty, 1b A
July 10, 1936, Chuck Klein, of* A
Apr. 17, 1976, MIKE SCHMIDT, 3b A
H—Home   A—Away   *Lefthanded Hitters   CAPS—Consecutive

Three Home Runs in One Game

Oct. 9, 1984, JOHN MANNING, of A
Sept. 15, 1922, Walt Henline, c-of H
May 11, 1923, Cy Williams, of* H
July 22, 1936, JOHN MOORE, of* H
June 2, 1949, Andy Seminick, c H
Aug. 27, 1951, DEL WILBER, c H
July 23, 1955, Del Ennis, of H
Sept. 12, 1961, DON DEMETER, of A
Sept. 27, 1964, JOHNNY CALLISON, of* H
June 6, 1965, Johnny Callison, of* A
Sept. 29, 1968, DICK ALLEN, of A
July 11, 1971, DERON JOHNSON, 1b H
July 7, 1979, MIKE SCHMIDT, 3b H
Aug. 29, 1989, Von Hayes, 1b* A
H—Home   A—Away   *Lefthanded Hitters   CAPS—Consecutive

Hitting for the Cycle

1922—Cy Williams	1931—Chuck Klein
1927—Cy Williams	1933—Chuck Klein
1929—Pinky Whitney	1963—Johnny Callison

Most Grand Slam Home Runs in One Season

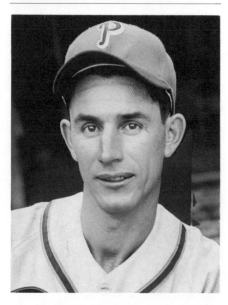

4	Vince DiMaggio, 1945	2	Del Ennis, 1950
3	Chuck Klein, 1929	2	Willie Jones, 1951
3	Chuck Klein, 1932	2	Don Demeter, 1962
3	Gene Freese, 1959	2	Dick Stuart, 1965
2	George Harper, 1924	2	Dick Allen, 1968
2	Cy Williams, 1925	2	Mike Schmidt, 1973
2	Cy Williams, 1926	2	Greg Luzinski, 1976
2	Russ Wrightstone, 1927	2	Greg Luzinski, 1977
2	Dolph Camilli, 1937	2	Dave Johnson, 1978
2	Andy Seminick, 1950	2	Mike Schmidt, 1983
2	Willie Jones, 1950	2	Darren Daulton, 1992

Vince DiMaggio blasted four grand slam home runs in 1945.

Extra-Inning Home Runs

9 Mike Schmidt
6 Dick Allen
5 Gavvy Cravath, Del Ennis, Cy Williams
4 Tony Gonzalez, Stan Lopata
3 Luis Aguayo, Johnny Callison, Wes Covington, Chuck Klein
2 John Briggs, Jack Clements, Ernie Courtney, Spud Davis, Bo Diaz, Granny Hamner, Rick Joseph, John Kruk, Hans Lobert, Greg Luzinski, Gary Matthews, Willie Montanez, Johnny Moore, Ron Northey, John Russell, Andy Seminick, Dick Sisler, Jim Tabor, Manny Trillo, Possum Whitted
1 Harry Anderson, Buzz Arlett, Morrie Arnovich, Bill Atwood, Dave Bancroft, Ed Bouchee, Bobby Bragan, Ollie Brown, Tommy Brown, Dolph Camilli, Gene Conley, Babe Dahlgren, Clay Dalrymple, Alvin Dark, Darren Daulton, Curt Davis, Bob Dernier, Vince DiMaggio, Red Dooin, Art Fletcher, Elmer Flick, Barry Foote, Chick Fraser, Barney Friberg, Charlie Frye, Mike Goliat, Billy Hamilton, George Harper, Von Hayes, Richie Hebner, Deron Johnson, Jay Johnstone, Ted Kazanski, Nap Lajoie, Phil Linz, Fred Luderus, Sherry Magee, Jack Manning, Bake McBride, Jack Meyer, John Morris, Dale Murphy, Bert Niehoff, Al Nixon, Lefty O'Doul, Lance Parrish, Eddie Pellagrini, Wally Post, Connie Ryan, Mike Ryan, Juan Samuel, Roy Sievers, Bill Sorrell, Jeff Stone, Tony Taylor, Derrel Thomas, Dickie Thon, Ozzie Virgil, Bucky Walters, George Watkins, Bill White, George Wood, Russ Wrightstone

Pinch-Hit Home Runs

9 Cy Williams
6 Gavvy Cravath, Rick Joseph, Del Unser
5 Gene Freese, Bill Nicholson
4 Bob Bowman, Ollie Brown, Johnny Callison, Dave Hollins, Wally Post, Rip Repulski
3 Luis Aguayo, Jeff Grotewold, Von Hayes, Tommy Hutton, Dave Johnson, Deron Johnson, Stan Lopata, Jerry Martin, Len Matuszek, John Russell, Tony Taylor
2 Marv Blaylock, Tommy Brown, Wes Covington, Spud Davis, Del Ennis, Tony Gonzalez, Johnny Herrnstein, Jim Hutton, Alex Johnson, Chuck Klein, Bevo LeBourveau, Cliff Lee, Joe Lefebvre, Bake McBride, Tim McCarver, Harry McCurdy, Dwayne Murphy, Lefty O'Doul, Dode Paskert, Mike Rogodzinski, Schoolboy Rowe, Juan Samuel, Mike Schmidt, Rick Schu, Johnny Schulte, Andy Seminick, Roy Sievers, Jeff Stone, Elmer Valo, Ozzie Virgil, Russ Wrightstone
1 Bert Adams, Buster Adams, Harry Anderson, Mike Anderson, Bill Atwood, Earl Averill, Beals Becker, Buddy Blattner, Bob Boone, Gib Brack, Bryon Browne, Earl Browne, Smoky Burgess, Sil Campusano, Jose Cardenal, Hal Carlson, Doug Clemens, Jack Clements, Jimmie Coker, Jacke Davis, Bobby Del Greco, Don Demeter, Vince DiMaggio, Vance Dinges, Clise Dudley, Bob Finley, Barney Friberg, Jimmie Foxx, Roger Freed, Charlie Frye, Oscar Gamble, Glen Gorbous, Bill Grabarkewitz, Earl Grace, Harry Hanebrink, George Harper, Don Hurst, Chris James, Stan Javier, Jay Johnstone, George Jumonville, John Kruk, Jim Lemon, Walt Lerian, Roy Leslie, Sixto Lezcano, Jim Lindeman, Phil Linz, Joe Lis, Mickey Livingston, Greg Luzinski, Joe Marty, Bob Molinaro, Bobby Morgan, Al Nixon, Ron Northey, John Peters, Dave Philley, Randy Ready, Ronn Reynolds, Johnny Rizzo, Bill Robinson, Ron Roenicke, Connie Ryan, Carl Sawatski, Tripp Sigman, Dick Sisler, Bobby Gene Smith, Gus Suhr, Frank Thomas, Earl Torgeson, Coaker Triplett, Bob Uecker, George Vukovich, George Watkins, Doc White, Glenn Wilson, Jimmie Wilson

Rick Joseph is among the Phillies' all-time leaders in pinch-hit home runs.

Home Runs Leading Off the Game

14   Juan Samuel

6   John Briggs, Bake McBride, Dode Paskert, Tony Taylor

4   Tony Gonzalez, Billy Hamilton, Heinie Sand

3   Phil Bradley, Bob Dernier, Lenny Dykstra, Garry Maddox, Leo Norris, George Wood

2   Richie Ashburn, Dave Cash, Duff Cooley, Bobby Del Greco, Bobby Malkmus, Jerry Martin, Joe Marty, Joe Morgan, Emmett Mueller, Randy Ready, Gary Redus, Connie Ryan, Denny Sothern, Jeff Stone, Roy Thomas

1   Ethan Allen, Dick Allen, Ruben Amaro, Jr., Stan Benjamin, Johnny Callison, Kiddo Davis, Len Dykstra, Bill Grabarkewitz, Granny Hamner, Von Hayes, Larry Hisle, Willie Jones, Joe Koppe, Ralph LaPointe, Bevo LeBourveau, Les Mallon, Jack Manning, Johnny Mokan, Bobby Morgan, Adolfo Phillips, Goldie Rapp, Bill Robinson, Cookie Rojas, Mike Schmidt, Lonnie Smith, Fresco Thompson, John Titus, Eddie Waitkus, Russ Wrightstone

Phillies Whose First Major League Hit Was a Home Run

Date	Player	Opponent
Apr. 21, 1898	Bill Duggleby	vs. New York
May 15, 1922	Tom Sullivan	at St. Louis
Apr. 19, 1938	Emmett Mueller	vs. Brooklyn
Aug. 21, 1940	Charlie Frye	at Chicago
Aug. 2, 1941	Jim Carlin	at St. Louis
July 5, 1943	Bob Finley	vs. St. Louis
Sept. 15, 1943	Andy Seminick	vs. New York
Sept. 28, 1949	Ed Sanicki	at Pittsburgh
July 11, 1954	Jim Command	at Brooklyn
Sept. 21, 1956	Bob Bowman	at New York
June 2, 1957	Dick Farrell	vs. Brooklyn
May 16, 1975	Larry Christenson	vs. Atlanta
Sept. 22, 1986	Jeff Bittiger	at Pittsburgh
July 17, 1988	Ricky Jordan	vs. Houston
Aug. 26, 1988	Ron Jones	vs. Los Angeles

Grand slam homers: Bill Duggleby, Jim Command

Pinch-hit homer: Charlie Frye

Homer leading off the game: Emmett Mueller

First time at bat in majors: Bill Duggleby, Emmett Mueller, Ed Sanicki

First official at bat in majors: Ricky Jordan

Emmett Mueller crosses the plate and gets a greeting from Hersh Martin after hitting a home run in his first major league at-bat in 1938.

Eddie Sanicki homered in his first big league trip to the plate in 1949.

Phillies 20–20 Club

Player	Year	HR	SB	Player	Year	HR	SB
Sam Thompson	1889	20	24	Mike Schmidt	1975	38	29
Chuck Klein	1932	38	20	Juan Samuel	1987	28	35
Dick Allen	1967	23	20	Von Hayes	1989	26	28
Mike Schmidt	1974	36	23				

Most Back-to-Back Home Runs in a Season

Club record for back-to-back homers in a season is 9 times in 1980.

9	Mike Schmidt/Greg Luzinski	(Schmidt hit the first homer seven times)
		(Luzinski hit the first homer two times)
9	Chuck Klein/Don Hurst	(Klein hit first homer all nine times)

Home Runs at Recreation Park

5	Charlie Bastian	(1885–86)		1	Ed Andrews	(1884–86)
3	Charlie Ferguson	(1884–86)			Jim Fogarty	(1884–86)
	Joe Mulvey	(1883–86)			Buster Hoover	(1884)
2	Ed Daily	(1885–86)			George Wood	(1886)
	Sid Farrar	(1883–86)				
	Deacon McGuire	(1886)				

Home Runs at Baker Bowl

156	Chuck Klein	(1928–33, 1936–38)		12	Billy Hamilton	(1890–95)
140	Cy Williams	(1918–30)		11	Ethan Allen	(1934–36)
92	Gavvy Cravath	(1912–20)			Elmer Flick	(1898–1901)
68	Don Hurst	(1928–34)			Hal Lee	(1931–33)
66	Sam Thompson	(1889–98)		10	Buzz Arlett	(1931)
62	Fred Luderus	(1910–20)			Roger Connor	(1892)
61	Dolph Camilli	(1934–37)			Heinie Sand	(1923–28)
46	Jack Clements	(1887–97)			George Watkins	(1935–36)
44	Ed Delahanty	(1888–89, 1891–1901)		9	Davey Bancroft	(1915–20)
42	Sherry Magee	(1904–14)			Art Fletcher	(1920–22)
	Russ Wrightstone	(1920–28)			Bob Grace	(1936–37)
					Walt Holke	(1923–25)
38	Johnny Moore	(1934–37)			Denny Sothern	(1926, 1928–30)
37	Pinky Whitney	(1928–33, 1936–38)		8	Morrie Arnovich	(1936–38)
33	Spud Davis	(1928–33, 1938)			Jack Boyle	(1893–98)
					Wes Schulmerich	(1933–34)
32	Lefty O'Doul	(1929–30)			Fresco Thompson	(1927–30)
29	Fred Leach	(1923–28)			George Whitted	(1915–19)
	Cliff Lee	(1921–24)		7	Kiddo Davis	(1932, 1934)
28	George Harper	(1924–26)			Bevo LeBourveau	(1919–22)
	Butch Henline	(1921–26)			Bert Niehoff	(1915–17)
26	Irish Meusel	(1918–21)			John Peters	(1921–22)
24	Dode Paskert	(1911–17)			Casey Stengel	(1920–21)
22	Johnny Mokan	(1922–27)		6	Lave Cross	(1892–97)
	Frank Parkinson	(1921–24)			Duff Cooley	(1896–99)
20	Beals Becker	(1913–15)			Clarence Huber	(1925–26)
17	George Wood	(1887–89)			Ed Konetchy	(1921)
16	Hans Lobert	(1911–14)			Roy Leslie	(1922)
15	Barney Friberg	(1925–32)			Al Orth	(1895–1901)
	Nap Lajoie	(1896–1900)			Walt Tragesser	(1919–20)
	John Titus	(1903–12)			Jimmy Walsh	(1910–13)
	Jimmie Wilson	(1923–28, 1934–38)		5	Bill Hallman	(1888–89, 1892–97, 1901–03)
14	Curt Walker	(1921–24)				
13	Leo Norris	(1936–37)				

	Hershel Martin	(1937–38)
	Al Todd	(1932–35)
4	Grover Alexander	(1911–17, 1930)
	Bob Allen	(1890–94)
	Ed Andrews	(1887–89)
	John Bates	(1909–10)
	Red Dooin	(1902–14)
	Jim Fogarty	(1884–89)
	Lew Fonseca	(1925)
	Chicken Hawks	(1926)
	Les Mallon	(1931–32)
	Harry McCurdy	(1930–33)
	Lee Meadows	(1919–23)
	Roy Thomas	(1899–1908, 1910–11)
	Cotton Tierney	(1923)
	Tuck Turner	(1893–96)
3	Frank Buggy	(1921)
	Eddie Burke	(1890)
	Phil Collins	(1929–35)
	Monte Cross	(1898–1901)
	Charlie Ferguson	(1887)
	Mickey Haslin	(1933–36)
	Lee King	(1921–22)
	Peck Lerian	(1928–29)
	Ed McFarland	(1897–1901)
	Ralph Miller	(1920–21)
	Joe Mulvey	(1887–89, 1892)
	Johnny Rawlings	(1920–21)
	Jimmy Ring	(1921–25, 1928)
	Johnny Schulte	(1928)
	Frank Shugart	(1897)
	Tripp Sigman	(1929–30)
	Jim Smith	(1921–22)
	Milt Stock	(1915–18)
	Jack Taylor	(1892–97)
	Bucky Walters	(1934–38)
	Mack Wheat	(1920–21)
2	Bert Adams	(1915–19)
	Dick Bartell	(1931–34)
	Fred Beck	(1911)
	Kitty Bransfield	(1905–11)
	Earl Browne	(1937–38)
	Hal Carlson	(1924–27)
	Pearce Chiles	(1899–1900)
	Gene Corbett	(1936–38)
	Johnny Couch	(1923–25)
	Wayland Dean	(1926–27)
	Mickey Doolan	(1905–13)
	Bill Duggleby	(1898, 1901–07)
	Sid Farrar	(1887–89)
	Horace Ford	(1924)
	Bill Keister	(1903)
	Bill Killefer	(1911–17)
	Otto Knabe	(1907–13)
	Emmett Mueller	(1938)
	Al Myers	(1889–91)
	Al Nixon	(1926–28)

	Claude Passeau	(1936–38)
	Tony Rensa	(1930–31)
	Joe Schultz	(1924–25)
	Ernie Sulik	(1936)
	Johnny Vergez	(1935–36)
	Phil Weintraub	(1938)
	Harry Wolverton	(1900–04)
1	Bill Atwood	(1936–38)
	Doug Baird	(1919)
	John Barry	(1901–04)
	Charlie Bastian	(1887–88)
	Chief Bender	(1916–17)
	Jack Bentley	(1920)
	Lena Blackburne	(1919)
	Joe Bowman	(1935)
	Fred Brickell	(1930–33)
	Dick Buckley	(1894–95)
	Bob Bryne	(1913–17)
	Forrest Cady	(1919)
	Leo Callahan	(1919)
	Kid Carsey	(1892–97)
	Dan Casey	(1887–89)
	Lou Chiozza	(1934–36)
	Bud Clancy	(1934)
	Frank Corridon	(1904–05, 1907–09)
	Ed Daily	(1887)
	Curt Davis	(1934–36)
	Ed Delker	(1932–33)
	Clise Dudley	(1931–32)
	Klondike Douglass	(1898–1904)
	Duke Esper	(1890–92)
	Bill Foxen	(1908–10)
	Chick Fraser	(1899–1900, 1902–04)
	Chick Fullis	(1933–34)
	Phil Geier	(1896–97)
	Kid Gleason	(1888–91, 1903–08)
	Wilbur Good	(1916)
	George Graham	(1912)
	Mike Grady	(1894–97)
	Ed Grant	(1907–10)
	Cliff Heathcote	(1932)
	Wilbur Hubbell	(1920–25)
	Harold Irelan	(1914)
	Arthur Irwin	(1887–89, 1894)
	Syl Johnson	(1934–38)
	Tony Kaufmann	(1927)
	Tim Keefe	(1891–93)
	Walt Kimmick	(1925–26)
	Ed Mayer	(1890–91)
	Erskine Mayer	(1912–18)
	Al Maul	(1887–1900)
	Patsy McGaffigan	(1917–18)
	Deacon McGuire	(1887–88)
	Billy Nash	(1896–98)
	Gene Paulette	(1919–20)

Buzzy Phillips	(1930)	
Charlie Reilly	(1892–95)	
Eppa Rixey	(1912–17, 1919–20)	
George Scharein	(1937–38)	
Pop Schriver	(1888–90)	
Frank Schulte	(1917)	

Jack Scott	(1927)	
Tom Seaton	(1912–13)	
Paul Sentelle	(1906–07)	
John Sharrott	(1893)	
Joe Sullivan	(1894–96)	
Poco Taitt	(1931–32)	
Doc White	(1901–02)	

Home Runs at Columbia Park

1	Kid Gleason
	Rudy Hulswitt

Home Runs at University of Pennsylvania

3	Lave Cross
1	Billy Hamilton
	Joe Sullivan
	Sam Thompson

Home Runs at Shibe Park/ Connie Mack Stadium

133	Del Ennis	(1946–56)
90	Willie Jones	(1947–49)
87	Dick Allen	(1963–69)
86	Johnny Callison	(1960–69)
67	Andy Seminick	(1943–51, 1955–57)
62	Stan Lopata	(1948–58)
53	Granny Hamner	(1944–59)
42	Tony Gonzalez	(1960–68)
29	Roy Sievers	(1962–64)
28	Wes Covington	(1961–65)
25	Harry Anderson	(1957–60)
	Deron Johnson	(1969–70)
23	Clay Dalrymple	(1960–68)
	Don Demeter	(1961–63)
22	Ron Northey	(1942–44, 1946–47, 1957)
	Tony Taylor	(1960–70)
21	Bill White	(1966–68)
19	Danny Litwhiler	(1940–43)
18	John Briggs	(1964–70)
17	Rip Repulski	(1957–58)
	Dick Stuart	(1965)
16	Buster Adams	(1943–45, 1947)
	Joe Marty	(1939–41)
	Wally Post	(1958–60)
	Cookie Rojas	(1963–69)
15	Larry Hisle	(1968–70)
14	Ed Bouchee	(1956–60)
	Bob Bowman	(1955–59)
	Bobby Morgan	(1954–57)
13	Pancho Herrera	(1958, 1960–61)
	Bobby Wine	(1960, 1962–68)

12	Gene Freese	(1959)
	Mike Goliat	(1949–51)
	Jim Greengrass	(1955–56)
	Don Lock	(1967–69)
	Bennie Warren	(1939–42)
11	Bobby Bragan	(1940–42)
	Don Money	(1968–70)
10	Nick Etten	(1941–42, 1947)
	Bill Nicholson	(1949–53)
	Mike Ryan	(1968–70)
9	Vince DiMaggio	(1945)
	Eddie Miller	(1948–49)
8	Chico Fernandez	(1957–59)
	Johnny Rizzo	(1940–41)
	Dick Sisler	(1948–51)
	Jim Tabor	(1946–47)
	Earl Torgeson	(1953–55)
	Coaker Triplett	(1943–45)
	Johnny Wyrostek	(1946–47, 1952–54)
7	Gib Brack	(1938–39)
	Tommy Brown	(1951–52)
	Smoky Burgess	(1952–55)
	Bobby Del Greco	(1960–61, 1965)
	Ted Kazanski	(1953–58)
	Schoolboy Rowe	(1943, 1946–49)
6	Richie Ashburn	(1948–59)
	Alex Johnson	(1964–65)
	Chuck Klein	(1938–44)
	Joe Koppe	(1959–61)
	Frank McCormick	(1946–47)
	Connie Ryan	(1952–53)
	Bobby Gene Smith	(1960–61)
	Frank Thomas	(1964–65)

	Ken Walters	(1960–61)		Buddy Blattner	(1949)
5	Johnny Blatnik	(1948–50)		Jackie Brandt	(1966–67)
	Marv Blaylock	(1955–57)		Bubba Church	(1950–52)
	Byron Browne	(1970)		Doug Clemens	(1966–68)
	Joe Lonnett	(1956–59)		Mike Compton	(1970)
	Bobby Malkmus	(1960–62)		Pat Corrales	(1964–65)
	Gene Oliver	(1967)		Billy Cowan	(1967)
	Carl Sawatski	(1958–59)		Babe Dahlgren	(1943)
	Roy Smalley	(1955–58)		Al Dark	(1960)
	Gus Triandos	(1964–65)		Jacke Davis	(1962)
	Lee Walls	(1960–61)		Dick Farrell	(1956–61, 1967–69)
	Del Wilber	(1951–52)			
4	Ruben Amaro	(1960–65)		Bob Finley	(1943–44)
	Chuck Essegian	(1958)		Charley Gilbert	(1946–47)
	Solly Hemus	(1956–58)		Alban Glossop	(1942)
	Don Hoak	(1963–64)		Dick Groat	(1966–67)
	Ted Savage	(1962)		Bert Haas	(1948–49)
	Danny Schell	(1954–55)		Jim Hutto	(1970)
	Elmer Valo	(1956, 1961)		Billy Klaus	(1962–63)
				Charlie Letchas	(1939, 1944, 1946)
3	Morrie Arnovich	(1938–40)			
	Stan Benjamin	(1939–42)			
	Don Cardwell	(1957–60)		Phil Linz	(1966–67)
	Jimmie Foxx	(1945)		Joe Lis	(1970)
	John Herrnstein	(1962–66)		Art Mahaffey	(1960–65)
	Rick Joseph	(1967–70)		Art Mahan	(1940)
	Al Lakeman	(1947–48)		Hershel Martin	(1938–40)
	Emmett Mueller	(1938–41)		Jackie Mayo	(1948–53)
	Cal Neeman	(1960–61)		Tim McCarver	(1970)
	Charlie Smith	(1961)		Bob Miller	(1949–58)
	Bob Uecker	(1966–67)		Skeeter Newsome	(1946–47)
	Cy Williams	(1927)		Lowell Palmer	(1969–70)
	Rick Wise	(1964, 1966–70)		Stan Palys	(1953–55)
				Ike Pearson	(1939–42, 1946)
2	Bill Atwood	(1938–40)			
	Jim Coker	(1958–62)		Eddie Pellagrini	(1951)
	Tony Curry	(1960–61)		Dave Philley	(1958–60)
	Glen Gorbous	(1955–57)		Jake Powell	(1945)
	Stan Hollmig	(1949–51)		Robin Roberts	(1948–61)
	Ernie Koy	(1942)		Saul Rogovin	(1955–57)
	Jim Lemon	(1963)		Eddie Sanicki	(1949, 1951)
	Ted Lepcio	(1960)			
	Mickey Livingston	(1941–43)		Jim Schaffer	(1966–67)
	Tony Lupien	(1944–45)		Howie Schultz	(1947–48)
	Earl Naylor	(1942–43)		Curt Simmons	(1947–50, 1952–60)
	Adolfo Phillips	(1964–66)			
	Ron Stone	(1969–70)		Gus Suhr	(1939–40)
	Jimmy Wasdell	(1943–46)		Gary Sutherland	(1966–68)
	Dave Watkins	(1969)		Eddie Waitkus	(1949–53, 1955)
	Sammy White	(1962)			
	Jim Woods	(1960–61)		Russ Wrightstone	(1927)
1	Stan Andrews	(1945)		Bobby Young	(1958)
	Earl Averill, Jr.	(1963)		Del Young	(1938–40)
	Hubert Bates	(1939)			

Home Runs at Veterans Stadium

265	Mike Schmidt	(1972–89)
130	Greg Luzinski	(1971–80)
77	Von Hayes	(1983–91)
52	Juan Samuel	(1983–89)
47	Garry Maddox	(1975–86)
38	Darren Daulton	(1983, 1985–92)
36	Bob Boone	(1972–81)
35	Willie Montanez	(1971–75, 1982)
29	Deron Johnson	(1971–73)
27	Richie Hebner	(1977–78)
24	Glenn Wilson	(1984–87)
23	Bo Diaz	(1982–85)
22	Bake McBride	(1977–81)
	Ricky Jordan	(1988–92)
21	Jay Johnstone	(1974–78)
	John Kruk	(1989–92)
20	Chris James	(1986–89)
	Ozzie Virgil	(1980–85)
19	Dave Hollins	(1990–92)
18	Luis Aguayo	(1980–88)
	Gary Matthews	(1981–83)
17	Bill Robinson	(1972–74, 1982–83)
	John Russell	(1984–88)
	Len Dykstra	(1989–92)
16	Mike Anderson	(1971–75, 1979)
	Lance Parrish	(1987–88)
15	Dick Allen	(1975–76)
	Don Money	(1971–72)
	Dickie Thon	(1989–91)
	Del Unser	(1973–74, 1979–82)
14	Tim McCarver	(1971–72, 1975–80)
	Manny Trillo	(1979–82)
13	Ollie Brown	(1974–77)
12	Wes Chamberlain	(1990–92)
	Charlie Hayes	(1989–91)
	Dale Murphy	(1990–92)
11	Tommy Hutton	(1972–77)
9	Sixto Lezcano	(1983–84)
	Joe Morgan	(1983)
	Rick Schu	(1984–87, 1991)
8	Phil Bradley	(1988)
	Ron Jones	(1988–91)
	Jerry Martin	(1974–78)
	Gary Redus	(1986)
	Jeff Stone	(1983–87)
	Milt Thompson	(1986–88)
7	Larry Bowa	(1971–81)
	Len Matuszek	(1981–84)
6	Joe Lefebvre	(1983–84, 1986)
	Joe Lis	(1971–72)
5	Ruben Amaro	(1992)
	Denny Doyle	(1971–73)

	Roger Freed	(1971–72)
	Dave Johnson	(1977–78)
	Mickey Morandini	(1990–92)
	Keith Moreland	(1978–81)
	John Wockenfuss	(1984–85)
4	Dave Cash	(1974–76)
	Bob Dernier	(1980–83, 1988–89)
	Carmelo Martinez	(1990)
	Dwayne Murphy	(1989)
	Randy Ready	(1989–91)
	Ron Roenicke	(1986–87)
	Mike Ryan	(1971–73)
	Ted Sizemore	(1977–78)
	Bobby Tolan	(1976–77)
3	Ken Brett	(1973)
	Steve Carlton	(1972–86)
	Larry Christenson	(1973–83)
	Ivan DeJesus	(1982–84)
	Mariano Duncan	(1992)
	Oscar Gamble	(1971–72)
	Tom Herr	(1989–90)
	Steve Jeltz	(1983–89)
	Jim Morrison	(1977–78)
	Tony Perez	(1983)
	Pete Rose	(1979–83)
	Lonnie Smith	(1978–81)
	Derrel Thomas	(1985)
	George Vukovich	(1980–82)
	Rick Wise	(1971)
2	Byron Browne	(1971–72)
	Sil Campusano	(1990–91)
	Tim Corcoran	(1983–85)
	Dick Davis	(1981–82)
	Tom Foley	(1985–86)
	Bill Grabarkewitz	(1973–74)
	Tommy Greene	(1990–92)
	Kevin Gross	(1983–88)
	Bobby Pfeil	(1971)
	Todd Pratt	(1992)
	Mike Rogodzinski	(1973–75)
	Alejandro Sanchez	(1982–83)
	Tony Taylor	(1971, 1974–76)
	Steve Lake	(1989–92)
1	Ramon Aviles	(1979–81)
	John Bateman	(1972)
	Juan Bell	(1992)
	Braulio Castillo	(1991–92)
	Jose Cardenal	(1978–79)
	Mike Easler	(1987)
	Darrin Fletcher	(1990–91)
	Woodie Fryman	(1971–72)
	Kiko Garcia	(1983–85)
	Jim Kaat	(1976–79)
	Randy Lerch	(1975–80, 1986)
	Jim Lindeman	(1991–92)
	Pete Mackanin	(1978–79)
	Tom Marsh	(1992)

John Morris	(1991)	Jim Vatcher	(1990)
John Oates	(1975–76)	John Vukovich	(1971,
David Palmer	(1988)		1976–77,
Dave Rader	(1979)		1979–81)
Ronn Reynolds	(1986)	Mike Young	(1988)
Ron Stone	(1971–72)		

Most RBI in One Season by Position

c	Darren Daulton, 1992 (109)	3b	Pinky Whitney, 1932 (124)
1b	Don Hurst, 1932 (143)	lf	Ed Delahanty, 1893 (146)
2b	Nap Lajoie, 1898 (127)	cf	Cy Williams, 1923 (114)
ss	Granny Hamner, 1952 (87)	rf	Chuck Klein, 1930 (170)

Most RBI in One Game

RBI	Player	Date	Opponent
8	Kitty Bransfield	July 11, 1910	at Pittsburgh
	Gavvy Cravath	Aug. 18, 1915	vs. Pittsburgh
	Willie Jones	Aug. 20, 1958	at St. Louis
	Mike Schmidt	Apr. 17, 1976 (10 inn.)	at Chicago
7	Ed Delahanty	July 13, 1894	at Chicago
	Lee King	Apr. 28, 1922	at Brooklyn
	Cy Williams	May 20, 1927	vs. Cincinnati
	Dolph Camilli	Apr. 19, 1935	vs. New York
	Granny Hamner	July 17, 1948	at St. Louis
	Del Ennis	July 27, 1950	vs. Chicago
	Del Ennis	July 23, 1955	vs. St. Louis
	Don Demeter	Sept. 12, 1961	at Los Angeles
	Dick Allen	Sept. 29, 1968	at New York
	Greg Luzinski	June 11, 1977	at Atlanta

Two Triples in One Game

1900	Klondike Douglass	May 7 at Brooklyn
	Ed Delahanty	May 28 at St. Louis
	Elmer Flick	July 14 vs. Boston
1901	Bill Hallman	May 16 vs. Pittsburgh
	Elmer Flick	June 17 at Boston
	Ed Delahanty	July 4 at St. Louis
1903	Harry Wolverton	Sept. 14 at Pittsburgh
	Harry Wolverton	Sept. 21 at Cincinnati
1904	Harry Wolverton	Aug. 24 at Pittsburgh
1905	John Titus	July 7 at Boston
1907	John Titus	May 25 vs. Brooklyn
1908	Sherry Magee	July 4 at Chicago
1909	Mickey Doolan	May 31 at New York
1910	Sherry Magee	June 9 vs. Chicago
	Kitty Bransfield	July 11 at Pittsburgh
	Mickey Doolan	Aug. 28 at Cincinnati
1911	Fred Luderus	May 12 vs. Pittsburgh
1912	John Titus	June 4 vs. Pittsburgh
	Gavvy Cravath	June 22 at Brooklyn
	Doc Miller	Sept. 26 at Brooklyn
1913	Gavvy Cravath	June 9 at Cincinnati
	Fred Luderus	June 23 at Boston
1914	Sherry Magee	July 12 at Cincinnati
	Ed Burns	Aug. 21 at Chicago
1916	Gavvy Cravath	May 16 at Cincinnati

Glen Stewart hit two triples in one game in 1944.

1917	Grover Alexander	June 6 at Chicago
	Possum Whitted	June 26 vs. New York
	Gavvy Cravath	Aug. 2 at St. Louis
	Gavvy Cravath	Aug. 24 at Cincinnati
1919	Dave Bancroft	July 31 at St. Louis
	Fred Luderus	Sept. 6 at Boston
1920	Gene Paulette	Apr. 15 at Brooklyn
1923	Russ Wrightstone	May 30 at Boston
	Clarence Mitchell	July 2 vs. New York
1924	Andy Woehr	May 4 at New York
	George Harper	July 1 at Boston
1925	Butch Henline	Apr. 22 vs. Brooklyn
1929	Pinky Whitney	July 30 at Pittsburgh
1930	Lefty O'Doul	June 22 at St. Louis
	Lefty O'Doul	June 27 at Pittsburgh
	Pinky Whitney	Aug. 3 at Boston
1933	Don Hurst	July 8 at Pittsburgh
1935	Dolph Camilli	July 4 at Brooklyn
	Mickey Haslin	July 22 at Pittsburgh
1936	Dolph Camilli	May 13 vs. Cincinnati
1939	Jim Shilling	Sept. 23 vs. Brooklyn
1940	Pinky May	May 20 vs. Pittsburgh
1941	Danny Litwhiler	Aug. 18 vs. Cincinnati
1943	Coaker Triplett	June 25 vs. Brooklyn
1944	Glen Stewart	July 5 at Pittsburgh
1948	Andy Seminick	Sept. 7 vs. New York
1952	Connie Ryan	Sept. 2 vs. Brooklyn
1955	Marv Blaylock	July 15 vs. Milwaukee
1956	Roy Smalley	July 29 vs. Milwaukee
1958	Chico Fernandez	May 28 vs. San Francisco
	Chico Fernandez	June 25 vs. Chicago
	Solly Hemus	July 27 vs. Los Angeles
1960	Pancho Herrera	May 31 vs. Milwaukee
1961	Lee Walls	July 14 at Los Angeles
	Tony Gonzalez	Aug. 25 vs. Milwaukee
1963	Tony Gonzalez	July 17 vs. Houston
1964	Johnny Callison	May 8 vs. Cincinnati
	Johnny Callison	Aug. 17 vs. Chicago
1965	Johnny Callison	June 12 vs. Houston
	Dick Allen	July 3 vs. Cincinnati
1966	Bill White	July 4 vs. New York
1974	Mike Schmidt	July 13 at San Francisco

1975	Terry Harmon	June 10 at San Diego
	Larry Bowa	Sept. 26 vs. New York
1976	Dave Cash	July 26 vs. New York
1977	Garry Maddox	July 30 vs. San Francisco
1979	Bake McBride	June 15 vs. Cincinnati
1980	Bake McBride	May 24 vs. Houston
	Mike Schmidt	July 11 vs. Chicago
1983	Jeff Stone	Oct. 1 vs. Pittsburgh
1984	Juan Samuel	May 18 at San Francisco
1986	Juan Samuel	June 5 at Montreal
	Gary Redus	Aug. 2 vs. Chicago
1990	John Kruk	Sept. 16 at New York
1991	John Kruk	June 9 at Cincinnati
		Aug. 14 at Pittsburgh
1992	Mickey Morandini	July 18 vs. Los Angeles
	Tom Marsh	Sept. 13 vs. Pittsburgh
	Ruben Amaro, Jr.	Sept. 26 vs. St. Louis

Three Doubles in One Game

1905	Sherry Magee	May 16 vs. St. Louis
	Mickey Doolan	May 30 at Boston
	Mickey Doolan	Sept. 4 at New York
1910	Johnny Bates	July 29 at Brooklyn
	Mickey Doolan	Aug. 5 vs. Pittsburgh
1912	Gavvy Cravath	Apr. 11 at Boston
	Dode Paskert	Sept. 30 at New York
1914	Gavvy Cravath	May 30 vs. Boston
	Sherry Magee	June 13 vs. Cincinnati
1917	Milt Stock	May 2 vs. Boston
1920	Cy Williams	Sept. 11 vs. Pittsburgh
1922	Goldie Rapp	Aug. 7 vs. Pittsburgh
1923	Cotton Tierney	June 29 vs. Brooklyn
1925	Chicken Hawks	May 18 vs. St. Louis
1926	Heinie Sand	Apr. 26 vs. New York
	Freddy Leach	July 8 at Pittsburgh
1929	Fresco Thompson	June 25 at Boston
1930	Lefty O'Doul	May 2 at Chicago
	Lefty O'Doul	May 7 at St. Louis
1931	Buzz Arlett	May 26 at Brooklyn
	Don Hurst	May 30 vs. Boston
	Dick Bartell	June 20 vs. Cincinnati
1932	Hal Lee	July 12 at St. Louis
	Pinky Whitney	Aug. 1 vs. Pittsburgh
1933	Don Hurst	May 23 at Chicago
1934	Johnny Moore	June 5 vs. Brooklyn
	Kiddo Davis	July 6 vs. Boston
	Johnny Moore	July 7 vs. Boston
	Ethan Allen	Aug. 10 vs. Brooklyn
1935	Jimmie Wilson	June 7 vs. Brooklyn
	Ethan Allen	June 26 vs. Cincinnati
	Al Todd	July 6 vs. Boston
	Ethan Allen	July 18 at Chicago
1936	Bill Atwood	July 21 vs. Pittsburgh
1937	Morrie Arnovich	Apr. 24 vs. Brooklyn
1938	Hershel Martin	May 20 vs. Chicago
	Gib Brack	July 20 at Pittsburgh
1939	Hershel Martin	May 22 at St. Louis
1940	Joe Marty	Sept. 18 vs. Cincinnati
1948	Johnny Blatnik	May 22 vs. Cincinnati
1950	Dick Sisler	June 29 at Boston
	Dick Sisler	July 5 vs. New York
1953	Willie Jones	June 25 at Chicago

1954	Granny Hamner	Sept. 3 at Pittsburgh
	Smoky Burgess	Sept. 8 vs. Cincinnati
1957	Harry Anderson	July 6 at Brooklyn
1958	Bob Bowman	July 3 at Milwaukee
	Ted Kazanski	Sept. 1 at Pittsburgh
	Ed Bouchee	Sept. 20 vs. Pittsburgh
1962	Tony Gonzalez	May 12 at Chicago
1963	Johnny Callison	Aug. 16 at Pittsburgh
1964	Dick Allen	June 23 vs. Chicago
	Frank Thomas	Aug. 11 at Chicago
	Dick Allen	Aug. 14 at New York
1965	Adolfo Phillips	Sept. 6 at St. Louis
1966	Johnny Callison	July 8 at Chicago
	Bill White	July 31 at Pittsburgh
1967	Johnny Callison	June 30 vs. San Francisco
1968	Tony Taylor	July 28 vs. Atlanta
1970	Deron Johnson	Aug. 2 vs. San Francisco
1971	Deron Johnson	July 17 at Chicago
1972	Willie Montanez	Apr. 21 vs. Pittsburgh
1980	Manny Trillo	July 6 at St. Louis
	Pete Rose	July 11 vs. Chicago
1981	Pete Rose	June 2 vs. New York
1982	Gary Matthews	Aug. 14 at Montreal
1983	Joe Morgan	Sept. 22 at Montreal
1985	Bo Diaz	June 11 vs. New York
1986	Von Hayes	May 12 at Houston
1988	Mike Young	June 2 vs. St. Louis
	Juan Samuel	July 26 vs. New York
	Juan Samuel	Sept. 28 vs. New York
1990	Tom Herr	May 2 vs. Houston
1991	Wally Backman	June 18 vs. Atlanta

200 or More Hits in One Season

1893	Sam Thompson	222
	Ed Delahanty	219
1894	Billy Hamilton	220
	Lave Cross	204
1895	Sam Thompson	211
	Billy Hamilton	201
1897	Ed Delahanty	200
1899	Ed Delahanty	238
1900	Elmer Flick	200
1929	Lefty O'Doul	254
	Chuck Klein	219
	Fresco Thompson	202
	Pinky Whitney	200

1930	Chuck Klein	250
	Pinky Whitney	207
	Lefty O'Doul	202
1931	Chuck Klein	200
1932	Chuck Klein	226
1933	Chuck Klein	223
	Chick Fullis	200
1951	Richie Ashburn	221
1953	Richie Ashburn	205
1958	Richie Ashburn	215
1964	Dick Allen	201
1974	Dave Cash	206
1975	Dave Cash	213
1979	Pete Rose	208

Chick Fullis had exactly 200 hits in 1933.

Five Hits in One Game (1883–1992)

Connie Ryan is one of only three Phillies ever to collect six hits in one game.

8	Ed Delahanty
6	Sam Thompson
4	Chuck Klein, Lefty O'Doul, Roy Thomas
3	Billy Hamilton, Eddie Waitkus
2	Larry Bowa, Kitty Bransfield, Jack Clements, Duff Cooley, Lave Cross, Eddie Grant, Bill Hallman, Nap Lajoie, Johnny Mokan, Joe Mulvey, Blondie Purcell, Joe Sullivan
1	Harry Anderson, Morrie Arnovich, Richie Ashburn, Beals Becker, Bob Boone, Phil Bradley, Dan Brouthers, Smoky Burgess, Johnny Callison, Mel Clark, Gavvy Cravath, Babe Dahlgren, Darren Daulton, Spud Davis, Bob Dernier, Bo Diaz, Del Ennis, Elmer Flick, Lew Fonseca, Chick Fullis, Kid Gleason, Mike Grady, George Harper, Chicken Hawks, Von Hayes, Richie Hebner, Tom Herr, Don Hurst, Deron Johnson, Ricky Jordan, Danny Litwhiler, Stan Lopata, Fred Luderus, Garry Maddox, Art Madison, Joe Marty, Bake McBride, Bill McClellan, Irish Meusel, Willie Montanez, Leo Norris, Gene Paulette, Charlie Reilly, Johnny Rizzo, Cookie Rojas, Pete Rose, Connie Ryan, Juan Samuel, Mike Schmidt, Dick Sisler, Jimmy Slagle, Lonnie Smith, Denny Sothern, Milt Thompson, John Titus, Emil Verban, Bill White, Cy Williams, Jimmie Wilson, Harry Wolverton, Russ Wrightstone, Johnny Wyrostek, George Watkins

Six Hits in One Game (1883–1992)

Jack Boyle—five singles, one double, July 6, 1898
Ed Delahanty—five singles, one double, June 16, 1894, vs. Cincinnati
Connie Ryan—four singles, two doubles, April 16, 1953, vs. Pittsburgh

100 or More RBI in One Season

Don Hurst drove in 143 runs in 1932.

1889	Sam Thompson	111	1929	Chuck Klein	145
1890	Sam Thompson	102		Don Hurst	125
1892	Sam Thompson	104		Lefty O'Doul	122
1893	Ed Delahanty	146		Pinky Whitney	115
	Sam Thompson	126	1930	Chuck Klein	170
1894	Sam Thompson	141		Pinky Whitney	117
	Ed Delahanty	131	1931	Chuck Klein	121
	Lave Cross	125	1932	Don Hurst	143
1895	Sam Thompson	165		Chuck Klein	137
	Ed Delahanty	106		Pinky Whitney	124
	Lave Cross	101	1933	Chuck Klein	120
1896	Ed Delahanty	126	1936	Dolph Camilli	102
	Sam Thompson	100	1944	Ron Northey	104
1897	Nap Lajoie	127	1949	Del Ennis	110
1898	Nap Lajoie	127	1950	Del Ennis	126
1899	Ed Delahanty	137	1952	Del Ennis	107
1900	Elmer Flick	110	1953	Del Ennis	125
	Ed Delahanty	109	1954	Del Ennis	119
1901	Ed Delahanty	108	1955	Del Ennis	120
1910	Sherry Magee	123	1962	Don Demeter	107
1913	Gavvy Cravath	128	1964	Johnny Callison	104
1914	Sherry Magee	103	1965	Johnny Callison	101
	Gavvy Cravath	100	1966	Dick Allen	110
1915	Gavvy Cravath	115		Bill White	103
1923	Cy Williams	114	1974	Mike Schmidt	116
1928	Pinky Whitney	103	1975	Greg Luzinski	120

Year	Player	
1976	Mike Schmidt	107
1977	Greg Luzinski	130
	Mike Schmidt	101
1979	Mike Schmidt	114
1980	Mike Schmidt	121
1983	Mike Schmidt	109
1984	Mike Schmidt	106
1985	Glenn Wilson	102
1986	Mike Schmidt	119
1987	Mike Schmidt	113
	Juan Samuel	100
1992	Darren Daulton	109

100 or More Runs Scored in One Season

Year	Player	
1887	George Wood	118
	Jim Fogarty	113
	Ed Andrews	110
1889	Jim Fogarty	107
	Sam Thompson	103
1890	Billy Hamilton	133
	Sam Thompson	116
1891	Billy Hamilton	141
	Sam Thompson	108
1892	Billy Hamilton	132
	Roger Connor	123
	Sam Thompson	109
	Bill Hallman	106
1893	Ed Delahanty	145
	Sam Thompson	130
	Bill Hallman	119
	Billy Hamilton	110
	Jack Boyle	105
1894	Billy Hamilton	192
	Ed Delahanty	147
	Lave Cross	123
	Sam Thompson	108
	Bill Hallman	107
1895	Billy Hamilton	166
	Ed Delahanty	149
	Sam Thompson	131
1896	Ed Delahanty	131
	Sam Thompson	103
1897	Duff Cooley	124
	Ed Delahanty	109
	Nap Lajoie	107
1898	Duff Cooley	123
	Ed Delahanty	115
	Nap Lajoie	113
	Klondike Douglass	105
1899	Roy Thomas	137
	Ed Delahanty	135
1900	Roy Thomas	132
	Jimmy Slagle	115
	Elmer Flick	106
1901	Elmer Flick	111
	Ed Delahanty	106
	Roy Thomas	102
1905	Roy Thomas	118
	Sherry Magee	100
1910	Sherry Magee	110
1912	Dode Paskert	102
1922	Curt Walker	102
1924	Cy Williams	101
1929	Lefty O'Doul	152
	Chuck Klein	126
	Fresco Thompson	115
	Don Hurst	100
1930	Chuck Klein	158
	Lefty O'Doul	122
1931	Chuck Klein	121
1932	Chuck Klein	152
	Dick Bartell	118
	Don Hurst	109
	Kiddo Davis	100
1933	Chuck Klein	101
1934	Dick Bartell	102
1936	Dolph Camilli	106
1937	Hershel Martin	102
	Dolph Camilli	101
1950	Eddie Waitkus	102
	Willie Jones	100
1953	Richie Ashburn	110
1954	Richie Ashburn	111
1962	Johnny Callison	107
1963	Tony Taylor	102
1964	Dick Allen	125
	Johnny Callison	101
1966	Dick Allen	112
1974	Mike Schmidt	108
1975	Dave Cash	111
1976	Mike Schmidt	112
1977	Mike Schmidt	114
1979	Mike Schmidt	109
1980	Mike Schmidt	104
1982	Mike Schmidt	108
1983	Mike Schmidt	104
1984	Juan Samuel	105
1985	Juan Samuel	101
1986	Von Hayes	107
1987	Juan Samuel	113
1990	Lenny Dykstra	106
1992	Dave Hollins	104

300 or More Total Bases in One Season

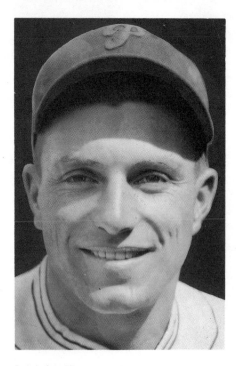

Dolph Camilli was an all-around slugger with the Phillies in the mid 1930s.

1893	Ed Delahanty	347	1948	Del Ennis	309
	Sam Thompson	318	1949	Del Ennis	320
1894	Sam Thompson	300	1950	Del Ennis	328
1895	Sam Thompson	352	1963	Johnny Callison	314
1896	Ed Delahanty	315	1964	Dick Allen	352
1897	Nap Lajoie	310		Johnny Callison	322
1899	Ed Delahanty	339	1965	Johnny Callison	315
1922	Cy Williams	300		Dick Allen	306
1923	Cy Williams	308	1966	Dick Allen	331
1924	Cy Williams	308	1974	Mike Schmidt	310
1929	Chuck Klein	405	1975	Greg Luzinski	322
	Lefty O'Doul	397	1976	Mike Schmidt	306
	Don Hurst	309	1977	Greg Luzinski	329
1930	Chuck Klein	445		Mike Schmidt	312
	Lefty O'Doul	319	1979	Mike Schmidt	305
1931	Chuck Klein	347	1980	Mike Schmidt	342
1932	Chuck Klein	420	1984	Juan Samuel	310
	Don Hurst	317	1986	Mike Schmidt	302
1933	Chuck Klein	365	1987	Juan Samuel	329
1936	Dolph Camilli	306			

10 or More Doubles, Triples, Home Runs, and Stolen Bases

Player	Year	2B	3B	HR	SB
George Wood	1887	22	19	14	19
Roger Connor	1892	37	11	12	22
Ed Delahanty	1893	35	18	19	37
Sam Thompson	1893	37	13	11	18
Sam Thompson	1894	29	27	13	24
Ed Delahanty	1895	49	10	11	46
Sam Thompson	1895	45	21	18	27
Ed Delahanty	1896	44	17	13	37
Elmer Flick	1900	32	16	11	35
Gavvy Cravath	1913	34	14	19	10
Sherry Magee	1914	39	11	15	25
Cy Williams	1920	36	10	15	18
Curt Walker	1922	36	11	12	11
Chuck Klein	1932	50	15	38	20
Johnny Callison	1962	26	10	23	10
Dick Allen	1965	31	14	20	15
Dick Allen	1966	25	10	40	10
Dick Allen	1967	31	10	23	20
Garry Maddox	1977	27	10	14	22
Mike Schmidt	1977	27	11	38	15
Bake McBride	1979	16	12	12	25
Juan Samuel	1984	36	19	15	72
Juan Samuel	1985	31	13	19	53
Juan Samuel	1986	36	12	16	42
Juan Samuel	1987	37	15	28	35

75 or More Extra-Base Hits in One Season

1895	Sam Thompson	84
1929	Chuck Klein	94
1930	Chuck Klein	107
1931	Chuck Klein	75
1932	Chuck Klein	103
1933	Chuck Klein	79
1949	Del Ennis	75
1964	Dick Allen	80
1966	Dick Allen	75
1975	Mike Schmidt	75
1977	Greg Luzinski	77
	Mike Schmidt	76
1980	Mike Schmidt	81
1987	Juan Samuel	80

150 or More Singles in One Season

1892	Billy Hamilton	152
1893	Sam Thompson	161
1894	Billy Hamilton	176
	Lave Cross	154
1895	Billy Hamilton	166
1897	Duff Cooley	155
1898	Duff Cooley	156
1899	Ed Delahanty	165
	Roy Thomas	162
1900	Roy Thomas	161
1905	Roy Thomas	161
1929	Lefty O'Doul	181
	Fresco Thompson	154
1930	Pinky Whitney	153
1933	Chick Fullis	162
1934	Dick Bartell	153
1949	Richie Ashburn	158
1951	Richie Ashburn	181
1953	Richie Ashburn	169
1954	Richie Ashburn	150
1956	Richie Ashburn	153
1957	Richie Ashburn	152
1958	Richie Ashburn	176
1974	Dave Cash	167
	Larry Bowa	154
1975	Dave Cash	166
1976	Dave Cash	162
1978	Larry Bowa	153
1979	Pete Rose	159

30 or More Doubles in One Season

1883	Jack Manning	31
1889	Sam Thompson	36
1890	Sam Thompson	41
1892	Roger Connor	37
	Ed Delahanty	30
1893	Sam Thompson	37
	Ed Delahanty	35
1894	Ed Delahanty	39
	Lave Cross	34
1895	Ed Delahanty	49
	Sam Thompson	45
1896	Ed Delahanty	44
1897	Ed Delahanty	40
	Nap Lajoie	40
1898	Nap Lajoie	43
	Ed Delahanty	36
1899	Ed Delahanty	55
1900	Nap Lajoie	33
	Elmer Flick	32
	Ed Delahanty	32
1901	Ed Delahanty	38
	Elmer Flick	32
1905	John Titus	36
1906	Sherry Magee	36
1908	Sherry Magee	30
1909	Sherry Magee	33
1910	Sherry Magee	39
	Mickey Doolan	31
1911	Sherry Magee	32
1912	Dode Paskert	37
	Fred Luderus	31
	Gavvy Cravath	30
1913	Sherry Magee	36
	Gavvy Cravath	34
	Fred Luderus	32
1914	Sherry Magee	39
1915	Fred Luderus	36
	Gavvy Cravath	31
1916	Bert Niehoff	42
	Dode Paskert	30
1919	Fred Luderus	30
1920	Cy Williams	36
1922	Curt Walker	36
	Cy Williams	30
1923	Walter Holke	31
	Cotton Tierney	31
1924	Cy Williams	31
1925	George Harper	35
	Lew Fonseca	30
	Heinie Sand	30
1926	Heinie Sand	30
1927	Fresco Thompson	32
	Freddy Leach	30
1928	Freddy Leach	36
	Pinky Whitney	35
	Fresco Thompson	34
1929	Chuck Klein	45
	Pinky Whitney	43
	Fresco Thompson	41
	Lefty O'Doul	35
1930	Chuck Klein	59
	Pinky Whitney	41
	Lefty O'Doul	37
	Fresco Thompson	34

Year	Player	Doubles		Year	Player	Doubles
1931	Dick Bartell	43		1964	Dick Allen	38
	Don Hurst	37			Johnny Callison	30
	Pinky Whitney	36		1965	Dick Allen	31
	Chuck Klein	34		1966	Johnny Callison	40
1932	Chuck Klein	50		1967	Dick Allen	31
	Dick Bartell	48			Johnny Callison	30
	Hal Lee	42		1972	Willie Montanez	39
	Don Hurst	41			Greg Luzinski	33
	Kiddo Davis	39		1973	Bill Robinson	32
	Pinky Whitney	33		1974	Willie Montanez	33
1933	Chuck Klein	44		1975	Dave Cash	40
	Chick Fullis	33			Greg Luzinski	35
1934	Ethan Allen	42			Mike Schmidt	34
	Johnny Moore	34		1976	Jay Johnstone	38
	Dick Bartell	30			Garry Maddox	37
1935	Ethan Allen	46			Mike Schmidt	31
	Johnny Moore	33		1977	Greg Luzinski	35
1936	Lou Chiozza	32		1978	Garry Maddox	34
	Chuck Klein	30			Greg Luzinski	32
1937	Hershel Martin	35			Larry Bowa	31
1938	Hershel Martin	36		1979	Pete Rose	40
1943	Ron Northey	31		1980	Pete Rose	42
1944	Buster Adams	35			Bake McBride	33
	Ron Northey	35			Garry Maddox	31
1946	Del Ennis	30		1982	Gary Matthews	31
	Johnny Wyrostek	30		1984	Juan Samuel	36
1948	Del Ennis	40		1985	Glenn Wilson	39
1949	Del Ennis	39			Juan Samuel	31
	Willie Jones	35			Mike Schmidt	31
	Granny Hamner	32			Von Hayes	30
1950	Del Ennis	34		1986	Von Hayes	46
	Eddie Waitkus	32			Juan Samuel	36
1951	Richie Ashburn	31			Glenn Wilson	30
1952	Richie Ashburn	31		1987	Juan Samuel	37
	Del Ennis	30			Von Hayes	36
	Granny Hamner	30		1988	Juan Samuel	32
1953	Granny Hamner	30			Phil Bradley	30
1954	Granny Hamner	39		1990	Lenny Dykstra	35
1955	Richie Ashburn	32			Darren Daulton	30
1956	Stan Lopata	33		1991	Dale Murphy	33
1957	Ed Bouchee	35		1992	Mariano Duncan	40
1958	Harry Anderson	34			Darren Daulton	32
1963	Johnny Callison	36			John Kruk	30
	Tony Gonzalez	36				

Ethan Allen was an outstanding doubles hitter in the 1930s.

10 or More Triples in One Season

Year	Player	Triples		Year	Player	Triples
1886	George Wood	15			Sam Thompson	11
	Charlie Bastian	11			Lave Cross	10
	Joe Mulvey	10			Bill Hallman	10
1887	George Wood	19		1893	Ed Delahanty	18
	Jim Fogarty	12			Sam Thompson	13
1889	Jim Fogarty	17			Bob Allen	12
1890	Bob Allen	11		1894	Sam Thompson	27
	Eddie Burke	11			Ed Delahanty	18
1891	Sam Thompson	10			Billy Hamilton	15
1892	Ed Delahanty	21			Jack Boyle	10
	Bob Allen	14		1895	Sam Thompson	21
	Roger Connor	11			Ed Delahanty	10

1896	Ed Delahanty	17
1897	Nap Lajoie	23
	Ed Delahanty	15
	Duff Cooley	13
1898	Elmer Flick	13
	Duff Cooley	12
	Nap Lajoie	11
1899	Elmer Flick	11
	Ed McFarland	10
1900	Elmer Flick	16
	Nap Lajoie	12
	Ed Delahanty	10
1901	Elmer Flick	17
	Ed Delahanty	16
1903	Harry Wolverton	12
1904	Sherry Magee	12
1905	Sherry Magee	17
	John Titus	14
	Mickey Doolan	11
1907	Sherry Magee	12
	John Titus	12
1908	Sherry Magee	16
	Fred Osborn	12
1909	Sherry Magee	14
	Mickey Doolan	10
1910	Sherry Magee	17
	Johnny Bates	11
1911	Fred Luderus	11
1913	Gavvy Cravath	14
	Hans Lobert	11
	Beals Becker	10
1914	Sherry Magee	11
1916	Possum Whitted	12
1917	Gavvy Cravath	16
	Dode Paskert	11
1920	Cy Williams	10
1922	Curt Walker	11
1924	Cy Williams	11
1927	Fresco Thompson	14

1928	Freddy Leach	11
	Fresco Thompson	11
1929	Pinky Whitney	14
	Barney Friberg	10
1931	Chuck Klein	10
1932	Chuck Klein	15
	Pinky Whitney	11
	Hal Lee	10
1936	Dolph Camilli	13
1947	Harry Walker	16
1949	Richie Ashburn	11
	Del Ennis	11
1950	Richie Ashburn	14
1952	Del Ennis	10
1954	Granny Hamner	11
1958	Richie Ashburn	13
1961	Johnny Callison	11
1962	Johnny Callison	10
1963	Tony Gonzalez	12
	Johnny Callison	11
	Tony Taylor	10
1964	Dick Allen	13
	Johnny Callison	10
1965	Johnny Callison	16
	Dick Allen	14
1966	Dick Allen	10
1967	Dick Allen	10
1972	Larry Bowa	13
1974	Dave Cash	11
	Larry Bowa	10
1976	Dave Cash	12
1977	Mike Schmidt	11
	Garry Maddox	10
1979	Bake McBride	12
	Larry Bowa	11
1980	Bake McBride	10
1984	Juan Samuel	19
1985	Juan Samuel	13
1986	Juan Samuel	12
1987	Juan Samuel	15

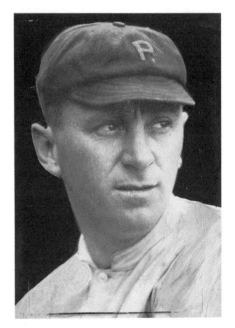

One of the swiftest Phillies of all time, Sherry Magee frequently led the club in triples.

One-Season Switch-Hitting Records

Games	Pete Rose	163	1979
At-bats	Larry Bowa	669	1974
Runs	Dave Hollins	104	1992
Hits	Pete Rose	208	1979
Singles	Pete Rose	159	1979
Doubles	Pete Rose	42	1980
Triples	Larry Bowa	13	1972
Home runs	Dave Hollins	27	1992
Home runs, rookie	Buzz Arlett	18	1931
Home runs, at home	Dave Hollins	14	1992
Home runs, on road	Dave Hollins	13	1992
Home runs, month	Buzz Arlett	7	1931
Home runs, pinch-hitter	Dave Hollins	3	1990
Total bases	Dave Hollins	275	1992
Extra-base hits	Dave Hollins	59	1992
Stolen bases	Larry Bowa	39	1974

Walks	Pete Rose	95	1979
Runs batted in	Dave Hollins	93	1992
Average	Pete Rose	.331	1979
Slugging percentage	Buzz Arlett	.538	1931

Buzz Arlett set a number of Phillies switch-hitting records in his one year with the club.

Dave Hollins now owns many of the Phillies switch-hitting records.

Most Pinch-Hits in One Season

20	Roy Miller	1913	16	Mike Rogodzinski	1973
19	Greg Gross	1982	15	Harry McCurdy	1933
18	Rene Monteagudo	1945		Schoolboy Rowe	1943
	Dave Philley	1958		Dave Philley	1959
17	Tony Taylor	1974		Greg Gross	1987

30 or More Stolen Bases in One Season

1887	Jim Fogarty	102	1897	Duff Cooley	31
	Ed Andrews	57		Tommy Dowd	30
	Joe Mulvey	43	1898	Ed Delahanty	58
1888	Jim Fogarty	58		Duff Cooley	31
	Ed Delahanty	38	1899	Roy Thomas	42
	Ed Andrews	35		Elmer Flick	31
1899	Jim Fogarty	99		Ed Delahanty	30
1890	Billy Hamilton	102	1900	Roy Thomas	37
	Al Myers	44		Elmer Flick	35
	Eddie Burke	38		Jimmy Slagle	34
1891	Billy Hamilton	111	1901	Elmer Flick	26
1892	Billy Hamilton	57	1905	Sherry Magee	48
1893	Billy Hamilton	43	1906	Sherry Magee	55
	Ed Delahanty	37	1907	Sherry Magee	46
1894	Billy Hamilton	98	1908	Sherry Magee	40
	Bill Hallman	36		Kitty Bransfield	30
1895	Billy Hamilton	97	1909	Sherry Magee	38
	Ed Delahanty	46	1910	Sherry Magee	49
1896	Ed Delahanty	37		Johnny Bates	31

1911	Hans Lobert	40
1912	Dode Paskert	36
	Sherry Magee	30
1913	Hans Lobert	41
1914	Hans Lobert	31
1948	Richie Ashburn	32
1958	Richie Ashburn	30
1974	Larry Bowa	39
1976	Larry Bowa	30
1977	Larry Bowa	32
1978	Garry Maddox	33
1980	Lonnie Smith	33

1982	Bob Dernier	42
1983	Bob Dernier	35
1984	Juan Samuel	72
	Von Hayes	48
1985	Juan Samuel	53
1986	Juan Samuel	42
1987	Milt Thompson	46
	Juan Samuel	35
1988	Juan Samuel	33
1990	Lenny Dykstra	33
1992	Lenny Dykstra	30

Speedy Bob Dernier was always a stolen base threat.

Three Steals in One Game

1901	Shad Barry	June 6 at Chicago
1904	Roy Thomas	Sept. 3 vs. Brooklyn
1906	Sherry Magee	June 9 vs. Pittsburgh
	Sherry Magee	Sept. 20 vs. St. Louis
1907	Sherry Magee	Sept. 9 at Brooklyn
	John Titus	Sept. 13 at Boston
1908	Eddie Grant	May 16 at Pittsburgh
	Otto Knabe	Sept. 12 vs. Boston (11 inn.)
1909	Johnny Bates	Aug. 8 at Cincinnati
	Johnny Bates	Sept. 23 at Cincinnati
1910	Sherry Magee	June 15 vs. Cincinnati (16 inn.)
1911	Hans Lobert	Sept. 20 at Chicago
1915	Dave Bancroft	May 31 at Boston
1921	Greasy Neale	May 4 at Boston
1927	Fresco Thompson	June 18 at Chicago
	Fresco Thompson	Aug. 16 vs. Cincinnati
1941	Stan Benjamin	Aug. 24 vs. Chicago
1948	Richie Ashburn	June 2 at Chicago (12 inn.)
1951	Richie Ashburn	July 28 at Chicago
1955	Richie Ashburn	Aug. 16 at Pittsburgh
1957	Chico Fernandez	July 11 vs. Chicago (11 inn.)
1960	Tony Taylor	June 12 at Chicago (10 inn.)
1966	Tony Taylor	Aug. 25 at Pittsburgh
1970	Larry Bowa	Aug. 28 vs. Atlanta
1976	Larry Bowa	May 25 vs. New York
1977	Larry Bowa	July 22 at San Francisco
	Bake McBride	Aug. 23 at Atlanta
1978	Mike Schmidt	May 30 vs. Pittsburgh
1980	Pete Rose	May 11 at Cincinnati
	Lonnie Smith	July 29 vs. Houston
1982	Bob Dernier	May 8 vs. San Diego
1983	Bob Dernier	July 2 vs. New York
1984	Juan Samuel	Apr. 8 at Cincinnati (11 inn.)
	Von Hayes	June 27 vs. New York
	Juan Samuel	Aug. 30 vs. San Francisco
	Juan Samuel	Sept. 2 vs. San Francisco
	Jeff Stone	Sept. 8 at Montreal

	Jeff Stone	Sept. 11 at Chicago
	Jeff Stone	Sept. 17 vs. New York
1985	Juan Samuel	Apr. 28 vs. Chicago
1986	Von Hayes	June 23 vs. Chicago
1987	Juan Samuel	Sept. 14 vs. St. Louis (11 inn.)
1990	John Kruk	July 13 at Houston
	Lenny Dykstra	Aug. 21 at New York
1991	Lenny Dykstra	Apr. 13 vs. St. Louis
1992	Stan Javier	July 31 at Montreal

Steals of Home (1946–1992)

Ted Savage stole home in 1962.

Date	Player	Location
Aug. 1, 1947	Harry Walker	at St. Louis
Sept. 12, 1947	Harry Walker	at Chicago
Sept. 16, 1947	Charlie Gilbert	at Pittsburgh
Apr. 23, 1948	Richie Ashburn	at Brooklyn
May 3, 1949	Eddie Waitkus	vs. St. Louis
Aug. 19, 1951	Richie Ashburn	vs. New York
Apr. 30, 1952	Granny Hamner	at Chicago
Aug. 30, 1952	Eddie Waitkus	at Boston
Aug. 30, 1952	Mel Clark	at Boston
Apr. 25, 1953	Connie Ryan	vs. Pittsburgh
June 11, 1956	Stan Lopata	at Milwaukee
Sept. 18, 1956	Elmer Valo	vs. Cincinnati
May 25, 1957	Chico Fernandez	vs. Pittsburgh
Aug. 27, 1957	Granny Hamner	vs. Cincinnati
July 2, 1959	Sparky Anderson	vs. Cincinnati
Aug. 3, 1960	Tony Taylor	at San Francisco
Aug. 19, 1960	Tony Taylor	vs. Milwaukee
June 29, 1961	Don Demeter	vs. San Francisco
July 8, 1962	Ted Savage	at Pittsburgh
Aug. 21, 1962	Billy Klaus	vs. Houston
June 5, 1963	Don Hoak	vs. St. Louis
Aug. 29, 1965	Tony Taylor	vs. Los Angeles
Aug. 25, 1966	Tony Taylor	at Pittsburgh
June 3, 1967	Dick Allen	at Houston
July 21, 1967	Tony Taylor	vs. Cincinnati
Aug. 15, 1967	Dick Allen	vs. New York
May 29, 1968	Roberto Pena	vs. Chicago
Aug. 24, 1968	Tony Taylor	at Atlanta
May 19, 1970	Larry Bowa	at Pittsburgh
Aug. 28, 1970	Larry Bowa	vs. Atlanta
June 19, 1971	Larry Bowa	at New York
Aug. 29, 1978	Jose Cardenal	at San Diego
May 11, 1980	Pete Rose	at Cincinnati
July 28, 1980	Larry Bowa	vs. Houston
June 18, 1982	Bo Diaz	at Pittsburgh
June 4, 1986	Ron Roenicke	vs. Los Angeles
Aug. 29, 1988	Bob Dernier	vs. San Francisco
Sept. 29, 1992	Ricky Jordan	at New York

100 or More Walks in One Season

Year	Player	Walks	Year	Player	Walks
1891	Billy Hamilton	102	1903	Roy Thomas	107
1892	Roger Connor	116	1904	Roy Thomas	102
1894	Billy Hamilton	126	1906	Roy Thomas	107
1899	Roy Thomas	115	1936	Dolph Camilli	116
1900	Roy Thomas	115	1954	Richie Ashburn	125
1901	Roy Thomas	100	1955	Richie Ashburn	105
1902	Roy Thomas	107	1974	Mike Schmidt	106

1975	Mike Schmidt	101
1976	Mike Schmidt	100
1977	Mike Schmidt	104
1978	Greg Luzinski	100
1979	Mike Schmidt	120

1982	Mike Schmidt	107
1983	Mike Schmidt	128
1987	Von Hayes	121
1989	Von Hayes	101

26	Mike Schmidt	1986
21	Ted Sizemore	1977
18	Dick Allen	1967
	Mike Schmidt	1981
	Ivan DeJesus	1983
17	Johnny Callison	1967
	Greg Luzinski	1975
	Mike Schmidt	1982
	Mike Schmidt	1983

16	Richie Hebner	1978
	Von Hayes	1990
	John Kruk	1990
	John Kruk	1991
15	Clay Dalrymple	1963
	Dick Allen	1968
	Greg Luzinski	1978
	Mike Schmidt	1987

Most Intentional Walks in One Season

All-Time Pitching Leaders

Games
Roberts	529
Carlton	499
McGraw	463
Short	459
Reed	458
Farrell	359
Alexander	338
Baldschun	333
Simmons	325
Konstanty	314
Collins	265
Garber	262

Losses
Roberts	199
Carlton	161
Short	127
Simmons	110
Rixey	103
Duggleby	101
Ring	98
Sparks	95
Alexander	91
Benge	85
Bunning	73

Runs
Roberts	1,591
Carlton	1,456
Short	949
Simmons	919
Ring	872
Alexander	812
Collins	782
Benge	683
Rixey	682
Duggleby	606

Strikeouts
Carlton	3,031
Roberts	1,871
Short	1,585

Alexander	1,409
Bunning	1,197
Simmons	1,052
Christenson	781
Ferguson	728
Wise	717
Ruthven	717
Rixey	690

Wins
Carlton	241
Roberts	234
Alexander	190
Short	132
Simmons	115
Orth	101
Ferguson	99
Sparks	94
Carsey	94
Duggleby	91
Bunning	89
Rixey	87

Hits
Roberts	3,661
Carlton	3,224
Alexander	2,131
Short	2,129
Simmons	1,865
Duggleby	1,711
Orth	1,687
Ring	1,610
Collins	1,533
Rixey	1,518

Walks
Carlton	1,252
Short	762
Roberts	718
Simmons	718
Ring	630
Alexander	561
E. Moore	537

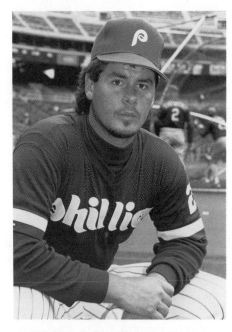

Mitch Williams has moved up among the Phillies' best relievers.

Collins	496
Gleason	482
Rixey	479
Ruthven	475
Duggleby	390

Complete Games

Roberts	272
Alexander	220
Carlton	185
Carsey	165
Ferguson	165
Duggleby	155
Sparks	150
Orth	149
Gleason	143
Casey	142
Buffinton	115
Simmons	112
Ring	102
Rixey	100
Short	88

Innings Pitched

Roberts	3,740
Carlton	3,696
Alexander	2,513
Short	2,252
Simmons	1,939
Sparks	1,691
Duggleby	1,642
Rixey	1,604
Bunning	1,520
Ferguson	1,514
Orth	1,505

Earned Runs

Roberts	1,437
Carlton	1,270
Short	845
Simmons	789
Collins	684

Alexander	603
Ring	599
Christenson	591
Ruthven	584
Benge	569
Rixey	504
Bunning	495

Shutouts

Alexander	61
Carlton	39
Roberts	35
Short	24
Bunning	23
Sparks	18
E. Moore	18
Simmons	18
McQuillan	17
Duggleby	16
Rixey	16

Saves

Bedrosian	103
McGraw	94
Reed	90
Farrell	65
Baldschun	59
Williams	59
Holland	55
Konstanty	54
Garber	51
McDowell	44
Selma	26
Tekulve	25
Roberts	24
Karl	23
Syl Johnson	23
Collins	22
J. Meyer	21
Hoerner	21

League Leaders in Pitching

Wins

1911	Alexander	28
1913	Seaton	27
1914	Alexander	27*
1915	Alexander	31
1916	Alexander	33
1917	Alexander	30
1931	J. Elliott	19*
1952	Roberts	28
1953	Roberts	23*
1954	Roberts	23
1955	Roberts	23
1972	Carlton	27
1977	Carlton	23
1980	Carlton	24
1982	Carlton	23
1983	Denny	19*

Games

1905	Pittinger	46*
1927	Scott	48*
1930	H. Elliott	48
1931	J. Elliott	52
1934	Davis	51
1935	Jorgens	53
1937	Mulcahy	56
1945	Karl	67
1950	Konstanty	74
1961	Baldschun	65
1975	Garber	71
1987	Tekulve	90

Complete Games

1911	Alexander	31
1914	Alexander	32
1915	Alexander	36

1916	Alexander	38
1917	Alexander	35
1952	Roberts	30
1953	Roberts	33
1954	Roberts	29
1955	Roberts	26
1956	Roberts	22
1972	Carlton	30
1973	Carlton	18*
1982	Carlton	19
1992	Mulholland	12

Innings Pitched

1911	Alexander	367
1912	Alexander	310*
1913	Seaton	322
1914	Alexander	355
1915	Alexander	376
1916	Alexander	389
1917	Alexander	388
1937	Passeau	292
1951	Roberts	315
1952	Roberts	330
1953	Roberts	347
1954	Roberts	337
1955	Roberts	305
1967	Bunning	302
1972	Carlton	346
1973	Carlton	293*
1980	Carlton	304
1982	Carlton	295
1983	Carlton	283

Earned Run Average

1886	Ferguson	1.98
1887	Casey	2.86
1899	Orth	2.48
1910	McQuillan	1.60
1915	Alexander	1.22
1916	Alexander	1.55
1917	Alexander	1.86
1972	Carlton	1.97

Shutouts

1887	Casey	4
1898	Piatt	6*
1901	Orth	6*
1911	Alexander	7*
1913	Alexander	9
1915	Alexander	12
1916	Alexander	16
1917	Alexander	8

1925	Carlson	4*
1936	Walters	4*
1949	Heintzelman	5*
1950	Roberts	5*
1951	Roberts	6
1952	Simmons	6*
1966	Bunning	5*
1966	L. Jackson	5*
1967	Bunning	6
1982	Carlton	6

Strikeouts

1910	Moore	185
1912	Alexander	195
1913	Seaton	168
1914	Alexander	214
1915	Alexander	241
1916	Alexander	167
1917	Alexander	201
1940	Higbe	137
1953	Roberts	198
1954	Roberts	185
1957	Sanford	188
1967	Bunning	253
1972	Carlton	310
1974	Carlton	240
1980	Carlton	286
1982	Carlton	286
1983	Carlton	275

Losses

1883	Coleman	48
1902	White	20
1911	E. Moore	19
1918	Oeschger	18
1920	Rixey	22
1921	Smith	20
1927	Scott	21
1936	Walters	21
1937	LaMaster	19
1938	Mulcahy	20
1940	Mulcahy	22
1944	Raffensberger	20
1945	Barrett	20
1948	Leonard	18
1954	Dickson	20
1956	Roberts	18
1957	Roberts	22
1961	Mahaffey	19
1973	Carlton	20
1989	Carman	15

*Tied for lead.

20-Game Winners

		Record			Record
1884	Charlie Ferguson	21–25	1887	Dan Casey	28–13
1885	Ed Daily	26–23		Charlie Ferguson	22–10
	Charlie Ferguson	26–20		Charlie Buffinton	21–17
1886	Charlie Ferguson	30–9	1888	Charlie Buffinton	28–17
	Dan Casey	24–18	1889	Charlie Buffinton	28–16

		Record			Record
1890	Kid Gleason	38–17	1913	Grover Alexander	22–8
	Tom Vickery	24–22		Tom Seaton	27–12
1891	Kid Gleason	24–22	1914	Grover Alexander	27–15
	Duke Esper	20–15		Erskine Mayer	21–19
1892	Gus Weyhing	32–21	1915	Grover Alexander	31–10
1893	Gus Weyhing	23–16		Erskine Mayer	21–15
	Kid Carsey	20–15	1916	Grover Alexander	33–12
1894	Jack Taylor	23–13		Eppa Rixey	22–10
1895	Jack Taylor	26–14	1917	Grover Alexander	30–13
	Kid Carsey	24–16	1950	Robin Roberts	20–11
1896	Jack Taylor	20–21	1951	Robin Roberts	21–15
1898	Wiley Piatt	24–14	1952	Robin Roberts	28–7
1899	Wiley Piatt	23–15	1953	Robin Roberts	23–16
	Red Donahue	21–8	1954	Robin Roberts	23–15
	Chick Fraser	21–12	1955	Robin Roberts	23–14
1901	Red Donahue	21–13	1966	Chris Short	20–10
	Al Orth	20–12	1972	Steve Carlton	27–10
1905	Charles Pittinger	23–14	1976	Steve Carlton	20–7
1907	Tully Sparks	22–8	1977	Steve Carlton	23–10
1908	George McQuillan	23–17	1980	Steve Carlton	24–9
1910	Earl Moore	22–15	1982	Steve Carlton	23–11
1911	Grover Alexander	28–13			

No-Hitters

By Phillies

1885	Charlie Ferguson, Providence, Aug. 29	1–0
1898	Red Donahue, Boston, July 8	5–0
1903	Charles Fraser, Chicago, Sept. 18	10–0
1906	John Lush, Brooklyn, May 1	6–0
1964	Jim Bunning, New York (perfect game), June 21 (1st)	6–0
1971	Rick Wise, Cincinnati, June 23	4–0
1990	Terry Mulholland, San Francisco, Aug. 15	6–0
1991	Tommy Greene, Montreal, May 23	2–0

The only Phillies no-hit pitchers in the last eight decades are (from left) Rick Wise and Jim Bunning (front row), and Tommy Greene and Terry Mulholland (top row).

Against Phillies

Year	Pitcher	Date	Score
1900	Frank Hahn, Cincinnati, July 12		4–0
1908	George Wiltse, New York, July 4 (10 inn.)		1–0
1912	Jeff Tesreau, New York, Sept. 6 (1st)		3–0
1914	George Davis, Boston, Sept. 9 (2nd)		7–0
1922	Jesse Barnes, New York, May 7		6–0
1925	Dazzy Vance, Brooklyn, Sept. 13 (1st)		10–1
1954	Jim Wilson, Milwaukee, June 12		2–0
1956	Sal Maglie, Brooklyn, Sept. 25		5–0
1960	Lew Burdette, Milwaukee, Aug. 18		1–0
1960	Warren Spahn, Milwaukee, Sept. 16		4–0
1963	Don Nottebart, Houston, May 17		4–1
1964	Sandy Koufax, Los Angeles, June 4		3–0
1968	George Culver, Cincinnati, July 29		6–1
1969	Bill Stoneman, Montreal, April 17		7–0
1970	Bill Singer, Los Angeles, July 20		5–0
1972	Burt Hooton, Chicago, April 16		4–0
1978	Bob Forsch, St. Louis, April 16		5–0

One-Hitters by Phillies Pitchers

Date	Pitcher	Opponent	Result
July 14, 1900	Chick Fraser	vs. Boston	W 1–0
May 30, 1906	Johnny Lush	vs. Boston	W 3–0
Aug. 13, 1906	Tully Sparks	vs. Cincinnati	W 4–0
Apr. 11, 1907	Frank Corridon (Game forfeited to Phillies after 8 innings)	at New York	W 9–0
May 7, 1907	Frank Corridon	at Boston	W 3–1 (10)
May 23, 1907	Togie Pittinger	vs. Pittsburgh	W 3–0
June 3, 1907	Tully Sparks	vs. Boston	W 2–0
June 8, 1907	Lew Moren	at St. Louis	W 3–0
Aug. 16, 1908	George McQuillan	at Chicago	W 1–0
Apr. 22, 1910	Earl Moore (7) (W) and Bert Humphries (2)	vs. Boston	W 3–0
Apr. 21, 1911	Earl Moore	vs. New York	W 3–0
July 25, 1911	George Chalmers	at St. Louis	W 2–0
Sept. 7, 1911	Grover Alexander	at Boston	W 1–0
Sept. 19, 1911	Bill Burns	at Chicago	W 2–0
June 5, 1915	Grover Alexander	at St. Louis	W 3–0
June 26, 1915	Grover Alexander	vs. Brooklyn	W 4–0
July 5, 1915	Grover Alexander	vs. New York	W 2–0
Sept. 29, 1915	Grover Alexander	at Boston	W 5–0
Aug. 21, 1917	Chief Bender	vs. Chicago	W 6–0
Aug. 30, 1931	Phil Collins	at New York	W 3–0
July 12, 1936	Joe Bowman (8) (W) and Claude Passeau (1)	at Cincinnati	W 4–0
June 3, 1941	Tommy Hughes	vs. Chicago	W 7–0
May 2, 1944	Charley Schanz	at New York	W 5–2
Aug. 15, 1948	Ken Heintzelman	vs. New York	W 8–1
Sept. 8, 1949	Russ Meyer	at Boston	W 3–1
July 1, 1951	Russ Meyer (7) (L) and Jim Konstanty (1)	at Brooklyn	L 2–0
Aug. 5, 1951	Bubba Church	at Pittsburgh	W 5–1
May 16, 1953	Curt Simmons	at Milwaukee	W 3–0
Apr. 29, 1954	Robin Roberts	at Milwaukee	W 4–0

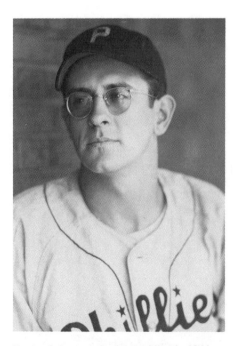

Charley Schanz pitched a one-hitter in 1944.

May 13, 1954	Robin Roberts	vs. Cincinnati	W 8–1
July 21, 1960	Robin Roberts	at San Francisco	W 3–0
Aug. 22, 1961	Art Mahaffey	vs. Chicago	W 6–0
May 18, 1964	Jim Bunning	at Houston	W 4–0
June 23, 1964	Ray Culp	vs. Chicago	W 9–0
June 20, 1967	Larry Jackson	vs. New York	W 4–0
Aug. 8, 1968	Rick Wise	at Los Angeles	W 1–0
Apr. 25, 1972	Steve Carlton	at San Francisco	W 3–0
Sept. 27, 1975	Steve Carlton	vs. New York	W 8–1
May 9, 1979	Dick Ruthven	at San Diego	W 2–0
June 5, 1979	Steve Carlton	at Houston	W 8–0
July 4, 1979	Steve Carlton	vs. New York	W 1–0
Sept. 3, 1979	Steve Carlton (7) (W) and Tug McGraw (2)	at Pittsburgh	W 2–0
Apr. 26, 1980	Steve Carlton	vs. St. Louis	W 7–0
Aug. 16, 1986	Tom Hume (6)(W) and Kent Tekulve (3)	vs. Pittsburgh	W 6–0
Aug. 20, 1986	Don Carman (9) (W) and Steve Bedrosian (1)	at San Francisco	W 1–0 (10)
Sept. 26, 1986	Marvin Freeman (6) (W) and Kent Tekulve (3)	at Montreal	W 5–0
Sept. 29, 1987	Don Carman	vs. New York	W 3–0
Aug. 2, 1988	David Palmer	at St. Louis	W 2–0
Sept. 9, 1992	Curt Schilling	vs. New York	W 2–1

Pitchers Who Beat All Clubs in One Season, (1900–92)

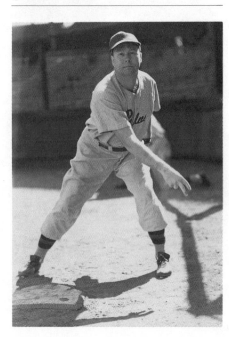

In 1945, Dick Barrett beat every club in the National League.

8-Team League (1900–61)

1900	Bill Bernhard
	Chick Fraser
1901	Red Donahue
	Al Orth
	Jack Townsend
1902	Doc White
1903	Bill Duggleby
1904	Chick Fraser
1905	Kid Nichols
	Togie Pittinger
1906	Tully Sparks
1907	Frank Corridon
	Tully Sparks
1908	George McQuillan
1909	Earl Moore
1910	Bob Ewing
	Earl Moore
	Lew Moren
1911	Grover Alexander
	George Chalmers
1912	Grover Alexander
1913	Grover Alexander
	Tom Seaton
1914	Grover Alexander
	Erskine Mayer
1915	Grover Alexander
	Erskine Mayer
1916	Grover Alexander
	Eppa Rixey
1917	Grover Alexander
	Joe Oeschger

1918	Mike Prendergast
1920	Lee Meadows
1923	Jimmy Ring
1924	Jimmy Ring
1925	Hal Carlson
	Jimmy Ring
1926	Hal Carlson
1929	Claude Willoughby
1930	Phil Collins
1931	Ray Benge
1932	Ray Benge
	Phil Collins
	Ed Holley
1934	Phil Collins
	Curt Davis
1935	Curt Davis
1936	Bucky Walters
1942	Tom Hughes
1944	Ken Raffensberger
1945	Dick Barrett
1947	Dutch Leonard
1950	Robin Roberts
	Curt Simmons
1951	Robin Roberts
1952	Karl Drews
	Robin Roberts
	Curt Simmons
1953	Jim Konstanty
	Robin Roberts
1954	Robin Roberts
	Curt Simmons
1955	Robin Roberts

1956	Robin Roberts
1957	Robin Roberts
1958	Robin Roberts
1959	Gene Conley
	Jim Owens

10-Team League (1962–68)

1962	Art Mahaffey
1964	Jim Bunning
1966	Jim Bunning
	Chris Short

1967	Jim Bunning
	Rick Wise

12-Team League (1969–92)

1971	Rick Wise
1972	Steve Carlton
1974	Jim Lonborg
1975	Steve Carlton
1978	Larry Christenson
1980	Steve Carlton
1982	Steve Carlton

Robin Roberts vs. Don Newcombe

Date	Site	WP	LP	Score
Oct. 2, 1949	Shibe Park	Banta	Heintzelman	9–7 (10)
	Newcombe started, Roberts relieved			
Apr. 18, 1950	Shibe Park	Roberts	Newcombe	9–1
June 30, 1950	Shibe Park	Konstanty	Newcombe	8–5
July 8, 1950	Ebbets Field	Konstanty	Newcombe	4–1
Aug. 8, 1950	Ebbets Field	Roberts	Newcombe	6–5
Sept. 23, 1950	Shibe Park	Newcombe	Roberts	3–2
Oct. 1, 1950	Ebbets Field	Roberts	Newcombe	4–1 (10)
May 30, 1951	Shibe Park	Newcombe	Roberts	5–3
Sept. 29, 1951	Shibe Park	Newcombe	Roberts	5–0
Sept. 30, 1951	Shibe Park	Podbielan	Roberts	9–8 (14)
	Newcombe and Roberts both pitched in relief			
July 11, 1954	Ebbets Field	Wehmeier	Newcombe	3–1
	Roberts saved it in relief			
Aug. 16, 1954	Ebbets Field	Roberts	Labine	9–6
	Newcombe pitched in relief			
Aug. 14, 1955	Ebbets Field	Roberts	Newcombe	3–2 (10)
Aug. 19, 1955	Connie Mack Stadium	Roberts	Newcombe	3–2
Apr. 17, 1956	Ebbets Field	Roberts	Newcombe	8–6
Sept. 26, 1956	Ebbets Field	Roberts	Newcombe	7–3
Apr. 16, 1957	Connie Mack Stadium	Labine	Roberts	7–6 (12)
Aug. 31, 1958	Crosley Field	Newcombe	Roberts	7–3
Sept. 6, 1958	Connie Mack Stadium	Newcombe	Roberts	8–4
Apr. 10, 1959	Connie Mack Stadium	Roberts	Newcombe	2–1
July 26, 1959	Crosley Field	Lawrence	Roberts	4–2
Apr. 24, 1960	Connie Mack Stadium	Newcombe	Owens	10–4
	Roberts pitched in relief			
July 5, 1960	Crosley Field	Roberts	Newcombe	2–0

Steve Carlton vs. Tom Seaver

Date	Site	WP	LP	Score
Apr. 12, 1970	Busch Memorial Stadium	Seaver	Carlton	6–4
May 21, 1972	Veterans Stadium	Seaver	Carlton	4–3
Sept. 24, 1972	Shea Stadium	Seaver	Carlton	2–1
Apr. 6, 1973	Shea Stadium	Seaver	Carlton	3–0
Apr. 6, 1974	Veterans Stadium	Scarce	McGraw	5–4
June 21, 1974	Veterans Stadium	Seaver	Carlton	3–1
Apr. 8, 1975	Shea Stadium	Seaver	Carlton	2–1
Sept. 3, 1976	Shea Stadium	Seaver	Carlton	1–0
Aug. 26, 1977	Riverfront Stadium	Seaver	Carlton	4–2
May 1, 1978	Riverfront Stadium	Carlton	Seaver	12–1

Date	Site	WP	LP	Score
May 11, 1978	Veterans Stadium	Carlton	Seaver	4–1
July 28, 1978	Riverfront Stadium	Seaver	Carlton	2–1
May 10, 1980	Riverfront Stadium	Seaver	Carlton	5–3
Apr. 8, 1981	Riverfront Stadium	Hume	Lyle	3–2
Aug. 18, 1981	Riverfront Stadium	Seaver	Carlton	3–1

Steve Carlton and Tom Seaver started against each other 15 times.

Seaver won 11 of 13 games, and there were two no decisions.

Carlton with St. Louis and Seaver with New York: Seaver led, 1–0.

Carlton with the Phillies and Seaver with New York: Seaver led, 6–0, 1 no decision.

Carlton with the Phillies and Seaver with Cincinnati: Seaver led, 4–2, 1 no decision.

Five of Seaver's wins have been by one run, 5 more by two runs, and 1 by three runs.

.650 Winning Percentage or Better in One Season

1886	Charlie Ferguson	.769	1950	Jim Konstanty	.696
1887	Charlie Ferguson	.688		Curt Simmons	.680
	Dan Casey	.683	1952	Robin Roberts	.800
1888	Ben Sanders	.655	1957	Jack Sanford	.704
1890	Kid Gleason	.691	1964	Jim Bunning	.704
1895	Jack Taylor	.650		Chris Short	.654
1896	Al Orth	.682	1965	Jim Bunning	.679
1899	Red Donahue	.724	1966	Chris Short	.667
1907	Tully Sparks	.733	1972	Steve Carlton	.730
1911	Grover Alexander	.683	1976	Steve Carlton	.741
1913	Grover Alexander	.733	1977	Larry Christenson	.760
	Tom Seaton	.692		Steve Carlton	.697
1915	Grover Alexander	.756	1980	Steve Carlton	.727
1916	Grover Alexander	.733	1981	Steve Carlton	.765
	Eppa Rixey	.688	1982	Steve Carlton	.676
1917	Grover Alexander	.698	1983	John Denny	.760
1949	Russ Meyer	.680	1984	Steve Carlton	.650
			1991	Tommy Greene	.650

300 or More Innings Pitched in One Season

Jimmy Ring worked 313 innings in 1923.

1883	John Coleman	538	1896	Jack Taylor	359
1884	Charlie Ferguson	417	1897	Jack Taylor	317
1885	Ed Daily	440	1898	Wiley Piatt	306
	Charlie Ferguson	405	1899	Wiley Piatt	305
1886	Charlie Ferguson	396	1901	Red Donahue	304
	Dan Casey	369	1902	Doc White	306
1887	Dan Casey	390	1904	Chick Fraser	302
	Charlie Buffinton	332	1905	Togie Pittinger	337
1888	Charlie Buffinton	400	1906	Tully Sparks	317
1889	Charlie Buffinton	380	1908	George McQuillan	360
	Ben Sanders	350	1909	Earl Moore	300
1890	Kid Gleason	506	1911	Grover Alexander	367
	Tom Vickery	382		Earl Moore	308
1891	Kid Gleason	418	1912	Grover Alexander	310
1892	Gus Weyhing	470	1913	Tom Seaton	322
	Kid Carsey	318		Grover Alexander	306
	Tim Keefe	313	1914	Grover Alexander	355
1893	Gus Weyhing	345		Erskine Mayer	321
	Kid Carsey	318	1915	Grover Alexander	376
1895	Kid Carsey	342	1916	Grover Alexander	389
	Jack Taylor	335	1917	Grover Alexander	388

1923	Jimmy Ring	313
1950	Robin Roberts	304
1951	Robin Roberts	315
1952	Robin Roberts	330
1953	Robin Roberts	347
1954	Robin Roberts	337

1955	Robin Roberts	305
1966	Jim Bunning	314
1967	Jim Bunning	302
1972	Steve Carlton	346
1980	Steve Carlton	304

200 or More Strikeouts in One Season

1886	Charlie Ferguson	212
1890	Kid Gleason	222
1892	Gus Weyhing	202
1911	Grover Alexander	227
1914	Grover Alexander	214
1915	Grover Alexander	241
1917	Grover Alexander	201
1964	Jim Bunning	219
1965	Jim Bunning	268
	Chris Short	237

1966	Jim Bunning	252
1967	Jim Bunning	253
1968	Chris Short	202
1972	Steve Carlton	310
1973	Steve Carlton	223
1974	Steve Carlton	240
1979	Steve Carlton	213
1980	Steve Carlton	286
1982	Steve Carlton	286
1983	Steve Carlton	275

10 or More Strikeouts in One Game (1900–92)

69	Steve Carlton
25	Jim Bunning
17	Chris Short
9	Ray Culp
8	Grover Alexander
7	Robin Roberts
6	Art Mahaffey, Earl Moore
5	Grant Jackson, Jack Sanford
4	Dennis Bennett, Larry Christenson, Kevin Gross, Curt Simmons, Rick Wise
3	John Denny, Woodie Fryman, Wayne LaMaster, Terry Mulholland
2	Ralph Caldwell, George Chalmers, Harvey Haddix, Ken Howell, Johnny Lush, Lee Meadows, Jimmy Ring, Dick Ruthven, Doc White
1	Bo Belinsky, Ray Benge, Ken Brett, Don Cardwell, Gene Conley, Harry Coveleski, Jose DeJesus, Murry Dickson, Chick Fraser, Tommy Greene, Jack Hamilton, Ken Heintzelman, Charles Hudson, Si Johnson, Syl Johnson, Johnny Lindell, Jack Meyer, Seth Morehead, Hugh Mulcahy, Lowell Palmer, Claude Passeau, Hub Pruett, Ken Raffensberger, Shane Rawley, Eppa Rixey, Tom Seaton, Wayne Twitchell

10 or More Saves in One Season

1945	Andy Karl	15
1950	Jim Konstanty	22
1955	Jack Meyer	16
1957	Dick Farrell	10
1958	Dick Farrell	11
1960	Dick Farrell	11
1962	Jack Baldschun	13
1963	Jack Baldschun	16
1964	Jack Baldschun	21
	Ed Roebuck	12
1966	Darold Knowles	13
1967	Dick Farrell	12
1968	Dick Farrell	12
1970	Dick Selma	22

1973	Mac Scarce	12
1975	Gene Garber	14
	Tug McGraw	14
1976	Ron Reed	14
	Gene Garber	11
	Tug McGraw	11
1977	Gene Garber	19
	Ron Reed	15
1978	Ron Reed	17
1979	Tug McGraw	16
1980	Tug McGraw	20
1981	Tug McGraw	10
1982	Ron Reed	14
1983	Al Holland	25

1984	Al Holland	29
1985	Kent Tekulve	14
1986	Steve Bedrosian	29
1987	Steve Bedrosian	40
1988	Steve Bedrosian	28

1989	Roger McDowell	19
1990	Roger McDowell	22
1991	Mitch Williams	30
1992	Mitch Williams	29

Pitchers with .270 Batting Average or Better in One Season (40 at Bats or More)

Pitcher	Year	Average	Hits	At Bats
Al Orth	1895	.356	16	45
Jack Taylor	1894	.333	48	144
Al Orth	1897	.329	50	152
Paul Weinert	1923	.322	19	59
Oscar Judd	1946	.316	25	79
Harry Keener	1896	.314	16	51
Lee Meadows	1922	.314	27	86
Dennis Cook	1990	.310	13	42
Harvey Haddix	1957	.309	21	68
Al Maul	1887	.304	17	56
Schoolboy Rowe	1943	.300	36	120
Al Orth	1898	.293	36	123
Les Sweetland	1929	.292	26	89
Kid Carsey	1895	.291	41	141
Steve Carlton	1978	.291	25	86
Jack Taylor	1895	.290	45	155
Jack Scott	1927	.289	33	114
Brad Hogg	1919	.283	17	60
Dick Ruthven	1978	.283	15	53
Claude Passeau	1936	.282	22	78
Al Orth	1901	.281	36	128
Les Sweetland	1930	.281	16	57
Phenomenal Smith	1890	.279	24	86
Chief Bender	1916	.279	12	43
Ben Sanders	1889	.278	47	169
Schoolboy Rowe	1947	.278	22	79
Herm Wehmeier	1955	.278	20	72
Bucky Walters	1937	.277	38	137
Doc White	1901	.276	27	98
Hal Carlson	1924	.276	21	76
Kid Carsey	1894	.272	34	125
Wiley Piatt	1899	.270	33	122
Rick Wise	1969	.270	20	74

Pitchers Hitting Home Runs

11	Larry Christenson, Rick Wise
9	Steve Carlton, Schoolboy Rowe
7	Al Orth
6	Bill Duggleby
5	Robin Roberts
4	Grover Alexander, Ken Brett, Jim Bunning, Don Cardwell, Hal Carlson, Phil Collins, Charlie Ferguson, Randy Lerch, Lee Meadows, Jimmy Ring, Jack Taylor
3	Johnny Couch, Wayland Dean, Kevin Gross, Art Mahaffey, Claude Passeau
2	Dennis Bennett, Ed Daily, Curt Davis, Jack Fifield, Woodie Fryman, Tommy Greene, Jack Knight, Erskine Mayer, Bob Miller, Clarence Mitchell, David Palmer, Bucky Walters, Doc White

1   Chief Bender, Jeff Bittiger, Joe Bowman, Ad Brennan, Kid Carsey, Dan Casey, Billy Champion, Bubba Church, Gene Conley, Dennis Cook, Frank Corridon, Murry Dickson, Clise Dudley, Duke Esper, Dick Farrell, Bill Foxen, Chick Fraser, Charlie Frye, Al Gerheauser, Ad Gumbert, Bill Hubbell, Grant Jackson, Larry Jackson, Syl Johnson, Oscar Judd, Jim Kaat, Tony Kaufmann, Tim Keefe, Jim Lonborg, Al Maul, Rube Melton, Jack Meyer, Russ Meyer, Elmer Miller, Frank O'Connor, Lowell Palmer, Ike Pearson, Buz Phillips, Steve Ridzik, Eppa Rixey, Saul Rogovin, Ben Sanders, Charley Schanz, Jack Scott, Tom Seaton, Curt Simmons, Tom Sullivan, Augie Walsh, George Wheeler

Nonpitchers who Pitched for the Phillies

Outfielder Earl Naylor had five losses in 20 games in 1942.

Player	Position	Year	W	L	ERA	G	GS	IP	H	BB	SO
Mike Anderson	of	1979	0	0	0.00	1	0	1	2	0	2
Jack Bentley	1b	1926	0	2	8.28	7	3	25	37	10	7
Bob Bowman	of	1959	0	1	6.00	5	0	6	5	5	0
Ben Chapman	3b-of	1945–46	0	0	6.67	4	0	8⅓	8	7	5
Bob Ferguson	2b	1883	0	0	9.00	1	0	1	2	0	0
Jim Fogarty	2b-ss	1884, 1886	0	1	4.50	7	0	14	16	3	5
	3b-of	1887, 1889									
Barney Friberg	c-2b-3b	1925	0	0	4.50	1	0	4	4	3	1
Jimmie Foxx	1b-3b	1945	1	0	1.59	9	2	22⅔	13	14	10
Greg Gross	1b-of	1986	0	0	0.00	1	0	1	1	1	2
Bud Hafey	of	1939	0	0	33.75	2	0	1⅔	7	1	1
Bill Hallman	2b	1896	0	0	18.00	1	0	2	4	2	0
Granny Hamner	2b-ss	1956–57	0	1	3.89	4	1	9⅓	11	2	5
Walter Holke	1b	1923	0	0	0.00	1	0	⅓	1	0	0
Arthur Irwin	2b-ss	1889	0	0	0.00	1	0	1	1	0	0
Al Lakeman	c	1948	0	0	13.50	1	0	⅔	1	0	0
Art Mahan	1b	1940	0	0	0.00	1	0	1	1	0	0
Joe Marty	of	1939	0	0	4.50	1	0	4	2	3	1
Tommy McCarthy	of	1886	0	0	0.00	1	0	1	0	1	1
Earl Naylor	of	1942	0	5	6.15	20	4	60	68	29	19
Blondie Purcell	of	1884	0	0	2.25	1	0	4	3	0	1
Cookie Rojas	c-2b-ss-3b-of	1967	0	0	0.00	1	0	1	1	0	0
Billy Sunday	of	1890	0	0	0.00	1	0	0	2	0	0
Roy Thomas	of	1900	0	0	3.38	1	0	2⅔	4	0	0
Tuck Turner	of	1894	0	0	7.50	1	0	6	9	2	3
Bucky Walters	2b-3b	1934	0	0	1.29	2	1	7	8	2	7
Glenn Wilson	of	1987	0	0	0.00	1	0	1	0	0	1
George Wood	ss-3b-of	1888–89	0	0	9.00	3	0	3	5	1	2

Club Fielding Records

First Base

Pct.	.999 by Frank McCormick, 1946
Putouts	1,597 by Fred Luderus, 1917
Assists	125 by Ed Bouchee, 1957
DPs	142 by Eddie Waitkus, 1950

Danny Litwhiler was the first major league outfielder to field a perfect 1.000 during a full season.

Second Base
Pct.	.994 by Manny Trillo, 1982
Putouts	450 by Emil Verban, 1947
Assists	562 by Frank Parkinson, 1922
DPs	141 by Dave Cash, 1974

Third Base
Pct.	.982 by Pinky Whitney, 1937
Putouts	229 by Ernie Courtney, 1905
Assists	404 by Mike Schmidt, 1974
DPs	40 by Mike Schmidt, 1974

Shortstop
Pct.	.991 by Larry Bowa, 1979
Putouts	395 by Mickey Doolan, 1906
Assists	560 by Larry Bowa, 1971
DPs	113 by Tom Thevenow, 1930

Catcher
Pct.	.994 by Ozzie Virgil, 1985; Spud Davis, 1931
Putouts	903 by Bo Diaz, 1983
Assists	199 by Red Dooin, 1909
DPs	17 by Red Dooin, 1908; Bill Killefer, 1912

Outfield
Pct.	1.000 by Danny Litwhiler, 1942; Tony Gonzalez, 1962; Don Demeter, 1963; Johnny Callison, 1968
Putouts	538 by Rich Ashburn, 1951
Assists	44 by Chuck Klein, 1930
DPs	11 by Sam Thompson, 1896

Fielding

Jim Kaat won two Gold Gloves while pitching with the Phillies.

Gold Glove Winners

1963	Bobby Wine, ss		1979	Garry Maddox, of
1964	Bobby Shantz, p			Mike Schmidt, 3b
	Ruben Amaro, ss			Bob Boone, c
1966	Bill White, 1b			Manny Trillo, 2b
1972	Larry Bowa, ss		1980	Garry Maddox, of
1975	Garry Maddox, of			Mike Schmidt, 3b
1976	Garry Maddox, of		1981	Garry Maddox, of
	Mike Schmidt, 3b			Mike Schmidt, 3b
	Jim Kaat, p			Manny Trillo, 2b
1977	Garry Maddox, of			Steve Carlton, p
	Mike Schmidt, 3b		1982	Garry Maddox, of
	Jim Kaat, p			Mike Schmidt, 3b
1978	Garry Maddox, of			Manny Trillo, 2b
	Mike Schmidt, 3b		1983	Mike Schmidt, 3b
	Larry Bowa, ss		1984	Mike Schmidt, 3b
	Bob Boone, c		1986	Mike Schmidt, 3b

All-Time Fielding Team

	Player	Year	Games	TC	E	Pct.
1b	Frank McCormick	1946	134	1,283	1	.999*
2b	Manny Trillo	1982	149	789	5	.994
ss	Larry Bowa	1979	146	683	6	.991
3b	Pinky Whitney	1937	130	374	7	.982
of	Danny Litwhiler	1942	151	317	0	1.000*
	Tony Gonzalez	1962	114	276	0	1.000
	Don Demeter	1963	119	172	0	1.000
	Johnny Callison	1968	109	197	0	1.000
c	Virgil Davis	1931	114	496	3	.994
c	Ozzie Virgil	1985	131	723	4	.994
p	Eppa Rixey	1917	39	108	0	1.000

*League record

Triple Plays

TURNED BY PHILLIES

Date	Opponent	Fielders	Batter
Sept. 8, 1890	vs. Brooklyn	Allen (ss) to Myers (2b) to McCauley (1b)	Smith
Apr. 23, 1891	vs. Brooklyn	Shindle (3b) to Allen (ss)	O'Brien
Sept. 5, 1908	vs. New York	Doolan (ss) to Knabe (2b) to Dooin (c) to Grant (3b) to Doolan to Dooin to Grant	Devlin
Sept. 4, 1909	vs. Brooklyn	Doolan (ss) to Ward (2b) to Bransfield (1b) to Dooin (c)	Bell
Aug. 12, 1916	vs. New York	Bancroft (ss) to Byrne (3b) to Bancroft	Robertson
May 26, 1918	at Cincinnati	Bancroft (ss) to Luderus (1b)	Magee
July 6, 1923	vs. Pittsburgh	Mokan (lf) to Henline (c) to Sand (ss)	Carey
July 4, 1924	at New York	Ford (3b) to Sand (ss) to Holke (1b)	Groh
May 1, 1925	vs. Boston	Schultz (lf) to Henline (c) to Fonseca (2b)	O'Neill
June 29, 1925	vs. Brooklyn	Carlson (p) to Sand (ss) to Hawks (1b)	DeBerry
June 3, 1929	at Pittsburgh	Thompson (2b) to Hurst (1b) to Friberg (ss)	Grimes
Sept. 16, 1930	vs. Pittsburgh	Thompson (2b) to Sherlock (1b)	Traynor
July 1, 1931	vs. Chicago	Mallon (2b) to Friberg (1b) to Bartell (ss)	Taylor
Apr. 26, 1935	at New York	Wilson (c) to Bivin (p) to Ryan (ss) to Camilli (1b)	Mancuso
July 23, 1948	at Cincinnati	Caballero (3b) to Hamner (2b) to Sisler (1b)	Stallcup
June 23, 1949	at Pittsburgh	Miller (2b) to Hamner (ss) to Sisler (1b)	Stevens
June 22, 1950	vs. Pittsburgh	Miller (p) to Hamner (ss) to Waitkus (1b) to Seminick (c)	Bell
Sept. 25, 1955	at New York	Kazanski (ss) to Morgan (2b) to Blaylock (1b)	Hoffman
June 28, 1958	vs. St. Louis	Hemus (2b) to Anderson (1b)	K. Boyer

TURNED BY PHILLIES

Date	Opponent	Fielders	Batter
May 17, 1964	at Houston	Herrnstein (1b) to Wine (ss) to Herrnstein to Triandos (c)	Grote
Aug. 15, 1964	at New York	Boozer (p) to Amaro (ss) to Thomas (1b)	Klaus
Oct. 2, 1964	at Cincinnati	Johnson (lf) to Wine (ss) to Taylor (2b) to Power (1b)	D. Johnson
Aug. 15, 1967	vs. New York	Allen (3b) to Rojas (2b) to White (1b)	Linz
May 4, 1968	vs. Pittsburgh	Wine (ss) to Rojas (2b) to White (1b)	Mota
Apr. 28, 1991	vs. San Diego	Ready (2b) to Jordan (1b)	T. Gwynn
Sept. 20, 1992	vs. Pittsburgh	Morandini (2b)	J. King

TURNED AGAINST PHILLIES

Date	Opponent	Fielders	Batter
Sept. 8, 1885	vs. New York	Connor (1b) to Gerhardt (2b)	Ferguson
Aug. 4, 1887	at Chicago	Pfeffer (2b) to Williamson (ss) to Burns (3b)	McGuire
Sept. 11, 1894	at Pittsburgh	Steere (ss) to Beckley (1b) to Sugden (c), to Bierbauer (2b)	Delahanty
June 26, 1902	vs. New York	Bean (ss) to Smith (2b) to O'Hagan (1b) to Yeager (c)	Jacklitsch
July 27, 1907	at Pittsburgh	Nealon (1b) to Wagner (ss) to Nealon (1b)	Courtney
Sept. 23, 1907	at Chicago	Howard (1b) to Tinker (ss)	Dooin
Sept. 3, 1908	vs. Brooklyn	Pastorius (p) to Alperman (2b) to Jordan (1b)	Dooin
Oct. 9, 1911	vs. Boston	Ingerton (ss) to Sweeney (2b) to Houser (1b)	Knabe
Apr. 24, 1914	at New York	Doyle (2b) to Merkle (1b) to Fletcher (ss) to McLean (c)	Luderus
July 17, 1919	vs. St. Louis	Lavan (ss) to Hornsby (3b)	Sicking
July 7, 1920	at Pittsburgh	Cooper (p) to Caton (ss) to Grimm (1b)	Wheat
Aug. 21, 1920	at Pittsburgh	Cooper (p) to McKechnie (3b) to Whitted (1b)	LeBourveau
July 27, 1921	at St. Louis	Hornsby (ss) to Toporcer (2b) to Fournier (1b)	Rapp
Sept. 3, 1922	at New York	Youngs (rf) to Bancroft (ss) to Groh (3b) to Kelly (1b)	Smith
Oct. 6, 1923	at Boston	Padgett (ss) unassisted	Holke
July 30, 1924	vs. St. Louis	Bottomley (1b) to Cooney (ss) to Hornsby (2b)	Mokan

TURNED AGAINST PHILLIES

Date	Opponent	Fielders	Batter
Sept. 6, 1924	vs. New York	Frisch (2b) to Terry (1b)	Schultz
May 18, 1929	vs. Brooklyn	Hendrick (1b) to Bancroft (ss)	O'Doul
May 25, 1929	at Brooklyn	Bancroft (ss) to Hendrick (1b) to Moore (2b)	Peel
May 29, 1934	at Boston	Frankhouse (p) to Jordan (1b) to Urbanski (ss)	Jeffries
Aug. 4, 1934	vs. New York	Critz (2b) to Terry (1b) to Jackson (ss)	Allen
Sept. 16, 1936	vs. St. Louis	Haines (p) to Mize (1b) to Durocher (ss)	Grace
July 12, 1937	vs. New York	Ott (rf) to Mancuso (c) to Bartell (ss) to Chiozza (3b)	Arnovich
Sept. 6, 1942	vs. Boston	Earley (p) to Miller (ss) to West (1b)	Murtaugh
Aug. 23, 1947	vs. St. Louis	Rice (c) to Marion (ss) to Musial (1b)	Gilbert
May 21, 1950	vs. St. Louis	Garagiola (c) to Glaviano (3b) to Marion (ss) to Musial (1b)	Waitkus
Aug. 30, 1953	vs. Cincinnati	Bridges (2b) to McMillian (ss) to Kluszewski (1b)	Hamner
July 6, 1960	at Milwaukee	Cottier (2b) to Adcock (1b) to Crandall (c) to Mathews (3b)	Smith
July 15, 1978	at Atlanta	Horner (3b) to Hubbard (2b) to Murphy (1b)	Cardenal
Apr. 11, 1981	at St. Louis	Templeton (ss) to Porter (c) to Hernandez (1b) to Herr (2b) to Oberkfell (3b)	Matthews

Top Phillies Fielders (Career)

	Pct.	PO	A	E	DP	Years Played
First Base						
Frank McCormick	.995	13,803	1,003	79	1,221	13
Eddie Waitkus	.993	9,193	716	73	886	11
Bill White	.992	13,015	966	115	1,160	13
Willie Montanez	.991	10,764	747	104	969	14
Dolph Camilli	.990	13,724	957	141	1,216	12
Second Base						
Dave Cash	.983	3,228	3,905	121	906	12
Manny Trillo	.981	3,977	4,855	169	1,029	17
Tony Taylor	.976	4,241	4,696	219	1,072	19
Emil Verban	.971	1,996	2,180	124	534	7
Shortstop						
Larry Bowa	.980	3,323	6,864	211	1,267	16
Bobby Wine	.972	1,795	3,030	141	708	12
Dick Bartell	.955	4,425	6,348	512	1,156	18
Granny Hamner	.955	2,811	4,304	334	888	17
Dave Bancroft	.944	4,673	6,604	666	1,027	16

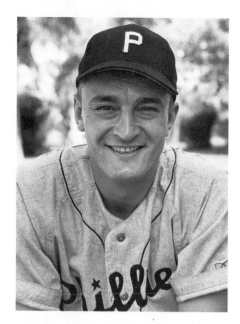

Frank McCormick holds the Phillies record for the top fielding percentage by a first baseman.

	Pct.	PO	A	E	DP	Years Played
Third Base						
Don Money	.975	2,697	3,242	150	554	16
Pinky Whitney	.964	1,828	3,019	180	268	12
Willie Jones	.963	2,050	2,934	192	273	15
Pinky May	.962	738	1,397	85	115	5
Mike Schmidt	.961	2,836	5,193	328	580	18
Outfield						
Tony Gonzalez	.986	2,613	73	38	15	12
Johnny Callison	.984	3,349	175	57	34	16
Richie Ashburn	.983	6,094	182	111	44	15
Garry Maddox	.983	4,449	94	78	21	15
Ethan Allen	.981	2,746	103	56	23	13
Danny Litwhiler	.981	1,942	99	39	13	11
Dode Paskert	.968	3,852	257	136	59	15
Chuck Klein	.962	3,250	194	135	39	17
Catcher						
Mike Ryan	.991	3,473	325	34	45	11
Bob Boone	.986	11,082	1,166	179	155	18
Spud Davis	.984	4,423	688	84	100	16
Jimmie Wilson	.977	4,972	935	142	158	18
Andy Seminick	.976	5,081	608	137	81	15
Pitcher						
Grover C. Alexander	.985	189	1,419	25	50	20
Rick Wise	.982	206	504	13	46	18
Eppa Rixey	.978	131	1,195	30	55	21
Claude Passeau	.977	130	583	17	44	13
Bobby Shantz	.976	174	468	16	48	16
Bucky Walters	.974	153	746	24	76	19
Curt Davis	.973	146	616	21	37	13
Robin Roberts	.967	316	601	31	45	19
Chris Short	.965	112	358	17	22	15
Larry Jackson	.960	257	656	38	46	14
Steve Carlton	.952	109	724	42	36	24
Jim Kaat	.947	262	744	56	65	25

League Leaders in Fielding

[(1) Club Record; (2) League Record]

First Basemen

Percentage

1886	Sid Farrar	.980
1891	Willard Brown	.989
1892	Roger Connor	.985
1909	Kitty Bransfield	.989
1932	Don Hurst	.993
1937	Dolph Camilli	.994
1946	Frank McCormick	.999 (1) (2)
1966	Bill White	.994
1980	Pete Rose	.997

Putouts

1912	Fred Luderus	1,421
1913	Fred Luderus	1,533
1917	Fred Luderus	1,597 (1)
1935	Dolph Camilli	1,442
1936	Dolph Camilli	1,446
1950	Eddie Waitkus	1,387
1959	Ed Bouchee	1,127

Assists

1884	Sid Farrar	42

1912	Fred Luderus	104
1913	Fred Luderus	92
1917	Fred Luderus	91
1918	Fred Luderus	98
1919	Fred Luderus	108
1929	Don Hurst	112
1933	Don Hurst	114
1957	Ed Bouchee	125 (1)
1959	Ed Bouchee	95

1960	Pancho Herrera	109
1966	Bill White	109
1980	Pete Rose	123

Double Plays

1905	Kitty Bransfield	75
1918	Fred Luderus	74
1923	Walt Holke	136
1950	Eddie Waitkus	142 (1)

Second Basemen

Manny Trillo has the Phillies' highest fielding percentage among second basemen.

Percentage

1886	Charlie Bastian	.945
1900	Nap Lajoie	.954
1901	Bill Hallman	.971
1940	Herman Schulte	.980
1963	Tony Taylor	.986
1968	Cookie Rojas	.987
1976	Dave Cash	.988
1982	Manny Trillo	.994 (1)

Putouts

1898	Nap Lajoie	442
1905	Kid Gleason	365
1908	Otto Knabe	344
1926	Barney Friberg	381
1927	Fresco Thompson	424
1929	Fresco Thompson	395
1947	Emil Verban	450 (1)
1968	Cookie Rojas	365
1975	Dave Cash	400
1980	Manny Trillo	360
1981	Manny Trillo	245
1985	Juan Samuel	389
1987	Juan Samuel	374
1988	Juan Samuel	343

Assists

1908	Otto Knabe	470
1913	Otto Knabe	466
1922	Frank Parkinson	562 (1)
1946	Emil Verban	381

1947	Emil Verban	453
1952	Connie Ryan	462
1974	Dave Cash	519

Double Plays

1890	Al Myers (tied)	62
1900	Nap Lajoie	69
1916	Bert Niehoff	65
1923	Cotton Tierney	104*
1968	Cookie Rojas	110
1974	Dave Cash	141 (1)
1975	Dave Cash	126
1976	Dave Cash	118
1977	Ted Sizemore	104
1988	Juan Samuel	92

400 or More Putouts a Season

450	Emil Verban	1947
442	Nap Lajoie	1898
424	Fresco Thompson	1927
409	Fresco Thompson	1928
407	Dave Cash	1976
400	Dave Cash	1975

500 or More Assists a Season

562	Frank Parkinson	1922
543	Hod Ford	1924
519	Dave Cash	1974
512	Barney Friberg	1926
512	Fresco Thompson	1929
509	Fresco Thompson	1928

Third Basemen

Percentage

1895	Lave Cross	.940
1901	Harry Wolverton	.921
1903	Harry Wolverton	.941
1904	Harry Wolverton	.925
1913	Hans Lobert	.974
1914	Hans Lobert	.943
1915	Bob Byrne	.969

1932	Pinky Whitney	.960
1935	Johnny Vergez	.953
1937	Pinky Whitney	.982 (1)
1939	Pinky May	.956
1941	Pinky May	.972
1943	Pinky May	.963

*Tierney's 104 double plays included 22 for Pittsburgh, 82 with the Phillies.

1953	Willie Jones	.975
1954	Willie Jones	.968
1955	Willie Jones	.960
1956	Willie Jones	.973
1958	Willie Jones	.967
1972	Don Money	.978
1986	Mike Schmidt	.980

Putouts

1884	Joe Mulvey	151
1885	Joe Mulvey	144
1905	Ernie Courtney	229 (1)
1910	Ed Grant	193
1911	Hans Lobert	202
1913	Hans Lobert	181
1929	Pinky Whitney	168
1930	Pinky Whitney	186
1932	Pinky Whitney	177
1935	Johnny Vergez	188
1941	Pinky May	194
1949	Willie Jones	181
1950	Willie Jones	190
1952	Willie Jones	216
1953	Willie Jones	176
1954	Willie Jones	184
1955	Willie Jones	202
1956	Willie Jones	202
1972	Don Money	139

Assists

1895	Lave Cross	308
1929	Pinky Whitney	333
1930	Pinky Whitney	313
1932	Pinky Whitney	276
1941	Pinky May	324
1949	Willie Jones	308
1950	Willie Jones	323
1974	Mike Schmidt	404 (1)
1976	Mike Schmidt	377
1977	Mike Schmidt	396
1980	Mike Schmidt	372
1981	Mike Schmidt	249
1982	Mike Schmidt	324
1983	Mike Schmidt	332
1990	Charlie Hayes	324

Double Plays

1891	Bill Shindle (tie)	24

1894	Lave Cross (tie)	24
1908	Ed Grant	22
1927	Barney Friberg (tie)	23
1929	Pinky Whitney	29
1930	Pinky Whitney	29
1932	Pinky Whitney	31
1935	Johnny Vergez	25
1941	Pinky May	31
1951	Willie Jones	33
1952	Willie Jones	31
1965	Dick Allen	29
1972	Don Money (tie)	31
1974	Mike Schmidt	40 (1)
1978	Mike Schmidt	34
1979	Mike Schmidt	36
1980	Mike Schmidt	31
1983	Mike Schmidt	29

200 or More Putouts a Season

229	Ernie Courtney	1905
216	Willie Jones	1952
202	Hans Lobert	1911
202	Willie Jones	1955
202	Willie Jones	1956

300 or More Assists a Season

404	Mike Schmidt	1974
396	Mike Schmidt	1977
377	Mike Schmidt	1976
372	Mike Schmidt	1980
368	Mike Schmidt	1975
361	Mike Schmidt	1979
333	Pinky Whitney	1929
332	Mike Schmidt	1983
325	Dick Allen	1964
324	Pinky May	1941
324	Mike Schmidt	1978
324	Mike Schmidt	1982
323	Willie Jones	1950
316	Don Money	1972
315	Tony Taylor	1968
313	Pinky Whitney	1930
310	Ed Grant	1909
308	Lave Cross	1895
308	Willie Jones	1949
307	Bill Lauder	1899
305	Dick Allen	1965

Shortstop

Percentage

1910	Mickey Doolan	.948
1924	Heinie Sand	.959
1927	Jimmy Cooney	.980 *
1967	Bobby Wine	.980
1971	Larry Bowa	.987
1972	Larry Bowa	.987
1974	Larry Bowa	.984
1978	Larry Bowa	.986
1979	Larry Bowa	.991 (1) (2)

Putouts

1884	Bill McClellan	165
1888	Arthur Irwin	204
1890	Bob Allen	337
1893	Bob Allen	302
1898	Monte Cross	404 (1)
1899	Monte Cross	370
1900	Monte Cross	339
1901	Monte Cross	343
1902	Rudy Hulswitt	318

*Cooney played 33 games for Chicago, 76 for the Phillies in 1927.

1903	Rudy Hulswitt	354
1906	Mickey Doolan	395
1907	Mickey Doolan	327
1909	Mickey Doolan	351
1913	Mickey Doolan	338
1918	Dave Bancroft	371
1924	Heinie Sand	333
1930	Tom Thevenow	344
1932	Dick Bartell	359
1933	Dick Bartell	381
1934	Dick Bartell	350
1937	George Scharein	335

Assists

1884	Bob McClellan	313
1890	Bob Allen	500
1899	Monte Cross	529
1906	Mickey Doolan	480
1909	Mickey Doolan	482
1910	Mickey Doolan	500
1912	Mickey Doolan	476
1913	Mickey Doolan	482
1930	Tom Thevenow	554
1932	Dick Bartell	529
1934	Dick Bartell	483
1949	Granny Hamner	506
1971	Larry Bowa	560 (1)

Double Plays

1890	Bob Allen	68
1892	Bob Allen	67
1907	Mickey Doolan	59
1909	Mickey Doolan (tie)	58
1910	Mickey Doolan	71
1911	Mickey Doolan	68

1913	Mickey Doolan	63
1930	Tom Thevenow	113 (1)
1931	Dick Bartell	96
1933	Dick Bartell	100
1934	Dick Bartell	93
1937	George Scharein	98
1949	Granny Hamner	101
1971	Larry Bowa (tie)	97

350 or More Putouts a Season

404	Monte Cross	1898
395	Mickey Doolan	1906
381	Dick Bartell	1933
371	Dave Bancroft	1918
370	Monte Cross	1899
359	Dick Bartell	1932
358	Heinie Sand	1926
354	Rudy Hulswitt	1905
352	Heinie Sand	1925
351	Mickey Doolan	1909
350	Dick Bartell	1934

500 or More Assists a Season

560	Larry Bowa	1971
554	Tom Thevenow	1930
537	Bob Allen	1891
529	Monte Cross	1899
529	Dick Bartell	1932
518	Larry Bowa	1977
513	Granny Hamner	1950
510	Dave Bancroft	1916
506	Monte Cross	1898
506	Granny Hamner	1949
502	Larry Bowa	1978
500	Bob Allen	1890
500	Mickey Doolan	1910

Dick Bartell led the National League in several different fielding categories.

Percentage

1889	Jim Fogarty	.961
1894	Sam Thompson	.977
1896	Sam Thompson	.974
1906	Roy Thomas	.986
1911	Sherry Magee	.981
1917	Dode Paskert	.984
1924	George Harper	.991 *
1927	Dick Spalding	.992
1942	Danny Litwhiler	1.000 (1) (2)
1962	Tony Gonzalez	1.000 (1)
1963	Don Demeter	1.000 (1)
1964	Tony Gonzalez	.996
1967	Tony Gonzalez	.993
1968	Johnny Callison	1.000 (1)
1973	Greg Luzinski	.993
1978	Bake McBride	.996
1982	Garry Maddox	.992

Putouts

1895	Jim Fogarty	227
1889	Jim Fogarty	302

1894	Billy Hamilton	361
1898	Duff Cooley	352
1903	Roy Thomas (tie)	318
1904	Roy Thomas	321
1905	Roy Thomas	373
1908	Wilfred Osborn	359
1933	Chick Fullis	410
1937	Hershel Martin	353
1941	Danny Litwhiler	393
1944	Buster Adams	449
1946	Johnny Wyrostek	388
1949	Richie Ashburn	514
1950	Richie Ashburn	405
1951	Richie Ashburn	538 (1)
1952	Richie Ashburn	428
1953	Richie Ashburn	496
1954	Richie Ashburn	483
1956	Richie Ashburn	503
1957	Richie Ashburn	502
1958	Richie Ashburn	495
1976	Garry Maddox	441
1978	Garry Maddox	444

Outfielders

*Harper played 28 games for Cincinnati, 109 for the Phillies in 1924.

Assists

1889	Jim Fogarty	42
1891	Sam Thompson	32
1896	Sam Thompson	28
1901	Elmer Flick (tie)	23
1905	Roy Thomas	27
1912	Gavvy Cravath (tie)	26
1914	Gavvy Cravath	34
1915	Gavvy Cravath	28
1921	Cy Williams	29
1927	Fred Leach	26
1928	Denny Sothern	19
1930	Chuck Klein	44 (1)
1932	Chuck Klein	29
1933	Chuck Klein	21
1935	Ethan Allen	26
1944	Ron Northey (tie)	24
1949	Del Ennis	16
1952	Richie Ashburn	23
1953	Richie Ashburn	18
1957	Richie Ashburn	18
1959	Harry Anderson	17
1962	Johnny Callison	24
1963	Johnny Callison	26
1964	Johnny Callison	19
1965	Johnny Callison	21
1972	Willie Montanez (tie)	15
1985	Glenn Wilson	18
1986	Glenn Wilson	20
1987	Glenn Wilson	18

Double Plays

1884	Jack Manning (tie)	7
1887	Jim Fogarty (tie)	9
1888	Jim Fogarty	9
1896	Sam Thompson	11
1906	John Titus (tie)	7
1910	John Bates	8
1913	Dode Paskert	8
1922	Curt Walker	8

1927	Fred Leach	10
1928	Denny Sothern	7
1930	Chuck Klein	10
1936	Lou Chiozza	10
1943	Buster Adams	8
1944	Ron Northey (tie)	7
1951	Richie Ashburn	6
1952	Richie Ashburn (tie)	5
1957	Richie Ashburn	7
1962	Johnny Callison	7
1981	Garry Maddox (tie)	4
1985	Glenn Wilson	4

400 or More Putouts a Year

538	Richie Ashburn	1951
514	Richie Ashburn	1949
503	Richie Ashburn	1956
502	Richie Ashburn	1957
496	Richie Ashburn	1953
495	Richie Ashburn	1958
483	Richie Ashburn	1954
449	Buster Adams	1944
444	Garry Maddox	1978
441	Garry Maddox	1976
433	Garry Maddox	1979
428	Richie Ashburn	1952
412	Ethan Allen	1935
411	Kiddo Davis	1932
410	Chick Fullis	1933
405	Richie Ashburn	1950
405	Garry Maddox	1980

30 or More Assists a Year

44	Chuck Klein	1930
42	Jim Fogarty	1889
39	Jim Fogarty	1887
37	Jack Manning	1883
34	Gavvy Cravath	1914
32	Sam Thompson	1891
31	Ed Delahanty	1893
31	Sam Thompson	1895

Catchers

Percentage

1900	Ed McFarland	.963
1916	Bill Killefer	.985
1917	Bill Killefer	.984
1922	Butch Henline	.983
1929	Peck Lerian	.986
1931	Virgil Davis	.994 (1)
1953	Smoky Burgess	.993
1955	Andy Seminick	.994
1978	Bob Boone	.991
1985	Ozzie Virgil	.994

Putouts

1888	Jack Clements	494
1890	Jack Clements	503
1892	Jack Clements	557
1917	Bill Killefer	617
1948	Andy Seminick	541
1963	Clay Dalrymple	881 (1)
1974	Bob Boone	825

Assists

1900	Ed McFarland	137
1908	Red Dooin	191
1909	Red Dooin	199 (1)
1913	Bill Killefer	166
1914	Bill Killefer	154
1931	Spud Davis	78
1941	Benny Warren	84
1948	Andy Seminick	74
1961	Clay Dalrymple	86
1963	Clay Dalrymple	90
1965	Clay Dalrymple	70
1969	Mike Ryan (tie)	79
1973	Bob Boone	89

Double Plays

Year	Player	
1891	Jack Clements (tie)	10
1899	Ed McFarland	14
1904	Red Dooin	12
1907	Fred Jacklitsch	15
1908	Red Dooin	17 (1)
1912	Bill Killefer	17 (1)
1913	Bill Killefer	16
1917	Bill Killefer	14
1919	Bert Adams	15
1932	Spud Davis	15
1938	Bill Atwood	12
1941	Benny Warren	16
1946	Andy Seminick (tie)	12
1956	Stan Lopata (tie)	10
1962	Clay Dalrymple (tie)	11
1963	Clay Dalrymple (tie)	16
1975	Johnny Oates	10

700 Putouts or More a Season

903	Bo Diaz	1983
881	Clay Dalrymple	1963
868	Bob Boone	1973
825	Bob Boone	1974
769	Mike Ryan	1969
741	Bob Boone	1980
737	Clay Dalrymple	1964

150 Assists or More a Season

199	Red Dooin	1909
191	Red Dooin	1908
166	Bill Killefer	1913
154	Bill Killefer	1914
152	Red Dooin	1905

Media

Phillies Broadcasters

Years	Broadcasters
1928–29	Andrew Stanton, Robert Paul
1936	Bill Dyer, Dolly Stark, Allen Scott, Harry McTigue
1937	Bill Dyer, Taylor Grant
1938	Taylor Grant, Byrum Saam, Walt Newton, Stoney McLinn
1939	Byrum Saam, Walt Newton
1940	Byrum Saam, Lee Vines
1941–42	Byrum Saam, Taylor Grant
1943–46	Byrum Saam, Roy Neal
1947–48	Byrum Saam, Chuck Thompson
1949	Byrum Saam, George Walsh
1950–51	Gene Kelly, Bill Brundige
1952	Gene Kelly, Claude Haring
1953–54	Gene Kelly, George Walsh
1955–59	Gene Kelly, Byrum Saam, Claude Haring
1960–62	Byrum Saam, Frank Sims, Claude Haring
1963–70	Byrum Saam, Rich Ashburn, Bill Campbell
1971–73	Harry Kalas, Byrum Saam, Rich Ashburn
1974–75	Harry Kalas, Byrum Saam, Rich Ashburn, Robin Roberts
1976	Harry Kalas, Rich Ashburn, Andy Musser, Robin Roberts
1977–79	Harry Kalas, Rich Ashburn, Andy Musser, Chris Wheeler
1980–82	Harry Kalas, Rich Ashburn, Andy Musser, Chris Wheeler, Tim McCarver
1983–86	Harry Kalas, Rich Ashburn, Andy Musser, Chris Wheeler
1987–89	Harry Kalas, Rich Ashburn, Andy Musser, Chris Wheeler, Garry Maddox
1990	Harry Kalas, Rich Ashburn, Andy Musser, Chris Wheeler, Garry Maddox, Jim Barniak, Mike Schmidt

| 1991 | Harry Kalas, Rich Ashburn, Andy Musser, Chris Wheeler, Garry Maddox, Jim Barniak, Jim Fregosi | 1992 | Harry Kalas, Rich Ashburn, Andy Musser, Chris Wheeler, Garry Maddox, Kent Tekulve, Jay Johnstone |

By Saam, Gene Kelly (top row from left), Harry Kalas, and Andy Musser (bottom row from left) have all broadcast Phillies games for many years.

Flagship Radio Stations

1937	WIP/WCAU
1938	WCAU
1939	WIP/WCAU
	WPEN (night games only)
1943–49	WIBG

Up until this point, only Phillies games at home were on radio.

| 1950–51 | WPEN (home games and away games) |
| 1952–53 | WIBG (home games and some road games) |

From here on, all home and away games were on radio.

1954	WIP
	WIBG
1955–59	WIP
1960–67	WFIL
1968–75	WCAU
1976	WIBG
1977–81	KYW
1982–90	WCAU
1991–92	WOGL

1947	WPTZ (3)		WFIL-TV (6)
1948	WPTZ (3)		WPFH-TV (12)
	WCAU-TV (10)	1958	WRCV-TV (3)
1949–54	WPTZ (3)		WFIL-TV (6)
	WFIL-TV (6)		WVUE-TV (12)
	WCAU-TV (10)	1959–70	WFIL-TV (6)
1955	WPTZ (3)	1971–82	WPHL-TV (17)
	WFIL-TV (6)	1983–92	WTAF (29)
1956–57	WRCV-TV (3)	1986–92	Prism

Sources

Baseball America

Baseball Digest

The Baseball Encyclopedia, Joseph L. Reichler, editor

Baseball Guide and Record Book by *The Sporting News*

Baseball's 100 by Maury Allen

Baseball Registers by *The Sporting News* (1941–92)

The Book of Sports Lists by Phil Pepe and Zander Hollander

The Boston Post

The Courier Post, Cherry Hill, N.J.

Diamond Greats by Rich Westcott

Even the Browns by William B. Mead

The Free Library of Philadelphia

The Great All-Time Baseball Record Book by Joseph L. Reichler

July 2, 1903, by Mike Sowell

The Little Red Book of Baseball

The National League 75th Anniversary Official History

The New York Times

1947—When All Hell Broke Loose in Baseball by Red Barber

Official Baseball Record Book by *The Sporting News*

Official World Series Records by *The Sporting News*

On a Clear Day, They Could See Seventh Place by George Robinson and Charles Salzberg

The Philadelphia Bulletin Library

The Philadelphia Daily News

The Philadelphia Evening and *Sunday Bulletin*

The Philadelphia Inquirer

The Philadelphia Phillies by Allen Lewis

The Philadelphia Phillies by Frederick G. Lieb and Stan Baumgartner

The Philadelphia Record

The Philadelphia Story by Frank Dolson

Phillies Media Guides

Phillies Report

Phillies Yearbooks

The Public Ledger

Reach Official Baseball Guides

Rochester Democrat and Chronicle

Rowdy Richard by Dick Bartell with Norman Macht

The Series by *The Sporting News*

Spaulding's Official Base Ball Guides

Sport Magazine

The Sporting News

The Sports Encyclopedia of Baseball by David S. Neft, Richard M. Cohen, and Jordan A. Deutsch

The Story of Baseball by John Durant

The Team That Wouldn't Die by Hal Bodley
Teenagers, Graybeards and 4-Fs by Harrington E. Crissey, Jr.
This Date in Philadelphia Phillies History by Allen Lewis and Larry Shenk
Total Baseball edited by John Thorn and Pete Palmer
Trade Him! edited by Jim Enright
The Ultimate Baseball Book by Daniel Okrent and Harris Levine
The Way It Is by Curt Flood with Richard Carter
The Whiz Kids by Harry T. Paxton
Who's Who in Baseball by Allan Roth
Who's Who in the Major Leagues (1936–55)

Photo Credits

Photos courtesy of the Philadelphia Phillies, *The Philadelphia Bulletin,* Philadelphia City Hall archives, the Free Library of Philadelphia, *Phillies Report,* the National Baseball Hall of Fame and Museum, Urban Archives of Temple University Libraries, Transcendental Graphics, Bob Bartosz, George Brace, Alan Kravetz, Roger Luce, Bruce Murray, Rosemary Rahn, Paul Roedig, and Jim Rowe.

Acknowledgments

The authors wish to thank the following people for their special assistance in compiling this encyclopedia: Craig Ammerman, Joe Bilovsky, Skip Clayton, Ed (Dutch) Doyle, Allen Lewis, John McAdams, Ernie Montella, Larry Shenk, and Lois Westcott. Special thanks to artist Andy Jurinko for the use of his painting of Shibe Park and to Peter Capolino of Mitchell and Ness Nostalgia Co.

About the Authors

Rich Westcott is publisher and editor of *Phillies Report,* a newspaper that covers the Phillies. He has served as a writer and editor on the staffs of a variety of newspapers and magazines in the Philadelphia and Baltimore areas, covering the Phillies during some of that time. Westcott is the author of *Diamond Greats,* a book of interviews and profiles of 65 former major league players. He wrote the Phillies chapter, "Often Last But Seldom Dull," in the National League edition of the *Encyclopedia of Major League Baseball Team Histories.* He is also a columnist for *Baseball Hobby News.* A native of Philadelphia, Westcott is a graduate of Drexel University and holds a master's degree from Johns Hopkins University. He and his wife Lois have four children and live in Springfield, Pa.

Frank Bilovsky is a business writer and columnist for the Rochester (N.Y.) *Democrat and Chronicle.* For 19 years, he covered the Phillies and other Philadelphia professional and college teams, including the 1980 World Series, for the now-defunct *Philadelphia Bulletin.* In 1982, he wrote *Lion Country: Inside Penn State Football,* which told the history of Nittany Lion football from 1947 to 1981. A native of Lebanon, Pa., and a graduate of La Salle University, Bilovsky has won numerous national and regional writing awards, including the Keystone Award for the best sports story written in Pennsylvania in 1970. He and his wife Rosemary have three sons and live in Pittsford, N.Y.